Hawaii

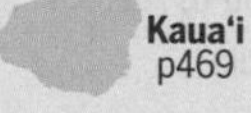

Kaua'i
p469

O'ahu
p62

Moloka'i
p437

Maui
p311

Lana'i
p422

Hawai'i
(Big Island)
p172

THIS EDITION WRITTEN AND RESEARCHED BY

Sara Benson,

Amy C Balfour, Adam Karlin, Craig McLachlan, Ryan Ver Berkmoes

PLAN YOUR TRIP

M SWIET PRODUCTIONS /GETTY IMAGES ©

WAIKIKI P105

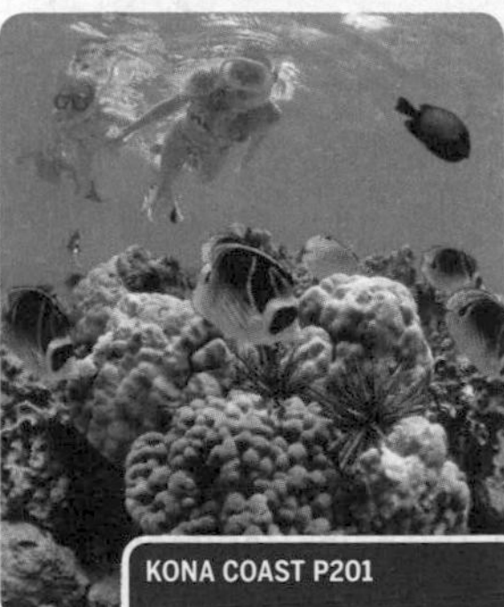
WATT JIM/GETTY IMAGES ©

KONA COAST P201

ON THE ROAD

THOMAS COLLINS /GETTY IMAGES ©

Contents

NA PALI COAST P531

ON THE ROAD

AARON BLACK/GETTY IMAGES ©

MAKAPU'U POINT P134

MAKENA STOCK MEDIA/GETTY IMAGES ©

KAPALUA P343

Contents

KA LANAKILA O KA MALAMALAMA CHURCH P434

LINDA CHING/GETTY IMAGES ©

LEI P615

UNDERSTAND

SURVIVAL GUIDE

SPECIAL FEATURES

Welcome to Hawaii

It's easy to see why Hawaii has become synonymous with paradise. Just look at these sugary beaches, Technicolor coral reefs and volcanoes beckoning adventurous spirits.

Natural Beauty

Snapshots of these islands scattered in a cobalt blue ocean are heavenly, without the need for any tourist-brochure embellishment. Sunrises and sunsets are so spectacular that they're cause for celebration all by themselves. As tropical getaways go, Hawaii couldn't be easier or more worth the trip, although visiting these Polynesian islands isn't always cheap. Whether you're dreaming of swimming in waterfall pools or lazing on golden-sand beaches, you'll find what you're looking for here.

Go Play Outside

Just as in days of old, life in Hawaii is lived outdoors. Whether it's surfing, swimming, fishing or picnicking with the *'ohana* (extended family and friends), encounters with nature are infused with the traditional Hawaiian value of *aloha 'aina* – love and respect for the land. Go hiking across ancient lava flows and fluted *pali* (sea cliffs). Learn to surf, the ancient Hawaiian sport of 'wave sliding,' and then snorkel or dive with giant manta rays and sea turtles. Kayak to a deserted offshore island or hop aboard a winter whale-watching cruise. Back on land, ride horseback with *paniolo* (Hawaiian cowboys).

Island Style

Floating all by itself in the middle of the Pacific, Hawaii proudly maintains its own identity apart from the US mainland. Spam, shave ice, surfing, ukulele and slack key guitar music, hula, pidgin, 'rubbah slippah' (flip-flops) – these are just some of the touchstones of everyday life, island style. Pretty much everything here feels easygoing, low-key and casual, bursting with genuine aloha and fun. You'll be equally welcome whether you're a globe-trotting surf bum, a beaming couple of fresh-faced honeymooners or a big, multigenerational family with rambunctious kids.

Modern Multiculturalism

Hawaii is as proud of its multicultural heritage as it is of island-born US President Barack Obama. On these islands, the descendants of ancient Polynesians, European explorers, American missionaries and Asian plantation immigrants mix and mingle. What's remarkable about contemporary Hawaii is that multiculturalism is the rule, not the exception. Boisterous arts and cultural festivals keep diverse community traditions alive, from Hawaiian hula and outrigger canoe races to Japanese *taiko* drumming.

Why I Love Hawaii

By Sara Benson, Coordinating Author

On my first trip to Hawaii, I landed on Maui almost broke and with my luggage lost in transit. No problem: I camped by the beach, plucked ripe guava from trees and spent days hiking in Haleakalā National Park. Since that serendipitous first island sojourn, I've lived and traveled around the archipelago, from the Big Island's geological wonderland to the emerald river valleys of Kaua'i to the big city of Honolulu, whose backstreets now seem as familiar as my own hometown. When it comes to Hawaii, I'm always ready to go again. *Hana hou!*

For more about our authors, see page 672

Above: Wailua Falls (p474), Kaua'i

Hawaii

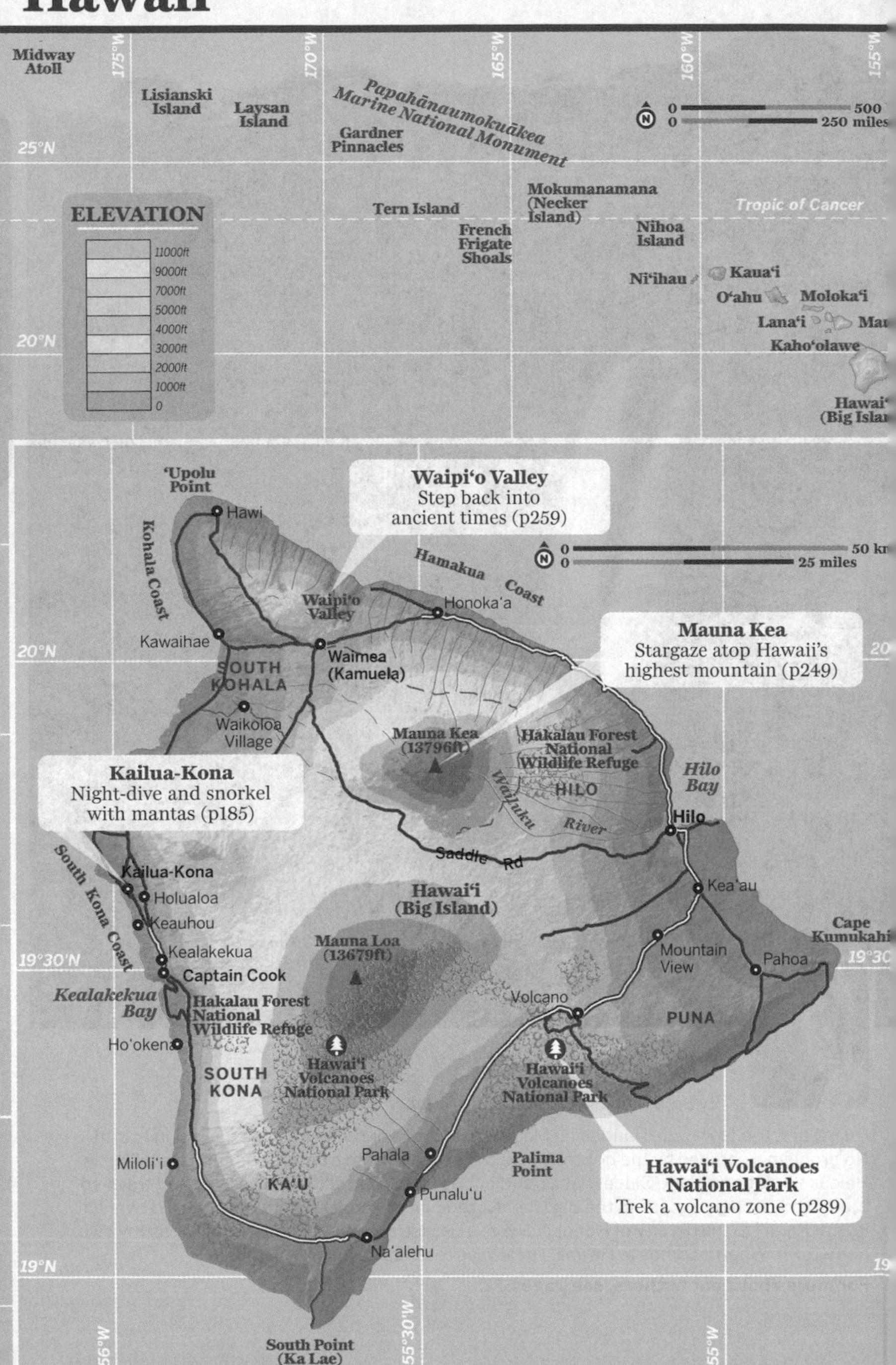

Midway Atoll
Lisianski Island
Laysan Island
Papahānaumokuākea Marine National Monument
Gardner Pinnacles
Mokumanamana (Necker Island)
Tern Island
French Frigate Shoals
Nihoa Island
Tropic of Cancer
Ni'ihau
Kaua'i
O'ahu
Moloka'i
Lana'i
Kaho'olawe
Hawai'i (Big Island)
ELEVATION
11000ft
9000ft
7000ft
5000ft
4000ft
3000ft
2000ft
1000ft
0
500 km
250 miles
'Upolu Point
Hawi
Kohala Coast
Waipi'o Valley
Step back into ancient times (p259)
Hamakua Coast
Honoka'a
Kawaihae
SOUTH KOHALA
Waimea (Kamuela)
Waikoloa Village
Mauna Kea
Stargaze atop Hawaii's highest mountain (p249)
Mauna Kea (13796ft)
Hakalau Forest National Wildlife Refuge
HILO
Wailuku River
Hilo Bay
Hilo
Saddle Rd
Kailua-Kona
Night-dive and snorkel with mantas (p185)
South Kona Coast
Kailua-Kona
Holualoa
Keauhou
Kealakekua
Captain Cook
Kealakekua Bay
Hawai'i (Big Island)
Kea'au
Cape Kumukahi
Mauna Loa (13679ft)
Mountain View
Pahoa
Volcano
PUNA
Ho'okena
SOUTH KONA
Hawai'i Volcanoes National Park
Pahala
Palima Point
Hawai'i Volcanoes National Park
Trek a volcano zone (p289)
Miloli'i
KA'U
Punalu'u
Na'alehu
South Point (Ka Lae)
50 km
25 miles

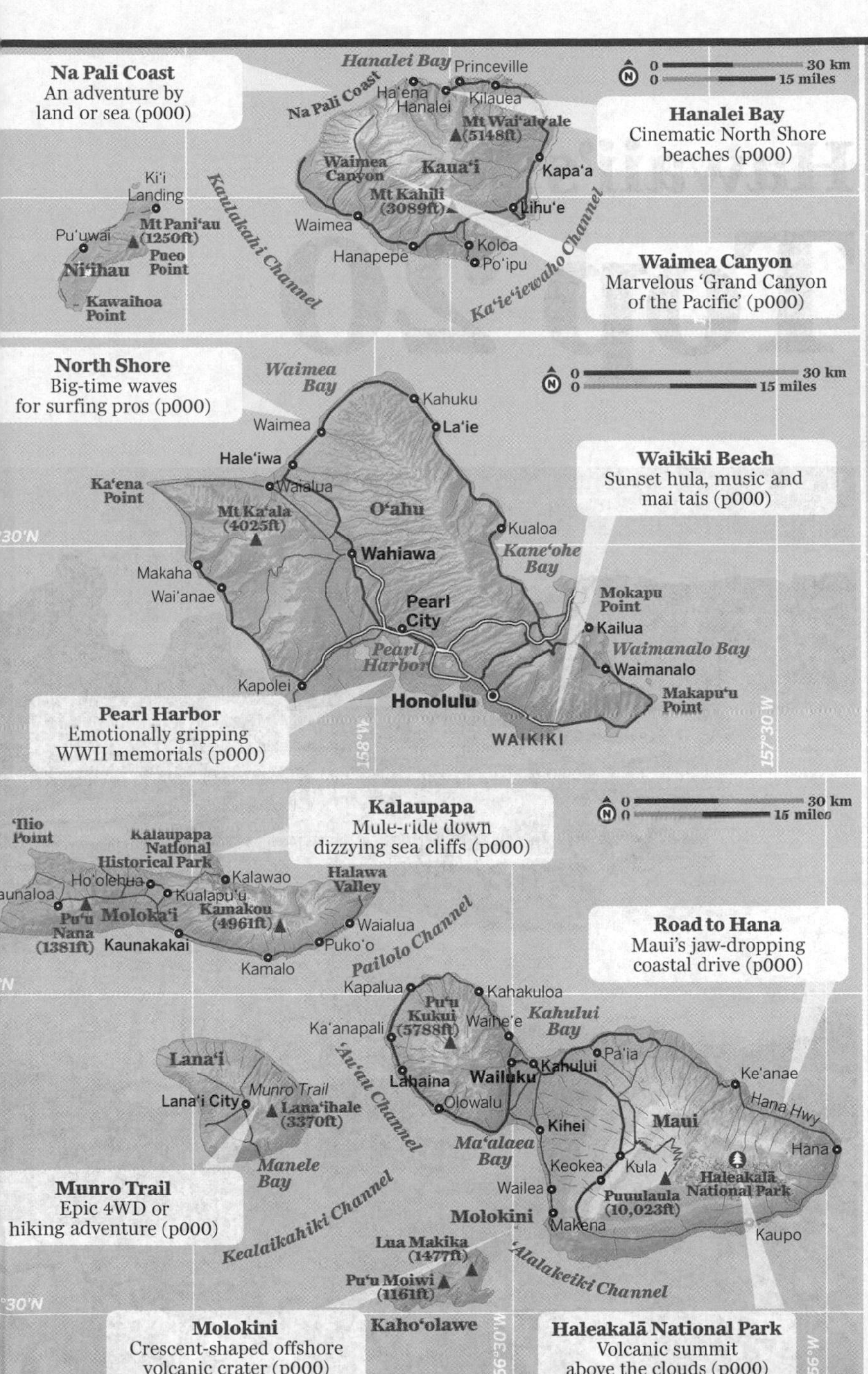

Na Pali Coast
An adventure by land or sea (p000)
Hanalei Bay
Cinematic North Shore beaches (p000)
Waimea Canyon
Marvelous 'Grand Canyon of the Pacific' (p000)
Hanalei Bay
Princeville
Na Pali Coast
Ha'ena
Hanalei
Kilauea
Mt Wai'ale'ale (5148ft)
Kaua'i
Waimea Canyon
Kapa'a
Mt Kahili (3089ft)
Lihu'e
Waimea
Hanapepe
Koloa
Po'ipu
Ka'ie'iewaho Channel
Kaulakahi Channel
Ki'i Landing
Mt Pani'au (1250ft)
Pu'uwai
Pueo Point
Ni'ihau
Kawaihoa Point
0 30 km
0 15 miles
North Shore
Big-time waves for surfing pros (p000)
Waikiki Beach
Sunset hula, music and mai tais (p000)
Pearl Harbor
Emotionally gripping WWII memorials (p000)
Waimea Bay
Kahuku
La'ie
Waimea
Hale'iwa
Ka'ena Point
Waialua
O'ahu
Mt Ka'ala (4025ft)
Kualoa
Kane'ohe Bay
Wahiawa
Makaha
Wai'anae
Pearl City
Mokapu Point
Kailua
Waimanalo Bay
Waimanalo
Pearl Harbor
Kapolei
Honolulu
Makapu'u Point
WAIKIKI
30'N
158°W
157°30'W
Kalaupapa
Mule-ride down dizzying sea cliffs (p000)
Road to Hana
Maui's jaw-dropping coastal drive (p000)
Munro Trail
Epic 4WD or hiking adventure (p000)
Molokini
Crescent-shaped offshore volcanic crater (p000)
Haleakalā National Park
Volcanic summit above the clouds (p000)
'Ilio Point
Kalaupapa National Historical Park
Kalawao
Halawa Valley
Ho'olehua
Kualapu'u
Pu'u Nana (1381ft)
Moloka'i
Kamakou (4961ft)
Waialua
Kaunakakai
Puko'o
Kamalo
Pailolo Channel
Kapalua
Kahakuloa
Pu'u Kukui (5788ft)
Ka'anapali
Waihe'e
Kahului Bay
Lana'i
Lahaina
Wailuku
Kahului
Pa'ia
Ke'anae
Munro Trail
Lana'i City
Lana'ihale (3370ft)
Olowalu
Hana Hwy
'Au'au Channel
Kihei
Maui
Ma'alaea Bay
Hana
Manele Bay
Keokea
Kula
Haleakalā National Park
Wailea
Puuulaula (10,023ft)
Molokini
Makena
Kaupo
Kealaikahiki Channel
Lua Makika (1477ft)
'Alalakeiki Channel
Pu'u Moiwi (1161ft)
Kaho'olawe
30'N
156°30'W
156°W

Hawaii's Top 20

1

Hawai'i Volcanoes National Park

1 And you thought Earth was firm ground. Set on the sloping hillside of the world's most active volcano, this fantastic park (p289) dramatically reminds you that nature is very much alive and in perpetual motion. An incredible network of hiking trails encompasses lava flows and tubes, steam vents and wild beaches. Alternatively, take in many of the major sights by car in one long, winding downhill drive. Don't miss the otherworldly overlook of Halema'uma'u, an enormous fiery crater that spews tons of ash into the sky.

Lava flowing from the Pu'u 'O'o vent (p289)

Na Pali Coast

2 The Na Pali Coast (p531) should top everyone's to-do list. Make the oceanic journey by sailing a catamaran, or, for true sea adventure, pit your paddle and kayak against the elements: wind, swells and sunshine. For hikers, Ke'e Beach is the entry point for the rugged, 11-mile-long Kalalau Trail. Hawaii's most famous trek will transport you to a place like no other, where verdant cliffs soar above a sloping valley abundant with fruit trees, waterfalls and solace seekers.

FRANS LANTING / GETTY IMAGES ©

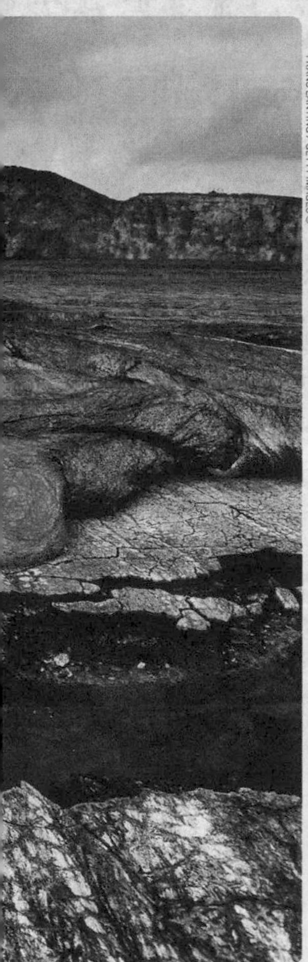

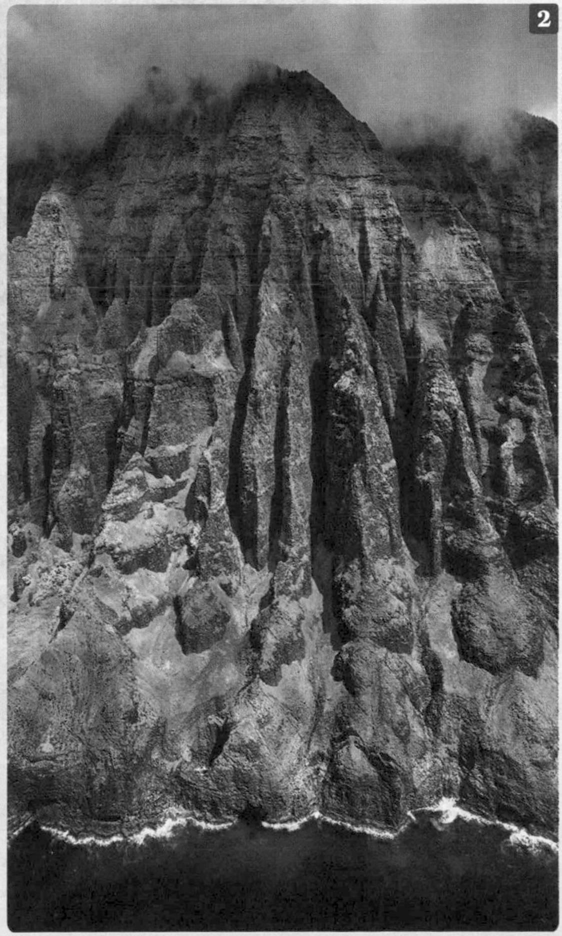

IGNACIO PALACIOS / GETTY IMAGES ©

Road to Hana

3 Hold on tight! Of all the jaw-droppingly dramatic drives in Hawaii, this is the Big Kahuna. A roller coaster of a ride, the Hana Hwy (p406) twists down into jungly valleys and back up towering cliffs, curling around 600 twists and turns along the way. Fifty-four one-lane bridges cross nearly as many waterfalls – some eye-popping torrents, others soothing and gentle. But the ride's only half the thrill. Get out and swim in a Zen-like pool, hike a ginger-scented trail and savor fresh guava and coconuts.

Waikiki Beach

4 Waikiki (p105) is back, baby! Hawaii's most famous beach resort may be a haven for tacky plastic lei, coconut-shell bikini tops and motorized, hip-shaking hula dolls. But real aloha and chic-modern style have remade this prototypical paradise. Beach boys and girls surf legendary waves by day, and after sunset tiki torches light up the sand. Every night hula dancers sway to ancient and modern rhythms – backed by famous island musicians strumming guitars and ukuleles – at oceanfront hotels, open-air bars and even shopping malls.

3

4

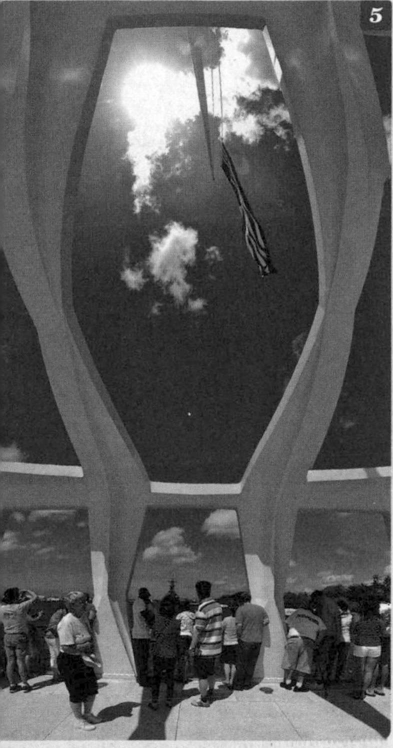

ED FREEMAN / GETTY IMAGES ©

M.M. SWEET / GETTY IMAGES ©

Pearl Harbor

5 Hawaii's active US military bases attest to the islands' continued strategic importance in the Pacific. For the most dramatic reminder of the reasons why, tour O'ahu's USS *Arizona* Memorial (p102), commemorating the 1941 attack on Pearl Harbor and its tragic cost in human lives. Nearby, military history buffs can clamber around inside a submarine, tour the aircraft hangars of the Pacific Aviation Museum and stand on the decks of the 'Mighty Mo' battleship, where Imperial Japan formally surrendered in 1945. USS *Arizona* Memorial

Haleakalā National Park

6 As you hike down into the belly of Haleakalā (p397), the first thing you notice is the crumbly, lunar-like landscape. Then you experience the eerie quiet – the only sound is the crunching of volcanic cinders beneath your feet. The path continues through an unearthly world, a tableau of stark lava, rainbow-colored cinder cones and ever-changing clouds. Looking back toward the summit, it's impossible not to be awed by the raw beauty of this ancient place, now a haven for wildlife and sure-footed hikers. Keonehe'ehe'e (Sliding Sands) Trail (p400)

Hanalei Bay

7 Voted one of the USA's best beaches many times over, this crescent-shaped bay (p517) will delight both lazy sunbathers and active beachgoers. Surfers can charge massive (and some beginner) waves while onlookers amble along the 2 miles of gloriously golden, sandy shore. Surf lessons go on near the pier, and most afternoons see locals and visitors alike firing up the BBQ, cracking open a brew and humbly watching the daylight fade. Without a doubt, beach life is *the* life here.

Molokini

8 Hawaiian legend says that Molokini was a beautiful woman turned to stone by a jealous Pele, goddess of fire and volcanoes. Today Molokini (p365) is the stuff of legends among scuba divers and snorkelers. The crescent-shaped rock, only about 3 miles off the South Maui coast, is the rim of an ancient volcanic crater that has eroded over eons and sunk back beneath the ocean's surface. The shallow waters cradled within are a more than hospitable spot for coral and a calling card for more than 250 species of tropical fish.

Kealakekua Bay

9 Whether you hike down, kayak across or slide from a catamaran into this blue gem of a bay (p208), the underwater wonderland is worth the trip. In depths akin to your average kiddie pool, brilliant-colored tangs, Moorish idols and unicorn fish teem around the historic shores where Captain Cook met his demise and ancient Hawaiians buried the bones of ali'i (royalty). Spinner dolphins and *honu* (green sea turtles) also swim in this bay, eliciting excited gasps – and big grins – from anyone lucky enough to spot them. Captain Cook Monument (p210)

Waimea Canyon

10 Formed by millions of years of erosion and the collapse of the volcano that formed Kaua'i, the 'Grand Canyon of the Pacific' (p552) stretches 10 miles long, 1 mile wide and more than 3600ft deep. Reached via a serpentine scenic drive, roadside lookouts provide panoramic views of rugged cliffs, crested buttes and deep valley gorges. Steep hiking trails allow the adventurous a chance to delve into the canyon floor and survey its interior, satisfying all curiosities – or creating even more. Waipo'o Falls (p568)

Surfing O'ahu's North Shore

11 When giant rollers come crashing in, head to O'ahu's North Shore (p152) for a glimpse of Hawaii's surfing rock stars (you can also spot them riding pro-worthy waves at Maui's Ho'okipa Beach and Kaua'i's own North Shore). No need to pull out a camera lens larger than a howitzer – you can practically look these surfers in the eye as they paddle into monster surf. Or experience the adrenaline rush for yourself by learning to ride *da kine* (the best kind of) waves. Hang loose, brah!

Waipi'o Valley

12 A stunning tropical valley at the end of the road. A mysterious green bowl full of ghosts and legends. A sacred site. A retreat from the outside world. Waipi'o's (p259) special distillation of all these makes it irresistible. Many choose to snap a photo from the panoramic overlook, one of the Big Island's most iconic views. Others trek down to the valley floor to stroll a black sand beach and peer at distant waterfalls. Access is limited beyond that, which only enhances the mystery.

Hulopo'e Beach

13 The main beach (p430) on the ex-pineapple island of Lana'i, this free public park is maintained by the same gardeners who manicure the Four Seasons resorts – so, predictably, it's gorgeous. A postcard-perfect crescent of curving white sand is enjoyed by all, from locals taking the kids for a swim to tourists on day trips from Maui who end up losing all track of time here. Take a break from lounging on the sand for some amazing snorkeling or to dive into the grottoes and lava tubes of the Cathedrals.

12

13

BRIT FINUCCI / SHUTTERSTOCK ©

GREG VAUGHN / GETTY IMAGES ©

Halawa Valley

14 Moloka'i's easternmost valley (p455) seems to be from another time. It enjoys end-of-the-road isolation and pristine scenery, which residents guard adamantly. In ancient Hawaiian times, this populous settlement was part sacred ground, where *heiau* (stone temples) loomed. Uninhabited and almost untouched today, here you can hike with a guide through dense tropical forest, where waterfalls and tropical flora vie for your attention. It's a lost part of a Hawaii you probably didn't think still existed. Stand still, stop talking and feel the pulsing *mana* (spiritual essence).

Night Diving & Snorkeling with Mantas

15 The alien wonders of the ocean become accessible to all on the Big Island. Take a night snorkeling or scuba diving trip near Kailua-Kona (p179) and come face to face, eye to eye and sometimes belly to belly with enormous Pacific manta rays. These graceful giants glide like dark angels beneath you, dancing a shadowy ballet that is heart-wrenchingly beautiful and utterly fascinating. Best of all, you need not be an expert in the water to enjoy this unforgettable adventure.

Munro Trail

16 The Munro Trail (p430), an exhilarating 12-mile 4WD dirt road, follows a surviving pine forest across the hills above Lana'i's one and only town. Open to hikers and mountain bikers, the trail passes through groves of rare native plants and imported Norfolk Island pines – the trail was once a Hawaiian footpath through a patchwork of taro farms, which drew on the frequent rainfall. On a clear day from up here, you can see all of the inhabited Hawaiian islands except for distant Kaua'i and Ni'ihau. Whoa.

ED DARACK / GETTY IMAGES ©

Stargazing atop Mauna Kea

17 Star light, star bright, the first star I see tonight…whoops, scratch that. Up on Mauna Kea (p249), where the night skies are brighter than almost anywhere on Earth, stars – even galaxies – sear the night white, and choosing the first is near impossible. Not to worry: with telescopes (free!) set up for visitors to browse the sky's celestial glory, you don't have to choose just one. Get here by sunset for a heavenly double feature or show up during meteor showers for all-night star parties.

WM Keck Observatory (p251)

Kalaupapa

18 From a lofty perch more than 1600ft above Moloka'i's Kalaupapa Peninsula (p461), you'll ride a trusty mule or hike down a steep trail with dizzying switchbacks, from where views of the Kalaupapa Peninsula below are spectacular. At the bottom you'll learn the dramatic tales of Hawaii's former colony for people with Hansen's disease (leprosy), now a unique national historical park. It's haunting and isolated, but also achingly beautiful, and you'll take heart from the stories of people who have lived here, including not one but two saints.

Old Lahaina Luau

19 Cold mai tais and sweet-smelling lei welcome guests to Maui's most authentic luau (p328), a place of warm aloha where Hawaiian history, culture and culinary prowess are the focus. A beachfront setting on Maui's sunny leeward coast sure doesn't hurt either. Highlights? The unearthing of the pig cooked in an *imu* (underground oven), the dancing of *hula kahiko* and, of course, the savoring of the island-style feast – a table-topping spread of fresh fish and grilled and roasted meats.

19

DEBRA BEHR / ALAMY ©

Farmers Markets

20 Wanna meet the locals? Just find the nearest farmers market. Besides being places to pick up the islands' freshest tropical fruits, macadamia nuts, wild honey and more, Hawaii's farmers markets (p598) are also celebrations of community. You might meet a traditional *kahuna lapa'au* (healer) extolling the virtues of *noni* (Indian mulberry); tipple a coconut-husk cup full of a mildly sedative brew made from *'awa* (kava); or find a handwoven *lauhala* (pandanus leaf) hat. If you're craving island-style fun and cultural authenticity, there's no better place to begin.

Waipa Farmers Market (p524)

Need to Know

For more information, see Survival Guide (p633)

Currency
US dollar ($)

Language
English, Hawaiian

Visas
Generally not required for Canadians or for citizens of Visa Waiver Program (VWP) countries for stays of 90 days or less with ESTA pre-approval.

Money
ATMs available in bigger towns. Credit cards widely accepted (except at some lodgings); often required for reservations. Traveler's checks occasionally accepted. Tipping customary.

Cell Phones
Coverage spotty in remote areas; US carriers Verizon and AT&T have best networks. International travelers need GSM multiband phones; buy prepaid SIM cards locally.

Time
Hawaiian–Aleutian Standard Time (GMT/UMC minus 10 hours)

When to Go

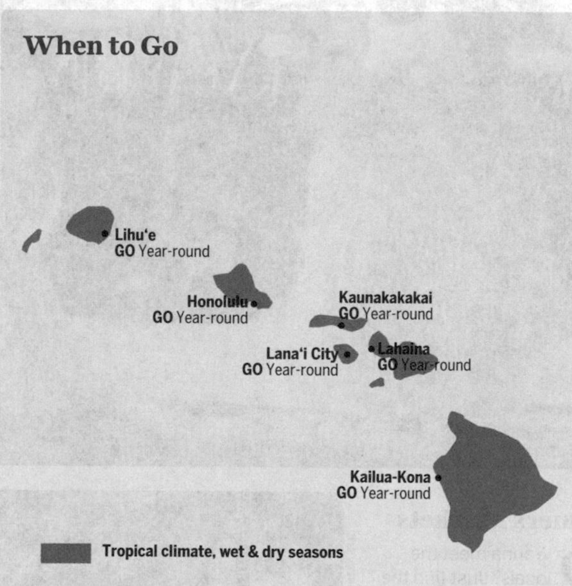

High Season
(Dec–Apr & Jun–Aug)

- ➡ Accommodations prices up 50–100%
- ➡ Christmas to New Year's and around Easter are most expensive and busy
- ➡ Winter is rainier (but best for whale-watching and surfing), summer slightly hotter

Shoulder
(May & Sep)

- ➡ Crowds and prices drop slightly between schools' spring break and summer vacation
- ➡ Temperatures mild, with mostly sunny, cloudless days
- ➡ Statewide Aloha Festivals throughout September

Low Season
(Oct & Nov)

- ➡ Fewest crowds, airfares to Hawaii at their lowest from US mainland and Canada
- ➡ Accommodations rates drop – around 50% less than in high season
- ➡ Weather is typically dry and hot (not ideal for hiking)

Useful Websites

Hawaii Visitors and Convention Bureau (www.gohawaii.com) Official tourism site; comprehensive events calendar and multilingual planning guides.

Hawai'i Magazine (www.hawaiimagazine.com) All-island news, features, festivals and travel tips.

Lonely Planet (www.lonelyplanet.com/usa/hawaii) Destination info, accommodations bookings, travelers' forums and more.

Important Numbers

Hawaii's area code (☎808) is not dialed for local calls, but must be used when calling between islands. Dial ☎1 before any toll-free or long-distance call, including to Canada (for which international rates apply).

USA's country code	☎1
International access code	☎011
Operator	☎0
Emergency (ambulance, fire & police)	☎911
Directory assistance	☎411

Exchange Rates

Australia	A$1	$0.80
Canada	C$1	$0.83
China	Y10	$1.61
Euro zone	€1	$1.14
Japan	¥100	$0.84
New Zealand	NZ$1	$0.74
UK	UK£1	$1.57

For current exchange rates see www.xe.com

Daily Costs

Budget: Less than $100

- Dorm bed: $20–35
- Local plate lunch: $5–10
- Bus fare (one way): $2–2.50

Midrange: $100–250

- Double room with private bath at midrange hotel or B&B: $100–250
- Rental car (excluding insurance and gas) per day/week: from $35/150
- Dinner at casual sit-down restaurant: $20–40

Top End: More than $250

- Beach resort hotel room or luxury condo rental: more than $250
- Three-course meal with a cocktail in a top restaurant: $75–120
- Guided outdoor adventure tour: $80–200

Opening Hours

Expect shorter hours in rural areas. Otherwise, standard opening hours year-round are as follows:

Banks 8:30am–4pm Mon-Fri, some to 6pm Fri & 9am–noon or 1pm Sat

Bars Usually noon–midnight daily, some to 2am Thu–Sat

Businesses (general) & government offices 8:30am–4:30pm Mon-Fri; some post offices 9am–noon Sat

Restaurants breakfast 6–10am, lunch 11:30am–2pm, dinner 5–9:30pm

Shops 9am–5pm Mon-Sat, some also noon–5pm Sun; shopping malls keep extended hours

Arriving in Hawaii

Honolulu International Airport (HNL p645)

- Most car-rental agencies are on-site. Drive takes 25 to 45 minutes to Waikiki via Hwy 92 (Nimitz Hwy/Ala Moana Blvd) or H-1 (Lunalilo) Fwy.
- Taxis are metered. It's around $35 to $45 to Waikiki, plus 35¢ per bag and 10% to 15% driver's tip.
- Door-to-door shuttles cost $16/30 one way/round trip to Waikiki; operate 24 hours (every 20 to 60 minutes).
- Bus 19 or 20 to Waikiki ($2.50) every 20 to 60 minutes from 6am to 11pm daily (large baggage prohibited).

Getting Around

Most interisland travel is by plane. Ferries only connect Maui with Moloka'i and Lana'i. Renting a car is usually necessary if you want to really explore.

Car Always reserve rental cars in advance; rates typically are lowest for airport pickups/drop-offs. You likely won't need a car if you're just staying in Honolulu and Waikiki on O'ahu.

Bus O'ahu's TheBus network is extensive but doesn't stop at some popular tourist sights, beaches and hiking trailheads. On Maui, Kaua'i, Hawai'i the Big Island and Moloka'i, infrequent public buses primarily serve commuters and residents.

Bicycle Not practical for island-wide travel due to narrow highways, heavy traffic, high winds and changeable weather.

For much more on **getting around**, see p646

What's New

Lana'i

On this ex-pineapple-plantation island, tech billionaire Larry Ellison has been keeping construction workers busy with upgrades to everything from the luxury Four Seasons resorts to the local supermarket. Even Lana'i City's historic movie theater has been transformed into a state-of-the-art media center. Pie-in-the-sky plans to spur 'green growth' include solar energy, a desalination plant and small farms. Things keep changing almost by the week, so stay tuned. (p428)

Puna's Lava Flow

Pele, the Hawaiian goddess of fire and volcanoes, has been up to her old tricks on the Big Island, sending lava creeping over roads toward Pahoa town. (p281)

Maui's New Resorts

The chic Andaz Maui beachfront hotel, with an Iron Chef Morimoto restaurant, and the airy residences of Montage Kapalua Bay have made a big splash on the island's sunny leeward coast. (p377; p347)

Interisland Flights

More shake-ups in the aviation biz have improved interisland air service, even to the smaller Neighbor Islands. Fares can be surprisingly high, unless you book ahead. (p646)

Kaka'ako

Redevelopment of Honolulu's waterfront is in the works, with even a presidential library bid. A creative batch of cutting-edge eateries, bars and coffee shops have already set up shop here.

Craft Beer & Spirits

More breweries and microdistilleries are popping up all around the bigger islands, including Maui's Ocean Vodka, Honolulu Beerworks and the Kauai Beer Company. (p393; p95; p483)

Makawao Forest Reserve

A welcome network of mountain-biking trails keeps expanding in Maui's Upcountry, thanks to local advocacy and state agency cooperation. (p390)

Mokuapapa Discovery Center

Relocated in downtown Hilo, the Big Island's marine educational center is bigger and better than ever. Stop by and take a virtual trip to the remote Northwestern Hawaiian Islands. (p272)

HART

Construction has finally begun on Honolulu's high-speed rail project, but the Honolulu Authority for Rapid Transportation (HART) won't start running trains to ease O'ahu's traffic woes until 2018.

Trail Closures

Some island hiking trails damaged during recent tropical storms have closed, including Maui's epic Skyline Trail and Kaua'i's Nualolo Cliffs Trail. Keep your fingers crossed that they'll reopen eventually.

For more recommendations and reviews, see lonelyplanet.com/hawaii

If You Like...

Beaches

Think of Hawaii, and you're instantly dreaming about golden sands backed by tropical palm trees. With six main islands and hundreds of miles of coastline, you'll be spoiled for choice.

Waikiki Learn to surf; board a sunset 'booze cruise'; and catch a hula show on O'ahu. (p105)

Mauna Kea Beach Kauna'oa Bay on Hawai'i (Big Island) reveals the most Hollywood-worthy crescent of white sand. (p230)

Hanalei Bay Kaua'i's postcard-perfect beach embraces surfers, paddlers, bodyboarders and beach bums alike. (p517)

Big Beach Arguably Maui's best beach, with its broad, mile-long golden sands and turquoise waters. (p380)

Hulopo'e Beach Ferries drop off day-trippers at this sun-kissed playground fronting gleaming Manele Bay on Lana'i. (p430)

Kawakiu Beach Trek into Moloka'i's wild west to have white sands all to yourself. (p466)

Surfing & Water Sports

The ancient Hawaiian sport of *he'e nalu* ('wave sliding') is reason enough to visit these islands. But there's also snorkeling with sea turtles and endless aquatic escapades to experience.

Banzai Pipeline & Sunset Beach The big barrels and winter swells of O'ahu's most famous surf breaks call to pros. (p154)

Ho'okipa Beach This beach on Maui is a pilgrimage for pro windsurfers and surfers – and gawking spectators, too. (p383)

Po'ipu Surfers show up for summer swells on Kaua'i's sunny South Shore, a hot spot for snorkelers and divers. (p537)

Kealakekua Bay See South Kona's marine-life conservation district by kayak and from behind a snorkel mask. (p208)

Cathedrals Dive into Lana'i's Manele Bay, where underwater grottoes, arches and a 100ft lava tube await. (p431)

Hanauma Bay O'ahu's giant outdoor tropical fishbowl lets even novice snorkelers get their fins wet. (p132)

Ni'ihau A boat ride from Kaua'i, the 'Forbidden Island' harbors Hawaii's best diving. (p564)

Adventures on Land

Hawaii's islands have as many adventures to offer landlubbers as water babies. Strap yourself into a zipline harness; lace up those hiking boots; or climb into the saddle.

Haleakalā National Park Cloud forest walks and volcano summit trails wind through Maui's high-altitude wilderness. (p397)

Ziplining Soar through forest canopies and down volcanic mountains, most thrillingly on Maui and Kaua'i. (p54)

Hawai'i Volcanoes National Park Trek through the geological wonderland ruled by Pele, goddess of fire and volcanoes. (p289)

Kalaupapa Bounce down sky-high sea cliffs to Moloka'i's remote peninsula on foot or by trusty mule. (p461)

Caving Descend underground into the world's longest lava tubes on the Big Island. (p49)

Kipu Ranch Ride an ATV to where *Jurassic Park* was filmed and Indiana Jones romped on Kaua'i. (p479)

Epic Views

No wonder hundreds of movies have been shot in Hawaii. Around every corner lies another glorious beach, lush jungle valley or towering mountains and sea cliffs. Soak it up.

Na Pali Coast Kaua'i's most impressive scenery, whether viewed on foot, from the air or at sea. (p531)

Sunrise on Haleakalā Mesmerizing clouds and heavenly light play atop Maui's tallest volcano. (p397)

Halema'uma'u Viewpoint Witness the Big Island's smoking volcanic crater and a fiery lava lake. (p292)

Waimea Canyon Waterfalls stream down colorful cliff faces in Kaua'i's 'Grand Canyon of the Pacific.' (p568)

Nu'uanu Pali State Wayside Lookout Peek over at the Windward Coast from a roadside viewpoint in O'ahu's mountains. (p135)

South Point (Ka Lae) Where ancient Polynesians first landed in Hawaii; today it's the USA's southernmost point. (p308)

Waterfalls & Swimming Holes

Wade through the mud and step over slippery tree roots on jungly trails, all so you can swim in (or just gaze upon) a crystal-clear pool under a rainforest cascade.

'Ohe'o Gulch In Haleakalā National Park, Maui's best-known waterfalls and natural pools tumble into the sea. (p405)

Uluwehi Falls Everyone knows about Kaua'i's pretty 'Secret Falls,' reached by paddling up the Wailua River. (p490)

Twin Falls Even kids can hike to this swimmable cascade on Maui's waterfall-strewn Road to Hana. (p406)

Moa'ula & Hipuapua Falls Hire a local guide to discover these falls deep inside Moloka'i's Halawa Valley. (p456)

Top: *Honu* (green sea turtle; p621)
Bottom: Ahi *poke* (raw tuna)

Hanakapi'ai Falls Trekkers earn the right to swim in this hidden gem on Kaua'i's Na Pali Coast. (p533)

'Akaka Falls Snap a photo of these plunging falls (no swimming, sorry!) on the Big Island's Hamakua Coast. (p266)

Extreme Thrills

Make your trip to Hawaii one to brag about for a lifetime. Jump out of an airplane; summit volcanic peaks; or bush-whack to wild beaches and ancient Hawaiian valleys.

Na Pali Coast Hawaii's most famous trek snakes along daunting sea cliffs and is also explorable by kayak. (p531)

Night dive with manta rays Don a wetsuit and join the underwater ballet on the Big Island's Kona Coast. (p184)

Waipi'o & Waimanu Valleys Earn awe-inspiring waterfall views by rugged hiking in the Big Island's emerald valleys. (p259)

Lava Viewing in Puna Hike or take a boat ride and, if your timing is lucky, see fiery lava flow into the ocean on the Big Island. (p280)

Waimea Bay Where only expert surfers paddle out to challenge monster winter waves on O'ahu. (p154)

Mauna Kea & Mauna Loa Reach the top of Hawaii's highest and most massive mountains on ancient paths. (p249) (p255)

Skydiving Leap from more than 10,000ft above O'ahu's North Shore or Kaua'i's Westside. (p163)

Kamakou Preserve In Moloka'i's almost impenetrable rainforest, unique flora and fauna thrive. (p457)

Flora & Fauna

Hawaii is bursting with biodiversity. Over eons, these geographically isolated islands have carved a unique ecological niche, with spectacular wildlife both on land and in the sea.

Nene (Hawiian goose) Back from the brink of extinction, this curious bird nests in Hawaii's national parks.

Hawaiian monk seals Critically endangered, these endearing marine mammals sometimes haul out on island beaches.

Honeycreepers Hawaii's spectacular diversity of birds includes these brightly colored forest flutterers.

Humpback whales Climb aboard a whale-watching boat to meet and greet Hawaii's most famous winter visitors.

Sea turtles You'll see them basking on beaches or spot their heads bobbing up like periscopes in the ocean.

Spinner dolphins Wild, playful and free, these acrobatic creatures often come into island bays to rest.

Koa trees These prized native hardwoods gracefully spread over island forests.

Scenic Drives

Ready to hit the road? These islands may be small, but you can still take long, unbelievably beautiful drives up volcano summits, into cloud forests and over high *pali* (cliffs).

Road to Hana Curving down East Maui's lush coast, you'll pass dozens of waterfalls and 54 stone bridges. (p406)

O'ahu's Windward Coast Leave behind the urban jungles of Honolulu for surf beaches and down-home countryside. (p135)

Haleakalā Crater Road From sea to summit, it's the steepest elevation gain of any road on the planet. Really. (p404)

Kaua'i's North Shore One-lane bridges squeeze between breathtaking *pali* and rollicking surf beyond Hanalei. (p505)

Chain of Craters Road Drop through the Big Island's active volcano zone to where lava has buried the road. (p294)

Mauna Kea Summit Road You'll need 4WD to reach the top of Hawaii's highest peak. (p251)

Food & Drink

There are so many *'ono grinds* (good eats) in Hawaii that you might find yourself eating more than three times a day!

Poke Pronounced *poh-kay*, it's Hawaii's chunky version of ceviche with island condiments.

Kalua pig & huli-huli chicken Get a mouthful of smokin' roasted and rotisserie meats – basically, Hawaii-style BBQ.

Loco moco The breakfast of champions: rice, fried egg and a hamburger patty doused in gravy.

Crack seed Got a sweet tooth? A salty, sour or spicy craving? Try Hawaii's Chinese-style dried fruit candy.

'Awa A mildly intoxicating traditional Polynesian brew made from the kava plant.

Shave ice Nothing tastes better after a hot day at the beach.

Month by Month

TOP EVENTS

Aloha Festivals, September

Triple Crown of Surfing, November & December

Merrie Monarch Festival, March/April

Koloa Plantation Days Celebration, July

Kona Coffee Cultural Festival, November

January

Typically Hawaii's wettest and coolest month, January is the month when tourist high season gets into full swing, with snowbirds escaping winter elsewhere. The Martin Luther King Jr holiday on the third Monday is especially busy.

Chinese New Year

On the second new moon after the winter solstice, usually between mid-January and mid-February, look for lion dances, firecrackers, street fairs and parades. Honolulu's Chinatown celebrations are the biggest; festivities on Hilo (Big Island) and Lahaina (Maui) are notable too. (p88)

February

Peak tourist season continues, with weekends around Valentine's Day (February 14) and Presidents Day (third Monday) usually booked solid at resorts. Winter storms bring more rainfall and cooler temperatures.

Waimea Town Celebration

Over a week in mid-February, more than 10,000 folks gather in Waimea (Kaua'i) to celebrate with canoe races, a rodeo, lei-making contests and live music. (p562)

March

It's another busy month to visit Hawaii, despite lingering rainfall. College students and families take a one- or two-week 'spring break' around Easter, falling in March or April.

Whale & Ocean Arts Festival

Throughout the winter, Maui welcomes its most famous visitors – migratory humpback whales – including with an annual whale count and an art show, live entertainment and kids' activities in early March. (p324)

Honolulu Festival

In mid-March, this three-day festival is a unique blend of Hawaii, Asia and Polynesia cultures, with an arts-and-crafts fair, live music and dance performances, culminating in a grand parade followed by a fireworks show. (p88)

Prince Kuhio Day

All islands honor the March 26 birthday of the man who would've become king if Queen Lili'uokalani hadn't been overthrown. Kaua'i bustles with a two-week arts and cultural festival, featuring a rodeo, canoe races, live music and Hawaiian storytelling, crafts and more. (p543)

April

Peak tourist season winds down as rainstorms lessen. Resorts are less busy after Easter, once college students and families finish taking their 'spring break' vacations.

Merrie Monarch Festival

On Hawai'i (Big Island), Easter Sunday (falling in late March or early April) kicks off Hilo's week-long celebration of Hawaiian arts and culture. The Olympics of hula competitions draws top troupes from all islands, the US mainland and abroad. (p274)

East Maui Taro Festival

On Maui, the rural town of Hana throws its biggest party for two weekend days in late April, with poi making, an arts-and-crafts fair, hula dancing and lots of island music. (p417)

Waikiki Spam Jam

How much does Hawaii love Spam? Residents consume almost seven million cans each year. Waikiki's wacky one-day street festival in late April, attended by thousands of folks, is all about *'ono kine grinds* (good eats). (p115)

May

Crowds thin and prices drop slightly between spring break and summer vacation. Temperatures remain mild, with mostly sunny and cloudless days. Hotels sell out for the Memorial Day holiday weekend in late May.

Mele Mei

O'ahu's month-long celebration of Hawaiian music, with ukulele and slack key guitar workshops, concerts and hula performances, leads up to Na Hoku Hanohano, Hawaii's version of the Grammy Awards.

Lei Day

Across Hawaii the traditional craft of lei making gets its own holiday on May 1. O'ahu crowns a lei queen in Waikiki; Lihu'e's Kaua'i Museum holds lei-making workshops and a contest; and Hilo hosts lei-making demonstrations and hula on the Big Island. (p480)

Moloka'i Ka Hula Piko

According to Hawaiian oral history, Moloka'i is the birthplace of hula. In early May, this three-day hula festival draws huge crowds to its sacred hula performances and Hawaiian *ho'olaule'a* (celebration). (p443)

June

Getting in before most families start taking summer vacations, visitors in early June can take advantage of warm, dry weather and discounts on hotels and flights.

Pan-Pacific Festival

In Honolulu, this three-day festival in early June combines family-friendly celebrations of Hawaiian, Japanese and other Pacific Rim cultures, with hula dancing, *taiko* drumming and live music, ending with a huge parade and block party in Waikiki. (p88)

King Kamehameha Day

On June 11, this state holiday is celebrated on all islands. North Kohala (Big Island), the king's birthplace, holds all-day festivities and a grand parade. Later in the month, Honolulu's King Kamehameha Hula Competition is one of Hawaii's biggest contests. (p242)

Kapalua Wine & Food Festival

Hawaii's longest-running culinary extravaganza attracts taste-makers to West Maui's Kapalua resort in mid-June. Show up for cooking demonstrations by TV celebrity chefs and wine tastings with master sommeliers. (p347)

July

Temperatures rise and rain is scarce. School summer vacations and the July 4 national holiday make this one of the busiest travel months. Book early and expect high prices.

Pineapple Festival

In early July this festival celebrating Lana'i's special relationship with the pineapple is the island's main bash, featuring kid-friendly activities, live music and food in Lana'i City. (Never mind that Lana'i no longer grows any of its own pineapples!) (p426)

Independence Day

Across the islands, Fourth of July celebrations inspire fireworks and fairs, but maybe the most fun is had at rodeos held in the *paniolo* (Hawaiian cowboy) towns of Waimea (Kamuela) on the

Big Island and Makawao on Maui. (p246)

Prince Lot Hula Festival

On the third Saturday in July, one of O'ahu's premier Hawaiian cultural festivals showcases noncompetitive hula performances in a garden setting at a former royal retreat, giving it a graceful, traditional feeling. (p89)

Koloa Plantation Days Celebration

On Kaua'i's south shore, this nine-day festival in mid-July is a huge celebration of the island's sugar-plantation and *paniolo* heritage. It's like a state fair, Hawaii-style, including a parade, rodeo, traditional games, live entertainment, movies and historical walks. (p535)

August

Families taking summer vacations keep things busy all around the islands. Hot, sunny weather prevails, especially on the islands' leeward sides. Statehood Day is a holiday observed on the third Friday of the month.

Hawaiian International Billfish Tournament

Kailua-Kona, on the Big Island, is the epicenter of big-game fishing, and for more than 50 years this has been Hawaii's grand tournament. It's accompanied by five days of festive entertainment in late July or early August. (p187)

Hawaiian Slack Key Guitar Festival

In Waikiki, free open-air concerts by ukulele and slack key guitar legends, with food and craft vendors and an arts-and-crafts fair, happen in mid-August. Spin-off events take place during other months on the Big Island, Maui and Kaua'i. (p115)

Music & Mango Festival

Kaua'i's North Shore sees a late-summer celebration of locally grown food and live music on Hanalei Bay in mid-August. Come back in December for the equally family-friendly *kalo* (taro) festival, held by an ancient Hawaiian fishpond. (p521)

September

After Labor Day weekend in early September, crowds start to fade away at beach resorts as students go back to school. Hotter weather continues.

Aloha Festivals

Begun in 1946, the Aloha Festivals are the state's premier Hawaiian cultural celebration, an almost non-stop series of events on all the main islands during September. On O'ahu, look for a Hawaiian royal court procession and Waikiki's block party. (p115)

Queen Lili'uokalani Canoe Race

In Hawaii, traditional outrigger canoeing is alive and well, and fall is the big season for long-distance events. Everything kicks off over Labor Day weekend with these races along the Big Island's Kona Coast. (p186)

Hawai'i Food & Wine Festival

Hawaii's hottest chefs and most lauded artisan farmers gather for this home-grown culinary celebration, with stellar farm-to-table food, and cocktail and wine tastings in Honolulu in early September. (p89)

Kaua'i Mokihana Festival

In mid-September, Kaua'i's week-long contemporary Hawaiian arts and cultural festival includes a three-day hula competition in ancient and modern styles, as well as the Kaua'i Composers Contest & Concert in Lihu'e. (p481)

Na Wahine O Ke Kai

Held in late September (weather permitting), this is the powerful all-women sister event of the all-male Moloka'i Hoe in early October. Both legendary long-distance outrigger canoe races traverse the 41-mile Ka'iwi Channel between Moloka'i and O'ahu. (p443)

Puna Culinary Festival

Go straight to the source of some of the Big Island's best farm bounty at this homegrown festival of cooking classes, markets, chef's dinners, art shows, films and talks. (p287)

October

The slowest month for tourism, October brings travel bargains on hotels and flights. Weather is reliably sunny, but very humid when the trade winds don't blow.

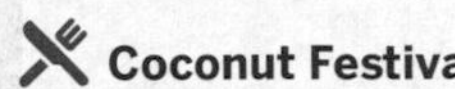

Coconut Festival

You can't call yourself a coconut festival and not get a little nutty. In fact, Kapa'a on Kaua'i gets downright silly, with two days of pie-eating contests, coconut crafts, recipe cook-offs, live entertainment and local food in early October. (p499)

Eo e Emalani I Alaka'i

On Kaua'i, Koke'e State Park reenacts Queen Emma's historic 1871 journey to Alaka'i Swamp during a powerful one-day festival in early October, with a royal procession, and Hawaiian music and hula performances. (p573)

Ironman Triathlon World Championship

This legendary triathlon on the Big Island's Kona coast is the ultimate endurance contest, combining a 2.4-mile ocean swim, 112-mile bike race and 26.2-mile marathon. Watch more than 2200 athletes push their own limits in mid-October. (p187)

Maui Ukulele Festival

Herald Hawaii's favorite stringed musical instrument outdoors at the Maui Arts & Cultural Center in mid-October, with guest appearances by stars such as Jake Shimabukuro and Kelly Boy De Lima. (p355)

Hawaii International Film Festival

In mid-October, this highly regarded festival of Pacific Rim cinema screens more than 200 Asian, Polynesian and Hawaii-made films, with the main action in Honolulu. (p89)

Halloween

On Maui, Lahaina's Halloween carnival was once so huge it was dubbed 'Mardi Gras of the Pacific.' It's been scaled back, but is still a great street party. Other places to get festive on October 31 include Waikiki on O'ahu. (p325)

November

Toward the end of the month, vacationing crowds (and scattered rainfall) start returning to Hawaii. Thanksgiving on the fourth Thursday is a popular and pricey time to visit.

Moku O Keawe

In early November, this three-day Big Island hula festival draws top hula *halau* (schools) from Hawaii, Japan and the US mainland to competitions, workshops, and a marketplace for hula fashions and traditional crafts in Waikoloa. (p225)

Kona Coffee Cultural Festival

For 10 days during the harvest season in early November, the Big Island honors Kona brews with a cupping competition, a coffee-picking contest, a recipe cook-off, coffee farm tours, art shows, live music, hula and more. (p187)

Kohala 'Aina Festival

In early November, the start of the traditional Hawaiian harvest season, Kohala shows off its agricultural pride at this festival with a 100% Big Island–grown feast, plus DIY workshops, live music and fun activities for kids. (p242)

Triple Crown of Surfing

O'ahu's North Shore – specifically Hale'iwa, Sunset Beach and Pipeline – hosts pro surfing's ultimate contest, known as the Triple Crown of Surfing. Thrill-a-minute competitions for women and men run from mid-November through mid-December, depending on when the surf's up. (p156)

December

As winter rainstorms return and temperatures cool slightly, peak tourist season begins in mid-December, making the Christmas to New Year's holiday period extremely busy – and expensive.

Honolulu Marathon

Held on the second Sunday in December, the Honolulu Marathon is Hawaii's biggest and most popular foot race. It attracts more than 30,000 runners every year (more than half of whom hail from Japan), making it one of the world's top 10 marathons. (p115)

Plan Your Trip
Itineraries

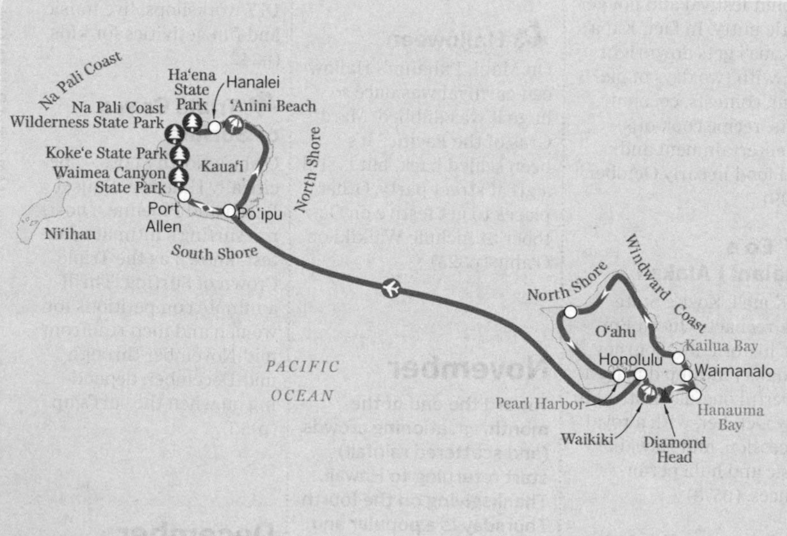

O'ahu & Kaua'i

Think of this as your 'town and country' trip to Hawaii. Start off in the breezy streets of Honolulu, sleeping in mod style at the classic beach resort of Waikiki. Then trade the big-city buzz for the small-town scene on verdant Kaua'i.

Touch down for four days on O'ahu amid the skyscrapers of **Honolulu**. Between sessions at the beaches of **Waikiki**, eat your heart out in the capital; go clubbing and art-gallery-hopping in Chinatown; visit the Bishop Museum and 'Iolani Palace; touch WWII history at **Pearl Harbor**; enjoy live Hawaiian music and hula at sunset; hike up **Diamond Head** and tour Doris Duke's incomparable Shangri La.

Now relax. Heading east, spend a morning snorkeling at **Hanauma Bay**. In the afternoon, swim off the white-sand beaches of **Waimanalo** or surf, kayak, windsurf and kiteboard at **Kailua Bay**. Wend your way along the **Windward Coast**, with its jungly hiking trails, ancient lava-rock fishponds and captivating offshore islands. Save at least an afternoon to savor the world-famous beaches of the

Lanikai Beach (p140), O'ahu

North Shore. In winter, watch big-wave surfers carving; in summer, snorkel with sea turtles.

Hop a plane over to Kaua'i, full of heart-stopping scenery, for the next six days. Start off nice and easy in **Po'ipu** with a lazy snooze on the sunny beaches of the **South Shore** or head straight to **Port Allen** for a snorkeling or scuba-diving boat trip. Then lace up your hiking boots and spend a day in **Waimea Canyon** and **Koke'e State Parks**, where you can traverse knife-edged 2000ft-high cliffs and peek into the 'Grand Canyon of the Pacific.'

Giddyap back around to Kaua'i's **North Shore**, which by itself deserves a couple of days. Get in some swimming, snorkeling or windsurfing at 'Anini Beach. Check out the beach-bum town of **Hanalei** for surfing and stand up paddle boarding on the bay or peaceful river kayaking. Road trips hardly get more scenic than the drive to the very end of the road at **Ha'ena State Park**.

OK, ready? **Na Pali Coast Wilderness State Park** is what's left. In summer, kayak 17 miles beside Kaua'i's epic sea cliffs. Otherwise, backpack 11 miles to Ke'e Beach. Either way, you've saved the best for last.

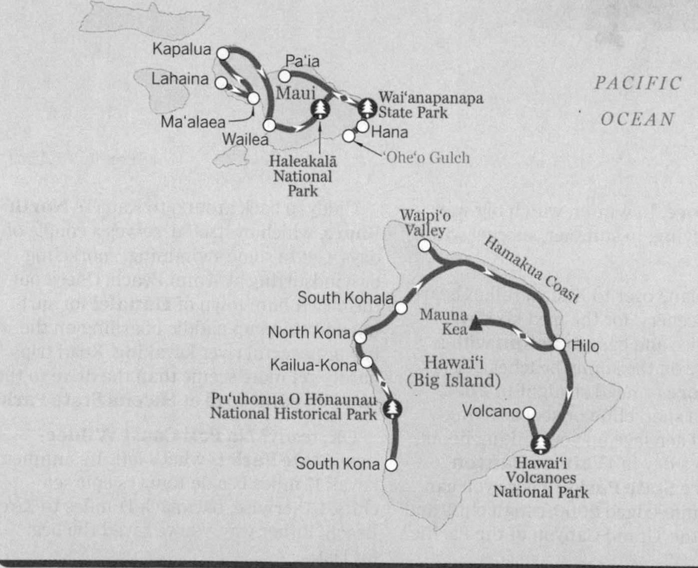
Kapalua
Lahaina
Ma'alaea
Wailea
Pa'ia
Maui
Haleakalā National Park
Wai'anapanapa State Park
Hana
'Ohe'o Gulch
PACIFIC OCEAN
Waipi'o Valley
Hamakua Coast
South Kohala
Mauna Kea
North Kona
Hilo
Kailua-Kona
Hawai'i (Big Island)
Pu'uhonua O Hōnaunau National Historical Park
Volcano
South Kona
Hawai'i Volcanoes National Park

GREG VAUGHN / GETTY IMAGES ©

Maui & Hawai'i

Looking for tropical adventures? Hit up Maui for its postcard-perfect honeymoon beaches, serpentine coastal drives and hang-loose surf scene. When you're ready for bigger thrills, jet over to the Big Island, where erupting volcanoes, mysterious valleys and deserted beaches await.

With just under a week to spend on Maui, start in the old whaling town of **Lahaina**, with its pirates' treasure chest of historical sites. In winter, spot whales breaching offshore or take a whale-watching boat tour from **Ma'alaea**. For golden-sand beaches that are idyllic for swimming and snorkeling, drive north up the coast to bayfront **Kapalua** and south to the resorts of **Wailea** and beyond.

Make sure you get to **Haleakalā National Park**. Spend a day hiking around an ancient volcano and catching sunrise from the summit. Then drive the cliff-hugging road to Hana, stopping to kick back on the black-sand beach at **Wai'anapanapa State Park**. Glide past sleepy **Hana** for a bamboo rainforest hike and a dip in the cascading waterfall pools of **'Ohe'o Gulch**. Backtrack up the coast to the surf town of **Pa'ia**, chowing *'ono grinds* (delicious food) and admiring the daredevil windsurfers at Ho'okipa Beach.

The Big Island can take a week and then some. Base yourself half the time in **Kailua-Kona**, alternating trips to the beaches – especially those in **North Kona** and on **South Kohala's** 'Gold Coast' – with feeling the ancient *mana* (spiritual essence) at **Pu'uhonua O Hōnaunau National Historical Park** and tasting the coffee farms of **South Kona**. Then take a leisurely drive along the **Hamakua Coast**, making sure to gaze out on **Waipi'o Valley** and hike down to the black-sand beach.

Walk around harborfront **Hilo**, exploring its historic architecture, the farmers market and the excellent astronomy center and museums. Don't miss detouring up to **Mauna Kea** for sunset views and an evening of stargazing. Spend at least a full day in **Hawai'i Volcanoes National Park**: hike the otherworldly Kilauea Iki Trail; drive along the Chain of Craters Road; and hopefully spy some hot lava glowing fiery red after dark. Afterward retreat to your own rainforest cottage B&B in nearby **Volcano**.

M.REMAGNUM / GETTY IMAGES ©

Top: Lava flowing into the ocean, Hawai'i Volcanoes National Park (p289)
Bottom: Best Western Pioneer Inn (p328), Lahaina

10 DAYS O'ahu & Hawai'i

Go big or go home – pair Hawaii's busiest island with its biggest for star chefs and beach resort life, ancient heiau (temples) set beside taro fields, mountainous hiking trails and deep blue bays with powdery white-sand beaches.

Start on the capital island of O'ahu, basing yourself in **Kailua** for five days. Among the many sights around **Honolulu**, don't miss Chinatown or the WWII memorials at **Pearl Harbor**. Snorkel one morning at **Hanauma Bay** and in the afternoon hike to Honolulu's Manoa Falls after visiting the Lyon Arboretum. Take a class in lei making, hula dancing or ukulele playing in **Waikiki**, where you can end the day with a sunset catamaran 'booze cruise' or live Hawaiian music at oceanfront bars.

Drive up the **Windward Coast**, stopping at panoramic beaches and to hike into the misty Ko'olau Mountains. Keep going past the white-sand coves of **Turtle Bay** to end up on the North Shore, famous for its big-wave surfing in winter. Stretch your legs and grab a shave ice in **Hale'iwa**, then take a joy-ride flight at Dillingham Airfield. Dip your toes into the lagoons at **Ko Olina** before cruising up the workaday **Wai'anae Coast** for a windy walk in **Ka'ena Point State Park**.

Mosey over to the Big Island and book a B&B in **South Kona** for a few nights. For ocean adventures, go scuba diving or snorkeling at night with manta rays around **Kailua-Kona** and paddle a kayak to snorkel at cobalt-colored **Kealakekua Bay**. Down in Ka'u, hike to Green Sands Beach near windswept **Ka Lae**, the USA's southernmost point. Next up, **Hawai'i Volcanoes National Park**, home of the world's longest-running volcanic eruption, offers alien-looking moonscapes for hiking.

Spend a night or two in **Hilo**, taking time to drive partway up **Mauna Kea** for stargazing after dark. After rolling up and down the **Hamakua Coast**, amble the old sugar-plantation town of **Honoka'a** before dropping into ancient **Waipi'o Valley**. Giddyup through **Waimea (Kamuela)**, a *paniolo* (Hawaiian cowboy) town. In the quiet countryside of North Kohala, hike into **Pololu Valley**, circle around **Mo'okini Heiau** and relax in quaint, artsy **Hawi**.

Top: Surfboards, Waikiki (p105)
Bottom: Kayaking, Kealakekua Bay (p208)

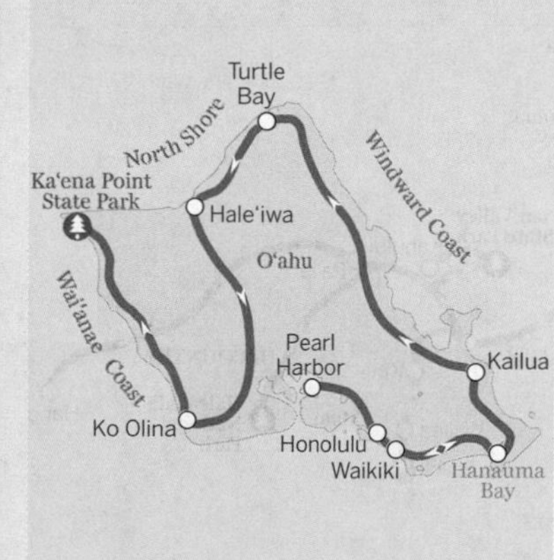
Turtle Bay
North Shore
Windward Coast
Ka'ena Point State Park
Hale'iwa
O'ahu
Wai'anae Coast
Pearl Harbor
Kailua
Ko Olina
Honolulu
Waikiki
Hanauma Bay
PACIFIC OCEAN

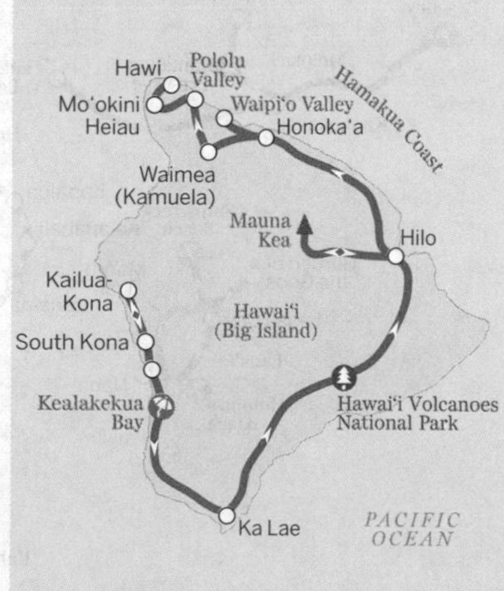
Hawi
Pololu Valley
Mo'okini Heiau
Waipi'o Valley
Hamakua Coast
Honoka'a
Waimea (Kamuela)
Mauna Kea
Hilo
Kailua-Kona
Hawai'i (Big Island)
South Kona
Kealakekua Bay
Hawai'i Volcanoes National Park
Ka Lae
PACIFIC OCEAN

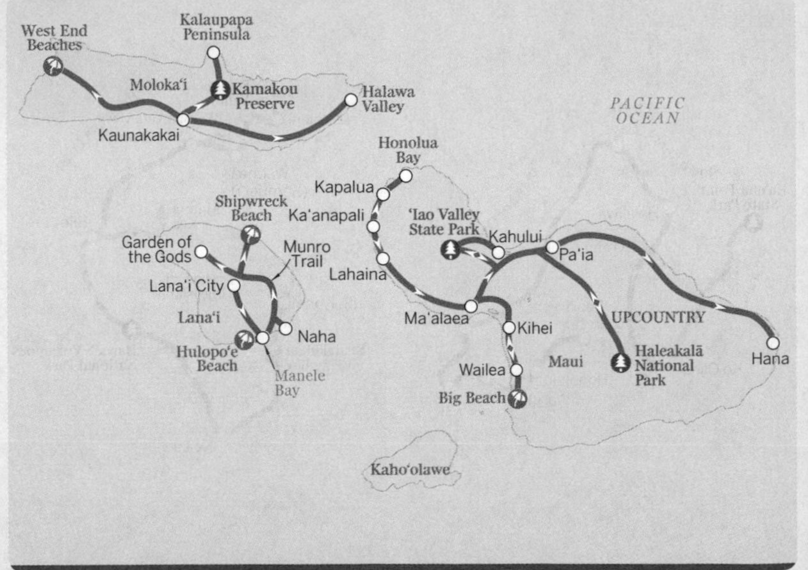
West End Beaches
Kalaupapa Peninsula
Moloka'i
Kamakou Preserve
Halawa Valley
Kaunakakai
PACIFIC OCEAN
Honolua Bay
Kapalua
Shipwreck Beach
Ka'anapali
'Iao Valley State Park
Kahului
Garden of the Gods
Munro Trail
Pa'ia
Lahaina
Lana'i City
Lana'i
Ma'alaea
UPCOUNTRY
Kihei
Naha
Hulopo'e Beach
Manele Bay
Wailea
Maui
Haleakalā National Park
Hana
Big Beach
Kaho'olawe

MONICA & MICHAEL SWEET / GETTY IMAGES ©

VICK JAURON, BABYLON AND BEYOND PHOTOGRAPHY / GETTY IMAGES ©

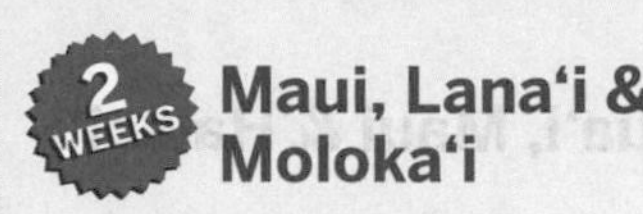

Maui, Lana'i & Moloka'i

You've got time, you've got money and you want outdoor adventures and tranquil relaxation in equal measure. But you're also willing to rough it when the rewards – hidden waterfalls, geological wonders – make it worthwhile. Mix up Maui, Lana'i and Moloka'i for an unforgettable island-hopping journey by airplane and possibly boat.

Spend five or six days on Maui first. Make it easy on yourself by getting a resort hotel room or a condo for your entire stay at **Ka'anapali** or **Kapalua** in West Maui or **Kihei** or **Wailea** in South Maui. Immerse yourself in the whaling history of **Lahaina** or take a whale-watching cruise from **Ma'alaea**. When it's beach time, some of Maui's most untamed coastal spots are nearby, like **Honolua Bay** or **Big Beach**.

Take one full day to hike around the summit of **Haleakalā National Park** and another to lazily drive down the road to **Hana**, stopping off for waterfall hikes and to buy fresh coconuts, before looping back to the laid-back surf town of **Pa'ia**. If you've got time to spare, visit the small farms, botanical gardens and ranches of Maui's Upcountry, where you can take a horse-back ride or go ziplining. Admire the legendary jungle spire at **'Iao Valley State Park** before you head back to the airport at **Kahului**.

Next, hop over to Lana'i and stay three nights at the world-class resort at **Manele Bay**. Things have been a little hectic so far, so laze on the sand before snorkeling at **Hulopo'e Beach**. To really get away from it all, take in the vistas on foot from the **Munro Trail** or rent a 4WD and head for the **Garden of the Gods**, **Shipwreck Beach** or down the dusty track to **Naha**.

Devote your last four or five days to Moloka'i. Check into a condo or beachfront B&B after arriving in small-town **Kaunakakai**. Day one: explore East Moloka'i, checking out waterfalls and heiau ruins in **Halawa Valley**. Day two: trek to the **Kalaupapa Peninsula** and munch macadamia nuts at Purdy's farm. Day three: head out to the remote beaches of the island's **West End** or penetrate the dense forests of the **Kamakou Preserve**. Days four and five: just hang out, blissfully doing nothing much at all.

Top: Humpback whale
Bottom: 'Iao Valley State Park (p360)

2 WEEKS Kaua'i, Maui & Hawai'i

If you want to live in the scenery – not just admire it – take two weeks to discover Kaua'i, Maui and Hawai'i. Find the truly off-the-beaten-track adventures of a lifetime and plenty of traditional and contemporary Hawaiian culture on these 'Neighbor Islands,' each with its own unique flavor.

Kaua'i is Hollywood's ready-made movie set. But these soul-inspiring canyons, cliffs, waterfalls, rivers, bays and beaches are more than just pretty backdrops. Kayak past sacred temples along the **Wailua River**, then glimpse rainy Mt Wai'ale'ale while hiking the rolling **Kuilau Ridge & Moalepe Trails**. Charming **Kapa'a** is worth a wander before bedding down in peaceful **Kilauea**, a jumping-off point to the backwaters of Kaua'i's **North Shore**. Turn around and head down to sunny **Po'ipu** on the South Shore, where the wild Maha'ulepu Coast beckons. Zip west to **Port Allen** and hop aboard a boat bound for the epic sea cliffs of the **Na Pali Coast**.

Hop over to Maui next. North of the old whaling port of **Lahaina**, laze on West Maui's beautiful beaches. Drive north around the peninsula, stopping to snorkel in summer at **Honolua Bay**, then get on the scenic, narrow cliffside Kahekili Hwy. Swing down to South Maui and book a snorkel cruise to **Molokini**, an eroded offshore volcanic crater, or spot migratory whales in winter at **Kihei**. Catch sunset on the beach by **Wailea's** resorts or at all-natural **Makena State Park**. After you ascend to the summit of **Haleakalā National Park** and snake down the Road to **Hana** all the way to the pools of **'Ohe'o Gulch**, find your way back to civilization on the rugged **Pi'ilani Highway**.

Less than a week on the Big Island is barely enough but it'll have to do. Soak up the sunshine north of **Kailua-Kona**, where you can hike or 4WD to gorgeous strands such as Makalawena Beach in **Kekaha Kai State Park**, and plunge into the **Puako Tide Pools** for snorkeling with tropical fish. After you drive past the lava deserts of **Ka'u** and round Hawaii's southernmost tip at **Ka Lae**, dig into **Hawai'i Volcanoes National Park** before losing track of time in the hippie paradise of **Puna**. Finish on top of the highest peak in the Hawaiian Islands, majestic **Mauna Kea**.

HOLGER LEUE / LOOK-FOTO / GETTY IMAGES ©

DEAGOSTINI / GETTY IMAGES ©

Top: Kalalau Trail (p532)
Bottom: 'Ohe'o Gulch (p405)

North Shore
Kilauea
Na Pali Coast
Kapa'a
Kaua'i
Kuilau Ridge & Moalepe Trails
Ni'ihau
Wailua River
Po'ipu Beach
Port Allen
O'ahu
Honolua Bay
Haleakalā National Park
Moloka'i
Lahaina
Maui
Lana'i
Kihei
Hana
'Ohe'o Gulch
Molokini
Pi'ilani Highway
Wailea
Makena State Park
Mauna Kea
Puako Tide Pools
Kekaha Kai State Park
Hawai'i (Big Island)
Kailua-Kona
PACIFIC OCEAN
Puna
Hawai'i Volcanoes National Park
Ka'u
Ka Lae

Hiking the Ka'iwa Ridge (Lanikai Pillboxes) Trail, O'ahu (p140)

Plan Your Trip

Outdoor Activities

Nature has given the Hawaiian Islands such awesome scenery, you could simply do nothing here but lie on your beach towel. But you didn't come all this way merely to rest on your elbows. If you're ready for the outdoor adventure of a lifetime, the real question is – how much time have you got?

DANA EDMUNDS / DESIGN PICS / GETTY IMAGES ©

Best Time for...

Kayaking May–Sep

Snorkeling & Scuba Diving Apr–Oct

Stand-Up Paddleboarding (SUP) Apr–Oct

Surfing Nov–Mar

Swimming Year-round

Whale-Watching Jan–Mar

Windsurfing & Kitesurfing Jun–Aug

Hiking Apr–Sep

Ziplining Year-round

Top Adrenaline-Fueled Sports

Surf the giant waves of Pipeline off O'ahu's North Shore

Kayak past the epic sea cliffs of the Na Pali Coast on Kaua'i

Night dive or snorkel with manta rays on the Kona Coast of Hawai'i, the Big Island

Hike and backpack around Haleakalā's volcanic summit on Maui

Dive into the lava tube and grottoes of the arched Cathedrals on Lana'i

Windsurf Moloka'i's fierce Pailolo and Ka'iwi Channels

Reel in a Pacific blue marlin 'grander' off the Big Island's Kona coast

At Sea

The Pacific Ocean – you probably noticed it on the flight over. Here are all the ways Hawaii lets you play in it.

Beaches & Swimming

When it comes to swimming beaches, your options seem endless in Hawaii. Coastal strands come in a rainbow of hues and an infinite variety of textures – with sand that's a sparkling white, tan, black, charcoal, green or orange, or scattered with sea-glass, pebbles and boulders, and cratered with lava-rock tide pools.

By law, all beaches in Hawaii are open to the public below the high-tide line. Private landowners can prevent access to their shoreline from land, but not by watercraft. Resort hotel beaches provide limited beach-access parking spots for the public, occasionally charging a small fee.

Most of Hawaii's hundreds of state and county beach parks have basic restrooms and outdoor cold-water showers; about half are patrolled by lifeguards. A few parks have gates that close during specified hours or they're signposted as off-limits from sunset until sunrise.

Nudity is legally prohibited on all public beaches in Hawaii. However, at a scant handful of beaches going nude or topless sunbathing by women is grudgingly tolerated. Law enforcement at de facto nude beaches can vary, from absolutely nothing to a stern verbal warning to a written ticket with a mandatory fine and possible court appearance.

Swimming with captive and wild dolphins (p631) is a controversial activity in Hawaii and deserves careful consideration due to safety and animal-welfare concerns.

Best Swimming Spots & Seasons

Water temperatures are idyllic, ranging from 71°F to 83°F year-round. It's almost always possible to find somewhere to swim, no matter what time of year you visit Hawaii: when it's rainy with high surf on one side of any island, it will usually be calm and clear on another. The only island on which swimming isn't great is Moloka'i: incessant winds often make ocean waters too rough year-round.

Each island has four distinct coastal areas – the north shore, south shore, leeward (west) coast and windward (east) coast – each with its own peculiar weather and water conditions. As a rule, the best places to swim in the winter are along the south shores, and in summer, along the north shores. Keep this in mind when deciding where to book your accommodations.

Ocean Safety Tips

Never turn your back on the ocean. Waves and water conditions can change abruptly, so pay attention and don't swim alone. Drowning is the leading cause of accidental death for tourists. To check on current beach hazard warnings, visit http://hawaii beachsafety.com.

Rogue waves All waves are not the same. They often come in sets: some bigger, some smaller. Sometimes one really big 'rogue wave' sweeps in and literally catches sunbathers napping.

Shore breaks Waves breaking close to shore are called shore breaks. Smaller sandy ones are great for bodysurfing. Large shore breaks, though, can slam down hard enough to knock you out.

Undertows Particularly on sloped beaches, undertows occur when large waves wash back directly into incoming surf. If one pulls you under the water, don't panic. Go with the current until you get beyond the wave.

Rip currents These fast-flowing ocean currents can drag swimmers out into deeper water. Anyone caught in a rip should either go with the flow until it loses power or swim parallel to shore to slip out of it.

Tsunami (p643) Infrequent but deadly natural disaster. If you hear the warning siren, head for higher ground immediately.

Bodysurfing & Bodyboarding

Sure, you might not be able to bodysurf like a ballet dancer, but anybody can give it a go and have some fun with it. Bodysurfing doesn't require any special equipment, and once you've found the groove for catching waves, it's good times ahead. Bodyboarding is even easier than bodysurfing, because you've got a three-foot-long piece of foam to hang on to. Some bodyboarders and bodysurfers wear webbed gloves and flipper-like fins to help propel themselves.

Except in the gnarliest or calmest surf, you can bodysurf or bodyboard on almost any beach. Ideal locations are beaches with sandy shorebreaks where the inevitable wipeouts will be less painful and/or dangerous. If you're new to either bodysurfing or bodyboarding, don't underestimate small-looking waves, because they can roll you just like intimidating five-footers.

Bodyboarder on the Pacific shore

DON'T GET STUNG!

Stings from jellyfish and Portuguese man-of-war (aka bluebottles) occur in Hawaii's tropical waters. Even touching a bluebottle hours after it has washed up onshore can result in burning stings. Jellyfish are often seen seven to 10 days after a full moon, when they float into Hawaii's shallow near-shore waters, especially on O'ahu at Waikiki. When this happens, some public beaches may be closed for safety. Check for current alerts: http://hawaiibeachsafety.com.

Best for Bodysurfing & Bodyboarding

O'ahu	Sandy Beach Park (p133)
	Makapu'u Beach Park (p134)
	Kapahulu Groin (Kuhio Beach Park; p111)
Hawai'i (Big Island)	White (Magic) Sands Beach (p179)
	Hapuna Beach State Recreation Area (p230)
Maui	Big Beach (Makena State Park; p380)
	DT Fleming Beach Park (p344)
	Slaughterhouse Beach (p344)
Kaua'i	Brennecke's Beach (p538)

Diving

Hawaii's underwater scenery is the equal of what's on land. Dive shipwrecks and 100ft-long lava tubes, listen to whales singing and go swim with sharks and manta rays.

Bodyboarding off Hawaii's coast

Ocean temperatures are perfect for scuba diving, averaging 71°F to 83°F at the surface year-round. Even better is the visibility, which is usually ideal for seeing the plethora of fish, coral and other sea creatures. November through March aren't the best months for diving, as winter brings rougher seas and higher waves to Hawaii.

Dive costs in Hawaii range widely depending on gear, dive length, location (especially shore versus boat dives) and so on. The average price for two-tank boat dives including all gear rental is $135 to $180. Remember to bring your dive certification card from home.

Some dive operators offer a beginners 'discover scuba' option, which includes brief instruction, and possibly swimming-pool practice, followed by a shallow beach or boat dive. No previous experience is necessary, but you must be a strong swimmer. These introductory dives generally cost $110 to $200, depending on your location and whether or not a boat is used.

If you don't already know how to dive, Hawaii is a great place to learn. **PADI** (Professional Association of Diving Instructors; www.padi.com) open-water certification courses can be completed in as few as three days, usually costing from $450 to $600 per person. Book classes ahead of your trip.

Best Scuba Diving Sites

O'ahu	Hanauma Bay (p132)
	Three Tables & Sharks Cove (Pupukea Beach Park; p154)
	Sunken ship & airplane wreck dives
Hawai'i (Big Island)	Off the Kona coast (p179)
	Night dives with manta rays
Maui	Offshore Molokini Crater (p365)
	Makena Landing (p379)
Lana'i	Cathedrals (p431; Manele Bay)
Moloka'i	Pala'au barrier reef (p459)
Kaua'i	South Shore (p534)
	Makua (Tunnels) Beach (p528)
	Neighboring Ni'ihau Island (p564)
Papahānaumokuākea Marine National Monument	Midway Atoll (p549)

DAVID FLEETHAM / GETTY IMAGES ©

Diving with a whitetip reef shark

To find more dive spots, pick up Lonely Planet's *Diving & Snorkeling Hawaii* or a waterproof, rip-proof *Franko's Dive Map* (http://frankosmaps.com), sold at island convenience shops, outdoor outfitters and bookstores.

Dive Safety Tips

➡ Ensure your travel medical kit contains treatment for coral cuts and tropical ear infections, as well as the standard problems.

➡ Have a dive medical before you leave your home country – local dive operators may not always ask about medical conditions that are incompatible with diving.

➡ Check that your travel and/or health insurance covers decompression illness, or get specialized dive insurance through the **Divers Alert Network** (DAN; www.diversalertnetwork.org).

➡ Don't go for a helicopter or plane ride or ascend to high altitudes on Hawaii's volcanoes (eg Haleakalā on Maui, Mauna Kea or Mauna Loa on the Big Island) for at least 24 hours before or after scuba diving.

Fishing

The sea has always been Hawaii's breadbasket. You'll see locals casting from shore, and no fishing license is required to join them (only freshwater or commercial fishing requires licensing). However, statewide regulations still govern exactly what you can catch and when. For details, check with Hawaii's **Division of Aquatic Resources** (http://dlnr.hawaii.gov/dar).

Most visiting anglers are more interested in deep-sea sportfishing for legendary quarry such as ahi (yellowfin tuna), swordfish, spearfish, mahimahi (dolphinfish) and, most famous of all, Pacific blue marlin, which can reach 1000lb ('granders'). Hawaii has some of the world's best sportfishing, chiefly off the Big Island's Kona coast, as well as at Penguin Banks off Moloka'i and all around Kaua'i. Expect to pay between $150 and $250 per person on a shared charter boat, or around $400 to $600 for a four-hour private charter trip for up to six people.

Kayaking

River kayaking is only possible on Kaua'i, but sea kayakers will find heavenly bits of coastline and offshore islets beckoning across the archipelago. Indeed, there are many beaches, bays and valleys that can be reached in no other way but from the open ocean. If it's your first time out, consider taking a guided kayaking tour (from $50), which usually includes some basic paddling instruction. DIY kayak rentals are available near popular put-ins, typically for $40 to $70 per day.

Best Places to Kayak

O'ahu	Kailua Beach Park (p140)
Hawai'i (Big Island)	Kealakekua Bay (p208)
	Puako (p229)
Maui	Makena Bay (p379)
	Honolua Bay (p344)
Moloka'i	Pali Coast (p456)
	South Shore (p439)
Kaua'i	Na Pali Coast (p531)
	Wailua River (p490)
	Hanalei River (p517)

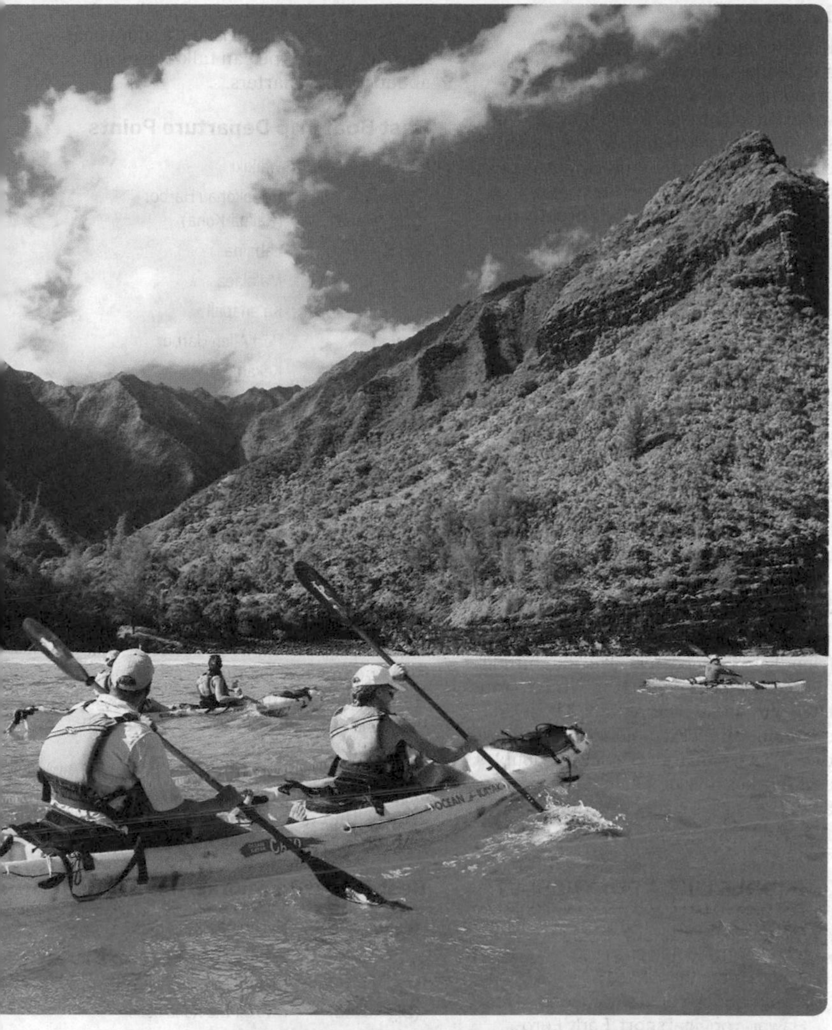

Top & Bottom: Kayaking the Na Pali Coast (p530)

DANITA DELIMONT / GETTY IMAGES ©

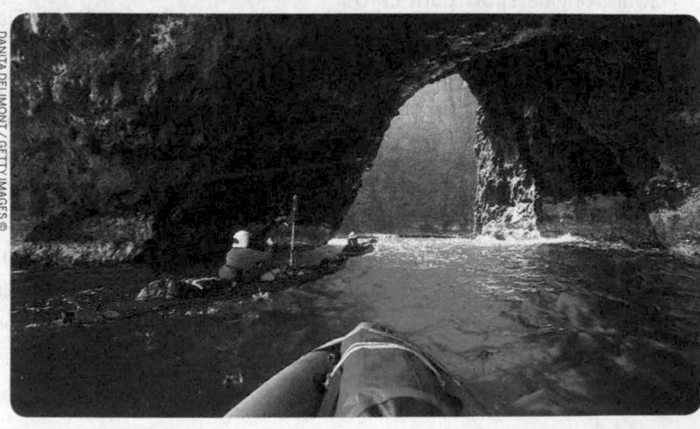

Kitesurfing

Kitesurfing, also called kiteboarding, is a little like strapping on a snowboard, grabbing a parachute and sailing over the water. If you already know how to windsurf, surf or wakeboard, there's a good chance you'll master it quickly. Any place that's good for windsurfing is also good for kitesurfing. The best winds usually blow in summer, but they vary depending on where you are on each island.

Maui dominates the attention of kitesurfers, aspiring or otherwise. Near Kahului's airport, windsurfing shops offer rentals and instruction at Kite Beach (Kanaha Beach Park (p351)), while experts brave Ho'okipa Beach Park (p383) in Pa'ia (during kiteboarding contests only). O'ahu's Kailua Beach Park (p140) is a great place to learn. On Kaua'i, 'Anini Beach Park (p510) and Kawailoa Bay (p539) are popular, while windy Moloka'i calls to pros – bring your own rigging.

Sailing

The mighty Pacific is no Caribbean Sea, friendly to bare boaters. The magnitude of the waves, particularly in winter, translates into no sailboat rentals. The most common sailing excursion in Hawaii is a two-fer: a catamaran cruise that doubles as a snorkel, dive or whale-watching tour. Sometimes passengers who don't snorkel or dive can pay a reduced ride-along fare. Tours leave from each island's small boat harbors, where you can talk to captains about private charters.

PADDLE LIKE A POLYNESIAN

Hawai'i was settled by ancient Polynesians who paddled outrigger canoes across more than 2000 miles of open ocean, so you could say canoeing was Hawaii's original sport. Early European explorers were awestruck at the skill Hawaiians displayed in their canoes – timing launches and landings perfectly, and paddling among the waves with the graceful agility of dolphins. Today traditional Hawaiian outrigger canoe clubs still race throughout the islands. The most impressive long-distance events happen in fall, starting with the Queen Lili'uokalani Canoe Race on the Big Island's Kona coast, followed by men's and women's races across the Ka'iwi Channel from Moloka'i all the way to O'ahu.

Best Boat Trip Departure Points

O'ahu	Waikiki
Hawai'i (Big Island)	Honokohau Harbor (Kailua-Kona)
Maui	Lahaina
	Ma'alaea
	Ka'anapali
Kaua'i	Port Allen Harbor
	Kekaha
	Nawiliwili Harbor (Lihu'e)

Snorkeling

Coming to Hawaii and not snorkeling is like climbing the Eiffel Tower and closing your eyes – the most bright and beautiful underwater city in the world lies at your feet and, if you can swim, Hawaii's magnificent coral reefs are yours. In addition to more than 500 species of often neon-colored tropical fish, endangered sea turtles are sometimes spotted, and you may see manta rays, spinner dolphins, jacks, sharks and other impressive predators.

Every island has fantastic shoreline snorkeling spots, in addition to snorkel cruises that deliver you to places you can't swim to.

Best Places to Snorkel

O'ahu	Hanauma Bay (p132)
	Pupukea Beach Park (p154)
Hawai'i (Big Island)	Night snorkeling with manta rays off the Kona coast
	Kapoho Tide Pools (p285)
	Two-Step (p214)
Maui	Molokini Crater (p365)
	Malu'aka Beach (p380)
	Honolua Bay (p344)
	Pu'u Keka'a (Black Rock; p336)
Lana'i	Hulopo'e Beach (p430)
Moloka'i	Dixie Maru Beach (p468)
	Twenty Mile Beach (p454)
Kaua'i	South Shore
	Makua (Tunnels) Beach (p528)

Snorkeling, Kealakekua (p205)

Snorkel Rental & Safety Tips

➡ Gear rental – including snorkel, mask, fins and usually a bag to carry them in – starts at as little as $6 a day or $20 per week. Quality gear costs more.

➡ It may be a worthwhile investment to bring or buy your own high-quality mask, if you plan on snorkeling more than once or twice.

➡ As a rule, snorkel early – morning conditions are often best, and if everyone else is sleeping, they won't be crowding the water and kicking up sand to mar visibility.

➡ Snorkelers often forget – whoops! – about putting sunblock on their back (or wearing a T-shirt) and, more importantly, watching the waves.

➡ Follow coral-reef etiquette: don't touch any corals, which are living organisms; watch your fins to avoid stirring up sand and breaking off pieces of coral; and finally, don't feed the fish.

Helpful Resources for Snorkelers

There are myriad marine life and snorkel guides to Hawaii but photographer John Hoover publishes some great ones. Snorkelers can pick up *Hawaii's Fishes* or the *Pocket Guide to Hawaii's Underwater Paradise,* while tide-pool enthusiasts might grab *Hawaii's Sea Creatures.* Hoover's *Ultimate Guide to Hawaiian Reef Fishes, Sea Turtles, Dolphins, Whales and Seals* covers everything. Island-hoppers can peruse Lonely Planet's *Diving & Snorkeling Hawaii.*

Stand-Up Paddleboarding (SUP)

Not quite ready to pop a stance on a surfboard? No worries. The latest trend is stand-up paddleboarding (SUP) – which, as the name implies, means standing on the surfboard and using a paddle to propel yourself along flat water or waves. It takes coordination to learn, but it's a lot easier than regular surfing.

For safety, always paddle with a buddy and use a leash. Carry enough water and a whistle or a cellphone in a waterproof case for emergencies. Don't forget about sun protection, including sunblock, sunglasses, a hat and a rash guard (surf shirt).

You'll see SUP fans paddling on all the main islands, anywhere from ocean beaches and calm bays to flat-water rivers, the latter on Kaua'i. Some outdoor outfitters specialize in SUP, offering instruction (two-hour lessons average $60 to $80), rentals (from $45 to $75 per day) and occasionally guided tours (from $120). Otherwise, ask at local surf shops and surf schools about SUP rentals and lessons.

Surfing

Ancient Hawaiians invented surfing (calling it *he'e nalu,* 'wave sliding'). In Hawaii today surfing is both its own intense subculture as well as a part of everyday island life. Hawaii's biggest waves roll in to the north shores of the islands from November through March. Summer swells, which break along the south shores, are smaller and more infrequent.

With its overwhelming variety and abundance of surf spots, O'ahu is where all the major pro surfing competitions happen; its North Shore is home to surfing's Triple Crown, which draws thousands of roadside spectators every November and December. All of the main islands have good, even great surfing breaks. Surf lessons and board rentals are available at just about every tourist beach that has rideable waves.

Surf Etiquette

As a visitor in Hawaii, there are some places you go, and some places you don't. Locals are usually willing to share surf spots that have become popular tourist destinations but they reserve the right to protect other 'secret' surf grounds. As a newbie in the lineup, don't expect to get every wave that comes your way. There's a definite pecking order and, frankly, tourists are at the bottom. That being said, usually if you give a wave, you'll get a wave in return. Be generous in the water, understand your place and surf with a smile. At famous breaks where surfers can be ferociously territorial, such as O'ahu's Banzai Pipeline, ask a local for an introduction.

BEST SURF BEACHES & BREAKS

- ➡ O'ahu (p157)
- ➡ Hawai'i, the Big Island (p209)
- ➡ Maui (p323)
- ➡ Lana'i (p431)
- ➡ Moloka'i (p467)
- ➡ Kaua'i (p475)

Windsurfing, Kihei (p366)

Helpful Resources for Surfers

Surf News Network (☎Kaua'i 808-241-7873, Maui 808-572-7873, O'ahu 808-596-7873; www.surfnewsnetwork.com) Comprehensive island weather-and-wave reports online or by phone.

Surfrider Foundation (www.surfrider.org) Nonprofit organization that helps protect the ocean and Hawaii's beaches and coastline.

Whale-Watching

Each winter about 10,000 North Pacific humpback whales migrate to the shallow coastal waters off the Hawaiian Islands to breed, calve and nurse, protected by the **Hawaiian Islands Humpback Whale National Marine Sanctuary** (http://hawaiihumpbackwhale.noaa.gov). Whale-watching cruises are a hot-ticket item, especially during the peak migration season (January through March). Maui's western coastline, Lana'i's eastern shore and Moloka'i's south shore are the whales' biggest birthing and nursing grounds, but the Big Island's west coast and Kaua'i's southern and northern

Surfing, Honolua Bay (p344)

shores also see activity, including the acrobatic breaching displays for which humpbacks are famous. The main islands offer whale-watching tours and have areas where you can spot whales from shore, including from Maui's sanctuary headquarters (p366) in Kihei.

Windsurfing

With warm waters and steady winds, Hawaii ranks as one of the world's premier spots for windsurfing. Generally, the best winds blow from June through September, but trade winds will keep windsurfers – somewhere, at least – happy all year.

As O'ahu's North Shore is to surfing, so Maui's Ho'okipa Beach (p383) is to windsurfing: a dangerous, fast arena where the top international windsurfing competitions sort out who's best. The other islands have windsurfing, but they don't reach Maui's pinnacle. Only Moloka'i, bracketed by wind-whipped ocean channels, provides an equivalent challenge for experts.

Mere mortals might prefer windsurfing Maui's Kanaha Beach (p351) or Ma'alaea Bay (p364). If you're looking to learn, O'ahu's Kailua Beach (p140) is consistently windy year-round and home to top-notch schools. Other windsurfing spots on O'ahu include Diamond Head, Fort DeRussy Beach (p111) in Waikiki and the North Shore's Backyards (p154) and Malaekahana State Recreation Area (p151). Kaua'i has only one prime spot for windsurfers: 'Anini Beach (p510). On the Big Island, check out 'Anaeho'omalu Beach (p223). Bring your own gear to windsurf Kaua'i's rugged Kawailoa Bay (p539) or Moloka'i's challenging Pailolo and Ka'iwi Channels.

On Land

As Hawaii's volcanoes rose above the ocean's surface, they evolved into one of the planet's richest and most varied ecosystems – no wonder some call it paradise.

Caving

Funny thing, lava. As the top of a flow cools and hardens, the molten rock beneath keeps moving. When the eruption stops and the lava drains, what's left behind is an underground maze of tunnels

AARON BLACK / GETTY IMAGES ©

Paragliding, Makapu'u Point (p467)

like some colossal ant farm. Many of these lava tubes are cultural as well as ecological wonders, since ancient Hawaiians used them as burial chambers, water caches, temporary housing and more.

Being the youngest island and still volcanically active, Hawai'i (Big Island) is a caving hot spot, with six of the world's 10 longest lava tubes. Ka'u's Kanohina cave system, managed by the **Cave Conservancy of Hawai'i** (www.hawaiicaves.org), has 35 miles of complex tunnels – take a peek at Kula Kai Caverns (p310). Kea'au's Kazumura Cave (p281) is even longer.

Other islands have fewer caving opportunities. Maui's Hana Lava Tube (p411), also called Ka'eleku Caverns, is a short cave system that even kids can explore.

Cycling & Mountain Biking

Quality trumps quantity when it comes to cycling and mountain biking in Hawaii. Cyclists will find the most bike-friendly roads and organizational support on O'ahu, but all of the main islands offer bicycle rentals, as well as trails and 4WD roads that double as two-wheel, pedal-powered adventures.

Best Places to Ride & Race

O'ahu	Ka'ena Point Trail (p171)
	Kuaokala Trail (p171)
	Maunawili Falls Trail (p135)
Hawai'i (Big Island)	Ironman Triathlon World Championship (p187)
	Kalopa State Recreation Area (p264)
	Chain of Craters Road
Maui	Haleakalā Crater Rd
	Skyline Trail (p402; temporarily closed)
	Makawao Forest Reserve Trails (p390)
Lana'i	Munro Trail (p430)
Moloka'i	Moloka'i Forest Reserve & Kamakou Preserve (p457)
Kaua'i	Hwy 550 (Waimea Canyon Dr/ Koke'e Rd; p568)
	Powerline Trail (p513)

Helpful Resources for Cyclists

➡ Check the **Hawaii Bicycling League** (www.hbl.org) website to find local bike shops, group rides and races, as well as links to cycling maps, regulations and safety tips.

➡ Mountain bikers can find out about island trails, volunteer opportunities and special events with **Mountain Bike Hawaii** (www.mtbhawaii.com), an O'ahu-based advocacy group.

Golf

Golfing is as popular with locals as with the PGA Tour, which always finds some excuse to visit Hawaii. Beach resorts host some of the most lauded, challenging and beautiful courses. While playing on one of these elite championship courses can easily cost more than $200 a round, Hawaii has dozens of well-loved, much more affordable municipal courses boasting scenery you probably can't get back home. Afternoon 'twilight' tee times are usually discounted. Club and shoe rentals are often available.

For discounts at privately owned courses and country clubs that are open to the public, visit **Hawaii Tee Times** (http://hawaiiteetimes.com).

Top: Manele Golf Course (p431)

Bottom: Mountain bikers in Waimea Canyon (p568)

MARK A JOHNSON / GETTY IMAGES ©

ANCIENT HAWAII'S EXTREME SPORTS

Never let it be said that ancient Hawaiians didn't know how to play. Every male ruler had to prove his prowess in sports – to demonstrate *mana* (spiritual essence) – and the greater the danger, the better. No contest topped the *holua* – an ancient sled just a little wider than a book, on which Hawaiians raced down mountains at speeds of up to 50mph. Not every sport was potentially deadly, though many involved gambling – like foot and canoe racing, wrestling and *'ulu maika* (stone bowling). Annual makahiki harvest celebrations featured four months of feasting, hula dancing, religious ceremonies and sports competitions.

Hang Gliding & Paragliding

Remove the engine and flying becomes an ecofriendly adrenaline rush. On O'ahu, glider rides (and skydiving) are offered at the North Shore's Dillingham Airfield (p163). On Maui, take a tandem paraglider ride on the slopes of Haleakalā volcano starting from Kula (p394) or Hana (p416).

Helicopter & Airplane Tours

Far and away the most popular places to visit by air are Kaua'i's remote Na Pali Coast (p514) and the Big Island's active volcanic zone. Flying over these areas provides unforgettable vantages and experiences you simply can't get any other way. Helicopter tours are also a popular way to see Maui, where some air tours include a jaunt over to Moloka'i's towering Pali Coast.

That said, helicopter and airplane tours negatively impact Hawaii's environment, both in noise generated and fuel burned.

Hiking & Backpacking

Hikers will find that, mile for mile, these tiny islands almost cannot be topped for heart-stopping vistas and soulful beauty. Being small, even the most rugged spots are usually accessible as day hikes. Backpacking is rarely necessary, though when it is, the rewards so outstrip the effort it's almost ludicrous. Start exploring Hawaii's public trails through **Na Ala Hele** (http://hawaiitrails.ehawaii.gov).

Trespassing on private land or government land not intended for public use is illegal, no matter how many people you see doing it. Show respect for all 'Kapu' or 'No Trespassing' signs – not just for legal reasons, but also for your own safety.

Best Islands for Hiking

For variety, **Hawai'i (Big Island)** wins by a nose. Hawai'i Volcanoes National Park contains an erupting volcano, plus steaming craters, lava deserts and rainforests. Then there are the two nearly 14,000ft mountains to scale – Mauna Loa and Mauna Kea.

On **Maui**, Haleakalā National Park provides awe-inspiring descents across the volcanic summit's eroded moonscape, while the Road to Hana tempts with short excursion hikes to waterfalls.

The legendary Kalalau Trail on **Kaua'i's** Na Pali Coast edges spectacularly fluted sea cliffs. An abundance of paths crisscross clifftop Koke'e State Park and cavernous Waimea Canyon.

On **O'ahu**, you can escape Honolulu in a hurry in the forests of the Manoa and Makiki Valleys around Mt Tantalus or lose the crowds entirely at Ka'ena Point.

Best Day Hikes with Views

O'ahu	Ka'ena Point Trail (p171)
	Kuli'ou'ou Ridge Trail (p131)
Hawai'i (Big Island)	Kilauea Iki Trail (p296)
	Pololu Valley Trail (p243)
Maui	Keonehe'ehe'e (Sliding Sands) Trail (p400)
	Halemau'u Trail (p400)
	Pipiwai Trail (p405)
	Waihe'e Ridge Trail (p350)
Lanai	Koloiki Ridge Trail (p426)
Moloka'i	Kalaupapa Trail (p461)
	Halawa Valley (p456)
Kaua'i	Cliff & Canyon Trails (p572)
	Ke'e Beach to Hanakapi'ai Beach (p533)
	Awa'awapuhi & Nu'alolo Trails (p572)

Horseback riding outside Po'ipu (p537)

Best Backcountry Hikes & Backpacking Treks

Hawai'i (Big Island)	Mauna Loa Trail (p298)
	Humu'ula–Mauna Kea Summit Trail (p252)
	Muliwai Trail (p261)
Maui	Kaupo Trail (p401)
Lana'i	Munro Trail (p430)
Moloka'i	Pepe'opae Trail (p457)
Kaua'i	Kalalau Trail (p532)

Hiking Safety Tips

➡ A hat, sunscreen and lots of water are always mandatory. Coastal trails can bake you to a crisp and cause heat exhaustion or life-threatening heatstroke, especially when walking across sun-reflective lava.

➡ If you're looking to spend hours (or days) on the trail, bring hiking boots and rainproof clothing – weather is changeable, and trails can be rocky, uneven and muddy.

➡ If you'll be tackling a mountain summit, carry a fleece or down jacket (even in summer).

➡ Always bring a flashlight. In the middle of the ocean it gets dark fast after sunset, and trails can take longer than expected to finish due to the uneven terrain or accidentally getting lost.

➡ All freshwater – whether flowing or from a pond – must be treated before drinking to avoid giardiasis (p638) and leptospirosis (p638).

➡ Depending on the hike, potential environmental hazards range from vog (p638) to flash floods and waterfalls, which are not always safe for swimming.

Horseback Riding

All of the main islands have ranches for memorable horseback rides. But the Big Island and Maui have the richest living *paniolo* (Hawaiian cowboy) culture and the most extensive riding opportunities. On Moloka'i, saddle up a mule for the switchbacking trail down the sea cliffs to the Kalaupapa Peninsula.

Running

Hawaii's scenery enhances almost any sport, and running is no exception.

Best Races & Fun Runs

Honolulu Marathon (p115) On O'ahu.

Volcano Rain Forest Runs (p302) On the Big Island.

Maui Marathon (www.mauimarathonhawaii.com; ⊙mid-Sep)

Kaua'i Marathon (www.thekauaimarathon.com; ⊙early Sep)

Best Triathlons

Ironman Triathlon World Championship (p187) On the Big Island's Kona coast; it's one of sport's ultimate endurance contests.

Ironman 70.3 Hawaii (www.ironman703hawaii.com; ⊙May/Jun) Half an Ironman in late May or early June on the Big Island's Kohala coast.

Tinman Hawaii Triathlon (www.tinmanhawaii.com; ⊙late Jul) At Waikiki on O'ahu.

Xterra World Championship (p347) Maui's off-road triathlon.

Helicopter tour, Na Pali Coast (p531)

Stargazing

Astronomers are drawn to Hawaii's night sky the way surfers are drawn to the islands' big waves. The view from Mauna Kea volcano on Hawai'i, the Big Island, is unmatched in clarity. Mauna Kea has more astronomical observatories than any mountain on earth. On Mauna Kea's summit road, the visitor information station (p250) hosts free public stargazing programs nightly (weather permitting). During the daytime, catch a family-friendly planetarium show at Hilo's educational 'Imiloa Astronomy Center (p270), also on the Big Island, or at Honolulu's Bishop Museum (p82) on O'ahu.

Astronomical observatories at Science City (p399) on Maui's Haleakalā volcano study the sun, not the stars, and they aren't open to the public. Haleakalā National Park rangers occasionally lead free stargazing programs, usually on summer weekends. Top-end resort hotels, especially on Maui and the Big Island, occasionally offer stargazing programs for guests that use high-quality telescopes.

Tennis

If you've brought your own racket and balls, you can use them at free public tennis courts in bigger island towns and cities. Upscale resorts really pull out the stops, and at many of these you'll find immaculate tennis courts, sometimes with pro shops, round-robin tournaments and partner-matching. Resorts and hotels typically reserve their courts for guests only, but may allow nonguests to rent equipment and court time.

Ziplining

This outdoor-activity fad has grown enormously popular in Hawaii. It's a thrilling ride among the treetops that was first developed as a tourist adventure in Costa Rica's rainforest canopy and is infiltrating jungles everywhere. The only skill required is the ability to hang on (including to your lunch), although riders must also meet minimum-age and maximum-weight requirements. Kaua'i, Maui, O'ahu and the Big Island all offer zipline thrills.

Plan Your Trip

Travel with Children

With its phenomenal natural beauty, Hawaii always appeals to families. Instead of hanging out in shopping malls, kids can play on sandy beaches galore, snorkel amid colorful tropical fish and even watch lava flow. You can then get them out of the sun for a spell by visiting museums, aquariums and historical attractions.

Hawaii for Kids

There's not too much to worry about when visiting Hawaii with kids, as long as you keep them covered in sunblock. Here, coastal temperatures rarely drop below 65°F and driving distances are relatively short. Just don't try to do or see too much, especially not if it's your first trip to Hawaii. Slow down and hang loose!

Eating Out & Entertainment

Hawaii is a family-oriented and unfussy place, so most restaurants welcome children; notable exceptions are some high-end resort dining rooms. Children's menus, booster seats and high chairs are usually available everywhere – but if it's a necessity at every meal, bring a collapsible seat.

If restaurant dining is inconvenient, no problem. Eating outdoors at a beach park is among the simplest and best island pleasures. Pack finger foods for a picnic, pick up fruit from farmers markets, stop for smoothies at roadside stands and order plate lunches at drive-in counters.

Grocery and convenience stores stock national brands. A kid who eats nothing but Cheerios will not go hungry here. But the local diet, with its variety of cuisines,

Best Islands for Kids

O'ahu

Waikiki Beach is stuffed full of family-friendly accommodations. Everything else on the island is less than a half-day's drive away, from hiking Diamond Head to snorkeling at Hanauma Bay to Matsumoto's shave ice on the North Shore.

Maui

Rent a family-sized condo and chill on Maui's sunny leeward shores. Kids' eyes will pop on a winter whale-watching cruise or when your family catches the sunrise high atop Haleakalā volcano.

Kaua'i

Baby beaches allow the pint-sized to get wet, and older kids can learn to surf. Be sure to peer into the 'Grand Canyon of the Pacific' and at the stunning sea cliffs of the Na Pali Coast before you leave.

Hawai'i, the Big Island

Horseback riding like a *paniolo* (Hawaiian cowboy), ziplining through forests and maybe even seeing red-hot lava flow are just a few of Hawai'i's unforgettable experiences for kids.

brightly colored fruit and plethora of sweet treats, may tempt kids away from mainland habits. Breastfeeding is usually done discreetly.

Commercial luau might seem like cheesy Vegas dinner shows to adults, but many kids love the flashy dances and fire tricks. Children typically get discounted tickets (and will sometimes get free admission when accompanied by a paying adult).

If parents need a night out to themselves, the easiest and most reliable way to find a babysitter is to ask a hotel concierge. Otherwise, contact **Nannies Hawaii** (808-754-4931; http://nannieshawaii.com).

Children's Highlights

Restaurants, hotels and attractions that especially welcome children and have good facilities for families are marked with the family-friendly icon throughout this guide.

Beaches

- **Kuhio Beach** (p111) Sand, surf and outrigger canoe rides at Waikiki.
- **Ko Olina Lagoons** (off Ali'inui Dr, Kapolei) Artificial pools for splashing around on O'ahu.
- **'Anaeho'omalu Beach** (p223) Sunsets on the Big Island's Kohala coast.
- **Wailea Beach** (p375) South Maui's gentlest crescent-shaped strand.
- **Baby Beach** (p539) Kaua'i's shallow South Shore waters beckon.

Water Adventures

- **Hanauma Bay** (p132) Snorkel in a giant outdoor fishbowl on O'ahu.
- **Ma'alaea Bay** (p632) Winter whale-watching cruises with Maui's Pacific Whale Foundation.
- **Hulopo'e Beach** (p430) Snorkeling and sailing in Lana'i's Manele Bay.
- **Na Pali Coast** (p552) Ride a catamaran sailboat to see Kaua'i's tallest sea cliffs.
- **Kailua-Kona** (p184) Take older kids snorkeling at night with manta rays on Hawai'i, the Big Island.

IS YOUR CHILD OLD ENOUGH?

Parents will find plenty of outdoor family fun for all ages on the bigger islands. However, some activities require that children be of a certain age, height or weight to participate. Always ask about restrictions when making reservations to avoid disappointment – and tears.

To learn to surf Kids who can swim comfortably in the ocean are candidates for lessons. Teens can usually join group lessons; younger kids may be required to take private lessons.

To take a snorkel cruise Depending on the outfit and type of boat (eg catamaran, raft), tours sometimes set minimum ages, usually from five to eight years. Larger boats might allow tots as young as two to ride along.

To go ziplining Minimum age requirements range from five to 12 years, depending on the company. Participants must also meet weight minimums (usually 50lb to 80lb).

To ride a horse For trail rides the minimum age ranges from seven to 10 years, depending on the outfitter. It helps if your child already has some riding experience. Short pony rides may be offered to younger kids.

To ride in a helicopter Most tour companies set minimum ages (eg two to 12 years) and some also set minimum body weights (eg 35lb). Toddlers must be strapped into their own seat and pay the full fare.

Aquariums, Zoos & Farms

➡ **Maui Ocean Center** (p364) USA's largest tropical aquarium has special kid-sized viewing ports.

➡ **Waikiki Aquarium** (p108) University-run aquarium sits beside O'ahu's most popular beach.

➡ **Ocean Rider Seahorse Farm** (☎808-329-6840; www.seahorse.com; 73-4388 Ilikai Place; tours adult/child 4-9yr $36/26; ⏱gift shop 9:30am-3:30pm, tours noon & 2pm Mon-Fri, also 10am Mon-Fri late Dec-Apr & Jun-late Aug; 👪) Unique family-friendly tour spot on Hawai'i, the Big Island.

➡ **Pana'ewa Rainforest Zoo & Gardens** (p272) Free kiddie zoo with walking trails, outside Hilo on Hawai'i, the Big Island.

➡ **Surfing Goat Dairy** (p393) Take a tour and pet the goats, or join in evening chores and milking duties, on Maui.

Hiking

➡ **Manoa Falls** (p85) O'ahu's family-favorite forest hike climbs above downtown Honolulu.

➡ **Diamond Head** (p130) Summit an extinct volcanic tuff cone outside Waikiki, on O'ahu.

➡ **Hawai'i Volcanoes National Park** (p289) Trek the Big Island's active volcanic moonscape or crawl through a lava tube.

➡ **Haleakalā National Park** (p397) Step onto Maui's biggest volcano above the clouds and through a bamboo forest by waterfall pools.

➡ **Waimea Canyon State Park** (p568) **& Koke'e State Park** (p570) Dizzying clifftop lookouts, native birds and flora await on Kaua'i's Westside.

Land Adventures

➡ **Kualoa Ranch** (p147) Movie and TV set tours and horseback trail rides on O'ahu's Windward Coast.

➡ **Pi'iholo Ranch** (p391) Maui's biggest zipline adventure on the slopes of Haleakalā volcano.

➡ **Dahana Ranch** (p245) Genuine *paniolo* (Hawaiian cowboy) trail rides on Hawai'i, the Big Island.

➡ **Silver Falls Ranch** (p511) Ride horseback to a hidden valley waterfall on Kaua'i.

HELPFUL BOOKS & WEBSITES

Travel with Children (Lonely Planet) Loaded with valuable tips and amusing tales, especially for first-time parents.

Lonelyplanet.com Ask questions and get advice from other travelers in the Thorn Tree's online 'Kids to Go' and 'USA' forums.

Go Hawaii (www.gohawaii.com) The state's official tourism site lists family-friendly activities, special events and more – easily search the site using terms such as 'kids' or 'family'.

Cultural & Historical Sites

➡ **Waimea Valley** (p157) Botanical gardens, archaeological sites and waterfall swimming on O'ahu's North shore, with poi-pounding, lei-making and hula-dancing lessons too.

➡ **Old Lahaina Luau** (p328) Hawaii's most authentic, aloha-filled luau comes with music, dancing and an *imu*-cooked whole roasted pig, on Maui.

➡ **Pearl Harbor** (p102) Squeeze inside a WWII-era submarine; pace a battleship's decks; or become a virtual-reality pilot, on O'ahu.

➡ **Kamokila Hawaiian Village** (p489) Outrigger canoe rides, traditional craft demonstrations and replicas of ancient Hawaiian houses, on Kaua'i.

➡ **Hawai'i Volcanoes National Park** (p289) Hike to petroglyph fields or watch traditional and sacred *hula kahiko* dancing and chanting on Hawai'i (Big Island).

Museums

➡ **Bishop Museum** (p82) Polynesian war clubs, feathered masks, an exploding faux-volcano and eye-opening planetarium sky shows in Honolulu, on O'ahu.

➡ **'Imiloa Astronomy Center of Hawai'i** (p270) Hands-on multimedia astronomy museum and 3D planetarium in Hilo, on Hawai'i, the Big Island.

➡ **Whalers Village Museum** (p335) Let kids imagine themselves aboard a 19th-century whaling ship, complete with harpoons and scrimshaw carvings, in West Maui.

➡ **Hawaii Children's Discovery Center** (p78) Best rainy-day indoor playground for tots and schoolchildren, not far from Waikiki Beach on O'ahu.

Planning

When choosing the time of year to visit, keep in mind that the windward sides of the islands get more rain and much higher waves during winter, which may nix swimming for kids.

What to Pack

Hawaii's small-town vibe means that few places – apart from top-chef's restaurants and five-star resorts – are formal, whether in attitude or attire. There's no need to pack your kids' designer jeans or collector-worthy kicks. Let 'em wear T-shirts, shorts and 'rubbah slippah' (flip-flops) just about everywhere you go. On the rainy windward sides of the islands or when visiting higher mountain elevations, rain gear, a warm hat and a sweater or fleece jacket will come in handy. Bring sun hats for everyone.

Hawaii's main islands have tourist convenience shops, such as the ubiquitous ABC Store, and beachfront stands where you can buy or rent inexpensive water-sports equipment (eg floaties, snorkel sets, boogie boards), so there's no need to lug them from home, unless your kids have superspecialized gear. Baby supplies, such as disposable diapers and infant formula, are sold everywhere, but for the best selection and prices, shop in bigger island towns and cities.

If you do forget some critical item, **Baby's Away** (☎ on Hawai'i, the Big Island 800-756-5800, on Maui & Lana'i 800-298-2745, on O'ahu 800-496-6386; www.babysaway.com) rents cribs, strollers, car seats, backpacks, beach toys and more. Major car-rental companies are required to provide infant and child-safety seats, but you must reserve them in advance (typically for $10 per day).

Where to Stay

When setting up a home base, choose your accommodations carefully based on your family's favorite activities and sightseeing priorities. Resorts offer spectacular swimming pools and other distractions, along with kids' activity day camps and on-call babysitting services. But parents might prefer the convenience and cost savings of having a full kitchen and washer-dryer, which many condominiums and vacation rentals offer.

Always ask about policies and bedding before booking any accommodations. Children often stay free when sharing a hotel or resort room with their parents, but only if they use existing bedding. Cots and rollaway beds may be available (usually for an additional fee). At condos, kids above a certain age might count as extra guests and receive an additional nightly surcharge; at a few condos, children are not allowed. Kids and even babies are welcome at many island B&Bs and vacation rentals, but not all.

Regions at a Glance

Ready to go island-hopping? Wherever you travel around the Hawaiian Islands, you'll find that fantastic beaches, friendly faces and *'ono grinds* (good eats) are practically guaranteed. Be swept up by the energy of the capital island, O'ahu. Hang loose on Maui, which offers a little something for everyone, from honeymooners to beach bums. Be awed by towering sea cliffs on ancient Kaua'i, then gape at new land being birthed by volcanoes on the Big Island, Hawaii's youngest island. Escape to total resort luxury on Lana'i or get back to the land on rural Moloka'i, where Hawaiian traditions run strong. Whatever kind of paradise you're seeking, the Aloha State has it – all you have to do is open your mind, and your heart.

O'ahu

Beaches
Food
Culture

Town & Country

Three-quarters of Hawaii residents call 'the Gathering Place' home. It's crowded – so everyone rubs elbows on the bus and city sidewalks. Yet miles of beaches and forest trails are just a short drive from Honolulu's museums and historical monuments.

Endless Feast

If you do nothing else on O'ahu, eat. And then eat some more. Food trucks, island farmers markets and fusion menus by Hawaii's star chefs – they're all here, waiting to be enjoyed.

Multicultural Modernism

O'ahu lets you take the pulse of multiracial Hawaii, which confounds census categories. East and West embrace as ancient Hawaiian traditions greet the 21st century.

p62

Hawai'i, the Big Island

Hiking
Culture
Wildlife

Trail Junkies Unite!

Kilauea, Earth's most active volcano, conjures up a dreamscape for hikers: emerald valleys, icy waterfall pools, lava flows crashing against rainforest and some of the loftiest summits your boots will ever struggle to top.

Cultural Border Crossing

On the Big Island culture is participatory – absorbed, rather than simply observed. You're invited to create a lei and dance a hula, but just beware the night marchers.

Undersea Adventures

Spinner dolphins leap, sea turtles glide and coral gardens are packed with brightly colored fish. In winter humpback whales steal the show.

p172

Maui

Beaches
Hiking
Food

Suntans & Surfboards

Maui's sandy shores are ready-made for beach towels, but the ocean encourages adventure – kayaking, kiteboarding, snorkeling, stand up paddling and, if you dare, surfing on some of the planet's biggest waves.

Trails Galore

The island's hiking trails wind through a bamboo forest, climb to lofty ridgetops, wander past waterfalls and crunch through a cindery volcanic national park.

Locavore Heaven

Grass-fed beef from Upcountry pastures, day-boat fish and bountiful organic gardens ensure Maui's chef-driven restaurants always have the raw ingredients to whip up their famed Hawaii Regional Cuisine creations.

p311

Lana'i

Remoteness
History
Beaches

South Pacific

Ignoring the great views of other islands, Lana'i feels like an isolated bit of subtropical pleasure far from the rest of the world. And given that new owner Larry Ellison wants to make the island self-sufficient, its sense of remoteness will only increase.

Pineapple Town

Nearly the entire island was planted with pineapples, which were exported around the world, for much of the 20th century. The crops are gone but the vintage plantation town of Lana'i City is timeless.

Hulopo'e Beach

Lana'i's one main beach is a beaut: a long crescent of sand on a bay good for snorkeling, and backed by a tidy, uncrowded park.

p422

Moloka'i

Culture
History
Activities

Most Hawaiian

More than 50% of Moloka'i's people have indigenous heritage. Locals favor preservation of land and culture over schemes promoting tourism. Yet there is aloha spirit everywhere and visitors find a genuine – rather than a paid-for – welcome.

St Damien

A young priest who traveled to Moloka'i's remote Kalaupapa Peninsula in 1873 to care for leprosy patients is the USA's first saint. Today the spectacular peninsula is a national park offering a time-travel adventure.

Halawa Valley

This end-of-the-road valley once was home to hundreds of sacred taro patches. Guides take you on a trail past ancient temples to waterfalls pounding into swimmable pools.

p437

Kaua'i

Beaches
Landscape
Lifestyle

Sunny Po'ipu

The most consistently sunny area of the island, Po'ipu is like a tropical version of sleep-away camp. Smiles abound on the South Shore, where beach days abound with plenty of postcard sunsets.

Canyons & Cliffs

The rugged terrain on the Garden Island ranges from gaping chasms to dramatic coastal cliffs, balanced by copious verdant flora. Peer into the 'Grand Canyon of the Pacific' or kayak Hawaii's only navigable river.

Tranquil Escapes

Surfing and an irresistibly laid-back vibe make up the lifestyle on this mostly rural island. The North Shore is home to many folks who came to check in and stayed to tune out.

p469

On the Road

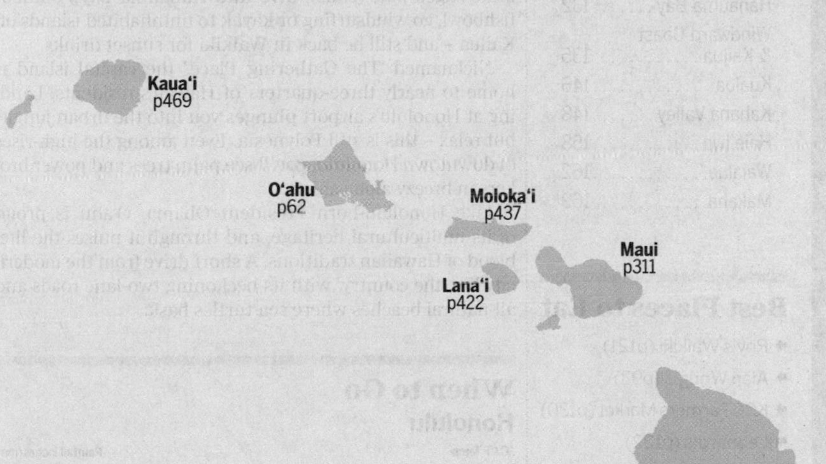

Kaua'i
p469

O'ahu
p62

Moloka'i
p437

Maui
p311

Lana'i
p422

Hawai'i
(Big Island)
p172

O'ahu

Includes ➡

Best Places to Eat

➡ Roy's Waikiki (p121)

➡ Alan Wong's (p93)

➡ KCC Farmers Market (p130)

➡ Leonard's (p122)

➡ Ted's Bakery (p158)

Best off the Beaten Track

➡ Waimanalo Bay Beach Park (p137)

➡ Shangri La (p130)

➡ Gyotaku by Naoki (p145)

➡ Malaekahana State Recreation Area (p151)

➡ Kuli'ou'ou Ridge Trail (p131)

Why Go?

O'ahu is much more than just a transit point en route to the Neighbor Islands. It's the thrill-of-a-lifetime adventure. Here you can surf the North Shore's giant waves, hike atop knife-edged *pali* (cliffs), dive into Hanauma Bay's outdoor fishbowl, go windsurfing or kayak to uninhabited islands off Kailua – and still be back in Waikiki for sunset drinks.

Nicknamed 'The Gathering Place,' the capital island is home to nearly three-quarters of Hawaii's residents. Landing at Honolulu's airport plunges you into the urban jungle, but relax – this is still Polynesia. Even among the high-rises of downtown Honolulu, you'll see palm trees and power brokers in breezy aloha shirts.

Like Honolulu-born President Obama, O'ahu is proud of its multicultural heritage, and through it pulses the lifeblood of Hawaiian traditions. A short drive from the modern city lies 'the country,' with its beckoning two-lane roads and all-natural beaches where sea turtles bask.

When to Go

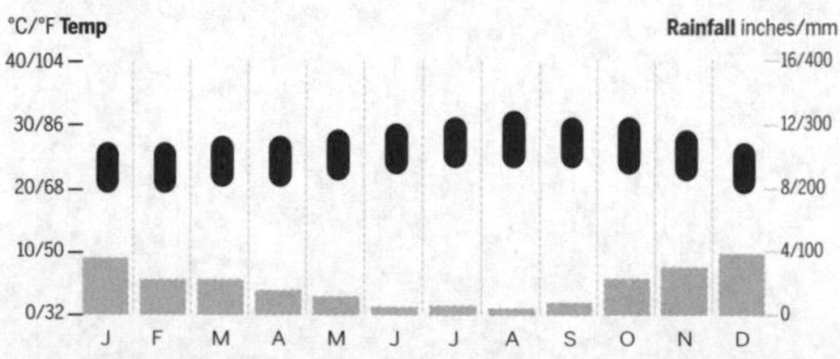

May–Jun Sunny skies; fewer crowds after Easter's spring break and before summer vacation.

Sep–Oct Low-season discounts; big festivals in Honolulu and Waikiki.

Nov–Dec Triple Crown of Surfing sweeps the North Shore.

History

Around AD 1450, Ma'ilikukahi, the ancient *mo'i* (king) of O'ahu, moved his capital to Waikiki, a coastal wetland known for its fertile farmlands and abundant fishing, as well as being a place of recreation and healing. O'ahu's fall to Kamehameha the Great in 1795 signaled the beginning of a united Hawaiian kingdom. Kamehameha later moved his royal court to Honolulu ('Sheltered Bay').

In 1793 the English frigate *Butterworth* became the first foreign ship to sail into what is now Honolulu Harbor. In the 1820s Honolulu's first bars and brothels opened to international whaling crews just as prudish Protestant missionaries began arriving from New England. Honolulu replaced Lahaina as the capital of the kingdom of Hawai'i in 1845. Today Hawaii's first church is just a stone's throw from 'Iolani Palace.

In the 1830s sugar became king of O'ahu's industry. Plantation workers from Asia and Europe were brought in to fill the labor shortage. The names of some of Honolulu's richest and most powerful plantation families – Alexander, Baldwin, Cooke and Dole – read like rosters from the first mission ships. The 19th century ended with the Hawaiian monarchy violently overthrown at Honolulu's 'Iolani Palace, creating a short-lived independent republic dominated by sugar barons and ultimately annexed by the USA.

After the bombing of Pearl Harbor on December 7, 1941, O'ahu was placed under martial law during WWII. As many civil rights were suspended, a detention center for Japanese Americans and resident aliens was established on Honolulu's Sand Island, and later an internment camp was built in the Honouliuli area of central O'ahu. The US federal government didn't apologize for these injustices until 1988.

After WWII, modern jet-age travel and baby-boom prosperity provided O'ahu with a thriving tourism business to replace its declining shipping industry. In the 1970s the Hawaiian renaissance flowered, especially on the University of Hawai'i at Manoa campus and after the successful wayfaring voyage of the *Hokule'a* canoe to Tahiti, first launched from O'ahu's Windward Coast.

By the 1980s rampant tourist development had overbuilt Waikiki and turned some of O'ahu's agricultural land into water-thirsty golf courses and sprawling resorts. The island's last sugar mills closed in the 1990s, leaving O'ahu more heavily dependent on tourism than ever. Debates about economic diversification and the continuing US military presence continue today.

National, State & County Parks

Although O'ahu is Hawaii's most populous island, nature awaits right outside Waikiki's high-rise hotels. About 25% of the island is

O'AHU IN...

One Day

Got only a day in the sun? Then it's all about you and **Waikiki**, baby. Laze on the sand, learn to surf, pose for a pic with the Duke Kahanamoku statue and catch the sunset torch lighting and hula show at **Kuhio Beach Park**. After dark, join the buzzing crowds for dinner and drinks along oceanfront Kalakaua Ave, or find local *grinds* (food) and watering holes on neighborhood side streets.

Three Days

The next day get up early to snorkel at **Hanauma Bay**, then hike up **Diamond Head** or to the lighthouse atop **Makapu'u Point** in the afternoon. Reward yourself with sunset mai tais on a **catamaran cruise** or at the Halekulani's **House Without a Key** beach bar. Spend a full morning or afternoon exploring the capital city of **Honolulu**, with its top-notch museums and historical sites, then dive into the arts, shopping, food and nightlife scenes of **Chinatown**. Take time to detour to the mighty WWII memorials at **Pearl Harbor**.

Five Days

Switch over to island time and take everything mo' slowly. Rent a car or hop on a bus over to the surf-kissed **North Shore** and **Windward Coast**. Stop off wherever white-sand beaches catch your eye, or to explore tiny towns like **Hale'iwa** and **Kailua**. Complete your circle-island tour by cruising past the wide-open horizons of the **Wai'anae Coast** for a windy walk out to **Ka'ena Point**.

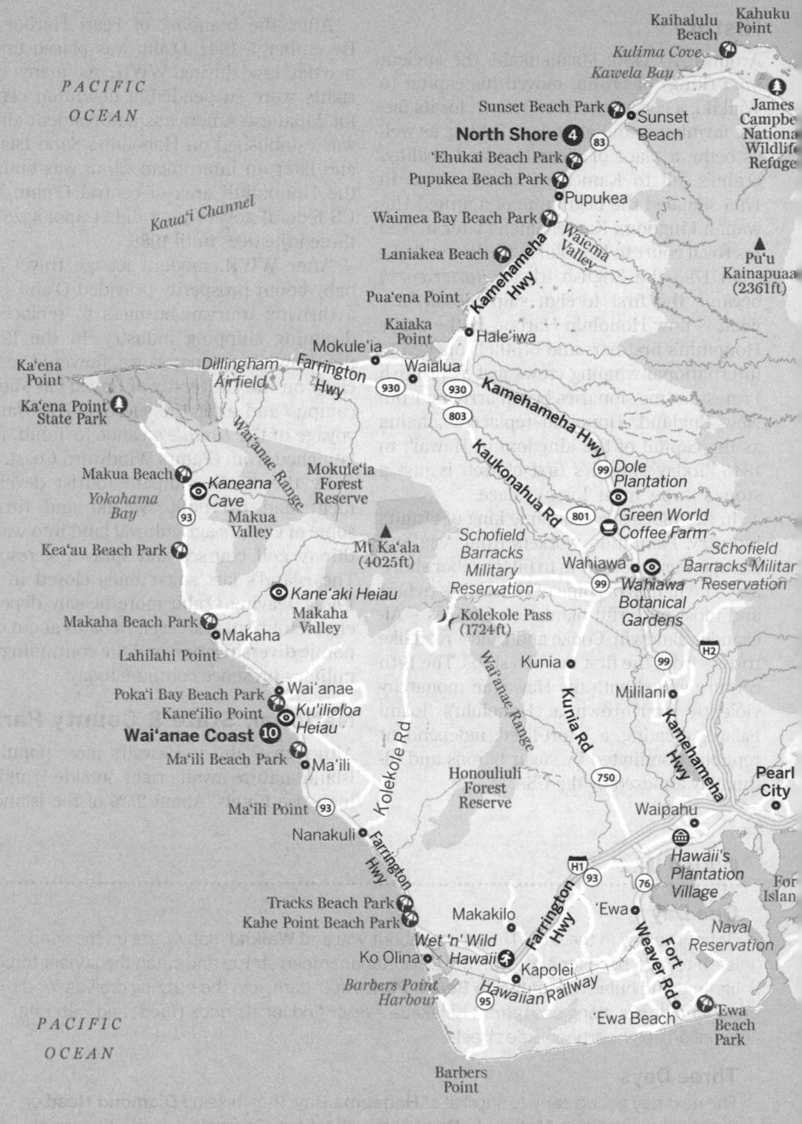

O'ahu Highlights

❶ Swizzle sunset mai tais while slack key guitars play at **Waikiki** (p124).

❷ Be moved by WWII history at **Pearl Harbor** (p102).

❸ Snorkel and dive with tropical marine life at **Hanauma Bay** (p132).

❹ Surf giant winter waves on the **North Shore** (p157).

❺ Cruise past rural valleys, wild beaches and roadside shrimp trucks on the **Windward Coast** (p135).

❻ Go gallery-hopping, shopping and clubbing in Honolulu's **Chinatown** (p76).

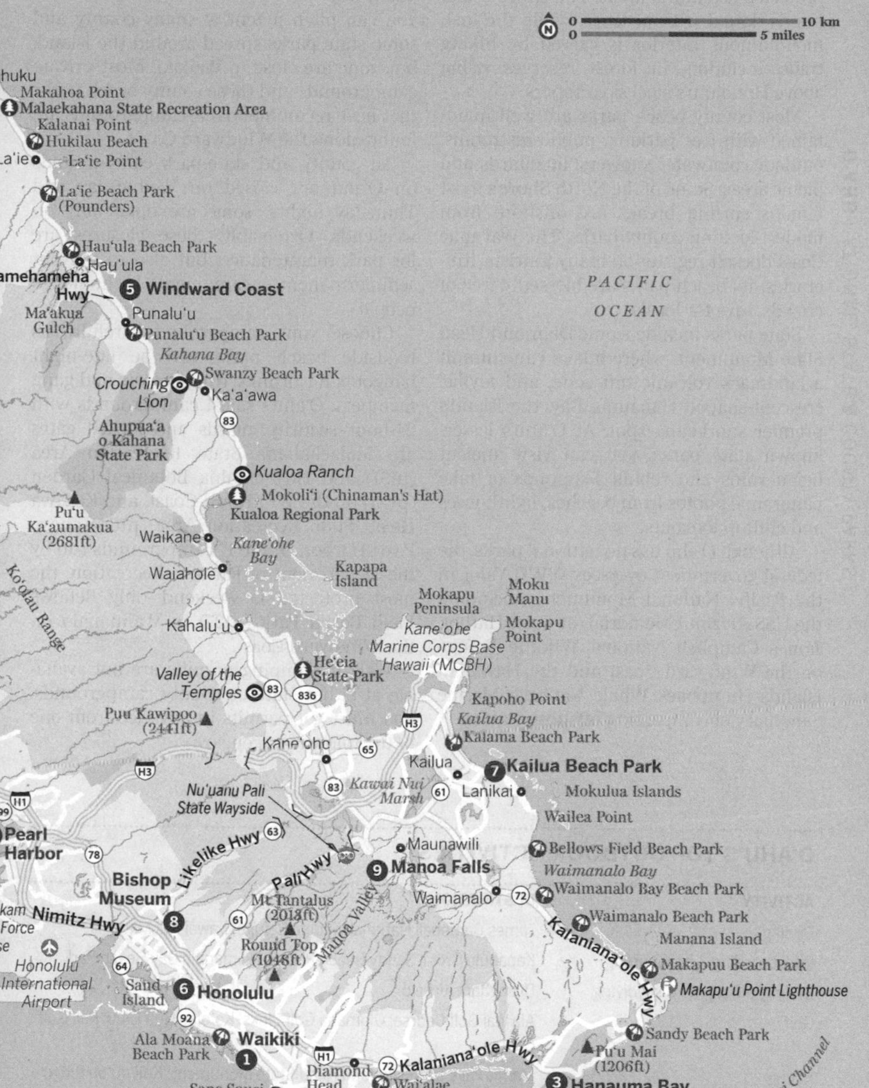

7 Kayak to deserted offshore islands from **Kailua Beach** (p140).

8 Inspect royal feathered capes and ancient Hawaiian temple carvings at the **Bishop Museum** (p82).

9 Hike into Honolulu's green belt to lacy **Manoa Falls** (p85).

10 Get lost on the untrammeled beaches of the **Wai'anae Coast** (p168).

protected as natural areas. The entire coastline is dotted with beaches, while the lush mountainous interior is carved by hiking trails, including in forest reserves rising above Honolulu's steel skyscrapers.

Most county beach parks are well maintained with free parking, public restrooms, outdoor cold-water showers, lifeguards and picnic areas. Some of the North Shore's most famous surfing breaks are offshore from modest-looking county parks. The Wai'anae Coast doesn't register on many tourists' itineraries; its beach parks are blessedly free of crowds, save for locals.

State parks include iconic Diamond Head State Monument, where hikers can summit a landmark volcanic tuff cone, and idyllic, crescent-shaped Hanauma Bay, the island's premier snorkeling spot. At O'ahu's lesser-known state parks, you can visit ancient heiau ruins and rebuilt fishponds or take panoramic photos from beaches, lighthouses and clifftop lookouts.

Although O'ahu has no national parks, the federal government oversees WWII Valor in the Pacific National Monument (including the USS *Arizona* Memorial) at Pearl Harbor, James Campbell National Wildlife Refuge on the Windward Coast and the Hawaiian Islands Humpback Whale National Marine Sanctuary encompassing offshore waters.

Camping

You can pitch a tent at many county and some state parks spread around the island, but none are close to Waikiki. Most private campgrounds and those county beach parks that have recommendable campgrounds are found along the Windward Coast.

All county and state-park campgrounds on O'ahu are closed on Wednesday and Thursday nights; some are open only on weekends. Ostensibly, these closures are for park maintenance, but also to prevent semipermanent encampments by homeless people.

Choose your campground carefully, as roadside beach parks can be late-night hangouts for drunks, drug dealers and gang members. O'ahu's safest campgrounds with 24-hour security guards and locked gates are Malaekahana State Recreation Area (p151) and Ho'omaluhia Botanical Garden (p145) on the Windward Coast, and Kea'iwa Heiau State Recreation Area (p104) above Pearl Harbor. Of the 17 campgrounds run by the Department of Parks & Recreation, the most protected is weekends-only Bellows Field Beach Park (p137) in Waimanalo on the Windward Coast.

Walk-in camping permits are not available at either state or county campgrounds. You must get permits in advance from one of the following agencies:

O'AHU'S TOP OUTDOOR ACTIVITIES

ACTIVITY	DESTINATION
Birding	James Campbell National Wildlife Refuge; Kawai Nui Marsh
Bodyboarding & bodysurfing	Kapahulu Groin; Sandy Beach Park & Waimanalo Bay Beach Park
Gliding, ultralights & skydiving	Dillingham Airfield
Golf	Ala Wai Golf Course; Olomana Golf Links, Ko'olau Golf Club; Pali Golf Course
Hiking	Manoa Falls Trail; Diamond Head State Monument; Kuli'ou'ou Ridge Trail; Ka'ena Point Trail
Horseback riding	Kualoa Ranch; Makaha Valley Riding Stables
Kayaking	Kailua Beach Park
Mountain biking	'Aiea Loop Trail; Ka'ena Point Trail
Scuba diving & snorkeling	Hanauma Bay Nature Preserve; Pupukea Beach Park
Surfing	Waikiki; North Shore; Makaha Beach Park
Swimming	Ala Moana Beach Park; Waikiki; Waimanalo; Kualoa; Ko Olina Lagoons
Tennis	Ala Moana Beach Park; Waikiki
Windsurfing & kiteboarding	Kailua Beach Park; Sunset Beach Park

Hawaii Division of State Parks BOOKING SERVICE
(☎808-587-0300; www.hawaiistateparks.org; Room 310, 1151 Punchbowl St, Honolulu; ⊙8am-3:15pm Mon-Fri) Apply for state-park camping permits (per night $12 to $30) in person or online up to 30 days in advance.

Honolulu Department of Parks & Recreation BOOKING SERVICE
(☎808-768-2267; https://camping.honolulu.gov) County-park camping permits (three-/five-night site permit $32/52) are issued online no sooner than two Fridays prior to the requested date.

Getting There & Around

The vast majority of flights into Hawaii land at Honolulu International Airport (p645), about 6 miles northwest of downtown Honolulu and 9 miles northwest of Waikiki. O'ahu's only commercial airport, it's a hub for domestic, international and interisland flights.

O'ahu itself is a fairly easy island to get around, whether by public bus or rental car.

TO/FROM THE AIRPORT

You can reach Honolulu or Waikiki by airport shuttle, public bus or taxi (average cab fare $35 to $45). For other points around O'ahu, it's more convenient to rent a car. Major car-rental agencies have desks or courtesy phones near the airport's baggage-claim areas.

Roberts Hawaii (☎808-441-7800; www.airportwaikikishuttle.com) operates 24-hour door-to-door shuttle buses to Waikiki's hotels, departing every 20 to 60 minutes. Transportation time depends on how many stops the shuttle makes before dropping you off. Fares average $12 to $15 one way, or $20 to $30 round-trip; surcharges apply for bicycles, surfboards, golf clubs and extra baggage. Reservations are helpful, but not always required for airport pickups. For return trips, reserve at least 48 hours in advance.

You can reach downtown Honolulu, Ala Moana Center and Waikiki via TheBus 19 or 20. Buses run every 20 minutes from 6am to 11pm daily; the regular fare is $2.50. Luggage is restricted to what you can hold on your lap or stow under the seat (maximum size 22in x 14in x 9in).

The easiest driving route to Waikiki is via the Nimitz Hwy (Hwy 92), which becomes Ala Moana Blvd. Although this route hits local traffic, it's hard to get lost. For the fast lane, take the H-1 (Lunalilo) Fwy eastbound, then follow signs 'To Waikiki.' On the return trip to the airport, beware of the poorly marked interchange where H-1 and Hwy 78 split; if you're not in the right-hand lane then, you could end up on Hwy 78 by mistake. The drive between the airport and Waikiki takes about 25 minutes without traffic; allow at least 45 minutes during weekday rush hours.

AVOIDING CAR BREAK-INS

When visiting O'ahu's beach parks, hiking trails or 'secret' spots off the side of the highway, take all valuables with you. Don't leave anything visible inside your car or stowed in the trunk. Car break-ins are common all over the island and can happen within a matter of minutes. Some locals leave their cars unlocked to avoid the hassles of broken windows or jimmied door locks.

BICYCLE

It's possible to cycle around O'ahu, but consider taking TheBus to get beyond Honolulu metro-area traffic. Hawaii's Department of Transportation publishes a Bike O'ahu route map available free online at http://hidot.hawaii.gov/highways/bike-map-oahu.

BUS

O'ahu's public-bus system, **TheBus** (☎808-848-5555; www.thebus.org; adult fare $2.50, 4-day visitor pass $35; ⊙infoline 5:30am-10pm), is extensive but most hiking trails and some popular viewpoints are beyond its reach, (necessitating access to a car). Ala Moana Center is Honolulu's central bus transfer point. Each bus route can have a few different destinations; buses generally keep the same number inbound and outbound.

Although buses are fast and frequent, you can't set your watch by them. Especially in Waikiki, buses sometimes bottleneck, with one packed bus after another passing right by crowded bus stops (you can't just flag a bus down anywhere along its route).

All buses are wheelchair-accessible and have front-loading racks that accommodate two bicycles at no extra charge – just let the driver know first.

Bus Fares & Passes

The one-way adult fare is $2.50 (children aged six to 17 $1.25). Use coins or $1 bills; bus drivers don't give change. One free transfer (two connections) is available from the driver.

A $35 visitor pass valid for unlimited rides over four consecutive days is sold at Waikiki's ubiquitous ABC Stores and **TheBus Pass Office** (Map p70; ☎808-848-4444; www.thebus.org; Kalihi Transit Center, cnr Middle St & Kamehameha Hwy; ⊙7:30am-4pm Mon-Fri).

A monthly bus pass ($60), valid for unlimited rides during a calendar month (not just any 30-day period), is sold at TheBus Pass Office,

7-Eleven convenience stores and Foodland and Times supermarkets.

Seniors (65 years and older) and anyone with a physical disability can buy a $10 discount ID card at TheBus Pass Office, entitling them to pay $1 per one-way fare or $5/30 for a pass valid for unlimited rides during one calendar month/year.

CAR, MOTORCYCLE & MOPED

Avis, Budget, Enterprise, Hertz and National have rental cars at Honolulu International Airport. Alamo, Dollar and Thrifty operate about a mile outside the airport off Nimitz Hwy (airport courtesy shuttles available). On the drive back to the airport, all highway signs lead to on-site airport car returns.

Most major car-rental agencies have multiple branch locations in Waikiki, usually in the lobbies of resort hotels. Although the best rental rates are usually offered at Honolulu's airport, Waikiki branches can be less hassle (and less expensive, given steep overnight parking costs at Waikiki hotels) if you're only renting a car for a day.

In Waikiki, independent car-rental agencies may offer much lower rates, especially for one-day rentals and 4WD vehicles. They're also more likely to rent to drivers under 25. Some also rent mopeds and motorcycles, and a few specialize in smart cars and hybrid vehicles.

Times vary depending upon traffic, but following are typical driving times and distances from Waikiki:

DESTINATION	MILES	TIME (MIN)
Diamond Head	3	10
Hale'iwa	37	55
Hanauma Bay	11	25
Honolulu International Airport	9	25
Ka'ena Point State Park	46	70
Kailua	17	30
Ko Olina	29	45
La'ie	38	65
Nu'uanu Pali Lookout	11	20
Sunset Beach	43	65
USS *Arizona* Memorial	15	30

TAXI

Taxis have meters and charge $3.10 at flagfall, plus $3.60 per mile and 50¢ per suitcase or backpack. They're readily available at the airport, resort hotels and shopping centers. Otherwise, you'll probably have to call for one. TheCab (p101) offers islandwide service.

TOURS

Prices usually include Waikiki pickups and drop-offs; ask when booking.

Roberts Hawaii (☎808-539-9400; www.robertshawaii.com) Conventional bus and van

USEFUL BUS ROUTES

ROUTE NO	DESTINATION
A City Express!	UH Manoa, Ala Moana Center, downtown Honolulu, Chinatown, Aloha Stadium
E Country Express!	Waikiki, Ala Moana Center, Waterfront Plaza, Aloha Tower, downtown Honolulu
2 & 13	Waikiki, Kapahulu Ave, Honolulu Convention Center, downtown Honolulu, Chinatown; also Honolulu Museum of Art and Bishop Museum (bus 2)
4	Waikiki, UH Manoa, downtown Honolulu, Queen Emma Summer Palace
6	UH Manoa, Ala Moana Center, downtown Honolulu
8	Waikiki, Ala Moana Center
19 & 20	Waikiki, Ala Moana Center, Ward Centers, Waterfront Plaza, Aloha Tower, downtown Honolulu, Chinatown, Honolulu International Airport; also USS *Arizona* Memorial (bus 20)
22 ('Beach Bus')	Waikiki, Diamond Head, Koko Marina, Sandy Beach, Hanauma Bay, Sea Life Park
23	Ala Moana, Waikiki, Diamond Head, Hawai'i Kai (inland), Sea Life Park
42	Waikiki, Ala Moana, Downtown Honolulu, Chinatown, USS *Arizona* Memorial (limited hours)
52 & 55 ('Circle Isle' buses)	Ala Moana Center, North Shore, Windward Coast
57	Ala Moana, Queen Emma Summer Palace, Kailua, Waimanalo, Sea Life Park

sightseeing tours, including marathon full-day 'Circle Island' trips (adult/child from $72/47) and 'Stars & Stripes' military-history itineraries (from $83/63).

E Noa Tours (☎808-591-2561; www.enoa.com) With knowledgeable guides certified in Hawaiiana, smaller buses circle the island (adult/child from $82/60) and explore Pearl Harbor (from $27/25).

Hawaiian Escapades (☎888-331-3668; www.hawaiianescapades.com) Waterfall walks, circle-island adventures, ghost-hunting trips and *Hawaii Five-O* and *Lost* TV location tours (half-/full day from $65/130) in minibuses and vans.

HONOLULU

POP 405,000

Here in Honolulu, away from the crowded haunts of Waikiki, you get to shake hands with the real Hawaii. A boisterous Polynesian capital, Honolulu delivers an island-style mixed plate of experiences. Eat your way through the pan-Asian alleys of Chinatown, where 19th-century whalers once brawled and immigrant traders thrived.

Gaze out to sea atop the landmark Aloha Tower, then sashay past Victorian-era brick buildings, including the USA's only royal palace. Ocean breezes rustle palm trees along the harborfront, while in the cool, mist-shrouded Ko'olau Range, forested hiking trails offer postcard city views.

At sunset, cool off with an amble around Magic Island or splash in the ocean at Ala Moana Beach. After dark, migrate to Chinatown's edgy art and nightlife scene.

Sights

Honolulu's compact downtown is just a lei's throw from the harborfront. Nearby, the buzzing streets of Chinatown are packed with food markets, antiques shops, art galleries and hip bars. Between downtown and Waikiki, Ala Moana has Hawaii's biggest mall and the city's best beach. The University of Hawai'i campus is a gateway to the Manoa Valley. A few outlying sights, including the Bishop Museum, are worth putting into your schedule.

Downtown

This area was center stage for the political intrigue and social upheavals that changed the fabric of Hawaii during the 19th century. Major players ruled here, revolted here, worshipped here and still rest, however restlessly, in the graveyards.

★'Iolani Palace PALACE

(Map p72; ☎info 808-538-1471, tour reservations 808-522-0832; www.iolanipalace.org; 364 S King St; grounds admission free, adult/child basement galleries $7/3, self-guided audiotour $15/6, guided tour $22/6; ⏲9am-5pm Mon-Sat, last entry 4pm) No other place evokes a more poignant sense of Hawaii's history. The palace was built under King David Kalakaua in 1882. At that time, the Hawaiian monarchy observed many of the diplomatic protocols of the Victorian world. The king traveled abroad meeting with leaders around the globe and received foreign emissaries here. Although the palace was modern and opulent for its time, it did little to assert Hawaii's sovereignty over powerful US-influenced business interests who overthrew the kingdom in 1893.

Two years after the coup, the former queen, Lili'uokalani, who had succeeded her brother David to the throne, was convicted of treason and spent nine months imprisoned in her former home. Later the palace served as the capitol of the republic, then the territory and later the state of Hawaii. In 1969 the government finally moved into the current state capitol, leaving 'Iolani Palace a shambles. After a decade of painstaking renovations, the restored palace reopened as a museum, although many original royal artifacts had been lost or stolen before work even began.

Visitors must take a docent-led or self-guided tour (no children under age five) to see 'Iolani's grand interior, including re-creations of the throne room and residential quarters upstairs. The palace was quite modern by Victorian-era standards. Every bedroom had its own bathroom with flush toilets and hot running water, and electric lights replaced the gas lamps years before the White House in Washington, DC, installed electricity. If you're short on time, you can independently browse the historical exhibits in the basement, including royal regalia, historical photographs and reconstructions of the kitchen and chamberlain's office.

The palace grounds are open during daylight hours and are free of charge. The former **barracks** of the Royal Household Guards, a building that looks oddly like the uppermost layer of a medieval fort, now houses the ticket booth. Nearby, a domed **pavilion**, originally built for the coronation of King Kalakaua in 1883, is still used for state governor inaugurations. Underneath

Greater Honolulu & Pearl Harbor

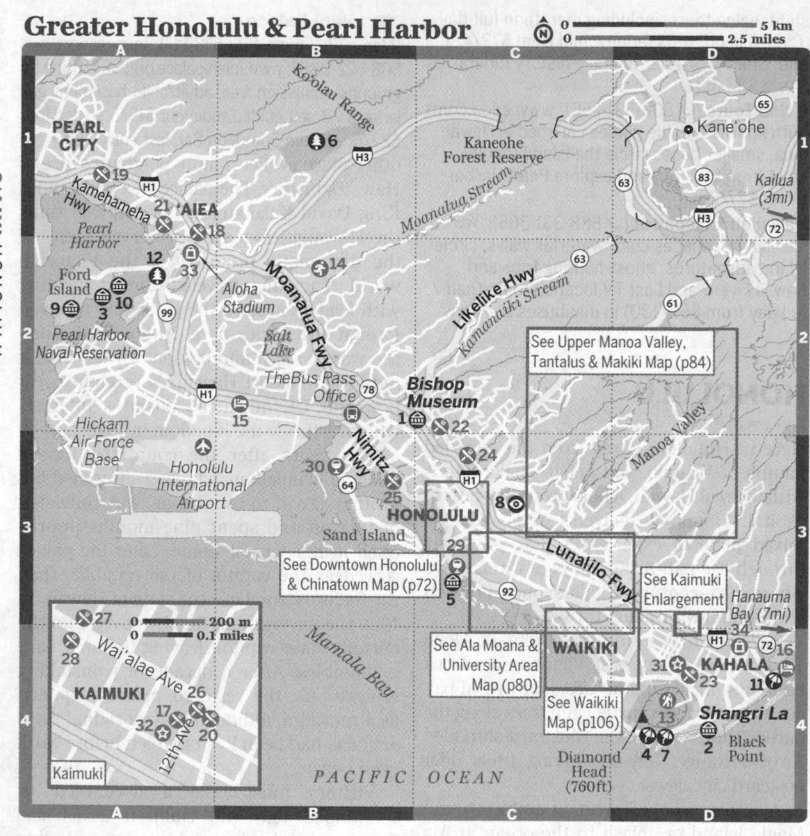

the huge banyan tree, allegedly planted by Queen Kapi'olani, the Royal Hawaiian Band gives free concerts on most Fridays from noon to 1pm, weather permitting.

Call ahead to confirm tour schedules and reserve tickets in advance during peak periods.

State Capitol BUILDING

(Map p72; ☎808-586-0178; 415 S Beretania St; ⏲7:45am-4:30pm Mon-Fri) FREE Built in the architecturally interesting 1960s, Hawaii's state capitol is a poster child of conceptual postmodernism: two cone-shaped legislative chambers have sloping walls to represent volcanoes; the supporting columns shaped like coconut palms symbolize the eight main islands; and a large encircling pool represents the Pacific Ocean surrounding Hawaii. Visitors are free to walk through the open-air rotunda and peer through viewing windows into the legislative chambers. Pick up a self-guided tour brochure on the 4th floor from Room 415.

Queen Lili'uokalani Statue STATUE

(Map p72) Pointedly positioned between the state capitol building and 'Iolani Palace is a life-size bronze statue of Queen Lili'uokalani, Hawaii's last reigning monarch. She holds a copy of the Hawaiian constitution she wrote in 1893 in an attempt to strengthen Hawaiian rule; 'Aloha 'Oe,' a popular song she composed; and 'Kumulipo,' the traditional Hawaiian chant of creation.

Father Damien Statue STATUE

(Map p72) In front of the capitol is a highly stylized statue of Father Damien, the Belgian priest who lived and worked with victims of Hansen's disease who were exiled to the island of Moloka'i during the late 19th century, before later dying of the disease himself. In 2009 the Catholic Church canonized Father Damien as Hawaii's first saint

Greater Honolulu & Pearl Harbor

Top Sights
1 Bishop Museum ... C2
2 Shangri La ... D4

Sights
3 Battleship Missouri Memorial ... A2
4 Diamond Head Beach Park ... D4
5 Hawaii Children's Discovery Center ... C3
6 Kea'iwa Heiau State Recreation Area ... B1
7 Kuilei Cliffs Beach Park ... D4
8 National Memorial Cemetery of the Pacific ... C3
9 Pacific Aviation Museum ... A2
10 USS Arizona Memorial ... A2
USS Bowfin Submarine Museum & Park ... (see 12)
11 Wai'alae Beach Park ... D4
12 WWII Valor in the Pacific National Monument ... A2

Activities, Courses & Tours
13 Diamond Head State Monument ... D4
14 Moanalua Golf Club ... B2

Sleeping
15 Airport Honolulu Hotel ... B2
16 Kahala Hotel & Resort ... D4

Eating
17 12th Avenue Grill ... A4
18 Alley Restaurant Bar & Grill ... A1
19 Buzz's Steakhouse ... A1
20 Crack Seed Store ... A4
21 Forty Niner Restaurant ... A1
22 Helena's Hawaiian Food ... C2
Hoku's ... (see 16)
23 KCC Farmers Market ... D4
24 Liliha Bakery ... C3
25 Nico's at Pier 38 ... B3
26 Salt Kitchen & Tasting Bar ... A4
27 Tamura's Poke ... A3
28 Town ... A4
Whole Foods ... (see 34)

Drinking & Nightlife
29 Honolulu Beerworks ... C3
30 La Mariana Sailing Club ... B3

Entertainment
31 Diamond Head Theater ... D4
Kahala Mall ... (see 34)
32 Movie Museum ... A4

Shopping
33 Aloha Stadium Swap Meet & Marketplace ... A2
34 Kahala Mall ... D4

after the allegedly miraculous recovery from cancer in 1988 of a Honolulu schoolteacher who had prayed over Damien's original grave site on Moloka'i.

Hawai'i State Art Museum MUSEUM
(Map p72; ☎808-586-0900; www.hawaii.gov/sfca; 2nd fl, No 1 Capitol District Bldg, 250 S Hotel St; ⊙10am-4pm Tue-Sat, also 6-9pm 1st Fri each month) FREE With its vibrant, thought-provoking collections, this public art museum brings together traditional and contemporary art from Hawaii's multiethnic communities. The museum inhabits a grand 1928 Spanish Mission Revival–style building, formerly a YMCA and today a nationally registered historic site.

Upstairs, revolving exhibits of paintings, sculptures, fiber art, photography and mixed media are displayed around themes, such as the island's Polynesian heritage, modern social issues or the natural beauty of land and sea. Hawaii's complex confluence of Asian, Pacific Rim and European cultures is evident throughout, shaping an aesthetic that captures the soul of the islands and the hearts of the people. Drop by at noon on the last Tuesday of the month for free 'Art Lunch' lectures or between 11am and 3pm on the second Saturday for hands-on Hawaiian arts and crafts, often designed with kids in mind.

Ali'iolani Hale HISTORIC BUILDING
(Map p72; ☎808-539-4999; www.jhchawaii.net; 417 S King St; ⊙8am-4.30pm Mon-Fri) FREE The first major government building ordered by the Hawaiian monarchy in 1874, the 'House of Heavenly Kings' was designed by Australian architect Thomas Rowe to be a royal palace, although it was never used as such. Today, it houses the Supreme Court of Hawai'i. Go through the security checkpoint and step inside the **King Kamehameha V Judiciary History Center**, where you can browse thought-provoking historical displays about martial law during WWII and the reign of Kamehameha I.

Kamehameha the Great Statue STATUE
(Map p72) Standing before the Ali'iolani Hale, a bronze statue of Kamehameha the Great faces 'Iolani Palace. Often ceremonially draped with layers of flower lei, the statue was cast in 1880 in Florence, Italy, by American sculptor Thomas Gould. The current

Downtown Honolulu & Chinatown

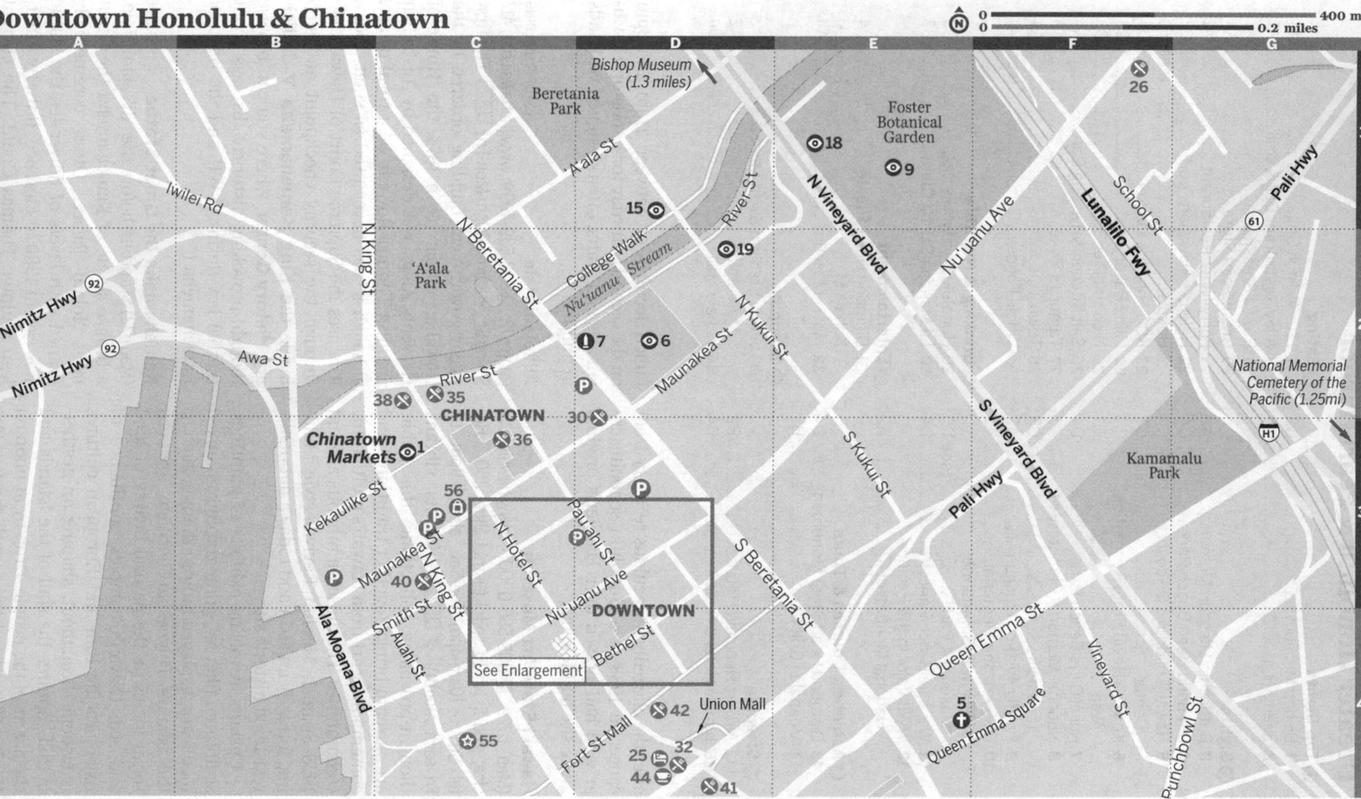

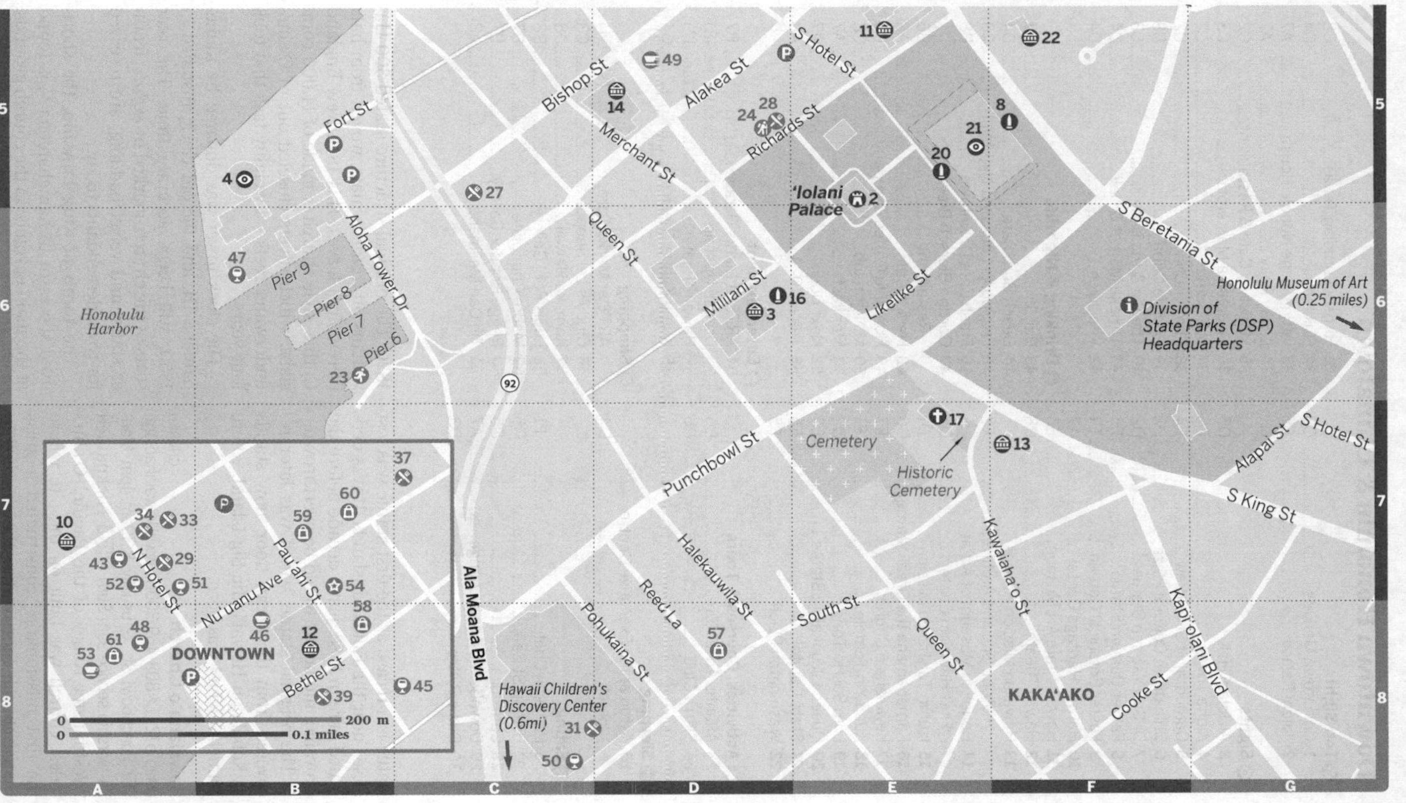

Honolulu Harbor
Pier 9
Pier 8
Pier 7
Pier 6
Fort St
Aloha Tower Dr
Bishop St
Alakea St
S Hotel St
Merchant St
Richards St
'Iolani Palace
Queen St
Mililani St
Likelike St
S Beretania St
Honolulu Museum of Art (0.25 miles)
Division of State Parks (DSP) Headquarters
Punchbowl St
Cemetery
Historic Cemetery
Alapai St
S King St
Kawaiaha'o St
Kapi'olani Blvd
Ala Moana Blvd
Hawaii Children's Discovery Center (0.6mi)
Pohukaina St
Reed La
Halekauwila St
South St
KAKA'AKO
Cooke St
N Hotel St
Nu'uanu Ave
Pau'ahi St
Bethel St
DOWNTOWN
0 200 m
0 0.1 miles

Downtown Honolulu & Chinatown

Top Sights
1 Chinatown Markets C3
2 'Iolani Palace E5

Sights
3 Ali'iolani Hale D6
4 Aloha Tower B5
5 Cathedral of St Andrew E4
6 Chinatown Cultural Plaza D2
7 Dr Sun Yat-sen Statue D2
8 Father Damien Statue F5
9 Foster Botanical Garden E1
10 Hawai'i Heritage Center A7
11 Hawai'i State Art Museum E5
12 Hawaii Theater B8
13 Hawaiian Mission Houses Historic Site and Archives F7
14 Honolulu Museum of Art at First Hawaiian Center D5
15 Izumo Taishakyo Mission D1
16 Kamehameha the Great Statue D6
17 Kawaiaha'o Church E7
18 Kuan Yin Temple E1
19 Lum Sai Ho Tong D2
20 Queen Lili'uokalani Statue E5
21 State Capitol E5
22 Washington Place F5

Activities, Courses & Tours
23 Atlantis Adventures B6
24 Sierra Club D5

Sleeping
25 Aston at the Executive Centre Hotel D4

Eating
26 Bangkok Chef F1
27 Bishop St Cafe C5
28 Cafe Julia D5
29 Downbeat Diner & Lounge A7
30 Duc's Bistro D3
31 Hiroshi Eurasian Tapas C8
32 Hukilau D4
33 Little Village Noodle House A7
34 Lucky Belly A7
35 Mabuhay Cafe & Restaurant C2
36 Maunakea Marketplace C3
37 Mei Sum C7
38 Pho To-Chau C2
39 Soul de Cuba B8
40 The Pig & the Lady C3
41 'Umeke Market & Deli D4
42 Vita Juice D4

Drinking & Nightlife
43 Bar 35 .... A7
44 Beach Bum Cafe D4
45 Fix Sports Lounge & Nightclub C8
46 Fresh Cafe Downtown B8
47 Gordon Biersch Brewery Restaurant B6
48 Hank's Cafe A8
49 Honolulu Coffee Company D5
50 M Nightclub C8
51 Manifest A7
52 Next Door A7
53 Tea at 1024 .... A8

Entertainment
54 ARTS at Marks Garage B7
Dragon Upstairs .... (see 48)
Hawaii Theater .... (see 12)
55 Kumu Kahua Theatre C4

Shopping
ARTS at Marks Garage .... (see 54)
56 Cindy's Lei Shoppe C3
57 Kamaka Hawaii D8
58 Louis Pohl Gallery B8
59 Madre Chocolate B7
60 Pegge Hopper Gallery B7
61 Tin Can Mailman A8

statue is a recast, as the first statue was lost at sea near the Falkland Islands. It was dedicated here in 1883, just a decade before the Hawaiian monarchy would be overthrown.

The original statue, which was later recovered from the ocean floor, now stands in Kohala on Hawai'i, the Big Island, where Kamehameha I was born.

Kawaiaha'o Church CHURCH
(Map p72; ☎808-469-3000; www.kawaiahao.org; 957 Punchbowl St; ⊙usually 8:30am-4pm Mon-Fri, worship service 9am Sun) FREE Nicknamed 'Westminster Abbey of the Pacific,' O'ahu's oldest church was built on the site where the first missionaries constructed a grass thatch church shortly after their arrival in 1820. The original structure seated 300 Hawaiians on *lauhala* mats, woven from hala (screwpine) leaves. This 1842 New England Gothic–style church is made of 14,000 coral slabs, which divers chiseled out of O'ahu's underwater reefs – a weighty task that took four years.

The clock tower was donated by Kamehameha III, and the old clock, installed in 1850, still keeps accurate time. The rear seats of the church, marked by *kahili* (feather staffs) and velvet padding, are reserved for royal descendants today.

The **tomb of King Lunalilo**, the short-lived successor to Kamehameha V, is found at the main entrance to the church grounds.

The **cemetery** to the rear of the church is almost like a who's who of colonial history: early Protestant missionaries are buried alongside other important figures, including infamous Sanford Dole, who became the first territorial governor of Hawaii after Queen Lili'uokalani was overthrown.

Hawaiian Mission Houses Historic Site and Archives MUSEUM

(Map p72; ☎808-447-3910; www.missionhouses.org; 553 S King St; 1hr guided tour adult/child 6-18yr & college student with ID $10/6; ⏰10am-4pm Tue-Sat, guided tours usually 11am, noon, 1pm, 2pm & 3pm) Occupying the original headquarters of the Sandwich Islands mission that forever changed the course of Hawaiian history, this modest museum is authentically furnished with handmade quilts on the beds and iron cooking pots in the stone fireplaces. You'll need to take a guided tour to peek inside any of the buildings.

Walking around the grounds, you'll notice that the first missionaries packed more than their bags when they left Boston – they brought a prefabricated wooden house, called the **Frame House**, with them around the Horn. Designed to withstand New England winter winds, the small windows instead blocked out Honolulu's cooling tradewinds, which kept the two-story house hellaciously hot and stuffy. Erected in 1821, it's the oldest wooden structure in Hawaii.

The 1831 coral-block **Chamberlain House** was the early mission's storeroom, a necessity because Honolulu had few shops in those days. Upstairs are hoop barrels, wooden crates packed with dishes, and the desk and quill pen of Levi Chamberlain. He was appointed by the mission to buy, store and dole out supplies to missionary families, who survived on a meager allowance – as the account books on his desk testify.

Mission Social Hall and Cafe, run by chef Mark 'Gooch' Noguchi, opened in December 2014 and promises foodie delights and family fun.

Nearby, the 1841 **Printing Office** houses a lead-type press used to print the first bible in the Hawaiian language.

Washington Place HISTORIC BUILDING

(Map p72; ☎808-586-0240; www.washingtonplacefoundation.org; 320 S Beretania St; ⏰tours by appointment only, usually at 10am Thu) FREE Formerly the governor's official residence, this colonial-style mansion was built in 1846 by US sea captain John Dominis. The captain's son became the governor of O'ahu and married the Hawaiian princess who later became Queen Lili'uokalani. After the queen was released from house arrest inside 'Iolani Palace in 1896, she lived here until her death in 1917. A plaque near the sidewalk is inscribed with the lyrics to 'Aloha 'Oe,' the patriotic anthem she composed.

Cathedral of St Andrew CHURCH

(Map p72; ☎808-524-2822; www.saintandrewscathedral.net; 229 Queen Emma Sq; ⏰usually 8:30am-4pm Mon-Fri, tours 11:50am Sun; P) FREE King Kamehameha IV, attracted to the royal Church of England, decided to build his own cathedral and founded the Anglican Church in Hawaii in 1861. The cathedral's cornerstone was laid in 1867, four years after his death on St Andrew's Day – hence the church's name. The architecture is French Gothic, utilizing stone and stained glass shipped from England. For a free lunchtime concert, the largest pipe organ in the Pacific is sonorously played every Friday at 12.15pm.

Aloha Tower LANDMARK

(Map p72; www.alohatower.com; 1 Aloha Tower Dr; ⏰9:30am-5pm; P) FREE Built in 1926, this 10-story landmark was once the city's tallest building. In the golden days when all tourists to Hawaii arrived by ship, this pre-WWII waterfront icon – with its four-sided clock tower inscribed with 'Aloha' – greeted every visitor. These days, Hawaii Pacific

HONOLULU'S BEST FREE THRILLS

- ➡ Catch sunset from Magic Island at Ala Moana Beach Park (p85).
- ➡ Gaze out to sea atop the Aloha Tower.
- ➡ Peruse downtown's Hawai'i State Art Museum (p71).
- ➡ Hike to Manoa Falls (p85) and the Nu'uanu Valley Lookout (p86).
- ➡ Hobnob on First Fridays in Chinatown (p97).
- ➡ Hear the Royal Hawaiian Band at 'Iolani Palace (p69).
- ➡ Learn to speak Hawaiian and make flower *lei* at Native Books/Nā Mea Hawaii (p88).
- ➡ Party at the Honolulu Festival (p88) or Pan-Pacific Festival (p88).

University has bought the Aloha Tower Marketplace and is revitalizing it for retail, dining and student housing. Take the elevator to the top-floor tower observation deck for 360-degree views of Honolulu and the waterfront.

Honolulu Museum of Art at First Hawaiian Center ART GALLERY
(Map p72; ☎808-526-0232; www.honoluluacademy.org; ⌚8:30am-4:30pm Mon-Thu, to 6pm Fri) FREE First Hawaiian Bank's high-rise headquarters also houses the downtown gallery of **Spalding House**, featuring fascinating mixed-media exhibits of modern and contemporary works by artists from around Hawaii. Even the building itself features a four-story-high art-glass wall incorporating 185 prisms. Free guided gallery tours typically meet at noon on the first Friday of the month while exhibitions are being held.

Chinatown

The location of this district is no accident. Between Honolulu's busy trading port and what was once the countryside, enterprises selling goods to city folks and visiting ships' crews sprang up in the 19th century. Many shops were established by Chinese laborers who had completed their sugarcane-plantation contracts. The most successful entrepreneurial families have long since moved out of this low-rent district to wealthier suburbs, making room for new waves of immigrants, mostly from Southeast Asia.

The scent of burning incense still wafts through Chinatown's buzzing markets, fire-breathing dragons spiral up the columns of buildings and steaming dim sum awakens even the sleepiest of appetites.

★**Chinatown Markets** MARKET
(Map p72; www.chinatownnow.com) The commercial heart of Chinatown revolves around its markets and food shops. Noodle factories, pastry shops and produce stalls line the narrow sidewalks, always crowded with cart-pushing grandmothers and errand-running families. An institution since 1904, the **O'ahu Market** sells everything a Chinese cook needs: ginger root, fresh octopus, quail eggs, jasmine rice, slabs of tuna, long beans and salted jellyfish. You owe yourself a bubble tea if you spot a pig's head among the stalls.

At the start of the nearby pedestrian mall is the newer, but equally vibrant, **Kekaulike Market**. At the top end of the pedestrian mall is **Maunakea Marketplace**, with its popular food court.

Foster Botanical Garden GARDENS
(Map p72; ☎808-522-7066; www.honolulu.gov/parks/hbg.html; 180 N Vineyard Blvd; adult/child 6-12yr $5/1; ⌚9am-4pm, guided tours usually 1pm Mon-Sat; P) Tropical plants you've only ever read about can be spotted in all their glory at this botanic garden, which took root in 1850. Among its rarest specimens are the Hawaiian *loulu* palm and the East African *Gigasiphon macrosiphon,* both thought to be extinct in the wild. Several of the garden's towering trees are the largest of their kind in the USA.

Oddities include the cannonball tree, the sausage tree and the double coconut palm capable of producing a 50lb nut – watch your head! Follow your nose past fragrant vanilla vines and cinnamon trees in the spice and herb gardens, then pick your way among the poisonous and dye plants. Don't miss the blooming orchids. A free self-guided tour booklet is available at the garden entrance.

Hawaii Theater HISTORIC BUILDING
(Map p72; ☎808-528-0506; www.hawaiitheatre.com; 1130 Bethel St) This neoclassical landmark first opened in 1922, when silent films were played to the tunes of a pipe organ. Dubbed the 'Pride of the Pacific', the theater ran continuous shows during WWII, but the development of Waikiki cinemas in the 1960s and '70s finally brought down the curtain. After multi-million-dollar restorations, this nationally registered historic site held its grand reopening in 1996.

Kuan Yin Temple TEMPLE
(Map p72; 170 N Vineyard Blvd; ⌚usually 7am-5pm) FREE With its green ceramic-tile roof and bright-red columns, this ornate Chinese Buddhist temple is Honolulu's oldest. The richly carved interior is filled with the sweet, pervasive smell of burning incense. The temple is dedicated to Kuan Yin, bodhisattva of mercy, whose statue is the largest in the interior prayer hall. Devotees burn paper 'money' for prosperity and good luck, while offerings of fresh flowers and fruit are placed at the altar. Respectful visitors welcome.

Izumo Taishakyo Mission TEMPLE
(Map p72; ☎808-538-7778; 215 N Kukui St; ⌚usually 8am-5pm) FREE This Shintō shrine was built by Japanese immigrants in 1906. It was confiscated during WWII by the city and wasn't returned to the community until the

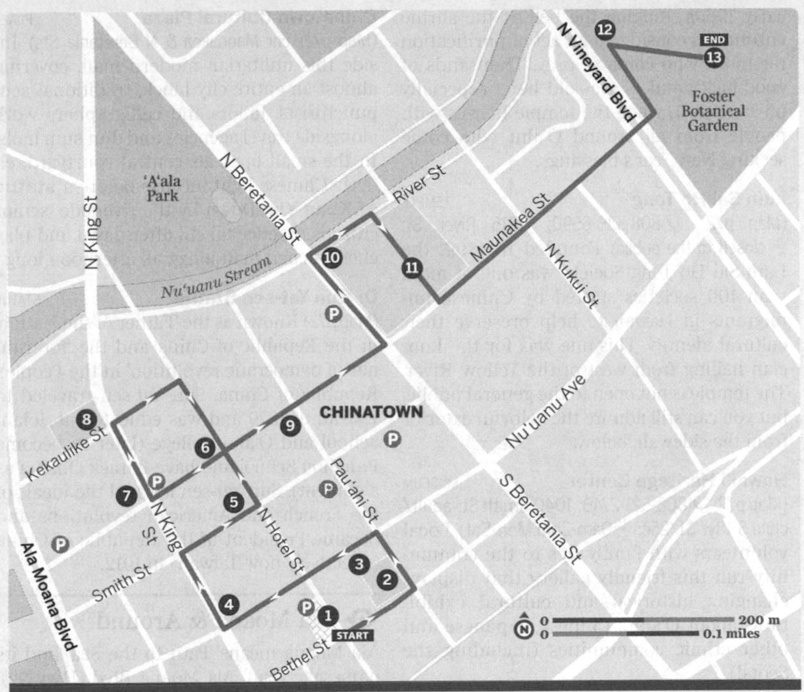

City Walk
Historical Chinatown

START DR SUN YAT-SEN MEMORIAL PARK
END FOSTER BOTANICAL GARDEN
LENGTH 1 MILE; ONE TO TWO HOURS

Honolulu's most foot-trafficked neighborhood, Chinatown is also its most historic. Start at ❶ **Dr Sun Yat-sen Memorial Park** at the stone lions. Walk northeast to the neoclassical 1922 ❷ **Hawaii Theater** (p76), nicknamed the 'Pride of the Pacific,' then continue around the corner.

On Nu'uanu Ave, the now-abandoned ❸ **Pantheon Bar** was a favorite of sailors in days past – even King David Kalakaua imbibed here. The avenue's granite-block sidewalks are themselves relics, built with the discarded ballasts of 19th-century trading ships. At the corner of King St, peek into the ❹ **First Hawaiian Bank**, with its antique wooden teller cages that cameoed in the TV show *Lost*.

Poke your head into the community-run ❺ **Hawai'i Heritage Center** (p78) before turning left onto seedy Hotel St, historically Honolulu's red-light district and now a row of trendy lounges, nightclubs, eateries and coffeehouses. At the corner of Maunakea St, the ornate facade of the ❻ **Wo Fat Building** resembles a Chinese temple. The building – and, incidentally, also the villain of the *Hawaii Five-O* TV series – is named after Honolulu's oldest restaurant, which opened here in 1882 (it's now closed).

On King St, continue past the red pillars coiled with dragons outside the ❼ **Bank of Hawaii** to the corner of Kekaulike St and venture inside the buzzing 1904 ❽ **O'ahu Market**. Heading north on Maunakea St, you'll pass ❾ **lei shops** where skilled artisans string and braid blossom after blossom, filling the air with the scent of *pikake*.

By the river, the ❿ **statue of Dr Sun Yat-sen** (p78), 'the Father of Modern China,' stands guard over the senior citizens playing checkers at stone tables outdoors. Cut through the courtyard of the ⓫ **Chinatown Cultural Plaza**. Back on Maunakea St, cross over Vineyard Blvd to the venerable ⓬ **Kuan Yin Temple** (p76), originally built in 1880. Finish with a peaceful stroll around the mid-19th-century ⓭ **Foster Botanical Garden** (p76).

early 1960s. Ringing the bell at the shrine entrance is considered an act of purification for those who come to pray. Thousands of good-luck amulets are sold here, especially on January 1, when the temple heaves with people from all around O'ahu who come seeking New Year's blessings.

Lum Sai Ho Tong TEMPLE
(Map p72; ☎808-536-6590; 1315 River St; ⊙closed to the public) Founded in 1899, the Lum Sai Ho Tong Society was one of more than 100 societies started by Chinese immigrants in Hawaii to help preserve their cultural identity. This one was for the Lum clan hailing from west of the Yellow River. The temple is not open to the general public, but you can still admire the colorful exterior from the sidewalk below.

Hawai'i Heritage Center MUSEUM
(Map p72; ☎808-521-2749; 1040 Smith St; adult/child 5-18yr $1/25¢; ⊙9am-2pm Mon-Sat) Local volunteers with family ties to the community run this friendly gallery that displays changing historical and cultural exhibitions about O'ahu's Chinese, Japanese and other ethnic communities (including the Scots!).

Chinatown Cultural Plaza PLAZA
(Map p72; cnr Maunakea & N Beretania Sts) Inside this utilitarian modern mall, covering almost an entire city block, traditional acupuncturists, tailors and calligraphers work alongside travel agencies and dim-sum halls. In the small open-air central courtyard, elderly Chinese light incense before a **statue of Kuan Yin**. Down by the riverside, senior citizens practice tai chi after dawn and play checkers and mah-jongg all afternoon long.

Dr Sun Yat-sen Statue STATUE
(Map p72) Known as the 'Father of the Nation' in the Republic of China and the 'forerunner of democratic revolution' in the People's Republic of China, Sun Yat-sen traveled to Hawaii in 1879 and was educated at 'Iolani School and O'ahu College (later to become Punahou School and have Barack Obama as a student). Sun Yat-sen learned the ideals of the French and American revolutions and became President of the Republic of China (effectively now Taiwan) in 1912.

Ala Moana & Around

Ala Moana means 'Path to the Sea' and its namesake road, Ala Moana Blvd (Hwy 92), connects the coast between Waikiki and

HONOLULU FOR CHILDREN

For endless sand and a children's playground, take your *keiki* (child) or teen to Ala Moana Beach Park (p85), where local families hang out. For more of Honolulu's great outdoors, head up to Manoa Valley's Lyon Arboretum (p80), then hike to Manoa Falls (p85). Indoors, the Bishop Museum (p82) is entertaining for kids of all ages, or drop by the interactive family art center in the basement of the Honolulu Museum of Art.

Hawaii Children's Discovery Center (Map p70; ☎808-524-5437; www.discoverycenter-hawaii.org; 111 'Ohe St; adult/child 1-17yr/senior $10/10/6; ⊙9am-1pm Tue-Fri, 10am-3pm Sat & Sun; P 🚸) On a rainy day when you can't go to the beach, consider dropping by this hands-on museum for families. Opposite Kaka'ako Waterfront Park, the building was once the city's garbage incinerator, as evidenced by the surviving smokestack. Interactive science and cultural exhibits are geared toward elementary-school-aged children, preschoolers and toddlers.

The Fantastic You! exhibit explores the human body, allowing kids to walk through a mock human stomach. In the Your Town section, kids can drive a play fire engine or conduct a TV interview. Hawaiian Rainbows and Your Rainbow World introduce Hawaii's multicultural heritage, while Rainforest Adventures highlights Hawaii's natural environment and conservation.

From Waikiki, take TheBus 19, 20 or 42, then walk around 530yd *makai* (seaward) from the nearest bus stop on Ala Moana Blvd at Kolua St. Limited free parking.

Hawai'i Nature Center (☎808-955-0100; www.hawaiinaturecenter.org; 2131 Makiki Heights Dr; program fees from $10; 🚸) Inside the woodsy Makiki Forest Recreation Area, this small nonprofit community center conducts family-oriented environmental education programs, day camps and guided weekend hikes for ages six and up. Reservations are usually required; check the online calendar or call ahead for details.

Honolulu. Although most people think of Ala Moana only for its shopping mall, **Ala Moana Beach Park**, which happens to be O'ahu's biggest beach park, makes a relaxing alternative to crowded Waikiki.

★Honolulu Museum of Art MUSEUM

(Map p80; ☎808-532-8700; www.honolulumuseum.org; 900 S Beretania St; adult/child $10/free, 1st Wed & 3rd Sun each month free; ⏲10am-4:30pm Tue-Sat, 1-5pm Sun; P) This exceptional fine-arts museum may be the biggest surprise of your trip to O'ahu. The museum, dating to 1927, has a classical facade that's invitingly open and airy, with galleries branching off a series of garden and water-fountain courtyards. Plan on spending a couple of hours at the museum, possibly combining a visit with lunch at the Honolulu Museum of Art Cafe. Admission tickets are also valid for same-day visits to Spalding House.

Stunningly beautiful exhibits reflect the various cultures that make up contemporary Hawaii, including one of the country's finest Asian art collections, featuring everything from Japanese woodblock prints by Hiroshige and Ming dynasty–era Chinese calligraphy and painted scrolls to temple carvings and statues from Cambodia and India. Another highlight is the striking contemporary wing with Hawaiian works on its upper level, and modern art by such luminaries as Henri Matisse and Georgia O'Keeffe below. Although the collections aren't nearly as extensive as at Honolulu's Bishop Museum, you can still be bewitched by the Pacific and Polynesian artifacts, such as ceremonial masks, war clubs and bodily adornments.

Check the museum website for upcoming special events, including gallery tours and art lectures; film screenings and music concerts at the Doris Duke Theatre; **ARTafterDARK** (www.artafterdark.org) parties with food, drinks and live entertainment on the last Friday of some months; and family-friendly arts and cultural programs on the third Sunday of every month.

Parking at the Museum of Arts Center at Linekona lot, diagonally opposite the museum at 1111 Victoria St (enter off Beretania or Young Sts), costs $5. From Waikiki, take bus 2 or 13 or B CityExpress!.

Water Giver Statue STATUE

(Map p80; 1801 Kalakaua Ave, Hawaii Convention Center) Fronting the Honolulu Convention Center, this magnificent statue symbolically acknowledges the Hawaiian people for their generosity and expressions of goodwill to newcomers. Its sister statue is the *Storyteller* in Waikiki.

University Area

In the foothills of Manoa Valley, the neighborhood surrounding the University of Hawai'i (UH) Manoa campus feels youthful, with a collection of cafes, eclectic restaurants and one-of-a-kind shops.

University of Hawai'i at Manoa UNIVERSITY

(UH Manoa; Map p80; ☎808-956-8111; http://manoa.hawaii.edu; 2500 Campus Rd; P) About 2 miles northeast of Waikiki, the main campus of the statewide university system was born too late to be weighed down by the tweedy academic architecture of the mainland. Today, its breezy, tree-shaded campus is crowded with students from islands throughout Polynesia. The university has strong programs in astronomy, oceanography and marine biology, as well as Hawaiian, Pacific and Asian studies.

From Waikiki or downtown Honolulu, take bus 4; from Ala Moana, catch bus 6 or 18.

East-West Center CULTURAL CENTER

(Map p80; ☎808-944-7111; www.eastwestcenter.org; 1601 East-West Rd) On the eastern side of the UH campus, the East-West Center aims to promote mutual understanding among the peoples of Asia, the Pacific and the US. Changing exhibitions of art and culture are displayed in the EWC Gallery. Spy the Japanese teahouse garden and royal Thai pavilion outside. The center regularly hosts multicultural programs, including lectures, films, concerts and dance performances.

John Young Museum of Art MUSEUM

(Map p80; ☎808-956-3634; www.hawaii.edu/johnyoung-museum; Krauss Hall, 2500 Dole St; ⏲11am-2pm Mon-Fri, 1-4pm Sun) FREE A short walk downhill from the UH Campus Center, the John Young Museum of Art features 20th-century Hawaii painter John Young's collection of artifacts from the Pacific islands, Africa and Asia, mostly ceramics, pottery and sculpture. Although it's not huge, it's worth a quick visit.

Upper Manoa Valley, Tantalus & Makiki

Welcome to Honolulu's green belt. Roads into the verdant upper Manoa Valley wind north of the UH Manoa campus, passing

Ala Moana & University Area

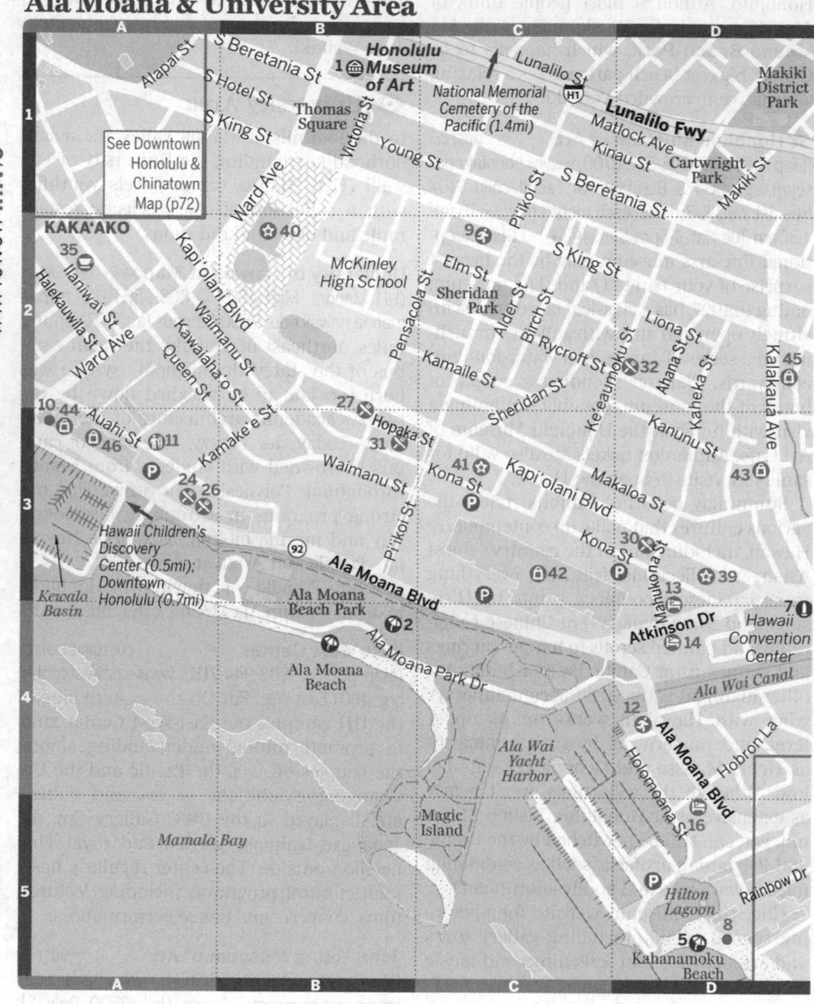

exclusive residential homes and entering forest reserve land in the hills above downtown's high-rises. Further west lies Makiki Heights, the neighborhood where President Barack Obama spent much of his boyhood.

Lyon Arboretum GARDENS

(☎info 808-988-0456, tour reservations 808-988-0461; www.hawaii.edu/lyonarboretum; 3860 Manoa Rd; donation $5, guided tour $10; ⏰8am-4pm Mon-Fri, 9am-3pm Sat, tours usually 10am Mon-Fri; P 👪) 🍃 Beautifully unkempt walking trails wind through this highly regarded 200-acre arboretum managed by the University of Hawai'i. It was originally founded in 1918 by a group of sugar planters growing native and exotic flora species to restore Honolulu's watershed and test their economic benefit. This is not your typical overly manicured tropical flower garden, but a mature and largely wooded arboretum, where related species cluster in a seminatural state. For a guided tour, call at least 24 hours in advance.

Key plants in the Hawaiian ethnobotanical garden are *'ulu* (breadfruit), *kalo* (taro) and *ko* (sugarcane) brought by early Polynesian settlers; *kukui,* once harvested to

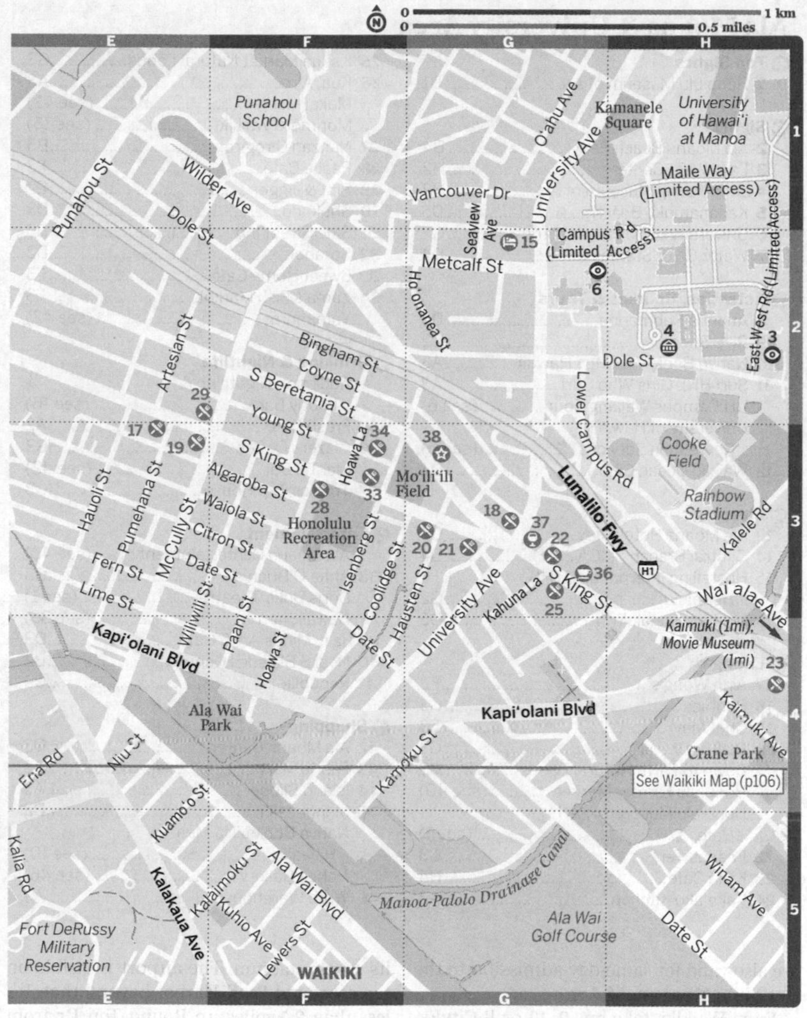

produce lantern oil; and *ti*, which was used for medicinal purposes during ancient times and for making moonshine after Westerners arrived. It's a short walk to **Inspiration Point**, or keep walking uphill for about 1 mile along a jeep road, then a narrow, tree-root-ridden path to visit seasonal **'Aihualama Falls**, a lacy cliffside cascade.

From Ala Moana Center, catch bus 5 toward Manoa Valley and get off at the last stop, then walk about half a mile uphill to the end of Manoa Rd. Limited free parking is available.

Spalding House MUSEUM

(☎808-526-1322; www.honoluluacademy.org; 2411 Makiki Heights Dr; adult/child 4-17yr $10/free, 1st Wed of the month free; ⏲10am-4pm Tue-Sat, noon-4pm Sun; P) Embraced by tropical sculpture gardens, this art museum occupies an estate house constructed in 1925 for O'ahu-born Anna Rice Cooke, a missionary descendant and wealthy arts patron. Inside the main galleries are changing exhibits of paintings, sculpture and other contemporary artwork from the 1940s through to today by international, national and island artists. There is a small cafe and gift shop on-site. Tickets

Ala Moana & University Area

Top Sights
1 Honolulu Museum of Art B1

Sights
2 Ala Moana Beach Park B4
3 East-West Center H2
4 John Young Museum of Art H2
5 Kahanamoku Beach D5
6 University of Hawai'i at Manoa G2
7 Water Giver Statue D4

Activities, Courses & Tours
8 Atlantis Submarine D5
9 Bike Shop C2
10 Native Books/Nā Mea Hawaii A3
11 Surf HNL Girls Who Surf A3
UH Campus Walking Tour .... (see 6)
University of Hawai'i Recreation Services .... (see 6)
12 Waikiki Ocean Club D4

Sleeping
13 Ala Moana Hotel D3
14 Central Branch YMCA D4
15 Hostelling International (HI) Honolulu G2
16 Modern Honolulu D5

Eating
17 Alan Wong's E3
18 Bubbies G3
19 Chef Mavro E3
20 Da Spot G3
21 Down to Earth Natural Foods G3
Honolulu Farmer Market .... (see 40)
Honolulu Museum of Art Cafe .... (see 1)
22 Imanas Tei G3
23 Kaila Cafe H4
24 Kaka'ako Kitchen A3
25 Kokua Market Natural Foods G3
26 Kua 'Aina A3
Makai Market .... (see 42)
Morimoto Waikiki .... (see 16)
27 Nanzan Girogiro B3
28 Peace Cafe F3
29 Pint & Jigger E2
30 Shokudo D3
31 Side Street Inn B3
32 Sorabol D2
33 Sweet Home Café F3
34 Yama's Fish Market F3
Yataimura .... (see 42)

Drinking & Nightlife
Addiction Nightclub & Lobby Bar .... (see 16)
35 Fresh Cafe A2
36 Glazers Coffee G3
Mai Tai Bar .... (see 42)
37 Tropics Tap House G3

Entertainment
Ala Moana Centertainment .... (see 42)
38 Anna O'Brien's G3
Doris Duke Theatre .... (see 1)
HawaiiSlam .... (see 35)
39 Jazz Minds Art & Café D3
40 Neal S Blaisdell Center B2
41 Republik C3

Shopping
42 Ala Moana Center C3
43 Fabric Mart D3
44 Island Slipper A3
45 Manuheali'i D2
Native Books/Nā Mea Hawaii .... (see 10)
Nohea Gallery .... (see 46)
46 Ward Warehouse A3

are also valid for same-day admission to the **Honolulu Museum of Art**.

From Waikiki, take bus 2, 13 or B CityExpress! toward downtown Honolulu and get off at the corner of Beretania and Alapa'i Sts; walk one block *makai* (seaward) along Alapa'i St and transfer to bus 15 bound for Pacific Heights, which stops outside Spalding House.

Pu'u 'Ualaka'a State Wayside LOOKOUT
(www.hawaiistateparks.org; 7am-7:45pm Apr-1st Mon in Sep, to 6:45pm 1st Tue in Sep-Mar; P) At this hillside park, sweeping views extend from Diamond Head on the left, across Waikiki and downtown Honolulu, to the Wai'anae Range on the right. The sprawling UH Manoa campus is easily recognized by its sports stadium. The airport is visible on the coast and Pearl Harbor beyond that. It's less than 2.5 miles up Round Top Dr from Makiki St to the park entrance, from where it's another half-mile drive to the lookout (bear left at the fork).

Greater Honolulu

★**Bishop Museum** MUSEUM
(Map p70; 808-847-3511; www.bishopmuseum.org; 1525 Bernice St; adult/child $20/15; 9am-5pm Wed-Mon; P) Like Hawaii's version of the Smithsonian Institute in Washington, DC, the Bishop Museum showcases a remarkable array of cultural and natural-history exhibits. It is often ranked as the finest Polynesian anthropological museum

in the world. Founded in 1889 in honor of Princess Bernice Pauahi Bishop, a descendant of the Kamehameha dynasty, it originally housed only Hawaiian and royal artifacts. These days it honors all of Polynesia.

The recently renovated main gallery, the **Hawaiian Hall**, resides inside a dignified three-story Victorian building. Displays covering the cultural history of Hawaii include a *pili* (grass) thatched house, carved *ki'i akua* (temple images), *kahili* (feathered royal staffs), shark-toothed war clubs and traditional *tapa* cloth made by pounding the bark of the paper mulberry tree. Don't miss the feathered cloak once worn by Kamehameha the Great, created entirely of the yellow feathers of the now-extinct *mamo* – some 80,000 birds were caught and plucked to create this single adornment. Meanwhile, upper-floor exhibits delve further into *ali'i* (royal) history, traditional life and relationships between Native Hawaiians and the natural world.

The fascinating two-story exhibits inside the adjacent **Polynesian Hall** cover the myriad cultures of Polynesia, Micronesia and Melanesia. You could spend hours gazing at astounding and rare ritual artifacts, from elaborate dance masks and ceremonial costumes to carved canoes. Next door, the **Castle Memorial Building** displays changing traveling exhibitions.

Across the Great Lawn, the eye-popping, state-of-the-art multisensory **Science Adventure Center** lets kids walk through an erupting volcano, take a minisubmarine dive and play with three floors of interactive multimedia exhibits.

The Bishop Museum is also home to O'ahu's only **planetarium**, which highlights traditional Polynesian methods of wayfaring (navigation), using wave patterns and the position of the stars to travel thousands of miles across the open ocean in traditional outrigger canoes, as well as modern astronomy and the cutting-edge telescope observatories atop Mauna Kea on the Big Island. Shows usually start at 11:30am, 1:30pm and 3:30pm daily except Tuesday, and are included in the museum admission price.

A gift shop off the main lobby sells books on the Pacific not easily found elsewhere, as well as some high-quality Hawaiian art, crafts and souvenirs. Check the museum website for special events, including popular 'Moonlight Mele' summer concerts, family-friendly Hawaiian cultural festivities and after-dark planetarium shows (buy tickets online or make reservations by calling ☎808-848-4168 in advance).

From Waikiki or downtown Honolulu, take bus 2 School St-Middle St to the intersection of School St and Kapalama Ave; walk one block *makai* on Kapalama Ave, then turn right onto Bernice St. By car, take eastbound H-1 Fwy exit 20, turn right on Houghtailing St, then take the second left onto Bernice St. Parking is free.

National Memorial Cemetery of the Pacific CEMETERY

(Map p70; ☎808-532-3720; www.cem.va.gov/cems/nchp/nmcp.asp; 2177 Puowaina Dr; ⏲8am-6:30pm Mar 2-Sep 29, to 5:30pm Sep 30-Mar 1; P) FREE Northeast of downtown Honolulu is a bowl-shaped crater, nicknamed the Punchbowl, formed by a long-extinct volcano. Hawaiians called the crater Puowaina ('hill of human sacrifices'). It's believed that at an ancient heiau here the slain bodies of kapu (taboo) breakers were ceremonially cremated upon an altar. Today the remains of ancient Hawaiians sacrificed to appease the gods share the crater floor with the bodies of nearly 50,000 soldiers, many of whom were killed in the Pacific during WWII.

The remains of Ernie Pyle, the distinguished war correspondent who was hit by machine-gun fire on Ie-shima during the final days of WWII, lie in section D, grave 109. Five stones to the left, at grave D-1, is the marker for astronaut Ellison Onizuka, the Hawai'i (Big Island) astronaut who perished in the 1986 *Challenger* space-shuttle disaster.

Even without the war sights, Punchbowl would be worth the drive up for the plum views of the city and Diamond Head. After entering the cemetery, bear left and go to the top of the hill, where there's a sweeping ocean-view lookout. Special events held at the cemetery include Memorial Day ceremonies to honor veterans and a traditional Easter sunrise Christian service.

From Waikiki, take bus 2, 13 or B CityExpress! toward downtown Honolulu and get off at Beretania and Alapa'i Sts. Walk one block *makai* along Alapa'i St and transfer to bus 15 Pacific Heights, which stops near the entrance at the corner of Puowaina Dr and Ho'okui St, then walk uphill for approximately 15 minutes. If you're driving, take the H1 Fwy westbound to the Pali Hwy; there's a marked exit on your right almost immediately as you start up the Pali Hwy. Then carefully follow the signs through winding, narrow residential streets.

Upper Manoa Valley, Tantalus & Makiki

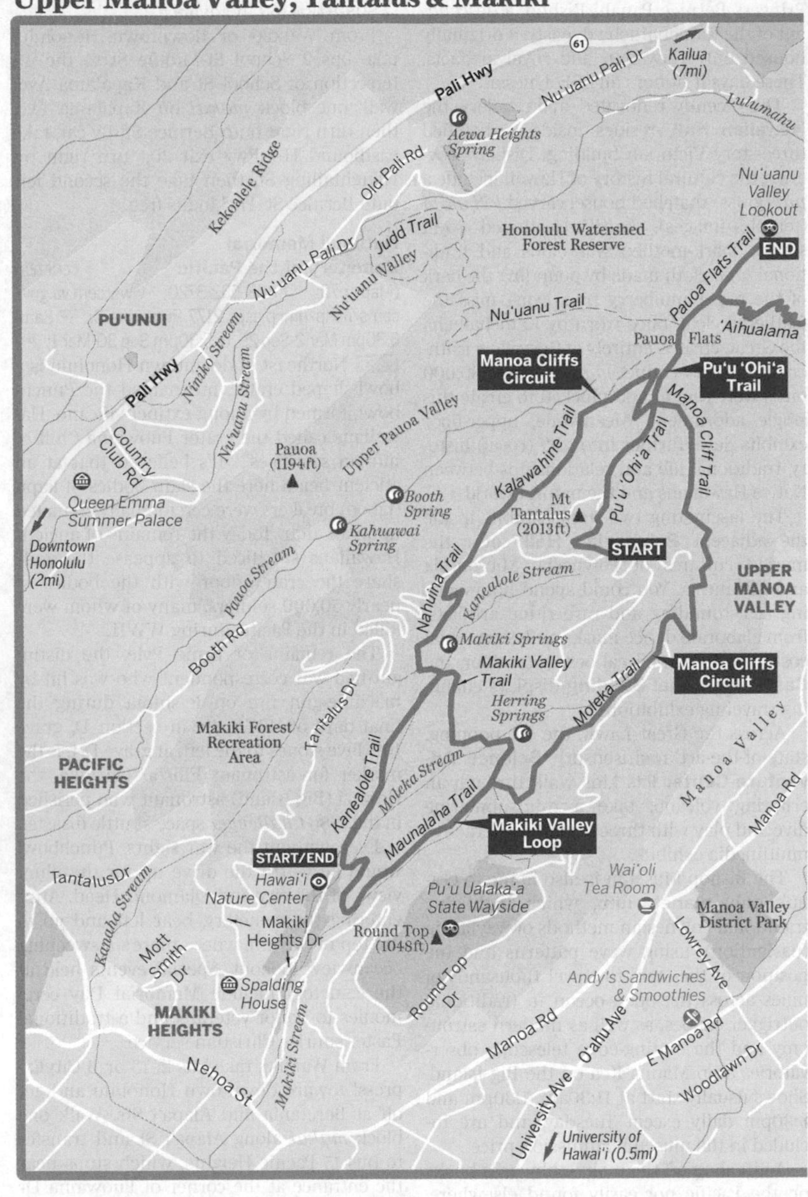

Queen Emma Summer Palace HISTORIC BUILDING
(☎808-595-3167; www.daughtersofhawaii.org; 2913 Pali Hwy; adult/child $8/1; ⏰9am-4pm, last guided tour 3pm; Ⓟ) In the heat and humidity of summer, Queen Emma (1836–85), the wife and royal consort of Kamehameha IV, used to slip away from her formal downtown Honolulu home to this cooler hillside retreat in Nu'uanu Valley. Gracious docents

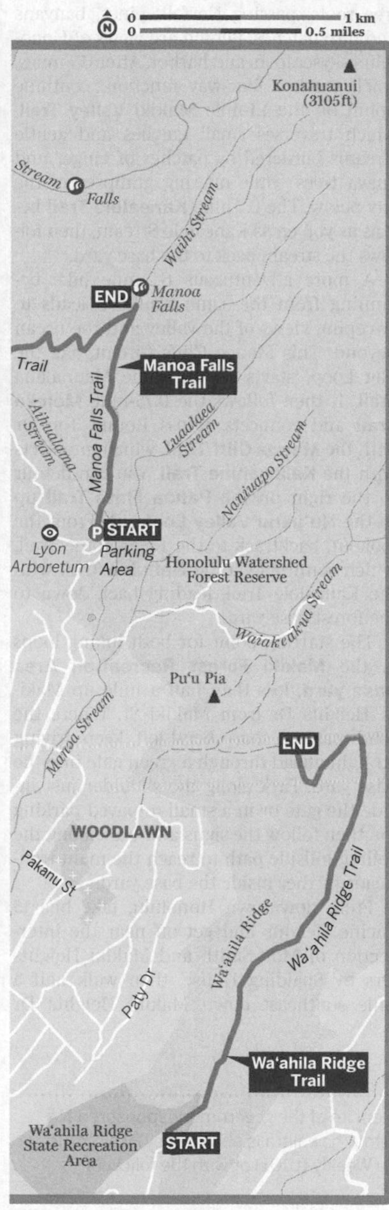

from the Daughters of Hawai'i society show off the cathedral-shaped koa cabinet that displays a set of china given by England's Queen Victoria, brightly colored feather cloaks and capes once worn by Hawaiian royalty, and more priceless antiques.

Built in Greek Revival style, the exterior recalls an old Southern plantation home, with its columned porch and high ceilings.

To get here, take bus 4 from Waikiki, the university area or downtown Honolulu, or bus 56, 57 or 57A from Ala Moana Center. Be sure to let the bus driver know where you're going, so you don't miss the stop. By car, look for the entrance on the northbound side of the Pali Hwy (Hwy 61), near the 2-mile marker.

Beaches

Ala Moana Beach Park — BEACH

(Map p80; 1201 Ala Moana Blvd; P) Opposite the Ala Moana Center shopping mall, this city park boasts a broad, golden-sand beach nearly a mile long buffered from passing traffic by shade trees. Ala Moana is hugely popular, yet big enough that it never feels too crowded. This is where Honolulu residents come to go running after work, play beach volleyball and enjoy weekend picnics. The park has full facilities, including lighted tennis courts, ball fields, picnic tables, drinking water, restrooms, outdoor showers and lifeguard towers.

The peninsula jutting from the southeast side of the park is **Magic Island**. Year-round, you can take an idyllic sunset walk around the peninsula's perimeter, within an anchor's toss of sailboats pulling in and out of neighboring Ala Wai Yacht Harbor.

Activities

Hiking & Walking

You could spend days enjoying the solitude of the forests and peaks around the city. Some of O'ahu's most popular hiking trails lead into the lush, windy Ko'olau Range just above downtown. For more info on O'ahu's trail system, see http://hawaiitrails.ehawaii.gov.

★ Manoa Falls Trail — HIKING

Honolulu's most rewarding short hike, this 1.6-mile round-trip trail runs above a rocky streambed before ending at a pretty little cascade. Tall tree trunks line the often muddy and slippery path. Wild orchids and red ginger grow near the falls, which drop about 100ft into a small, shallow pool. It's illegal to venture beyond the established viewing area.

Falling rocks and the risk of leptospirosis (a waterborne bacterial infection) make even wading dangerous.

On public transport, take bus 5 Manoa Valley from Ala Moana Center or the university area to the end of the line; from there, it's a half-mile walk uphill to the trailhead. By car, drive almost to the end of Manoa Rd, where a privately operated parking lot charges $5 per vehicle. Free on-street parking may be available just downhill from the bus stop.

Nu'uanu Valley Lookout HIKING

Just before Manoa Falls, the marked **'Aihualama Trail** heads up to the left and scrambles over boulders. The trail quickly enters a bamboo forest with some massive old banyan trees, then contours around the ridge, offering broad views of Manoa Valley.

Another mile of gradual switchbacks brings hikers to an intersection with the **Pauoa Flats Trail**, which ascends to the right for more than half a mile over muddy tree roots to the spectacular Nu'uanu Valley Lookout. High atop the Ko'olau Range, with O'ahu's steep *pali* visible all around, it's possible to peer through a gap over to the Windward Coast. The total round-trip distance to the lookout from the Manoa Falls trailhead is approximately 5.5 miles.

Makiki Valley Loop & Manoa Cliffs Circuit HIKING

A favorite workout for city dwellers, the 2.5-mile Makiki Valley Loop links three Tantalus-area trails. The loop cuts through a diverse tropical forest, mainly composed of non-native species introduced to reforest an area denuded by the 19th-century *'iliahi* (sandalwood) trade. Keep watch for the tumbledown remains of ancient Hawaiian stone walls and a historic coffee plantation.

Starting just past the Hawai'i Nature Center, the **Maunalaha Trail** crosses a small stream and climbs over a giant staircase of tree roots, passing Norfolk pines, banyans and taro patches. Behind are views of Honolulu's skyscrapers and harbor. After 0.7 miles, you'll reach a four-way junction: continue uphill on the 1.1-mile **Makiki Valley Trail**, which traverses small gulches and gentle streams bordered by patches of ginger and guava trees while offering glimpses of the city below. The 0.7-mile **Kanealole Trail** begins as you cross Kanealole Stream, then follows the stream back to the base yard.

A more adventurous 6.2-mile hike beginning from the same trailhead leads to sweeping views of the valley and the ocean beyond. This Manoa Cliffs Circuit, aka the 'Big Loop,' starts on the same Maunalaha Trail. It then follows the 0.75-mile **Moleka Trail** and connects across Round Top Dr with the **Manoa Cliff Trail**, which intersects with the **Kalawahine Trail**. You can detour to the right on the **Pauoa Flats Trail** up to the **Nu'uanu Valley Lookout**. From the lookout, backtrack to the Kalawahine Trail, which connects via the **Nahuina Trail** with the Kanealole Trail, leading back down to the forest base yard.

The starting point for both hiking loops is the **Makiki Forest Recreation Area base yard**, less than half a mile up Makiki Heights Dr from Makiki St. Where the road makes a sharp bend left, keep driving straight ahead through a green gate into the base yard. Park along the shoulder just inside the gate or in a small unpaved parking lot, then follow the signs and walk along the rolling hillside path to reach the main trailheads further inside the base yard.

From downtown Honolulu, take bus 15 Pacific Heights and get off near the intersection of Mott-Smith and Makiki Heights Drs by Spalding House, then walk half a mile southeast down Makiki Heights Dr

HIKE LIKE A LOCAL

To find more hiking trails island-wide, visit the website of the government sponsored **Na Ala Hele Hawaii Trail & Access System** (http://hawaiitrails.ehawaii.gov). For group hikes, check the calendar published by Honolulu Weekly (p101) or with the following organizations:

Hawaiian Trail & Mountain Club (http://htmclub.org; donation per hike $3) Volunteer-run hiking club that arranges intermediate to challenging group hikes on weekends all over the island. Trail descriptions and safety tips available online.

Sierra Club (Map p72; 808-537-9019; www.hi.sierraclub.org/oahu; 1040 Richards St; donation per hike adult/child under 14yr $5/1;) The Hawaii chapter of this nonprofit national organization leads weekend hikes and other outings around O'ahu, including volunteer opportunities to rebuild trails and combat invasive plants.

to the base yard. From Waikiki, take bus 4 Nu'uanu to the corner of Wilder Ave and Makiki St, then walk 528yd northeast up Makiki St, veering left onto Makiki Heights Dr and continuing another 704yd uphill to the base yard.

Wa'ahila Ridge Trail HIKING

Popular even with novice hikers, this boulder-strewn trail offers a cool retreat amid Norfolk pines and endemic plants, with ridgetop views of Honolulu and Waikiki. Rolling up and down a series of small saddles and knobs before reaching a grassy clearing, the 4.8-mile round-trip trail covers a variety of terrain in a short time, making an enjoyable afternoon's walk.

Look for the Na Ala Hele trailhead sign beyond the picnic tables inside Wa'ahila Ridge State Recreation Area, at the back of the St Louis Heights subdivision, east of Manoa Valley.

If you are traveling by car, turn left off Wai'alae Ave onto St Louis Dr at the stoplight. Heading uphill, veer left onto Bertram St, turn left onto Peter St, then turn left again onto Ruth Pl, which runs west into the park. From Waikiki, bus 14 St Louis Heights stops at the intersection of Peter and Ruth Sts, which is about a half-mile walk from the trailhead.

UH Campus Walking Tour WALKING TOUR

(Map p80; ☎808-956-7236; www.hawaii.edu/campuscenter; 2465 Campus Rd; ⏲8:30am-4:30pm Mon-Fri) The UH Campus Center is your departure point for free one-hour walking tours of campus, emphasizing history and architecture. Tours usually leave at 2pm Monday, Wednesday and Friday; no reservations are necessary, but check in 10 minutes beforehand at the ticket, information and ID office upstairs.

Ask for a free *Campus Art* brochure, which outlines a self-guided walking tour of outdoor sculptures and other works by notable Hawaii artists.

Cycling

Bike Shop CYCLING

(Map p80; ☎808-596-0588; www.bikeshophawaii.com; 1149 S King St; per day rental bicycle $20-85, car rack $5; ⏲9am-8pm Mon-Fri, 9am-5pm Sat, 10am-5pm Sun) Rents a variety of high-quality bicycles and can give you maps of cycling routes to match your skill level. Road cyclists looking for an athletic workout should pedal the Tantalus–Round Top scenic loop.

OFF THE BEATEN TRACK

TANTALUS–ROUND TOP SCENIC DRIVE

Offering skyline views to drivers and cyclists alike, the Tantalus–Round Top Scenic Drive climbs almost to the top of Mt Tantalus (2013ft), aka Pu'u 'Ohi'a. Bamboo, ginger, elephant-eared taro and eucalyptus trees make up the roadside profusion of tropical plants, as vines climb to the tops of telephone poles and twist their way across the wires. Starting above downtown Honolulu and the H-1 Fwy, this 10-mile circuit is a two-way loop called Tantalus Dr on its western side, Round Top Dr to the east. Many hiking trails branch off the loop, which passes by Pu'u 'Ualaka'a State Wayside with its magnificent views.

Surfing

Surf HNL Girls Who Surf SURFING, SUP

(Map p80; ☎808-772-4583; http://surfhnl.com/; 1020 Auahi St; 2hr lesson from $99, rental per hour/day SUP sets $18/47; ⏲8am-6pm) Award-winning girl-powered surf and stand up paddling (SUP) lessons are on offer in Ala Moana Beach Park and Ko Olina. Free hotel transportation to/from Waikiki for Ala Moana, $20 to Ko Olina. For surfboard, bodyboard and SUP rentals, delivery to Ala Moana Beach costs $15, to Ko Olina $40.

Whale-Watching

Atlantis Adventures WHALE-WATCHING

(Map p72; ☎800-381-0327; www.atlantisadventures.com/waikiki/whale-watch-cruises; Pier 6, Aloha Tower Dr; 2hr tour adult/child 7-12yr from $74/32) From mid-December through mid-April, Atlantis runs whale-watching cruises with an onboard naturalist on the *Navatek*, a high-tech catamaran designed to minimize rolling, twice daily at 9am and 12.30pm. Reservations are essential; book online for discounts, or look for coupons in free tourist magazines.

Golf

Moanalua Golf Club GOLF

(Map p70; ☎808-839-2311; www.mgchawaii.com; 1250 Ala Aolani St; green fees $45; ⏲by reservation only) The oldest golf course in Hawaii was built in 1898 by a Protestant missionary family and has the distinction of once having Amelia Earhardt land her aircraft on it! It's a fairly quick par-72 course with elevated greens, straight fairways and nine holes that are played twice around from different tees.

Tennis

Ala Moana Beach Park TENNIS
(1201 Ala Moana Blvd) Municipal park has 10 free first-come, first-served public tennis courts. If you hit balls during the day, you can cool off with a dip in the ocean afterwards; if you come at night, the courts are lit.

Courses

★ Native Books/ Nā Mea Hawaii ARTS, CULTURE
(Map p80; 808-596-8885; www.nativebookshawaii.com; Ward Warehouse, 1050 Ala Moana Blvd) Highly recommended community-oriented bookstore, art gallery and gift shop hosts free classes, workshops and demonstrations in hula dancing, Hawaiian language, traditional feather lei making and *lauhala* weaving, ukulele playing and more. Call for schedules and to check if preregistration is required.

University of Hawai'i Recreation Services OUTDOORS
(Map p80; 808-956-6468; www.manoa.hawaii.edu/studentrec/outdoored/classes.html) The University of Hawai'i at Manoa offers a variety of inexpensive outdoor sports, 'leisure classes' and group activities that are open to the public, from hiking ($12) and kayaking ($32) excursions around O'ahu, to half-day introductory bodyboarding ($27) and learn-to-sail classes ($27). Advance sign-up is required; check class schedules online or call ahead to register.

Tours

Architectural Walking Tour WALKING TOUR
(808-628-7243; www.aiahonolulu.org; tours $10; usually 9-11:30am Sat) Led by professional architects, these historical-minded walking tours will literally change your perspective on downtown Honolulu's capitol district. Reservations required; register online.

Hawaii Food Tours TOUR
(808-926-3663; www.hawaiifoodtours.com; tours from $119) These guys offer two extremely popular tours. The five-hour 'Hole-in-the-Wall' tour hits all sorts of spots around Honolulu, such as Chinatown, island plate-lunch stops, beloved bakeries, crack-seed candy shops and more. The seven- to eight-hour 'North Shore Food Tour' heads to the other side of the island. Tours include food, fun and transportation. Reservations are essential.

Festivals & Events

Some of Honolulu's biggest festivals spill over into Waikiki.

Chinese New Year CULTURAL
(http://chinatownhonolulu.org; late Jan–mid-Feb) Taking place between late January and mid-February, Chinatown's swirling festivities include a parade with lion dances and crackling firecrackers.

Great Aloha Fun Run SPORTS
(www.greataloharun.com; Feb) A popular 8.15-mile race from the harborfront Aloha Tower to Aloha Stadium on the third Monday in February.

★ Honolulu Festival CULTURAL
(www.honolulufestival.com; Mar) Three days of Asian-Pacific cultural exchange with music, dance and drama performances, an arts-and-crafts fair, a parade and fireworks, all in early to mid-March.

Lantern Floating Hawaii CULTURAL
(www.facebook.com/lanternfloatinghawaii; May) On the last Monday in May, the souls of the dead are honored with a Japanese floating-lantern ceremony after sunset at Magic Island in Ala Moana Beach Park.

Pan-Pacific Festival ART, CULTURAL
(www.pan-pacific-festival.com; early Jun) Three days of Japanese, Hawaiian and South Pacific entertainment in early to mid-June, with music, dancing and *taiko* (traditional Japanese drumming) at Waikiki and the Ala Moana Center.

King Kamehameha Hula Competition DANCE
(http://hulacomp.webstarts.com; Jun) One of Hawaii's biggest hula contests, with hundreds of dancers competing at downtown's Neal S Blaisdell Center in late June.

Queen Lili'uokalani Keiki Hula Competition DANCE
(www.kpcahawaii.com/Site/Queen_Liliuokalani_Keiki_Hula_Comp.html; Jul) Children's hula troupes from throughout Hawaii take over the stage at the Neal S Blaisdell Center in mid-July.

Prince Lot Hula Festival DANCE
(www.mgf-hawaii.org; ⏲Jul) The state's oldest and largest noncompetitive hula event invites Hawaii's leading hula *halau* (schools) to the royal Moanalua Gardens on the third Saturday in July.

Hawaii Dragon Boat Festival SPORTS, MUSIC
(www.dragonboathawaii.com; ⏲Jul) Colorful Chinese dragon boats race to the beat of island drummers at Ala Moana Beach Park in late July.

★ **Hawai'i Food & Wine Festival** FOOD
(www.hawaiifoodandwinefestival.com; ⏲Sep) Star chefs, sustainable farms and food lovers come together for a weekend of wining and dining in early September.

Talk Story Festival LITERATURE
(⏲Oct; 👪) Storytellers gather at Ala Moana Beach Park over a long weekend in mid-October; Friday is usually spooky stories.

★ **Hawaii International Film Festival** FILM
(www.hiff.org; ⏲Oct) This celebration of celluloid packs the city's movie theaters with homegrown and imported Pacific Rim, Asian, mainland American and European films for 11 days from late October.

King Kalakaua's Birthday MUSIC, CULTURAL
(www.iolanipalace.org; ⏲Nov) Victorian-era decorations and a concert of traditional monarchy-era music by the Royal Hawaiian Band at 'Iolani Palace on November 16.

Sleeping

Honolulu doesn't have much in the way of accommodations. Most visitors sleep by the beach at Waikiki.

Hostelling International (HI) Honolulu HOSTEL $
(Map p80; ☎808-946-0591; www.hostelsaloha.com; 2323-A Seaview Ave; dm/r $22/85; ⏲reception 8am-noon & 4pm-midnight; P @ 📶) Along a quiet residential side street near the UH Manoa campus, this tidy, low-slung house just a short bus ride from Waikiki has same-sex dorms and basic private rooms kept cool by the tradewinds. Some students crash here while looking for apartments, so it's often full. It has a kitchen, a laundry room, lockers and two free parking spaces.

Central Branch YMCA HOSTEL $
(Map p80; ☎808-941-3344; www.ymcahonolulu.org; 401 Atkinson Dr; s/d $55/75, with shared bathroom $45/65; @ 📶 🏊) Opposite the Ala Moana Center, the ol' Y lets unfussy budget travelers book basic, well-worn rooms with shared bathrooms or slightly larger en suite rooms on single-sex or co-ed floors. Perks include an Olympic-sized swimming pool and a gym. Traffic noise, a general lack of cleanliness and an institutional atmosphere are downers.

Ala Moana Hotel HOTEL $$
(Map p80; ☎808-955-4811, 866-956-4262; www.alamoanahotelhonolulu.com; 410 Atkinson Dr; r/ste from $139/285; P ❄ @ 📶 🏊) Looming over the Ala Moana Center mall and convenient to the convention center, this high-rise offers bland hotel rooms without island flavor. Upper floors may have straight-on views of the beach – request the Waikiki Tower for a lanai (balcony). Parking costs $20.

Airport Honolulu Hotel HOTEL $$
(Map p70; ☎818-836-0661, 866-956-4262; www.outrigger.com; 3401 N Nimitz Hwy; r from $110; P ❄ @ 📶 🏊) If you need to be next to the airport (although Waikiki hotels are only a 20-minute taxi ride away), this nondescript hotel sleeps underneath the noisy freeway. Rates include infrequent 24-hour airport-shuttle service and free wi-fi.

Aston at the Executive Centre Hotel HOTEL $$$
(Map p72; ☎808-539-3000; www.resortquesthawaii.com; 1088 Bishop St; 📶) Honolulu's only downtown hotel is geared for business travelers and extended stays. Large, modern suites with floor-to-ceiling windows get kitchenettes, while one-bedroom condos add a full kitchen and washer/dryer. A fitness center, heated lap pool and complimentary continental breakfast round out the executive-class amenities. Free wi-fi.

Eating

If O'ahu weren't so far away from the US mainland, you'd hear a lot more buzz about this multiethnic chowhound capital. Watch for **Eat the Street** (www.streetgrindz.com), an outdoor rally for food trucks and street-food vendors on the last Friday of each month. During **Restaurant Week Hawaii** (www.restaurantweekhawaii.com), usually happening in mid-November, dozens of locally owned restaurants offer serious discounts for dining out, including prix-fixe dinner menus.

MR OBAMA'S NEIGHBORHOOD

During the 2008 race to elect the 44th president of the United States, Republican vice-presidential candidate Sarah Palin kept asking the country, 'Who is Barack Obama?' It was Obama's wife, Michelle, who had an answer ready: 'You can't really understand Barack until you understand Hawaii.'

Obama, who grew up in Honolulu's Makiki Heights neighborhood, has written that 'Hawaii's spirit of tolerance…became an integral part of my world view, and a basis for the values I hold most dear.' The local media and many *kama'aina* (those who were born and grew up in Hawaii) agree that Hawaii's multiethnic social fabric helped shape the leader who created a rainbow coalition during the 2008 election.

Obama has also said Hawaii is a place for him to rest and recharge. Back in 1999 he wrote: 'When I'm heading out to a hard day of meetings and negotiations, I let my mind wander back to Sandy Beach, or Manoa Falls… It helps me, somehow, knowing that such wonderful places exist and I'll always be able to return to them.'

If you want to walk in Obama's boyhood and presidential footsteps on O'ahu, here are some places you can visit:

- Manoa Falls (p85)
- Alan Wong's (p93)
- Kapi'olani Beach Park (p112)
- Rainbow Drive-In (p122)
- Waiola Shave Ice (p122)
- Hanauma Bay Nature Preserve (p132)
- Sandy Beach Park (p133)
- National Memorial Cemetery of the Pacific (p83)
- Nu'uanu Pali State Wayside (p135)
- Olomana Golf Links (p137)

Downtown

Weekday cafes for office workers and students abound downtown.

Vita Juice HEALTH FOOD $

(Map p72; ☎808-526-1396; www.freewebs.com/vitajuice; 1111-C Fort St Mall; items $3-7; ⏰7am-5pm Mon-Fri;) Flooded with Hawai'i Pacific University students, this orange-walled juice and smoothie bar takes the concept of 'brain food' seriously. Healthy ingredients range from Amazonian acai and Tibetan goji berries to green tea and ginseng.

'Umeke Market & Deli SUPERMARKET $

(Map p72; ☎808-522-7377; www.umekemarket.com; 1001 Bishop St; mains $4-10; ⏰7am-4pm Mon-Fri;) Fresh, organic island produce, natural-foods groceries and a vegetarian- and vegan-friendly takeout deli counter for healthy pick-me-ups such as kale and quinoa salads, hummus sandwiches, hoisin turkey meatloaf and iced *kombucha* (effervescent tea).

Bishop St Cafe JAPANESE, ITALIAN $

(Map p72; ☎808-537-6951; www.facebook.com/bishopstreetcafe; 725 Bishop St; mains $7-15; ⏰11am-3pm Mon-Fri) Offering up lunches to downtown workers in an extremely convivial setting, Bishop St Cafe is one of those lovely fusion places, serving equally good Japanese and Italian cuisine. There's outside courtyard seating in the historic Dillingham Transportation Building. Choices range from Japanese udon or soba noodles to panini and pastas.

★Cafe Julia CAFE $$

(Map p72; ☎808-533-3334; http://cafejuliahawaii.com; 1040 Richards St; mains $10-28; ⏰11am-2pm Mon-Fri, plus 4-9pm Wed-Fri, 9am-1pm & 4-9pm Sun) In the charming old YWCA Laniakea building opposite Iolani Palace, Cafe Julia is a gem. Named after Julia Morgan (one of America's first female architects, who designed the building), the service and cuisine is superb in an open-air setting. Perfect for *poke* tacos or garlic ahi for lunch; settle into a few cocktails in the evening.

Hiroshi Eurasian Tapas FUSION $$

(Map p72; ☎808-533-4476; www.hiroshihawaii.com; Waterfront Plaza, 500 Ala Moana Blvd; shared plates $9-17, mains $26-29; ⏰5:30-9:30pm; 🅿) A serious player on the Honolulu culinary scene, chef Hiroshi Fukui puts a Japanese twist on Pacific Rim fusion style, from crab cannelloni swirled with miso sauce to smoked *hamachi* (yellow-tail) with a garlicky habanero pepper kick. Order foamy tropical martinis and fresh-fruit sodas at the bar. Make reservations for dinner.

Hukilau HAWAIIAN $$

(Map p72; ☎808-523-3460; www.dahukilau.com/honolulu; Executive Centre, 1088 Bishop St; mains $11-20; ⏰11am-2pm & 3-9pm Mon-Fri) Underground at downtown's only high-rise hotel, this sports bar and grill serves an aloha-shirt-wearing business crowd. Huge salads, sandwiches and burgers aren't as tempting as only-in-Hawaii specialties such as miso butterfish, kimchi (Korean seasoned vegetable pickle dish) and *kalua* (cooked in an underground pit) pig *saimin* (noodle soup) and ahi *poke*. Live music on most Friday nights.

Chinatown

Chinese restaurants are plentiful, but the cavalcade doesn't stop there – dishes from all across Asia and around the Pacific Rim are cooked in this historic downtown neighborhood, packed with hole-in-the-wall kitchens, dim-sum palaces and trendy fusion eateries.

Maunakea Marketplace FAST FOOD $

(Map p72; 1120 Maunakea St; meals from around $6; ⏰5.30am-4pm; 👪) In the food court of this open-air marketplace, you'll find about 20 stalls dishing out authentic Chinese, Filipino, Thai, Vietnamese and Korean fare. Chow down at tiny wooden tables crowded into the walkway. Cash only.

Bangkok Chef THAI $

(Map p72; ☎808-585-8839; http://bangkokchefexpress.com; 1627 Nu'uanu Ave; mains $8-10; ⏰10:30am-9pm Mon-Sat, noon-8pm Sun) It feels strangely like you're eating out of someone's garage, but who cares when the Thai curries, noodle dishes and savory salads taste exactly like those from a Bangkok street cart? Dessert is either mango ice cream over warm sticky rice topped with salty peanuts, or tapioca pudding cups in a rainbow of flavors.

Pho To-Chau VIETNAMESE $

(Map p72; ☎808-533-4549; 1007 River St; mains $7-10; ⏰8:30am-2:30pm) Always packed, this Vietnamese restaurant holds fast to its hard-earned reputation for serving Honolulu's best *pho* (Vietnamese noodle soup). With beef, broth and vegetables, the dish is a complete meal in itself. It's so popular that you may have to queue underneath the battered-looking sign outside to score one of a dozen or so rickety wooden tables.

Downbeat Diner & Lounge DINER $

(Map p72; ☎808-533-2328; www.downbeatdiner.com; 42 N Hotel St; mains $5-15; ⏰11am-midnight Mon, to 3am Tue-Thu, to 4am Fri & Sat, to 10pm Sun; 🌶👪) Shiny late-night diner with lipstick-red booths posts a vegetarian- and vegan-friendly menu of salads, sandwiches, grilled burgers and heaping island-style breakfasts such as *loco moco* (rice, fried egg and hamburger patty) and Portuguese sweet-bread French toast. The lounge, running a full bar, features live music three to four times per week.

Mei Sum CHINESE $

(Map p72; ☎808-531-3268; 1170 Nu'uanu Ave; dim-sum dishes $2-4, mains $8-23; ⏰8am-9pm Mon-Fri, from 7am Sat & Sun) Where else can you go to satisfy that crazy craving for dim sum in the afternoon or evening (though maybe not as fresh as it is in the morning)? For over a decade, this no-nonsense corner stop has been cranking out a multitude of cheap little plates and a full spread of Chinese mains.

Mabuhay Cafe & Restaurant FILIPINO $

(Map p72; ☎808-545-1956; 1049 River St; mains $6-13; ⏰10am-9pm Mon-Sat) The tablecloths, well-worn counter stools and jukebox should clue you in that this is a mom-and-pop joint. They've been cooking pots of succulent, garlic-laden pork *adobo* (meat marinated in vinegar and garlic) and *kare-kare* (oxtail stew) on this corner by the river since the 1960s.

★**The Pig & the Lady** ASIAN, FUSION $$

(Map p72; ☎808-585-8255; http://thepigandthelady.com; 83 N King St; mains $10-25; ⏰10.30am-2pm Mon-Sat plus 5.30-9.30pm Tue-Thu, to midnight Fri & Sat) An award-winning Vietnamese fusion restaurant that you'll need to reserve a table at in the evening, The Pig & the Lady is one of the hottest new places to dine on the island. Imaginative lunch sandwiches come with shrimp chips or *pho* broth, while delicious dinner options include Laotian fried chicken and dipping-style *pho tsukumen*.

★ Lucky Belly ASIAN, FUSION $$
(Map p72; ☎808-531-1888; www.luckybelly.com; 50 N Hotel St; mains $8-14; ⏲11am-2pm & 5pm-midnight Mon-Sat) Where Japanese pop art hangs over sleek bistro tables packed elbows-to-shoulders, this arts-district noodle bar crafts hot and spicy Asian fusion bites, knock-out artisanal cocktails and amazingly fresh, almost architectural salads that the whole table can share. A 'Belly Bowl' of ramen soup topped with buttery pork belly, smoked bacon and pork sausage is carnivore heaven.

Duc's Bistro FUSION $$
(Map p72; ☎808-531-6325; www.ducsbistro.com; 1188 Maunakea St; mains $16-26; ⏲11am-2pm Mon-Fri, 5-10pm daily) Honolulu's bigwigs hang out after work at this swank French-Vietnamese bistro with a tiny bar. Ignore the surrounding seedy streets and step inside this culinary oasis for buttery escargot, *bánh xèo* (Vietnamese crepes), pan-fried fish with green mango relish, and fire-roasted eggplant. A small jazz combo serenades diners some evenings. Reservations recommended.

Little Village Noodle House CHINESE $$
(Map p72; ☎808-545-3008; 1113 Smith St; mains $8-22; ⏲10:30am-10:30pm Sun-Thu, to midnight Fri & Sat; ❄) Forget about chop suey. If you live for anything fishy in black-bean sauce, this is Honolulu's gold standard. On the eclectic pan-Chinese menu, regional dishes are served up garlicky, fiery or with just the right dose of saltiness. For a cross-cultural combo, fork into sizzling butterfish or roasted pork with island-grown taro. Reservations recommended.

Soul de Cuba CUBAN $$
(Map p72; ☎808-545-2822; www.souldecuba.com; 1121 Bethel St; mains $10-24; ⏲11am-10pm Mon-Thu, to 11pm Fri & Sat, to 9pm Sun) Nowhere else in Honolulu can you sate your craving for Afro-Cuban food and out-of-this-world mojitos except at this hip resto-lounge near Chinatown's art galleries. Stick with family-recipe classics such as *ropa vieja* (shredded beef in tomato sauce), *bocadillos* (sandwiches, served until 5pm) and black-bean soup. Reservations recommended.

Ala Moana & Around

Shopping-mall food courts are ground zero for this neighborhood, but surprisingly many kitchens of star chefs are spread out along trafficked thoroughfares or on dumpy-looking side streets.

Honolulu Farmer Market MARKET $
(Map p80; http://hfbf.org/markets; Neal S Blaisdell Center, 777 Ward Ave; ⏲4-7pm Wed; 🌶👪) 🍃 Pick up anything from aquacultured seafood and O'ahu honey to fresh fruit and tropical flowers, all trucked into the city by Hawaii Farm Bureau Federation members. Graze food stalls set up by island chefs, food artisans and Kona coffee roasters too.

Yataimura JAPANESE $
(Map p80; www.shirokiya.com; 2nd fl, Shirokiya, Ala Moana Center, 1450 Ala Moana Blvd; items $2-12; ⏲10am-10pm) Head to the upper level of the Ala Moana Center's Japanese department store Shirokiya to unlock a beer garden and boisterous food-stall marketplace that's a gold mine of takeout meals, from bento boxes to hot *takoyaki* (fried minced-octopus balls).

Makai Market FAST FOOD $
(Map p80; 1st fl, Ala Moana Center, 1450 Ala Moana Blvd; mains $6-12; ⏲8am-8pm; 👪) Let your preconceptions about mall food courts fly out the window at these Asian-fusion-flavored indoor food stalls. Dig into Yummy Korean BBQ, Donburi Don-Don for Japanese rice bowls or the island-flavored Lahaina Chicken Company and Ala Moana Poi Bowl.

Kaka'ako Kitchen FAST FOOD $
(Map p80; ☎808-596-7488; http://kakaakokitchen.com; Ward Center, 1200 Ala Moana Blvd; meals $7-15; ⏲10am-9pm Mon-Thu, to 10pm Fri & Sat, to 5pm Sun; 🅿👪) As '*ono* (delicious) as always, this popular counter joint still dishes up healthy-minded plate lunches with brown rice and organic greens. For a local deli twist, get the tempura mahimahi sandwich on a homemade taro bun. Anticipate lines at lunchtime.

Kua 'Aina FAST FOOD $
(Map p80; ☎808-591-9133; www.kua-aina.com; Ward Center, 1200 Ala Moana Blvd; burgers & sandwiches $5-10; ⏲10:30am-9pm Mon-Sat, to 8pm Sun; 🅿👪) Shopping-mall outpost of Hale'iwa's gourmet burger joint serves crispy matchstick fries, pineapple and avocado beef burgers, and grilled ahi and veggie sandwiches for hungry crowds. Also in Kapolei.

Side Street Inn HAWAIIAN $$
(Map p80; ☎808-591-0253; http://sidestreetinn.com; 1225 Hopaka St; mains $7-20; ⏰2pm-midnight Sun-Thu, to 1am Fri & Sat) This late-night mecca is where you'll find Honolulu's top chefs hanging out after their own kitchens close, along with partyin' locals who come for hearty portions of *kalbi* (short ribs) and pan-fried pork chops. Make reservations and bring friends, or join the construction-worker crews ordering plate lunches at the takeout counter. Warning: big portions!

Honolulu Museum of Art Cafe MODERN AMERICAN $$
(Map p80; ☎808-532-8734; www.honoluluacademy.org; Honolulu Museum of Art, 900 S Beretania St; mains $11-22; ⏰11:30am-1:30pm Tue-Sat) Market-fresh salads and sandwiches made with O'ahu-grown ingredients, a decent selection of wines by the glass and tropically infused desserts make this an indulgent way to support the arts. Romantic tables facing the sculpture courtyard fountain and underneath a monkeypod tree are equally well suited to dates or power-broker lunches. Reservations recommended.

Sorabol KOREAN $$
(Map p80; ☎808-947-3113; www.sorabolhawaii.com; 805 Ke'eaumoku St; set meals $11-38; ⏰24hr) Sorabol feeds lunching Korean ladies by day and bleary-eyed clubbers before dawn. Detractors often sniff that its reputation is undeserved, but the rest of the city has undying gratitude for this around-the-clock joint, often visited after midnight in a drunken stupor. Marinated *kalbi* and steamed butterfish are specialties. Watch out for a late-night service charge (20%).

Shokudo JAPANESE $$
(Map p80; ☎808-941-3701; www.shokudojapanese.com; 1585 Kapi'olani Blvd; shared plates $5-25; ⏰11:30am-midnight Sun-Thu, to 1am Fri & Sat) Knock back lychee sake-tinis at this sleek, modern Japanese restaurant (*shokudō* means 'dining room') that's always filled to the rafters. A mixed-plate traditional Japanese and island-fusion menu depicts dozens of dishes, from *mochi* (rice cake) cheese gratin to lobster dynamite rolls, more traditional noodles and sushi, and silky house-made tofu. Reservations recommended.

★ Alan Wong's HAWAII REGIONAL CUISINE $$$
(Map p80; ☎808-949-2526; www.alanwongs.com; 1857 S King St; mains $35-60; ⏰5-10pm) One of O'ahu's big-gun chefs, Alan Wong offers his creative interpretations of Hawaii Regional Cuisine with emphasis on fresh seafood and local produce. Order Wong's time-tested signature dishes such as ginger-crusted *onaga* (red snapper), Kona lobster seafood stew and twice-cooked *kalbi*. Make reservations for in-demand tables weeks in advance. Valet parking $5.

Chef Mavro FUSION $$$
(Map p80; ☎808-944-4714; www.chefmavro.com; 1969 S King St; multicourse tasting menus from $95; ⏰6-9pm Wed-Sun) At Honolulu's most avant-garde restaurant, maverick chef George Mavrothalassitis creates conceptual dishes, all paired with Old and New World wines. Unfortunately the cutting-edge experimental cuisine, like the half-empty atmosphere, sometimes falls flat, although some will swear they've had the meal of a lifetime. Reservations essential.

Nanzan Girogiro JAPANESE $$$
(Map p80; ☎808-521-0141; www.guiloguilo.com; 560 Pensacola St; chef's tasting menu $50-60; ⏰6pm-midnight Thu-Mon) Traditional *kaiseki ryōri* (seasonal small-course) cuisine infused with Hawaii-grown fruits and vegetables, fresh seafood and, frankly, magic. Inside an art gallery, bar seats ring the open kitchen. Ceramic turtles hide savory custard in their shells and pottery bowls harbor tea-soaked rice topped with delicately poached fish. Reservations essential.

University Area

Internationally flavored restaurants that'll go easy on your wallet cluster south of the UH Manoa campus near the three-way intersection of University Ave and S King and Beretania Sts.

Kokua Market Natural Foods SUPERMARKET $
(Map p80; ☎808-941-1922; www.kokua.coop; 2643 S King St; ⏰8am-9pm;) Hawaii's only natural-food co-op has an organic hot-and-cold salad bar and a vegetarian- and vegan-friendly deli for takeout meals on S King St near UH. Free parking off Kahuna Lane behind the store.

Down to Earth Natural Foods SUPERMARKET $
(Map p80; ☎808-947-7678; www.downtoearth.org; 2525 S King St; ⏰7:30am-10pm;) Emphasizing organic and natural foods, this always-busy store has a vegetarian- and vegan-friendly salad bar, a deli for made-to-order sandwiches, a juice and smoothie

bar, and a few sidewalk tables for chowing down. Free garage parking on the 2nd floor.

Da Spot INTERNATIONAL $

(Map p80; ☎808-941-1313; http://daspot.net; 2469 S King St; smoothies $3-5, plate lunches $6-10; ⌚10:30am-9:30pm Mon-Sat) An enterprising duo of chef-owners set up kiosks at farmers markets and on the UH Manoa campus, but this converted auto mechanic's garage is home base for their world fusion and island-flavored plate lunches, plus dozens of smoothie combinations. Egyptian chicken, Southeast Asian curries and homemade baklava will leave you as stuffed as a dolma.

Bubbies ICE CREAM $

(Map p80; www.bubbiesicecream.com; Varsity Center, 1010 University Ave; items $1.50-6; ⌚noon-midnight Mon-Thu, to 1am Fri & Sat, to 11:30pm Sun; 👪) Homemade ice cream in tropical flavors such as papaya-ginger plus unique bite-sized frozen *mochi* (Japanese pounded-rice cakes) ice-cream treats. Very, very difficult to walk past without going in once you've tried a mango *mochi* ice cream!

Yama's Fish Market SEAFOOD, FAST FOOD $

(Map p80; www.yamasfishmarket.com; 2332 Young St; mains $5-10; ⌚9am-7pm Mon-Sat, to 5pm Sun; P) Swing by this side-street seafood market for heaping island-style plate lunches – eg *kalua* pig, *mochiko* chicken, *lomilomi* salmon – and freshly mixed *poke* by the pound with sour poi (fermented taro paste) and sweet *haupia* (coconut) pudding on the side.

Peace Cafe HEALTH FOOD $

(Map p80; ☎808-951-7555; www.peacecafehawaii.com; 2239 S King St; mains $8-10; ⌚11am-9pm Mon-Sat, to 3pm Sun; 🌱) Vegan home cooking is the theme at this strip-mall kitchen, where daily dishes get handwritten on the chalkboard. Pick a Popeye spinach or cilantro hummus sandwich to go, or a substantial lunch box with Moroccan stew. *Mochi* and soy ice creams are dairy-free delights.

Sweet Home Café TAIWANESE $

(Map p80; ☎808-947-3707; 2334 S King St; shared dishes $2-8; ⌚4-10pm) You won't believe the lines snaking outside this strip-mall eatery's door. On long wooden family-style tables squat heavily laden, steaming-hot pots filled with lemongrass beef, sour cabbage, mixed tofu or Asian pumpkin squash, plus spicy dipping sauces and extra lamb, chicken or tender beef tongue as side dishes. Bonus: complimentary shave ice for dessert!

★ Kaila Cafe CAFE $$

(Map p80; ☎808-732-3330; www.cafe-kaila-hawaii.com; 2919 Kapi'olani Blvd, Market City Shopping Center; mains $8-18; ⌚7am-3pm) This place has racked up Best Breakfast gold medals in local culinary awards and Kaila is so successful that she has opened her second shop... in Tokyo! Expect to line up to get in for the legendary lineup of incredibly well-presented breakfast specials. A tad out of the way, but well worth the effort.

Pint & Jigger PUB FOOD $$

(Map p80; ☎808-744-9593; http://pintandjigger.com; 1936 S King St; shared plates $4-13; ⌚4:30pm-midnight Sun-Wed, to 2am Thu-Sat) Red-brick walls and high-top tables make this gastropub, not too far west of the UH Manoa campus, trendy enough for aspiring 20- and 30-something foodies, who mix and match craft beers and cocktails with creative nosh like guava wood-smoked sausage sliders and Scotch eggs.

Imanas Tei JAPANESE $$$

(Map p80; ☎808-941-2626; 2626 S King St; shared dishes $5-30; ⌚5-11:30pm Mon-Sat) Look for the orange sign outside this long-standing *izakaya,* where staff shout their welcome *('Irrashaimase!')* as you make your way to a low-slung tatami-mat booth. Sake fans come here for the liquid version of rice, then graze their way through a seemingly endless menu of sushi and epicurean and country-style Japanese fare.

Reserve days, if not weeks, in advance or stand in line for open seating after 7pm.

Greater Honolulu

Kaimuki is making its mark on Honolulu's cuisine scene by sprouting trendy restaurants along Wai'alae Ave, east of the university area.

★ Andy's Sandwiches & Smoothies SANDWICHES $

(☎808-988-6161; www.andyssandwiches.com; 2904 E Manoa Rd; items $4-12; ⌚7am-5pm Mon-Thu, to 4pm Fri, to 2.30pm Sun) Andy's is a hidden gem up the Manoa valley that doesn't see too many tourists. Opposite the Manoa Shopping Centre, it's a squeeze to get in, but worth the effort. The sandwiches, smoothies and salads are superb, especially the Bird's Nest salad.

★ Helena's Hawaiian Food HAWAII REGIONAL CUISINE $

(Map p70; ☎808-845-8044; http://helenashawaiianfood.com; 1240 N School St; dishes $3-8; ⏲10am-7:30pm Tue-Fri) Walking through the door is like stepping into another era. Even though long-time owner Helena Chock has passed away, her relatives still command the family kitchen, which opened in 1946. Most people order à la carte and Helena's is good! It's just a few blocks southeast of the Bishop Museum.

★ Tamura's Poke SEAFOOD $

(Map p70; ☎808-735-7100; www.tamurasfinewine.com/pokepage.html; 3496 Waialae Ave, Kaimuki; ⏲11am-8:45pm Mon-Fri, 9:30am-8:45pm Sat, 9:30am-7:45pm Sun; P) Arguably the best *poke* on the island is up on Waialae Rd in undistinguished-looking Tamura's Fine Wines & Liquors. Head inside, turn right, wander down to *poke* corner and feast your eyes. The 'spicy *ahi*' and the smoked marlin are to die for. Ask for tasters before you buy and take away.

Liliha Bakery BAKERY $

(Map p70; ☎808-531-1651; www.lilihabakeryhawaii.com; 515 N Kuakini, cnr Liliha St; items from $2, mains $6-10; ⏲6am-5.30am Tue-Sat, to 8pm Sun) Not far northwest of Chinatown, this old-school island bakery and diner causes a neighborhood traffic jam for its coco-puff and green-tea cream pastries. Still hungry? Grab a counter seat and order a hamburger steak or other hearty lumberjack faves in Liliha's retro coffee shop.

Crack Seed Store SWEETS $

(Map p70; ☎818-737-1022; 1156 Koko Head Ave; ⏲9.30am-6pm Mon-Sat, noon-4pm Sun; 👪) Mom-and-pop candy store on a side street in Kaimuki vends overflowing glass jars of made-from-scratch crack seed, plus addictive frozen slushies spiked with *li hing mui* (salty dried plums).

12th Avenue Grill MODERN AMERICAN $$

(Map p70; ☎808-732-9469; http://12thavegrill.com; 1120 12th Ave; mains $18-36; ⏲5:30-10pm Sun-Thu, to 11pm Fri & Sat) Hidden in a side road off Waialae Ave, this Kaimuki grill has been picking up a number of best-restaurant awards of late. Combining the efforts of an impressive team and using as much local produce as possible, 12th Ave Grill has the locals drooling.

Town FUSION $$

(Map p70; ☎808-735-5900; www.townkaimuki.com; 3435 Wai'alae Ave; mains breakfast & lunch $5-16, dinner $16-26; ⏲7am-2:30pm daily, plus 5:30-9:30pm Mon-Thu, to 10pm Fri & Sat) At this hip modern coffee shop and bistro hybrid in Kaimuki, the motto is 'local first, organic whenever possible, with aloha always.' On the daily-changing menu of boldly flavored cooking are burgers and steaks made from North Shore free-range cattle and salads that taste as if the ingredients were just plucked from a backyard garden.

Salt Kitchen & Tasting Bar MODERN AMERICAN $$

(Map p70; ☎808-744-7567; http://salthonolulu.com; 3605 Wai'alae Ave; shared plates $5-21, mains $10-25; ⏲5pm-midnight Sun-Thu, to 1am Fri & Sat) Mexican oxtail empanadas, Italian ravioli made with Hawaii-grown squash, and Indian naan with pickled eggplant fill the tapas-sized plates lined up all along the lacquered bar top. Bartenders shake up grapefruit daiquiris and tequila martinis for a chic crowd of urbane revelers during afternoon happy hours in the Kaimuki neighborhood.

BREWPUBS

If you're searching for that perfect pint glass from the USA's westernmost state, you can round out your souvenir collection at the Big Island's Kona Brewing Company (p132) in Hawai'i Kai, or stop by these two Honolulu brewpubs.

Honolulu Beerworks (Map p70; ☎808-589-2337; www.honolulubeerworks.com; 328 Cooke St; ⏲11am-10pm Mon-Thu, to midnight Fri & Sat) This new kid on the microbrewery scene is fast building up a following with 12 brews on tap and barrel-aged beers. Based in a warehouse with recycled wooden walls, chairs and benches, the menu of 'beer food' may be limited, but it certainly hits the spot as you work your way through the beers on offer.

Gordon Biersch Brewery Restaurant (Map p72; ☎808-599-4877; www.gordonbiersch.com; 1st fl, 1 Aloha Tower Dr; ⏲10am-11pm Sun-Thu, to midnight Fri & Sat) Down fresh lagers made according to Germany's centuries-old purity laws, often with live music by the waterfront.

Nico's at Pier 38 SEAFOOD $$
(Map p70; ☎808-540-1377; www.nicospier38.com; 1133 N Nimitz Hwy; breakfast & lunch plates $6-13, dinner mains $13-16; ⏰6:30am-9pm Mon-Sat, 10am-9pm Sun) Chef Nico was inspired by the island-cuisine scene to merge his classical French training with Hawaii's humble plate lunch. French standards such as *steak frites* appear alongside market-fresh fish sandwiches and local belly-fillers such as *furikake*-crusted ahi and hoisin BBQ chicken. Tables with chairs are positioned near the waterfront and Honolulu's fish auction. Happy hour 4pm to 6pm daily.

Mitch's Fish Market & Sushi Bar SEAFOOD $$$
(☎808-837-7774; www.mitchsushi.com; 524 Ohohia St; small plates $5-35, set meals $25-40, chef's tasting menu $110; ⏰11:30am-8:30pm) A hole-in-the-wall sushi bar near the airport for cashed-up connoisseurs, who come for the chef's superbly fresh *omakase* tasting menu and rarely seen fishy delicacies shipped in from around the globe. Reservations essential; BYO.

Drinking & Nightlife

Every self-respecting bar in Honolulu has a *pupu* (snacks) menu to complement the liquid sustenance, and some bars are as famous for their appetizers as their good-times atmosphere. A key term to know is *pau hana* (literally 'stop work'), Hawaiian pidgin for 'happy hour.' Chinatown's edgy nightlife scene revolves around N Hotel St, which was the city's notorious red-light district not so long ago.

Downtown

Beach Bum Cafe COFFEE
(Map p72; ☎808-521-6699; www.beachbumcafe.com; 1088 Bishop St; ⏰6:30am-5pm Mon-Fri; 📶) Right in downtown's high-rise financial district, this connoisseur's coffee bar serves 100% organic, grown-in-Hawaii beans, roasted in small batches and hand-brewed just one ideal cup at a time. Chat up the baristas while you sip the rich flavors of the Big Island, Maui, Kaua'i and even Moloka'i. Also has an outpost at the First Hawaiian Center down the road.

Honolulu Coffee Company COFFEE
(Map p72; ☎808-521-4400; www.honolulucoffee.com; 1001 Bishop St; ⏰6am-5:30pm Mon-Fri, 7am-noon Sat; 📶) Overlooking Tamarind Sq with city skyline views, here you can take a break from tramping around Honolulu's historical sites for a java jolt brewed from handpicked, hand-roasted 100% Kona estate-grown beans. Also at Ala Moana Center and in Waikiki.

M Nightclub CLUB, LOUNGE
(Map p72; ☎808-529-0010; http://mnlhnl.com; Waterfront Plaza, 500 Ala Moana Blvd; admission after 10pm Fri & Sat $10; ⏰4:30pm-2am Tue-Thu, 4:30pm-4am Fri, 8pm-4am Sat) Flickering votive candles, bartenders who juggle bottles of Grey Goose and Patron and table service at sexy white couches backlit with purple hues – this restaurant-nightclub hybrid is as close as Honolulu gets to Vegas. An insider crowd of dressed-to-kill locals bumps shoulders on the dance floor ruled by electronica DJs.

Chinatown

Fresh Cafe Downtown CAFE
(Map p72; ☎808-953-7374; www.freshcafehi.com; 1121 Nu'uanu Ave; ⏰7am-11pm Mon-Sat) Fresh Cafe's new bright and breezy Chinatown place is proving just as popular as its original location. With everything from breakfast to lunch to dinner and bar, with options to sit inside or out, Fresh hits the spot with its 'garden-fresh and local' attitude to food. Dedicated to promote local music, culture and art too!

Manifest BAR, CAFE
(Map p72; http://manifesthawaii.com; 32 N Hotel St; ⏰8am-2am Mon-Fri, 10am-2am Sat; 📶) Smack in the middle of Chinatown's art scene, this lofty apartment-like space adorned with provocative photos and paintings doubles as a serene coffee shop by day and a cocktail bar by night, hosting movie and trivia nights and DJ sets (no cover). Foamy cappuccinos and spicy chais are daytime perfection.

Tea at 1024 TEAHOUSE
(Map p72; ☎808-521-9596; www.teaat1024.net; 1024 Nu'uanu Ave; ⏰11am-2pm Tue-Fri, to 3pm Sat) Tea at 1024 takes you back to another era. Cutesy sandwiches, scones and cakes accompany your choice of tea as you relax and watch the Chinatown crowd rush by the window. It even has bonnets for you to don to add to the ambience. Set menus run from $20.95 per person; reservations recommended.

Hank's Cafe BAR
(Map p72; ☎808-526-1410; http://hankscafehawaii.com; 1038 Nu'uanu Ave; ⏰7am-2am) You can't get more low-key than this neighbor-

hood dive bar on the edge of Chinatown. Owner Hank is a jack-of-all-trades when it comes to the barfly business: the walls are decorated with Polynesian-themed art, live music rolls in some nights and regulars practically call it home.

Next Door CLUB, LOUNGE

(Map p72; 808-852-2243; www.facebook.com/nextdoorhi; 43 N Hotel St; 7pm-2am Wed-Sat) Situated on a skid-row block of N Hotel St where dive bars are still the order of the day, this svelte cocktail lounge is a brick-walled retreat with vivid red couches and flickering candles. DJs spin house, hip-hop, funk, mash-ups and retro sounds, while on other nights loud, live local bands play just about anything.

Fix Sports Lounge & Nightclub CLUB

(Map p72; 808-728-4416; http://thefixsportsloungeandnightclub.com; 80 S Pau'ahi St; 11am-2am Mon-Fri, 5pm-2am Sat) These guys have got the bases covered with a cavernous sports lounge full of large flat-screens offering the standard sports-lounge fare…morphing into a raging nightclub later on with DJs and dancing. One of the largest venues on O'ahu.

Bar 35 BAR

(Map p72; 808-537-3535; http://bar35hawaii.com; 35 N Hotel St; 4pm-2am Mon-Fri, 6pm-2am Sat) Filled with aloha, this indoor-outdoor watering hole has a dizzying 100 domestic and international bottled beers to choose from, plus addictive chef-made gourmet fusion pizzas to go with all the brews. There's live music or DJs some weekend nights.

Ala Moana & Around

Fresh Cafe CAFE

(Map p80; 808-688-8055; http://freshcafehi.com; 831 Queen St; 8am-11pm Mon-Sat, 9am-6pm Sun;) At this alternative coffeehouse in an industrial warehouse area just west of Ala Moana Center, artists, bohemians and hipster hangers-on sip Vietnamese coffee, *pikake* (jasmine flower) iced tea, and Thai or *haupia*-flavored lattes. Evening special events vary.

Mai Tai Bar BAR

(Map p80; 808-947-2900; www.maitaibar.com; Ho'okipa Tce, 3rd fl, Ala Moana Center, 1450 Ala Moana Blvd; 11am-1am;) A happening bar in the middle of a shopping center? We don't make the trends, we just report 'em. During sunset and late-night happy hours, this enormous circular tropical bar is packed with a see-and-flirt crowd. Island-style live music plays nightly.

> DON'T MISS
>
> **FIRST FRIDAYS IN CHINATOWN**
>
> Chinatown's somewhat seedy Nu'uanu Ave and Hotel St have become surprisingly cool places for a dose of urban art and culture, socializing and bar-hopping from 5pm on the first Friday of each month (www.firstfridayhawaii.com). What was once a low-key art walk has become almost too big for its britches, according to local naysayers. A giant block party now rocks out to live music and DJs, with food trucks and over-21 wristbands required for getting into Chinatown's most popular bars and clubs – be prepared to queue behind velvet ropes.

University Area

Glazers Coffee CAFE

(Map p80; 808-391-6548; www.glazerscoffee.com; 2700 S King St; 7am-11pm Mon-Thu, 7am-9pm Fri, 8am-11pm Sat & Sun;) They're serious about brewing strong espresso drinks and batch-roasted coffee at this university students' hangout, where you can kick back on comfy living-room sofas next to jazzy artwork and plentiful electrical outlets.

Tropics Tap House SPORTS BAR

(Map p80; 808-955-5088; www.tropicstaphouse.com; 1019 University Ave; 2pm-2am Mon-Fri, 11am-2pm Sat & Sun) Relive your college days at this open-air sports bar on University that couldn't be called fancy, but gets the job done. Standard sports-bar fare, but lots of beers to choose from and even beer cocktails. Lots of big screens for sports.

Upper Manoa Valley, Tantalus & Makiki

Wai'oli Tea Room TEAHOUSE

(808-988-5800; www.thewaiolitearoom.com; 2950 Manoa Rd; 8am-2pm) If 19th-century author Robert Louis Stevenson were still hanging around Honolulu today, this is where you'd find him. Set in the verdant Manoa Valley, this open-air teahouse overlooks gardens of red ginger and birds-of-paradise and serves excellent breakfasts and lunches. Afternoon high tea by reservation only.

Greater Honolulu

★La Mariana Sailing Club BAR
(Map p70; ☎808-848-2800; www.lamarianasailingclub.com; 50 Sand Island Access Rd; ⏲11am-9pm) Time warp! Who says all the great tiki bars have gone to the dogs? Irreverent and kitschy, this 1950s joint by the lagoon is filled with yachties and long-suffering locals. Classic mai tais are as killer as the other signature tropical potions, complete with tiki-head swizzle sticks and tiny umbrellas. Grab a waterfront table and dream of sailing to Tahiti.

☆ Entertainment

For what's going on after dark this week, from live music and DJ gigs to theater, movies and cultural events, check the TGIF section of the *Honolulu Star-Advertiser* (www.honolulupulse.com), which comes out every Friday, and the free alternative tabloid *Honolulu Weekly* (http://honoluluweekly.com), published every Wednesday.

Live Music

If traditional and contemporary Hawaiian music is what you crave, don't look any further than Waikiki. But if it's jazz, alt-rock and punk sounds you're after, venture outside the tourist zone into Honolulu's other neighborhoods.

Republik LIVE MUSIC
(Map p80; ☎808-941-7469; http://jointherepublik.com; 1349 Kapi'olani Blvd; ⏲lounge 6pm-2am Mon-Sat, concert schedules vary) Honolulu's most intimate concert hall for touring and local acts – indie rockers, punk and metal bands, and more – has a graffiti-bomb vibe and backlit black walls that trippily light up. Buy tickets for shows in advance, to make sure you get in and also to save a few bucks.

Dragon Upstairs LIVE MUSIC
(Map p72; ☎808-526-1411; http://thedragonupstairs.com; 2nd fl, 1038 Nu'uanu Ave; ⏲usually 7pm-2am) Right above Hank's Cafe in Chinatown, this claustrophobic hideaway with a sedate older vibe and lots of funky artwork and mirrors hosts a rotating lineup of jazz cats, blues strummers and folk singers, usually on Thursday, Friday and Saturday nights. Occasional $5 cover charge.

Anna O'Brien's LIVE MUSIC
(Map p80; ☎808-946-5190; http://annaobriens.com; 2440 S Beretania St; ⏲2pm-2am) A college dive bar, part roadhouse and part arthouse, the reincarnation of Anna Bananas, goes beyond its retro-1960s 'Summer of Love' atmosphere to book reggae, alt-rock, punk and metal bands. Regular DJs, comedy nights and Sunday reggae. Check the online calendar for what's on and cover charges.

Jazz Minds Art & Café LIVE MUSIC
(Map p80; ☎808-945-0800; www.honolulujazzclub.com; 1661 Kapi'olani Blvd; cover charge $10; ⏲9pm-2am Mon-Sat) Don't let the nearby strip clubs turn you off this place. This tattered brick-walled lounge with an almost speakeasy ambience pulls in the top island talent – fusion jazz, funk, bebop, hip-hop, surf rock and minimalist acts. However, you will need to be prepared for a stiff two-drink minimum.

Performing Arts

★Hawaii Theater PERFORMING ARTS
(Map p72; ☎808-528-0506; www.hawaiitheatre.com; 1130 Bethel St) Beautifully restored, this grande dame of O'ahu's theater scene is a major venue for dance, music and theater. Performances include top Hawaii musicians, contemporary plays, international touring acts and film festivals. The theater also hosts the annual Ka Himeni Ana competition of singers in the traditional *nahenahe* style, accompanied by ukuleles.

Neal S Blaisdell Center PERFORMING ARTS
(Map p80; ☎808-768-5252; www.blaisdellcenter.com; 777 Ward Ave) A cultural linchpin, this modern performing-arts complex stages symphony and chamber-music concerts, opera performances and ballet recitals, prestigious hula competitions, Broadway shows and more. Occasionally big-name pop and rock touring acts play here instead of at Aloha Stadium. Parking costs from $6.

ARTS at Marks Garage PERFORMING ARTS
(Map p72; ☎808-521-2903; www.artsatmarks.com; 1159 Nu'uanu Ave; ⏲11am-6pm Tue-Sat) On the cutting edge of the Chinatown arts scene, this community gallery and performance space puts on a variety of live shows, from stand-up comedy, burlesque cabaret nights and conversations with island artists to live jazz and Hawaiian music.

Kumu Kahua Theatre PERFORMING ARTS
(Map p72; ☎808-536-4441; www.kumukahua.org; 46 Merchant St) In the restored Kamehameha V Post Office building, this little 100-seat

treasure is dedicated to premiering works by Hawaii's playwrights, with themes focusing on contemporary multicultural island life, often richly peppered with Hawaiian pidgin.

Ala Moana Centertainment PERFORMING ARTS
(Map p80; ☎808-955-9517; www.alamoanacenter.com; Ground fl, Center Court, 1450 Ala Moana Blvd; 👪) The mega shopping center's courtyard area is the venue for all sorts of island entertainment, including music by O'ahu musicians and the Royal Hawaiian Band, Japanese *taiko* drumming and Sunday-afternoon *keiki* (children's) hula shows.

HawaiiSlam PERFORMING ARTS
(Map p80; www.hawaiislam.com; Fresh Cafe, 831 Queen St; admission before/after 8:30pm $3/5; ⏲8:30pm 1st Thu of each month) One of the USA's biggest poetry slams, here international wordsmiths, artists, musicians, MCs and DJs share the stage. For aspiring spoken-word stars, sign-up starts at 7:30pm.

Cinemas

★Doris Duke Theatre CINEMA
(Map p80; ☎808-532-8768; www.honolulumuseum.org; Honolulu Museum of Art, 900 S Beretania St; tickets $10) Shows a mind-bending array of experimental, alternative, retro-classic and art-house films, especially ground-breaking documentaries, inside the Honolulu Museum of Art. For weekday matinees, validated parking costs $3 (evenings and weekends free).

Movie Museum CINEMA
(Map p70; ☎808-735-8771; www.kaimukihawaii.com; 3566 Harding Ave; tickets $5; ⏲noon-9pm Thu-Mon) In the Kaimuki neighborhood, east of the UH Manoa campus, this sociable spot screens classic oldies, foreign flicks and indie films, including some Hawaii premieres, in a tiny theater equipped with digital sound and just 20 comfy Barca-loungers. Reservations recommended.

Shopping

Ala Moana Center MALL
(Map p80; www.alamoanacenter.com; 1450 Ala Moana Blvd; ⏲9.30am-9pm Mon-Sat, 10am-7pm Sun; 👪) This open-air shopping mall and its nearly 300 department stores and mostly chain stores could compete on an international runway with some of Asia's famous megamalls. A handful of Hawaii specialty shops, such as Crazy Shirts for tees, Reyn Spooner's for aloha shirts, Loco Boutique for swimsuits, Local Motion surfwear and Na Hoku jewelry, are thrown into the mix.

HONOLULU'S BEST HAWAIIANA SHOPS

- Native Books/Nā Mea Hawaii (p99)
- Bailey's Antiques & Aloha Shirts (p126)
- Cindy's Lei Shoppe (p100)
- Manuheali'i (p99)
- Kamaka Hawaii (p100)
- Tin Can Mailman (p100)
- Honolulu Museum of Art (p79)
- Bishop Museum (p82)

Ward Warehouse MALL
(Map p80; www.wardcenters.com; 1050 Ala Moana Blvd; ⏲10am-9pm Mon-Sat, to 6pm Sun) Across the street from Ala Moana Beach, this mini-mall has many one-of-a-kind island shops and eateries. There's a threat that it will all be bowled over to make way for glitzy towers, but at the time of research, Ward Warehouse survives!

★Native Books/ Nā Mea Hawaii BOOKS, GIFTS
(Map p80; ☎808-597-8967; www.nativebookshawaii.com; Ward Warehouse, 1050 Ala Moana Blvd; ⏲10am-8:30pm Mon-Thu, to 9pm Fri & Sat, to 6pm Sun) So much more than just a bookstore stocking Hawaiiana tomes, CDs and DVDs, this cultural gathering spot also sells beautiful silk-screened fabrics, koa-wood bowls, Hawaiian quilts, fishhook jewelry and hula supplies. Call or check online for special events, including author readings, live local music and cultural classes.

Nohea Gallery ARTS, CRAFTS
(Map p80; www.noheagallery.com; Ward Warehouse, 1050 Ala Moana Blvd; ⏲10am-9pm Mon-Sat, to 6pm Sun) A meditative space amid the shopping-mall madness, this high-end gallery sells handcrafted jewelry, glassware, pottery and woodwork, all of it made in Hawaii. Local artisans occasionally give demonstrations of their crafts on the sidewalk outside.

Manuheali'i CLOTHING
(Map p80; ☎808-942-9868; www.manuhealii.com; 930 Punahou St; ⏲9:30am-6pm Mon-Fri, 9am-4pm Sat, 10am-3pm Sun) Look to this island-born

CHINATOWN ART GALLERIES

Pick up a free map from any of Chinatown's two dozen art galleries, most within a two-block radius of the Hawaii Theater.

ARTS at Marks Garage (Map p72; ☎808-521-2903; www.artsatmarks.com; 1159 Nu'uanu Ave; ⊙noon-5pm Tue-Sat) Performance art and eclectic works by up-and-coming island artists.

Pegge Hopper Gallery (Map p72; www.peggehopper.com; 1164 Nu'uanu Ave; ⊙11am-4pm Tue-Fri, to 3pm Sat) Represents the namesake artist's distinctive prints and paintings depicting voluptuous island women.

Louis Pohl Gallery (Map p72; www.louispohlgallery.com; 1142 Bethel St; ⊙11am-5pm Tue, to 3pm Wed-Sat) Paintings by contemporary island artists and a former 'living treasure' of Hawaii.

shop for original and modern designs. Hawaiian musicians often sport Manuheali'i's bold-print silk aloha shirts. Flowing synthetic print and knit dresses and wrap tops take inspiration from the traditional muumuu but are transformed into spritely contemporary looks. Also in Kailua.

Cindy's Lei Shoppe ARTS, CRAFTS

(Map p72; ☎808-536-6538; www.cindysleishoppe.com; 1034 Maunakea St; ⊙usually 6am-6pm Mon-Sat, to 5pm Sun) At this inviting little shop, a Chinatown landmark, you can watch aunties craft flower lei made of orchids, plumeria, twining maile, lantern *'ilima* (flowering ground-cover) and ginger. Several other lei shops clustered nearby will also pack lei for you to carry back home on the plane.

Kamaka Hawaii MUSIC

(Map p72; ☎808-531-3165; www.kamakahawaii.com; 550 South St; ⊙8am-4pm Mon-Fri) Skip right by those tacky souvenir shops selling cheap plastic and wooden ukuleles. Kamaka specializes in handcrafted ukuleles made on O'ahu since 1916, with prices starting at around $500. Its signature is an oval-shaped 'pineapple' ukulele, which has a more mellow sound. Call ahead for free 30-minute factory tours, usually starting at 10:30am Tuesday through Friday.

Tin Can Mailman ANTIQUES, BOOKS

(Map p72; http://tincanmailman.net; 1026 Nu'uanu Ave; ⊙11am-5pm Mon-Thu, to 9pm Fri, to 4pm Sat) If you're a big fan of vintage tiki wares and 20th-century Hawaiiana books, you'll fall in love with this little Chinatown antiques shop. Thoughtfully collected treasures include jewelry and ukuleles, silk aloha shirts, tropical-wood furnishings, vinyl records, rare prints and tourist brochures from the post-WWII tourism boom. No photos allowed.

Fabric Mart ARTS, CRAFTS

(Map p80; ☎808-947-4466; www.fmart.com; 1631 Kalakaua Ave; ⊙9am-7pm) This fabric store has masses of Hawaiian print materials that can be used for everything from cushion covers to dresses to aloha shirts. Buy them at best prices by the yard. The only place on the island with more fabric is the main store out in Aiea.

Island Slipper SHOES

(Map p80; www.islandslipper.com; Ward Warehouse, 1050 Ala Moana Blvd; ⊙10am-9pm Mon-Sat, to 8pm Sun) Across Honolulu and Waikiki, scores of stores sell flip-flops (aka 'rubbah slippah'), but nobody else carries such ultra-comfy suede and leather styles – all made in Hawaii since 1946 – let alone such giant sizes (as one clerk told us, 'We fit *all* the island people.'). Try on as many pairs as you like until your feet really feel the aloha.

Madre Chocolate FOOD

(Map p72; ☎808-377-6440; http://madrechocolate.com; 8 N Pau'ahi St; ⊙11am-8pm Tue-Sat, to 6pm Mon) The Honolulu outpost of this Kailua chocolate company is serving up a storm in Chinatown with free samplings of such innovative flavors as Lili'koi Passionfruit and Coconut Milk & Caramelized Ginger Chocolate. A must for chocolate lovers, but it don't come cheap! If you're really keen, it even offers a five-day 'Experience Hawaiian Cacao & Chocolate Bootcamp' on O'ahu.

Lion Coffee GIFTS, SOUVENIRS

(☎808-847-3600; www.lioncoffee.com; 1555 Kalani St; ⊙6am-5pm Mon-Sat; 📶) In an out-of-the-way warehouse west of downtown en route to the airport, this discount grown-in-Hawaii coffee giant roasts myriad flavors from straight-up strong (100% Kona 24-Karat and

Diamond Head espresso blend) to outlandishly wacky (chocolate macnut, toasted coconut). Friendly baristas pour free tastes.

Information

DANGERS & ANNOYANCES

Drug dealing and gang activity are prevalent on the north side of Chinatown, particularly along Nu'uanu Stream and the River St pedestrian mall, which should be avoided after dark.

EMERGENCY

Honolulu Police Department (☎808-529-3111; www.honolulupd.org; 801 S Beretania St) For nonemergencies (eg stolen property reports necessary for insurance claims).

INTERNET ACCESS

Cheaper cybercafes on King St near the UH Manoa campus stay open late.

FedEx Office (www.fedex.com/us/office; per hour $12; wi-fi) Ala Moana (1500 Kapi'olani Blvd; ⏰7:30am-9pm Mon-Fri, 10am-6pm Sat, noon-6pm Sun); Downtown (590 Queen St; ⏰7am-11pm Mon-Fri, 9am-9pm Sat & Sun); University Area (2575 S King St; ⏰24hr; wi-fi) Self-serve computer terminals (20¢ to 30¢ per minute), pay-as-you-go digital photo-printing and CD-burning stations and free wi-fi.

Hawaii State Library (☎808-586-3500; www.librarieshawaii.org; 478 S King St; ⏰10am-5pm Mon & Wed, 9am-5pm Tue, Fri & Sat, 9am-8pm Thu; wi-fi) Free wi-fi and internet terminals (temporary nonresident library card $10) downtown that may be reserved by calling ahead.

MEDIA

Newspapers & Magazines

Honolulu Magazine (www.honolulumagazine.com) Glossy monthly magazine covering arts, culture, fashion, shopping, lifestyle and cuisine. Also with online edition.

Honolulu Star-Advertiser (www.staradvertiser.com) Honolulu's daily newspaper; look for 'TGIF,' Friday's special events and entertainment pull-out section. Also with online edition.

Honolulu Weekly (www.honoluluweekly.com) Free weekly arts-and-entertainment tabloid has a local events calendar listing museum and gallery exhibits, cultural classes, outdoor activities, farmers markets, volunteering meet-ups and 'whatevas.'

Radio & TV

KHET (cable channel 10) Hawaii public TV (PBS).

KHPR (88.1FM) Hawaii Public Radio; classical music.

KIKU (cable channel 9) Multicultural community TV programming.

KINE (105.1FM) Contemporary Hawaiian music.

KIPO (89.3FM) Hawaii Public Radio; news, jazz and world music.

KQMQ (91.3FM) Island-style music and Hawaiian reggae.

KTUH (90.3FM) UH Manoa student-run radio.

MEDICAL SERVICES

Longs Drugs (www.cvs.com/longs) Convenient 24-hour drugstores with pharmacies in a number of locations.

Queen's Medical Center (☎808-691-7000; www.queensmedicalcenter.net; ⏰24hr) O'ahu's biggest, best-equipped hospital has a 24-hour emergency room downtown.

Straub Clinic & Hospital (☎808-522-4000; www.straubhealth.org; 888 S King St; ⏰24hr) Operates a 24-hour emergency room downtown and a nonemergency clinic open weekdays (call ahead to check hours).

Getting There & Around

BUS

Just northwest of Waikiki, the Ala Moana Center mall is the central transfer point for TheBus, O'ahu's public-transportation system. Several direct bus routes run between Waikiki and Honolulu's other neighborhoods.

CAR

Major car-rental companies are found at Honolulu International Airport and in Waikiki.

Traffic jams up during rush hours, roughly from 7am to 9am and 3pm to 6pm weekdays. Expect heavy traffic in both directions on the H-1 Fwy during this time, as well as on the Pali and Likelike Hwys headed into Honolulu in the morning and away from the city in the late afternoon.

Parking

Downtown and Chinatown have on-street metered parking; it's reasonably easy to find an empty space on weekends but nearly impossible on weekdays. Bring lots of quarters.

Pay parking is also available at several municipal garages and there are a lot scattered around Chinatown and downtown. On the outskirts of the downtown core, the private Neal S Blaisdell Center offers all-day parking from $6, depending on special events.

Most shopping centers, including the Ala Moana Center, provide free parking for customers.

TAXI

Charley's Taxi (☎808-233-3333, 877-531-1333; www.charleystaxi.com)

City Taxi (☎808-524-2121; www.citytaxihonolulu.com)

TheCab (☎808-422-2222; www.thecabhawaii.com)

PEARL HARBOR AREA

Pearl Harbor

The WWII-era rallying cry 'Remember Pearl Harbor!' that once mobilized a nation dramatically resonates on O'ahu. It was here that the surprise Japanese attack on December 7, 1941, hurtled the US into war in the Pacific. Every year about 1.6 million tourists visit Pearl Harbor's unique collection of war memorials and museums, all clustered around a quiet bay where oysters were once farmed.

Sights

WWII Valor in the Pacific National Monument PARK

(Map p70; www.nps.gov/valr/; admission free, 7-day Passport to Pearl Harbour adult/child $65/35) One of the USA's most significant WWII sites, this National Park Service monument narrates the history of the Pearl Harbor attack and commemorates fallen service members. The monument is entirely wheelchair accessible. The main entrance also leads to Pearl Harbor's other parks and museums.

The monument grounds are much more than just a boat dock for the USS *Arizona* Memorial. Be sure to stop at the two museums, where multimedia and interactive displays bring to life the Road to War and the Attack & Aftermath through historic photos, films, illustrated graphics and taped oral histories. A shoreside walk passes signs illustrating how the attack unfolded in the now-peaceful harbor.

The bookstore sells just about every book and movie ever produced on the Pearl Harbor attack and WWII's Pacific theater, as well as informative illustrated maps of the battle. If you're lucky, the few remaining, 90-plus-year-old Pearl Harbor veterans who volunteer might be out front signing autographs and answering questions.

Various ticket packages are available for the three attractions that have admission fees. The best deal is a seven-day pass that includes admission to all. Tickets are sold online at www.pearlharborhistoricsites.org, at the main monument ticket counter and at each attraction.

USS Arizona Memorial MUSEUM, MEMORIAL

(Map p70; ☎808-422-3300; www.nps.gov/valr; 1 Arizona Memorial Pl; boat-tour reservation fee $1.50; ⏲7am-5pm, boat tours 8am-3pm) FREE One of the USA's most significant WWII sites, this somber monument commemorates the Pearl Harbor attack and its fallen service members with an offshore shrine reachable by boat.

The USS *Arizona* Memorial was built over the midsection of the sunken USS *Arizona*, with deliberate geometry to represent initial defeat, ultimate victory and eternal serenity. In the furthest of three chambers inside the shrine, the names of crewmen killed in the attack are engraved onto a marble wall. In the central section are cutaways that allow visitors to see the skeletal remains of the ship, which even now oozes about a quart of oil each day into the ocean. In its rush to recover from the attack and prepare for war, the US Navy exercised its option to leave the servicemen inside the sunken ship; they remain entombed in its hull, buried at sea. Visitors are asked to maintain respectful silence at all times.

Boat tours to the shrine depart every 15 minutes from 8am until 3pm (weather permitting). For the 75-minute tour program, which includes a 23-minute documentary film on the attack, make reservations online (fee per ticket $1.50) at www.recreation.gov at least a few days before your visit. Free first-come, first-served tickets are also available in person at the visitor center's Aloha Court, but during peak season when more than 4000 people take the tour daily, the entire day's allotment of tickets may be gone by 10am and waits of a few hours are not uncommon, so arrive early.

Battleship Missouri Memorial MUSEUM, MEMORIAL

(Map p70; ☎808-455-1600; www.ussmissouri.com; 63 Cowpens St, Ford Island; admission incl tour adult/child from $25/13; ⏲8am-4pm, to 5pm Jun-Aug) The last battleship built at the end of WWII, the USS *Missouri* provides a unique historical 'bookend' to the US campaign in the Pacific during WWII. Nicknamed the 'Mighty Mo' this decommissioned battleship saw action during the decisive WWII battles of Iwo Jima and Okinawa.

The USS *Missouri* is now docked on Ford Island, just a few hundred yards from the sunken remains of the USS *Arizona*. During a self-guided audiotour, you can poke about the officers' quarters, browse exhibits on the ship's history and stride across the deck where General MacArthur accepted the Japanese surrender on September 2, 1945. Guided battle-station tours, which are sometimes led by knowledgeable US military veterans, are worth the extra time and expense.

To visit the memorial, board the mandatory Ford Island visitor shuttle bus (bring photo ID) outside the visitor center's Aloha Court.

USS Bowfin Submarine Museum & Park MUSEUM, PARK

(Map p70; ☎808-423-1341; www.bowfin.org; 11 Arizona Memorial Dr; museum adult/child $5/3, incl self-guided submarine tour $12/5; ⏰7am-5pm, last entry 4:30pm) If you have to wait an hour or two for your USS *Arizona* Memorial tour to begin, this adjacent park harbors the moored WWII-era submarine USS *Bowfin* and a museum that traces the development of submarines from their origins to the nuclear age, including wartime patrol footage. Undoubtedly, the highlight is clambering aboard a historic submarine.

Launched on December 7, 1942, one year after the Pearl Harbor attack, the USS *Bowfin* sank 44 enemy ships in the Pacific by the end of WWII. A self-guided audiotour explores the life of the crew – watch your head below deck! Children under age four are not allowed aboard the submarine for safety reasons.

Pacific Aviation Museum MUSEUM

(Map p70; ☎808-441-1000; www.pacificaviationmuseum.org; 319 Lexington Blvd, Ford Island; adult/child $25/15, incl guided tour $35/25; ⏰9am-5pm, last entry 4pm) This military aircraft museum covers WWII through the US conflicts in Korea and Vietnam. The first aircraft hangar has been outfitted with exhibits on the Pearl Harbor attack, the Doolittle Raid on mainland Japan in 1942 and the pivotal Battle of Midway, when the tides of WWII in the Pacific turned in favor of the Allies.

Authentically restored planes on display here include a Japanese Zero and a Dauntless navy dive bomber. Walk next door to explore the MiG Alley Korean War exhibit or take a guided tour to look behind the scenes at restoration work in Hangar 79's replica WWII-era maintenance shop.

To visit the museum, board the mandatory Ford Island visitor shuttle bus (bring photo ID) outside the visitor center's Aloha Court.

Tours

Private tours of Pearl Harbor from Waikiki don't add much, if anything, to the experience of visiting the memorials and museums. Besides, tourist boats aren't allowed to disembark at the USS *Arizona* Memorial.

Festivals & Events

Memorial Day COMMEMORATION

(⏰May) On the last Monday in May, this national public holiday honors military personnel killed in battle. The USS *Arizona* Memorial, dedicated on Memorial Day in 1962, has a special ceremony.

Veterans Day COMMEMORATION

(⏰Nov) On November 11, this national public holiday honors US military veterans; the USS *Missouri* hosts a sunset ceremony and tribute.

Pearl Harbor Day COMMEMORATION

(⏰Dec) On December 7, ceremonies at Pearl Harbor include a Hawaiian blessing and heartfelt accounts from survivors of the 1941 Japanese attack.

PEARL HARBOR: A SURPRISE ATTACK

December 7, 1941 – 'a date which will live in infamy,' President Franklin D Roosevelt later said – began at 7:55am with a wave of more than 350 Japanese planes swooping over the Ko'olau Range headed toward the unsuspecting US Pacific Fleet in Pearl Harbor. The battleship USS *Arizona* took a direct hit and sank in less than nine minutes, trapping most of its crew beneath the surface. The average age of the 1177 enlisted men who died in the attack on the ship was just 19 years. It wasn't until 15 minutes after the bombing started that American anti-aircraft guns began to shoot back at the Japanese warplanes. Twenty other US military ships were sunk or seriously damaged and 347 airplanes were destroyed during the two-hour attack.

The offshore shrine at the sunken USS *Arizona* doesn't tell the only story. Nearby are two other floating historical sites: the USS *Bowfin* submarine, aka the 'Pearl Harbor Avenger,' and the battleship USS *Missouri*, where General Douglas MacArthur accepted the Japanese surrender at the end of WWII. Together, for the US, these military sites represent the beginning, middle and end of the war. To visit all three, as well as the Pacific Aviation Museum, dedicate at least a day.

Eating

All four sights have concession stands or snack shops. The cafe at the Pacific Aviation Museum is the biggest, with the best selection; the hot dogs at Bowfin Park are the cheapest. For a full meal, detour to nearby 'Aiea or go a little further to the Kapolei area on the Leeward Coast.

Information

Strict security measures are in place at Pearl Harbor. You are not allowed to bring in *any* items that allow concealment (eg purses, camera bags, fanny packs, backpacks, diaper bags). Personal-sized cameras and camcorders are allowed. Don't lock valuables in your car. Instead use the storage facility outside the main park gate.

Getting There & Away

The entrance to the Valor in the Pacific Monument and the other Pearl Harbor historic sites is off the Kamehameha Hwy (Hwy 99), southwest of Aloha Stadium. From Honolulu or Waikiki, take H-1 west to exit 15A (Arizona Memorial/Stadium), then follow the highway signs for the monument, not the signs for Pearl Harbor (which lead onto the US Navy base). There's plenty of free parking.

From Waikiki, bus 42 ('Ewa Beach) is the most direct, running twice hourly between 6am and 3pm, taking just over an hour each way. The 'Arizona Memorial' stop is right outside the main memorial entrance.

'Aiea

Just north of Pearl Harbor lies the town of 'Aiea. Beyond Aloha Stadium and its famous flea market, the crowded old community climbs the hill to a historic heiau (stone temple).

Sights

Kea'iwa Heiau State Recreation Area PARK

(Map p70; www.hawaiistateparks.org; off 'Aiea Heights Dr; 7am-7:45pm Apr-1st Mon in Sep, to 6:45pm 1st Tue in Sep-Mar) FREE In the mountains north of Pearl Harbor, this state park protects Kea'iwa Heiau, an ancient *ho'ola* (healing or medicinal) temple. Today people wishing to be cured may still place offerings here. The 4ft-high terraces are made of stacked rocks that enclose an approximately 16,000-sq-ft platform; the construction may date to the 16th century.

The scenic, 4.8-mile (2½-hour) 'Aiea Loop Trail starts from the top of the park's paved loop road. There are some steep, sometimes muddy switchbacks, but you'll enjoy sweeping vistas of Pearl Harbor, Diamond Head and the Ko'olau Range. About two-thirds of the way, the wreckage of a plane that crashed in 1944 can be spotted through the foliage on the east ridge.

The park has picnic tables, covered pavilions with barbecue grills, restrooms, showers, a payphone and drinking water. The four tent sites at the campground (tent sites by permit $5; 8am Friday to noon Wednesday) are well tended but don't have much privacy. Permits must be obtained in advance. Bring waterproof gear; rains are frequent at this elevation. There's a resident caretaker by the front gate, which is locked at night.

To get here from Honolulu, take exit 13A 'Aiea off Hwy 78 onto Moanalua Rd. Turn right onto 'Aiea Heights Dr at the third traffic light. The road winds up through a residential area for over 2.5 miles to the park. From downtown Honolulu, bus 11 ('Aiea Heights; 35 minutes, hourly) stops about 1.3 miles downhill from the park entrance.

Eating

Tamura's Poke SEAFOOD $

(808-488-7444; http://tamurasfinewine.com; 98-302 Kamehameha Hwy; poke per pound $8-16; 9.30am-9pm Mon-Sat, to 8pm Sun) The sign may read Tamura's Fine Wine & Liquor, but what you're really here for is the huge selection of tasty *poke*, claimed by many to be the best on the island. It's strictly takeout, so pick some up on the way to the beach.

Forty Niner Restaurant DINER $

(Map p70; 808-484-1940; 98-110 Honomanu St; mains $4-9; 7am-8pm Mon-Thu, to 9pm Fri & Sat, to 2pm Sun) Don't judge a book by its cover. This little 1940s diner may look abandoned, but its old-fashioned *saimin* (local-style noodle soup) is made with a secret-recipe broth. The garlic chicken and hamburgers aren't half bad either. Ask the locals.

★Alley Restaurant Bar & Grill HAWAIIAN $$

(Map p70; 808-486-3499; www.aieabowl.com; 99-115 'Aiea Heights Dr; breakfast $5-10, mains $9-17; 7am-9:30pm Sun-Wed, to 10pm Thu-Sat) A bowling-alley-attached restaurant seems an unlikely place to get great food, but that's what makes it so fun. You can dig into a scrumptious *furikake 'ahi* sandwich with supercrispy fries, or Asian braised pork with brown rice, and then bowl a few rounds. Head to Tasty Tuesday for a $42 five-course tasting menu! There is a full bar available.

Buzz's Steakhouse STEAK **$$$**
(Map p70; ☎808-487-6465; http://buzzsoriginalsteakhouse.com; 98-751 Kuahoa Pl, Pearl City; mains $18-36; ⏲5-9pm) Just west of 'Aiea, Buzz's classic island surf-and-turf steakhouse sits atop a bluff off Moanalua Rd, with sunset views of Pearl Harbor. Buzz's salad bar is as popular as the steaks. You will need to make reservations.

Shopping

Aloha Stadium Swap Meet & Marketplace MARKET
(Map p70; www.alohastadiumswapmeet.net; 99-500 Salt Lake Blvd, Aiea; adult/child $1/free; ⏲8am-3pm Wed & Sat, from 6.30am Sun) Aloha Stadium's parking lot contains the island's biggest flea market. Don't expect to find any antiques or vintage goods, but there are endless stalls of cheap island-style souvenirs, including Hawaiian-style quilts. By car, take the H-1 west to Stadium/Halawa exit 1E. **VipTrans** (☎808-836-0317; www.viptrans.com; round-trip $14) runs shuttle buses from Waikiki hotels by reservation, every 30 minutes on meet days.

WAIKIKI

Once a Hawaiian royal retreat, Waikiki is riding high on a new wave of effortlessly chic style these days. No longer just a beach destination for package tourists, this famous strand of sand is flowering, starting with a renaissance of Hawaiian music at beachfront hotels and resorts. In this concrete jungle of modern high-rises, you can, surprisingly, still hear whispers of Hawaii's past, from the chanting of hula troupes at Kuhio Beach to the legacy of Olympic gold medalist Duke Kahanamoku.

Take a surfing lesson from a bronzed beachboy, then spend a lazy afternoon lying on Waikiki's golden sands. Before the sun sinks below the horizon, hop aboard a catamaran and sail off toward Diamond Head. Sip a sunset mai tai and be hypnotized by the lilting harmonies of slack key guitar, then mingle with the locals, who come here to party after dark too.

History

Looking at Waikiki today, it's hard to imagine that less than 150 years ago this tourist mecca was almost entirely wetlands filled with fishponds and *kalo lo'i* (taro fields). Fed by mountain streams from the Manoa Valley, Waikiki (Spouting Water) was once one of O'ahu's most fertile farming areas. In 1795, Kamehameha I became the first *ali'i* (chief) to successfully unite the Hawaiian Islands under one sovereign's rule, bringing his royal court to Waikiki.

By the 1880s Honolulu's more well-to-do citizens had started building gingerbread-trimmed cottages along the narrow beachfront. Tourism started booming in 1901 when Waikiki's first luxury hotel, the Moana, opened its doors on a former royal compound. Tiring quickly of the pesky mosquitoes that thrived in Waikiki's wetlands, early beachgoers petitioned to have the 'swamps' brought under control. In 1922 the Ala Wai Canal was dug to divert the streams that flowed into Waikiki and to dry out the wetlands. Tourists quickly replaced the water buffalo.

In the 'Roaring '20s' the Royal Hawaiian hotel opened to serve passengers arriving on luxury ocean liners from San Francisco. The Depression and WWII put a damper on tourism, but the Royal Hawaiian was turned into an R & R playground for sailors on shore leave. From 1935 to 1975 the classic radio show *Hawaii Calls*, performed live at the Moana Hotel, broadcast dreams of a tropical paradise to the US mainland and the world. As late as 1950 surfers could still drive their cars right up to the beach and park on the sand – hard to imagine nowadays!

Sights

Let's be honest: you're probably just here for the beach, but Waikiki does offer a number of other points of interest.

Duke Kahanamoku Statue STATUE
On the waterfront on Kalakaua Ave, this wonderful statue of Duke Kahanamoku is always draped in colorful lei. The Duke (1890–1968) was a real Hawaiian hero, winning numerous Olympic swimming medals, breaking the world record for the 100yd freestyle in his first competitive event, and becoming known as 'the father of modern surfing.' He even had stints as sheriff of Honolulu and as a Hollywood actor. Duke also pioneered the Waikiki Beach Boys, teaching visitors how to surf.

Waikiki

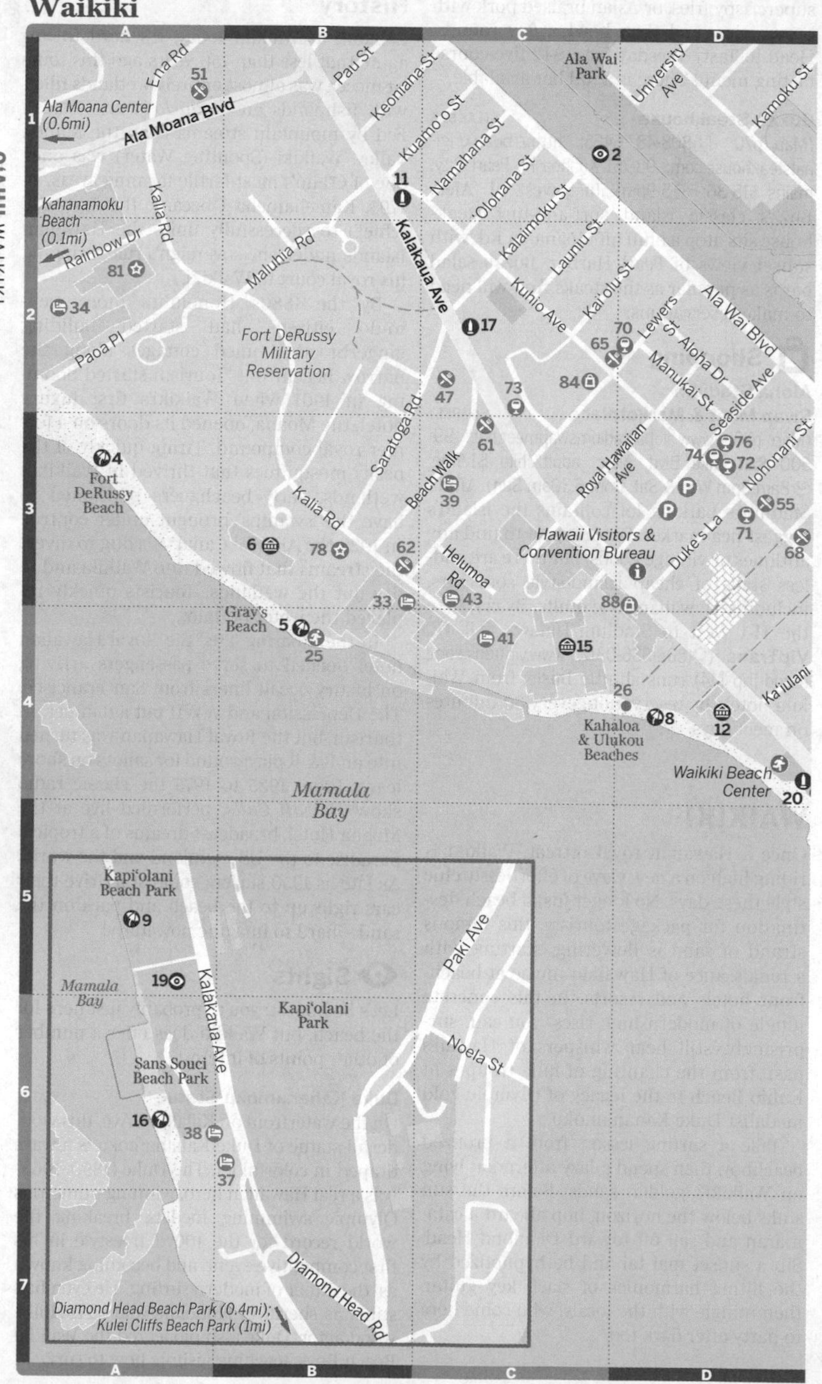

Ala Moana Center (0.6mi)
Ala Moana Blvd
Ena Rd
Pau St
Keoniana St
Kuamo'o St
Namahana St
'Olohana St
Kalaimoku St
Launiu St
Kai'olu St
Lewers St
Aloha Dr
Manukai St
Seaside Ave
Nohonani St
Ala Wai Park
University Ave
Kamoku St
Ala Wai Blvd
Kahanamoku Beach (0.1mi)
Rainbow Dr
Kalia Rd
Maluhia Rd
Kalakaua Ave
Kuhio Ave
Paoa Pl
Fort DeRussy Military Reservation
Saratoga Rd
Beach Walk
Royal Hawaiian Ave
Fort DeRussy Beach
Hawaii Visitors & Convention Bureau
Duke's La
Helumoa Rd
Gray's Beach
Ka'iulani
Kahaloa & Ulukou Beaches
Waikiki Beach Center
Mamala Bay
Kapi'olani Beach Park
Paki Ave
Kapi'olani Park
Noela St
Sans Souci Beach Park
Diamond Head Rd
Diamond Head Beach Park (0.4mi); Kulei Cliffs Beach Park (1mi)

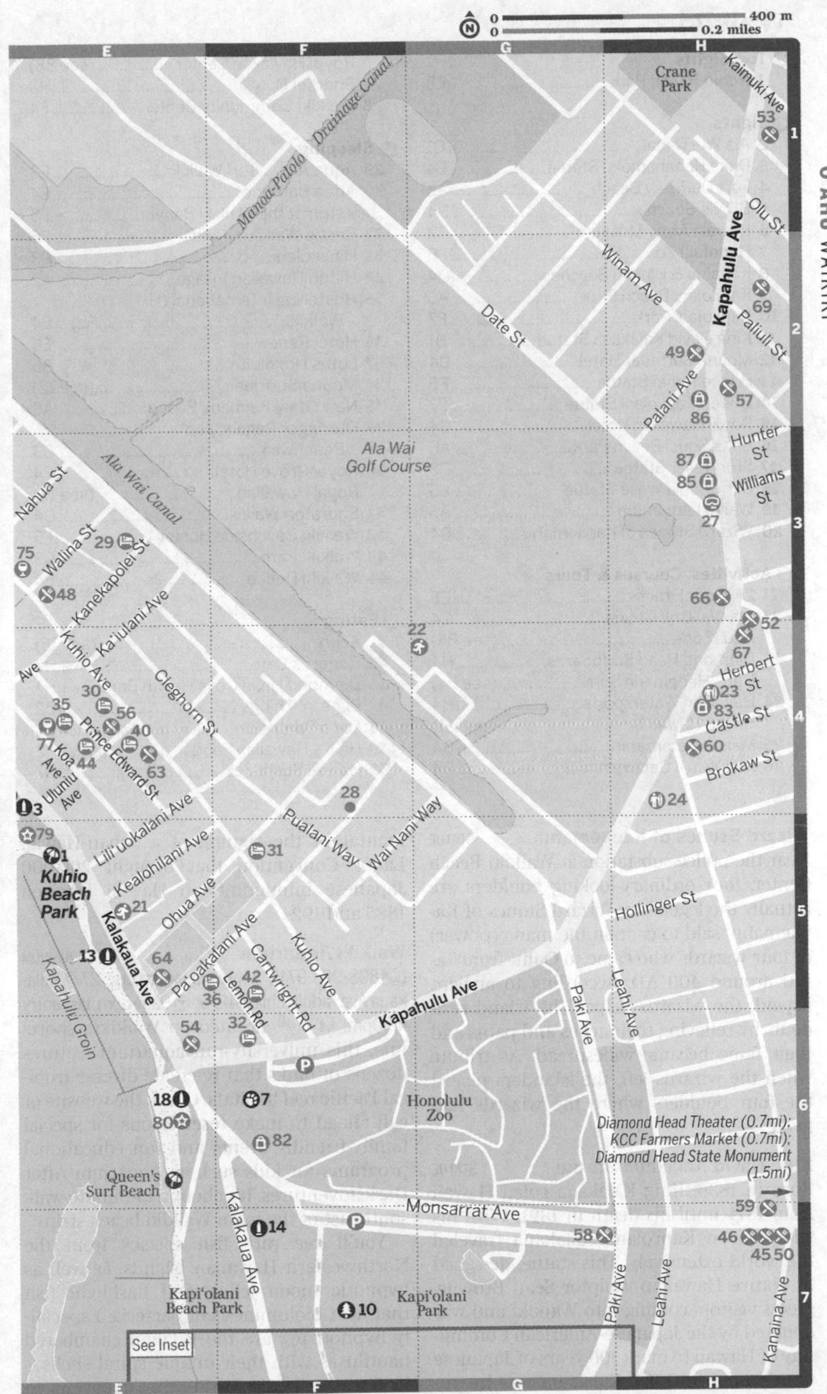

0 400 m
0 0.2 miles
Crane Park
Kaimuki Ave
Manoa-Palolo Drainage Canal
Olu St
Kapahulu Ave
Winam Ave
Date St
Paliuli St
Palani Ave
Hunter St
Williams St
Ala Wai Golf Course
Ala Wai Canal
Nahua St
Walina St
Kanekapolei St
Ka'iulani Ave
Kuhio Ave
Cleghorn St
Herbert St
Castle St
Brokaw St
Prince Edward St
Koa Ave
Uluniu Ave
Pualani Way
Wai Nani Way
Lili'uokalani Ave
Kealohilani Ave
Kuhio Beach Park
Ohua Ave
Kalakaua Ave
Hollinger St
Pa'oakalani Ave
Cartwright Rd
Lemon Rd
Kapahulu Groin
Paki Ave
Leahi Ave
Honolulu Zoo
Diamond Head Theater (0.7mi); KCC Farmers Market (0.7mi); Diamond Head State Monument (1.5mi)
Queen's Surf Beach
Monsarrat Ave
Kapi'olani Beach Park
Kapi'olani Park
Kanaina Ave
See Inset

Waikiki

Top Sights
1 Kuhio Beach Park E5

Sights
2 Ala Wai Canal C1
3 Duke Kahanamoku Statue E4
4 Fort DeRussy Beach A3
5 Gray's Beach B4
6 Hawai'i Army Museum B3
7 Honolulu Zoo F6
8 Kahaloa & Ulukou Beaches D4
9 Kapi'olani Beach Park A5
10 Kapi'olani Park F7
11 King David Kalakaua Statue B1
12 Moana Surfrider Hotel D4
13 Prince Kuhio Statue E5
14 Queen Kapi'olani Statue F7
15 Royal Hawaiian Hotel C4
16 Sans Souci Beach Park A6
17 Storyteller Statue C2
18 Surfer on a Wave Statue E6
19 Waikiki Aquarium A5
20 Wizard Stones of Kapaemahu D4

Activities, Courses & Tours
21 24-Hour Fitness E5
22 Ala Wai Golf Course G4
AquaZone .... (see 64)
23 Diamond Head Surfboards H4
Hans Hedemann Surf .... (see 54)
24 Hawaiian Watersports H4
Hiking Hawaii .... (see 51)
25 Maita'i Catamaran B4
26 Na Hoku II Catamaran D4
Royal Hawaiian Center .... (see 88)
27 Snorkel Bob's H3
28 Waikiki Community Center F4

Sleeping
29 Aqua Aloha Surf Waikiki E3
30 Aqua Bamboo E4
31 Aston at the Waikiki Banyan F5
32 Castle Waikiki Grand F6
33 Halekulani B3
34 Hilton Hawaiian Village A2
35 Hostelling International (HI) Waikiki E4
36 Hotel Renew E5
37 Lotus Honolulu B6
Moana Surfrider .... (see 12)
38 New Otani Kaimana Beach A6
39 Outrigger Regency on Beachwalk C3
40 Royal Grove Hotel E4
Royal Hawaiian .... (see 15)
41 Sheraton Waikiki C4
42 Waikiki Beachside Hostel F5
43 Waikiki Parc C3
44 Waikiki Prince E4

Eating
Azure .... (see 15)
45 Bogart's Cafe H7
46 Diamond Head Cove Health Bar H7
47 Eggs 'n' Things C2
48 Food Pantry E3
49 Haili's Hawaiian Foods H2
50 Hawaii Sushi H7

Wizard Stones of Kapaemahu STATUE

Near the police substation at Waikiki Beach Center, four ordinary-looking boulders are actually the legendary Wizard Stones of Kapaemahu, said to contain the mana (power) of four wizards who came to Oahu from Tahiti around 400 AD. According to ancient legend, the wizards helped the island residents by relieving their aches and pains and their fame became widespread. As tribute when the wizards left, the islanders placed the four boulders where the wizards had lived.

King David Kalakaua Statue STATUE

Born in 1836, King Kalakaua ruled Hawaii from 1874 until his death in 1891. With his wife, Queen Kapi'olani, Kalakaua traveled the world extensively. This statue, designed by Native Hawaiian sculptor Sean Browne, greets visitors coming into Waikiki and was donated by the Japanese-American Community of Hawaii to mark 100 years of Japanese immigration in 1985. Kalakaua was instrumental in the signing of a Japan-Hawaii Labor Convention that brought 200,000 Japanese immigrants to Hawaii between 1885 and 1924.

Waikiki Aquarium AQUARIUM

(808-923-9741; www.waquarium.org; 2777 Kalakaua Ave; adult/child $12/5; 9am-5pm, last entry 4:30pm;) Located on Waikiki's shoreline, this university-run aquarium features dozens of tanks that re-create diverse tropical Pacific reef habitats. Check the website or call ahead to make reservations for special family-friendly events and fun educational programs for kids such as Aquarium After Dark adventures. It's about a 15-minute walk southeast of the main Waikiki beach strip.

You'll see rare fish species from the Northwestern Hawaiian Islands, as well as hypnotic moon jellies and flashlight fish that host bioluminescent bacteria. Especially hypnotizing are the Palauan chambered nautiluses with their unique spiral shells – in fact, this is the world's first aquarium to

51 Hiking Hawaii Cafe A1
52 Irifune H3
53 Leonard's H1
54 LuLu's Surf Club E6
55 Marukame Udon D3
Me's BBQ .... (see 40)
56 Musubi Cafe Iyasume E4
Nobu .... (see 43)
57 Ono Seafood H2
58 People's Open Market G7
59 Pioneer Saloon H7
60 Rainbow Drive-In H4
61 Ramen Nakamura C3
62 Roy's Waikiki B3
63 Ruffage Natural Foods E4
64 Sansei Seafood Restaurant & Sushi Bar E5
65 Siam Square C2
66 Side Street Inn on Da Strip H3
67 Uncle Bo's Pupu Bar & Grill H4
68 Veggie Star Natural Foods D3
Veranda .... (see 12)
69 Waiola Shave Ice H2

Drinking & Nightlife

70 Bacchus Waikiki D2
71 Da Big Kahuna D3
Five-O Bar & Lounge .... (see 88)
72 Fusion Waikiki D3
Genius Lounge .... (see 84)
Hula's Bar & Lei Stand .... (see 32)
73 In Between C2
Lewers Lounge .... (see 33)
74 Lo Jax Waikiki D3
Lulu's Waikiki .... (see 54)
75 Nashville Waikiki E3
RumFire .... (see 41)
76 Tapa's Restaurant & Lanai Bar D3
77 Wang Chung's E4

Entertainment

'Aha 'Aina .... (see 15)
Beach Bar .... (see 12)
House Without a Key .... (see 33)
78 Kani Ka Pila Grille B3
79 Kuhio Beach Torch Lighting & Hula Show E5
Mai Tai Bar .... (see 15)
Moana Terrace .... (see 64)
Royal Grove .... (see 88)
80 Sunset on the Beach E6
81 Tapa Bar A2
Waikiki Starlight Luau .... (see 34)

Shopping

82 Art on the Zoo Fence F6
83 Bailey's Antiques & Aloha Shirts H4
84 Genius Outfitters C2
85 Island Paddler H3
86 Na Lima Mili Hulu No'eau H2
Newt at the Royal .... (see 15)
87 Peggy's Picks H3
Reyn Spooner .... (see 41)
88 Royal Hawaiian Center D3
Ukulele PuaPua .... (see 12)

breed these endangered creatures in captivity, a ground-breaking achievement. An outdoor pool is home to rare and endangered Hawaiian monk seals.

Kapi'olani Park PARK

(off Kalakaua & Paki Aves) **FREE** In its early days, horse racing and band concerts were the biggest attractions at Waikiki's favorite green space. Although the racetrack is long gone, this park named after Queen Kapi'olani is still a beloved outdoor venue for live music and local community gatherings, from farmers markets to arts-and-crafts fairs to festivals to rugby matches. The tree-shaded Kapi'olani Bandstand is ideal for catching a concert by the time-honored Royal Hawaiian Band, which performs classics here on many Sunday afternoons.

Queen Kapi'olani Statue STATUE

This bronze statue depicts Queen Kapi'olani, the wife of King David Kalakaua – his statue at the other end of Waikiki greets visitors to Waikiki. The Queen was a beloved philanthropist, known as the queen who loved children. Among other accomplishments, she founded a maternity home in 1890 for disadvantaged Hawaiians and today you'll hear her name often – the park, a hospital, a major boulevard and a community college are named for her.

Moana Surfrider Hotel HISTORIC BUILDING

(☎808-922-3111; www.moana-surfrider.com; 2365 Kalakaua Ave; ⏲tours 11am Mon, Wed & Fri) **FREE** Christened the Moana Hotel when it opened in 1901, this beaux-arts plantation-style inn was once the haunt of Hollywood movie stars, aristocrats and business tycoons. The historic hotel embraces a seaside courtyard with a big banyan tree and a wraparound veranda, where island musicians and hula dancers perform in the evenings.

Upstairs from the lobby you'll find displays of memorabilia from the early days: everything from scripts of the famed *Hawaii Calls* radio show broadcast live from the courtyard here between 1935 and 1975 to woolen bathing suits, historical period photographs and a short video of Waikiki back in the days when the Moana was the only hotel on the oceanfront horizon.

Royal Hawaiian Hotel HISTORIC BUILDING

(☎808-923-7311; www.royal-hawaiian.com; 2259 Kalakaua Ave; ⏲tours 2pm Tue & Thu) FREE With its Moorish-style turrets and archways, this gorgeously restored 1927 art-deco landmark, dubbed the 'Pink Palace,' is a throwback to the era when Rudolph Valentino was *the* romantic idol and travel to Hawaii was by Matson Navigation luxury liner. Its guest list read like a who's-who of A-list celebrities, from royalty to Rockefellers, along with luminaries such as Charlie Chaplin and Babe Ruth. Today, historic tours explore the architecture and lore of this grande dame.

Ask the concierge for a self-guided walking-tour brochure.

Honolulu Zoo ZOO

(☎808-971-7171; www.honoluluzoo.org; cnr Kapahulu & Kalakaua Aves; adult/child 4-12yr $14/6; ⏲9am-4:30pm; P) Honolulu Zoo does a great job on limited finances of showcasing tropical animals from around the globe. There are 40-plus acres of tropical greenery, happy-looking animals and a petting zoo for kids. Hawaii has no endemic land mammals, but in the aviary near the entrance you can see some native birds, including the *nene* (Hawaiian goose) and *'apapane*, a bright-red Hawaiian honeycreeper. Make reservations for family-oriented twilight tours, dinner safaris, zoo campouts and stargazing nights.

Prince Kuhio Statue STATUE

This statue of Prince Jonah Kuhio Kalaniana'ole sits at Kuhio Beach in Waikiki. It celebrates the man who was prince of the reigning House of Kalakaua when the Kingdom of Hawaii was overthrown in 1893. When Hawaii was annexed as territory of the United States, Kuhio was elected as Hawaii's congressional delegate for 10 consecutive terms. Kuhio was often called Ke Ali'i Makaainana (Prince of People), and is well known for his efforts to preserve and strengthen the Hawaiian people.

Hawai'i Army Museum MUSEUM

(www.hiarmymuseumsoc.org; 2161 Kalia Rd; donations welcome, audiotour $5; ⏲9am-5pm Tue-Sat, last entry 4:45pm; P) FREE At Fort DeRussy, this museum showcases an almost mind-numbing array of military paraphernalia as it relates to Hawaii's history, starting with shark-tooth clubs that Kamehameha the Great used to win control of the island more than two centuries ago. Fascinating old photographs and stories help bring an understanding of the influence of the US military presence in Hawaii.

Extensive exhibits include displays on the 442nd, the Japanese American regiment that became the most decorated regiment in WWII, and on Kaua'i-born Eric Shinseki, a retired four-star army general who spoke out against the US invasion of Iraq and has served as President Barack Obama's Secretary of Veterans Affairs.

Surfer on a Wave Statue STATUE

Opposite the entrance to Honolulu Zoo and right on the beach, the 'Surfer on a Wave' statue celebrates surfing as a major part of the culture of Waikiki. Cast in bronze by Robert Pasby, it was unveiled in 2003.

Ala Wai Canal CANAL

The Ala Wai Canal was created in 1922 to drain the rice paddies, marshes and swamps that would become present-day Waikiki. Running from Kapahulu Ave, the waterway runs in a straight line down the back of Waikiki before turning left and out to sea between the Ala Wai Yacht Harbor and Ala Moana Beach Park's Magic Island. The canal is a popular spot with kayakers and outrigger canoe teams.

Storyteller Statue STATUE

This bronze statue just off Kalakaua Ave represents 'the storytellers,' the keepers of Hawaiian culture. For centuries, women have been at the top of Hawaiian oral traditions, and the storytellers preserve the identity of their people and land by reciting poems, songs, chants and genealogies. The *Storyteller's* brother statue is the *Water Giver* at the Hawaiian Convention Center.

Beaches

The 2-mile stretch of white sand that everyone calls Waikiki Beach runs from Hilton Hawaiian Village all the way to Kapi'olani Beach Park. Along the way, the beach keeps changing names and personalities. In the early morning, quiet seaside paths belong to walkers and runners, and strolling toward Diamond Head at dawn can be a meditative experience. By midmorning it looks like any resort beach – packed with water-sports

DON'T MISS

O'AHU'S BEST BEACHES

- Kuhio Beach – Waikiki's always-busy oceanfront carnival.
- Hanauma Bay (p132) – snorkeling even kiddies can enjoy.
- Sandy Beach (p133) – bodyboarding only for the fearless.
- Waimanalo (p137) – O'ahu's longest, calmest golden strand.
- Kailua (p140) – swimming, kayaking, paddle surfing, windsurfing and kiteboarding.
- Kualoa (p146) – the Windward Coast's prettiest ocean views.
- Malaekahana State Recreation Area (p151) – wild, untamed windward O'ahu beach.
- Sunset Beach (p154) – the North Shore's epic surfing beach.
- Pupukea (p154) – superb summertime snorkeling and diving.
- Makaha (p169) – the Wai'anae Coast's big-wave beach.

concessionaires and lots of tourist bodies. By noon it's a challenge to walk along the packed beach without stepping on anyone.

Waikiki is good for swimming, bodyboarding, surfing, sailing and other water sports most of the year, and there are lifeguards, restrooms and outdoor showers scattered along the beachfront. Between May and September, summer swells make the water a little rough for swimming, but great for surfing. For snorkeling, head to Sans Souci Beach Park or Queen's Surf Beach. The following beaches are listed geographically from northwest to southeast.

Kahanamoku Beach BEACH

(Map p80) Fronting the Hilton Hawaiian Village, Kahanamoku Beach is Waikiki's westernmost beach. It takes its name from Duke Kahanamoku, the legendary Waikiki beachboy whose family once owned the land where the resort now stands. Hawaii's champion surfer and Olympic gold-medal winner learned to swim right here. The beach offers calm swimming conditions and a gently sloping, if rocky bottom. Public access is at the end of Paoa Pl, off Kalia Rd.

Fort DeRussy Beach BEACH

(👪) Seldom crowded, this often-overlooked beauty extends along the shore of a military reservation. Like all beaches in Hawaii, it's free and open to the public. The water is usually calm and good for swimming, but it's shallow at low tide. When conditions are right, windsurfers, bodyboarders and board surfers all play here. Usually open daily, beach-hut concessionaires rent bodyboards, kayaks and snorkel sets. A grassy lawn with palm trees offers some sparse shade, an alternative to frying on the sand.

Gray's Beach BEACH

Nestled up against the Halekulani luxury resort, Gray's Beach has suffered some of the Waikiki strip's worst erosion. Because the seawall in front of the Halekulani hotel is so close to the waterline, the beach sand fronting the hotel is often totally submerged by the surf, but the offshore waters are shallow and calm, offering decent swimming conditions. Public access is along a paved walkway. It was named after Gray's-by-the-Sea, a 1920s boarding house that stood here.

Kahaloa & Ulukou Beaches BEACH

The beach between the Royal Hawaiian and Moana Surfrider hotels is Waikiki's busiest section of sand and surf, great for sunbathing, swimming and people-watching. Most of the beach has a shallow bottom with a gradual slope. The only drawback for swimmers is its popularity with beginning surfers, and the occasional catamaran landing hazard. **Queens** and **Canoes**, Waikiki's best-known surf breaks, are just offshore. Paddle further offshore over a lagoon to **Populars** (aka 'Pops'), a favorite of long-boarders.

★ **Kuhio Beach Park** BEACH

(👪) If you're the kind of person who wants it all, this beach offers everything from protected swimming to outrigger-canoe rides, and even a free sunset-hula and Hawaiian-music show. You'll find restrooms, outdoor showers, a snack bar, surfboard lockers and beach-gear-rental stands at **Waikiki Beach Center**, near the friendly police substation.

The beach is marked on its opposite end by Kapahulu Groin, a walled storm drain with a walkway on top that juts out into the ocean. A low stone breakwater, called the Wall, runs out from Kapahulu Groin, parallel to the beach. It was built to control sand erosion and, in the process, two nearly enclosed swimming pools were formed.

The pool closest to Kapahulu Groin is best for swimming. However, because circulation is limited, the water gets murky with a noticeable film of sunscreen oils, especially later in the day.

Kapahulu Groin is one of Waikiki's hottest bodyboarding spots. If the surf's right, you can find a few dozen bodyboarders, mostly teenagers, riding the waves. These experienced local kids ride straight for the groin's cement wall and then veer away at the last moment, thrilling the tourists watching them from the little pier above.

Kapi'olani Beach Park BEACH

Where did all the tourists go? From Kapahulu Groin south to the Natatorium, this peaceful stretch of beach, backed by a green space of banyan trees and grassy lawns, offers a relaxing niche with none of the frenzy found on the beaches fronting the Waikiki hotel strip. Facilities include restrooms and outdoor showers. Kapi'olani Beach is a popular weekend picnicking spot for local families, who unload the kids to splash in the ocean while adults fire up the BBQ.

The widest northern end of Kapi'olani Beach is nicknamed Queen's Surf Beach. The stretch in front of the pavilion is popular with Waikiki's gay community. Its sandy bottom offers decent swimming. Long-boarders favor the offshore left-handed surf break **Publics**.

Sans Souci Beach Park BEACH

At the Diamond Head edge of Waikiki, Sans Souci is a prime sandy stretch of oceanfront that's far from the frenzied tourist scene. It's commonly called Kaimana Beach, as it's next door to the New Otani Kaimana Beach Hotel. Local residents often come here for their daily swims. A shallow reef close to shore makes for calm, protected waters and provides good snorkeling.

Activities

Waikiki's beaches steal the spotlight, but landlubbers can also find plenty of fun in the sun. In the early mornings and late afternoons, runners pound the pavement next to Ala Wai Canal, while Kapi'olani Park has tennis courts and sports fields for soccer and rugby, even cricket.

Waikiki has good surfing year-round, with the largest waves rolling in during winter. Gentler summer surf breaks are best for beginners. Surfing lessons (from $75 for a two-hour group class) and surfboard, SUP and bodyboard rentals (from $10 to $80 per day) can be arranged at the concession stands along the sand at Kuhio Beach Park, near the bodyboarding hot spot of Kapahulu Groin. Some surf outfits offer outrigger-canoe rides ($75 for two people) that take off from the beach and ride the tossin' waves home – kids especially love those thrills.

Water Sports

Waikiki Ocean Club WATER SPORTS

(Map p80; ☎808-539-9481; www.waikikioceanclub.com; 1651 Ala Moana Blvd; adult/child $39/30; 👪) Zip on a shuttle over from Ala Wai Yacht Harbor to this aquatic theme park moored offshore. Bounce on the ocean trampoline, swivel down the water slide or test the triple-level diving deck, then go snorkeling or swimming in the Pacific. Add-on activities such as banana boat, jet skiing, scuba

O'AHU FOR CHILDREN

- Outrigger canoe rides, swimming and a free sunset torch-lighting and hula show at Waikiki's Kuhio Beach Park (p111).
- Touch tanks at the educational, eco-conscious Waikiki Aquarium (p108).
- Planetarium shows and exploding faux volcanoes at Honolulu's Bishop Museum (p82).
- Hiking to Manoa Falls (p85) or summiting Diamond Head (p130).
- Snorkeling at Hanauma Bay Nature Preserve (p132).
- Wading into Ko Olina Lagoons near Disney's Aulani (p166) resort.
- Steam-train rides and a giant maze at the Dole Plantation (p164).
- Movie and TV filming tours at Kualoa Ranch (p147).
- Walking the decks of Pearl Harbor's Battleship Missouri Memorial (p102).

diving and parasailing all cost extra. Reservations advised.

Hawaiian Watersports SURFING, SUP
(☎808-739-5483; www.hawaiianwatersports.com; 415 Kapahulu Ave; ⌚9am-5pm) Inland on Kapahulu Ave, this shop offers surfing and SUP rentals and lessons away from the crowds at Diamond Head beaches (transportation to/from Waikiki included for lessons, $10 surcharge for rental delivery).

Hans Hedemann Surf SURFING
(☎808-924-7778; www.hhsurf.com; Park Shore Waikiki, 2586 Kapahulu Ave; 2hr group/semiprivate/private lesson $75/125/150; ⌚8am-5pm) You can take baby steps and learn to board or paddle surf at this local pro surfer's well-established school, which is conveniently opposite the main beach strip in the lobby of the Park Shore Hotel. Rentals are also available.

Hawaii Surfboard Rentals SURFING, SUP
(☎808-672-5055; www.hawaiisurfboardrentals.com) Free surfboard, SUP, bodyboard and car-rack delivery and pickup with a two-day minimum rental; weekly rates are an especially good deal.

Diamond Head Surfboards SURFING
(☎808-691-9599; http://diamondheadsurfboards.com; 525 Kapahulu Ave; ⌚10am-6pm Mon-Wed, to 7pm Thu-Sat, 9am-1pm Sun) Check out Ben's place on Kapahulu for all your surfing requirements. As well as renting out surfboards, stand up paddleboards and body boards by the hour, day or week, it has excellent personalized surfing lessons based out of its well-stocked and attractive shop.

Snorkeling & Scuba Diving

Waikiki's crowded central beaches are not particularly good for snorkeling, so pick your spot carefully. Two top choices are Sans Souci Beach Park and Queen's Surf Beach, where you'll find some live coral and a decent variety of tropical fish. But to really see the gorgeous stuff – coral gardens, manta rays and more exotic tropical fish – head out on a boat. You can easily rent snorkel sets (from $10 to $20 per day) and scuba-diving equipment (from $35), or book ahead for boat trips (from $110) and PADI Open Water certification courses (from $350).

AquaZone DIVING, SNORKELING
(☎808-923-3483, 866-923-3483; www.aquazonescuba.com; Marriott Waikiki Beach Resort, 2552 Kalakaua Ave) Dive shop and tour outfitter on Kalakaua Ave behind the Harley Davidson shop in the front of the Waikiki Beach Marriott. Sign up for a beginner's scuba-diving pool lesson (no PADI certification required), a sea-turtle snorkeling tour or a morning deep-water boat dive, including out to WWII shipwrecks. Rental snorkel and diving gear available.

O'ahu Diving DIVING
(☎808-721-4210; www.oahudiving.com) Specializes in first-time experiences for beginning divers without certification, as well as deep-water boat dives offshore and PADI refresher classes if you're already certified and have some experience under your diving belt.

Snorkel Bob's SNORKELING
(☎808-735-7944; www.snorkelbob.com; 702 Kapahulu Ave; ⌚8am-5pm) A top spot to get your gear. Rates vary depending on the quality of the snorkeling gear and accessories packages, but excellent weekly discounts are available and online reservations taken. You can even rent gear on O'ahu, then return it on another island.

Hiking

Hiking Hawaii HIKING
(☎855-808-4453; http://hikinghawaii808.com; 1910 Ala Moana Blvd; per person from $40) Based out of Hiking Hawaii Cafe, these guys offer a number of hiking options daily all over O'ahu, from a Makap'u Lighthouse walk ($40) to a hike to Manoa Falls ($45) to a full-day trip to the North Shore ($165). Check out the options online. Hotel pickups, transportation and guide are included.

Golf

Ala Wai Golf Course GOLF
(☎reservations 808-296-2000; www.honolulu.gov/des/golf/alawai.html; 404 Kapahulu Ave; green fees $22-55) With views of Diamond Head and the Ko'olau Range, this flat 18-hole, par-70 layout scores a Guinness World Record for being the world's busiest golf course. Local golfers are allowed to book earlier in the week and grab most of the starting times, leaving few for visitors (who may call to reserve up to three days in advance).

If you get there early in the day and put yourself on the waiting list – and as long as your entire party waits at the course – you'll probably get to play. Driving range and club rentals available.

Health & Fitness

24-Hour Fitness GYM

(☎808-923-9090; www.24hourfitness.com; 2490 Kalakaua Ave; daily/weekly pass $25/75; ⊙24hr) For an indoor workout in Waikiki, 24-Hour Fitness is a modern gym with cardio and weight machines and group classes.

Tennis

If you've brought your own rackets, the Diamond Head Tennis Center, at the Diamond Head end of Kapi'olani Park, has 10 courts. For night play, go to the Kapi'olani Park Tennis Courts, opposite the aquarium; all four courts are lit. All of these public courts are free and first-come, first-served.

Courses

Waikiki Community Center HAWAIIANA, ARTS & CRAFTS

(☎808-923-1802; www.waikikicommunitycenter.org; 310 Pa'oakalani Ave; most classes $5-15) Try your hand at mah-jongg, the ukulele, hula, tai chi or a variety of island arts and crafts. Instructors at this homespun community center are brimming with aloha. Although most students are locals, visitors are welcome too. Preregistration may be required.

Royal Hawaiian Center HAWAIIANA, ARTS & CRAFTS

(☎808-922-2299; www.royalhawaiiancenter.com; 2201 Kalakaua Ave) Gargantuan shopping mall that offers free cultural classes and demonstrations in Hawaiian arts and crafts, such as quilting and flower lei-making, plus hula dancing, ukulele playing and even lomilomi traditional body massage.

Tours

Atlantis Submarine TOUR

(Map p80; ☎800-548-6262; www.atlantissubmarines.com; ⊙90min tour adult $124, child under 13yr & taller than 36in $53) See the world from a porthole aboard the sub that dives to a depth of 100ft near a reef off Waikiki, offering views of sea life otherwise reserved for divers – though honestly, it's not nearly as exciting as it sounds. There are several sailings daily; you should book ahead online for discounts. Check-in is at the Hilton Hawaiian Village's pier in front of the Ali'i Tower.

Festivals & Events

Waikiki loves to party year-round. Every Friday night, usually starting around 7:45pm, the Hilton Hawaiian Village shoots off a big ol' **fireworks show**, sounding like thunder inside hotel rooms all across Waikiki.

Duke Kahanamoku Challenge CULTURAL, SPORTS

(http://waikikicommunitycenter.org/Events.html; ⊙Mar;) Outrigger-canoe and SUP races, island-style local food, traditional Hawaiian games, arts-and-crafts vendors and live entertainment all happen on a Sunday in early March at the Duke Kahanamoku Lagoon & Beach.

Honolulu Festival ART, CULTURAL

(www.honolulufestival.com; ⊙Mar) In early March, free Asian and Pacific arts and cultural performances are staged at Waikiki Beach Walk and Waikiki Shopping Plaza, with a festive parade along Kalakaua Ave followed by a fireworks show.

SAIL AWAY!

Several catamaran cruises leave right from Waikiki Beach – just walk down to the sand, step into the surf and hop aboard. A 90-minute, all-you-can-drink 'booze cruise' will typically cost you $25 to $40 per adult. Reservations are recommended for sunset sails, which sell out fast.

Na Hoku II Catamaran (☎808-554-5990; www.nahokuii.com; incl drinks $30) With its unmistakable yellow-and-red-striped sails, this catamaran is so famous you'll see a photo of it on the Waikiki edition of the Monopoly board game. These hard-drinkin' tours set sail four times daily (11:30am, 1:30pm, 3:30pm and 5:30pm), shoving off from in front of Duke's Waikiki bar. The sunset sail usually sells out, so book early.

Maita'i Catamaran (☎808-922-5665; www.leahi.com; adult/child from $28/14;) Ahoy! Pulling up on the beach between the Halekulani and Sheraton hotels, this white catamaran with green sails offers the biggest variety of boat trips. Reserve ahead for a 90-minute daytime or sunset booze cruise (children allowed) or a moonlight sail to take in the Hilton's Friday fireworks show. Looking for something a bit different? On weekdays, family-friendly reef-snorkeling tours include an onboard picnic lunch.

Waikiki Spam Jam FOOD
(www.spamjamhawaii.com;) On a Saturday in late April or early May, join thousands of Spam aficionados celebrating at this street festival devoted to Hawaii's favorite tinned meat product.

Pan-Pacific Festival ART, CULTURAL
(www.pan-pacific-festival.com; mid-Jun) In mid-June, this Asian and Polynesian cultural festival puts on a performing-arts showcase at the Royal Hawaiian Center, outdoor hula shows at Kuhio Beach Park, and a huge *ho'olaule'a* (celebration) block party and parade along Kalakaua Ave.

Na Hula Festival ART, CULTURAL
(https://www.facebook.com/pages/Na-Hula-Festival/157159837738728; Aug) Local hula *halau* gather for a full day of music and dance celebrations at Kapi'olani Park in early August.

Hawaiian Slack Key Guitar Festival MUSIC, ART
(www.slackkeyfestival.com; mid-Aug) A day-long celebration of traditional Hawaiian slack key guitar and ukulele music with food vendors and an arts-and-crafts fair at Kapi'olani Park in mid-August.

Aloha Festivals ART, CULTURAL
(www.alohafestivals.com; mid-Sep) During Hawaii's premier statewide cultural festival in mid-September, Waikiki is famous for its royal court ceremonies and also its *ho'olaule'a* evening block party and float parade along Kalakaua Ave, with food vendors, live music and hula dancers.

Na Wahine O Ke Kai SPORTS, CULTURAL
(www.nawahineokekai.com; Sep) Hawaii's major annual women's outrigger-canoe race is held near the end of September. It starts at sunrise on the island of Moloka'i and ends 42 miles later at Waikiki's Kahanamoku Beach.

Moloka'i Hoe SPORTS, CULTURAL
(www.molokaihoe.com; mid-Oct) Taking place in mid-October, the men's outrigger-canoe world-championship race starts just after sunrise on Moloka'i and then finishes at Waikiki's Kahanamoku Beach less than five hours later.

Honolulu Marathon SPORTS
(www.honolulumarathon.org; Dec) The USA's third-largest marathon runs from downtown Honolulu to Diamond Head on the second Sunday of December.

Sleeping

Waikiki's main beachfront strip, along Kalakaua Ave, is lined with hotels and sprawling resorts. Some of them are true beauties with quiet gardens, seaside courtyards and either historic or boutique atmosphere, while others are generic high-rises, which cater to the package-tour crowd.

If stepping out of your room and digging your toes in the sand isn't a must, look for inviting small hotels on Waikiki's backstreets. Some hotels off Kuhio Ave and near Ala Wai Canal have rooms as good as many of the beachfront hotels, but at half the price. If you don't mind walking to the beach, you can save a bundle.

Be aware that 'ocean view' and its cousins 'ocean front' and 'partial ocean view' are all liberally used and may require a periscope to spot the waves. 'City,' 'garden' or 'mountain' views may be euphemisms for rooms that overlook the parking lot.

Increasingly, Waikiki's bigger hotels are also charging mandatory 'resort fees,' which could tack another $25 or more per day onto your final bill. Resort fees may cover internet connections, local and toll-free phone calls and fitness-room entry, or no extra perks at all, but regardless, you're gonna have to pay. Parking usually costs $15 to $30 per night.

Hostelling International (HI) Waikiki HOSTEL $
(808-926-8313; www.hostelsaloha.com; 2417 Prince Edward St; dm/r from $28/60, all with shared bath; reception 7am-midnight; P @) Occupying a converted low-rise apartment building, this tidy hostel is just a few blocks from the beach. Inside are fan-cooled single-sex dormitories and simple private rooms, a self-catering kitchen, coin-op laundry and free bodyboards to borrow. No smoking or alcohol allowed, but no daytime lockout or curfew either. Reservations are strongly recommended (seven-night maximum stay). Limited self-parking ($5 per night).

Waikiki Prince HOTEL $
(808-922-1544; www.waikikiprince.com; 2431 Prince Edward St; r from $79; P) Forget about ocean views and never mind the cramped check-in office at this six-story, 1970s-era apartment complex on an anonymous side street. Inside this standout budget option are two dozen compact yet cheery rooms with kitchenettes that feel fresh and reasonably modern. Free wi-fi and

weekly rates available year-round. A good option if you are on a budget.

Waikiki Beachside Hostel HOSTEL $
(808-923-9566, 866-478-3888; www.waikikibeachsidehostel.com; 2556 Lemon Rd; dm $25-35, semiprivate r from $70; P @) This private hostel attracts an international party crowd and offers plenty of perks, from an internet cafe to surfboard and moped rentals. Like most hostels on sketchy, back-alley Lemon Rd, this one occupies an older apartment complex. Each dorm has its own kitchen, bathroom and telephone, but no air-con.

Royal Grove Hotel HOTEL $
(808-923-7691; www.royalgrovehotel.com; 161 Uluniu Ave; r from $60; @) No frills but plenty of aloha characterize this kitschy, candy-pink hotel that attracts so many returning snowbirds it's nearly impossible to get a room in winter without advance reservations. Retro motel-style rooms in the main wing are basic but do have lanai. All rooms have kitchenettes. Inquire about discounted weekly off-season rates. It's a great budget option.

Hotel Renew BOUTIQUE HOTEL $$
(808-687-7700, 888-485-7639; www.hotelrenew.com; 129 Pa'oakalani Ave; r from $180; P @) At this fabulous find, just a half-block from the beach, a $25 per room 'amenity fee' brings a slew of services, from chilled drinks upon arrival to daily continental breakfast to free beach mats and bodyboards to borrow. Design-savvy, ecofriendly accommodations come with mod platform beds, projection-screen TVs, spa robes, earth-toned furnishings and Japanese-style *shōji* (sliding paper-screen doors).

It's romantic enough for honeymooners, and also gay friendly. No swimming pool. Valet parking only.

Outrigger Regency on Beachwalk HOTEL $$
(808-922-3871, 866-956-4262; www.outrigger.com; 255 Beach Walk; 1/2 bedrooms from $199/269; P @) This sleek, modern high-rise has more-than-respectable family-size rooms, with earth-toned furnishings, marble baths and bold, modern artwork. Spacious condo-style suites have full kitchens and some have private lanai with peek-a-boo ocean views. Step outside the downstairs lobby and you're right on Waikiki Beach Walk – then keep walking five minutes to the beach or the off-site swimming pool.

Waikiki Parc BOUTIQUE HOTEL $$
(808-921-7272; www.waikikiparc.com; 2233 Helumoa Rd; r from $295; P @) Epitomizing new-wave Waikiki, this hip hangout mixes nostalgic touches such as plantation-shuttered windows with minimalist contemporary furnishings. The staff are top class, and although guest rooms are cool and modern, they're not nearly as spacious or as chic as Nobu Waikiki lounge and restaurant downstairs. For serenity, swim in the rooftop pool with oceanview cabanas.

Hilton Hawaiian Village RESORT $$
(808-949-4321; www.hiltonhawaiianvillage.com; 2005 Kalia Rd; r from $215; P @) On the Fort DeRussy side of Waikiki, the Hilton is Waikiki's largest resort hotel – practically a self-sufficient tourist fortress of towers, restaurants, bars and shops. It's geared almost entirely to families and package tourists, with standard-issue hotel rooms, swimming pools and a lagoon, and tons of kid-centric activities by the beach, including kayak and surfboard rentals.

Aqua Bamboo BOUTIQUE HOTEL $$
(808-954-7412, 866-326-8423; www.aquabamboo.com; 2425 Kuhio Ave; r from $149, studio/1-bedroom ste from $169/199; P @) Looking for a meditative retreat in Waikiki's concrete jungle? This refreshed boutique hotel with an intimate cabana spa has a small saltwater pool, should you tire of the ocean. Stylishly minimalist rooms include suites with kitchenettes or full kitchens. A $15 amenity fee includes wi-fi, coffee, beach gear and newspaper.

Aston at the Waikiki Banyan HOTEL $$
(808-922-0555, 855-718-9908; www.astonwaikikibanyan.com; 201 Ohua Ave; 1-bedroom ste from $145; P @) Perfect for families, this all-suites high-rise hotel is a short walk from the aquarium, the zoo and, of course, the beach. Roomy if sometimes beat-up suites have a handy sofabed in the living room. The pool deck has a playground, as well as a tennis and basketball court. A mandatory nightly resort fee of $18 includes in-room wi-fi. Stacks of parking on-site for $15 per night.

Aqua Aloha Surf Waikiki BOUTIQUE HOTEL $$
(808-923-0222, 866-970-4160; www.alohasurfhotelwaikiki.com; 444 Kanekapolei St; r from $107; @) If you don't mind a shoebox-size room, or being next to Ala Wai Canal, this youth-

ful hotel can be a real bargain. The lobby is lively, with surf videos playing an endless-summer loop and hanging surfboards on the walls. The $15 hospitality fee includes wi-fi in lobby, wired internet in rooms, breakfast, coffee and beach gear.

Castle Waikiki Grand HOTEL **$$**
(☎808-923-1814; www.WaikikiGrandCondos.com; 134 Kapahulu Ave; r with/without kitchenette from $130/103; P❄@📶🏊) Small, gay-friendly condo hotel best known as the home of Hula's Bar & Lei Stand. Standard-issue rooms are compact, with limited kitchenette rooms available. Each vacation-rental condo is individually owned, so they can vary in quality – view online photos with some skepticism. Free in-room wi-fi. Ask about weekly and low-season discounts. There is limited self-parking available on-site.

★Royal Hawaiian RESORT **$$$**
(☎866-716-8110, 808-923-7311; www.royal-hawaian.com; 2259 Kalakaua Ave; r from $400; P❄@📶🏊) Waikiki's original luxury hotel, this pink Spanish-Moorish-style landmark is loaded with charm, especially since recent splendid, multi-million-dollar renovations. The historic section of the aristocratic 'Pink Palace' maintains its classic appeal, although you may prefer the modern high-rise tower for its ocean views.

Spa suites are adorned in carved teak, bamboo and mosaic glass, with cabana day beds on the lanai to help you unwind.

★Moana Surfrider HISTORIC HOTEL **$$$**
(☎866-716-8112, 808-922-3111; www.moana-surfrider.com; 2365 Kalakaua Ave; r from $350; P❄@📶🏊) Waikiki's most historic beachfront hotel, this grand, colonial-style establishment has been painstakingly restored. A line of rocking chairs beckons on the front porch and Hawaiian artwork hangs on the walls, while wedding parties sweep through the bustling lobby every 10 minutes. Graceful yet compact guest rooms no longer retain much of their period look, having been upgraded with 21st-century amenities and style.

Sheraton Waikiki RESORT **$$$**
(☎808-922-4422, 866-716-8109; www.sheraton-waikiki.com; 2255 Kalakaua Ave; r from $325; P❄@📶🏊) Looming over the Royal Hawaiian, this high-rise has plenty of room to accommodate families, package-tour groups and conferences. No-surprises rooms are clean and crisp, with a well-equipped gym and drop-off day-care center downstairs. By the beach, an amphibious playground keeps kids entertained with a 'superpool' and 70ft-long waterslide, while adults retreat to the infinity pool.

Lotus Honolulu BOUTIQUE HOTEL **$$$**
(☎808-922-1700, 866-970-4166; www.lotushonoluluhotel.com; 2885 Kalakaua Ave; r from $215; ❄📶) This hip boutique hotel is a lovely sanctuary by Sans Souci Beach, at the calm southern edge of Waikiki. Mingle with honeymooners looking for a romantic escape at wine social hours in a lobby that's more like a living room. Included in the $25 boutique fee are morning coffee, afternoon wine, wi-fi, beach gear and cruiser bicycle use.

Halekulani RESORT **$$$**
(☎808-923-2311; www.halekulani.com; 2199 Kalia Rd; r from $490; P❄@📶🏊) Evincing modern sophistication, this resort hotel lives up to its name, which means 'House Befitting Heaven.' It's an all-encompassing experience of gracious living, not merely a place to crash. Meditative calm washes over you immediately as you step onto the lobby's cool stone tiles.

Peaceful rooms are equipped with all mod cons such as hi-tech entertainment centers, as well as deep soaking tubs and expansive lanai. Eclectic luxury suites include one personally designed by Vera Wang. Find ultimate relaxation in the Halekulani's pampering spa.

Modern Honolulu BOUTIQUE HOTEL **$$$**
(Map p80; ☎808-943-5800, 866-970-4161; www.themodernhonolulu.com; 1775 Ala Moana Blvd; r $345-525; P❄@📶🏊) Terraced ocean-view rooms and suites are elementally chic, showing off teak doors, Frette linens and marble baths. The lanai deck pool overlooks Ala Wai Yacht Harbor, as does an Iron Chef's sushi bar, Morimoto Waikiki. The only downside to staying at this mod spa oasis is the 10-minute walk to a sandy beach.

New Otani Kaimana Beach BOUTIQUE HOTEL **$$$**
(☎808-923-1555; www.kaimana.com; 2863 Kalakaua Ave; r $170-505; P❄@📶) Location, location, location. Right? Small rooms will leave you wanting more space, but the soothing setting right on Sans Souci Beach makes this 1960s-era hotel special. There's no pool, but with a beach this gorgeous, who needs one?

O'ahu

Gaze at royal Hawaiian feathered capes and ancient temple carvings in Honolulu, then swizzle sunset mai tais while listening to the strumming of slack key guitars at Waikiki Beach. Set your watch to island time to snorkel in Hanauma Bay, cruise the waterfall-laden Windward Coast and hit the North Shore's world-renowned surf beaches.

2

JEFF WHYTE / SHUTTERSTOCK ©

4

DANA EDMUNDS / GETTY IMAGES ©

1. Waimanalo (p135)
White sand stretches for miles to form O'ahu's longest beach, near the proudly Hawaiian community of Waimanalo.

2. Waikiki (p105)
Famous Waikiki Beach has been attracting surfers for decades.

3. Hanauma Bay (p132)
Beneath these sapphire and turquoise waters lies a 7000-year-old coral reef, perfect for snorkeling.

4. Kualoa (p146)
Once one of the most sacred places on Oahu, Kualoa has magnificent mountain scenery.

3

MAURO TANDOI / ROBERT HARDING ©

Eating

By the Beach

Along Kalakaua Ave, chains such as the Cheesecake Factory overflow with hungry tourists. A block inland, Kuhio Ave is great for cheap grazing, especially at multiethnic takeout joints.

★Hiking Hawaii Cafe CAFE $
(☎855-808-4453; http://hikinghawaii808.com/cafe.php; 1910 Ala Moana Blvd; ⏰7am-9pm Tue-Sat, to 3pm Sun & Mon; 📶) This downstairs eco-cafe serves up healthy meals such as panini, wraps and smoothies using fresh local produce. Worth trying is the Pitaya (Dragonfruit) Bowl for $8.95. There's complimentary wi-fi and the cafe serves as base for Hiking Hawaii's various daily tours on O'ahu. A great spot to hang out.

★Marukame Udon JAPANESE $
(☎808-931-6000; www.facebook.com/marukameudon; 2310 Kuhio Ave; mains $2-8; ⏰7am-9am & 11am-10pm; 👪) Everybody loves this Japanese noodle shop, which is so popular there is often a line stretching down the sidewalk. Watch those thick udon noodles get rolled, cut and boiled fresh right in front of you, then stack mini plates of giant tempura and *musubi* (rice balls) stuffed with salmon or a sour plum on your cafeteria tray.

Wash it all down with iced barley or green tea.

Food Pantry SUPERMARKET $
(2370 Kuhio Ave; ⏰6am-1am) It's more expensive than chain supermarkets found elsewhere in Honolulu, but cheaper than buying groceries at Waikiki's convenience stores; look for a Coffee Bean & Tea Leaf coffee bar inside.

Ruffage Natural Foods HEALTH FOOD $
(☎808-922-2042; www.facebook.com/ruffage.naturalfoods; 2443 Kuhio Ave; mains $4-8; ⏰9am-9pm; 🖉) This pint-sized health-food store whips up taro burgers, veggie burritos, deli sandwiches with fresh avocado and real-fruit smoothies that will revitalize your whole body. At night, the grocery shop shares space with a tiny, backpacker-friendly sushi bar run by a Japanese expat chef.

Me's BBQ HAWAIIAN, KOREAN $
(☎808-926-9717; 151 Uluniu Ave; mains $5-12; ⏰7am-8:45pm Mon-Sat; 👪) The streetside takeout counter may be a tad short on atmosphere, but there are plastic tables sitting in the sunshine where you can chow down on Korean standards such as *kimchi* and *kalbi*. The wall-size picture menu offers a mind-boggling array of mixed-plate combos including chicken *katsu* (deep-fried fillets), Portuguese sausage and eggs, and other only-in-Hawaii tastes.

Musubi Cafe Iyasume JAPANESE $
(www.tonsuke.com/eomusubiya.html; Pacific Monarch Hotel, 2427 Kuhio Ave; menu items $2-8; ⏰6:30am-8pm) This hole-in-the-wall keeps busy making fresh *onigiri* (rice balls) stuffed with seaweed, salmon roe, sour plums and even Spam. Other specialties include salmon-roe rice bowls, bizarre Japanese curry and island-style *mochiko* fried chicken. In a hurry? Grab a *bentō* (boxed lunch) to go.

Veggie Star Natural Foods HEALTH FOOD $
(☎808-922-9568; 417 Nahua St; ⏰10am-6pm Mon-Sat; 🖉) For organic, all-natural and health-conscious groceries, plus tropical smoothies and monster-sized vegetarian burritos, fake-meat burgers, salads and 'airplane ready' sandwiches wrapped to go, visit this little side-street shop. It's the vegan chili that makes the most people rave.

Siam Square THAI $$
(☎808-923-5320; 2nd fl, 408 Lewers St; mains $11-16; ⏰11am-10.30pm; 🖉) It's Waikiki's most authentic Thai restaurant, although that's not saying much. You want it spicy? You won't have to work too hard to convince your waiter that you can handle the heat when you order pork *larb* (salad) or fried fish with chili sauce. Service is standoffish, but the kitchen works so fast and furiously that you probably won't mind.

Ramen Nakamura JAPANESE $$
(☎808-922-7960; 2141 Kalakaua Ave; mains $9-14; ⏰11am-11:30pm) Hit this urban connoisseurs' noodle shop at lunchtime and you'll have to strategically elbow aside Japanese tourists toting Gucci and Chanel bags just to sit down. Then you're free to dig into hearty bowls of oxtail or *tonkatsu* (breaded and fried pork cutlets) or *kimchi* ramen soup with crunchy fried garlic slices on top. Cash only.

Eggs 'n' Things BREAKFAST $$
(www.eggsnthings.com; 343 Saratoga Rd; mains $9-18; ⏰6am-2pm & 4-10pm; 👪) Never empty, this bustling diner dishes straight-up comfort food: banana-macnut pancakes with trop-

ical syrups (guava, honey or coconut), sugary crepes topped with fresh fruit, or fluffy omelets scrambled with Portuguese sausage. You'll fit right in with the early-morning crowd of jet-lagged tourists lined up outside the door – and sometimes around the block.

LuLu's Surf Club AMERICAN **$$**
(☎808-926-5222; www.luluswaikiki.com; Park Shore Waikiki, 2586 Kalakaua Ave; mains breakfast $6-15, dinner $10-24; ⏰7am-2am; 🚸) Surfboards on the wall and an awesome ocean view set the mood at this gregarious open-air restaurant, bar and nightclub. Lulu's filling breakfasts, complete with 'dawn patrol' omelets, eggs Benedict, stuffed French toast, *loco moco* and fruit bowls, are legendary. Sunset Happy Hour runs every day from 3pm to 5pm.

Sansei Seafood Restaurant & Sushi Bar JAPANESE, FUSION **$$**
(☎808-931-6286; www.sanseihawaii.com; 3rd fl, Marriott Waikiki Beach Resort, 2552 Kalakaua Ave; most shared plates $5-20, mains $16-35; ⏰5:30-10pm Sun-Thu, to 1am Fri & Sat) From the mind of one of Hawaii's hottest chefs, DK Kodama, this Pacific Rim menu rolls out everything from 'new look' fusion sushi and sashimi to Dungeness crab ramen with black-truffle broth – all to rave reviews. Tables on the torch-lit verandah equal prime sunset views.

★**Roy's Waikiki** HAWAII REGIONAL **$$$**
(☎808-923-7697; www.royshawaii.com; 226 Lewers St; mains $30-60; ⏰11am-9:30pm Mon-Thu, to 10pm Fri-Sun) This contemporary incarnation of Roy Yamaguchi's island-born chain is perfect for a flirty date or just celebrating the good life. The ground-breaking chef doesn't actually cook in the kitchen here, but his signature *misoyaki* butterfish, blackened ahi and macadamia-nut-encrusted mahimahi are always on the menu (vegans and vegetarians have options too). Molten-chocolate soufflé for dessert is a must.

Azure SEAFOOD **$$$**
(☎808-921-4600; www.azurewaikiki.com; Royal Hawaiian, 2259 Kalakaua Ave; mains from $38, 5-course tasting menu $79; ⏰5:30-9pm) 🍃 Azure is the signature restaurant at the Royal Hawaiian Hotel. Seafood fresh from the pier, such as Kona abalone, red snapper and *ono* (white-fleshed mackerel), are all exquisitely prepared island-style, with finishing touches such as red Hawaiian sea salt and Moloka'i purple sweet potatoes on the side.

Morimoto Waikiki ASIAN FUSION **$$$**
(Map p80; ☎808-943-5900; www.morimotowaikiki.com; Modern Honolulu, 1775 Ala Moana Blvd; lunch $18-35, dinner mains $22-50; ⏰11am-2:30pm & 5-10pm; 🅿) In Modern Honolulu boutique hotel, Iron Chef Morimoto's ocean-front dining room seduces with coconut cocktails and yacht-harbor views from a sunny poolside patio. Sink back against a mod sea-green pillow banquette and fork into cubic seafood *poke* and sushi rolls, ginger-soy braised black cod, wagyu beef *loco moco* or curried whole roasted lobster. Complimentary valet parking with restaurant validation.

Nobu JAPANESE, FUSION **$$$**
(☎808-237-6999; www.noburestaurants.com/waikiki; Waikiki Parc, 2233 Helumoa Rd; shared dishes $5-48, mains $30-40; ⏰restaurant 5:30-10pm Sun-Thu, to 10:30pm Fri & Sat, lounge 5pm-midnight daily) Nobu Matsuhisa's first Japanese-fusion restaurant and sushi bar in Hawaii has made a big splash, and his elegant seafood tapas taste right at home by the beach. Broiled black cod with miso sauce, new-style sashimi with spicy sauce drizzled on top and Japanese-Peruvian *tiradito* (ceviche) rank among Nobu's signature tastes. A low-lit cocktail lounge serves appetizing small bites and 'sake-tinis.'

Veranda CAFE **$$$**
(☎808-921-4600; www.moana-surfrider.com; Moana Surfrider, 2365 Kalakaua Ave; afternoon tea from $34; ⏰6-11am & noon-3pm; 🅿) For colonial atmosphere that harks back to early-20th-century tourist traditions, traditional

O'AHU'S BEST SWEET TREATS

Leonard's (p122) Hot-out-of-the oven, sugary *malasadas*.

Liliha Bakery (p95) Coco-puff pastries that cause traffic jams.

Bubbies (p94) Rainbow-colored *mochi* ice cream.

Crack Seed Store (p95) Salty, sweet and sour dried fruit.

Lanikai Juice (p142) O'ahu's premier fresh-fruit smoothies.

Matsumoto's (p161) North Shore's classic shave-ice stand.

Dole Plantation (p164) Cones of frozen-pineapple soft-serve whip.

afternoon tea comes complete with finger sandwiches, scones with pillowy Devonshire cream and tropically flavored pastries. Portions are small, but the oceanfront setting and house-blended teas are memorable. Make reservations and come prepared to shoo away those pesky beggar birds.

Kapahulu Ave

On the outskirts of Waikiki, Kapahulu Ave is always worth a detour for its standout neighborhood eateries, drive-ins and bakeries, cooking up anything from Hawaiian soul food to Japanese country fare.

★ Leonard's BAKERY $

(808-737-5591; www.leonardshawaii.com; 933 Kapahulu Ave; snacks from $1; 5:30am-10pm Sun-Thu, to 11pm Fri & Sat;) It's almost impossible to drive by the Leonard's eye-catching, vintage 1950s neon sign without stopping in. This bakery is famous on O'ahu for its *malasadas,* sweet fried dough rolled in sugar, Portuguese-style – like a doughnut without the hole. Order ones with *haupia* or *liliko'i* (passion fruit) filling, and you'll be hooked for life.

Pick up a souvenir 'got malasadas?' T-shirt for even sweeter island memories.

Waiola Shave Ice DESSERTS $

(808-949-2269; www.waiolashaveice.com; 3113 Mokihana St; shave ice $2-5; 11am-5:30pm Mon-Thu, to 6pm Fri-Sun; P) This clapboard corner shop has moved locations but still makes the same superfine shave ice as it did back in 1940, and we'd argue that it's got the formula exactly right. Get yours doused with 20-plus flavors of syrup and topped by azuki beans, *liliko'i* cream, condensed milk, Hershey's chocolate syrup or spicy-sweet *li hing mui* (crack seed).

It's one building in on Mokihana St and a tad hard to spot from Kapahulu Ave.

Rainbow Drive-In HAWAIIAN $

(808-737-0177; www.rainbowdrivein.com; 3308 Kanaina Ave; meals $4-9; 7am-9pm;) Started by an island-born US army cook after WWII, this classic Hawaii drive-in wrapped in rainbow-colored neon is a throwback to another era. Construction workers, surfers and gangly teens order all their down-home favorites such as burgers, mixed-plate lunches, *loco moco* and Portuguese sweet-bread French toast from the takeout counter.

The owners' family donates part of the profits to Hawaiian schools and local charities. Factoid: President Barack Obama eats here.

Ono Seafood SEAFOOD $

(808-732-4806; 747 Kapahulu Ave; mains $7-12; 9am-6pm Mon-Sat, 10am-3pm Sun) Arrive early at this addictive, made-to-order *poke* shop, before it runs out of fresh fish marinated in *shōyu* (soy sauce), house-smoked *tako* (octopus), spicy ahi rice bowls or boiled peanuts spiked with star anise. Limited free parking.

Haili's Hawaiian Foods HAWAIIAN $$

(808-735-8019; http://hailishawaiianfood.com; 760 Palani Ave; meals $11-16; 10am-7pm Tue-Thu, to 8pm Fri & Sat, 11am-3pm Sun) Haili's has been cooking up homegrown Hawaiian fare since the 1950s. Locals cheerfully shoehorn themselves into kid-friendly booths and tables, then dig into heaping plates of *kalua* pig, *lomilomi* salmon and *laulau* (meat wrapped in ti leaves and steamed) served with poi or rice.

For a little variety, try the grilled ahi plate lunches, bowls of tripe stew, poke bowls or fat tortilla wraps.

Irifune JAPANESE $$

(808-737-1141; 563 Kapahulu Ave; mains $10-15; 11:30am-1:30pm & 5:30-9:30pm Tue-Sat) This bustling kitchen decorated with Japanese country kitsch may look very odd, especially when staff turn off the lights so you can see those glow-in-the-dark stars on the ceiling. But it's locally beloved for garlic ahi and crab dinners. With bargain-priced *bentō*-box lunches and combo dinner plates, you'll never walk away hungry. BYOB (bring your own beer).

Side Street Inn on Da Strip HAWAIIAN $$

(808-739-3939; http://sidestreetinn.com; 614 Kapahulu Ave; shared plates $7-15, mains $12-25; 3pm-midnight Mon-Fri, 1pm-midnight Sat & Sun; P) This is a Hawaiian-style sports bar with meal portions so huge that virtually everyone walks out with a bag containing what they couldn't eat. The good news is that the food is great. Pan-fried pork chops, *kimchi* fried rice and 'Side' soba are all tops, but you might have to wait a while for a table. Valet parking $5.

Uncle Bo's Pupu Bar & Grill ASIAN, FUSION $$

(808-735-8311; www.unclebosrestaurant.com; 559 Kapahulu Ave; shared plates $8-15, mains $19-27; 5pm-1am) Inside this chic storefront, boisterous groups devour the inventive chef's encyclopedic list of fusion *pupu* crafted with island flair, such as *kalua* pig nachos with wonton chips and Maui onions or baby back ribs basted in pineapple BBQ sauce. For dinner, focus on market-fresh seafood such as baked *opah* (moonfish) or steamed *opakapaka* (pink snapper). Reservations recommended.

Monsarrat Ave

Wander down past the zoo and Waikiki School to reach some great eating options up on Monsarrat.

★Diamond Head Cove Health Bar CAFE $
(www.diamondheadcove.com; 3045 Monsarrat Ave, Ste 5; 10am-8pm Mon & Sat, 9am-11pm Tue-Thu, 9am-8pm Fri, 10am-11pm Sun) This place specialises in acai bowls, fruit smoothies, healthy wraps, fresh *poke* and sashimi. Chill out with a coconut-husk dose of *'awa* (kava), Polynesia's mildly intoxicating elixir, and enjoy a relaxed vibe on *'awa* nights, when local musicians play until late.

Bogart's Cafe CAFE $
(808-739-0999; http://bogartscafe.webs.com; 3045 Monsarrat Ave, Ste 3; 6am-6.30pm Mon-Fri, to 6pm Sat & Sun) The taro-banana pancakes get rave reviews at Bogart's. This cafe uses fresh local produce to keep the locals happy with a full menu from breakfast right through to the early evening.

Pioneer Saloon JAPANESE FUSION $
(808-732-4001; www.facebook.com/pages/Pioneer-Saloon/339130739445778; 3046 Monsarrat Ave; 11am-8pm Tue-Sun) It's simple stuff, but the locals can't get enough of Pioneer Saloon's Japanese-fusion plate lunches, with everything from grilled ahi to fried baby octopus to *yakisoba* (fried noodles). On the opposite side of the road from Waikiki School.

Hawaii Sushi SUSHI $
(3045 Monsarrat Ave, Ste 1; 10am-8pm Mon-Sat, to 6pm Sun) This new place up Monsarrat Ave in the strip mall just past Waikiki School is a winner for Hawaiian-style fresh sushi with rolls and bowls such as the Spicy Ahi Bowl for $11. There's parking outside and a few seats inside.

People's Open Market MARKET $
(www.honolulu.gov/parks/dprpom.html; cnr Monsarrat & Paki Aves, Kapi'olani Park; 10-11am Wed;) City-sponsored farmers market in Kapi'olani Park trades in fresh bounty from *mauka* (inland) to *makai*. Only a short walk from Waikiki.

Drinking & Nightlife

If you're looking for a frosty cold beer or a fruity cocktail to help you recover from a day at the beach, don't worry, there are endless options in Waikiki. Sip a sunset mai tai and be hypnotized by the lilting harmonies of slack key guitars, then mingle with locals who come here to party too.

★RumFire BAR
(www.rumfirewaikiki.com; Sheraton Waikiki, 2255 Kalakaua Ave; noon-midnight) The collection of vintage rum is mighty tempting at this lively hotel bar at the Sheraton Waikiki, with flirty fire pits looking out onto the beach and live contemporary Hawaiian (or jazz) music. Or wander over to the resort's cabana-like Edge of Waikiki Bar for knockout views, designer cocktails and more live Hawaiian and pop-rock music poolside.

Addiction Nightclub & Lobby Bar CLUB, BAR
(Map p80; 808-943-5800; www.addictionnightclub.com; Modern Honolulu, 1775 Ala Moana Blvd; nightclub 10:30pm-3am Thu-Sun, beach club noon-4pm Sat, lobby bar 6pm-late daily) Superstar mainland DJs and island dynamos spin at this boutique hotel's chic nightspot with an upscale dress code (no shorts, flip-flops or hats). On special weekends, Addiction's daytime beach club lets you hang out on the pool deck with the sounds of electronica and techno grooves.

Lulu's Waikiki BAR, CLUB
(808-926-5222; www.luluswaikiki.com; Park Shore Waikiki, 2586 Kalakaua Ave; 7am-2am) Brush off your sandy feet at Kuhio Beach, then step across Kalakaua Ave to this surf-themed bar and grill with 2nd-story lanai views of the Pacific Ocean and Diamond Head. Lap up sunset happy hours (3pm to 5pm daily), then chill out to acoustic acts and local bands later most evenings. DJs crank up the beats after 10pm on Saturday.

Five-O Bar & Lounge SPORTS BAR
(808-922-0550; www.five-o-bar.com; 2nd fl, Bldg B, Royal Hawaiian Center, 2233 Kalakaua Ave; noon-midnight Mon-Thu, to 2am Fri & Sat, 11am-11pm Sun) You won't spot any *Hawaii Five-0* stars hiding out among the tropical lanai greenery inside this shopping-mall bar, but it's still loads of fun with friends. Boogie down on the dance floor or twirl the swizzle

stick in your mai tai while listening to live bands, then belly up to the polished native-wood bar for *kalua* pork sliders.

Lewers Lounge LOUNGE
(www.halekulani.com/dining/lewers-lounge-bar; 2199 Kalia Rd, Halekulani; ⏲7:30pm-1am) The nostalgic dream of Waikiki as an aristocratic playground is kept alive at this Halekulani hotel bar. We're talking contemporary and classic cocktails, tempting appetizers and desserts, and smooth jazz combos that serenade after 8:30pm nightly.

Genius Lounge LOUNGE
(☎808-626-5362; www.geniusloungehawaii.com; 3rd fl, 346 Lewers St; ⏲6pm-2am) Like a Japanese speakeasy, this glowing candlelit hideaway is a chill retreat for ultracool hipsters and lovebird couples. East-West tapas bites let you nibble on squid tempura, *loco moco* or banana cake while you sip made-in-Japan sake brews and retro jazz or cutting-edge electronica tickles your ears.

Da Big Kahuna BAR
(☎808-923-0033; www.dabigkahuna.net; 2299 Kuhio Ave; ⏲10:30am-3am) Do you dream of a kitschy tiki bar where fruity, Kool Aid–colored drinks are poured into ceramic mugs carved with the faces of Polynesian gods? To get soused fast, order Da Fish Bowl – just don't try picking up a pool cue or shimmying on the small dance floor once you've drained it. Full food menu served till 3am.

Nashville Waikiki BAR, CLUB
(www.nashvillewaikiki.com; 2330 Kuhio Ave; ⏲4pm-4am) Like Waikiki's own little honky-tonk, this country-and-western dive bar can get as rowdy as a West Texas brawl. Homesick Southerners show up for sports TVs, billiards, darts, pool tournaments, and free line-dancing and two-steppin' lessons. Afternoon, evening and late-night happy hours seem endless.

☆ Entertainment

Whether you want to linger over one of those cool, frosty drinks with the little umbrellas or are craving live Hawaiian music and hula dancing, you're in the right place. For what's going on tonight, from DJ and live-music gigs to special events, check the TGIF section of the *Honolulu Star-Advertiser* (www.honolulupulse.com), which comes out every Friday, and the free alternative tabloid *Honolulu Weekly* (www.honoluluweekly.com), published every Wednesday.

Hawaiian Music & Hula

★Kuhio Beach Torch Lighting & Hula Show LIVE MUSIC
(☎808-922-5331; www.honolulu.gov/moca; Kuhio Beach Park; ⏲6.30-7.30pm Tue, Thu & Sat, weather

GAY & LESBIAN WAIKIKI

Waikiki's LGBT community is tightly knit, but full of aloha for visitors. The free monthly magazine *Odyssey* (www.odysseyhawaii.com) covers the scene. It's available at the friendly, open-air **Hula's Bar & Lei Stand** (☎808-923-0669; www.hulas.com; 2nd fl, Castle Waikiki Grand, 134 Kapahulu Ave; ⏲10am-2am; 📶), which has ocean views of Diamond Head. Stop by for drinks and to meet a variety of new faces, play pool and boogie. More svelte **Bacchus Waikiki** (☎808-926-4167; www.bacchus-waikiki.com; 2nd fl, 408 Lewers St; ⏲noon-2am) is an intimate wine bar and cocktail lounge with happy-hour specials, shirtless bartenders and Sunday-afternoon beer busts. For nonstop singalongs, seek out **Wang Chung's** (☎808-921-9176; http://wangchungs.com; 2424 Koa Ave; ⏲5pm-2am), a living-room-sized karaoke bar.

Tiki-themed **Tapa's Restaurant & Lanai Bar** (☎808-921-2288; www.tapaswaikiki.com; 2nd fl, 407 Seaside Ave; ⏲2pm-2am Mon-Sat, from 9am Sun) is a bigger chill-out spot with bear-y talkative bartenders, pool tables, a jukebox and karaoke nights. Around the corner, **Lo Jax Waikiki** (www.lojaxwaikiki.com; 2256 Kuhio Ave; ⏲noon-2am; 📶) is a gay sports bar with drag shows and weekend DJs. Next door **Fusion Waikiki** (☎808-924-2422; www.fusionwaikiki.com; 2260 Kuhio Ave; ⏲10pm-4am) is a divey nightclub with weekend drag shows. Hidden up an alley a few blocks away, **In Between** (☎808-926-7060; www.facebook.com/inbetween.waikiki; 2155 Lau'ula St; ⏲noon-2am), a laid-back neighborhood bar, attracts an older crowd for 'the happiest of happy hours.'

By day, have fun in the sun at Queen's Surf Beach (p112) and (illegally clothing optional) Diamond Head Beach (p129). At night, check into the gay-friendly Castle Waikiki Grand (p117) or Hotel Renew (p116).

permitting, 6-7pm Nov-Jan; 👪) It all begins at the Duke Kahanamoku statue with the sounding of a conch shell and the lighting of torches after sunset. At the nearby hula mound, lay out your beach towel and enjoy the authentic Hawaiian music and dance show. It's full of aloha!

★ House Without a Key LIVE MUSIC, HULA
(☎808-923-2311; www.halekulani.com; Halekulani, 2199 Kalia Rd; ⊙7am-9pm) Named after a 1925 Charlie Chan novel set in Honolulu, this genteel open-air hotel lounge sprawled beneath a century-old kiawe tree simply has no doors to lock. A sophisticated crowd gathers here for sunset cocktails, Hawaiian music and solo hula dancing by former Miss Hawaii pageant winners. Panoramic ocean views are as intoxicating as the tropical cocktails.

Mai Tai Bar LIVE MUSIC, HULA
(☎808-923-7311; www.royal-hawaiian.com; Royal Hawaiian, 2259 Kalakaua Ave; ⊙10am-midnight) At the Royal Hawaiian's low-key bar (no preppy resort wear required), you can catch some great acoustic island music acts and graceful solo hula dancers some nights. Even if you don't dig who's performing, the signature Royal Mai Tai still packs a punch and romantic views of the breaking surf extend down to Diamond Head.

Beach Bar LIVE MUSIC, HULA
(☎808-922-3111; www.moana-surfrider.com; Moana Surfrider, 2365 Kalakaua Ave; ⊙10:30am-midnight) Inside this historic beachfront hotel bar, soak up the sounds of classical and contemporary Hawaiian musicians playing underneath the old banyan tree where the *Hawaii Calls* radio program was broadcast nationwide during the mid-20th century. Live-music schedules vary, but hula soloists dance from 6pm to 8pm most nights.

Tapa Bar LIVE MUSIC
(☎808-949-4321; www.hiltonhawaiianvillage.com; Ground fl, Tapa Tower, Hilton Hawaiian Village, 2005 Kalia Rd; ⊙10am-11pm) It's worth navigating through the gargantuan Hilton resort complex to this Polynesian-themed open-air bar just to see some of the best traditional and contemporary Hawaiian groups performing on O'ahu today. There is live music nightly from 7.30pm or 8pm.

Moana Terrace LIVE MUSIC
(☎808-922-6611; 2nd fl, Marriott Waikiki Beach Resort, 2552 Kalakaua Ave; ⊙11am-11pm; 👪) If you're in a mellow mood, come for sunset happy-hour drinks at this casual poolside bar, just a lei's throw from Kuhio Beach. Slack key guitarists, ukulele players and *ha'i* falsetto singers make merry for a family-friendly crowd.

Kani Ka Pila Grille LIVE MUSIC
(☎808-924-4990; www.outriggerreef.com; Outrigger Reef on the Beach, 2169 Kalia Rd; ⊙11am-10pm) Once happy hour ends, the Outrigger's lobby bar sets the scene for some of the most laid-back live-music shows of any of Waikiki's beachfront hotels, with traditional and contemporary Hawaiian musicians playing their hearts out and cracking jokes.

Royal Grove LIVE MUSIC, HULA
(☎808-922-2299; www.royalhawaiiancenter.com/info/entertainment; Ground fl, Royal Hawaiian Center, 2201 Kalakaua Ave; ⊙schedules vary) This shopping mall's open-air stage may lack oceanfront views, but Hawaiian music and hula performances by top island talent happen here almost every evening, along with twice-weekly lunchtime shows by performers from the Windward Coast's Polynesian Cultural Center and concerts by the Royal Hawaiian Band.

Luau & Dinner Shows

'Aha 'Aina LUAU
(☎808-921-4600; www.royal-hawaiian.com/dining/ahaaina; Royal Hawaiian, 2259 Kalakaua Ave; adult/child 5-12yr from $179/101; ⊙5:30-8pm Mon) This oceanfront sit-down dinner show is like a three-act musical play narrating the history of Hawaiian *mele* (songs) and hula. The food is top-notch and there's an open bar.

Waikiki Starlight Luau LUAU
(☎808-947-2607; www.hiltonhawaiianvillage.com/luau; Hilton Hawaiian Village, 2005 Kalia Rd; adult/child 4-11yr from $99/50; ⊙5:30-8pm Sun-Thu, weather permitting; 👪) Enthusiastic pan-Polynesian show, with buffet meal, outdoor seating, Samoan fire dancing and *hapa haole* (literally 'half foreign') hula.

Shopping

Hundreds of shops in Waikiki are vying for your tourist dollars. Not feeling flush? You'll never be far from Waikiki's ubiquitous ABC Stores, conveniently cheap places to pick up vacation essentials such as beach mats, sunblock, snacks and sundries, not to mention plastic flower and shell lei, 'I got lei'd in Hawaii' T-shirts and motorized, grass-skirted hula girls for the dashboard of your car back home.

★Bailey's Antiques & Aloha Shirts CLOTHING, ANTIQUES
(http://alohashirts.com; 517 Kapahulu Ave; ⌚10am-6pm) Bailey's has, without a doubt, the finest aloha-shirt collection on O'ahu, possibly the world! Racks are crammed with thousands of collector-worthy vintage aloha shirts in every conceivable color and style, from 1920s kimono-silk classics to 1970s polyester specials to modern offerings. Prices dizzyingly vary from five bucks to several thousand dollars. 'Margaritaville' musician Jimmy Buffett is Bailey's biggest fan.

Royal Hawaiian Center MALL
(www.royalhawaiiancenter.com; 2201 Kalakaua Ave; ⌚10am-10pm) Not to be confused with the Royal Hawaiian resort hotel next door, Waikiki's biggest shopping center has four levels and houses more than 80 breezily mixed stores. Look for Hawaii-born labels such as Noa Noa for Polynesian-print sarongs, sundresses and shirts. Art galleries display high-quality koa carvings, while jewelers trade in Ni'ihau shell-lei necklaces, and flower lei stands sell fresh, wearable art.

Reyn Spooner CLOTHING
(☎808-923-7896; www.reynspooner.com; Sheraton Waikiki, 2259 Kalakaua Ave; ⌚8am-10:30pm) Since 1956, Reyn Spooner's subtly designed, reverse-print preppy aloha shirts have been the standard for Honolulu's businessmen, political power brokers and social movers and shakers. Reyn's Waikiki flagship is a bright, mod and clean-lined store, carrying colorful racks of men's shirts and board shorts, too. Also at Kahala Mall and Ala Moana Center. Ask about Reyn's Rack downtown for discounts on factory seconds.

SUNSET ON THE BEACH

On a number of Saturdays, Queen's Surf Beach turns into a festive scene. Dubbed **Sunset on the Beach** (www.sunsetonthebeach.net), almost everything is free – except for the food sold by local vendors, and even that's a bargain.

Tables and chairs are set up on the sand and live Hawaiian music acts perform on a beachside stage for about two hours before show time. When darkness falls, a huge screen is unscrolled and a feature movie is shown, starting around 7pm. Sometimes it's a film with island connections, while other nights it's a Hollywood blockbuster. Check the website for schedules.

Ukulele PuaPua UKULELE
(☎808-924-2266; www.hawaiianukuleleonline.com; Sheraton Waikiki, 2255 Kalakaua Ave; ⌚9am-10pm) Avoid those flimsy souvenir ukuleles and head to one of PuaPua's two locations, one at the Sheraton Waikiki, the other at the Moana Surfrider (p117), to find the real thing. These guys are passionate and offer free group beginner lessons every day.

Newt at the Royal CLOTHING
(www.newtattheroyal.com; Royal Hawaiian, 2259 Kalakaua Ave; ⌚9am-9pm) With stylish flair and panache, Newt specializes in Montecristi Panama hats – classic men's fedoras, plantation-style hats and women's *fino*. It also has fine reproductions of aloha shirts using 1940s and '50s designs. Everything's tropical, neat as a pin and top-drawer quality.

Genius Outfitters ARTS, CRAFTS
(☎808-922-2822; www.geniusoutfitters.net; 346 Lewers St; ⌚10.30am-10pm) This cutesy arts, crafts and clothing store on Lewers specializes in locally made goods. It covers the first two floors of an attractive three-story building with Genius Lounge on top.

Peggy's Picks COLLECTIBLES
(☎808-737-3297; www.facebook.com/PeggysPicks; 732 Kapahalu Ave; ⌚11am-7pm Mon-Sat) Peggy's Picks on Kapahulu Ave is the place to go for Hawaiiana, treasures and collectibles from all over the world. It's a bit ramshackle and can get a tad crowded, but well worth it for the collectors among us.

Island Paddler CLOTHING
(☎808-737-4854; www.islandpaddlerhawaii.com; 716 Kapahulu Ave; ⌚10am-6pm) Besides having a great selection of paddles and paddling gear, these guys have T-shirts, aloha shirts, beachwear and everything you might need for a day at the beach – along with a friendly and relaxed atmosphere.

Na Lima Mili Hulu No'eau CRAFTS
(☎808-732-0865; 762 Kapahulu Ave; ⌚usually 9am-4pm Mon-Sat) The late Aunty Mary Louise Kaleonahenahe Kekuewa's daughter and granddaughter keep alive the ancient craft of feather lei-making at this small storefront, whose name means 'the skilled hands that touch the feathers.' It can take days to produce a single feather lei, prized by collectors. Call ahead to check opening hours or make an appointment for a personalized lesson.

Art on the Zoo Fence ARTS, CRAFTS

(www.artonthezoofence.com; Monsarrat Ave, opposite Kapi'olani Park; ⌚9am-4pm Sat & Sun) Dozens of artists hang their works along the fence on the south side of the Honolulu Zoo every weekend, weather permitting. Browse the contemporary watercolor, acrylic and oil paintings and colorful island photography as you chat with the artists themselves.

Information

DANGERS & ANNOYANCES

Never leave your valuables unattended on the beach. At night, it's risky to walk on the beach or along Ala Wai Canal. After dark, prostitutes stroll Kuhio Ave, preying on naive-looking male tourists.

EMERGENCY

Waikiki Police Substation (☎808-723-8562; www.honolulupd.org; 2405 Kalakaua Ave; ⌚24hr) If you need nonemergency help, or just friendly directions, stop here next to Kuhio Beach Park.

INTERNET ACCESS

These days the internet is everywhere. All Waikiki hotels have wired internet or wi-fi connections in guest rooms (for which a surcharge may apply), with wi-fi also in the lobby or poolside. Cybercafes on Kuhio and Kalakaua Aves provide pay-as-you-go Internet terminals, charging $6 to $12 per hour.

Waikiki-Kapahulu Public Library (☎808-733-8488; www.librarieshawaii.org; 400 Kapahulu Ave; ⌚10am-5pm Tue, Wed, Fri & Sat, noon-7pm Thu; wi-fi) Free wi-fi and internet terminals (temporary nonresident library card $10) that may be reserved by calling ahead.

Waikiki Beachside Hostel (www.waikikibeachsidehostel.com; 2556 Lemon Rd; per hour $7; ⌚24hr; wi-fi) Internet-cafe terminals available to nonguests.

LAUNDRY

Many accommodations have coin-operated laundry facilities for guests.

Campbell Highlander Laundry (3340 Campbell Ave; ⌚6:30am-9pm) Self-serve washers and dryers; same-day laundry service available. Inland off Kapahulu Ave.

Waikiki Laundromat (☎808-351-5331; http://waikikilaundromathi.com; 2450 Prince Edward St; ⌚6am-8pm) Clean and simple in the heart of Waikiki.

MEDICAL SERVICES

Doctors on Call (www.straubhealth.org) North Waikiki (☎808-973-5250; 2nd fl, Rainbow Bazaar, Hilton Hawaiian Village, 2005 Kalia Rd; ⌚8am-4:30pm Mon-Fri); South Waikiki (☎808-971-6000; ground fl, Sheraton Princess Kaiulani, 120 Ka'iulani Ave; ⌚24hr) Nonemergency walk-in medical clinics that accept some travel-health-insurance policies.

MONEY

There are 24-hour ATMs all over Waikiki, including at the following full-service banks near Waikiki Beach Walk.

Bank of Hawaii (www.boh.com; 2155 Kalakaua Ave; ⌚8:30am-4pm Mon-Thu, 8:30am-6pm Fri, 9am-1pm Sat) International banking and currency exchange.

First Hawaiian Bank (www.fhb.com; 2181 Kalakaua Ave; ⌚8:30am-4pm Mon-Thu, to 6pm Fri) Lobby displays Hawaii history murals by French artist Jean Charlot.

TOURIST INFORMATION

Freebie tourist magazines containing discount coupons, such as *This Week O'ahu* and *101 Things to Do*, can be found in street-corner boxes and hotel lobbies and at Honolulu's airport.

Hawaii Visitors & Convention Bureau (☎808-923-1811; www.gohawaii.com; Suite 801, Waikiki Business Plaza, 2270 Kalakaua Ave; ⌚8am-4:30pm Mon-Fri) This business office hands out free tourist maps and brochures.

Getting There & Around

Technically, Waikiki is a district of the city of Honolulu. Three parallel roads cross Waikiki: one-way Kalakaua Ave (northwest to southeast) alongside the beach; two-way Kuhio Ave, the main drag inland for pedestrians and buses; and one-way Ala Wai Blvd (southeast to northwest), which borders Ala Wai Canal.

BICYCLE

You can rent beach cruisers and commuter bikes all over Waikiki.

Big Kahuna Motorcycle Tours & Rentals (☎808-924-2736; www.bigkahunarentals.com; 407 Seaside Ave; per 4hr/9hr/24hr/week $10/15/20/100) Rents commuter-style mountain bikes only.

EBikes Hawaii (☎808-722-5454; www.ebikeshawaii.com; 3318 Campbell Ave; 4/7hr $40/50) These guys are passionate about E-bikes and are based just off Kapahulu Ave. They have half-, full- and multiday rentals available.

Hawaiian Style Rentals (☎866-916-6733; www.hawaiibikes.com; Waikiki Beachside Hostel, 2556 Lemon Rd; per day $20-30) Multiday and monthly discounts on both beach cruiser and 'comfort bike' rentals.

BUS

Most public bus stops in Waikiki are found inland along Kuhio Ave. The Ala Moana Center mall, just northwest of Waikiki, is the island's main bus-transfer point.

CAR

Major car-rental companies have branches in Waikiki. If you're renting a car for the entire time you're on O'ahu, you may be better off picking up and dropping off at Honolulu's airport, where rates are usually cheaper, but then you'll also have to pay for parking at your hotel (averaging $15 to $30 per night).

Independent rental agencies in Waikiki include the following:

808 Smart Car Rentals (☎808-735-5000; http://smartcartours.com; 444 Niu St) Rents smart cars with convertible roofs that get over 40mpg on island highways; being smaller, they're also easier to park.

Paradise Rent-a-Car (☎808-946-7777; www.paradiserentacar.com; 1837 Ala Moana Blvd; ⏰8am-5pm) Rents sedans, SUVs, jeeps and convertibles; drivers aged 18 to 24 accepted with a hefty cash deposit (no credit card required).

VIP Car Rental (☎808-922-4605; http://vipcarrentalhawaii.com; 234 Beach Walk; ⏰7am-5pm) Rents compacts, sedans, jeeps, minivans and convertibles; drivers aged 18 to 24 accepted with a hefty cash deposit (no credit card required).

Parking

Most hotels charge $15 to $30 per night for either valet or self-parking. The **Waikiki Trade Center Parking Garage** (2255 Kuhio Ave, enter off Seaside Ave) and next-door **Waikiki Parking Garage** (333 Seaside Ave) usually offer Waikiki's cheapest flat-rate day, evening and overnight rates. At the less-trafficked southeast end of Waikiki, there's a free parking lot along Monsarrat Ave beside Kapi'olani Park with no time limit.

MOTORCYCLE & MOPED

You can ride around on a motorcycle or moped, but don't expect to save any money that way – two-wheeled vehicles can be more expensive to rent than a car.

Chase Hawaii Rentals (☎808-942-4273; www.chasehawaiirentals.com; 355 Royal Hawaiian Ave) Rents Harley-Davidson, Kawasaki and Honda motorcycles and Vespa scooters (drivers over 21 with valid motorcycle license and credit card only).

Cruzin Hawaii (☎808-945-9595, 877-945-9595; http://cruzinhawaii.com; 444 Niu St) Rents mostly Harley-Davidson motorcycles (drivers over 21 with valid motorcycle license and credit card only).

TAXI

Taxi stands are found at Waikiki's bigger resort hotels and shopping malls.

TROLLEY

The motorized **Waikiki Trolley** (☎808-593-2822; www.waikikitrolley.com; adult/child 4-11yr 4-day pass $54/37, 7-day pass $59/41) runs four color-coded lines designed for tourists that connect Waikiki with the Ala Moana Center, downtown Honolulu, Chinatown, Diamond Head and Kahala Mall. Passes allow you to jump on and off the trolley as often as you like, but they don't offer much in the way of value compared with buses. Purchase trolley passes at **DFS Galleria** (330 Royal Hawaiian Ave) or **Royal Hawaiian Center** (2201 Kalakaua Ave), or buy them online in advance at a discount.

SOUTHEAST O'AHU

Cue the *Hawaii 5-0* theme music and pretend to be the star of your own TV show or Hollywood blockbuster on O'ahu's most glamorous stretch of coastline. It looks a lot like Beverly Hills by the beach, with cherry-red convertibles cruising past private mansions with drop-dead ocean views. But you'll also find more natural thrills that are open to the public on these scenic shores: the snorkeling hot spot of Hanauma Bay, hiking trails to the top of Diamond Head and the windblown lighthouse at Makapu'u Point, and O'ahu's most famous bodysurfing and bodyboarding beaches are all just a short ride east of Waikiki.

Diamond Head & Kahala

A dramatic backdrop for Waikiki Beach, Diamond Head is one of the best-known landmarks in Hawaii. Ancient Hawaiians called it Le'ahi and at its summit they built a *luakini heiau,* a temple dedicated to the war god Ku and used for human sacrifices. Ever since 1825, when British sailors found calcite crystals sparkling in the sun and mistakenly thought they'd struck it rich, the sacred peak has been called Diamond Head.

Beaches

Kuilei Cliffs Beach Park BEACH

(Map p70; 3450 Diamond Head Rd) In the shadow of Diamond Head, this rocky beach draws experienced windsurfers when the tradewinds are blowing. When the swells are up, surfers take over the waves. The

Southeast Coast

Southeast Coast

Top Sights

1 Sandy Beach Park C3

Sights

2 Fishing Shrine C3
Halona Blowhole .... (see 3)
3 Halona Cove C3
4 Hanauma Bay Nature Preserve B4
5 Koko Crater Botanical Garden C3
6 Lana'i Lookout C4
7 Makapu'u Beach Park D2
8 Makapu'u Point Lighthouse D2
9 Marine Educational Center B4
10 Sea Life Park C2

Activities, Courses & Tours

11 H²0 Sports Hawaii B3
Island Divers .... (see 11)
12 Koko Crater Trail B3
13 Kuli'ou'ou Ridge Trail A2
14 Makapu'u Point Lighthouse Trail D2

Eating

Bubbie's .... (see 15)
Fatboy's .... (see 15)
Kokonuts Shave Ice & Snacks .... (see 15)
15 Kona Brewing Company B3

Shopping

Island Treasures at the Marina .... (see 15)

little beach has outdoor showers but no other facilities. You'll find paved parking lots off Diamond Head Rd, just east of the lighthouse.

Diamond Head Beach Park BEACH

(Map p70; 3300 Diamond Head Rd) Bordering the lighthouse, this rocky beach occasionally draws surfers, snorkelers and tide-poolers,

DON'T MISS

O'AHU'S TOP FARMERS MARKET

At O'ahu's premier gathering of farmers and their fans, **KCC Farmers Market** (Map p70; http://hfbf.org/markets; parking lot C, Kapi'olani Community College, 4303 Diamond Head Rd; 7:30-11am Sat;), everything sold is locally made or grown and has a loyal following, from Nalo greens to Kahuku shrimp and corn. Restaurants and vendors sell all kinds of tasty takeout meals, with Hawaii coffee brewed fresh and cold coconuts cracked open on demand. Get there early for the best of everything.

plus a few picnickers. The narrow strand nicknamed Lighthouse Beach is popular with gay men, who pull off Diamond Head Rd onto short, dead-end Beach Rd, then walk east along the shore to find a little seclusion and (illegally) sunbathe au naturel.

Wai'alae Beach Park BEACH
(Map p70; 4925 Kahala Ave) At this picturesque sandy beach, a gentle stream meets the sea. Local surfers challenge Razors, a break off the channel's west side. Swimming conditions are usually calm, though not the best due to the shallow reef. A favorite of wedding parties, the beach park has shady picnic tables, restrooms and outdoor showers. The parking lot is often full.

Sights & Activities

★Shangri La HISTORIC BUILDING
(Map p70; 808-532-3853; www.shangrilahawaii.org; 2½hr tour incl transportation $25; tours 9am, 10:30am & 1:30pm Wed-Sat, closed early Sep-early Oct) Celebrity Doris Duke had a lifelong passion for Islamic art and architecture, inspired by a visit to the Taj Mahal during her honeymoon voyage to India at the age of 23. During that same honeymoon in 1935, she stopped at O'ahu, fell in love with the island and decided to build Shangri La, her seasonal residence, on Black Point in the shadow of Diamond Head.

Over the next 60 years she traveled the globe from Indonesia to Istanbul, collecting priceless Islamic art objects. Duke appreciated the spirit more than the grand scale of the world wonders she had seen, and she made Shangri La into an intimate sanctuary rather than an ostentatious mansion. One of the true beauties of the place is the way it harmonizes with the natural environment. Finely crafted interiors open to embrace gardens and the ocean, and one glass wall of the living room looks out at Diamond Head. Throughout the estate, courtyard fountains spritz. Duke's extensive collection of Islamic art includes vivid gemstone-studded enamels, glazed ceramic paintings and silk suzanis (intricate needlework tapestries). Art often blends with architecture to represent a theme or region, as in the Damascus Room, the restored interior of an 18th-century Syrian merchant's house.

Shangri La can only be visited on a guided tour departing from downtown's Honolulu Museum of Art, where you'll watch a brief background video first, then travel as a group by minibus to the estate. Tours often sell out weeks ahead of time, so make reservations as far ahead as possible. Children under eight are not allowed.

★Diamond Head State Monument HIKING
(Map p70; www.hawaiistateparks.org; off Diamond Head Rd btwn Makapu'u & 18th Aves; admission per pedestrian/car $1/5; 6am-6pm, last trail entry 4:30pm;) The extinct crater of Diamond Head is now a state monument, with picnic tables and a hiking trail up to the 760ft-high summit. The trail was built in 1908 to service military observation stations located along the crater rim. Although a fairly steep trail, it's partly paved and only 1408yd to the top, taking about an hour round-trip. Plenty of people of all ages make the hike.

The trail, which passes through several tunnels and up head-spinning staircases, is mostly open and hot, so wear a hat and sunscreen and bring plenty of water. The windy summit affords fantastic 360-degree views of the southeast coast to Koko Head and the Leeward Coast to the Wai'anae Range.

The state park has restrooms, drinking fountains, vending machines and a picnic area. From Waikiki, catch bus 23 or 24; from the closest bus stop, it's about a 20-minute walk to the trailhead. By car, take Monsarrat Ave to Diamond Head Rd and turn right immediately after passing Kapi'olani Community College (KCC).

Sleeping

Kahala Hotel & Resort RESORT $$$
(Map p70; 808-739-8888; www.kahalaresort.com; 5000 Kahala Ave; r from $495;) Facing a private beach, this luxury resort is a favorite of celebs, royalty and other

rich-and-famous types who crave Kahala's paparazzi-free seclusion. The grande dame still maintains an appealing island-style casualness: staff who have been working here for decades and guests who return every year know each other by name, and it's that intimacy that really separates it from the Waikiki pack.

A lei greeting at check-in, Hawaiian cultural classes, rental bicycles and SUP lessons are all complimentary, but overnight parking costs $25.

Eating

Whole Foods SUPERMARKET $

(Map p70; http://wholefoodsmarket.com; Kahala Mall, 4211 Wai'alae Ave; 7am-10pm;) Fill your picnic basket with organic produce and locally made specialty foods, hot and cold deli items, takeout sushi and salads, made-to-order hot pizzas and imported wines.

Hoku's PACIFIC RIM $$$

(Map p70; 808-739-8760; www.kahalaresort.com; Kahala Hotel & Resort, 5000 Kahala Ave; Sun brunch adult/child 6-12yr $65/33, dinner mains $30-65; 10am-2pm Sun, 5:30-10pm Wed-Sun) Chef Wayne Hirabayashi is revered for his elegant East-West creations such as braised short ribs with avocado tempura and wok-fried market-fresh fish paired with a world-ranging wine list. The Sunday-brunch buffet stars a seafood raw bar piled high with all-you-can-eat king-crab legs and a chocolate dessert fountain. Make reservations; collared shirts and slacks for men and evening attire for women are required.

Entertainment

Diamond Head Theater THEATER

(Map p70; 808-733-0277; www.diamondheadtheatre.com; 520 Makapuu Ave) Opened in 1915 and known as 'the Broadway of the Pacific,' this lovely old theater is the third-oldest continuously running community theater in the USA. Runs a variety of high-quality shows throughout the year with everything from *Mary Poppins* to *Spamalot* to *South Pacific*. Also runs acting, dancing and singing classes.

Kahala Mall CINEMA

(Map p70; movie infoline 808-593-3000; www.kahalamallcenter.com; 4211 Wai'alae Ave) Eight-screen multiplex that frequently screens independent art-house and foreign films.

Shopping

Kahala Mall MALL

(Map p70; www.kahalamallcenter.com; 4211 Wai'alae Ave; 10am-9pm Mon-Sat, to 6pm Sun) It's no competition for the Ala Moana Center, but this neighborhood mall has a noteworthy mix of only-in-Hawaii shops, including Cinnamon Girl clothing boutique, Reyn Spooner and Rix Island Wear for aloha shirts, and Sanrio Surprises selling collectible, hard-to-find imported Hello Kitty toys and logo gear.

Hawai'i Kai

With its yacht-filled marina and breezy canals surrounded by mountains, bays and gentle beach parks, this meticulously planned suburb designed by the late steel tycoon Henry J Kaiser (he's the Kai in Hawai'i Kai) is a nouveau-riche scene. All the action revolves around the three shopping centers off Kalaniana'ole Hwy (Hwy 72) and Keahole St.

Activities

The marina is flush with tour operators and water-sports outfitters that can hook you up with jet skis, banana and bumper boats, parasailing trips, wakeboarding, scuba dives, speed sailing and more.

Kuli'ou'ou Ridge Trail HIKING, MOUNTAIN BIKING

(https://hawaiitrails.ehawaii.gov) West of town, this 5-mile round-trip route is open to both hikers and mountain bikers. The trail winds up forest switchbacks before making a stiff but ultimately satisfying climb along a ridgeline to a windy summit offering 360-degree views of Koko Head, Makapu'u Point, the Windward Coast, Diamond Head and downtown Honolulu.

The trail is not always well maintained and may be partly overgrown with vegetation. Start from the Na Ala Hele trailhead sign at the end of Kala'au Pl, which branches right off Kuli'ou'ou Rd, just over 1 mile north of the Kalaniana'ole Hwy.

Island Divers DIVING, SNORKELING

(808-423-8222; www.oahuscubadiving.com; Hawai'i Kai Shopping Center, 377 Keahole St) Five-star PADI operation offers boat dives for all levels, including expert-level wreck dives. If you're a novice, staff can show you the ropes and take you to calm, relatively shallow waters. Snorkelers can ride along on the dive boats ($40 per person, including equipment rental), which visit all sides of the island.

H$_2$O Sports Hawaii WATER SPORTS
(808-396-0100; www.h2osportshawaii.com; Hawai'i Kai Shopping Center, 377 Keahole St) These guys can hook you up with jet packs (the first commercial operation of H$_2$O jet packs in the US), water skis, banana boats, bumper tubes, parasailing trips, wakeboarding, scuba dives, speed sailing – whatever gets your adrenaline pumping. Just be prepared to pay plenty; check online for advance booking discounts.

Koko Crater Trail HIKING
This nerve-rattling trail is not for anyone with a fear of heights! The fully exposed route leads for almost a mile along an abandoned wooden-tie rail bed to reach the summit of Pu'u Mai (1206ft). There's no shade, but don't worry: the panoramic views from atop the extinct crater's rim are worth your sweat.

Turn north off the Kalaniana'ole Hwy onto Lunalilo Home Rd, which borders the east side of Koko Marina Center, then turn right onto Anapalau St, which leads into the community park where you'll find the trailhead.

Eating & Drinking

Bubbie's ICE CREAM $
(808-396-8722; www.bubbiesicecream.com; Koko Marina Center, 7192 Kalaniana'ole Hwy; items $1.50-6; 10am-11pm;) Could it possibly get any better than a Bubbie's *mochi* ice cream? We don't think so! There are so many great flavors to try that it will be hard to stop, especially after a day at the beach.

Kokonuts Shave Ice & Snacks SWEETS $
(808-396-8809; Koko Marina Center, 7192 Kalanianaole Hwy; 10.30am-9pm) After a tough day at Hanauma Bay, do as President Obama has done (attested to by photos of Obama in a Kokonuts Shave Ice T-shirt!) and drop into Kokonuts at Koko Marina for some tasty refreshments. The acai and pitaya bowls are top notch, the shave ice really hits the spot, and the welcome is friendly. Good aloha here!

Fatboy's HAWAIIAN $
(808-394-2373; http://fatboyshawaii.com; Koko Marina Center, 7192 Kalanianaole Hwy; 8am-8pm) Slightly indelicately named, Fatboy's handle says it all. If you're into Hawaiian-style plate lunches, then Fatboy's at Koko Marina ticks all the boxes. The Garlic Chicken ($8.99) gets rave reviews, but it's the Fatboy's Bento ($7.99) that has sold over 500,000 plates through the Fatboy's O'ahu stores. The full tables are testament to Fatboy's popularity.

Kona Brewing Company PUB
(808-396-5662; www.konabrewingco.com; Koko Marina Center, 7192 Kalaniana'ole Hwy; 11am-10pm;) On the docks of Koko Marina, this Big Island import is known for its microbrewed beers, especially the Longboard Lager, the Pipeline Porter and the Big Wave Golden Ale. There's live Hawaiian music some nights, and the brewpub's island-style *pupu* (appetizers), wood-fired pizzas, burgers, seafood and salads are filling (mains $12 to $28). But it's the beer that makes this place!

Shopping

Island Treasures at the Marina ARTS, CRAFTS
(808-396-8827; Koko Marina Center, 7192 Kalaniana'ole Hwy; 10am-6pm Mon-Sat, 11am-4pm Sun) Near the waterfront at Koko Marina, this locally owned shop displays high-quality artisan handiwork such as koa wood carvings, etched glass, pottery and island paintings. Handmade soaps, lotions and jewelry make memorable gifts.

Hanauma Bay

A wide, curved bay of sapphire and turquoise waters protected by a rugged volcanic ring, **Hanauma Bay Nature Preserve** (808-396-4229; www.honolulu.gov/parks/facility/hanaumabay; adult/child under 13yr $7.50/free; 6am-6pm Wed-Mon Nov-Mar, to 7pm Wed-Mon Apr-Oct) is a gem. You come here for the scenery, you come here for the beach, but above all you come here to snorkel – and if you've never been snorkeling before, it's a perfect place to start.

From the overlook, you can peer into crystal waters and view the 7000-year-old coral reef that stretches across the width of the bay. You're bound to see schools of glittering silver fish, the bright-blue flash of parrotfish and perhaps sea turtles so used to snorkelers they're ready to go eyeball-to-mask with you. Feeding the fish is strictly prohibited, to preserve the delicate ecological balance of the bay. Despite its protected status as a marine-life conservation district, this beloved bay is still a threatened ecosystem, constantly in danger of being loved to death.

Activities

Past the entrance ticket windows is an award-winning **educational center** (http://hbep.seagrant.soest.hawaii.edu/;) run by the University of Hawai'i. Interactive, family-friendly displays teach visitors about the unique geology and ecology of the bay. Everyone should watch the informative 12-minute video about environmental precautions before snorkeling. Down below at beach level are snorkel and beach-gear rental concessions, lockers, lifeguards and restrooms.

The bay is well protected from the vast ocean by various reefs and the inlet's natural curve, making conditions favorable for **snorkeling** year-round. The fringing reef closest to shore has a large, sandy opening known as the Keyhole Lagoon, which is the best place for novice snorkelers. It's also the most crowded part of the bay and later in the day visibility can be poor. The deepest water is 10ft, although it's very shallow over the coral. Be careful not to step on the coral or to accidentally knock it with your fins. Feeding the fish is strictly prohibited.

For confident snorkelers and strong swimmers, it's better on the outside of the reef, where there are large coral heads, bigger fish and fewer people; to get there follow the directions on the signboards or ask the lifeguard at the southern end of the beach. Because of the channel currents on either side of the bay, it's generally easier getting outside the reef than it is getting back in. Don't attempt to swim outside the reef when the water is rough. Not only are the channel currents too strong, but the sand will be stirred up and visibility poor.

If you're **scuba diving**, you'll have the whole bay to play in, with crystal-clear water, coral gardens and sea turtles. Beware of currents when the surf's up, especially those surges near the shark-infested **Witches Brew**, on the bay's right-hand side, and the amusingly named **Moloka'i Express**, a treacherous current on the left-hand side of the bay's mouth.

Information

Hanauma Bay is both a county beach park and a nature preserve. To beat the crowds, arrive as soon as the park opens.

All built park facilities are wheelchair accessible. Beach wheelchairs for visitors with mobility issues are available free of charge from the information kiosk between 8am and 4pm on a first-come, first-served basis.

Getting There & Away

CAR

Hanauma Bay is about 10 miles east of Waikiki via the Kalaniana'ole Hwy (Hwy 72). Self-parking costs $1. As soon as the parking lot fills (sometimes before noon), drivers will simply be turned away, so get there early or take the bus.

BUS

Bus 22 (the 'Beach Bus') runs between Waikiki and Hanauma Bay (50 minutes, every 30 to 60 minutes). Buses leave Waikiki between 8am and 4pm (4:45pm on weekends and holidays). Buses back to Waikiki pick up at Hanauma Bay from 10:50am until 5:20pm (5:50pm on weekends and holidays).

Koko Head Regional Park

With mountains on one side and a sea edged by bays and beaches on the other, the drive along this coast rates among O'ahu's best. The highway rises and falls as it winds around the eastern tip of the Ko'olau Range, looking down on stratified rocks, lava sea cliffs and other fascinating geological formations.

Beaches

Halona Cove BEACH

Take your lover down for a roll in the sand at this sweet pocket cove made famous in the steamy love scene between Burt Lancaster and Deborah Kerr in the 1953 movie *From Here to Eternity*. You can peer down at the cove from the Halona Blowhole parking lot, from where you'll just be able to make out a path leading down to the beach.

★ Sandy Beach Park BEACH

(8800 Kalaniana'ole Hwy) Here the ocean heaves and thrashes like a furious beast. This is one of O'ahu's most dangerous beaches, with a punishing shorebreak, powerful backwash and strong rip currents. Expert bodysurfers and bodyboarders spend hours trying to mount the skull-crushing waves, as crowds gather to watch the daredevils being tossed around. Sandy Beach is wide, very long and, yes, sandy, but this is no place for the inexperienced to frolic – dozens of people are injured every year.

Sights & Activities

Lana'i Lookout LOOKOUT

FREE Less than a mile east of Hanauma Bay, roadside Lana'i Lookout offers a panorama on clear days of several Hawaiian islands: Lana'i to the right, Maui in the middle and Moloka'i to the left. It's also a good vantage point for getting a look at lava-rock formations that form the sea cliffs along this coast.

Fishing Shrine SHRINE

(Kalaniana'ole Hwy) FREE As you drive east, make sure to keep your eyes toward the ocean. At the highest point, you should spot a templelike mound of rocks. The rocks surround a statue of Jizō, who is a Japanese Buddhist deity and a guardian of fishers. The fishing shrine is often decked out in flower lei and surrounded by sake cups. There is a little roadside pull-off in front of the shrine, about a half-mile east of the Lana'i Lookout.

Halona Blowhole LOOKOUT

FREE Just watch where all the tour buses are turning off to find this one. Here, ocean waves surge through a submerged tunnel in the rock and spout up through a hole in the ledge. It's preceded by a gushing sound, created by the air that's being forced out of the tunnel by rushing water. The action depends on water conditions – sometimes it's barely discernible, while at other times it's a real showstopper.

Koko Crater Botanical Garden GARDENS

(www.honolulu.gov/parks/hbg.html; end of Kokonani St; ⌚9am-4pm, closed Dec 25 & Jan 1) FREE According to Hawaiian legend, Koko Crater is the imprint left by the magical flying vagina of Kapo, sent from the Big Island to lure the pig-god Kamapua'a away from her sister Pele, the Hawaiian goddess of fire and volcanoes. Inside the crater today is a quiet, county-run botanical garden abloom with flowering aloe plants and *wiliwili* trees, fragrant plumeria, spiny cacti and other native and exotic dryland species. Connecting loop trails lead through the lonely garden.

To get here, turn inland on Kealahou St off the Kalaniana'ole Hwy, opposite Sandy Beach. After about 0.5 miles, turn left onto Kokonani St. From Waikiki, bus 23 stops every hour or so near the intersection of Kealahou and Kokonani Sts, just over 528yd from the garden entrance.

Makapu'u Point

Makapu'u Point and its coastal **lighthouse** mark the easternmost point of O'ahu. On the north side of the point, a roadside **lookout** gives you an exhilarating view down onto Makapu'u Beach Park, its aqua-blue waters outlined by diamond-white sand and jet-black lava. It's an even more spectacular sight when hang gliders or paragliders take off from the cliffs above.

Two islands, the larger of which is **Manana Island** (aka Rabbit Island), can be seen offshore. Once populated by feral rabbits, this aging volcanic crater now harbors burrowing wedge-tailed shearwaters. Curiously, it looks vaguely like the head of a rabbit with its ears folded back. In front is smaller, flat **Kaohikaipu Island**, another seabird sanctuary.

Beaches

Makapu'u Beach Park BEACH

(41-095 Kalaniana'ole Hwy) Opposite Sea Life Park, Makapu'u Beach is one of O'ahu's top winter bodyboarding and bodysurfing spots, with waves reaching 12ft and higher. It also has the island's best shorebreak. As with Sandy Beach Park, Makapu'u is strictly the domain of experts who can handle rough water and dangerous currents. In summer, when the wave action disappears, calmer waters allow swimming. The beach park has restrooms, outdoor showers, drinking water and lifeguards.

Sights & Activities

Sea Life Park THEME PARK

(☎808-259-2500; www.sealifeparkhawaii.com; 41-202 Kalaniana'ole Hwy; adult/child 3-11yr $30/20; ⌚10:30am-5pm; 👪) Hawaii's only marine-life park offers a small mixed bag of run-down attractions. The theme-park entertainment features animals that aren't found in Hawaiian waters, though it also maintains a breeding colony of green sea turtles, releasing young hatchlings back into the wild every year.

★ **Makapu'u Point Lighthouse Trail** HIKING

(www.hawaiistateparks.org; off Makapu'u Lighthouse Rd; ⌚7am-7:45pm Apr-1st Mon in Sep, 7am-6:45pm 1st Tue in Sep-Mar) South of the lookout on the *makai* side of the road, a mile-long paved service road climbs toward the red-roofed Makapu'u Lighthouse. You can park in the lot just off the main road. Although not difficult, the uphill walk can be hot and extremely windy – take drinks and hang onto your hat!

Along the way stop to take in the stellar coastal views of Koko Head and Hanauma Bay and, in winter, migrating whales who might just happen to be swimming by below. The trail itself is part of the Ka Iwi State Scenic Shoreline.

WINDWARD COAST & KAILUA

Welcome to O'ahu's lushest, most verdant coast, where turquoise waters and light-sand beaches share the dramatic backdrop of misty cliffs in the Ko'olau Range. Cruise over the *pali* from Honolulu and you first reach Kailua, aka adventure central. Many repeat visitors make this laid-back community their island base, whether they intend to kayak, stand up paddle, snorkel, dive, drive around the island or just laze on the sand. To the south, more beautiful beaches await in Waimanalo. North up the coast, Kamehameha Hwy narrows into a winding two-lane road with a dramatic oceanfront on one side and small rural farms and towns on the other.

The Pali Highway

Slicing through the spectacular emerald Ko'olau Range, the Pali Hwy (Hwy 61) runs between Honolulu and Kailua. If it's been raining heavily, every fold and crevice in the jagged cliffs will have a fairyland waterfall streaming down it.

Once upon a time, an ancient Hawaiian footpath wound its way perilously over these cliffs. In 1845 the path was widened into a horse trail and later into a cobblestone carriage road. In 1898 the Old Pali Hwy (as it's now called) was built along the same route but was abandoned in the 1950s after tunnels were blasted through the Ko'olau Range.

Sights & Activities

★Nu'uanu Pali State Wayside LOOKOUT

(Map p136; www.hawaiistateparks.org; per car $3; ⊙sunrise-sunset) About 5 miles northeast of Honolulu, turn as indicated to the popular ridge-top lookout with a sweeping vista of Windward O'ahu from a height of 1200ft. Standing at the edge, Kane'ohe lies below straight ahead, Kailua to the right, Mokoli'i Island and the coastal fishpond at Kualoa Point to the far left. The winds that funnel through the *pali* here are so strong you can sometimes lean against them; it's usually so cool that you'll want a jacket.

Maunawili Falls Trail HIKING

(Map p136; http://hawaiitrails.ehawaii.gov) The most popular, and populated, trail on Windward O'ahu ascends and descends flights of wooden stairs and crosses a stream several times before reaching the small, pooling Maunawili Falls amid the tropical vegetation. When the trail forks, veer left; straight ahead is the connector to the much longer **Maunawili Trail**.

Even with the moderate elevation change, this 2.5-mile round-trip is kid friendly and you'll see lots of families on the trail at weekends. Just be prepared, as the way can be muddy and mosquitoes are omnipresent.

To reach the trailhead, driving east on the Pali Hwy from Honolulu, take the second right-hand exit onto A'uloa Rd. At the first fork, veer left onto Maunawili Rd, which ends in a residential subdivision; look for a gated trailhead-access road on the left. Note that this road is accessible only to pedestrians (and by residents' vehicles); non-residents may not drive or park along this road. Instead, park along nearby residential streets that aren't gated.

Waimanalo

POP 5450

The proudly Hawaiian community of Waimanalo sprawls alongside O'ahu's longest beach, where the white sands stretch for miles, within view of offshore islands and a coral reef that keeps breaking waves at a comfortable distance. Small hillside farms in 'Nalo, as it's often called, grow many of the fresh leafy greens served in Honolulu's top restaurants.

Sights

Akebono Statue STATUE

(Map p136) Posed in fighting form outside East Honolulu Clothing Company in Waimanalo Town Center is one of Waimanolo's most famous sons. Chad Rowan was born here in 1969 and went on to make history by becoming the first non-Japanese-born sumo wrestler ever to reach *yokozuna*, the highest rank

Windward Coast (South)

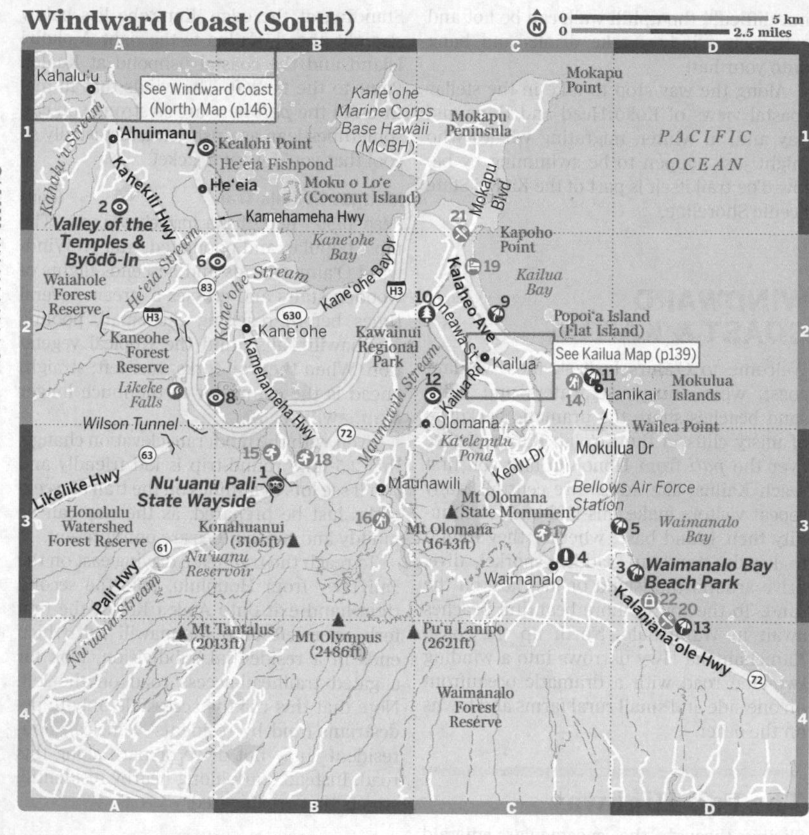

Windward Coast (South)

Top Sights

1 Nu'uanu Pali State Wayside B3
2 Valley of the Temples & Byōdō-In A1
3 Waimanalo Bay Beach Park D3

Sights

4 Akebono Statue C3
5 Bellows Field Beach Park D3
6 Gyotaku by Naoki B2
7 He'eia Pier A1
8 Ho'omaluhia Botanical Garden B2
9 Kalama Beach Park C2
10 Kawai Nui Marsh C2
11 Lanikai Beach C2
12 Ulupo Heiau State Monument C2
13 Waimanalo Beach Park D4

Activities, Courses & Tours

Captain Bob's Picnic Sails .... (see 7)
14 Ka'iwa Ridge (Lanikai Pillboxes) Trail C2
15 Ko'olau Golf Club B3
16 Maunawili Falls Trail B3
17 Olomana Golf Links C3
18 Pali Golf Course B3

Sleeping

Bellows Field Beach Park .... (see 5)
Ho'omaluhia Botanical Garden .... (see 8)
19 Manu Mele Bed & Breakfast C2
Waimanalo Bay Beach Park .... (see 3)

Eating

20 Serg's Mexican Kitchen Nalo D3
Sweet Home Waimanalo .... (see 22)
21 Tamura's Poke C2

Shopping

22 Naturally Hawaiian Gallery D3
Waimanalo Market Co-op .... (see 22)

in sumo. At 6ft 8in (203cm) in height and a hefty 514lb (233kg) in weight, Akebono was a *yokozuna* for eight years, winning 11 championships before his retirement in 2001.

Beaches

As elsewhere at O'ahu's beaches, don't leave any valuables in your car; petty theft is not uncommon.

★Waimanalo Bay Beach Park BEACH
(Map p136; Kalaniana'ole Hwy) A wide forest of ironwoods hides a broad sandy beach with little development in sight. This 75-acre county park has Waimanalo Bay's biggest waves and is popular with board surfers and bodyboarders. Even if you're not planning to hit the water, just take a walk along the cream-colored sand and try to imagine the feeling of old Hawaii. Countless weddings take place on this enchanting beach. There are lifeguards, campsites and restrooms. Entrance is opposite the Honolulu Polo Club.

Waimanalo Beach Park BEACH
(Map p136; Kalaniana'ole Hwy) By the side of the roadway south of the main business area, this sloping strip of soft white sand has little puppy waves that are excellent for swimming. Manana Island and Makapu'u Point are visible to the south. The facilities include a huge grassy picnic area, restrooms, ball-sports courts, a playground and a rather unappealing campground. Lifeguards are on watch here.

Bellows Field Beach Park BEACH
(Map p136; Tinker Rd, off Kalaniana'ole Hwy); open to public noon Fri-8am Mon, gates closed 8pm-6am) With fine sand and a natural setting backed by ironwood trees in places, this is a great beach. The only problem is that the park is only open to civilians on weekends (and national holidays) because it fronts Bellows Air Force Station. The small shorebreak waves are good for beginning bodyboarders and board surfers. Lifeguards, showers, restrooms, drinking water and camping are all available on-site. The park entrance is just north of Waimanalo Bay Beach Park.

Activities

Olomana Golf Links GOLF
(Map p136; 808-259-7926; www.pacificlinks.com/olomana; 41-1801 Kalaniana'ole Hwy; green fees $100) LPGA star Michelle Wie got her start here, and President Obama regularly swings through these two challenging nine-hole courses on his holidays. Played together they form a regulation 18-hole, par-72 course beneath the dramatic backdrop of the Ko'olau Range. The facilities include a driving range and a restaurant.

Sleeping

There are fewer private house and apartment-suite vacation rentals around Waimanalo than near Kailua; check with consolidators such as **VRBO** (www.vrbo.com) and **HomeAway** (www.homeaway.com). **Beach House Hawaii** (808-224-6213, 866-625-6946; www.beachhousehawaii.com) has a number of properties in Waimanalo ranging from studios to five-bedroom estates; check out the website and see what is available. All three Waimanalo beach parks have campgrounds (see https://camping.honolulu.gov).

★Bellows Field Beach Park CAMPGROUND $
(Map p136; tent sites by permit free; noon Fri-8am Mon) The nearby army base guard shack makes this the most secure of area campgrounds. Some of the 40 sites are beneath the ironwood trees, some by the beach. Barbecue grills, showers and restrooms available. Note that buses stop in front of the entrance road, about 1.5 miles from the beach itself.

Waimanalo Bay Beach Park CAMPGROUND $
(Map p136; tent sites by permit free; 8am Fri-8am Wed) The 10 tree-shaded sites are a good choice if Bellows isn't open. It has BBQ grills and restrooms with showers.

Eating

★Sweet Home Waimanalo HAWAIIAN
(Map p136; 808-259-5737; http://sweethome-waimanalo.com; 41-1025 Kalaniana'ole Hwy; mains $8-13; 9:30am-6.30pm Wed-Mon) FREE
Taste local Waimanalo's back-to-the-earth farm goodness from this family kitchen, where local chicken gets sauced with honey and citrus, and fresh corn tortillas wrap lime cream and grilled fish for tacos. Even the island standards get a twist: the *kalua* pork sandwich is topped with bok choy slaw.

Take it to go for the beach or chow down in the colorful picnic area out front next to the highway.

Serg's Mexican Kitchen Nalo MEXICAN $
(Map p136; ☎808-259-7374; 41-865 Kalanianaole Hwy; mains $6-11; ⏲10am-8pm) Whether you're heading to the beach or are cruising on a round-island trip, Serg's offers an excellent roadside option for take-out or eat-in Mexican favorites. Try the fish tacos.

Tersty Treats SEAFOOD $
(☎808-259-3474; 41-1540 Kalaniana'ole Hwy; mains $6-12; ⏲10am-7pm Mon-Thu, to 8pm Fri & Sat, to 5pm Sun) This locally owned fish market lets you sample a dozen different flavors of freshly made *poke,* including old-school luau tastes like crab, squid and *opihi* (Hawaiian limpet). Keep filling up your beach cooler with deli faves like *char siu* pork and seared ahi belly.

Shopping

Naturally Hawaiian Gallery ARTS, CRAFTS
(Map p136; www.patrickchingart.com; 41-1025 Kalaniana'ole Hwy; ⏲9:30am-5:30pm) Since it shares space inside a converted gas station with Sweet Home Waimanalo, you can browse island artists' paintings and handmade crafts while you wait for a kale smoothie. Naturalist Patrick Ching's prints are especially good.

Waimanalo Market Co-op MARKET
(Map p136; ☎808-690-0390; www.waimanalo-market.com; 41-1029 Kalaniana'ole Hwy; ⏲9am-6pm Thu-Sun) A local co-operative selling everything from art to kitchenware to fruit and vegetables. Next to Sweet Home Waimanalo.

East Honolulu Clothing Company CLOTHING, SOUVENIRS
(www.doublepawswear.com; Waimanalo Town Shopping Center, 41-537 Kalaniana'ole Hwy; ⏲9am-5pm) The striking, graphic one-color tropical prints on the clothing here are all designed and silk screened in-house. This company provides many local hula schools with their costumes. There's plenty of local artwork to peruse as well.

Getting There & Away

Waimanalo is about a 35-minute drive (17 miles) from Waikiki via Hwy 61; it's 10 minutes (6 miles) down the coast from Kailua.

Bus 57 travels between Honolulu's Ala Moana Center and Waimanalo (one hour) via Kailua (25 minutes). It makes stops along the Kalaniana'ole Hwy (Hwy 72) through town.

Kailua

POP 40,000

A long, graceful bay protected by a coral reef is Kailua's claim to fame. The nearly 4-mile-long shoreline stretch of ivory sand is made for strolling, and the weather and wave conditions can be just about perfect for swimming, kayaking, windsurfing and kitesurfing. None of this has gone unnoticed. Decades ago expatriates from the mainland bought up cottages crowded into the little neighborly lanes; the ones near the beachfront were often replaced with megahouses. South along the shore lies the exclusive enclave of Lanikai, with million-dollar views – and mansions that may be valued at 10 times that much.

In ancient times Kailua (meaning 'two seas') was a home to Hawaiian chiefs, including briefly Kamehameha the Great after he conquered O'ahu. Today it's the Windward Coast's largest suburban town, where you'll find the vast majority of the coast's restaurants and retail.

Sights

Ulupo Heiau State Monument TEMPLE
(Map p136; www.hawaiistateparks.org; ⏲sunrise-sunset) FREE Rich in stream-fed agricultural land, abundant fishing grounds and protected canoe landings, Kailua was an ancient economic center that supported at least three temples. Ulupo, once bordered by 400 acres of cultivated fishponds and taro fields, is the only one left to visit.

Construction of this imposing platform temple was traditionally attributed to *menehune,* the 'little people' who legend says created much of Hawaii's impressive stonework, finishing each project in one night. It's thought the temple's final use may have been as a *luakini,* a place for human sacrifice dedicated to the war god Ku. Interpretive panels provide an artist's rendition of the site as it probably looked in the 18th century.

The heiau is a mile southwest of downtown Kailua, behind the YMCA at 1200 Kailua Rd. Coming over the Pali Hwy from Honolulu, take Uluoa St, the first left after passing the Kalaniana'ole Hwy junction, then turn right on Manu Aloha St and right again on Manu O'o St.

Kailua

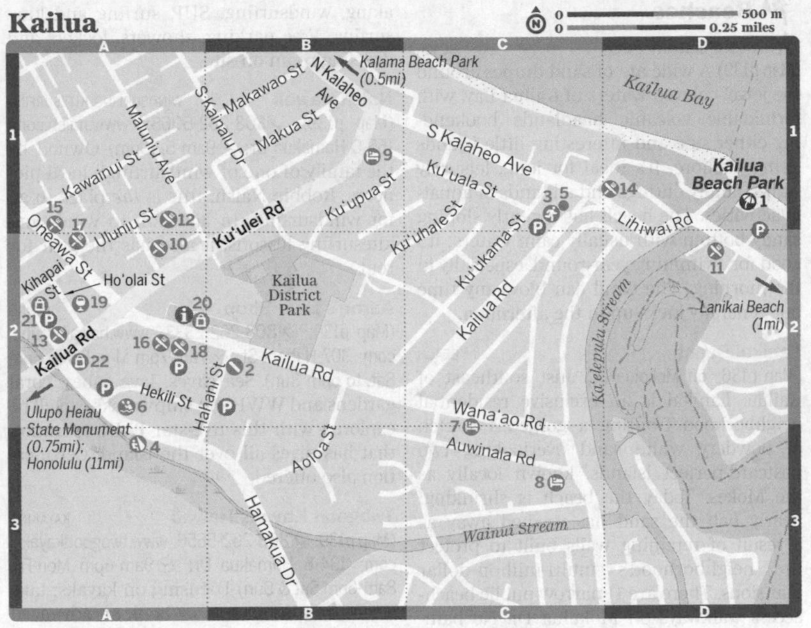

Kailua

Top Sights
1 Kailua Beach Park D1

Activities, Courses & Tours
2 Aaron's Dive Shop B2
3 Kailua Sailboards & Kayaks, Inc C1
4 Naish Hawaii A3
5 Segway Hawaii-Kailua C1
6 Twogood Kayaks Hawaii A2

Sleeping
7 Kailua Guesthouse C3
8 Papaya Paradise Bed & Breakfast C3
9 Sheffield House B1

Eating
10 Baci Bistro A2
11 Buzz's D2
12 Cinnamon's Restaurant A1
13 Kalapawai Cafe A2
14 Kalapawai Market D1
15 Rai Rai Ramen A1
16 Thursday Farmers Market A2
17 Tokoname Sushi Bar & Restaurant A2
18 Whole Foods A2

Drinking & Nightlife
19 Kailua Town Pub & Grill A2
Lanikai Juice .... (see 20)
Morning Brew Coffee House & Bistro .... (see 20)

Shopping
Bookends .... (see 20)
20 Kailua Shopping Center A2
Lily Lotus .... (see 18)
21 Madre Chocolates A2
22 Mu'umu'u Heaven A2

Kawai Nui Marsh PARK

(Map p136; www.kawainuimarsh.com; off Kaha St; 7am-7pm) FREE One of Hawaii's largest freshwater marshes, Kawai Nui provides flood protection for the town, a habitat for endangered waterbirds, and is also one of the largest remaining fishponds used by ancient Hawaiians. You may see rare birds including the *koloa maoli* (Hawaiian duck), *ae'o* (Hawaiian stilt), *'alae kea* (Hawaiian coot) and *kolea* (Pacific golden plover). Several local groups work to preserve and restore the marsh.

To access the area, park in the lot at the end of Kaha St, off Oneawa St, just over a mile northwest of Kailua Rd.

Beaches

★Kailua Beach Park BEACH

(Map p139) A wide arc of sand drapes around the jewel-colored waters of Kailua Bay, with formidable volcanic headlands bookending either side and interesting little islands rising offshore. It's ideal for long, leisurely walks, family outings and all kinds of aquatic activities. The beach has a gently sloping sandy bottom with usually calm waters; it's good for swimming year-round, especially in the morning. The wind can blow any time but generally kicks up in the afternoon.

Lanikai Beach BEACH

(Map p136; off Mokolua Dr) Just southeast of Kailua, Lanikai is an exclusive residential neighborhood fronting a gorgeous stretch of powdery white sand overlooking two postcard-perfect islands, known locally as the Mokes. Today the beach is shrinking: nearly half the sand has washed away as a result of retaining walls built to protect the neighborhood's multi-million-dollar mansions. There are 11 narrow public beach-access walkways off Mokulua Dr. No bathrooms, no lifeguards.

Kalama Beach Park BEACH

(Map p136; 248 N Kalaheo Ave) Kalama Beach Park, 1 mile north of Kailua Beach Park on Kalaheo Ave, is the best place to park for a great walk. Climb over the grassy lawn to a much more residential stretch of sand. Weekdays there's hardly a soul besides tan, fit locals walking their dogs and the occasional group of mums with their infants. Restrooms and outdoor shower available. No lifeguards.

Activities

There are a handful of water-sports outfitters that have in-town shops, where you can arrange private or group lessons (from $130) and guided tours (from $100), and rent gear, including kayaks (single/tandem from $45/55), SUP sets (from $59), windsurfing rigs (from $70), surfboards (from $20), snorkel sets (from $12) and boogie boards (from $8).

★Kailua Sailboards & Kayaks, Inc WATER SPORTS

(Map p139; ☎808-262-2555; www.kailuasailboards.com; Kailua Beach Center, 130 Kailua Rd; ⊙8:30am-5pm) Good all-purpose outfitter with energetic staff and great kayak tours, near the beach. Lots of options such as kayaking, windsurfing, SUP, surfing and kitesurfing. Free parking, showers, lockers and dressing room on-site.

Naish Hawaii WINDSURFING, KITESURFING

(Map p139; ☎808-262-6068; www.naish.com; 155-C Hamakua Dr; ⊙9am-5:30pm) Owned by the family of one of windsurfing's local pioneers, Robbie Naish, this is *the* place to go for windsurfing. In addition to wind- and kitesurfing lessons, it also has the gear for rent.

Aaron's Dive Shop DIVING

(Map p139; ☎808-262-2333; www.hawaii-scuba.com; 307 Hahani St; ⊙7am-7pm Mon-Fri, to 6pm Sat, to 5pm Sun) Sea caves, lava tubes, coral gardens and WWII-era shipwrecks can all be explored with this five-star PADI operation that has dives all over the island. Certification also offered.

Twogood Kayaks Hawaii KAYAKING

(Map p139; ☎808-262-5656; www.twogoodkayaks.com; 134-B Hamakua Dr; ⊙9am-6pm Mon-Fri, 8am-6pm Sat & Sun) Focusing on kayaks: take a tour, rent your own or book an advanced lesson and learn to surf the waves or race in the craft. Snorkel gear and SUPs are also available.

Ka'iwa Ridge (Lanikai Pillboxes) Trail HIKING

(Map p136; http://hawaiitrails.ehawaii.gov; off Kaelepulu Dr) Though officially named for Ka'iwa Ridge, this 1.25-mile (one way), half-hour trek is better known for the several WWII 'pillboxes', aka concrete bunkers, it passes. The barren trail is steep and often slippery. Make it to the top and you're rewarded with head-spinning views of the Mokulua Islands in Kailua Bay, Lanikai and the Ko'olau Range.

The trailhead is in Lanikai: turn right off A'alapapa Dr onto Ka'elepulu Dr; park uphill just beyond the country club. On the side road across the street, you'll see a trail marker and a dirt track beginning next to a chain-link fence.

Tours

Segway Hawaii-Kailua TOUR

(Map p139; ☎808-262-5511; www.segwayofhawaii-kailua.com; Kailua Beach Center, 130 Kailua Rd; tours $59-129; ⊙9am-5pm) Quiet and electric-powered, Segway provides an ecofriendly open-air ride. Take a tour along Kailua Beach, into Lanikai, out to Ulupo Heiau or through Kawanui Marsh.

THE BATTLE OF NU'UANU

O'ahu was the lynchpin conquered by Kamehameha the Great during his campaign to unite the Hawaiian Islands under his rule. In 1795, on the quiet beaches of Waikiki, Kamehameha landed his fearsome fleet of canoes to battle Kalanikupule, the *mo'i* (king) of O'ahu.

Heavy fighting started around Puowaina ('Hill of Sacrifice,' now nicknamed Punchbowl), and continued up Nu'uanu Valley. O'ahu's spear-and-stone warriors were no match for Kamehameha's troops, which included a handful of Western sharpshooters. O'ahu's defenders made their last stand at the narrow ledge near the current-day Nu'uanu Pali lookout. Hundreds were driven over the top to their deaths. A century later, during the construction of the Old Pali Hwy, more than 500 skulls were found at the base of the cliffs.

Some O'ahu warriors, including their king, escaped into the forest. When Kalanikupule surfaced a few months later, he was sacrificed by Kamehameha to the war god Ku. Kamehameha's taking of O'ahu marked the last battle ever fought between Hawaiian warriors.

Festivals & Events

'I Love Kailua' Town Party CULTURAL

(www.lanikailuaoutdoorcircle.org/index/Kailua_Town_Party; Kailua Rd; Apr) One Sunday in April the whole community turns out for a giant block party, with hula schools and bands performing, local artists selling wares and local restaurants feeding the masses.

'I Love Hula' CULTURAL

(http://castlefoundation.org/ilovehula; Kailua Rd) See a rotating schedule of area hula schools perform the second Sunday of every month at 3pm, behind Long's Drugs in Kailua Town.

Sleeping

Kailua has no hotels, but suburban home-style B&Bs and vacation rentals abound, some just a short walk from the beach. Most are nonsmoking, don't accept credit cards, require an advance deposit and multiple-night stays, charge a one-time cleaning fee and are legally prohibited from offering hot breakfasts. The majority are unlicensed, whether they're managed by local vacation-rental agencies or listed on websites such as **Vacation Rentals by Owner** (VRBO; www.vrbo.com), **HomeAway** (www.homeaway.com) and **Airbnb** (www.airbnb.com). Book online or call ahead (not just from the airport!) a few weeks or even months in advance.

Manu Mele Bed & Breakfast B&B $$

(Map p136; 808-262-0016; www.manumele.net; 153 Kailuana Place, Kailua; d $110-130;) Just 100 steps from the beach, Manu Mele enjoys a peaceful location west from town. The simple, island-contemporary guest rooms feel light and bright. Creature comforts include private entrances, Hawaiian quilts, plush seven-layer beds, and a pool available for guest use – very rare. Free wi-fi, beach accessories and complimentary baked goods and fruit on your first morning.

Kailua Guesthouse B&B $$

(Map p139; 808-261-2637, 888-249-5848; www.kailuaguesthouse.com; d $139-159;) Not far from downtown, two large apartment studio-style suites feel bright and breezy. Helpful amenities include flat-screen TVs with DVD players, free wi-fi, digital in-room safes and shared washer and dryer access. The owner is an excellent source of local lore. It's a healthy 10-minute walk to the beach. Coffee only provided.

Sheffield House B&B $$

(Map p139; 808-262-0721; www.hawaiisheffieldhouse.com; d $139-169;) Bring the family: the two private-entrance apartment-suites here welcome kids. The beach is an easy, 10-house walk down the road. And the suitably cottagey decor fits right in with the lush tropical gardens created by landscape designer and architect owners. Pastries and fruit for the first day included.

Papaya Paradise Bed & Breakfast B&B $$

(Map p139; 808-261-0316; www.kailuaoahuhawaii.com; d incl breakfast from $100;) The giant covered patio with comfortable sofas, reading nook and a dining table is more like a living room than a lanai – with views of Mt Olomana. The quiet atmosphere here is best suited to more mature travelers. Rooms are simple with free wi-fi and self-catered breakfast. Shared kitchen available.

Eating

★ **Kalapawai Market** SUPERMARKET, DELI $
(Map p139; www.kalapawaimarket.com; 306 S Kalaheo Ave; items $2-12; ⏲6am-9pm) A don't-miss 1930s landmark market near the beach that stocks picnic supplies and serves the same fancy, made-to-order sandwiches and market-fresh salads as its in-town sister. Good coffee, too.

Thursday Farmers Market MARKET $
(Map p139; http://hfbf.org/markets/markets/kailua; 609 Kailua Rd; ⏲5-7:30pm Thu) An incredible spread of vendors sell not only fruit and veggies but a bevy of hot meals to take out: organic pizza, Portuguese stew, BBQ, Filipino dishes, Thai curries – you name it. Located in the parking lot by Longs Drugs.

Tamura's Poke SEAFOOD $
(Map p136; ☎808-254-2000; www.tamurasfinewine.com; 25 Kane'ohe Bay Dr; per lb $7-15; ⏲10:30am-7:45pm) The wine is fine, but you're really here for the *poke*. Tucked into the back of Tamura's Fine Wines & Liquors is a deli with a top *poke* selection. Some say this is the best on the island!

Whole Foods SUPERMARKET $
(Map p139; ☎808-263-6800; http://wholefoodsmarket.com/stores/kailua; Kailua Town Center, 629 Kailua Rd; ⏲7am-10pm; 📶) 🍃 Emphasizing organic, natural and locally sourced food, this supermarket offers deliciously healthy options. Grab a hot meal from the full-service deli – sandwiches, BBQ meats or tacos, anyone? – or graze the pizza, *poke*, sushi and salad bars. Island-made gelato is sold at the coffee kiosk up front. Come for happy-hour drinks and *pupu* at the supermarket's Windward Bar.

Rai Rai Ramen JAPANESE $
(Map p139; ☎808-230-8208; 124 Oneawa St; mains $7-10; ⏲11am-8:30pm Wed-Mon) Look for the red-and-white banner written in kanji outside this brightly lit noodle shop. The menu of ramen styles ranges from Sapporo south to Hakata, all with rich broth and topped with tender pork, if you like. The *gyōza* (dumplings) are grilled or steamed bundles of heaven.

Kalapawai Cafe BISTRO, DELI $$
(Map p139; ☎808-262-2354; www.kalapawaimarket.com; 750 Kailua Rd; dinner mains $14-24; ⏲6am-9pm Mon-Thu, to 9:30pm Fri & Sat, from 7am Sun) A gourmet, self-serve deli by day, after 5pm it transforms into an inviting, eclectic bistro. The eggplant bruschetta and other share dishes are excellent paired with a wine flight (a series of tasting-sized pours). But it's hard to resist the creative, ingredient-driven mains. Dine streetside on the lanai or in the intimate candlelit dining room.

Cinnamon's Restaurant BREAKFAST $$
(Map p139; ☎808-261-8724; www.cinnamons808.com; Kailua Sq, 315 Uluniu St; mains $7-13; ⏲7am-2pm; 👪) Locals pack this family cafe decorated like Grandma's house for the airy chiffon pancakes drowning in guava syrup, Portuguese sweet-bread French toast, eggs Benedict mahimahi, curried-chicken-and-papaya salad, and Hawaiian plate lunches. Waits are long on weekends; only the breakfast menu is available Sunday.

Tokoname Sushi Bar & Restaurant JAPANESE $$
(Map p139; ☎808-262-8656; www.tokonamehawaii.com; 442 Uluniu St; sushi $5-10, dinner mains $10-16; ⏲4-11pm) Surprisingly good sushi considering the suburban location in Kailua. Daily early-bird and late-night sushi power hour (9pm to 10pm) specials help keep the costs down, too.

Baci Bistro ITALIAN $$
(Map p139; www.bacibistro.com; 30 Aulike St; mains lunch $10-15, dinner $15-25; ⏲11:30am-2pm & 5:30-10pm Mon-Fri, 5:30-10pm Sat & Sun) Homegrown Italian cooking, where the owner knows most patrons by name. Don't miss the white chocolate mascarpone cheesecake. The ravioli is made fresh daily.

Buzz's STEAK $$$
(Map p139; ☎808-261-4661; http://buzzsoriginalsteakhouse.com; 413 Kawailoa Rd; mains lunch $9-17, dinner $16-38; ⏲11am-3pm & 4:30-9:30pm) Classic mainlander expat territory; beachfront home-owning regulars here definitely get the best service. But the old-school kitschy island decor, surf-and-turf menu (complete with throwback salad bar) and proximity to the beach make it worth the stop. Book ahead, but still expect a wait.

Drinking

★ **Lanikai Juice** CAFE
(Map p139; ☎808-262-2383; www.lanikaijuice.com; Kailua Shopping Center, 600 Kailua Rd; ⏲6am-8pm Mon-Sat, 7am-7pm Sun) With fresh fruit gathered from local farmers, this ad-

dictive juice bar blends a tantalizing assortment of smoothies with names such as Ginger 'Ono or Kailua Monkey. Early in the morning, local yoga fanatics hang out at sunny sidewalk tables with overflowing bowls of granola topped with acai berries, bananas, blueberries and grated coconut.

Morning Brew Coffee House & Bistro CAFE
(Map p139; ☎808-262-7770; http://morningbrewhawaii.com; Kailua Shopping Center, 600 Kailua Rd; ⌚6am-8pm Tue-Sat, to 7pm Sun & Mon; 📶) Baristas at this pleasant cafe cup everything from chai to 'Funky Monkey' mochas with banana syrup. Swing by for an espresso or for bagel breakfasts, hot-pressed panini lunches and ahi kebabs and wine at dinner.

Kailua Town Pub & Grill PUB
(Map p139; ☎808-230-8444; http://kailuatownpub.com; 26 Ho'olai St; ⌚10am-2am Mon-Sat, 7am-2am Sun) This casual Irish pub wannabe has tasty from-scratch Bloody Marys, sports on the TV and a friendly mixed-age crowd. Best burgers in town too, not to mention the fish and chips.

Shopping

Kailua Shopping Center GIFTS, BOOKS
(Map p139; 600 Kailua Rd) Start your souvenir shopping downtown at this strip mall opposite Macy's department store. Pick up Hawaiiana books and beach reads at **Bookends** (☎808-261-1996; ⌚9am-8pm Mon-Sat, to 5pm Sun), tropically scented lotions and soaps at **Lanikai Bath & Body** (☎808-262-3260; http://lanikaibathandbody.com; ⌚10am-6pm Mon-Fri, to 5pm Sat, to 4pm Sun) or beachy home accents, tote bags and kids' toys at **Sand People** (☎808-261-8878; www.sandpeople.com; ⌚10am-6pm Mon-Sat, to 5pm Sun).

Mu'umu'u Heaven CLOTHING, HOMEWARES
(Map p139; ☎808-263-3366; www.muumuuheaven.com; 767 Kailua Rd; ⌚10am-6pm Mon-Sat, 11am-4pm Sun) Recycling at its most fabulous: all the fun and funky, tropical-print dresses, skirts, tops and accessories are sewn using at least a little fabric from vintage muumuus. A second set of rooms contains equally colorful and eccentric homewares and original island art, some muumuu-inspired.

Madre Chocolates FOOD & DRINK
(Map p139; ☎808-377-6440; http://madrechocolate.com; 20-A Kainehe St; ⌚11am-7pm Tue-Fri, to 6pm Sat) Aficionados will be wowed by these award-winning Hawaiian-made boutique chocolates infused with island flavors – coconut and caramelized ginger, passion fruit, kiawe-smoked sea salt. Kailua is home, but has a new store in Honolulu's Chinatown.

Lily Lotus CLOTHING
(Map p139; ☎808-888-3564; www.lilylotus.com; Suite 102, 609 Kailua Rd; ⌚10am-6pm Mon-Sat, 11am-4pm Sun) Outfit for the yoga lifestyle with breathable and organic clothing from a Honolulu-local designer. You can also buy mats, jewelry and accessories by Lily and other makers.

Information

Kailua Information Center (Map p139; ☎808-261-2727, 888-261-7997; www.kailuachamber.com; Kailua Shopping Center, 600 Kailua Rd; ⌚10am-4pm Mon-Fri, to 2pm Sat) Retiree-run chamber-of-commerce center with limited info, good $1 maps. Open occasional Sundays 10am to 1pm.

Getting There & Around

Outside the morning and evening commutes, it's normally a 30-minute drive between Waikiki and Kailua along the Pali Hwy (Hwy 61), about the same from the airport via the H-3 Fwy.

TO/FROM THE AIRPORT

SpeediShuttle (☎877-242-5777; www.speedishuttle.com) Shared-ride shuttle service from Honolulu International Airport (HNL).

WHOSE LAND IS IT ANYWAY?

Not everything on the Windward Coast is as peaceful as the *lo'i kalo* (taro fields) seen alongside the Kamehameha Hwy. Large tracts of these rural valleys were taken over by the US military during WWII for training and target practice, which continued into the 1970s.

After decades of pressure from locals, cleanup of ordnance and chemicals by the military is slowly getting underway. Not surprisingly, you'll encounter many Hawaiian sovereignty activists here. Spray-painted political banners and signs, Hawaii's state flag flown upside down (a sign of distress) and bumper stickers with antidevelopment slogans like 'Keep the Country Country' are seen everywhere.

BICYCLE

Avoid parking headaches by cycling around town.

Bike Shop (808-261-1553; www.bikeshophawaii.com; 270 Ku'ulei Rd; rentals per day/week from $20/100; 10am-8pm Mon-Fri, 9am-5pm Sat, 10am-5pm Sun) Full-service sales, rental and repair shop. In addition to cruisers, it rents performance street and mountain bikes ($40 to $85 per day).

Hawaii B-Cycle (http://hawaii.bcycle.com; 24hr/30-day pass $5/30; 5am-10pm) Davis Building (Davis Building, 767 Kailua Rd; 5am-10pm); Hahani Plaza (Hahani Plaza, 515 Kailua Rd; 5am-10pm) Kailua's bicycle-exchange program was the first in the state. Pay for a pass online or at the kiosk, borrow the shiny-white cruiser bicycle with basket for a quick trip around town, and then return to any B-station.

BUS

Though having a car is most convenient, especially if you're visiting the rest of the Windward Coast, riding buses to, and around, Kailua is possible.

The following are useful routes:

56 and 57 Honolulu's Ala Moana Center to downtown Kailua (corner Kailua Rd and Oneawa St, 45 to 60 minutes, every 15 minutes); all continue to Waimanalo (25 minutes), some go on to Sea Life Park (30 minutes).

70 Downtown Kailua to Kailua Beach Park (five minutes) and Lanikai (15 minutes); runs only every 90 minutes.

Kane'ohe Bay Area

POP 37,000

The state's largest bay and reef-sheltered lagoon, Kane'ohe Bay is largely silted and not great for swimming. The town itself is a Marine-base suburb, populated by chain restaurants and stores. It just doesn't pack the eating and sleeping appeal of neighboring town Kailua, which is only 6 miles (15 minutes) south.

Sights & Activities

★Valley of the Temples & Byōdō-In TEMPLE
(Map p136; www.byodo-in.com; 47-200 Kahekili Hwy; temple admission adult/child under 13yr/senior $3/1/2; 9am-5pm) So peaceful and park-like, it might take you a minute to realize Valley of the Temples is an interdenominational cemetery. Up at the base of the Ko'olau mountain's verdant fluted cliffs sits Byōdō-In, a replica of a 900-year-old temple in Uji, Japan. The symmetry is a classic example of Japanese Heian architecture, with rich vermillion walls. The 3-ton brass bell is said to bring peace and good fortune to anyone who rings it.

Bus 65 stops near the cemetery on Kahekili Hwy, but from there it's a winding 1232yd hike up to the temple.

Ho'omaluhia Botanical Garden GARDENS
(Map p136; 808-233-7323; www.honolulu.gov/parks/hbg.html; 45-680 Luluku Rd; 9am-4pm) FREE Beneath the dramatic ridged cliffs of the Ko'olau Range, O'ahu's largest botanical garden encompasses 400 acres of trees and shrubs from around the world. Plants are arranged in six regionally themed areas accessible by car. Pick up a map at the small visitor center, located at the far end of Luluku Rd, over 1 mile *mauka* from the Kamehameha Hwy. Call ahead to register for free two-hour guided nature walks (10am Saturday and 1pm Sunday).

He'eia Pier HARBOR
(Map p136) Just north of, and run in conjunction with, the state park is one of the Windward Coast's only small boat harbors. It's fun just to watch the comings and goings of local boat owners. On weekends they head out to the 'sandbar', a raised spit in the bay that becomes a mooring party place for people to kick back and relax.

Captain Bob's Picnic Sails BOAT TOUR
(Map p136; 808-942-5077; www.captainbobpicnicsail.com; 4hr cruise $95) Captain Bob's catamaran tour launches at He'eia Pier and stops at a sandbar, as well as for reef snorkeling and lunch. Free transportation from Waikiki.

Ko'olau Golf Club GOLF
(Map p136; 808-236-4653; www.koolaugolfclub.com; 45-550 Kionaole Rd; green fees $55-145) Considered the toughest and one of the most picturesque golf courses on O'ahu. This tournament course is scenically nestled beneath the Ko'olau Range. For practice, there's a driving range and both chipping and putting greens.

Pali Golf Course GOLF
(Map p136; info 808-266-7612, reservations 808-296-2000; www.honolulu.gov/des/golf/pali.html; 45-050 Kamehameha Hwy; green fees $22-55) This municipal 18-hole hillside course has stunning mountain views, stretching across to Kane'ohe Bay. Club and handcart rentals are available. Reserve tee times in advance.

Sleeping

Ho'omaluhia Botanical Garden CAMPGROUND $

(Kahua Nui-Makai Campsites; Map p136; 808-233-7323; https://camping.honolulu.gov; 45-680 Luluku Rd; 3-night campsite permit $32; 9am Fri-4pm Mon) The grassy, botanical-garden-surrounded tent sites at the base of the Ko'olau Range are cool and green, fed by frequent mists. With an overnight guard and gates that close, it's among O'ahu's most petty-theft-free campgrounds. Reserve your permit online for one of 15 campsites.

Paradise Bay Resort HOTEL $$

(Map p146; 808-239-6658; http://paradisebayresorthawaii.com; 47-039 Lihikai Dr; studio/1 bedroom/2 bedroom incl continental breakfast from $229/250/280;) The Windward Coast's only resort property is a step above area rentals. Casual, earth-tone contemporary rooms with kitchenettes are just the beginning. Here, bayside breakfasts, a Wednesday Hawaiian-food happy hour, evening mai tais and Hawaiian music, and a Saturday-morning bay cruise are all complimentary. Stand-up paddling lessons, kayaking, eco-tours and spa services are available, but cost extra.

Getting There & Around

Two highways run north–south through Kane'ohe. The slower but more scenic Kamehameha Hwy (Hwy 836) hugs the coast. Further inland, the Kahekili Hwy (Hwy 83) intersects the Likelike Hwy (Hwy 63) and continues north past the Valley of the Temples. Kane'ohe Marine Corps Base Hawaii (MCBH) occupies the entire Mokapu Peninsula.

TheBus Route 55 runs from Honolulu's Ala Moana Center to downtown Kane'ohe (one hour, departs every 20 minutes), then continues along Kamehameha Hwy toward the North Shore. Route 56 connects Kailua and Kane'ohe (20 minutes) every 30 minutes or so.

Kahalu'u & Waiahole

Driving north along the Kamehameha Hwy, you'll cross a bridge near Kahulu'u's Hygienic Store (formerly owned by the Hygienic Dairy Company). There you'll make a physical and cultural departure from the gravitational pull of Honolulu. Now you've officially crossed into 'the country,' where the highway becomes a two-laner and the ocean shares the shoulder.

WORTH A TRIP

GYOTAKU FISH PRINTS

Gyotaku by Naoki (Map p136; 1-866-496-8258; http://gyotaku.com; 46-020 Alaloa St, Unit D, Kane'ohe) You'll probably have seen Naoki's magnificent *gyotaku* (Japanese-style fish prints) all over O'ahu in galleries, restaurants and bars, but there's nothing like watching him print up a freshly caught fish in his own studio in Kane'ohe. All the fish he prints are eaten later and the spectacular art on hand is for sale. Call ahead to check the studio is open because Naoki is often out fishing. It's a little hard to find, but well worth the effort.

Sights

Senator Fong's Plantation & Gardens GARDENS

(Map p146; 808-239-6775; www.fonggarden.com; 47-285 Pulama Rd, Kahalu'u; adult/child 5-12yr $14.50/9; tours 10:30am & 1pm Sun-Fri) A labor of love by Hiram Fong (1907–2004), the first Asian American elected to the US Senate, these flowering gardens aim to preserve Hawaii's plant life for future generations. The lush 700-acre grounds are accessible only on the 1½-hour, 1-mile guided walking tours.

Eating

★**Waiahole Poi Factory** HAWAIIAN $

(Map p146; 808-239-2222; http://waiaholepoifactory.com; 48-140 Kamehameha Hwy, Waiahole; meals $7-11; 11am-5pm) This family-owned roadside landmark sells *'ono* traditional Hawaiian plate lunches, baked *laulau* and squid, freshly pounded poi and seafood *poke* by the pound, and homemade *haupia* for dessert. Get here early at lunchtime, as food sells out fast.

Mike's Huli Huli Chicken FOOD TRUCK $

(Map p146; 808-277-6720; https://sites.google.com/site/mikeshulihulichicken/; 47-525 Kamehameha Hwy, Kahalu'u; meals $7-11; 10.30am-7pm) At the convergence of Kamehameha and Kahekili Hwys, a cluster of food trucks have taken up residence. As seen on TV's Food Network, 'Monkey Mike' not only rotisserie roasts birds, but also bakes *kalua* pork and minces *lomilomi* salmon.

Windward Coast (North)

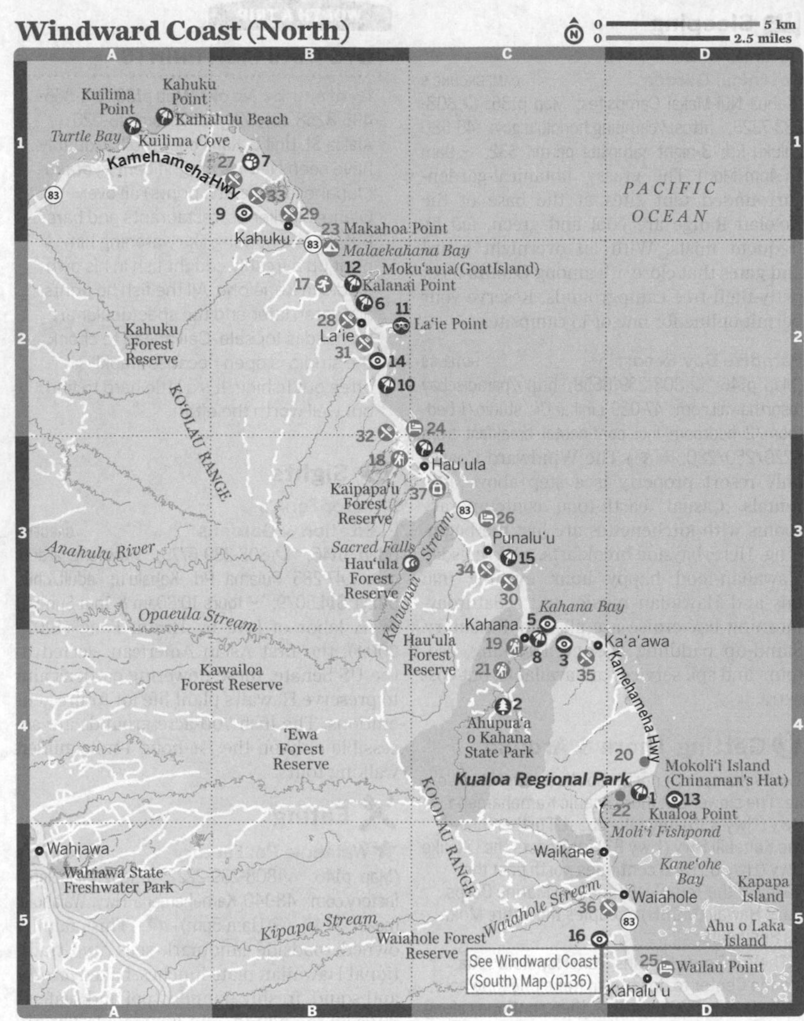

Kualoa

Although nowadays there is not a lot of evidence, in ancient times Kualoa was one of the most sacred places on O'ahu. When a chief stood on Kualoa Point, passing canoes lowered their sails in respect.

Beaches

★ Kualoa Regional Park BEACH
(Map p146; 49-479 Kamehameha Hwy) Huge extended-family groups gather for weekend picnics on the wide, grassy field that fronts the narrow white-sand beach here. There's good swimming, with magnificent mountain scenery as a backdrop. Stroll south along the beach to **'Apua Pond**, a 3-acre brackish salt marsh on Kualoa Point that's a nesting area for the endangered *ae'o* (Hawaiian stilt).

Sights & Activities

Tropical Farms TOUR
(Map p146; ☎808-237-1960; www.macnutfarm.com; 49-227 Kamehameha Hwy; tours $20; ⏲9:30am-5pm, tours 11am Mon-Sat) Sure, it's a bit of a kitschy tourist trap, but everything

Windward Coast (North)

Top Sights
1 Kualoa Regional Park D4

Sights
2 Ahupua'a o Kahana State Park C4
3 Crouching Lion C4
4 Hau'ula Beach Park C3
5 Huilua Fishpond C3
6 Hukilau Beach B2
7 James Campbell National Wildlife Refuge B1
8 Kahana Bay C4
9 Kahuku Farms B1
10 La'ie Beach Park B2
11 La'ie Point State Wayside B2
12 Malaekahana State Recreation Area B2
13 Mokoli'i Island D4
14 Polynesian Cultural Center B2
15 Punalu'u Beach Park C3
16 Senator Fong's Plantation & Gardens C5

Activities, Courses & Tours
17 Gunstock Ranch B2
18 Hau'ula Loop Trail B3
19 Kapa'ele'ele Trail C4
20 Kualoa Ranch D4
21 Nakoa Trail C4
22 Tropical Farms D4

Sleeping
23 Friends of Malaekahana Campground B2
24 Hale Ko'olau C2
Kalanai Point Campground .... (see 12)
25 Paradise Bay Resort D5
26 Pat's at Punalu'u C3
Paul Comeau Condos .... (see 26)

Eating
Aunty Pat's Café .... (see 20)
27 Fumi's Kahuku Shrimp B1
Giovanni's .... (see 29)
28 Hukilau Cafe B2
29 Kahuku Grill B1
30 Keneke's Grill C3
31 La'ie Shopping Center B2
Mike's Huli Huli Chicken .... (see 25)
32 Papa Ole's Kitchen B2
33 Romy's Kahuku Prawns & Shrimp B1
34 Shrimp Shack C3
35 Uncle Bobo's C4
36 Waiahole Poi Factory D5

Shopping
37 Kim Taylor Reece Gallery C3

for sale at this family-owned business is homegrown Hawaiian. The open-air store overflows with various flavored macadamia nuts, local jams and sauces, as well as natural remedies and arts and crafts.

Kualoa Ranch TOUR
(Map p146; ☎808-237-7321; www.kualoa.com; 49-560 Kamehameha Hwy; tours adult/child from $27/16; ⏱tours 9am-3pm; 👪) In the 1800s the Judd family purchased the roughly 4000 acres that make up today's Kualoa Ranch from Kamehameha III and Queen Kalama. It's still O'ahu's largest cattle ranch (with 1500 head), but the family's descendants expanded the business into a slick tourist sight to help support the land.

If you want to see where Hurley built his *Lost* golf course, Godzilla left his footprints and the *Jurassic Park* kids hid from dinosaurs, take the movie tour that covers the many films and TV shows shot in the Ka'a'awa Valley. All-terrain vehicle (ATV) and horseback rides also mosey along in this busy area. Go a bit more off the beaten trail with the recommended 6WD jungle tour into Hakipu'u Valley's steep slopes covered with tropical vegetation. Hakipu'u is also where most of the ranch's ancient sites are located; you may have a bit more luck seeing some if you book a private Ali'i tour ($130, four hours). Other options include hula lessons, a guided Hakipu'u hike and a fishpond boat and garden tour. Book all tours at least a couple days in advance; they fill up. There's a cafe on-site.

Eating

Aunty Pat's Café CAFE $$
(Map p146; www.kualoa.com/amenities/aunty-pats-cafe; 49-560 Kamehameha Hwy; meals $7-15, lunch buffet adult/child 4-11yr $16/11; ⏱7:30am-3pm; 👪) At Kualoa Ranch's visitor center, this cafeteria lays out a filling midday buffet. Banana pancakes for breakfast and grass-fed beef burgers for lunch are cooked à la carte.

Ka'a'awa

Here the road tightly hugs the coast and the *pali* move right on in, with barely enough space to squeeze a few houses between the base of the cliffs and the highway. A narrow neighborhood beach used mainly by fishers has a grassy lawn fronted by a shore wall.

A LEGENDARY LIZARD

That eye-catching islet you see offshore from Kualoa Regional Park is called **Mokoli'i Island** (Map p146; Little Lizard). In ancient Hawaiian legend, it's said to be the tail of a *mo'o* (lizard spirit) slain by the goddess Hi'iaka and thrown into the ocean. Following the immigration of Chinese laborers to Hawaii, this cone-shaped island also came to be called Chinaman's Hat, a nickname that predominates today, regardless of any political incorrectness.

Sights

Crouching Lion MOUNTAIN

(Map p146) The Crouching Lion is a landmark rock formation just north of mile marker 27 on the Kamehameha Hwy. According to legend, the rock is a demigod from Tahiti who was cemented to the mountain during a jealous struggle between the volcano goddess Pele and her sister Hiiaka. When he tried to free himself by crouching, he was turned to stone.

To spot the lion, stand at the Crouching Lion Inn restaurant sign with your back to the ocean and look straight up to the left of the coconut tree at the cliff above.

Eating

Uncle Bobo's HAWAIIAN $

(Map p146; 808-237-1000; www.unclebobos.com; 51-480 Kamehameha Hwy; mains $5-13; 11am-5pm Tue-Fri, to 6pm Sat & Sun) You don't usually find buns baked from scratch at a Hawaiian BBQ joint. Here a local family dishes up smoked brisket and ribs, grills mahimahi tacos and other island faves done right. The cheery yellow dining room is small, but the beach park across the street has ocean-view picnic tables.

Kahana Valley

In ancient Hawai'i, all of the islands were divided into *ahupua'a* – pie-shaped land divisions that ran from the mountains to the sea – providing everything Hawaiians needed for subsistence. Modern subdivisions and town boundaries have erased this traditional organization almost everywhere except here, O'ahu's last publicly owned *ahupua'a*.

Before Westerners arrived, the Kahana Valley was planted with wetland taro, which thrived in the rainy valley. Archaeologists have identified the remnants of over 120 agricultural terraces and irrigation canals, as well as the remains of a heiau, fishing shrines and numerous *hale* (house) sites.

In the early 20th century the lower valley was planted with sugarcane, which was hauled north to Kahuku via a small railroad. During WWII the upper valley was taken over by the US military and used to train soldiers in jungle warfare.

Beaches

Kahana Bay BEACH

(Map p146; www.hawaiistateparks.org; Kamehameha Hwy) Although many of Kahana's archaeological sites are inaccessibly deep in the valley, impressive **Huilua Fishpond** (Map p146) is visible from the highway and can be visited simply by walking down to the beach. The beach itself offers mostly safe swimming with a gently sloping sandy bottom. Watch out for the riptide near the bay's southern reef break. There are restrooms, outdoor showers, picnic tables and usually drinking water. Ten roadside campsites (advance state-park camping permit required) don't offer much privacy.

Sights & Activities

Ahupua'a o Kahana State Park PARK

(Map p146; www.hawaiistateparks.org; Kamehameha Hwy; sunrise-sunset) FREE In spite of over 40 years of political controversy and failed plans for a living-history village, this park is currently still open to visitors.

Starting near the community center, the gentle, 1.2-mile round-trip **Kapa'ele'ele Trail** (Map p146) runs along a former railbed and visits a fishing shrine and a bay-view lookout, then follows the highway back to the park entrance.

Park before the private residential neighborhood, then walk 1056yd further up the valley road to the start of the **Nakoa Trail** (Map p146), a 3.5-mile rainforest loop that confusingly crisscrosses Kahana Stream and bushwhacks through thick vegetation.

Both of these trails can be very slippery and muddy when wet. Don't attempt the Nakoa Trail if any rain is forecast or dark clouds are visible in the sky, due to the danger of flash floods.

The signposted park entrance is a mile north of Crouching Lion Inn. Turn *mauka* past the picnic tables and drive up the valley road to an unstaffed orientation center, where hiking pamphlets with trail maps are available outside by the educational boards.

Punalu'u

This sleepy seaside community consists of a string of houses and businesses lining the highway.

Beaches

Punalu'u Beach Park BEACH
(Map p146; Kamehameha Hwy) At this long, narrow swimming beach, an offshore reef protects the shallow waters in all but stormy weather. Be cautious of strong currents near the mouth of the stream and in the channel leading out from it, especially during high surf. The roadside park has restrooms, outdoor showers and picnic tables.

Sleeping

Check **VRBO** (www.vrbo.com) and other online sites; this part of the coast has some good deals on beachfront vacation rentals.

Pat's at Punalu'u CONDO $$
(Map p146; ☎808-255-9840; 53-567 Kamehameha Hwy; studio/1 bedroom from $100/125;) An older, seven-story residential condominium complex, Pat's houses spacious, sometimes well-worn, units – all with ocean views. Rentals here are privately owned and listed; some are available through VRBO and **Paul Comeau Condo Rentals** (Map p146; ☎808-293-2624; www.paulspunaluucondos.com; studio/1 bedroom from $100/125, plus cleaning fee $50;).

Eating

Keneke's Grill HAWAIIAN $
(Map p146; ☎808-237-1010; www.kenekes.net; 53-138 Kamehameha Hwy; mains $4-10; 10am-8pm) Right on the road and with plenty of parking out front, Keneke's comes complete with Christian sayings and quotes on the wall. Hawaiian plate lunches, such as *loco moco* and teriyaki steak, plus burgers and daily specials, fill the menu. Don't miss having shave ice or Dave's ice cream for dessert.

Shrimp Shack SEAFOOD $$
(Map p146; ☎808-256-5589; http://shrimpshackoahu.com; 53-360 Kamehameha Hwy; meals $10-18; 10am-5pm) The shrimp are fried in garlic and dipped in butter, or you could order mussels or crab legs at this legendary sunny, yellow-painted food truck parked outside Ching's c 1946 general store. You can't miss it roadside – the menu is on a yellow surfboard.

Shopping

Kim Taylor Reece Gallery ART
(Map p146; ☎808-293-2000; www.kimtaylorreece.com; 53-866 Kamehameha Hwy; noon-5pm Mon-Wed, by appointment Thu-Sun) Reece's sepia-toned photographs of traditional Hawaiian *hula kahiko* dancers in motion are widely recognized, but it's his images of Kalaupapa, a place of exile on Moloka'i, that haunt. The artist's gallery inhabits an airy, light-filled two-story house on the *mauka* side of the highway.

Hau'ula

A small coastal town sitting against a scenic backdrop of hills and majestic Norfolk pines, Hau'ula has a main drag with not much more than a general store, a modern strip mall and a convenience store, but there are hiking possibilities in the area.

Beaches

Hau'ula Beach Park BEACH
(Map p146; Kamehameha Hwy) Across the road from the middle of town, this ironwood-shaded beach has a shallow, rocky bottom that isn't too appealing for swimming but does attract snorkelers. It occasionally gets waves big enough for local kids to ride. The grassy lawn is popular for family picnics on weekends. The 15 roadside campsites here won't give you a good night's sleep.

Activities

Hau'ula Loop Trail HIKING
(Map p146; http://hawaiitrails.ehawaii.gov; Ma'akua Rd; sunrise-sunset) Open to hikers and mountain bikers, the tranquil Hau'ula Loop Trail is a 2.5-mile loop (1½ hours) that clambers through Waipilopilo Gulch onto a ridge over Kaipapa'u Valley. The trail forks off to the right immediately after the road enters the forest reserve, and then rises quickly through a native forest of ohia and hala trees.

The signposted trailhead appears at a sharp bend in Hau'ula Homestead Rd above the Kamehameha Hwy, north of Hau'ula Beach Park. Trailhead parking is unsafe due to vehicle break-ins, so leave your car by the beach and instead walk up 440yd from the highway to the trailhead.

Sleeping

Hale Ko'olau APARTMENT $$
(Map p146; ☎808-536-4263, 888-236-0799; www.halekoolau.com; 54-225 Kamehameha Hwy; 1-/2-/3-bedroom apt from $115/205/340;) Beachfronts, lawns, hot tubs and washer-driers are all shared at this wonderfully comfy, slightly timeworn community of bungalows and residential buildings. Prices vary depending on unit size and location (not all have water views); there's even a five-bedroom house (from $370). Hawaiian-family owned and operated.

Eating

Papa Ole's Kitchen HAWAIIAN $
(Map p146; ☎808-293-2292; Hau'ula Shopping Center, 54-316 Kamehameha Hwy; mains $5-12; ⌚7am-9pm Thu-Mon, to 3pm Tue) When billing itself as 'da original, with *ono grinds*,' Papa Ole's doesn't lie. Opt for sautéed veggies or a green salad instead of macaroni and you've made your Hawaiian plate lunch a tiny bit healthier. Dine inside the small cafe, outside at parking-lot picnic tables or take it to-go to the beach park.

La'ie

POP 4150

Bustling and busy, La'ie is quite a contrast to its rural neighbors. This is the center of the Mormon community in Hawaii, so you are just as likely to see white-collared shirts as board shorts in town. Life here revolves around resident Brigham Young University (BYU) – Hawaii, where scholarship programs recruit students from islands throughout the Pacific. Many students help pay for their living expenses by working as guides at the local Polynesian Cultural Center (PCC), the tourist complex that draws gazillions of visitors each year (second only to Pearl Harbor among O'ahu's attractions).

La'ie is thought to have been the site of an ancient Hawaiian *pu'uhonua* – a place where kapu (taboo) breakers could escape being put to death. And it was a refuge for the Mormon missionaries as well; after an attempt to create a 'City of Joseph' on Lanai failed, the church purchased a 6000-acre plantation here in 1865. In 1919 construction began on a smaller version of the Salt Lake City, Utah, temple at the foot of the Ko'olau Range. This dazzling, formal white edifice – open only to practicing Latter Day Saint (LDS, also known as Mormon) church members – stands at the end of a wide boulevard and may be one of the most incongruous sights on O'ahu.

Beaches

La'ie Beach Park BEACH
(Map p146; Kamehameha Hwy) A half-mile south of the PCC's main entrance, this is an excellent bodysurfing beach, but the shorebreak can be brutal, thus its nickname Pounders Beach. Summer swimming is generally good, but watch out for strong winter currents. The area around the old landing is usually the calmest.

Hukilau Beach BEACH
(Map p146; Kamehameha Hwy) North of La'ie Shopping Center is a pocket of white sand that's a leisurely place for swimming when summer waters are calm. Just beware any time the surf's up.

Sights & Activities

Polynesian Cultural Center THEME PARK
(PCC; Map p146; ☎808-293-3333; www.polynesia.com; 55-370 Kamehameha Hwy; adult/child from $40/36; ⌚11.30am-9pm Mon-Sat;) A nonprofit cultural park owned by the Mormon Church, the PCC revolves around eight Polynesian-themed 'villages' representing Hawaii, Rapa Nui (Easter Island), Samoa, Aotearoa (New Zealand), Fiji, Tahiti and Tonga. The admission price is steep, but this includes frequent village shows and a park-wide boat parade showcasing native dances.

BYUH students dressed in native garb demonstrate poi pounding, coconut-frond weaving, handicrafts, music and games. You'll learn a bit more if you add on the Ambassador option, which includes a personal guide. The evening Ali'i Luau show and buffet, another add-on, is one of the island's biggest and best, with some authentic Hawaiian dances and foods. Afterwards you can see Ha: Breath of Life, a Polynesian song-and-dance revue that's partly authentic, partly Bollywood-style extravaganza. Check online for ticket packages; advance discounts are sometimes offered.

La'ie Point State Wayside LOOKOUT
(Map p146; www.hawaiistateparks.org; end of Naupaka St; ⌚sunrise-sunset) Crashing surf, a lava arch and a slice of Hawaiian folk his-

tory await at La'ie Point. The tiny offshore islands are said to be the surviving pieces of a *mo'o* (lizard spirit) slain by a legendary warrior. To get here from the highway, head seaward on Anemoku St, opposite La'ie Shopping Center, then turn right onto dead-end Naupaka St.

Gunstock Ranch HORSEBACK RIDING
(Map p146; ☎808-341-3995; http://gunstock-ranch.com; 56-250 Kamahameha Hwy; trail rides from $89; 👪) Take a small-group horseback ride across a working ranch at the base of the Ko'olau Mountains. Options include scenic mosey-alongs, advanced giddyaps, picnic and moonlight trail rides, plus there's a kiddie experience that includes a 30-minute guide-led ride (ages two to seven, $39).

Eating

Hukilau Cafe HAWAIIAN $
(Map p146; ☎808-293-8616; 55-662 Wahinepe'e St; mains $4-9; ⏰6am-2pm Tue-Fri, 7-11:30am Sat) In a backstreet in town, this small cafe is the kind of place locals would rather keep to themselves. Local *grinds* (food) – such as Portuguese sweet-bread French toast and a teriyaki burger lunch – are right on. In case you're wondering, this isn't the restaurant featured in the movie *50 First Dates*, though it's said to be the inspiration for it.

La'ie Shopping Center FAST FOOD, SUPERMARKET $
(Map p146; 55-510 Kamehameha Hwy; ⏰most shops closed Sun) Fast-food restaurants, shops and services cluster in this minimall, about a half-mile north of the PCC. Foodland supermarket has a takeout deli and bakery, but doesn't sell alcohol and it's closed Sunday (this is Mormon country).

Malaekahana State Recreation Area

Just north of La'ie, a long, narrow strip of sand stretches between Makahoa Point to the north and Kalanai Point to the south with a thick inland barrier of ironwoods.

Sights

Malaekahana State Recreation Area BEACH
(Map p146; www.hawaiistateparks.org; Kamehameha Hwy; ⏰7am-7:45pm Apr-early Sep, to 6:45pm early Sep-Mar) FREE The long, slightly steep, but relatively uncrowded beach is popular with families. Swimming is generally good here year-round, although there are occasionally strong currents in winter. Bodyboarding, board surfing and windsurfing are also possible. When the tide is low, you can wade over to Moku'auia (Goat Island), a state bird sanctuary about 400yd offshore. It has a small sandy cove with good swimming and snorkeling.

Sleeping

Friends of Malaekahana Campground CAMPGROUND $
(Map p146; ☎808-293-1736; www.malaekahana.net; 56-335 Kamehameha Hwy; tent sites per person $12, rental units $40-150; ⏰gates open 7am-7pm only; @) 🌿 Let the surf be your lullaby and the roosters your wake-up call at Makahoa Point, about 1232yd north of the park's main entrance. Here the nonprofit Friends of Malaekahana maintains tent sites by the beach, very rustic 'little grass shacks,' canvas yurts and duplex cabins, providing 24-hour security, outdoor hot showers and internet access at the campground office. Make reservations at least two weeks in advance; there's usually a two-night minimum stay.

Kalanai Point Campground CAMPGROUND $
(Map p146; ☎808-293-1736; www.hawaiistateparks.org; tent sites $18; ⏰8am Fri-8am Wed) Kalanai Point, the main section of the park, is less than a mile north of La'ie. It has picnic tables, BBQ grills, restrooms, showers and good public camping – advance permits are required.

Kahuku

Kahuku is a former sugar-plantation town. Much of the old sugar mill that operated here until 1996 was knocked down, but the remnants of the smokestack and the old iron gears can be seen behind the post office. The rest of the former mill grounds have been transformed into a small shopping center containing the town's bank, post office, grocery store and eateries.

Sights & Activities

Kahuku Farms FARM
(Map p146; ☎808-628-0639; http://kahukufarms.com; 56-800 Kamehameha Hwy; tours adult/child 5-12yr $22/15; ⏰11am-4pm Wed-Mon, tours 2pm, call for reservations; 👪) 🌿 Take a tractor-pulled wagon tour through the taro patch and fruit orchards at this family

farm – sampling included. Then stop at the gift shop for bath products and foodstuffs made from the farm's bounty.

James Campbell National Wildlife Refuge WILDLIFE RESERVE
(Map p146; ☎808-637-6330; www.fws.gov/jamescampbell; off Kamehameha Hwy; ⌚tours by reservation only) FREE A few miles northwest of Kahuku town heading toward Turtle Bay, this rare freshwater wetland provides habitat for four of Hawaii's six endangered waterbirds – the *'alae kea* (Hawaiian coot), *ae'o* (Hawaiian black-necked stilt), *koloa maoli* (Hawaiian duck) and *'alae 'ula* (Hawaiian moorhen). During stilt nesting season, normally mid-February through mid-October, the refuge is off-limits to visitors.

The rest of the year you may only visit by taking a volunteer-guided tour. Finding the refuge is tricky, so ask for directions when you call ahead for tour reservations.

Kahuku Land Farms MARKET
(☎808-232-2202; 56-781 Kamehameha Hwy; ⌚10am-7pm) A number of local farm stands group together just west of the Turtle Bay Resort entrance. Stop here for a fresh-cold coconut water ($3) and to peruse the unexpected selection of fruits (pitaya, pomelo...).

Eating

Kahuku is a favorite eating stop on circle-island road trips. Shrimp ponds at the north side of town supply O'ahu's top restaurants, while colorful food trucks that cook up the crustaceans are thick along the highway. They are usually open from 10am to 6pm or 6:30pm daily, depending upon supply and demand. Expect to pay at least $13 per dozen shrimp with two-scoop rice. Chow down at outdoor picnic tables.

Kahuku Grill BURGERS, SEAFOOD $
(Map p146; ☎808-852-0040; http://kahukugrill.com; 55-565 Kamehameha Hwy; mains $8-12; ⌚11am-9pm Mon-Sat; 👪) Serving from a window in one of the old wooden mill buildings near the center of the small town, this outdoor cafe has real aloha spirit. The pancakes are fluffy, the handmade beef burgers juicy and the island-style plates piled high. It's well worth the wait, especially for coconut-and-macadamia-crusted shrimp with organic Pupukea greens.

Giovanni's SEAFOOD $$
(Map p146; http://giovannisshrimptruck.com; 56-505 Kamehameha Hwy; plates $13; ⌚10:30am-6:30pm) The original, graffiti-covered shrimp truck that spawned an empire. No longer a lonely little vehicle, Giovanni's is flanked by a covered patio and surrounded by a bevy of other food trucks serving different meals, smoothies, fro-yo and shave ice.

Romy's Kahuku Prawns & Shrimp SEAFOOD $$
(Map p146; ☎808-232-2202; www.romyskahukuprawns.org; 56-781 Kamehameha Hwy; plates $12-17; ⌚10am-6pm) Eat overlooking the aquaculture farm where your giant, and pricey, prawns are raised. Steamed shrimp and whole fish available too. Try the *pani popo* (Samoan coconut buns) for dessert.

Fumi's Kahuku Shrimp SEAFOOD $$
(Map p146; ☎808-232-8881; 56-777 Kamehameha Hwy; plates $10-13; ⌚10am-7pm) Shrimp is sold from its original truck and just up the road from an added building; both have picnic tables. Alternative eating options include tempura shrimp, fried fish and burgers.

NORTH SHORE

Pipeline, Sunset, Waimea... You don't have to be a surfer to have heard of the North Shore; the epic breaks here are known worldwide. Sure, winter brings giant swells that can reach 15ft to 40ft in height, but there is more to this coast than monster waves. The beaches are gorgeous year-round, perfect for swimming in summer. And there are so many activities besides surfing. Try SUP or kayaking, take a snorkeling or whale-watching tour, go hiking or horseback riding – jump out of an airplane, even.

Turtle Bay

Idyllic coves and coastal rock beds define the island's northeastern tip, where the North Shore and the Windward Coast meet. Dominating the area is Turtle Bay Resort, with its low-key, view-perfect hotel and restaurants, golf course, condo village and public access to the nearby beaches. So far, it's the only large-scale tourist development on this side of the island, and locals have fought to keep it that way.

Beaches

Kuilima Cove BEACH
(👪) Just east of the Turtle Bay Resort on Kuilima Point is beautiful little Kuilima Cove

and its perfect, protected **Bayview Beach**. On the bay's right-hand side is an outer reef that not only knocks down the waves but facilitates great snorkeling in summer – and, in winter, some moderate surf. Rent bodyboards, snorkel sets and beach gear at the resort's on-site Sand Bar.

Kaihalulu Beach BEACH

A mile's walk along the beach east of Kuilima Cove is this beautiful, curved, white-sand beach backed by ironwoods. The rocky bottom makes for poor swimming, but the shoreline attracts morning beachcombers. Continue another mile east, detouring up onto the bluff by the golf course, to reach scenic **Kahuku Point**, where fishers cast throw-nets and pole-fish from the rocks.

★**Kawela Bay** BEACH

West of the Turtle Bay Resort, a 1.5-mile shoreline trail runs over to Kawela Bay. In winter you might spy whales cavorting offshore. After walking round **Protection Point**, named for its WWII bunker, voila! You've found Kawela Bay, with its thicket of banyan trees as seen on TV's *Lost*. For the best swimming and snorkeling, keep walking to the middle of the bay.

Activities

Turtle Bay Golf GOLF

(808-293-8574; www.turtlebayresort.com; Turtle Bay Resort, 57-091 Kamehameha Hwy; green fees $75-185; by reservation only) Turtle Bay's two top-rated, par-72 courses abound in water views. The more challenging Palmer Course is the site of the PGA Championship Tour. The Fazio Course is host of the LPGA Tour's SBS Open. Discounts for hotel guests and twilight play.

Hans Hedemann Surf School SURFING

(808-447-6755; http://hhsurf.com/hh/en/turtlebay.html) Located in the Turtle Bay Resort, this surfing and SUP school is an extension of Hans Hedemann's well-known Waikiki school. It offers lessons for beginners and intermediates for both disciplines virtually right outside the hotel.

Guidepost OUTDOORS

(808-293-6020; http://tbrapp.com/activities; Turtle Bay Resort, 57-091 Kamehameha Hwy;) Swimming and snorkeling not exciting enough for you? Guidepost, the Turtle Bay Experience Center, can organize everything from horseback rides to surfing lessons to Segway rentals, plus kayaking, fishing and helicopter tours.

Sleeping

A good number of the privately owned Turtle Bay area condos are available for vacation rental on websites such as **VRBO** (www.vrbo.com).

Turtle Bay Resort RESORT $$$

(808-293-6000; www.turtlebayresort.com; 57-091 Kamehameha Hwy; r from $259, cottages/villas from $659/1090;) Situated on a dramatic point, Turtle Bay Resort boasts impressive 800-acre surrounds. Each of the slightly dated guest lodgings has an ocean view; deluxe rooms come with private lanai. Ocean villas ($550 to $1200) have high ceilings, deep soaking tubs and a villa-guest-only private pool, in addition to sharing the resort's many other amenities. Check for package discounts online.

Eating & Drinking

Ola SEAFOOD $$

(808-293-0801; www.olaislife.com; Turtle Bay Resort, 57-091 Kamehameha Hwy; mains lunch $10-24, dinner $19-58; 11am-10pm) Reserve in advance and you might get to dine by torchlight with your toes in the sand. This open-air cabana bar and restaurant stakes out an unparalleled position beachside. The menu is regular surf and turf; *pupu* such as *kalua* pork nachos and ahi *poke* are a bit more interesting.

Pa'akai SEAFOOD $$$

(808-293-6000; www.turtlebayresort.com; Turtle Bay Resort, 57-091 Kamehameha Hwy; mains $30-75; 5.30-10pm) Turtle Bay Resort's top seafood restaurant, with a name that means 'sea salt'. The best in local fish, prawns, lobster and scallops as well as steak and lamb from the land. Try the pan-seared *kampachi* (yellowtail) for a can't-miss dish. Full bar and nightly live entertainment. Casual wear is fine; reservations recommended.

Surfer, The Bar BAR

(808-293-6000; www.turtlebayresort.com; Turtle Bay Resort, 57-091 Kamehameha Hwy) Big-name North Shore musicians occasionally play live sets at the resort's Surfer, The Bar, where the stage is set for anything from open-mic nights to surf-film screenings. Happy-hour coconut margaritas and 'lychee-tinis' are a bargain. Plenty of tasty *pupu* and bar food options (mains $10 to $20).

North Shore

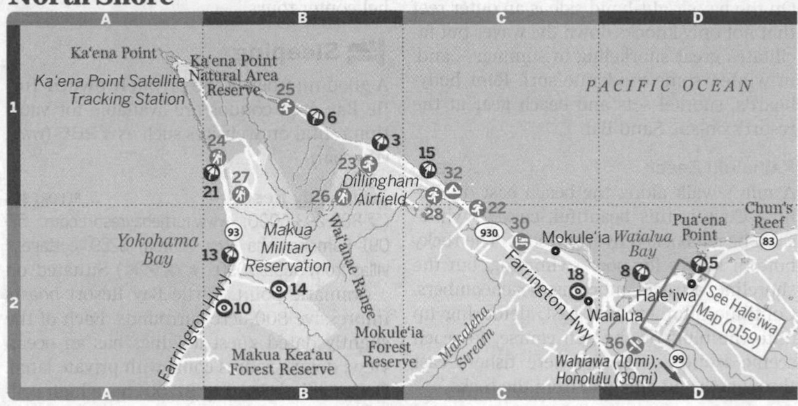

Sunset Beach to Hale'iwa

Revered for monster winter waves and having some of the best surf breaks on the planet, the stretch of coastline running from Sunset Beach all the way to Waimea Bay is a sort of loose gathering point for the world's best surfers, ardent fans and enthusiastic wannabes.

Waimea Bay is so stunning that it's hard not to catch your breath when you round the highway curve and see it. Captain Cook's men, the first Westerners to sail into Waimea Bay, had the same reaction. An entry in the 1779 ship's log noted its uncommon beauty. Back then the valley was heavily settled; the lowlands terraced in taro, the valley walls dotted with house sites and the ridges topped with heiau. In those days the Waimea River emptied into the bay and served as a passage for canoes traveling to upstream villages. Post contact, logging and plantation clearing resulted in a devastating 1894 flood, after which residents abandoned the settlement.

Beaches

Sunset Beach Park BEACH

(59-104 Kamehameha Hwy) Like many beaches on the North Shore, Sunset Beach has a split personality. In winter big swells come in for pro wave riders and the posse of followers these rock stars of the sea attract. The second leg of the Triple Crown of Surfing takes place here in late November and early December. In summer, Sunset is a prime place to log beach time. Waves calm down, there's a swimming channel before the reef and trees for shade.

In winter the tremendous surf activity causes the slope of the beach to become increasingly steep as the season goes on. Though the water looks more inviting in summer, be aware there are still some nasty currents about.

Backyards is a smokin' hot reef break off Sunset Point on the northeastern side of the beach.

'Ehukai Beach Park BEACH

(59-337 Ke Nui Rd) **Banzai Pipeline**, aka Pipeline, aka Pipe – call it whatever you want, this place is known the world over as one of the biggest, heaviest and closest-to-perfect barrels in all of wave riding. When the strong westerly swells kick up in winter, the waves can reach over 15ft before breaking on the ultrashallow reef below. The final leg of the Triple Crown of Surfing is held here in early to mid-December.

For expert board riders who know what they're doing (no, a day of lessons at Waikiki Beach doesn't count), this could be surfing's holy grail. The waves break only a few yards offshore, so spectators are front-row and center. In the summer months everything calms down and there's even some decent snorkeling off this beach.

★ **Pupukea Beach Park** BEACH

(59-727 Kamehameha Hwy) With deep-blue waters, a varied coastline and a mix of lava and white sand, Pupukea, meaning 'white shell,' is a very scenic stretch. The long beach encompasses three areas: Shark's Cove to the north, Old Quarry in the center and Three

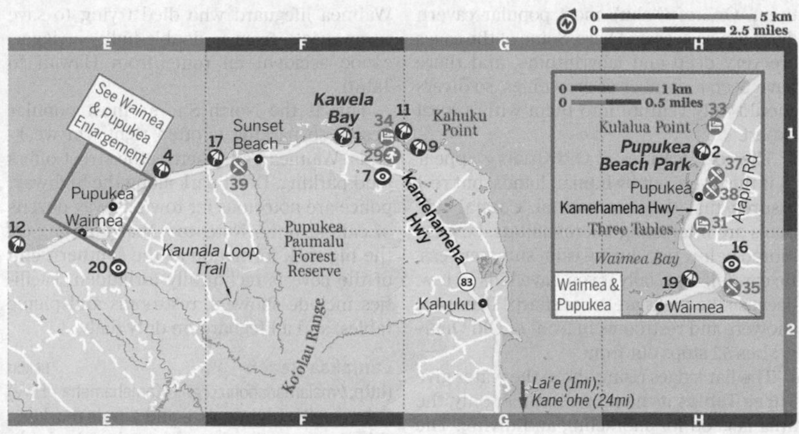

North Shore

Top Sights
1 Kawela Bay ... F1
2 Pupukea Beach Park ... H1

Sights
3 Army Beach ... B1
4 'Ehukai Beach Park ... E1
5 Hale'iwa Beach Park ... D2
6 Ka'ena Point State Park ... B1
7 Kahuku Land Farms ... F1
8 Kaiaka Bay Beach Park ... D2
9 Kaihalulu Beach ... G1
10 Kaneana Cave ... B2
11 Kuilima Cove ... F1
12 Laniakea Beach ... E2
13 Makua Beach ... B2
14 Makua Valley ... B2
15 Mokule'ia Beach Park ... C1
16 Pu'u o Mahuka Heiau State Historic Site ... H2
17 Sunset Beach Park ... F1
18 Waialua Sugar Mill ... C2
19 Waimea Bay Beach Park ... H2
20 Waimea Valley ... E2
21 Yokohama Bay ... B1

Activities, Courses & Tours
Guidepost ... (see 34)
Hans Hedemann Surf School ... (see 34)
22 Hawaii Polo ... C2
23 Honolulu Soaring ... B1
24 Ka'ena Point Trail ... B1
25 Ka'ena Point Trail ... B1
26 Kealia Trail ... B1
27 Kuaokala Trail ... B1
28 Pacific Skydiving Center ... C1
Paradise Air ... (see 23)
Pipeline ... (see 4)
Stearman Biplane Rides ... (see 23)
29 Turtle Bay Golf ... F1

Sleeping
30 Anna Banana's Country Cottage ... C2
31 Backpackers Vacation Inn & Hostel ... H1
32 Camp Mokule'ia ... C1
Kaiaka Bay Beach Park ... (see 8)
33 Ke Iki Beach Bungalows ... H1
34 Turtle Bay Resort ... F1

Eating
35 Hale'iwa Farmers Market ... H2
Ola ... (see 34)
Pa'akai ... (see 34)
36 Pa'ala'a Kai Bakery ... D2
37 Pupukea Grill ... H1
Scoop of Paradise Ice Cream Factory ... (see 36)
38 Sharks Cove Grill ... H1
39 Ted's Bakery ... F1

Drinking & Nightlife
Surfer, The Bar ... (see 34)

Tables to the south. The waters off Pupukea Beach are all protected as a marine-life-conservation district.

The reef formation at **Shark's Cove** provides an excellent habitat for marine life, including sea turtles, and is good for snorkeling. When seas are calm, this is a great area for water exploring; just make sure you always wear shoes to protect from sharp coral. Despite the cove's name, the white-tipped reef sharks aren't usually a problem; just keep your distance and don't provoke them. One of O'ahu's most popular cavern dives is also accessed here. Some of the caves are very deep and labyrinthine, and there have been a number of drownings, so divers should only venture into them with a local expert.

The rock features at **Old Quarry** appear as if they were cut by human hands, but rest assured that they are natural. Coastal tide pools are interesting microhabitats, best explored at low tide during calm summer seas. Be careful, especially if you have kids in tow, because the rocks are razor sharp. There are showers and restrooms in front of Old Quarry; bus 52 stops out front.

The flat ledges rising above the water give **Three Tables** its name. In summer only, the area is good for snorkeling and diving. The best coral and fish, as well as some small caves, lava tubes and arches, are in deeper water further out. Access to Three Tables is just beyond Old Quarry, where there are a few unmarked parking spots.

Waimea Bay Beach Park BEACH
(61-031 Kamehameha Hwy) It may be a beauty, but it's certainly a moody one. Waimea Bay changes dramatically with the seasons: it can be tranquil and flat as a lake in summer, then savage in winter, with the island's meanest rip currents. Typically, the only time it's calm enough for swimming and snorkeling is from June to September, maybe October. Winter water activities at this beach are *not* for novices – the waves at Waimea can get epically huge.

The beach plays host to the annual Quiksilver Eddie Aikau memorial surf competition between December and February. Eddie Aikau was a legendary waterman and Waimea lifeguard who died trying to save compatriots from a double-hull outrigger-canoe accident en route from Hawaii to Tahiti.

This is the North Shore's most popular beach, so parking is often tight. On weekends, Waimea Valley across the street offers paid parking. Don't park along the highway; police are notorious for towing away dozens of cars at once. Note, too, that jumping off the big rock formation at the southern end of the cove is technically forbidden. Facilities include showers, restrooms and picnic tables, and a lifeguard on duty daily.

Laniakea Beach BEACH
(http://malamanahonu.org; Kamehameha Hwy) Between the highway's 3- and 4-mile markers, this narrow spit of sand is visited by basking *honu* (green sea turtles), who migrate here from French Frigate Shoals in the remote Northwestern Hawaiian Islands. Stay back at least 20ft from these endangered sea creatures, which are very sensitive to noise and human disturbance. Volunteers are on hand to answer questions. Most people park alongside the highway opposite the beach, but vehicle break-ins and theft are a risk.

TRIPLE CROWN OF SURFING

During the North Shore's **Triple Crown of Surfing championships** (http://vanstriplecrownofsurfing.com; Nov-Dec), touring pros compete for pride – and megabucks in prizes. The kickoff is the Reef Hawaiian Pro at Hale'iwa Ali'i Beach Park in mid-November. The competition's second challenge, the Vans World Cup of Surfing (late November to early December), takes place at Sunset Beach. The final leg, the Billabong Pipe Masters, happens in early to mid-December at Pipeline.

Sights & Activities

Pu'u o Mahuka Heiau State Historic Site TEMPLE
(www.hawaiistateparks.org; off Pupukea Rd; sunrise-sunset) FREE A cinematic coastal panorama and a stroll around the grounds of O'ahu's largest temple reward those who venture up to this national historic landmark, perched on a bluff above Waimea Bay. It's a dramatically windswept and lonely site. Though the ruined walls leave a lot to be imagined, it's worth the drive for the commanding views, especially at sunset.

Pu'u o Mahuka means 'hill of escape' – but this was a *luakini* heiau, where human sacrifices took place. Likely dating from the 17th century, the temple's stacked-stone construction is attributed to the legendary *menehune* (the 'little people' who, according to legend, built many of Hawaii's fishponds, heiau and other stonework), who are said to have completed their work in just one night.

To get here, turn *mauka* onto Pupukea Rd by the Foodland supermarket; the monument turnoff is about 880yd uphill, from where it's another roughshod 1232yd to the heiau.

LOCAL KNOWLEDGE

O'AHU'S BEST SURF BEACHES & BREAKS

O'ahu has some of the most diverse surf breaks in all of the Hawaiian Islands, so boarders of all skill levels can find what they're looking for.

In Waikiki, slow and mellow combers provide the perfect training ground, allowing beginners to gain some confidence. Board-rental outfits abound on Waikiki Beach, where beachboys are always on hand to give lessons at spots like nice-and-mellow **Queens**, mushy left- and right-handed **Canoes**, gentle but often crowded **Populars** and ever-popular **Publics**. In Honolulu proper, **Ala Moana** offers a heavy tubing wave. Waves in these places are biggest during summer, when south swells arrive from New Zealand and Tahiti.

Reckon yourself a serious surfer? A pilgrimage to the famed North Shore is mandatory. In winter, when the waves can reach heights of more than 30ft, spots like **Waimea Bay**, **Pipeline** and **Sunset Beach** beckon to the planet's best professional surfers. Watch out for turf-protective locals, some organized into surfer gangs.

While home to some great waves, O'ahu's Wai'anae Coast has even more turf issues; the locals who live and surf here cherish this area and are trying to hold onto their Hawaiian culture and community. In the winter, large west swells can make for big surf at places like **Makaha Beach**, but tread lightly: locals know each other, so there will be no question that you're from out of town.

If you're looking for a multipurpose wave, **Diamond Head Beach** is friendly to shortboarders, long-boarders, windsurfers and kiteboarders. For adrenaline-charged bodysurfing, **Sandy Beach** and **Makapu'u Beach** near the island's southeast point are ideal. If you go out there, do so with caution: the pounding waves and shallow bottom have caused serious neck and back injuries. **Waimanalo Bay Beach Park** provides a safer alternative.

Surf News Network (www.surfnewsnetwork.com) runs an online surf report with webcams.

Waimea Valley GARDENS, PARK
(☎808-638-7766; www.waimeavalley.net; 59-864 Kamehameha Hwy; adult/child 4-12yr $15/7.50; ⏰9am-5pm; 👪) Craving land instead of sea? This 1800-acre Hawaiian cultural and nature park, just inland from Waimea Bay, is a sanctuary of tropical tranquillity. Among the junglelike foliage you'll find up to 5000 native and exotic plant species. Wander the numerous paths alongside Kamananui Stream and up to different cultural stations, which may have demonstrations of ancient Hawaiian games and practices.

The valley is home to numerous ancient sites, but few are on the paths. Equally interesting are the replicas of buildings ancient Hawaiians dwelled in and a restored heiau dedicated to Lono, the traditional god of fertility and agriculture. Guided hikes ($10 to $15) lead into otherwise inaccessible parts of the valley and are worth making time for; reservations required.

Ke Ala Pupukea Bike Path CYCLING
A partly shaded bike path provides an excellent link between the beaches along part of the North Shore. Pie-in-the-sky plans are to expand it from Turtle Bay to Waialua. In the meantime, the trail runs roughly 3 miles on the *makai* side of Kamehameha Hwy, from O'opuola St in Sunset Beach to the northern end of Waimea Bay.

Sleeping

Rentals abound around Sunset Beach, check both the big online sites, such as **VRBO** (www.vrbo.com), plus local ones such as Team Real Estate in Hale'iwa.

Backpackers Vacation Inn & Hostel HOSTEL $
(☎808-638-7838; http://backpackers-hawaii.com; 59-788 Kamehameha Hwy; dm $27-30, d $62-85, studio/2-bedroom/3-bedroom cabins from $120/170/215; @📶) The only budget option on the North Shore. If you care more about money and location than the odd bit of peeling paint or modest-to-the-point-of-ramshackle furnishings, this friendly, backpacker-style village is for you. Hostel rooms are mostly located in the two large main buildings. Our preferred location is Plantation Village, a groovy collection of beach cabins, some private, some shared. You don't have to do much more than cross the street to get to the beach from either. Studio 'condos' directly overlook the ocean but are way too spartan for the price. Shared kitchens and laundry on-site.

★Ke Iki Beach Bungalows APARTMENT $$
(☎808-638-8229, 866-638-8229; http://keikibeach.com; 59-579 Ke Iki Rd; 1-/2-bedroom apt from $205/230; ❄📶) Smartly updated tropical decor adds to the retreat feel of this bungalow community on the white-sand beach just north of Pupukea Beach Park. Grassy lawns and a garden full of tropical trees complete the picture. Kick back on the shared beachfront lanai, nap in a hammock beneath the palm trees or head out for a swim.

Though not all of the full-kitchen units have ocean views, none is more than a minute's walk from the water. The on-site manager is a font of area info.

O'ahu Family Rental APARTMENT $$
(www.oahufamilyrentals.com; studios $90, 1-bedroom apt $150-165; ❄📶) A local surfer family owns several rentals that are an easy bike ride from the beach (cruiser usage included). The smallest studio doesn't have much floor space but is fresh and cheery; a loft-like one bedroom has exposed-beam ceilings and original hula stained glass. Shared laundry facilities; insider beach advice included.

Eating

★Ted's Bakery HAWAIIAN $
(☎808-638-8207; www.tedsbakery.com; 59-024 Kamehameha Hwy; meals $7-16; ⏰7am-8pm; 👪) Quintessential North Shore, Ted's is the place surfers load up for breakfast, laid-back locals grab a snack, suntanned vacationers dig into plate lunches – and everybody goes for dessert. The chocolate-*haupia* cream pie is legend all across the island. Favorites include the meat-filled fried rice with eggs at breakfast and melt-in-your-mouth, lightly pan-fried garlic shrimp any other time.

Sharks Cove Grill HAWAIIAN $$
(☎808-638-8300; www.sharkscovegrill.com; 59-712 Kamehameha Hwy; dishes $4-8, meals $11-16; ⏰8:30am-8:30pm) Order your taro burger or ahi skewers from the food-truck window, pull up a rickety covered-patio seat and watch the waves as a chicken pecks the ground nearby. The food's OK; the experience is totally North Shore.

Pupukea Grill HAWAIIAN $$
(☎808-779-7943; www.pupukeagrill.com; 59-680 Kamehameha Hwy; meals $9-15; ⏰11am-5pm Tue-Sun) Grilled-fish tacos, panini sandwiches and *poke* bowls aren't typical food-truck fare. Take yours to go; the parking-lot picnic tables aren't appetizing.

Hale'iwa

POP 4000

Originally a plantation-era supply town in the 1900s, Hale'iwa today is the de facto surf city of the North Shore. It's all about the waves here and everyone knows it. If the town is all hustle and bustle, chances are the ocean is flat. If the swells are breaking, it could take you an hour to travel the 8 miles through rubber-necking traffic to Sunset Beach.

Sights

Lili'uokalani Protestant Church CHURCH
(66-090 Kamehameha Hwy) Hale'iwa's historic 1832 church takes its name from Queen Lili'uokalani, who spent summers on the shores of the Anahulu River and attended services here. As late as the 1940s services were held entirely in Hawaiian.

Beaches

Hale'iwa Ali'i Beach Park BEACH
(66-167 Hale'iwa Rd) Home to some of the best surf on the North Shore, waves here can be huge and the beach is a popular spot for surf contests. In mid-November the Triple Crown of Surfing gets under way on this break. When it's relatively flat, the local kids rip it up with their bodyboards and mere mortals test their skills on the waves. The 20-acre beach park has restrooms, showers, a wide grassy area with picnic tables and lifeguards.

Hale'iwa Beach Park BEACH
(62-449 Kamehameha Hwy) On the northern side of the harbor, this park is protected by a shallow shoal and breakwater so is usually a good choice for swimming. There's little wave action, except for the occasional north swells that ripple into the bay. Although the beach isn't as pretty as others, the 13-acre park has basketball and volleyball courts, an exercise area, a softball field and a large parking lot.

Kaiaka Bay Beach Park BEACH
(66-449 Hale'iwa Rd) Beachside trees a mile or so west of town offer shade, and turtles sometimes show up. But the swimming is better at the other local beaches, so look elsewhere if you're wanting to get wet.

Activities

If you're a beginner board rider, the North Shore has a few tame breaks such as **Pua'ena Point**, just north of Hale'iwa Beach Park, and **Chun's Reef**, north of town.

Hale'iwa

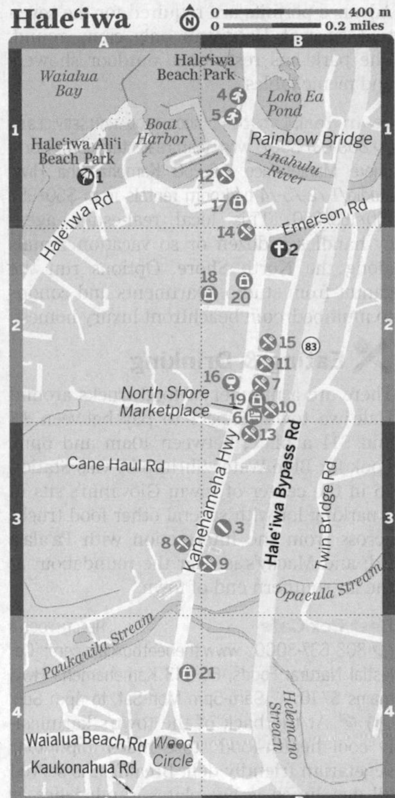

Hale'iwa

Sights

1 Hale'iwa Ali'i Beach Park A1
2 Lili'uokalani Protestant Church B2

Activities, Courses & Tours

3 Deep Ecology B3
4 Rainbow Watersports B1
5 Surf 'n' Sea B1

Sleeping

6 Team Real Estate B2

Eating

7 Banzai Sushi Bar B2
8 Beet Box Cafe A3
9 Cafe Haleiwa B3
10 Coffee Gallery B2
11 Grass Skirt Grill B2
12 Haleiwa Joe's B1
13 Kono's Restaurant B3
14 Matsumoto's Shave Ice B2
15 Waialua Bakery & Juice Bar B2

Drinking & Nightlife

16 Lanikai Juice B2

Shopping

17 Growing Keiki B1
18 Guava B2
19 Hale'iwa Art Gallery B2
20 Kai Ku Hale B2
21 Ukulele Site A4

Even if you've caught a few waves in Waikiki, it's smart to take a lesson with one of the many freelancing surfers to get an introduction to local underwater hazards. Ask around the beach, where surf school vans rent gear and offer same-day instruction, or book ahead for surf or SUP lessons. Expect to pay from $75 to $90 for two-hour group lessons, $100 to $180 for a private lesson and $30 to $45 to rent a board for the day ($60 with paddle).

Surf 'n' Sea WATER SPORTS
(808-637-9887; www.surfnsea.com; 62-595 Kamehameha Hwy; 9am-7pm) The big daddy of all surf shops, this colorful wooden building by the sea rents most any kind of water gear you can think of: surfboards, paddleboard setups, wetsuits, car racks, snorkel sets, kayaks, beach umbrellas and chairs... Lessons, tours and bicycle rental too.

Rainbow Watersports SUP
(808-372-9304; www.rainbowwatersports.com; by reservation only) The local SUP specialist offers calm-water classes, lessons for braving the waves and four-hour coastal paddle tours (from $189), with snorkeling and lunch included. Rentals available, too. These guys wrote the *Stand Up Paddle Book*.

North Shore Surf Girls SURFING
(808-637-2977; www.northshoresurfgirls.com; by reservation only) Some of the instructors here were featured in the movie *Blue Crush*, and they're all especially great teaching kids and other women to bodyboard, surf and stand up paddle. Packages include a sunset Hawaiian-BBQ surfing tour.

Sunset Surratt Surf Academy SURFING, SUP
(808-783-8657; www.surfnorthshore.com) 'Uncle Bryan,' born and raised on the North Shore, has been coaching pro surfers for decades. He and his staff teach all levels from beginner to advanced, and stand up paddlers. Rentals offered.

Deep Ecology DIVING
(☎808-637-7946; www.deepecologyhawaii.com; 66-456 Kamehameha Hwy; dives from $95) If you're keen to get under the waves, the folks here can help. Summer shore dives explore Shark's Cove and Three Tables, while offshore lava tubes, coral reefs, arches and cathedrals await boat divers. With a strong ecological bent, these divers are conscious about the ocean and create ecodive boat trips with that in mind. Summer snorkel trips and winter whale-watching cruises offered.

North Shore Shark Adventures ADVENTURE SPORTS
(☎808-228-5900; http://sharktourshawaii.com; Hale'iwa Small Boat Harbor; 2hr tour adult/child $120/60) Submerge in a cage surrounded by sharks about 3 miles offshore. Shark sightings guaranteed. Return transport for a fee from Waikiki.

Tours

The visitor center sells illustrated tour maps ($2) that describe all the old structures of town and can be followed at your own pace.

Historic Hale'iwa Tour WALKING TOUR
(☎808-637-4558; www.gonorthshore.org; 66-434 Kamehameha Hwy; tour $10; ⏲3pm Wed & 9:30am Sat) Reserve in advance for the 90-minute walking tours that take in the scattered historic buildings of town.

North Shore Ecotours HIKING
(☎877-521-4453; http://northshoreecotours.com; hiking tour adult/child $90/60, driving tour $65/45) Native Hawaiian guides lead three different, easy to difficult hikes on private land. All begin with a ride to the trailhead in a Swiss military off-road vehicle; taking a tour in the Pinzgauer is also possible.

Festivals & Events

Hale'iwa Arts Festival ART
(www.haleiwaartsfestival.org; ⏲Jul) More than 100 artists gather at Hale'iwa one weekend in July to sell their wares. Music, food, cultural tours and hands-on demonstrations are also scheduled.

Sleeping

Hale'iwa has no hotels, but there are a number of vacation rentals in the area.

Kaiaka Bay Beach Park CAMPGROUND $
(https://camping.honolulu.gov; 66-449 Hale'iwa Rd; 5-night campsite permit $52; ⏲8am Fri-8am Wed) Advance permits are required for the seven tent sites at Hale'iwa's only campground. The park has restrooms, outdoor showers and picnic tables.

Team Real Estate ACCOMMODATION SERVICES $$
(☎808-637-3507; www.teamrealestate.com; North Shore Marketplace, 66-250 Kamehameha Hwy; studio/1-/2-/3-/4-bedroom rentals from $60/95/150/165/250) This local real-estate agency handles a dozen or so vacation rentals along the North Shore. Options run the gamut from studio apartments and condos to multibedroom beachfront luxury homes.

Eating & Drinking

There are a number of food trucks around Hale'iwa town. Expect to pay between $8 and $14 a plate, between 10am and 6pm. Look for Blue Water Shrimp by Gas Station 76 in the center of town; Giovanni's sits in a parking lot with several other food trucks across from the intersection with Pa'ala'a Rd; and Macky's is near the roundabout at the far southern end of town.

Beet Box Cafe HEALTH FOOD $
(☎808-637-3000; www.thebeetboxcafe.com; Celestial Natural Foods, 66-443 Kamehameha Hwy; mains $7-10; ⏲9am-5pm Mon-Sat, to 4pm Sun; ✎) At the back of the town's karmically cool health-food store hides a popular vegetarian-friendly deli. Breakfast is served all day, lunch is hot plates, sandwiches or salads.

Waialua Bakery & Juice Bar BAKERY, DELI $
(☎808-341-2838; 66-200 Kamehameha Hwy; items $1-8; ⏲10am-5pm Mon-Sat; ✎) Many of the ingredients for the smoothies here come from the owners' farm in Waialua. Breads for the piled-high sandwiches, cookies and treats are all made from scratch.

Kono's Restaurant HAWAIIAN $
(☎808-637-9211; www.kaluapork.com; 66-250 Kamehameha Hwy; mains $6-12; ⏲7am-2.30pm Mon-Sat, 8am-3pm Sun) If you like pork, this is as good as it gets – legendary Kalua pork cooked daily for over 15 hours! The Triple Crown Sandwich ($15) features three kinds of pork, but we think the Pork Rice Bowl ($8.99) with Kalua pig, rice and guava BBQ sauce tops the selection.

Kono's is right on the main road. Look for the logo of a pig on a surfboard!

Hale'iwa Farmers Market MARKET $
(www.haleiwafarmersmarket.com; Waimea Valley, 59-864 Kamehameha Hwy; ⏲3-7pm Thu;) So much more than produce; here 40 vendors sell artisan crafts and organic, seasonal edibles. At the time of research, the market was being held at Waimea Valley, but intentions are to move back to Hale'iwa.

Coffee Gallery CAFE $
(☎808-637-5571; www.roastmaster.com; North Shore Marketplace, 66-250 Kamehameha Hwy; snacks & drinks $2-6; ⏲6:30am-8pm;) Coffee lovers rejoice over the house-roast beans and brews here.

Grass Skirt Grill HAWAIIAN $
(☎808-637-4852; 66-214 Kamehameha Hwy; mains $6-13; ⏲11am-6pm) Retro surf decor covers every square inch! The names of the island-style plate lunches seem familiar – teriyaki chicken, *ono* (a type of mackerel) burgers – but the results are way above average, using brown rice, local greens and homemade sauces. These are great takeout meals when you're beach-bound. Cash only.

Cafe Haleiwa BREAKFAST $$
(☎808-637-5516; 66-460 Kamehameha Hwy; mains breakfast & lunch $5-12, dinner $18-30; ⏲7am-2pm daily, plus 6-10pm Wed-Sat;) Locals have been fueling up at this laid-back surf-style diner since the 1980s. A daily menu of fresh preparations focuses on local ingredients and may feature mains such as lamb or mahimahi. Here even the side-dish vegetables are stars. Grab a bottle of wine from Bonzers Wine Shop next door.

Banzai Sushi Bar JAPANESE $$
(☎808-637-4404; http://banzaisushibarhawaii.com; 66-246 Kamehameha Hwy, North Shore Marketplace; mains $10-20; ⏲noon-9:30pm) It's all about the atmosphere at Banzai Sushi Bar. This open-air sushi bar has surf videos scrolling on the walls and live bands jamming on Saturday evenings. We like its mantra – keep it real, keep it raw.

Haleiwa Joe's SEAFOOD $$$
(☎808-637-8005; www.haleiwajoes.com; 66-011 Kamehameha Hwy; mains lunch $11-19, dinner $19-40; ⏲11:30am-9:30pm) With a superb location overlooking the marina, Joe's is the place for romantic dinners. Lunches are just so-so; we much prefer the inventive *pupu,* discounted at happy hour.

DON'T MISS

MATSUMOTO'S SHAVE ICE

Matsumoto's Shave Ice (☎808-637-4827; www.matsumotoshaveice.com; 66-087 Kamehameha Hwy; snacks $3-5; ⏲9am-6pm;) O'ahu's classic circle-island drive just isn't complete without stopping for shave ice at this legendary tin-roofed 1920s general store, locally known as Matsumoto's. Some families drive from Honolulu to the North Shore with one goal in mind: to stand in line here for a cone drenched with island flavors, such as *liliko'i*, banana, mango and pineapple.

Lanikai Juice HEALTH FOOD
(☎808-637-7774; www.lanikaijuice.com; 66-215 Kamehameha Hwy; snacks & drinks $4-8; ⏲8am-7pm) Kailua's favorite smoothie and fresh-juice bar has branched out. You can expect the same commitment to fresh ingredients and creative combos.

Shopping

From trendy to quirky, most of the North Shore's boutiques and galleries can be found in Hale'iwa. The central shopping hub is in the North Shore Marketplace in the center of town.

Hale'iwa Art Gallery ARTS, CRAFTS
(www.haleiwaartgallery.com; North Shore Marketplace, 66-250 Kamehameha Hwy; ⏲10am-6pm) Featuring works by 20-plus local and regional painters, photographers, sculptors, glass-blowers and mixed-media artists.

Guava CLOTHING
(www.guavahawaii.com; Hale'iwa Town Center, 66-165 Kamehameha Hwy; ⏲10am-6pm) A chic, upscale boutique for beachy women's apparel such as gauzy sundresses and strappy sandals.

Kai Ku Hale HOMEWARES, GIFTS
(http://kaikuhale.com; Hale'iwa Town Center, 66-145 Kamehameha Hwy; ⏲10am-7pm) Bring island style home with Hawaiian art, wood wall carvings, homewares and jewelry.

Growing Keiki CLOTHING, CHILDREN
(http://thegrowingkeiki.com; 66-051 Kamehameha Hwy; ⏲10am-6pm;) This kids' shop has gear for junior surf grommets and budding beach bunnies, including mini aloha shirts, trunks and toys.

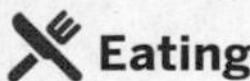

Ukulele Site MUSIC
(☎808-622-8000; www.theukulelesite.com; 66-560 Kamehameha Hwy; ⏲11am-6pm Mon-Sat, to 5pm Sun) The North Shore's top ukulele store, this place also has a top online site and ships all over the world. Head to the store to see and try out a mind-boggling array of ukuleles.

Getting There & Around

From Honolulu's Ala Moana Center, TheBus 52 runs to Hale'iwa via Wahiawa once or twice hourly; the one-way ride from Honolulu takes 1¾ hours. Every hour, TheBus 55 trundles from Hale'iwa up to Turtle Bay, then down the Windward Coast, taking over two hours to reach the Ala Moana Center.

Waialua

POP 3800

If you find the relatively slow pace of life on the North Shore just too hectic, head over to Waialua. This sugar-mill town ground to a halt in 1996, when production ended. Since then, creative locals have transformed the old mill into a crafty, island-born shopping complex.

Sights & Activities

Waialua Sugar Mill HISTORIC SITE
(www.sugarmillhawaii.com; 67-106 Kealohanui St; ⏲9am-5pm Mon-Sat, 10am-5pm Sun) The now-defunct sugar mill that was the genesis of the town in the 1900s has been redeveloped to house a number of shops and businesses. You can still see the old smoke stack and plenty of history. The rambling **Waialua Coffee – Island X Hawaii** warehouse is stuffed full of everything from vintage aloha shirts to wooden handicrafts and pieces of original art.

In addition to buying its Waialua-local, estate-grown coffee as beans or grounds, you can pick up a hot cup o' joe (or shave ice) from a little coffee stand in the corner.

The **North Shore Soap Factory** features sugar-mill history displays. While you're there, peek through the glass and watch the soap makers craft the all-natural bars they sell, made with local ingredients such as *kukui* (candlenut tree) nuts and coconut cream.

On Saturday and Wednesday mornings, the **Waialua Farmers Market** sets up in the sugar-mill parking lot. Surfboard-makers and craft vendors keep this market lively.

Eating

Pa'ala'a Kai Bakery BAKERY $
(☎808-637-9795; www.pkbsweets.com; 66-945 Kaukonahua Rd; snacks & pastries $2-4; ⏲5:30am-7pm) Take a detour down a country road to find this family-run bakery, a pilgrimage for anyone craving a 'snow puffy' (flaky chocolate cream puff dusted with powdered sugar) or hot *malasada*.

Scoop of Paradise Ice Cream Factory ICE CREAM $
(☎808-637-3020; www.facebook.com/scoopofparadisefactory; 66-935 Kaukonahua Rd; ⏲9am-6pm) Exquisite homemade ice cream, coffees, cakes and smoothies in an old building next to Pa'ala'a Kai Bakery. After careful research, we recommend the chocolate and macadamia-nut ice cream. It also has a shop in Haleiwa, but this is the factory.

Mokule'ia to Ka'ena Point

The further down the road you go, the fewer signs of habitation you'll see in this desolate corner of the island. Farrington Hwy finally dead ends into a rocky, undeveloped patch short of the island's edge.

Beaches

Mokule'ia Beach Park BEACH
(68-919 Farrington Hwy) The beach itself is a nice sandy stretch, but the rocky seabed makes for poor swimming. When waters are calm and flat in summer, snorkelers swim out along the shallow reef. Keen windsurfers often congregate on this stretch of shore, taking advantage of the consistent winds. The park has a large grassy area with picnic tables, restrooms and outdoor showers; but there aren't any lifeguards.

Army Beach BEACH
(Farrington Hwy) Opposite the western end of Dillingham Airfield, this is the widest stretch of sand on the Mokule'ia shore, although it's not maintained and there are no facilities. The beach also has very strong rip currents, especially during high winter surf. If the beach looks familiar, it might be because it appeared in the pilot of the hit TV drama *Lost*.

Ka'ena Point State Park BEACH
(www.hawaiistateparks.org; Farrington Hwy; ⏲sunrise-sunset) From Army Beach you can drive further down the road, passing still more white-sand beaches with aqua-blue

waters. The bit of sand off the pull-out just beyond the first Ka'ena State Park sign has a small rock-free swimming area accessible in calm surf. The large parking area is not only desolate but can also be a bit trashed. Car break-ins are commonplace.

Activities

Honolulu Soaring SCENIC FLIGHTS
(808-637-0207; www.honolulusoaring.com; Dillingham Airfield, Farrington Hwy; rides from $79; 10am-5:30pm) Plenty of great options. Take a scenic tour over the North Shore; go for an aerobatic thrill ride; or have a mini-lesson in a glider plane. Return transport from Waikiki to Dillingham Airfield costs $40.

Pacific Skydiving Center SKYDIVING
(808-637-7472; www.pacificskydivinghonolulu.com; Dillingham Airfield, 68-760 Farrington Hwy; tandem jumps from $139; 7.30am-2.30pm) Want to jump out of a perfectly good airplane? Tandem jumps attached to an instructor range from the relatively sedentary 10,000ft jump with 15 to 20 seconds of free fall right up to 'the Challenge', a monster jump from 24,000ft with over 100 seconds of free fall. Your budget may well choose your jump for you! Jumps include free Waikiki pickup.

Paradise Air GLIDING
(808-497-6033; www.paradiseairhawaii.com; Dillingham Airfield, Farrington Hwy (Hwy 930); flights from $175; by reservation only) Soar like a bird in an ultralight-powered hang glider called a trike, accompanied by an instructor who may even let you pilot.

Stearman Biplane Rides SCENIC FLIGHTS
(808-637-4461; www.stearmanbiplanerides.com; Hangar B6, Dillingham Airfield, Farrington Hwy; flights from $175; by reservation only) Loop-de-loop on an aerobatic flight, take a short scenic tour (20 minutes) or retrace the route the Japanese took to Pearl Harbor (40 minutes) – all in a restored 1941 Boeing biplane.

Ka'ena Point Trail MOUNTAIN BIKING, HIKING
(www.hawaiistateparks.org; sunrise-sunset) A mountain-bike-friendly hiking path leads from the end of Farrington Hwy along the remaining 2.5 miles out to Ka'ena Point. The terrain is scrubland reaching up to the base of the Wai'anae Range, while the shoreline is wild and windswept. December to May you may be able to spot whales from this area.

NOT LOST AFTER ALL

Does Army Beach look familiar? It appeared in the pilot of the hit TV drama *Lost*. When *Lost* first started filming here, tourists driving along the highway would see the smoking wreckage of a crashed plane sitting on the beach. Needless to say, a burned-out jetliner is an alarming sight, and many called 911 to mistakenly report an emergency.

We recommend doing the full hike from the other side of the point, on the Wai'anae Coast.

Kealia & Kuaokala Trails HIKING
(http://hawaiitrails.ehawaii.gov) Beyond the Gate D entrance above Dillingham Airfield, the 2.5-mile, one-way Kealia Trail switchbacks steeply up (1660ft elevation change) through exposed country with ocean views along the way. It connects to the 2.5-mile, one-way Kuaokala Trail (p171), which brings hikers to a justly celebrated ridge-top viewpoint over Makua Valley and the Wai'anae Range.

Note that access to Kuaokala Trail is physically easier from the Wai'anae Coast but requires an advance permit to approach via the Ka'ena Point Satellite Tracking Station. Both trails are open to mountain bikes. Print out a topo map if you go; allow six hours for both.

Hawaii Polo HORSEBACK RIDING
(808-220-5153; http://hawaii-polo.org; 68-539 Farrington Hwy; rides from $85; by reservation only) When the polo ponies aren't playing, you can take a ride around their 100-acre stomping grounds at the polo club. Sunset beach rides recommended. You can even take a polo lesson!

Sleeping

Anna Banana's Country Cottage COTTAGE $
(808-754-6461; www.vrbo.com/425288; per night $95) Want a secluded, quiet place to stay for two in Mokule'ia just back from the beach? Then Anna Banana's Country Cottage is the place to go. If there are more of you, opt for **Carly's Country Cottage** (www.vrbo.com/422422; per night $115) on the same site. There's a three-night minimum stay, but you may want to stay for weeks.

DON'T MISS

GREEN WORLD COFFEE FARM

A must for coffee nuts, **Green World Coffee Farm** (808-622-2326; http://greenworldcoffeefarm.com; 71-101 N Kamehameha Hwy; 6am-6pm Mon-Fri, 7am-6.30pm Sat & Sun) roasts all its coffee on-site with home-grown beans and beans bought from throughout the Hawaiian Islands. There is free sampling, free wi-fi and a great vibe in this roadside coffee extravaganza. It ships all over the world with a huge range of products including a huge variety of flavored coffee.

Camp Mokule'ia CAMPGROUND **$**

(808-637-6241; www.campmokuleia.com; 68-729 Farrington Hwy; campsites per person $18; office 8:30am-5pm Mon-Fri, 10am-5pm Sat) Looking for solace and solitude? This church-run seaside camp is open to travelers – by reservation only – as long as there isn't a prebooked group. Amenities are ultrabasic, with outdoor showers and chemical toilets. It also has well-worn lodge rooms, cabins and beach cottage.

CENTRAL O'AHU

Central O'ahu is the island's forgotten backwater. It's squeezed by enormous military bases: don't be surprised if you get passed on the highway by camo-painted Humvees or Black Hawk choppers buzzing overhead. A few highways head north to Wahiawa, the region's central town: the H-2 Fwy is the fastest option, while Kunia Rd (Hwy 750), the furthest west, is the most scenic.

Wahiawa

POP 18,000

Wahiawa itself isn't the sort of place that travelers seek out, unless you're looking for a military buzz cut, a tattoo or a pawn shop. Yet the land around town was considered sacred by ancient Hawaiians, who built temples, gave birth to royal chiefs and clashed in fierce battles here.

Sights

Dole Plantation THEME PARK

(808-621-8408; www.dole-plantation.com; 64-1550 Kamehameha Hwy; visitor center admission free, adult/child 4-12yr maze $6/4, train ride $8.50/6.50, walking tour $5/4.25; 9:30am-5.30pm;) Expect a sticky-sweet overdose of everything *ananas* (pineapples) when you walk into Dole Plantation's visitor-center gift shop. After you've watched fruit-cutting demonstrations and bought your fill of pineapple potato chips and fruity trinkets, take your pineapple ice-cream sundae outside for more pineapple educational fun.

The small ornamental garden showcasing different species – including pink pineapple – is free; to see more, you'll have to pay to take the Garden Tour. On the 20-minute Pineapple Express open-air train ride, you chug along through the upland scenery while more of Dole's story is narrated. The Pineapple Garden Maze is meant purely as fun, as you find (or lose) your way among 14,000 Hawaiian plants on 1.5 miles of pathways. If you're hungry after that, you can stop at the plantation's self-service grill restaurant, which is surprisingly well priced.

Wahiawa Botanical Gardens GARDENS

(808-522-7064; www.honolulu.gov/parks/hbg.html; 1396 California Ave; 9am-4pm, closed Dec 25 & Jan 1) FREE Started 80 years ago as an experiment by the local sugarcane farmers, the unstaffed 27-acre garden has evolved to showcase plants that thrive in a cool and moist climate. There's a mix of the manicured, with lawns and pruned ornamental plants, and the wild, with a gully of towering hardwoods, tropical ferns and forests of bamboo. Several paths, some wheelchair friendly, weave their way through the garden. It's located 1 mile east of Kamehameha Hwy (Hwy 99).

Eating

Maui Mike's BARBECUE, FAST FOOD **$**

(808-622-5900; http://mauimikes.com; 96 S Kamehameha Hwy; meals $6-9; 10:30am-8:30pm;) At Mike's you have the choice of chicken, chicken or chicken – all free range, fire roasted and superfresh. Even the Cajun-spiced fries are 100% natural and trans-fat free. There are a few tables inside, but most people grab and go.

Poke Stop SEAFOOD **$$**

(http://poke-stop.com; 95-1840 Meheula Pkwy, Mi'ilani; meals $8-14; 8am-8:30pm Mon-Sat, to 7pm Sun) This excellent fisherman-owned seafood outlet is 5 miles south of Wahiawa, off the H-2. Load up for a picnic of incredible *poke* or a gourmet plate lunch of blackened fish and garlic shrimp. You can also eat in.

LEEWARD O'AHU & WAI'ANAE COAST

O'ahu's lost coast is full of contradictions. There is a collective feeling of the forgotten here, with the wealthier citizens of Honolulu sweeping what they don't want in their backyard under the leeward rug.

In some ways the Wai'anae Coast is the heart and soul of O'ahu. You'll find more Native Hawaiians here than anyplace else on the island, and cultural pride is alive. The land may look parched, with mountains that almost push you into the sea, but the beaches are wide, and relatively untouched by development.

Beyond Ko Olina's luxury resorts, the stop-and-go Farrington Hwy (Hwy 93) runs the length of the Wai'anae Coast, rolling past working-class neighborhoods and strip malls on one side and gorgeous white-sand beaches on the other. Human habitation eventually gives way to velvet-tufted mountains and rocky coastal ledges near Ka'ena Point.

Kapolei Area

Times they are a-changin' in the southwestern corner of O'ahu, once the stomping ground of sugarcane plantations and the US navy. You'll still find a few run-down beach houses, but this is the fastest-growing residential area on the island today, with housing and super megamarts being built.

Beaches

'Ewa Beach Park BEACH

(91-050 Fort Weaver Rd) A huge grassy lawn and sizable pavilion attract large Hawaiian families to this pleasant western beachfront on weekends. There's always a spare table or two for a picnic, and a good view of Honolulu from the spit of sand.

Sights & Activities

Hawaii's Plantation Village MUSEUM

(☎808-677-0110; www.hawaiiplantationvillage.org; Waipahu Cultural Garden Park, 94-695 Waipahu St; 90min tours adult/child 4-11yr $13/5; ⊙tours on the hour 10am-2pm Mon-Sat) Waipahu was one of O'ahu's last plantation towns and this outdoor museum tells the story of life on the sugar plantations. Though the village is definitely showing its age, you can still learn plenty about the lives of plantation workers on the 90-minute tour.

It starts on the hour and takes in buildings typical of an early-20th-century plantation: a Chinese cookhouse, a Japanese shrine and replicated homes of the seven ethnic groups – Hawaiian, Japanese, Chinese, Korean, Portuguese, Puerto Rican and Filipino – that worked the fields. To get there by car from Honolulu, take the H-1 Fwy to exit 7, turn left onto Paiwa St, then right onto Waipahu St.

Hawaiian Railway HISTORIC SITE

(www.hawaiianrailway.com; 91-1001 Renton Rd, 'Ewa; adult/child $12/8; ⊙1pm & 3pm Sun) For half a century from 1890 to 1940 a railroad carried sugarcane and passengers from Honolulu all the way around the coast through to Kahuku. The railway closed and the tracks were torn up after WWII and the automobile boom in Hawaii. Thanks to the historical society, trains run again along a segment of restored track between 'Ewa and Kahe Point. The 90-minute round-trip chugs along through sometimes pastoral, sometimes industrial scenery, and past the Ko Olina resorts.

Displayed in the abandoned-looking yard is the coal engine that pulled the first O'ahu Railway and Land Company (OR&L) train in 1889. To get here, take exit 5A off the H-1, drive south 2.5 miles on Fort Weaver Rd and turn right at the 7-Eleven onto Renton Rd.

Wet 'n' Wild Hawaii AMUSEMENT PARK

(☎808-674-9283; www.wetnwildhawaii.com; 400 Farrington Hwy, Kapolei; adult/child $48/38; ⊙10:30am-3:30pm Mon, Thu & Fri, to 4pm Sat

TASTY TIDBITS

- In 1901 James Dole planted O'ahu's first pineapple patch in Wahiawa.
- Today, each acre of a pineapple field can support around 30,000 plants.
- The commercial pineapple variety grown in Hawaii is smooth cayenne.
- It takes nearly two years for a pineapple plant to reach maturity.
- Each plant produces just two pineapples, one in its second year and one in its third year.
- Pineapples are harvested year-round, but the long, sunny days of summer produce the sweetest fruit.
- Pineapples won't continue to ripen after they've been picked.

& Sun) Every temperament from timid to thrill-seeking is served at this 25-acre water park. Float on a lazy river or brave a seven-story waterslide and the football-field-sized wave pool with bodysurfable rides. Such splashy fun doesn't come cheap; some activities and parking ($10) are extra.

Bus 40 takes 1¼ hours to get here from the Ala Moana Center in Honolulu; it runs every half hour between 8:30am and 6:30pm.

Shopping

Waikele Premium Outlets SHOPPING CENTRE

(808-676-5656; www.premiumoutlets.com/waikele; 94-790 Lumiania Street, Waipahu; 9am-9pm) The mother lode in terms of outlet stores. Lots of big brands are here and the place is so popular that there is direct transport from Waikiki. Prepare to battle the shopper crowds for the deals.

Ko Olina

Don't have a beach? No problem. All it takes is a couple thousand tons of imported sand. When Kapolei's luxury resort was still on the drawing board, it lacked one key feature – a beach. In exchange for public beach access, investors were allowed to carve out four kidney-shaped lagoons from the coastline and line them with soft white sand. Disney's Aulani resort has made quite a splash here.

Beaches

Lagoons BEACH

(off Ali'inui Dr) A wide, paved recreational path connects all four lagoons, inviting a lazy stroll from beach to beach. Extremely limited free public beach-access parking can be found at each. The largest and most elaborately landscaped and serviced lagoon fronts the Four Seasons Resort and Disney Aulani.

Both resorts offer daytime beach-equipment rentals of snorkeling gear and such. The rocks that block the open sea from the lagoons are great places for spotting fish. Keep an eye on the kiddies, though – the current picks up near the opening. At dusk a Disney outrigger canoe enters the cove as a conch shell sounds the end to the day. The nearest free parking is north of the Ihilani. The hotels each charge $30 a day for valet parking but will validate if you spend at least an equivalent amount at one of their restaurants – easy to do.

The southern two lagoons are probably our favorite. Though they're smaller, the water and the sand are just as beautiful, and there are fewer people to contend with. The nearby free public parking is just before the marina at the end of the drive.

Activities

Ko Olina Marina FISHING, CRUISE

(808-853-4300; www.koolinamarina.com; 92-100 Waipahe Pl, Kapolei; cruises adult/child 2-13yr from $119/99) The marina will hook you up with snorkeling tours, sunset cruises, whale-watching (December through March) and sport-fishing charters. A five-hour boat tour ranges from $120 to $150 per person.

Ko Olina Golf Club GOLF

(808-676-5300; www.koolinagolf.com; 92-1220 Ali'inui Dr, Kapolei; green fees $139-199; by reservation only) Both the LPGA and the senior PGA tour have held tournaments at this highly acclaimed course and driving range. Mere golf mortals can also enjoy the landscaped oasis of green among the barren brown hills. Check online for special rates and packages; free transportation from Waikiki available.

Sleeping

Aulani RESORT $$$

(808-674-6200, reservations 714-520-7001; http://resorts.disney.go.com/aulani-hawaii-resort/; 92-1185 Ali'inui Dr, Kapolei; r from $450;) The daily activity list at Aulani is mind-boggling. Tone up at beach-body boot camp, take a Hawaiian craft class or hula the day away. All the while the little ones will be listening to Hawaiian tales at Aunty's House kids club and the older kids will be off on a treasure hunt or tasting a treat at the teen spa.

In the evening you can attend a free Hawaiian dance and music revue, or listen to Hawaiian music at a lounge, as the teens and tweens karaoke. That's not to mention the stingray interactive experience, character meet-and-greets, the water-park-like pools – and oh, yeah, the beach. Good thing there's so much to do. Maybe you won't notice that the Hawaii-inspired, casually luxe and characteristically understated (no giant Mickeys here) accommodations are a full 35 minutes from Honolulu – without traffic.

Four Seasons Resort Oahu at Ko Olina RESORT $$$

(www.fourseasons.com; 92-1001 Olani St, Kapolei;) Formerly the JW Marriott Ihilani

Resort, the newly renovated Four Seasons resort should be open by the time you read this. Right on the beach, it should be popular with those wanting to avoid the Waikiki scene, but still have all the trappings of top-end luxury. When it was the Ihilani, Hollywood even checked in here – the Ihilani starred in the surfer-girl movie *Blue Crush* as the hotel in which the girls worked.

Eating

Though both the Four Seasons and Aulani have dining outlets, don't expect cheap eats. There are a few more reasonable places in the **Ko Olina Station shopping center** (92-1047 Olani St).

★ Pizza Corner PIZZA $

(☎808-380-4626; http://pizzacornerhawaii.com; Ko Olina Station, 92-1047 Olani St; pizzas from $24; ⊙11am-9pm) These innovators are earning raves from locals for their new Hawaiian-style pizzas. We're talking about their Poke Pizza with spicy ahi and *lomilomi* chopped tomato and red onions on a thin-crust hand-tossed base, and the Kalua Pork pizza with mango salsa and chutney. There's takeout and they deliver to the Ko Olina resorts.

Kahe

If few nonislanders make it to southwest O'ahu, fewer still round the corner and follow the Farrington Hwy (Hwy 93) north up the Wai'anae Coast. Touring around here is best done by car and your first potential stop is Kahe. A hulking power plant complete with towering smoke stacks isn't the best neighbor for a beach – but, as they say, you can't pick your neighbors.

Beaches

Kahe Point Beach Park BEACH

(92-301 Farrington Hwy) At a rocky point that's popular with snorkelers and anglers. There are, however, great coastal views, as well as running water, picnic tables and restrooms.

Tracks Beach Park BEACH

(off Farrington Hwy) Just north of Kahe Point Beach Park and sometimes called Hawaiian Electric Beach, Tracks Beach Park has sandy shores that are good for swimming in the summer and great for surfing in the winter. Its name stems from the train-transported beachgoers who frequented the beach prior to WWII.

Nanakuli

It's hard to find much that qualifies as aesthetic in this seaside town that's essentially a strip of fast-food joints along the highway. There's so little opportunity to experience the culture, you probably won't even realize there's a Hawaiian Homesteads settlement here with one of the largest Native Hawaiian populations on O'ahu.

Beaches

Nanakuli Beach Park BEACH

(89-269 Farrington Hwy) This beach park lines the town in a broad, sandy stretch that offers swimming, snorkeling and diving during the summer. In winter, high surf can create rip currents and dangerous shorebreaks. The park has a playground, sports fields and beach facilities. To get to the beach park, turn *makai* at the traffic lights on Nanakuli Ave.

Ma'ili

There's not much to see in Ma'ili other than its enticing beach park.

Beaches

Ma'ili Beach Park BEACH

(87-021 Farrington Hwy) This attractive beach has the distinction of being one of the longest stretches of snow-white sand on the island. The grassy park that sits adjacent to the beach is popular with families having weekend barbecues and island-style parties. Like other places on the Wai'anae Coast, the water conditions are often treacherous in winter but usually calm enough for swimming in summer. The park has a lifeguard station, a playground, beach facilities and a few coconut palms that provide limited shade.

Sleeping

Ma'ili Cove CONDO

(☎808-696-4186; www.mailicove.org; 87-561 Farrington Hwy; 1-bedroom condos per week $675; 📶🏊) Walk out the patio door and right onto the beach if you stay at a one-bedroom Ma'ili Cove condo. The two condos for rent are clean, comfortable and eclectically decorated. There is a barbecue available for your use. One-week minimum stays.

Wai'anae

POP 13,500

A little rough around the edges, Wai'anae is this coast's hub for everyday services, with grocery stores, gas stations, a commercial boat harbor and a well-used beach park.

Beaches

Poka'i Bay Beach Park

BEACH

(85-037 Wai'anae Valley Rd;) Protected by Kane'ilio Point and a long breakwater, the beach is a real beauty. Waves seldom break inside the bay, and the sandy beach slopes gently. Calm, year-round swimming conditions make it perfect for children, as evidenced by the number of Hawaiian families here on weekends. The park has showers, restrooms and picnic tables, and a lifeguard is on duty daily.

Sights & Activities

Ku'ilioloa Heiau

TEMPLE

Along the south side of the bay, Kane'ilio Point is the site of a terraced-stone platform temple, partly destroyed by the army during WWII, then later reconstructed by local conservationists. The site was used in part as a teaching and blessing place for navigation and fishing. Wai'anae was one of the last places on the island to accept Christianity, and the heiau continued to be used after the kapu system was overthrown in 1819.

Today the area around the terraces still affords superb coastal views all the way to Makaha in the north. To get here, start at the parking lot of Poka'i Bay Beach Park, walk straight across the lawn with the outrigger canoes at your right and take the path half a mile out to the point.

Hawaii Nautical

BOAT TOUR

(808-234-7245; www.hawaiinautical.com; Waianae Harbor, 85-491 Farrington Hwy; tours adult/child $109/79) Set sail on a deluxe catamaran to look at marine life and go snorkeling on the southwest coast. You can either upgrade to snuba, or opt for a scuba-dive trip, but don't expect to be frolicking with Flipper; this is a Dolphin Smart–certified boat that cares about all of the ocean's inhabitants. There are shuttle rides available from both Ko Olina and Waikiki.

Wild Side Specialty Tours

WHALE-WATCHING, CRUISE

(808-306-7273; http://sailhawaii.com; Wai'anae Boat Harbor, 85-371 Farrington Hwy; tours from $175;) Recognized by the Hawaiian Ecotourism Association, Wild Side Tours caters to the naturalist in you. For respectful snorkeling, take a morning wildlife cruise and stay near the shore or go further to less-frequented sites with the Best of the West excursion for more dolphin and whale-watching.

Paradise Isle

WATER SPORTS

(808-695-8866; 84-1170 Farrington Hwy; rentals per day $15-50; 9am-5pm) Across from the beach, this island shop rents all things water-sport related: surfboards, SUP setups, kayaks, snorkels...plus it sells local crafts and dispenses free area information.

Hale Nalu Surf & Bike

WATER SPORTS, CYCLING

(808-696-5897; www.halenalu.com; 85-876 Farrington Hwy; 10am-5pm) This sports shop sells and rents mountain bikes, surfboards, snorkel sets and such.

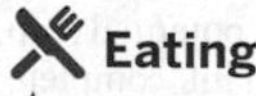

Eating

★Coquitos Latin Cuisine

LATIN AMERICAN $$

(808-888-4082; 85-773 Farrington Hwy; mains $8-18; 11am-9pm Tue-Sat, to 4pm Sun) Inside a breezy green plantation-style house that looks like it belongs in the Caribbean or Key West, this Puerto Rican kitchen has hooked

HOMELESS IN PARADISE

Living on the beach sounds like paradise, right? Estimates indicate that around 4500 homeless people live on O'ahu. There are shelters and temporary encampments all over the island, but it is thought that one-third of that number reside on the Wai'anae Coast. Locals say this is because there are fewer rich residents and tourists here, and there's a not-in-my-backyard mentality on other parts of the island.

The homeless issue is a complex one. While many believe that mainland states send their homeless to Hawaii with a one-way ticket, the fact is that most of the disenfranchised are local. The state has a long-term goal of ending homelessness in Hawaii by 2021, but to date, little new monies have been allocated for the project.

locals with its *mofongo* (mashed plantains with garlic and bacon), grilled Cuban sandwiches, shredded beef empanadas and tall *tres leches* (sponge cake) for dessert.

Kahumana Cafe HEALTH FOOD **$$**
(☎808-696-8844; www.kahumana.org; 86-660 Lualualei Homestead Rd; mains $10-15; ⏰11.30am-2pm & 6-8pm Tue-Sat; 🥗) 🌿 Way off the beaten track, this organic farm's cafe inhabits a cool, tranquil hardwood-floored dining room with green-field views. Fork into fresh daily specials, bountiful salads and sandwiches or macadamia-nut pesto pasta with fish or fowl. Don't forget the homemade *liliko'i* and mango cheesecake. The cafe is about 2 miles inland from Farrington Hwy via Ma'ili'ili Rd.

Makaha

POP 8300

Relatively free of tourists even today, this is where big-wave surfing got its start in the 1950s. Makaha means 'ferocious,' and long ago the valley was notorious for bandits who waited along the cliffs to ambush passing travelers, but the word could just as easily describe the stark, rugged landscape.

Sights

Kane'aki Heiau TEMPLE
(☎808-695-8174; end of Maunaolu St; ⏰call for hours) FREE Hidden within a gated residential community in Makaha Valley, this quietly impressive heiau is one of O'ahu's best-restored sacred sites. Originally an agricultural temple dedicated to Lono, the Hawaiian god of agriculture and fertility, the site was later used as a *luakini*.

Kamehameha the Great worshipped here and the temple remained in use until his death in 1819. Restorations by the Bishop Museum added two prayer towers, a kapu house, drum house, altar and *ki'i* (deity statues), while the heiau was reconstructed using traditional ohia tree logs and *pili*.

To get here, turn *mauka* off Farrington Hwy (Hwy 93) onto Makaha Valley Rd. Just over a mile later, follow Huipu Dr as it briefly curves left, then right. Turn right again onto Maunaolu St, which enters Mauna Olu Estates. Sign in at the security gatehouse (bring your driver's license and car-rental contract).

At the time of writing, public access was closed indefinitely due to vandalism. Call ahead to ask if the site has since reopened.

Beaches

Makaha Beach Park BEACH
(84-369 Farrington Hwy) This beautifully arching beach invites you to spread out your towel and spend the day. Except for weekends and big surf days, you'll likely have the place to yourself. Snorkeling is good during the calmer summer months. There are showers and restrooms, and lifeguards on duty daily. Winter brings big swells that preclude swimming.

In December 1969 legendary surfer Greg Noll rode what was thought to be the biggest wave in surfing history (to that point) at Makaha. Speculation still rages as to exactly how big the monster wave was, but it is commonly accepted that it was at least a 30ft face – a mountain of water for the era. The long point break at Makaha still produces waves that inspire big-wave surfers.

Turtle Beach BEACH
Another beautiful, mostly deserted half-mile of sand sits behind the Hawaiian Princess and Makaha Beach Cabana condos. If you're lucky, you may see green sea turtles in the surf early mornings or late evenings. There are sea caves and rocks they use as a cleaning station offshore. Though the area is protected somewhat by Lahilahi Point to the south, be cautious if you have kids – the beach's sandy bottom has a quick and steep drop-off.

Activities

Makaha Valley Riding Stables HORSEBACK RIDING
(☎808-779-8904; http://makahastables.com; 84-1042 Maunaolu St; rides from $50) 🌿 Saddle up at this historic ranch for a sunset trail ride with a BBQ dinner and s'mores by the fire pit, or an afternoon horseback ramble through the valley as you learn about Hawaiian culture, including traditional games and crafts. Advance reservations required.

Sleeping

Makaha has the majority of the vacation rentals available on the Wai'anae Coast; check out **VRBO** (www.vrbo.com), **Home Away** (www.homeaway.com), **Airbnb** (www.airbnb.com) and others. Beachside condos are the most popular (one bedrooms run from $100 to $200, two bedrooms from $250 to $350). You should be wary of house rentals as they could be in sketchier neighborhoods. Three-night minimums are usually required.

SOUL'S LEAP

Ancient Hawaiians believed that when people went into a deep sleep or lost consciousness, their souls would wander. Souls that wandered too far were drawn west to Ka'ena Point. If they were lucky, they were met here by their *'aumakua* (guardian spirit), who led their souls back to their bodies. If unattended, their souls would be forced to leap from Ka'ena Point into the endless night, never to return.

The four beachfront condo complexes are Makaha Shores, Makaha Cabanas, Makaha Surfside and Hawaiian Princess.

Affordable Oceanfront Condos ACCOMMODATION SERVICES $$
(www.hawaiibeachcondos.com) Rents condos at both Makaha Cabanas and Hawaiian Princess on Turtle Beach; 30-day bookings available at lower-lying Makaha Surfside.

Inga's Realty, Inc ACCOMMODATION SERVICES $$
(☎808-696-1616; www.ingasrealty.com; 85-910 Farrington Hwy, Wai'anae) Has vacation rentals at Makaha Shores, Makaha Beach Cabanas and at Ma'ili Cove further down the coast.

Eating

Basic places to eat are 3 miles south in Wai'anae. Drive on to Ko Olina (13 miles, 25 minutes) for fine dining.

Makaha to Ka'ena Point

As you travel north of Makaha, you leave development behind.

Sights

Kaneana Cave HISTORIC SITE
The waves that created this giant stone amphitheater receded long ago. Now the highway sits between the ocean and this cave, about 2 miles north of Kea'au Beach. *Kahuna* (priests) performed rituals inside the cave's inner chamber, which was the legendary abode of a vicious shark-man, a shapeshifter who lured human victims into the cave before devouring them. Hawaiians consider it a sacred place and won't enter the cave for fear that it's haunted by the spirits of deceased chiefs.

Makua Valley VALLEY
The scenic Makua Valley opens up wide and grassy, backed by a fan of sharply fluted mountains. It serves as the ammunition field of the Makua Military Reservation. The seaside road opposite the southern end of the reservation leads to a little graveyard that's shaded by yellow-flowered be-still trees. This site is all that remains of the valley community that was forced to evacuate during WWII when the US military took over the entire valley for war games.

After several ground fires, and lawsuits charging that not enough environmental-impact studies had been done, live-fire exercises were discontinued in 2011.

Ka'ena Point State Park

You don't have to be well versed in Hawaiian legends to know that something mystical occurs at this dramatic convergence of land and sea in the far northwestern corner of the island. Powerful ocean currents altered by O'ahu's landmass have been battling against each other for millennia here. The watery blows crash onto the long lava-bed fingers, sending frothy explosions skyward.

Running along both sides of the westernmost point of O'ahu, Ka'ena Point State Park is a completely undeveloped coastal strip with a few beaches. Until the mid-1940s the O'ahu Railway ran up here from Honolulu and continued around the point, carrying passengers on to Hale'iwa on the North Shore. Now the railbed serves as an excellent hiking trail.

Those giant white spheres that are perched on the hillsides above the park belong to the air force's Ka'ena Point Satellite Tracking Station.

Beaches

Makua Beach BEACH
Way back in the day, this beach was a canoe-landing site for interisland travelers. In the late '60s it was used as the backdrop for the movie *Hawaii*, which starred Julie Andrews. Today there is little here beyond a nice, gated stretch of sand and trees opposite the Makua Military Reservation.

Yokohama Bay BEACH
(www.hawaiistateparks.org; Farrington Hwy; ⏲sunrise-sunset) Some say this is the best sunset spot on the island. It certainly has the right

west-facing orientation and a blissfully scenic mile-long sandy beach. You'll find restrooms, showers and a lifeguard station at the park's southern end. Swimming is limited to the summer and then only when calm. When the water's flat, it's also possible to snorkel. The best spot with the easiest access is on the south side of the bay.

Winter brings huge, pounding waves, making Yokohama a popular seasonal surfing and bodysurfing spot that's best left to the experts because of submerged rocks, strong rips and a dangerous shorebreak.

Activities

Ka'ena Point Trail HIKING, MOUNTAIN BIKING

(www.hawaiistateparks.org; end of Farrington Hwy) An extremely windy, mostly level coastal trail runs along the old railbed for 2.5 miles from Yokohama Bay to Ka'ena Point, then continues another 2.5 miles around the point to the North Shore. Most hikers take the trail from the end of the paved road at Yokohama Bay as far as the point, then return the same way.

This hike offers fine views the entire way, with the ocean on one side and craggy cliffs on the other. Along the trail are tide pools, sea arches and blowholes that occasionally come to life on high surf days. In addition to native and migratory seabirds, you might spot Hawaiian monk seals hauled out on the rocks or the sand – but do not approach or otherwise disturb these endangered creatures.

The trail is extremely exposed and lacks any shade, so take sunscreen and plenty of water, and hike during the cooler parts of the day. Be cautious near the shoreline, as there are strong currents, and rogue waves can reach extreme heights.

Kuaokala Trail HIKING, MOUNTAIN BIKING

(https://hawaiitrails.ehawaii.gov; off Farrington Hwy) Hawaii's Division of Forestry & Wildlife issues advance permits for the hiking and mountain-biking trail system surrounding Ka'ena Point's satellite tracking station. From a dirt parking lot, the dusty 2.5-mile one-way Kuaokala Trail climbs a high ridge into Mokule'ia Forest Reserve. On a clear day you can see Mt Ka'ala (4025ft), O'ahu's highest peak.

Check in with your hiking permit at the station guardhouse opposite Yokohama Bay. Without a permit, the Kuaokala Trail can still be accessed via the Kealia Trail, starting from the North Shore's Dillingham Airfield.

Hawai'i, the Big Island

Includes ➜

Best Beaches

- ➜ Hapuna Beach (p230)
- ➜ Mau'umae Beach (p230)
- ➜ Waipi'o Valley (p259)
- ➜ Manini'owali Beach (p220)
- ➜ Makalawena Beach (p220)

Best Snorkeling

- ➜ Two-Step (p214)
- ➜ Mau'umae Beach (p230)
- ➜ Kapoho Tide Pools (p285)
- ➜ Hapuna Beach (p230)

Why Go?

If you're lucky enough, you might see lava pouring into the ocean next to black rock cliffs as the wind howls overhead on the Big Island. Remember the four classic elements: wind, water, earth and fire? It's rare to see all four occurring naturally at once but when they do, creation – of the island itself – quite literally takes place in front of your eyes.

And yet, the Big Island, which is as large as the other Hawaiian islands combined, isn't just where raw creation occurs. It's where the fruits of that process are presented in dizzying diversity. Eight of the world's 13 climate zones exist here, encompassing Martian-like lava deserts, emerald jungle, paradisaical valleys that front black-, white- and even green-sand beaches, snowcapped mountains, coral forests and an enchanting population of locals, hippies, transplants and more.

You can easily laze away your time, but the Big Island really shines for adventurers. Its beauty is astounding, and for a little effort you'll get enormous rewards.

When to Go

Kailua-Kona

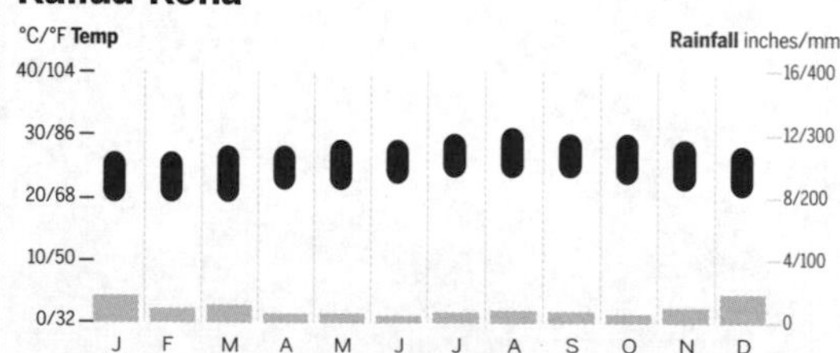

Jan Surf's up and summits are snowcapped during the Big Island 'winter.'

Late Mar–early Apr Catch the world's greatest hula at Hilo's Merrie Monarch Festival.

Oct Tenacious triathletes compete in the legendary swim-bike-run race born in Kailua-Kona.

History

The modern history of the Big Island is a tale of two cities – Kailua-Kona and Hilo – which represent the island's split personality: West Hawai'i and East Hawai'i. Kamehameha the Great, born in West Hawai'i, lived out the end of his life in Kailua, and throughout the 19th century Hawaiian royalty enjoyed the town as a leisure retreat, using Hulihe'e Palace as a crash pad.

Yet, during the same period, Hilo emerged as the more important commercial harbor. The Hamakua Coast railroad connected Hilo to the island's sugar plantations, and its thriving wharves became a hub for agricultural goods and immigrant workers. By the 20th century the city was the Big Island's economic and political center, and Hilo remains the official seat of island government.

On April 1, 1946 the Hamakua Coast was hit by an enormous tsunami, which crumpled the railroad and devastated coastal communities (such as Laupahoehoe). Hilo got the worst of it: its waterfront was completely destroyed and 96 people were killed. The city was rebuilt, but in 1960 it happened again: another deadly tsunami splintered the waterfront. This time Hilo did not rebuild, but left a quiet expanse of parks separating the downtown area from the bay.

After that the sugar industry steadily declined (sputtering out in the 1990s), and the Big Island's newest income source – tourism – focused quite naturally on the sun-drenched, sandy western shores where Hawaiian monarchs once gamboled. Since the 1970s, resorts and real-estate barons have jockeyed for position and profit along the leeward coast, turning West Hawai'i into the de facto seat of power.

Today, despite escalating home prices, the Big Island is considered the most affordable island to live on (and travel around), attracting young people from across the state; and it is diversifying its economy with small farm-based agriculture and renewable energy.

In 2014, Kilauea erupted, sending lava flows within a few hundred feet of the Pahoa village road in Puna. Some 50 homes were evacuated but, despite the destruction, many Puna residents objected to suggestions that the flow be diverted, arguing that Mother Pele's fire should move unimpeded.

National, State & County Parks

The Big Island's main attraction, Hawai'i Volcanoes National Park, is one of the USA's most interesting and varied national parks. More than a million visitors come annually to drive and hike this lava and rainforest wonderland.

The Big Island is also notable for its wealth of ancient Hawaiian sights, which are preserved in several national and state historical parks. The most famous is Pu'uhonua o

HAWAI'I, THE BIG ISLAND IN...

Two Days

If you arrive in **Kona**, spend your days leeward, starting with a swim at **Hapuna Beach**, a kayak and snorkel at **Two-Step** and a visit to ancient Hawai'i at Pu'uhonua o Honaunau. Save day two for exploring the galleries in **Holualoa**, followed by a **coffee-farm tour**.

If you arrive in **Hilo**, browse the **farmers markets** and explore **historic downtown** before visiting **'Imiloa Astronomy Center**. If the lava is flowing into the ocean, head to **Puna** at night to check it out. Then spend a day hiking **Hawai'i Volcanoes National Park**.

Four Days

If you've got double the time, double your fun by linking the leeward and windward itineraries with a twilight visit to **Mauna Kea** for sunset and stargazing, or a hike in **Waipi'o Valley**. En route you'll pass through **Waimea**, restaurant capital of the island: give casual **Pau** or powerhouse **Merriman's** a try.

One Week

To really make the most of the Big Island, you should give yourself a week. On top of our four-day itinerary, spend an extra day exploring **Kona Coast** beaches including **Kekaha Kai State Park** and **Kiholo Bay** before snorkeling or diving with manta rays at night. Bookend these experiences with a visit north to quaint **Hawi** and a hike in the **Pololu Valley**. Close out your adventures with a trip to **South Point** and **Green Sands Beach**.

Hawai'i, the Big Island Highlights

1. Gaze at stars from the summit of the world's tallest mountain, **Mauna Kea** (p251).
2. Explore black-sand nooks and crannies and chill with sea turtles at isolated **Kiholo Bay** (p222).
3. See how dramatic Eden can be in the rugged, emerald vistas of the **Waipi'o Valley** (p259).
4. Get happily lost amid magical coral gardens and multicolored reefs while snorkeling at **Two-Step** (p214).
5. Take in **Halema'uma'u Crater** (p294), the smoldering home of Pele, goddess of fire, at Hawai'i Volcanoes National Park.
6. Get in touch with the local side of Hawai'i while perusing the many museums of **Hilo** (p269).
7. Find hidden **Makalawena Beach** (p220), take pictures of its perfection, then make your friends envious.
8. Bodysurf till the waves pound you into submission at **White (Magic) Sands Beach** (p179).
9. Perform a surreal underwater dance with manta rays on a nighttime snorkeling trip off **Kailua-Kona** (p179).
10. Witness the raw power of creation on a lava-flow tour in **Puna** (p281).

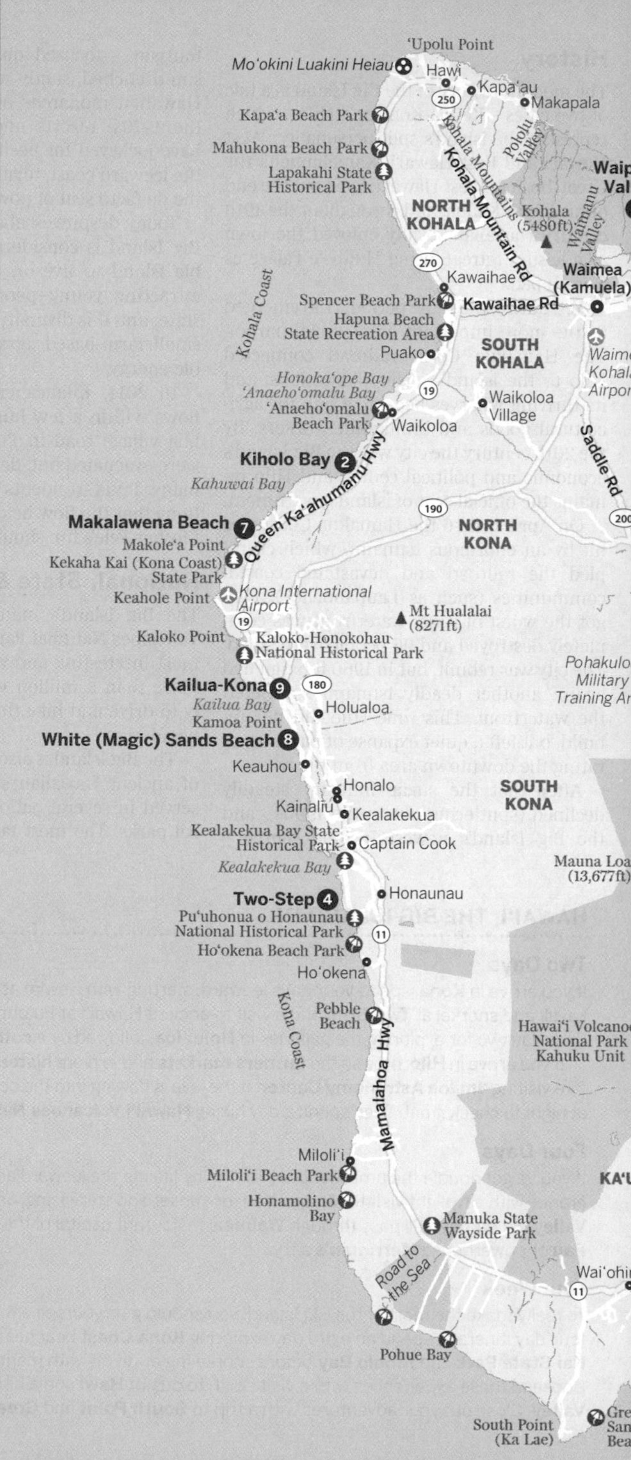

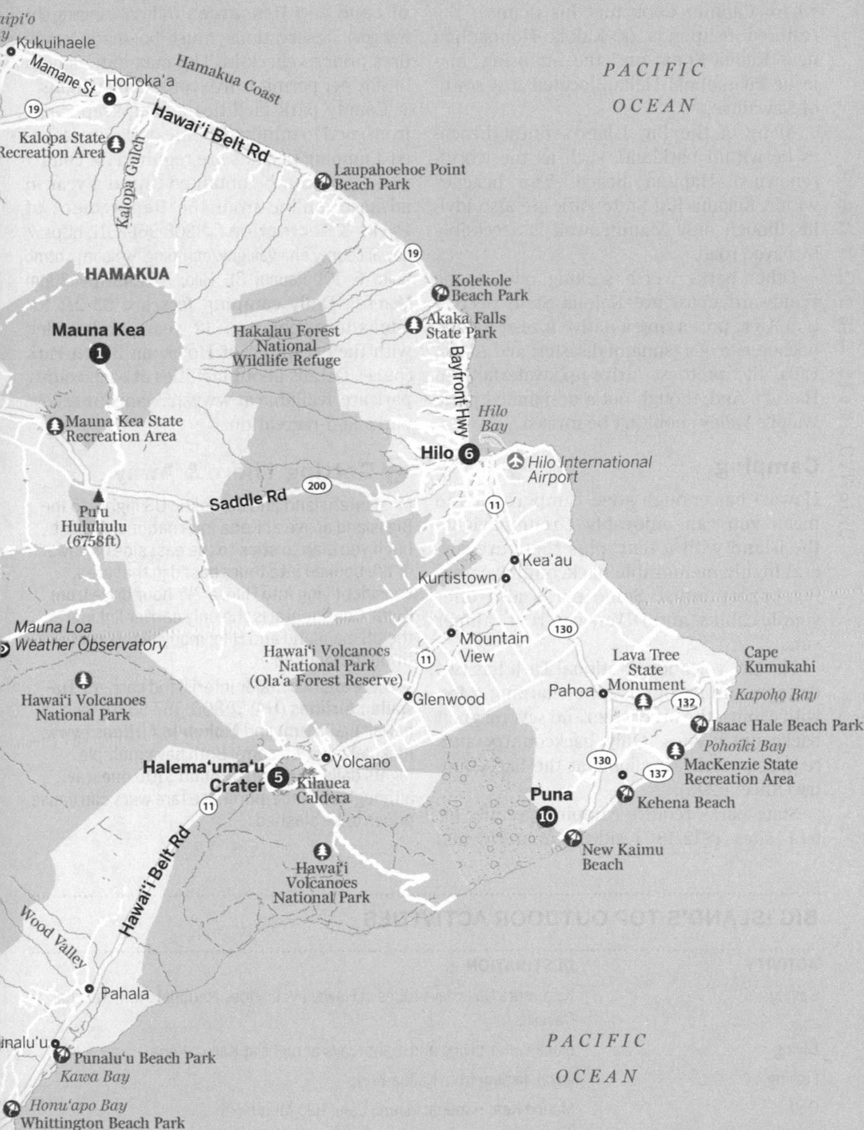

0 20 km
0 10 miles
PACIFIC OCEAN
Kukuihaele
Mamane St
Honoka'a
Hamakua Coast
Hawai'i Belt Rd
Kalopa State Recreation Area
Kalopa Gulch
Laupahoehoe Point Beach Park
HAMAKUA
Kolekole Beach Park
Akaka Falls State Park
Mauna Kea
1
Hakalau Forest National Wildlife Refuge
Bayfront Hwy
Mauna Kea State Recreation Area
Hilo Bay
Hilo
6
Hilo International Airport
Saddle Rd
200
Pu'u Huluhulu (6758ft)
11
Kea'au
Kurtistown
Mauna Loa Weather Observatory
Mountain View
130
Hawai'i Volcanoes National Park (Ola'a Forest Reserve)
Cape Kumukahi
Lava Tree State Monument
Pahoa
Hawai'i Volcanoes National Park
Glenwood
Kapoho Bay
132
Isaac Hale Beach Park
Pohoiki Bay
Halema'uma'u Crater
5
Volcano
Kilauea Caldera
MacKenzie State Recreation Area
137
Puna
10
Kehena Beach
Hawai'i Belt Rd
New Kaimu Beach
Hawai'i Volcanoes National Park
Wood Valley
Pahala
Punalu'u Beach Park
Kawa Bay
Honu'apo Bay
Whittington Beach Park
19
PACIFIC OCEAN

Honaunau, an ancient place of refuge in South Kona. But Native Hawaiian history and moody landscapes can also be found at remote Mo'okini Luakini Heiau in North Kohala; snorkeling mecca Kealakekua Bay, where Captain Cook met his demise; the restored fishponds of Kaloko-Honokohau near Kailua-Kona; and the imposing, majestic Pu'ukohola Heiau, located just south of Kawaihae.

Many of the Big Island's finest beaches lie within parkland, such as the world-renowned Hapuna Beach. The beaches within Kekaha Kai State Park are also idyllic, though only Manini'owali is accessible by paved road.

Other parks worth seeking out on the Windward Coast are Kalopa State Recreation Area, preserving a native forest; Laupahoehoe, site of a tsunami disaster; and Akaka Falls, the prettiest 'drive-up' waterfalls in Hawai'i. And, though not a designated park, Waipi'o Valley shouldn't be missed.

Camping

Hawai'i has enough good campgrounds to mean you can enjoyably circumnavigate the island with a tent, plus there are several highly memorable backcountry camping opportunities. Some parks also offer simple cabins, and DIYers can rent camper vans.

Hawai'i Volcanoes National Park has two drive-up campgrounds (one charging a fee, with cabins; the other free) and several great backcountry sites. Only backcountry sites require permits (available at the Backcountry Office; p296).

State parks require camping permits for tent sites ($12/18 residents/nonresidents) and cabins. The easiest way to make a reservation and obtain a permit for state-park cabins and campgrounds (plus those in Waimanu Valley) is via the online reservation system for the **State of Hawaii Department of Land and Resources** (https://camping.ehawaii.gov); reservations must be made seven days prior to check-in. The maximum length of stay per permit is five consecutive nights.

County park facilities and upkeep range from good to minimal. Some parks are isolated. Camping permits are required for county parks, and can be obtained (up to a year in advance) online from the **Department of Parks & Recreation** (808-961-8311; https://hawaiicounty.ehawaii.gov/camping/welcome.html; Suite 6, 101 Pauahi St, Hilo; 7:45am-4:30pm Mon-Fri). Daily camping fees are $5/2/1 for adults/teens/children 12 years and under, with the exception of Ho'okena Beach Park (p214). Details about facilities at each county park are available at www.hawaiicounty.gov/parks-and-recreation.

Getting There & Away

Most interisland and domestic US flights to the Big Island arrive at Kona International Airport, but if you plan to stick to the east side of Hawai'i or are booked into tours based in that area, consider flying into Hilo, a 2½-hour drive from Kona. Continental is the only carrier linking the US mainland and Hilo; many flights route through Honolulu.

There are two major interisland carriers: **Hawaiian Airlines** (HA; 800-367-5320; www.hawaiianair.com) and **Mokulele Airlines** (www.mokuleleairlines.com). Both have multiple flights daily. Fares are around $100 one way, although advance-purchase fare wars can cause prices to be slashed.

BIG ISLAND'S TOP OUTDOOR ACTIVITIES

ACTIVITY	DESTINATION
Caving	Kazumura Cave; lava tubes in Hawai'i Volcanoes National Park; Kula Kai Caverns
Diving	black-water diving and manta rays at night at Kailua-Kona
Fishing	kayak fishing from Kailua-Kona
Golf	Mauna Kea; Hapuna; Mauna Lani; Hilo Municipal
Hiking	Hawai'i Volcanoes National Park; Waipi'o Valley; Mauna Kea
Kayaking	Kealakekua Bay; Puako; Pebble Beach
Snorkeling	Kapoho Tide Pools; Kealakekua Bay; Two-Step
Stand-up paddleboarding	Kailua-Kona; Kahalu'u Beach
Ziplining	Hamakua Coast

Kona International Airport at Keahole (p194) is on Hwy 19, 7 miles north of Kailua-Kona.

Hilo International Airport (p280) is off Hwy 11, just under a mile south of the intersection of Hwys 11 and 19.

Getting Around

The Big Island is divided into six districts: Kona, Kohala, Waimea, Hilo, Puna and Ka'u. The Hawai'i Belt Rd circles the island, connecting the main towns and sights. It's possible but neither efficient nor convenient to get around by bus. If you really want to explore, you'll need a car.

The best foldout map is the *Hawaii Street Guide Big Island Manini Map*. The colorful *Franko's Hawai'i (Big Island) Guide Map* features water-sports info and is sold at dive shops. For longer visits, consider getting the Ready Mapbook series of encyclopedic books covering East and West Hawai'i.

TO/FROM THE AIRPORTS

Most visitors rent cars at the airport; car-hire booths for the major agencies line the road outside the arrivals area at both airports.

Shuttle-bus services typically cost as much as taxis. Speedi Shuttle (p195) will get you to destinations up and down the Kona Coast; it costs $31.90/124 for a shared/private shuttle to Kailua-Kona and $59.10/185.80 to the Mauna Lani resort area. Book in advance.

Taxis are curbside. The approximate fare from Hilo International Airport to downtown is $20. From Kona airport to Kailua-Kona it's $30, and to Waikoloa it's $55.

BICYCLE

Cycling around the Big Island as a primary form of transportation is easiest with the support of a tour. Though doable on one's own, it's a challenge, particularly if the weather doesn't cooperate. Kona – the hub for the famous Ironman

BIG ISLAND PARK CAMPGROUNDS

Apart from those specified as backcountry, all these campgrounds are drive-up.

PARK/CAMPSITE	FEATURES
Hawai'i Volcanoes National Park	
'Apua Point	backcountry; no water; shelter
Halape Shelter	backcountry; closes during drought; turtle nesting site
Ka'aha Shelter	backcountry; shelter
Keauhou Shelter	backcountry; shelter
Kulanaokuaiki Campground	pit toilets; no water; views
Namakanipaio Campground & Cabins	shelter; water; toilets; no showers
Napau Crater	backcountry; no water
State Parks	
Hapuna Beach State Recreation Area	cabins only
Kalopa State Recreation Area	full facilities; cabins
MacKenzie State Recreation Area	full facilities
Manuka Natural Area Reserve	full facilities
County Parks	
Ho'okena Beach Park	full facilities
Isaac Hale Beach Park	full facilities; surfing
Kapa'a Beach Park	full facilities
Kolekole Beach Park	full facilities; surfing
Laupahoehoe Point Beach Park	full facilities
Mahukona Beach Park	showers; toilets; no potable water
Miloli'i Beach Park	showers
Punalu'u Beach Park	full facilities; turtle nesting site
Spencer Beach Park	full facilities
Whittington Beach Park	no potable water

A DRIVER'S PARADISE

Not only a tropical paradise, the Big Island is also a driver's paradise. From the ocean to the top of Mauna Kea, and from the dry side to the wet, this is one enormous area with nicely paved roads, very few people on them, and staggering views all around. It is absolutely screaming for a convertible. So, without further ado, here are some of the island's greatest drives.

Saddle Road (Highway 200) Drive between the world's two highest peaks.

Kohala Mountain Road (Highway 250) An exhilarating trip down the spine of the Kohala Peninsula.

Old Mamalahoa Highway A winding journey through the backcountry of Ahualoa.

Kawaihae to Hawi (Highway 270) Ring the surreal, windswept hills of North Kohala.

Hamakua Coast (Highway 19) Twist and turn across deep tropical valleys plunging toward the ocean.

Hilina Pali Road Coast beneath a big sky through the volcanic wastes of Hawai'i Volcanoes National Park.

Ka'alaiki Road Only Ka'u locals know about this freshly paved jaunt amid green hills and distant sea.

Pohoiki and Kapoho Roads These adjacent Puna roads are like a jaunt into the Platonic ideal of jungle.

Napoopoo Road In South Kona, this road traverses the wet jungle mountain slope to the savannah bottomlands.

Triathlon – has good bike shops that sell and repair high-caliber equipment.

BUS

The islandwide Hele-On Bus (p223) will get you (most) places on the Big Island, but Sunday and holiday service is limited. Fares are $2 per ride, and a monthly pass is $60 (two rides per day for 20 days). Always check the website for current routes and schedules. Most buses originate from Mo'oheau terminal in Hilo.

You cannot board with a surfboard or bodyboard, and luggage, backpacks and bicycles are charged $1 apiece.

CAR & MOTORCYCLE

There are companies with car-hire booths at Kona and Hilo airports. Reserve well in advance for decent rates.

At the time of research, **Harper Car & Truck Rentals** (☎800-852-9993, 808-969-1478; www.harpershawaii.com) was the only outfit that let you drive 4WDs up Mauna Kea. Damage to a vehicle entails a high deductible, rates are generally steeper than at major agencies, and Harper is thorough about the condition of your ride when you return it.

To circumnavigate the island on the 225-mile Hawai'i Belt Rd (Hwys 19 and 11), you'll need at least five hours.

DESTINATION	DISTANCE (MILES)	TIME (HR)
From Hilo		
Hawai'i Volcanoes National Park	30	¾
Hawi	76	1¾
Honoka'a	41	1
Kailua-Kona	86	2
Na'alehu	66	1½
Pahoa	20	½
Waikoloa	72	1¾
Waimea	55	1¼
Waipi'o Lookout	50	1¼
From Kailua-Kona		
Hawai'i Volcanoes National Park	98	2¼
Hawi	53	1¼
Hilo	86	2
Honoka'a	53	1¼
Na'alehu	59	1½
Pahoa	102	2¼
Waikoloa	26	¾
Waimea	40	1
Waipi'o Lookout	63	1½

KAILUA-KONA & THE KONA COAST

Kailua-Kona

Kailua-Kona, also known as 'Kailua,' 'Kona Town' and sometimes just 'Town,' is a love-it-or-leave-it kind of place. On the main drag of Ali'i Dr, along the shoreline, Kailua works hard to evoke the nonchalance of a sun-drenched tropical getaway, but in an injection-molded, bargain-priced way.

But we like it. Spend enough time here and you'll scratch past the souvenirs to an oddball identity built from a collision of two seemingly at-odds forces: mainlanders who want to wind down to Hawaiian time, and ambitious Big Islanders who want to make it in one of the few local towns worthy of the title. Somehow, this marriage works. Kailua-Kona can be tacky, but it's got character.

Additional pros: it's an easy place to book tours, what nightlife exists on the Big Island is here and the waterfront can be attractive in the right light (ie sunset). Cons: many restaurants are overrated, traffic can be a pain and there's no sense of residential civic pride like you get in Hilo.

At the end of the day, Kailua has the most hotels and condos, the most tourists, the most souvenirs per square foot and is the most likely place on the island to have businesses open on Sunday. It's a convenient base from which to enjoy the Kona Coast's beaches, snorkeling, water sports and ancient Hawaiian sites, so you'll likely spend at least a day here.

Beaches

Kailua-Kona might act like a beach town, but most of its in-town beaches don't rank among the Kona Coast's showstoppers.

★White (Magic) Sands Beach BEACH
(La'aloa Beach Park; Ali'i Dr; P) This small but gorgeous beach (also called La'aloa Beach) has turquoise water, great sunsets, little shade and possibly the best bodysurfing and bodyboarding on the Big Island. Waves are consistent and just powerful enough to shoot you across the water into a sandy bay (beware: the north side of the bay has more rocks). During high winter surf the beach can vanish literally overnight, earning the nickname 'Magic Sands.' The park is about 4 miles south of central Kailua-Kona.

When the rocks and coral located past the disapearing sands are exposed, the beach becomes too treacherous for most swimmers. Gradually the sand returns, transforming the shore back into its former beachy self. Facilities include restrooms, showers, picnic tables and a volleyball court; a lifeguard is on duty.

White Sands is almost always packed but there's little proprietary attitude from locals.

Old Kona Airport State Recreation Area BEACH
(www.hawaiistateparks.org; Kuakini Hwy; ⏲7am-8pm; P 👪) Visitors often overlook this quiet park, located a mile from downtown. The swimming isn't great but it's a grand spot for a picnic. The beach area is studded with lava rock and tide pools, the latter occasionally occupied by napping sea turtles. Jogging and fishing are the main activities, but scuba divers and confident snorkelers can make for Garden Eel Cove, a short walk from the north end of the beach. To get here, follow Kuakini Hwy to its end.

Just inside the southern entrance gate is one tidal pool large and sandy enough to be the perfect *keiki* (child) pool. When the surf's up, local surfers flock to an offshore break here.

Facilities include restrooms, showers and covered picnic tables on a lawn dotted with beach heliotrope and short coconut palms. Oh, and you know what makes getting to the beach better? Barreling down an unused airport runway. There's still a tarmac at Old Airport Park, which was the area's airport until it was deemed too small.

Kamakahonu Beach BEACH
(👪) Kailua-Kona's only swimmable in-town beach is this teeny-tiny strand between Kailua Pier and Ahu'ena Heiau, where ocean waters are calm and usually safe for kids. Concession stands rent all kinds of beach gear.

Sights

Ali'i Dr bombards you with surf shops and ABC Stores, but amid the tourist kitsch is a handful of historic buildings and landmarks worth seeking out.

Hulihe'e Palace HISTORIC BUILDING
(☎808-329-1877; www.huliheepalace.net; 75-5718 Ali'i Dr; adult/child $8/1; ⏲9am-4pm Mon-Sat) 🍃 This palace is a fascinating study in the rapid shift the Hawaiian royal family made from Polynesian god-kings to Westernized monarchs. Here's the skinny: Hawai'i's second

Kailua-Kona

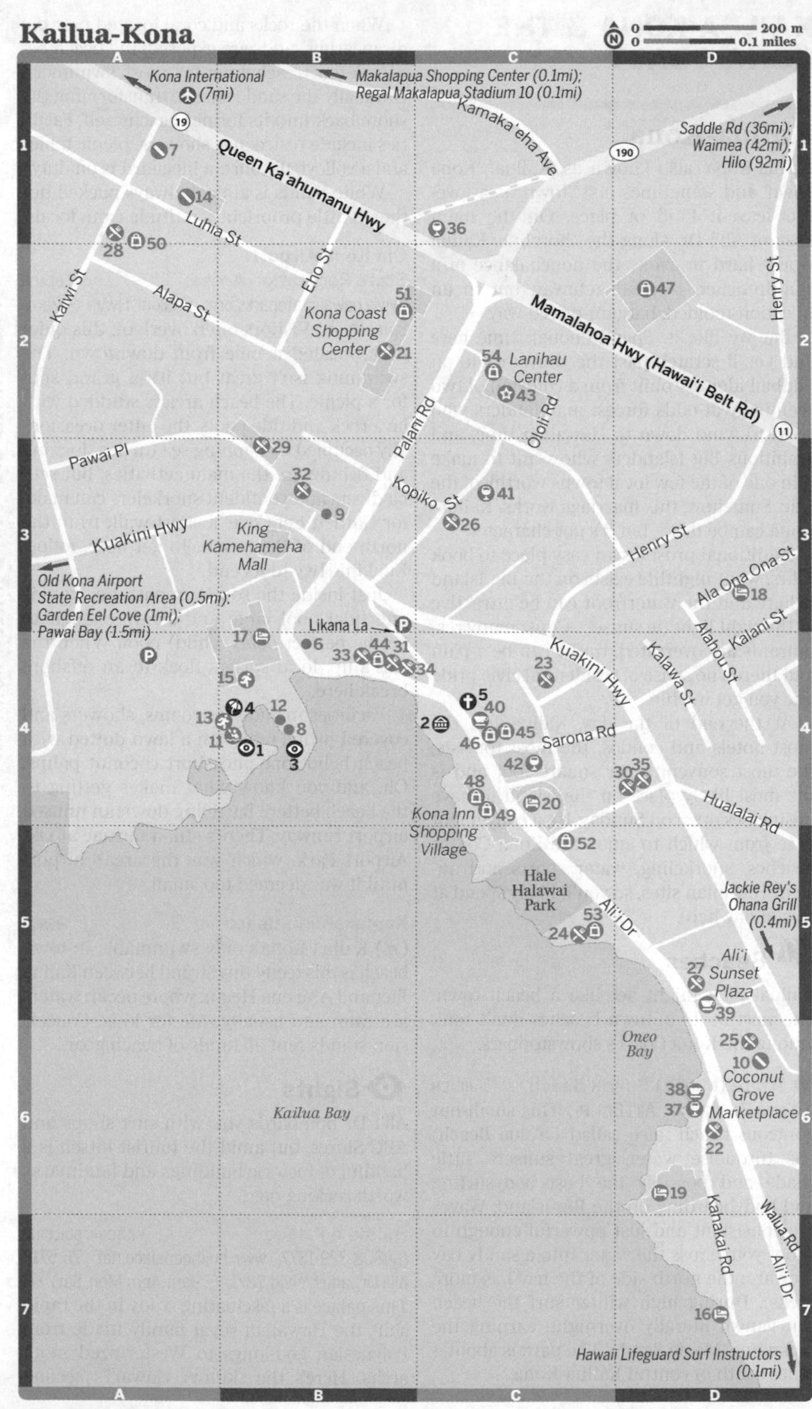

0 200 m
0 0.1 miles
Kona International (7mi)
Makalapua Shopping Center (0.1mi); Regal Makalapua Stadium 10 (0.1mi)
Saddle Rd (36mi); Waimea (42mi); Hilo (92mi)
Queen Ka'ahumanu Hwy
Kamaka'eha Ave
Luhia St
Alapa St
Kaiwi St
Eho St
Kona Coast Shopping Center
Mamalahoa Hwy (Hawai'i Belt Rd)
Henry St
Lanihau Center
Palani Rd
Ololi Rd
Pawai Pl
Kopiko St
Kuakini Hwy
King Kamehameha Mall
Old Kona Airport State Recreation Area (0.5mi); Garden Eel Cove (1mi); Pawai Bay (1.5mi)
Likana La
Ala Ona Ona St
Alahou St
Kalani St
Kalawa St
Sarona Rd
Hualalai Rd
Kona Inn Shopping Village
Hale Halawai Park
Ali'i Dr
Jackie Rey's Ohana Grill (0.4mi)
Ali'i Sunset Plaza
Oneo Bay
Coconut Grove Marketplace
Kailua Bay
Kahakai Rd
Walua Rd
Hawaii Lifeguard Surf Instructors (0.1mi)

Kailua-Kona

Sights
1 Ahu'ena Heiau B4
2 Hulihe'e Palace C4
3 Kailua Pier B4
4 Kamakahonu Beach B4
5 Moku'aikaua Church C4

Activities, Courses & Tours
6 Atlantis Submarines B4
7 Big Island Divers A1
8 Blue Sea Cruises B4
9 Body Glove Hawaii B3
10 Jack's Diving Locker D6
11 Kai 'Opua Canoe Club B4
12 Kailua Bay Charter Company B4
Kona Boys Beach Shack .... (see 13)
13 Kona Boys Beach Shack B4
Kona Brewing Company .... (see 29)
14 Kona Honu Divers A1
Lotus Center .... (see 19)
Snorkel Bob's .... (see 22)
15 UFO Parasailing B4

Sleeping
16 Hale Kona Kai D7
17 King Kamehameha's Kona Beach Hotel B4
18 Koa Wood Hale Inn/Patey's Place D3
19 Royal Kona Resort D6
20 Uncle Billy's Kona Bay Hotel C4

Eating
21 Ba-Le Kona B2
22 Basik Acai D6
23 Big Island Grill C4
24 Daylight Mind C5
25 Evolution Bakery & Cafe D6
26 Hayama C3
27 Island Lava Java D5
28 Island Naturals Market & Deli A1
29 Kona Brewing Company B3
KTA Super Store .... (see 21)
30 Lemongrass Bistro D4
31 Metal Mike's Twisted Pretzels B4
32 Original Thai B3
33 Rapanui Island Cafe B4
34 Scandinavian Shave Ice B4
35 Umeke D4

Drinking & Nightlife
36 Dolphin Spit Saloon C1
Don's Mai Tai Bar .... (see 19)
37 Huggo's on the Rocks D6
Humpy's Big Island Alehouse .... (see 10)
38 Java on the Rock D6
39 Kanaka Kava D5
40 Kope Lani C4
41 Mask-Querade Bar C3
42 Sam's Hideaway C4

Entertainment
Island Breeze Lu'au .... (see 17)
43 KBXtreme C2
Lava Legends & Legacies – Journeys of the South Pacific .... (see 19)

Shopping
44 Big Island Jewelers B4
45 Conscious Riddims Records C4
46 Crazy Shirts C4
47 Crossroads Shopping Center D2
48 Honolua Surf Co C4
49 J. Lambus Photography C4
50 Kona Bay Books A1
51 Kona Coast Shopping Center B2
52 Kona Farmers Market C5
53 Kona Oceanfront Gallery C5
54 Lanihau Center C2

governor, 'John Adams' Kuakini, built a simple two-story, lava-rock house as his private residence in 1838. After Kuakini's death, the house became the favorite vacation getaway for Hawaiian royalty. The palace contains Western antiques collected on royal jaunts to Europe and ancient Hawaiian artifacts, most notably several of Kamehameha the Great's war spears.

Hard times befell the monarchy in the early 20th century, and the house was sold and the furnishings and artifacts auctioned off by Prince Kuhio. Luckily his wife and other royalty numbered each piece and recorded the names of bidders.

In 1925 the Territory of Hawaii purchased the house to be a museum run by the Daughters of Hawai'i, a women's group dedicated to the preservation of Hawaiian culture and language. This group tracked down the furnishings and royal memorabilia, such as a table inlaid with 25 kinds of native woods, several of Kamehameha the Great's war spears and the (surprisingly small) bed of 6ft, 440lb Princess Ke'elikolani.

You'll learn these and other stories on 40-minute guided tours ($2 extra charged on adult tickets only) given by Daughters of Hawai'i docents. The free concert series, held at 4pm on the third Sunday of each month, is a treat, with Hawaiian music and hula performed on the grass facing sparkling Kailua Bay.

Ahu'ena Heiau TEMPLE
(75-5660 Palani Rd) FREE After uniting the Hawaiian Islands in 1810, Kamehameha the Great established the kingdom's royal court in Lahaina on Maui, but he continued to return to the Big Island. After a couple of years, he restored this sacred site as his personal retreat and temple. Notice the towering carved *ki'i* (deity image) with a golden plover atop its helmet: these long-distance flying birds may have helped guide the first Polynesians to Hawaii.

When Kamehameha I died at Ahu'ena Heiau on May 8, 1819, his body was prepared for burial here. In keeping with ancient Hawaiian tradition, the king's bones were secreted elsewhere, hidden so securely no one has ever found them (though some theorists point to a cave near Kaloko Fishpond).

Step inside **King Kamehameha's Kona Beach Hotel** nearby to view historical paintings and a mural by legendary artist and Hawaiian historian Herb Kawainui Kane. Also on display are a rare feathered helmet and cloak once worn by *ali'i* (royalty), ancient Hawaiian war weapons and musical instruments, and a whale's-tooth pendant strung on a braided cord made of human hair.

Moku'aikaua Church CHURCH
(☎808-329-0655; www.mokuaikaua.org; 75-5713 Ali'i Dr; ⏲7:30am-5:30pm) FREE Completed in 1836, this church is a handsome building with walls of lava rock held together by sand and coral-lime mortar. The posts and beams, hewn with stone adzes and smoothed with chunks of coral, are made from ohia, and the pews and pulpit are made of koa, the most prized native hardwood. The steeple tops out at 112ft, making this the tallest structure in Kailua. Contemporary services are held at 9am on Sundays, with traditional services at 11am.

Often referred to as 'the big stone church on Ali'i,' Moku'aikaua is the gestation point of Hawaiian Christianity. On April 4, 1820, the first Christian missionaries to the Hawaiian Islands sailed into Kailua Bay. When they landed they were unaware that Hawai'i's kapu (taboo) system had been abolished on that very spot just a few months before.

The church is popular for weddings, and inside is a dusty model of the missionaries' ship, *Thaddeus,* and a history of their arrival.

Kailua Pier LANDMARK
Kailua Bay was once a major cattle-shipping area, where animals were stampeded into the water and forced to swim to steamers waiting to transport them to Honolulu slaughterhouses. Now locals come to swim at lunchtime and canoe clubs launch their vessels. The Hawaiian International Billfish Tournament (p187) kicks off here, continuing a sportfishing tradition begun in 1915, when the pier was built.

Kona Cloud Forest Sanctuary FOREST
(www.konacloudforest.com) Above 3000ft on the slopes of Mt Hualalai, the Kaloko Mauka subdivision is the home of this spectacular 70-acre sanctuary. It's not just any forest – a cloud forest is a moist woodland where mist and fog are constants. The sanctuary is a lush haven for native plants and birds, and thanks to a consistent carpet of ropy gray-green fog, it always feels as mysterious as it is beautiful.

It also contains demonstration gardens of non-native species, including more than 100 varieties of bamboo, which local experts study for their viability for use. Sustainable-agriculture types and horticulturists won't want to miss a visit to this well-kept Kona secret most locals don't even know about.

Hawaiian Walkways (p186) leads a daily morning tour to the sanctuary, including a stop at adjacent Mountain Thunder Coffee.

Activities

Several activity outfitters and tour companies are based at Keauhou, about 5 miles south of Kailua-Kona.

Swimming

With rocky shores and rough waters, Kailua-Kona isn't ideal for swimming – for that head to North Kona Coast beaches. Still, Kahalu'u Beach Park (p196), 5 miles south, is a good bet when conditions are calm, as is Old Kona Airport State Recreation Area (p179), especially with kids in tow.

Bodyboarding, Surfing, Stand-Up Paddling & Parasailing

White (Magic) Sands Beach (p179) is a favorite spot for bodyboarding and bodysurfing. Local experts surf at Banyans, north of White Sands, and Pine Trees (p220), south of the airport near Wawaloli (OTEC) Beach. Newbies can surf at Lymans, south of Banyans.

It's hard to explain the appeal of stand-up paddling (SUP) to someone who's completely new to the concept. Initially the sport con-

OFF THE BEATEN TRACK

THREE RING RANCH

Dr Ann Goody is as close to a real life Dr Doolittle as you'll ever be lucky to meet. She doesn't just talk to the animals, she also fixes their broken bones and psyches. When she can, she then sets them free, but if they can't cut it in the wild they become residents of this sanctuary on five lovely acres in upland Kona.

Visiting **Three Ring Ranch Exotic Animal Sanctuary** (☎808-331-8778; www.threeringranch.org; 75-809 Keaolani Dr, Kailua-Kona; suggested donation $35; ⏲tours 11am-1pm, by reservation) is one of the most fascinating animal encounters you can experience...well, anywhere.

Licensed by the US Department of Agriculture and accredited by the American Association of Sanctuaries, Three Ring currently hosts South African crowned cranes, lesser flamingos, giant tortoises and much more, including native endangered species such as the Hawaiian owl.

Dr Goody – who, incredibly, has been struck by lightning, tossed by a shark and is a breast-cancer survivor – is as good with people as she is with animals. This has led to enormously successful educational initiatives, including an after-school program, a resident-intern program and a residency placement program for pre-veterinarian students. Since the sanctuary's primary commitment is to the animals and their welfare, it leads two-hour tours by prior arrangement only; booking via email preferred. See the website for details.

sisted of people standing balanced on surfboards, paddling them about. This might appear to make surfing slower and paddling more difficult but, in fact, it's a sweet blend of intense exercise, aquatic adventure and marine-biology lesson. SUP delivers a core workout accompanied by dolphins, turtles, tropical fish and very meditative, Zen-like paddling techniques.

It's the perfect way to slow down and drink up the mana (spiritual essence) of the Big Island, although, be warned, your first day on a board may be less about relaxing and more about tumbling into the drink. Give it a spin in Kailua Bay or Kahalu'u Bay.

Kona Boys Beach Shack SUP

(☎808-329-2345; www.konaboys.com; Kamakahonu Beach; surfboard/SUP rental from $29, SUP lesson & tours per person group/private $99/150; ⏲8am-5pm; 🐾) Organizes SUP lessons for beginners as well as more ambitious coastal paddling tours, and rents SUP sets and surfboards right on the beach. Call in advance to arrange group or private surfing or SUP lessons. You can also book through the shop in Kealakekua (p205).

Hawaii Lifeguard Surf Instructors SURFING, SUP

(HLSI; ☎808-324-0442; www.surflessonshawaii.com; 75-5909 Ali'i Dr; group/private lessons from $75/110; ⏲8am-5pm) Skilled, professional HLSI instructors have a minimum of 15 years surfing experience and are all certified lifeguards. Join a group surfing or SUP lesson, or book a private one-on-one session (which is the only way that kids aged three to 10 years are taught at this school). Offers lessons in Japanese. Call in advance to book.

Kona Surf Adventures SURFING

(☎808-334-0033; www.konasurfadventures.com; 75-6129 Ali'i Dr, Ali'i Gardens Marketplace; surfing lesson $99-150) This surf school is run by California-born 'Kona Mike,' who comes with endorsements from novice students and veteran wave riders alike.

FBI Surf School SURFING

(☎808-557-7089; www.fbisurfschool.com; 74-4966 Mamalahoa Hwy; group/semiprivate/private lesson per person $99/125/165) While the name implies you'll be hitting the waves with Mulder and Scully while wearing a trenchcoat, FBI actually stands for 'From Big Island.' This friendly outfit is run by Ossian (Ocean), a big surf dude who's a beloved local instructor. While FBI's office is in Holulaloa, lessons are done on Ali'i Drive or Kaloko-Honokohau National Historical Park (p218). Call in advance to book.

UFO Parasailing PARASAILING

(☎800-359-4836; www.ufoparasail.net; 75-5660 Palani Rd, Suite 111; flights from $75) Harness the wind and the water and parasail your way through paradise via trips with UFO, which operates out of the King Kamehameha hotel. You can opt for single or tandem 'flights.'

Snorkeling

For easy-access snorkeling, Kahalu'u Beach Park (p196), 5 miles south in Keauhou, is your closest and best option. To snorkel further afield, take a cruise from Honokohau Harbor or Keauhou Pier. Opt to depart in the morning, when conditions are calmer and clearer. Tour prices typically include snorkel gear, beverages and snacks; book ahead online for discounts.

Zodiac rafts are zippy and thrilling, capable of exploring sea caves, lava tubes and blowholes, but expect a bumpy ride and no shade or toilets. Catamarans are much larger, smoother and comfier but can't get as close into coves. Alternatively, many dive boats let snorkelers ride along at a cheaper rate.

Sea Paradise SNORKELING
(☎800-322-5662; www.seaparadise.com; 78-6831 Ali'i Dr; snorkel cruise adult/child 5-12yr from $72/42) Highly recommended outfitter offering morning snorkel cruises to Kealakekua Bay and nighttime manta-ray trips (free rebooking if you don't spot any the first time out) on a smaller 46ft-long catamaran with a friendly, professional crew.

Fair Wind SNORKELING, DIVING
(☎800-677-9461, 808-322-2788; www.fair-wind.com; 78-7130 Kaleiopapa St; snorkel cruise adult/child 4-12yr from $75/45) The *Fair Wind II,* a two-story catamaran with two 15ft-long waterslides, sails to Kealakekua Bay every morning. Longer daytime cruises on the luxury hydrofoil catamaran *Hula Kai* explore less-trafficked waters ($149), while nighttime manta-ray snorkel cruises are hugely popular ($105; minimum seven years old), so book ahead.

Captain Zodiac SNORKELING, WHALE-WATCHING
(☎808-329-3199; www.captainzodiac.com; 74-425 Kealakehe Pkwy, Honokohau Harbor; snorkel cruise adult/child 4-12yr from $99/78) In business with a jaunty pirate theme since 1974, Captain Zodiac makes daily trips down the coast in 24ft-long rigid-hull inflatable rafts that each carry up to 16 passengers.

Kamanu Charters SNORKELING
(☎800-348-3091, 808-329-2021; www.kamanu.com; 74-381 Kealakehe Pkwy, Honokohau Harbor; adult/child under 13yr $95/50) Snorkel without crowds in the protected waters of Pawai Bay, just north of Old Kona Airport State Recreation Area. This 36ft catamaran maxes out at 24 people. Kamanu also offers a nighttime manta-ray snorkel, but skip the dolphin swim – state law prohibits swimmers from getting closer then 150yd to these wild creatures to avoid disturbing them.

Snorkel Bob's SNORKELING
(☎800-262-7725, 808-329-0770; www.snorkelbob.com; 75-5831 Kahakai Rd; ⊙8am-5pm) Enthusiastic, friendly staff rent snorkel masks (including corrective lenses for near-sighted folks), fins, reef walkers, wetsuits and flotation aids. They're pretty lenient about returning gear after hours, which is a plus.

Sea Quest SNORKELING
(☎808-329-7238; www.seaquesthawaii.com; 78-7106 Kamehameha III Rd; 2-snorkel cruise adult/child $99/83; ⊙7am-9pm) Sea Quest has rigid-hull inflatable rafts that take up to six or 14 passengers. On offer are one- and two-stop snorkel adventures that take in much of the South Kona Coast.

Diving

The Kona Coast is known for calm, clear waters, unique lava formations and coral reefs. Near shore, divers can see steep drop-offs with lava tubes, caves and diverse marine life. In deeper waters there are dozens of popular boat-dive areas, including an airplane wreck off Keahole Point.

Most dive boats launch from Honokohau Harbor but have bricks-and-mortar offices in Kailua-Kona. Including all gear, the cost of a standard two-tank morning dive or one-tank night dive to see manta rays ranges from $110 to $150. Multiday PADI Open Water certification programs cost around $500 or more.

★ **Jack's Diving Locker** DIVING, SNORKELING
(☎808-329-7585; www.jacksdivinglocker.com; 75-5813 Ali'i Dr, Coconut Grove Marketplace, Bldg H; ⊙8am-8pm Mon-Sat, to 6pm Sun) With top-notch introductory dives and courses, plus extensive programs for kids, this eco-conscious dive outfitter has a 5000-sq-ft facility with a store, classrooms, tank room and Hawaii's only 12ft-deep indoor dive pool. Sign up for a boat or shore dive, as well as a night manta-ray dive. Snorkelers are welcome on many dive-boat trips.

Sandwich Isle Divers DIVING
(☎888-743-3483, 808-329-9188; www.sandwichisledivers.com) This small charter dive-boat outfit run by a husband-and-wife team organizes personalized trips (six-person maximum). These folks have decades of ex-

perience in Kona waters, Captain Steve has a marine-biology degree, and the pair are particularly wonderful with new divers. Contact them for boat and launch location.

Big Island Divers DIVING, SNORKELING
(808-329-6068; www.bigislanddivers.com; 74-5467 Kaiwi St; 8am-6pm) Personable staff, an expansive shop and boat dives that are open to snorkelers all score big. This outfit specializes in night and manta-ray dives. Black-water boat trips ($150, or $24 if you combine with a manta-ray excursion) are for experienced divers only.

Kona Honu Divers DIVING, SNORKELING
(888-333-4668, 808-324-4668; www.konahonudivers.com; 74-5583 Luhia St; 7:30am-5:30pm) Dive company with a good reputation that schedules diverse boat trips, including manta-ray night dives and Nitrox trips.

Fishing

Kailua-Kona is legendary for its big-game fishing, especially Pacific blue marlin (June to August are the best months), which can grow into 1-ton 'granders.' It's also home to ahi (yellowfin tuna), aku (bonito or skipjack tuna), swordfish, spearfish and mahimahi (white-fleshed fish also called 'dolphin'). Most of the world records for catches of these fish belong to Kona fishers.

On average, charter boats run around $550/725/875 for a four-/six-/eight-hour excursion, not including tax. That cost is for the whole boat and can be split among individuals. Ask whether the captain shares the catch.

Agencies book for so many boats that it's impossible to guarantee quality or consistency, but **Charter Desk** (888-566-2487, 808-326-1800; www.charterdesk.com; Honokohau Marina; 6am-6pm) is reputable and can match you with 60 boats.

BLACK-WATER MAGIC

For many, a night snorkel or dive with Pacific manta rays is the capstone experience to their time in Hawaii. The ocean at night is spooky enough, but to see these graceful, gentle creatures with 8ft to 14ft wing spans glide out of the darkness and spin cartwheels as they feed is unforgettable. There are two main dive locations: the original site in front of the Sheraton Keauhou Bay Resort and a more northerly site near Garden Eel Cove. If you snorkel, you'll likely be put in the water with a floating metal ladder-rig that you'll hang onto as mantas whir beneath you. A powerful light is attached to the ladder-rigs, which attracts a buffet of plankton and, subsequently, mantas.

While clutching the rig you may feel a little like someone is holding your hand, but it is illegal in the state of Hawaii to touch manta rays, and the floating ladders are a good preventative tool that guards against accidental contact. Some kayak outfits lead night manta dives that do not include the floating ladder rigs. While it is possible to enter the water on your own from an access point near the Sheraton, we do not recommend trying to do so. The currents in this area are unpredictable, the nearby rocks are sharp and the waves can become powerful in the blink of an eye; throw in the cover of night and you're asking for trouble.

Most manta night dives are two-tank dives exploring one mediocre site during sunset before heading to the manta grounds. Operators tend to offer manta dive and snorkel excursions; the former run around $150 (not including gear), the latter around $100 (mask and fins included). Check the Manta Pacific Research Foundation website (www.mantapacific.org) for manta-sighting data and guidelines for responsible manta-watching.

If you *really* want a nighttime underwater adventure, try a black-water dive. Sound ominous and creepy? It kind of is, but it's also surreal and beautiful. You'll be boated to a site offshore where you dive into the cold black waters of the open ocean. At night, the strange, bioluminescent animals of the deep rise to the surface, creating a glow-in-the-dark rave of alien underwater life feeding all around you. Occasionally much larger, strange beasts, such as 900lb bug-eyed marlin, will dart past your astonished eyes. Trust us when we say black-water dives are one of the most fascinating experiences available in Hawaii. They don't take just anyone on these excursions; Jack's Diving Locker (p184), which runs an excellent Pelagic Magic black-water excursion, requires night divers to have a previous night dive under their belt, as well as 10 logged dives, including one within the last year.

Outrigger Canoeing & Kayaking

To see how outrigger canoeing pros do it, check out the January-to-May race schedule of the **Hawaii Island Paddlesports Association** (http://hipa.squarespace.com). Over Labor Day weekend in late August and/or early September, don't miss the **Queen Lili'uokalani Canoe Race** (www.kaiopua.org) from Kailua Bay south to Honaunau.

Kona Boys Beach Shack CANOEING, KAYAKING
(808-329-2345; www.konaboys.com; Kamakahonu Beach; kayak tours $120-170, rentals per hour/day from $19/54; 8am-5pm) Experience what the original Polynesian settlers must have felt with the water rushing under their hull as they approached the volcanic shores of the Big Island. Paddle an outrigger canoe around Kamakahonu Bay or all the way from Keauhou to snorkel in Kealakekua Bay. Sea-kayaking tours often stop to snorkel too.

Kai 'Opua Canoe Club CANOEING
(www.kaiopua.org; Kamakahonu Beach) This local club is dedicated to traditional Hawaiian outrigger canoeing; visitors are welcome to join recreational paddling excursions leaving at 6am every morning except Sunday. There is no club office, so check its website or Facebook page for schedules and contact details. Trips launch next to Ahu'ena Heiau.

Ocean Safaris SNORKELING, KAYAKING
(808-326-4699; www.oceansafariskayaks.com; 78-7128 Kaleiopapa Rd; night snorkeling with mantas per person $55; 8am-5pm) Based in Keauhou, just south of Kailua-Kona, this place conducts kayak tours of local sea caves and can take you out on a nighttime manta-ray trip.

Whale-Watching

Although snorkeling, diving and fishing tours often give you whale-watching opportunities during humpback season (December to April), you're more likely to see, and learn, more on specialized tours.

Dan McSweeney's Whale Watch WHALE-WATCHING
(808-322-0028, 888-942-5376; www.ilovewhales.com; Honokohau Harbor; 2½hr cruise adult/child under 12yr $110/99; 7am-10am & 11am-2pm Mon, Tue, Thu & Fri;) Captain McSweeney's winter excursions focus on humpback-whale sightings, marine conservation and education. Several other species of whales and dolphins can be seen in Kona waters year-round. Hydrophones allow passengers to listen in on whale songs.

Tours

Body Glove Hawaii CRUISE
(808-326-7122, www.bodyglovehawaii.com; 75-5629 Kuakini Hwy; adult/child 6-17yr historical cruise incl dinner $115/83, incl lunch $88/68; 8am, 9am, 1pm & 4pm;) These popular historical cruises along the Kona Coast last three hours and feature a so-so buffet, live music and engaging historical narration. Also offers snorkeling excursions (adult/child $128/78). The crew show off some genuine aloha, and the boat is wheelchair accessible.

Kona Brewing Company TOUR
(808-334-2739; http://konabrewingco.com; 74-5612 Pawai Place; 30min tours 10:30am & 3pm) FREE Since 1994, this eco-conscious company has anchored Hawai'i's microbrewery scene. The once-small, family-run operation is now one of the nation's fastest-growing microbreweries – from Maine to California, you can sip 'liquid aloha.' Complimentary tours include tasting samples. No reservations accepted; sign up in person at the pub.

Hawaiian Walkways WALKING TOUR
(808-322-2255; www.hawaiianwalkways.com; tours $129-190) Leads a number of walking tours, including trips to Hawai'i Volcanoes National Park (p289), the Pololu Valley (p243) and through the upland Kona Cloud Forest Sanctuary (p182). Guides are knowledgeable about botany and geology. All tours for children from seven to 11 years are $99. Wear sturdy shoes. Will pick you up from your hotel.

Kailua Bay Charter Company CRUISE
(808-324-1749; www.konaglassbottomboat.com; Kailua-Kona Pier; 50min tour adult/child under 12yr $40/20; usually 10:30am, 11:30am & 12:30pm;) Gain a new perspective on Kailua-Kona's coastline, its underwater reef and sea life from a 36ft glass-bottomed boat with a cheery crew and onboard naturalist. Easy boarding available for passengers with mobility issues.

Blue Sea Cruises CRUISE
(808-331-8875; 75-5660 Palani Rd; dinner cruise adult/child $110/84; 8:30am-6pm;) If you want to add a little fine dining – well, OK, decent buffet dinner – to a glass-bottom-boat excursion, consider a trip with Blue Sea. Along with sunset dinner cruises, it also offers a nighttime manta snorkel or, if you don't want to get wet, a manta cruise (both adult/child $90/67).

Atlantis Submarines BOAT TOUR
(808-329-3175; www.atlantisadventures.com; 75-5669 Ali'i Dr; adult/child under 13yr $109/45; 10am daily;) You read that right: a real-deal submarine descends up to 100ft into a coral-reef crevice and explores nearby shipwrecks. The battery-powered sub has 26 portholes and carries 48 passengers. Children must be at least 36in tall.

Festivals & Events

★ **Kokua Kailua** ART, FOOD
(http://historickailuavillage.com; 1pm-sunset, 3rd Sunday of month;) Local food vendors, artists and craftspeople set up booths along Ali'i Dr, which closes to vehicular traffic. Free Hawaiian music and hula dancing at Hulihe'e Palace start at around 4pm.

Kona Brewers Festival BEER, FOOD
(www.konabrewersfestival.com) On the second Saturday in March, Kona Brewing Company throws its annual beer bash, with proceeds benefiting local charities. Sample dozens of craft beers and island chefs' gourmet *grinds* (local food). Buy tickets in advance online.

Hawaiian International Billfish Tournament FISHING
(www.hibtfishing.com) Hawaii's most prestigious sportfishing contest encompasses five days of fishing followed by weigh-ins and festivities at Kailua Pier. The tournament starts in late July or early August.

Ironman Triathlon World Championship SPORTS
(www.ironman.com; Oct) On the second Saturday in October, all traffic on Ali'i Dr halts for this human-powered endurance test that starts and finishes at Kailua Pier.

★ **Kona Coffee Cultural Festival** COFFEE
(www.konacoffeefest.com;) For 10 days in early November during the harvest season, the community celebrates Kona coffee pioneers and their renowned beans. Dozens of events include a cupping competition, art shows, live music and hula performances, farm tours, coffee tastings, a recipe cook-off and a coffee-cherry-picking contest.

Sleeping

The quality of hotels and condos in walkable downtown Kailua-Kona is fair to middling. Many condos and vacation rentals are either along or near Ali'i Dr heading toward Keauhou, the beachy resort area just south of Kailua-Kona, or several miles upland on the cool slopes of Mt Hualalai.

Wherever you stay, remember that oceanfront in Kona doesn't necessarily mean a sandy beach, because there's little sand along the rocky shoreline. Make reservations, especially during high season. Booking online in advance usually nets you the biggest savings.

Koa Wood Hale Inn/Patey's Place HOSTEL $
(808-329-9663; 75-184 Ala Ona Ona St; dm/r with shared bath from $25/55; reception 8am-noon & 5-10pm; @) Kailua-Kona's only

IRONMAN TRIATHLON WORLD CHAMPIONSHIP

When thousands of athletes and fans swoop into Kailua-Kona each October, locals gripe about traffic and crowds. But nobody can deny the thrilling spectacle of the Ironman Triathlon World Championship. The granddaddy of triathlons is a brutal combination of a 2.4-mile ocean swim, 112-mile bike race and 26.2-mile run. And it has to be done in under 17 hours. Australian Craig Alexander set the current course record at eight hours, three minutes and 56 seconds in 2011.

Harsh conditions make the event the ultimate endurance test. Heat bouncing off the lava commonly exceeds 100°F (38°C), making dehydration and heat exhaustion major challenges. Many contenders arrive on the island weeks before to acclimatize. On race day, the world's toughest athletes are pushed to the max – in the past, they've included a 75-year-old nun, an Iraq war veteran amputee, and father-son Team Hoyt, with Rick pushing son Dick in a wheelchair (they're six-time finishers).

Begun in 1978 by a US Navy man on a dare, the Ironman was labeled 'lunatic' by *Sports Illustrated*. Only 15 people competed the first year, and three didn't even cross the finish line. With that kind of crazy drama, the sports world was hooked. Today the event draws up to 2000 athletes from more than 50 countries, everyone seeking the rights to 'Brag for the rest of your life!'.

hostel is a backpacker crash pad, with fan-cooled dorms and private rooms, a common kitchen and the usual crowd of backpackers, misfits and the globally road-weary. As with many hostels, it's as enjoyable as the crowd that is staying there. It's on a residential street within walking distance of Ali'i Dr. No drugs, alcohol or shoes indoors.

★**Kona Tiki Hotel** HOTEL $$
(808-329-1425; www.konatikihotel.com; 75-5968 Ali'i Dr; r $85-159; P) You can find affordable oceanfront views at this retro three-story hotel, a quirky, well-kept complex south of downtown Kailua-Kona. The motel-style rooms are forgettably basic (no TVs, phones or air-con), but all have a fridge and enchanting lanai. Book well ahead, because the hotel regularly fills with nostalgic repeat guests. No credit cards.

Nancy's Hideaway B&B $$
(866-325-3132, 808-325-3132; www.nancyshideaway.com; 73-1530 Uanani Pl; studio/cottage incl breakfast $130/150;) At this lush peaceful retreat, 6 miles upslope from town, take your pick of a freestanding studio or a one-bedroom cottage, each contemporary in design, with its own kitchenette and jungly garden surroundings (plus some curious cats). The views to the ocean are stupendous. No children under 13 years allowed.

Bear's Place Guest House GUESTHOUSE $$
(808-990-1383; www.bearsplacekona.com; 72-1071 Puukala Rd; s/d from $95/105) Located north of town, up the slope from the airport, Bear's Place is a cool upland retreat with good-value apartments that get plenty of light, a breezy lanai for enjoying coffee, and a gorgeous view to the big blue ocean. The owners are fantastically helpful and hospitable (and speak German, for what it's worth).

Hale Kona Kai APARTMENT $$
(808-329-6402; www.halekonakai-hkk.com; 75-5870 Kahakai Rd; apt $190-215; P) All condos overlook crashing surf at this well-managed, oceanfront complex off the busy commercial stretch of Ali'i Dr. The one-bedroom units vary in style, but each has a separate living room, full kitchen and ocean-view lanai. Poolside wi-fi only. Minimum-night stay varies, and prices drop in the low season.

Casa de Emdeko APARTMENT $$
(808-329-2160; www.casadeemdeko.org; 75-6082 Ali'i Dr; apt from $100; P) With Spanish-tile roofs, white stucco, immaculate gardens and two pools, this enormous condo complex south of downtown Kailua-Kona is stylish and restful. The individually owned units are mostly up to date, peacefully quiet and reasonably priced.

Mango Sunset B&B B&B $$
(808-325-0909; www.mangosunset.com; 73-4261 Mamalahoa Hwy; r with private/shared bath $130/115; P@) Hawaiiana-bedecked teak furnishings and bamboo accents spruce up the snug accommodations on this family-owned organic coffee farm. The best rooms offer sweeping ocean views from a shared lanai, and there's a common kitchenette. It's about a 15-minute drive from downtown

VACATION RENTALS

Condos tend to be cheaper than hotels for longer stays, and offer more independence for DIY types and families. Condo vacation rentals are handled directly by owners or property-management agencies. Check listings for condos and vacation rentals on the following websites:

Affordable Paradise (808-261-1693; www.affordable-paradise.com)

Airbnb (www.airbnb.com)

HomeAway (www.homeaway.com)

Kona Hawaii Vacation Rentals (808-329-3333; www.konahawaii.com)

Kona Rentals (800-799-5662; www.konarentals.com)

Knutson & Associates (808-329-6311; www.konahawaiirentals.com)

Luxury Retreats Hawaii (877-993-0100; www.fabulous-homes.com)

SunQuest Vacations (from Canada 800-367-5168, from USA 808-329-6438; www.sunquest-hawaii.com)

Vacation Rentals by Owner (www.vrbo.com)

Kailua-Kona, closer to the airport. Breakfast included.

Kona Hawaii Guest House GUESTHOUSE **$$**
(808-557-1420; www.konahawaiiguesthouse.com; 77-362 Paulina Place; r from $113) This cozy house, on a quiet cul-de-sac, could be a good base for exploring the west coast of the Big Island. We say 'base' because minimum stays are usually a week. Rooms are fine, with silly-if-cute jungle and seaside themes, and the owners organize yoga retreats and New Age healing sessions, complete with drum circle and couples massage.

Honu Kai B&B B&B **$$**
(808-292-1775, 808-329-8676; www.honukaibnb.com; 74-1529 Hao Kuni St; d incl breakfast $220-255; P @) Amid tropical gardens, this plush, romantic four-room B&B is filled with rich fabrics, carved bedframes and Asian and Hawaiian decor. Guests share a hot tub, outdoor kitchen and rooftop lanai. Enclosed by rock walls, the private gated property is a 10-minute drive from downtown Kailua-Kona. Adults only.

Royal Sea-Cliff Resort APARTMENT **$$**
(info 866-733-0659, reservations 800-688-7444; www.outrigger.com; 75-6040 Ali'i Dr; 1/2 bedroom apt from $220/295; P @) This seven-floor timeshare complex feels almost like a hotel, giving you the best of both worlds. Immaculate units are generously sized and appointed with tropical furniture and lots of amenities: well-stocked kitchens, washer/dryers, two oceanfront pools, tennis courts and outdoor BBQ grills. The minimum two-night stay comes with a hefty mandatory cleaning fee ($125).

King Kamehameha's Kona Beach Hotel HOTEL **$$**
(808-329-2911; www.konabeachhotel.com; 75-5660 Palani Rd; r $140-240, ste from $340; P @) A prime beachfront location and spiffy renovations are watchwords for the historic 'King Kam,' anchoring the north end of Ali'i Dr. Chic decor by the Courtyard Marriott chain, Herb Kawainui Kane's artwork and Hawaiian historical artifact exhibits in the lobby, a 24-hour fitness center and free wi-fi are all draws at this favorite with both vacationers and business types.

Kona Magic Sands Resort APARTMENT **$$**
(808-329-3333; www.konahawaii.com/ms.htm; 77-6452 Ali'i Dr; apt $150-195; P) Large studios have oceanfront lanai, but the 2nd- and especially 3rd-floor units are best. The location south of downtown Kailua-Kona is good for beachgoers, but some rooms are stale and uninspired. An all-concrete building keeps out some noise and heat, but not all units have air-con.

Uncle Billy's Kona Bay Hotel HOTEL **$$**
(808-329-1393; www.unclebilly.com; 75-5739 Ali'i Dr; r $99-135; P @) In a pinch, head to this low-rent waterfront hotel. The good: it's right downtown and has complimentary continental breakfast. The bad: street noise, frumpy interiors and kooky folks.

Kona Sugar Shack SUITE **$$$**
(877-324-6444, 808-895-2203; www.konasugarshack.com; 77-6483 Ali'i Dr; ste $225-400, weekly from $1050; P) The beach-adjacent Sugar Shack hits the sweet spot for vacation rentals, but almost all rooms, except the anniversary suite, are rented on a weekly basis. The friendly, artistic hosts have created a solar-powered oasis with funky, colorful and eclectic decor and relaxing, kid-friendly vibes. Extras include a shared outdoor kitchen, coin-op laundry, miniscule pool, and beach and baby gear to borrow.

Expect a one-time cleaning fee ($125 to $275). Ouch.

Royal Kona Resort RESORT **$$$**
(808-329-3111; www.royalkona.com; 75-5852 Ali'i Dr; r $130-300; P @) Spread over three ship-shaped towers, this breezy, 1970s Polynesian fantasy has a tropical theme that lets you know you're in Hawaii. Although all rooms are remodeled, those in the pricier Ali'i and Lagoon Towers are worth an upgrade. A protected, saltwater lagoon is perfect for kids. Check out the long menu of spa services at the **Lotus Center** (www.konaspa.com).

Eating

You don't have to spend a lot to eat *'ono kine grinds* (good food), but you'll usually have to venture further afield than Ali'i Dr, where most waterfront restaurants are disappointing and overpriced.

★ **Da Poke Shack** SEAFOOD **$**
(808-329-7653; http://dapokeshack.com; 76-6246 Ali'i Dr, Castle Kona Bali Kai; mains & meals $5-10; 10am-6pm;) *Poke* is a local specialty that blends ceviche and sushi: raw, marinated cubes of fish mixed with soy sauce, sesame oil, chiles, seaweed and...well, really, the sky's the limit. The point is, *poke* is

RED-HOT GREEN ISSUES

Understanding the issues that impassion locals – invasive species, resort developments, renewable energy, sovereignty – provides insight into what makes this island tick. You'll see placards, squatters, DIY projects and graffiti (for example, 'No Spray,' a plea to keep pesticides off crops) addressing all these hot topics in your travels.

10% Kona coffee blends These cheaper blends using foreign beans threaten local farmers, who are currently fighting for recognition of Kona coffee as a Product of Designated Origin. This would protect the name and origin of Kona coffee à la Napa Valley wines and Parmigiano-Reggiano cheese.

Coffee berry borer This destructive beetle, which first began ravaging Kona farms in 2010, has been devastating to the area's small-scale coffee industry. Some of the insects have already made their way to O'ahu.

Kealakekua Bay At the time of writing, a moratorium was in place on unlicensed watercraft entering Kealakekua Bay. Pods of spinner dolphins sleep in these waters, but locals and biologists have claimed that this sleep is being disturbed by the presence of hordes of snorkelers.

Thirty Meter Telescope Mauna Kea, Hawai'i's most sacred spot, will be home to the TMT, slated for completion by 2018. The community is divided over this project, which will be bigger than all current observatories combined. See http://kahea.org/issues/sacred-summits for info on opposition to the TMT, and www.tmt.org for the argument in favor of the facility.

Dolphin encounters Whether in captivity or the wild, human-dolphin encounters carry potential risks for the latter. Wild dolphins may become too tired to feed, while captive 'show' dolphins can suffer from stress, infections and damaged dorsal fins.

Renewable energy Hawaii has the highest electricity costs in the USA, and also happens to be a tropical state that sits in the path of Pacific breezes and a blazing sun. The Big Island has a large population of eco-conscious, counterculture types and, as such, the idea of using solar power is a popular one here. Solar panels have been fast to spread across the island, and enormous wind farms can be seen in places such as Ka'u and North Kohala.

wonderful, and Da Poke Shack is the spot to get it. You'll be eating at a picnic table or, better, bring it to the beach.

★Umeke HAWAII REGIONAL CUISINE $
(808-329-3050; www.umekespoke808.com; 75-143 Hualalai Rd; mains $5-10; 10am-8pm;) Umeke takes Da Poke Shack's eat-delicious-food-for-dirt-cheap-on-picnic-tables concept to the next level of Hawaiian-centric cuisine. Local ingredients such as ahi, spicy crab salad and salted Waimea beef are served plate-lunch-style with excellent, innovative sides such as seasoned seaweed and cucumber kimchi (along with heaping scoops of rice). Some of the best-value *grinds* on the island.

Ba-Le Kona VIETNAMESE $
(808-327-1212; 74-5588 Palani Rd, Kona Coast Shopping Center; mains $5-10; 10am-9pm Mon-Sat, 11am-7pm Sun;) Don't let the fluorescent-lit dining room and polystyrene plates fool you: Ba-Le serves the sort of Vietnamese that makes you want to pack it all up and move to Hanoi. Flavors are simple, refreshing and bright, from the green-papaya salad to traditional *pho* (noodle soup), and rice plates of spicy lemongrass chicken, tofu, beef or roast pork.

The *banh mi* (baguette sandwiches) are a perfect choice for a Big Island picnic.

Evolution Bakery & Cafe BAKERY $
(808-331-1122; www.evolutionbakerycafe.com; 75-5813 Ali'i Dr; mains $5-10; 6am-8pm;) Kailua-Kona has always had room for a spot that's hip enough for a MacBook, and crunchy enough for dreadlocks. Enter Evolution. There's wi-fi, smoothies, vegan bagels, pancakes and sandwiches, Kona coffee and some seriously good mac nut (served to the Macnuts, get it? Never mind) banana bread. Much of the menu is vegan friendly and gluten free.

Basik Acai CAFE $
(www.basikacai.com; 75-5831 Kahakai Rd; snacks & drinks $6-13; 7am-4pm Mon-Fri, 8am-4pm Sat & Sun;) Healthy, wholesome acai bowls bursting with tropical fruity goodness, granola, nuts, shredded coconut and even cacao nibs, along with fresh juice smoothies, are made to order at this tiny upstairs kitchen that sources organic, local ingredients. It's expensive but worth it.

Metal Mike's Twisted Pretzels FAST FOOD $
(Likana Lane; snacks $3-5; usually 11:30am-10pm Mon-Thu, 11:30am-midnight Fri & Sat, noon-10pm Sun;) Metal Mike, who seriously looks like he spent time as a roadie, runs this rock-and-roll pretzel stand on a narrow alley by a parking lot just above Ali'i Dr. Go gaga over a dozen kinds of pretzels and dipping sauces, from cheesy jalapeño to white chocolate macnut.

Scandinavian Shave Ice DESSERT $
(www.scandinavianshaveice.com; 75-5699 Ali'i Dr; snacks & drinks $3-8; 11am-8pm Sun-Thu, to 9pm Fri & Sat;) Shave ice is piled up here in huge, psychedelic-colored mounds that are as big as your head. Dither over a rainbow variety of flavored syrups, then borrow a board game to while away an hour.

KTA Super Store SUPERMARKET $
(www.ktasuperstores.com; 74-5594 Palani Rd, Kona Coast Shopping Center; 5am-11pm) The Big Island's best grocery chain, featuring many Hawaii-made products, anything from lavosh crackers to *liliko'i* (passion fruit) jam.

Island Naturals Market & Deli SUPERMARKET $
(www.islandnaturals.com; 74-5487 Kaiwi St; 7:30am-8pm Mon-Sat, 9am-7pm Sun;) This health-conscious grocery store has a fantastic deli making sandwiches, wraps and salads to go, plus a hot-and-cold takeout bar. Some organic and gluten-free options too.

Big Island Grill HAWAIIAN $$
(808-326-1153; 75-5702 Kuakini Hwy; mains $10-20; 7am-9pm Mon-Sat, to noon Sun;) The grill serves fresh and flavorful Hawaiian soul food such as plate lunches and *loco moco* (rice, fried egg and hamburger patty topped with thick gravy). Choose from fried chicken katsu (deep-fried fillets), fried mahimahi, shrimp tempura and more. All meals come with two scoops of rice, potato-mac salad and rich gravy. Service is swift and warm with aloha.

Lemongrass Bistro ASIAN $$
(808-331-2708; www.lemongrassbistrokona.com; 75-5742 Kuakini Hwy; mains $13-25; 11am-3pm Mon-Fri, noon-3pm Sat & Sun, 5-9pm daily;) The food at Lemongrass is clean and elegant but also hearty enough to stick to your ribs, just like the best comfort food. Try the meaty oxtail or crispy duck shellacked in a garlic soy glaze and you'll agree this is the tastiest local bridge between Eastern and Western gastronomy.

Kona Brewing Company AMERICAN $$
(808-334-2739; http://konabrewingco.com; 75-5629 Kuakini Hwy; mains $13-18; 11am-9pm Sun-Thu, to 10pm Fri & Sat;) Expect a madhouse crowd at this sprawling, eco-sustainable brewpub, with tiki-torch-lit outdoor seating and laid-back waitstaff. Everyone's here for the handcrafted 'liquid aloha' made on-site (Pipeline Porter and Castaway IPA are our faves). Pizza toppings verge on gourmet, but crusts can be soggy; BBQ sandwiches and fish tacos are better bets. Enter the parking lot off Kaiwi St.

Island Lava Java CAFE $$
(808-327-2161; www.islandlavajava.com; 75-5799 Ali'i Dr, Ali'i Sunset Plaza; breakfast & lunch mains $7-20; 6:30am-9:30pm;) A convivial gathering spot for Sunday brunch or a sunny breakfast (served until 11:30am) with ocean-view dining on the sidewalk patio. This upscale diner is a little too fancy to be a greasy spoon; maybe it's a greasy complete cutlery set. Anyways, there are huge portions, Big Island–raised meats and fish, farm-fresh produce and 100% Kona coffee.

Rapanui Island Cafe ASIAN $$
(808-329-0511; 75-5695 Ali'i Dr, Kona Banyan Court; mains lunch $6-10, dinner $13-19; 11am-2pm Tue-Fri, 5-9pm Mon-Sat) The New Zealand owners know Polynesian and Indonesian curries, which they prepare with tongue-tingling warmth. Various salads and satays, spiced pork and pawpaw chicken also make an appearance. Order the house coconut rice and wash it down with lemongrass-ginger tea.

Original Thai THAI $$
(808-329-3459; 75-5629 Kuakini Hwy; mains $8-20; 11am-3pm & 5-9pm) Run by a friendly Thai family, this place does a mean line of Thai classics (as the name implies), including the standard rainbow of curries. There's a particularly strong depth of dishes from the Isan region – the *larb* (a kind of spicy and savory salad) is quite excellent.

Jackie Rey's Ohana Grill HAWAII REGIONAL CUISINE $$
(808-327-0209; www.jackiereys.com; 75-5995 Kuakini Hwy; mains lunch $10-16, dinner $15-33; 11am-9pm Mon-Fri, 5-9pm Sat & Sun;) Jackie Rey's is a casual, family-owned grill with a delightfully retro-kitsch Hawaii vibe. Haute versions of local *grinds* include guava-glazed ribs, wasabi-seared ahi and *mochiko* (rice-flour-battered) fish with Moloka'i purple sweet potatoes. Locals, tourists, kids, aunties – pretty much everyone loves it. Pop by between 3pm and 5pm on weekdays for half-price *pupu* (snack or appetizer), tropical cocktails and island microbrews. Reservations recommended for dinner.

Hayama JAPANESE $$
(808-331-8888; 75-5660 Kopiko St; mains $14-35; 11am-2pm & 5-9pm Tue-Sat) Hayama imparts that feeling of authenticity you get when the kitchen and service staff don't speak much English, and most of the clientele speaks fluent Japanese. This *izakaya* (Japanese pub-eatery), tucked into a nondescript strip mall, serves heaping platters of mouth-watering sushi, strong sake, and a tempura fried in heaven's own cooking oil.

Daylight Mind FUSION $$$
(808-339-7824; http://daylightmind.com; 75-5770 Ali'i Dr; brunch $11-23, dinner $23-33; 8am-9pm) A pretty perch over the water and an airy dining space is complemented by fare that runs the gamut from Hawaii Regional (short ribs braised in local coffee) to Pacific fusion (Hamakua mushroom polenta). It's all delicious, but the morning brunch stands out as a particularly excellent start to a Kona day.

Drinking

Kailua-Kona's bar scene is pretty touristy, but there are a handful of places for a cocktail or a beer. Always a good fallback, Kona Brewing Company (p191) usually has live Hawaiian music from 5pm to 8pm on Sundays.

Kope Lani CAFE
(www.kopelani.com; 75-5719 Ali'i Dr; snacks & drinks $3-7; 7am-9pm;) Ali'i Dr is chockablock with coffee shops vending 100% Kona brews from upcountry coffee plantations. This sweet spot stands out, not just for its ocean views and ice-blended espresso drinks, but also its two-dozen flavors of Big Island–made ice cream.

Sam's Hideaway BAR
(75-5725 Ali'i Dr; 9am-2am) Sam's is a dark, cozy (OK, maybe 'dank') little nook of a bar. You'll rarely find tourists but there are always locals, especially on karaoke nights. Trust us: you haven't done Kailua-Kona until you've seen a 7ft Samoan guy tear up as he belts out 'The Snows of Mauna Kea.' Located a little off Ali'i Dr, behind shops that front the main road.

Humpy's Big Island Alehouse BAR
(808-324-2337; http://humpys.com/kona; 75-5815 Ali'i Dr, Coconut Grove Marketplace; 11am-2am Mon-Fri, 8am-2am Sat & Sun) With its enviable location on the strip overlooking Kailua Bay, Alaskan Humpy's would probably survive in touristy Kailua-Kona even without having dozens of craft beers on tap. Perch on the upstairs balcony, with its sea breezes and views, while live bands rock out. Regular happy hours, pub quizzes, open mics and an eclectic musical lineup round out the Humpy's experience.

Humpy's opens at 7am on Sundays if an NFL game is going, and has multiple screens so you can catch most games.

Don's Mai Tai Bar BAR
(808-930-3286; www.royalkona.com; 75-5852 Ali'i Dr, Royal Kona Resort; 10am-10pm) For pure kitsch, nothing beats the lounge-lizard fantasy of Don's inside the Royal Kona Resort. Soak up the killer ocean views of the crashing surf – then lament the fact that the 10 varieties of mai tai are all pretty lackluster (at least the little blue plastic monkey is yours to keep). Real tiki fans roll in for **Don's Mai Tai Festival** (www.donsmaitaifest.com) in mid-August.

Huggo's on the Rocks BAR
(808-329-1493; http://huggosontherocks.com; 75-5828 Kahakai Rd; 11:30am-11:30pm) Huggo's is as adjacent to the water as you can get in Kailua-Kona (ordinances now prevent other bars from getting this close to the waves). You'll be drinking under thatch with live music, sunsets and occasionally a spray of surf dusting your hair. In the mornings this place reverts to **Java on the Rock** (808-324-2411; www.javaontherock.com; 75-5828 Kahakai Rd; 6-11am;), serving coffee and espresso.

Mask-Querade Bar GAY, BAR
(Mask Bar; 808-329-8558; 75-5660 Kopiko St; 10am-2am) Hidden away in a strip mall is 'the Mask,' Kailua-Kona's only dedicated

gay bar. In a town where drinking options run from tourist traps to sports bars to fratty hook-up joints, it's nice to find a place that feels a little playfully kitschy. On some nights it can get pretty sexy; on others it's a cozy neighborhood joint.

Dolphin Spit Saloon BAR
(808-326-7748; 75-5626 Kuakini Hwy, Unit F; 10am-2am) In a city full of transplants and tourists, the Dolphin Spit (yum!) is where the locals are: smoking, drinking till they're merry, rubbing elbows, giving each other crap, watching sports and generally pickling themselves in the Pacific sun. Located in a strip mall on a hill overlooking Kuakini Hwy.

Kanaka Kava CAFE
(75-5803 Ali'i Dr, Coconut Grove Marketplace; bar 10am-11pm, kitchen to 9:30pm) This tiny, locals' grass-shack hangout is the place to try Hawaiian-style kava (the mildly sedative juice of the *'awa* plant) or organic *noni* (Indian mulberry) juice, another herbal elixir. *Pupu* such as squid luau and ahi *poke* are just an afterthought. Cash only.

Entertainment

Kailua-Kona's two hokey, cruise-ship-friendly luau include a ceremony, a buffet dinner with Hawaiian specialties, an open bar and a Polynesian dinner show featuring a cast of flamboyant dancers and fire twirlers. Forego if any rain is forecast – an indoor luau ain't worth it.

Regal Makalapua Stadium 10 CINEMA
(808-327-0444; Makalapua Shopping Center, 74-5469 Kamaka'eha Ave; adult/child $10.75/7.50) Catch first-run Hollywood movies on 10 screens. Matinee showings before 6pm are discounted.

KBXtreme BOWLING, KARAOKE
(808-326-2695; www.kbxtreme.com; 75-5591 Palani Rd; 9am-2am;) Make a rainy day or dull night fun for families with a bowling alley, arcade games, a sports bar and a karaoke lounge. 'Xtreme' black-light bowling parties take over Friday and Saturday nights; weekday afternoon bowling is discounted.

Island Breeze Lu'au LUAU
(808-329-8111; www.islandbreezeluau.com; 75-5660 Palani Rd, Courtyard Marriott King Kamehameha's Kona Beach Hotel; adult/child 5-12yr $88/45; 5pm Tue, Thu & Sun;) Family-friendly luau benefitting from a scenic oceanfront setting, but crowds can reach 400.

Lava Legends & Legacies – Journeys of the South Pacific LUAU
(808-329-3111; www.royalkona.com/luaus; 75-5852 Ali'i Dr, Royal Kona Resort; adult/child 6-11yr $67/33; 6pm Mon, Tue, Wed & Fri;) Assuage your disappointment in the buffet by taking a photo with the lissome dancers.

Shopping

Ali'i Dr is swamped with run-of-the-mill, dubious-quality Hawaiiana and souvenir shops. Beware of 'Made in China' fakes.

Kona Bay Books BOOKS, MUSIC
(808-326-7790; http://konabaybooks.com; 74-5487 Kaiwi St; 10am-6pm) The Big Island's largest selection of used books, CDs and DVDs, including Hawaiiana titles.

J. Lambus Photography ARTS
(808-989-9560; www.jlambus.com; 75-5744 Ali'i Dr, Kona Inn Shopping Village; 11am-8pm Tue-Sat, to 4pm Mon) Josh Lambus' celebrated underwater photography has been exhibited by the Smithsonian, and he has taken some of the first recorded snaps of several deep-sea species. Pop into his gallery, then check his blog for Big Island adventure stories.

Big Island Jewelers JEWELRY
(888-477-8571, 808-329-8571; http://bigislandjewelers.com; 75-5695A Ali'i Dr; 9am-5:30pm Mon-Sat) Family owned for nearly four decades, with master jeweler Flint Carpenter at the helm, this storefront sells high-quality Hawaiiana bracelets, pendants, earrings and rings, including pieces made with Tahitian pearls. Custom orders welcome.

Honolua Surf Co CLOTHING
(808-329-1001; www.honoluasurf.com; 75-5744 Ali'i Dr, Kona Inn Shopping Village; 9am-9pm) This island-grown surfwear shop is split right down the middle between styles for *kane* (men) and *wahine* (women). Board shorts, bikinis, hoodies, T-shirts and beach cover-ups will last you as long as an endless summer.

Kona Oceanfront Gallery ARTS
(Wyland Kona Oceanfront Gallery; 808-334-0037; http://wylandbigisland.com; 75-5770 Ali'i Dr; 9:30am-9pm) Robert Wyland is known for his maritime-themed, neon-palette artwork. His originals, and the works of many Big Island locals, are for sale in this huge space, which regularly hosts art events and special gallery nights.

Crazy Shirts CLOTHING
(☎808-329-2176; www.crazyshirts.com; 75-5719 Ali'i Dr, Kona Marketplace; ⏰9am-9pm) Once maverick, now mainstream, Crazy Shirts are worn mainly by tourists these days. The best designs feature natural dyes such as Kona coffee, hibiscus, *ti* leaves and volcanic ash.

Conscious Riddims Records MUSIC
(☎808-322-2628, 808-326-7685; www.conscious-riddims.org; 75-5719 Ali'i Dr, Kona Marketplace; ⏰10am-7pm Mon-Fri, to 5pm Sun) Drop by for reggae and Jawaiian (Hawaii-style reggae) music and dope clothing.

Kona Farmers Market SOUVENIRS
(www.konafarmersmarket.com; Hualalai Rd, cnr Ali'i Dr; ⏰7am-4pm Wed-Sun) Sells a lotta phony shell jewelry and pseudo-Hawaiian knick-knacks, but also fresh produce and flower lei.

ℹ Information

MEDIA

Popular radio stations:

KAGB 99.1 FM (www.kaparadio.com) West Hawai'i home of Hawaiian and island music.

KKUA 90.7 FM (www.hawaiipublicradio.org) Hawaii Public Radio; classical music, talk and news.

KLUA 93.9 FM Native FM plays island tunes and reggae beats.

Hawaii Tribune-Herald (www.hawaiitrib une-herald.com) The Big Island's main daily newspaper.

West Hawaii Today (www.westhawaiitoday.com) Kona Coast's daily newspaper covers Kohala to Ka'u.

MEDICAL SERVICES

Kona Community Hospital (☎808-322-9311; www.kch.hhsc.org; 79-1019 Haukapila St; ⏰24hr) West Hawai'i's most advanced (level-III) trauma center, about 10 miles south of Kailua-Kona.

ℹ PARKING LOT PROBLEMS

The parking lot behind Humpy's Big Island Alehouse is convenient if you've got a designated driver and want to park near Ali'i Dr's most popular boozing strip. With that said, be careful walking back to your car later in the evening, given the level of alcohol/testosterone around and the sometime problem of locals picking fights with tourists. If you're in a group you should be fine; just keep your wits about you.

CVS (☎808-329-1632; www.cvs.com; 75-5595 Palani Rd; ⏰store 7am-10pm daily, pharmacy 7am-8pm Mon-Fri, 8am-7pm Sat, 8am-6pm Sun) Centrally located drugstore and pharmacy.

MONEY

The following banks have 24-hour ATMs and islandwide branches:

Bank of Hawaii (☎808-326-3900; www.boh.com; 74-5457 Makala Blvd; ⏰8:30am-4pm Mon-Thu, 8:30am-6pm Fri, 9am-1pm Sat)

First Hawaiian Bank (☎808-329-2461; www.fhb.com; Lanihau Center, 74-5593 Palani Rd; ⏰8:30am-4pm Mon-Thu, 8:30am-6pm Fri, 9am-1pm Sat)

WEBSITES

Big Island Visitors Bureau (www.gohawaii.com/big-island) Travel planning info and comprehensive listings for festivals and special events.

KonaWeb (www.konaweb.com) Homegrown website for locals and visitors, with an island-wide calendar of events.

ℹ Getting There & Away

AIR

Kona International Airport at Keahole (KOA; ☎808-327-9520; http://hawaii.gov/koa; 73-200 Kupipi St) Mostly interisland and some US mainland and Canada flights arrive at Hawai'i's main airport, 7 miles northwest of Kailua-Kona.

BUS

Hele-On Bus (☎808-961-8744; www.hele-onbus.org; adult 1-way $2, 10-ride ticket $15, monthly pass $60) Public buses run between Kailua-Kona and Captain Cook in South Kona (one to 1¾ hours) up to 10 times daily except Sunday; one or two also stop at the airport. Buses connect Kailua-Kona with Hilo (three hours) via Waimea (1¼ to 1¾ hours) three times daily except Sunday; one goes via South Kohala's resorts.

Buses on the long-distance Pahala–South Kohala route (four hours) make stops in Kailua-Kona, South Kona, Ka'u and sometimes at Kona's airport and in Keauhou; service is three times daily Monday through Saturday, once on Sunday.

All schedules and fares are subject to change; check the website. A $1 surcharge applies for luggage, backpacks or bicycles; no surfboards or boogie boards allowed on board. Children under six years old ride free.

Keauhou Trolley (☎808-329-1688; www.sheratonkona.com; 1-way $2; ⏰9am-9:15pm) Also called the 'Honu Express,' this tourist trolley makes six daily round-trips between Keauhou and Kailua-Kona. Stops include White

(Magic) Sands Beach, Kona Brewing Company, Kailua Pier and various shopping centers and resort hotels. Check current schedules and fares online.

Kona Trolley (http://historickailuavillage.com; ⏲9am-9:15pm) This breezy trolley service makes six trips a day with stops running from central Kailua-Kona to the Keahou resort area.

CAR

The drive from Kailua-Kona to Hilo is 75 miles and takes at least 1¾ hours via Saddle Rd, 95 miles (two hours) via Waimea and 125 miles (three hours) via Ka'u and Volcano.

To avoid snarly commuter traffic on Hwy 11 leading into and away from Kailua-Kona, try the Mamalahoa Hwy Bypass Rd. It connects Ali'i Dr in Keauhou with Haleki'i St in Kealakekua, between mile markers 111 and 112 on Hwy 11.

Getting Around

TO/FROM THE AIRPORT

A car is almost necessary on Hawai'i, but for those who are not renting one upon arrival at the airport, taxis are available curbside (book late-night pickups in advance). Taxi fares average $25 to Kailua-Kona or $35 to Keauhou, plus tip.

Speedi Shuttle (☎877-242-5777, 808-329-5433; www.speedishuttle.com; airport transfer Kailua-Kona shared/private $31.90/124, Mauna Lani $59.10/185.80; ⏲9am-last flight) Economical if you're in a group. Book in advance.

BICYCLE

Home of the Ironman Triathlon World Championship, Kailua-Kona is a bike-friendly town.

Bike Works (☎808-326-2453; www.bikeworkskona.com; 74-5583 Luhia St, Hale Hana Center; bicycle rental per day $40-80; ⏲9am-6pm Mon-Sat, 10am-4pm Sun) Full-service bike shop renting high-quality mountain and road-touring bikes; rates include helmet, lock, pump and patch kit. Multiday and weekly discounts available. Second location in Waikoloa.

BUS

Both the public Hele-On Bus and privately operated Keauhou and Kona Trolleys make stops within Kailua-Kona.

CAR

Ali'i Dr in downtown Kailua-Kona is almost always congested. Free public parking is available in a lot between Likana Lane and Kuakini Hwy. Many shopping centers along Ali'i Dr have free parking lots for customers.

> **BORED WAITING TO BOARD**
>
> They were clever, the people who located the Astronaut Ellison S Onizuka Space Center (p219) at the Kona International Airport. This little museum paying tribute to the Big Island native who perished in the 1986 *Challenger* space-shuttle disaster collects celestial ephemera such as moon rocks and space suits; it makes an interesting way to spend some time before takeoff.

MOPED & MOTORCYCLE

Doesn't it look fun zipping down Ali'i Dr on a moped? And what a breeze to park!

Big Island Harley Davidson (☎888-904-3155, 808-217-8560; www.bigislandharley.com; 75-5633 Palani Rd; per day/week $179/763; ⏲8:30am-6pm Mon-Fri, 8:30am-5pm Sat, 10am-4pm Sun) Well-maintained Harley motorcycles come with helmets and rain gear to borrow. Book ahead online.

Scooter Brothers (☎808-327-1080; www.scooterbrothers.com; 75-5829 Kahakai Rd; per 4hr/8hr/day $40/50/60; ⏲10am-6pm Mon-Sat, 9am-6pm Wed, by reservation Sun) Got around town like a local, on a moped or electric scooter. The official riding area is from Hapuna Beach up north to Honaunau down south. Honda motorcycle rentals cost from $95 per 24 hours.

TAXI

Call ahead for pickups from local taxi companies:

Dakine Taxi (☎808-329-4446; www.dakinetaxi.com)

Laura's Taxi (☎808-326-5466; www.laurastaxi.com)

Around Kailua-Kona

Keauhou Resort Area

With its wide streets and manicured landscaping, Keauhou feels like a US mainland suburb: easy, pleasant and bland. Like most suburbs, there's no town center (unless you count the shopping mall). Rather, it's a collection of destinations: Keauhou Harbor for boat trips, beaches for snorkeling and surfing, condos and resort hotels for sleeping, and farmers markets for local flavor.

Beaches

Kahalu'u Beach Park
BEACH

(👪) Whether young or old, triathlete or couch potato, everyone appreciates the island's most thrilling, easy-to-access (and admittedly busy) snorkeling spot. Protected by an ancient breakwater (which, according to legend, was built by the *menehune* – 'little people'), the bay is pleasantly calm and shallow. You'll spot tropical fish and *honu* (green sea turtles) without even trying. The lifeguard-staffed park has outdoor showers, restrooms, drinking water, snorkel and locker rentals and picnic tables.

Kahalu'u can be too popular for its own good, with snorkelers literally bumping into one another. The salt-and-pepper beach (composed of lava and coral sand) is often a mass of humanity, which you may find sociable or nauseating. Come early; the parking lot may fill by 10am. Treading lightly is also important: follow coral-reef etiquette (p630) and stay at least 50yd in the water (20ft on land) from all sea turtles.

When the surf's up (and it can rage here), expert surfers challenge the offshore waves and avoid strong rip currents on the bay's north side near the church. When conditions are mellow, beginners can learn to surf or stand-up paddle.

Sights & Activities

Kahulu'u Manowai
ARCHAEOLOGICAL SITE

(78-6740 Ali'i Dr) FREE On the former grounds of the Outrigger Keauhou Beach Resort, just south of Kahalu'u Beach Park, three restored heiau (temples) and ancient Hawaiian petroglyphs are the centerpiece of a planned outdoor-education and Hawaiian cultural center, sponsored by Kamehameha Schools and still under development with the local community. For now, respectful visitors can explore the archaelogical sites during daylight hours. Check in at the security guardhouse and ask for a map.

At the north end of the complex is **Kapuanoni Heiau**, a restored fishing temple. Just south, **Hapaiali'i Heiau** was built 600 years ago – its construction aligns the temple with seasonal equinoxes and solstices. Both of these temples were painstakingly restored by Hawaiian cultural practitioners, archaeologists and students in 2007.

Furthest south is **Ke'eku Heiau**, also recently restored. Legends say that Ke'eku was a *luakini* (temple of human sacrifice). Most famously, a Maui chief who tried to invade the Big Island was sacrificed here, and the spirits of his grieving dogs are said to still guard the site. Along the shoreline look for teeming tide pools and *ki'i pohaku* (petroglyphs) visible among the rocks at low tide.

Keauhou Kahalu'u Heritage Center
GALLERY

(www.keauhouresort.com; 78-6831 Ali'i Dr, Keauhou Shopping Center; ⏲10am-5pm) FREE To learn more about the restoration of Keauhou's heiau, visit this unstaffed cultural center, where small exhibits and videos also describe *holua,* the ancient Hawaiian sport of lava-rock sledding, at nearby He'eia Bay. The center is on the KTA Super Store side of the mall, hidden behind the post office near the public restrooms.

Keauhou Bay
HARBOR

Many tour cruises launch from the small pier at this protected bay. While not worth going very far out of your way for, the small beach, picnic tables and sand volleyball courts bring out locals. Facilities include restrooms and outdoor showers. Against the hillside, a **plaque** marks the site where Kamehameha III was born in 1814. The prince is said to have been stillborn and brought back to life by a visiting kahuna who dunked him in a healing freshwater spring here.

To get here, turn *makai* (seaward) off Ali'i Dr onto Kaleiopapa St.

St Peter's Church
CHURCH

Ever popular for weddings, the much-photographed 'Little Blue Church' practically sits in Kahulu'u Bay. Made of clapboard and a corrugated-tin roof in the 1880s, the church was moved here from White (Magic) Sands Beach in 1912. The church is on the *makai* side of Ali'i Dr, north of mile marker 5.

Incidentally, an ancient Hawaiian temple, Ku'emanu Heiau, once stood here. Hawaiian *ali'i* (royalty), who surfed at the northern end of Kahalu'u Bay, prayed at the temple before hitting the waves.

Original Hawaiian Chocolate Factory
FARM

(☎888-447-2626; www.ohcf.us; 78-6772 Makenawai St; tour adult/child under 12yr $15/free; ⏲usually 9am Wed, 9am & 11am Fri, by reservation; 👪) A must for chocolate fans, these one-hour farm tours detail how the *only* Hawaiian chocolate is grown, harvested, processed and packaged, followed by chocolate sampling and sales. Book tours by phone or email at least a week ahead. The factory is inland from Hwy 11 and King Kamehameha III Rd.

OFF THE BEATEN TRACK

END OF THE WORLD

Rarely do geographic titles so convincingly live up to their names, but then comes Keauhou's **End of the World** (Kuamo'o Bay; Ali'i Dr). A Mordor-esque lava plain of jagged *'a'a* rock crinkles to the deep blue coast, and then drops steeply into the ocean. To get here, drive all the way to the end of Ali'i Dr and look for a trailhead to the water. It's a short, rocky hike to the cliffs.

Sometimes waves crash like thunderheads on the rocks, sometimes the ocean is calm as a pond and, often, local teenagers jump off the cliffs into the water. It's a lot of fun but is best not attempted unless you're a strong swimmer and are with a group of friends.

The End of the World marked the end of an era. When Kamehameha the Great's son Liholiho (Kamehameha II) was crowned king, the new monarch took major steps to abolish the rigid kapu, the taboo system that regulated daily life. So Liholiho took the then-drastic step of eating at a table with women. His cousin Chief Kekauokalani was incensed (or perhaps he coveted the crown, or maybe a bit of both) and challenged Liholiho to battle at the End of the World. In the resulting Battle of Kuamo'o some 300 were killed, including Kekauokalani and his wife. The dead were interned in cairns on the lava field, Liholiho's rule was firmly established and the kapu system was broken.

Sleeping

Cheaper rates may be available by booking ahead online.

Outrigger Kanaloa at Kona APARTMENT $$$
(866-956-4262, 808-322-9625; www.outrigger-kanaloaatkonacondo.com; 78-261 Manukai St; 1/2 bedroom apt from $219/269; P ❄ @ ≋) These tropical townhouse-style condos feel exclusive, sitting behind a private gate on an oceanfront lava ledge. Incredibly spacious, immaculate and fully equipped units gather in small clusters. One-bedroom condos easily fit a family of four. With three pools, night-lit tennis courts and an adjacent golf course, you can practically stay put. Multiple-night minimum stay (cleaning fee from $50).

Sheraton Kona Resort & Spa at Keauhou Bay RESORT $$$
(866-716-8109, 808-930-4900; www.sheratonkona.com; 78-128 'Ehukai St; r/ste from $199/399; P ❄ @ ≋) The family-friendly Sheraton has a sleek modern design with hip boutique-hotel appeal. Despite having more than 500 rooms, an oceanfront bar and restaurant with fire pits and live music (usually 6pm to 9pm nightly), and a massive pool with a spiral waterslide, unfortunately there's no beach. Manta rays gather off the rocky shoreline at night.

A mandatory resort fee (over $30 per night) covers self-parking, wi-fi, unlimited Keauhou Trolley rides, a morning yoga class and Hawaiian cultural activities.

Eating & Drinking

Drop by Keahou's twice-weekly farmers markets for tasty, cheap *grinds*.

KTA Super Store SUPERMARKET $
(78-6831 Ali'i Dr, Keauhou Shopping Center; 7am-10pm) Locally owned supermarket chain stocking groceries, beach snacks and drinks, with a full-service deli and bakery.

Peaberry & Galette CAFE $
(808-322-6020; www.peaberryandgalette.com; 78-6831 Ali'i Dr, Keauhou Shopping Center; mains $7-14; 7am-5pm Mon-Sat, 8am-5pm Sun) Brewing 100% Kona estate-grown coffee and Illy espresso, this cafe with Euro-bistro style also dishes up sweet and savory French crepes, plus satisfying salads, sandwiches, quiches and *liliko'i*-lemon bars for dessert.

Bianelli's ITALIAN $$
(808-322-0377; http://bianellis.com; 78-6831 Ali'i Dr, Keauhou Shopping Center; pizzas $13.50-19; 3-9pm Mon-Sat;) Is Bianelli's the best pizza in Keahou? More to the point, it's about the only pizza we found in Keahou. And, honestly, it's quite good; the Bufala, layered with garlic sauce and white mozarella, is pretty perfect after a day of snorkeling.

Sam Choy's Kai Lanai HAWAII REGIONAL CUISINE $$
(808-333-3434; www.samchoy.com; 78-6831 Ali'i Dr, Keauhou Shopping Center; mains lunch $10-14, dinner $17-38; 11am-9pm Mon-Thu, 11am-9:30pm Fri, 8am-9:30pm Sat, 8am-9pm Sun;) Sam Choy is one of the pioneers of Hawaii Regional Cuisine, an island-grown version

of Pacific Rim fusion. At this casual eatery with dynamite sunset panoramas, the dinner menu is stuffed with haute fusion gastronomy such as lamb chops broiled with soy, ginger and local bird peppers, although execution falls short of the chef's sterling reputation. During happy hour (3pm to 5pm daily), nosh on *pupu* on the breezy ocean-view lanai.

Kenichi Pacific JAPANESE, FUSION $$$
(☎808-322-6400; www.kenichihawaii.com; 78-6831 Ali'i Dr, Keauhou Shopping Center; dishes $3-18, mains $23-38; ⊙5-9pm Sun-Thu, to 9:30pm Fri & Sat) Ignore the mall setting. Just savor the beautifully presented Pacific Rim fusion cuisine, including tender miso black cod, Hawaiian *ono* (white-fleshed wahoo) topped with a cloud of *ponzu* (Japanese citrus sauce) and macadamia-nut-encrusted lamb. Sushi and sashimi cuts are fresh and generous. Happy hour (4:30pm to 6:30pm daily) brings half-price sushi rolls and drinks (hello, sake!) to the bar.

☆ Entertainment

Haleo Luau LUAU
(☎866-482-9775; www.haleoluau.com; 78-128 'Ehukai St, Sheraton Keauhou Bay Resort; adult/child 6-12yr $95/45; ⊙4:30pm Mon) The Sheraton's touristy luau weaves together Hawaiian themes and tales of ancient kings and battles, along with fiery dances from across Polynesia. The buffet is about as generic as you'd expect, but there's an open bar.

Regal Keauhou Stadium 7 CINEMA
(☎808-324-0172; 78-6831 Ali'i Dr, Keauhou Shopping Center) Hollywood flicks fill seven screens. Showings before 6pm are discounted.

Keauhou Shopping Center MUSIC, DANCE
(www.keauhouvillageshops.com; 78-6831 Ali'i Dr) FREE This shopping mall has hula shows from 6pm to 7pm most Friday nights. It also usually runs free Hawaiian craft workshops from 10am to noon every Thursday. Check the website for more cultural activities and special events.

Shopping

★Ho'oulu Community Farmers Market MARKET
(www.hooulufarmersmkt.com; 78-128 Ehukai St, Sheraton Keauhou Bay Resort; ⊙9am-2pm Wed) Unlike the touristy Kailua-Kona farmers market selling knickknacks from who-knows-where, this weekly event focuses on small-scale farm and fishing bounty, including genuine Kona coffee and flower lei. Live music, island artists and takeout food vendors make this a must-do lunchtime stop.

Keauhou Farmers Market MARKET
(www.keauhoufarmersmarket.com; 78-6831 Ali'i Dr, Keauhou Shopping Center; ⊙8am-noon Sat) At this parking-lot farmers market with live Hawaiian music and a neighborly spirit, everything is Big Island–grown including seasonal fruits and veggies, organic coffee, homemade preserves and fresh flowers.

Kona Stories BOOKS
(☎808-324-0350; www.konastories.com; 78-6831 Ali'i Dr, Keauhou Shopping Center; ⊙10am-6pm Mon-Fri, 10am-5pm Sat, 11am-5pm Sun) Independent bookstore with a strong Hawaiiana section, which hosts community events for kids and adults. It's near KTA Super Store.

Information

Bank of Hawaii (www.boh.com; 78-6831 Ali'i Dr, Keauhou Shopping Center, Suite 131; ⊙9am-6pm Mon-Fri, to 2pm Sat & Sun) ATM available inside KTA Super Store.

Keauhou Urgent Care Center (☎808-322-2544; www.konaurgentcare.com; 78-6831 Ali'i Dr, Suite 418, Keauhou Shopping Center; ⊙9am-7pm) Walk-in clinic for nonemergency medical matters.

Longs Drugs (www.cvs.com; 78-6831 Ali'i Dr, Keauhou Shopping Center; ⊙store 7am-10pm, pharmacy 8am-8pm Mon-Fri, 9am-7pm Sat, 9am-6pm Sun) Convenient drugstore and pharmacy.

Getting There & Around

Nicknamed the 'Honu Express,' Keauhou Trolley (p194) makes five daily round-trips between Keauhou and Kailua-Kona, stopping at White (Magic) Sands Beach, Kailua Pier, various shopping centers, resort hotels and elsewhere. Check current schedules and fares online.

Holualoa

POP 8540

The further up the mountain you get from Kailua-Kona, the artsier, more residential, more rural (not to mention cooler and damper) it gets until all of these qualities mush into one misty bohemian village: Holualoa. Perched at 1400ft on the lush slopes of Mt Hualalai, this town has come a long way from its days as a tiny, one-donkey coffee crossroads. Today Holualoa's ramshackle

OFF THE BEATEN TRACK

UPCOUNTRY KONA COFFEE FARMS

Kona coffee has had gourmet cachet for decades, and today many coffee farms have opened roadside visitor centers and gift shops, where they give free samples and quickie tours. The best time to visit is during the harvest season, running from August through February, when 'Kona snow' (white blossoms) and 'cherries' (mature berry fruit) cluster on the coffee trees.

Mountain Thunder Coffee Plantation (888-414-5662, tours 808-345-6600; www.mountainthunder.com; 73-1944 Hao St; 20min tour free, 3hr VIP tour adult/child under 6yr $135/free; tours hourly 10am-4pm, VIP tours 10am Mon-Fri) This award-winning farm lies upland in lush Kaloko Mauka, a 20-minute drive from downtown Kailua-Kona or Holualoa village. VIP tours (call to reserve at least one day in advance) give you a more in-depth look at Kona coffee, and let you roast half a pound of beans to take home.

Hula Daddy Kona Coffee (808-327-9744; www.huladaddy.com; 74-4944 Mamalahoa Hwy, Holualoa; 10am-4pm Mon-Sat) With jaw-dropping ocean views from a breezy lanai, this epicurean tasting room and eco-conscious farm is the place to learn about cupping. Ask about unusual coffee-production techniques used to create its signature Kona Oli and Kona Sweet beans. It's less than 5 miles north of Holualoa.

Holualoa Kona Coffee Company (808-322-9937; www.konalea.com; 77-6261 Mamalahoa Hwy, Holualoa; 8am-4pm Mon-Fri) Kona Le'a Plantation does not use pesticides or herbicides on its small organic-certified farm, less than 2 miles south of Holualoa. As you drive up, watch out for the free-ranging geese, who do double duty as lawn mowers and fertilizers.

Kona Blue Sky Coffee (877-322-1700; www.konablueskycoffee.com; 76-973 Hualalai Rd, Kailua-Kona; visitor center & gift shop 8:30am-4pm Mon-Sat, tours 9am-3:30pm Mon-Sat) A convenient choice if your time is limited, this tiny coffee estate in Holualoa village offers a free walking tour that passes traditional open-air drying racks and includes an educational video.

buildings hold a stunning collection of sophisticated artist-owned galleries.

Most businesses close on Sunday and Monday.

Sights & Activities

Donkey Mill Art Center ARTS CENTER
(808-322-3362; www.donkeymillartcenter.org; 78-6670 Mamalahoa Hwy; 10am-4pm Tue-Sat Aug-May, 9am-3pm Mon-Fri Jun & Jul;) FREE The Holualoa Foundation for Arts & Culture created this community art center in 2002. There are free exhibits, plus lectures and workshops – taught by recognized national and international artists – open to visitors. If you're wondering where the name comes from, the center's building, built in 1953, was once a coffee mill with a donkey painted on its roof. It puts on lots of family-friendly arts-education programs. Located 3 miles south of the village center.

Malama I'ka Ola Holistic Health Center HEALTH & FITNESS
(808-324-6644; www.malamatherapy.com; 76-5914 Mamalahoa Hwy) Inside a 19th-century doctor's office, this alternative-minded oasis offers yoga and Pilates classes, as well as massage, acupuncture, Chinese herbal medicine and organic skin treatments.

Festivals & Events

Coffee & Art Stroll ART, FOOD
(www.konacoffeefest.com) During early November's Kona Coffee Cultural Festival (p187), Holualoa hosts an incredibly popular, daylong block party.

Music & Light Festival ART, MUSIC
(www.holualoahawaii.com) A small-town Christmas celebration with live music and a tree-lighting ceremony in mid-December.

Sleeping

Lilikoi Inn B&B $$
(510-364-4700, 808-333-5539; www.lilikoiinn.com; 75-5339 Mamalahoa Hwy; r incl breakfast $135-195;) All four rooms have an airy, modern-art-gallery-in-the-tropics kind of vibe, blending cool monochromes with tasteful Hawaiiana. Each has a private entrance and access to a hot tub, guest laundry,

kitchen and pick-your-own avocado and fruit trees. Enjoy the chef's restaurant-worthy breakfasts on a garden lanai. It's 3 miles north of Holualoa village.

Hale Maluhia Country Inn B&B $$
(808-329-1123; www.hawaii-bnb.com; 76-770 Hualalai Rd; r $95-124, cottages $147-175; P) Take an exuberant grab-bag run by a friendly couple and stuff it with Japanese, Hawaiian and bohemian style and sensibility. Put it all on a jungle mountain abutting some coffee plantations and boom, there's Hale Maluhia. We're not fans of the smallest, cheapest rooms, so go up a little in price or opt for one of the excellent private cottages.

The cottages feel like Shintō-tropical retreats designed by a Zen monk who was really into the *Swiss Family Robinson* story.

Haleakala B&B B&B $$
(808-322-6053; www.haleakalabedbreakfast.com; 78-6612A Mamalahoa Hwy; d $130-150;) Setting this breezy, welcoming B&B apart are the breathtaking views – over coffee farms and macnut orchards all the way to the startling blue Pacific – from your private lanai or the shared hot tub. For *ipo* (sweethearts), the Kokua Nest is a private cottage suite with an outdoor garden shower. Rates include a local cafe breakfast voucher.

★ **Holualoa Inn** B&B $$$
(808-324-1121; www.holualoainn.com; 76-5932 Mamalahoa Hwy; r/ste/cottages from $355/395/495;) From gleaming eucalyptus floors to river-rock showers, serene beauty shines in every soul-soothing detail. Common rooms are graced with Polynesian and Asian art and exquisite carved furniture that segue seamlessly into outdoor gardens and a pool, while the rooftop gazebo surveys the ocean. It's a peaceful retreat you'll long remember. No TVs, phones or children under 13 years old. Breakfast included.

Eating

★ **Holuakoa Gardens & Café** HEALTH FOOD $$
(808-322-2233; www.holuakoacafe.com; 76-5900 Mamalahoa Hwy; mains brunch $12-20, dinner $17-32; cafe 6:30am-3pm Mon-Fri, 8am-3pm Sat & Sun, restaurant 10am-2:30pm Mon-Fri, 9am-2:30pm Sat & Sun, 5:30-8:30pm Mon-Sat;) The storefront cafe serves 100% Kona coffee, baked goods and sandwiches. Out back, an organic, slow-food restaurant dishes a sophisticated yet casual bistro-style menu that makes the most of fresh, Big Island–grown produce. Book ahead for dinner.

As this is one of Hawai'i's establishments most dedicated to supporting local farmers, it's no surprise there's a seasonal **farmers market** (9am-noon Sat Apr-Oct) here.

Shopping

Holualoa is a tiny village but don't underestimate the quality of its artists. Along the Mamalahoa Hwy (Hwy 180) you'll find internationally known, highly commissioned artists creating art beyond the stereotypical tropical motifs. Most galleries and shops are closed on Sunday and Monday.

Studio 7 Fine Arts ARTS, CRAFTS
(808-324-1335; http://studio7hawaii.com; 76-5920 Mamalahoa Hwy; 11am-5pm Tue-Sat) A serene, museum-like gallery featuring prominent artist-owner Hiroki Morinoue's watercolor, oil, woodblock and sculpture pieces, and the pottery of his accomplished wife, Setsuko.

ISLAND INSIGHTS: LAUHALA

Hawaiians wove the dried *lau* (leaves) of the *hala* (pandanus) tree into floor mats, hats, baskets, fans and other household items. Strong and flexible, *lauhala* is surprisingly hardy and long-lasting. Today, most *lauhala* is actually mass-produced in the Philippines and sold cheaply to unwitting tourists.

But Holualoa's **Kimura Lauhala Shop** (808-324-0053; www.holualoahawaii.com/member_sites/kimura.html; Hwy 180, cnr Hualalai Rd; 9am-5pm Mon-Fri, to 4pm Sat), run by the Kimura family's fourth generation, sells high-quality, genuine Hawaiian *lauhala*, from traditional hats to signature lined tote bags. In the 1930s the Kimuras originally purchased *lauhala* products from Hawaiian weavers to sell. When demand increased they took on the production themselves, assisted by local farming wives, who do piecework at home outside of coffee season. Don't fall prey to cheap imports – the *lauhala* hats, placemats, baskets and floor mats sold here are the real deal.

Ipu Hale Gallery ARTS, CRAFTS
(808-322-9069; www.holualoahawaii.com/member_sites/ipu_hale.html; 76-5893 Mamalahoa Hwy; 10am-4pm Tue-Sat) Magnificent *ipu* (gourds) are decoratively carved with Hawaiian imagery and dyed using an ancient method unique to Ni'ihau island, knowledge of which had been lost for over a century until a scholar rediscovered it in 1980.

Holualoa Ukulele Gallery MUSIC
(808-324-4100; www.konaweb.com/ukegallery/index.html; 76-5942 Mamalahoa Hwy; 11am-4:30pm Tue-Sat, other times by appointment) Inside a historic post office, owner Sam Rosen displays beautifully handcrafted ukuleles made by himself and other island luthiers. He's happy to show you his workshop and, if you've got 10 days, he'll even teach you how to build your own uke.

Dovetail Gallery & Design ARTS, CRAFTS
(808-322-4046; www.dovetailgallery.net; 76-5942 Mamalahoa Hwy; 10am-4pm Tue-Sat) Showcases elegant contemporary work by Big Island sculptors, painters, photographers and furniture designers.

Getting There & Away

Holualoa village straggles along Hwy 180 (Mamalahoa Hwy), north of the Hualalai Rd intersection. Parking in the free village lot or along the highway's shoulder is easy most of the time, except during special events.

South Kona Coast

South Kona, more than any other district of Hawai'i, embodies the many strands that make up the geo-cultural tapestry of the Big Island. There is both the dry lava desert of the Kohala Coast and the wet, misty jungles of Puna and Hilo; fishing villages inhabited by countrified Hawaiian locals next to hippie art galleries established by counterculture exiles from the mainland, next to condos plunked down by millionaire land developers.

In addition, the dozen or so miles heading south from Kailua-Kona to Kealakekua Bay are among Hawai'i's most action packed, historically speaking. It's here that ancient Hawaiian *ali'i* secretly buried the bones of their ancestors, kapu breakers braved shark-infested waters to reach the *pu'uhonua* (place of refuge), and British explorer Captain Cook and his crew fatally first stepped ashore in Hawaii.

This is the acclaimed Kona Coffee Belt, consisting of 22 miles patchworked with more than 600 small coffee farms. That there is no cost-efficient way to industrialize the handpicking and processing of the beans contributes to the time-warp quality of local life. But the reasons are also cultural: at the turn of the 20th century, thousands of Japanese immigrants arrived to labor as independent coffee farmers, and their influence – along with that of Chinese, Filipino and Portuguese workers – remains richly felt in Buddhist temples, fabric stores and restaurant menus.

Note that the main island belt road also goes by the names Hwy 11 and Mamalahoa Hwy. Southbound Hele-On (p194) buses departing from Kailua-Kona for Kau can drop travelers at sights along the way.

Honalo

At a bend in the road where Hwys 11 and 180 intersect, little time-warped Honalo is your first sign that more than miles separate you from touristy Kailua-Kona.

Sights & Activities

Daifukuji Soto Mission TEMPLE
(808-322-3524; www.daifukuji.org; 79-7241 Mamalahoa Hwy; usually 8am-4pm Mon-Sat) The first building you see in Honalo resembles a cross between a low-slung red barn, a white-roofed villa and a Japanese shrine. Well, one out of three ain't bad: this is the Buddhist Daifukuji (Temple of Great Happiness) Soto Mission. Slip off your shoes and admire the two ornate, lovingly tended altars. Everyone is welcome to join Zen meditation sessions, tai-chi lessons and *taiko* (Japanese drum) practices, which are held across the week; call or check the website for details.

Higashihara Park PARK
(7am-8pm;) If you have young kids, head north a mile or so from Honalo and enjoy shady Higashihara Park. Its unique Hawaii-themed wooden play structure is both attractive and endlessly climbable. It is on the *makai* side, between mile markers 114 and 115.

Aloha Kayak Co KAYAKING
(808-322-2868; www.alohakayak.com; 79-7248 Mamalahoa Hwy; kayak per 24hr single/double/triple $35/60/85, tours $50-130; usually 7:30am-5pm) This Hawaiian-owned outfit knows

South Kona Coast

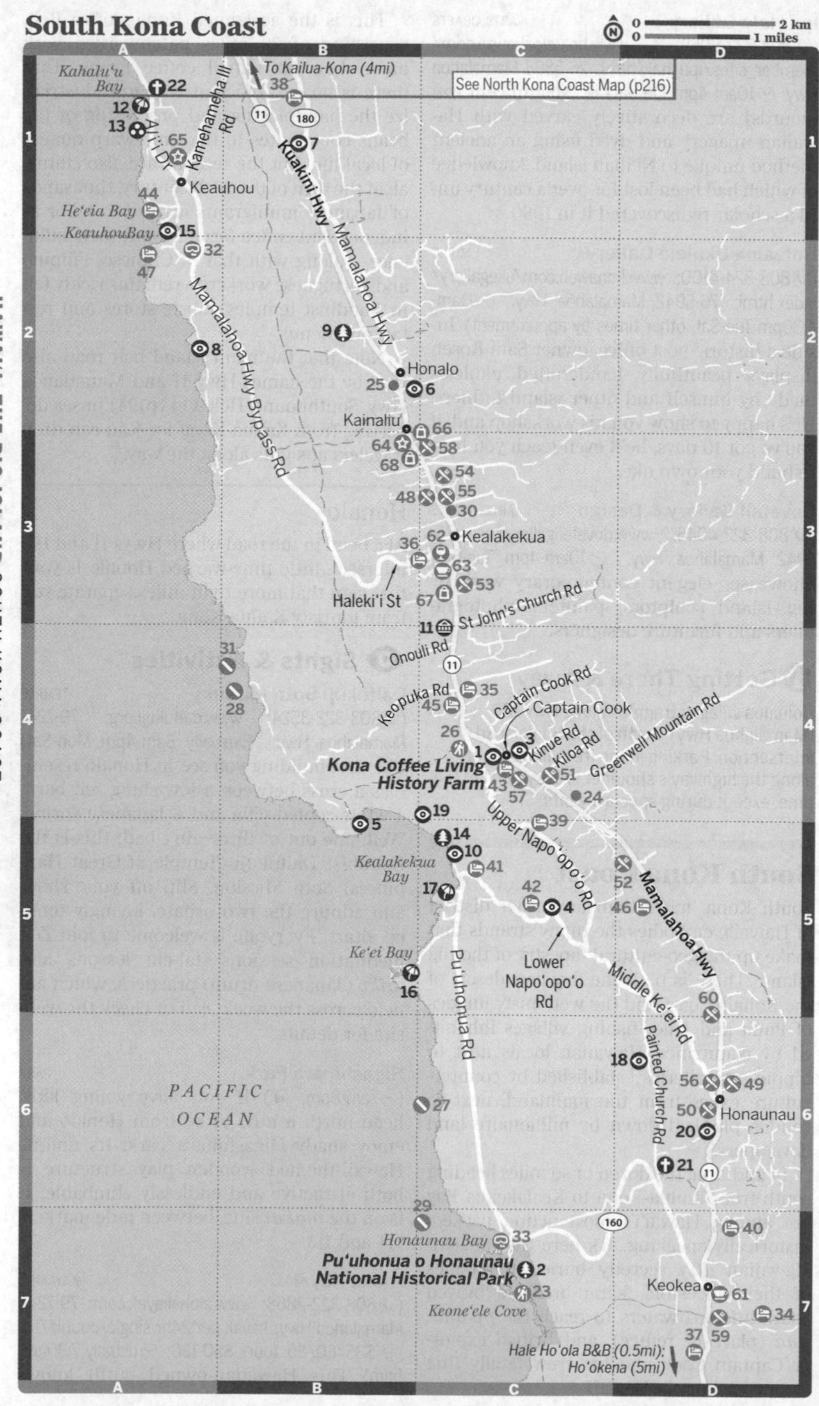

South Kona Coast

Top Sights

1 Kona Coffee Living History Farm C4
2 Pu'uhonua o Honaunau National Historical Park C7

Sights

3 Amy BH Greenwell Ethnobotanical Garden C4
4 Big Island Bees C5
5 Captain Cook Monument B5
6 Daifukuji Soto Mission B2
7 Donkey Mill Art Center B1
8 End of the World A2
Greenwell Farms .... (see 11)
9 Higashihara Park B2
10 Hiki'au Heiau C5
11 HN Greenwell Store Museum C4
12 Kahalu'u Beach Park A1
13 Kahulu'u Manowai A1
14 Kealakekua Bay State Historical Park C5
15 Keauhou Bay A1
Keauhou Kahalu'u Heritage Center .... (see 65)
16 Ke'ei Beach B5
17 Manini Beach C5
18 Paleaku Gardens Peace Sanctuary D6
19 Pali Kapu o Keoua C4
20 Society for Kona's Education & Art D6
21 St Benedict's Painted Church D6
22 St Peter's Church A1

Activities, Courses & Tours

23 1871 Trail C7
24 Adventures in Paradise C4
25 Aloha Kayak Co B2
26 Captain Cook Monument Trail C4
27 Coral Dome C6
28 Driftwood B4
Fair Wind .... (see 15)
29 Hammerhead C7
30 Kona Boys C3
31 Long Lava Tube B4
Mamalahoa Hot Tubs & Massage .... (see 35)
32 Ocean Safaris A2
Sea Paradise .... (see 15)
Sea Quest .... (see 15)
33 Two-Step C7

Sleeping

34 Aloha Guest House D7
35 Areca Palms Estate B&B C4
36 Banana Patch B3
37 Hale Ho'ola B&B D7
38 Haleakala B&B B1
39 Ka'awa Loa Plantation & Guesthouse C5
40 Kane Plantation D7
41 Kealakekua Bay Bed & Breakfast C5
42 Luana Inn C5
43 Manago Hotel C4
44 Outrigger Kanaloa at Kona A1
45 Pineapple Park C4
46 Pomaika'i 'Lucky' Farm B&B D5
47 Sheraton Kona Resort & Spa at Keauhou Bay A2

Eating

48 Annie's Island Fresh Burgers C3
Bianelli's .... (see 65)
49 Big Jake's Island B-B-Q D6
50 Bong Brothers & Sistahs D6
51 ChoiceMart C4
52 Coffee Shack D5
53 Dave's Hawaiian Ice Cream C3
54 Donkey Balls C3
55 Ke'ei Café C3
Kenichi Pacific .... (see 65)
56 Keoki's Roadside Cafe D6
KTA Super Store .... (see 65)
57 Mahina Cafe C4
Manago Restaurant .... (see 43)
Mi's Italian Bistro .... (see 35)
Patz Pies .... (see 57)
Peaberry & Galette .... (see 65)
58 Rebel Kitchen C3
Sam Choy's Kai Lanai .... (see 65)
59 South Kona Fruit Stand D7
60 Super J's D5
Teshima's Restaurant .... (see 6)

Drinking & Nightlife

61 Kona Coffeehouse & Cafe D7
62 Korner Pocket Bar & Grill C3
63 Orchid Isle Café C3

Entertainment

64 Aloha Theatre B3
Haleo Luau .... (see 47)
65 Keauhou Shopping Center A1
Regal Keauhou Stadium 7 .... (see 65)

Shopping

66 Blue Ginger Gallery C3
67 Discovery Antiques C3
Ho'oulu Community Farmers Market .... (see 47)
Keauhou Farmers Market .... (see 65)
Kiernan Music .... (see 58)
Kimura Store .... (see 58)
Kona Stories .... (see 65)
68 Lavender Moon Gallery B3
South Kona Green Market .... (see 51)

local waters, offers half-day (noon to 5pm) kayak rentals and SUP gear rental. Kayak-snorkel tours go to Kealakekua Bay and other spots along the coast, seeking out sea caves and manta rays at night.

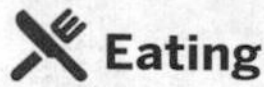

Eating

Teshima's Restaurant JAPANESE $$
(808-322-9140; www.teshimarestaurant.com; 79-7251 Mamalahoa Hwy; dinner mains $13-23; 6:30am-1:45pm & 5-9pm;) For a real window into local life, grab a table at this family-run restaurant, which has been dishing up Japanese comfort food since the 1950s. The vintage atmosphere and the country-style Japanese home cooking come together into a lovely whole; the sashimi is always superfresh and the tempura lightly crisp and golden.

Kainaliu

Packed with antiques shops, art galleries and eclectic boutiques, Kainaliu is a lunch-and-linger town – handy if you get caught in the infamous 'Kainaliu crawl' traffic jam along the two-lane Mamalahoa Hwy.

Eating

★ **Annie's Island Fresh Burgers** BURGERS $
(808-324-6000; www.anniesislandfreshburgers; 79-7460 Mamalahoa Hwy, Mango Court; burgers $9-14; 11am-8pm;) Sometimes you just need a burger. The sort of burger that makes you sigh and smile and go 'Damn' and feel slightly uncomfortably full afterwards. Enter Annie's, which uses local veggies and grass-fed Big Island beef to make some of the Big Island's best burgers. Vegetarian? No worries – dig into a portobello mushroom stuffed with parmesan cheese.

Rebel Kitchen SANDWICHES $$
(808-322-0616; http://rebelkitchen.com; 79-7399 Mamalahoa Hwy; mains $9-16; 11am-5:30pm Mon-Fri;) There's a sense of playful anarchy here, from the young counter staff to the punk and reggae coming out of the kitchen. You know what else comes out of the kitchen? Amazing sandwiches. We'll fight you for the blackened *ono* with cajun mayo, although you could pacify us with the jerk-chicken sandwich served on a rosemary roll.

Entertainment

Aloha Theatre THEATER, CINEMA
(808-322-9924; www.apachawaii.org; 79-7384 Mamalahoa Hwy; tickets $10-25; box office 10am-4pm Mon-Fri) Meet one of the liveliest little community theater troupes in the islands: the Aloha Performing Arts Company, with quality plays, indie films and live music on its program. Budget tip: buy tickets in advance to save money. Pro tip: on the opening night of locally produced shows, the cast cooks the audience dinner.

Shopping

Kiernan Music MUSIC
(808-323-4939; www.kiernanmusic.com; 79-7401 Mamalahoa Hwy; 10am-6pm Tue-Fri, to 5pm Sat) Friendly owner Brian Kiernan has a talent for restoring vintage ukuleles and guitars, and he's a wonderful resource whether you're a curious beginner or a serious musician looking to buy a custom-made uke or archtop guitar.

Blue Ginger Gallery ARTS
(808-322-3898; http://mybluegingergallery.com; 79-7391 Mamalahoa Hwy; 10am-5pm Tue-Sat) This quirky little gallery is supremely eclectic and friendly. There's a definite blue-turquoise aura about, as well as plenty of paintings, prints and crafts produced by local artists and artisans.

Lavender Moon Gallery ARTS, CRAFTS
(808-324-7708; www.lavendermoongallery.com; 79-7404 Mamalahoa Hwy; 11am-6pm Tue-Fri, to 5pm Sat) High-quality original paintings, prints, jewelry, pottery and handmade bags by Big Island artists fill the colorful storefront windows.

DON'T MISS

DONKEY BALLS

When it comes to sweets and Kainaliu, we love **Donkey Balls** (808-322-1475; www.alohahawaiianstore.com; 79-7411 Mamalahoa Hwy; 8am-6pm), and we promise it's not just for the saucy name, but for the excellent quality and diverse varieties of these beefy chocolates. Sure, the pure version is amazing enough, but check out the Jitter Balls, coated in 100% Kona coffee, or the Hot Board Balls, rolled in cayenne pepper, or the Blue Balls, which come in a layer of blue-colored white chocolate… OK, maybe we're a little enamored of the saucy names.

The local factory store also contains a pretty excellent cafe if you need some espresso to go with your punny chocolates.

Kimura Store ARTS, CRAFTS
(79-7408 Mamalahoa Hwy; ⏰9am-5pm Mon-Sat) This long-standing family shop rolls out yards of colorfully patterned Hawaiian and Japanese fabrics.

Kealakekua

Hawaiian heiau and the secret burial caves of *ali'i* sat high upon these cliffs centuries ago. Today, the workaday town of Kealakekua, spread along the busy Mamalahoa Hwy, is South Kona's commercial center. It is a sacred place whose name means 'pathway of the gods.'

Sights

HN Greenwell Store Museum MUSEUM
(808-323-3222; www.konahistorical.org; 81-6551 Mamalahoa Hwy; adult/child 5-12yr $7/3; ⏰10am-2pm Mon & Thu) Housed in one of Kona's oldest buildings, this museum is a taste of 19th-century Hawai'i. Built in 1875 and meticulously restored, it has educational docents in period dress who bring Kona's multicultural and agricultural history to life as they wield dry goods and talk story. You'll usually smell sweet bread baking in the traditional Portuguese bread oven outside after 11am on Thursdays.

The museum is between mile markers 111 and 112 on Hwy 11.

Greenwell Farms FARM
(808-323-2295, 888-592-5662; www.greenwell-farms.com; 81-6581 Mamalahoa Hwy; ⏰8am-5pm, tours 8:30am-4:30pm) FREE This 150-acre family farm, established in 1850, is run by fourth-generation Greenwells and is one of Kona's oldest and best-known coffee plantations. It currently roasts coffee cherries from more than 200 local growers. Take a free tour and sample coffee and fruit at a shady picnic table. You can also purchase Kona Red (www.konared.com), a juice made from coffee-cherry pulp. The farm is between mile markers 110 and 111.

Activities

Adventures in Paradise WATER SPORTS
(info 808-447-0080, reservations 888-210-5365; www.bigislandkayak.com; 82-6020 Mamalahoa Hwy; kayak-snorkel tour $90; ⏰usually 8am-5pm) At this professional water-sports outfitter, guides look after beginners and lead excellent kayak-snorkeling trips to Kealakekua Bay.

Kona Boys WATER SPORTS
(808-328-1234; www.konaboys.com; 79-7539 Mamalahoa Hwy; single/double kayak rental per day $54/74, tours $119-169; ⏰7am-5pm) This laid-back pro water-sports outfitter is South Kona's largest, and a fixture of the local tourism scene. Kayaking, snorkeling and outrigger-canoe sailing trips visit Kealakekua Bay, and you can learn surfing and SUP from these *brahs* (brothers). Snorkel gear, SUP, surfboard and kayak rentals available. Call ahead for tour and gear-rental reservations.

Mamalahoa Hot Tubs & Massage SPA
(808-323-2288; www.mamalahoa-hottubs.com; 81-1016 St John's Church Rd; hot tub per hour 2 people $35-50; ⏰noon-9pm Wed-Sat, by appointment) Soak away your blisters or blues in a lush garden mini-oasis. The two teak tubs, sheltered by thatched roofs that allow for stargazing, are open-sided yet private. Many types of massage, from Swedish to traditional Hawaiian *lomilomi* and hot stone, are available. Reservations required; ask about discount packages.

Sleeping

Areca Palms Estate B&B B&B $$
(808-323-2276; www.konabedandbreakfast.com; 81-1031 Keopuka Mauka Rd; d incl breakfast $120-145; @) Country comfort and aloha spirit seamlessly combine in this spotless, wooden home. The airy rooms are meticulously outfitted, with lots of pillows and lush robes, and your hosts share their local knowledge freely. Kick back in the family room or watch a sunset from the hot tub. You'll eat like royalty with the fresh breakfasts. Guests can borrow beach and snorkel gear.

Banana Patch COTTAGE $$
(800-452-9017, 808-322-8888; www.banana-banana.com; Mamao St; studios $125, cottages from $145; @) Let it all hang out in one of these comfortable, clothing-optional cottages secluded amid tropical foliage. The rustic retreats are terrific for DIY naturists, who share a full kitchen and hot tub. A two bedroom cottage is available for stays of longer than a week but you may be able to talk your way into shorter stays.

Eating & Drinking

Dave's Hawaiian Ice Cream ICE CREAM $
(808-345-8042; www.daveshawaiianicecream.com; 81-6592 Mamalahoa Hwy; snacks $3-6; ⏰11:30am-9pm;) Made on O'ahu, Dave's

BYPASS THE TRAFFIC

If you need to get between Keauhou and Kealakekua, consider skipping the belt road and using the Mamalahoa Hwy Bypass Rd that connects the two communities. This cut-through allows savvy drivers to avoid the worst of commuter traffic in and out of Kailua-Kona. The road connects Haleki'i St in Kealakekua (seaward off Hwy 11 between mile markers 111 and 112) to Kamehameha III Rd in Keauhou and Ali'i Dr and Hwy 11 (Mamalahoa) beyond.

creamy concoctions are bursting with island flavors: *poha* (cape gooseberry), guava, *lilikoʻi,* coconut, *ube* (purple yam), chocolate macnut, Kona coffee and more. Get a scoop inside a cup of rainbow shave ice.

Ke'ei Café BISTRO $$
(808-322-9992; www.keeicafe.net; 79-7511 Mamalahoa Hwy; mains $15-29; 5-9pm Tue-Sat;) If you're craving some fine dining while in South Kona, it's hard to do better than Keʻei Cafe, which has carved a name for itself as an excellent outpost of haute Hawaiian cuisine. Cracking peanut miso salad sets the stage for powerful mains like roasted chicken served with red-curry sauce – or, if you're in the mood, a more Western peppercorn gravy. Reservations recommended; request a lanai table. No credit cards.

Mi's Italian Bistro ITALIAN $$
(808-323-3880; www.misitalianbistro.com; 81-6372 Mamalahoa Hwy; mains $14-35; 4:30-8:30pm;) This intimate eatery, run by husband-and-wife team chef Morgan Starr and Ingrid Chan, does a great job of filling South Kona's need for upscale Italian laced with local ingredients. Settle into a romantic nook and devour homemade pasta, organic veggies, wickedly good seafood corn chowder and thin-crust pizza amid a laid-back, classy vibe.

Orchid Isle Café CAFE
(808-323-9730; www.orchidislecoffee.com; 81-6637 Mamalahoa Hwy; 6:30am-2pm;) Hang out on the ocean-view lanai, surf the internet and refuel with Kona coffee at this cozy coffeehouse. Eat elswhere.

Korner Pocket Bar & Grill BAR
(808-322-2994; 81-970 Haleki'i St; 11am-1am) This is about it when it comes to bar options in South Kona. It's a pretty local joint, and sees live music on weekends and packed pool tables any day of the week. On slow nights, it may close earlier.

Shopping

Discovery Antiques ANTIQUES
(808-323-2239; 81-6593 Mamalahoa Hwy; 10am-5pm Mon-Sat, 11am-4pm Sun) Tin toys and aloha shirts, bric-a-brac and vintage Hawaiiana – who knows what you'll find at this secondhand antiques and curiosities shop. Bonus: it sells scoops of Tropical Dreams ice cream, made in Hilo.

South Kona Green Market MARKET
(www.skgm.org; 9am-2pm Sun;) Currently setting up at the Amy BH Greenwell Ethnobotanical Garden, this small farmers market with live music vends organic island-grown produce, artisanal foodstuffs and funky crafts.

Information

First Hawaiian Bank (808-322-3484; www.fhb.com; 81-6626 Mamalahoa Hwy; 8:30am-4pm Mon-Thu, to 6pm Fri)

Kona Community Hospital (808-322-9311; www.kch.hhsc.org; 79-1019 Haukapila St) Level-III trauma center with a 24-hour emergency room.

Captain Cook

As Hwy 11/Mamalahoa Hwy winds southward, the greenery thickens, the ocean views become more compelling and it can be hard to tell where towns start and stop. Captain Cook is signaled by the historic Manago Hotel, which began in 1917 as a restaurant catering to salesmen on the then-lengthy journey between Hilo and Kona. The stout building remains a regional touchstone for travelers and residents alike.

Captain Cook is also where you access Kealakekua Bay, plus a great selection of B&Bs and down-home cooking. Sinewy Napoʻopoʻo Rd, which eventually becomes Middle Keei Rd, webs between the mountain and the ocean and is a pretty place to drive without an agenda. The many 'No Spray' signs are put up by organic farms (or even just home owners) that are warding against state pesticide spraying.

Sights

★Kona Coffee Living History Farm
HISTORIC SITE

(808-323-2006; www.konahistorical.org; 82-6199 Mamalahoa Hwy; 1hr tour adult/child 5-12yr $15/5; 10am-2pm Mon-Fri, hourly tours 10am-1pm) Many coffee-farm tours are perfunctory 15-minute affairs. This tour run by the Kona Historical Society, an affiliate of the Smithsonian Institute, is different and deep. More than just an exploration of how coffee is grown and harvested, it's an evocative look at rural Japanese immigrant life in South Kona. Restored to Hawai'i's prestatehood era, this 5.5-acre working coffee farm once belonged to the Uchida family, who lived here until 1994.

Several of the docents grew up on area coffee farms, so they speak from experience as they show you around the orchards, processing mill, drying roofs and main house. On easy walking tours, you'll learn how to pick coffee cherries and prepare a traditional *bentō* (Japanese boxed lunch).

The farm is between mile markers 110 and 111.

Amy BH Greenwell Ethnobotanical Garden
GARDENS

(808-323-3318; www.bishopmuseum.org/greenwell; 82-6160 Mamalahoa Hwy; adult/child under 12yr $7/free; 9am-4pm Tue-Sun, guided tours 1pm Tue-Sat) Without pottery or metals, ancient Hawaiians fashioned most of what they needed from plants. This ethnobotanical garden preserves Hawai'i's endemic species dating from before Western contact and Polynesian-introduced plants in an *ahupua'a* (land division). Wander along unlandscaped paths or take a guided tour to go more in-depth. Bring insect repellent.

The garden is between mile markers 110 and 111.

Big Island Bees
FARM

(808-328-7318; www.bigislandbees.com; 82-5780 Napo'opo'o Rd; 10am-4pm) At this roadside gift shop and tiny historical museum, genial staff will let you in on all the secrets of beekeeping, then give you a peek inside a living apiary and teach you how their award-winning, single-varietal and certified organic honey gets made. Taste a free sample of *'ohi'a lehua* (blossom honey spiced with cinnamon), or the macnut-blossom honey, and you'll be hooked.

Sleeping

There are a lot of rental properties in this area; check out www.vrbo.com and www.airbnb.com for updated listings.

Managa Hotel
HOTEL $

(808-323-2642; www.managohotel.com; 82-6151 Mamalahoa Hwy; s/d from $56/59, with shared bath from $33/36;) This no-frills, historical hotel has been hosting travelers and islanders since 1917. Run by the family's third generation, the Manago has clean, spare, motel-style rooms without air-con; the best are on the 3rd floor, with private bathrooms and ocean-view lanai. Book far ahead, especially for the Japanese-style tatami room with futons and a *furo* (Japanese bathtub).

A koi pond and garden add to the breezy tropical atmosphere. This local landmark is between mile markers 110 and 111.

Pineapple Park
HOSTEL $

(877-800-3800, 808-323-2224; www.pineapple-park.com; 81-6363 Mamalahoa Hwy; dm $30, r shared/private bath $79/89; office 8am-8pm;) South Kona's only hostel is your basic backpacker crash pad, run by a friendly if iron-willed proprietor. A sociable vibe makes up for cramped dorms (No 10 is best) and more comfortable (but still overpriced) private rooms. Look for colorful kayaks out front, between mile markers 110 and 111.

★Ka'awa Loa Plantation & Guesthouse
B&B $$

(808-323-2686; www.kaawaloaplantation.com; 82-5990 Upper Napo'opo'o Rd; r $129-149, cottages/ste $159/199, incl breakfast;) Some places embody Hawaii's beauty effortlessly – like this guesthouse with wraparound lanai, unparalleled coastal views and gracious hosts who show genuine aloha. Exquisitely decorated rooms (not all have private baths) with fine linens and cottages set amid organic coffee and macadamia orchards are ideal for romance; so is soaking in the outdoor hot tub watching the sunset.

Luana Inn
B&B $$

(808-328-2612; www.luanainn.com; 82-5856 Lower Napo'opo'o Rd; d $169-199, ste $209, all incl breakfast;) Welcome to spotless Luana Inn, where each spacious, uncluttered and tastefully understated room has its own private entrance and kitchenette. Two rooms open right onto the pool and hot tub with jaw-dropping bay views, while two spacious suites share a sunny cottage. Over a lavish breakfast, pick your hosts' brains for Hawai'i travel tips – they've been around.

Pomaika'i 'Lucky' Farm B&B B&B $$
(☎808-328-2112; www.luckyfarm.com; 83-5465 Mamalahoa Hwy; d incl breakfast $90-140;) Rustic, bohemian charm oozes from this macadamia-and-fruit farm. Two simple rooms share the main house, with two airy 'Greenhouse' rooms with queen beds and screened windows attached. Hidden by banana plants, the Barn is a tastefully unadorned shack with screened, half-open walls and outdoor shower. Families are particularly welcome, and breakfast is a social occasion. Two-night minimum stay.

Eating

★Super J's HAWAIIAN $
(☎808-328-9566; 83-5409 Mamalahoa Hwy; plates $8-12; ⏲10am-6:30pm Mon-Sat) The full title of this place is 'Ka'aloa's Super J's Hawaiian Food,' but everyone calls it Super J's. They also call it freakin' delicious. The *laulau* (pork, chicken or fish wrapped inside taro or *ti* leaves) is steamed until it's so tender it melts under your fork, the *lomilomi* salmon is perfectly salty – you'll even want second helpings of *poi* (mashed taro).

Best of all is the setting: you're basically eating in a welcoming Hawaiian family's kitchen. It's on the *makai* side of Hwy 11, between mile markers 106 and 107.

Manago Restaurant JAPANESE $
(☎808-323-2642; www.managohotel.com; 82-6155 Mamalahoa Hwy; mains breakfast $4-6, lunch & dinner $6-14; ⏲7-9am, 11am-2pm & 5-7:30pm Tue-Sun;) The bingo-parlor dining room of the Manago is an iconic Big island experience. It feels like an early-20th-century diner, but one made for South Kona's ethnic blend: a mix of Japanese, Chinese, Portuguese, Filipino, a few mainlanders and Native Hawaiians. Thus, the Manago's meals are hearty, American-size portions, yet come with bowls of rice and diced Japanese vegetables.

Mahina Cafe CAFE $
(☎808-323-3200; 82-6123 Mamalahoa Hwy; breakfast & lunch mains $6-12; ⏲7am-4pm Mon-Fri, to 3pm Sat & Sun) Just south of the Manago Hotel, this simple diner run by two sisters serves excellent, made-from-scratch comfort food such as pancakes slathered in *haupia* (coconut cream), *loco moco* bowls and mixed-plate lunches. Grab fresh, hot *malasadas* (Portuguese doughnuts) from the drive-through window. Ingredients tend to be sourced locally (and assembled with expert care).

Patz Pies PIZZA $
(☎808-323-8100; 82-6127 Mamalahoa Hwy; slices/whole pizzas from $3/17; ⏲10am-9pm) Thin crust, zesty sauce. Claims to authentic NYC pizza are only slightly exaggerated at this native New Yorker's kitchen, just south of the Manago Hotel.

ChoiceMart SUPERMARKET $
(82-6066 Mamalahoa Hwy; ⏲5am-10pm) South Kona's largest grocery store lets you stock up on beach picnic supplies.

Coffee Shack CAFE $$
(☎808-328-9555; www.coffeeshack.com; 83-5799 Mamalahoa Hwy; meals $10-15; ⏲7:30am-3pm) Perched precariously next to the highway, the Shack is famous for insane views of Kealakekua Bay from its open-air deck. We can say, with no hyperbole, you may never have a cup of coffee with a better vista. The food – sandwiches, salads and the like – is pretty kick-butt too, especially homemade desserts such as *liliko'i* cheesecake.

Look for the historic building on the *makai* side of Hwy 11, between mile markers 108 and 109.

Keoki's Roadside Cafe SEAFOOD $$
(☎808-328-2259; 83-5293 Mamalahoa Hwy; mains $8-18; ⏲9am-6:30pm Mon-Sat, to 6pm Sun) This little roadside stand dishes out solid fish and chips made with locally caught seafood species such as *ono* and mahimahi. And do you need some corny island art? There's corny island art for sale too!

Kealakekua Bay

Kealakekua Bay is one of Hawai'i's seminal sites, a location that manages to blend incredible natural beauty with supreme historical importance. Besides being one of the major religious sites of Native Hawaiians, the bay marks the spot where Captain Cook and, by extension, the outside world first set foot in the archipelago, irrevocably altering the fate of the islands and their residents.

A wide, calm bay is shouldered by a low lava point to the north, tall reddish *pali* (cliffs) in the center and miles of green mountain slopes to the south. The bay is both a state park and a marine-life conservation district, and is famous for its rich variety of sea life, including spinner dolphins. This entire area is considered sacred, and deserves your respect.

Napo'opo'o Rd, off Hwy 11, winds 4.5 miles down to the bay, leaving behind the lush foliage of the rainier uplands for the perpetually sunny coast (never assume that rain on the highway means rain in the bay). The road ends at the parking lot for Napo'opo'o Beach and Wharf.

Beaches

Manini Beach BEACH

On its southern side, Kealakekua Bay is rocky and exposed to regular northwest swells, so swimming and snorkeling conditions are poor. That said, Manini Beach makes a scenic, shady picnic spot. If you do want to take a dip, despite the scattered, sharp coral and *a'a* (rough, jagged lava) along the shoreline, the best ocean access is to your right upon arriving at the beach.

From Napo'opo'o Rd, turn left onto Pu'uhonua Rd, then right onto Manini Rd. There's limited roadside parking.

Ke'ei Beach BEACH

South of Kealakekua Bay, Ke'ei Beach is an attractive cove that's mostly too rough and rocky for swimming, except for a narrow sandy stretch at its northern end. When conditions are right, local surfers ride the long reef break. Bayside, there's a small canoe and kayak launch and a few fishing shacks but no public facilities. Be respectful of local residents – you're essentially walking in their front yards.

To get here, take the ragged 4WD road leading *makai* off Pu'uhonua Rd, about 528yd south of Manini Beach Rd (if you hit Ke'ei Transfer Station, you've gone too far). Paved Pu'uhonua Rd continues another few miles south to Place of Refuge.

BIG ISLAND SURF BEACHES & BREAKS

Because Hawai'i, the Big Island is the youngest of Hawaii's islands and its coastline is still quite rugged, it's often assumed there isn't much in the way of surfable waves. As a result, places like O'ahu and Kaua'i have stolen the surf spotlight, but archaeologists and researchers believe that Kealakekua Bay is probably where ancient Polynesians started riding waves. It is currently not possible for visitors to follow in the footsteps of the ancient Hawaiians and surf there, due to a moratorium on unlicensed visitors.

Unlike neighboring islands, where the north and south shores are the primary centers of swell activity, the Big Island's east and west shores are its focal points. Because swells are shadowed by the other islands, as a general rule the surf doesn't get as big here. The Kona Coast offers the best opportunities, with north and south swell exposures, as well as offshore trade winds. **Kawaihae Harbor** is surrounded by several fun, introductory reefs near the breakwall, while further south, near Kekaha Kai (Kona Coast) State Park (p220), is a considerably more advanced break that challenges even the most seasoned surfers. If you have a 4WD vehicle or don't mind an hour-long hike, be sure to check out heavy reef breaks such as Mahai'ula (p221) and Makalawena (p220). They break best on northwest swells, making the later winter months the prime season. A hike or 4WD is also necessary to reach popular Pine Trees (p220) at Keahole Point, near Kailua-Kona's airport.

In East Hawai'i, just outside of Hilo, there are several good intermediate waves. Richardson Ocean Park (p269) is a good option within Hilo, and just west of town is Honoli'i (p270), a fast left and right peak breaking into a river mouth. Further up the Hamakua Coast is Waipi'o Bay (p261) – access to the beach requires a long walk or a 4WD vehicle but the waves are worth the effort. Puna's Pohoiki Bay (p286), meanwhile, boasts three breaks and offers the island's best surfing, according to many. This is decidedly not a beginner's break – the waves crash right up on some rough rocks.

In Ka'u, locals brace a rough paddle out to catch long rides on the nearly perfect left break at Kawa Bay (p306).

In Kailua-Kona, newbies take lessons and test the waves at Kahalu'u Beach Park (p196).

Top bodyboarding and bodysurfing spots include Hapuna Beach (p230), White (Magic) Sands Beach (p179), near Kailua-Kona, and the beaches at Kekaha Kai State Park.

Sights

Captain Cook Monument HISTORIC SITE

This tall white obelisk is visible a mile away at Ka'awaloa Cove. It marks the spot where Captain Cook was killed in an armed confrontation with Hawaiians in 1779. In 1877, as an act of diplomacy, the Kingdom of Hawai'i deeded the land that the monument stands on to Britain. Behind lie some scattered stones and foundation marks, the ruins of the ancient village of Ka'awaloa.

Hiki'au Heiau TEMPLE

Veer right at the base of Napo'opo'o Rd to reach this large platform temple. In front of the heiau, a stone beach makes a moody perch from which to observe the stunning scenery, but the surf is too rough to swim in. Climbing on the ruins is kapu.

Pali Kapu o Keoua HISTORIC SITE

Above Kealakekua Bay, the 'sacred cliffs of Keoua' were named for a chief and rival of Kamehameha I. Several high, inaccessible caves in these cliffs served as burial places for Hawaiian royalty, and it's speculated that some of Captain Cook's bones ended up here as well.

Activities

Snorkeling

At Kealakekua Bay's northern end, protected **Ka'awaloa Cove** ranks among Hawai'i's premier snorkeling spots. Protected from ocean swells, its aquamarine waters are especially clear. Tropical fish and coral are brilliantly abundant, and those with iron stomachs can swim 100ft from shore to hang over the blue abyss of an underwater cliff.

If you're lucky, *honu* (green sea turtles) and spinner dolphins might join you, but remember not to approach these wild animals. By law, you must remain at least 50yd away from turtles, dolphins, whales and seals in the water. All Hawaiian sea turtles are endangered, so give 'em a break and never touch or try to ride them.

At the time of research, you could only visit Ka'awaloa Cove on a snorkel cruise leaving from Kailua-Kona or Keahou, on a guided kayaking tour by a South Kona outfitter or by hiking the Captain Cook Monument Trail.

Kayaking

Controversy over overcrowding and environmental impact on the bay has resulted in new legal regulations for kayakers. Special recreational permits for transiting the bay, but not for landing at Ka'awaloa Cove or launching from Napo'opo'o Wharf, are currently available to individual kayakers in advance from the **Division of State Parks** (☎808-951-9540; www.hawaiistateparks.org; 75 Aupuni St, Hilo; ⌚8:30am-3:30pm Mon-Fri).

Otherwise, your only other option (for now) is a guided kayaking tour by a state-permitted outfitter; check www.hawaiistateparks.org for a current list. Most tours launch from Napo'opo'o Wharf, paddling 30 to 45 minutes across the bay to Ka'awaloa Cove. Prevailing winds are from the northwest, so returning is usually faster and easier.

At the time of research, the only outfitters permitted to lead guided kayaking tours of Kealakekua Bay were Kona Boys (p205) in Captain Cook, Aloha Kayak Co (p201) in Honalo and Adventures in Paradise (p205) in Kealakekua.

Diving

There are many good dive sites clustered around Kealakekua Bay, including **Ka'awaloa Cove**, with its exceptionally diverse coral and fish. Other sites further north include **Hammerhead**, a deep dive with pelagic action; **Coral Dome**, a big, teeming cave with a giant skylight; and **Driftwood**, featuring lava tubes and whitetip reef sharks.

In the aptly named **Long Lava Tube**, an intermediate site just north of Kealakekua Bay, lava 'skylights' shoot light through the ceiling of the 70ft-long tube, and you may see crustaceans, morays and maybe even Spanish dancers. Outside are countless lava formations sheltering conger eels, triton's trumpet shells and squirrelfish.

Hiking

Captain Cook Monument Trail HIKING

Your only land access to the Captain Cook Monument is this trail, which offers nice lookouts on the way down and leads right to the snorkeling cove. The descending path is an easy (if buggy) hour, but after snorkeling, the uphill return seems twice as steep (in reality it's a 1300ft elevation gain in 1.8 miles); allow two hours to return.

To get to the trailhead, turn *makai* off the Mamalahoa Hwy onto Napo'opo'o Rd; within the first tenth of a mile, park along the narrow road shoulder, wherever it's safe and legally signposted to do so. To find the trailhead, count five telephone poles from

THE CAPTAIN COOK STORY

On January 17, 1779, Captain Cook sailed into Kealakekua Bay, kicking off one of the most controversial months in Hawaii's history.

Cook's visit coincided with the annual makahiki festival, a four-month period when all warfare and heavy work was suspended to pay homage to Lono – the god of agriculture and peace. Makahiki was marked by an islandwide procession to collect the chief's annual tribute, which set off celebrations, sexual freedom and games.

Cook's welcome in Kealakekua Bay was spectacular: more than 1000 canoes surrounded his ships and 9000 people hailed him from shore. Once landed, Cook was treated with supreme deference – feted as any ruling chief would be, with huge celebrations and overwhelming offerings. The Hawaiians also bartered for goods – particularly for metals, which they'd never seen before. Though Cook tried to keep his sailors from fraternizing with Hawaiian women, he failed utterly and ultimately gave up: Hawaiian women flocked to the boats, having sex freely and frequently in exchange for nails.

On February 4, restocked and ready to go, Cook departed Kealakekua Bay. But only a short way north he encountered a huge storm, and the *Resolution* broke a foremast. Unable to continue, Cook returned to the safety of Kealakekua Bay on February 11.

This time, no canoes rowed out in greeting. Chief Kalaniopu'u instead seemed to indicate Cook had worn out his welcome. For one, captain and crew had already depleted the Hawaiians' supplies of food, plus the makahiki season had ended; the party was over.

As Hawaiian generosity decreased, petty thefts increased, and insults and suspicion replaced politeness on both sides. After a rowboat was stolen, Cook ordered a blockade of Kealakekua Bay and took Chief Kalaniopu'u hostage until the boat was returned.

Cook convinced Kalaniopu'u to come to the *Resolution* to resolve their disputes. But as they walked to shore, Kalaniopu'u learned that sailors had killed a lower chief attempting to exit the bay in his canoe. At this, Kalaniopu'u apparently sat and refused to continue, and a large angry crowd gathered.

Thinking to frighten the Hawaiians, Cook fired his pistol, killing one of the chief's bodyguards. Incensed, the Hawaiians attacked. In the deadly melee, Captain Cook was stabbed with a dagger and clubbed to death.

Cook's death stunned both sides and ended the battle. In the days afterward, the Hawaiians took Cook's body and dismembered it in the custom reserved for high chiefs. The Englishmen demanded Cook's body back, and in a spasm of gruesome violence torched homes and slaughtered Hawaiians – women and children included.

Eventually the Hawaiians returned some bits and pieces – a partial skull, hands and feet – which the English buried at sea, per naval tradition. The Hawaiians kept the bones that held the most mana (spiritual essence), such as his femurs.

the start of the road – it's *makai* across from three tall palm trees.

The route is fairly easy to follow; when in doubt, stay to the left. For the uphill return, you should stay alert for the trail's right-hand turn back up onto the lava ledge, or you'll end up on a 4WD road heading north along the coast – for miles.

Sleeping

Kealakekua Bay Bed & Breakfast B&B **$$**
(808-328-8150; www.keala.com; 82-6002 Lower Napo'opo'o Rd; r/ste/cottage $165/240/360;) Gourmet breakfasts served in a Mediterranean-style villa are reason enough to stay here. Local goat cheese, macadamia-nut pancakes, fresh fruit plucked from the garden – you can't go wrong. That goes for the property itself too: three bright, sun-kissed rooms filled with tropical accents, and the six-person Ohana Kai Guest House, a hill-perched cottage with postcard views of Kealakekua Bay.

Honaunau

Little more than some scattered, friendly businesses hidden amid thick coffee and macadamia-nut groves, Honaunau is fun to explore without a guidebook. The nearby 'Place of Refuge' remains the star attraction, but for another type of retreat meander down Painted Church Rd, stopping at fruit stands and coffee shacks with sea views.

Sights & Activities

St Benedict's Painted Church CHURCH
(☎808-328-2227; www.thepaintedchurch.org; 84-5140 Painted Church Rd, Captain Cook; ⊙services 7am Tue, Thu & Fri, 4pm Sat, 7:15am Sun) A pulpit with a view, gravestones cradled by tropical blooms and a little chapel with floor-to-ceiling 'outsider art' make this church a picturesque side trip. A self-taught artist and Catholic priest, John Velghe, came to Hawai'i from Belgium in 1899 and he modeled the vaulted nave on a Gothic cathedral in Burgos, Spain. His trompe l'oeil artwork is delightful, in a naive art kind of way. Come early or late, when the light is softer and birds sing out.

Paleaku Gardens Peace Sanctuary GARDENS
(☎808-328-8084; www.paleaku.com; 83-5401 Painted Church Rd; adult/child 6-12yr $10/3; ⊙9am-4pm Tue-Sat) Near the church on Painted Church Rd, these tranquil 7-acre gardens contain shrines to the world's major religions and a frankly staggeringly impressive 'Galaxy Garden,' in which famous space painter Jon Lomberg has created a scale model of the Milky Way – in plants. You'll also find yoga and tai chi classes and plenty of general interfaith good vibes.

Society for Kona's Education & Art ARTS CENTER
(SKEA; ☎808-328-9392; www.skea.org; 84-5191 Mamalahoa Hwy) SKEA is a hotbed of activity, with Pilates, Polynesian dance, tai chi and Japanese ink painting classes, art shows and poetry readings; check the online calendar. Around back at the **Kona Potter's Guild**, you can watch potters at work and buy their handmade creations. It's between mile markers 105 and 106.

Sleeping

Aloha Guest House B&B $$
(☎808-328-8955; www.alohaguesthouse.com; 84-4780 Mamalahoa Hwy; r incl breakfast $125-230; @📶) If you're coming all the way to Hawai'i, you should have the finest digs. Heady views from the shared lanai, guest living room and, for the lucky ones, a king-size bed will make you swoon, guaranteed. Ocean vistas are complemented by luxurious amenities such as organic bath products and full breakfasts with local fruit and estate-grown coffee. Access is via an unpaved one-lane farm road that's very steep and bumpy.

Hale Ho'ola B&B B&B $$
(☎877-628-9117, 808-328-9117; www.hale-hoola.com; 85-4577 Mamalahoa Hwy; r incl breakfast $125-165; @📶) This remarkably hospitable roadside B&B provides a homey, relaxed stay with three small but comfortable rooms downstairs in the main house. Despite comfy beds and private lanai with ocean views, the unfortunately thin-walled rooms are jammed together – they're not recommended for honeymooners or antisocial types. Robust breakfasts somewhat compensate.

★**Kane Plantation** B&B $$$
(☎808-328-2416; http://kaneplantationhawaii.com; 84-1120 Telephone Exchange Rd; d incl breakfast $190-280; 📶) You'll be in excellent hands at this upscale historic home, where renowned Hawaiian artist Herb Kane once lived. Perched on a lush *mauka* (inland) hillside, the B&B shares the grounds with an avocado farm. Upstairs, the most spacious Kanaloa Suite boasts a king-size canopy bed and views of Kealakekua Bay from a private lanai. Breakfasts are gourmet, and the hosts are charming.

Eating & Drinking

South Kona Fruit Stand MARKET, CAFE $
(☎808-328-8547; www.southkonafruitstand.com; 84-4770 Mamalahoa Hwy; items $3-10; ⊙9am-6pm Mon-Sat, 10am-4pm Sun; ✎) Baskets overflow with everything from tart apple bananas to filling breadfruit, creamy *abiu* (sapote) and purple jaboticaba berries. Slurp a smoothie on the outdoor patio with gorgeous coastal views. Look for the pineapple flags on the *mauka* side of Hwy 11, between mile markers 103 and 104.

Bong Brothers & Sistahs HEALTH FOOD, DELI $
(www.bongbrothers.com; 84-5227 Mamalahoa Hwy; items $3-8; ⊙9am-6pm Mon-Fri, noon-6pm Sun; ✎) Food is politics at this small organic health-food store, vegetarian takeout deli and coffee shop inside a historic 1929 building.

Big Jake's Island B-B-Q BARBECUE $
(☎808-328-1227; 83-5308 Mamalahoa Hwy; most mains $7-12; ⊙11am-6pm Sun-Thu, to 7pm Fri & Sat) Barbecued ribs, pork and chicken are slowly cooked in the barrel smoker parked by mile marker 106. Chow down at picnic tables out back, or for DIY surf-and-turf, pick up some *poke* from the seafood shop next door.

Kona Coffeehouse & Cafe CAFE
(☎808-328-2524; http://konahomesteadcoffee.com; 84-4830 Mamalahoa Hwy; ⏲7am-4pm Tue-Sat, 8:30am-2pm Sun; 👪) On the *mauka* side of Hwy 11, at the turnoff to Place of Refuge, this coffee shop is serious about 100% Kona brews, espresso and delicious sandwiches. Gooey macnut caramel pies and *liliko'i* bars are homemade.

Pu'uhonua o Honaunau National Historical Park

Standing at the end of a long semidesert of thorny scrub and lava plains, the **national park** (☎808-328-2326, 808-328-2288; www.nps.gov/puho; off Hwy 160, Honaunau; 7-day entry per car $5; ⏲park 7am-sunset, visitor center 8:30am-4:30pm) 🍃 fronting Honaunau Bay provides one of the state's most evocative experiences of ancient Hawai'i, and easy access to some of the best snorkeling anywhere. In short, Pu'uhonua o Honaunau combines a seminal historical experience with some of the best wildlife-spotting on the island, and to access all this, you just need to be able to fit a snorkel in your mouth. The park's tongue-twister name simply means 'place of refuge at Honaunau.'

To get here, turn *makai* (seaward) on to City of Refuge Rd (about 17 miles south of Kailua-Kona). Follow the signs along the curvy road for about 2 miles to Pu'uhonua o Honaunau.

Early morning or late afternoon is an optimal time to visit to avoid the midday heat and crowds. On the weekend closest to July 1, show up for the park's annual **cultural festival**, an extravaganza of traditional food, hula dancing, Hawaiian crafts and cultural demonstrations.

History

In ancient Hawai'i the kapu system regulated every waking moment. A *maka'aina* (commoner) could not look at *ali'i* or walk in their footsteps. Women couldn't cook for men, nor eat with them. Fishing, hunting and gathering timber was restricted to certain seasons. And on and on.

Violators of kapu were hunted down and killed. After all, according to the Hawaiian belief system, breaking kapu infuriated the gods. And gods wrought volcanic eruptions, tidal waves, famine and earthquakes, which could be devastating to the entire community.

There was one loophole, however. Commoners who broke kapu could stave off death if they reached the sacred ground of a *pu'uhonua*. A *pu'uhonua* also gave sanctuary to defeated warriors and wartime noncombatants (men who were too old, too young or unable to fight).

To reach the *pu'uhonua* was no small feat. Since royals and their warriors lived on the grounds surrounding the refuge, kapu breakers had to swim through violent, open ocean, braving currents and sharks, to safety. Once inside the sanctuary, priests performed ceremonies of absolution to placate the gods. Kapu breakers could then return home to start afresh.

The *pu'uhonua* at Honaunau was used for several centuries until 1819, when Hawai'i's old religious ways were abandoned after King Kamehameha II and regent Queen Ka'ahumanu ate together in public, overthrowing the ancient kapu system forever.

👁 Sights

A half-mile walking tour encompasses the park's major sites – the visitor center provides a brochure map with cultural information. At midday, the park gets hot and is only partially shaded. While most of the sandy trail is accessible by wheelchair, sites near the water require traversing rough lava rock.

You enter the national park in the village-like royal grounds, where Kona *ali'i* and their warriors lived; this area's quiet spiritual atmosphere is greatly enhanced by the gently breaking waves and wind-rustled palms. **Hale o Keawe Heiau**, the temple on the point of the cove, was built around 1650 and contains the bones of 23 chiefs. It was believed that the mana of the chiefs remained in their bones and bestowed sanctity on those who entered the grounds. A fishpond, lava tree molds, a hand-carved koa canoe and a few thatched huts and shelters are scattered through here. The royal canoe landing, a tongue of sand called **Keone'ele Cove**, is a favorite resting spot for sea turtles.

Carved wooden *ki'i* standing up to 15ft high front an authentic-looking heiau reconstruction. Leading up to the heiau is the **Great Wall**, separating the royal grounds from the *pu'uhonua*. Built around 1550, this stone wall is over 1000ft long and 10ft high. Inside the wall are two older heiau platforms and legendary standing stones.

Just south of the park's central village area, an oceanfront palm-tree grove holds one of South Kona's choicest picnic areas. Parking, picnic tables and BBQs face a wide slab of *pahoehoe* (smooth-flowing lava), which is littered with wave-tumbled lava-rock boulders and pockmarked with busy tide pools where you may encounter sea turtles. Swimming is possible but can be dicey; judge the surf and entry for yourself. Note that it's kapu to snorkel here.

After wandering the self-guided trail, you might try some wildlife-watching: humpback whales can be seen offshore in winter, and turtles and dolphins and even hoary bats can be seen (after sunset is best for the bats).

Activities

★Two-Step SNORKELING, DIVING

Immediately north of Pu'uhonua o Honaunau National Historical Park, concealed within a (usually) placid bay, are a series of ridiculously vibrant and beautiful coral gardens where the reef and marine life seem locked in a permanent race to outstrip each other with the gaudiest color palette. From above the water, your only indication of the action is the presence of boats leading snorkeling, diving, kayaking and SUP tours, plus the crowds gathering at the titular two steps.

There's no beach here – snorkelers use a stepped lava ledge beside the boat ramp to access about 10ft of water, which quickly drops to about 25ft.

Once you're in the water you'll feel like a supporting cast player in Disney's *The Little Mermaid*. Visibility is usually excellent, especially with the noon sun overhead; good-size reef fish and a fine variety of coral are close to shore. The predatory 'crown of thorns' starfish can be seen feasting on live coral polyps. Cool, freshwater springs seep out of the ground, creating blurry patches in the water. Divers can investigate a ledge a little way out that drops off about 100ft.

The best time to go is during a rising tide, when there are more fish. High winter surf means rough waters.

A privately operated parking lot costs $3, or try to squeeze in along the road's shoulder.

1871 Trail HIKING

A 2-mile round-trip oceanfront hike leads to the abandoned village of Ki'ilae, where there's very little left to see. The visitor center stocks trail guides describing ancient Hawaiian archaeological sites along the way; among other things, you pass a collapsed lava tube and a tremendous, if overgrown, *holua* (lava-sledding course) that *ali'i* raced sleds down. Watch out for feral goats (but they're usually benign).

The steep **Alahaka Ramp** once allowed riders on horseback to travel between villages; halfway up the ramp, the **Waiu o Hina** lava tube (closed for safety reasons) opens to the sea. From the top of the ramp, the incredible vista of ocean coves and ragged cliffs is a trail highlight; for confident snorkelers, some of these coves can provide water access in calm seas. Continuing, you reach a gate that once marked the park's boundary; this is the current Ki'ilae Village site – the ruins are pretty, well, ruined, with almost nothing to see.

Fit hikers can walk all the way to Ho'okena Beach on this 3.5-mile trail, though it becomes increasingly rough after the Alahaka Ramp.

Ho'okena & Around

Most tourists zip right by the turnoff for Ho'okena, between mile markers 101 and 102 on Hwy 11. But meander just a couple of miles downhill to this fishing community and you'll be surprised by a gorgeous bayfront beach that locals love and, more importantly, are willing to share.

Ho'okena was once a bustling Hawaiian village. Novelist Robert Louis Stevenson wrote about his 1889 visit in *Travels in Hawaii*. In the 1890s, Chinese immigrants moved in, a tavern and a hotel opened, and the town got rougher and rowdier. In those days, Big Island cattle were shipped from the Ho'okena landing, but when the circle-island road was built, Honolulu-bound steamers stopped coming and most people moved away.

Beaches

★Ho'okena Beach Park BEACH

This modest, charcoal-colored beach is backed by a steep green hillside. When calm, the bay's waters are good for swimming, kayaking and snorkeling (although the bottom drops off quickly). Coral abounds, as do strong currents further out. When the winter surf is up, local kids hit the waves with bodyboards. You might spot dolphins and humpback whales offshore between December and April. Facilities include restrooms, outdoor showers, drinking water, campsites, a picnic pavilion and a concession stand.

Camping is right on the sand at the base of the cliffs. Ongoing security issues have been addressed by implementing a guard patrol and through the activism of the **Friends of Ho'okena Beach Park** (808-328-7321; http://hookena.org); you can obtain required camping permits and rent camping gear from them online or in person. Camping permits can also be obtained in advance from the county.

Pebble Beach BEACH

Not quite pebbles, the smoky stones of this nonsandy beach at the bottom of the Kona Paradise subdivision range from gumdrop- to palm-size. It's a popular kayak put-in and offers a good dose of peace and quiet. Lounge for a bit, paddle a while or just watch the sun go down. If you enter the water, watch out for potentially fatal 'sneaker' waves.

The beach is a mile down very steep, winding Kaohe Rd, accessed between mile markers 96 and 97 on Hwy 11. Signs say 'private road' and 'keep out,' although the subdivision is ungated. Always ask permission from locals before entering.

Miloli'i

Miloli'i is a fishing village fighting to maintain its traditional ways while an upscale subdivision rises from the lava landscape around it. Miloli'i means 'fine twist,' and historically the village was known for skilled sennit twisters, who used coconut-husk fibers to make fine cord and highly valued fishnets. Villagers still live close to the sea, and many continue to make a living from it.

Privacy is paramount in these parts and curious tourists are tolerated – barely. The turnoff to Miloli'i is just south of mile marker 89 on Hwy 11; the village is 5 miles down a steep, winding, single-lane road that cuts across a 1926 lava flow. Avoid Miloli'i Beach Park; it has a locals-only vibe and facilities are limited.

Beaches

★Honomalino Beach BEACH

Instead of feeling like an unwanted guest at Miloli'i Beach Park, head to Honomalino Bay, less than a mile's walk south. With sand the color of all Big Island beaches crushed into one – green, gold, tawny and black – this beach has gentle swimming (for kids too) and reef snorkeling. Look for the marked public path beginning just beyond Miloli'i's public basketball courts by the yellow church and up the rocks.

When in doubt, keep to the right fork along the trail. Respect all private property and kapu signs.

North Kona Coast

If you thought the Big Island was all jungle mountains and white-sand beaches, the severe North Kona Coast and its beige deserts and black-and-rust lava fields will come as a shock. Yet always, at the edge of your eyesight, is the bright blue Pacific, while bits of green are sprinkled like jade flecks amid the dry. Turn off the Queen Ka'ahumanu Hwy and make your way across the eerie lava fields to snorkel with sea turtles, bask on almost deserted black-sand beaches and catch an iconic Kona sunset. On clear days, gaze *mauka* at panoramas of Mauna Kea and Mauna Loa volcanoes, both often snow-dusted in winter, and in the foreground between the two, Mt Hualalai.

North Kona technically runs 33 miles along Queen Ka'ahumanu Hwy (Hwy 19) from Kailua-Kona up the Kona Coast to Kawaihae. Honokohau Harbor is an easy 2-mile drive from downtown Kailua.

Honokohau Harbor

Almost all of Kona's catch comes in at this harbor, about 2 miles north of downtown Kailua-Kona, including granders (fish weighing over 1000lb). Most fishing charters, dive boats and snorkeling and whale-watching cruises booked out of Kailua-Kona depart here.

To reach the harbor, turn *makai* on Kealakehe Pkwy, just north of mile marker 98 on Hwy 19. The harbor provides public access to Honokohau Beach (p218) inside Kaloko-Honokohau National Historical Park.

Activities

Diving & Surfing

From Honokohau Harbor south to Kailua Bay is a marine-life conservation district, accessible only by boat. This stretch of coast is littered with dive sites, including **Turtle Pinnacle**, a premier turtle-spotting site straight out from the harbor. Northbound toward the airport is **Garden Eel Cove**, aka 'Manta Heaven.'

North Kona Coast

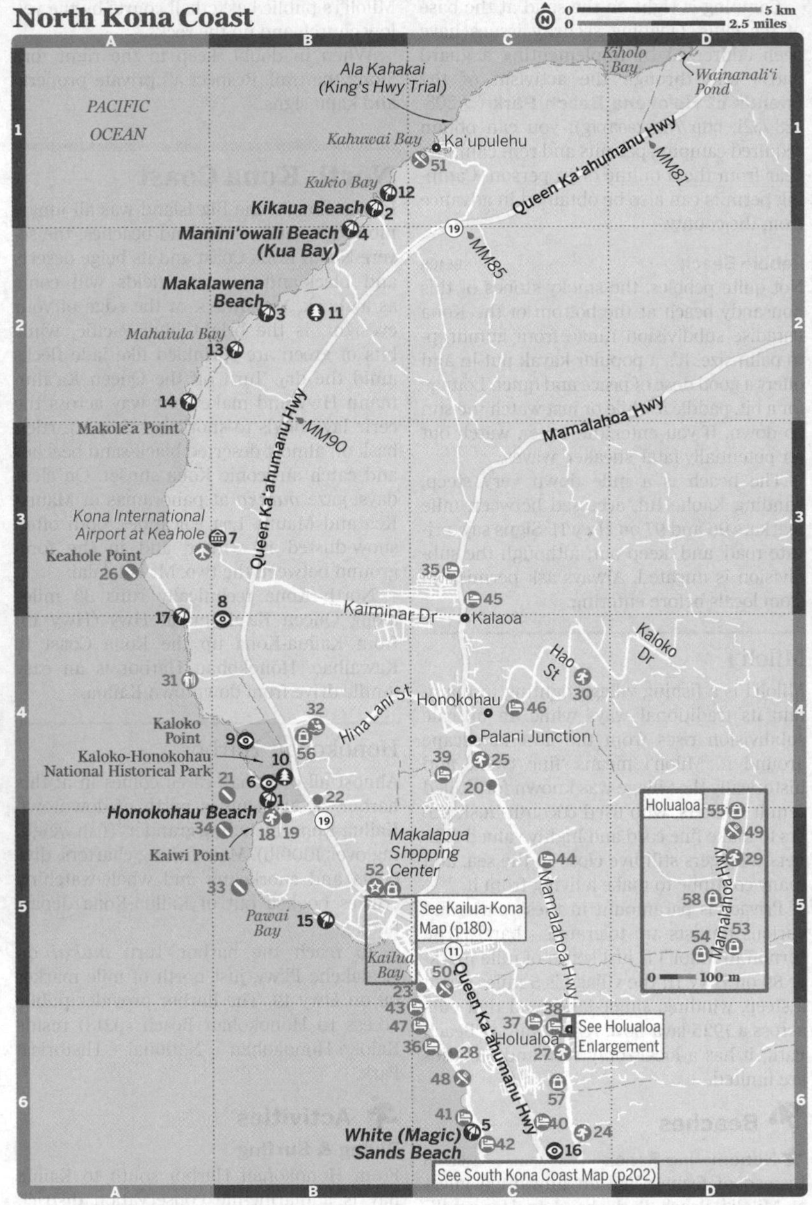

Another good diving spot is off **Kaiwi Point**, south of Honokohau Harbor, where sea turtles, large fish and huge eagle rays swim around some respectable drop-offs. Nearby is **Suck 'Em Up**, a couple of lava tubes you can swim into, letting the swell pull you through.

Ocean Eco Tours DIVING, SURFING
(☎808-324-7873; www.oceanecotours.com; 74-425 Kealakehe Pkwy, Honokohau Harbor; snorkel/

North Kona Coast

Top Sights
1 Honokohau Beach ... B4
2 Kikaua Beach ... B1
3 Makalawena Beach ... B2
4 Manini'owali Beach (Kua Bay) ... B2
5 White (Magic) Sands Beach ... C6

Sights
6 'Aimakapa Fishpond ... B4
7 Astronaut Ellison S Onizuka Space Center ... B3
8 Hawaii Ocean Science & Technology Park ... B4
9 Kaloko Fishpond ... B4
10 Kaloko-Honokohau National Historical Park ... B4
Kampachi Farms ... (see 8)
Ka'upulehu Cultural Center ... (see 12)
11 Kekaha Kai (Kona Coast) State Park ... B2
Kona Cloud Forest Sanctuary ... (see 30)
12 Kukio Beach ... B1
13 Mahai'ula Beach ... B2
14 Makole'a Beach ... A2
Ocean Rider Seahorse Farm ... (see 8)
15 Old Kona Airport State Recreation Area ... B5
16 Original Hawaiian Chocolate Factory ... C6
17 Wawaloli (OTEC) Beach ... A4

Activities, Courses & Tours
Captain Zodiac ... (see 1)
18 Charter Desk ... B5
19 Dan McSweeney's Whale Watch ... B5
20 FBI Surf School ... C4
21 Garden Eel Cove ... B4
22 Hawaii Forest & Trail ... B4
23 Hawaii Lifeguard Surf Instructors ... C5
24 Holualoa Kona Coffee Company ... C6
25 Hula Daddy Kona Coffee ... C4
26 Kaiwi Point ... A3
Kamanu Charters ... (see 1)
27 Kona Blue Sky Coffee ... C6
28 Kona Surf Adventures ... C6
29 Malama I'ka Ola Holistic Health Center ... D5
30 Mountain Thunder Coffee Plantation ... C4
Ocean Eco Tours ... (see 1)
31 Pine Trees ... A4
32 Plenty Pupule ... B4
33 Suck 'Em Up ... B5
34 Turtle Pinnacle ... B5

Sleeping
35 Bear's Place Guest House ... C3
36 Casa de Emdeko ... C6
Four Seasons Resort Hualalai ... (see 12)
37 Hale Maluhia Country Inn ... C6
38 Holualoa Inn ... C6
39 Honu Kai B&B ... C4
40 Kona Hawaii Guest House ... C6
41 Kona Magic Sands Resort ... C6
42 Kona Sugar Shack ... C6
43 Kona Tiki Hotel ... C6
44 Lilikoi Inn ... C5
45 Mango Sunset B&B ... C3
46 Nancy's Hideaway ... C4
47 Royal Sea-Cliff Resort ... C6

Eating
Beach Tree ... (see 51)
Bite Me Fish Market Bar & Grill ... (see 1)
48 Da Poke Shack ... C6
49 Holuakoa Gardens & Café ... D5
50 Jackie Rey's Ohana Grill ... C5
51 'Ulu Ocean Grill + Sushi Lounge ... C1

Drinking & Nightlife
Kona Coffee & Tea Company ... (see 22)

Entertainment
52 Regal Makalapua Stadium 10 ... B5

Shopping
53 Dovetail Gallery & Design ... D5
Holualoa Farmers Market ... (see 49)
54 Holualoa Ukulele Gallery ... D5
55 Ipu Hale Gallery ... D5
56 Kailua Candy Company ... B4
57 Kimura Lauhala Shop ... C6
58 Studio 7 Fine Arts ... D5

dive boat trip from $99/150, group/private surfing lesson $95/150) This is the only operator permitted to run surfing lessons within the boundaries of Kaloko-Honokohau National Historical Park. It also guides snorkeling and scuba trips along the coast, including night dives with manta rays. Stop by the small shop at the harbor to rent surfboards, boogie boards and snorkel or scuba gear.

Fishing

Scads of fishing charters leave from Honokohau Harbor. If you're just after the money shot, you can watch the boats as they pull up and weigh their haul at around 11:30am and 3:30pm. Entering the harbor area, take the first right, park near the gas station and walk toward the dock behind Bite Me Fish Market Bar & Grill.

Kayaking

Plenty Pupule KAYAKING
(☎808-880-1400; www.plentypupule.com; 73-4976 Kamanu St, Kaloko Industrial Park; kayak rental per day single/double $25/38, tours $80-250; ⏲10am-5:30pm Mon-Fri, to 5pm Sat) One of the island's top outfitters for adventure kayaking, these folks can recommend the best put-ins and snorkel spots, customize tours, teach you to kayak surf or take you kayak sailing, the latter particularly memorable during winter whale-watching season.

Tours

Hawaii Forest & Trail TOUR
(☎808-331-8505; www.hawaii-forest.com; 74-5035B Queen Ka'ahumanu Hwy; tours adult/child from $159/139) This multi-award-winning outfitter caters to active travelers who want to delve into the Big Island's greenest depths. From the always-popular Mauna Kea summit and stargazing van tours to exclusive guided bird-watching hikes in Hakalau Forest National Wildlife Refuge, you won't regret an adventure with these expert naturalists and eco-sustainability stewards.

Eating & Drinking

Bite Me Fish Market Bar & Grill SEAFOOD $$
(☎808-327-3474; www.bitemefishmarket.com; 74-425 Kealakehe Pkwy, Honokohau Harbor; mains $8-23; ⏲6am-9pm;) Stop into this bamboo-fenced place steps from the harbor boat ramp for a bottle of Longboard Lager and to spin yarns after a day of fishing. At dockside picnic tables, chow down on just all-right fish sandwiches, tacos, ceviche, *poke* and seafood and *pupu* platters. Service from the tatted-out servers can be lackadaisical.

Kona Coffee & Tea Company CAFE
(☎808-329-6577; www.konacoffeeandtea.com; 74-5035 Queen Ka'ahumanu Hwy; ⏲6:30am-5pm Mon-Sat, 7am-5pm Sun;) Life is too short for bad coffee: head here for award-winning 100% Kona grown on sustainable farms. Freshly roasted beans and toothsome macnut pies mitigate the location behind a gas station.

Shopping

Kailua Candy Company FOOD
(☎808-329-2522; http://kailua-candy.com; 73-5612 Kauhola St, Kaloko Industrial Park; ⏲9am-5pm Mon-Sat) A detour to this chocolate factory shop is mandatory for every sweet tooth. Savor free samples of Mauna Kea 'snowballs' (white chocolate with shredded coconut), Kona coffee swirls, Hawaiian 'turtles' and tropically flavored truffles. To get here, turn *mauka* onto Hina Lani St off Hwy 19, then right on Kamanu St.

Kaloko-Honokohau National Historical Park

Just north of Honokohau Harbor, this 1160-acre **national park** (☎808-326-9057; www.nps.gov/kaho; ⏲visitor center 8:30am-4pm, park 24hr) FREE may be the Kona Coast's most underappreciated ancient Hawaiian site. Hidden among lava fields lies evidence of the innovations that allowed Hawaiians to thrive in this hostile landscape: fish traps, lava planters used to grow taro and other staples, plus the *ahupua'a* between Kaloko and Honokohau that gives the park its name. There are also heiau, burial caves and petroglyphs.

Despite the seemingly endless expanse of lava rock and unbearable midday heat, this is a good place to explore. Go in the early morning, late afternoon or when skies are overcast. *Kokua* (please) remember not to climb on, move, alter or deface any rock structures. Take special care not to disturb the endangered *honu*, who haul out here to rest, feed and bask in the sun – it's illegal to approach them closer than 20ft away on land, or 50yd in the water.

The park's main entrance is off Hwy 19 between mile markers 96 and 97, where there's a parking lot and a small but informative ranger-staffed visitor center.

Beaches

★**Honokohau Beach** BEACH
At this beautiful hook-shaped beach with a mix of black lava, white coral and wave-tossed shells, the water is usually too cloudy for snorkeling, but just standing on shore you'll see *honu*. You may spot more *honu* munching on *limu* (seaweed) around the ancient **'Ai'opio fishtrap**, bordered by a Hawaiian **heiau** at the beach's southern end. Inland are **anchialine ponds** – pools of brackish water that make unique habitats for marine and plant life.

To get here, turn right into the first parking lot at Honokohau Harbor (look for the small public coastal access sign). Near the end of the road is the signposted trailhead; a five-minute walk on a well-beaten path leads to the beach. You could also take the more scenic, if longer, route by hiking to the beach along the 1320yd **Ala Hele Iki Trail** from the visitor center.

Sights

Kaloko Fishpond HISTORIC SITE

At the northern end of Kaloko-Honokohau National Historical Park, this fishpond is one of the most interesting sites because its massive rock retaining wall is being completely rebuilt, so it can once again be fished in the traditional way. Some speculate that the bones of Kamehameha the Great were secretly buried in a cave nearby.

From the park's visitor center, drive north on Hwy 19 until you reach a separate gated entrance at Ala Kaloko Rd. Alternatively, it's about a 1-mile hike north from the visitor center along the coastal Ala Kahakai National Historic Trail (p231), a restored ancient Hawaiian footpath.

'Aimakapa Fishpond HISTORIC SITE

Located in the southern section of Kaloko-Honokohau National Historical Park, 'Aimakapa is the largest fishpond on the Kona Coast. It's home to *ae'o* (Hawaiian black-necked stilt) and *'alae kea* (Hawaiian coot), both of which are endangered native waterbirds. Nearby look for the ancient remains of a *holua* (lava-sledding course).

Keahole Point

Funny place, Keahole Point. Just offshore, the seafloor drops abruptly, providing a continuous supply of both cold water from 2000ft depths and warm surface water. These are ideal conditions for ocean thermal-energy conversion (OTEC), deep sea water extraction and aquaculture. All of this is happening here, plus there's a beach and one of the island's best surf breaks.

Beaches

Wawaloli (OTEC) Beach BEACH

(Makiko Bay Dr; 6am-8pm) At the *makai* end of the access road to the Natural Energy Laboratory of Hawaii Authority, this quiet locals' beach is perfectly positioned for sunsets – never mind the jets flying overhead. Swimming isn't good, except at high tide when the oodles of protected tide pools along the lava-rock coastline overflow. Bring a picnic and the kids. Facilities include restrooms and outdoor showers.

KONA COAST FOR KIDS

- Turtle-spotting at Makalawena Beach (p220)
- Swimming and beachcombing at Kiholo Bay (p222)
- Snorkeling in Ka'awaloa Cove (p210) or Two-Step (p214)
- Meeting other kids at Manini'owali Beach (p220)

Sights & Activities

Hawaii Ocean Science & Technology Park NOTABLE BUILDING

(HOST Park; 808-329-8073, 808-327-9585; http://nelha.hawaii.gov; 73-4660 Queen Ka'ahumanu Hwy; lecture & tour adult/child under 9yr $10/free, grand tour adult/child under 9yr $32/free) That funny-looking building with the gigantic solar panels is the Natural Energy Laboratory of Hawaii Authority (NELHA). This 'zero-net energy facility' was voted one of the USA's 10 greenest buildings in 2007. Learn about OTEC and research into alternative- and renewable-energy technologies at NELHA's public presentations, which are followed by an abalone-farm tour and tasting on Monday, Wednesday and Thursday or a solar-energy plant tour on Tuesday. Friday's 'Grand Tour' (reservations required) visits OTEC Tower and kampachi and abalone farms.

About 40 businesses call NELHA's HOST Park home, including **Kampachi Farms** (www.kampachifarm.com), the aquaculture gurus responsible for yellowfin tuna seen on haute island restaurant menus.

The turnoff is just over a mile south of Kona International Airport, between mile markers 94 and 95.

Astronaut Ellison S Onizuka Space Center MUSEUM

(808-329-3441; www.aloha.net/~tashima; Kona International Airport; adult/child under 12yr $3/1; 8:30am-4:30pm) This little museum pays tribute to the Big Island native who perished in the 1986 *Challenger* space-shuttle disaster. Between the aiport's departure and arrival buildings, you'll find kid-friendly exhibits and educational videos about space and astronauts. Items on display include a moon rock, a NASA space suit and scale models of spacecraft.

AVOIDING CAR BREAK-INS

For many, the Big Island's remote beaches and hikes are the main event – but they also make your rental car a prime target for thieves. Follow local advice: leave nothing of value in your car (yes, this includes in the trunk). It's smart to get all your gear packed up before arriving at your destination.

Another local tip is to leave your doors unlocked so would-be ne'er-do-wells know there's nothing of value in the car. In this way, you can avoid a smashed window – which, as the confetti of broken glass in beach and trailhead parking areas proves, occurs fairly frequently. Check your rental-car insurance policy before considering doing this though. This strategy can backfire, as it leaves your car wide open to stinky feral animals who may hop inside and make a huge mess that's impossible to clean up.

Pine Trees SURFING

Pine Trees is one of West Hawai'i's best surfing breaks. The break stretches along a pretty beach that is rocky enough to make swimming difficult. The final bay gets the most consistent, more forgiving waves. An incoming midtide is favorable, but as the swell picks up in winter these breaks often close out.

Get friendly with local regulars if you want in on the action – this hot spot draws crowds, especially on weekends. Where the access road to NELHA veers to the right, look left for a rutted dirt road leading about 2 miles further south. You'll need a high-clearance 4WD to make it, or you can walk, but it's hot. The access road gates are locked between 8pm and 6am.

Kekaha Kai (Kona Coast) State Park

The gorgeous beaches of **Kekaha Kai** (www.hawaiistateparks.org; 9am-7pm) FREE are all the more memorable for being tucked on the far side of a vast desert of unforgiving black lava. This nearly undeveloped 1600-acre park has four beaches, only one of which has paved access. The others are best approached with a 4WD or on foot; but if you hike, come prepared with good shoes, food and lots of water. It can be brutally hot, and once you reach the sand you'll want to stay till the last drop of sunlight. The park is 11 miles north of Kailua-Kona.

Hard-core hikers can tackle a section of the coastal Ala Kahakai National Historic Trail (p231) from Kua Bay north via Kikaua Beach to Kukio Beach (2 miles each way), or south via Makalawena Beach to Mahai'ula Beach (4.5 miles each way). But beware that temperatures by midmorning can be boiling, and the trail has painful stretches of nothing but *a'a* lava.

Beaches

★Manini'owali Beach (Kua Bay) BEACH

(www.hawaiistateparks.org; 9am-7pm) This crescent-shaped white-sand beach is fronted by sparkling turquoise waters that offer first-rate swimming and bodyboarding (especially in winter), and good snorkeling when waters are calm. And unlike Makalawena, a paved road leads right up to it. Thus Manini'owali draws major crowds, especially on weekends. Arrive late and cars will be parked half a mile up the road. That's reason aplenty for locals to continue grumbling about the easy access the paved road provides. The parking area has bathrooms and showers.

To get here, take the paved road between mile markers 88 and 89 (north of the main Kekaha Kai entrance). Hikers will enjoy the scenic coastal trail from here to Kukio Beach.

★Makalawena Beach BEACH

If what you're after is an almost deserted, postcard-perfect scoop of soft, white-sand beach cupping brilliant blue-green waters (are you sold yet?), head to 'Maks.' Although popular, this string of idyllic coves absorbs crowds so well you'll still feel like you've found paradise. The northernmost cove is sandier and gentler, while the southernmost cove is (illegally) a naked sunbathing spot. Swimming is splendid, but beware of rough surf and rocks in the water. Bodyboarding and snorkeling are more possibilities.

Practice aloha during your visit by packing out all trash and respecting the privacy of others. For locals, this is an unofficial camping and fishing getaway, and the growing popularity of these beaches among outsiders is contentious for some. Always give endangered sea turtles a wide berth – it's illegal to approach them closer than 20ft on land or 50yd in the water.

Getting to Makalawena requires extra effort. Take the unpaved Kekaha Kai (Kona Coast) State Park access road (4WD recommended, although many locals drive it in a standard passenger car), off Hwy 19 between mile markers 90 and 91. Less than 1.5 miles later, at the road junction before the parking lot for Mahai'ula Beach, turn right. Park on the road shoulder near the cables restricting vehicle access to a service road, then walk north for 30 minutes across the lava flow and sand dunes to the beach, either following the service road or a rougher footpath over crunchy *a'a* lava.

Mahai'ula Beach BEACH

Kekaha Kai (Kona Coast) State Park's largest beach has salt-and-pepper sand, rocky tide pools, shaded picnic tables and pit toilets. Swimming usually isn't good, but during big winter swells, surfing happens. Walk a few minutes north along the coast to find a second, less rocky beach with soft tawny sands (nicknamed Magoon's), perfect for sunbathing and swimming. Access to Mahai'ula is via a chunky lava road between mile markers 90 and 91 on Hwy 19.

Although a 4WD is recommended, many locals drive the unpaved beach-access road in a standard passenger car. If you want to attempt this, drive very carefully. Alternatively, you could traverse the 1.5 miles on foot from Hwy 19. Park at an improvised lot just inland from the highway and start walking or thumb it – drivers may take pity on your sun-beaten head and give you a lift. The end of this road is the junction for Makalawena and Makole'a Beaches.

Makole'a Beach BEACH

Amazingly, this secluded black-sand beach belongs to Kekaha Kai (Kona Coast) State Park. Although there's no shade and it's too rocky for swimming, its natural beauty rewards those who make the effort to visit (which is usually some local fisherfolk). To reach this small, dark treasure on foot, head south along Mahai'ula Beach and either follow the road or the coastline while making toward a lone tree. With a 4WD, turn left at the road junction by Mahai'ula Beach, drive south for about 1000yd until you reach a path marked by white coral, then get out and hoof it as the lava becomes too rough.

Ka'upulehu

Once a thriving fishing village among many dotting this length of coast, Ka'upulehu was wiped out by the 1946 tsunami and abandoned until the Kona Village Resort opened here in 1965. The resort closed indefinitely in 2011 after more tsunami damage caused by a massive earthquake in Japan. The luxurious Four Seasons Resort Hualalai remains open and, by law, these and other resorts must provide public coastal access, meaning you can enjoy some fine beaches without the resort price tag.

Beaches

★Kikaua Beach BEACH

(👪) Though obviously artificial (a thin layer of sand laid over concrete is hard on the feet), Kikaua Beach has some things going for it. There's lots of shade, and a completely protected cove is perfect for teaching *na keiki* (children) to swim and even snorkel. Around the kiawe-covered point are gaggles of sea turtles. Facilities include restrooms, outdoor showers and drinking water.

Public beach access is through a private country club and residential development. It's limited to 28 cars per day, so it never feels that crowded. To get here, turn *makai* onto Kuki'o Nui Rd near mile marker 87 on Hwy 19. Drive to the security guardhouse and request a parking pass and directions to the beach.

Kukio Beach BEACH

From Kikaua Beach you can walk north to the scalloped, palm-fringed coves of Kukio Bay, officially part of the Four Seasons Resort Hualalai. There the sand is soft, the swimming is good (even for kids) and there's a paved trail leading north along the rocky coastline to another beach. Facilities include restrooms, outdoor showers and drinking water.

To drive here, turn onto Ka'upulehu Rd (unsigned) between mile markers 86 and 87 on Hwy 19. Drive straight ahead to the Four Seasons security guardhouse and request a beach parking pass. The 50-car beach parking lot almost never fills up.

Sights

Ka'upulehu Cultural Center GALLERY

(☎808-325-8520; 72-100 Ka'upulehu Dr, Four Seasons Resort Hualalai; ⏰8:30am-4pm Mon-Fri) FREE Inside the Four Season's Hawaiian cultural center is a small, museum-quality exhibit organized around a collection of 11 original paintings by Herb Kawainui Kane. Each painting is accompanied by a hands-on exhibit about traditional Hawaiian culture: shake an *'uli'uli* (feathered hula rattle), test the heft of a *kapa* (bark-cloth) beater or examine stone adze heads. On-site Hawaiian cultural practitioners link the present with the past by teaching classes (usually reserved for resort guests only) and giving impromptu Hawaiian arts-and-crafts demonstrations.

At the Four Seasons security guardhouse, tell them you're visiting the cultural center. Drive all the way downhill to the resort's self-parking lot, from where it's a short walk to the center.

Sleeping

Four Seasons Resort Hualalai RESORT **$$$**
(808-325-8000; www.fourseasons.com/hualalai; 72-100 Ka'upulehu Dr; r/ste from $895/1795;) The island's only five-diamond resort earns its accolades with top-flight service and lavish attention to details like fresh orchids in every room, embracing lush gardens and an ocean-view infinity pool. Some poolside rooms have rejuvenating lava-rock garden outdoor showers. The golf course and spa are both outstanding, or snorkel with 75 species of tropical fish in the King's Pond.

Eating & Drinking

'Ulu Ocean Grill + Sushi Lounge HAWAII REGIONAL CUISINE **$$$**
(808-325-8000; www.uluoceangrill.com; 72-100 Ka'upulehu Dr, Four Seasons Resort Hualalai; mains $24-48, tasting menu from $65; restaurant 6:30-11am & 5:30-9pm, sushi lounge 5:30-10pm) 'Ulu means 'breadfruit,' and this sustainably minded restaurant is all about locally sourced produce, seafood and meat – in fact, 75% of its dishes are made with Hawai'i-grown ingredients. The menu mixes tastes from *makai* to *mauka:* currried Kona mussels, kiawe-smoked potatoes and wild boar glazed with *liliko'i*. Too bad the food doesn't live up to the hype – or the sky-high prices.

The atmosphere is casually elegant, with glass-ball partitions and island artwork. Soak up sunset views from the 10-seat bar inside the sushi lounge. Dinner reservations are recommended for the restaurant.

Beach Tree CALIFORNIAN **$$$**
(808-325-8000; www.fourseasons.com/hualalai; 72-100 Ka'upulehu Dr, Four Seasons Resort Hualalai; mains lunch $14-22, dinner $16-39; 11:30am-8:30pm;) Do you know what's better than enjoying *pupu* or one of the island's best burgers on the breezy, beachside porch of the Beach Tree on a perfect Hawaiian day? Not much. Thin-crust brick-oven pizzas come with toothsome toppings and sit alongside a variety of surf-and-turf delights, including a fierce paella. Also, you can eat barefoot. Bonus!

Kiholo Bay

With its pristine turquoise waters and shoreline fringed with coconut trees, Kiholo Bay is yet another off-the-beaten-track Big Island beauty. It's more of a series of beaches than one contiguous stretch of sand, and as for tourists, it's relatively unvisited.

The main beach (near the parking lot) is pebbly and swimming is fine when seas are calm. Follow a trail south (left if facing the water) over the lava to find secluded pockets of fine black sand and, further south, a coconut grove surrounding **Luahinewai**, a pretty spring-fed pool.

Walking north at low tide reveals tide pools that are popular feeding and napping grounds for sea turtles and offer plenty of snorkeling possibilities. Inland near the end of the gravel path is a **lava tube/Queen's Bath** filled with clear freshwater; adventurous swimmers can check it out. Rumor has it other tubes in the area are some of the longest in the island. Lots of folks stop here to wash off salt water, but please note there is an actual ecosystem within the pond, and coming in while wearing suncreen can harm said environment. Just past the Queen's Bath is a sandy patch with a **keiki pool** perfect for the little ones.

Keep going north. You'll pass a gargantuan private estate with a yellow mansion and tennis courts, then a huge **Balinese house**. This estate was built in Indonesia, then taken apart and reassembled here. Keep a respectful distance from this private residence, then continue to the north end of Kiholo.

You'll see more black sand fronted by smooth *pahoehoe*. Follow a circular bay, crossing a bridge over a fishpond, and you'll come to **Wainanali'i Pond**, also known as the Blue Lagoon (Brooke Shields was absent when we visited). Green sea turtles love this spot; on our last visit we saw no less than 10 sunbathing on the sand. You may see them swimming around if you want to snorkel, although the presence of freshwater stream outflow clouds underwater visibility.

To get to Kiholo, turn seaward on the unmarked, graded gravel road between mile markers 82 and 83. Follow the road for a mile, taking the left-hand fork, and park at the roundhouse. An alternate way in, which we prefer for the scenery, is hiking from a trailhead located by a small, rocky parking lot just north of mile marker 81. Hike along the trail at the bottom of the lot for 20 to 30 minutes (bring water), and say hi to the goats. You'll pop out just north of the Balinese house. Kiholo is a popular camping spot for locals, and you can join them with a permit from Hawaii state parks; just be aware that there's no potable water.

Keawaiki Beach is just north of Kiholo Bay. This secluded black-sand strand fronts the former estate of Francis I'i Brown, an influential 20th-century Hawaiian businessperson. It's fine for swimming when calm, but wear reef shoes, because sea urchins like the rocks. To get here, park between mile markers 78 and 79 on Hwy 11; there's a small lot in front of a boulder-blocked gravel road. Walk the road to the estate's fence, then follow the trail to the right around the fence to the beach.

KOHALA & WAIMEA

South Kohala

The Queen Ka'ahumanu Hwy (Hwy 19) cuts through stark fields of lava. But a series of sumptuous resorts have created tropical oases along the water's edge, some containing the island's best beaches, some building their own. Meet the Gold Coast. In contrast to the very modern world of the resorts, South Kohala also contains numerous ancient Hawaiian sights. Apparently, the Kohala Coast (including North Kohala) was more populated at the time of their creation than it is now, and the region is packed with village sites, heiau, fishponds, petroglyphs and historic trails.

The waters off the Kohala Coast are pristine and teeming with marine life – and they're relatively uncrowded. The reef drops off more gradually here than along the Kona Coast, so you see sharks, dolphins, turtles and manta rays, but not large schools of tuna and other deepwater fish. Kohala is the oldest area of the Big Island, with lush coral growth and lots of lava tubes, arches and pinnacles.

A car is essential to get around South Kohala. While **Hele-On Bus** (☎808-961-8744; www.heleonbus.org) routes stop at the major hotels, they're geared for commuting hotel staff and run very early in the morning.

Waikoloa Resort Area

POP 6362

Among South Kohala's resort areas, the **Waikoloa Beach Resort** (www.waikoloabeachresort.com) is the most affordable and bustling. Its two megahotels and golf courses aren't as prestigious as those further up the coast but it does offer two shopping malls and the lion's share of events.

Note that the Waikoloa Beach Resort is not Waikoloa Village, a residential community further inland. To get to the resort area, turn *makai* just south of mile marker 76 on Hwy 19. To get to the village for general services, such as a post office, turn *mauka* onto Waikoloa Rd north of mile marker 75.

Beaches

'Anaeho'omalu Beach Park BEACH

(Waikoloa Beach Dr; ⏲6am-8pm; 👪) 'A Bay' boasts easy access, salt-and-pepper sand and calm waters; it's the only place suited to windsurfing on Hawai'i. Classically beautiful, it's backed by hundreds of palm trees and makes for fantastic sunset viewing. Drinking water, showers and restrooms are available.

The Waikoloa Beach Marriott fronts the beach's north end, but ancient fishponds add a buffer zone between the two. In that area, there's decent snorkeling directly in front of the sluice gate, where you'll find coral formations, a variety of fish and possibly sea turtles.

Archaeologists have found evidence of human habitation dating back more than 1000 years. A short footpath with interpretive plaques starts near the showers.

To get here, turn left off Waikoloa Beach Dr opposite the Kings' Shops.

Sights

Waikoloa Petroglyph Preserve HISTORIC SITE

(Waikoloa Beach Dr; ⏲site dawn-dusk, tour 9:30am) FREE This collection of petroglyphs carved in lava rock is so easy access that it merits a stop, although the Puako Petroglyph Preserve (p227) further north is more spectacular and doesn't neighbor a shopping mall. Many petroglyphs date back to the 16th century; some are graphic (humans, birds, canoes) and others cryptic (dots, lines). Western influences appear in the form of horses and English initials.

South Kohala

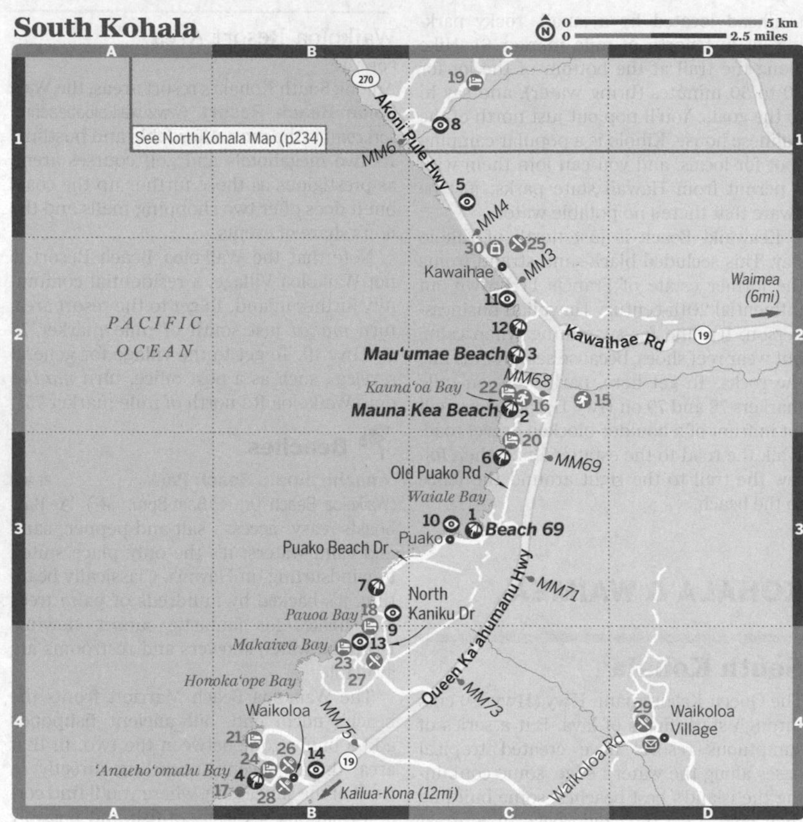

To get here, park at the Kings' Shops and walk for five minutes on the signposted path. Free one-hour guided tours of the petroglyphs are offered most Thursdays and Fridays, starting at the mall.

Activities

Ocean Sports WATER SPORTS
(☎888-724-5924, 808-886-6666; www.hawaiioceansports.com; 69-275 Waikoloa Beach Dr; ⏲7am-9:30pm) Ocean Sports monopolizes the ocean-activity market in South Kohala. Fortunately the company is well run, if slightly steep in its pricing. Cruises include whale-watching ($119) and snorkeling tours ($147) aboard a 49-passenger catamaran. Departures are from 'Anaeho'omalu Bay and Kawaihae Harbor.

At Anaeho'omalu Beach Park and the Hilton Waikoloa Village, this outfit also rents beach equipment.

Waikoloa Beach & Kings' Courses GOLF
(☎808-886-7888; www.waikoloabeachgolf.com; 69-275 Waikoloa Beach Dr, Waikoloa Beach Marriott; green fees guest/nonguest $145/180) The Waikoloa Beach Marriott boasts two top golf courses: the coastal Beach course is known for its par-five 12th hole; the Kings' course is more challenging and offers Scottish-style links. Tee off later and pay less (11:30am/1pm/2pm $120/119/95). Carts are mandatory.

Star Gaze Hawaii STARGAZING
(☎808-323-3481; http://stargazehawaii.biz; adult/child 5-11yr $40/20) Take advantage of Kohala's consistently clear night skies with professional astronomers and equipment. Locations include **Fairmont Orchid** (1 North Kaniku Dr; ⏲7:30-8:30pm Fri), **Hapuna Beach Prince Hotel** (62-100 Kauna'oa Dr; ⏲8-9pm Sun & Wed) FREE and **Hilton Waikoloa Village** (425 Waikoloa Beach Dr; ⏲8-9pm Tue & Thu). Reservations are required.

South Kohala

Top Sights
- 1 Beach 69 ..... C3
- 2 Mauna Kea Beach C2
- 3 Mau'umae Beach C2

Sights
- 4 'Anaeho'omalu Beach Park B4
- 5 Hamakua Macadamia Nut Company C1
- 6 Hapuna Beach State Recreation Area C3
- 7 Holoholokai Beach Park B3
- Kalahuipua'a Fishponds ..... (see 23)
- Kalahuipua'a Historic Trail ..... (see 23)
- 8 Pua Mau Place Botanic & Sculpture Garden C1
- 9 Puako Petroglyph Preserve B3
- 10 Puako Tide Pools C3
- 11 Pu'ukohola Heiau National Historic Site C2
- 12 Spencer Beach Park C2
- 13 Waikoloa Beach Resort B4
- 14 Waikoloa Petroglyph Preserve B4

Activities, Courses & Tours
- Francis I'i Brown North & South Golf Courses ..... (see 23)
- 15 Hapuna Golf Course C2
- Kohala Divers ..... (see 30)
- 16 Mauna Kea Golf Course C2
- Mauna Lani Sea Adventures ..... (see 23)
- Mauna Lani Spa ..... (see 23)
- 17 Ocean Sports B4
- Spa Without Walls ..... (see 18)
- Star Gaze Hawaii ..... (see 18)
- Star Gaze Hawaii ..... (see 21)
- Star Gaze Hawaii ..... (see 20)
- Waikoloa Beach & Kings' Courses ..... (see 24)

Sleeping
- 18 Fairmont Orchid B4
- 19 Hale Ho'onanea C1
- 20 Hapuna Beach Prince Hotel C3
- 21 Hilton Waikoloa Village B4
- 22 Mauna Kea Beach Hotel C2
- 23 Mauna Lani Bay Hotel & Bungalows B4
- 24 Waikoloa Beach Marriott B4

Eating
- Anuenue ..... (see 30)
- 25 Blue Dragon Musiquarium C2
- Brown's Beach House ..... (see 18)
- Cafe Pesto ..... (see 30)
- CanoeHouse ..... (see 23)
- Foodland Farms ..... (see 27)
- Hau Tree ..... (see 22)
- Island Gourmet Markets ..... (see 28)
- 26 Kings' Shops B4
- Kohala Burger & Taco ..... (see 30)
- 27 Monstera B4
- Original Big Island Shave Ice Co, Inc. ..... (see 25)
- Pueo's Osteria ..... (see 29)
- 28 Queens' MarketPlace B4
- Sansei Seafood Restaurant & Sushi Bar ..... (see 28)
- Sushi Shiono ..... (see 28)
- 29 Waikoloa Highlands Shopping Center D4
- Waikoloa Kings' Shops Farmers Market ..... (see 26)
- Waikoloa Village Market ..... (see 29)

Drinking & Nightlife
- Luana Lounge ..... (see 18)

Entertainment
- Gathering of the Kings ..... (see 18)
- Legends of the Pacific ..... (see 21)
- Mauna Kea Hawaiian Luau ..... (see 22)
- Waikoloa Beach Marriott Sunset Luau ..... (see 24)

Shopping
- 30 Kawaihae Shopping Center C2

Festivals & Events

★ **A Taste of the Hawaiian Range** FOOD
(www.tasteofthehawaiianrange.com; Hilton Waikoloa Village; admission advance/door $40/60) Celebrated Big Island chefs work magic with local range-fed meats and local produce in late September or early October.

Moku O Keawe HULA
(www.mokif.com; Waikoloa Resort Area; admission per night $15-25) This early November hula competition includes *kahiko* (ancient), *'auana* (modern) and *kupuna* (elder) categories. A decent alternative to the sell-out Merrie Monarch Festival in Hilo around Easter.

Sleeping

★ **Waikoloa Beach Marriott** HOTEL $$$
(808-886-6789, 888-924-5656; www.waikoloabeachmarriott.com; 69-275 Waikoloa Beach Dr; r $220-460, ste from $570; P ❄ @ 🛜 ≋) This airy, enormous hotel fronts 'Anaeho'omalu Bay and thus boasts an awesome beach setting, plus three oceanfront pools. Renovated in late 2013, rooms feature quality beds (down comforters and high-thread-count linens), tastefully muted decor and standard amenities, from cable TV to refrigerator. Internet access is wi-fi in public areas and

wired in rooms. Book ahead and online for deep discounts. There's a $25 resort fee.

Hilton Waikoloa Village RESORT $$$

(☎808-86-1234; www.hiltonwaikoloavillage.com; 425 Waikoloa Beach Dr; r from $229; P ❄ @ 📶 🏊) You'll either love or hate the showy, theme-park features of this megahotel. There's no natural beach, so its highlights are artificial. Rooms are comfy enough but they're standard business class and neither luxury nor oceanfront. Due to sheer property size, getting around can be a hike and service somewhat impersonal.

The hotel is showing its age, but its larger-than-life decor, including monorail and boats navigating between three towers, could be a diversion for kids. Visitors must shell out $15/21 per day for self/valet parking. Resort fee is $25.

Eating

Increase your dining options at Kings' Shops and Queens' MarketPlace, both located near the resort areas, and at Waikoloa Highlands Shopping Center, across the highway in Waikoloa Village. On Wednesdays, another option is the **Waikoloa Kings' Shops Farmers Market** (www.kingsshops.com; Kings' Shops; ⏲8:30am-2pm Wed), which sells locally grown and produced edibles.

★Island Gourmet Markets MARKET $

(Queens' MarketPlace; ☎808-886-3577) Spectacularly maintained and stocked, this is a one-stop shop for takeout food, freshly made sushi, basic and specialty groceries, magazines, gifts and more. It's a great option for healthy eats, and there's a small patio for diners. Inside the market, an excellent little sushi bar called **Sushi Shiono** (☎808-886-3588; www.sushishiono.com; Queens' MarketPlace; sushi $5-12; ⏲7am-9:30pm) prepares rolls and *nigiri* (oblong-shaped sushi) by request, as well as packs to go.

Waikoloa Village Market SUPERMARKET $

(☎808-883-1088; 68-3916 Paniolo Ave, Waikoloa Highlands Shopping Center; ⏲6am-9pm) Located *mauka* of the highway in Waikoloa Village, this branch of the excellent KTA Super Stores is a full-service grocery store with deli, bakery and ATM.

★Pueo's Osteria ITALIAN $$

(☎808-339-7566; http://pueososteria.com; 68-1845 Waikoloa Rd, Waikoloa Highlands Shopping Center; pizzas $14-18, mains $17-31; ⏲5pm-midnight Mon-Sat, 8:30am-1:30pm & 5-9pm Sun) Run by a former top resort chef, this hidden gem will satisfy your cravings for gourmet-rustic Italian fare: pizzas, pastas and classics, including a yummy gorgonzola gnocchi. Everything is homemade and it's obvious. The Sunday brunch menu, from lemon-ricotta pancakes to a cherrywood bacon BLT, surpasses the standard buffet line.

Located in the Waikoloa Highlands Shopping Center, inland of the highway.

Sansei Seafood Restaurant & Sushi Bar JAPANESE $$$

(☎808-886-6286; www.sanseihawaii.com; Queens' MarketPlace; mains $25-45, rolls $5-20; ⏲5:30-10pm Sun-Thu, 5:30pm-1am Fri & Sat) Local celebrity chef DK Kodama is known for innovative, fusion Japanese cuisine, such as his signature flash-fried ahi roll, and an extensive wine list. This newest branch might be a letdown to fans, with inconsistent service and less impressive execution. But it's worth a try, especially with the fantastic 50%

ANCIENT HAWAIIAN ART

Ancient Hawaiians carved *ki'i pohaku* (stone images), called petroglyphs, into *pahoehoe* (smooth lava). These mysterious carvings are most common on the Big Island, perhaps because it is the youngest island, with the most extensive fields of *pahoehoe*. The simple images include human figures, animals and important objects such as canoes and sails. No one can prove why the Hawaiians made *ki'i pohaku* or placed them where they did. Many petroglyph fields are found along major trails or on the boundaries of *ahupua'a* (land divisions).

In addition to the Waikoloa petroglyphs (p223), a large field remains further north along the South Kohala coast in Puako (p227); they're also found at Hawai'i Volcanoes National Park (p295).

Touching the petroglyphs will damage them, so never step on or make rubbings of them. Photography is fine and is best done in the early morning or late afternoon, when the sun is low.

early-bird discount. Free karaoke on Friday and Saturday after 10pm.

Entertainment

Check www.waikoloanights.com for special nightlife events, from rock concerts to hula shows. Free early-evening concerts featuring slack key guitar, ukulele and hula can be had at the Kings' Shops and Queens' MarketPlace shopping malls.

Waikoloa Beach Marriott Sunset Luau LUAU
(☎808-886-6789; www.waikoloabeachmarriott.com; 69-275 Waikoloa Beach Dr; adult/child 6-12yr $103/48; ⊙5pm Wed & Sat) This oceanfront luau features a Hawaiian-style dinner buffet, open bar and various Polynesian performances, including the Samoan fire dance.

Legends of the Pacific LUAU
(☎808-886-1234; www.sunsetluau.com; Hilton Waikoloa Village; adult/child $112/102; ⊙5:30pm Tue, Fri & Sun) Features various South Pacific dances and includes a dinner buffet and one cocktail.

Mauna Lani Resort Area

Constructed in 1983 by a Japanese company, the Mauna Lani Resort Area resembles its neighbors, with high-end hotels, condos and golf courses. But it deserves special attention for its significant historical sites and for the Mauna Lani Bay Hotel & Bungalows' open attitude toward nonguests who come to explore its fishponds and trails.

Beaches

The best beaches for swimming or snorkeling are small and located around the two large hotels.

The beach fronting the Mauna Lani Bay Hotel & Bungalows is protected and relatively calm, but the water is shallow. Just 10 minutes south of the hotel by foot, in **Makaiwa Bay**, there's a small, calm lagoon fronting the Mauna Lani Beach Club condo. To get here, park at the hotel and walk south along the path past the fishponds.

One mile south of the hotel, there's a small salt-and-pepper beach at **Honoka'ope Bay**. When seas are calm, swimming and snorkeling are fine but not fantastic. The resort development fronting the beach reserves 20 daily parking spaces for nonresidents. To get here, drive toward the golf courses, turn left at Honoka'ope Place and check in at the entry gate.

KOHALA & WAIMEA FOR KIDS

- Horseback riding in Waimea (p245) or North Kohala (p235)
- Paddling with Kohala Kayak (p229)
- Splashing around at Spencer Beach Park (p231)
- Ziplining in Kapa'au (p239)
- Exploring the Puako Tide Pools (p229)
- Cooling off with shave ice at Anuenue (p232)

Located at the Fairmont Orchid, **Pauoa Bay** is an excellent, little-known snorkeling spot, which unfortunately is accessible only to hotel guests.

Holoholokai Beach Park BEACH
(⊙6:30am-6:30pm) Forget about sand and swimming and instead enjoy picnicking and strolling at this pleasantly uncrowded beach, blanketed by chunks of white coral and black lava. Facilities include restrooms, showers, drinking water, picnic tables and grills.

To get here, take Mauna Lani Dr and veer right at the circle; turn right on the marked road immediately before the Fairmont Orchid. The trail to the Puako petroglyphs starts here.

Sights

Puako Petroglyph Preserve HISTORIC SITE
With more than 3000 petroglyphs, this preserve is among the largest collections of ancient lava carvings in Hawaii. The simple pictures might not make sense to you, but viewed together, they are fascinating and worth a visit.

The ¾-mile walk from Holoholokai Beach Park to the preserve adds to the experience: take the well-marked trail at the parking lot. The walk is easy but rocky; wear sturdy footwear and expect blazing sun.

Kalahuipua'a Historic Trail HISTORIC SITE
(68-1400 Mauna Lani Dr, Mauna Lani Bay Hotel & Bungalows; P) FREE The first segment of this easy trail meanders through a 16th-century Hawaiian settlement, passing **lava tubes** once used as cave shelters and a few other archaeological and geological sites marked by interpretive plaques.

The trail then skirts ancient **fishponds** lined with coconut palms and continues to the beach, where there's a thatched shelter with an outrigger canoe and a **historic cottage**. Continue southwest past the cottage to loop around the fishponds and back to the start (about 1.5 miles, round-trip).

Located on Mauna Lani Bay Hotel & Bungalows grounds, this trail starts at a marked parking lot opposite the hotel convenience store.

Kalahuipua'a Fishponds HISTORIC SITE
These ancient fishponds are among the island's few remaining working fishponds and, as in ancient times, they're stocked with *awa* (Hawaiian milk fish). Water circulates from the ocean through traditional *makaha* (sluice gates), which allow small fish to enter but keep mature, fattened catch from escaping.

To access the fishponds directly (without taking the trail), exit the hotel lobby and go south toward the beach.

Activities

Mauna Lani Sea Adventures WATER SPORTS
(808-885-7883; http://maunalaniseaadventures.com; 68-1400 Mauna Lani Dr, Mauna Lani Bay Hotel & Bungalows; snorkeling tour adult/child 3-12yr $99/45, whale-watching cruise $85/45) For snorkeling, whale-watching and diving, this outfit offers almost daily tours at decent prices. While Kailua-Kona is the Big Island's hub for snorkeling and scuba diving, the waters off Mauna Lani are excellent and much less crowded. You can also try SUP (rental and instruction $30/50 per 30/60 minutes).

Francis I'i Brown North & South Golf Courses GOLF
(808-885-6655; 68-1400 Mauna Lani Dr, Mauna Lani Bay Hotel & Bungalows; green fees guest/nonguest $170/225) Mauna Lani boasts two world-class golf courses. The South course is more scenic and popular, with its signature 15th hole featuring a tee shot over crashing surf. The North course is more challenging and interesting, with a par-three 17th hole within an amphitheater of black lava.

Sleeping

★ Mauna Lani Bay Hotel & Bungalows RESORT $$$
(808-885-6622; www.maunalani.com; 68-1400 Mauna Lani Dr; r/ste from $390; P ❄ ☎ ≋) The Mauna Lani has a loyal clientele for its unfussy vibe and commitment to Hawaiian cultural stewardship. The grounds feature well-tended tropical gardens, hundreds of towering coconut palms and precious historic sites. Geared more for couples than kids, this is a solid upscale, if shy of luxurious, hotel.

Rates include basic services (eg parking, phone, internet access). Eco policies include use of solar power, drought-resistant grass and recycled water for irrigation. The **Mauna Lani Spa** (808-881-7922; massages & facials from $165; treatments 10am-4pm) boasts lush landscaping and a lava-rock sauna; treatments are pricey, perhaps overpriced, but a memorable splurge.

Fairmont Orchid HOTEL $$$
(808-885-2000; www.fairmont.com/orchid-hawaii; 1 North Kaniku Dr; r/ste from $360/820; P ❄ @ ☎ ≋) Elegant and almost formal (for Hawai'i), the Orchid never lets you forget that you're at an exclusive, luxury hotel. The architecture feels rather continental, but the meticulously maintained grounds are buoyantly tropical. Rooms are clean, modern and comfortable. The resort fee is $25.

Spa fans can experience outdoor treatments at **Spa Without Walls** (808-885-2000; www.fairmont.com/orchid-hawaii/spa; massages & facials from $159; 7am-6pm), hidden amid orchids, palms and waterfalls.

Eating

Foodland Farms SUPERMARKET $
(808-887-6101; 68-1330 Mauna Lani Dr, Shops at Mauna Lani; 6am-11pm) Full-service gourmet supermarket that has an impressive deli selection.

★ Monstera JAPANESE $$
(808-887-2711; www.monsterasushi.com; 68-1330 Mauna Lani Dr; plates $16-30, sushi rolls $13-20; 5:30-10pm) Chef Norio Yamamoto left his namesake restaurant at the Fairmont Orchid to launch his own *izakaya*. It's a looser, cooler place, where the menu ranges from classic *nigiri* sushi and tuna *tataki* (tuna seared and seasoned with ginger) to sizzling plates of kimchi stir-fried pork loin and teriyaki chicken.

★ Brown's Beach House HAWAII REGIONAL CUISINE $$$
(808-887-7368; 1 North Kaniku Dr, Fairmont Orchid; mains $41-69; 5:30-8:30pm Thu-Mon, 5:30-9pm Tue & Wed) The prices might deter you, but Brown's remains a standout for those willing to pay. Expect gracious service

and the finest local ingredients: the surf and turf features locally raised beef and Kona lobsters, wild boar ribs are served with local fern shoots and the fresh caught *ono* comes with Hamakua mushrooms.

CanoeHouse HAWAII REGIONAL CUISINE **$$$**
(808-881-7911; 68-1400 Mauna Lani Dr, Mauna Lani Bay Hotel & Bungalows; mains $32-48; 6-9pm) The Mauna Lani's flagship restaurant showcases local ingredients creatively but simply. Those seeking a huge punch might find the dishes lackluster. A decadent option is the 'Captain's Table' (two to eight diners; per person $100), a five-course meal specially designed in collaboration with the chef. The setting and service are lovely.

Drinking & Entertainment

Luana Lounge BAR
(808-885-2000; 1 North Kaniku Dr, Fairmont Orchid; 5pm-midnight) A nice spot to unwind at sunset, with specialty drinks and tapas (small plates). The fish or burger sliders (three per order for under $20) make for a light, relatively affordable meal.

Gathering of the Kings LUAU
(808-326-4969; www.gatheringofthekings.com; 1 North Kaniku Dr, Fairmont Orchid; adult/child 6-12yr $109/75; 4:30pm Sat) This luau spins a thread of storytelling to highlight slightly modernized versions of Polynesian and Hawaiian dance and music. It's notable for its above-average Polynesian dinner buffet and open bar.

Puako

POP 772

Standing in contrast to the megaresorts to the south, Puako is essentially a mile-long row of homes. The single road through 'town' is marked with numerous 'shoreline access' points. To get here, turn *makai* down Puako Beach Dr between mile markers 70 and 71.

Heading towards Puako 'town' you'll pass the **Hokuloa United Church** on your right. This may be the cutest little white seaside church on the Big Island. Originally built in 1860, the structure fell apart and was then restored in 1990.

Vacation rentals abound: check www.2papayas.com and www.hawaiianbeachrentals.com for listings.

Beaches

★ **Beach 69** BEACH
(7am-8pm;) This lovely crescent of white sand is a local favorite but remains somewhat off the tourist radar. Both family-friendly and gay-friendly, its calm, protected waters are ideal for morning snorkeling. Around the boundary, shady trees provide welcome relief. Restrooms and showers are available; no lifeguards.

From Puako Beach Dr, take the first right turn onto Old Puako Rd. Find telephone pole No 71 (originally numbered No 69) to the left and park. Follow the 'road' to its end, and then tramp along the footpath that runs parallel to a wooden fence.

Sights & Activities

For diving tours, book with Kawaihae-based Kohala Divers (p232).

Puako Tide Pools LANDMARK
Puako is known for giant tide pools, some deep enough to shelter live coral and other marine life. There's no sandy beach, but a narrow strip of pulverized coral and lava covers the shore. It's ideal for beach walks and you might even see *honu* sunning on the rocks. To get to the pools, park along the road near one of six signposted 'beach access' paths.

★ **Kohala Kayak** KAYAKING
(808-882-4678; www.kohalakayak.org; 3hr tour $70; depart 9am) Paddle and snorkel in Puako's pristine, less-traveled waters with knowledgeable, customer-service-oriented guides. Water depth is about 20ft; swim through underwater arches 10ft below. All levels are welcome; pedal kayaks are available for more stability.

ONE FISH, TWO FISH, ROYAL FISH, NOT-FOR-YOU FISH

In ancient Hawaii, the fish raised in fishponds were reserved for the *ali'i* (chiefs and royalty). Commoners who stole fish for their own consumption could be punished by death. When a chief wanted fish, the pond caretaker would simply net the biggest as they gathered for feeding. Sometimes, trained runners would transport fresh fish to distant royal tables. According to legend, they were wrapped in wet *limu* (seaweed) and arrived still wriggling, proof of freshness.

Hapuna Beach State Recreation Area

Hapuna Beach is world famous for its magnificent half-mile sweep of white powder sand and fabulously clear waters. In summer, waves are calm and allow good swimming, snorkeling and diving, although the fish population has declined woefully since the 1980s. When the surf's up in winter, bodyboarding is awesome, thanks to reliable swells from the northwest. In general, Hapuna waters are too choppy for tots or non-swimmers. Waves over 3ft should be left for experts; drownings are not uncommon here.

The restrooms and picnic area at this **state recreation area** (www.hawaiistateparks.org/parks/hawaii; gate 7am-8pm; P) can be crowded and, at worst, grungy. Lifeguards are on duty. For nonresidents, parking costs $5 per vehicle.

To get here, take Hapuna Beach Rd just south of mile marker 69. Arrive early to snag a parking space and a good spot. Bring industrial-strength sunscreen because there's virtually no shade.

Stay overnight in one of six state-owned **A-frame cabins** (www.hawaiistateparks.org/camping/hawaii.cfm; per night residents/nonresidents $30/50) near the beach, an awesome location for sunset-watching. While rather makeshift for the price, each sleeps four people on wooden platforms (bring your own bedding). Restrooms, showers and a cooking pavilion are available.

Mauna Kea Resort Area

The Mauna Kea may not have the historical heritage of resorts to the south, but it does have proximity to two of the Big Island's great beaches. Development began here when the late Laurance Rockefeller obtained a 99-year lease on the land around Kauna'oa Bay. 'Every great beach deserves a great hotel,' Rockefeller apparently said. Not everyone would agree, but he got his way here.

For dining options beyond hotel fare, head to Waimea, Kawaihae or the Waikoloa Resort Area for more variety.

Beaches

★ Mauna Kea Beach BEACH

Crescent-shaped Kauna'oa Bay (nicknamed 'Mauna Kea Beach' after Rockefeller built his landmark hotel on it) is blanketed in powdery white sand, while the clear waters are calm and shallow (generally less than 10ft). Snorkeling is best at the north end along the rocky ledge. This wonderfully uncrowded beach is open to the public through 40 parking spaces set aside daily for nonguests. Arrive by 9am and stop at the entry gate for a parking pass and directions.

★ Mau'umae Beach BEACH

White sand, teal water, shady trees and protected waters – and it's even more private and local than Kauna'oa Bay. What's not to love about Mau'umae? Locals are proprietary about this gem, and for good reason. There's great snorkeling on either end of the bay. Only 10 parking spots are given out, so arrive by 9am on weekdays, and possibly earlier on weekends.

To get here, go toward Mauna Kea Beach Hotel, turn right on Kamahoi and cross two wooden bridges. Look for telephone pole No 22 on the left and park next to the other cars. Walk down the trail to the Ala Kahakai sign and turn left toward the beach. You can also walk here from Spencer Beach Park to the north.

Activities

Mauna Kea Golf Course GOLF

(808-882-5400; www.princeresortshawaii.com; Mauna Kea Beach Hotel; green fees resort guest/nonguest $275/235) A 72-par championship course that consistently ranks among the top courses in the USA. Designed by Robert Trent Jones, Sr, it was remodeled in 2008 by his son, Rees Jones.

Hapuna Golf Course GOLF

(808-880-3000; www.princeresortshawaii.com; Hapuna Beach Prince Hotel; resort guest/nonguest $150/130) Has a 700ft elevation gain and was designed by Arnold Palmer and Ed Seay.

Sleeping

Room rates vary significantly by season.

Hapuna Beach Prince Hotel HOTEL $$$

(808-880-1111, 888-977-4623; www.princeresortshawaii.com; 62-100 Kauna'oa Dr; r $225-435, ste from $700;) The Mauna Kea Beach Hotel's 'sister' hotel offers good value and a primo beach setting. The architectural design is rather heavy-handed and rooms could use a face-lift, but they're clean and come with large bathrooms. This hotel shares amenities with Mauna Kea Beach, and buses transport guests between the two.

Mauna Kea Beach Hotel HOTEL $$$
(808-882-7222, 866-977-4589; www.maunakeabeachhotel.com; 62-100 Mauna Kea Beach Dr; r $425-760;) This grand hotel on the Gold Coast is understated, quietly confident of its reputation. At first glance it might not wow you, but there is history here, among loyal returning guests and longtime staff. Rooms are regularly renovated and nicely maintained. The hotel's crowning jewel is simply its location on Kauna'oa Bay, arguably the island's best beach.

Eating

Hau Tree HAWAIIAN $$
(808-882-5707; lunch mains $10-22, dinner mains $18-29; 11am-3:30pm daily, 5:30-8:30pm Sun, Mon & Wed) Casual dining and outdoor dress codes, all overlooking the deep blue Pacific. The solid if uninspiring menu includes grilled mahi with miso butter, pork BBQ with guava sauce and a kick-butt brunch that gets the week started right.

Entertainment

Mauna Kea Hawaiian Luau LUAU
(808-882-5707; www.princeresortshawaii.com; 62-100 Mauna Kea Beach Dr, Mauna Kea Beach Hotel; adult/child 5-12yr $96/48; 6pm Tue & Fri) This outdoor luau features standard entertainment (thrilling fire dance, group hula) and a gorgeous beach setting. The buffet is generous and above average.

Kawaihae & Around

Kawaihae is more functional than recreational, a working port 'town' (if such can be said for a settlement that's a couple of blocks long) where fuel tanks and cargo containers give off an industrial vibe. For all its compact utilitarianism, there is noteworthy dining, a family beach and a historic heiau toward the south. For an insider's view of Kawaihae, see the Pacific Worlds Kawaihae site: www.pacificworlds.com/kawaihae.

Beaches

Spencer Beach Park BEACH
() Shallow, sandy and gentle, this beach lacks the dramatic sweep of Mauna Kea or Hapuna, but it's ideal for kids and popular with local families. Come to swim rather than to snorkel; the waters are slightly silty due to being close to Kawaihae Harbor (to the north).

OFF THE BEATEN TRACK

ALA KAHAKAI TRAIL FROM KAWAIHAE TO PUAKO

Die-hard sun worshippers access South Kohala's signature beaches via a 6-mile stretch of the 175-mile **Ala Kahakai National Historic Trail** (www.nps.gov/alka/index.htm). You'll also pass pristine shoreline and natural anchialine ponds (pools of brackish water that provided the ancients with drinking water).

From the north, start at the southern end of Spencer Beach Park, where you'll pass thick kiawe groves until you reach Mau'umae Beach and eventually the Mauna Kea Resort Area, including the renowned golf course. After you navigate the Hapuna Beach, the trail continues down to Beach 69. The whole hike, especially the last leg, is scorching. Of course, you can turn back at any point, and can start at any point along the way.

Located off the Akoni Pule Hwy just north of the 2-mile marker, the park has a lifeguard, picnic tables, barbecue grills, restrooms, showers, drinking water and campsites (permit required). The campsites are exposed and crowded together, but it's the best camping beach north of Kona.

Sights

Pu'ukohola Heiau National Historic Site HISTORIC SITE
(808-882-7218; www.nps.gov/puhe; 62-3601 Kawaihae Rd; 7:45am-4:45pm) FREE By 1790 Kamehameha the Great had conquered Maui, Lana'i and Moloka'i. But power over his home island of Hawai'i was a challenge. When told by a prophet that he'd rule all of the Hawaiian Islands if he built a heiau dedicated to his war god Kuka'ilimoku atop Pu'ukohola (Whale Hill) in Kawaihae, Kamehameha built this massive structure.

He and his men formed a human chain 20 miles long, transporting rocks hand to hand from Pololu Valley in North Kohala. After finishing the heiau by summer 1791, Kamehameha held a dedication ceremony and invited his cousin and rival Keoua, chief of Ka'u. When Keoua came ashore, he was killed and taken to the *luakini* heiau as the first offering to the gods. With Keoua's death, Kamehameha took sole control of the Big Island and by 1810 ruled the Hawaiian Islands.

Back then Pu'ukohola Heiau was adorned with wooden *ki'i* and thatched structures, including an oracle tower, an altar, a drum house and shelter for the high priest. After Kamehameha's death in 1819, his powerful widow Ka'ahumanu and son Liholiho, who abolished the kapu system, destroyed the deity images and the heiau was abandoned.

Today, only the basic rock foundation remains, but it's still a massive 224ft by 100ft, with 16ft- to 20ft-high walls. To get here, turn *makai* off the Akoni Pule Hwy halfway between mile markers 2 and 3.

Hamakua Macadamia Nut Company FACTORY

(☎808-882-1690, 888-643-6688; www.hawnnut.com; 61-3251 Maluokalani St; ⊙8am-5pm) FREE It's a tourist stop, but a darned good one, featuring a spanking-clean factory, gift shop and generous free samples. This eco-conscious company generates 75% of its energy needs from solar power and 10% from ground macnut shells. The Hamakua-grown nuts are excellent in quality and reasonably priced. To get here, turn *mauka* just north of mile marker 4.

Activities

★Kohala Divers WATER SPORTS

(☎808-882-7774; www.kohaladivers.com; 61-3665 Akoni Pule Hwy, Kawaihae Shopping Center; 1-/2-/3-tank dive $100/139/239; ⊙8am-6pm) This long-running outfit leads excellent diving trips throughout Kohala waters, plus snorkeling and seasonal whale-watching. One memorable trip visits a *honu* 'cleaning' station where the turtles allow fish to pick parasites off their bodies.

Sleeping & Eating

Hale Ho'onanea B&B $$

(☎808-882-1653, 877-882-1653; www.houseofrelaxation.com; Ala Kahua Dr; r $100-130;) About 5 miles north of Kawaihae is this terrific-value B&B atop peaceful grassy knolls 900ft above sea level. The Bamboo Suite includes kitchenette, private lanai, satellite TV, wi-fi, high ceiling, hardwood floor and stunning 180-degree horizon view.

★Anuenue DESSERTS $

(☎808-882-1109; Akoni Pule Hwy, Kawaihae Shopping Center; cones from $2.50, fast food $3.50) Since 1998, Tim Termeer has delighted all comers with snowy shave ice and premium ice cream. Among his 35 flavors are ginger lemongrass, citrus mint and lavender lemonade. He also offers hot dogs, veg burgers and chili bowls.

★Kohala Burger & Taco BURGERS, MEXICAN $

(☎808-880-1923; www.kohalaburgerandtaco.com; Akoni Pule Hwy, Kawaihae Shopping Center; mains under $11; ⊙8am-7pm Mon-Fri, to 4pm Sat & Sun) When only a real burger will do, come here for local grass-fed quarter-pounders with specialty toppings. But the real standouts are the fish tacos, quesadillas and dreamy shakes and malts.

Original Big Island Shave Ice Co, Inc. DESSERTS $

(61-3616 Kawaihae Rd; shave ice $3.75; ⊙11am-5:30pm Tue-Sat, 1:30-5:30pm Sun) Kawaihae's only food truck, parked in the lot of the Blue Dragon, is also a supremely good shave ice stand. The flavors are good and the ice texture is smooth, but we say the standout is the ice cream and the *halo-halo*, with *ube* (sweet potato) ice cream, azuki beans, taro, coconut and jelly. It's oddly delicious.

SACRED SITES

Ancient Hawaiians built a variety of heiau (temples) for different gods and different purposes: healing the sick, sharing the harvest, changing the weather, offering human sacrifice and succeeding in warfare.

While some were modest thatched structures, others were enormous stone edifices, which today exist in eroded ruins that only hint at their original grandeur. After Kamehameha II (Liholiho) abolished the kapu (taboo) system in 1819, many were destroyed or abandoned. But on the Big Island, two of the largest and best-preserved heiau remain: Pu'ukohola Heiau (p231) and Mo'okini Luakini Heiau (p236).

Luakini heiau, for human sacrifice, were always dedicated to Ku, the war god. Only Ku deserved the greatest gift, a human life, and only the highest chiefs could order it. An enemy slain in battle was an acceptable sacrifice. But the victim had to be a healthy man, never a woman, a child or an aged or deformed man.

Cafe Pesto BISTRO **$$**
(☎808-882-1071; www.cafepesto.com; Akoni Pule Hwy, Kawaihae Shopping Center; lunch $11-14, pizzas $9-20, dinner mains $17-33; ⏰11am-9pm Sun-Thu, to 10pm Fri & Sat) This well-loved favorite serves eclectic, innovative cuisine you might call Mediterranean with an Asian twang or Italian with an island twist. Choose from curries and Greek salads, seafood risotto and smoked-salmon alfredo, piping-hot calzones and thin-crust gourmet pizzas.

Blue Dragon Musiquarium HAWAII REGIONAL CUISINE **$$$**
(☎808-882-7771; www.bluedragonhawaii.com; 61-3616 Kawaihae Rd; mains $18-36; ⏰5-10pm Wed-Thu & Sun, to 11pm Fri & Sat) This roofless restaurant under towering palms features great live music five nights a week, starting at 6pm. The cuisine is hard to pin down, from stir-fries to curries to rib-eye steaks, but generally good. It's a convivial, family-oriented place for dinner; later, the potent specialty cocktails might tempt you to the dance floor.

North Kohala

Where the winds scream out of the Pacific, bending the tall grass into stiff yellow prairies that drop to a frothy ocean held adjacent to a black lava rock coastline – there, friend, you've reached North Kohala, and North Kohala is a world unto itself. This is the birthplace of Kamehameha, 'the Lonely One,' a fitting nickname given the austerity of this landscape, in some ways utterly removed from the lush garden cliché you may have of the Hawaiian Islands. This applies to the west side of North Kohala, anyways; drive east and the rains lash out with the winds, greening the hills until you reach the fertile jungle cleft of the Pololu Valley.

Where Keahou is mainlanders in condos, and Hilo is fierce localism, this area has a distinct flavor all its own – a charming, successful mix of rural farmers and local artists, Native Hawaiians and mainland transplants, and plantation-era storefronts. While still relatively untouristed, word of its charms has leaked, and the area is slowly moving onto the beaten track. In recent years several wealthy individuals have purchased major tracts of land, helping to limit future development.

The North Kohala peninsula is the oldest part of the Big Island, and it shows: driving up the coast from Kona, you see a mountain range deeply cut with ravines, as opposed to the smooth slopes found elsewhere. In modern times North Kohala was sugar country, until the Kohala Sugar Company closed in 1975. Today the small historic towns of Hawi and Kapa'au contain enough art galleries, boutiques and distinctive eateries to succeed as tourist attractions, particularly when you take them as a whole.

The refreshing **Kohala Welcome Center** (☎808-889-5523; www.northkohala.org; 55-3393 Akoni Pule Hwy; ⏰loosely 9am-4pm Mon-Fri, 10am-2pm Sat, 11am-1pm Sun), located in the North Kohala Community Center at the western entrance to Hawi, offers an excellent map to the entire area, some local history, and friendly advice from a tribe of doting mavens.

Akoni Pule Highway (Hwy 270)

The land along the Akoni Pule Hwy (Hwy 270) remains largely undeveloped, affording spectacular views of the Pacific (and Maui in the distance).

Sights & Activities

Pua Mau Place Botanic & Sculpture Garden GARDENS
(☎808-882-0888; www.puamau.com; 10 Ala Kahua Dr; adult/student $15/5; ⏰9am-4pm) In a region that receives only 3in to 10in of annual rainfall, this 13-acre botanic and sculpture garden is a questionable endeavor, but is of interest to botanophiles and those who appreciate a giant statue of a praying mantis and the stubborn will to grow green out of the desert. To get here, turn inland on Ala Kahua Dr just north of the 6-mile marker.

Lapakahi State Historical Park HISTORIC SITE
(☎808-882-6207; www.hawaiistateparks.org; ⏰8am-4pm, closed state holidays) FREE This park was a remote fishing village 600 years ago. An unshaded, 1-mile loop trail traverses the 262-acre grounds, passing the remains of stone walls, house sites, canoe sheds and fishing shrines. Visitors can try their hand at Hawaiian games, with game pieces and instructions laid out for *'o'o ihe* (spear throwing), *konane* (checkers) and *'ulu maika* (stone bowling). Nothing is elaborately presented, so visitors need an imagination to appreciate the modest remains. Located just south of the 14-mile marker.

The village of Lapakahi grew into an *ahupua'a*, a wedge-shaped division of land radiating from the mountains to the sea. When the freshwater table dropped in the 19th century, the village was abandoned. Lapakahi's clear waters are loaded with tropical fish and

North Kohala

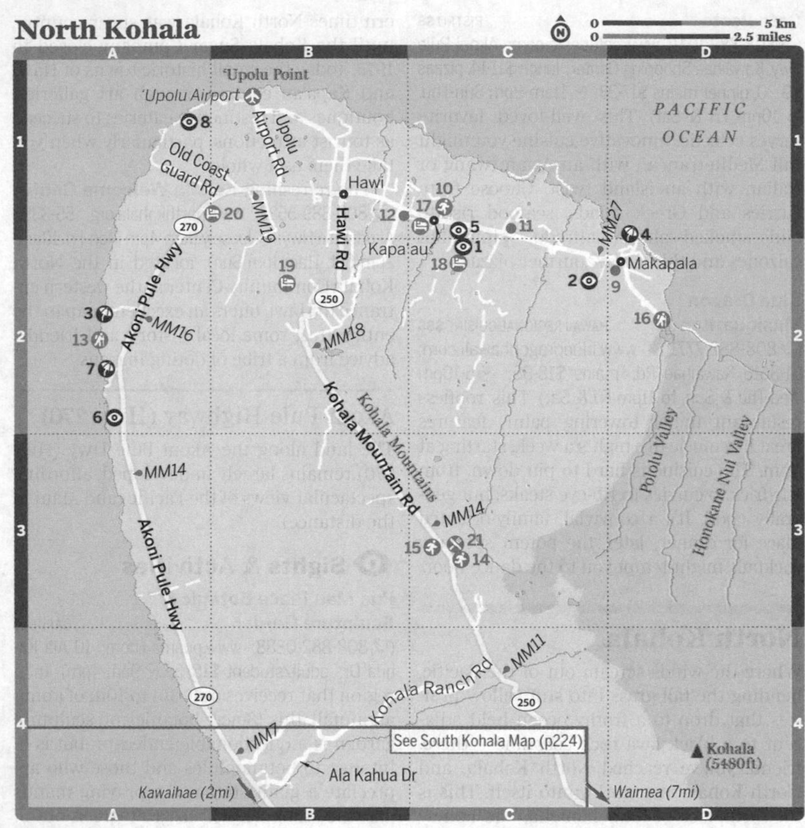

See South Kohala Map (p224)

North Kohala

Sights

1 Bond Historic District C2
Kalahikiola Church .... (see 1)
2 Kamehameha Rock C2
3 Kapa'a Beach Park A2
4 Keokea Beach Park D1
5 Kohala Institute C1
6 Lapakahi State Historical Park A2
7 Mahukona Beach Park A2
8 Mo'okini Luakini Heiau A1

Activities, Courses & Tours

9 Hawaii Paso Finos D2
10 Kamehameha Park & Golf Learning Center C1
11 Kohala Ditch Adventures C1
12 Kohala Zipline B1
13 Mahukona to Kapa'a Walking Trail A2
14 Na'alapa Stables C3
15 Paniolo Riding Adventures C3
16 Pololu Valley Lookout & Trail D2

Sleeping

17 Kohala Club Hotel C1
18 Kohala Country Adventures Guest House C2
19 Kohala Lodge B2
20 Puakea Ranch B1

Eating

21 Kahua Ranch C3

belong to a marine-life conservation district. But this is a historical, not recreational, park, with historically sacred waters. Park staff may grant permission for snorkeling, but they generally discourage it.

Mahukona Beach Park BEACH

This abandoned harbor offers no sandy beach, so what's the appeal? Some very fine snorkeling and diving. Head into the blue and you'll see coral-encrusted underwater mooring chains that lead to the wreckage of an old ship in the center of the harbor; said ship is home to multicolored fish and creeping eels. The left side of the park leads into a county park, where a shabby cluster of picnic tables and restrooms overlooks a scenic, if formidable, beach.

Kapa'a Beach Park BEACH

This lovely seaside park offers a covered picnic area with welcome shade, few people and public toilets. It is simple and clean, with nice coastal and Maui views and a little scalloped bay of blue water. The water is often clear, but the coast is rocky; thus, fishing, snorkeling and diving are popular, but swimming is not recommended. Camping by permit. Turn at mile marker 16.

Mahukona to Kapa'a Walking Trail HIKING

Mahukona and Kapa'a Beach Parks are linked by a beautiful, little-known, 2-mile oceanside walking trail. From Kapa'a Beach Park, start by the old railway bed on the left, visible on the way in. From Mahukona Beach Park, go past the two-story brown metal building and park at the turnout on the right. Scoot left around the metal pipe gate to find the trail sign. Bring water and a hat and stay on the trail.

Kohala Mountain Road (Highway 250)

Arguably the Big Island's best scenic drive, Kohala Mountain Rd (Hwy 250) affords stupendous views of the Kohala–Kona coastline and three majestic volcanic mountains: Mauna Kea, Mauna Loa and Hualalai. Start from Waimea, climb past an overlook, and then follow the spine of the peninsula through green pastures until you finally descend to the sea at Hawi. The name changes to Hawi Rd close to town.

Activities

Paniolo Riding Adventures HORSEBACK RIDING

(808-889-5354; www.panioloadventures.com; Kohala Mountain Rd, Mile 13.2; rides $69-175) Paniolo Adventures offers five different horseback rides ranging from one to four hours, enough for anyone to find their comfort level, whether it's walking or cantering. Of particular note is the Sunset Ride, allowing you to finally – ahem – ride off into the sunset.

The terrain is the beautiful 1000-acre Ponoholo Ranch, a working cattle ranch. Horses are selected for the rider's experience and all necessary equipment is provided. This is the best choice on the island for an experienced rider.

Na'alapa Stables HORSEBACK RIDING

(808-775-0419, 808-889-0022; www.naalapastables.com; Kahua Ranch Rd; rides $73-94) Na'alapa Stables organizes rides both into the Waipi'o Valley, and across the rolling hills and pastures of the 8500-acre Kahua Ranch, which affords exceptionally fine views of the coast from its 3200ft elevation. Either way, this is mostly a nose-to-tail ride, set at the level of the most inexperienced rider. Na'alapa's guides are personable and knowledgeable.

Turn off Route 250 between mile marker 11 and 12; it's the first building on the right.

Eating

Kahua Ranch BARBECUE $$$

(808-882-7954; www.exploretheranch.com; Kahua Ranch Rd; with transportation $119, without $95, child 6-11yr/under 5yr half-price/free; 6-9pm Wed summer, 5:30-8:30pm Wed winter;) Looking for a down-home country BBQ? Well they've got a doozy at the Kahua Ranch. One of the ranch owners, who missed his calling in stand-up comedy, gets things rolling with jokes on ranching life. Busloads of lei-wearing tourists then line up for a hearty buffet dinner of meat and beer in a nearby Quonset hut.

The feast is followed by country music, line dancing, s'mores over the campfire and, best of all, Piggly Wiggly, the performing pig. The cheerful, long-standing event takes place on a gorgeous piece of sloping pasture with wide-open views, making sunset and stargazing by telescope a natural highlight. There's a 15% online discount.

Hawi & Around

POP 1081

Hawi (hah-vee) is a little slice of picturesque North Kohala that's been massaged by mainlanders (and their money) into a bohemian enclave of cafes, locavore dining, galleries and artisan gifts: all in about two blocks, which is as big as this town gets. Rarely will you see a 'snowbird' community settle into such a permanent nest; transplants and locals have built something special in Hawi, and it's quite simply one of the nicest places to stop and smell the organic coffee.

This was once a major plantation town for the Kohala Sugar Company, and many local residents are descendants of sugar workers. For all the town has evolved from

WORTH A TRIP

MO'OKINI LUAKINI HEIAU & THE BIRTHPLACE OF KAMEHAMEHA

On a micro-continent full of raw beauty, a land of lava flows and crystal fish grottos and volcanic cliffs, **Mo'okini Luakini Heiau** (808-373-8000; 9am-8pm Thu-Tue) FREE still manages to make an impression. Located at 'Upolu Point, at Hawai'i's northernmost tip, this is among the oldest (c AD 480) and most historically significant of Hawaiian sites.

Measuring about 250ft by 125ft, with walls ascending some 6ft, the temple draws the eye. But the location – a solitary and brooding perch on a wind-rustled grassy plain – is even more powerful. In general, North Kohala is a landscape impregnated with spirits, but this particular area feels like a ghost convention.

According to legend, the heiau was built from 'sunrise to first light' by up to 18,000 'little people' passing water-worn basalt stones in complete silence from Pololu Valley – a distance of 14 miles – under the supervision of Kuamo'o Mo'okini. It is a 'closed' temple, reserved only for *ali'i nui* (high chiefs).

Five hundred years later Pa'ao, a priest from Samoa, raised the walls to 30ft and rebuilt the altar as his *ho'okupu* (offering) to the gods. He initiated human sacrifice, to stem dilution of the royal bloodlines and to enforce stricter moral codes of conduct, making this the first *luakini* (sacrificial) heiau.

Wander outside the main heiau to a large boulder next to an upturned stone. This rock was where sacrificial victims were skinned and deboned and turned into fishing implements and other tools. Geographically and conceptually, the northerly Mo'okini creates a fascinating counterbalance to the southerly Pu'uhonua o Honaunau (*pu'uhonua* means 'place of refuge'; p213); one place was where the kapu (taboo) system was enforced in its most violent iterations, while the other was a potential escape from the most brutal excesses of traditional law.

In 1963 the National Park Service designated Mo'okini Heiau as Hawaii's first registered National Historic Landmark. Fifteen years later, it was deeded to the state. Leimomi Mo'okini Lum, the seventh high priestess of the Mo'okini bloodline to serve the temple, lifted the kapu that restricted access to the site in 1978, thereby opening it to visitors.

To get here, drive toward 'Upolu Airport, past a cluster of wind farms, then turn south onto the gutted coastal road, which is impassable after rains. You'll either have to walk around 3.5 miles to get here, or use a 4WD.

Along the way, you'll pass a plaque marking the spot where Kamehameha the Great was born, an area also marked by stone-walled foundations. According to legend, when Kamehameha was born on a stormy winter night in 1758, his mother received a kahuna's prophecy that her son would be a powerful ruler who would conquer all the islands. Upon hearing this, the high chief of Hawai'i ordered all male newborns killed. After Kamehameha was taken to the Mo'okini Heiau for his birth rituals, he was spirited away into hiding.

rustic boondocks to tourist destination, there is still a very Kohala-esque sense of feisty isolation, an independent streak that's easy to love.

Note that Kohala Mountain Rd (Hwy 250) is called Hawi Rd close to town.

Sights & Activities

Hawi Farmers Market MARKET

(Hwy 250; 8am-2pm Sat, 2-6pm Tue;) All of the funky, organic, crunchy goodness of North Kohala is presented and sold by all of its funky, organic, crunchy characters at this weekly farmers market, held under the shade of the huge banyan tree off Hwy 250. Pick up honey or mushrooms or sweet potatoes, listen to live, local music and generally revel in the region's idiosyncrasies.

Kohala Grown Farm Tours TOUR

(808-937-4930; www.kohalagrownfarmtours.com; 55-3419 Akoni Pule Hwy; tour adult/child $125/60; Wed-Fri 10am-2pm;) On this enjoyable little agricultural adventure, you'll be ushered through multiple small Kohala farms, get a peak at the local lush countryside (unlike the coast near Kawaihae, this area gets lots of rain), enjoy a farm-to-table lunch and basically immerse yourself in all kinds of locally grown goodness. It can arrange transport from South Kohala resorts for a fee.

Sleeping

Kohala Village Inn INN $

(808-889-0404; www.kohalavillageinn.com; 55-514 Hawi Rd; r $75-85, ste $130;) For budget travelers or those seeking digs in the heart of Hawi, this inn offers terrific value. In a plantation-era, motel-style building, no-frills rooms are clean and cozy, with wood-plank floors, pleasant lighting and cable TV. Walls are rather thin and there's no view, but it's a fine place to rest your head.

Hawi Plantation House B&B B&B $$

(888-465-8565; www.hawiplantationhousebandb.com; r $230;) In a magnificently restored plantation house there are six lovely bedrooms of various sizes and sleeping configurations to choose from. All are smartly appointed and share a kitchen, a laundry room, a swimming pool, a gym and a tennis court.

★Kohala Lodge RENTAL HOUSE $$$

(808-884-5105; www.vacationhi.com; 56-867 Kamalei St; $300;) Tucked away in a tree line with sweeping views, this reproduction 19th-century *paniolo* (Hawaiian cowboy) ranch house (formerly known as Cabin in the Treeline) is unique in every way. The owner has showered attention on every architectural detail, from the lava-rock fireplace to the period plumbing to retro-style appliances (which are actually high tech). It enforces a two-night minimum-stay policy. The house is located about 2 miles from Hawi, off Kohala Mountain Rd. Book well in advance.

★Puakea Ranch COTTAGE $$$

(808-315-0805; www.puakearanch.com; 56-2864 Akoni Pule Hwy; cottages $289-639;) Live the *paniolo* estate dream in one of four meticulously restored cottages. Ranging from two to six bedrooms, each cottage enjoys its own bucolic grounds and includes kitchen, laundry facilities, and detached bathhouse with Japanese-style *furo* hot tub. Striking the right balance of luxury and authenticity, Puakea Ranch is located off a gated dirt road 3 miles from Hawi center.

Eating & Drinking

Kohala Coffee Mill CAFE $

(808-889-5577; 55-3412 Akoni Pule Hwy; drinks $2-4, sandwiches $6-10; 6am-6pm Mon-Fri, 7am-6pm Sat & Sun) A comfy place to hang out and treat yourself to muffins, fresh-brewed Kona coffee and heavenly Tropical Dreams ice cream. For breakfast, the souffléd eggs with cheese, onion, tomato, pesto and/or bacon are a winner. Frequently hosts live music on Sunday mornings.

Sweet Potato Kitchen VEGETARIAN $

(808-345-7300; http://sweetpotatokitchen.com; 55-3406 Akoni Pule Hwy; $5-12; 9am-3:30pm Tue-Sat, 10am-2pm Sun;) This cozy kitchen serves heaping plates of vegetarian and vegan fare, from congee (rice porridge) cooked with black rice, garlic and local greens to a 'BeetSteak' patty burger that's as hearty as any Waimea steer. Dairy-free coconut ice cream, banana bread and some sinful mushroom gravy round out the offerings.

★Sushi Rock SUSHI $$$

(808-889-5900; http://sushirockrestaurant.net; 55-3435 Akoni Pule Hwy; sushi rolls $7-19, mains $18-32; noon-3pm daily, 5:30-8pm Sun-Tue & Thu, 5:30-9pm Fri & Sat) This ever-popular sushi bar is famous all over the island for its fusion tropical rolls, which might include papaya, macnuts, Fuji apple or goat cheese. Some work better than others, but we always leave satisfied. The menu also includes vegetarian/vegan rolls, creative salads and sandwiches, plus a wild selection of cocktails.

★Bamboo HAWAII REGIONAL CUISINE $$$

(808-889-5555; www.bamboorestaurant.info; 55-3415 Akoni Pule Hwy, Kohala Trade Center; lunch $11-16, dinner $25-35; 11:30am-2:30pm Tue-Sun, 6-8pm Tue-Sat;) Always-packed Bamboo offers interesting takes on old standbys, such as mahimahi on focaccia with shredded papaya. It shares space with a gallery and gift shop, making you feel like you're eating in a general store – which you are. The inviting interior – suspended Balinese umbrellas, twinkling Christmas lights and warm wood walls – is cheerful and pure Hawi.

Trio FUSION $$$

(808-889-5900; www.sushirockrestaurant.net; 55-3435 Akoni Pule Hwy; 3-course menu $29; noon-3pm daily, 5:30-8pm Sun-Tue & Thu, 5:30-9pm Fri & Sat) Trio, attached to and operated by Sushi Rock, specializes in three-course, creative Hawaiian-fusion cuisine. The menu has a lot of variation; eg on one night you may mix Indonesian chicken with Waimea beef sliders finished with some vegetarian *poke*. For a town as small as Hawi, this is a heady gastronomic adventure.

Shopping

Living Arts Gallery ARTS, CRAFTS
(808-889-0739; www.livingartsgallery.net; 55-3435 Akoni Pule Hwy; 10:30am-5pm, to 8pm Fri) To appreciate the Big Island's extraordinary amount of artistic talent, come to this artists' co-op. Members staff the gallery, giving you firsthand contact with some of the 65 artists represented.

L Zeidman Gallery ARTS, CRAFTS
(808-889-1400; http://zeidmangallery.wix.com/aloha; 55-3419 Akoni Pule Hwy; 10am-5pm) The exquisitely crafted, museum-quality wood bowls made by the owner are mesmerizing en masse. Take one home for between $150 and $2500.

Hawi Gallery MUSIC
(206-452-3697; www.hawigallery.com; 55-3406 Akoni Pule Hwy; 10am-5pm Mon-Sat, 11am-3pm Sun) The ukulele as a work of art? Definitely, as this fascinating collection proves. In addition to gorgeous classics, check out the Cuban model made from a cigar box and the curvaceous Polk-a-lay-lee, a rare 1960s promotional item from a Chicago furniture store.

Elements JEWELRY, ACCESSORIES
(808-889-0760; www.elementsjewelryandcrafts.com; 55-3413 Akoni Pule Hwy; 10am-6pm) This jewelry and gift shop carries an eclectic collection of locally made finery.

Kapa'au

POP 1734

Kapa'au isn't quite as bohemian and consciously crunchy as Hawi, and thus feels more authentically rustic and/or undeveloped and quiet, depending on your point of view. Either way, this is another former sugar town refashioned into an attractive tourist destination. Although more scattered than Hawi, Kapa'au has a few good eateries and serves as a meeting point for several outdoor adventure tours.

Beaches

Keokea Beach Park BEACH
(off Akoni Pule Hwy; gate 7am-11pm) While it has no beach to speak of, this park, about 3.5 miles from Kapa'au, has the best picnic spot around: an elevated pavilion with smashing views of a rocky bay and the motley crew of local surfers brave enough to test its dangerous shorebreaks and strong currents. Besides picnic tables, there are barbecue grills, showers, drinking water and portable toilets. The marked turnoff is about 1.5 miles before the Pololu Valley Lookout.

Sights

Kamehameha the Great Statue MONUMENT
The statue on the front lawn of the North Kohala Civic Center has a famous twin in Honolulu, standing across from Iolani Palace. The Kapa'au one was the original, constructed in 1880 in Florence, Italy, by American sculptor Thomas Gould. When the ship delivering it sank off the Falkland Islands, a duplicate statue was cast from the original mold and erected in downtown Honolulu in 1883. Later the sunken statue was recovered and sent here, Kamehameha's childhood home.

Kamehameha Rock LANDMARK
According to legend, Kamehameha carried this rock uphill from the beach to demonstrate his prodigious strength. Much later, when a road crew attempted to move it elsewhere, the rock stubbornly fell off the wagon – a sign that it wanted to stay put. Not wanting to upset Kamehameha's mana, the workers left it alone. Don't blink or you'll miss it, on the inland roadside about 2 miles east of Kapa'au, on a curve just past a small bridge.

Kohala Institute FARM
(808-889-5151; www.kohalainstitute.org; 53-496 'Iole Rd; farm tour adult/child $30/15; 10am-noon Mon-Fr;) The Kohala Institute manages some 2400 acres that are part of a traditional tract of land known as 'Iole. This community organization hosts a number of courses related to both New Age pursuits (yoga) and traditional Hawaiian culture (hula courses). It also conducts family-friendly walking farm tours which show off the techniques of Polynesian agriculture and the beauty of 'Iole's preserved acreage.

Kalahikiola Church CHURCH
In 1855, Protestant missionaries Elias and Ellen Bond built this church on their vast estate. It's not a must-see, but the towering banyan trees and peaceful macadamia-nut orchards surrounding the church make it a scenic detour, and history and religion scholars will appreciate this preserved slice of 19th-century early Hawaii Christianity. The church is 900yd up 'Iole Rd, which is on the *mauka* side of the highway between the 23- and 24-mile markers.

THE KOHALA COASTLINE

The breeze-bent grass, choppy waters and jagged rock shoreline that runs from Kawaihae to Hawi is a beautiful, largely undeveloped coast that is perfect for those seeking an escape from it all. Some areas are given over to subdivisions and others to ranching, but there are large swaths of open space overlooking the waves that roll north to Maui.

Speckled across the dry hills and red soil are the most numerous intact, precontact archaeological and cultural sites in the state. Don't think this means that huge temples and structures are ubiquitous; what you'll more often find are the crumbling remnants of a wall or fortification sitting vacant in the isolated breeze. It's honestly an eerie experience when you come upon a stretch of crumbling temple walls amid acres of empty land.

Unmarked roads lead to the jagged coastline. You can usually get down these in a 4WD, although it can be nice to walk. Once you reach the water you can try and snorkel amid the huge schools of yellow tang but, fair warning, there are no lifeguards on duty and the seas can be roiling.

Activities

★Kohala Zipline ZIPLINING

(☎808-331-3620; www.kohalazipline.com; 54-3676 Akoni Pule Hwy; adult/child 8-12yr $169/139) Once you're up in the trees, you stay up for the whole canopy tour, which includes nine easy zips, five elevated suspension bridges between platforms, and two rappels. There are no superlong zips, but also no walking between elements. The course is built to blend with nature and cause no harm to trees.

Maximum number of eight per group; mandatory weight range 70lb to 270lb (kids must be at least eight years old). A dozen three-hour tours go out daily.

★Hawaii Paso Finos HORSEBACK RIDING

(☎808-884-5625; rides $85-130) Paso Finos are incredibly smooth riding horses. Experience their bounceless gait and engaging demeanor with this outfit; it's obsessive about the care and treatment of its horses, and you'll engage your equine charge on a deep level that's unique on the Big Island. Learn horse handling, riding, therapeutic communication and even yoga on horseback. A unique activity, even for experienced equestrians.

Kohala Ditch Adventures KAYAKING

(☎808-889-6000, 888-288-7288; www.kohaladitchadventures.com; 53-324 Lighthouse Rd, btwn Miles 24 & 25; adult/child 5-11yr $139/75; ⏱7-11am & 12:15-4pm Mon-Sat) After an off-road excursion by Pingauer, a six-wheel Austrian military vehicle, you embark on a leisurely 2.5-mile kayaking trip through historic plantation irrigation ditches or flumes, including 10 tunnels. Guides are well versed in island history, and the entire experience comes off as a unique cultural journey, as opposed to a fast-paced action adventure.

Kamehameha Park & Golf Learning Center GOLF

(☎golf center 808-345-4393, gym 808-889-6505; 54-540 Kapa'au Rd; ⏱pool 10-11:45am & 1-4:45pm, golf 8am-7pm, gym noon-8pm Mon-Thu, 7:45am-1:30pm Fri, 10am 4pm Sat) This county park includes a huge pool (call for schedule updates), tennis courts, gym with basketball courts and weight room, and playground. In back there's a privately run six-hole golf learning center where you can rent equipment and play all day for $10.

Festivals & Events

North Kohala Kamehameha Day Celebration CULTURAL

(www.kamehamehadaycelebration.org) FREE On June 11 join islanders in honoring Kamehameha the Great in his birthplace. The spectacular parade of floral-bedecked horseback riders and floats culminates in an all-day gathering with music, crafts, hula and food.

Kohala Country Fair FAIR

(www.kohalacountryfair.com; Akoni Pule Hwy opp 'Iole Rd) FREE This old-fashioned fair, held in the first week in October, brings together a smorgasbord of local artists and food, plus events including a Spam-carving contest, frog catching, equestrian demonstrations, tug of war and who knows what else.

Hawaii, the Big Island

The Big Island, larger than all of the other Hawaiian islands combined, contains a staggering diversity of landscapes. Moonscape lava deserts spread across the western side of the island, while thick groves of hardwood jungle cling to black sea cliffs in the east, all separated by snowcapped Mauna Kea.

1

2

ROSENBERG PHILIP / GETTY IMAGES ©

4

WATT JIM / GETTY IMAGES ©

1. The South Coast
The Big Island's south coast, with lush forest, arid lava fields and endless sky over the deep-blue Pacific, has a palpable end-of-the-world feel.

2. Mauna Kea (p249)
The unmatched clarity of Mauna Kea's views draws hikers by day and stargazers by night.

3. 'Akaka Falls (p266)
These grand falls plunge 442ft into a deep green basin.

4. Snorkeling
Snorkelers will explore a colorful underwater world of tropical fish and coral reefs.

3

FENG WEI PHOTOGRAPHY / GETTY IMAGES ©

THE KOHALA INSTITUTE & BOND HISTORIC DISTRICT

A pioneering blend of indigenous cultural activity, historical preservation and environmental education is taking root in North Kohala. 'Iole, a 2400-acre tract extending from the Pacific Ocean into the Kohala Mountains, is now owned and managed by the Kohala Institute at 'Iole.

The Kohala Institute offers a large range of educational activities on this huge parcel of traditional land, many of which are aimed at families. Kids and parents are taught, on traditional farms, about sustainable cultivation and native Hawaiian folkways. Check the Kohala Institute website, www.kohalainstitute.org, for more information on its ever-changing program schedule.

The area also encompasses the 54-acre **Bond Historic District** ('Iole), which contains three historic properties all built by missionary Elias Bond (1813–62), a seminal figure in numerous aspects of Kohala life, from education to roads to the sugar industry. The Bond Homestead (1889) was the original base for Elias' work. The Kohala Girls School is in excellent condition and is an atmospheric throwback to the merger of New England missionary sensibilities with Hawaii. So too is the Kalahikiola Congregational Church, a vital part of the Kohala community since 1855.

Kohala 'Aina Festival FOOD

(www.hipagriculture.org/events/kohalaaina;) Put on by the Hawaiian Institute of Pacific Agriculture in early November, this festival, held at the Kohala Fairgrounds, is a celebration of the Big Island's considerable agricultural output. Expect lots of music, family-friendly activities and 100% Big Island–grown food and produce.

Sleeping

Kohala Club Hotel INN $

(808-889-6793; www.kohalaclubhotel.com; 54-3793 Akoni Pule Hwy; r/cottage $56/90) Less than half a mile from Kapa'au, this laid-back inn offers spotless rooms with private bathrooms for an unbelievable price. The main house contains four small, no-frills rooms with either a queen bed or two twins. The two-bedroom cottage is perfect for families. It's 'Old Hawaii' and decidedly charming over chic, and we mean that as an enthusiastic compliment.

Kohala Country Adventures Guest House INN $$

(808-889-5663, 866-892-2484; off Akoni Pule Hwy; r $85-175;) For country livin', try this relaxed, lived-in house on 10 acres of ungroomed tropical gardens, with fruit trees, livestock and coastal views. The Sundeck Suite is comfy for families, with kitchenette, three beds and an open loft layout. Host Bobi Moreno is a gracious community fixture, and works hard to make your stay comfortable.

Hawaii Island Retreat HOTEL $$$

(Hawaii Island Retreat at Ahu Pohaku Hòomaluhia; 808-889-6336; www.hawaiiislandretreat.com; 54-250 Lokahi Rd; d $290-340, yurts $130) Set on acres of Zen-like gardens in an isolated, end-of-the-world corner north of Kapaau town, the Island Retreat lives up to its name. Individually appointed rooms are airy and colorful, and a long list of amenities include a decadent infinity pool, yoga sessions and massage. Want a tented accomodation experience? Opt for the well-appointed on-site yurts.

Eating

Gill's Lanai CAFE $

(808-315-1542; 54-3866 Akoni Pule Hwy; mains $6-9; 11am-5pm;) With its umbrella-shaded patio and tiny kitchen, this avocado-colored roadside cafe offers a beach vibe and unfairly good food, given Kapa'au's small size. Favorites include fish tacos, fish and chips, savory sandwiches, bowls of 'ahi *poke* and veg quesadillas. Service can definitely run on island time.

Minnie's DINER $

(808-889-5288; 54-3854 Akoni Pule Hwy; meals $7-9; 11am-8pm Mon-Thu, 11am-3pm Fri & Sat, 6-8:30pm Fri) This local-favorite family restaurant serves generous portions of Hawaiian and American comfort food: burgers, sandwiches and plate lunches, including *ono,* mahimahi and Korean chicken, dished with heaping sides of rice. The house specialty is roast pork – if you're a dedicated carnivore it is not to be missed.

Fig's Mix Plate HAWAIIAN $

(☎808-889-1989; 54-3785 Akoni Pule Hwy; mains $5-9; ⏰10:30am-3:30pm Mon-Sat, 7-11:30am Sun) Home cooking, Hawaiian-style: big plate lunches and big aloha. Bring a big appetite, because they don't skimp on da portions here, *brah*. For such a small spot, it has an impressively varied menu; the burgers are excellent, the *kalbi* is great and the garlic chicken is just silly delicious.

Nambu Courtyard CAFE $

(☎808-889-5546; 54-3885 Akoni Pule Hwy; mains $9-12; ⏰6:30am-2:30pm Mon-Fri, 7am-noon Sun;) Pleasantly low-key, this owner-run cafe is friendly to the point that it positively radiates aloha. Nambu serves freshly made salads and sandwiches, espresso, moist carrot cake and an unbelievable blueberry bread pudding. With lots of seating, indoor and outdoor, it manages to be both airy and cozy.

Shopping

Dunn Gallery ARTS, CRAFTS

(☎808-884-5808; dunngallerywoodart.com; 54-3862 Akoni Pule Hwy; ⏰11am-4pm Tue-Sat) Of the many wood art shops on the island, this one stands alone. The distinctive works, gathered from 30 Big Island artists, represent a museum-quality collection. Contemporary, traditional and functional pieces range from $20 to five figures. You can call to visit by appointment outside of regular hours.

Ackerman Galleries ARTS, CRAFTS

(☎808-889-5971, 808-889-5138; www.ackermangalleries.com; 55-3897 Akani Pule Hwy; ⏰11am-5pm Tue-Sat) The Ackerman family has managed to combine art and commerce for 30 years. They have two galleries: the Gift Gallery has an excellent array of wooden bowls, glasswork and jewelry; the Fine Art Gallery across the street (open from October to March and by request) displays Gary Ackerman's impressionistic paintings of Hawaii and France.

Pololu Valley

Followed to its absolute terminus, Hwy 270 takes you from the sparse habitation and gale-driven semidesert north of Kawaihae to an utterly fecund emerald vision: the Pololu (Long Spear) Valley, a toothy hump of jungle ribboned by a black-sand beach that together form an utterly unforgettable vista.

The area was once abundant with wetland taro, when Pololu Stream carried water from the deep, wet interior to the valley floor. When the Kohala Ditch was built in 1906, it diverted the water for sugar production. Unlike its sister valley, Waipi'o, Pololu Valley has not been inhabited since the 1940s. So, instead of territorial residents, you are met by a forest reserve.

Activities

★**Pololu Valley Lookout & Trail** HIKING

From the lookout, you can admire the spectacular coastline toward the east, but you must hike down to see Pololu Valley. The steep trail is doable for most, thanks to switchbacks and its 1320yd distance.

At the valley's mouth lies a rugged black-sand beach. The surf is rough, and swimming is a terrible idea, even if you see local surfers testing the waves. Deeper valley explorations are blocked by a pond, beyond which cattle roam (so don't drink the water).

Avoid trekking down after rainfall, because the mud-slicked rocks will be precarious. Makeshift walking sticks are often left at the trailhead.

Hawaii Forest & Trail HIKING, SWIMMING

(☎808-331-8505; www.hawaii-forest.com; adult/child under 12yr $169/139) The Kohala Waterfalls Adventure includes a leisurely 1.5-mile loop trail to waterfalls (swimming included). Transportation from the Waikoloa Resort Area is included.

Waimea (Kamuela)

POP 9212

The misty rolling pastureland surrounding Waimea is perhaps Hawai'i's most unexpected face. This is *paniolo* country, and nearly all of it, including Waimea itself, is controlled by Parker Ranch, the fifth-largest cow-calf ranch in the USA.

But don't leap to any conclusions: this is no company town. For its size, Waimea contains extraordinary depths, and one of the joys of visiting is to plumb them. From the highway all you see are bland strip malls, but closer inspection finds an extraordinary art scene, a long list of dining options, outstanding shopping, farmers markets and a rich cowboy heritage. Then there are all the fascinating transplants: organic farmers, astronomers, artists, teachers – a most enlightened, well-traveled bunch. Old West courtesy and small-town pace prevail, making it easy to strike up a conversation.

Waimea (Kamuela)

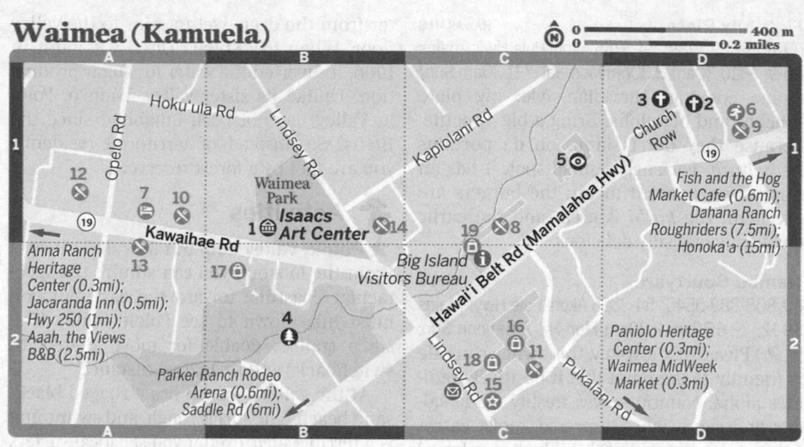

Waimea (Kamuela)

Top Sights
1 Isaacs Art Center....B1

Sights
2 Imiola Congregational Church....D1
3 Ke Ola Mau Loa Church....D1
4 Waimea Nature Park....B2
5 WM Keck Observatory Office....C1

Activities, Courses & Tours
6 Mountain Road Cycles....D1

Sleeping
7 Kamuela Inn....A1

Eating
8 Aka Sushi Bar....C1
9 Big Island Brewhaus & Taqueria....D1
10 Hawaiian Style Cafe....A1
Healthways II....(see 16)
KTA Super Store....(see 19)
11 Lilikoi Cafe....C2
Merriman's....(see 12)
12 Pau....A1
13 Redwater Cafe....A2
Village Burger....(see 16)
14 Waimea Town Farmers Market....B1

Entertainment
15 Kahilu Theatre....C2

Shopping
Gallery of Great Things....(see 17)
16 Parker Ranch Center....C2
17 Parker Square....B2
18 Reyn's....C2
19 Waimea Center....C2
Waimea General Store....(see 17)
Wishard Gallery....(see 16)

The town has some wonderfully wacky weather. It is split into the 'dry side' and the 'wet side,' the boundary being roughly the center of town. So while Kawaihae Rd is a desert, if you drive past the malls along Mamalahoa Hwy you'll find yourself in green fields. Days are warm and nights are cool up here at 2670ft, necessitating jeans and sweaters. And it can go from sun to rain in the swish of a horse's tail, so make sure that convertible top is up overnight.

Sights

★Isaacs Art Center GALLERY
(808-885-5884; http://isaacsartcenter.hpa.edu; 61-1268 Kawaihae Rd; 10am-5pm Tue-Sat) FREE Set in a meticulously relocated 1915 schoolhouse, this series of bright, charming galleries displays a diverse collection of local and international fine art. The permanent collection features mostly renowned late masters, while the pieces for sale are by living artists. Works include paintings, pottery, furniture, jewelry and Hawaiian arts. As you enter, take note of Herb Kawainui Kane's classic *The Arrival of Captain Cook at Kealakekua Bay in January 1779*. For deep pockets seeking the ultimate gift, this gallery is not to be missed. All proceeds go to the Hawai'i Preparatory Academy Scholarship Fund.

Anna Ranch Heritage Center HISTORIC SITE
(808-885-4426; www.annaranch.org; 65-1480 Kawaihae Rd; 10am-3pm Tue-Fri) The life and

times of Hawaii's 'first lady of ranching,' Anna Leialoha Lindsey Perry-Fiske, are celebrated at this lovingly restored 14-room historic ranch house, which contains impressive koa furniture, Perry-Fiske's bountiful wardrobe and other memorabilia. Tours (10am and 1pm, $10) must be booked in advance. Located 1 mile west of the town center.

Paniolo Heritage Center MUSEUM
(808-854-1541; www.paniolopreservation.org; Pukalani Rd; 9am-4pm Wed) FREE The Paniolo Preservation Society is developing this museum at Pukalani Stables, where Parker Ranch once bred horses. It's a work in progress, currently housing a photo exhibit and a saddle-making operation. The real reward is the personal touch: staffers are happy to talk story about *paniolo* history.

The **Waimea MidWeek Market** (Pukalani Stables; 9am-4pm Wed) is held at the stables on the same day the museum is open.

WM Keck Observatory Office OBSERVATORY
(808-885-7887; www.keckobservatory.org; 65-1120 Mamalahoa Hwy; 10am-2pm Tue-Fri) The lobby of this working office is open to the public. See models of the twin 10m (33ft) Keck telescopes, fascinating photos and a telescope trained on Mauna Kea. Informative volunteers prep you for a trip to the Mauna Kea summit.

Church Row CHURCH
Home to Christians, Buddhists and Mormons, Church Row is a living history of religious life on the island. There are several noteworthy, if humble, structures along this curved street, including the much-photographed, all-Hawaiian **Ke Ola Mau Loa Church**. Look for the green steeple.

Next door is **Imiola Congregational Church** (www.imiolachurch.com; services 9:30am), Waimea's first Christian church, which originated as a grass hut in 1830 and was built entirely of koa in 1857.

Here lies the grave of missionary Lorenzo Lyons, who arrived in 1832 and spent 54 years in Waimea. He wrote many hymns in Hawaiian, including the classic 'Hawai'i Aloha.'

Waimea Nature Park PARK
(Ulu La'au; 808-443-4482; 7am-5:30pm) Not to be confused with adjacent Waimea Park, this is a 10-acre green space in the center of town with picnic tables and free wi-fi. It's also a native plant restoration project. An excellent booklet on said plants and efforts to re-establish them in the region is available on-site ($3 or free if you return it). The park is surprisingly easy to miss: follow the road by the side of the large Canada France building.

Activities

Dahana Ranch Roughriders HORSEBACK RIDING
(808-885-0057; www.dahanaranch.com; 90min ride adult/child $80/70; rides 9am, 11am, 1pm & 3pm;) Ride American quarter horses bred, raised and trained by third- and fourth-generation *paniolo*. On offer are open-range rides for kids as young as three years, as well as advanced rides ($115) and a cattle drive ($150) for those who can canter. The ranch, owned and operated by a Native Hawaiian family, is 7.5 miles east of Waimea, off Mamalahoa Hwy. Reservations required.

Mountain Road Cycles CYCLING
(808-885-7943; www.mountainroadcycles.com; 64-1066 Mamalahoa Hwy; bikes per day $30-45; 9:30am-5:30pm Mon-Fri, 10am-3pm Sat) In addition to renting bicycles, this full-service bike shop arranges mountain-biking and road tours starting at $50. It prefers small groups and serious riders.

Festivals & Events

Waimea Ocean Film Festival FILM
(808-854-0095; www.waimeaoceanfilm.org) In early January films, speakers, receptions and art exhibits showcase the beauty, power and mystery of the ocean. Multiple venues in Waimea, Kohala and Kona.

Waimea Cherry Blossom Heritage Festival CULTURAL
(808-961-8706; waimeacherryblossom@gmail.com; Parker Ranch Center & Church Row Park) FREE Dark-pink blossoms are greeted with

KAMU-WHERE-AH?

Waimea is also known as Kamuela, which is the Hawaiian spelling of Samuel, apparently for Samuel Parker of Parker Ranch. Maps generally list both names; the post office and phone book use Kamuela to distinguish this Waimea from those on O'ahu and Kaua'i.

Also: curious about where the word *paniolo* comes from? The first cowboys who came to the Big Island, c 1830, hailed from the Spanish part of North America. In the local diction, these *españoles* soon became *paniolos*.

taiko drumming, *mochi* (sticky rice cake) pounding and other Japanese cultural events on the first Saturday in February.

Fourth of July Rodeo RODEO

(☎808-885-2303; 67-1435 Mamalahoa Hwy, Parker Ranch Rodeo Arena; admission $6) Celebrating over 45 years of ranching, this event includes cattle roping, bull riding and other hoopla.

Waimea Paniolo Parade and Hoʻolauleʻa PARADE

(www.waimeatown.org) This mid-September parade of authentic *paniolo,* island princesses and beautiful steeds begins at historic Church Row Park and makes its way through town, followed by a lively fair in Waimea Park. In conjunction with statewide Hawaii Island Festivals.

Round-Up Rodeo RODEO

(☎808-885-5669; www.parkerranch.com; 67-1435 Mamalahoa Hwy, Parker Ranch Rodeo Arena; admission $5) This whip-cracking event is held on the first Monday in September after Labor Day weekend.

★Waimea Ukulele & Slack Key Guitar Institute Concert MUSIC

(☎808-885-6017; www.kahilutheatre.org; admission $20-64) This annual concert in mid-November is a dream opportunity to see Hawaii's musical greats. Past headliners include Ledward Kaʻapana and Cyril Pahinui.

Christmas Twilight Parade CHRISTMAS

In early December the town gets into the Kalikimaka (Christmas) spirit with a block party.

Sleeping

★Kamuela Inn INN $

(☎808-885-4243; https://thekamuelainn.com; 65-1300 Kawaihae Rd; r $79-99, ste $109-189, all incl breakfast; 📶) Resembling a typical motor inn, this local institution is awesome value. Nothing's fancy but rooms are clean and comfy, with a range of bed configurations and kitchen amenities. Rooms in the renovated Mauna Kea Wing are worth the extra cost, with open-beam ceilings and spiffier decor. The spacious Executive Suite ($189) with full kitchen is ideal for families.

★Waimea Garden Cottages COTTAGE $$

(☎808-885-8550; www.waimeagardens.com; 65-1632 Kawaihae Rd; studios $160, cottages $175-190, all incl breakfast; 📶) On a well-tended property, find three spruce, well-equipped, country cottages around the owners' home. The largest, Kohala Cottage, has a full kitchen, enormous bath and adjacent walled garden. The cozy Waimea Cottage offers a fireplace, kitchenette and private patio. There's also a spacious studio near a seasonal stream.

Located a quick 2 miles west of town, near the intersection of Kawaihae Rd and Hwy 250. Three-day minimum stay.

★Aaah, the Views B&B B&B $$

(☎808-885-3455; www.aaahtheviews.com; 66-1773 Alaneo St; r incl breakfast 1/2-plus nights $209/189; 📶) Run by a welcoming family, this B&B takes advantage of a uniquely designed house with lots of windows, peaceful mountain views and charming ladder-accessible lofts. The two-bedroom Treetop Suite is an especially sweet deal, with four beds and a private deck. Enjoy generous breakfasts in your room or on a pleasant shared lanai. Located 3 miles west of town.

Jacaranda Inn INN $$

(☎808-885-8813; www.jacarandainn.com; 65-1444 Kawaihae Rd; r/ste/cottages from $129/179/250; 📶) Built in 1897 as a home for the manager of the Parker Ranch, the Jacaranda divides opinions. Some find the home and its eight rooms historically cozy and indulgent. Others find the antiquey aesthetic (four-poster beds, opulent tiled baths, carved furniture and oriental rugs) a little musty and unironically aged for the price.

Eating

You can stock up on groceries at **KTA Super Store** (☎808-885-8866; 65-1158 Mamalahoa Hwy, Waimea Center; ⏰6am-11pm), a large supermarket with a pharmacy, and at **Healthways II** (Kona Natural Foods; ☎808-885-6775; www.konanaturalfoods.net; 67-1185 Mamalahoa Hwy, Parker Ranch Center; ⏰9am-7pm Mon-Sat, to 5pm Sun), a natural food store; both have deli. Be sure to visit the **Waimea Homestead Farmers Market** (www.waimeafarmersmarket.com; Hwy 19; ⏰7am-noon Sat) and MidWeek Market (p245).

★Waimea Town Farmers Market MARKET $

(http://waimeatownmarket.com; 65-1224 Lindsey Rd; ⏰8am-1pm Sat) 🌿 With a circle of vendors around a grassy field, this farmers market has a friendly, cohesive vibe. Find artisan edibles, including handcrafted pasta and sausages and bread freshly baked in a mobile oven. While the specialty items like

OF CATTLE & COWBOYS

Parker Ranch (808-885-7311; www.parkerranch.com; 66-1304 Mamalahoa Hwy) was once the nation's largest privately owned ranch, peaking at 250,000 acres. Recently, however, the ranch has had to sell off parcels, including 24,000 acres to the US military in 2006. Today it's the fifth-largest cow-calf ranch in the USA, with at least 12,000 mother cows on 130,000 acres, and producing 12 million pounds of beef annually.

Big Island ranching goes back to 1793, when British Captain George Vancouver gifted King Kamehameha with a herd of long-horned cattle. Protected by the king's kapu (taboo), the herd proliferated and by 1815 was a menace.

Massachusetts mariner John Palmer Parker, who arrived here in 1809 at age 19, was deft with a rifle and was hired to control the cattle problem. After successfully cutting the herd down to size, he received not only top-quality cows, but also the hand of one of Kamehameha's granddaughters and a prime piece of land. Parker Ranch was born in 1847.

tea, jam and honey are delightful, the selection of basic produce is surprisingly limited. Located in front of Parker School.

★Village Burger BURGERS $

(808-885-7319; www.villageburgerwaimea.com; 67-1185 Mamalahoa Hwy, Parker Ranch Center; burgers $8-12; 10:30am-8pm Mon-Sat, to 6pm Sun;) Burger connoisseurs, prepare to be impressed. Big Island beef, veal and lamb burgers are juicy and tender, while vegetarian options (Waipi'o Valley taro or Hamakua mushroom) are equally scrumptious. All major ingredients pass muster with locavores, and freshly cut fries and aptly named 'Epic Shakes' top it off. Seating is very limited, but there's ample space in the adjacent food court.

★Hawaiian Style Cafe DINER $

(808-885-4295; 64-1290 Kawaihae Rd, Hayashi Bldg; dishes $7.50-10; 7am-1:30pm Mon-Sat, to noon Sun) Think you can eat a lot? If the portions at this local favorite greasy spoon don't satisfy you, we nod our heads in awe (and maybe a little in disgust). Expect enormous portions of *loco moco*, pancakes, fried rice, burgers and more. Health nuts and dieters need not apply.

Big Island Brewhaus & Taqueria MEXICAN $

(808-887-1717; www.bigislandbrewhaus.com; 64-1066 Mamalahoa Hwy; mains $7.50-16; 11am-8:30pm Mon-Sat, noon-8:30pm Sun) This quality brewpub nails the intersection of booze and belly-busting meals. Owner Thomas Kerns has created more than a dozen memorable beers, including White Mountain Porter, rich with coffee and coconut, and Golden Sabbath Belgian Ale, which has a tremendous aroma. The setting is casual verging on sloppy. Much of the food is locally sourced.

Lilikoi Cafe CAFE $

(808-887-1400; 67-1185 Mamalahoa Hwy, Parker Ranch Center; meals $9-12; 7:30am-4pm Mon-Sat;) This cheery cafe serves healthy, innovative food such as a breakfast burrito with eggs, tofu and sweet red pepper, and hearty vegetable lasagne. Drink the fresh carrot, apple, beet and ginger 'House Cocktail' ($5.50) and conquer the world. Hidden in the back of the shopping center.

★Aka Sushi Bar SUSHI $$

(808-887-2320; www.bigakasushi.com; 65-1158 Mamalahoa Hwy, Waimea Shopping Center; sushi $5-10, bowls $12-16; 10:30am-2:30pm & 5-8:30pm Tue-Sat) Ignore the strip-mall setting: this is a gem for reasonably priced or takeout sushi, and a beloved local instutiton. *Nigiri* and rolls have a high fish-to-rice ratio, and everything is fresh. Be sure to try the succulent *hamachi kama* (grilled yellowtail collar).

Fish and the Hog Market Cafe BARBECUE $$

(808-885-6268; 64-957 Mamalahoa Hwy; sandwiches $10-13, barbecue $15-24; 11:30am-8pm Mon-Sat, 8am-8pm Sun) Barbecue isn't the first food genre folks tend to associate with Hawaii, but this is an island that loves smoked meat. This sit-down restaurant serves ribs, pulled pork, beef brisket and other kiawe-smoked meats with its signature BBQ sauces. Fish dishes, from gumbo to tacos, are well done. Save room for the famous banana cream pie.

Pau SANDWICHES, PIZZA $$

(808-885-6325; www.paupizza.com; 65-1227 Opelo Rd, Opelo Plaza; pizzas $17-28; 11am-8pm)

This casual eatery serves reliably creative, tasty and healthful salads, sandwiches, pastas and more than a dozen crisp, thin-crust pizzas.

★ **Merriman's** HAWAII REGIONAL CUISINE $$$
(☎808-885-6822; www.merrimanshawaii.com; 65-1227 Opelo Rd, Opelo Plaza; lunch $11-15, dinner $29-50; ⏲11:30am-1:30pm Mon-Fri, 5:30-8pm daily) Chef-owner Peter Merriman's Waimea namesake has long wowed diners with its creative use of organic, island-grown ingredients. Today there are four sister restaurants anchored by this, the original flagship. It's still the best fine-dining spot in town. The mahimahi marinated in *ponzu* (Japanese citrus sauce), wok-charred ahi and crispy molten chocolate 'purse' are classics. Lunch offers good value.

Redwater Cafe HAWAII REGIONAL CUISINE $$$
(☎808-885-9299; www.redwatercafe.com; 65-1299 Kawaihae Rd; mains $22-38; ⏲noon-2:30pm Mon-Fri, 5-9pm daily) Redwater has quickly risen to the top of many lists, propelled in part by the reputation of owner/chef David Abrahams, a 25-year veteran of resort kitchens on the West Coast. The decor is saloon simple, the menu a tasty playground of excellent sushi, plus local ingredients and fusion influences; think guava braised short ribs and *liliko'i* chicken curry.

A sushi bar (5pm to 9pm) and outdoor garden area provide some variety. Extensive kids' menu.

☆ Entertainment

★ **Kahilu Theatre** THEATER
(☎808-885-6868; www.kahilutheatre.org; 67-1185 Mamalahoa Hwy, Parker Ranch Center; admission from $20; ⏲box office 9am-3pm Mon-Fri, show times vary) A hot spot for music and dance, this theater has its finger on the pulse of the Big Island, and offers a variety of top performances – for example, from Hawaii icons the Brothers Cazimero, the latest Van Cliburn winner and the annual Waimea Ukulele & Slack Key Guitar Institute Concert. Check the website for upcoming shows.

Shopping

Three shopping malls line Hwy 19 through town: **Parker Ranch Center** (67-1185 Mamalahoa Hwy), where the stop signs say 'Whoa'; **Waimea Center** (65-1158 Mamalahoa Hwy); and **Parker Square** (65-1279 Kawaihae Rd). The first two have groceries and basics, plus restaurants and fast food; Parker Square aims for discriminating, upscale gift buyers.

Gallery of Great Things ARTS, CRAFTS
(☎808-885-7706; www.galleryofgreatthingshawaii.com; 65-1279 Kawaihae Rd, Parker Square; ⏲9am-5.30pm Mon-Sat, 10am-4pm Sun) This unpretentious gallery is crammed with antiques, high-quality art and collectibles from Hawaii, Polynesia and Asia. Among the Hawaiian crafts for sale is *kapa*, bark cloth painstakingly handmade by traditional methods. There's something for every budget.

Waimea General Store GIFTS, HOMEWARES
(☎808-885-4479; www.waimeageneralstore.com; 65-1279 Kawaihae Rd, Parker Square) Shoppers, browsers and homemakers will enjoy the eclectic mix of kitsch, kook and Hawaiiana, from Le Creuset and Japanese tableware to fancy toiletries and vintage hula-girl cards.

Reyn's CLOTHING
(www.reyns.com; Parker Ranch Center; ⏲9:30am-5:30pm Mon-Sat, to 4pm Sun) If you want to dress like a local, shop at Reyn's. Its classic, understated aloha shirts (which use Hawaiian fabrics in reverse) never go out of style.

Wishard Gallery ARTS
(☎808-887-2278; www.wishardgallery.com; 67-1185 Mamalahoa Hwy, Parker Ranch Center; ⏲9am-7pm Mon-Sat, to 2pm Sun) Apart from Harry Wishard's own work (imaginative landscapes that pop up in houses and restaurants around the island), this gallery represents 20 other artists. Of note are Ethan Tweedie's stunning panoramas of Mauna Kea transferred to aluminum.

Information

North Hawaii Community Hospital (☎808-885-4444; 67-1125 Mamalahoa Hwy) Emergency services available 24 hours.

Post office (☎808-885-6239; 67-1197 Mamalahoa Hwy; ⏲8am-4:30pm Mon-Fri, 9am-noon Sat) Address all Waimea mail to Kamuela.

Getting There & Around

Kailua-Kona is 37 miles along Hwy 190; Hilo is 51 miles away on Hwy 19.

On Monday to Saturday the Hele-On Bus (p223) goes from Waimea (Parker Ranch Center) to Kailua-Kona on its 16 Kailua-Kona route (65 minutes) and to Hilo on its 7 Downtown Hilo route (80 minutes).

MAUNA KEA & SADDLE ROAD

Mauna Kea

Mauna Kea (White Mountain) is called Mauna O Wakea (Mountain of Wakea) by Hawaiian cultural practitioners. While all of the Big Island is considered the first-born child of Wakea (Sky Father) and Papahanaumoku (Earth Mother), the deity progenitors of the Hawaiian race, Mauna Kea is the sacred *piko* (navel) connecting the land to the heavens.

For the scientific world, it all began in 1968 when the University of Hawai'i (UH) began observing the universe from atop the mountain. The summit is so high, dry, dark and pollution free that it allows investigation of the furthest reaches of the observable universe. Today, astronomers from 11 countries staff 13 observatories on Mauna Kea's summit – the largest conglomeration of high-powered telescopes anywhere in the world. They huddle in a small area of the Mauna Kea Science Reserve, a chunk of land leased by UH that encompasses almost everything above 12,000ft.

Many Hawaiians are opposed to the summit 'golf balls' – the white observatories. While not antiscience, they believe that unchecked growth on the mountain threatens the *wahi pana* (sacred places) there, including heiau and burial sites. In a dramatic episode in 2006, an *ahu lele* (spiritual altar) built for ceremonies on the mountain was desecrated. Toxic mercury spills from some observatories have occurred, and damage to the mountain's fragile ecosystem is another arrow in the activists' antidevelopment quiver.

Nevertheless, in 2011 plans were approved to build the Thirty Meter Telescope (TMT) here, and in October of 2014, construction officially began. The TMT will be the world's most advanced and powerful

Mauna Kea & Mauna Loa

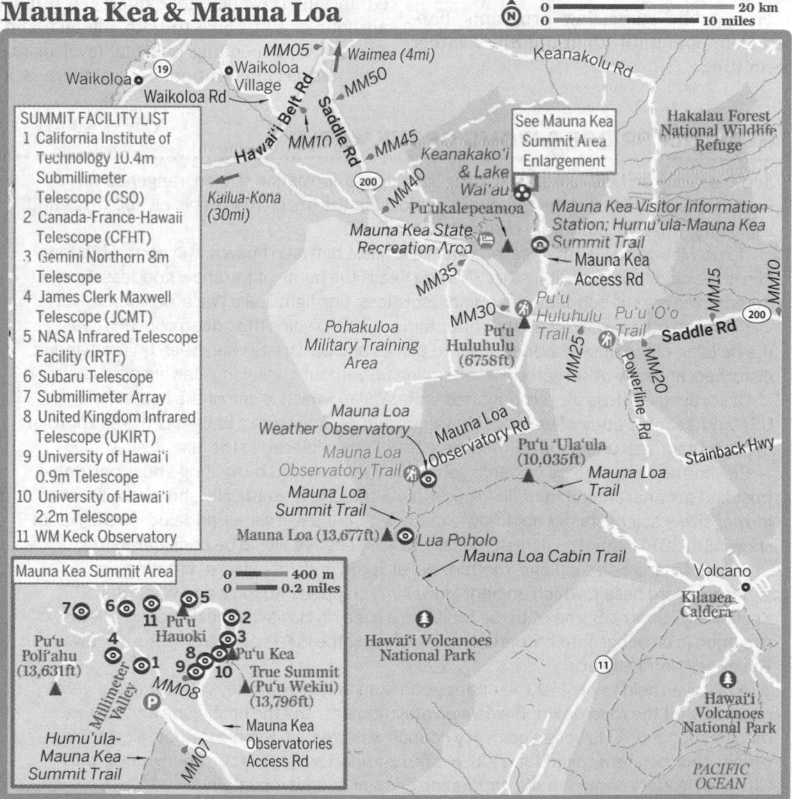

telescope, offering 10 times the resolution of the Hubble telescope. With that said, its structural footprint will be larger than all the observatories currently on the summit (around 5 acres), with the possible disruptions of natural and cultural resources that implies.

Sights

★Mauna Kea Visitor Information Station TOURIST INFORMATION

(MKVIS; ☎808-961-2180; www.ifa.hawaii.edu/info/vis; ⏲9am-10pm) FREE Modestly sized, MKVIS packs a punch with astronomy and space-exploration videos, virtual observatory tours and exhibits on the mountain's history, ecology and geology. Budding astronomers of all ages geek out in the gift shop, where knowledgeable staff will help you pass the time acclimatizing to the 9200ft altitude. Check the website for upcoming special events, such as lectures about science and Hawaiian culture, typically held on Saturday nights.

Free public stargazing programs happen from 6pm until 10pm nightly, weather permitting.

Inside the gift shop you can buy hot chocolate, coffee, packets of instant noodles and freeze-dried astronaut food to munch on; hoodies, hats and gloves to stay warm; and books about science and Hawaiian culture.

Across from MKVIS, a 15-minute uphill hike crests **Pu'u Kalepeamoa** (9394ft), a cinder cone offering glorious sunset views. Directly off the MKVIS parking lot is a small enclosed area where rare and endangered **silversword plants** grow.

As you drive the 6 miles uphill (gaining 2500ft in altitude) from Saddle Rd to the MKVIS, you'll break through the cloud cover. The road is paved and normally accessible by 2WD vehicles as far as MKVIS.

★Keanakako'i & Lake Wai'au ARCHAEOLOGICAL SITE

Just after the 6-mile marker en route to Mauna Kea's summit area from MKVIS, pull into a paved parking area. Below is the trailhead to Lake Wai'au, the third-highest lake in the USA, and Keanakako'i, a protected ancient Hawaiian adze quarry. It'll take an hour or so to hike to both the lake and the quarry, depending on your level of fitness and acclimatization. To say there is a

HEAVENLY BRIDGE & WOMB OF THE WORLD

Snow is falling on Mauna Kea and, near the visitor information station, ranger James Keali'i Pihana – 'Kimo,' as he's known – is blocking the frozen road in his pickup truck and explaining what the mountain means to Hawaiians.

'To us, Mauna Kea is "the heavens." It is the place between heaven and earth…Mauna Kea is the center of our "Biblestory." Mauna Kea is the home of the snow goddess, Poliahu. Ceremonies are still conducted: equinox, solstices, first light. Lake Wai'au is sacred water.'

Kimo and others walked up the mountain in 1998 to voice their deep concern over the building of the observatories. Sacred places and burial sites had been built on and disturbed, and new observatories were going up without consulting Hawaiians.

Of particular note is aforementioned Lake Wai'au, which is one of the highest in the USA and a sacred body of water in Hawaiian culture. To ensure a baby has the strength of the mountain, real umbilical stumps were traditionally placed in the lake.

Clay formed long ago by volcanic ash holds the water, fed by melting snow, permafrost and minimal annual rainfall. Around 2010, the lake dramatically shrunk to 2% of its former size – scientists did not know exactly why, but a wet winter and decent blanket of snowfall in 2014 helped replenish the lake to 75% of what would be considered full.

During Mauna Kea's ice age, molten lava erupted under its glacier, creating an extremely hard basalt, which ancient Hawaiians chipped into tools and weapons at Keanakako'i quarry. Some of these tools were used on Hawai'i to peck massive fields of symbolic drawings into hardened lava, including the Pu'u Loa petroglyphs in Hawai'i Volcanoes National Park.

A rally was held to protest the changes on Mauna Kea. Kimo says, 'Our people were ready to shut the road down.' It was a pivotal moment, and the politicians and astronomers responded. A Hawaiian advisory council was created, Kimo conducted cleansing rituals, and then he applied for a job. His most important task is communicating with Hawaiian leaders about what's happening on their sacred mountain.

palpable sense of the sacred here would be an understatement.

Entering the quarry is discouraged, because it's a fragile archaeological site of importance to Hawaiians, but the views from the trail are still worth seeing.

★ **Mauna Kea's Summit Area** LANDMARK

If measured from the sea floor, you are 13,808ft in the air, on top of, technically, the tallest mountain in the world. Massive observatories rise around you, shining silver on the stark terrain, like a human colony on an alien planet. These observatories comprise the greatest collection of telescopes on earth; the summit is above 40% of the earth's atmosphere and 90% of its water vapor, resulting in many cloudless nights. Be sure to bring long pants, a thick coat (or lots of layers), a warm hat and gloves. It gets cold up here.

It's a veritable UN on the mountaintop, with a bevy of countries administering different telescopes: Taiwan and the USA collaborate on the **Submillimeter Array** (www.cfa.harvard.edu/sma); the UK and Canada run the **James Clerk Maxwell Telescope** (JCMT; www.eaobservatory.org/jcmt); and six nations share the **Gemini Northern 8m Telescope** (www.gemini.edu). The **University of Hawai'i 0.9m Telescope** (www.astro.uhh.hawaii.edu) is now used mostly for training undergraduates. Most of these observatories are closed to the public, and none allow public viewing through their telescopes.

Sunsets are phenomenal from around the summit. All of Hawai'i lies below as the sun sinks into an ocean of clouds – while the telescopes silently unshutter and turn their unblinking eyes to the heavens. Look east to see 'the shadow' – the gigantic silhouette of Mauna Kea looming over Hilo. Moonrises can be equally as impressive: the high altitude may make the moon appear squashed and misshapen, or sometimes resemble a brushfire.

If you have a 4WD, you may drive to the summit in the daytime, but you must descend 30 minutes after sunset. It takes about half an hour to drive the 8-mile summit road, the first 4.5 miles of which are slippery gravel. Just before the pavement picks up again, the area on the east side of the road is dubbed **Moon Valley**, where Apollo astronauts rehearsed with their lunar rover before their journey to the real moonscape.

BEST MAUNA KEA WEBCAMS

- CFH Telescope Timelapse Webcam (www.cfht.hawaii.edu/webcam)
- Joint Astronomy Centre Webcam (www.jach.hawaii.edu/weather/camera/jac)
- MKVIS Live Allsky Cam (www.ifa.hawaii.edu/info/vis/photo-gallery/live-webcam.html)
- NASA Infrared Telescope Facility Cameras (http://irtfweb.ifa.hawaii.edu/~irtfcameras)
- Subaru Telescope Webcams (www.naoj.org/Weather)

WM Keck Observatory OBSERVATORY

(☎808-935-6268; www.keckobservatory.org; ⏲visitors' gallery 10am-4pm Mon-Fri) FREE Near Mauna Kea's summit, this observatory has a visitors' gallery with scientific displays, public restrooms and partial views inside the Keck I dome. The world's largest and most powerful optical and infrared telescopes are housed here, a joint project of the California Institute of Technology (CalTech), the University of California and NASA. The two interchangeable telescopes can function as one – like a pair of binoculars searching the sky – allowing them to study incredibly distant galaxies.

In 1992, **Keck I** made a breakthrough in telescope design using a unique honeycomb feature made up of 36 hexagonal mirror segments that function as a single piece of glass. A replica of the first telescope, **Keck II**, went online in 1996. In 2013, scientists using Keck I discovered the most distant galaxy ever observed, a mere 13.1 billion light years away.

Subaru Telescope OBSERVATORY

(☎808-934-7788; http://subarutelescope.org; ⏲tours usually 10:30am, 11:30am & 1:30pm Tue-Thu) FREE When it was built in 1999, Japan's Subaru Telescope was the most expensive observatory constructed, until ground was broken on the nearby Thirty Meter Telescope. The 22-ton mirror, reaching 27ft in diameter, is one of the largest optical mirrors in existence. Observatory tours, which don't include looking through the telescope, are given in Japanese or English but not both, so sign up early for your preferred language. Reserve tours online at least one week in advance.

Children under 16 years old are not allowed on tours and there are no public restrooms. Incidentally, Subaru is the Japanese word for the Pleiades constellation.

Pu'u Wekiu MOUNTAIN

The short trail up this cinder cone to Mauna Kea's true summit (13,796ft) begins opposite the UH 2.2m Telescope. The hike is harder than it looks, and it's not necessary to go just to watch the sunset. Hawaiian cultural practitioners counsel against hiking due to the area's environmental fragility and cultural significance. At the true summit is a US Geological Survey (USGS) marker and an *ahu* (altar). Given the biting winds, high altitude and extreme cold, most people don't linger.

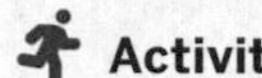

Activities

Stargazing

The Mauna Kea Visitor Information Station (p250) offers a terrific nightly stargazing program. Numerous telescopes are set up outside the station, each one trained on a different celestial object.

On an average night you might move from the Ring Nebula to the Andromeda Galaxy to a galactic cluster to Jupiter's moons. It is a unique and profoundly memorable experience.

The program begins at 6pm with the film *First Light,* a documentary on Mauna Kea as both cultural and astronomical entity. How much you'll see through the telescopes depends on cloud cover and moon phase, but you can call ahead if you want to double check. The busiest nights are Friday and Saturday but there are no reservations. Special 'scope attachments accommodate visitors in wheelchairs.

During big meteor showers, the station staffs its telescopes for all-night star parties; call for details. And every Saturday night at 6pm it hosts a rotating series of lectures and events: 'The Universe Tonight' is an astronomy lecture held on the first Saturday; on the second Saturday students from the UH Hilo Astrophysics Club assist with stargazing; 'Malalo I Ka Lani Po' is a culture lecture on the third Saturday; and the fourth Saturday is a multigenre international music night.

> **STARGAZING PLANNER**
>
> Here are some tips from the experts about the best times – celestially speaking – to visit Mauna Kea.
>
> ➡ Lunar eclipses and meteor showers are special events in this rarefied air; the Leonides in November are particularly impressive. Check **StarDate** (http://stardate.org/nightsky/meteors) for the year's meteor showers, eclipses, moon phases and more.
>
> ➡ The Milky Way streaks the night sky bright and white between January and March.
>
> ➡ Don't forget the monthly full moon. It's simply spectacular as it rises over you, seemingly close enough to touch.

Hiking

For sunset views without going to the summit, take the 15-minute, steep hike up **Pu'u Kalepeamoa**, starting across the road from MKVIS (p250). Heading toward Mauna Kea's summit area, you can hike to Keanakako'i & Lake Wai'au (p250).

★Humu'ula–Mauna Kea Summit Trail HIKING

This daunting, all-day hike starts at 9200ft, then climbs almost 4600ft over the next 6 miles to Mauna Kea's summit. Expect thin air, steep grades and biting weather on this utterly exposed trail, where it often feels like you're going to step off the mountain into the sky. Plan on eight hours for the round-trip hike and bring a gallon of water per person – dehydration is a real danger at these altitudes. Don't hike in inclement weather.

Start very early – by 6am if possible. It typically takes five hours to reach the summit, and half as long coming down, and you want time to explore in between. Consult rangers for advice, and get a map and register at the Visitor Information Station's outdoor trail kiosk before hiking. Be prepared for serious weather – snow and 100mph winds are possible.

Park at the Visitor Information Station and walk 1000ft up the road. Where the pavement ends, go left on the dirt road, following several Humu'ula Trail signs to the trail proper. Reflective T-posts and cairns mark the route. After about an hour the summit road comes back into view on your right, and the vegetation starts to disappear. As you weave around cinder cones and traipse over crumbled *'a'a* and slippery scree, you pass various spur trails, which all lead back to the access road.

LOCAL KNOWLEDGE

Name Rob Pacheco

Occupation Owner, Hawai'i Forest & Trail

Residence Holualoa

How Many Times Have You Summited Mauna Kea?

I've been up there more times than I can count – hundreds of times. We all need beauty, awe and wonder in our lives. Mauna Kea does that for me.

What's the Best View in Your Opinion?

Now my favorite view is from outside the University of Hawai'i 2.2m Telescope, where you get unobstructed views to the western horizon; turn around and you have the same to the eastern horizon. Logistically, I like it because you can tuck yourself into the telescope when the wind is howling.

What Hike Would You Recommend?

Off Saddle Rd, Pu'u Huluhulu is a great introduction to Hawai'i's native forests. You'll see rare endemic species, plus trees like sandalwood and koa. The views of the entire region are great too.

Skiing on Mauna Kea: Your Take?

For me, Mauna Kea is not a recreational playground. On good snow days, of which there are only a handful each year, hundreds of people are up there skiing and sledding. Too many people. The Hawaiian-ness of the mountain is not on everyone's radar. My job is to help connect visitors to this land in deeper ways, to convert them from simple thrill seekers into stakeholders.

Most of the way you will be passing through the Mauna Kea Ice Age Natural Area Reserve. After about three hours a sharp, short ascent leads to Keanakako'i. The hardest, steepest part of the trail is now behind you. After another mile you reach a four-way junction, where a 10-minute detour to the left brings you to Lake Wai'au. Return to the four-way junction and head north (uphill) for the final push to meet the Mauna Kea Summit Rd at a parking area. Suddenly the observatories are visible on the summit, and straight ahead is 'Millimeter Valley,' nicknamed for its submillimeter and millimeter observatories. The trail officially ends at the access road's mile marker 7, but the true summit still snickers at you another 1.5 miles away.

For Native Hawaiians, the summit is a region, a realm, not a point on a map. But if you really need to place a boot toe on Pu'u Wekiu, Mauna Kea's true summit, soldier on till you reach the UH 2.2m Telescope, where the short spur trail to the summit begins.

When descending, return along the shoulder of the access road rather than retracing the trail. Though the road is 2 miles longer, it's easier on the knees and easier to follow as sunlight fades. Also, it's common for hikers to get offered a lift downhill; sticking to the road increases your chances.

Alternatively, save time and energy by hitching a lift to the top from the Visitor Information Station and just walking down (about three hours).

Skiing & Snowboarding

In January or February, enough snow may fall on Mauna Kea's heights to allow for winter sports. The so-called 'slopes' are crowded with locals using skis, snowboards, surfboards, bodyboards, inner tubes – whatever!

What concerns activists and conservationists is increased mountaintop usage during snowfall, combined with the degradation caused by monster trucks used to access the 'slopes,' which erode natural habitat and culturally significant sites.

For those chasing this trophy experience, know that skiing Mauna Kea is entirely DIY. There are no groomed trails, no lifts, no patrols; exposed rocks and ice sheets are constant dangers.

Tours

MKVIS Escorted Summit Tour GUIDED TOUR (808-935-6268; www.ifa.hawaii.edu/info/vis; usually 1pm Sat & Sun) You must provide your own low-gear 4WD vehicle to take

TO BUY A SUMMIT TOUR OR NOT, THAT IS THE QUESTION

Tours have many positives: transportation from other parts of the island to the visitor station, 4WD to the summit, warm clothing, a box dinner, excellent guides with deep knowledge of astronomy, and the ease of it all. The negatives to consider include the considerable cost (up to $200 per individual), a fixed and limited schedule, and the herd factor.

Itinerary-wise, a typical sunset tour starts in the early afternoon, stops for dinner, arrives at the summit just before sunset, stays about 40 minutes (this is not long enough to allow for hiking), descends to the visitor station for private stargazing with a single telescope, and gets you home after 9pm. There is no tour of summit telescopes.

Now assess the DIY alternative. If you have a 4WD rental, you can do some hiking on your own, then take the summit tour from the Visitor Information Station. This includes a movie, a talk at the summit and a visit to one of the observatories (if you only have a 2WD rental, you will need to hitch a round-trip ride from the station to the summit). Finally, you can come back down to the visitor station for a smorgasbord of stargazing amid multiple telescopes. You'll have to pack your dinner and bring warm clothing, but the total cost is zero, apart from the car (a rental 4WD is less than $200 a day), which you might have rented anyway.

advantage of these free guided summit tours (no reservations accepted). You'll spend the first hour acclimatizing and watching astronomy videos. After the orientation, you'll caravan up to the summit, where a docent talks about the telescopes, their history and what they're typically looking at. Tours visit at least one of the summit observatories, ending around 4:30pm.

Most people stay for the sunset, then drive back down on their own. Tours don't run when bad weather closes the road, so call ahead to check weather and road conditions. Children must be at least 16 years old.

Hawaii Forest & Trail TOUR
(☎808-331-8505; www.hawaii-forest.com; tour $199; ⏲tours nightly, weather permitting) This top-notch, ecotour outfitter hosts a sunset and stargazing tour, with parkas, gloves and a picnic dinner at a private location. Knowledgeable guides take you to the summit, then conduct a tour of the heavens with an 11in Celestron telescope outside MKVIS. Pickups are from near Kailua-Kona, Waikoloa and the Hwys 190/200 junction. Participants must be at least 16 years old. Book early.

Mauna Kea Summit Adventures TOUR
(☎888-322-2366, 808-322-2366; www.maunakea.com; tour $212) The granddaddy of Mauna Kea tours has been taking folks to the summit for over 30 years. Distinguishing this outfit are vans with extra-tall windows and spacious seating. A hot dinner outside MKVIS, cold-weather parkas to borrow and stargazing through a 11in Celestron telescope are included. Pickups from Kailua-Kona, Waikoloa and Hwys 190/200 junction. Children must be at least 13 years old.

Arnott's Mauna Kea Adventures TOUR
(Map p268; ☎808-339-0921; www.arnottslodge.com; 98 Apanane Rd, Hilo; tours $180; ⏲Wed & Fri-Mon) Arnott's Lodge tours are for budget travelers, not serious stargazers. They're cheaper, leave from Hilo (or you can drive your own car and meet them on Saddle Rd for $160) and the astronomy is bare bones, with guides relying on laser pointers. BYO food and warm clothes. If you're staying at Arnott's (p275), the tour is $130.

Sleeping

The closest accommodations besides camping are in Waimea and Hilo.

Mauna Kea State Recreation Area CABIN $
(☎808-961-8311; Saddle Rd) At the 35-mile marker is this public recreation area, which at the time of writing had been taken over by the County of Hawaii. Plans are to extensively renovate the grounds and on-site cabins, which should be open when you read this. In previous years, military maneuvers at nearby Pohakuloa Training Area meant it could be very noisy.

Information

There are no restaurants, gas stations or emergency services anywhere on Mauna Kea or along Saddle Rd. Come prepared with a full tank of gas, warm clothing, sunglasses, sunscreen, snacks and plenty of water.

Even at the MKVIS (9200ft), some visitors experience shortness of breath and mild 'altitude sickness' (acute mountain sickness, or AMS). At the 13,796ft summit, atmospheric pressure is less than 60% what it is at sea level, and AMS is common. The risk increases with faster ascents and greater exertion; being physically fit offers no protection. All travelers to the summit should stop first at MKVIS for at least 30 minutes to acclimatize.

Symptoms of AMS include nausea, headaches, drowsiness, impaired reason, loss of balance, breathlessness and dehydration. AMS can lead to life-threatening pulmonary or cerebral edema. If you feel ill, descend immediately. Children under 16 years, pregnant women and those with high blood pressure or circulatory conditions should not go to the summit. Do not scuba dive for 24 hours before or after visiting Mauna Kea.

Be prepared for rapidly changing (and possibly severe) weather conditions, with daytime temperatures anywhere from 50°F (10°C) to below freezing and possible high winds. In winter, several feet of snow can fall, with road closures on the morning following a storm. Check weather and road conditions with the **Mauna Kea Weather Center** (http://mkwc.ifa.hawaii.edu) before heading up. Even when the fog's as thick as pea soup on Saddle Rd, it's crystal clear at the mountaintop 325 days a year.

Getting There & Around

Coming from Kona or Waimea, Saddle Rd (Hwy 200) starts just south of mile marker 6 on Hwy 190. From Hilo, drive *mauka* (inland) on Kaumana Dr (Hwy 200) or Puainako Extension (Hwy 2000), both of which become Saddle Rd. Start with a full tank of gas – Saddle Rd has no gas stations.

To get to MKVIS and the summit beyond, turn onto Mauna Kea Access Rd, near mile marker 28 on Saddle Rd. It takes about an hour to get to MKVIS from Hilo, Waimea or Waikoloa, or around 90 minutes from Kailua-Kona. MKVIS is 6 miles uphill from Saddle Rd; the summit is another 8 miles beyond the information station. Call ☎808-935-6268 for current road conditions.

Driving to the summit requires a low-gear 4WD vehicle – there have been many accidents that underscore this point. Over half of the summit road is gravel, sometimes at a 15% grade. The upper road can be covered with ice, and loose cinders are always challenging. Drive in low gear and be particularly careful on the way down *not* to ride your vehicle's brakes, which can overheat and fail. Driving when the sun is low – in the hour after sunrise or before sunset – can create hazardous, blinding conditions. Plan to drive up to the summit during the daytime: vehicle headlights between sunset and sunrise interfere with astronomical observations.

Saddle Road

Off Saddle Rd you'll discover a few exceptional wilderness hikes, as well as one high-altitude scenic drive.

Sights & Activities

Mauna Loa Observatory Road SCENIC DRIVE

Mauna Loa is somewhat of an enigma for visitors – it looms large all around, but how do you actually get there? The answer is simple: drive up Mauna Loa Observatory Rd. This unsigned road starts near mile marker 28 on Saddle Rd, almost opposite Mauna Kea Access Rd and next to Pu'u Huluhulu. Delivering kicking views, the single-lane, 17.5-mile asphalt road ends at a parking area just below the Mauna Loa Observatory (11,150ft).

★ **Mauna Loa Observatory Trail** HIKING

The easiest way to summit Mauna Loa (Long Mountain) is via this trail. Drive up to the **Mauna Loa Observatory** at 11,150ft, then pick up the 6.4-mile walking trail for the remaining 2500ft to the top. It's a steep, exhausting, all-day adventure, but also an exceptional one that allows experienced hikers to conquer a 13,000ft mountain in one day. There are no visitor facilities or bathrooms at the observatory.

Begin hiking by 8am; you want to be off the mountain or descending if afternoon clouds roll in. The trail is marked by *ahu* (cairns), which disappear in the fog. If fog does roll in, stop hiking; find shelter in one of several small tubes and hollows along the route until you can see again, even if this means waiting till morning.

It is nearly 4 miles to the trail junction with the Mauna Loa Trail (p298; an alternative multiday backpacking route to the summit). Allow three hours for this gradual ascent of nearly 2000ft. If it weren't for the altitude, this would be a breeze. Proceed slowly but steadily, keeping breaks short. If you feel the onset of altitude sickness, descend. About two hours along, you re-enter the national park, and the old lava flows appear in a rainbow of sapphire, turquoise, silver, ochre, orange, gold and magenta.

Once at the trail junction, the majesty of the summit's **Moku'aweoweo Caldera** overwhelms you. Day hikers have two choices: proceed another 2.6 miles and three hours along the **Summit Trail** to the tippy-top at 13,677ft (visible in the distance), or explore the caldera by following the 2.1-mile **Mauna**

Loa Cabin Trail. If you can stand not summiting, the second option is extremely interesting, leading to even grander caldera views and a vertiginous peek into the awesome depths of **Lua Poholo** – a craterlike hole in the landscape.

Descending takes half as long as ascending; depending on how far you go, prepare for a seven- to 10-hour round-trip hike. Bring copious amounts of water, food, a flashlight and rain gear, and wear boots, a winter coat and a cap – it's cold and windy year-round.

Day hikers do not need a permit, but if you would like to overnight at Mauna Loa Cabin, register the day before at Hawai'i Volcanoes National Park's Backcountry Office (p296), where rangers can inform you about current trail conditions and water-catchment levels at the cabin.

Pu'u Huluhulu Trail HIKING

The easy 1056yd trail up the cinder cone **Pu'u Huluhulu** (Shaggy Hill, 6758ft) makes a piquant appetizer before going up Mauna Kea. Inside a *kipuka* (volcanic oasis), the 20-minute hike climbs through native forest to the hilltop, from where there are panoramic views of Mauna Kea, Mauna Loa and Hualalai on clear days.

The trailhead parking area is almost opposite the turnoff to Mauna Kea, near mile marker 28 on Saddle Rd. Don't confuse this hike with the Pu'u Huluhulu Trail (p298) in Hawai'i Volcanoes National Park.

DON'T MISS

MAUNA KEA POLO CLUB

After a long hiatus the Big Island once again has polo, and the field alone is worth the trip. The games are sponsored by **Mauna Kea Polo Club** (808-960-5098; www.maunakeapoloclub.com; Waiki'i Ranch, off Waikii Rd; adult/child 12yr & under $5/free; 1-4pm Sun Oct-Dec) and held 6.4 miles up Saddle Rd from Waimea on exclusive Waikii Ranch. More Big Island than Long Island, the games are very low key, with BBQ eats and T-shirts for sale, and tailgating encouraged. It's the perfect excuse for a beautiful drive and picnic, and you might even learn something about polo. Turn right at Saddle Rd mile marker 59; the gatehouse attendant will let you in.

Pu'u 'O'o Trail HIKING

For a peaceful yet substantial ramble, take this 7.5-mile loop traversing meadows, old lava flows and pretty *kipuka* forests filled with koa and ohia trees and the songs of Hawaiian honeycreepers and other native birds. The signed trailhead parking area is almost exactly halfway between mile markers 22 and 23 on Saddle Rd.

The trail is marked by *ahu* (stone cairns); it's easy to follow in good weather, less so in rain or fog. If in doubt, retrace your steps to find your way back. Eventually the trail connects with Powerline Rd (marked with a sign), a 4WD road that can be used as a return route, although this road dumps you about a mile from the trailhead parking area.

HAMAKUA COAST

Honoka'a & Around

POP 2258

A sleepy main street primarily inhabited by wide-eyed day trippers and bored local teens belies Honoka'a's long history – this was once the third-largest town in Hawaii, after Honolulu and Hilo. Honoka'a was the hub for the powerful cattle and sugar industries, but was forced to reinvent itself when those industries crashed; by the time Honoka'a Sugar Company processed its last harvest in 1993, the town had dwindled in size and struggled to find new economic niches. Eventually, entrepreneurial farmers diversified their crops and found success with niche edibles, such as mushrooms, tomatoes and lettuces, sold at farmers markets and prized by gourmet chefs.

You can catch Hele-On Bus (p223) to Honoka'a from Hilo or Kailua-Kona, but service is infrequent. In and around town, you'll definitely need a car.

Sights

There are small, family-run farms in pastoral **Pa'auilo** and **Ahualoa**, on the *mauka* side of the highway. They are working farms so you must book ahead for tours.

★**Hawaiian Vanilla Company** FARM

(808-776-1771; www.hawaiianvanilla.com; 43-2007 Paauilo Mauka Rd, Pa'auilo; tasting $25, afternoon tea $29, lunch per adult/child $39/19; tasting 10:30am Mon-Fri, afternoon tea 3pm Sat, lunch

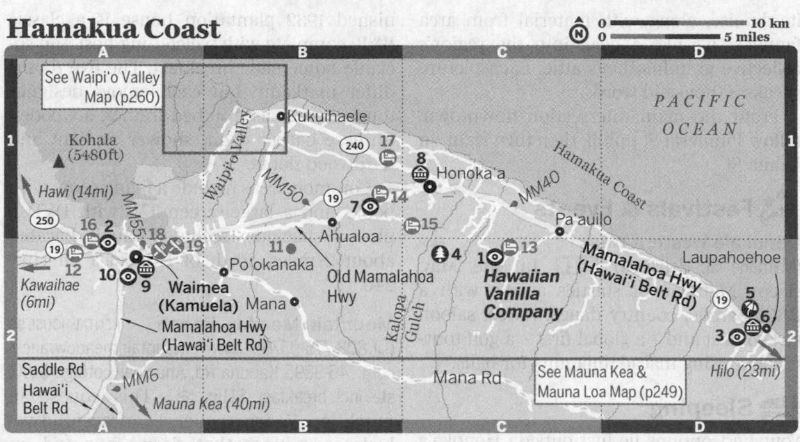

Hamakua Coast

Top Sights
1 Hawaiian Vanilla Company C2

Sights
2 Anna Ranch Heritage Center A2
3 Hamakua Mushrooms..................... D2
4 Kalopa State Recreation Area..................... C2
5 Laupahoehoe Point Beach Park D2
6 Laupahoehoe Train Museum D2
7 Mauna Kea Tea B1
8 NHERC Heritage Center C1
9 Paniolo Heritage Center A2
10 Parker Ranch..................... A2

Activities, Courses & Tours
11 Dahana Ranch Roughriders B2

Sleeping
12 Aaah, the Views B&B A2
Jacaranda Inn .... (see 2)
13 Keolamauloa C2
14 Mountain Meadow Ranch B1
15 Waianuhea B&B..................... C1
16 Waimea Garden Cottages A2
17 Waipi'o Wayside B&B B1

Eating
18 Fish and the Hog Market Cafe A2
19 Waimea Homestead Farmers Market A2
Waimea MidWeek Market .... (see 9)

12:30pm Mon-Fri) The first commercial vanilla operation in the USA, this family-run farm is a model for successful agritourism. All of the edible tours are decently priced and worth your time. If time is short, stop by the gift shop (10am to 5pm) for vanilla-infused coffee, tea, bath and body products and, of course, prime beans and extracts.

Mauna Kea Tea FARM

(808-775-1171; www.maunakeatea.com; 46-3870 Old Mamalahoa Hwy, Ahualoa; 60-90min tour per person with 2/3/4-plus people $30/25/20) If you're into tea, organic farming and philosophical inquiry, arrange a tour at this small-scale, family-run plantation. Its green and oolong teas are intended to represent the inherent 'flavor' of the land rather than artificial fertilizers. You can also meet the farmers at the Waimea Homestead Farmers Market (p246) on Saturday mornings.

Long Ears Coffee FARM

(808-775-0385; www.longearscoffee.com; tour $35) Try unique three-year 'aged' Hamakua coffee at this family farm. Wendell and Irmanetta Branco process their own and other Hamakua farms' beans, creating a sustainable agricultural economy for farmers. On tour, you'll see the entire process: growing trees, harvesting cherries, pulping, drying, husking and roasting. Directions to the farm are given upon booking a tour.

NHERC Heritage Center MUSEUM

(808-775-8890; http://hilo.hawaii.edu/academics/nherc/HeritageCenter.php; 45-539 Plumeria St, Honoka'a; 8am-4pm Mon-Fri, 9am-1pm Sat) FREE Honoka'a will make a lot more sense if you visit this museum. Sponsored by the Northern Hawai'i Education and Research Center, it's mainly a large photo collection documenting the plantation era and its demise, along with material from area families; it's like a peak into the region's collective grandmother's attic. Each picture speaks a thousand words.

From the main intersection downtown, follow Plumeria St uphill, then turn right on Lehua St.

Festivals & Events

Honoka'a Western Week FAIR
(Mamane St; Honoka'a) FREE In late May, sleepy Mamane St startles awake with a BBQ, parade, country dance, rodeo, saloon girl contest and – a global first – a golf tournament using macadamia nuts for balls.

Sleeping

Your best options lie just outside Honoka'a town, in misty upcountry Ahualoa and Pa'auilo pastureland. If money's not an issue, consider Kukuihaele and its incomparable views of Waipi'o Valley.

★ **Keolamauloa** RENTAL HOUSE $$
(808-776-1294; www.keolamauloa.com; 43-1962 Pa'auilo Mauka Rd, Pa'auilo; house per 2/3/4 people $100/125/150;) This well-tended family homestead in Pa'auilo offers a modern 'farmstay.' Don't think you'll be roughing it, though; the comfy two-bedroom house includes full kitchen, laundry facilities and access to the grounds, replete with koa and fruit trees, vegetable gardens, pond and livestock. Guests are encouraged to participate in farm life. Discounts for long stays; surcharge for stays shorter than four nights and for cleaning.

★ **Waipi'o Wayside B&B** B&B $$
(808-775-0275; www.waipiowayside.com; Hwy 240, Honoka'a; r incl breakfast $110-200;) Loaded with character, this attractively furnished 1932 plantation house is a classic B&B, complete with welcoming host and sociable homemade breakfast. The five rooms differ markedly, but each enjoys designer touches, such as iron bed frames, a wooden Chinese barber chair, shower skylight and hardwood floors.

Common areas include a living room with books and a large-screen TV (with DVDs), plus a spacious, secluded lanai. Located about 2 miles north of Honoka'a on Hwy 240.

Mountain Meadow Ranch RENTAL HOUSE $$
(808-775-9376; www.mountainmeadowranch.com; 46-3895 Kapuna Rd, Ahualoa; cottage $150, ste incl breakfast $115;) This equestrian ranch on 7 acres offers a peaceful two-bedroom cottage that sleeps four and includes full kitchen, wood stove and washer/dryer. The B&B suite, attached to the main house, is ideal for two and, though lacking a kitchen, has a microwave, small fridge and soothing dry sauna.

Waianuhea B&B B&B $$$
(808-775-1118, 888-775-2577; www.waianuhea.com; 45-3503 Kahana Dr, Ahualoa; r $225-350, ste $400, all incl breakfast;) This striking inn combines eco thinking (solar power) with fine art and design (Tiffany lamps, Philippe Starck chairs, bright skylights and gleaming hardwood floors). You get excellent hotel professionalism in rural solitude, with the majesty of the Big island forming a lovely backdrop. Gourmet dinners are served onsite with 48 hours' notice.

AHUALOA PASTORAL

For a peaceful meander, turn off Hwy 19 onto the Old Mamalahoa Hwy, just west of the 52-mile marker. (Coming from Hilo, turn left at the 43-mile marker opposite Tex Drive-In and then take the next immediate right.) This 10-mile detour winds through hill country, with small roadside ranches, old wooden fences and grazing horses. Take it slow, snap some pictures and get a taste of old-time Waimea. It's even more picturesque by bike.

Eating

Much of Honoka'a is closed on Sundays and possibly Mondays too.

★ **Tex Drive-In** BAKERY $
(808-775-0598; www.texdriveinhawaii.com; 45-690 Pakalana St, Honoka'a; mains $5-10; 6am-8pm) A *malasada* is just a donut, but Tex is famous for serving them hot and fresh. They come plain or filled; either way, folks drive across the island to enjoy them. Tex also serves decent plate lunches and *loco moco*, with fish options and seasonal taro burgers.

Simply Natural CAFE $
(808-775-0119; 45-3625 Mamane St, Honoka'a; dishes $5-12; 9am-3pm Mon-Sat, 11am-3pm Sun;) A cozy go-to spot for wholesome eats, from taro pancakes to an open-faced spicy tuna melt. A kiddie menu, biodegrada-

ble takeout containers and a mural showing the whole world coming together to enjoy healthy food adds to the appeal.

Honoka'a People's Theatre Cafe CAFE $
(☎808-775-9963; www.honokaapeople.com; 45-3574 Mamane St, Honoka'a; espresso $2.50-4.50, sandwiches $5.50-8; ⊙7am-7:30pm Tue-Sun) In the theater lobby, this friendly cafe serves espresso, sandwiches and other light meals. A cozy hangout spot with counter or table seating.

Café il Mondo ITALIAN $$
(☎808-775-7711; www.cafeilmondo.com; 45-3626a Mamane St, Honoka'a; pizzas $12-24; ⊙11am-8pm Mon-Sat; ✎) Honoka'a's gathering place specializes in pizzas, pastas and enormous calzones packed to bursting point. Sit at the convivial central table and mingle with locals. Bring your own wine and don't hesitate to share it.

☆ Entertainment

★Honoka'a People's Theatre THEATER
(☎808-775-0000; www.honokaapeople.com; 45-3574 Mamane St, Honoka'a; movie tickets adult/child/senior $6/3/4; ⊙showings 5pm & 7pm Tue-Sun) In a historic building dating from 1930, this theater shows movies and hosts special events. If you're curious about what's going on locally, hang out here; the theatre has its finger on the pulse of the Hamakua Coast in the way little local arts organizations are wont to do.

Shopping

Honoka'a Trading Company ANTIQUES
(☎808-775-0808; Mamane St, Honoka'a; ⊙10:30am-5pm) If some of Honoka'a's aunties emptied their attics, basements and garages, the results would look like this hangar-size store. Weave through a worthy collection of vintage aloha wear, antiques, used books (great Hawaiiana selection), rattan and koa furniture, and real Hawaiian artifacts. Then talk story with the owner, quite a character herself (it must be noted, she keeps pretty adjustable hours).

Big Island Grown GIFTS
(☎808-775-9777; www.bigislandgrown.com; 45-3626 Mamane St, Honoka'a; ⊙9am-5pm Mon-Sat) Support local! This store carries an assortment of Big Island items, including bamboo T-shirts, koa jewelry, coffee and tea, and natural soap (made by unforgettably named island brand Filthy Farmgirl).

Taro Patch GIFTS
(☎808-775-7228; Mamane St, Honoka'a; ⊙9am-5pm) With a little of everything, this welcoming place is a one-stop shop for souvenirs, from colorful ceramic dishes and breezy island apparel to Waipi'o Valley mouse pads and organic soaps. The shopkeeper's organic macadamia nuts, roasted in the shell, are awesome.

Waipi'o Valley

The Waipi'o Valley occupies a special place on an already special island. Reaching the end of Hwy 240, you look out across a spectacular natural amphitheater, as if an enormous scoop was scalloped from the emerald coastline. The Waipi'o is one of seven valleys carved into the windward side of the Kohala Mountains; the last (or first, depending on where you start counting) is the Polulu Valley in North Kohala. The valley goes back 6 miles, its flat floor an emerald patchwork of jungle, huts and taro patches crowned by the awesome sight of Hi'ilawe, a distant ribbon of white falling 1450ft, making it the longest waterfall in the state. A river winds through it all (Waipi'o means 'curving water'), to a black-sand beach squeezed between dramatic running cliffs that disappear around the corner of the island.

The valley has ever been a sacred spot, closed to outsiders, and a voluntarily enforced policy of isolationism continues to this day. Taro cultivation and poi production are building blocks of Hawaiian identity, and both valley residents and Native Hawaiians across the island fiercely guard Waipi'o Valley – its residents have a long history of disagreement with the outside world. Said residents point out that their home is sacred in traditional Hawaiian culture, contains an intangible spiritual energy, holds a special place in Hawaii's history, is limited in space and has a natural beauty that must be protected. Others above the rim say the valley's residents simply wish to separate themselves from the outside world for reasons ranging from misanthropy to marijuana growing.

For visitors, all of this has a practical impact: it is strongly advised that you stick to established trails and avoid trespassing on private property if you enter the valley. You can explore Waipi'o Beach and take the King's Trail to Nanewe Falls, but that is it, unless you pay for a tour (and even those

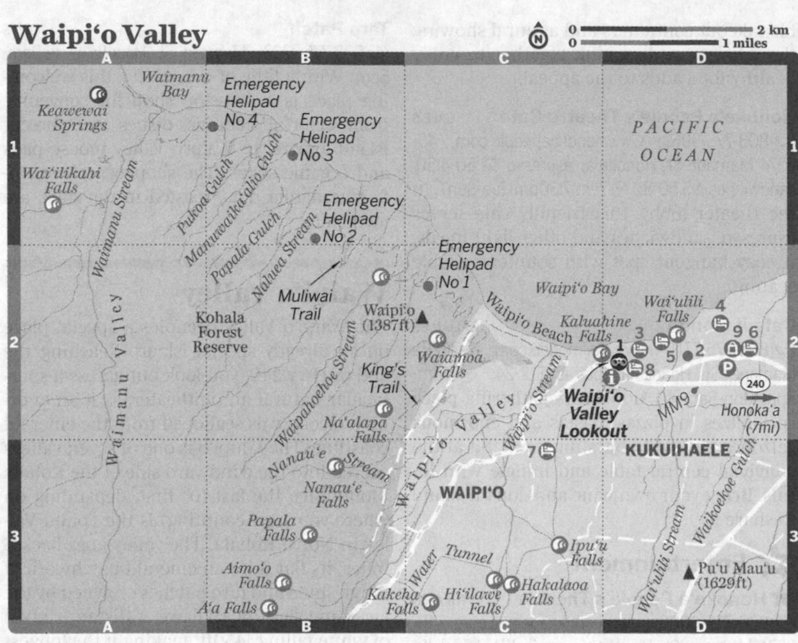

Waipi'o Valley

Top Sights
1 Waipi'o Valley Lookout D2

Activities, Courses & Tours
2 Ride the Rim D2

Sleeping
3 Cliff House Hawaii D2
4 Hale 'Io D2
5 Hale Kukui Orchard D2
Hawaii Oceanview House .... (see 3)
6 Waipio Hostel/Alegre Plantation Cottage D2
7 Waipio Rim B&B C3
8 Waipi'o Valley Nanea D2

Shopping
9 Waipi'o Valley Artworks D2

are limited in range). Hiking along Waipi'o Stream to Hi'ilawe is no longer recommended as you must either traverse private land or walk in the stream itself, which is difficult and somewhat hazardous. Having said that, for the average person the beach and the King's Trail are enough, and if you want more, you can head over the ridge toward Waimanu on the Muliwai Trail and explore to your heart's content. At the moment there is a workable treaty in place if everyone adheres to it.

For those content with a photograph from afar, the scenic lookout on the rim of the valley is your destination. There's plenty of information to be had from the **information booth** (8am-dusk).

History

Known as the Valley of the Kings, Waipi'o was the island's ancient breadbasket and also its political and religious center, home to the highest *ali'i*. According to oral histories, several thousand people lived here before Westerners arrived, and the remains of heiau can still be seen. In 1823 William Ellis, the first missionary to descend into Waipi'o, estimated the population to be around 1300. In the 1880s Chinese immigrants began to settle in the valley's green folds, adding rice to the native taro cultivation.

In 1946 Hawai'i's most devastating tsunami struck the valley, traveling over a mile inland. No one perished despite the massive flooding but, once the waters receded, most people resettled 'topside' in Kukuihaele. The valley floor has been sparsely populated ever since, attracting only a few dozen nature lovers, recluses, pot farmers, hippies, and *kama'aina* (people born and raised in Hawaii; literally 'child of the land') seeking to reclaim their history.

Sights

★Waipi'o Valley Lookout VIEWPOINT

Located at the end of Hwy 240, this lookout provides a jaw-dropping view across the valley. It's one of Hawaii's iconic images.

Activities

Experienced sea kayakers can arrange custom tours with Plenty Pupule (p218) in Kona. Waipi'o Beach isn't swimmable due to rip currents and treacherous undertow.

Hiking

Less-experienced hikers should consider exploring Waipi'o backcountry with guides.

★Waipi'o Valley Hike HIKING

To reach the valley floor, you must walk or drive the incredibly steep road from the lookout, leading to Waipi'o Beach. To explore further, the adventurous can follow the King's Trail to Nanau'e Falls.

The road down from the lookout is to be taken seriously, no matter how you tackle it. If by car, you must have a 4WD, and use your gears for braking. Do not attempt it otherwise, as the road has a 25% grade and ends in a rutted mess that becomes a quagmire when wet. The trip is about 15 minutes. If you hike down (45 minutes), make sure you have tightly fitted shoes, as the pitch of the pavement will tend to jam your toes. If you can't hitch a ride back up, the return trip can be exhausting for those not used to strenuous effort. There's no shade, so bring water.

Once on the valley floor, follow the road to **Waipi'o Beach**, passing the twisted remains of some vehicles that took the quick way down. There are bathrooms near the beginning of the black-sand beach, which has rip currents and a treacherous undertow, so don't even think of swimming, even if you see local surfers in search of its daunting break.

Look for spinner dolphins and whales offshore, and views of **Hi'ilawe** in the distance. Midway down you'll have to cross **Waipi'o Stream**, which flows into the sea; best to do so by wading in the ocean, where there are no rocks. If there has been rain, you'll see **Kaluahine Falls** cascading down the cliffs from whence you came. High surf makes getting to the falls more challenging than it looks. Ahead you'll see the Muliwai Trail zigzagging up the cliffs on the other side of the valley, on its way to distant Waimanu.

Once you near the base of the far cliffs, you will see a trail that heads inland, next to a gate. The trail forks shortly thereafter, with the Muliwai Trail heading upwards, and the **King's Trail** further inland, along a fence. If you don't mind a good workout, it's an excellent idea to climb the Muliwai to the ridgeline for an outstanding view, then return to the fork before heading along the King's Trail.

As it parallels the valley walls the King's Trail passes through a natural botanic garden. You'll encounter coffee plants, *liliko'i*, massive monkeypods, papaya, elephant ear, avocado and lots more, making you realize what a cornucopia the valley really is. You'll also come across small groups of friendly wild horses, the descendants of domesticated animals left behind after the tsunami.

After 45 minutes or so you'll reach a wire fence, which you can pass through because the trail is public. Shortly thereafter the trail reaches Nanau'e Falls, a stepped series of three pools, which are a popular swimming hole for residents, not all of whom see the necessity for clothes. This is the end of the public trail, so take a dip and head back. Don't forget your bathing suit.

★Muliwai Trail HIKING, CAMPING

For expert trekkers only, this 8-mile backcountry trail goes from Waipi'o Valley to Waimanu Valley, traversing steep, slippery and potentially treacherous ground. It takes 6½ to eight hours one way and crosses 13 gulches – brutal to ascend and descend, but lovely, with little waterfalls and icy pools for swimming. Plan on camping in Waimanu Valley for at least two nights. *Don't attempt this hike during or after rains*. For detailed hiking information, contact **Na Ala Hele** (☎808-974-4382; http://hawaiitrails.ehawaii.gov) in Hilo.

You can park your car at the signposted 24-hour parking area. The Muliwai Trail begins at the base of the cliffs on the far side of the valley; you can see it zigzagging up the cliff face as you approach. A shaded path at the end of the beach takes you to a dual trailhead: head right and up for Muliwai (straight ahead leads to the King's Trail). The ancient Hawaiian footpath now rises over 1200ft in a mile of hard laboring back and forth up the cliff face; it's nicknamed 'Z-Trail' for the killer switchbacks. Hunters still use this trail to track feral pigs. The hike is exposed and hot, so cover this stretch early.

Eventually the trail moves into ironwood and Norfolk pine forest, and tops a little knoll before gently descending and becoming muddy and mosquito-ridden. The view of the ocean gives way to the sounds of a rushing stream. The trail crosses a gulch and ascends past a sign for Emergency Helipad No 1. For the next few hours the trail finds a steady rhythm of gulch crossings and forest ascents. A waterfall at the third gulch is a source of fresh water; treat it before drinking. For a landmark, look for Emergency Helipad No 2 at about the halfway point from Waipi'o Beach. Beyond that, there's an open-sided emergency shelter with pit toilets and Emergency Helipad No 3.

Rest here before making the final difficult descent. Leaving the shelter, hop across three more gulches and pass Emergency Helipad No 4, from where it's less than a mile to **Waimanu Valley**. This final section of switchbacks starts out innocently enough, with some artificial and natural stone steps, but over a descent of 1200ft the trail is poorly maintained and hazardous later. A glimpse of **Wai'ilikahi Falls** (accessible by a 45-minute stroll) on the far side of the valley might inspire hikers to press onward, but beware: the trail is narrow and washed out in parts, with sheer drop-offs into the ocean and no handholds apart from mossy rocks and spiny plants. If the descent is questionable, head back to the trail shelter for the night.

HIKING ETIQUETTE IN WAIPI'O VALLEY

The first rule of backpacking etiquette is to leave no trace. This is particularly critical in pristine, sacred places such as Waipi'o Valley. Inexcusably, some stick their garbage into crevices in the lava-rock walls surrounding the campsites. This attracts roaches and other pests. Some even abandon unneeded gear in the valley: tents, mattress pads, beach chairs, reef shoes, rope, canned goods, you name it. Always carry out what you carry in.

Waimanu Valley is...well, this is as good as God's green earth gets. It's a mini Waipi'o, minus the tourists. There was once a sizable settlement here, and the valley contains many ruins, including house and heiau terraces, stone enclosures and old *lo'i* (taro patches). In the early 19th century an estimated 200 people lived here, but the valley was abandoned by its remaining three families after the 1946 tsunami. Today you'll bask alone amid a stunning deep valley framed by cliffs, waterfalls and a boulder-strewn beach.

From the bottom of the switchbacks, **Waimanu Beach** is 10 minutes past the camping-regulations signboard. To ford the stream to reach the campsites on its western side, avoid the rope strung across the water, which is deep there. Instead, cross closer to the ocean entry where it is shallower. Camping requires a state permit from the **Division of Forestry & Wildlife** (☎808-974-4221; http://camping.ehawaii.gov; 19 E Kawili St, Hilo, HI 96720; per night nonresident/resident $18/12; ⏰8am-4:30pm Mon-Fri) for a maximum of six nights.

There are nine campsites: recommended are No 2 (full valley views, proximity to stream, grassy spot), No 6 (view of Wai'ilikahi Falls, access to the only sandy beach) and No 9 (very private at the far end of the valley, lava-rock chairs and a table). Facilities include fire pits and composting outhouses. There's a spring about 10 minutes behind campsite No 9, with a PVC pipe carrying water from a waterfall; all water must be treated.

On the return trip, be careful to take the correct trail. Walking inland from Waimanu Beach, don't veer left on a false trail-of-use that attempts to climb a rocky streambed. Instead keep heading straight inland past the camping-regulations sign to the trail to the switchbacks. It takes about two hours to get to the trail shelter, and another two to reach the waterfall gulch: refill your water here (again, treat before drinking). Exiting the ironwood forest soon after, the trail descends back to the floor of Waipi'o Valley.

Hawaiian Walkways HIKING
(☎808-457-7759; www.hawaiianwalkways.com; guided hikes adult/child $119/99; ⏰tours 9:30am) Go to waterfalls and swimming holes via a private trail.

Walking Waipi'o HIKING
(☎808-345-9505; www.walkingwaipio.com; adult/child 7-12yr $120/75; ⏰tours 8am Mon-Fri) An un-

common five-hour hiking trip on the valley floor, including swimming, led by a valley resident.

Other Activities

★ Ride the Rim DRIVING TOUR

(☎808-775-1450; www.ridetherim.com; adult/child $159/85; ⊙tours 9am & 1pm) If you want to ride an all-terrain vehicle (ATV), what better place to do it than the rim of Waipi'o Valley? Much of the trail takes you through a private forest, with a refreshing stop at a swimming hole. The highlight is a panoramic overlook stretching from Hi'ilawe across the valley to the sea.

Drivers must be at least 16 years old but children may ride with a guide. Tours depart from Waipi'o Valley Artworks.

Waipi'o Ridge Stables HORSEBACK RIDING

(☎808-775-1007, 877-757-1414; www.waipioridgestables.com; rides $85-165; ⊙tours 8:45am) Tour the valley rim to the top of Hi'ilawe Falls (2½ hours) or combine with a forest trail ride (five hours), ending with a picnic and waterfall swim. Caters for all abilities.

Na'alapa Stables HORSEBACK RIDING

(☎808-775-0419; www.naalapastables.com; rides $85; ⊙tours 9am & 12:30pm Mon-Sat) Visit the valley on a 2½-hour horseback ride; children eight and over are welcome. Caters for all abilities.

Waipi'o Valley Wagon Tours TOUR

(☎808-775-9518; www.waipiovalleywagontours.com; adult/child $60/30; ⊙tours 10:30am, 12:30pm & 2:30pm Mon-Sat) This 1½-hour jaunt in a mule-drawn wagon carts visitors around the valley floor.

Sleeping

You'll find excellent options in Kukuihaele, the residential community on the rim of the valley, including cliffside properties with spectacular views.

Waipio Hostel/Alegre Plantation Cottage COTTAGE, HOSTEL $

(☎808-775-1533, 808-989-1533; 48-5380 Kukuihaele Rd; r/cottage $50/145; 📶) This simply furnished former plantation house, in largely original condition, contains a three-bedroom top floor with full kitchen and large living spaces (rented as the Alegre Plantation Cottage) and three private rooms on the lower level (the hostel) with shared bath and a choice of beds. In a residential neighborhood, but with sea views out back.

NIGHT MARCHERS

Kukuihaele means 'light that comes and goes' in Hawaiian, referring to the *huaka'ipo* ('night marchers') – torch-bearing ghosts of Hawaiian warriors who pass through Kukuihaele to Waipi'o. As the legend goes, if you look at the night marchers or get in their way, you die. Survival is possible only if one of your ancestors is a marcher – or if you lie face down on the ground.

Waipi'o Valley Nanea APARTMENT $$

(☎808-775-9194; http://waipiovalleynanea.com; 48-5530 Waipi'o Rd; studio $110-125 ; 📶) Located three houses back from the lookout, this private and cozy studio doesn't offer cliff views (except from the adjacent yard) but there's a nice four-poster bed and plenty of tranquillity. Laundry access too. Cleaning fee $35.

★ Hale 'Io RENTAL HOUSE $$$

(☎808-775-0118; www.vrbo.com/381655; 48-5484 Kukuihaele Rd; per week $5000, extra night $750; 📶🏊) What can we say? This may be the greatest vacation rental on the Big Island. The completely private five-bedroom house sits atop a 600ft bluff with a panoramic view of the Waipi'o cliffs, Maui and a vast expanse of ocean. The house itself is like a sexy temple, bursting with color and evocative artworks inside and out.

Loads of covered outdoor space harbors alluring couches. The knockout master bedroom with attached office, dressing room, bathroom and outdoor lava-rock shower is the palace within the palace. The expansive kitchen is a chef's delight, and could have fed Captain Cook's crew. The pool replicates a tropical jungle swimming hole, replete with waterfall, lava tube slide (which will keep the kids entertained all day) and beach entry. The cherry on top: the secret staircase that ascends to a rooftop room with four-poster bed. Add hawks, whales, sunsets and endless tranquillity, and you have a big problem: you won't want to leave. Ever.

★ Waipio Rim B&B B&B $$$

(☎808-775-1727; www.waipiorim.com; 48-5561 Honokaa-Waipio Rd; studio $220) Get away from it all at this handsome studio, gloriously perched on a cliff near the lookout. On the private deck, all-around windows maintain what may well be the best view on this side of the island. There's a microwave and refrigerator, and the fifth night is free.

Hale Kukui Orchard RENTAL HOUSE **$$$**
(808-775-1701; http://halekukui.com; 48-5460 Kukuihaele Rd; studio/unit/cottage $199/249/249;) You can't go wrong with these three rentals: each includes a full kitchen, spacious living area, private deck, outdoor hot tub and, best of all, fantastic views of the Waipi'o Valley cliffs (which is what you're paying for). The grounds include trees with papaya, banana, star fruit and citrus, all for the taking. Classy owners ensure a great stay.

Cliff House Hawaii RENTAL HOUSE **$$$**
(808-775-0005; www.cliffhousehawaii.com; Waipi'o Rd; house $199, additional person $35; @) Set on sprawling acres of pastureland, this house assures privacy and space. It's well equipped with two bedrooms, full kitchen, living and dining rooms, wrap-around lanai, satellite TV, washer/dryer and even a telescope for whale-watching. The same parcel of land contains the less dramatic but still beautifully situated **Hawaii Oceanview House** (808-775-9098; www.hawaiioceanviewhouse.com; house $165, additional person $35). Minimum two-night stay.

Shopping

★ **Waipi'o Valley Artworks** ARTS, CRAFTS
(808-775-0958; www.waipiovalleyartworks.com; 48-5416 Kukuihaele Rd; 8am-5pm) This inviting little shop wears many hats: stop for ice cream, sandwiches and snacks, or just browse the koa-wood furniture, bowls and other crafts. It's also the best place to park your car overnight, if camping in Waimanu Valley (per day $15).

Kalopa State Recreation Area

Kalopa State Recreation Area STATE PARK
(www.hawaiistateparks.org/parks/hawaii/index.cfm?park_id=45; dawn-dusk) FREE Don't miss this idyllic 100-acre state park, with camping (first left as you enter), cabins (second left) and various gentle trails. Set in a quiet, native forest at 2000ft, it's fantastically lush and a great place for beginner or family camping. Group cabins (eight people max) have bunk beds, linen and blankets, plus hot showers and a fully equipped kitchen. Permits ($60/90 for residents/nonresidents) are required.

The park comprises two overall trail systems (see the large map near the cabins). The first starts where the road by the cabins ends. The easy 1320yd **Nature Trail** passes through old ohia forest, where some trees measure over 3ft in diameter. The path can be overgrown so watch for the established trail. Skip the Dryland Forest Trail, which only goes 100yd, and the Arboretum Trail, which is so overgrown that you might get lost. A small **Polynesian garden** contains a dozen of the original 25 canoe plants, introduced to Hawaii by the original Polynesian voyagers for food, medicine and clothing.

The second, more-interesting, trail system leads into the adjoining forest reserve with old-growth forest and tremendous tree ferns. It starts along Robusta Lane, on the left between the caretaker's house and the campground, and goes about 600yd to the edge of Kalopa Gulch, through a thick eucalyptus forest. The trail continues along the gulch rim for another mile, while several side trails branch off and loop back into the recreation area via the **Perimeter Trail**. Signage is confusing so you should sketch the map near the cabins for reference along the way. You can go over 4 miles on these scenic but spottily maintained trails.

To get to the park, turn *mauka* off the Hawai'i Belt Rd near mile marker 42, at Kalopa Dr. Follow park signs for 3 miles.

Laupahoehoe

Laupahoehoe had its heyday when sugar was king, but it remains a solid village community with a pleasant beach park and a handful of attractions.

On April 1, 1946, tragedy hit the small plantation town when a 30ft-high tsunami wiped out the schoolhouse on the point, killing 20 children and four adults. After the tsunami the whole town moved uphill.

Laupahoehoe Point Beach Park BEACH
Only real crazy *buggahs* would swim at windy, rugged Laupahoehoe, where the fierce surf sometimes crashes over the rocks and onto the parking lot. But it's strikingly pretty, with a scenic breakwater and fingers of lava rock jutting out of the waves. It's popular with local families for picnics and camping (full facilities available).

The 1.5-mile scenic drive to the point winds through dense tropical jungle and past long-standing plantation houses. Stop to view the memorial for the students and teachers who died in the 1946 tsunami. The school stood around the colossal banyan tree toward your right as you approach the park.

Hamakua Mushrooms FARM
(☎808-962-0305; www.hamakuamushrooms.com; 36-221 Manowaiopae Homestead Rd; 70min tour per adult/child 3-11yr/senior $20/10/17.50; ⊙tours 9:30am & 11:30am Mon-Fri) A hugely successful boutique crop, Hamakua Mushrooms is favored by top chefs statewide. Its specialty mushrooms are cultivated in bottles and are immediately recognizable, especially the hefty Ali'i Oyster. The husband-and-wife owners give informative guided tours with a personal touch, including sauteéd samples. Their passion for mushrooms is oddly contagious.

Laupahoehoe Train Museum MUSEUM
(☎808-962-6300; www.thetrainmuseum.com; 36-2377 Mamalahoa Hwy; adult/student/senior $6/3/5; ⊙10am-5pm Thu-Sun, by appt Mon-Wed; P) If you love little quirks of history, make sure to pop into this unassuming museum. It's essentially a house (specifically an old station agent's house) of cool stuff, brimming with fascinating artifacts and photographs of the plantation railroad era. Don't miss the video of the long-gone coastal train, which showcases the amazing bridges that once curved along (and across) Hamakua gulches, until demolished by tsunami. Located between mile markers 25 and 26.

Old Jodo Temple B&B $$
(☎808-962-6967; www.vrbo.com/236574; r per night/week $150/950; 🛜) This historic Buddhist temple (c 1899) is a gem hidden in the tropical valley near Laupahoehoe Point. Nicely restored by the owner-hosts, it's simple, retro and downright charming. Downstairs, the B&B area has two large bedrooms (sleeps up to seven), spacious living and dining rooms, airy porches and full kitchen.

For an additional charge, you can rent the entire house, which includes a large yoga space (formerly the temple), bedroom and bathroom upstairs. Washer and dryer available. Directions to the B&B are given upon booking.

Hakalau & Around

It's a stretch to call Hakalau a 'town,' but it's home to an active residential community of old-timers and newcomers. There are no restaurants, but stock up on homemade taro chips and other snacks at **Aaron's Blue Kalo** (Map p268; ☎808-963-6929; 29-2110 Hwy 19; chips $5-10; ⊙9:30am-2pm Mon, Wed & Fri).

Kolekole Beach Park PARK
(Map p277) Beneath a highway bridge, this park sits alongside Kolekole Stream in a verdant tropical valley. The river-mouth break is a local surfing and bodyboarding hot spot, but ocean swimming is dangerous. There are small waterfalls and full facilities. Camping is allowed with a county permit, but the narrow area can get crowded and boisterous with picnicking local families, and might not be the best choice at night.

To get here, turn inland off the Hawai'i Belt Rd at the southern end of the Kolekole Bridge, about 1300yd south of mile marker 15, right before the bridge.

World Botanical Gardens GARDENS
(Map p277; ☎808-963-5427; www.worldbotanicalgardens.com; 31-240 Old Mamalahoa Hwy; adult/teen 13-17yr/child 5-12yr $15/6/3; ⊙9am-5:30pm) Under development since 1995, this garden remains a work in progress, and includes a shrubbery maze, waterfall, arboretum and a nice zipline adventure ($147). It is an admirable effort but plays second fiddle to the Hawaii Tropical Botanical Garden closer to Hilo. To get here from Hwy 19, turn *mauka* (inland) near mile marker 16, at the posted sign.

★Akiko's Buddhist Bed & Breakfast B&B, RENTAL HOUSE $
(Map p277; ☎808-963-6422; www.akikosbnb.com; 29-2091 Old Mamalahoa Hwy; s/d incl breakfast from $65/75, cottage $65-85, house from $150; 🛜) Immersed in tropical foliage, this

HAMAKUA COAST FOR KIDS

- See Waipi'o Valley by horseback (p263)
- Eat Tex Drive-In (p258) *malasadas* (donuts) with abandon
- Stay on a family farm at Keolamauloa (p258)
- Go ziplining (p266)

peaceful retreat offers a variety of lovely, fashionably austere accommodations. The B&B rooms, with shared bath, are simple and clean, while two off-the-grid studio cottages allow a rare indoor-outdoor experience. For those seeking more space and privacy, the well-kept Hale Aloha house, with full kitchen, three bedrooms and two baths, is great value.

Most compelling might be owner Akiko Masuda, who invites guests to join morning meditation and coordinates a popular New Year's Eve *mochi* (Japanese rice cake) pounding festival. To get here, turn inland toward Wailea-Hakalau between mile markers 15 and 16.

Honomu

Honomu is a quaint old sugar town that might be forgotten today if it weren't for its proximity to 'Akaka Falls. Life remains rural and slow paced, but now with retro wooden buildings sprouting shops and eateries.

★'Akaka Falls State Park PARK
(Map p277; www.hawaiistateparks.org; 'Akaka Falls Rd; entry per car/pedestrian $5/1) This outstanding and convenient little park features an easily navigable concrete path that loops along the lush cliffs above a river, first passing scenic **Kahuna Falls** (100ft), then reaching the truly grand **'Akaka Falls**, which plunge 442ft into a deep green basin. These are the best of the 'tourist falls' on this coast so don't miss them. You'll also enjoy a natural botanic garden that goes wildly into bloom during certain times of year (June to July is heliconia season).

To get here turn onto Hwy 220 between mile markers 13 and 14, and head 4 miles inland. You can avoid the parking fee if you park outside the lot, but you must still pay the walk-in fee. Cash or credit cards accepted.

Palms Cliff House Inn B&B $$$
(866-963-6076, 808-963-6076; www.palmscliffhouse.com; 28-3514 Mamalahoa Hwy; r incl breakfast $299-449;) As elegant as a fine hotel, this well-run inn is warm and welcoming. The eight ocean-view rooms are spacious, with old-school if elegant furnishings, and guests rave about the full hot breakfasts. Rates are steep, but if you opt out of said breakfast, the price makes a major drop.

Hilo Sharks Coffee CAFE $
(808-963-6706; www.hilosharkscoffee.com; 28-1672 Old Mamalahoa Hwy; sandwiches $6-7; 8am-6pm Mon-Sat, to 4pm Sun;) This is *the* place to hang out in Honomu: great locally grown coffee, outdoor seating, wi-fi, creative sandwiches, refreshing smoothies, homemade chocolate and rock-bottom prices.

Woodshop Gallery & Cafe CAFE $
(808-963-6363; www.woodshopgallery.com; Hwy 220; lunch dishes $6-9; 11am-5:30pm) From burgers and lemonade to homemade ice cream and espresso, it's all good Americana served with a side of aloha here. Following lunch, browse or splurge on the extraordinary collection of handcrafted bowls, photos and blown glass.

HAMAKUA ZIPLINES

Ziplines are being strung all over Hamakua's rainforests and waterfalls. Which course is best for you?

Skyline EcoAdventures Akaka Falls (Map p277; 808-878-8400, 888-864-6947; www.zipline.com; 28-1710 Honomu Rd; $170; 10am-3pm) Skyline has the single best zip and it's a jaw dropper. The seven zips on this course get progressively longer and higher until you whoosh directly over a 250ft waterfall on a 3350ft ride! Weight 80lb to 260lb, ages 10 and up.

Umauma Falls & Zipline Experience (Map p277; 808-930-9477; http://umaumaexperience.com; 31-313 Old Mamalahoa Hwy; $189; 8am-3pm) The most consistently thrilling of Hamakua's ziplines. None of its nine zips has the grandeur of Skyline's magnificent climax, but there are no bunny-slope lines and you'll see 18 waterfalls. Weight 35lb to 275lb, ages four and up.

Zip Isle Zipline Adventures (Map p277; 808-963-5427, 888-947-4753; www.zipisle.com; $147; 9:30am-2:30pm) A good choice for kids and anxious first-timers. There are seven gentle zips, including a dual line, and a 150ft suspension bridge. Located at World Botanical Gardens, which you can enter for free. Weight 70lb to 270lb.

Mr Ed's Bakery BAKERY $
(808-963-5000; www.mredsbakery.com; Hwy 220; 6am-6pm Mon-Sat, 9am-4pm Sun) Check out the staggering selection of homemade preserves featuring local fruit (jar $7.50). Pastries are hit or miss; some are cloyingly sweet, but the Portuguese sweet bread is a winner.

Onomea Bay & Around

Pepe'ekeo, Onomea and Papaikou are three plantation villages admired for their gorgeous landscapes and views.

★Pepe'ekeo 4-Mile Scenic Drive SCENIC DRIVE
The gorgeous rainforest jungle along this stretch of the Old Mamalahoa Hwy proves that those annoying showers are worth it. Cruising the narrow road, you cross a series of one-lane bridges spanning little streams and waterfalls, under a tangle of trees, a green yin to the dry yang of the western side of the island. By far the best way to get to Hilo.

Although with that said, while you can begin the drive from either end, approaching from the south (Hilo side) involves an easy right turn between the 7- and 8-mile markers on the main highway.

★Hawaii Tropical Botanical Garden GARDENS
(Map p277; 808-964-5233; www.hawaiigarden.com; 27-717 Old Mamalahoa Hwy, Papaikou; adult/child $15/5; 9am-5pm, last tours at 4pm) This is a fabulous botanic garden, beautifully situated by the ocean and superbly managed. A paved trail meanders through 2000 species of tropical plants set amid streams and waterfalls. Give yourself at least an hour for the walk, which ends at Onomea Bay. The garden is located halfway along the Pepe'ekeo 4-Mile Scenic Drive. Park and buy your ticket at the yellow building on the *mauka* side of the road. A guided tour ($5) is offered on Saturday at noon.

Hawaii Plantation Museum MUSEUM
(Map p277; 808-964-5151; http://memoriesofhawaiibigisland.com; 27-246 Old Mamalahoa Hwy, Papaikou; adult/child/senior $8/3/6; 10am-3pm Tue-Sat) This well-done museum highlights Hawai'i's sugar industry, which spanned the period from the mid-1880s to 1996. Museum curator Wayne Subica has single-handedly amassed this collection, which includes plantation tools, memorabilia from 'Mom & Pop' shops, vintage photos and retro signage. To get here from Hilo, turn left just past the 6-mile marker on the main highway; from Kona, turn right just past the 8-mile marker.

Onomea Tea Company FARM
(Map p277; 808-964-3283; www.onomeatea.com; 27-604 Alakahi Pl, Papaikou; tasting $30) This 9-acre tea plantation offers tea tastings and tours. It's a small-scale operation, allowing for friendly chatting about tea and its cultivation. Website reservations are required.

Onomea Bay Hike HIKING
For a quick, scenic hike to the bay, take the Na Ala Hele trailhead on the *makai* side of the road, along the Pepe'ekeo 4-Mile Scenic Drive. From Hilo, turn onto the scenic drive and go about 1.75 miles; look for a small sign marking the trailhead. Parking is tricky, but there's a small pull-over spot just north of the sign.

After a 10-minute hike down a slippery jungle path, you'll come to a finger of lava jutting into the sea. A spur to the right leads to a couple of small waterfalls and a cove. Continuing straight brings you to the diminutive bluffs overlooking the batik blues of Onomea Bay. Hawaiian monk seals have been sighted here.

★What's Shakin' HEALTH FOOD $
(Map p277; 808-964-3080; 27-999 Old Mamalahoa Hwy; smoothies $6; 10am-5pm;) Your fondest memory of the Pepe'ekeo 4-Mile Scenic Drive might be this roadside eatery. Just over a mile from the north end, look for the cheerful yellow cottage, which pumps out fantastic homemade food and killer smoothies (all fruit, no filler).

HILO

POP 43,263

Kailua-Kona may host more visitors, but Hilo is the beating heart of the Big Island. Hidden beneath its daily drizzle lies deep soil and soul, from which sprouts the unique, natural, holistic, organic, local, personal and artistic. The result is the social version of a botanic garden, where the endless color, variety and quirkiness of all forms never ceases to amaze.

Perhaps this ongoing celebration of life's boundless creativity has something to do with local demographics. Like other former sugar towns in Hawaii, Hilo is a diverse mix of Native Hawaiians, Japanese, Chinese,

Hilo

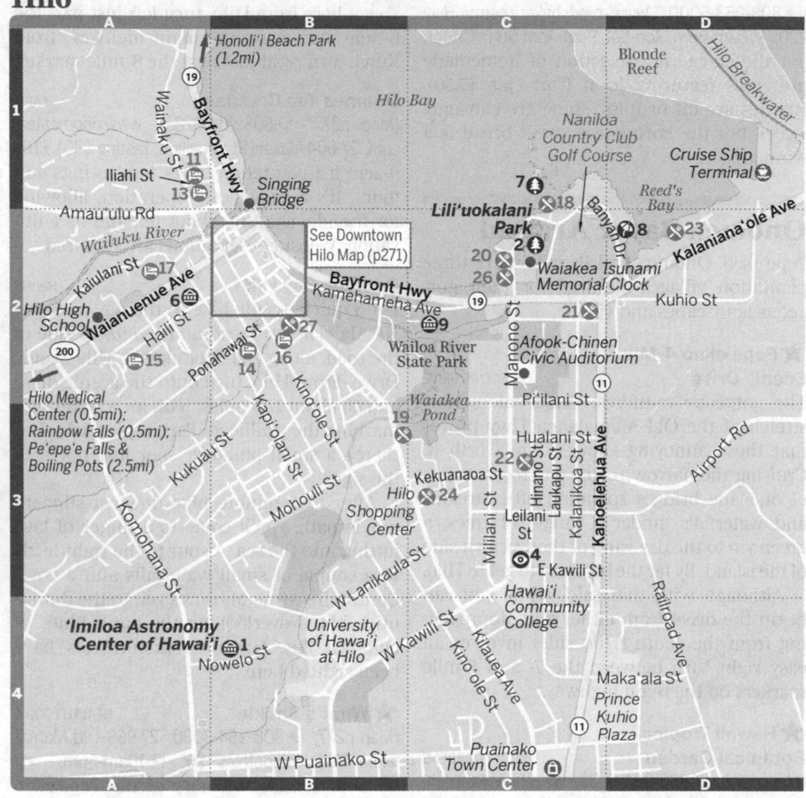

Hilo

Top Sights

1 'Imiloa Astronomy Center of Hawai'i B4
2 Lili'uokalani Park C2
3 Onekahakaha Beach Park E1

Sights

4 Hawai'i Nui Brewing C3
5 James Kealoha Beach Park F1
6 Lyman House Memorial Museum A2
7 Mokuola (Coconut Island) C1
8 Reeds Bay Beach Park D2
9 Wailoa Center & Wailoa River State Park C2

Activities, Courses & Tours

10 Arnott's Mauna Kea Adventures E1

Sleeping

11 Annex A1
12 Arnott's Lodge E1
13 Dolphin Bay Hotel A1
14 Hilo Bay Hale B2
15 Hilo Honu Inn A2
16 Quirky Cottage B2
17 Shipman House B&B A2

Eating

18 Aaron's Blue Kalo C1
19 Cafe 100 .... B3
20 Hilo Bay Cafe C2
21 Ken's House of Pancakes C2
22 Miyo's C3
23 Ponds D2
24 Restaurant Miwa C3
25 Seaside Restaurant F1
26 Suisan Fish Market C2
Takenoko Sushi .... (see 22)
27 Two Ladies Kitchen B2

Drinking & Nightlife

Mehana Brewing Company .... (see 4)

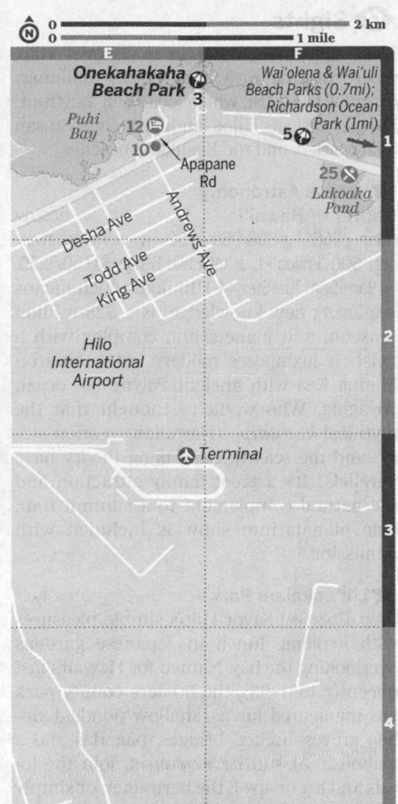

Koreans, Filipinos, Portuguese, Puerto Ricans and Caucasians, many of them descended from plantation workers. Or perhaps it has to do with living on the edge. Knocked down by two tsunamis, threatened with extinction by Mauna Loa lava flows (most recently in 1984), and subject to the highest annual rainfall in the USA, Hilo knows more than most that life is a gift from the gods, and you can see this reflected in the vivacious attitude of the locals.

In any case, Hilo is sunny Kona's alter ego, which is why you ought to visit. The town had a life before tourism, a culture influenced by the many communities of the Pacific Rim, and remains the Big Island's commercial center. What else is available? Some quirky museums, a walkable downtown and what may be the island's best farmers market. Set on a calm bay, Hilo also makes an ideal base for exploring Hawai'i Volcanoes National Park, Mauna Kea, Puna and the Hamakua Coast. Drizzle aside, the state's second-largest city makes a compelling argument for at least a day trip, if not making it your home base.

History

Since its first Polynesian settlers farmed and fished along the Wailuku River, Hilo has been a busy port town. In the 20th century it was the trading hub for sugarcane grown in Puna and Hamakua, connecting in both directions with a sprawling railroad, the Hawaii Consolidated Railway.

Back then, townsfolk set up homes and shops along the bay. But after being slammed by disastrous tsunami in 1946 and 1960, no one wanted to live downtown anymore. Today, you'll find parks, beaches and open space along Kamehameha Ave.

When the sugar industry folded in the 1980s and '90s, Hilo focused its economy on diversified agriculture, the university, retail and, of course, tourism. While downtown Hilo is still the charming heart of town, the main retail destinations are the big chain stores (Walmart, Target, Home Depot etc) south of the airport.

Beaches

Except for Honoli'i Beach Park, Hilo's beaches are located in the Keaukaha neighborhood. On weekends, expect jammed parking lots and steady traffic along Kalaniana'ole Ave.

★Richardson Ocean Park BEACH

(Map p277) Near the end of Kalaniana'ole Ave, this pocket of black sand is Hilo's best all-round beach. During calm surf, the protected waters are popular for swimming and snorkeling, with frequent sightings of friendly sea turtles (keep your distance, at least 50yd in the water). High surf attracts local bodyboarders. Shaded by lots of coconut trees, the beach also makes a sweet picnic spot. Has daily lifeguards, restrooms, showers and picnic areas.

★Onekahakaha Beach Park BEACH

(Map p268; [family icon]) Popular with local families, this beach has a broad, shallow, sandy-bottomed pool, protected by a boulder breakwater. The water is only 1ft to 2ft deep in spots, creating the perfect 'baby beach.' An unprotected cove north of the protected pool is deeper but can be hazardous due to spiny *wana* (sea urchins) and rough surf. Has lifeguards on weekends and holidays, as well as restrooms, showers and picnic areas.

Reeds Bay Beach Park BEACH
(Map p268) At the end of Banyan Dr, this calm little cove is ideal for kids or stand-up paddleboard (SUP) beginners. While centrally located, within sight of buildings and passing cars, it's a picturesque spot. Warning: a behemoth cruise ship might be docked in the distance. The beach has restrooms, showers and picnic areas.

James Kealoha Beach Park BEACH
(Carlsmith Beach Park; Map p268) Best for older kids and snorkelers, this county beach is nicknamed 'Four Miles' (the distance between the park and the downtown post office). For swimming and snorkeling, head to the eastern side, which has a deep, protected basin with generally calm, clear water and pockets of white sand. The park's western side is open ocean and much rougher. Locals surf in winter or net fish. No lifeguards but it has restrooms, showers and picnic areas.

Wai'olena & Wai'uli Beach Parks BEACH
(Map p277) Rocky and ruggedly pretty, these side-by-side beaches (commonly known by their former name, **Leleiwi Beach**) are Hilo's best shore-dive site. You might see turtles, interesting coral growth and a variety of butterfly fish. The water is freezing until you go past the reef, and the entrance is tricky (ask for advice at Nautilus Dive Center). Lifeguards on weekends and holidays, plus restrooms, showers and picnic areas.

Honoli'i Beach Park BEACH
(Map p277) Less than 2 miles north of downtown Hilo, this protected cove is Hilo's best surfing and bodyboarding spot. When surf's up, it's jammed with locals and not a place for novices. Don't expect a sandy beach or ideal swimming conditions. It's all about the waves. Has daily lifeguards, restrooms, showers and picnic areas.

HILO FOR KIDS

- Picnic at Lili'uokalani Park
- Cross a footbridge to Mokuola (Coconut Island)
- Splash around at Onekahakaha Beach Park (p269)
- Stroll the Pana'ewa Rainforest Zoo & Gardens (p272)
- Learn about voyaging at 'Imiloa Astronomy Center of Hawai'i

Sights

Most sights are found in downtown Hilo, where historic early-20th-century buildings overlook the coast, which locals call 'bayfront.' Further east sits Hilo's landmark dock, Suisan Fish Market, and the Keaukaha beaches.

★ 'Imiloa Astronomy Center of Hawai'i MUSEUM
(Map p268; ☎808-969-9700; www.imiloahawaii.org; 600 'Imiloa Pl; adult/child 6-17yr $17.50/9.50; ⏰9am-5pm Tue-Sun; 👪) 'Imiloa, which means 'exploring new knowledge,' is a $28-million museum and planetarium complex with a twist: it juxtaposes modern astronomy on Mauna Kea with ancient Polynesian ocean voyaging. Who would've thought that the mythical *kumulipo* (Hawaiian creation story) and the scientific big bang theory have parallels? It's a great family attraction and the natural complement to a summit tour. One planetarium show is included with admission.

★ Lili'uokalani Park PARK
(Map p268; 👪) Savor Hilo's simple pleasures with a picnic lunch in Japanese gardens overlooking the bay. Named for Hawaii's last queen (r 1891–93), the 30-acre county park has manicured lawns, shallow ponds, bamboo groves, arched bridges, pagodas and a teahouse. At sunrise or sunset, join the locals and jog or stroll the perimeter, or simply admire the Mauna Kea view. Cross the paved footbridge to **Mokuola (Coconut Island)** (Map p268), a tiny island always lively with families, picnicking and swimming.

Adjacent to the park is Banyan Dr, Hilo's mini 'hotel row,' best known for the giant banyan trees lining the road. Royalty and celebrities planted the trees in the 1930s and, if you look closely, you'll find plaques beneath the trees identifying Babe Ruth, Amelia Earhart and Cecil B DeMille.

★ Pacific Tsunami Museum MUSEUM
(Map p271; ☎808-935-0926; www.tsunami.org; 130 Kamehameha Ave; adult/child 6-17yr $8/4; ⏰10am-4pm Tue-Sat) You cannot understand Hilo without knowing its history as a two-time tsunami survivor (1946 and 1960). This seemingly modest museum is chock-full of riveting information, including a section on the Japanese tsunami of 2011, which damaged Kona. Allow enough time to experience the multimedia exhibits, including chilling computer simulations and heart-wrenching first-person accounts.

Downtown Hilo

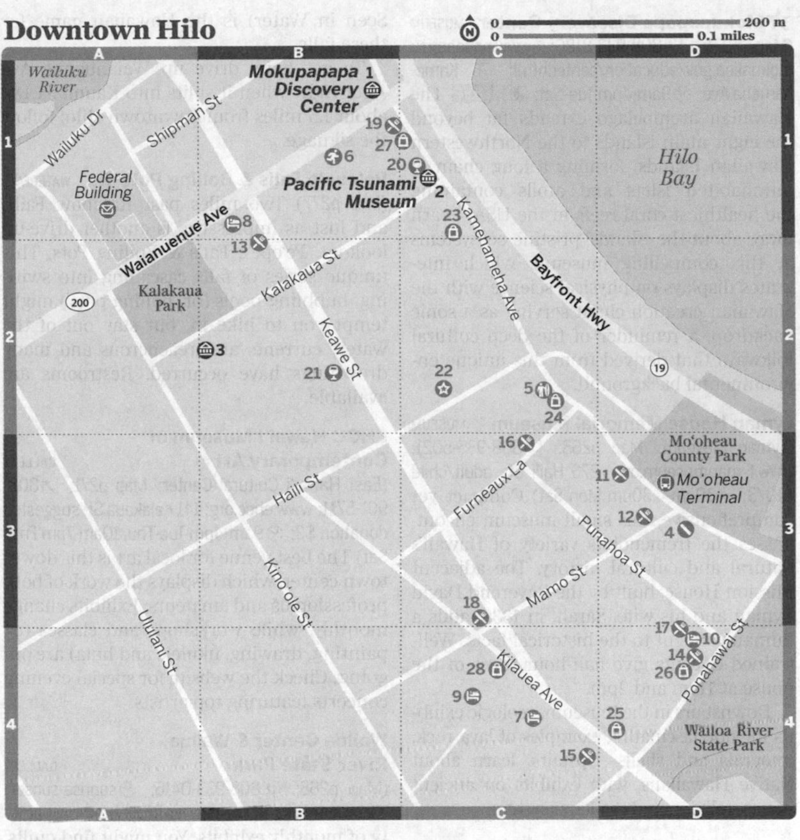

Downtown Hilo

Top Sights

1 Mokupapapa Discovery Center B1
2 Pacific Tsunami Museum C1

Sights

3 EHCC Hawai'i Museum of Contemporary Art B2

Activities, Courses & Tours

4 Nautilus Dive Center D3
5 Orchidland Surfboards C2
6 Yoga Centered B1

Sleeping

7 D&S Bed & Breakfast C4
8 Hilo Bay Hostel B1
9 Lotus Garden of Hilo C4
10 Pakalana Inn D4

Eating

11 Cafe Pesto D3
12 Hilo Farmers Market D3
13 Kanpai B2
14 Koji's Bento Korner D4
15 Lucy's Taqueria C4
16 Moonstruck Patisserie C3
17 Paul's Place D4
18 Pineapple's C3
19 Tina's Garden Gourmet B1

Drinking & Nightlife

20 Bayfront Kava Bar C1
21 Hilo Town Tavern B2

Entertainment

22 Palace Theater C2

Shopping

23 Basically Books C1
24 Dragon Mama C2
25 Grapes: A Wine Store D4
26 Hilo Guitars & Ukuleles D4
27 Sig Zane Designs C1
28 Still Life Books C4

★Mokupapapa Discovery Center MUSEUM (Map p271; ☎808-933-8180; www.papahanaumokuakea.gov/education/center.html; 76 Kamehameha Ave; ⌚9am-4pm Tue-Sat; 👪) FREE The Hawaiian archipelago extends far beyond the eight main islands to the Northwestern Hawaiian Islands, forming a long chain of uninhabited islets and atolls containing the healthiest coral reefs in the USA. Learn more about the islands' pristine ecosystems at this compelling museum, which integrates displays on physical science with the Hawaiian creation chant serving as a sonic backdrop, a reminder of the deep cultural folkways that derived from this unique environmental background.

Lyman House Memorial Museum MUSEUM (Lyman Museum; Map p268; ☎808-935-5021; www.lymanmuseum.org; 276 Haili St; adult/child $10/3; ⌚10am-4:30pm Mon-Sat) Compact yet comprehensive, this small museum encompasses the tremendous variety of Hawaii's natural and cultural history. The adjacent Mission House, built by the Reverend David Lyman and his wife, Sarah, in 1839, adds a human element to the historical facts. Well-trained docents give half-hour tours of the house at 11am and 2pm.

Downstairs in the museum, geologic exhibits include fascinating examples of lava rock, minerals and shells. Upstairs, learn about Native Hawaiians, with exhibits on ancient sports, religion and the kapu system.

Pana'ewa Rainforest Zoo & Gardens ZOO (Map p277; ☎808-959-9233; www.hilozoo.com; ⌚9am-4pm, petting zoo 1:30-2:30pm Sat; 👪) FREE Four miles south of town, Hilo's sprawling 12-acre zoo is a nice freebie. Amid well-kept tropical gardens, see a global collection of monkeys, reptiles, sloths, parrots and more. The star is a white Bengal tiger named Namaste. Two play structures and a shaded picnic area make this a good family outing.

To get here, turn *mauka* off the Volcano Hwy onto W Mamaki St, just past the 4-mile marker.

Rainbow Falls WATERFALL (Map p277) A regular stop for tour buses, the lookout for this 'instant gratification' cascade is just steps from the parking lot. Depending on rainfall, the lovely 80ft waterfall can be a torrent or a trickle. Go in the morning and you'll see rainbows if the sun and mist cooperate. Waianuenue (Rainbow Seen in Water) is the Hawaiian name for these falls.

To get here, drive up Waianuenue Ave (veer right when it splits into Kaumana Dr) about 1.5 miles from downtown Hilo; follow the signage.

Pe'epe'e Falls & Boiling Pots WATERFALL (Map p277) Two miles past Rainbow Falls, and just as impressive, is another drive-up lookout, Pe'epe'e Falls & Boiling Pots. This unique series of falls cascading into swirling, bubbling pools (or 'boiling pots') might tempt you to hike in, but stay out of the water; currents are treacherous and many drownings have occurred. Restrooms are available.

EHCC Hawai'i Museum of Contemporary Art GALLERY (East Hawai'i Cultural Center; Map p271; ☎808-961-5711; www.ehcc.org; 141 Kalakaua St; suggested donation $2; ⌚9am-4pm Tue-Thu, 10am-7pm Fri & Sat) The best venue for local art is this downtown center, which displays the work of both professionals and amateurs. Exhibits change monthly, while workshops and classes (eg painting, drawing, ukulele and hula) are ongoing. Check the website for special evening concerts featuring top artists.

Wailoa Center & Wailoa River State Park GALLERY (Map p268; ☎808-933-0416; ⌚sunrise-sunset) This eclectic, state-run gallery hosts a variety of monthly exhibits. You might find quilts, bonsai, Chinese watercolors or historical photos, all done by locals. Surrounding the center is a quiet state park on the Wailoa River.

The main park landmark is a 14ft, Italian-made bronze statue of Kamehameha the Great, erected in 1997 and restored with gold leaf in 2004. There is also a tsunami memorial and a Vietnam War memorial.

Mauna Loa Macadamia-Nut Visitor Center FACTORY (Map p277; ☎808-966-8618, 888-628-6256; www.maunaloa.com; Macadamia Rd; ⌚8:30am-5pm) FREE Hershey-owned Mauna Loa provides a self-guided tour of its working factory, where you can watch the humble macnut as it moves along the assembly line from cracking to roasting to chocolate dipping and packaging. The gift shop sells the finished product at decent prices.

To get here, follow signage about 5 miles south of Hilo; along the 3-mile access road, see acres of macadamia trees.

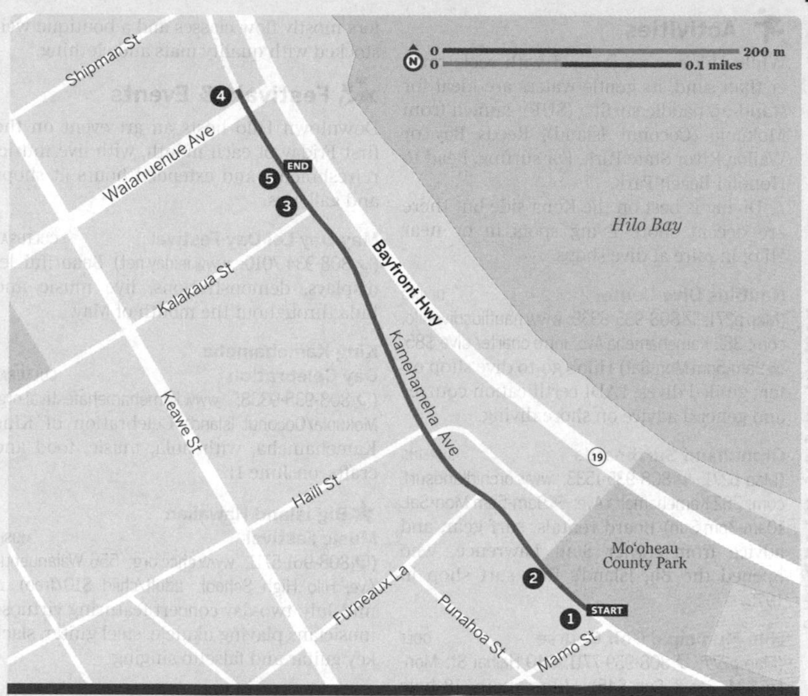

City Walk
Bayfront Hiloism

START HILO FARMERS MARKET
END BAYFRONT KAVA BAR
LENGTH 400YD; HALF TO FULL DAY

Unite things that don't normally go together, and you get the creativity, the surprise, the mystery, the quirkiness and, ultimately, the pleasure that defines Hilo. It's hard to put your finger on it sometimes, but by the time you've finished walking the bayfront, you'll know Hiloism when you see it. Just be sure to talk to the locals: they'll happily weigh in.

The tour begins at ground zero: ❶ **Hilo Farmers Market** (p276), where the most surprising combinations end up in the same container on Wednesdays and Sundays. Goat's-milk soap, anyone? After surveying the local produce, duck into ❷ **Cafe Pesto** (p278) for a fine brunch. But even as you relax, the questions keep coming. Is it a French bistro? An Italian pizzeria? A Spanish tapas bar? Or more Hawaii Regional Cuisine? Feeling a bit full, you make a move to your next stop, only to receive the double whammy of the ❸ **Pacific Tsunami Museum** (p270). This is a place dedicated to revisiting Hilo's own destruction – twice. No wonder they show the movies in the bank vault. Then get ready for a deeper shock at ❹ **Mokupapapa Discovery Center** (p272). Did you think there were only eight Hawaiian Islands? Guess again – they go on for another 1500 miles. By now you have lost your moorings so completely that you need pharmaceutical support. Head back down the street, the way you have come, to ❺ **Bayfront Kava Bar** (p279), where you'll find Hilo's own licit substance, kava, ladled out at the bar. Grasp half a coconut shell – clearly, it's time to give in – and raise a toast to this wonderfully eclectic town. Just don't be surprised when your mouth turns numb.

Activities

While Hilo's coast is lined with reefs rather than sand, its gentle waters are ideal for stand-up paddle surfing (SUP); launch from Mokuola (Coconut Island), Reeds Bay or Wailoa River State Park. For surfing, head to Honoli'i Beach Park.

Diving is best on the Kona side but there are decent shore-diving spots in or near Hilo; inquire at dive shops.

Nautilus Dive Center DIVING

(Map p271; ☎808-935-6939; www.nautilusdivehilo.com; 382 Kamehameha Ave; intro charter dive $85; ⏲9am-5pm Mon-Sat) Hilo's go-to dive shop offers guided dives, PADI certification courses and general advice on shore diving.

Orchidland Surfboards SURFING

(Map p271; ☎808-935-1533; www.orchidlandsurf.com; 262 Kamehameha Ave; ⏲9am-5pm Mon-Sat, 10am-3pm Sun) Board rentals, surf gear, and advice from owner Stan Lawrence, who opened the Big Island's first surf shop in 1972.

Hilo Municipal Golf Course GOLF

(Map p277; ☎808-959-7711; 340 Haihai St; Mon-Fri $34, Sat & Sun $45) Hilo's main 18-hole course (locally known as 'Muni') offers a well-designed layout, friendly staff and good clubhouse restaurant. Morning tee times are favored by the local contingent; call ahead to avoid waiting. While it's reasonably maintained, expect weeds and mud, thanks to Hilo rain.

Yoga Centered YOGA

(Map p271; ☎808-934-7233; www.yogacentered.com; 37 Waianuenue Ave; drop-in class $14) In an attractive space downtown, this studio offers mostly flow classes and a boutique well stocked with quality mats and clothing.

Festivals & Events

Downtown Hilo hosts an art event on the first Friday of each month, with live music, refreshments and extended hours at shops and galleries.

May Day Lei Day Festival CULTURAL

(☎808-934-7010; www.leiday.net) Beautiful lei displays, demonstrations, live music and hula throughout the month of May.

King Kamehameha Day Celebration CULTURAL

(☎808-935-9338; www.kamehamehafestival.org; Mokuola/Coconut Island) Celebration of King Kamehameha, with hula, music, food and crafts, on June 11.

★ **Big Island Hawaiian Music Festival** MUSIC

(☎808-961-5711; www.ehcc.org; 556 Waianuenue Ave, Hilo High School; adult/child $10/free) A mid-July, two-day concert featuring virtuoso musicians playing ukulele, steel guitar, slack key guitar and falsetto singing.

Hawai'i County Fair FAIR

(www.hilojaycees.org; 799 Pi'ilani St, Afook-Chinen Civic Auditorium; adult/student $6/2.50) Pure nostalgia comes to town in September, with carnival rides, games and cotton candy.

Black & White Night FAIR

(www.downtownhilo.com; ⏲5-9pm) Downtown Hilo comes alive on the first Friday of November, with shops and galleries open late, artist and author appearances, and lots of live music.

CHAMPIONSHIP HULA

The **Merrie Monarch Festival** (☎808-935-9168; www.merriemonarch.com; Afook-Chinen Civic Auditorium; 3-night admission $20-30) swoops into town around Easter (late March or early April) and turns laid-back Hilo into *the* place to be. Forget about booking a last-minute room! This sellout three-day hula competition was established in 1964 to honor King David Kalakaua (1836–91), who almost single-handedly revived Hawaiian culture and arts, which had been forbidden by missionaries for 70 years.

Top hula troupes from all the islands vie in *kahiko* (ancient) and *'auana* (modern) categories. *Kahiko* performances are strong and serious, accompanied only by chanting. *'Auana* is closer to the mainstream style, with sinuous arm movements, smiling dancers and melodious accompaniment that includes string instruments. The primal chanting, meticulous choreography and traditional costumes are profoundly moving.

The competitions are televised, but to see it live, order tickets by mail on December 26 (no earlier postmarks accepted); see the website for seating and payment info. The 2700 tickets sell out within a month. Book accommodations and car a year in advance.

Sleeping

In true Hilo style, there are few hotels, but a gamut of indie B&Bs, inns and hostels. Note that many proprietors charge extra for one-night stays.

★**Quirky Cottage** INN $
(Map p268; ☎770-530-8788; www.thequirkycottage.net; 577 Kinoʻole St; r $40-80) Simple, clean, private and affordable. If these are your priorities, this no-frills inn is perfect. The two suites each include private bath and two separate sleeping areas ($80 for up to four guests); one even has a kitchen. The studio ($40), with fridge and microwave, is a budget traveler's dream.

Hilo Bay Hostel HOSTEL $
(Map p271; ☎808-933-2771; www.hawaiihostel.net; 101 Waianuenue Ave; dm with shared bath $29, r with private/shared bath $79/69; 📶) Perfectly situated downtown, this well-managed hostel occupies an airy, historic building with hardwood floors, remarkably clean restrooms and a kitchen in which you could cook Thanksgiving dinner.

Arnott's Lodge HOSTEL, CAMPGROUND $
(Map p268; ☎808-339-0921; www.arnottslodge.com; 98 Apapane Rd; dm $28, r with private/shared bath $75/65, ste from $99; 📶) Hilo's longest-running hostel remains solid value, with a variety of lodging options close to beaches. The $75 rooms are especially nice, with private garden views and bathrooms.

★**Lotus Garden of Hilo** RENTAL HOUSE $$
(Map p271; ☎808-936-5212; www.lotusgardenhawaii.com; 140 Kilauea Ave; r $95-130, cottages $160; 📶) These brightly painted buildings exemplify Hilo at its funky bohemian best. Of the two cottages, the Sugar Shack is available by room (shared kitchen and bathroom), while the Lotus is rented as a whole. The fantastically romantic Lohi apartment has a Balichic tropical vibe. All accommodations are comfortable and within walking distance of everything you need.

★**Dolphin Bay Hotel** HOTEL $$
(Map p268; ☎877-935-1466, 808-935-1466; www.dolphinbayhotel.com; 333 Iliahi St; studios $119, apt from $169; 📶) This family-run hotel attracts countless loyal, repeat guests. No surprise. The 18 apartment units, each with full kitchen, are clean and conveniently located within a five-minute walk of downtown Hilo. Enjoy free coffee and locally grown fruit for breakfast amid tropical foliage. For longer stays, ask about the one-bedroom apartments in the **Annex** (Map p268; per day/week/month $119/763/1600) across the street.

MONARCHY IS JUST A STONE'S THROW AWAY

According to Hawaiian legend, young prospective chiefs faced a ritual challenge: could they lift the 3.5-ton **Naha Stone**? The man with enough strength to budge the boulder was destined to reign all of the Hawaiian Islands. Along came teenage boy Kamehameha, who reputedly flipped the stone – and proceeded to conquer and unite the Hawaiian kingdom.

Today the Naha Stone, along with the upright **Pinao Stone**, are landmarks fronting the **Hilo Public Library** (☎808-933-8888; www.librarieshawaii.org; 300 Waianuenue Ave; ⏲11am-7pm Tue & Wed, 9am-5pm Thu & Sat, 10am-5pm Fri).

★**Hilo Honu Inn** B&B $$
(Map p268; ☎808-935-4325; www.hilohonu.com; 465 Haili St; r incl breakfast $140-250; 📶) In a lovely retro home, three custom-designed guest rooms accommodate different budgets. A worthy splurge, the Samurai Suite is utterly memorable, with genuine Japanese detailing, plus tatami floor, *furo* (soaking tub), tea room and sweeping (if distant) views of Hilo Bay.

★**Hilo Bay Hale** B&B $$
(Map p268; ☎808-640-1113; www.hilobayhale.com; 301 Ponahawai St; r incl breakfast $139-159; ❄📶) In a gorgeously restored 1912 plantation home, two main-floor rooms feature private lanai overlooking charming koi ponds, while a ground-floor room boasts more privacy and space. Guests have access to the kitchen and laundry facilities. With two personable hosts, proximity to town and weekly discounts ($99 to $119 per night), you can't go wrong.

D&S Bed & Breakfast B&B $$
(Map p271; ☎808-934-9585; www.dnsbnb.com; 150 Kilauea Ave; r/ste $115/125; 📶) Located downtown, this B&B is convivial, casual and family friendly, run by a welcoming young couple. While simple (almost spartan), the rooms include a minifridge and dining table and chairs, and open to a shared patio. An economy unit can cramp in three travelers, and goes for singles/doubles/triples $75/85/95.

Orchid Tree B&B B&B $$
(Map p277; 808-961-9678; www.orchidtree.net; 6 Makakai Pl; r incl breakfast $150;) A few miles outside Hilo, this perennial favorite combines B&B friendliness with space and privacy. Couples will appreciate the stylish Koi Room with a gleaming hardwood floor and, yes, koi pond outside. The Hula Room is larger, containing two beds plus lounging area with plump, inviting sofas. Breakfast is served ouside in a communal 'surfer shack' patio.

To get here from Hilo, head north and turn right just past the 4-mile marker on Nahala St.

Pakalana Inn INN $$
(Map p271; 808-935-0709; www.pakalanainn.com; 123 Punahoa St; r $129-159;) With hardwood floors and clean-lined furnishings, this boutique inn is an oasis just a block from the downtown farmers market. Rooms are average size but immaculate and airy.

Hale Kai Hawaii B&B $$
(Map p277; 808-935-6330; www.halekaihawaii.com; 111 Honoli'i Pl; r incl breakfast $169-179;) Four rooms below the main house enjoy panoramic ocean views and shared lanai. The Pele Suite is the best value, offering more space and kitchenette. Gourmet breakfasts are served on the upper lanai. Kids 13 and older only.

Inn at Kulaniapia Falls INN $$
(Map p277; 808-935-6789; www.waterfall.net; 1 Kulaniapia Dr; r incl breakfast $179-199, guesthouses $279;) Drive up, up, up 4 miles past acres of macadamia orchards to 850ft above sea level. Your reward? Ten rooms (in two buildings) and a pagoda guesthouse, exquisitely appointed with Asian antiques, in a fantastically verdant setting, complete with waterfall. All power is hydroelectric.

Shipman House B&B B&B $$$
(Map p268; 808-934-8002; www.hilo-hawaii.com; 131 Kaiulani St; r incl breakfast $219-249;) Staying at the Shipman family's grand Victorian mansion is pricey, albeit peerless in historical significance. Queen Lili'uokalani played the grand piano, and Jack London slept in the guest cottage. Surrounded by museum-quality antiques, three rooms in the main house are sedate and finely (although not luxuriously) furnished. In a separate cottage, two rooms are more casual and private.

Eating

★**Suisan Fish Market** FISH $
(Map p268; 808-935-9349; 93 Lihiwai St; poke per pound $13; 8am-6pm Mon-Fri, 8am-4pm Sat, 10am-4pm Sun) For a fantastic variety of *poke* (sold by the pound), you can't beat Suisan, where you know the fish is freshly caught. Honestly, a bowl of fresh takeout *poke* and rice ($5 to $7) is as good as food gets on the Big Island.

★**Two Ladies Kitchen** DESSERTS $
(Map p268; 808-961-4766; 274 Kilauea Ave; 8-piece boxes $6; 10am-5pm Wed-Sat) A hole-in-the-wall it may be, but it's a hole that makes superlatively good Japanese *mochi* (sticky rice dessert).

★**Moonstruck Patisserie** BAKERY $
(Map p271; 808-933-6868; www.moonstruck-patisserie.com; 16 Furneaux Lane; pastries & cake slices $4-5; 8:30am-4pm Wed-Sat) It's kind of ridiculous that a European-style bakery this good is plopped in the middle of the Pacific Ocean. Pastry chef Jackie Tan-DeWitt specializes in classic pastries and unique cakes, cheesecakes and fruit tarts.

★**Paul's Place** CAFE $
(Map p271; 808-280-8646; 132 Punahoa St; mains $8-12; 7am-3pm Tue-Sat) In a three-table dining room, Paul serves absolutely scrumptious renditions of the classics, including Belgian waffles, robust salads, and eggs Benedict featuring his special sauce. Everything's healthy, with lots of fresh fruit and veggies. If the place is full, wait or try again. You won't regret it.

Hilo Farmers Market MARKET $
(Map p271; 808-933-1000; www.hilofarmers-market.com; Kamehameha Ave, cnr Mamo St; 6am-4pm Wed & Sat) Hilo's gathering place is its downtown farmers market, which opened in 1988 with four farmers selling from trucks. Today, the market is bustling and attracts sizable crowds. A single pass through the food tent unearths luscious mangoes and papayas but, fair warning, the produce sold here is not 100% locally grown.

If you miss Wednesday or Saturday market days, you'll still find a row of daily vendors selling produce and flowers.

Kino'ole Farmers Market MARKET $
(Map p277; 808-557-2780; Kahaopea St, cnr Kino'ole Ave; 6am-noon Sat) Hilo's 'other' farmers market is low-key and attracts main-

Around Hilo

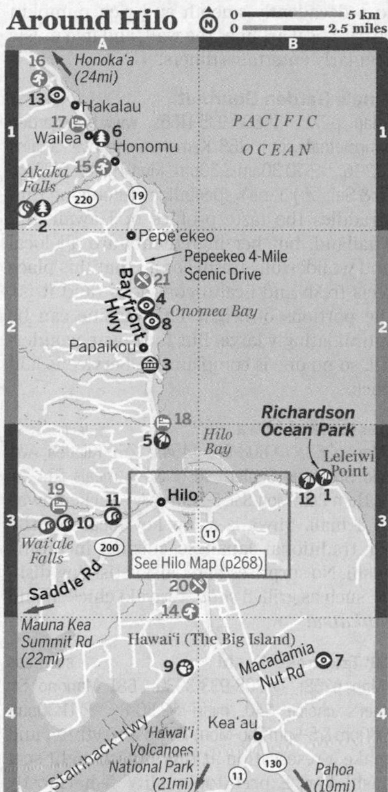

Around Hilo

Top Sights
1 Richardson Ocean Park B3

Sights
2 'Akaka Falls State Park A1
3 Hawaii Plantation Museum A2
4 Hawaii Tropical Botanical Garden A2
5 Honoli'i Beach Park A3
6 Kolekole Beach Park A1
7 Mauna Loa Macadamia-Nut Visitor Center B4
8 Onomea Tea Company A2
9 Pana'ewa Rainforest Zoo & Gardens A4
10 Pe'epe'e Falls & Boiling Pots A3
11 Rainbow Falls A3
12 Wai'olena & Wai'uli Beach Parks B3
13 World Botanical Gardens A1

Activities, Courses & Tours
14 Hilo Municipal Golf Course A3
15 Skyline EcoAdventures Akaka Falls A1
16 Umauma Falls & Zipline Experience A1
Zip Isle Zipline Adventures .... (see 13)

Sleeping
17 Akiko's Buddhist Bed & Breakfast A1
18 Hale Kai Hawaii A2
19 Inn at Kulaniapia Falls A3
Orchid Tree B&B .... (see 5)

Eating
20 Kino'ole Farmers Market A3
21 What's Shakin' A2

ly locals, with its 100% locally grown and made products sold by the farmers themselves. The 15 to 20 vendors supply all you need, including fresh produce, baked goods, taro chips, poi, plants and flowers. Parking is plentiful.

Cafe 100 FAST FOOD $
(Map p268; ☎808-935-8683; 969 Kilauea Ave; loco moco $3-5, plate lunches $5-7; ⏰6:45am-8:30pm Mon-Thu, to 9pm Fri, to 7:30pm Sat) Locals love this drive-in for its generous plate lunches and 20 rib-sticking varieties of *loco moco*, including fish and veggie-burger options. With a clean seating area and efficient service, it's local fast food at its finest.

Lucy's Taqueria MEXICAN $
(Map p271; ☎808-315-8246; http://lucystaqueria.com; 194 Kilauea Ave; mains $5-10; ⏰10:30am-9pm Sun, Mon, Wed & Thu, to 10pm Fri & Sat;) Hilo is a pretty chill spot, but Lucy's can be a divisive issue. People either find the no-frills atmosphere and lack of service tolerable, or hate the same qualities. It comes down to the food, which we like: cheap, tasty, family-size Mexican portions of carne asada, prawns, tofu *pastor*, wet burritos and the like. Oh, and $4 margaritas.

Koji's Bento Korner HAWAIIAN $
(Map p271; ☎808-935-1417; 52 Ponahawai St; loco moco $3.25-7.50; ⏰7am-2pm Mon-Fri, 9am-2pm Sat) The Koji *loco moco* – with two homemade hamburger patties, teriyaki sauce and gravy, one egg, two Portuguese sausages, macaroni salad and kimchi – is the stuff of local cravings.

Ken's House of Pancakes DINER $
(Map p268; 1730 Kamehameha Ave; meals $6-12; ⏰24hr) There's something comforting about

a 24-hour diner with a mile-long menu. Choose from macadamia-nut pancakes, Spam omelettes, slow-cooked *kalua* pig plates and steaming bowls of saimin.

★Cafe Pesto BISTRO **$$**

(Map p271; ☎808-969-6640; www.cafepesto.com; 308 Kamehameha Ave, S Hata Bldg; pizzas $10-20, dinner $18-30; ⏲11am-9pm Sun-Thu, to 10pm Fri & Sat) Café Pesto is a safe choice, whether for business lunches or dinner with your mother-in-law. Set downtown in a lovely historic building, the versatile kitchen covers all bases with creative salads, risotto, stir-fries, pasta, seafood and chicken.

★Hilo Bay Cafe AMERICAN, SUSHI **$$**

(Map p268; ☎808-935-4939; www.hilobaycafe.com; 123 Lihiwai St; mains $18-30; ⏲11am-9pm Mon-Thu, 11am-9:30pm Fri & Sat, 5-9pm Sun) Since 2003, this casually sophisticated eatery has wowed critics and put Hilo on the foodie map. The eclectic menu features gourmet versions of comfort food, such as Hamakua mushroom pot pie and a local beef burger with garlic-salted fries.

Miyo's JAPANESE **$$**

(Map p268; ☎808-935-2273; http://miyosrestaurant.com; 681 Manono St; dinner $11-15; ⏲11am-2pm & 5:30-8:30pm Mon-Sat) A longtime local favorite, Miyo's is known for home-style Japanese meals and nightly crowds. Try classics such as grilled ahi or *saba* (mackerel), tempura or *tonkatsu* (breaded and fried pork cutlets). Reservations are a must.

Kanpai JAPANESE **$$**

(Map p271; ☎808-969-1000; www.kanpaihilo.com; 190 Keawe St; sushi $7-12, mains $12-18; ⏲5pm-1am Mon-Sat) Hip Kanpai looks slick enough for Brooklyn, but overlaid with Hilo's appealing mix of small-town camaraderie, experimental attitude and Pacific-fusion soul. It specializes in ramen, sushi and sake (three words inscribed on the grave of a person who died well fed and happy). Ahi macnut rolls and pulled pork ramen are served till surprisingly late.

Pineapple's FUSION **$$**

(Map p271; ☎808-238-5324; http://pineappleshilo.com; 332 Keawe St; mains $14-24; ⏲11am-9:30pm Sun & Tue-Thu, to 10pm Fri & Sat; 🖉) Pineapple's is carving a name for itself as a bastion of locavore, sit-down dining offered at midrange prices. The food ranges from island tacos stuffed with shrimp or *kalua* pork, to a half-pound burger topped with local pineapple, to a decadently smooth and rich pumpkin curry. Local art lines the wall, and live music regularly entertains diners.

Tina's Garden Gourmet THAI **$$**

(Map p271; ☎808-935-1166; www.tinasgardengourmetcafe.com; 168 Kamehameha Ave; mains $12-16; ⏲10:30am-3:30pm Mon-Thu,to 9:30pm Fri & Sat; 🖉) Tina's specializes in cuisine that straddles the taste profiles of Hawaii and Thailand, but her ingredients are all local and wonderfully fresh. For all that this place feels fresh and health conscious (and it is), the portions of bright Thai cuisine can be intimidatingly large. But they taste wonderful, so no one is complaining. Service is laid back.

Restaurant Miwa JAPANESE **$$**

(Map p268; ☎808-961-4454; 1261 Kilauea Ave, Hilo Shopping Center; sushi $5-8, meals $14-28; ⏲11am-2pm Mon-Sat, 5-9pm daily) Tucked away in a mall, Miwa is a low-key local favorite for traditional Japanese cuisine, including sushi. No surprises here, just satisfying dishes, such as grilled *saba*, teriyaki chicken and *tonkatsu*.

★Takenoko Sushi SUSHI **$$$**

(Map p268; ☎808-933-3939; 681 Manono St; chef's choice $40, nigiri $2.50-8; ⏲11:30am-1:30pm & 5-9pm Thu-Mon) Drop everything and make a reservation at this superb eight-seat sushi bar. Expect top-quality fish (mostly flown fresh from Japan), a spotlessly clean setting, expert sushi chef and gracious service. Each bite is a memorable experience. The three dinner seating times: 5pm, 7pm and 9pm.

Ponds AMERICAN **$$$**

(Map p268; ☎808-934-7663; www.pondshilohi.com; 135 Kalaniana'ole Ave; mains $20-25; ⏲11am-9:30pm Sun-Thu, to midnight Fri & Sat) This steak/seafood/pasta restaurant will suit those hankering for familiar American food with an island twist. A big plus is the airy dining room overlooking 'Ice Pond.'

Seaside Restaurant SEAFOOD **$$$**

(Map p268; ☎808-935-8825; www.seasiderestaurant.com; 1790 Kalaniana'ole Ave; meals $25-30; ⏲4:30-8:30pm Tue-Thu, to 9pm Fri & Sat) 🍃 This old-school seafood restaurant specializes in fresh fish, from locally caught mahimahi to pan-size *aholehole* (flagtail fish) raised in on-site Hawaiian-style fishponds. It's a sit-down restaurant, but the vibe is homey and retro.

Drinking & Nightlife

Hilo Town Tavern BAR
(Map p271; 168 Keawe St; mains $9-11; ⏲2pm-2am) This friendly neighborhood tavern has an outdoor area, a pool hall, and is pretty much the spot for the discerning Hilo resident looking for a cold beer and nightlife action.

Mehana Brewing Company BREWERY
(Map p268; ☎808-934-8211; http://mehanabrewing.com; 275 E Kawili St; ⏲noon-5pm Mon-Thu, to 6pm Fri, to 4pm Sat) Mehana, which also owns popular Hawaii Nui beers, is Hilo's very own brewery. It doesn't offer brewery tours yet, but its tasting room is open to the public. The folks behind the counter are generous with the aloha, as well as their pours.

Bayfront Kava Bar BAR
(Map p271; ☎808-345-1698; www.bayfrontkava.com; 116 Kamehameha Ave; cup $5; ⏲4-10pm Mon-Sat) If you're curious about kava (*'awa* in Hawaiian), try a cup at this minimalist bar. Friendly bar staff serve freshly brewed, locally grown kava root in coconut shells. Get ready for tingling tastebuds and a calm buzz. Live music and art exhibitions kick off on a regular basis.

Entertainment

Palace Theater THEATER
(Map p271; ☎808-934-7010, box office 808-934-7777; www.hilopalace.com; 38 Haili St) This historic theater is Hilo's cultural crown jewel. Its eclectic programming includes arthouse and silent films (accompanied by the house organ), music and dance concerts, Broadway musicals and cultural festivals. On Wednesday morning (11am to noon) it hosts 'Hawai'iana Live' (adult/child $5/free), a touching, small-town intro to Hawaiian culture through storytelling, film, music, *oli* (chant) and hula.

Shopping

★**Basically Books** BOOKS
(Map p271; ☎808-961-0144; www.basicallybooks.com; 160 Kamehameha Ave; ⏲9am-5pm Mon-Sat, 11am-3:30pm Sun) A browser's paradise, this shop specializes in maps, travel guides and books about Hawaii. Good selection for kids too.

Grapes: A Wine Store WINE
(Map p271; ☎808-933-1471; www.grapeshawaii.com; 207 Kilauea Ave; ⏲noon-6pm Tue-Sat) This hidden treasure is owned by a true aficionado and packed to the rafters with global stock. There are free wine tastings every other Thursday.

Still Life Books BOOKS
(Map p271; ☎808-756-2919; http://stillifebooks.blogspot.com; 134 Kilauea Ave; ⏲11am-3pm Tue-Sat) Come for quality used books – primarily literary works – and to browse and talk ideas with the owner, a keen bibliophile.

Hilo Guitars & Ukuleles MUSIC
(Map p271; ☎808-935-4282; www.hiloguitars.com; 56 Ponahawai St; ⏲10am-5pm Mon-Fri, to 4pm Sat) Find a wide selection of quality ukuleles, from koa or mahogany collectibles to fine entry-level instruments.

Sig Zane Designs CLOTHING
(Map p271; ☎808-935-7077; www.sigzane.com; 122 Kamehameha Ave; ⏲9:30am-5pm Mon-Fri, 9am-4pm Sat) Legendary in the hula community, Sig Zane creates iconic custom fabrics, marked by rich colors and graphic prints of Hawaiian flora. You can spot a 'Sig' a mile away.

Dragon Mama HOMEWARES
(Map p271; ☎808-934-9081; www.dragonmama.com; 266 Kamehameha Ave; ⏲9am-5pm Mon-Fri, to 4pm Sat) Go home with exquisite bedding custom-made from imported Japanese fabric.

Information

DANGERS & ANNOYANCES

While Hilo is relatively safe, be careful downtown and avoid Kalakaua Park at night.

MEDICAL SERVICES

Hilo Medical Center (☎808-932-3000; www.hilomedicalcenter.org; 1190 Waianuenue Ave; ⏲24hr emergency) Near Rainbow Falls.

Longs Drugs General store and pharmacy; store hours run longer than pharmacy hours. Branches at Kilauea Ave (☎808-935-3357, pharmacy 808-935-9075; 555 Kilauea Ave; ⏲7am-7pm Mon-Fri, 7am-6pm Sat, 8am-5pm Sun) and Prince Kuhio Plaza (☎808-959-5881, pharmacy 808-959-4508; 111 E Puainako St, Prince Kuhio Plaza; ⏲pharmacy 8am-8pm Mon-Fri, to 7pm Sat, to 5pm Sun).

MONEY

Bank of Hawaii Branches at Kawili St (☎808-961-0681; 417 E Kawili St) and Pauahi St (☎808-935-9701; 120 Pauahi St).

First Hawaiian Bank (☎808-969-2211; 1205 Kilauea Ave)

POLICE

Police (☎808-935-3311; 349 Kapi'olani St) For nonemergencies.

POST

Downtown post office (Map p271; ☎808-933-3014; 154 Waianuenue Ave; ⏲9am-4pm Mon-Fri, 12:30-2pm Sat) Located in the Federal Building.

Getting There & Away

AIR

Hilo International Airport (ITO; Map p268; ☎808-961-9300; http://hawaii.gov/ito; 2450 Kekuanaoa St) Almost all flights to Hilo are interisland, mostly from Honolulu.

BUS

Hele-On Bus (☎808-961-8744; www.hele-onbus.org; adult/senior/student $2/1/1) All buses originate at **Mo'oheau Terminal** (Map p271; 329 Kamehameha Ave) in downtown Hilo. From there, buses go around the island, but service is infrequent, sometimes only very early in the morning (for work commuters) or only a few times daily. If you're going to a major destination (such as Kailua-Kona or a South Kohala resort) and are staying within the area, the bus is a feasible option. Check the website for current routes and schedules.

CAR

The drive from Hilo to Kailua-Kona (via Waimea) is 95 miles and averages 2½ hours. Driving on Saddle Rd can cut travel time by about 15 minutes.

Getting Around

BICYCLE

Cycling is more recreation than transportation in Hilo. **Mid-Pacific Wheels** (☎808-935-6211; www.midpacificwheelsllc.com; 1133-C Manono St; ⏲9am-6pm Mon-Sat, 11am-5pm Sun) rents mountain and road bikes for $25 to $45 per day.

BUS

The Hele-On Bus covers much of Hilo, although service can be infrequent.

CAR

Free parking is generally available. Downtown street parking is free for two hours; finding a spot is easy except during Saturday and Wednesday farmers markets.

TAXI

The approximate cab fare from the airport to downtown Hilo is $15.

AA Marshall's Taxi (☎808-936-2654)

PUNA

The Polynesian word 'mana' is tough to translate. 'Life force,' 'energy' and other terms are usually bandied about. But if you really want to learn mana's meaning, come to Puna, because everyone on this island agrees it is overflowing with the stuff.

Here, at Hawai'i's eastern tip, the primal soul of the island manifests in an unrestrained display of eco-bravado. The rain blends with black volcanic soil to engender a fertility that is frankly astounding. Green bursts through the soil and weaves itself into thick forests of wood rooted in lava soil. The ocean beats like a hammer on the Big Island's easternmost cliffs, and edges back as lava flows into the ocean.

Who lives here? Hippies, funky artists, alternative healers, Hawaiian sovereignty activists, *pakalolo* (marijuana) growers, organic farmers and off-the-grid survivalists. A nickname for all these folks, which they have adopted themselves, is Puna-tics. They exhibit a disconcerting blend of laid-back apathy to the world and intense emotions.

Kea'au & Around

POP 2253

Between Hilo and Volcano is a series of former sugar plantations and mini-villages. The main town, Kea'au, is just a cluster of gas stations and stores, including a supermarket, off Volcano Hwy (Hwy 11). Past Kea'au toward Pahoa, however, burgeoning residential subdivisions have transformed Puna into sprawling suburbs. If you want to explore Hawai'i Volcanoes National Park from a balmier home base than Volcano, consider the lodgings tucked away here.

Sights & Activities

Fuku-Bonsai Cultural Center GARDENS

(☎808-982-9880; www.fukubonsai.com; 17-856 Ola'a Rd; ⏲8am-4pm Mon-Sat) FREE This bonsai nursery is mostly a salesroom for its commercial specialty: dwarf schefflera that can be grown indoors. That said, the folks who run the place are passionate about bonsai, and love giving visitors a verbal primer (and then some) on the plants. To get here from Kea'au, drive south on Hwy 11 and turn left on Ola'a Rd between mile markers 9 and 10.

★**Kazumura Cave Tours** TOUR
(808-967-7208; http://kazumuracave.com; off Volcano Hwy, past Mile 22; tours from $30; Mon-Sat by appointment) Since discovering that his property lies atop Kazumura Cave (the world's longest lava tube), Harry Schick has become an expert on lava caves and gives small tours (six people maximum) of the underworld kingdom that exists under his living room. All this, and at a reasonable cost! Be prepared to climb ladders and walk over rocky terrain, even on the shortest, easiest tour. Minimum age is 11 years; English proficiency is required. Make reservations at least a week ahead.

Kilauea Caverns of Fire TOUR
(808-217-2363; www.kilaueacavernsoffire.com; off Volcano Hwy, before Mile 11; tours $29-79; by appointment) These tours through Kazumura Cave can run a bit large – up to 20 for the one-hour walk and up to eight for the three-hour adventure – but it's a pretty impressive spelunking adventure for all that. It's worth noting that the shorter tour is a decent option for families; the minimum age is five years.

Sleeping & Eating

For groceries, stock up at **Foodland** (808-966-9316; 16-586 Old Volcano Rd; 6am-10pm) or **Kea'au Natural Foods** (808-966-8877; 16-586 Old Volcano Rd; 8:30am-8pm Mon-Fri, 8:30am-7pm Sat, 9:30am-5pm Sun), both at Kea'au Shopping Center, at the junction of Volcano Hwy and Kea'au-Pahoa Rd.

Eco Hostel Hawaii HOSTEL $
(808-315-2202; www.ecohostelhawaii.com; 16-1925 9 Rd; camping/yurts $28/65;) This is a lovely green garden of a hostel that has more than a little bit of a hippie vibe. You can camp in tented accommodations plunked in the jungle, or opt for a more cozy yurt. There's a permaculture farm where you can work for accommodation; solar panels; and lots of bookable tours of the Big Island.

Butterfly Inn INN $$
(808-966-7936; www.thebutterflyinn.com; Kurtistown; s/d with shared bath $100/125) Geared for women travelers, this long-standing inn is a safe, supportive place in a comfortable home in Kurtistown. Two tidy rooms with private entrances share an ample kitchen, living room, dining deck, bathroom and outdoor hot tub.

★**Hilo Coffee Mill** CAFE $
(808-968-1333; www.hilocoffeemill.com; 17-995 Hwy 11; mains $4-10; 7am-4:30pm Mon, Tue, Thu & Fri, to 2pm Wed, to 4pm Sat;) This tidy cafe makes for a pleasant stop, with ample seating, light meals, friendly staff, coffee (brewed and beans) and adjacent roasting room. Owners give personal, informative, 90-minute farm tours (with/without meal, $20/15). Located roadside between mile markers 12 and 13.

Shopping

Dan De Luz's Woods ARTS, CRAFTS
(808-968-6607; Hwy 11, past Mile 12;) Master woodworker Dan passed away in 2012, but the grandson whom he trained is carrying on the family craft. The shop still carries numerous calabashes by this much-loved local talent.

THE JUNE 27 LAVA FLOW

At the time of writing, a lava flow that erupted from Kilauea on June 27, 2014 was still creeping across Puna.

The volcanic activity had a mixed impact on local life and tourism in the area. The speed of the lava flow, pouring like slow syrup, meant that daily life was not dramatically affected. School groups were visiting the outward edge on field trips.

The lava rolled through a relatively unpopulated part of the region, destroying one house as of this writing. A traffic diversion in Pahoa village closed off the area between Post Office Rd and Kahakai Blvd; a relatively minor inconvenience as traffic goes, but a hard impact on the businesses and residences that occupied this small stretch of pavement.

Some businesses have actually thrived. Civil defense employees and contractors flooded Pahoa, and the usual counterculture crowd of repeat Puna visitors was all about witnessing the wrath of Pele.

As of press time, the lava flow was still live. Thus, we recommend you check active updates on the situation on the ground via the USGS Hawaiian Volcano Observatory website, http://hvo.wr.usgs.gov.

Puna

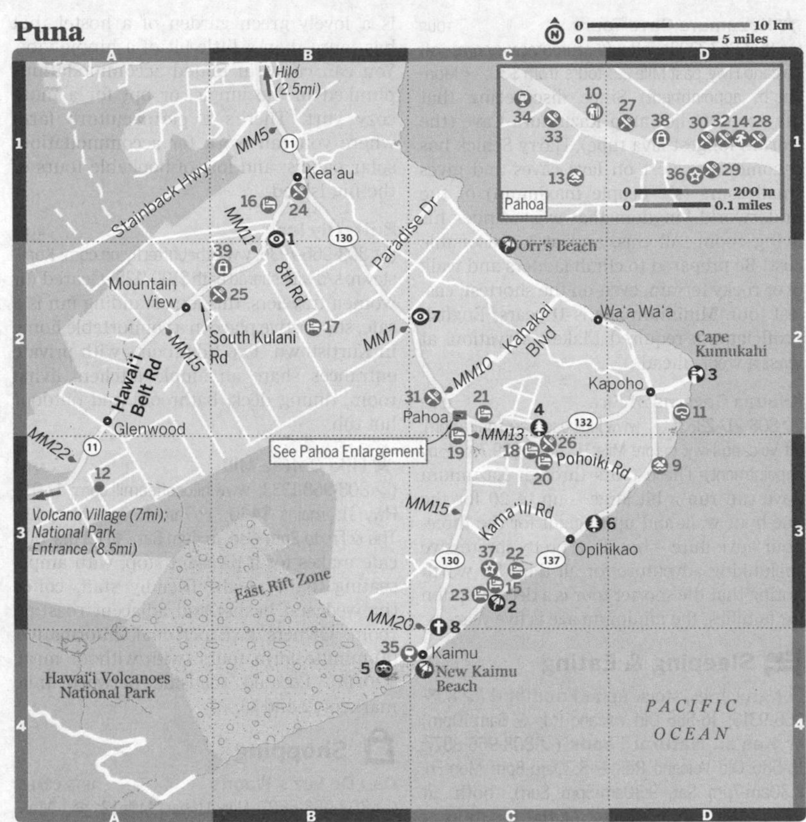

Pahoa

POP 945

Like a weird mix of Wild West frontier town and hippie commune, Pahoa is the beating original, eclectic heart of Puna. This ramshackle, ragamuffin town, with its raised wooden sidewalks, peeling paint and unkempt bohemian edge, can easily capture your heart. It's full of oddballs and eccentrics.

The main thoroughfare is signposted as Pahoa Village Rd. As you enter town, there are two shopping malls on either side of the highway: one with a supermarket and a hardware store, the other with Longs Drugs. In town, you'll find banks, gas stations, a post office and **Big Island BookBuyers** (☎808-315-5335; 15-2901 Pahoa Village Rd; ⏰10am-5pm Mon-Sat), a well-run used bookshop.

Sights & Activities

★**Maku'u Craft & Farmers Market** MARKET
(Hwy 130; ⏰8am-2pm Sun) Crowds converge here for wide-ranging offerings, including psychic readings, massage, surfboard repairs, orchids, jewelry and, yes, fruits and vegetables. Freshly cooked food includes Hawaiian, Mexican and Thai cuisine. Morning cultural workshops (9am) give way to live music through the afternoon. You can't miss it on the *makai* side of Hwy 130 between mile markers 7 and 8.

★**Lava Ocean Adventures** BOAT TOUR
(☎808-966-4200; http://lavaoceanadventures.com; adult/child from $145/119) The crew on the *Lava Kai* get you close enough to the lava to feel the heat and smell the sulfur. It's an unforgettable experience – assuming the lava is flowing. These expertly narrated tours motor from Isaac Hale Beach Park to the sea

Puna

Sights
1 Fuku-Bonsai Cultural Center ... B1
2 Kehena Beach ... C3
3 Kumukahi Lighthouse ... D2
4 Lava Tree State Monument Park ... C2
5 Lava Viewing Area ... B4
6 MacKenzie State Recreation Area ... C3
7 Maku'u Craft & Farmers Market ... C2
8 Star of the Sea Church ... C3

Activities, Courses & Tours
9 Ahalanui Beach Park ... D3
10 Jeff Hunt Surfboards ... C1
11 Kapoho Tide Pools ... D2
12 Kazumura Cave Tours ... A3
Kilauea Caverns of Fire ... (see 25)
13 Pahoa Community Aquatic Center ... C1
14 Paradissimo Tropical Spa ... D1

Sleeping
15 Absolute Paradise B&B ... C3
16 Butterfly Inn ... B1
17 Eco Hostel Hawaii ... B2
18 Hale Moana B&B ... C3
19 Hawaiian Sanctuary ... C2
20 Hedonisia ... C3
21 Jungle Farmhouse ... C2
22 Kalani Oceanside Retreat ... C3
23 Ramashala ... C3

Eating
24 Foodland ... B1
25 Hilo Coffee Mill ... B2
26 Hot Dog Guy ... C3
27 Island Naturals ... D1
28 Kaleo's Bar & Grill ... D1
Kea'au Natural Foods ... (see 24)
29 Luquin's Mexican Restaurant ... D1
30 Ning's Thai Cuisine ... D1
31 Pahoa Fresh Fish ... C2
32 Paolo's Bistro ... D1
33 Sirius Coffee Connection ... C1

Drinking & Nightlife
34 Black Rock Cafe ... C1
35 Uncle Robert's Awa Bar ... B4

Entertainment
36 Akebono Theater ... D1
37 SPACE ... C3

Shopping
38 Big Island BookBuyers ... D1
39 Dan De Luz's Woods ... B2
SPACE Farmers Market ... (see 35)

entry near Kalapana, where lava gushes into the ocean, boiling it on contact.

For 90 minutes watch as live lava chunks explode underwater, getting churned into a water-molten-rock 'smoothie' while a new black-sand beach is built – simply awesome. Go for the sunrise tour and you'll be escorted by flying fish, leaping dolphins and maybe a rainbow. Warning: you may get seasick.

★ Jeff Hunt Surfboards SURFING
(808-965-2322; http://jeffhuntsurfboards.com; 15-2883 Pahoa Village Rd; rental per day $20; 10am-5pm Mon-Sat, 11am-3pm Sun) Jeff Hunt is one of the island's best board shapers, and at his little hut you can buy one, talk surfing and rent soft-top boards.

Paradissimo Tropical Spa SPA
(808-217-2202; www.spaparadissimo.com; 15-2958 Pahoa Village Rd; facials from $25; 11am-5pm Tue & Thu-Sat) In our estimation, there's no better way to spend a rainy afternoon than getting a good pampering here. Owner Olivia is a tender soul with talented hands, and the organic spa products she uses feel like a magical alchemy for the skin. Sauna and massages available.

Pahoa Community Aquatic Center SWIMMING
(808-965-2700; 15-2910 Puna Rd; 9am-5:30pm Mon-Fri, to 4:30pm Sat & Sun) For lap swimming, try this fantastic outdoor Olympic-size pool behind the Pahoa Neighborhood Facility.

Sleeping

★ Hedonisia HOSTEL $
(808-430-2545, 808-430-9903; http://hedonisiahawaii.com; 13-657 Hinalo St; dm from $25, r with shared bath $40-60, cottages $65-95;) This spot, by Lava Tree State Monument, ranks up there among the world's friendliest, funkiest hostels. This former junkyard has been converted into an organic farm/ramshackle accommodation compound, with Technicolor murals, simple, cozy chalets, 'dorms' where you can sleep in a comfy common area in a tent, wild pigs and a school bus. Anyone who wants to volunteer in the hostel gets discounted stays.

Hawaiian Sanctuary FARMSTAY $
(800-309-8010; http://sustainable-hawaii.org; Mile 12, Hwy 130; r with shared bath $75-95) This permaculture farm offers internships for those interested in sustainable agriculture

NOISY NEIGHBORS – COQUI FROGS

Hawaii's most wanted alien is the Puerto Rican coqui frog, only an inch long, but relentlessly loud. At sunset, coquis begin their nightly chirping (a two-tone 'ko-kee' call), which can register between 90 and 100 decibels from 2ft away. Even at a distance, their chorus maintains 70 decibels, equivalent to a vacuum cleaner.

Coquis accidentally reached the Hawaiian Islands around 1988, and they've proliferated wildly on the Big Island. Around Lava Tree State Monument, densities are the highest in the state and twice that of Puerto Rico. Besides causing a nightly racket, coquis are disrupting the ecosystem by eating the bugs that feed native birds. Light sleepers: bring ear plugs.

and going back to nature. Nightly stays are also offered, so visitors can eat vegan food and soak up the vibe. Located about 1.5 miles from central Pahoa.

★Jungle Farmhouse RENTAL HOUSE **$$**
(808-640-1113; http://pahoa.info; 15-3001 Mako Way; per night/week $139/700) Kick back at this beautifully maintained house, full of handpicked vintage furnishings, with three bedrooms, 1.5 bathrooms, laundry facilities and an airy screened patio. Outside, enjoy fruit trees, chickens (fresh eggs!) and ducks. It's fantastic value: there's no extra charge for extra guests (maximum four total), and the weekly rate is a steal.

★Hale Moana B&B B&B **$$**
(808-965-7015; www.bnb-aloha.com; 13-3315 Makamae St; studios $110, ste $140-170; @) In a clean-cut neighborhood, this B&B is immaculate, family friendly and a bargain to boot. Suites are especially comfy, with well-equipped kitchenettes and enough space to kick back. All accommodations have a separate entrance onto lush gardens. Hot breakfast is served in a breakfast room bursting with orchids. The hosts are fluent in German.

Eating & Drinking

For such a small town, Pahoa has a decent bunch of eateries.

★Pahoa Fresh Fish FISH & CHIPS **$**
(808-965-8248; 15-2670 Pahoa Village Rd; mains $5-7; 8am-7pm) This utterly unassuming spot, which has the atmosphere of the moon and is slotted in an ugly strip mall, serves, hands down, the best fish and chips around. We don't know what the friendly woman behind the counter is doing and we don't care; we'll come back for her perfectly battered and fried ono and mahimahi anytime, all the time.

Sirius Coffee Connection CAFE **$**
(15-2874 Pahoa Village Rd; 7am-6pm Mon-Sat, to 3pm Sun;) This simple space offers good coffee, internet and computer access, friendly service and baked goodies.

Island Naturals MARKET **$**
(15-1403 Pahoa Village Rd; sandwiches $6-10; 7:30am-7:30pm Mon-Sat, 8am-7pm Sun;) You'll find organic produce, healthy sandwiches, hot mains and the local nouveau hippie crowd.

★Kaleo's Bar & Grill HAWAII REGIONAL CUISINE **$$**
(808-965-5600; www.kaleoshawaii.com; 15-2969 Pahoa Village Rd; lunch mains $9-16, dinner mains $14-32; 11am-9pm;) Pahoa's top sitdown restaurant serves island-fusion fare – such as tempura ahi roll, orzo pasta salad, and coconut chicken curry – in a relaxed, family-friendly atmosphere. There's live music most nights and a consistent local buzz. Definitely make a reservation on weekends.

★Paolo's Bistro ITALIAN **$$**
(808-965-7033; Pahoa Village Rd; mains $13-26; 5:30-9pm Tue-Sun) With all due respect to Puna, we weren't expecting fantastic Italian food out here in the jungle. Then along comes Paolo's. Brilliant. This intimate place serves a well-executed menu of authentic northern-Italian cooking. Bring your own vino.

Ning's Thai Cuisine THAI **$$**
(15-2955 Pahoa Village Rd; mains $10-14; noon-9pm Mon-Sat, 5-9pm Sun;) Reliable Thai curries, lively salads and an emphasis on local, organic ingredients.

Luquin's Mexican Restaurant MEXICAN **$$**
(808-965-9990; 15-2942 Pahoa Village Rd; mains $10-19; 7am-9pm;) If you're craving Mexican fare, go to Luquin's for a fix, but it's nothing to write home about. The *liliko'i* margaritas are memorable (though after

a few, you won't be remembering much of anything). These guys do breakfast best, so consider starting your day here.

Black Rock Cafe BAR
(15-2872 Pahoa Village Rd; ⌚7am-9pm) Half the Black Rock is an average restaurant serving passable burgers and breakfast. The other half is a bar popular with Punatics who are a little more Harley-Davidson than hippie. Not that it gets rough (and hippies do show up too); the Black Rock is just a little salty, smoky and sweaty.

☆ Entertainment

Akebono Theater LIVE MUSIC
(☎808-965-9990; Pahoa Village Rd; tickets $10-20) This historical theater hosts all kinds of music, from Big Island Elvis to visiting jam bands. It's located behind Luquin's Mexican Restaurant.

ℹ Getting There & Away

Traffic between Hilo and Puna is a nightmare during commuting hours. By all means, avoid driving toward Hilo in the early morning or toward Kea'au and Pahoa in the late afternoon.

Hele-On Bus (☎808-961-8745; www.heleonbus.org; adult/senior/student $2/1/1) goes from Hilo to Kea'au and Pahoa several times daily.

Highway 132

A good way to explore Puna is to navigate the triangle formed by three highways: Hwy 132, Red Road (Hwy 137) and the Kalapana Hwy (Hwy 130). It's even better on a bike.

Lava Tree State Monument Park PARK
(⌚dawn-dusk) FREE Entering this park, located beneath a tight-knit canopy of (invasive) albizia trees is an otherworldly experience. A short, easy loop trail passes through a tropical vision of Middle Earth, full of ferns, orchids and bamboo, and takes you past unusual 'lava trees,' which were created in 1790 when a rainforest was engulfed in *pahoehoe* from Kilauea's East Rift Zone. The lava enveloped the moisture-laden ohia trees and then receded, leaving lava molds of the destroyed trees.

These mossy shells now lie scattered like dinosaur bones, adding to the park's ghostly aura. In the late afternoon the love songs of coqui frogs reverberate among the trees.

To get here follow Hwy 132 about 2.5 miles east of Hwy 130.

Red Road (Highway 137)

Winding Hwy 137 is nicknamed Red Rd because its northern portion is paved with red cinder. It's a swooping, atmospheric drive that periodically dips beneath tunnel-like canopies of *milo* and *hala* (pandanus) trees. There are many discreet paths to the shore along this road – take one for a private piece of coast.

Two side roads make intriguing detours or shortcuts back to Pahoa: **Pohoiki Road** connects Hwy 137 with Hwy 132, and is another shaded, mystical mana path winding through thick forest dotted with papaya orchards and wild noni (Indian mulberry). Further south, **Kama'ili Road**, connecting with Hwy 130, is not quite as dramatic, but still makes for a pleasant country ramble.

When hunger strikes, pull up to the **Hot Dog Guy** (Pohoiki Rd, cnr Hwy 132; hotdogs $5-7; ⌚daily, weather permitting) for some bison, reindeer or all-beef hotdogs grilled to order and nestled in a whole-wheat bun.

Kapoho Tide Pools

The best snorkeling on the Big Island's windward side is in this sprawling network of **tide pools** (Wai Opae Tide Pools Marine Life Conservation District; suggested donation $3; ⌚7am-7pm). Here Kapoho's lava-rock coast is a mosaic of protected, shallow, interconnected pools containing a rich variety of sea life. It's easy to pool-hop for hours, tracking saddle wrasses, Moorish idols, butterfly fish, sea cucumbers and much more. For interesting coral gardens, head straight out from the blue house; sea turtles like the warm pocket a bit further south and octopuses are known to visit.

BEST PUNA VIEWS

- The underground world in Kazumura Cave (p281), the world's longest lava tube
- Marine life in the Kapoho Tide Pools
- Molten lava by land (p288) or by sea (p282)
- People-watching at Kehena Beach (p286)
- Towering foliage in and around Lava Tree State Monument Park

Wear reef shoes to avoid cutting your soles on the lava rock. From Hwy 137, a mile south of the lighthouse, turn onto Kapoho Kai Dr, which winds a little and dead-ends at Wai Opae; turn left and park in the lot. Sometimes, locals put out a portable toilet.

This area is also peppered with vacation rentals. **Pualani** (☎805-225-1552; www.bigislandhawaiivacationhomes.com; Kapoho Beach Lots; house $150; @), an airy house with hot tub and wraparound lanai, is lovely. Check www.vrbo.com and www.airbnb.com for listings.

If you stay here, you'll have access to **Champagne Pond**, a tranquil pool with sandy shores frequented by green turtles. It drew controversy when increased use by those driving here (on a rough 4WD-only road from Kumukahi Lighthouse) caused sanitation problems and other issues. Tread lightly.

Ahalanui Beach Park

Ahalanui Beach Park (⏰7am-7pm) is called 'the hot pond' because of its main attraction – a large, spring-fed thermal pool that's set in lava rock and deep enough for swimming. It's a pretty sweet bathtub: water temperatures average 90°F (cooler with the incoming tide), cement borders make for easy access, tropical fish abound and, though the ocean pounds the adjacent seawall, the pool is always calm. However, despite being regularly flushed by the sea, the pond contains a risk of bacterial infection.

The park gates are never locked – early and late soaking is the best crowd-beating strategy. The park has picnic tables, portable toilets and a lifeguard daily. Don't leave valuables in your car.

HIDDEN DANGERS IN THE WATER

Frolicking in tide pools and hot ponds has a potential downside – bacteria, including staphylococcus. To minimize risk, go early in the morning when fewer people have entered the pools; go during high tide; and avoid Mondays and after holidays. Most important, do not enter pools if you have open cuts and shower immediately after swimming.

Isaac Kepo'okalani Hale Beach Park

This beach park, which goes by **Isaac Hale** (pronounced *ha*-lay), is a rocky locals' beach along **Pohoiki Bay**. Waters are too rough for swimming but are addictive to experienced bodyboarders and surfers, who regard Pohoiki as the island's top break, despite the omnipresence of sharp *wana*. It's a scenic spot to witness pounding waves and local talent. The boat-ramp area is still a popular fishing spot, and beyond that a well-worn path leads (past a private house) to a small natural **hot pond**.

Across the road from the beach, the camping area consists of a pristine lawn, trim as a putting green, with picnic tables, BBQs, and bathrooms with flush toilets and drinking water. A security guard checks permits (folks used to squat here). Lava boat tours leave from the camping area.

MacKenzie State Recreation Area

MacKenzie State Recreation Area PARK

This grove of ironwood trees edging sheer 40ft cliffs above a restless ocean is a moody, windswept location. During the day the quiet, secluded park makes an unforgettable picnic spot, and exploring the lava tube just back from the precipitous ledge a moment's walk from the pavilion makes a memorable post-lunch adventure.

Head into the forest facing the ledge to find the entrance (this requires a short, steep descent and a little boulder scrambling); after about 20 minutes walking on uneven lava rock you'll emerge a little way down and across the road from the park entrance.

Camping at MacKenzie is allowed, but not recommended due to the area's unsettling isolation. It was the site of violent crimes in the past – a long time ago, but the place retains an eerie vibe.

Kehena Beach & Around

If any place captures the friendly uninhibited intensity of Puna, it's this beautiful black-sand **beach** at the base of rocky cliffs, shaded by coconut and ironwood trees. All types and persuasions mix easily – hippies, Hawaiians, gays, families, teens, seniors, tourists. Many come to doff their clothes but, truly, no one cares if you don't. As the drum circle plays, old guys dance

OFF THE BEATEN TRACK

CAPE KUMUKAHI LIGHTHOUSE

Hwy 132 goes east until it meets Red Road at **Four Corners** near Kapoho. Once a small farming village, Kapoho became the victim of Pele (Hawaiian goddess of fire and volcanoes) in January 1960 when a volcanic fissure let loose a half-mile-long curtain of fiery lava in a nearby sugarcane field. The main flow of *pahoehoe* (smooth, flowing lava) ran toward the ocean, but an offshoot of *'a'a* (rough, crumbly lava) crept toward the town, burying orchid farms in its path. Two weeks later Kapoho's nearly 100 homes and businesses were buried.

When the lava approached **Cape Kumukahi**, however, it parted around the **lighthouse**, which survived. Old-timers say that the lighthouse keeper offered a meal to Pele, who appeared disguised as an old woman on the eve of the disaster, and so she spared the structure. Today, the lighthouse is just a tall piece of white-painted metal scaffolding, at the end of an unpaved 1.5-mile road from Four Corners. This is the easternmost point in the state, where you can breathe some of the freshest air in the world.

From the lighthouse, trek 10 minutes over *'a'a* to a rugged beach – too rough for swimming, but starkly memorable.

with their eyes closed while parents chase their kids in the surf and others meditate, drink, swim and hang out. For a quieter experience, come early to greet the rising sun and watch the resident dolphin pod leap into the air.

The surf is powerful, even when 'calm,' so swim with caution. Deaths occur every year, and you shouldn't venture beyond the rocky point at the southern end. Kehena is immediately south of mile marker 19. From the small parking lot a short, steep path leads down to the beach. Don't leave valuables in your car.

Festivals & Events

Puna Culinary Festival FOOD
(http://punaculinaryfestival.com; Kalani Oceanside Retreat & various farms; classes & tours $25, dinners $24) In September, feast on Puna's farm-to-fork bounty at gourmet dinners, tours, markets and cooking classes.

Sleeping & Eating

Kalani Oceanside Retreat RESORT $$
(808-965-7828; www.kalani.com; camping from $40, r $140-245, r with shared bath $99;) Immerse yourself in the Puna mindset at this rustic 120-acre compound that hums with communal energy. Daily programs include yoga, meditation, dance and alternative healing. Note that workshops/retreats by visiting teachers are separate from ongoing programs. Nonguests can enjoy facilities on a day pass ($20; 7:30am to 8pm). Weekly Ecstatic Sun-Dance (admission $15; 10:30am to 12:30pm Sunday) gatherings attract the dreadlocked and tattooed.

An outdoor dining lanai (open to nonguests) serves healthy buffet-style meals (breakfast/lunch/dinner $13/15/24). Rooms are simple, with plywood floors covered in *lauhala* mats, and the camping area is peaceful. To get here, turn inland from Hwy 137 between mile markers 17 and 18.

Ramashala RENTAL HOUSE $$
(808-965-0068; www.ramashala.com; 12-7208 Hwy 137; r $50-125, ste $150-200;) Almost directly across from Kehena Beach, this architecturally delightful retreat offers six rooms in three sizes: the smallest come with twin beds and shared bath, while the largest are mini-apartments with full kitchens. High ceilings, hardwood floors, numerous windows, tropical grounds and two yoga studios make for an elegant private retreat.

Absolute Paradise B&B B&B $$
(888-285-1540, 808-965-1828; http://absoluteparadise.tv; Kipuka St; r $99-135, ste $164;) Be treated as family at this gay-oriented, clothing-optional B&B a five-minute walk from Kehena Beach. The house and rooms, which vary in size and price, aren't extravagant, but are very comfy and clean.

Entertainment

SPACE PERFORMING ARTS
(Seaview Performing Arts Center for Education; www.hawaiispace.com; 12-247 West Pohakupele Loop; 8-11:30am Sat) Kalapana Seaview Estates, near mile marker 18, is home to the

SPACE. Frequent performances and creative classes are held here, from adult aerial ballet to circuses for the kids. Essentially, this spot serves as an unofficial community center for many Punatics. Note that the old SPACE Farmers Market is now held at Uncle Robert's Awa Bar.

Kalapana (Former Village)

For generations, Kalapana was a close-knit fishing village near **Kaimu Beach**, the island's most famous black-sand beach. When Kilauea began erupting in 1983, the lava flowed downslope west of Kalapana. But in 1990 the flow inched toward Kalapana's 100 buildings. When Star of the Sea Church was threatened, the community moved it to safety in the nick of time.

Within the year, the village and beach were destroyed. Hawaiian residents were remarkably accepting of losing their homes, commenting that 'Pele's taking back the land' or 'She gave it to us and now she's reclaiming it.'

Today Hwy 137 ends abruptly at the eastern edge of the former village. At the dead end, a makeshift **tourist stop** includes photos of the eruption and an outpost of the Hawaiian sovereignty movement. From here, you can take a short, but hot and rocky, walk across lava desert to **New Kaimu Beach** (aka Coconut Beach), where hundreds of baby coconut palms surround a black arc of sand. The water is too rough for swimming but it's a contemplative spot to stare across the ocean.

SPACE Farmers Market (Outer SPACE Ho'olaule'a; www.hawaiispace.com/farmersmarket; Hwy 130; 7am-noon Sat) is a small but varied and lively market. Browse tarot readers and tie-dyes, green smoothies, homemade soups and gluten-free breads.

In the afternoon, sidle up to **Uncle Robert's Awa Bar** (3-10pm), where you can try kava, listen to live music and rub elbows with local characters.

DON'T BE THAT GUY

You know: the one who says, 'Pele wants me to see the lava! I don't need any help!', who we all read about in a newspaper obituary section while shaking our heads. Do not attempt to trek to the lava without a guide. We can't stress it enough: people die and are seriously injured out here. There are areas where the ground can give way and others with trapped bubbles of poison gas. Instead, take a tour guide from Kalapana.

Highway 130

From Kalapana, Hwy 130 makes its way north to Pahoa and on to Kea'au.

Sights

Lava Viewing Area VIEWPOINT
(808-961-8093; 3-9pm, car entry by 8pm) At the end of Hwy 130 there's a parking lot staffed by informative personnel, plus souvenir vendors and a few portable toilets. From the lot, you can walk over rocky terrain to a public lava-viewing area, but you might see only a plume of hot steam or absolutely nothing. The flow is unpredictable, so call the hotline for current info and keep your expectations in check.

Star of the Sea Church CHURCH
(9am-4pm) This historic tiny Catholic church (built in 1929 and also known as 'Painted Church') is noted for its trompe l'oeil murals that create an illusion of depth and expansiveness. Its first priest was Father Damien, legendary for his work on Moloka'i with people suffering from leprosy. Originally in Kalapana, it's now off Hwy 130 at the 20-mile marker.

Activities

At the end of Hwy 130, there's nothing but vast fields of lava rock. Here, the main activity is lava-viewing. Whether you see glowing, red lava depends on luck and timing. If lava is flowing into the ocean, a lava-watching boat tour is possible. If the flow is remote, the only option is a strenuous hike, covering miles of rugged terrain, in pitch darkness on the way back.

Bear in mind, the entire lava flow covers private land, and trespassing is illegal (although no one is cracking down on those crossing their property). If you walk across the flow – guided or unguided – you do so at your own risk. It's prudent to join a guided tour if you decide to hike to see the flow.

★ **Ahiu Hawaii** HIKING
(808-769-9453; www.ahiuhawaii.com; tour per person $195; departures 9am & noon) When

the flow is too remote for most tours, these intrepid guides slog through muddy jungle and sharp lava rock to find it. For very strong hikers only.

Native Guide Hawaii HIKING
(808-982-7575; www.nativeguidehawaii.com; tour incl lunch per person up to $300; by appointment) For the personal touch, Native Hawaiian and cultural practitioner Warren Costa offers customized all-day tours that reveal gems you wouldn't find on your own. The per-person price drops to $150 for parties of two or more.

Poke A Stick Lava Tours HIKING
(808-987-3456; www.pokeastick.com; tour $100; 7:30am-4:30pm) When the flow is accessible from their Kalapana property, this versatile couple takes groups out. They also offer vacation rentals.

Kalapana Cultural Tours HIKING
(808-936-0456; www.kalapanaculturaltours.com; tour approximately $100) Run by a local family, this is a solid choice for evening hikes when the flow cooperates.

HAWAI'I VOLCANOES NATIONAL PARK & AROUND

If each Hawaiian island has a representative element, the Big Island, people will tell you, is defined by fire. Fire, after all, creates and destroys and, most of all, is active. For all that it can be as laid-back as its archipelagic siblings, the Big Island is an active, energetic place, where creation's drama is played out against the stunning backdrop of a micro-continent.

With this in mind, **Hawai'i Volcanoes National Park** (HAVO; 808-985-6000; www.nps.gov/havo; 7-day entry per car/bicycle $10/5) is the searing heart of the Big Island's heat. This is the land at its most raw and elemental; indeed, the entire island chain is the result of the volcanic processes on display in this region.

The elder sibling is Mauna Loa, whose recumbent bulk slopes as gently as Buddha's belly, as if the earth's largest volcano (which constitutes over half of the Big Island's land mass) were nothing more than an overgrown hill. But, at 13,677ft, its navel is a frigid alpine desert that's snow-covered in winter.

The younger sibling is Kilauea – the earth's youngest and most active volcano. Since 1983 Kilauea's East Rift Zone has been erupting almost nonstop from the Pu'u 'O'o vent (southeast of the caldera), adding nearly 500 acres of new land to the island and providing residents and visitors with a front-row seat at one of the best shows on earth. In 2008 new action erupted within Halema'uma'u Crater, located within the larger Kilauea Caldera (like a bubble within a cauldron). The lava lake here still glows molten red every night, drawing people from far and wide. In traditional Hawaiian spirituality, this is the home of the goddess Pele.

In geologic terms, Hawai'i's shield volcanoes lack the explosive gases of other volcanoes. Bomb-like explosions and geysers of lava aren't the norm: most of the time lava simply oozes and creeps till it reaches the sea, creating arcs of steamy fireworks. Naturally, whenever Pele does send up dramatic curtains of fire, people stream in from everywhere to watch.

Ka wahine 'ai honua – 'the earth-eating woman,' as Pele is known – exacts a price for this entertainment. Since 1983, this side of the island has been remade several times over. Lava blocked the coastal road to Puna in 1988, and covered the village of Kalapana in 1990. Flows then crept further west, engulfing Kamoamoa Beach in 1994, and later claiming an additional mile of road and most of Wahaula Heiau. In 2008, in addition to the Halema'uma'u eruption, a Thanksgiving Breakout vent sent lava back through Kalapana, and in 2014 and 2015 an eruption blocked the roads of Pahoa, Puna's main village. There is truly no telling how (or even if) lava will be flowing by the time you read this.

No matter what the lava is doing, there is still plenty to see. When the enormous Kuhuku Unit in Ka'u is factored in, HAVO is nearly the size of O'ahu, and contains a highly varied landscape – black-lava deserts, rainforests, grassy coastal plains, snowy summits and more. The park is the Big Island's best place for hiking and camping, with about 150 miles of trails, but you don't have to break a sweat: good roads circle the caldera and take in the main highlights.

Hawai'i Volcanoes National Park

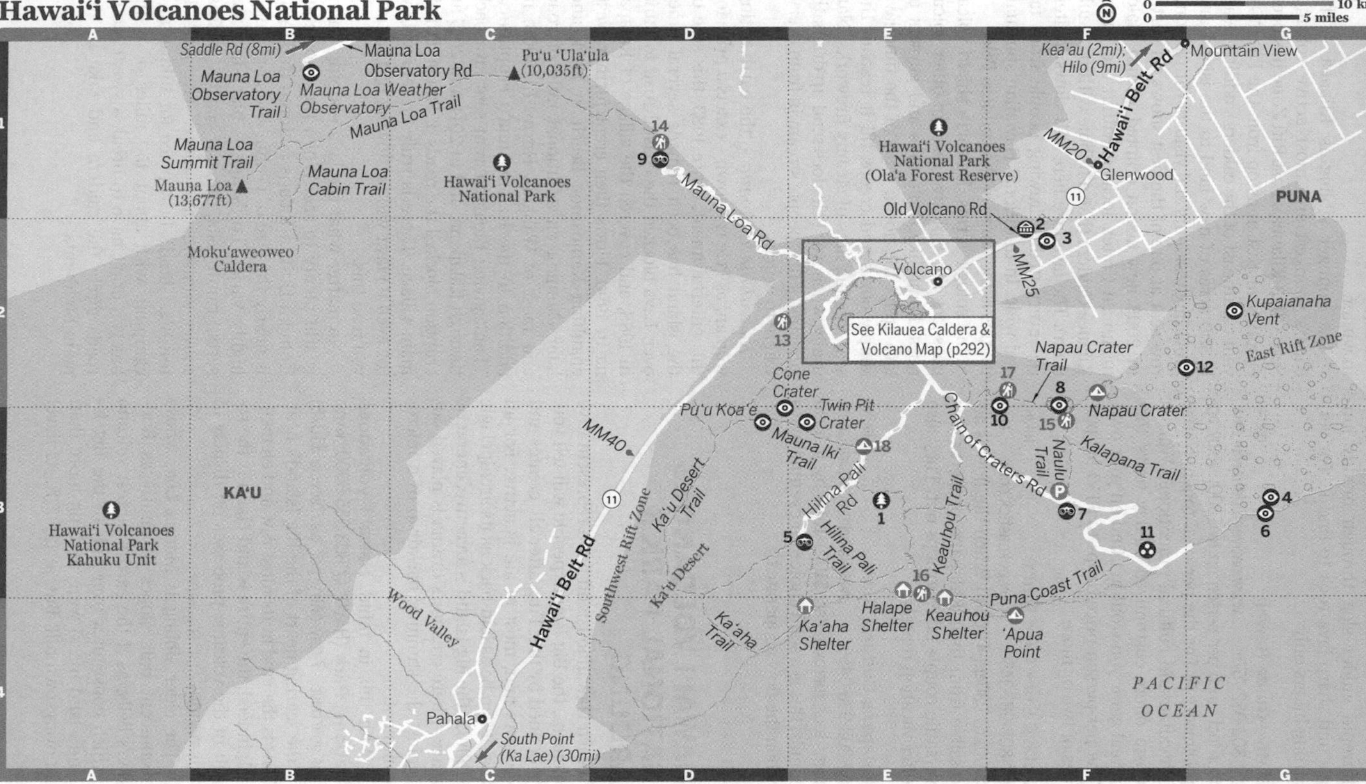

Hawai'i Volcanoes National Park

Sights

This vast and varied park can fill as many days as you give it, particularly if you enjoy hiking. Or you can drive it all in one long downhill 50-mile journey, from Jaggar Museum to the suitably named End of the Road, with only one detour (Hilina Pali Rd). Even less time? Stick to Crater Rim Dr, where many of the key sites are located. In any case, start at the Kilauea Visitor Center, just past the entrance.

Crater Rim Drive

This incredible 11-mile paved loop road starts at Kilauea Visitor Center and skirts the rim of Kilauea Caldera, passing steam vents and rifts, hiking trailheads and amazing views of the smoking crater. At the time of research, the road beyond the Jaggar Museum and Halema'uma'u Overlook to the Chain of Craters Road intersection was closed indefinitely due to eruption activity.

Kilauea Visitor Center & Museum MUSEUM
(Map p292; 808-985-6000; www.nps.gov/havo; Crater Rim Dr; 7:45am-5pm, film screenings hourly 9am-4pm;) Make this your first stop. Rangers and volunteers can advise you about volcanic activity, air quality, road closures and hiking-trail conditions. Interactive museum exhibits are small but family friendly, and will teach even science-savvy adults a lot about the park's delicate ecosystem and Hawaiian heritage. Pick up fun junior-ranger program activity books for your kids before leaving.

Geology talks are given twice daily by the outdoor signboards, where ranger-led hikes and other activities are posted. A well-stocked nonprofit bookstore inside the visitor center sells souvenirs, rain ponchos, walking sticks and flashlights. Wheelchairs are free to borrow upon request. There are restrooms and a payphone.

Volcano Art Center GALLERY
(Map p292; 808-967-7565; www.volcanoart-center.org; Crater Rim Dr; 9am-5pm) Near the visitor center, this innovative local art gallery spotlights museum-quality pottery, paintings, woodwork, sculpture, jewelry, Hawaiian quilts and more. The nonprofit shop, housed in the historic 1877 Volcano House hotel, is worth a visit just to admire its solid artisanship. Ask about upcoming art classes and cultural workshops.

Sulphur Banks PARK
(Map p292; off Crater Rim Dr) Wooden boardwalks weave through to steaming Sulphur Banks, where rocky vents and holes are stained chartreuse, yellow, orange and other weird colors by tons of sulfur-infused steam rising from deep within the earth. That rotten-egg stench is from noxious hydrogen sulfide wafting out of the vents. The easy 1232yd one-way trail connects to Crater Rim Dr near the parking lot for Steaming Bluff. The latter half of the trail is wheelchair-accessible.

Steam Vents & Steaming Bluff VIEWPOINT
(Map p292; Crater Rim Dr) Pumping impressive plumes of steam in the cool early morning, these vents make a convenient drive-up photo op. Steam is created when rainwater percolates into the earth, is heated by the hot rocks below and then released upward. For an even more evocative experience, take the short walk to the crater rim at Steaming Bluff, where the view looks like an inferno with steam pouring over the cliffs.

Kilauea Caldera & Volcano

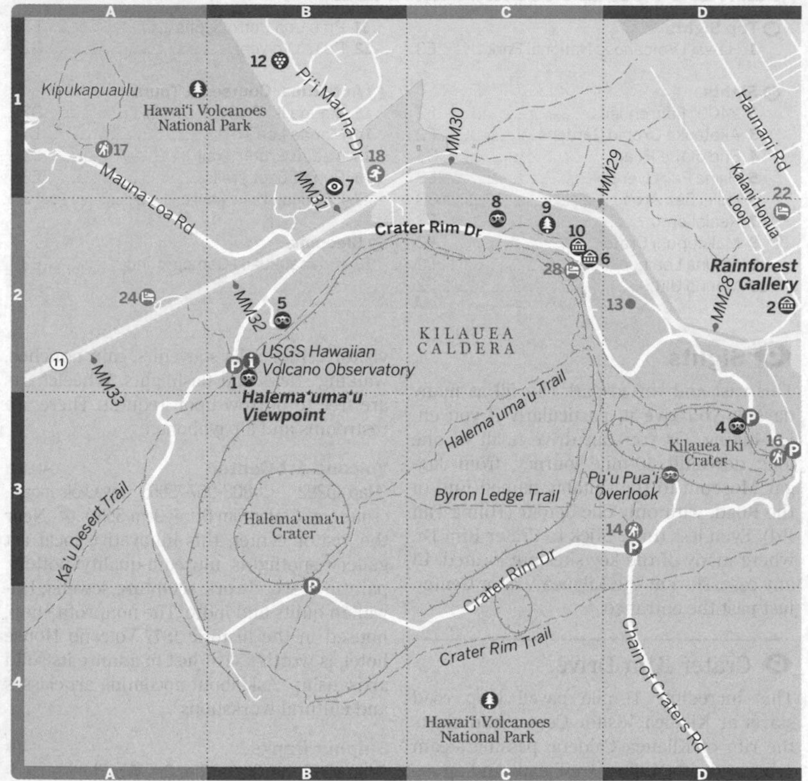

Kilauea Overlook VIEWPOINT

(Map p292; Crater Rim Dr) This parking lot and picnic area provides a pause-worthy panorama, including views of Halema'uma'u Crater and the Southwest Rift. The latter's rocky fissure is bigger and longer than it looks: it slices from the caldera summit all the way to the coast.

Jaggar Museum MUSEUM

(Map p292; ☎808-985-6051; Crater Rim Dr; ⏲8:30am-7:30pm; 👪) The big draws at this small one-room museum are the views and the real-time seismographs and tiltmeters recording earthquakes inside the park. Other exhibits introduce Hawaiian gods and goddesses and give a short history of the neighboring Hawai'i Volcano Observatory, founded by famed geologist Dr Thomas A Jaggar. Park rangers frequently give geology talks inside the museum. Wheelchairs are free to borrow.

★Halema'uma'u Viewpoint VIEWPOINT

(Map p292; Crater Rim Dr) The original Halema'uma'u Overlook off Crater Rim Dr has been closed since 2008 due to ongoing volcanic activity. The next best vantage point is the patio outside the Jaggar Museum. But don't worry, this new viewpoint is still extraordinary: there's absolutely nothing like witnessing a huge smoking volcanic crater or roiling lava lake, especially after dark when the flickering hellfire glow is mesmerizing.

Halema'uma'u is really a crater within the crater of Kilauea Caldera. About 3000ft across and almost 300ft deep, it spews a rising column of volcanic ash and gases, such as sulfur dioxide, which emerges from the great hole and billows into the sky, partly creating the vog (volcanic fog) that increasingly carpets the island (Kilauea's Pu'u 'O'o vent adds the rest).

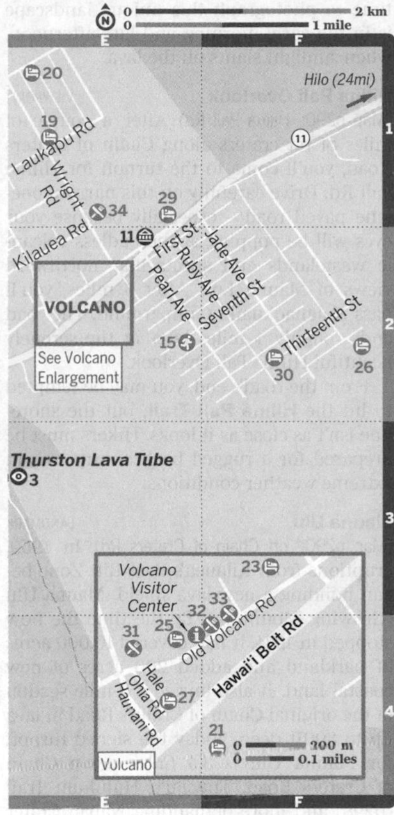

How active Kilauea Volcano will be when you visit is subject to the whims of Pele, the Hawaiian goddess of fire and volcanoes who makes her home here, so don't count on a dramatic lake of fire. It's most advantageous to show up on clear nights after sunset. For more distant views of the crater, visit Volcano House near Kilauea Visitor Center.

Kilauea Iki Overlook VIEWPOINT

(Map p292; Crater Rim Dr) When Kilauea Iki (Little Kilauea) burst open in a fiery inferno in November 1959, it turned the crater into a roiling lake of molten lava and sent 1900ft-high fountains of lava into the night sky. At its peak, the eruption gushed 2 million tons of lava an hour and the landscape glowed an eerie orange for miles.

From the overlook, you can view the steaming mile-wide crater below, used for filming the 2001 remake of *Planet of the Apes*.

Kilauea Caldera & Volcano

Top Sights

1 Halema'uma'u Viewpoint ...B2
2 Rainforest Gallery ...D2
3 Thurston Lava Tube ...E3

Sights

Jaggar Museum ...(see 1)
4 Kilauea Iki Overlook ...D3
5 Kilauea Overlook ...B2
6 Kilauea Visitor Center & Museum ...C2
7 Lava Tree Molds ...B1
8 Steam Vents & Steaming Bluff ...C2
9 Sulphur Banks ...C2
10 Volcano Art Center ...C2
11 Volcano Garden Arts ...E2
12 Volcano Winery ...B1

Activities, Courses & Tours

13 Backcountry Office ...D2
14 Devastation Trail ...D3
15 Hale Ho'ōla ...E2
16 Kilauea Iki Trail ...D3
17 Kipuka Puaulu (Bird Park) ...A1
Niaulani Rain Forest Tour ...(see 2)
18 Volcano Golf & Country Club ...B1

Sleeping

Artist Cottage ...(see 11)
19 Chalet Kilauea Collection ...E1
20 Enchanted Rainforest Cottages ...E1
21 Hale Ohia Log Cabin ...F4
22 Holo Holo In ...D2
23 Kilauea Lodge ...F3
24 Namakanipaio Cabins & Campground ...A2
25 Volcano Country Cottages ...E4
26 Volcano Guest House ...F2
27 Volcano Hideaways ...E4
28 Volcano House ...C2
29 Volcano Inn ...E1
30 Volcano Rainforest Retreat ...F2

Eating

31 Café Ohi'a ...E4
Café Ono ...(see 11)
Kilauea Lodge Restaurant ...(see 23)
32 Lava Rock Café ...F4
Rim Restaurant ...(see 28)
33 Thai Thai Restaurant ...F3
34 Volcano Farmers Market ...E1

Drinking & Nightlife

Uncle George's Lounge ...(see 28)

★ Thurston Lava Tube CAVE

(Map p292; off Crater Rim Dr;) On Kilauea's eastern side, Crater Rim Dr passes through rainforest *kipuka* thick with tree ferns and ohia trees. An often overflowing parking lot is the access point for the ever-popular Thurston Lava Tube. All the tour buses stop here and it's a favorite with kids, so plan to come early or late in the day. A 528yd loop walk starts in ohia forest filled with birdsong before heading underground through a gigantic lava tube that's artificially lit.

Lava tubes are formed when the outer crust of a lava river starts to harden but the liquid lava beneath the surface continues to flow through. After the flow drains out, the hard shell remains.

Chain of Craters Road

This is it: possibly the most scenic road trip on an island packed with really scenic road trips. Turning south off Crater Rim Dr, paved Chain of Craters Road winds almost 20 miles and 3700ft down the southern slopes of Kilauea, ending abruptly at the volcano's East Rift Zone on the coast. Allow at least 90 minutes for the round-trip drive *excluding* stops; if you're going to get out and wander and snap pictures (spoiler alert: you're going to get out and wander and snap pictures), bank on a few more hours. Drive slowly, especially in foggy or rainy conditions, and watch out for endangered nene (Hawaiian goose) along the way.

From the paved road you'll have striking vistas of the coastline far below, but for miles and miles the predominant view is of hardened lava. You can sometimes find thin filaments of volcanic glass, known as Pele's hair, in the cracks and crevices. The best time to photograph this unique landscape is in the early morning and late afternoon, when sunlight slants off the lava.

Hilina Pali Overlook VIEWPOINT

(Map p290; Hilina Pali Rd) After a couple of miles of pit craters along Chain of Craters Road, you'll come to the turnoff for Hilina Pali Rd. Drive carefully on this narrow, one-lane paved road – especially because your eyes will be popping at the endless volcanic wastelands and spectacular northward views of Mauna Loa. After 5 miles, you'll pass Kulanaokuaiki Campground. The road ends roughly 4 miles later at the serenely beautiful Hilina Pali Overlook.

From the road's end, you may be tempted to hit the **Hilina Pali Trail**, but the shoreline isn't as close as it looks. Hikers must be prepared for a rugged backcountry trek in extreme weather conditions.

Mauna Ulu LANDMARK

(Map p290; off Chain of Craters Rd) In 1969, eruptions from Kilauea's East Rift Zone began building a new lava shield, Mauna Ulu (Growing Mountain). By the time the flow stopped in 1974, it had covered 10,000 acres of parkland and added 200 acres of new coastal land. It also buried a 6-mile section of the original Chain of Craters Road in lava up to 300ft deep. Today the signed turnoff for Mauna Ulu is 3.5 miles down Chain of Craters Road. The Pu'u Huluhulu Trail (p298) and more demanding Napau Crater Trail (p296) begin here.

HALEMA'UMA'U CRATER: A LAKE OF FIRE

On March 19, 2008, Halema'uma'u Crater shattered a quarter-century of silence with a huge steam-driven explosion that scattered rocks and Pele's hair (strands of volcanic glass) over 75 acres. A series of explosions followed, widening a 300ft vent in the crater floor which, as of this writing, has continued to spew a muscular column of gas and ash. The vent bubbles molten lava, which *usually* doesn't spurt, although a 'splatter' did reach the old, now closed, Halema'uma'u Lookout in October 2014.

In 1823, missionary William Ellis first described the boiling goblet of Halema'uma'u to a wide audience, and this prodigious sight attracted travelers from all over the world. Looking in, some saw the fires of hell, others primeval creation, but none left the crater unmoved. Mark Twain wrote that he witnessed: '[C]ircles and serpents and streaks of lightning all twined and wreathed and tied together…I have seen Vesuvius since, but it was a mere toy, a child's volcano, a soup kettle, compared to this.'

Then, in 1924, the crater floor subsided rapidly, touching off a series of explosive eruptions. Boulders and mud rained for days. When it was over, the crater had doubled in size – to about 300ft deep and 3000ft wide. Lava activity ceased and the crust cooled.

Since then, Halema'uma'u has erupted 18 times; it's the most active area on the volcano's summit. All of Hawai'i is the territory of Pele, goddess of fire and volcanoes, but Halema'uma'u is her home, making it a sacred site for Hawaiians.

Kealakomo VIEWPOINT
(Map p290; Chain of Craters Rd) About halfway along Chain of Craters Road is this coastal lookout (elevation 2000ft), with picnic tables and commanding views. Below Kealakomo, the road descends in long, sweeping switchbacks, some cut deeply through lava flows.

★ **Pu'u Loa Petroglyphs** ARCHAEOLOGICAL SITE
(Map p290; off Chain of Craters Rd) The gentle, 1.5-mile round-trip **Pu'u Loa Trail** leads to one of Hawai'i's largest concentrations of ancient petroglyphs. Here Hawaiians chiseled more than 23,000 drawings into *pahoehoe* with adze tools quarried from Keanakako'i (p250). Stay on the boardwalk at all times – not all petroglyphs are obvious, and you are likely to trample and damage some if you walk over the rocks. The trailhead parking area is signed between mile markers 16 and 17.

There are abstract designs, animal and human figures, as well as thousands of dimpled depressions (or cupules) that were receptacles for *piko* (umbilical cords). Placing a baby's *piko* inside a cupule and covering it with stones was intended to bestow health and longevity on the child. Rangers occasionally lead hikes exploring petroglyphs beyond the boardwalk; inquire at Kilauea Visitor Center.

Holei Sea Arch LANDMARK
(Map p290) Constantly brutalized by unrelenting surf, the coastal section of Chain of Craters Road has sharply eroded lava-rock *pali*. Visible from near the road's end, this high rock arch is a dramatic landmark, carved out of a cliff by crashing waves.

End of the Road LANDMARK
(Map p290; Chain of Craters Rd) Quite. The road ends where the lava says it ends, having swamped this coastal section of Chain of Craters Road repeatedly between 1969 and 1996. The 'Road Closed' sign, almost entirely buried in lava, is a classic photo op. There's a simple info board and portable toilets, plus a ranger outpost – but don't count on it being staffed unless lava starts flowing again within hiking distance.

Mauna Loa Road

If you really want to escape the crowds, drive 11.5-mile Mauna Loa Rd past hiking trailheads, majestic views and *kipuka* spared by massive lava flows. The road begins off Hwy 11 near mile marker 31, just over 2 miles west of the park's main entrance. After a mile or so, before reaching Kipuka Puaulu, roadside picnic tables and pit toilets are the only facilities.

Lava Tree Molds OUTDOORS
(Map p292; off Mauna Loa Rd) Near the start of Mauna Loa Rd, there's a turnoff to some neglected lava tree molds, deep tube-like apertures formed when lava flows engulfed the rainforest and hardened around the waterlogged trees instead of burning them upon contact. As the trees disintegrated, they left deep holes where the trunks once stood.

Mauna Loa Lookout VIEWPOINT
(Map p290; Mauna Loa Rd) It's a narrow, winding and potholed drive to the very top of lonely Mauna Loa Rd, passing heavily forested *kipuka* as you come ever closer to the world's most massive active volcano. Mauna Loa has erupted more than 18 times in the past century – the last eruption, in March 1984, lasted three weeks. At the end of the road lies epic Mauna Loa Lookout (6600ft) and the start of the exceptionally challenging, multiday Mauna Loa Trail (p298).

For the best views, wander a short way down the trail for vistas that encompass smoking Kilauea far below.

Kahuku Unit

In 2003, the National Park Service (NPS) and the Nature Conservancy jointly purchased Kahuku Ranch, part of Hawai'i's largest traditional *ahupua'a*. The biggest conservation land purchase in the state's history, this deal added a whopping 116,000 acres to the national park, increasing its size by over 50%.

Today, the park's **Kahuku Unit** (☎808-985-6011; www.nps.gov/havo/planyourvisit/kahuku-hikes.htm; ⏲9am-3pm Sat & Sun) remains largely wild, undeveloped and undervisited. This is a real get-away-from-it-all destination, with no amenities besides outhouses. Four hiking trails – Pu'u o Lokuana (p299), Palm (p299), Glover (p299) and Kona (p299) – lead through green pastures and around volcanic cinder cones, lava tree molds, rainforest and lava flows. The 12-mile round-trip **scenic drive** is unpaved, but usually passable just over halfway in a standard car. Beyond the Palm Trail's upper trailhead, a high-clearance, 4WD vehicle is advised.

Double check opening hours at Kilauea Visitor Center (p291) before making the trip. The entrance is about 4 miles west of

Wai'ohinu, between mile markers 70 and 71 on Hwy 11. Ranger-guided hikes are offered some weekends (advance reservations not usually required).

Activities

Hiking

Dust off your hiking boots: rainforest oases, lava deserts, secluded beaches, crater walks and the world's most active volcano all await on the park's 150-mile trail network, rising from sea level to the summit of Mauna Loa.

Be prepared for highly changeable weather: a hot sunny stroll can turn cold and wet in an instant. Despite that chance of clamminess, this is a dry area and dehydration comes easily. No drinking water is available, except possibly at primitive campgrounds (where it must be treated before drinking); plan to pack at least 3 quarts of water per person per day. Campfires are prohibited. A compass and binoculars are handy, because misty or 'voggy' conditions and intense sunlight reflecting off lava can impede navigation.

All overnight hikes require a free permit, available in person up to one day ahead from the **Backcountry Office** (Map p292; ☎808-985-6178; Crater Rim Dr, Visitor Emergency Operations Center; ⏲8am-4pm). Ask at Kilauea Visitor Center (p291) for directions, or check the park website, which has a downloadable backcountry trip planner covering potential hazards with safety tips and advice for protecting wildlife and archaeological sites.

If you prefer to join a group, the nonprofit **Friends of Hawai'i Volcanoes National Park** (☎808-985-7373; www.fhvnp.org; annual membership adult/student/family $30/15/45) leads weekend hikes and field trips, and organizes volunteer activities such as native forest restoration.

★Kilauea Iki Trail HIKING

(Map p292) If you can only do one day hike, make it this one. Beginning at the Kilauea Iki Overlook (p293) parking lot off Crater Rim Dr, this 4-mile, clockwise loop takes you through a jaw-dropping microcosm of the park. It quickly descends 400ft through fairy-tale ohia forest, then cuts across mile-wide Kilauea Iki crater. Scattered vents lace the crater's surface with ethereal steam plumes, while the wrinkly, often iridescent lava surface is peppered with *ohelo* shrubs, ohia trees and ferns.

Hitting the trail before 8am is a good way to beat the day-tripping crowds. The faint footpath across the crater floor is marked by *ahu* (stone cairns) to aid navigation. Don't wander off-trail to explore any steaming vents, lava tubes or caves without an experienced guide.

Geology-oriented trail brochures ($2) are sold at Kilauea Visitor Center.

★Napau Crater Trail HIKING

(Map p290) This incredibly varied and satisfying all-day hike passes lava fields, immense craters and thick native forest, ending with distant views of Pu'u O'o, the source of Kilauea's ongoing eruption. It's a 14-mile round-trip backcountry hike over rugged terrain, starting from the Mauna Ulu (p294) parking area off Crater Rim Dr. Backcountry permits are required for both day and overnight hikes.

Self-registration is available at the trailhead, but it's smarter to pick up your free permit from the Backcountry Office, where you can ask about trail conditions and closures in this geologically unstable area. The trail's first 5 miles follow what was formerly Chain of Craters Road, before lava swamped it; reticulite and Pele's hair (strands of volcanic glass) are strewn over the flows.

You'll pass lava trees and **Pu'u Huluhulu** cinder cone before veering left (east). On clear days the view is magnificent, with Mauna Loa to the northwest, Mauna Kea to the north and the volatile **Pu'u 'O'o vent** (Map p290) to the east. After descending across *pahoehoe* flows, you'll reach the south rim of jaw-dropping, mile-long **Makaopuhi Crater** (Map p290).

Exiting a cool fern forest, you'll come to the rock walls of an old depository for *pulu*, the golden, silky 'hair' found at the base of *hapu'u* (tree fern) fiddlehead stems, with which ancient Hawaiians embalmed the dead. Tour helicopters whir overhead as fantastic views of the partially collapsed Pu'u 'O'o cone appear. Beyond the **Napau Crater lookout** junction is primitive Napau Campground (pit toilets, no water).

You can shave off about 4 miles round-trip if you start on the Naulu Trail from Kealakomo down Chain of Craters Road. However, you'll miss some of the grandest views and the huffing vents and cracks peppering the active rift.

OFF THE BEATEN TRACK

VIEWING THE LAVA FLOW UP CLOSE

Lucky travelers can view live lava making the 64-mile journey from the Pu'u O'o Vent to the ocean. Where the lava will be flowing when you visit and whether or not you can reach it are impossible to predict. Sometimes it's an arduous 13-mile round-trip hike from the end of Chain of Craters Road. Ask at the Kilauea Visitor Center (p291), call the park or check the NPS website (www.nps.gov/havo) for updates.

It's usually a much easier hike to the flow from the free, county-run lava-viewing area (p288) outside park boundaries at the end of Hwy 130 in Puna. If the show is really on, there will be surface flows, lava 'skylights' and flaming trees. When the flow mellows or changes course, you'll be able to see a steam plume during the day, and an unearthly red glow after dark. Bring a flashlight and water, and plan to stick around after sunset. You might be able to get even closer to the lava flow on a guided hiking tour or lava boat cruise leaving from Puna. Of course, all of this information is highly changeable – staying informed about the flow helps manage expectations (especially those of kids).

Lava entering the ocean is wondrous but extremely dangerous. The explosive clash between seawater and 2100°F lava can spray scalding water hundreds of feet into the air and throw flaming lava chunks well inland. Unstable ledges of lava crust (lava benches) sometimes collapse without warning. Several observers have been injured, some fatally, over the past decade. Always stay at least 500yd inland from the lava flow and heed all official warnings.

★Puna Coast Trails HIKING

(Map p290) You'll experience secluded snorkeling, white-sand beaches, soaring cliffs and savagely beautiful landscapes on these rugged backcountry trails. The main approaches – the Hilina Pali, Keauhou and Puna Coast Trails – are all hot, steep and strenuous, so bring lots of extra water. With an interconnecting trail network, you can design your own overnight trek.

Pick up your free overnight hiking permit (required) at the Backcountry Office, where rangers have information on current trail closures and conditions, and, just as importantly, water-catchment levels at primitive backcountry shelters and campgrounds.

With swimming and snorkeling, white sand and coconut trees, **Halape** is the most popular overnight destination, followed by **Keauhou**. Endangered hawksbill sea turtles nest all along the coast here, so travel responsibly.

The easiest route to the coast is the gently sloping **Keauhou Trail** (6.8 miles one way); the trailhead is past mile marker 6 on Chain of Craters Road. The shortest route to Ka'aha is the **Hilina Pali Trail** (3.6 miles one way), which continues to Halape (8 miles), but it begins with a brutal cliff descent; the trail starts at Hilina Pali Overlook (p294).

★Kipuka Puaulu (Bird Park) HIKING

(Map p292; 👪) If you're looking for a shady, 1.2-mile loop hike easy enough for young kids, this is it. This 100-acre sanctuary is a prime specimen of a rainforest *kipuka*, with more native tree species per acre than anywhere in Hawai'i Volcanoes National Park. The trailhead is just over a mile up Mauna Loa Rd.

This hike is best done in the early morning or at dusk, when you'll be enveloped by birdsong. You'll see honeycreepers – the *'amakihi, 'apapane* and *'i'iwi* – plus the inquisitive *'elepaio*. The trees soar, so bring binoculars and park yourself on a forest bench. You'll also pass a lava tube inhabited by a unique species of big-eyed hunting spider and lava-tree crickets.

Flora-and-fauna trail guides ($2) are sold at Kilauea Visitor Center.

Halema'uma'u Trail HIKING

At the time of writing, this was a 1.8-mile path that traversed a lovely stretch of volcanic rainforest that includes groves of swaying ohia trees. One day in the future, a full 7-mile loop may take in the entirety of Halema'uma'u Crater, but for now, the geologic situation around the crater is quite literally too explosive.

Devastation Trail HIKING

(Map p292) Only half a mile long, this paved, wheelchair-accessible trail offers fantastic views of Mauna Loa looming over the sulfur-encrusted caldera. The 1959 eruption of Kilauea Iki toasted this rainforest, leaving trees dead, stripped bare and sun-bleached white, along with tree molds and scars of ashen gray and black dirt. Now ohia trees, *ohelo* shrubs and ferns are colonizing the area anew.

The prominent cinder cone you'll see along the way is **Pu'u Pua'i** (Gushing Hill), formed during the eruption. You can start the trail from either end, at the Pu'u Puai Overlook parking lot or the Devastation Trail parking area further west, where Crater Rim Dr turns south.

Crater Rim Trail HIKING

At the time of writing, a large section of this trail, from the Jaggar Museum south to the Chain of Craters Road junction, was closed. When the volcano is calm, this 11.5-mile loop hike showcases just how dramatically the volcano has altered the landscape over time. Ask at Kilauea Visitor Center about which trail sections are currently open.

Pu'u Huluhulu Trail HIKING

(Map p290) The easy trail up the cinder cone Pu'u Huluhulu (Shaggy Hill; 6758ft), an ancient *kipuka* created more than 10,000 years ago, makes a piquant appetizer before going up Mauna Kea. The 20-minute hike climbs through secondary growth to the top of the hill, from where there are panoramic views of Mauna Kea, Mauna Loa and Hualalai.

A self-guiding trail brochure ($2), which includes perilous eyewitness accounts of the 1969–74 eruption, is sold at Kilauea Visitor Center.

HIKING & BACKPACKING SAFETY TIPS

In Hawai'i Volcanoes National Park, both lava desert and coastal trails can be extremely hot and dehydrating. Heat exhaustion is a real danger. Sunscreen, sunglasses and a wide-brimmed hat are essential. When weather conditions turn windy and wet, hypothermia is possible even if temperatures stay above freezing. Always pack extra insulating, waterproof layers.

Only fit and experienced high-altitude hikers should attempt Mauna Loa. It's critically important to acclimatize first. For 'altitude sickness' (acute mountain sickness, or AMS), descent is the only remedy.

Mauna Loa Trail HIKING

(Map p290; off Mauna Loa Rd) This trail begins at the end of Mauna Loa Rd, off Hwy 11. All in all, it's an extremely challenging (though nontechnical) 19.6-mile hike that ascends 7000ft and takes at least three days, although four is better for acclimatization and exploring the summit area. Rain, fog, snow and whiteouts can make the trail's *ahu* hard to follow.

Two simple bunk-bed cabins are available on a first-come, first-served basis at Pu'u'ula'ula (Red Hill) and closer to the summit. Potable water might be available, but must be treated; inquire at the Backcountry Office (p296) when picking up your free (required) permit. Be prepared for severe winter conditions year-round, as well as wildfires and volcanic eruptions (very unlikely).

The trail begins rising through an ohia forest then above the tree line. After 7.5 miles you'll reach **Pu'u'ula'ula (Red Hill)** at 10,035ft, offering views of Mauna Kea to the north and Maui's Haleakalā to the northwest. The next day, the 11.6-mile hike to the summit cabin (13,250ft) crosses a stark, stirring landscape of multicolored cinder fields, spatter cones and gaping lava fissures. Two miles before arriving at the cabin, turn left at the **Moku'aweoweo Caldera** trail junction for the summit cabin. The other fork leads to the 2.6-mile **Summit Trail**, for tackling the summit (13,679ft) on day three.

To summit the mountain in just one day, there's the Mauna Loa Observatory Trail (p255) off Saddle Rd.

Mauna Iki Trail HIKING

(Map p290) For solitude in a mesmerizing lava landscape, follow this trail into Ka'u Desert. Start off Hwy 11 along what's commonly called the **Footprints Trail**. Your initial commitment is low and variations allow for great route extensions.

The entire trail section from the Jaggar Museum to Hwy 11 was closed at the time of research due to ongoing volcanic activity.

Look for the Ka'u Desert Trailhead parking area between mile markers 37 and 38 on Hwy 11. Start early, because midday can be brutally hot and dry. Initially, the trail is very clear, level and partly paved, threading through sand-covered *pahoehoe* flows to reach a structure protecting ancient Hawaiian footprints preserved in hardened ash.

Beyond here the trail is marked by easy-to-follow cairns. As you gradually ascend, views expand, with Mauna Loa behind and the immense Ka'u Desert in front. Less than 2 miles from the trailhead, you'll crest **Mauna Iki** and stand likely alone in the middle of a vast lava field.

Pu'u o Lokuana Trail HIKING

Near the entrance to the park's remote Kahuku Unit, this easy 2-mile loop follows historic ranch roads through verdant pasture lands. After passing lava tree molds, the route wanders around spatter ramparts from Mauna Loa's 1868 eruption. Follow an abandoned airstrip back to the road and climb the cinder cone that gives this trail its name – you'll catch spectacular views.

Palm Trail HIKING

A lonely semi-loop inside the park's detached Kahuku Unit, this 2.6-mile ramble traverses pasture land with panoramic views over rolling hills and swishy tall grass prairie. Highlights include ranching-era relics, remnants of native forest and striking volcanic features along a fissure from Mauna Loa's 1868 eruption. Start at the lower trailhead, an 1408yd walk downhill from the upper trailhead.

Glover & Kona Trails HIKING

Deep inside the park's wilderness Kahuku Unit await these two trails. The highlight of the 3-mile Glover Trail semi-loop is standing at the edge of a huge forested pit crater, a deep bowl full of trees looking like the entrance to the underworld. Another semi-loop hike nearby, the 3.8-mile Kona Trail passes through ranch lands and borders an 1887 lava flow.

The Lower Glover trailhead is on the right about 3 miles uphill beyond the Upper Palm trailhead (high-clearance 4WD recommended). The Glover Trail loops back to the upper trailhead near the end of Kahuku Rd, from where it's a 1584yd walk back downhill on the road to the lower trailhead. Alternatively, extend your hike by cutting west to the Upper Kona trailhead and ending at the Lower Kona trailhead, a short walk from the Lower Glover trailhead.

Cycling

Volcano Bike Tours CYCLING

(☎888-934-9199, 808-934-9199; http://bikevolcano.com; tours $105-129) If you're into pedal power, try these guided cycling tours of the park on hybrid comfort bikes. Tours, which take off rain or shine and last three to five hours, follow Crater Rim Dr and Chain of Craters Road.

Festivals & Events

Check the park website or ask at Kilauea Visitor Center (p291) about free (or low-cost) special events, including **After Dark in the Park** natural-history lectures, **'Ike Hana No'eau** cultural demonstrations and craft workshops, **Nā Leo Manu** evening concerts and **Stewardship at the Summit** daytime volunteer activities.

Volcano Art Center MUSIC, DANCE

(☎808-967-7565; www.volcanoartcenter.org) Free Hawaiian craft demonstrations are given one Friday each month. The center also hosts arts, music and cultural events year-round, including popular concert, dance and theater performances here and at its Niaulani Campus in Volcano.

Hula Arts at Kilauea ARTS, CULTURE

(www.volcanoartcenter.org;) A free series of outdoor *kahiko* hula performances happens near the Volcano Art Center on one Saturday morning each month.

★**Kilauea Cultural Festival** CULTURE, ARTS

(www.nps.gov/havo/planyourvisit/events.htm;) This annual cultural festival in July has celebrated traditional Hawaiian arts, crafts, music and hula. Free entrance to the park during the festival.

Sleeping & Eating

The park's two drive-up campgrounds are relatively uncrowded outside summer. Nights can be crisp and cool, however; you should bring rainproof gear. Campsites operate on a first-come, first-served basis (and with a seven-night limit).

Kulanaokuaiki Campground CAMPGROUND

(Map p290; www.nps.gov/havo; Hilina Pali Rd; campsites free) About 5 miles down Hilina Pali Rd, this minimally developed campground has eight campsites, pit toilets and picnic tables, but no water. Campfires are prohibited.

Namakanipaio Cabins & Campground CABIN, CAMPGROUND $

(Map p292; ☎info 808-756-9625, reservations 866-536-7972; www.hawaiivolcanohouse.com; campsites/cabins $15/80) The park's busiest campground is off Hwy 11, about 3 miles west of the visitor center. Tent camping is in a small, unshaded meadow with little privacy. Facilities include restrooms, drinking water, picnic tables and BBQ grills. Book ahead for simple, A-frame wooden cabins

HAWAI'I VOLCANOES NATIONAL PARK AT NIGHT

- Lava-lake viewing from Jaggar Museum (p292)
- 'After Dark in the Park' evening programs
- Nā Leo Manu music concerts
- Walking to Thurston Lava Tube (p293) by flashlight
- Toasting your tootsies by the Volcano House fireplace
- Live music and drinks at Uncle George's Lounge

with shared communal bathrooms and hot showers; check-in at Volcano House.

★**Volcano House** LODGE **$$**
(Map p292; ☎866-536-7972, 808-756-9625; www.hawaiivolcanohouse.com; Crater Rim Dr; r $185-385;) With an unforgettable location perched on the rim of Kilauea Caldera, the reborn Volcano House has long enjoyed its unique status as the park's only hotel. Eco-conscious renovations have brought long overdue upgrades to the restaurant, bar, fireplace lobby areas, gift shops and 33 spacious, if quite plain and thin-walled, guest rooms. Reserve well in advance.

Both the refurbished **Rim Restaurant** (Map p292; www.hawaiivolcanohouse.com/dining; Crater Rim Dr, Volcano House; breakfast buffet adult/child $18/9, lunch mains $11-19, dinner mains $19-39; ⏱7-10am, 11am-2pm & 5-9pm), serving better-than-average Hawaii Regional Cuisine crafted from local ingredients, and **Uncle George's Lounge** (Map p292; Crater Rim Dr, Volcano House; mains $11-19; ⏱11am-9pm), a pint-size bar with live music and food, have enormous windows that afford absolutely staggering volcano views (as do certain guest rooms). If you can't spring for the room, just sip a beer. Slowly.

Information

The park is open 24 hours a day, except when eruption activity and volcanic gases necessitate temporary closures. For current lava flows, and trail, road and campground status, check the website or call ahead.

The park's main entrance sits at almost 4000ft, with varying elevation and climates inside the park boundaries. Chilly rain, wind, fog and vog typify the fickle weather, which can go from hot and dry to a soaking downpour in a flash. Near Kilauea Caldera, temperatures average 15°F cooler than in Kona, so bring a rain jacket and pants, just in case.

DANGERS & ANNOYANCES

Although few people have died due to violently explosive eruptions at Kilauea (the last was in 1924), come prepared if you plan to walk about or hike: bring hiking shoes or sneakers, long pants, a hat, sunscreen, water (and snacks), and a flashlight with extra batteries. For more information see the excellent safety film at the visitor's center (p291).

Lava

As for less mortal dangers, remember that hardened lava is uneven and brittle; rocks can be glass-sharp. Thin crusts can give way over unseen hollows and lava tubes; the edges of craters and rifts crumble easily. Deep earth cracks may be hidden by plants. When hiking, abrasions, deep cuts and broken limbs are all possible. So, it's even more important than most places to stay on marked trails and take park warning signs seriously. Blazing paths into unknown terrain can damage fragile areas, lead to injuries and leave tracks that encourage others to follow.

Vog & Sulfuric Fumes

Another major, constant concern is air quality. Halema'uma'u Crater and Pu'u 'O'o vent belch thousands of tons of sulfur dioxide daily. Where lava meets the sea it creates a 'steam plume,' where sulfuric and hydrochloric acid mix with airborne silica (or glass particles): all this combines to create 'vog' which, depending on the winds, can settle over the park. People with respiratory and heart conditions, pregnant women, infants and young children should take care when visiting.

Dehydration

Vast areas of the park qualify as desert, and dehydration is common. Carrying 2 quarts of water per person is the standard advice, but bring more and keep a gallon in the trunk: you'll drink it.

WEBSITES

Air Quality (www.hawaiiso2network.com) Air-quality updates in the park.

Hawai'i County Civil Defense (☎808-935-0031; www.hawaiicounty.gov/civil-defense) Information on lava flows and volcanic activity.

Trail & Road Closures (www.nps.gov/havo/closed_areas) Updated information on trail and road closings.

USGS Hawaiian Volcano Observatory (Map p292; http://hvo.wr.usgs.gov) Kilauea Volcano eruption updates, current earthquake and atmospheric conditions, and hypnotizing web cams.

Getting There & Around

The park is 30 miles (45 minutes) from Hilo and 95 miles (2¼ hours) from Kailua-Kona via Hwy 11. The turnoffs for Volcano village are a couple miles east of the main park entrance. Hwy 11 is prone to flooding, washouts and closures during rainstorms. Periods of drought may close Mauna Loa Rd and Hilina Pali Rd due to wildfire hazards.

The public **Hele-On Bus** (808-961-8744; www.heleonbus.org; adult 1 way $2) departs fives times daily (except Sunday) from Hilo, arriving at the park visitor center about 1¼ hours later, with one bus continuing to Ka'u.

In the park, cyclists are permitted only on paved Crater Rim Dr, Chain of Craters Road, Hilina Pali Rd and Mauna Loa Rd.

Volcano

POP POP 2231

The primal power of Hawai'i's volcanoes has a strong pull on the eccentric, the oddball and the countercultural. That demographic, plus an assortment of park rangers and folks drawn to mindblowing natural beauty, has settled in the village of Volcano, hidden in a forest of giant ferns, *sugi* (Japanese evergreen) and ohia trees (the main drag is an exception) on the edge of Hawai'i Volcanoes National Park. Artists and writers find inspiration in this quiet and remote setting. Their annual coming-out party is the Volcano Village Artists' Hui, an open-studios extravaganza held the three days after Thanksgiving. There's no better time to visit.

Sights

★Rainforest Gallery GALLERY

(Niaulani Campus; Map p292; 808-967-8211; www.volcanoartcenter.org; 19-4074 Old Volcano Rd; 9am-4pm) This campus of the Volcano Art Center (p291) in Hawai'i Volcanoes National Park showcases local artists working in many different media, unencumbered by the park's thematic requirements. The adjacent shop offers some remarkable handcrafted works for sale. Art workshops and performing arts events are sometimes held here too.

Volcano Garden Arts GALLERY

(Map p292; 808-985-8979; www.volcanogardenarts.com; 19-3834 Old Volcano Rd; 10am-4pm Tue-Sun) Get inspired at charming artist-owner Ira Ono's working studio in the fern forest. You'll also discover an art gallery representing dozens of island craftspeople and fine artists, rotating art installations, gardens, Café Ono (p304) and a cottage (p302) that serves as a creative crash pad. Check the online calendar for art workshops and special events.

2400° Fahrenheit GALLERY

(Map p290; 808-985-8667; www.2400f.com; 11-3200 Old Volcano Rd; 10am-4pm Thu-Mon) Drop by to watch Michael and Misato Mortara blow hot glass into mind-boggling bowls and vases. A tiny gallery displays their finished masterpieces (don't ask how much). It's off Hwy 11 at the village's eastern end.

Akatsuka Orchid Gardens GARDENS

(Map p290; 808-967-8234; www.akatsukaorchid.com; 11-3051 Volcano Rd; 9:30am-5pm) Famous for its unique hybrid orchids, this touristy showroom bursts with 200,000 blooming plants, shippable all over the world. Drop in for an olfactory awakening. It's off Hwy 11 between mile markers 22 and 23.

Volcano Winery WINERY

(Map p292; 808-967-7772; http://volcanowinery.com; 35 Pi'i Mauna Dr; tasting flight $5; 10am-5:30pm) With grapes grown in Mauna Loa's volcanic soil, this winery inland from Hwy 11 pours bottles with some *very* unusual (read: supersweet) flavor infusions: tea, macadamia nuts, honey and guava.

Activities

Hale Hoʻōla SPA

(Map p292; 808-756-2421; www.halehoola.net; 11-3913 7th St; treatments $35-160; by appointment) This is a professional Hawaiian massage center with a full menu of body and skin treatments: the perfect complement to a long day's hike. Located in the wing of a private home in the fern forest, it combines indigenous ingredients, traditional methods and holistic spirituality for therapeutic ends. A perfect place to experience authentic *lomilomi*. Appointments required.

Volcano Golf & Country Club GOLF

(Map p292; 808-967-7331; www.volcanogolfshop.com; 99-1621 Pi'i Mauna Dr; greens fees $56, club rental $20) With a lush setting beneath Mauna Loa and Mauna Kea, this straightforward 18-hole, par-72 course is a local favorite. At 4000ft above sea level, it's the most elevated course in the state.

Tours

★Niaulani Rain Forest Tour WALKING TOUR

(Map p292; 808-967-8211/22; www.volcanoartcenter.org; 19-4074 Old Volcano Rd, Volcano Art

Center; tours 9:30am Mon & 11am Sat;) **FREE** Join an hour-long, half-mile guided nature walk through Volcano's rainforest. Guides cover the ecological importance and protection of old-growth koa and ohia forests, traditional Hawaiian uses of plants, and the role of birds in the forest. Call to ask about forest restoration volunteer workdays.

Tea Hawaii & Company WALKING TOUR
(808-967-7637; http://teahawaii.com; 1hr tour $25) Get an insider's look at Hawai'i's specialty-tea cultivation at this sustainable farm and forest sanctuary, where you'll tour the tea gardens before tasting handpicked black, white and oolong brews. Reservations required.

Hawaii Photo Retreat WALKING TOUR
(808-985-7487; www.hawaiiphotoretreat.com; 1-/2-/3-day tour $345/690/1035; by reservation) Seriously aspiring photographers experience unbridled natural beauty on customized tours with professional shooters Ken and Mary Goodrich, who live in Volcano. Meals and transportation not included.

Festivals & Events

Volcano Rain Forest Runs SPORTS
(http://volcanorainforestruns.com; Aug) In August, this half-marathon, 10km run or 5km run/walk passes through Volcano village and nearby ranch lands.

Volcano Village Artists Hui ARTS
(www.volcanovillageartistshui.com) **FREE** Tour pottery, fiber-work, wood-sculpture, ceramics, woodblock-prints, glass-blowing and photography studios over a three-day weekend in late November.

Sleeping

Tranquil B&Bs and vacation-rental cottages grow around Volcano like mushrooms. Most require a two-night minimum stay, or else add a one-night surcharge or cleaning fee. For more listings, check **Vacation Rentals by Owner** (www.vrbo.com), **HomeAway** (www.homeaway.com), **Airbnb** (www.airbnb.com) and local rental agent **Volcano Gallery** (808-987-0920; www.volcanogallery.com).

Holo Holo In HOSTEL $
(Map p292; 808-967-8025, 808-967-7950; www.volcanohostel.com; 19-4036 Kalani Honua Rd; dm $24, r with private/shared bath $75/60;) Don't be put off by this hostel's exterior. Inside, the two six-bed dorms and four private rooms are sizable and cabinlike. The hostel, which has a well-equipped kitchen, is locked from 11am to 4:30pm daily, and guests must vacate. No credit cards, or shoes indoors. Book ahead. The Hele-On Bus stops two blocks away.

★ **Enchanted Rainforest Cottages** RENTAL HOUSE $$
(Map p292; 808-443-4930; http://erc-volcano.com; 19-4176 Kekoa Nui Blvd; d $85-140;) Private, well-designed and impeccably kept, these cottages are harbored in a fern forest landscaped with footpaths and koi ponds. Both the light-filled Apapane Guesthouse – with a skylit bathroom, gas stove and full kitchen – and the smaller Hikers' Retreat studio attached to the main house have private lanai, immersing you in a leafy world of bird calls.

Volcano Country Cottages RENTAL HOUSE $$
(Map p292; 808-967-7960; www.volcanocottages.com; 19-3990 Old Volcano Rd; d $105-155;) Nestled in the rainforest, each of these cozy, centrally located cottages has a full kitchen with modern appliances (except for the studio, which has no kitchen). Privacy is assured, and there's outdoor space too, including a candlelit hot tub hidden among ohia trees and ferns. Rates include self-catering breakfast fixin's.

Volcano Hideaways RENTAL HOUSE $$
(Map p292; 808-985-8959, 808-936-3382; www.volcanovillage.net; 6 Hale Ohia Rd; cottages $140-160;) On a quiet lane in Volcano town, all three of these historic cottages are spotless and expertly outfitted by energetic hosts, who provide everything from robes and a DVD library to freshly roasted coffee from the owner's farm. Depending upon which cottage you choose, perks include rain showers, whirlpool tubs, gas fireplaces, laundry rooms and kitchens.

Artist Cottage RENTAL HOUSE $$
(Map p292; 808-985-8979, 808-967-7261; www.volcanoartistcottage.com; 19-3834 Old Volcano Rd; cottage incl breakfast $129-149;) To the artists and writers reading this: make your creative retreat here. On the grounds of Volcano Garden Arts (p301), this refurbished redwood cottage full of original art has a sky-lit bedroom and bathroom with a giant walk-in shower. There's a full kitchen and a private outdoor hot tub. It's small – best for one or an intimate pair.

Chalet Kilauea Collection LODGE $$
(Map p292; ☎808-937-7786; www.volcano-hawaii.com; 19-4178 Wright Rd; r $110-225, r with shared bath $63-75, bungalows $265;) Three properties target three kinds of travelers. Volcano Hale is basic and aimed at hikers, with shared baths, a kitchen and wood-burning fireplace lounge. A bit motel-ish, Lokahi Lodge works well for families and has a garden hot tub. Romantic Chalet Kilauea evinces a cozy country-cottage atmosphere, with unique rooms and a treehouse suite. Breakfast buffet served (surcharge applies).

Volcano Inn GUESTHOUSE $$
(Map p292; ☎808-967-7773; www.volcanoinnhawaii.com; 19-3820 Old Volcano Rd; r $99-149;) Apart from aesthetic blunders (glaring signage, photos tacked to walls), this inn offers outstanding value. The main building contains immaculate rooms (corner rooms enjoy fern-forest views) and a positive community atmosphere. Family cottages come with kitchenettes and hot tubs. Rates drop for multiple-night stays. Takeout breakfasts and lunches available à la carte.

Hale Ohia Log Cabin CABIN $$
(Map p292; ☎808-735-9191; www.homeaway.com/vacation-rental/p206956; Hale Ohia Rd; q $200;) Step back in time to 'Old Hawaii' with a couple of nights at this sweet log cabin built in 1906. Century-old *sugi* pine trees grow in the yard, and notice the Hilo's Boy School carving on the cabin wall (the first headmaster built this cabin). There's a king and double bed in an upstairs loft, a modern kitchen and a wood-burning stove.

Volcano Guest House B&B $$
(Map p292; ☎866-886-5226, 808-967-7775; www.volcanoguesthouse.com; 11-3733 Ala Ohia St; r & ste $95-145, cottages $140-220, all incl breakfast;) At this eco-conscious, family-run property, heart-warming rooms, suites and cottages with kitchenettes sit among rainforest gardens, with a hot tub and laundry for guests' use. It's a value pick for families.

Lotus Garden Cottages B&B $$
(☎808-345-3062; www.volcanogetaway.com; 194245 Kekoa Nui Blvd; r incl breakfast $185-195;) Choose among three sweet cottage rooms with rainforest views. The Aloha Moon and Hula Moon suites have cedar-plank walls, gas fireplaces, rattan furnishings and tall ceilings, while the unique Lotus Suite is outfitted with Asian antiques. Directions will be provided upon booking; no walk-in guests accepted.

★**Volcano Rainforest Retreat** RENTAL HOUSE $$$
(Map p292; ☎808-985-8696; www.volcanoretreat.com; 11-3832 12th St; cottages incl breakfast $180-295;) Serenity abounds at these four individually designed cedar cottages, each artfully positioned with huge windows to take advantage of fern-forest views. Each has an outdoor hot tub or Japanese-style soaking tub. For added romance, in-room massage can be arranged in advance. Breakfast supplies provided. A winning integration of Volcano's natural beauty and modern, artistic interior design.

Kilauea Lodge B&B $$$
(Map p292; ☎808-967-7366; www.kilauealodge.com; 19-3948 Old Volcano Rd; r & cottages incl breakfast $195-205, houses $230-300;) A tastefully renovated 1930s YMCA camp, this 12-room lodge is like a small hotel. Rooms embody upscale country chic with romantic accents such as gas fireplaces, Hawaiian quilts and stained-glass windows. The honeymoon room has a wood-burning fireplace and private balcony, but even newlyweds have to share the garden hot tub. For more privacy, rent one of four off-property houses.

Eating

Despite all the tourist traffic, Volcano has only limited eating options.

Café Ohi'a CAFE $
(Map p292; 19-4005 Haunani Rd; items $3-9; usually 7am-5pm;) This humble cafe's daily fresh soups in bread bowls, giant sandwiches and baked goods (try the chocolate-pecan tart) are all perfect for devouring on a hike or at picnic tables right outside. Breakfast croissants and cinnamon rolls kick off the day right.

★**Volcano Farmers Market** MARKET $
(Map p292; http://thecoopercenter.org; 1000 Wright Rd, Cooper Community Center; 7-10am Sun;) The whole community comes out to this weekly market to buy farm-fresh produce, takeout meals, flowers, local crafts and more.

Thai Thai Restaurant THAI $$
(Map p292; ☎808-967-7969; 19-4084 Old Volcano Rd; dinner mains $15-26; noon-9pm Thu-Tue, 4-9pm Wed;) Locals claim it's the best Thai on the island, and classic curries are authentically flavored and well portioned, but they're a bit overpriced. Good thing there

are eight other Thai restaurants in town… oh, wait, there aren't. The dining-hall atmosphere can get crowded and stressed (dinner reservations recommended). Avoid tables in the kitschy gift shop or, better yet, call ahead for takeout.

Lava Rock Café DINER $$

(Map p292; ☎808-967-8526; www.volcanoslavarockcafe.com; 19-3972 Old Volcano Rd; mains breakfast & lunch $7-11, dinner $11-24; ⏰7:30am-9pm Tue-Sat, to 4pm Sun, to 5pm Mon;) This roadhouse joint is nearly always jumping, although the stick-to-your-ribs menu of huge burgers, seafood and pasta won't wow you, whenever it finally arrives at your table. For breakfast (served until 3pm), try the sweet French toast with house-made *liliko'i* butter. Local musicians often play on Wednesday and Saturday nights.

Café Ono CAFE $$

(Map p292; http://volcanogardenarts.com/cafeono.html; 19-3834 Old Volcano Rd, Volcano Garden Arts; mains $12-18; ⏰11am-3pm Tue-Sun;) At an art gallery with a lovely garden for dining, here you can lunch on organic vegetarian and vegan salads, sandwiches, soups, pasta and cakes. For what you get, it's slightly overpriced. Expect slowed-down service.

Kilauea Lodge Restaurant INTERNATIONAL $$$

(Map p292; ☎808-967-7366; www.kilauealodge.com; 19-3948 Old Volcano Rd; mains breakfast & lunch $8-14, dinner $24-39; ⏰7:30am-2pm & 5-9:30pm) Volcano's only high-end kitchen puts out a daily-changing dinner menu that oddly (and sometimes unsuccessfully) mixes European continental classics like duck l'orange and *hasenpfeffer* (braised rabbit) with fresh local seafood. Hardwood floors and a huge stone fireplace make the dinner atmosphere date-worthy. Service is outstanding; too bad the food is mostly mediocre. Make reservations.

Information

Most services are along Old Volcano Rd, including gas and a post office. Some businesses are cash only.

Volcano Visitor Center (Map p292; 19-4084 Old Volcano Rd; ⏰usually 7am-7pm) Unstaffed tourist-information kiosk with brochures aplenty. Next door is a coin laundromat, ATM and hardware store selling some camping gear.

KA'U

Ka'u, the southernmost district in Hawai'i (the island), Hawaii (the state) and the United States as a whole, has a palpable end-of-the-world feel. The black, lava-laced soil of the highlands supports lush forests which, as they descend in elevation, give way to plains of thorny brush, then windswept grasslands that smooth themselves into arid lava fields. This sparse littoral zone abuts the deep blue Pacific, itself a hazy band under an endless sky.

We'll be frank: this isn't where you go for tons of warm aloha or, at least, not the openly given sort you find in more touristed areas. Here at the under-tip, locals fiercely protect their rural, stay-away-from-it-all culture, quashing coastal resorts, lobbying for protected land, pioneering off-the-grid living, and speaking lots of pidgin. In many ways this is an island within an island, adding intrigue to any itinerary.

Pahala

POP 1356

A former sugar-plantation town now making a living growing coffee and macadamia nuts, Pahala dozes just inland from Hwy 11, south of mile marker 51. Its quiet streets are lined with unrestored early-20th-century plantation houses – just squint to imagine the past. The unhurried town center, with a gas station, bank and post office, is at the corner of Kamani and Pikake Sts.

Ka'u Coffee Mill FARM

(☎808-928-0550; www.kaucoffeemill.com; 96-2694 Wood Valley Rd; ⏰8:30am-4:30pm) This down-to-earth coffee farm roasts its own award-winning beans. Taste a variety of brews, which some connoisseurs rate as highly as Kona coffee, at the gift shop stocked with bags of beans to take home.

From Hwy 11, follow Kamani St inland, turn right onto Pikake St, then continue on Wood Valley Rd for about 1.5 miles.

Wood Valley Temple TEMPLE

(Nechung Dorje Drayang Ling; ☎808-928-8539; www.nechung.org; Wood Valley Rd; requested donation $5; ⏰usually 10am-5pm) Just outside Pahala, this century-old, colorful Tibetan Buddhist temple is wonderfully juxtaposed against a lush 25-acre retreat center where peacocks roam free. The temple's official name, which translates to 'Immutable Is-

Ka'u

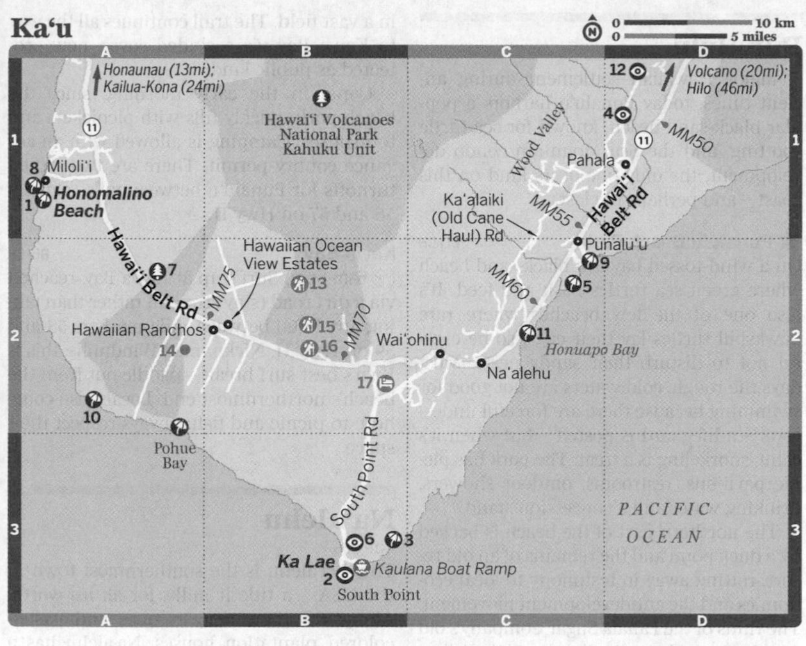

Ka'u

Top Sights

1 Honomalino Beach A1
2 Ka Lae B3

Sights

3 Green Sands Beach B3
Kalalea Heiau .... (see 2)
4 Ka'u Coffee Mill D1
5 Kawa Bay C2
6 Lua 'O Palehemo B3
7 Manuka State Wayside & Natural Area Reserve A2
8 Miloli'i Beach Park A1
9 Punalu'u Beach Park C2
10 Road to the Sea A2
11 Whittington Beach Park C2
12 Wood Valley Temple D1

Activities, Courses & Tours

13 Glover & Kona Trails B2
14 Kula Kai Caverns A2
15 Palm Trail B2
16 Pu'u o Lokuana Trail B2

Sleeping

17 Kalaekilohana B2

land of Melodious Sound,' perfectly captures the valley's wind and birdsong.

Visitors are welcome to join daily chanting and meditation sessions (8am and 6pm), or to just visit the temple and gift shop. A meditative **guesthouse** (s $65-75, d $85; wi-fi) lets you stay for a few nights.

Turn off Hwy 11 onto Kamani St, then right into Pikake St, which becomes Wood Valley Rd; the retreat is about 5 miles inland. It's a meandering drive up the valley with farms, forest and one-lane bridges crossing babbling creeks.

Ka'u Coffee Festival CULTURAL
(www.kaucoffeefest.com) In mid-May, Pahala wakes up with music, coffee, hula, coffee-farm and mill tours, farm-to-fork food, more coffee and even stargazing. No decaf allowed.

Getting There & Away

One or two daily **Hele-On Bus** (808-961-8744; www.heleonbus.org; adult one-way $2) services run between Pahala, Na'alehu and Ocean View, continuing up the Kona Coast to South Kohala's resorts. There's also one bus daily except Sunday between Hilo and Ka'u, stopping in Volcano.

Punalu'u

A major Hawaiian settlement during ancient times, today Punalu'u harbors a popular black-sand beach, known for sea-turtle spotting, and the Sea Mountain condo development, the only one of its kind on this coast – and perhaps the last.

★ Punalu'u Beach Park BEACH

On a wind-tossed bay is a black-sand beach where green sea turtles bask and feed. It's also one of the few beaches where rare hawksbill turtles lay their eggs, so be careful not to disturb their sandy nests. Most days the rough, cold waters are not good for swimming because there are forceful undertows – a lifeguard is posted – but when it's calm, snorkeling is a treat. The park has picnic pavilions, restrooms, outdoor showers, drinking water and a concession stand.

The northern part of the beach is backed by a duck pond and the remains of an old resort, rotting away in testimony to local economics and the antidevelopment movement. The ruins of the Pahala Sugar Company's old warehouse and pier lie slightly north. Follow a trail up the hill past the cement pier to find the ruins of **Kane'ele'ele Heiau**, an ancient temple where human sacrifices took place, in a vast field. The trail continues all the way to Kawa Bay via secluded coves, now protected as public land.

Come in the early morning, since the beach park quickly fills with picnickers and tour buses. Camping is allowed with an advance county permit. There are two signed turnoffs for Punalu'u between mile markers 56 and 57 on Hwy 11.

Kawa Bay BEACH

(⏲6am-6pm) Surf's up at Kawa Bay, reached via a dirt road (stay straight, rather than taking any lefts) between mile markers 58 and 59 off Hwy 11. Nicknamed Windmills, this is Ka'u's best surf break – paddle out from the beach's northernmost end. Locals also come here to picnic and fish; always respect their space.

Na'alehu

POP 866

Tiny Na'alehu is the southernmost town in the USA – a title it milks for all it's worth. Alongside giant banyan trees and pastel-colored plantation houses, Na'alehu has a lost-in-time rural feel that's underscored by the beautiful, but boarded-up, Na'alehu Theatre, a 1940s movie house along the main

PROTECTING HAWAII'S HONU

Hawai'i's gorgeous beaches and warm tropical waters attract more than tourists, they also draw *honu* (green sea turtles). Traditionally revered by Hawaiians, these magnificent creatures can be seen feeding, sunning and even nesting on Big Island beaches. Often considered an *'aumakua* (family deity or guardian spirit), *honu* appear in ancient petroglyphs.

Sea turtles were once a prized source of food, but their capture and consumption was governed by ancient Hawai'i's strict religious laws. In modern times, governance has once again become necessary to prevent further damage to the beaches turtles depend on to reproduce. Development, tourism, hunting and harvesting of their shells have all contributed to a dangerously dwindling population.

Green sea turtles now abound in Hawai'i (look for them munching on seaweed in shallow, rocky areas). Less common are hawksbill sea turtles, called *honu 'ea*. The rarest turtles in the Pacific Ocean, they're easily recognized by their plated shells, beaked noses and clawed flippers. Spot them at Punalu'u or in remote coastal areas of Hawai'i Volcanoes National Park.

Before you get too close to the turtles, consider that only a very small percentage survive hatching, live to maturity and return to reproduce. All Hawaiian sea turtles are endangered species protected by law and you must not approach them any closer than 50yd in the water and 20ft on land (this means kids, too!) – don't imitate tourists who crowd closely around, hassling these gentle reptiles.

To learn more about sea turtles and efforts to preserve critical habitat in Hawaii, visit **Save Punalu'u** (www.savepunaluu.org) and Maui-based **World Turtle Trust** (www.world-turtle-trust.org) online.

road. Na'alehu is northern Ka'u's commercial center, with a supermarket, hardware store, laundromat, library, playground, post office, gas station and ATM.

One or two daily Hele-On Bus (p305) services run between Pahala, Na'alehu and Ocean View.

Beaches

Whittington Beach Park BEACH

North of Na'alehu, this small beach park has tide pools to explore, a fishpond frequented by birds, and the ruins of an old pier. Despite its name, there's no beach and the ocean is usually too rough for swimming, but hawksbill sea turtles can often be spotted. Facilities include restrooms, outdoor showers and picnic pavilions (no drinking water). Camping on the grass requires an advance county permit, but proximity to the highway means little privacy.

The turnoff to the park is between mile markers 60 and 61 on Hwy 11.

Sleeping & Eating

Ka'u Coffee House & Guesthouse HOSTEL $

(Historic Main Street Guesthouse; 808-747-4142; www.airbnb.com/rooms/606561; 95-5587 Hwy 11; s/d $35/50;) This well-run hostel does practically everything right. An upstairs area offers clean and tidy rooms and a relaxing community space, while the downstairs cafe (11am to 6pm Monday to Friday) serves a cooked breakfast (from $5 for guests), Ka'u coffee, and veggie burgers and sandwiches at lunch. The Hele-On Bus stops out front. Helpful owner Shane is a treasure trove of information.

Punalu'u Bake Shop BAKERY $

(808-929-7343; www.bakeshophawaii.com; 95-5642 Hwy 11; items $3-8; 9am-5pm) Famous islandwide, this landmark bakery packs in locals and busloads of tourists, who come for sandwiches and a variety of flavored, doughy Portuguese sweet bread (purple taro!). Free samples aid in decision-making. Bonus: clean restrooms and a picnic area outside.

Ka'u Farmers Market MARKET $

(7am-noon Wed & Sat) A small but quality farmers market sets up in front of Ace Hardware.

Island Market SUPERMARKET $

(95-5657 Hwy 11, Na'alehu Shopping Center; 8am-7pm Mon-Sat, 9am-6pm Sun) This well-stocked grocery store is the best between Hilo and Captain Cook.

> **DON'T MISS**
>
> **KA'ALAIKI ROAD**
>
> If traveling between Pahala and Na'alehu, get off Hwy 11 and take the *mauka* (inland) backroad. Freshly paved Ka'alaiki Rd (also called Old Cane Haul Rd) is a beautiful drive that loops through green hills with distant sea views, and you'll have it to yourself. In Na'alehu turn near Punalu'u Bakeshop; in Pahala take Pikake St to Huapala St, turn right and follow it out of town.

Hana Hou Restaurant DINER $$

(808-929-9717; http://naalehurestaurant.com; 95-1148 Na'alehu Spur Rd; mains $8-16; 8am-7pm Sun-Thu, to 8pm Fri & Sat;) Here's your chance to eat 'the southernmost plate lunch in the USA' at a 1940s plantation-era family restaurant. Stuffed sandwiches and wraps are great for picnicking, and the home-baked pies, such as banana cream and macadamia nut, are a treat. The burger is great fuel after cliff jumping off Ka Lae. There's often live music on Friday and Saturday nights.

Shaka Restaurant AMERICAN $$

(808-929-7404; 95-5673 Hwy 11; mains breakfast & lunch $8-14, dinner $12-22; 7am-9pm) This sports bar dishes up big plates of grilled burgers, pizza and pub grub (the deep fryer works overtime). Cleanliness is questionable, service is hit or miss, but if you want to experience Ka'u 'nightlife,' (or at least grab a beer next to the locals), this is the scene, as it were. Live music on most Fridays.

Wai'ohinu & Around

Blink and you'll miss sleepy little Wai'ohinu ('sparkling water,' population 230) between mile markers 65 and 66 on Hwy 11. The village's claim to fame is its **Mark Twain monkeypod tree**, planted by the peripatetic author in 1866. The original tree fell during a hurricane in 1957, but hardy shoots sprang up and it's once again full-grown. There's a gas station and general store along the road through town.

Four miles west of Wai'ohinu, between mile markers 70 and 71 on Hwy 11, lies the entrance to Hawai'i Volcanoes National Park's Kahuku Unit (p295), which offers

HONU'APO BAY

For killer coastal views, pull off at the scenic lookout above Honu'apo Bay just northeast of Na'alehu. From the lookout you can see a broad sweep of cliffs and arid scrub; you could fall off the edge of the earth here. Adding to the finality of the landscape are the cast-off cement pilings of the old Whittington Pier, which was used for shipping sugar and hemp until the 1930s. At the turn of the 21st century, it had a more scientific purpose for a few years, when a fiber-optic cable measuring the rising Lo'ihi Seamount, Hawai'i's active underwater volcano, was temporarily attached to the pier's pylons.

hikers the chance to explore historic ranch lands and lava flows.

The fabulous studio apartment digs at **South Point Banyan Tree House** (☎808-929-8515, 808-217-2504; www.southpointbth.com; Hwy 11, cnr Pinao St; d $100; 📶), equipped with a full kitchen and a hot-tub deck, seem to float in the branches of a giant banyan tree. Flooded with light, the octagonal two-story house is a private escape in a jungle of mango, lychee and *'ulu* trees.

South Point (Ka Lae)

The southernmost tip of the Big Island, and of the USA, Ka Lae (literally 'the Point') feels like the end of the earth in a region where there's a lot of spots that feel like *terra finite*.

Beaches

Green Sands Beach BEACH

Also known as Papakolea Beach, this legendary beach on Mahana Bay isn't really *that* green, but it is a secluded, sandy strand. Its rare color comes from the semiprecious olivine crystals (a type of volcanic basalt) eroded from a cinder cone above, worn smooth by the relentless surf and then mixed with black sand until it sparkles in the sun. Swimming isn't advisable (even on calm days) due to strong waves, with frequent high surf and howling winds.

To get here take South Point Rd, turning left after 10 miles. Follow this road until it dead ends at a grassy parking area (don't leave any valuables in your car). At this point you can hike – it's a dusty, hot and long 2.5-mile trek each way, so bring plenty of water – or pay around $10 to $15 for a ride in one of the local 4WD 'taxis' waiting to transport tourists.

If you choose to hike, start by walking toward the water, past the Kaulana boat ramp, and follow the rutted dirt road left through the metal gate. Then just keep going, enjoying the gorgeous undulating coastline and aiming for the uplifted, striated cliff face in the distance.

Whether you arrive on foot or by 4WD, you'll have to scramble down the cliff to the beach, which has become a major tourist attraction despite the difficulty of reaching it. Go early, late or when it's overcast to beat the crowds.

Sights

★Ka Lae HISTORIC SITE

(South Point Rd) Hawai'i's southernmost tip, Ka Lae feels like the utter end of the earth. Even with rushing wind filling your ears, an odd stillness steals over this sacred spot pulsing with potent mana. But don't expect to be alone on the path, which is well worn by visitors heading south from the dirt parking area toward the light beacon. Standing near the actual point, you can imagine what it must have been like for ancient Polynesians to land here, fighting violent surf after months at sea.

The confluence of ocean currents just offshore makes this one of Hawai'i's most bountiful fishing grounds. Wooden platforms built onto the cliffs have hoists and ladders for the small boats anchored below, while local fishers brace themselves on lava-rock ledges partway down.

Daredevil locals like to cliff-jump into the surging waters, but you might want to just peek over the edge, as you're many miles from help and hospitals. Behind the platforms, inside a large *puka* (hole), spy on the ocean raging upward and receding with the waves.

There are no facilities except portable toilets.

Kalalea Heiau TEMPLE

Near the dirt parking area for Ka Lae is this ancient temple and fishing shrine where Hawaiians left offerings in hopes of currying favor for a bountiful catch. A standing rock below the heiau is pocked with canoe mooring holes. Enterprising ancient Hawaiians would tether their canoes here with ropes, then let strong currents pull them out into deeper waters to fish.

Lua 'O Palehemo HISTORIC SITE

A short distance inland from the Kalalea Heiau is Lua 'O Palehemo, marked with a tree bent nearly horizontal by battering winds. From this brackish watering hole (*lua* means 'hole' or 'pit' in Hawaiian), views take in the massive flanks of Mauna Loa and the entire coast from South Kona to Puna.

Sleeping

★ Kalaekilohana B&B $$$

(☎808-939-8052; www.kau-hawaii.com; 94-2152 South Point Rd; d incl breakfast $309;) It's a rare place that's so welcoming you feel like a special guest and part of the family. But the *ho'okipa* (hospitality) here has just that effect. Upstairs, airy rooms feature gleaming hardwood floors, luxurious beds, rainfall showers and private lanai. Downstairs, the gracious library and music room, a wide porch and complimentary drinks invite lingering. Directions given upon booking.

Ocean View & Around

Ah. Ocean View. Sounds nice, right? It depends on your point of view. For some, this is a rugged, wild land, a frontier of the Pacific. To others, it feels lonely and forlorn. See, the relatively lush Hawaiian Ocean View Estates (HOVE) that sit *mauka* and the arid Hawaiian Ranchos that are *makai*, together make up the largest subdivision in the USA, but the lots never seem to get fully settled. When you look out over the black lava desert, with its accompanying persistent lack of jobs, blankets of vog and reputation for illegal drugs, it's easy to see why. The people who stay here either have a sense of adventure, or greatly value their privacy, or both.

On either side of Hwy 11 near mile marker 76, two shopping centers – Pohue Plaza and Ocean View Town Center – make up southern Ka'u's thriving commercial center (nope, just kidding, it's quiet out here), with gas stations, supermarkets, fast food, ATMs and a laundromat. One or two daily Hele-On Bus (p305) services run between Pahala, Na'alehu and Ocean View.

LOCAL KNOWLEDGE

Name John Replogle

Occupation Conservation practitioner, Nature Conservancy

Residence Ocean View

Why Is Ka'u Such a Special Place?

Geographically, it's the largest region in Hawai'i. It also has Ka'u Forest Reserve, the largest intact native forest in the state. Most importantly, it's home to Ka Lae (p308) and Kapalaoa – Hawaii's oldest archaeological site (currently closed to the public). Ka'u was once the seat of the Hawaiian Kingdom.

What Are Some of Your Favorite Spots in Ka'u?

I like to go to South Point to fish and hang out. The road down is an excellent cycling route. Lua 'O Palehemo is a place I like to share with people, especially in the early morning when you can see all the way down the coast. I take my grandchildren there a lot.

How about Green Sands Beach?

This is a beautiful, windblown piece of coastline worth visiting. But it's also fragile – do you see how many people drive there? It's eating away the land and accelerating erosion – it's better to hike anyway to get the full experience.

Visiting Punalu'u & Seeing the Turtles Is a Perennial Favorite. Any Tips for Visitors?

There's the black-sand beach and the *honu* (green sea turtles), but the Kane'ele'ele Heiau is also there. Punalu'u (p306) was a prominent place in ancient Hawai'i. As for visitors, they should be very careful when swimming – there are major undertows at Punalu'u. While encountering *honu* is a unique experience, the turtles should never be hassled. Stand back and enjoy.

OFF THE BEATEN TRACK

ROAD TO THE SEA

This high-clearance 4WD road crosses enough loose *'a'a* (rough, jagged lava) to shake your fillings loose. Once only for adventurers, these remote black- and green-sand beaches with looming cliffs are no longer human-free pockets. You may find, after all the trouble of getting here, that the sea is too rough to swim and the beach too windy to enjoy. Even so, it's worth the trip for the scenery alone.

To find the Road to the Sea, turn *makai* (seaward) off Hwy 11 at the row of mailboxes between mile markers 79 and 80 (look for the 'Taki Mana/Ka Ulu Malu Shady Grove Farm' sign). From there you'll drive 6 miles over rudimentary, seemingly never-ending lava. To reach the first and smaller of the two beaches at the road's end takes 45 minutes or so, depending on how rough you like your ride.

To reach the second beach, drive a half-mile back inland. Skip the first left fork (it's a dead end) and take the second left fork instead. Look for arrows painted on lava rock. The road jogs inland before heading toward the shore again, and the route isn't always readily apparent. There are many places you can lose traction or get lost. Almost a mile from the fork, you'll reach a red *pu'u* (hill). Park here and walk down to the ocean. You can hike the whole distance to the second beach from the split in the road, it's about 1.5 miles each way. Bring as much water as you can carry, because it's a mercilessly hot and shadeless walk.

Sights & Activities

Manuka State Wayside & Natural Area Reserve PARK

(www.hawaiistateparks.org; Hwy 11) FREE This 13-acre reserve offers an exceptionally well-done nature trail. Proceeding through native forest on a lava rock path, and assisted by an interpretive trail guide, you'll identify 30 species of plant, and see a pit crater and lava flows. The entrance to the park and picnic area is off Hwy 11, just north of mile marker 81.

Uninviting camping in an open shelter with concrete floors is allowed with an advance state-park permit, but it's isolated, not always safe and there's no drinking water.

★ **Kula Kai Caverns** TOUR

(☎808-929-9725; www.kulakaicaverns.com; 92-8864 Lauhala Dr; tours adult/child 6-12yr from $20/10) Top-notch underground tours are led by local experts who emphasize respectful stewardship of these 'living museums.' The geologically astounding caves belong to the world's longest lava-tube system, reaching back into the bowels of Mauna Loa volcano. On the basic 30-minute tour, you'll enter a short, lighted cave section, where guides present Hawai'i's cultural and ecological history. Reservations are required.

There's also a longer 'crawling' tour ($60) and a two-hour extended twilight tour ($95). Group sizes are kept small, usually with a two- or four-person minimum. Children (minimum age six or eight years) are allowed on most tours.

Sleeping & Eating

Leilani Bed & Breakfast B&B $$

(☎808-929-7101; www.leilanibedandbreakfast.com; 92-8822 Leilani Pkwy; r incl breakfast $99-124; 📶) On a tropical lot in the Hawaiian Ocean View Estates subdivision, these three plain-Jane guest rooms are a bit tight, but the well-tended grounds, complete with a covered BBQ area, and lanai (which doubles as an art gallery) more than compensate.

Ocean View Pizzaria PIZZA $

(☎808-929-9677; Hwy 11, Ocean View Town Center; pizza slices/pies from $3/13, sandwiches $7-12; ⏰11am-7pm Sun-Thu, to 8pm Fri & Sat) The submarine sandwiches are filling, the pizza just OK. It's a place to eat or get takeout from, not linger at.

Malama Market SUPERMARKET $

(☎808-939-7560; 92-8701 Hwy 11, Pohue Plaza; ⏰6:30am-8pm) Standard groceries, hot *huli-huli* (rotisserie-cooked) chicken, teriyaki-glazed Spam *musubi* (rice balls) and basic supplies.

Ocean View Market SUPERMARKET $

(Hwy 11, Ocean View Town Center) By the post office and an auto-parts store, this community grocery store sells hot food and sandwiches. It's got a decent variety of goods and fresh produce, considering how far out this spot is.

Maui

Includes ➡

Best Places to Eat

- Lahaina Grill (p327)
- Mama's Fish House (p386)
- Star Noodle (p326)
- Geste Shrimp Truck (p355)
- Choice Health Bar (p326)

Best Snorkeling

- Honolua Bay (p344)
- 'Ahihi-Kina'u Natural Area Reserve (p381)
- Molokini Crater (p365)
- Malu'aka Beach (p380)
- Ulua Beach (p375)

Why Go?

When it comes to outdoor adventure, Maui wins best in show. Just check out that zipliner launching into a canopy of green. Or the mountain biker hurtling past eucalyptus and pine. Hikers have it darn good too, with trails winding through lava flows and bamboo forests. Along the coast, surfers barrel through waves, windboarders skim across whitecaps and snorkelers glide beside green turtles.

And we haven't even mentioned Maui's most iconic adventures – all of them flanked by once-in-a-lifetime backdrops. Along the Road to Hana, lofty waterfalls plunge into shimmering pools. A mesmerizing sunrise illuminates the cindery summit of Haleakalā. And the view from Makena Bay? Downright sublime in winter when kayakers share the sea with frolicking humpback whales.

Top-notch restaurants and lodging enhance the island's natural charms. From food trucks to white-linen dining, eateries embrace local food and its traditions. Resorts wow guests with impeccable service and prime seaside locations.

When to Go

Lahaina

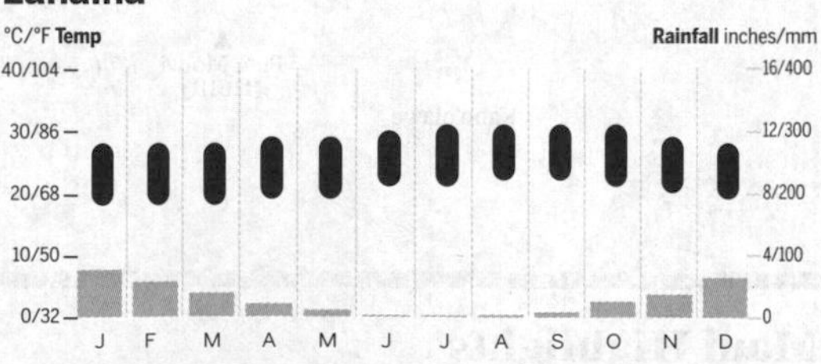

Jan–Mar Watch humpback whales frolic along the coast in winter.

Jul Maui celebrates July 4 with a big rodeo and *paniolo* (cowboy) parade.

Oct–Nov A quiet season with good weather and lower hotel prices.

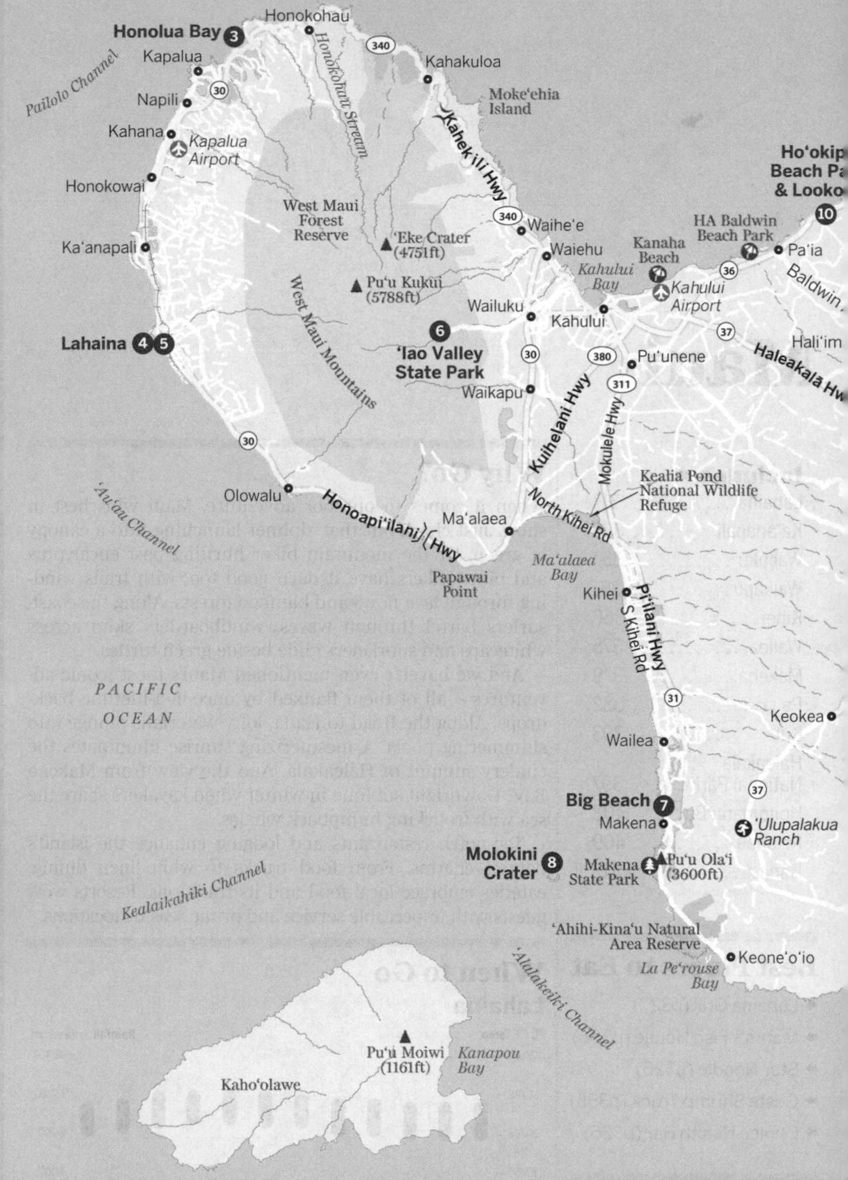

Maui Highlights

❶ Catch a soulful crater-rim sunrise at **Haleakalā National Park** (p397).

❷ Swoop across 54 one-lane bridges on the dramatic **Road to Hana** (p406).

❸ Snorkel the pristine waters of **Honolua Bay** (p344).

❹ Sail among breaching humpbacks on a **whale-watching cruise** (p324).

❺ Savor a traditional feast at **Old Lahaina Luau** (p328).

❻ Photograph Maui's favorite green landmark at **'Iao Valley State Park** (p360).

❼ Soak up the sun on golden **Big Beach** (p380) (Oneloa), Makena State Park.

❽ Dive the crystal-clear waters of **Molokini Crater** (p365).

❾ Hike through a bamboo forest on the **Pipiwai Trail** (p405).

❿ Watch windboarders zip across waves at **Ho'okipa Beach Park & Lookout** (p383).

History

Maui's early history mirrors the rest of Hawaii's, with warring chiefs, periods of peace, missionaries, whalers and sugarcane. At the time of statehood in 1959, Maui's population was a mere 35,000. In 1961 Maui retained such a backwater appearance that director Mervyn LeRoy filmed his classic *The Devil at 4 O'Clock* in Lahaina, where the dirt roads and untouristed waterfront doubled for the sleepy South Pacific isle depicted in his adventure movie. Spencer Tracy and Frank Sinatra not only shot many of their scenes at Lahaina's Pioneer Inn, but stayed there too.

Enter sugar giant Amfac in 1962, which sweetened its pot by transforming 600 acres of canefields in Ka'anapali into Hawaii's first resort destination outside Waikiki. Things really took off in 1974 with the first nonstop flight between mainland USA and Kahului. Maui soon blossomed into the darling of Hawaii's tourism industry.

Its growth spurt hasn't always been pretty. In the mid-1970s developers pounced on the beachside village of Kihei with such intensity that it became a rallying call for anti-development forces throughout Hawaii. Recent years have been spent catching up with Kihei's rampant growth, mitigating traffic and creating plans intent on sparing the rest of Maui from willy-nilly building sprees.

In the 21st century Maui has been a leader in eco-activism. Parks, forest reserves and watersheds cover nearly half of the island. Maui approved a ban on single-use plastic bags, the first Hawaiian island to do so. Thirty-four wind turbines line the slopes above wind-whipped Ma'alaea Harbor, enough to power more than 18,000 homes annually. In 2012 eight more windmills went online in east Maui. Citizens voted in 2014 to ban temporarily the planting of genetically modified organisms until environmental and health impacts could be analyzed. At press time, the ban had not been implemented due to legal challenges from large-scale GMO producers.

Climate

Maui's west coast typically boasts dry, sunny weather, with conditions improving as you continue south from occasionally rainy Kapalua to consistently sunny Kihei and Makena. Hana and the jungle-covered east Maui offer rainforests and gushing waterfalls. The Upcountry slopes, beneath Haleakalā, commonly have intermittent clouds, making for a cooler, greener respite and ideal conditions for land-based activities such as hiking and horseback riding.

National, State & County Parks

The commanding Haleakalā National Park, with its steep slopes and cloud-capped volcanic peaks, gives rise to east Maui. The park has two distinct faces. The main section encompasses Haleakalā's summit with its breathtaking crater-rim lookouts and lunarlike hiking trails. In the park's rainforested Kipahulu section you're in the midst of dramatic waterfalls, swimming holes and ancient Hawaiian archaeological sites.

Top among Maui's state parks is 'Iao Valley State Park, whose towering emerald pinnacle rises picture-perfect from the valley floor. For the ultimate stretch of unspoiled beach, head to Makena State Park. On the east side of Maui, Wai'anapanapa State Park sits on a distinctive black-sand beach.

MAUI'S TOP OUTDOOR ACTIVITIES

ACTIVITY	DESTINATION
Hiking	Haleakalā National Park, Waihe'e Ridge Trail, Kapalua Resort
Horseback Riding	Pony Express, Piiholo Ranch, Mendes Ranch, Thompson Ranch
Kayaking	Makena, Honolua-Mokule'ia Bay Marine Life Conservation District
Kitesurfing	Kite Beach (Kanaha Beach Park)
Scuba Diving	Molokini Crater, Makena Landing
Snorkeling	Honolua-Mokule'ia Bay Marine Life Conservation District, 'Ahihi-Kina'u Natural Area Reserve, Molokini Crater, Malu'aka Beach, Ulua Beach, Pu'u Keka'a (Black Rock)
Surfing	Lahaina, Ma'alaea Pipeline, Honolua Bay, Ho'okipa Beach
Windsurfing	Kanaha Beach, Ho'okipa Beach
Ziplining	Kapalua Ziplines, Piiholo Ranch Zipline, Skyline Eco-Adventures

MAUI IN...

Three Days

Splash into the scene with a dip into the sea at **Ka'anapali**, followed by a sunset cruise. On day two, stroll the historic whaling town of **Lahaina** then treat yourself to the **Old Lahaina Luau**. Still got jet lag? Good. Set the alarm early for the drive to **Haleakalā National Park** to catch a breathtaking sunrise and hike into the crater. On the way back, stop in **Pa'ia** for Maui's hippest cafe scene and to check the surf action at **Ho'okipa Beach Park**.

Six Days

For your first three days, follow the three-day itinerary. Day four is all about those gorgeous beaches. Begin by snorkeling with turtles at **Malu'aka Beach**, followed by a picnic at magnificent **Big Beach**. In the afternoon pop by **'Iao Valley State Park** to ogle central Maui's emerald gem, and then head to **Kanaha Beach** for the sailboarding scene. Day five winds past waterfalls galore on the most legendary drive in Hawaii, the wildly beautiful **Road to Hana**. It's going to be a big day – start early, and bring a bathing suit and a sense of adventure. On your last day look out for leviathans on a whale-watching cruise or savor a fine dinner on the **western coast**.

Maui's county parks center on beaches and include the windsurfing meccas of Kanaha Beach Park and Ho'okipa Beach Park. Details about county parks and beaches, including contact information and lifeguard availability, can be found on the Maui County government website: www.mauicounty.gov.

Camping

On Maui there's a clear pecking order in camping. At the top, offering the best and most unique options, are the campgrounds at Haleakalā National Park. After that, the state parks – most notably Wai'anapanapa State Park – are a better option than the county parks.

National Parks Haleakalā National Park has excellent drive-up camping at the summit area and in the seaside Kipahulu section. No fees, reservations or permits are required for drive-up camping. Haleakalā also offers free backcountry camping on the crater floor with a permit, as well as $75 cabin rentals, though the cabins are in high demand and difficult to score.

State Parks Maui has campgrounds and cabins at Wai'anapanapa State Park and Polipoli Spring State Recreation Area. Each park allows a maximum stay of five consecutive nights and requires a permit. Tent camping is $18 per night per site. Cabins cost $90. For reservations contact the **Division of State Parks** (Map p358; ☎808-984-8109; www.hawaiistateparks.org; 54 S High St, Room 101, Wailuku; ⊙8am-3:30pm Mon-Fri) in person or online.

County Parks Maui County permits camping at Kanaha Beach Park in Kahului (closed Monday and Tuesday) and at Papalaua Wayside Park south of Lahaina (closed Wednesday and Thursday). Camping is allowed for three consecutive nights and costs $5 to $8 per day ($2 to $3 for children under 18). For reservations and permits for either site, contact the **Department of Parks & Recreation – Central District** (Map p354; ☎808-270-7389; www.mauicounty.gov; 700 Halia Nakoa St, War Memorial Gymnasium, Wailuku; ⊙8am-1pm & 2:30-4pm Mon-Fri) or the **Department of Parks & Recreation – West District** (☎808-661-4685; www.mauicounty.gov; 1840 Honoapi'ilani Hwy; ⊙8am-noon Mon-Sat, 1:30-4pm Mon-Fri).

Getting There & Away

AIR

Most mainland flights to Maui involve at least one stopover, but direct flights to Maui are offered from some cities, including Los Angeles, San Diego, San Francisco, Seattle and Vancouver, BC.

Kahului International Airport (p645) All trans-Pacific flights to Maui arrive in Kahului, the island's main airport.

Kapalua Airport (www.hawaii.gov/jhm) Off Hwy 30, south of Kapalua, this regional airport has flights to other Hawaiian islands on chartered planes and small carrier Mokulele Airlines (www.mokuleleairlines.com).

Hana Airport (Map p413; ☎808-248-4861; www.hawaii.gov/hnm) **Mokulele Airlines** (☎866-260-7070; www.mokuleleairlines.com) offers three daily flights from Kahului to this small airport, cutting a two-hour drive to a 20-minute flight.

SEA

Interisland ferries connect Lahaina with its sister islands of Moloka'i and Lana'i. For information about these ferries, see Lana'i and Moloka'i.

Getting Around

To explore Maui thoroughly and reach off-the-beaten-path sights, you'll need your own wheels. Public transportation, while improving, is still limited to the main towns and tourist resorts.

The most comprehensive road atlas available is *The Ready Mapbook of Maui County*, which shows every road on the island; it's sold in bookstores.

TO/FROM THE AIRPORTS

To speed things up on arrival at Kahului Airport, make advance reservations with the two companies listed below. No reservations? **Roberts Hawaii** (☎808-954-8630; www.robertshawaii.com) shuttle service has a counter in the baggage-claim area open from 5:30am until the last flight. Reserve in advance for your return to the airport – don't wait till the last minute.

The **Maui Visitors Bureau** (Map p358; www.gohawaii.com/maui) runs a staffed Visitor Information Desk in the baggage claim area that's open 7:45am to 10pm daily. There are racks of local travel brochures beside the desk.

Shuttles

Speedi Shuttle (☎877-242-5777; www.speedishuttle.com) A big Speedi plus is that they've converted some vehicles to bio-diesel, using recycled vegetable oil for fuel – a green-friendly innovation. Fares for one person from Kahului airport cost about $50 to Lahaina, $54 to Ka'anapali, $74 to Kapalua, $33 to Kihei and $39 to Wailea. Add $5 to $10 more per additional person.

Hawaii Executive Transportation (☎808-669-2300; www.hawaiiexecutivetransportation.com; ⏲reservations 7am-11pm) Fares for one person traveling from Kahului airport cost $47 to Lahaina, $49 to Ka'anapali, $66 to Kapalua, $31 to Kihei and $34 to Wailea. Add $2 to $7 more per additional person.

BUS

Maui Bus (☎808-871-4838; www.mauicounty.gov/bus; $2 per boarding) offers the most extensive public bus system of any Hawaiian island, except O'ahu. But don't get too excited – the buses can take you between the main towns, but they don't run to prime out-of-the-way places, such as Haleakalā National Park or Hana. Buses come with front-load bike racks.

The main routes run once hourly, every day of the week.

Routes The handiest buses for visitors are the Lahaina Islander (Kahului–Lahaina), Kihei Islander (Kahului–Wailea), Wailuku Loop (Kahului–Wailuku), Haiku Islander (Kahului–Ha'iku), Kihei Villager (Ma'alaea–Kihei), Ka'anapali Islander (Lahaina–Ka'anapali) and Napili Islander (Ka'anapali–Napili) routes.

The Upcountry Islander and Haiku Islander routes stop at Kahului Airport.

Costs Fares are $2 per ride, regardless of distance. There are no transfers; if your journey requires two separate buses, you'll have to buy a new ticket when boarding the second bus. Best deal is a daily pass for just $4.

Carry-on All buses allow you to carry on only what fits under your seat or on your lap, so forget the surfboard.

Resort Shuttle The Ka'anapali Resort Shuttle runs a complimentary service between Whalers Village and the major resorts in Ka'anapali. Many resorts run a guest shuttle to nearby destinations.

CAR & MOTORCYCLE

Alamo, Avis, Budget, Dollar, Enterprise, Hertz, National and Thrifty all have operations at Kahului Airport. Check the the airport website (http://hawaii.gov/ogg) for contact information. Most of these rental companies also have branches in Ka'anapali and will pick you up at the nearby Kapalua Airport. For a green option, consider Bio-Beetle (p357) in Kahului. Also check out Kihei Rent A Car (p375).

Be sure to check for any road restrictions on your vehicle rental contract. Some car rental agencies, for instance, may prohibit driving on the Kahekili Hwy between Honokohau and Waihe'e and in the Kaupo district of the Pi'ilani Hwy.

Average driving times and distances from Kahului are as follows. Allow more time during weekday morning and afternoon rush hours, and any time the surf is up on the North Shore if you're heading that way.

DESTINATION	MILES	DURATION
Haleakalā Summit	36	1½ hours
Hana	51	2 hours
Ka'anapali	26	50 minutes
Kapalua	32	1 hour
Kihei	12	25 minutes
La Pe'rouse Bay	21	50 minutes
Lahaina	23	40 minutes
Makawao	14	30 minutes
'Ohe'o Gulch	61	2¾ hours
Pa'ia	7	15 minutes
Wailuku	3	15 minutes

TAXI

Taxis pick up passengers in front of the baggage claim. The drop charge is $3.50 and each additional mile is $3. Expect to pay about $78 for a cab to Lahaina, $87 to Ka'anapali, $33 to $55 to Kihei and $57 to Wailea.

TOURS

A number of tour bus companies operate half-day and full-day sightseeing tours on Maui, covering the most visited island destinations. Popular routes include daylong jaunts to Hana, and Haleakalā trips that take in the major Upcountry sights.

Polynesian Adventure Tours (☎808-833-3000; www.polyad.com; tours adult $102-155, child 3-11yr $61-134) Part of Gray Line Hawaii, it's a big player among Hawaiian tour companies; offers tours to Haleakalā National Park, Central Maui and 'Iao Valley State Park, and the Road to Hana. Also runs short trips from Maui to Pearl Harbor in O'ahu (from adult/child $378/357).

Roberts Hawaii (☎800-831-5541; www.robertshawaii.com; tours adult $74-106, child 4-11yr $55-63) In operation for more than 70 years, Roberts Hawaii runs three tours: Hana, 'Iao Valley and Lahaina, and Haleakalā National Park.

Valley Isle Excursions (☎808-661-8687; www.tourmaui.com; tours adult/child 2-12yr $142/104) Costs a bit more but hands-down the best Road to Hana tour. Vans take just 12 passengers and guides offer more local flavor and less canned commentary. Includes continental breakfast and, in Hana, a BBQ chicken lunch.

LAHAINA

POP 11,700

With its weathered storefronts, narrow streets and bustling harbor, plus a few chattering parrots, Maui's most historic town looks like a port-of-call for Captain Ahab. Is this the 21st century, or an 1850s whaling village? In truth, it offers an inviting mix of of both.

Tucked between the West Maui Mountains and a tranquil sea, sunny Lahaina has long been a popular convergence point. Ancient Hawaiian royals were the first to gather here, followed by missionaries, whalers and sugar plantation workers. Today it's a base for eco-minded chefs, passionate artists and dedicated surf instructors.

Near the harbor, storefronts that once housed saloons, dance halls and brothels now teem with art galleries, souvenir shops and, well, still plenty of watering holes. As for the whalers, they've been replaced by a new kind of leviathan hunter: photo-snapping whale-watchers as dedicated as Ahab in their search for a spout. Fortunately, between January and March, they don't have to look very hard.

History

In ancient times Lahaina – then known as Lele – housed a royal court for high chiefs and was the breadbasket (or, more accurately, the breadfruit basket) of West Maui. After Kamehameha the Great unified the islands, he chose the area as his base, and the capital remained here until 1845. The first Christian missionaries arrived in the 1820s and within a decade Hawaii's first stone church, missionary school and printing press were in place.

Lahaina became the dominant port for whalers, not only in Hawaii but in the entire Pacific. The whaling years reached their peak in the 1840s, with hundreds of ships pulling into port each year. When the whaling industry fizzled in the 1860s, Lahaina became all but a ghost town. In the 1870s sugarcane came to Lahaina and it remained the backbone of the economy until tourism took over in the 1960s.

Sights

Lahaina's top sights cluster around the harbor, with other sights either on Front St or withi7n a few blocks of it. This makes Lahaina an ideal town to explore on foot. The top free sight? The sunset view from Front St, at its intersection with Lahainaluna Rd.

★Old Lahaina Courthouse MUSEUM

(☎visitor center 808-667-9193; www.visitlahaina.com; 648 Wharf St; ⌚9am-5pm) FREE Tucked in the shadows of a banyan tree, Lahaina's 1859 courthouse is a repository of history and art, housing a museum, the town visitor center and two art galleries. Its location beside the harbor is no coincidence. Smuggling was so rampant during the whaling era that officials deemed this the ideal spot for customs operations, the courthouse and the jail – all neatly wrapped into a single building. It also held the governor's office, and in 1898 the US annexation of Hawaii was formally concluded here.

Gifts and a walking tour map, with details about historic sites ($2), are available at the 1st-floor visitor center (p330). On the 2nd

Lahaina

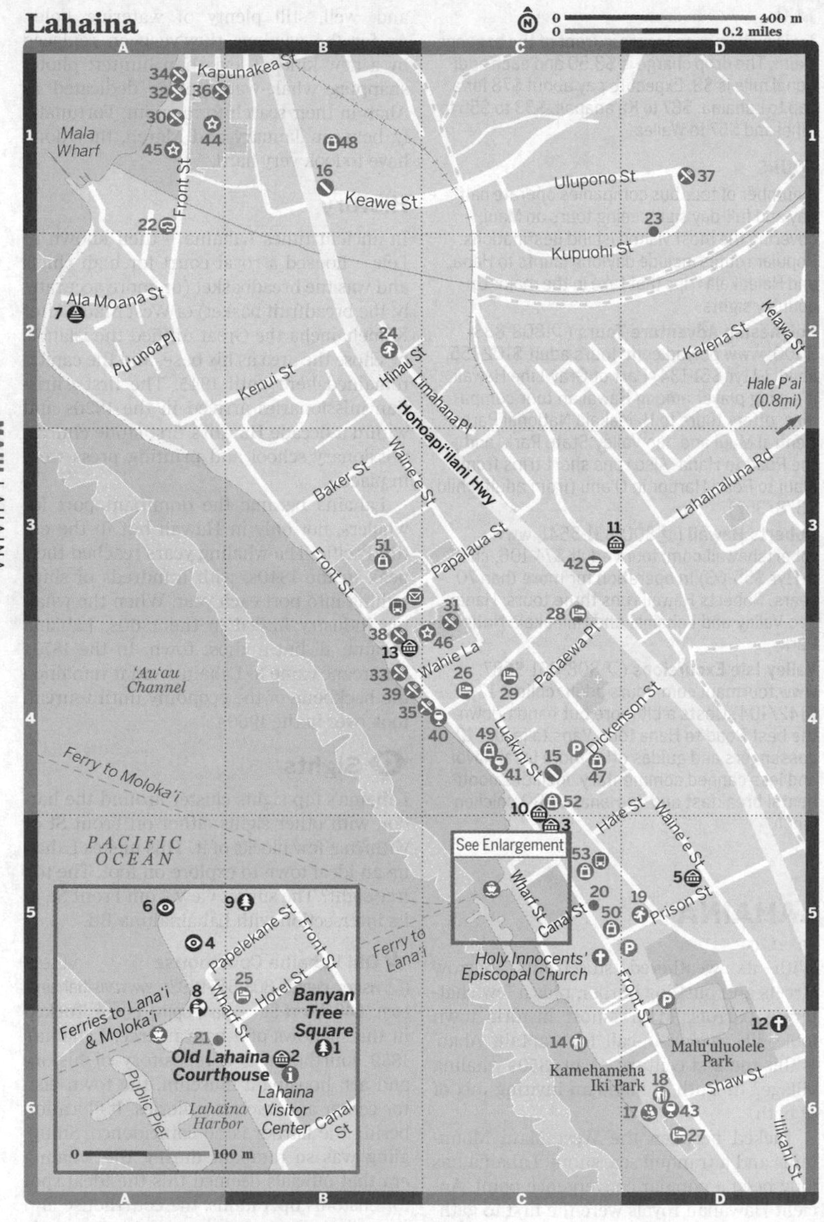

floor, the **Lahaina Heritage Museum** (www.lahainarestoration.org; ⏲9am-5pm) FREE celebrates Lahaina's prominent role in Maui's history. Exhibits spotlight ancient Hawaiian culture, 19th-century whaling, and local plantations and mills. Check out the lemon-shaped sling stones. Made from volcanic rock, they were deadly projectiles used in early Hawaiian warfare.

There are also two art galleries in the building, both operated by the Lahaina Arts Society (p329), an artists' cooperative. The

Lahaina

Top Sights
1 Banyan Tree Square B6
2 Old Lahaina Courthouse B6

Sights
3 Baldwin House C5
4 Brick Palace A5
5 Hale Pa'ahao Prison D5
6 Hauola Stone A5
Lahaina Heritage Museum .... (see 2)
7 Lahaina Jodo Mission A2
8 Lahaina Lighthouse A5
9 Library Grounds B5
10 Masters' Reading Room C4
11 Pioneer Mill Company C3
12 Waine'e (Waiola) Church D6
13 Wo Hing Museum B4

Activities, Courses & Tours
Atlantis Submarine .... (see 25)
Goofy Foot Surf School .... (see 18)
14 Lahaina Breakwall C6
15 Lahaina Divers C4
16 Maui Dive Shop B1
17 Maui Kayaks D6
18 Maui Surf Clinics D6
19 Maui Wave Riders D5
20 Pacific Whale Foundation C5
21 Reefdancer A6
22 Snorkel Bob's A1
23 Trilogy Excursions D1
24 West Maui Cycles B2

Sleeping
25 Best Western Pioneer Inn B5
26 Lahaina Inn C4
27 Lahaina Shores D6
28 Lahaina's Last Resort C3
29 Plantation Inn C4

Eating
30 Aloha Mixed Plate A1
Choice Health Bar .... (see 24)
Cool Cat Cafe .... (see 53)
31 Foodland C3
Gerard's .... (see 29)
32 Honu Seafood & Pizza A1
33 Kimo's B4
Lahaina Grill .... (see 26)
34 Mala Ocean Tavern A1
35 Ono Gelato Co C4
Pacific'O .... (see 18)
Prison Street Pizza .... (see 19)
36 Safeway A1
37 Star Noodle D1
38 Thai Chef B4
39 Ululani's Hawaiian Shave Ice B4

Drinking & Nightlife
Aloha Mixed Plate .... (see 30)
Best Western Pioneer Inn .... (see 25)
40 Cheeseburger In Paradise C4
Cool Cat Cafe .... (see 53)
41 Fleetwood's on Front St C4
42 MauiGrown Coffee C3
43 Spanky's Riptide D6

Entertainment
Burn'n Love .... (see 46)
Feast at Lele .... (see 43)
44 Lahaina Cannery Mall A1
45 Old Lahaina Luau A1
46 'Ulalena C4

Shopping
47 Hale Zen Home Decor & More C4
Lahaina Arts Society .... (see 2)
Lahaina Cannery Mall .... (see 44)
48 Lahaina Gateway B1
49 Lahaina Printsellers C4
50 Maui Hands Center C5
51 Outlets of Maui B3
52 Village Galleries C4
Village Gifts & Fine Arts .... (see 10)
53 Wharf Cinema Center C5

Banyan Tree Gallery is on the 1st floor, in the former post office. The Old Jail Gallery is in the basement, where cells that once held drunken sailors now display paintings. The entrance to the jail is outside, on the north side of the building.

★ Banyan Tree Square — PARK

(cnr Front & Hotel Sts) This leafy landmark, which marks the center of Lahaina, sprawls across an entire town square. Planted as a seedling on April 24, 1873, to commemorate the 50th anniversary of missionaries in Lahaina, the tree has become a virtual forest unto itself, with 16 major trunks and scores of horizontal branches reaching across the better part of an acre. It ranks as the largest banyan tree in Hawaii.

The songs of thousands of mynah birds keep things lively at night. Most weekends artists and craftsmen set up booths beneath the tree's shady canopy.

Baldwin House — MUSEUM

(www.lahainarestoration.org/baldwin-home-museum; 120 Dickenson St; adult/child under 13yr $7/free, incl admission to Wo Hing Museum; ⏲10am-4pm, candlelit tours 6-8:30pm Fri) Reverend Dwight Baldwin, a missionary doctor, built this house in 1834–35, making it the oldest surviving Western-style building in Lahaina. It served as both his home and the community's first medical clinic. The coral-and-rock walls are a hefty 24in thick, which keeps the house cool year-round. The exterior walls have been plastered over, but you can get a sense of how they originally appeared next door at the **Masters' Reading Room**, which now houses an art gallery.

It took the Baldwins 161 days to get here from their native Connecticut, sailing around Cape Horn at the southern tip of South America. Dr Baldwin's passport and representative period furniture are on display. A doctor's 'scale of fees' states that $50 was the price for treating a 'very great sickness', while a 'very small sickness' cost $10. It's only a cold, Doc, I swear.

Wo Hing Museum MUSEUM

(www.lahainarestoration.org/wo-hing-museum; 858 Front St; adult/child under 13yr $7/free, incl admission to Baldwin House; ⏲10am-4pm) This two-story temple, built in 1912 as a meeting hall for the benevolent society Chee Kung Tong, provided Chinese immigrants with a place to preserve their cultural identity, celebrate festivities and socialize in their native tongue. After WWII, Lahaina's ethnic Chinese population spread far and wide and the temple fell into decline. Now restored and turned into a cultural museum, it houses ceremonial instruments, a teak medicine cabinet c 1900, jade pieces dating back thousands of years and a Taoist shrine.

The tin-roof cookhouse out back holds a tiny theater showing films of Hawaii shot by Thomas Edison in 1898 and 1906, soon after he invented the motion-picture camera. These grainy black-and-white shots capture poignant images of old Hawaii, including *paniolo* (cowboys) herding cattle, cane workers in the fields and everyday street scenes.

Hale Pa'ahao Prison MUSEUM

(Stuck-in-Irons House; www.lahainarestoration.org/hale-paahao-prison; 187 Prison St; ⏲10am-4pm Mon-Fri) FREE A remnant of the whaling era, this coral stone jail was built in 1852 and looks much as it did 150 years ago. One of the tiny reconstructed cells displays a list of arrests in 1855. The top three offenses were drunkenness (330 arrests), 'furious riding' (89) and lascivious conduct (20). Other transgressions of the day included profanity, aiding deserting sailors and drinking *'awa* (kava).

Library Grounds PARK

(680 Wharf St) Three historic sites surround the Lahaina library: the foundation of Kamehameha I's 'palace,' a birthing stone and an early 1900s lighthouse. The yard itself was once a royal taro field where Kamehameha II toiled in the mud to instill in his subjects the dignity of labor.

The first Western-style building in Hawaii, the **Brick Palace** was erected by Kamehameha I around 1800 so he could keep watch on arriving ships. Despite the name, this 'palace' was a simple two-story structure built by a pair of ex-convicts from Botany Bay, Australia. All that remains is the excavated foundation, which can be found behind the library.

From this foundation, walk to the northern shoreline and look down. There lies the **Hauola Stone**, a chair-shaped rock that the ancient Hawaiians believed emitted healing powers to those who sat upon it. It sits just above the water's surface, the middle of three lava stones. In the 14th and 15th centuries royal women sat here while giving birth to the next generation of chiefs and royalty.

About 100ft to the south stands the **Lahaina Lighthouse**, the site of the first lighthouse in the Pacific. It was commissioned in 1840 to aid whaling ships pulling into the harbor. The current structure dates from 1916.

Lahaina Jodo Mission BUDDHIST TEMPLE

(www.lahainajodomission.org; 12 Ala Moana St; ⏲sunrise-sunset) FREE A 12ft-high bronze Buddha sits serenely in the courtyard at this Buddhist mission, looking across the Pacific toward its Japanese homeland. Cast in Kyoto, the Buddha is the largest of its kind outside Japan and was installed here in 1968 to celebrate the centennial of Japanese immigration to Hawaii. The grounds also hold a 90ft pagoda and a whopping 3.5-ton temple bell, which is rung 11 times each evening at 8pm. Inside the temple are priceless Buddhist paintings by Haijin Iwasaki.

Pioneer Mill Company MUSEUM

(www.lahainarestoration.org; ⏲sunrise-sunset) FREE Anchored by the hard-to-miss Pioneer Mill smokestack, this new outdoor exhibit spotlights equipment and vehicles used on the company's sugar plantation, in operation from 1860 until 1999. Train buffs will get a kick out of the two 1800s mini-locomotives, formerly used by Pioneer Mill.

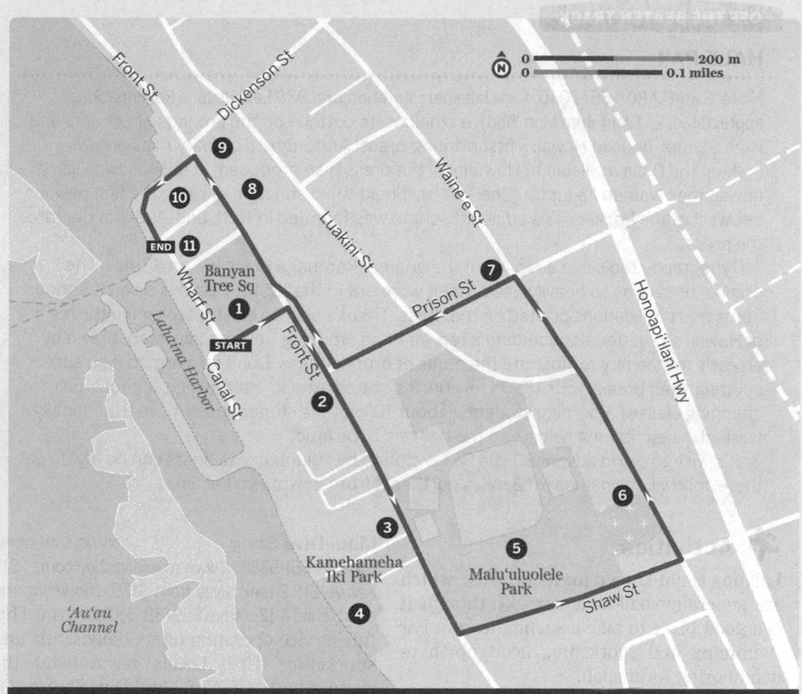

City Walk
Historic Lahalna

START BANYAN TREE SQUARE
END PIONEER INN
LENGTH 1.5 MILES; TWO TO THREE HOURS

Downtown Lahaina is packed with historic sights. Stop by the visitor center for a brochure ($2) describing Lahaina's historic sites. Interpretative markers are placed in front of many historic sites throughout downtown.

Begin at ❶ **Banyan Tree Square** (p319) with its landmark banyan and the Old Lahaina Courthouse. Turn right onto Front St to reach ❷ **Holy Innocents' Episcopal Church**, at No 561, which has a colorful interior depicting a Hawaiian Madonna, an outrigger canoe and Hawaiian farmers harvesting taro. The site was once a summer home of Hawaii's last monarch, Queen Lili'uokalani.

Just south is the foundation of ❸ **Hale Piula**, Lahaina's attempt at a royal palace. It was abandoned mid-construction because Kamehameha III preferred sleeping in a Hawaiian-style thatched house. Fronted by ❹ **Kamehameha Iki Park**, the site is now used by local woodcarvers to build traditional outrigger canoes.

Across the street is ❺ **Malu'uluolele Park**, which once held a pond-encircled island, Moku'ula, home to ancient kings and site of an ornate burial chamber. In 1918 it was landfilled to make a county park.

Pivotal figures in 19th-century Maui are buried in the cemetery beside ❻ **Waine'e Church**. Evocative inscriptions and cameos adorn many of the old tombstones. Just north, ❼ **Hale Pa'ahao Prison** (p320) held drunken whalers serving time.

Back on Front St, ❽ **Baldwin House** (p319) is the oldest surviving Western-style building on Maui. The adjacent coral-block ❾ **Masters' Reading Room** was an officers' club during whaling days.

Near the harbor, stop by the ❿ **Library Grounds** (p320) for a look at the Brick Palace and Hauola Stone. End with a drink at the ⓫ **Pioneer Inn** (p328). For many years this was Lahaina's only hotel; Jack London slept here.

OFF THE BEATEN TRACK

HALE PA'I

Hale Pa'i (808-667-7040; www.lahainarestoration.org; 980 Lahainaluna Rd; donations appreciated; 10am-4pm Mon-Wed), a small white cottage on the grounds of Lahainaluna High School, housed Hawaii's first printing press. Although its primary mission was making the Bible available to Hawaiians, the press also produced, in 1834, Hawaii's first newspaper. Named *Ka Lama* (The Torch), it held the distinction of being the first newspaper west of the Rockies. The adjacent school was founded in 1831, and students operated the press.

Typography tools and a replica of the original Rampage Press are on display. The original press was so heavily used that it wore out in the 1850s. Displays discuss various items and publications printed on the press. There's also an exhibit explaining the history of Hawaii's 12-letter alphabet and a reprint of an amusing 'Temperance Map,' drawn by an early missionary to illustrate the perils of drunkenness. Don't be alarmed if an ear-splitting siren breaks your 1850s reverie; it's not an attack, just the high school's 'bell' for changing classes. Boarding students, about 10% of the student body, have traditionally worked in neighboring fields – so the bell has to be loud.

It's wise to call in advance. Hale Pa'i is staffed by volunteers so hours can be iffy. To get there, follow Lahainaluna Rd 2 miles northeast from downtown Lahaina.

Activities

Lahaina is not known for its beaches, which are generally shallow and rocky, though it is a good place to take a surfing lesson. For swimming and snorkeling, head north to neighboring Ka'anapali.

For a sunset cruise, a whale-watching tour or other maritime adventures, head to Lahaina Harbor, located directly behind the Old Lahaina Courthouse. Here, tour operators angle for your business from small kiosks. This is also the departure point for the ferries to Lana'i and Moloka'i.

Hours for activities may vary seasonally.

Cycling

West Maui Cycles BICYCLE RENTAL
(808-661-9005; www.westmauicycles.com; 1087 Limahana Pl; per day $15-60; 9am-5pm Mon-Sat, 10am-4pm Sun) Rents quality hybrid and mountain bikes, as well as cheaper cruisers fine for kicking around town. Check the website for route maps and trail locations.

Diving & Snorkeling

Dive boats leave from Lahaina Harbor, offering dives suitable for all levels.

Lahaina Divers DIVING
(808-667-7496; www.lahainadivers.com; 143 Dickenson St; 2-tank dives from $129; 8am-8pm) Maui's first PADI five-star center offers a full range of dives, from night dives to 'discover scuba' dives for newbies. The latter go to a reef thick with green sea turtles – a great intro to diving.

Maui Dive Shop DIVING, SNORKELING
(808-661-5388; www.mauidiveshop.com; 315 Keawe St; 2-tank dives from $120, snorkeling trip adult/child 4-12yr from $69/39; 7am-9pm) This full-service operation offers daily scuba and snorkeling trips. Locals recommend the custom-built *Alii Nui*, Maui Dive Shop's 65ft catamaran available for small-group snorkeling excursions. The company has seven shops across Maui; this branch, located in Lahaina Gateway, also rents scuba and snorkel gear.

Snorkel Bob's SNORKELING
(808-661-4421; www.snorkelbob.com; 1217 Front St; 8am-5pm) If you're driving from downtown Lahaina to Ka'anapali to snorkel, stop by Snorkel Bob's for cheap snorkel-set rentals on your way. The store is on Front St north of downtown.

Kayaking

Maui Kayaks KAYAKING
(808-874-4000; www.mauikayaks.com; 505 Front St; guided tour per person $69-99; store 8am-4pm, reservations 8am-6pm) This locally owned operation takes guided kayaking and kayaking-snorkel tours along the western coast of Maui. The Lahaina Paddle trip doubles as a whale-watching excursion in season (adult $59, child five to 11 years $49). Kayak rentals are also available (two hours/day $25/35).

Stand-Up Paddle Surfing

Everybody's trying to stand-up paddle surf (SUP) these days, as a quick glance at Maui's western coast quickly confirms. The graceful sport – which requires a longboard, a paddle and some balance – is easy to learn, but Maui's currents can be tricky for newcomers. Beginners should consider a lesson.

Maui Wave Riders SUP
(☎808-875-4761; www.mauiwaveriders.com; 133 Prison St; 90min class adult/child 8-12yr from $60/50; ⏰7am-3:30pm) Limits class size to six students per instructor. Also offers surfing lessons.

Surfing

If you've never surfed before, Lahaina is a great place to learn, with first-class instructors, gentle waves and ideal conditions for beginners. The section of shoreline known as **Lahaina Breakwall**, north of Kamehameha Iki Park, is a favorite spot for novices. Surfers also take to the waters just offshore from Launiupoko Beach Park.

Several companies in Lahaina offer surfing lessons. Rates vary depending upon the number of people in the group and the length of the lesson, but for a two-hour class expect to pay about $65 in a small group or $150 for private instruction.

Maui Surf Clinics SURFING
(☎808-244-7873; www.mauisurfclinics.com; 505 Front St, Suite 201; 2hr lesson from $78; ⏰lessons 9am, noon & 2:30pm) The oldest surfing school on the island was started by Nancy Emerson, who was winning international surfing contests by the time she was 14. Now under new ownership, this welcoming school still implements her techniques. Also offers SUP lessons.

Goofy Foot Surf School SURFING
(☎808-244-9283; www.goofyfootsurfschool.com; 505 Front St, Suite 123; 2hr lesson from $65; ⏰6:30am-8pm Mon-Sat, 8am-8pm Sun; 👪) This top surf school combines fundamentals with fun. In addition to lessons, it runs daylong surf camps. Pick up a free beginner surf map with safety guidelines at the shop. SUP lessons also offered. Also rents surfboards and SUP boards to experienced surfers and paddlers – if you've taken a lesson or been on a board, you're good.

☞ Tours

Catamarans and other vessels in Lahaina Harbor cater to tourists, and outfitters staff booths along the harbor's edge. Most companies offer discounts or combo deals on their websites. Check with the company for the specifics about where to meet pre-trip.

During whale season, cocktail cruises often double as whale-watching excursions.

The ferries to Lana'i (p425) and Moloka'i (p444) dock behind the Best Western Pioneer Inn.

★**Trilogy Excursions** BOAT TOUR
(☎888-225-6284, 808-874-5649; www.sailtrilogy.com; 207 Kupuohi St; adult/teen 13-18yr/child 3-12yr from $49/37/25; ⏰8:30am-4:30pm Mon-Thu, 8:30am-4pm Fri, noon-3pm Sun) Offering snorkeling tours in Maui for more than 40 years, this family-run operation specializes in personable ecofriendly catamaran tours. The 10am trip from Lahaina to Lana'i's Hulopo'e Beach Park & Marine Preserve (adult $199, teen 13 to 18 years $149, child three to 12 years $100) includes morning cinnamon rolls and fruit, deli wraps, optional van tour of Lana'i City, snorkeling and a barbecue

MAUI SURF BEACHES & BREAKS

For action sports, head to Maui's beaches. On the north shore, near the town of Ha'iku, is the infamous big-wave spot known as Pe'ahi, or Jaws (p389). Determined pro surfers, such as Laird Hamilton, Dave Kalama and Derrick Doerner, helped put the planet's largest, most perfect wave on the international map. Jaws' waves are so high that surfers must be towed into them by wave runners.

Not into risking your life? No worries, there are plenty of other waves to ride. Maui's west side, especially around Lahaina, offers a wider variety of surf. The fun reef breaks at Lahaina Breakwall (p323) and Harbor cater to both beginner and intermediate surfers. To the south is Ma'alaea Pipeline (p364), a fickle right-hand reef break that is often considered one of the fastest waves in the world. On the island's northwest corner is majestic Honolua Bay (p344). Its right point break works best on winter swells and is considered one of the premier points not just in Hawaii, but around the world.

Gentler shorebreaks good for bodysurfing can be found around Pa'ia, Kapalua and the beaches between Kihei and Makena.

dinner. In winter there's whale-watching along the way and you can spot spinner dolphins year-round.

Pacific Whale Foundation ECOTOUR
(☎reservations 800-942-5311, store 808-667-7447; www.pacificwhale.org; 612 Front St; whale-watching adult/child 7-12yr from $26/19; ⊙reservations 6am-9pm, snorkel tours from 7am;) The Lana'i Snorkel & Dolphin Watch Cruise and several whale-watching excursions leave from Lahaina Harbor. Other trips depart from Ma'alaea Harbor to the south. The whale-watching cruises, which depart several times a day in winter, are immensely popular. In the unlikely event you don't spot whales, your next trip is free. Well-versed naturalists add context to the trips.

For the standard whale-watching trips, one child under six is free for every one adult. For a small group experience, try the Raft Whalewatch Cruise (adult $45, child seven to 12 years $33) on a smooth, anti-slamming raft.

The company also offers half-day volunteering opportunities in Maui through its Volunteering on Vacation (p400) program. Visit the website for a program calendar.

Atlantis Submarine BOAT TOUR
(☎808-661-7827; www.atlantisadventures.com; 658 Wharf St, Best Western Pioneer Inn; adult/child under 13yr $109/45; ⊙tours 9am, 10am, noon, 1pm & 2pm;) To see Maui's undersea wonders without getting wet, consider a trip on the *Atlantis*. The price is steep, but this 65-footer is a real sub, and it dives to a depth of more than 100ft. Sights include coral, tropical fish and the sunken *Carthaginian*, a sailing brig that played a leading role in the 1965 movie *Hawaii*.

Check in at the office, which is inside the Pioneer Inn building. The office opens onto Front St. One child under 13 years free with adult.

Reefdancer BOAT TOUR
(☎808-667-2133, 855-249-0087; www.mauiglass-bottomboat.com; Slip 6, Lahaina Harbor; adult/child 6-12yr 1hr $35/19, 90min $45/25; ⊙reservations 7am-10pm, departures 10am-2:15pm;) A nice option if you're traveling with young children, this glass-bottomed boat has a submerged lower deck lined with viewing windows. The views aren't as varied as on a submarine, but the underwater scenes are still eye candy and you won't feel claustrophobic.

Festivals & Events

Lahaina's top festivals draw huge crowds, with Front St closed to traffic during many of these events. For updated details on Lahaina festivities, contact the **Lahaina Town Action Committee** (☎event hotline 808-667-9194; www.visitlahaina.com) or check the events calendar on its website.

★**Whale & Ocean Arts Festival** CULTURAL
(⊙Mar) Fete the annual humpback whale migration in early March at Banyan Tree Sq during this weekend-long celebration with Hawaiian music, hula and games. Naturalists are on hand to share their knowledge about whales. Also features marine-themed art.

Banyan Tree Birthday Party FESTIVAL
(⊙Apr) Lahaina's favorite tree gets a two-day birthday party, complete with a birthday cake, music and art, plus piñatas for the *nā keiki* (children). It's held on the weekend closest to April 24. The tree celebrated its 142nd birthday in 2015.

RIGHTEOUS & ROWDY

Two diametrically opposed groups of New Englanders clashed in Lahaina in the 1820s – missionaries and whalers.

In 1823 William Richards, Lahaina's first missionary, converted Maui's native governor, Hoapili, to Christianity and persuaded him to pass laws against 'drunkenness and debauchery.' However, after months at sea, sailors weren't looking for a prayer service when they pulled into port – to them there was 'no God west of the Horn.' Missionaries and whalers almost came to battle in 1827 when Governor Hoapili arrested a whaler captain for allowing women to board his ship. The crew retaliated by shooting cannonballs at Richards' house. The captain was released, but laws forbidding liaisons between seamen and Hawaiian women remained in force.

It wasn't until Governor Hoapili's death in 1840 that laws prohibiting liquor and prostitution were no longer enforced and whalers began to flock to Lahaina. Among the sailors who roamed Lahaina's streets was Herman Melville, who later penned *Moby Dick*.

King Kamehameha Celebration PARADE
(⌚mid-Jun) Traditionally dressed Hawaiian riders on horseback, marching bands and floral floats take to Front St to honor Kamehameha the Great on this public holiday in mid-June. An awards ceremony and arts festival follow at Kamehameha Iki Park.

Fourth of July PUBLIC HOLIDAY
(⌚4 Jul) Enjoy a concert on the lawn of the public library from 5pm then watch fireworks light up the sky over the harbor at 8pm.

Plantation Days CULTURAL
(www.lahainarestoration.org/plantationdays; ⌚mid-Oct) Beneath the Pioneer Mill smokestack, this two-day festival in mid-October spotlights Lahaina's plantation past, with displays about life and work at the former sugar mill. Food booths, live music and Maui-brewed beer add to the fun.

Halloween in Lahaina CARNIVAL
(⌚Oct 31) Front St morphs into a costumed street festival on Halloween night. The party is fun for families in the late afternoon, with a *keiki* costume parade, but things get a bit wilder as the night goes on – although a strong police presence keeps rowdiness in check. Forget parking; take a shuttle or taxi to this one.

Holiday Lighting of the Banyan Tree CHRISTMAS
(⌚Dec) Lahaina lights Hawaii's biggest tree on the first weekend in December with thousands of colorful lights, accompanied by hula performances, carolers, cookie decorating and a craft show. And, of course, Santa shows up for the *nā keiki*.

Friday Town Party CARNIVAL
(www.mauifridays.com) This outdoor festival features music and food vendors. It's held the second Friday of the month from 5pm to 8pm at Campbell Park, which is across from the Pioneer Inn on Front St.

Sleeping

Despite the throngs of tourists filling its streets, Lahaina is surprisingly sparse on places to stay. West Maui's resort hotels are to the north, where the beaches are better. On the other hand, Lahaina's accommodations tend to be less crowded. Between Lahaina and Ma'alaea Harbor, to the south, are an oceanside campground and a stylish hillside B&B. Prices typically jump during the height of whale season (January and February).

Lahaina's Last Resort HOSTEL $
(☎808-661-6655; www.lahainaslastresort.com; 252 Lahainaluna Rd; dm/r $39/50; P❄📶) Decide what's important to you before booking a bed at this small hostel. On the plus side, the staff are outgoing and helpful, and the hostel – housed in a compact cottage – is just two blocks from Front St. On the flip side, the small co-ed bathroom and overall tight quarters may be a turnoff.

Rooms have mini-refrigerators and microwaves. The kitchen/common area is outside.

Plantation Inn B&B $$
(☎808-667-9225; www.theplantationinn.com; 174 Lahainaluna Rd; r/ste incl breakfast from $160/248; P❄📶🏊) Alohas are warm at this genteel oasis, which is set back from the hustle and bustle of Lahaina's waterfront. Inside the stylish lanai rooms, flat-screen TVs and DVD players blend seamlessly with plantation-era decor. Victorian-style standard rooms come with four-poster beds. The highlight? Complimentary breakfast from Gerard's (p327) served by the pool – the savory eggs Florentine are delicious.

The property is not on the beach, but guest privileges are provided at its sister property Ka'anapali Beach Hotel (p338).

Best Western Pioneer Inn HOTEL $$
(☎808-661-3636; www.bestwestern.com; 658 Wharf St; r $188; P❄@📶🏊) The historic Pioneer Inn may look salty and sea-worn at first glance, but step inside for a pleasant surprise. Rooms have undergone a stylish revamp, which includes new flat-screen TVs. The accommodating staff keep the sailing smooth. Ship figureheads and the saloon's swinging doors give a nod to Lahaina's whaling past.

To avoid the nightly chatter of mynah birds in Banyan Park and noise from Front St, ask for a courtyard room. All rooms are on the 2nd floor, with no elevators.

Lahaina Inn INN $$
(☎808-661-0577; www.lahainainn.com; 127 Lahainaluna Rd; r from $159; P📶) Small, spare and a bit worn out – yep, the rooms at the Lahaina Inn sound akin to an orphan in a Dickens novel. But if budget and a central location are your primary goals, this 12-room

inn near Front St is a solid choice. All rooms have a lanai if you need more space. Reception is not staffed overnight. Per day parking is $15. Wi-fi is $10 per day.

Gourmands take note: the inn is perched above the highly recommended Lahaina Grill (p327).

Lahaina Shores CONDO **$$$**
(808-661-4835, 866-934-9176; www.lahainashores.com; 475 Front St; r from $225;) This seven-story property, the only oceanfront condo complex in central Lahaina, operates hotel-style with a front desk and full services. All the units are roomy, and even the studios have a full kitchen and lanai. Remodeled Premier rooms shine with a breezy island style. The adjacent beach is good for beginner surfers, and the neighboring shopping village offers dining, entertainment and surf lessons.

Parking is $8 per day. Guest laundry available.

Eating

Lahaina has the finest dining scene on Maui and a range of choices. But remember, fine food draws hungry hordes. Many folks staying in Ka'anapali pour into Lahaina at dinnertime and traffic jams up. Allow extra time.

Need to stock up? **Foodland** (808-661-0975; www.foodland.com; 878 Front St, Old Lahaina Center; 6am-midnight) and **Safeway** (808-667-4392; www.safeway.com; 1221 Honoapi'ilani Hwy, Lahaina Cannery Mall; 24hr) supermarkets have everything you need for self-catering, as well as good delis. For discounts, you can use your phone number in place of a customer card in Foodland, and Safeway accepts customer club cards from the mainland.

★ **Choice Health Bar** HEALTH FOOD **$**
(808-661-7711; www.choicehealthbar.com; 1087 Limahana Pl; mains $8-16; 8am-4pm Mon-Sat;) This breezy box of healthy deliciousness whips up addictive organic fare. The chilly, fruit-stuffed acai bowls, loaded with berries, greens and granola, are invigorating. The Buddha Bowl, one of our favorite lunch dishes on Maui, is a triple-layered nirvana of grains topped by soup then a salad – trust us, it works. Smoothies, juices and health shots are perfect for travelers on the go.

Aloha Mixed Plate HAWAII REGIONAL CUISINE **$**
(808-661-3322; www.alohamixedplate.com; 1285 Front St; breakfast $8-12, lunch & dinner $6-17; 8am-10pm) Aloha Mixed Plate is the Hawaii you came to find: friendly, open-air and beside the beach. The food's first-rate, the prices affordably local. For a thoroughly Hawaiian experience, order the Ali'i Plate, packed with *laulau, kalua* pig, *lomilomi* salmon, poi and *haupia* – and, of course, macaroni salad and white rice.

The restaurant now serves breakfast, which stays Hawaiian with dishes such as *loco moco* and and *kalua* pig omelets.

★ **Star Noodle** ASIAN **$$**
(808-667-5400; www.starnoodle.com; 286 Kupuohi St; shared plates $3-30, mains $7-15; 10:30am-10pm) This hillside hot spot is constantly busy – and rightfully so. Inside this sleek noodle shop, grazers can nibble on an eclectic array of Asian-fusion share plates. Those seeking heartier fare can dive into garlic noodles, *kim chee ramen* and a local saimin (local-style noodle soup; Spam included). A central communal table and the chatty bar keep the vibe lively.

Kimo's HAWAII REGIONAL CUISINE **$$**
(808-661-4811; www.kimosmaui.com; 845 Front St; mains lunch $12-18, dinner $24-34; 11am-10pm;

SWEET TREATS IN DOWNTOWN LAHAINA

The best way to enjoy a stroll on Front St? With a colorful shave ice or a silky gelato, of course. If you'd prefer to savor your dessert indoors, we recommend the hula pie at Kimo's (p326) or a slice of triple berry pie at Lahaina Grill (p327).

Ululani's Hawaiian Shave Ice (www.ululanisshaveice.com; 819 Front St; small $5; 12:30-10pm) For over-the-top (literally) shave ice, amble up to the counter at Ululani's Hawaiian Shave Ice and take your pick of tropical flavors. A second location has opened one block south at 790 Front St (open 10:30am to 9pm).

Ono Gelato Co (808-495-0203; www.onogelatocompany.com; 815 Front St; small $5; 8am-10pm) At Ono Gelato Co there's always a crowd gazing at the sinful array of smooth gelatos.

(👪) This is our favorite oceanside patio on Front St. A locally beloved standby, Hawaiian-style Kimo's keeps everyone happy with reliably good food, a superb water view and a family-friendly setting. Try one of the fresh fish dishes and the towering hula pie. At lunch, if you're seeking lighter fare, order the delicious Caesar salad. Mai tais are served in glass totems.

Cool Cat Cafe DINER **$$**
(☎808-667-0908; www.coolcatcafe.com; 658 Front St, Wharf Cinema Center; mains $9-27; ⏰10:30am-10:30pm; 👪) It's a hunka-hunka burger love at Cool Cat Cafe, a lively doo-wop diner where most of the burgers, sandwiches and salads are named for 1950s icons, honoring the likes of Marilyn Monroe, Chubby Checker and, of course, Elvis Presley. The 6½oz burgers, which are made with 100% Angus beef, consistently rank as Maui's best. The view overlooking Banyan Tree Sq isn't bad either.

Honu Seafood & Pizza SEAFOOD, PIZZA **$$**
(☎808-667-9390; www.honumaui.com; 1295 Front St; mains lunch $14-33, dinner $14-48; ⏰11am-10pm) Named for Maui's famous green sea turtles, this stylish venture from restaurateur Mark Ellman is wowing crowds with expansive ocean views and a savory array of wood-fired pizzas, out-of-this-world salads and comfort-food dishes. And we haven't even mentioned the fish, with ahi, *ono* and Hawaiian snapper seasoned with global flavors. Beer connoisseurs can choose from more than 50 brews.

As you dine, scan the water beside the rocky coast – you might just glimpse a green sea turtle.

Thai Chef THAI **$$**
(☎808-667-2814; www.thaichefrestaurantmaui.com; 878 Front St, Old Lahaina Center; most mains $12-22; ⏰11am-2pm Mon-Fri, 5-9pm Mon-Sat) Tucked in the back of an aging shopping center, this place looks like a dive from the outside, but the food's incredible. Start with the fragrant ginger coconut soup and the fresh summer rolls and then move on to savory curries that explode with flavor. It's BYOB so pick up a bottle from the nearby Foodland.

Prison Street Pizza PIZZA **$$**
(☎808-662-3332; 133 Prison St; pizza $8-28; ⏰9:30am-10pm Mon-Sat, noon-9pm Sun) For cheap eats in Lahaina, the $7 daily surfer's special – two slices of cheese pizza and a soda – is the way to go. This low-key new pizza joint is just a few steps from Banyan Tree Sq. Also delivers.

LOCAL KNOWLEDGE

FOODLAND POKE

The ahi *poke* (raw tuna) is served fresh, cheap and in numerous varieties at the Foodland (p326) grocery store seafood counter. It's one of the best culinary deals on the island. Our favorite part? The free samples! If you want a meal to-go, ask for a *poke* bowl, which comes with a hefty helping of rice. The spiced ahi *poke* is outstanding.

★Lahaina Grill HAWAII REGIONAL CUISINE **$$$**
(☎808-667-5117; www.lahainagrill.com; 127 Lahainaluna Rd; mains $39-86; ⏰from 5:30pm) The windows at the Lahaina Grill frame a simple but captivating tableau: beautiful people enjoying beautiful food. Trust us (and the crowd gazing in from the sidewalk) – there's something special about this restaurant. Once inside, expectations are confirmed by the service and the food. The menu relies on fresh local ingredients given innovative twists and presented with artistic style.

A seafood standout is the Maui onion-seared ahi with vanilla-bean jasmine rice. The finishing brushstroke? Always the triple berry pie.

Mala Ocean Tavern FUSION **$$$**
(☎808-667-9394; www.malaoceantavern.com; 1307 Front St; mains brunch $8-15, lunch $15-26, dinner $19-45; ⏰11am-10pm Mon-Fri, 9am-10pm Sat, 9am-9pm Sun) This smart bistro from chef Mark Ellman fuses Mediterranean and Pacific influences with sophisticated flair. Recommended tapas include the Kobe beef cheeseburger slathered with caramelized onions and smoked applewood bacon, and the 'adult' mac and cheese with mushroom cream and three fancy fromages. For main meals, anything with fish is a sure pleaser. At sunset, tiki torches on the waterfront lanai add a romantic touch.

Gerard's FRENCH **$$$**
(☎808-661-8939; www.gerardsmaui.com; 174 Lahainaluna Rd; mains from $39, 8-course prix fixe per person $105; ⏰seatings 6-8pm) Where has all the romance gone? To the front porch of Gerard's, where white linens and flickering shadows are an invitation for murmurings of love. Or exclamations of culinary bliss.

Chef Gerard Reversade, who infuses fresh Lahaina-caught seafood with flavors from the French countryside, has earned top-of-the-line accolades across Maui. The extensive wine lists are also noteworthy.

Pacific'O ASIAN FUSION, SEAFOOD **$$$**
(808-667-4341; www.pacificomaui.com; 505 Front St; lunch $15-18, dinner $30-42; 11:30am-9:30pm) Enjoy Pacific Rim cuisine prepared with contemporary flourishes at Chef James McDonald's chic oceanside restaurant. Bold and innovative seafood and beef dishes are accompanied by the best of Maui's garden bounty. Lunch is a slightly tamer affair, with island-inspired salads, sandwiches and tacos – but the same up-close ocean view.

Drinking & Nightlife

Front St is the center of the action. Check the entertainment listings in the free *MauiTime Weekly,* published on Thursdays, or just stroll the streets. Many of Lahaina's waterfront restaurants have live music at dinnertime.

★ Fleetwood's on Front St BAR
(808-669-6425; www.fleetwoodsonfrontst.com; 744 Front St; 11am-10pm Sun-Thu, to 11pm Fri & Sat) With its comfy pillows, cushy lounges and ornate accents, this rooftop oasis – owned by Fleetwood Mac drummer Mick Fleetwood – evokes Morocco. But views of the Pacific and the West Maui mountains keep you firmly rooted in Hawaii. At sunset, a conch-shell blast announces a tiki-lighting ceremony that's followed by a bagpipe serenade – from a kilt-wearing Scot! It's all great fun, and it works.

After the sunset ceremony stick around for live music. All drinks are 50% off during happy hour (2pm to 5pm). If you see the red flag flying, it means Mick is on the island.

Aloha Mixed Plate BAR
(808-661-3322; www.alohamixedplate.com; 1285 Front St; 8am-10pm;) Let the sea breeze whip through your hair while lingering over a heady mai tai – come between 2pm and 6pm and they're $3.50. After sunset, you can listen to Old Lahaina Luau's music beating next door.

Best Western Pioneer Inn PUB
(808-661-3636; 658 Wharf St; 7am-10pm) Ahoy matey! If Captain Ahab himself strolled through the swinging doors, no one would look up from their grog. With its whaling-era atmosphere and harborfront lanai, the captain would blend right in at this century-old landmark. For us landlubbers, the afternoon happy hour (3pm to 6pm) keeps it light on the wallet.

Spanky's Riptide SPORTS BAR
(505 Front St; 11am-1:30am) Want to catch the big game? Try the loveably rowdy Spanky's Riptide. Follow the whoops and cheers, stroll right in, step around the dog, pick your brew, then look up at the wall of action-packed TV screens.

Cheeseburger In Paradise BAR
(808-661-4855; www.cheeseburgerland.com; 811 Front St; 8am-10pm) Perched above the sea at the corner of Front St and Lahainaluna Rd, this open-air spot is a lively – and lovely – spot to watch the sunset. The music's Jimmy Buffett–style, and the setting is pure tropics, from the rattan decor to the homemade piña coladas. Live soft rock from 4:30pm to 10:30pm nightly.

Cool Cat Cafe CAFE
(808-667-0908; 658 Front St, Wharf Cinema Center; 10:30am-10:30pm) Whether you're looking for fountain drinks or hard-hitting cocktails, this breezy, '50s-inspired cafe is an easygoing spot to wet your whistle as the sun sets over the harbor, just beyond the banyan tree. Live music nightly (7:30pm to 10pm) and rotating list of $4 daily cocktails.

MauiGrown Coffee COFFEE
(808-661-2728; www.mauigrowncoffee.com; 277 Lahainaluna Rd; 6:30am-5pm Mon-Sat) Your view from the lanai at MauiGrown's historic bungalow? A sugar plantation smokestack and the cloud-capped West Maui Mountains. With 100% Maui-grown coffee, life can be good at 7am. A 12oz coffee is only $1.50.

☆ Entertainment

When it comes to hula and luau (Hawaiian feast), Lahaina offers the real deal. Catching a show is sure to be a vacation highlight. You can also enjoy free hula shows at **Lahaina Cannery Mall** (www.lahainacannery.com; 1221 Honoapi'ilani Hwy) at 7pm Tuesday and Thursday, and hula shows for the *nā keiki* at 1pm Saturday and Sunday.

★ Old Lahaina Luau LUAU
(808-667-1998; www.oldlahainaluau.com; 1251 Front St; adult/child under 13yr $105/75; 5:15-8:15pm Oct-Mar, 5:45-8:45pm Apr-Sep;) From

the warm aloha greeting to the extravagant feast and the mesmerizing hula dances, everything here is first rate. No other luau on Maui comes close to matching this one for its authenticity, presentation and all-around aloha. The feast is outstanding, with high-quality Hawaiian fare that includes *kalua* pork, ahi *poke*, *pulehu* (broiled) steak and an array of salads and sides.

It's held on the beach at the north side of town. One caveat: it often sells out a month in advance, so book ahead.

Feast at Lele LUAU
(☎808-667-5353, 866-244-5353; www.feastatlele.com; 505 Front St; adult/child under 13yr $120/90; ⏲from 5:30pm (Oct-Jan), 6pm (Feb-Apr, Sep) or 6:30pm (May-Aug)) Food takes center stage at this intimate Polynesian luau held on the beach. Dance performances in Hawaiian, Maori, Tahitian and Samoan styles are each matched to a food course. With the Hawaiian music, you're served *kalua* pork and *pohole* ferns; with the Maori, duck tenderloin salad with *poha* berry dressing. A true gourmet feast.

'Ulalena MODERN DANCE
(☎808-856-7900; www.mauitheatre.com; 878 Front St, Old Lahaina Center; adult/child 6-12yr from $60/30, ⏲6.30pm Mon, Tue, Thu & Fri) This Cirque du Soleil–style extravaganza has its home at the 680-seat Maui Theatre. The theme is Hawaiian history and storytelling; the medium is modern dance, brilliant stage sets, acrobatics and elaborate costumes. An entertaining, high-energy performance.

Burn'n Love LIVE MUSIC
(☎808-856-7900; www.burnnlove.com; 878 Front St, Old Lahaina Center; adult/child 6-12yr from $60/30; ⏲8pm Mon, Tue, Thu & Fri) This rave-winning ode to Elvis celebrates the King's time in the Hawaiian Islands. Led by Elvis impressario Darren Lee.

Shopping

Classy boutiques, tacky souvenir shops and flashy art galleries run thick along Front St. You'll find lots of shops in one location at the **Wharf Cinema Center** (☎808-661-8748; www.thewharfcinemacenter.com; 658 Front St) and **Lahaina Cannery Mall** (☎808-661-5304; www.lahainacannery.com; 1221 Honoapi'ilani Hwy; ⏲9:30am-9pm Mon-Sat, to 7pm Sun).

★**Lahaina Arts Society** ARTS, CRAFTS
(☎808-661-0111; www.lahainaarts.com; 648 Wharf St, Old Lahaina Courthouse; ⏲9am-5pm) A non-profit collective representing more than 90 island artists, this extensive gallery covers two floors in the Old Lahaina Courthouse. Works range from avant-garde paintings to glassworks. Many of Maui's best-known artists got their start here, and there are some gems among the collection.

Village Gifts & Fine Arts ARTS, CRAFTS
(☎808-661-5199; www.villagegalleriesmaui.com; cnr Front & Dickenson Sts; ⏲10am-6pm, to 9pm Fri) This one-room shop in the Masters' Reading Room sells prints, wooden bowls and other crafts. For fine art, visit the shop's sister property, the **Village Galleries** (www.villagegalleriesmaui.com; 120 Dickenson St; ⏲9am-9pm), which is located in a separate building behind the store, across the parking lot.

Lahaina Printsellers ART, MAPS
(☎808-667-5815; www.printsellers.com; 764 Front St; ⏲9am-10pm) Hawaii's largest purveyor of antique maps, including fascinating originals dating back to the voyages of Captain Cook. The shop also sells affordable reproductions. This location shares space with Lahaina Giclee, a gallery selling a wide range of fine quality Hawaiian *giclée* (zhee-clay) digital prints.

Maui Hands Center ARTS, CRAFTS
(☎808-667-9898; www.mauihands.com; 612 Front St; ⏲10am-7:30pm Mon-Sat, to 7pm Sun) Excellent selection of island-made crafts from more than 300 fine artists, jewelers and craftspeople.

LOCAL KNOWLEDGE

FRIDAY TOWN PARTIES

If it's Friday night, suit up for a party in the street. The **Maui Friday Town Parties** (www.mauifridays.com) celebrate local art, food and musicians. On the first Friday of the month the party is held in downtown Wailuku. It moves to Lahaina the second Friday, followed by Makawao and Kihei on the third and fourth Fridays respectively. For exact locations, check the website. Festivities typically start at 6pm.

Local food trucks are a town party highlight. At the Wailuku and Kihei town parties, keep an eye out for the chunky and delicious cookies from the Maui Cookie Lady (www.themauicookielady.com) and tasty fruit-filled popsicles from Shaka Pops (p419).

Hale Zen Home Decor & More HOMEWARES
(808-661-4802; www.halezen.com; 180 Dickenson St; 10am-6pm Mon-Sat, to 5pm Sun) This inviting shop embraces stylish island living with candles, lotions and gifts as well as crafted furniture and cute children's clothes.

Outlets of Maui MALL
(www.theoutletsofmaui.com; 9:30am-10pm) The factory-store retailers at this new, open-air outlet mall include Banana Republic, Brooks Brothers, Coach and Guess.

Lahaina Gateway MALL
(www.lahainagateway.com; 305 Keawe St; 9:30am-10pm) Across Hwy 30 from the Lahaina Cannery Mall is Lahaina Gateway strip mall. Here you'll find Barnes & Noble (www.barnesandnoble.com) and a branch of Maui Dive Shop (p322).

Information

The Maui Memorial Medical Center in Wailuku is the nearest hospital in case of emergencies. For serious accidents you may want to ask to be transported to O'ahu.

Bank of Hawaii (www.boh.com; 130 Papalaua St, Old Lahaina Center; 8:30am-4pm Mon-Thu, to 6pm Fri)

Downtown Post Office Station (132 Papalaua St, Old Lahaina Center; 10am-4pm Mon-Fri)

Lahaina Visitor Center (808-667-9193; www.visitlahaina.com; 648 Wharf St, Old Lahaina Courthouse; 9am-5pm) Located inside the old courthouse.

Longs Drugs (808-667-4390; www.cvs.com; 1221 Honoapi'ilani Hwy, Lahaina Cannery Mall; store 7am-midnight, pharmacy 8am-8pm Mon-Fri, 8am-5pm Sat & Sun)

Minit-Medical (808-667-6161; www.minit-medical.com; 305 Keawe St, Lahaina Gateway; 8am-6pm Mon-Sat) Urgent-care clinic. Takes walk-ins.

Police (808-244-6400) Contact for nonemergencies.

Getting There & Away

The Honoapi'ilani Hwy (Hwy 30) connects Lahaina with Ka'anapali and points north, with Ma'alaea to the south and Wailuku to the east. The second phase of the five-phase Lahaina Bypass opened in late 2013. The bypass swings east around downtown congestion and runs parallel to Hwy 30.

The **Maui Bus** (808-871-4838; www.mauicounty.gov; per boarding $2, daily pass $4) runs between Kahului and Lahaina (one hour) on the Lahaina Islander route. This bus stops at Ma'alaea Harbor. At Ma'alaea Harbor a connection can be made to Kihei (various stops) via the Kihei Villager. Another route, the Ka'anapali Islander, connects Lahaina and Ka'anapali (30 minutes). Both Islander routes depart from the Wharf Cinema Center hourly from 6:30am to 8:30pm.

Ferries to Lana'i and Moloka'i dock at Lahaina Harbor.

Getting Around

TO/FROM THE AIRPORT

To get to Lahaina from the airport in Kahului, take Hwy 380 south to Honoapi'ilani Hwy (Hwy 30); the drive takes about 45 minutes. If you're not renting a car, Executive Shuttle (p316) provides service between the airport and Lahaina, charging $47 for one person and $54 for two. From the airport to Lahaina, taxi fare is about $78.

BUS

In Lahaina, the Lahaina Villager route for the Maui Bus runs along Front St downtown and connects to Lahaina Cannery Mall and Lahaina Gateway.

CAR & MOTORCYCLE

Most visitors can rent cars upon arrival at Kahului Airport. For a sport bike try **Maui Motorsports** (808-445-9071; www.mauisportbikerentals.com; 1429 Front St). This low-profile agency offers various specialty motorcycles. Rent a Harley Davidson from **Lahaina Harley Davidson Rentals** (808-667-2800; www.cyclecitymaui.com; 602 Front St) from $139 per day, helmet included.

PARKING

Front St has free on-street parking, but there's always a line of cruising cars competing for spots. There's one free lot on tiny Luakini St between Lahainaluna Rd and Dickenson St – but get there early, it fills fast. Your best bet is the large lot at the corner of Front and Prison Sts where there's free public parking with a three-hour limit. At private lots near downtown, you may pay as much as $5 for up to two hours and $10 for two to eight hours. Otherwise, park at one of the shopping centers and get your parking ticket validated by making a purchase.

TAXI

For a taxi in Lahaina, call **Maui Pleasant Taxi** (808-344-4661; www.mauipleasanttaxi.com) or **West Maui Taxi** (808-661-1122, 888-661-4545; www.westmauitaxi.com). Expect to pay $14 to $20 one way between Lahaina and Ka'anapali.

WEST MAUI

For sun-kissed fun, West Maui is the place to be. Whether you want to snorkel beside lava rocks, zipline down the mountains, thwack a golf ball, hike through the jungle or sail beneath the setting sun, the adventures are as varied as the landscape. Ka'anapali is West Maui's splashy center, a look-at-me town luring travelers with world-class golf courses, stylish resorts, oceanfront dining and a dazzling, mile-long crescent of beach.

Further north, Hawaiian history and swanky exclusivity have formed an intriguing, sometimes uneasy, alliance in Kapalua, where luxurious lodgings and a PGA golf course preen near a lush mountain watershed, an ancient burial ground and several gorgeous beaches. To escape this glittery scene, hunker down in Kahana or Napili, lovely seaside communities known for their condos and budget-friendly prices. For off-the-grid excitement, only one adventure will do – a breezy, sometimes hair-raising, drive around the untamed northern coast.

Lahaina to Ma'alaea

The drive between Lahaina and Ma'alaea offers fine mountain scenery, but in winter everyone is craning their necks seaward to spot humpback whales cruising just offshore. Stand-up paddle surfers are also a common sight.

Beaches

Launiupoko Beach Park BEACH

Beginner and intermediate surfers head to this beach park, a popular surf spot 3 miles south of Lahaina. The southern side of the beach has small waves ideal for beginning surfers, while the northern side ratchets it up a notch for those who have honed their skills. You're also likely to see stand-up paddle surfers plying through Launiupoko's surf. The park is an ideal spot for families; *nā keiki* have a blast wading in the large rock-enclosed shoreline pool and good picnic facilities invite you to linger. Launiupoko is at the traffic lights at the 18-mile marker.

Puamana Beach Park BEACH

This shady beach park, 1.5 miles south of Lahaina, is rocky but sometimes has good conditions for beginner surfers – otherwise it's mostly a quick stop for a seaside view, particularly at sunset. Not a great spot for lying out.

Sleeping

For B&Bs on Maui, remember to reserve a room ahead of time. Showing up late at night, unannounced and without reservations is strongly discouraged.

★Ho'oilo House B&B $$$

(☎808-667-6669; www.hooilohouse.com; 138 Awaiku St; r $329; ❄📶🏊) 🌿 Up the road from Launiupoko Beach Park, this Zen-ful retreat on the slopes of the West Maui Mountains is a place for relaxation. Six Asian- and Maui-themed rooms hug an A-framed community area with a sweeping view of Lana'i. Stylish furnishings differ by room – many contain Balinese imports – but all have a private lanai and an eclectically designed outdoor shower.

Breakfast includes fresh muffins and bread, cereal, granola and fruit, which is often plucked from the 2-acre property's pesticide-free orchard. Solar panels generate 85% to 90% of the house's power, and soap products are recycled in partnership with Clean the World.

Olowalu

POP 80

The West Maui Mountains provide the scenic backdrop and give Olowalu its name, which means 'many hills.' For the moment, the tiny village is marked by the Olowalu General Store, Leoda's Kitchen & Pie Shop and a juice and fruit stand. The controversial Ol7owalu Town Project calls for the development of 1500 housing units on land just south of the village. The good news? If completed, half of the housing will be set aside as affordable housing. The bad? Environmental groups are concerned that the project will harm Olowalu's famed coral reef at the 14-mile marker.

Sights

Olowalu Petroglyphs ARCHAEOLOGICAL SITE

A short walk behind the general store leads to petroglyphs (ancient Hawaiian stone carvings) dating back 200 to 300 years. To get to them, park just beyond the water tower at the back of the store. It's a 440yd or so walk up an open road to the petroglyph site. The road is easy to follow; just keep the cinder cone straight ahead of you as you go. Bear left at the Olowalu Cultural Reserve sign.

As with most of Maui's petroglyphs, these figures are carved into the vertical sides of cliffs (rather than on horizontal lava as they

West Maui

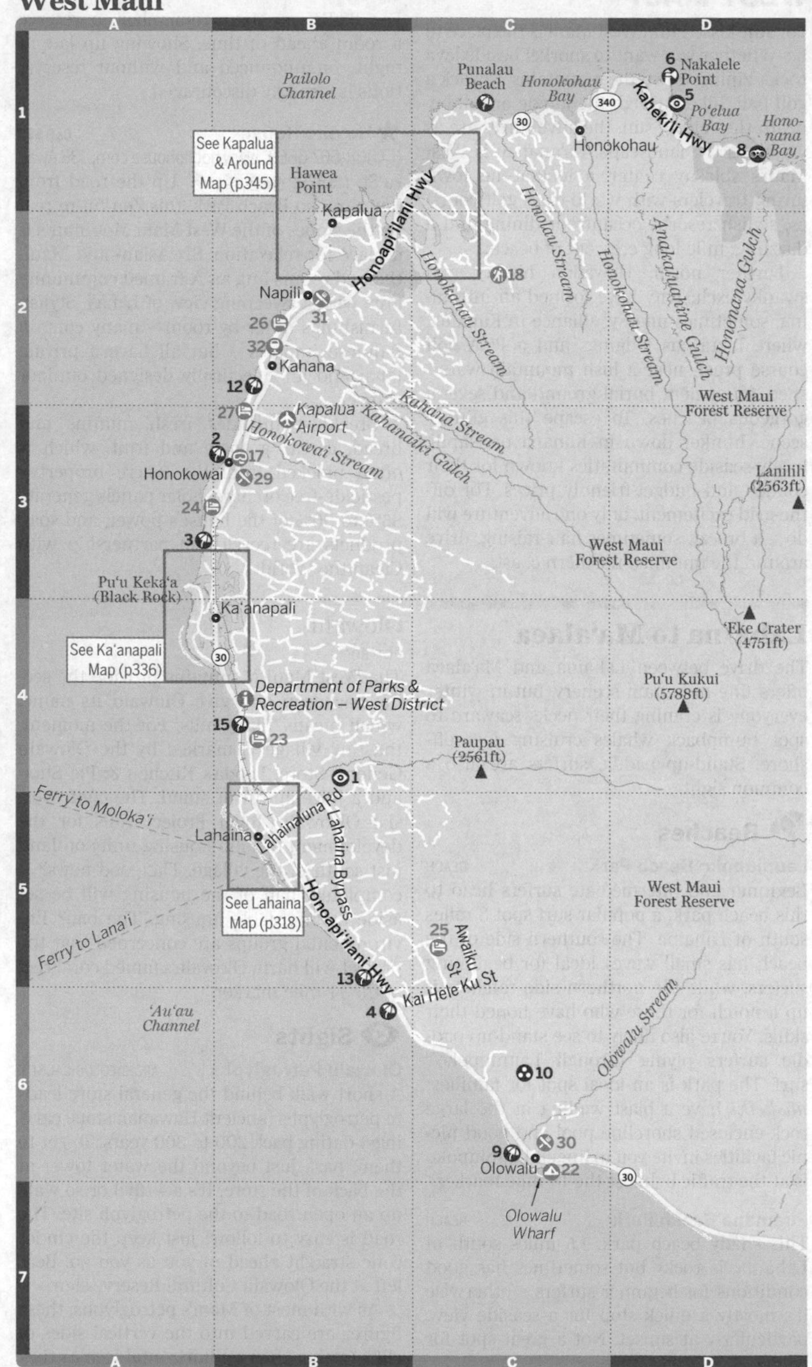

A
B
C
D
1
2
3
4
5
6
7
Pailolo Channel
Punalau Beach
Honokohau Bay
340
30
6
Nakalele Point
5
Po'elua Bay
Kahekili Hwy
Hono-nana Bay
8
Honokohau
See Kapalua & Around Map (p345)
Hawea Point
Kapalua
Honoapi'ilani Hwy
Honokahau Stream
Honolau Stream
Honokohau Stream
Anakaluahine Gulch
Honokohau Gulch
18
Napili
31
26
32
Kahana
12
27
Kapalua Airport
Kahana Stream
Kahanaiki Gulch
Honokowai Stream
West Maui Forest Reserve
2
17
Honokowai
29
Lanilili (2563ft)
24
3
West Maui Forest Reserve
Pu'u Keka'a (Black Rock)
Ka'anapali
See Ka'anapali Map (p336)
30
'Eke Crater (4751ft)
Department of Parks & Recreation – West District
Pu'u Kukui (5788ft)
15
23
Paupau (2561ft)
1
Ferry to Moloka'i
Lahaina
Lahainaluna Rd
Lahaina Bypass
West Maui Forest Reserve
See Lahaina Map (p318)
Ferry to Lana'i
25
Awaiku St
13
Kai Hele Ku St
4
'Au'au Channel
Olowalu Stream
10
30
9
Olowalu
22
Olowalu Wharf
MAUI LAHAINA TO MA'ALAEA

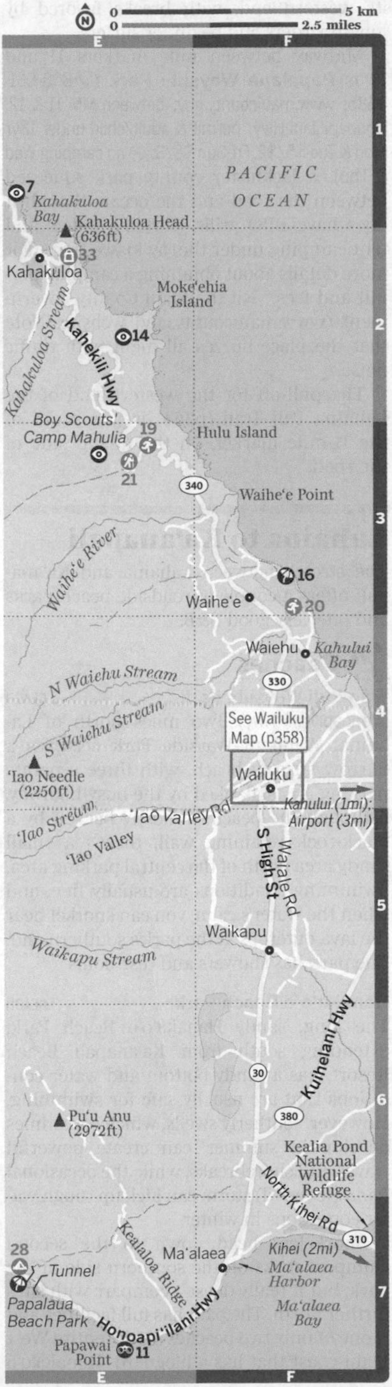

West Maui

Sights

1 Hale Pa'i B4
2 Honokowai Beach Park B3
3 Kahekili Beach Park A3
4 Launiupoko Beach Park B6
5 Nakalele Blowhole D1
6 Nakalele Point Light Station D1
7 Natural Ocean Baths E1
8 Ohai Viewpoint D1
9 Olowalu Beach C6
10 Olowalu Petroglyphs C6
11 Papawai Point E7
Pohaku Kani .... (see 7)
12 Pohaku Park B2
13 Puamana Beach Park B5
14 Turnbull Studios & Sculpture Garden E2
15 Wahikuli Wayside Park B4
16 Waihe'e Beach Park F3

Activities, Courses & Tours

17 Boss Frog B3
Maui Dive Shop .... (see 32)
18 Maunalei Arboretum Trail C2
19 Mendes Ranch E3
20 Waiehu Municipal Golf Course F3
21 Waihe'e Ridge Trailhead E3

Sleeping

22 Camp Olowalu C6
23 Guest House B4
24 Honua Kai Resort & Spa A3
25 Ho'oilo House C5
26 Kahana Village B2
27 Noelani B3
28 Papalaua Wayside Park E7

Eating

Farmers Market Deli .... (see 17)
Hawaiian Village Coffee .... (see 32)
29 Honokowai Okazuya B3
30 Leoda's Kitchen & Pie Shop C6
31 Maui Tacos B2

Drinking & Nightlife

32 Maui Brewing Co B2
Napili Coffee Store .... (see 31)

Shopping

33 Kaukini Gallery & Gift Shop E2

are on Hawai'i, the Big Island). Most of the Olowalu figures have been damaged, but you can still make out some of them. Don't climb the rocks for a better look, however. And watch for falling rocks. There's a picnic table and interpretive signage at the site.

If you have mobility issues it's OK to drive to the site, instead of walking, but be respectful of neighboring landowners.

Beaches

Olowalu Beach BEACH

The coral reef of Olowalu Beach, which is popular with snorkelers, is shallow and silty, and the 'Sharks may be present' signs lining the beach are the real thing. There were three shark attacks off Olowalu between 1993 and 2002. Located at the 14-mile marker.

Sleeping & Eating

Camp Olowalu CAMPGROUND $

(808-661-4303; www.campolowalu.com; 800 Olowalu Village Rd; campsites per adult/child 6-12yr $15/5; P Wi-Fi) Bordered by the ocean on one side and a dense thicket of gnarled trees on the other, the setting here is pure *Survivor.* But simple amenities – cold-water showers, outhouses, picnic tables, drinking water – kick things up a notch. With its tightly packed sites, port-o-johns and slightly scruffy appearance, this place may not work for travelers who prefer more polished campgrounds.

Enter across the highway from the Olowalu General Store then drive southeast beside Hwy 30 to the campground. Wi-fi available at the checkout window. Fourteen-night maximum stay.

★**Leoda's Kitchen & Pie Shop** SANDWICHES, BURGERS $

(808-662-3600; www.leodas.com; 820 Olowalu Village Rd, on Honoapi'ilani Hwy; breakfast $6-19, lunch & dinner $6-16, dessert pies $5-9; 7am-8pm; Wi-Fi) Wear your stretchy pants to Leoda's. Diet-busters at this simple-but-stylish restaurant include savory pot pies, topping-laden burgers and rich sandwiches such as the 'pork, pork...mmm pork.' Save room for one of the mini dessert pies – gorgeous creations vying for attention at the front counter. It's also a great breakfast spot on your way into or out of Lahaina. Located at the 15-mile marker.

Ukumehame Beach Park & Around

Heading south from Lahaina, look for Ukumehame Beach Park at the 12-mile marker. Shaded by ironwood trees, this sandy beach is OK for a quick dip, but because of the rocky conditions most locals stick with picnicking and fishing. Dive and snorkel boats anchor offshore at Coral Gardens. This reef also creates Thousand Peaks toward its western end, with breaks favored by long-boarders and beginner surfers.

Midway between mile markers 11 and 12 is **Papalaua Wayside Park** (808-661-4685; www.mauicounty.gov; between MM 11 & 12, Honoapi'ilani Hwy; permit & adult/child under 18yr Mon & Tue $5/$2, Fri-Sun $8/3; no camping Wed & Thu), a lackluster county park squeezed between the road and the ocean, though it does have BBQ grills, portable toilets and tent camping under thorny kiawe trees. For more details about obtaining a camping permit and fees, visit the Maui County government (www.mauicounty.gov) website. Note that the place buzzes all night with traffic noise.

The pull-off for the western end of the Lahaina Pali Trail (p364) is just south of the 11-mile marker, on the inland side of the road.

Lahaina to Ka'anapali

The stretch between Lahaina and Ka'anapali offers a couple of roadside beach parks and one very good B&B.

Beaches

Wahikuli Wayside Park BEACH

(Honoapi'ilani Hwy) Two miles north of Lahaina, Wahikuli Wayside Park occupies a narrow strip of beach, with three separate parking areas, flanked by the busy highway. Although the beach is mostly backed by a black-rock retaining wall, there's a small sandy area north of the central parking area. Swimming conditions are usually fine, and when the water's calm, you can snorkel near the lava outcrops at the park's southern end. The park has showers and restrooms.

Hanaka'o'o Beach Park BEACH

The long, sandy Hanaka'o'o Beach Park, extending south from Ka'anapali Beach Resort, has a sandy bottom and water conditions that are usually safe for swimming. However, southerly swells, which sometimes develop in summer, can create powerful waves and shorebreaks, while the occasional *kona* (leeward) storm can kick up rough water conditions in winter.

Snorkelers head down to the second clump of rocks on the southern side of the park, but it really doesn't compare with sites further north. The park has full facilities and is one of only two beaches on the entire West Maui coast that has a lifeguard. Hanaka'o'o

WHALE SPOTTING

During the winter humpback whales occasionally breach as close as 100yd from the coast, and 40 tons of leviathan suddenly exploding straight up through the water can be a real showstopper!

Beach parks and pull-offs along the road offer great vantage points for watching the action. The very best spot is **Papawai Point**, a cliffside perch jutting into the western edge of Ma'alaea Bay, and a favored humpback nursing ground (not to mention a great place to catch a sunset). The Pacific Whale Foundation posts volunteers at the parking lot to share their knowledge and point out the whales (8am to 2pm mid-December to mid-April).

Papawai Point is midway between the 8- and 9-mile markers, about 3 miles north of Ma'alaea. Note that the road sign simply reads 'scenic point,' not the full name, but there's a turning lane into it, so slow down and you won't miss it.

Beach is also called 'Canoe Beach,' as West Maui outrigger canoe clubs practice here in the late afternoon.

A small immigrant cemetery dating from the 1850s marks the entrance.

Sleeping

Guest House B&B $$

(☎808-661-8085; www.mauiguesthouse.com; 1620 Ainakea Rd; s/d incl breakfast $169/189; P❄@🛜🏊) The welcoming Guest House, which has hosted travelers for more than 25 years, provides amenities that put nearby resorts to shame. Every room has its own hot tub and 42in plasma TV. Stained-glass windows reflect a tropical motif, and a roof-top deck offers ocean views. Perks include beach towels, snorkel gear, salt-water pool, community kitchen and a guest shower you can use before your midnight flight.

In 2012 this eco-minded B&B went 100% solar after installing a 113-panel photovoltage solar system. Guest House is located in a residential neighborhood, inland of Hwy 30. The beach is a five-minute drive away.

Ka'anapali

POP 1045

Honeymoons, anniversaries, girlfriend getaways – Ka'anapali is a place to celebrate. Maui's flashiest resort destination welcomes guests with 3 miles of sandy beach, a dozen oceanfront hotels, two 18-hole golf courses and an ocean full of water activities. You can sit at a beachfront bar with a tropical drink, soak up the gorgeous views of Lana'i and Moloka'i across the channel and listen to guitarists strum their wiki-wacky-woo.

Sights

★ **Whalers Village Museum** MUSEUM

(☎808-661-5992; www.whalersvillage.com/museum.htm; 2435 Ka'anapali Pkwy, Whalers Village; adult/child 6-18yr $3/1; ⏲10am-4pm; 👪) Lahaina was a popular stop for whaling ships traveling between Japan and the arctic during the Golden Age of whaling (1825–60). The ships would also restock here before the long voyage home to New England. At this small but fascinating museum the hardships and routines of life at sea are revealed in authentic period photographs, ship logs, harpoons and intriguing interpretive plaques that sound the depths of whaling history.

Particularly eye-opening is the life-size whaling ship forecastle. How 20 crewmen could live for weeks in this tiny room – without coming to blows or losing their minds – is a mystery.

Museum hours may extend until 6pm during the winter whale season. A free humpback whale talk is offered Monday, Wednesday and Friday at 11am; whale talks may also occur on Tuesday and Thursday during whale season. Talks are based on docent availability, so call ahead. A full-size sperm whale skeleton welcomes guests at the front entrance to the shopping center. Parking tickets validated with $6 admission.

Ka'anapali Beach Walk WATERFRONT

For people-watching and a bit of exercise, stroll the mile-long beachfront walk that runs between the Sheraton Maui and Hyatt Regency Maui hotels. In addition to the action on the shore, both the Hyatt and the Westin Maui, located at the midpoint of the walk, are worth a detour for their dazzling garden statuary and landscaping replete with free-form pools and rushing waterfalls.

At the Hyatt, pampered black African penguins love to waddle beside their four-star penguin cave, found in the rambling lobby.

At the southern end of the walk, beyond the Hyatt, the graceful 17ft-high bronze sculpture *The Acrobats,* by Australian John Robinson, makes a dramatic silhouette at sunset.

In the early evening you'll often be treated to entertainment from the beachside restaurants.

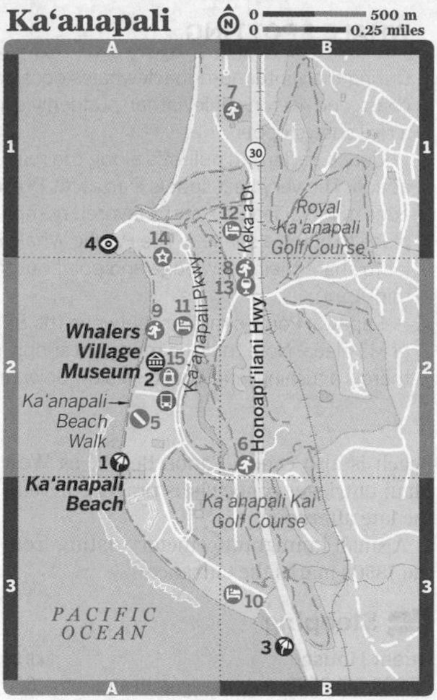

Beaches

★Ka'anapali Beach BEACH

Home to West Maui's liveliest beach scene, this gorgeous stretch of sand unfurls alongside Ka'anapali's resort hotels, linking the Hyatt Regency Maui with the Sheraton Maui 1 mile north. Dubbed 'Dig-Me Beach' for all the preening, it's a vibrant spot. Surfers, boogie boarders and parasailers rip across the water, snorkelers admire the sea life, and sailboats pull up on shore. Check with the hotel beach huts before jumping in, however, as water conditions vary with the season and currents are sometimes strong.

For the best snorkeling, try the underwater sights off **Pu'u Keka'a** (Black Rock). This lava promontory protects the beach in front of the Sheraton Maui. Novices stick to the sheltered southern side of the landmark rock – where there's still a lot to see – but the shallow coral here has been stomped to death. If you're a confident swimmer, the less-frequented horseshoe cove cut into the tip of the rock is the real prize, teeming with tropical fish, colorful coral and sea turtles. There's often a current to contend with off the point, which can make getting to the cove a bit tricky, but when it's calm you can swim right in. Pu'u Keka'a is also a popular shore-dive spot.

There are no lifeguards along Ka'anapali Beach.

Kahekili Beach Park BEACH

This idyllic golden-sand beach at Ka'anapali's less-frequented northern end is a good place to lose the look-at-me crowds strutting their stuff further south. The swimming's better, the snorkeling's good and the park has everything you'll need for a day at the beach – showers, restrooms, a covered picnic pavilion and barbecue grills. Access is easy and there's ample free parking.

Snorkelers will find plenty of coral and marine life right in front of the beach. Sea turtle sightings are common. To go a bit further afield, swim north to **Honokowai Point** and then ride the mild current, which runs north to south, all the way back.

The wide beach, backed by swaying palms and flowering morning glory, is also ideal for strolling. It's a 15-minute walk south to Pu'u Keka'a. Or you could walk north along the beach for about 20 minutes to Honokowai Point and have lunch in the village.

To get to the beach from the Honoapi'ilani Hwy, turn *makai* (seaward) 350yd north of the 25-mile marker onto Kai Ala Dr, then bear right.

Activities

Teralani Sailing SAILING

(☎808-661-7245; www.teralani.net; 2435 Ka'anapali Pkwy, Whalers Village; outings adult/teen 13-20yr/child 3-12yr from $61/50/40; ⊙hours vary; 👪) This friendly outfit offers a variety of sails on two custom-built catamarans that depart from the beach beside Whalers Village. The easygoing sunset sail offers an inspiring introduction to the gorgeous West Maui coast. Snorkel sails and whale-watching outings are additional options, but no matter which you choose, you'll find an amiable crew, refreshing cocktails and decent food.

Note the 24-hour cancellation policy and the $5 fuel charge per person.

Ka'anapali

Hula Girl SAILING, SNORKELING

(808-665-0344; www.sailingmaui.com; snorkeling tour adult/child 2-12yr $100/85; reservations 7am-9pm) You'll sail in style from Ka'anapali to Honolua Bay, one of Maui's top snorkeling spots, on the 65ft *Hula Girl* catamaran. Divers are welcome too. Food and cocktails are not included in trip rates, but the prices are reasonable and choices may be more impressive than what you'll find on all-inclusive trips. Honolua Bay trips are five hours (departures 9:30am and 2pm). See website for additional tours.

Trips depart from the beach in front of Leilani's at Whalers Village.

Ka'anapali Dive Company DIVING

(808-661-2179; www.goscubamaui.com; Westin Maui Resort & Spa; 1-tank dive $79; reservations 7am-5pm) Want to learn to scuba dive? These are the people you want to see. The introductory two-tank dive ($110) for novices, with equipment, starts with instruction in a pool and moves on to a guided dive from the beach. It also offers one-tank beach dives for certified divers. No separate rentals. Walk up or call to make reservations (the Starwood Activities line).

Trilogy Ocean Sports WATER SPORTS

(808-661-7789; www.sailtrilogy.com; Ka'anapali Beach Walk; 2hr lesson surfing $70, SUP $89; 8am-5pm) From its beach hut in front of the Ka'anapali Beach Hotel, Trilogy can get you up and riding a board with a two-hour surfing or 90-minute stand-up paddleboarding (SUP) lesson. Snorkel sets rent for $20 a day, and SUP boards are $25 for the first hour then $15 per hour. Don't want to work so hard? Try the sunset catamaran cruise (adult $69, teen 13 to 18 years $52, child three to 12 years $35).

Skyline Eco-Adventures ZIPLINING

(808-878-8400; www.zipline.com; 2580 Keka'a Dr, Fairway Shops; 4hr outing $150; departs on the hour 7am-2pm) The Ka'anapali course takes you 2 miles up the wooded cliffsides of the West Maui Mountains and drops you on a free-glide along eight separate lines above waterfalls, stream beds and valleys. If it's drizzly and windy? Hold on tight and no cannonballs! Drop from a line into a mountain pool on the new Zip & Dip tours ($140).

Skyline is 100% carbon neutral and donates 1% of sales to ecofriendly causes as a member of 1% for the Planet.

Ka'anapali Golf Courses GOLF

(808-661-3691; www.kaanapaligolfcourses.com; 2290 Ka'anapali Pkwy; greens fee $205-249, after 1pm $119-139; hours vary seasonally, opens about 6:30am) The more demanding of the two courses is the Royal Ka'anapali Golf Course, designed by Robert Trent Jones. It's tournament grade with greens that emphasize putting skills. The Ka'anapali Kai Golf Course is shorter and more of a resort

SPIRIT'S LEAP

According to traditional Hawaiian beliefs, Pu'u Keka'a (p336), the westernmost point of Maui, is a place where the spirits of the dead leap into the unknown to be carried to their ancestral homeland. The rock is said to have been created during a scuffle between the demigod Maui and a commoner who questioned Maui's superiority. Maui chased the man to this point, froze his body into stone then cast his soul out to sea. Today, daring teens wait their turn to leap off the rock for a resounding splash into the cove below.

course. The setting isn't as spectacular as the courses in Kapalua, but it tends to be less windy and the rates are a relative bargain.

If you're staying in a hotel or condo at the Ka'anapali Resort, ask for the guest rate which will save you about $70.

Tour of the Stars STARGAZING
(808-667-4727; www.maui.hyatt.com; 200 Nohea Kai Dr, Hyatt Regency Maui Resort & Spa; adult/child guest 6-12yr $25/15, nonguest $30/20) Enjoy stellar stargazing atop the Hyatt resort. These 50-minute viewings are limited to 14 people, use a 14in-diameter telescope and are held at 8pm and 9pm on clear nights. Romantic types should opt for the couples-only viewing at 10pm Friday and Saturday, which rolls out champagne and chocolate-covered strawberries (guest/nonguest $40/45).

Royal Lahaina Tennis Ranch TENNIS
(808-667-5200; www.royallahaina.com/activities.cfm; 2780 Keka'a Dr; per person per half-day $10; pro shop 8am-noon daily & 2-6pm Mon-Fri, 2-5pm Sat & Sun) Named the 2010 Facility of the Year by the United States Tennis Association, this is the largest tennis complex in West Maui, with four courts lit for night play. Rackets and shoes can be rented. Private lessons and group clinics are available. Courts open until 9pm

Festivals & Events

Maui Onion Festival FOOD
(www.whalersvillage.com/events.htm; 1st Sat May) This popular celebration highlights all that can be done with Maui's famed Kula onions. Look for chef demonstrations and an onion-eating competition.

Hula O Na Keiki DANCE
(www.kbhmaui.com; Nov) Children take center stage at this hula dance competition in early to mid-November, which features some of the best *keiki* dancers in Hawaii. It's held at the Ka'anapali Beach Hotel.

Sleeping

The following accommodations are on the beach or within walking distance of it.

Ka'anapali Beach Hotel RESORT $$
(808-661-0011; www.kbhmaui.com; 2525 Ka'anapali Pkwy; r $176-299; P) This welcoming property feels like summer camp – but in the best possible way. The hotel is a little older than its neighbors and the style is more comfy than posh, but it has its own special charms: warm staff, hula shows, an outdoor tiki bar, tidy grounds framed by palm trees and an enviable location on a gorgeous stretch of beach.

Family-friendly activities include lei making and ukulele lessons. For churchgoers there's a nondenominational outdoor service on Sunday mornings. On your last day, bring a camera and a hankie to your farewell lei ceremony. One drawback? Wi-fi (free) is available in the courtyard only, although it may reach some rooms. Parking is $11 per day.

Outrigger Maui Eldorado CONDO $$
(808-661-0021, 866-956-4262; www.outrigger.com; 2661 Keka'a Dr; studio/1 bedroom/2 bedroom from $165/189/395; P) Have a golfer in your family? Then consider this quiet condo development bordering the Royal Ka'anapali Golf Course. The best rooms are the large studios, which have kitchens set apart from the bedroom area. All units have washers and dryers. The condos are not on the beach, but the complex isn't far from the ocean, and the resort shuttle stops out front.

The resort fee is $12 per day and includes parking. There is a mandatory cleaning charge per stay ($95 to $175).

★ **Honua Kai Resort & Spa** CONDO $$$
(808-662-2800; www.honuakai.com; 130 Kai Malina Pkwy; r from $514;) This breezy oasis in northern Ka'anapali feels less frenetic than similar properties along Ka'anapali Beach 2 miles south. From the open-air lobby with its well-placed couches to the aesthetically pleasing pools to the extra spacious lanai adjoining the units – there's a consistent and effective blending of style, functionality and comfort. Units are individ-

ually owned so decor varies. The Spa offers honeymoon massage packages.

In each unit, Bosch appliances, Maui-made coffee, and washers and dryers round out the appeal. Check the website for deals and packages that reduce the nightly rate. One quibble – the front desk has a teensy lack of aloha on the phone. So busy! Daily resort fee is $29.

Hyatt Regency Maui Resort & Spa RESORT **$$$**
(☎808-661-1234; www.maui.hyatt.com; 200 Nohea Kai Dr; r/ste from $389/889; P ❄ @ ☉ ≋) Exotic birds and extravagant artwork fill the airy lobby atrium while gardens and swan ponds catch the eye across the grounds. Kids of all ages will thrill in the water world of meandering pools, swim-through grottoes and towering water slides. As part of a $12 million renovation project, guest rooms have been 'refreshed' – picture monochromatic walls, chocolate-brown furniture and bold splashes of color. The daily resort fee of $30 includes wi-fi, but parking is a separate $16 per day.

Eating

Don't limit yourself to Ka'anapali's restaurants as many of Maui's top chefs are just a skip down the road in Lahaina.

★Hula Grill & Barefoot Bar HAWAII REGIONAL CUISINE **$$**
(☎808-667-6636; www.hulagrillkaanapali.com; 2435 Ka'anapali Pkwy, Whalers Village; bar lunch $14-20, dining room mains $25-33; ⊙bar 10:45am-10pm, dining room 4:45-9:30pm) Coconut-frond umbrellas, sand beneath your sandals and the guy strumming guitar. The Barefoot Bar is the best spot on the beach walk to sip mai tais and nibble *pupu* (snacks). The Kapulu Joe pork sandwich with macnut slaw (add a dash of chili water) is reliably good. Dinner inside at the restaurant kicks it up a notch with spicy kiawe-grilled seafood.

Japengo SUSHI, STEAKS **$$$**
(☎808-661-1234; www.maui.hyatt.com; 200 Nohea Kai Dr, Hyatt Regency Maui Resort & Spa; sushi $7-24, mains $24-44; ⊙5-10pm) Got the sun-kissed tan and the windswept hair? Japengo is the place to show off your Ka'anapali glow. On the tiki-lit patio, enjoy an artist's array of tropical cocktails and delectable sushi as the sun goes down. Roasted meat and seafood dishes, such as the grilled ahi (yellowfin tuna) with Hamakua mushrooms and wasabi butter, are prepared with Pacific Rim flair.

Roy's Ka'anapali HAWAII REGIONAL CUISINE **$$$**
(☎808-669-6999; www.royshawaii.com; 2290 Ka'anapali Pkwy, Ka'anapali Resort; lunch $14-25, dinner $16-45; ⊙lunch 11am-2pm, bar pupus 2-5pm, dinner from 5pm) The Maui outpost of Chef Roy Yamaguchi's upscale dining empire sits inside the golf course clubhouse at the Ka'anapali Resort. Here, big-windowed views of the greens are a pleasant backdrop for the exquisitely prepared island and regional fare. Main meals include sashimi-like blackened ahi with Chinese mustard and Roy's meatloaf with Maui cattle beef onion rings and mushroom gravy.

Drinking & Entertainment

Bars in Whalers Village and at many resorts offer live music in the evening. Luau and hula shows are also popular. Check www.mauitime.com for performers and schedules.

Bars

Sangrita Grill & Cantina BAR
(☎808-662-6000; www.sangritagrill.com; 2580 Keka'a Dr, Fairways Shops; mains $15-23; ⊙11am-10pm Mon-Fri, 10am-midnight Sat, 11am-9pm Sun) The chicken enchiladas, like the parking lot view, are somewhat uninspiring at this new Mexican restaurant in the Fairways Shops. But the cocktails? Now we're having some fun. The Ruby Red martini includes Maui's Organic Ocean Vodka and the Lilikoi margarita blends tequila with passionfruit. The lengthy tequila menu and the sultry interior? Also worth a look.

Live Music

Many Ka'anapali bars have live music regularly. It's typically Jimmy Buffett–style guitar tunes, occasionally spiced up with some ukulele strumming.

Leilani's LIVE MUSIC
(☎808-661-4495; www.leilanis.com; 2435 Ka'anapali Pkwy, Whalers Village; ⊙10:30am-10:30pm) This open-air bar and restaurant beside the beach is a pleasant place to linger over a cool drink while catching a few rays. It also has a good grill and *pupu* menu. Live music Wednesday through Sunday from 3pm to 5pm.

Japengo LIVE MUSIC
(☎808-661-1234; www.maui.hyatt.com; 200 Nohea Kai Dr, Hyatt Regency Maui Resort & Spa; ⊙5-11pm) There's low-key live music on the patio at Japengo from 5:30pm to 7:30pm nightly.

Hula, Luau & Theater

Ka'anapali Beach Hotel HULA

(808-661-0011; www.kbhmaui.com; 2525 Ka'anapali Pkwy; 6-9pm;) Maui's most Hawaiian hotel cheerfully entertains anyone who chances by between 6pm and 9pm (Tuesday to Sunday) with a free hula show and Hawaiian music. Enjoy mai tais and brews at the adjacent Tiki Bar (10am to 10pm), with music and dancing nightly in the Tiki Courtyard.

Sheraton Maui LIVE PERFORMANCE

(808-661-0031; www.sheraton-maui.com; 2605 Ka'anapali Pkwy; sunset) Everybody swings by to watch the torch-lighting and cliff-diving ceremony from Pu'u Keka'a (Black Rock) that takes place at sunset. Afterwards, there's live music at the Cliff Dive Grill.

Drums of the Pacific LUAU

(808-667-4727; www.maui.hyatt.com; 200 Nohea Kai Dr, Hyatt Regency Maui Resort & Spa; adult/child 6-12yr from $95/65; from 5pm Oct-Mar, from 5:30pm Apr-Sep;) Ka'anapali's best luau includes an *imu* ceremony (unearthing of a roasted pig from an underground oven), an open bar, a Hawaiian-style buffet and a South Pacific dance and music show.

Whalers Village HULA, DANCE

(808-661-4567; www.whalersvillage.com; 2435 Ka'anapali Pkwy; hula shows 7-8pm Mon & Wed, dance shows 7-8pm Sat) Ka'anapali's shopping center hosts Polynesian and Tahitian dance and hula performances. Check the website for a monthly calendar of events and classes.

Shopping

You'll find more than 60 shops and restaurants at **Whalers Village** (808-661-4567; www.whalersvillage.com; 2435 Ka'anapali Pkwy; 9:30am-10pm) shopping center.

ABC Store ACCESSORIES

(808-667-9700; www.abcstores.com; Whalers Village; 7am-11pm) Stop here for sunblock and great beach totes.

Honolua Surf CLOTHING

(808-661-5455; www.honoluasurf.com; Whalers Village; 9am-10pm) The place to pick up Maui-style board shorts as well as bikinis.

Lululemon SPORTS

(808-661-0468; www.lululemon.com; Whalers Village; 11am-6pm Wed-Sun) Called a showroom, this is a smaller version of the typical Lululemon yoga retail store.

Martin & MacArthur ARTS, CRAFTS

(808-667-7422; www.martinandmacarthur.com; Whalers Village; 9:30am-10pm) Has museum-quality Hawaiian-made wood carvings, paintings and other crafts.

Sand People CLOTHING, HOMEWARES

(808-662-8785; www.sandpeople.com; Whalers Village; 9:30am-10pm) Boutique with women's apparel and Hawaii-inspired cottage decor.

Getting Around

BUS

The **Maui Bus** (808-871-4838; www.mauicounty.gov; per trip $2; most routes 6:30am-8pm) currently connects Whalers Village shopping center in Ka'anapali with the Wharf Cinema Center in Lahaina hourly on the Ka'anapali Islander from 6am to 9pm and on the half-hour between 2pm and 6pm. The Napili Islander runs north up the coast to Kahana and Napili from 6am to 8pm.

The free Ka'anapali Trolley loops between the Ka'anapali hotels, Whalers Village and the golf courses about every 20 to 30 minutes (times can vary) between 10am and 8pm. The trolley schedule is posted at the Whalers Village stop.

CAR & MOTORCYCLE

For Harley-Davidson motorcycle rentals, try **Eagle Rider** (808-667-7000; www.eaglerider.com; 30 Halawai Dr A-3; motorcyle per day incl helmet from $99; 9am-5pm), located just north of Ka'anapali off the Honoapi'ilani Hwy. The company shares space with Aloha Motorsports (www.alohamotorsport.com), which rents scooters.

PARKING

The resort hotels offer free beach parking to the public, but the spaces allotted are so limited they commonly fill by mid-morning. Your best bet for beach parking is at the Hyatt, which has more public slots than other hotels.

Another option is the pay parking lot at Whalers Village (7am to midnight) but beware: at $3 per 30 minutes, parking here can be an expensive proposition. You can get three hours validated with a purchase from a merchant in the mall, but the minimum purchase requirement varies by merchant and can be steep. The Whalers Village Museum validates with $6 admission. The daily maximum at the lot is $40.

TAXI

Cabs often line up beside the trolley and Maui bus stop in front of Whalers Village on Ka'anapali Pkwy.

Honokowai

POP HONOKOWAI-NAPILI 7261

Condo-laden Honokowai may not have the glamour of pricier Ka'anapali to the south, but it has its virtues. It's convenient, affordable and low-rise, and the ocean views are as fine as in the upscale resorts. Another perk: in winter this is the best place in West Maui to spot passing whales right from your room lanai.

The main road, which bypasses the condos, is Honoapi'ilani Hwy (Hwy 30). The parallel shoreline road is Lower Honoapi'ilani Rd, which leads into Honokowai and continues north into Kahana and Napili.

Sights & Activities

Honokowai Beach Park BEACH

( ) The real thrills here are on land, not in the water. This family-friendly park in the center of town has playground facilities and makes a nice spot for a picnic. Forget swimming, though. The water is shallow and the beach is lined with a submerged rock shelf. Water conditions improve at the southern side of town, and you could continue walking along the shore down to lovely Kahekili Beach Park (p336) at the northern end of Ka'anapali.

Boss Frog SNORKELING

(808-665-1200; www.bossfrog.com; 3636 Lower Honoapi'ilani Rd; snorkel set per day from $1.50; 8am-6pm) Offers great prices for rental mask, snorkel and fins.

Sleeping

Noelani CONDO $$

(808-669-8374; www.noelanicondoresort.com; 4095 Lower Honoapi'ilani Rd; studio $182, 1 bedroom $227-237, 2/3 bedroom $339/403;) Meet your neighbors at the weekly mai tai party at this compact hideaway, a small condo complex that's so close to the water you can sit on your lanai and watch turtles swimming in the surf. Units range from cozy studios to three-bedroom suites, all with ocean views. Two pools, a Jacuzzi, a small exercise room and concierge services are additional perks.

Eating

Farmers Market Deli DELI $

(808-669-7004; 3636 Lower Honoapi'ilani Rd; sandwiches $6; 7am-7pm;) For healthy and tasty takeout fare, stop at this welcoming market. The salad bar (with free samples; $9 per pound) includes organic goodies and hot veggie dishes. The smoothies are first-rate. The place becomes even greener on Monday, Wednesday and Friday mornings (7am to 11am), when vendors sell locally grown produce in the parking lot.

★ **Honokowai Okazuya** INTERNATIONAL $$

(808-665-0512; 3600 Lower Honoapi'ilani Rd; mains $10-18; 11am-2:30pm & 4:30-8:30pm Mon-Sat) The appeal is not immediately apparent. The place is tiny, prices are high and the choices seem weird (*kung pao* chicken *and* spaghetti with meatballs?). Then you nibble the Mongolian beef. Hmm, it's OK. Chomp chomp. That's pretty interesting. Gulp gulp. What is that spice? Savor savor – until the whole meal is devoured. Here, plate lunches take a delicious gourmet turn. Primarily takeout. Cash only.

Kahana

Trendy Kahana, the village north of Honokowai, boasts million-dollar homes, upscale beachfront condominiums and Maui's only microbrewery.

Sights & Activities

The sandy **beach** fronting the village offers reasonable swimming. Park at seaside **Pohaku Park** and walk north to reach the beach. Pohaku Park itself has an offshore break called S-Turns that attracts surfers.

Maui Dive Shop DIVING, SNORKELING

(808-669-3800; www.mauidiveshop.com; 4405 Honoapi'ilani Hwy, Kahana Gateway; 2-tank dives from $130, snorkel sets per day $6-9; 8am-9pm) Come here for information about a full range of dives and to rent snorkel gear.

Sleeping

Kahana Village CONDO $$$

(808-669-5111; www.kahanavillage.com; 4531 Lower Honoapi'ilani Rd; 2/3 bedroom from $300/510;) With A-frame ceilings, airy lofts and oceanfront views, the 2nd-story units have a fun 'vacation' vibe. The breezy appeal of the interior is well-matched outside with lush tropical flora and weekly mai tai parties with live Hawaiian music. Some condos have views of Lana'i while others face Moloka'i. Every unit has a full kitchen and washer and dryer.

Eating & Drinking

Hawaiian Village Coffee CAFE $
(808-665-1114; www.hawaiianvillagecoffee.com; 4405 Honoapi'ilani Hwy, Kahana Gateway shopping center; pastries under $6, sandwiches $8-10; 6am-6pm;) Off-duty surfers shoot the breeze at this low-key coffee shop. Use computers in back to surf the net (20 minutes for $3, then 20¢ per minute) and print documents (35¢ per page).

Maui Brewing Co BREWERY
(808-669-3474; www.mauibrewingco.com; 4405 Honoapi'ilani Hwy, Kahana Gateway shopping center; mains $12-25; 11am-10pm) From burgers sourced with local beef to the *kalua* pork pizza, bar food takes a Hawaiian spin at this cavernous brewpub. The company, which has been honored as one of Hawaii's top green businesses, implements sustainable practices where it can. The Bikini Blonde lager, Mana Wheat, Big Swell IPA and Coconut Porter are always on tap, supplemented by seasonal and specialty brews.

In 2015, ever-growing Maui Brewing added a new production facility and taproom to its line-up, housed together in Kihei (p374).

Napili

Napili is a bayside oasis flanked by the posh grounds of Kapalua to the north and the hustle and bustle of Kahana and Ka'anapali to the south. For an oceanfront retreat that's a bit more affordable – and not far from the action – we highly recommend this sun-blessed center of calm.

Beaches

Napili Beach BEACH
The deep golden sands and gentle curves of Napili Beach offer good beachcombing at any time and excellent swimming and snorkeling when it's calm. Look for green sea turtles hanging out by the rocky southern shore. Big waves occasionally make it into the bay in winter, and when they do it's time to break out the skimboards – the steep drop at the beach provides a perfect run into the surf.

Sleeping

Napili Bay is surrounded by older condos and small, mellow resorts. Come here to escape the Ka'anapali crowds and to enjoy low-cost proximity to Kapalua. Most don't have air-conditioning but ocean breezes typically keep rooms cool.

Napili Sunset Beachfront Resort CONDO $$
(808-669-8083; www.napilisunset.com; 46 Hui Dr; studio/1 bedroom/2 bedroom $170/330/490, 1 bedroom with loft $350;) The Napili Sunset is a little well-worn around the edges, but it is also well loved. With welcoming staff and repeat guests who enjoy talking story, the place has a small-town feel. But this small town is on the beach, or just a few steps away. The 26 units, which are spread across two buildings, have kitchens and lanai. Guest laundry.

★ **Hale Napili** CONDO $$$
(8089-669-6184, 800-245-2266; www.halenapili.com; 65 Hui Dr; studio $199-299, 1 bedroom $349;) A welcome throwback to an earlier era, this small and personable place will win you over with its island hospitality. Guests receive a list of occupants, making it easier to strike up conversations, and there's a central Keurig coffee machine so you can chat over morning coffee. The 18 neat-as-a-pin units have tropical decor, full kitchens and oceanfront lanai.

Mauian HOTEL $$$
(808-669-6205; www.mauian.com; 5441 Lower Honoapi'ilani Rd; studio with kitchen from $225, r $205;) Most Napili condos wear their age gracefully, but not the sassy Mauian, a 44-room condo-hotel hybrid kicking up her stylish heels like a teenager. Bamboo ceilings, frond prints, crisp whites and browns, Tempur-Pedic mattresses – rooms are sharp, stylish and comfortable. Enjoy the breeze from the lanai.

Units do not have TVs or phones, but both are available in the common area. Hotel rooms do not have kitchens.

Napili Kai Beach Resort CONDO, HOTEL $$$
(808-669-6271; www.napilikai.com; 5900 Lower Honoapi'ilani Rd; r/studio/ste from $280/375/555; @) This low-key yet sophisticated resort covers 10 acres at the northern end of Napili Bay. The units, which tastefully blend Polynesian decor with Asian touches, have private lanai, and the studios and suites have kitchenettes. For modern style and decor, reserve a room in the Puna Point, Puna 2 or Lani 1 buildings. Some units have air-con, so check when booking.

There are complimentary children's activities during holidays and in summer. The Monday 'putting party' offers 50¢ cocktails on the resort's 18-hole green.

Eating & Drinking

★Gazebo CAFE $

(☎808-669-5621; 5315 Lower Honoapi'ilani Rd, Outrigger Napili Shores; mains $8-12.25; ⏲7:30am-2pm) Locals aren't kidding when they advise you to get here early to beat the crowds. But a 7:10am arrival is worth it for this beloved open-air restaurant – a gazebo on the beach – with a gorgeous waterfront setting. The tiny cafe is known for its breakfasts, and those with a sweet tooth love the white chocolate macnut pancakes.

Meal-size salads, hearty sandwiches and the *kalua* pig plate steal the scene at lunch. The restaurant is behind Outrigger Napili Shores.

Maui Tacos MEXICAN $

(☎808-665-0222; www.mauitacos.com; 5095 Napilihau St, Napili Plaza; mains $5-11; ⏲9am-9pm Mon-Sat, to 8pm Sun) The burritos are huge at Maui Tacos, where the Mexican fare is island-style healthy. The salsas and beans are prepared fresh daily, trans-fat-free oil replaces lard, and fresh veggies and local fish feature on the menu. It's fast-food style and good for a quick meal.

Sea House Restaurant HAWAII REGIONAL CUISINE $$

(☎808-669-1500; www.seahousemaui.com; 5900 Lower Honoapi'ilani Rd, Napili Kai Beach Resort; breakfast $8-15, lunch $11-16, dinner $22-36; ⏲7am-9pm, cocktails to 10pm) Pssst, want an $8 meal framed by a million dollar view? Sidle up to the bar at this tiki-lit favorite, order a bowl of the smoky seafood chowder then watch as the perfectly framed sun drops below the horizon in front of you. Bravo! If you stick around, and you should, seafood and steak dishes are menu highlights.

Happy hour (2pm to 5pm) draws crowds for $3 to $7 *pupu* and $6 to $8 cocktails.

Napili Coffee Store CAFE

(☎808-669-4170; www.facebook.com/thecoffeestorenapili; 5095 Napilihau St, Napili Plaza; pastries $4-5, sandwiches & salads $7-14; ⏲6am-6pm; 📶) The ice-blended mocha at Napili's favorite coffee shop is nothing less than aloha in a cup. Utterly delicious. Locals also line up for the pleasant service and the pastries, from banana bread to pumpkin-cranberry muffins and chocolate peanut butter bars. For heartier fare try a slice of quiche or a turkey sandwich with basil pesto.

Entertainment

★Masters of Hawaiian Slack Key Guitar Concert Series LIVE MUSIC

(☎808-669-3858; www.slackkeyshow.com; 5900 Lower Honoapi'ilani Rd, Napili Kai Beach Resort; admission $38-45; ⏲7:30pm Wed & Thu) Ledward Kaapana and other top slack key guitarists appear regularly at this exceptional concert series, and George Kahumoku Jr, a slack key legend in his own right, is the weekly host. As much a jam session as a concert, this is a true Hawaiian cultural gem that's worth going out of your way to experience. Reservations recommended.

Kapalua & Northern Beaches

POP 353

Kapalua has long been a sacred place for Native Hawaiians. In the 1900s it was also the site of a productive pineapple plantation. Currently the home of a posh resort with several top-notch lodging options and two world-class golf courses, Kapalua is making an all-out effort to lure in guests. A new zipline company is taking people skyward, an adrenaline-fueled off-road triathlon has relocated here and a swanky hotel opened its doors in the summer of 2014. And the dining scene? Still among the island's best. The nightlife doesn't exactly sizzle, but the beaches – all with public access – sure do.

If you want to avoid the well-manicured glitz, swoop past the resort and take a winding drive along the rugged northern coast. The untamed views are guaranteed to replenish your soul.

If uninterrupted sunshine is your goal, note that Kapalua can be a bit rainier and windier than points south.

Sights

Makaluapuna Point CULTURAL SITE

Razor-sharp spikes crown rocky Makaluapuna Point, known informally by the nickname Dragon's Teeth. The formation does look uncannily like the mouth of an imaginary dragon. The 3ft-high spikes are the work of pounding winter waves that have ripped into the lava rock point, leaving the pointy 'teeth' behind.

Signage states that the outcropping is sacred to Native Hawaiians. Although the public is allowed access to the ocean by law, visitors are strongly discouraged from walking onto the formation out of respect for native customs. The adjacent **Honokahua burial site** is off-limits to the general public.

Both sites are of cultural significance to Native Hawaiians and should not be inspected up close. Respect the signage. The point is also potentially hazardous. It is subject to powerful waves, particularly the northern winter swells, and covered by uneven, sometimes sharp, rocks.

For a view of Makaluapuna Point, you can skirt along the outside of the 13-acre burial site below the parking area, but don't enter areas marked 'Please Kokua,' which are easily visible islets of stones bordering the Ritz's manicured golf greens. Do not walk across the greens.

Get here by driving north to the very end of Lower Honoapi'ilani Rd, where you'll find parking and a plaque detailing the burial site. The path to the point leads down from the plaque along the northern edge of the Kapalua Bay Golf Course.

Beaches

The following beaches are listed geographically, beginning at the southwestern tip of Kapalua then heading north.

★Kapalua Beach BEACH

For a long day on the beach, it's hard to beat this crescent-shaped strip at the southwestern tip of Kapalua. Snorkel in the morning, grab lunch at the Sea House, try stand-up paddle surfing, then sip cocktails at Merriman's next door. Or simply sit on the sand and gaze across the channel at Moloka'i.

Long rocky outcrops at both ends of the bay make Kapalua Beach the safest year-round swimming spot on this coast. You'll find colorful snorkeling on the right side of the beach, with abundant tropical fish and orange slate-pencil sea urchins. There's a rental hut here for beach gear.

Take the drive immediately north of Napili Kai Beach Resort to get to the beach parking area, where there are restrooms and showers. A tunnel leads from the parking lot north to the beach. This is also a starting point for the Coastal Trail.

Oneloa Beach BEACH

Fringed by low sand dunes covered in beach morning glory, this white-sand jewel is a picturesque place to soak up the rays. On calm days swimming is good close to shore, as is snorkeling in the protected area along the rocky point at the northern side of the beach. When there's any sizable surf, strong rip currents can be present.

The half-mile strand – Oneloa means 'long sand' – sits beside the Coastal Trail and is backed by gated resort condos and restricted golf greens. Beach access requires a sharp eye. Turn onto Ironwood Lane and then left into the small parking lot opposite the Ironwoods gate. Arrive early or at lunchtime, when people are heading out.

DT Fleming Beach Park BEACH

(Honoapi'ilani Hwy) Surrounded by ironwood trees and backed by an old one-room schoolhouse, this sandy crescent looks like an outpost from another era. In keeping with its Hawaiian nature, the beach is the domain of wave riders. Experienced surfers and bodysurfers find good action here, especially in winter. The shorebreaks can be brutal, however, and the beach is a hot spot for injuries. The reef on the right is good for snorkeling in summer when the water is very calm.

Fleming has restrooms, showers, grills, picnic tables and a lifeguard. The access road is off Honoapi'ilani Hwy (Hwy 30), immediately north of the 31-mile marker.

The Coastal Trail and the Mahana Ridge Trail intersect here.

Slaughterhouse Beach & Honolua Bay BEACH

The narrow Kalaepiha Point separates **Slaughterhouse Beach** and **Honolua Bay**. Together they form the Honolua–Mokule'ia Bay Marine Life Conservation District, which is famed for its snorkeling and surfing.

Honolua Bay is a surfer's dream. It faces northwest and when it catches the winter swells it has some of the gnarliest surfing in the world. In summer snorkeling is excellent in both bays, thanks in part to prohibitions on fishing in the preserve. Honolua Bay is the favorite, with thriving reefs and abundant coral along its rocky edges.

Spinner dolphins sometimes hang near the mouth of the bays, swimming just beyond snorkelers. When it's calm, you can snorkel around Kalaepiha Point from one bay to the other, but forget it after heavy rains: Honolua Stream empties into Honolua Bay and the runoff clouds the water.

The land fronting Honolua Bay has long been owned by Maui Land & Pineapple. The company has allowed recreational access to the bay for no fee. A few families have the right to live on this land, but they cannot charge an access fee or restrict visiting

Kapalua & Around

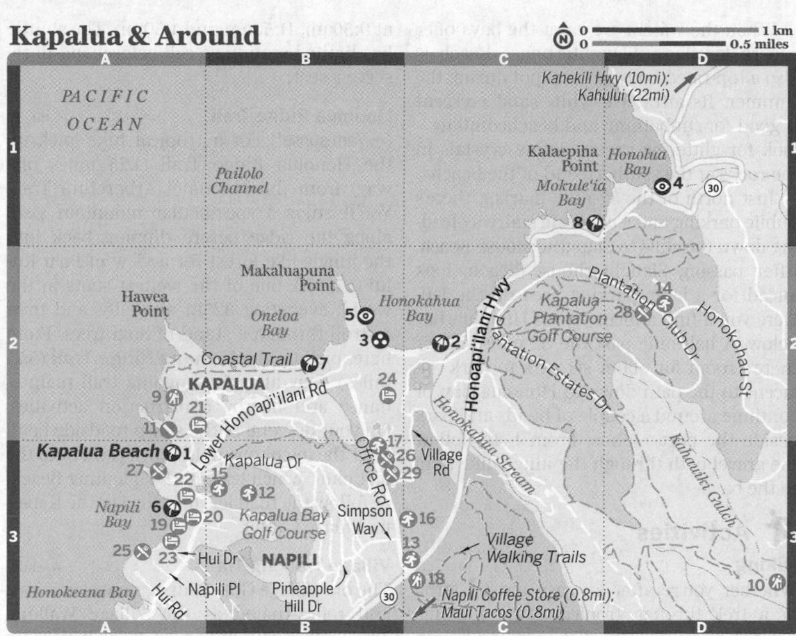

Kapalua & Around

Top Sights
1 Kapalua Beach A3

Sights
2 DT Fleming Beach Park C2
3 Honokahua Burial Site B2
4 Honolua Bay Entry Point D1
5 Makaluapuna Point B2
6 Napili Beach A3
7 Oneloa Beach B2
8 Slaughterhouse Beach C1

Activities, Courses & Tours
9 Coastal Trail A2
10 Honolua Ridge Trail D3
11 Kapalua Bay Beach Crew A2
12 Kapalua Bay Golf Course B3
13 Kapalua Golf Academy C3
14 Kapalua Plantation Golf Course D2
15 Kapalua Tennis Garden B3
16 Kapalua Village Center C3
17 Kapalua Ziplines B3
Spa Montage Kapalua Bay .... (see 21)
18 Village Walking Trails C3

Sleeping
19 Hale Napili A3
20 Mauian A3
21 Montage Kapalua Bay A2
22 Napili Kai Beach Resort A3
23 Napili Sunset Beachfront Resort A3
24 Ritz-Carlton Kapalua B2

Eating
25 Gazebo A3
26 Honolua Store B3
27 Merriman's Kapalua A3
28 Plantation House D2
29 Sansei Seafood Restaurant & Sushi Bar B3
Sea House Restaurant .... (see 22)

Entertainment
Masters of Hawaiian Slack Key Guitar Concert Series .... (see 22)

hours. In 2013, with community support, the state set aside funds to purchase 280 acres beside the bay to protect them from development (p346).

Once you reach the bay, read the signage about protecting the coral then enter via the rocky coastline. Sunscreen, for example, should be avoided in order to safeguard the coral. Do not enter the water via the concrete boat ramp, which is very slippery and potentially hazardous.

When the waters are calm the bays offer superb kayaking. Slaughterhouse Beach is also a top-rated bodysurfing spot during the summer. Its attractive white-sand crescent is good for sunbathing and beachcombing – look for glittering green olivine crystals in the rocks at the southern end of the beach.

Just north of the 32-mile marker, there's public parking and a concrete stairway leading down the cliffs to Slaughterhouse Beach. After passing Slaughterhouse Beach, look ahead for a large parking area on the left. Here you'll find a nice view of Honolua Bay below. A half-mile past the 32-mile marker there's room for about six cars to park adjacent to the path down to Honolua Bay, or continue around a couple of bends and park beside the port-o-johns. From here, follow the gravel path through the jungle-like flora to the bay.

Activities

Hiking

Whether you're after an easy coastal stroll or a trek through tropical flora, Kapalua has got a trail for you. For maps and shuttle pickups, check in at the Kapalua Village Center.

Maunalei Arboretum Trail HIKING

The Maunalei Arboretum Trail cuts through a forest planted by DT Fleming, the arborist who developed Maui's pineapple industry. Access is strictly via a free shuttle (665-9110) that departs from the **Kapalua Village Center** (☎808-665-4386; www.kapalua.com/adventures; 2000 Village Rd) located between the Ritz-Carlton Kapalua and the Honoapi'ilani Hwy. Shuttles depart at 9:30am, 11:30am and 1:30pm, and return from the arboretum at 9:50am, 11:50am and 1:50pm. The shuttle has limited seating so call beforehand to reserve a seat.

Honolua Ridge Trail HIKING

(⏲7am-sunset) For a tropical hike, pick up the Honolua Ridge Trail (1.25 miles one way) from the Maunalei Arboretum Trail. You'll enjoy a spectacular mountain vista along the ridge before dipping back into the jungle-like forest for a view of Pu'u Kukui (5788ft), one of the wettest spots in the world, averaging 325in annually, and then a stroll through a stand of Sugi trees. From here, pick up the **Mahana Ridge Trail** (5.75 miles). Stay alert for ongoing trail maintenance and nearby construction activities. On your descent, at the sharp roadside bend after the telephone poles, turn right onto the dirt path, which leads to DT Fleming Beach, or follow the road left to return to the Kapalua Village Center.

Village Walking Trails WALKING

The old Village Golf Course, now overgrown and reincarnated as the Village Walking Trails, offers stunning scenery as it rises up the mountain slopes.

Coastal Trail HIKING

The easy Coastal Trail (1.76 miles) links Kapalua Beach with Oneloa Beach, then crosses below the Ritz-Carlton to end at DT Fleming Beach. During your walk, be sure to stay on the designated path to avoid disturbing nesting birds. The Coastal Trail passes ancient burial grounds and Makaluapuna Point, both located north of the Ritz-Carlton and the trail. These sites are of cultural significance to Native Hawaiians and should not be inspected up close. Respect the signage.

SAVING HONOLUA BAY

What do snorkelers, surfers, environmentalists and native Hawaiians have in common in West Maui? Their love for Honolua Bay, a sparkling inlet sitting about 2 miles north of Kapalua. The bay is a marine conservation area famed for its hollow, right-breaking point surf and its coral reef, which teems with marine life.

In 2007 the owner of the land surrounding the bay, Maui Land & Pineapple Company, submitted development plans to Maui County. Its vision for the property? Forty luxury homes, a golf course, a cultural area and a surf park. The Save Honolua Coalition (www.savehonolua.org) formed in response, and gathered 16,000 signatures calling for the land's preservation. Maui Land dropped its plans, but the energized community called for a more permanent protection plan. After years of negotiating, the state agreed in 2013 to allocate $20 million for the purchase of 280 acres beside the bay, which will be managed by the state. According to news reports, proceeds from the sale will help fund pensions of Maui Land & Pineapple Company retirees. Planning continues as regulatory requirements and eco-concerns are addressed.

Golf

Kapalua Golf GOLF
(☎808-669-8044, 877-527-2582; www.golfatkapalua.com; Bay/Plantation greens fee $215/295, twilight (1pm) $155/195, late afternoon $105/135; ⏰1st tee around 6:40am) Kapalua boasts two of the island's top championship golf courses, both certified by Audubon International as sanctuaries for native plants and animals. How's that for green greens? The **Bay course** (☎808-662-7720; 300 Kapalua Dr) is the tropical ocean course, meandering across a lava peninsula. The challenging **Plantation course** (☎808-662-7710; 2000 Plantation Club Dr) sweeps over a rugged landscape of hills and deep gorges.

Kapalua Golf Academy GOLF
(☎808-662-7740; www.golfatkapalua.com; 1000 Office Rd; 1hr private lesson $180, half-day school $250; ⏰7am-5pm) Hawaii's top golf academy is staffed by PGA pros.

Spas

Spa Montage Kapalua Bay SPA
(☎808-665-8282; www.spamontage.com; 1 Bay Dr) This soothing place, with top-of-the line facilities and aesthetically pleasing treatment areas, embraces native Hawaiian ingredients and traditions from both the *mauka* (mountain) and the *makai* (sea). This is the place for a couple's massage. Post-treatment, continue invigorating with a fresh fruit juice or smoothie from the on-site cafe and juice bar (6am to 5pm; juices and smoothies under $10).

Tennis

Kapalua Tennis Garden TENNIS
(☎808-662-7730; www.kapaluatennis.com; 100 Kapalua Dr; per person per day $15, racket rental $6; ⏰8am-6pm) Maui's premier full-service tennis club has 10 Plexipave courts, with four lit for evening games, and an array of clinics. If you're on your own, give the club a ring and they'll match you with other players for singles or doubles games.

Water Sports

Kapalua Bay Beach Crew DIVING
(☎808-649-8222; Kapalua Bay; ⏰8am-5pm) Rent a basic snorkel set for $15 per day and an SUP board for $40 per hour. An SUP lesson is $139 for two hours. Look for its hut at the northern end of Kapalua Beach.

Ziplining

Kapalua Ziplines ZIPLINING
(☎808-756-9147; www.kapaluaziplines.com; 500 Office Rd; 4-/7-line zip $177/208; ⏰6:30am-6pm) Ready to soar across the West Maui Mountains for nearly 2 miles? On the signature tour (four hours, 15 minutes) you'll glide down seven zip lines, two of them extending a breathtaking 2000ft in length. The tour has a dual track, allowing you to zip beside a friend. The seven-line tour includes lunch.

Festivals & Events

Hyundai Tournament of Champions SPORTS
(www.pgatour.com; ⏰Jan) Watch Tiger and friends tee off at the PGA Tour's season opener in early January at the Plantation course, vying for a multimillion-dollar purse.

Celebration of the Arts ART
(www.celebrationofthearts.org; ⏰May) This festival held in early May at the Ritz-Carlton celebrates traditional Hawaiian culture with art, hula, music, films and cultural panels.

Kapalua Wine & Food Festival FOOD, WINE
(www.kapaluawineandfoodfestival.com; ⏰Jun) This culinary extravaganza is held over four days in mid-June at the Ritz-Carlton. It features renowned winemakers and Hawaii's hottest chefs, offering cooking demonstrations and wine tastings.

Xterra World Championship SPORTS
(www.xterraplanet.com/maui; ⏰Oct) Held in October, this race is a major off-road triathlon. Based out of the Ritz-Carlton, it boasts a $105,000 purse. The race moved from Makena to Kapalua in 2013.

Sleeping

★ **Montage Kapalua Bay** RESORT $$$
(☎808-662-6600; www.montagehotels.com; 1 Bay Dr; ste from $775; P ❄ @ 🛜 ≋) Whoa, nice work Montage Kapalua Bay. Swanky yet inviting, this 24-acre resort, which opened in 2014, takes style and comfort to an utterly pleasing level. With only 50 units, all of them suites, the property feels more intimate and less hectic than other resorts across Maui. Bright pillows add a colorful splash to the subdued but appealing in-room furnishings.

Suites come with kitchens, washer and dryer, and spacious lanai. And beyond your suite? You can relax beside the three-tiered pool, enjoy pampering at the tranquil spa or hop into the bright blue waters lapping below the 1940 Cliff House, once used by the Honolua Plantation. Condo-style residences will be available for rent in 2015. The resort fee is $30 per day and valet-only parking is $20 per day.

Ritz-Carlton Kapalua RESORT HOTEL **$$$**
(808-669-6200; www.ritzcarlton.com; 1 Ritz-Carlton Dr; r/ste from $499/659;) Understated elegance attracts the exclusive golf crowd to this luxe northern outpost. On a hillside fronting the greens and the sea, the hotel has a heated multilevel swimming pool flanked by palm trees, a spa and a fitness club. Rooms dazzle with simple but sleek island style: dark-wood floors, low-key Hawaiiana and oversize marble bathrooms.

The $30 daily resort fee covers wi-fi, and use of the fitness center and resort shuttle. Self-parking is $18 per day.

Eating

Honolua Store SANDWICHES, PLATE LUNCH **$**
(808-665-9105; 502 Office Rd; breakfast $6-9, lunch $5-13; store 6am-8pm, deli 6am-3pm) This porch-wrapped bungalow, which was revamped and expanded in 2013, opened in 1929 as the general store for the Honolua Pineapple Plantation. Today, the place is a nod to normalcy in the midst of lavish exclusiveness. The deli is known for its reasonable prices and fantastic plate lunches. Grab-and-go sandwiches and bento items are available in the deli case.

Merriman's Kapalua HAWAII REGIONAL CUISINE **$$$**
(808-669-6400; www.merrimanshawaii.com/kapalua; 1 Bay Club Pl; restaurant mains $28-65, happy hour menu $9-24; restaurant 5:30-9pm, bar 3pm until close) We especially like Merriman's at happy hour (3pm to 5pm). Perched on a scenic point between Kapalua Bay and Napili Bay, the tiki- and palm-dotted Point Bar is a gorgeous place to unwind after braving the Kahekili Hwy. At the acclaimed restaurant, Maui-caught fish and locally sourced meats and produce are the highlights.

Sansei Seafood Restaurant & Sushi Bar JAPANESE **$$$**
(808-669-6286; www.sanseihawaii.com; 600 Office Rd; sushi from $3, mains from $16; dinner 5:15-10pm Sat-Wed, to 1am Thu & Fri) The innovative sushi menu is the draw, but the non-sushi house specials, which often blend Japanese and Pacific Rim flavors, shouldn't be overlooked. The spicy Dungeness crab ramen with truffle broth is a noteworthy prize. Order between 5:15pm and 6pm Tuesday to Saturday and food is discounted by 25%. No reservation? Queue up early for one of the seats at the sushi bar.

Sushi, soup and appetizers are 50% off from 10pm to 1am on Thursday and Friday nights.

Plantation House HAWAII REGIONAL CUISINE **$$$**
(808-669-6299; www.theplantationhouse.com; 2000 Plantation Club Dr, Plantation Golf Course Clubhouse; breakfast $9-19, lunch $15-20, dinner $29-47; 8am-9pm) The crab cake Benedict at this open-air eatery is a fluffy, hollandaise-splashed affair that will have you kissing your plate and plotting your return. Adding to the allure are stellar views of the coast and Moloka'i, as well as the world-famous golf course below. For dinner, fresh fish and beef dishes are prepared with global flair.

Kahekili Highway

Bring your hat, your scrambling shoes and your sense of adventure on this challenging road trip, which hugs the rugged northern tip of Maui. Optimistically called a highway (Route 340), it charges around hairpin turns, careens over one-lane bridges and teeters beside treacherous cliffs. It's one of Maui's most adventurous drives. The area is so ravishingly rural that it's hard to imagine trendy West Maui could hold such untouched countryside.

Not for the faint of heart, sections slow to just 5mph as the road wraps around blind curves; a lengthy stretch around the village of Kahakuloa is a mere one lane with cliffs on one side and a sheer drop on the other – if you hit oncoming traffic here you may be doing your traveling in reverse! But if you can handle that, this largely overlooked route offers all sorts of adventures, with horse and hiking trails, a mighty blowhole and delicious banana bread.

Don't be fooled by car rental maps that show the road as a dotted line – it's paved and open to the public the entire way. There are no services, so gas up beforehand. Give yourself a good two hours' driving time, not counting stops.

Property between the highway and the coast is both privately and publicly owned. Trails to the shore are often uneven, rocky and slippery, and the coast is subject to dangerous waves. If you decide to explore, take appropriate precautions, and get access permission when possible.

Many of the trails and viewpoints are exposed, with little shade, so bring water, sunscreen and hat if you plan to explore.

Punalau Beach

Manicured golf courses and ritzy enclaves drop away and the scenery gets wilder as you drive toward the island's northernmost point. Ironwood-lined Punalau Beach, 0.7 miles after the 34-mile marker, makes a worthy stop if you're up for a solitary stroll. Swimming is a no-go though, as a rocky shelf creates unfavorable conditions for water activities.

Nakalele Point

The terrain turns hilly after Punalau Beach, with rocky cattle pastures punctuated by tall sisal plants. At a number of pull-offs, you can stop and explore. Lush pastures are quite enticing, willing you to traipse down the cliffs and out along the rugged coastline.

At the 38-mile marker, a mile-long trail leads to a **light station** at the end of windswept Nakalele Point. Here you'll find a coastline of arches and other formations worn out of the rocks by the pounding surf. There are several worn paths leading toward the light station, but you can't really get lost – just walk toward the point. Bring water and wear a hat because there's little shade.

The **Nakalele Blowhole** roars when the surf is up but is a sleeper when the seas are calm. To check on its mood, park at the boulder-lined pull-off 0.6 miles beyond the 38-mile marker. You can glimpse the action, if there is any, a few hundred yards beyond the parking lot. It's a 15-minute scramble down a jagged moonscape of lava rocks to the blowhole, which can shoot up to 100ft. Keep a safe distance and watch your footing carefully. A tourist fell into the hole and vanished in 2011. Another died after falling from a cliff in the area in 2013. And it probably goes without saying, but don't sit on, or peer into, the blowhole!

Eight-tenths of a mile after the 40-mile marker look for the **Ohai Viewpoint**, on the *makai* side of the road. The viewpoint won't be marked but there's a sign announcing the start of the Ohai Trail, a 1.2-mile loop with interpretative signage and views off the coast. For the best views, bear left from the trailhead and walk to the top of the point for a jaw-dropping coastal panorama that includes a glimpse of the Nakalele Blowhole. If you have kids, be careful – the crumbly cliff has a sudden drop of nearly 800ft!

Natural Ocean Baths & Bellstone

After the 42-mile post the markers change; the next marker is 16 and the numbers drop as you continue.

One-tenth of a mile before the 16-mile marker, look seaward for a large dirt pull-off and a well-beaten path that leads 15 minutes down lava cliffs to **natural ocean baths** on the ocean's edge. Cut out of slippery lava rock and encrusted with olivine minerals, these incredibly clear pools sit in the midst of roaring surf. Some have natural steps, but if you're tempted to go in, size it up carefully – people unfamiliar with the water conditions here have been swept into the sea and drowned. If the rocks are covered in silt from recent storm runoffs, or the waves look high, forget about it – it's dangerous. Although the baths are on public land, state officials do not recommend accessing them due to the hazardous conditions, including slippery rocks, large and powerful surf, waves crashing over ledges and strong currents.

The huge boulder with concave marks on the inland side of the road just before the pull-off is a bellstone, **Pohaku Kani**. If you hit it with a rock on the Kahakuloa side, where the deepest indentations are, you might be able to get a hollow sound. It's a bit resonant if you hit it just right, though it takes some imagination to hear it ring like a bell.

Kahakuloa

An imposing 636ft-tall volcanic dome guards the entrance to Kahakuloa Bay like a lurking, watchful dragon. They say this photogenic landmark, known as **Kahakuloa Head**, was a favorite cliff-diving spot of Chief Kahekili. Before the road drops into the valley, there's a pull-off above town providing a bird's-eye view.

The bayside village of Kahakuloa, tucked at the bottom of a lush valley and embraced by towering sea cliffs, retains a solidly Hawaiian character. Kahakuloa's isolation has protected it from the rampant development found elsewhere on Maui. Farmers tend taro patches, dogs wander across the road, and a missionary-era Protestant church marks the village center. One of Hawaii's most accomplished ukulele players, Richard Ho'opi'i, grew up here.

You won't find any stores, but villagers set up hard-to-miss roadside stands selling fruit and snacks to day-trippers. For shave ice, hit Ululani's hot-pink stand. For free samples of macadamia nuts, coconut candy and *'ono* (delicious) banana bread, stop at **Julia's lime-green shack** (www.juliasbananabread.com; ⌚9am-5:30pm or until sold out). After one taste of the banana bread and some talk story on the porch, we bet you'll buy a loaf for the road ($9). It tastes fresh for days and makes a terrific no-fuss breakfast.

Kahakuloa to Waihe'e

On the outskirts of Kahakuloa, after a heart-stopping, narrow climb, you'll reach the hilltop **Kaukini Gallery & Gift Shop** (☎808-244-3371; www.kaukinigallery.com; ⌚10am-5pm), near the 14-mile marker. The gallery sells works by more than 120 island artists, with watercolors, jewelry, native-fiber baskets, koa boxes, vintage postcards and more. From here, it's 11 miles back to Kapalua or 13 miles onward to Wailuku.

Look for the towering giraffe statue after the 10-mile marker. It marks the entrance for **Turnbull Studios & Sculpture Garden** (☎808-244-0101; www.turnbullstudios.org; 5030 Kahekili Hwy; ⌚10am-5pm Mon-Sat). Here you can view Bruce Turnbull's ambitious bronze and wood creations, peer into a working studio and wander through a small gallery selling an attractive collection of work by area artists.

Continuing around beep-as-you-go blind turns, the highway gradually levels out atop sea cliffs. For an Eden-like scene, stop at the pull-off 175yd north of the 8-mile marker and look down into the ravine below, where you'll see a cascading **waterfall** framed by double pools.

For a real *paniolo* experience, saddle up at **Mendes Ranch** (☎808-871-5222; www.mendesranch.com; 3530 Kahekili Hwy; 1½hr rides $110; ⌚rides 8:45am & 12:15pm), a working cattle ranch near the 7-mile marker, just past the road to Waihe'e Ridge Trail. The picture-perfect scenery on these rides includes everything from jungle valleys to lofty sea cliffs.

Waihe'e Ridge Trail

This fabulous **trail** has it all: tropical flora, breezy ridgelines, lush valley landscapes and lofty views of Maui's wild northern coast and the central valley. The best part? The well-defined trail is less than 5 miles round-trip and only takes about three hours to complete.

The path is a bit steep, but it's a fairly steady climb and not overly strenuous. It's best to tackle this one before 8am in order to beat the clouds, which can obscure the view from the top later in the morning.

Starting at an elevation of 1000ft, the trail, which crosses reserve land, climbs a ridge, passing from pasture to forest. Guava trees and groves of eucalyptus are prominent, and the aroma of fallen fruit may accompany you after a rainstorm. From the 0.75-mile post, panoramic views open up, with a scene that sweeps clear down to the ocean along the **Waihe'e Gorge** and deep into pleated valleys.

As you continue on, you'll enter ohia forest with native birds and get distant views of waterfalls cascading down the mountains. The ridge-top views are similar to those you'd see from a helicopter, and you'll probably see a handful of them dart into the adjacent valley like gnats on a mission.

There are several benches along the trail to stop and soak in the scenery and the remarkable stillness. Birdsong, chirping insects, a rushing stream, muffled bits of hiker conversation below – these are the only interruptions. The trail ends at a small clearing and picnic table on the 2563ft peak of **Lanilili**. Here you'll find awesome views in all directions. If it's foggy, wait about 10 minutes or so because it may blow off.

Solos, seniors and in-shape kids should be fine on this hike. If you have access to hiking poles, bring them. The trail gets muddy and steep in spots.

To get to the trailhead, take the one-lane paved road that starts on the inland side of the highway just south of the 7-mile marker. It's almost directly across the road from the big gate to Mendes Ranch. After passing through an entrance gate (currently open 7am to 5pm), the road climbs 1 mile through open pasture to the **Boy Scouts' Camp Maluhia**. Keep an eye out for cattle that mosey across the road. The trailhead, marked with a Na Ala Hele sign, is on the left just before the camp. Take a right for the parking lot. According to the Division of Forestry & Wildlife, 50 to 100 people hike the trail per day, so expect company.

For complete details, visit www.hawaiitrails.org, the state's trail and access website.

Waihe'e to Wailuku

Soon after the Waihe'e Ridge Trail, the Kahekili Hwy runs through the sleeper towns of Waihe'e and Waiehu before arriving in Wailuku. There's not much to do here, but if you're up for a round of golf, the county-run **Waiehu Municipal Golf Course** (808-243-7400; www.mauicounty.gov; 200 Halewaiu Rd; greens fee $55, optional cart $20; 6:45am-5pm Mon-Fri, 6am-5pm Sat & Sun) offers an affordable and easily walkable 18 holes on the coast. On-site are a small cafe, pro-shop and public restrooms. Cash or travelers check only for greens fees although credit cards are accepted at the pro shop for cart and club rentals.

'IAO VALLEY & CENTRAL MAUI

Welcome to the flat bit. Central Maui is the isthmus connecting the West Maui Mountains to mighty Haleakalā, giving the island its distinctive three-part shape. This odd wedge of topography, Maui's most arable piece of land, was once known only for its fields of waving sugarcane, but it now boasts a potpourri of attractions. To the north, the island's commercial center, Kahului, contains windswept Kanaha Beach, a hub for water sports. Sister-city Wailuku is a funky up-and-comer with the best lunch scene, and the gateway to the lush 'Iao Valley. On the southern coast, Ma'alaea is home to a top-notch aquarium and its harbor is the launchpad for a Molokini cruise.

Kahului

POP 26,337

Most Hawaiian islands have a working town like Kahului, full of warehouses, strip malls, shopping centers, and that island-wide magnet, the big-box store. Like its counterparts, Kahului also contains Maui's main harbor and airport, turning it, in the eyes of many, into a transit stop. But at the same time, you'll find a great swath of local life here. You can talk story with the locals at the Saturday swap meet, watch a concert on the lawn of the cultural center and join the wave-riders at Kanaha Beach.

Sights

Kanaha Pond Bird Sanctuary NATURE RESERVE
(Map p354; Hwy 37; sunrise-sunset) FREE You wouldn't expect a wildlife sanctuary to be so close to a main road, but a short walk leaves it behind. This shallow marsh is a haven for rare Hawaiian birds, including native coots, black-crowned night herons, and the *ae'o* (Hawaiian black-necked stilt), a graceful wading bird with long, orange legs that feeds along the pond's marshy edges.

According to various Fish and Wildlife surveys the *ae'o* population probably hovers around 1500 statewide, but you can count on spotting some here.

Schaefer International Gallery MUSEUM
(Map p354; 808-242-2787; www.mauiarts.org; 1 Cameron Way; 10am-5pm Tue-Sun) FREE This art gallery at the Maui Arts & Cultural Center features six different exhibitions per year, ranging from native Hawaiian arts to contemporary local artists working in all mediums.

Kahului Harbor HARBOR
(Map p354) Kahului's large protected harbor is the island's only deep-water port, so all boat traffic, from cruise ships to cargo vessels, docks here. But it's not all business. Late afternoon you're likely to see outrigger canoe clubs like Na Kai 'Ewalu (www.nakaiewalucanoeclub.org) practicing at **Ho'aloha Park** – a timeless scene.

Maui Nui Botanical Gardens GARDENS
(Map p354; 808-249-2798; www.mnbg.org; 150 Kanaloa Ave; adult/child under 13yr $5/free, all guests on Sat free; 8am-4pm Mon-Sat) For botanophiles interested in native Hawaiian plants, this garden on the grounds of a former zoo is a wealth of knowledge. An excellent new audio tour ($5) brings it to life. Don't expect the exotic tropicals that dominate most Hawaiian gardens; do expect dedicated staff. Staff also lead personal guided tours from 10am to 11:30am Tuesday to Friday (suggested donation $5).

Beaches

★**Kanaha Beach Park** BEACH
(Map p352) Well, you can't judge a beach by its cover. Wedged between downtown Kahului and the airport, and hidden behind a strip of ironwood trees, this mile-long stretch of

Central Maui

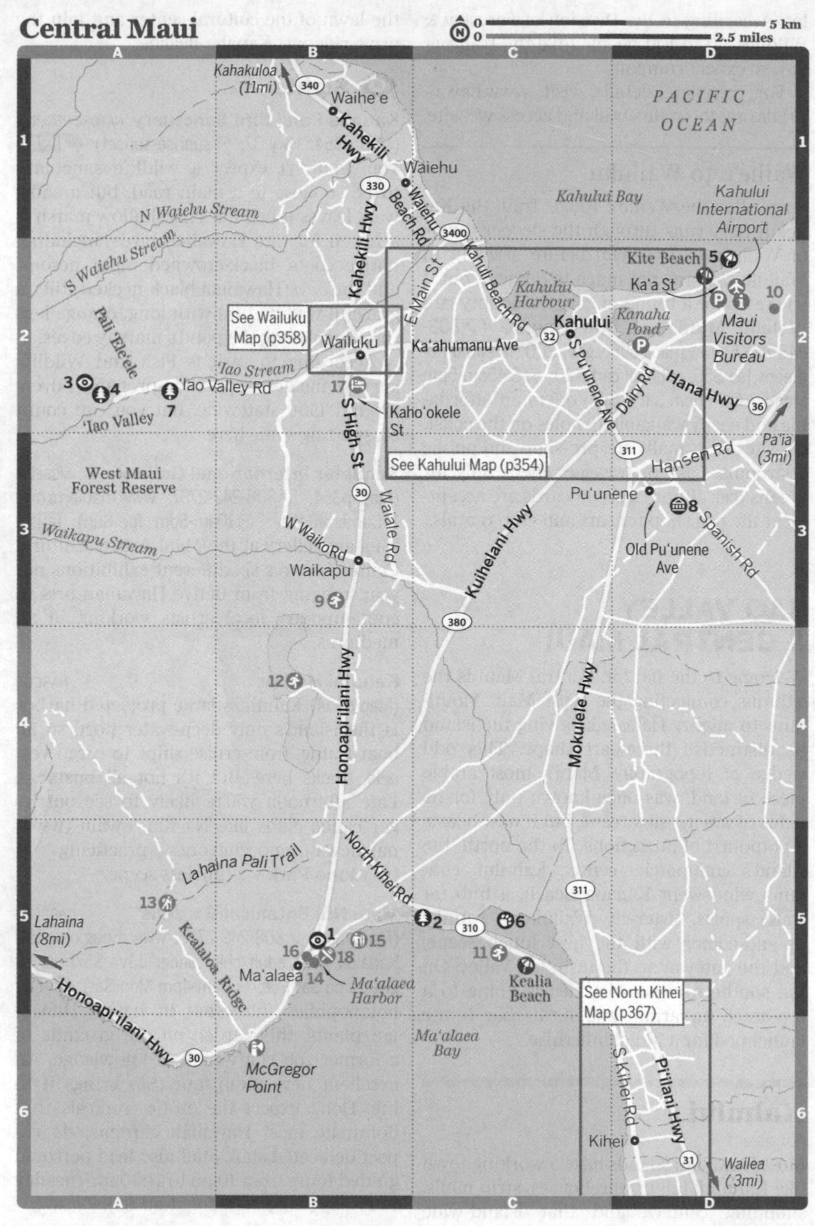

sand is surf city, with scores of brilliant sails zipping across the waves. Kitesurfers converge at the southwest end, known as **Kite Beach**, while windsurfers head northeast. A roped-off swimming area lies in-between. Facilities include restrooms, showers and shaded picnic tables.

There's no better place to learn how to ride the wind – or just to watch the action.

Central Maui

Top Sights
1 Maui Ocean Center.............................B5

Sights
2 Haycraft Park.....................................C5
3 'Iao Needle...A2
4 'Iao Valley State Park..........................A2
5 Kanaha Beach Park..............................D2
6 Kealia Pond National Wildlife Refuge.....C5
7 Kepaniwai Park & Heritage Gardens.......A2
8 Old Pu'unene Bookstore......................D3

Activities, Courses & Tours
Air Maui Helicopter Tours.......... (see 10)
Blue Hawaiian Helicopters .... (see 10)
9 Flyin Hawaiian Zipline..........................B3
10 Kahului Heliport..................................D2
11 Kealia Coastal Boardwalk....................C5
12 King Kamehameha Golf Club...............B4
13 Lahaina Pali Trail.................................A5
14 Ma'alaea Harbor Activities..................B5
15 Ma'alaea Pipeline................................B5
16 Pacific Whale Foundation....................B5
Quicksilver.................................. (see 14)
Shark Dive Maui ....(see 1)
Sunshine Helicopters................ (see 10)

Sleeping
17 Old Wailuku Inn....................................B2

Eating
Beach Bums Bar & Grill .... (see 16)
18 Ma'alaea General Store & Cafe...........B5

Activities

Kanaha Beach Park is the best place to windsurf on Maui, unless you're an aspiring pro ready for Ho'okipa. Board-and-rig rentals start at $55/335 per day/week, while two-hour introductory classes cost around $90. For more info see www.mauiwindsurfing.net.

Kitesurfing (or kiteboarding) is enormously popular in Kahului. The action centers on Kite Beach, the southwest end of Kanaha Beach Park. Here you can learn the ropes from some real pros, and you're likely to see vans from different water-sports companies parked in the lot. Expect to pay about $255 for a half-day intro course. Check out the scene live at www.kitebeachcam.com.

Be sure to shop around and ask about discounts.

Kanaha Kai WATER SPORTS
(Map p354; ☎808-877-7778; www.kanahakai.com; 96 Amala Pl; ⏲9am-6pm mid-Oct–Jan, to 5pm Feb–mid-Oct) Windsurfing, SUP, kitesurfing and surfing rentals and lessons. Very competitive pricing.

Second Wind WATER SPORTS
(Map p354; ☎808-877-7467; www.secondwindmaui.com; 111 Hana Hwy; ⏲9am-6pm) Full range of kiteboarding, windsurfing, SUP and surfing rentals.

Hawaiian Island Surf & Sport WATER SPORTS
(Map p354; ☎808-871-4981; www.hawaiianisland.com; 415 Dairy Rd; ⏲8:30am-6pm) Full range of water-sports rentals: kiteboarding, windsurfing, SUP, surfing, bodyboarding, diving and snorkeling. Website describes fundamentals and gear for each sport.

Aqua Sports Maui KITESURFING
(Map p354; ☎808-242-8015; www.mauikiteboardinglessons.com) Specializes in kitesurfing lessons. A one-hour intro is $39.

Crater Cycles MOUNTAIN BIKING
(Map p354; ☎808-893-2020; www.cratercycleshawaii.com; 358 Papa Pl; downhill bikes per day $65-85; ⏲9am-5pm Mon-Sat) Rents quality full-suspension downhill and road bikes, complete with helmet, pads and a roof rack. Provides good trail maps on its website.

Tours

Helicopter

In Hawaii the best helicopter tours operate out of Maui and Kaua'i. So if you aren't visiting the latter, this is your shot at the top. Various tour routes are available, but the finest combines the West Maui Mountains with the eastern end of Moloka'i, a jaw-dropping, uninhabited region of unspoiled emerald-green valleys and waterfalls.

Several tour companies operate out of **Kahului Heliport** (Map p352; 1 Kahului Airport Rd), alongside the airport. Check online and in free tourist magazines for significant discounts and ask about fuel surcharges.

★ **Blue Hawaiian Helicopters** SCENIC FLIGHTS
(Map p352; ☎808-871-8844; www.bluehawaiian.com; 1 Kahului Airport Rd, Hangar 105; tours $169-500) Industry-leader Blue Hawaiian uniquely flies the hi-tech Eco-Star, with its enclosed tail rotor. Excellent visibility means you see everything, while noise-cancelling headsets let you hear everything, and digital in-flight video brings the entire experience home. Tour prices depend on the itinerary and chopper; it also flies A-Stars, the industry workhorse.

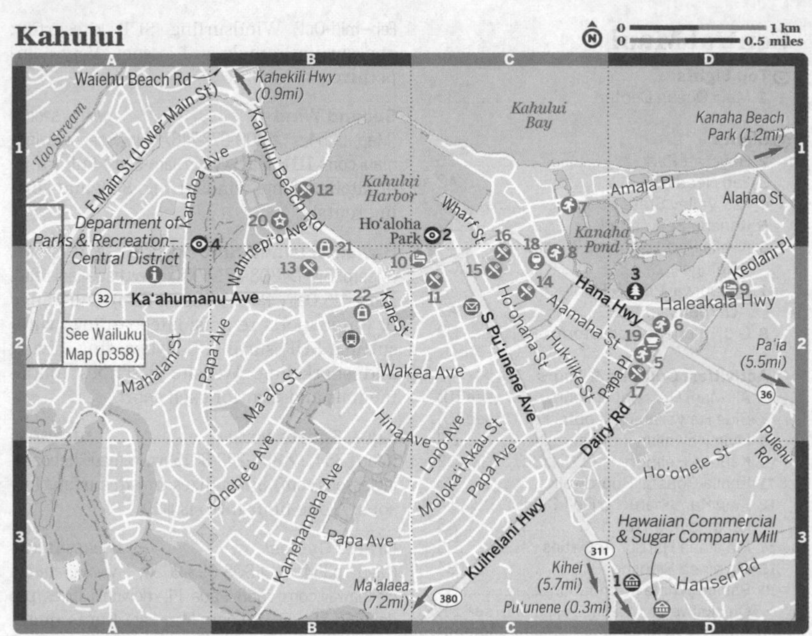

Kahului

Sights
1 Alexander & Baldwin Sugar Museum D3
2 Kahului Harbor C1
3 Kanaha Pond Bird Sanctuary D2
4 Maui Nui Botanical Gardens A1
Schaefer International Gallery .... (see 20)

Activities, Courses & Tours
Aqua Sports Maui .... (see 8)
5 Crater Cycles D2
6 Hawaiian Island Surf & Sport D2
7 Kanaha Kai C1
8 Second Wind C2

Sleeping
9 Courtyard Marriott Kahului Airport D2
10 Maui Seaside Hotel C2

Eating
11 Bistro Casanova C2
Da Kitchen .... (see 6)
12 Geste Shrimp Truck B1
13 Leis Family Class Act B2
Pa'ina Food Court .... (see 21)
14 Safeway Kahului C2
15 Tasaka Guri-Guri C2
16 Whole Foods C2
17 Wow-Wee Maui's Kava Bar & Grill D2

Drinking & Nightlife
18 Kahului Ale House C2
19 Maui Coffee Roasters D2

Entertainment
20 Maui Arts & Cultural Center B1

Shopping
Bounty Music .... (see 8)
21 Maui Swap Meet B2
22 Queen Ka'ahumanu Center B2

The signature West Maui Mountains & Moloka'i tour by Eco-Star is $300 (50 minutes). The professional staff operate like clockwork.

Air Maui Helicopter Tours SCENIC FLIGHTS
(Map p352; ☎808-877-7005; www.airmaui.com; 1 Kahului Airport Rd, Hangar 110; tours $188-338) A full range of tour options in A-Stars. Professionally run and good value.

Sunshine Helicopters SCENIC FLIGHTS
(Map p352; ☎808-270-3999; www.sunshinehelicopters.com; 1 Kahului Airport Rd, Hangar 107; tours $260-515) Well-established firm operating on four islands.

Hiking

Hike Maui HIKING
(☎808-879-5270; www.hikemaui.com; tours $85-229) To learn more about your natural surroundings as you hike through the rainforest and splash beneath waterfalls, consider a guided hike with this well-established company, which opened its doors in 1983! Also leads hikes into the crater at Haleakalā National Park. Hike Maui won the Hawaii Ecotourism Association's Operator of the Year award in 2010. Check website for departure locations.

Festivals & Events

★Ki Ho'alu Slack Key Guitar Festival MUSIC
(www.mauiarts.org; Jun) FREE Top slack key guitarists take the stage at this 30-year-old event, held on the lawn of the Maui Arts & Cultural Center each June.

Maui Ukulele Festival MUSIC
(www.ukulelefestivalhawaii.org; mid-Oct) FREE Held outdoors at the Maui Arts & Cultural Center on a Sunday in mid-October, this aloha event showcases uke masters from Maui and beyond.

Na Mele O Maui MUSIC
(www.kaanapaliresort.com; Dec) FREE This celebration of Hawaiian culture features children's choral groups singing native Hawaiian music. This aloha-rich event is held in early December at the Maui Arts & Cultural Center.

Sleeping

Maui Seaside Hotel HOTEL $$
(Map p354; ☎808-877-3311; www.mauiseasidehotel.com; 100 W Ka'ahumanu Ave; r $99-185;) If you want to stay on the beach, this aging hotel is the only decent option. It's a plain Jane but the rooms are clean.

★Courtyard Marriott Kahului Airport HOTEL $$$
(Map p354; ☎808-871-1800; www.marriott.com; 532 Keolani Pl; r/ste from $269/339;) Hands-down your best option in Kahului, and just a stone's throw from the airport. The stylish Modern Aloha lobby contains a breezy bistro, complete with media booths, that serves breakfast and dinner. Large rooms, including family suites, offer crisp white bedding and lots of light (pay up for a deluxe).

Other beneficial amenities include a guest laundry, a fitness center, a pleasant pool with fire pit and, best of all, a free shuttle serving a 3-mile radius (including the airport). Parking is $10 per day.

Eating

★Geste Shrimp Truck FOOD TRUCK $
(Map p354; ☎808-298-7109; www.gesteshrimp.com; Kahului Beach Rd, beside Kahului Harbor; meals $6-15; 10:30am-5:30pm Tue-Sat) This small white food truck – emblazoned with a giant shrimp – serves the tastiest shrimp on Maui – maybe even the world! $13 buys a dozen with a scoop of crab mac salad and rice. It's a messy meal so bring handi-wipes, don't wear white and don't eat in your car! The nearby Maui Nui Botanical Gardens has picnic tables.

Pa'ina Food Court FOOD COURT $
(Map p354; www.mauiculinary-campusdining.com; 310 W Ka'ahumanu Ave, Maui College; mains $6-9; 7:30am-4:30pm Mon-Thu, to 1pm Fri) With tenants like Paniolo Grill and World Plate, this multistall food court isn't your average campus fare. Run by students from Maui College's acclaimed culinary arts program, it's worth a detour for choice alone. The food court is inside the Pa'ina Building, which borders the parking lot beside the easy-to-find Maui Swap Meet grounds off Wahinepio Ave.

Tasaka Guri-Guri ICE CREAM $
(Map p354; 70 E Ka'ahumanu Ave, Maui Mall; 2 scoops/quart $1.20/5.50; 9am-6pm Mon-Thu & Sat, 9am-8pm Fri, 10am-4pm Sun) For the coolest treat in town, queue up at this hole-in-the-wall shop dishing up homemade pineapple sherbet. The *guri-guri*, as it's called, is so popular that locals take it to friends on neighboring islands. Cash only.

Safeway Kahului SUPERMARKET $
(Map p354; ☎808-877-3377; www.safeway.com; 170 E Kamehameha Ave; 24hr) For groceries, the Safeway in the town center never closes.

Whole Foods SUPERMARKET $
(Map p354; ☎808-872-3310; www.wholefoodsmarket.com; 70 E Ka'ahumanu Ave, Maui Mall; 7am-9pm) Whole Foods carries island-grown produce, fish and beef, and is a good place to pick up lei.

★Bistro Casanova MEDITERRANEAN $$
(Map p354; ☎808-873-3650; www.casanovamaui.com; 33 Lono Ave; lunch $8-20, dinner $14-34; ⏰11am-9:30pm Mon-Sat) An offshoot of the popular Casanova in Makawao, this is Kahului's classiest dining, with a solid tapas menu (from 3pm; $5 to $14), good seafood and steaks and plenty of Kula veggies. The setting is upscale and urban. Reservations are recommended at dinner, when the bistro can fill with a pre-theater crowd en route to a show at the Maui Arts & Cultural Center.

Da Kitchen HAWAIIAN $$
(Map p354; ☎808-871-7782; www.da-kitchen.com; 425 Koloa St, Triangle Sq; mains $10-26; ⏰11am-9pm Mon-Sat) Tasty local *grinds* attract all kinds to this strip mall eatery. The *kalua* pork is, as they say, 'so tender it falls off da bone,' while the more expensive plate lunches are big enough to feed two. Expect a crowd at lunch but the service is quick.

Wow-Wee Maui's Kava Bar & Grill BURGERS, SUSHI $$
(Map p354; www.wowweemaui.com; 333 Dairy Rd; sushi $7-17, mains $7-16; ⏰11am-9pm) The grill dominates the kava at this buzzing local joint, but it's still your best chance to try *piper methysticum,* a ceremonial drink made from the kava plant that has an earthy taste and numbs your mouth. The rest of the restaurant unites a sushi bar with a regular bar, and offers good burgers and wraps.

Leis Family Class Act INTERNATIONAL $$
(Map p354; ☎808-984-3280; www.mauiculinary-campusdining.com; 310 W Ka'ahumanu Ave, Maui College; prix fixe per person $29-39; ⏰11am-12:30pm Wed & Fri) Maui Culinary Academy's fine-dining restaurant connects an ocean view with the opportunity to watch up-and-coming chefs create a four-course locavore meal. The menu rotates between countries. Reserve online.

Drinking & Nightlife

Maui Coffee Roasters CAFE
(Map p354; ☎800-645-2877; www.mauicoffeeroasters.com/cafe; 444 Hana Hwy; pastries $4-9, sandwiches & wraps $7-10; ⏰7am-6pm Mon-Sat, 8am-4pm Sun; 📶) Enjoy good vibes and good java at this bright and upbeat cafe where locals sip lattes and nibble wraps while surfing free w-ifi. Kitchen hours 7am to 5pm Monday to Saturday and 8am to 2:30pm Sunday.

Kahului Ale House SPORTS BAR
(Map p354; ☎808-877-0001; www.alehouse.net; 355 E Kamehameha Ave; ⏰11am-12:30am Mon-Thu, to 2am Fri-Sun) With 35 flat-screens, Maui's top sports bar won't let you miss a single play. Pub grub includes burgers, sandwiches and pizzas. Live music from about 5pm to 8pm or so daily. The kitchen is open until midnight.

Entertainment

Maui Arts & Cultural Center CONCERT VENUE
(MACC; Map p354; ☎808-242-7469; www.mauiarts.org; 1 Cameron Way) This snazzy performance complex boasts two indoor theaters and an outdoor amphitheater. As Maui's main venue for music, theater and dance, 'the MACC' hosts everything from ukulele jams to touring rock bands. Don't miss the Slack Key Masters on the third Thursday of the month.

Shopping

Kahului hosts Maui's big-box discount chains of the Wal-Mart and Costco variety, as well as its reigning shopping mall, **Queen Ka'ahumanu Center** (Map p354; ☎808-877-3369; www.queenkaahumanucenter.com; 275 W Ka'ahumanu Ave; ⏰9:30am-9pm Mon-Sat, 10am-5pm Sun).

★Maui Swap Meet MARKET
(Map p354; ☎808-244-3100; www.mauiexposition.com; 310 Ka'ahumanu Ave, Maui College; adult/child 12yr & under 50¢/free; ⏰7am-1pm Sat) Don't be misled by 'swap meet.' This outdoor market is not a garage sale, nor a farmers market, but an arts and crafts show of the highest order. Scores of white tents, set up behind Maui College, are chock-full of fascinating, high-quality merchandise, most of it locally made, including jewelry, sculptures, clothing and Hawaii memorabilia. Visit here for a meaningful souvenir.

Bounty Music MUSIC
(Map p354; ☎808-214-1591; www.bountymusicmaui.com; 111 Hana Hwy; ⏰9am-6pm Mon-Sat, 10am-4pm Sun) Hawaiian music lovers, step inside for all sorts of ukuleles, from inexpensive imported models to handcrafted masterpieces. Rentals, too. And you might catch some impromptu live music.

Information

Bank of Hawaii (☎808-871-8250; www.boh.com; 27 S Pu'unene Ave; ⏰8:30am-4pm Mon-Thu, to 6pm Fri)

Longs Drugs (☎808-877-0068; 70 E Ka'ahumanu Ave, Maui Mall; ⏰24hr; pharmacy 8am-10pm Mon-Fri, to 7pm Sat & Sun) More than just a pharmacy – a local institution offering everything from flip-flops to souvenirs.

Maui Visitors Bureau (Map p352; ☎808-872-3893; www.gohawaii.com/maui; Kahului Airport; ⏰7:45am-10pm) This staffed booth in the airport's arrivals area has tons of tourist brochures.

Post Office (Map p354; 138 S Pu'unene Ave; ⏰8am-4:30pm Mon-Fri, 9am-noon Sat)

Getting There & Around

TO/FROM THE AIRPORT

Kahului International Airport (p645) is at the eastern side of town. Most visitors pick up rental cars at the airport.

The Haiku Islander and Upcountry Islander routes of the Maui Bus pass through the airport throughout the day. One medium-sized suitcase allowed.

BUS

The **Maui Bus** (Map p354; www.mauicounty.gov) connects Kahului with Ma'alaea, Kihei, Wailea and Lahaina, and these routes run hourly. Maui Bus routes also connect with Wailuku, Pa'ia and Ha'iku. Each route costs $2.

CAR

Bio-Beetle (☎808-873-6121; www.bio-beetle.com; 55 Amala Pl; per day $50-90, per week $199-399) Offers a spread of ecofriendly vehicles, including biodiesel VW bugs, gas and electric Chevy Volts, and the purely electric Nissan Leaf. Free airport pickup/drop-off.

Wailuku

POP 15,313

Four streams feed the lush landscape surrounding Wailuku, which made the area an important food source and land holding for Maui chieftains. Missionaries took up residence here in the 1800s. Today, while offering more sights on the National Register of Historic Places than any other town on Maui, Wailuku sees few tourists. And that is its appeal. An earthy mishmash of curio shops, galleries and mom-and-pop stores surround the modern center of the county capital, all begging to be browsed. If you're here at lunchtime you're in luck. Thanks to a combination of low rent and hungry government employees, Wailuku dishes up tasty eats at prices that shame more touristy towns.

Sights

A cluster of historic buildings anchor the small downtown. Hawaii's best-known architect, Maui-born CW Dickey, left his mark here before moving on to fame in Honolulu. The c 1928 **Wailuku Public Library** (Map p358; 251 High St, cnr High & Aupuni Sts; ⏰9am-5pm Mon-Wed & Fri, 1-8pm Thu) is a classic example of his distinctive regional design. Another Dickey creation, the **Territorial Building** (Map p358), sits across the street. To learn more, pick up a copy of the free Wailuku Historic District walking map at the Bailey House Museum or download it at www.mauimuseum.org. Five buildings along the walk are on the National Register of Historic Places.

★**Bailey House Museum** MUSEUM

(Map p358; ☎808-244-3326; www.mauimuseum.org; 2375 W Main St; adult/child 7-12yr $7/2; ⏰10am-4pm Mon-Sat) This small but historically evocative museum occupies the 1833 home of Wailuku's first Christian missionary, Edward Bailey. He was the second missionary to occupy the house and lived there nearly 50 years. The home gives you a sense of what it was like to live in missionary times while also containing a collection of interesting artifacts, including a shark-tooth dagger and a notable collection of native wood bowls, stone adzes, feather lei and tapa cloth.

Outside there's an historic koa canoe (c 1900) and a 10ft redwood board used by surfing legend Duke Kahanamoku.

Ka'ahumanu Church CHURCH

(Map p358; 103 S High St) This handsome missionary church is named for Queen Ka'ahumanu, who cast aside the old Hawaiian gods and allowed Christianity to flourish. The clock in the steeple, brought around the Horn in the 19th century, still keeps accurate time. The church is usually locked, but hymns still ring out in Hawaiian at Sunday services.

Festivals & Events

★**Wailuku First Friday** CARNIVAL

(www.mauifridays.com) On the first Friday of every month, from 6pm to 9pm, Market St turns into a pedestrian zone and laid-back street party, with several bands, lots of tasty food options, and even a beer garden. This is Wailuku at its finest, so don't miss it if you're nearby.

Wailuku

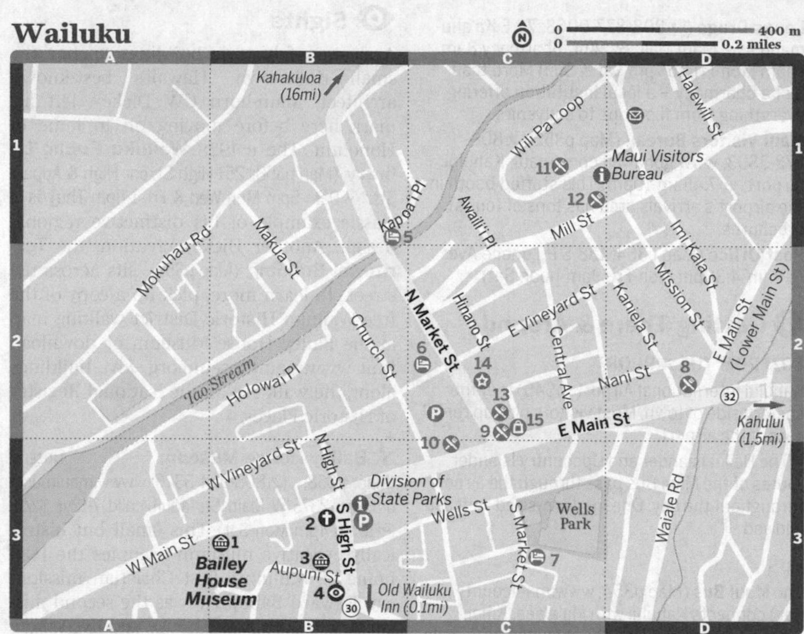

Wailuku

Top Sights
1 Bailey House Museum B3

Sights
2 Ka'ahumanu Church B3
3 Territorial Building B3
4 Wailuku Public Library B3

Sleeping
5 Banana Bungalow B1
6 Northshore Hostel C2
7 Wailuku Guesthouse C3

Eating
8 A Saigon Café D2
9 Farmacy Health Bar C2
10 Giannotto's Pizza C3
11 Sam Sato's C1
12 Tasty Crust C1
13 Wailuku Coffee Co C2

Entertainment
14 'Iao Theater C2

Shopping
15 Native Intelligence C2

Maui County Fair FAIR

(www.mauifair.com; Sep or Oct) Get a feel for Maui's agricultural roots at this venerable fair held in late September or early October, with farm exhibits, tasty island *grinds* and a dazzling orchid display.

E Ho'oulu Aloha CULTURAL

(www.mauimuseum.org; Nov) This old-Hawaii-style festival held in November at the Bailey House Museum features hula, music, crafts, food and more. You won't find a friendlier community scene.

Sleeping

Northshore Hostel HOSTEL $

(Map p358; 808-986-8095, 866-946-7835; www.northshorehostel.com; 2080 W Vineyard St; dm $33, r $79-99, all with shared bath; reception 8am-2pm & 5-11pm;) This quiet and traditional hostel attracts all ages. Located in an old building with a fresh coat of paint, it has separate male and female dorms as well as private rooms, a full kitchen, rental beach gear and valuable freebies, including an airport shuttle, international calls and breakfast.

Banana Bungalow HOSTEL $
(Map p358; ☎808-846-7835; www.mauihostel.com; 310 N Market St; dm $39, s/d $89/99; @ 📶) A free keg party every Friday night? If you're young, or young at heart, few hostels can compare with the vitality of this one. A constantly changing, international crowd of 20-somethings generates more pure fun here than anywhere else on the island.

But there's more: where else do you get a free tour to a different part of Maui? Or a free pancake breakfast every morning? Did we mention the hot tub? And for women travelers, a women-only dorm is available.

Wailuku Guesthouse GUESTHOUSE $
(Map p358; ☎808-986-8270; www.wailukuhouse.com; 210 S Market St; 1br $109-149, 2br $209; ❄ 📶 🏊) This affordable family-run guesthouse has simple, clean, midsized en-suite rooms, each with its own private entrance and a refrigerator. There's no art to the decor, unless you include the macaws in the aviary. All rooms except the Hibiscus Room have air-con. Complimentary use of chairs, towels and coolers for the beach.

★ **Old Wailuku Inn** B&B $$
(Map p352; ☎808-244-5897; www.mauiinn.com; 2199 Kaho'okele St; r incl breakfast $165-195; ❄ 📶) Hawaiian hospitality is a highight at this elegant period home. With its classic verandah and lightly vintage style, it transports you back to a breezy 1920s, while discreetly adding modern amenities. Each room has its own personality, but all are large and comfy, with traditional Hawaiian quilts, and come with a full breakfast. This is the best B&B in Central Maui. See website for specials.

Eating & Drinking

★ **Sam Sato's** JAPANESE $
(Map p358; ☎808-244-7124; 1750 Wili Pa Loop; mains under $10; ⏲restaurant 7am-2pm Mon-Sat, takeout pickup to 4pm) On busy days, Sam Sato's may use 350lb of noodles to keep the crowds sated. A Hawaii classic, this place packs them in with steaming bowls of noodles and delicious *manju* (Japanese cakes filled with sweet bean paste, offered for takeout until 4pm). You'll find yourself waiting for a table at lunchtime, but there's often room at the counter. The dry mein is the signature dish.

Takeout orders must be placed by 2pm.

Farmacy Health Bar HEALTH FOOD $
(Map p358; ☎808-866-4312; www.facebook.com/farmacyhealthbar; 12 Market St; smoothies $8, mains $7-14; ⏲9am-5pm Mon-Sat) The acai creations are so cold they chill your teeth at this spare but inviting health food eatery where you'll feel invigorated just reading the menu. Smoothies and acai bowls, both packed with fruit, are highlights, but a handful of good-for-you salads and sandwiches are also on offer. Best for carry-out. And check out those bright green walls!

Tasty Crust DINER $
(Map p358; ☎808-244-0845; www.tastycrust.com; 1770 Mill St; breakfast $2-13, lunch & dinner $5-16; ⏲6am-3pm Mon, to 10pm Sun & Tue-Thu, to 11pm Fri & Sat) The old-school American diner gets a Hawaiian twist at this low-frills locals' joint. Breakfast standbys like Denver omelets and banana pancakes jostle for attention with *loco moco,* Spam, and fried rice with egg. Settle in among the aunties, crying babies and breakfast-steak-eating businessmen for a solid budget meal on your way to 'Iao Valley. Cash and debit cards only.

Giannotto's Pizza ITALIAN $
(Map p358; ☎808-244-8282; www.giannottospizza.com; 2050 Main St; pizza slice $2-4, mains $7-26; ⏲11am-9pm Mon-Sat, to 8pm Sun) Brando, Sinatra and the Sopranos look down in approval from the cluttered walls of Giannotto's, a helpful family-run pizza joint known for its home recipes.

Wailuku Coffee Co CAFE $
(Map p358; ☎808-495-0259; www.wailukucoffee-co.com; 26 N Market St; mains under $9; ⏲7am-5pm Mon-Fri, 8am-3pm Sat & Sun; 📶 ✍) Located in the bays of a 1920s gas station, this is (as a sign proclaims) 'where the hip come to sip.' But if you're a few years behind the times, don't worry: in Wailuku this means surfing the web in your T-shirt while downing a toddy (iced coffee). Enjoy the smoothies, sandwiches, salads and pita pizzas too.

A Saigon Café VIETNAMESE $$
(Map p358; ☎808-243-9560; cnr Main & Kaniela Sts; mains $10-28; ⏲10am-9:30pm Mon-Sat, to 8:30pm Sun) The oldest and best Vietnamese restaurant on Maui is out of the way, but rewards the search. Menu stars include Buddha rolls in spicy peanut sauce and aromatic lemongrass curries.

Entertainment

'Iao Theater THEATER
(Map p358; ☎808-242-6969; www.mauionstage.com; 68 N Market St; ⏰box office 11am-3pm Mon, Wed & Fri) Nicely restored after years of neglect, this 1928 art-deco theater, which once hosted big names such as Frank Sinatra, is now the venue for community theater productions.

Shopping

Head to N Market St for fun and ecelectic browsing, with antique stores and locally made offerings tucked between the 'Iao Theater and Main St.

Native Intelligence GIFTS
(Map p358; ☎808-249-2421; www.native-intel.com; 1980 Main St; ⏰10am-5pm Mon-Fri, to 4pm Sat) Hula instruments, koa bowls and finely handcrafted items.

Information

Wailuku can get rough at night. The public parking lot on W Main St gets more police calls than any other spot on Maui. Avoid this and the area north of 'Iao Stream after dark.

First Hawaiian Bank (www.fhb.com; 27 N Market St)

Maui Memorial Medical Center (☎808-244-9056; www.mauimemorialmedical.org; 221 Mahalani St; ⏰24hr) The island's main hospital. Mahalani St is off W Kaahumanu Ave, right between Kahului and Wailuku. For extreme emergencies, flying to Queen's Medical Center in Honolulu may be preferable.

Post Office (Map p358; ☎808-244-1653; www.usps.com; 250 Imi Kala St; ⏰9am-4pm Mon-Fri, to noon Sat)

Getting There & Around

The Maui Bus runs between Wailuku and Kahului hourly between 6:30am and 9:30pm. Wailuku stops include the state office building and the post office. Fare is $2 per ride.

Wailuku to 'Iao Valley State Park

It's hard to believe today, but the route from Wailuku to 'Iao Valley was the site of Maui's bloodiest battle. In 1790 Kamehameha the Great invaded Kahului by sea and drove the defending Maui warriors up 'Iao Stream. As the valley walls closed in, those unable to escape over the mountains were slaughtered. The waters of 'Iao Stream were so choked with bodies that the area was named Kepaniwai (Dammed Waters).

Sights

Kepaniwai Park & Heritage Gardens PARK
(Map p352; www.mauicounty.gov; 870 'Iao Valley Rd; ⏰7am-7pm; 👪) This unique and beautiful park celebrates the various ethnic groups of Hawaii by displaying a building for each one. Sharing the compact grounds are a traditional Hawaiian *hale* (house), a New England–style missionary home, a Filipino farmer's hut, Japanese gardens and a Chinese pavilion, all of which can be seen in a 15-minute walk. But you'll want to linger. Enlivened by 'Iao Stream, this a perfect picnic spot and a refreshing monument to social harmony.

A lone pine, or *matsu,* was planted atop the small hill overlooking the gardens. A symbol of longevity and perseverance, it honors the victims of the devastating Japanese earthquake and tsunami in 2011.

'Iao Valley State Park

As you drive out of Wailuku, 'Iao Valley's emerald lushness envelops you, concluding with an explosion of riparian and mountain greenery at **'Iao Valley State Park** (Map p352; www.hawaiistateparks.org; admission per car $5; ⏰7am-7pm), deep inside the bosom of the West Maui Mountains. The scenery is dramatic, with sheer peaks rising in all directions, most notably 'Iao Needle. Rising above the lush rainforest, and caressed by passing mist, this rock pinnacle stands as a monument to your journey, while marking the entrance to the mysterious, uninhabited valley beyond. Most will never go beyond the viewpoint, but the park extends clear up to Pu'u Kukui (5788ft), Maui's highest and wettest place.

You'll arrive first at a parking lot, beyond which is a small bridge. If the water is high you'll see local kids taking bravado jumps from the bridge to the rocky stream below. Don't even think about doing this. Take your dip further on, remembering that flash floods do occur here.

After you cross the bridge you'll come to two short trails that start opposite each other. Both take just 10 minutes to walk and shouldn't be missed. The upper path leads skyward up a series of steps, ending

A FRANK LLOYD WRIGHT MASTERPIECE

The clubhouse at the King Kamehameha Golf Club (p361) is Maui's great anomaly: a building that should be known worldwide is hardly mentioned on the island, or visited by anyone save its members.

The spectacular rose building looks like a set from *Star Wars*, and is beautifully sited in the Waikapu Valley, at the foot of the West Maui Mountains. A whopping 75,000 sq feet in size, it can be seen from the slopes of Haleakalā. Originally designed as a much smaller home by famed American architect Frank Lloyd Wright, it contains many artistic flourishes, including art glass, etched designs and an elegant Hawaiian art collection.

Wright adapted the design for three successive clients, including Marilyn Monroe, but never broke ground. In 1988, three decades after his death, Japanese investors purchased the plans, intent on building a clubhouse in Maui. They poured $35 million into the project, including further adaptation by one of Wright's apprentices. Then the Japanese economy collapsed in 1999, the club closed and the greens turned brown. In 2004 another Japanese investor bought the property, and spent $40 million more. Today the club is working to fill its roster, but this is no reflection on the course, or the magnificent building that crowns it.

The public is welcome to tour the building free of charge, and to use the restaurant. A brochure about the building and the art collection is available at the entrance. Note that the clubhouse is a short drive up the hill beyond the proshop.

at a sheltered lookout with a close-up view of 'Iao Needle. The lower path leads down along 'Iao Stream, skirting the rock-strewn streambed past native hau trees with their fragrant hibiscus-like flowers. Look around and you'll be able to spot fruiting guava trees as well. The lower path returns to the bridge by way of a garden of native Hawaiian plants, including patches of taro: a beautiful round-trip.

Sights

'Iao Needle PINNACLE

(Map p352) Rising straight up 2250ft, this velvety green pinnacle is Maui's iconic landmark. Most people shoot their mandatory photos from the bridge near the parking lot. A better idea is to take the walkway just before the bridge that loops downhill by 'Iao Stream. This leads to the nicest angle, one that captures the stream, bridge and 'Iao Needle together.

The pinnacle takes its name from 'Iao, the daughter of Maui. According to legend, Maui and the goddess Hina raised their beautiful daughter deep in this hidden valley to shelter her from worldly temptations. But a merman (half-man, half-fish) swam into the valley one night and took 'Iao as a lover. When Maui discovered the affair he snatched the merman and threatened to cast him out to sea. 'Iao pleaded that she could not live without the sight of her beloved, so instead Maui turned him into a needle of stone.

Waikapu

Located in the foothills of the West Maui Mountains and beyond, Waikapu is a large tract of land with only 1100 people in it, most of them in one planned community. For visitors, highlights include a top-notch golf course and a thrilling zipline.

Activities

★King Kamehameha Golf Club GOLF

(Map p352; ☎808-249-0033; www.kamehamehagolf.com; 2500 Honoapi'ilani Hwy; 1-day guest $170; ⊙6:30am-6:30pm) The only 18-hole private club on Maui is surprisingly friendly to the public. One-day guests can enjoy a round of golf on Maui's most challenging course for less than most resort courses. The extraordinary bi-coastal vistas are matched only by the spectacular Frank Lloyd Wright clubhouse (p361), considered by *Golf Digest* as 'perhaps the best in the country.'

★Flyin Hawaiian Zipline ZIPLINING

(Map p352; ☎808-463-5786; www.flyinhawaiianzipline.com; 1670 Honoapi'ilani Hwy, office located inside Maui Tropical Plantation; per person $185) Wheeeee! Adrenaline junkies will revel in this new addition to a crowded field. Located high in the crumpled folds of the West Maui Mountains, this course spans nine valleys with eight lines, including one 3200ft monster, and achieves speeds more than 50mph. Allow four to five hours. There is a 10-year-old, 75lb-to-250lb limit.

Maui

There's a thrill for every adventurer on the Valley Isle. Adrenaline junkies surf and soar while take-it-easy explorers snorkel the coast or drive past waterfalls. Armchair adventurers might glimpse a whale from the comforts of their cushy lounge chair. And for culinary explorers? From food truck to four-star, Maui has it all.

2

SHARE YOUR EXPERIENCES / GETTY IMAGES ©

ROBINSON ED / GETTY IMAGES ©

1. Big Beach (p380), Makena
Experienced bodysurfers ride the turquoise waves at what is arguably Maui's finest beach.

2. Humpback whale
In winter, humpback whales breach as close as 100yds from Maui's coast.

3. Pipiwai Trail (p405)
Meander through the bamboo forest, where thick groves of bamboo bang together musically in the wind.

4. Molokini (p365)
Home to more than 250 species of tropical fish, this volcanic crater is the stuff of legends among scuba divers and snorkelers.

MICHELE FALZONE / GETTY IMAGES ©

Ma'alaea

POP 352

Wind defines Ma'alaea. Prevailing trade winds sweep from the north, funneling down between the two great rises of Haleakalā and the West Maui Mountains straight at Ma'alaea Bay. It's no coincidence that Maui's first windmill farm marches up the slopes here. By midday you'll need to hold on to your hat.

Sights

★Maui Ocean Center AQUARIUM

(Map p352; ☎808-270-7000; www.mauioceancenter.com; 192 Ma'alaea Rd; adult/child 3-12yr $26/19; ⊙9am-5pm Sep-Jun, to 6pm Jul & Aug; 👪) This midsize aquarium showcases Hawaii's dazzling marine life, including many species found nowhere else. The floorplan takes you on an ocean journey, beginning with nearshore reefs teeming with colorful tropical fish and ending with deep-ocean sealife. The grand finale is a 54ft clear acrylic tunnel that leads you through a large tank as sharks and rays glide by. Local ordinance prevents exhibition of live cetaceans, so there's no dolphin show. The rest is family friendly, but pricey.

Beaches

Ma'alaea Bay BEACH

Ma'alaea Bay is fronted by a 3-mile stretch of sand, running from Ma'alaea Harbor south to Kihei. Access is from **Haycraft Park** (Map p352; www.co.maui.hi.us; 399 Hauoli St) at the end of Hauoli St in Ma'alaea and from several places along N Kihei Rd including **Kealia Beach**, which parallels the Kealia Coastal Boardwalk. Parking is limited, but the beach is mostly deserted.

SWIM WITH THE SHARKS

No, this is not a trip to Wall Street. We mean *real* sharks. Some 20 of them, to be exact, from a blacktip reef shark to a hammerhead and, gasp, a tiger shark. And you can jump in and join them. **Shark Dive Maui** (Map p352; ☎808-270-7075; www.mauioceancenter.com; 2hr dive $199, incl admission to aquarium for diver & viewing guest; ⊙8:15am Mon, Wed & Fri) takes intrepid divers on a daredevil's plunge into Maui Ocean Center's 750,000-gallon deep-ocean tank to swim with the toothy beasts as aquarium visitors gaze on in disbelief. You do need to be a certified diver over 15, and since it's limited to only four divers per day, advance reservations are essential.

Activities

Wicked winds from the north shoot straight out toward Kaho'olawe, creating excellent windsurfing conditions that, unlike elsewhere, persist throughout the winter. The bay also has a couple of hot surfing spots. The **Ma'alaea Pipeline** (Map p352) freight-trains right and is the fastest surf break in all Hawaii. Summer's southerly swells produce huge tubes.

Lahaina Pali Trail HIKING

(Map p352; https://hawaiitrails.ehawaii.gov) This dry and rugged trail, part of the ancient King's Trail that circles Maui, runs from Ma'alaea up over Kealaoloa Ridge (the unmissable wind farm on the edge of the West Maui Mountains), down through Ukumehame Gulch, and on to long and sandy **Papalaua Beach** (www.co.maui.hi.us; between MP 11 & 12 Honoapi'ilani Hwy), where you can snorkel and picnic.

Along the way you'll enjoy great views of Kaho'olawe and Lana'i, ancient petroglyphs, and whales in season. For explanations of the 16 numbered markers en route, download the excellent trail guide from www.mauiguidebook.com/adventures/lahaina-pali-trail.

The 5.5-mile trail ranges 1500ft in elevation, making it strenuous, and takes about 2½ hours one way. Drop a car at one end if you don't want to hike or hitch back. The eastern trailhead access road, marked by a Na Ala Hele sign, is on Hwy 30, just south of its intersection with N Kihei Rd. Starting early here will keep you ahead of the blistering sun. The western trailhead is also on Hwy 30, 200yd south of the 11-mile marker. For a shorter hike with excellent views, take the eastern trailhead to the wind farm and back.

Tours

The tour operators at Ma'alaea Harbor have consolidated reservations at the **Ma'alaea Harbor Activities** (Map p352; ☎808-280-8073; www.maalaeaharboractivities.com; Ma'alaea Harbor; ⊙9am-8pm) hut, facing Slip 47. Here you can book fishing trips, snorkeling excursions, dinner/cocktail/sunset cruises, and seasonal whale-watching trips. They're great at comparison shopping.

Pacific Whale Foundation BOAT TOUR
(Map p352; ☎808-249-8811; www.pacificwhale.org; 300 Ma'alaea Rd, Ma'alaea Harbor Shops; adult/child 7-12yr from $26/19; ⏰6am-6pm) Led by naturalists, these tours do it right, with onboard snorkeling lessons and wildlife talks. Snacks are provided; it's free for kids under six. Half-day tours concentrate on Molokini; full-day tours add Lana'i. There's also a great variety of other tours, including whale-watching, dinner and cocktail cruises, and for the explorer, raft tours to Lana'i. Prices vary.

Quicksilver BOAT TOUR
(Map p352; ☎808-662-0075; www.quickilver.com; Slip 44, Ma'alaea Harbor; adult/child 7-12yr $90/60) If you want more of a party scene, hop aboard this sleek double-decker catamaran. Once you're done snorkeling off Molokini, your crew cranks up Jimmy Buffett and breaks out a barbecue lunch.

Eating

★**Ma'alaea General Store & Cafe** CAFE $
(Map p352; ☎808-242-8900; www.maalaeastore.com; 132 Ma'alaea Rd; mains $2-13; ⏰6am-6pm Mon-Sat, to 5pm Sun; 📶🌶) Located in the only original building left from the days when Ma'alaea was a small Japanese fishing village, this friendly general store and cafe offers deli eats, fresh-baked bread, and a rare focus on veggie and gluten-free solutions. Plus $2 Red Hot hot dogs! The porch is a great place to dive into its signature Reuben while watching the world go by.

Beach Bums Bar & Grill BARBECUE $$
(Map p352; ☎808-243-2286; www.beachbumshawaii.com; 300 Ma'alaea Rd, Ma'alaea Harbor Shops; breakfast $8-13, lunch & dinner $8-30; ⏰8am-9pm) For harbor views and barbecue, settle in at this lively eatery. Beach Bums uses a wood-burning rotisserie smoker to grill up everything from burgers and ribs to turkey and Spam. Come from 3pm to 6pm for $3.25 drafts. Enjoy live local music nightly from 5pm to 8pm.

Getting There & Away

Ma'alaea has good connections to the rest of Maui's public bus system. The Maui Bus ($2) connects the Harbor Shops at Ma'alaea with Lahaina, Kahului and Kihei. Service depends on the route, but buses operate hourly from around 6am to 8pm.

OFF THE BEATEN TRACK

MOLOKINI

Molokini is a **volcanic crater** (per person $140) sitting midway between the islands of Maui and Kaho'olawe. Half of the crater has eroded, leaving a pretty, 18-acre crescent moon that rises 160ft above the sea. But what lies beneath is the main attraction. Steep walls, ledges and an extraordinary fringing reef attract white-tipped reef sharks, manta rays, turtles, abundant fish – and some 1000 visitors per day, most armed with a snorkel and mask. Basic snorkeling trips from Ma'alaea Harbor cost about $90 per person. For more info call or visit the Ma'alaea Harbor Activities Hut (p364). Trips also leave from Kihei. Avoid discounted afternoon tours: the water is calmest and clearest in the morning, but can get rough and murky later.

Kealia Pond National Wildlife Refuge

A magnet for both birds and bird-watchers, this **refuge** (Map p352; ☎808-875-1582; www.fws.gov/refuge/kealia_pond/; Mokulele Hwy, MP 6; ⏰7:30am-4pm Mon-Fri) FREE harbors native waterbirds year-round and migratory birds from August to April. In the rainy winter months Kealia Pond swells to 400 acres, making it one of the largest natural ponds in Hawaii. In summer it shrinks to half that size, creating the skirt of crystalline salt that gives Kealia (meaning 'salt-encrusted place') its name.

Birding is excellent from the coastal boardwalk and the refuge's **headquarters** (Map p352; ⏰7:30am-4pm Mon-Fri) off Mokulele Hwy (Hwy 311) at the 6-mile marker, where there's a small, child-friendly visitors center. In both places you're almost certain to spot wading *ae'o* (Hawaiian black-necked stilts) and Hawaiian coots, two endangered species that thrive here. In winter ospreys can sometimes be seen diving for fish. The coastal marsh and dunes nestling Kealia Pond are also a nesting site for the endangered hawksbill sea turtle.

Activities

★**Kealia Coastal Boardwalk** BOARDWALK
(Map p352; www.fws.gov/refuge/kealia_pond; Kealia Pond National Wildlife Refuge) This wonderful

elevated boardwalk by Ma'alaea Bay seems to go on forever. It traverses over 2000ft of wetlands, making it a magnet for birders but also a great nature walk for anyone. Interpretive plaques and benches help along the way. In winter you may spot humpback whales. Located 350yd north of the 2-mile marker on N Kihei Rd.

Pu'unene

Sugar is the lifeblood of Pu'unene. Fields of cane expand out from the Hawaiian Commercial & Sugar (C&S) Company's rusty old **mill** (Map p354), the last of its kind in Hawaii. Its industrial hulk looms high, belching smoke; if you smell molasses, they're boiling down sugarcane. Hidden nearby are the remains of a barely surviving plantation village, including an old schoolhouse, a long-abandoned church, and a shack that's served as a used **bookstore** (Map p352; 9am-4pm Tue-Sat) since 1913. It's a bit musty, but still sells books for a quarter!

To see the mill and village turn off Mokulele Hwy (Hwy 311) onto Hansen Rd and take the first right onto Old Pu'unene Ave, continuing past the old Pu'unene Meat Market building (c 1926) and the unmissable mill. Turn left after 0.6 miles, past a little bridge. Just before the pavement ends, turn right and drive behind the old school to reach the bookstore.

Sights

Alexander & Baldwin Sugar Museum MUSEUM

(Map p354; 808-871-8058; www.sugarmuseum.com; 3957 Hansen Rd; adult/child 6-12yr $7/2; 9:30am-4:30pm) This homespun museum occupies the former residence of the sugar mill's superintendent. There's the usual display of industrial machinery, including a working model of a cane-crushing plant, but what lingers afterward is the human story.

One exhibit traces how the sons of missionaries took control of Maui's fertile valleys and dug the amazing irrigation system that made large-scale plantations viable. Compelling black-and-white photographs spotlight the labor and recreational aspects of plantation life. An early-20th-century labor contract on display, from the Japanese Emigration Company, committed laborers to work the cane fields 10 hours a day, 26 days a month, for $15.

KIHEI & SOUTH MAUI

Sunsets are a communal affair in South Maui – just look at the throngs crowding the beach wall at Kama'ole Beach Park II in the late afternoon. It's a scene repeated up and down the coast here every day.

Dubbed Haole-wood for its LA-style strip malls and white-bread resorts, the region is a bit shiny and overbuilt. But dig deeper and you'll find a mixed plate of scenery and adventure, from Kihei to Wailea, Makena and beyond, that's truly unique. You can snorkel reefs teeming with turtles, kayak to remote bays or sail in an outrigger canoe. The coral gardens are so rich you can dive from the shore. And the beaches are undeniably glorious, whether you're looking to relax beneath a resort cabana or to discover your own pocket of sand. Add reliably sunny weather, quiet coastal trails and a diverse dining scene and South Maui's a pretty irresistible place to strand yourself.

Kihei

POP 20,881

Want to maximize your beach time and your budget? And maybe throw in an adventure or two? Set your sights on Kihei, an energetic beach town that works well for short-trip vacationers in a hurry. Yes, it's overrun with strip malls and traffic, but with 6 miles of sunny beaches, loads of affordable accommodations and a variety of dining options, it offers everything you need for an enjoyable seaside vacation.

To zip from one end of Kihei to the other, take the Pi'ilani Hwy (Hwy 31). It runs parallel to and bypasses the stop-start traffic of S Kihei Rd. Well-marked crossroads connect these two routes.

Sights

Hawaiian Islands Humpback Whale National Marine Sanctuary Headquarters MUSEUM

(Map p367; 808-879-2818; http://hawaiihumpbackwhale.noaa.gov; 726 S Kihei Rd; 10am-3pm Mon-Fri, plus 10am-1pm Sat early Jan-Mar;) FREE The oceanfront deck at the revamped marine sanctuary headquarters, which sits just north of the ancient Ko'ie'ie Fishpond, is an ideal spot for viewing the humpback whales that frequent the bay during winter. Free scopes are set up for viewing. Inside, displays and videos provide background, and there are lots of informative brochures

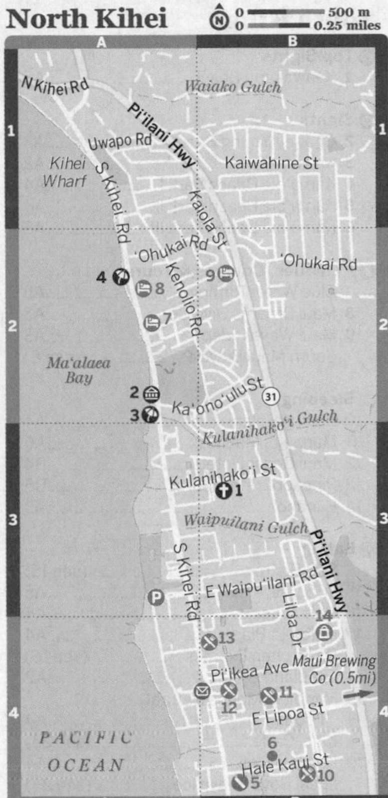

North Kihei

Sights

1 David Malo's Church B3
2 Hawaiian Islands Humpback Whale National Marine Sanctuary Headquarters A2
3 Kalepolepo Beach Park A2
Ko'ie'ie Fishpond .... (see 3)
4 Mai Poina 'Oe Ia'u Beach Park A2

Activities, Courses & Tours

5 Maui Dive Shop B4
6 South Pacific Kayaks & Outfitters B4

Sleeping

7 Maui Sunseeker A2
8 Nona Lani Cottages A2
9 Ocean Breeze Hideaway B2

Eating

Coconut's Fish Cafe .... (see 12)
10 Eskimo Candy B4
11 Fabiani's Bakery & Pizza B4
12 Roasted Chiles B4
13 Yee's Orchard B4

Drinking & Nightlife

Diamonds Ice Bar .... (see 12)

Shopping

14 Pi'ilani Village B4

about whales and other Hawaiian wildlife. Swing by at 11am on Tuesday or Thursday for the free '45-Ton Talks' about whales.

Congress created the marine sanctuary in 1992 with a mission to protect humpback whales and their habitat. The sanctuary extends from the shoreline to ocean depths of 600ft in the waters surrounding the Hawaiian Islands.

David Malo's Church CHURCH
(Map p367; www.trinitybts.org; 100 Kulanihako'i St) Philosopher David Malo, who built this church in 1852, was the first Hawaiian ordained to the Christian ministry. He was also co-author of Hawaii's first Constitution and an early spokesperson for Hawaiian rights. While most of Malo's original church has been dismantled, a 3ft-high section of the wall still stands beside a palm grove. Pews are lined up inside the stone walls. It's really quite beautiful.

Outdoor services are held at 9am on Sunday by Trinity Episcopal Church By-the-Sea. All are welcome.

Kalama Park PARK
(Map p368; 1900 S Kihei Rd;) Athletes, skate rats and toddlers who need to roam will appreciate this expansive seaside park. Sports facilities include tennis and basketball courts, ball fields and a skateboard park. Also on-site are a playground, picnic pavilions, restrooms and showers. Although there is a small beach, behind the whale statue, a runoff ditch carries wastewater here after heavy rains so best swim elsewhere.

The park is across Kihei Rd from the busy bar and restaurant scene at Kihei Kalama Village.

Kihei Coastal Trail WATERFRONT
This short trail meanders along coastal bluffs ideal for whale-watching and quiet meditation. You might even see an outrigger canoe glide past. At the start of the trail look for the burrows of *'ua'u kani* (wedge-tailed shearwaters), ground-nesting seabirds that return to the same sites each spring.

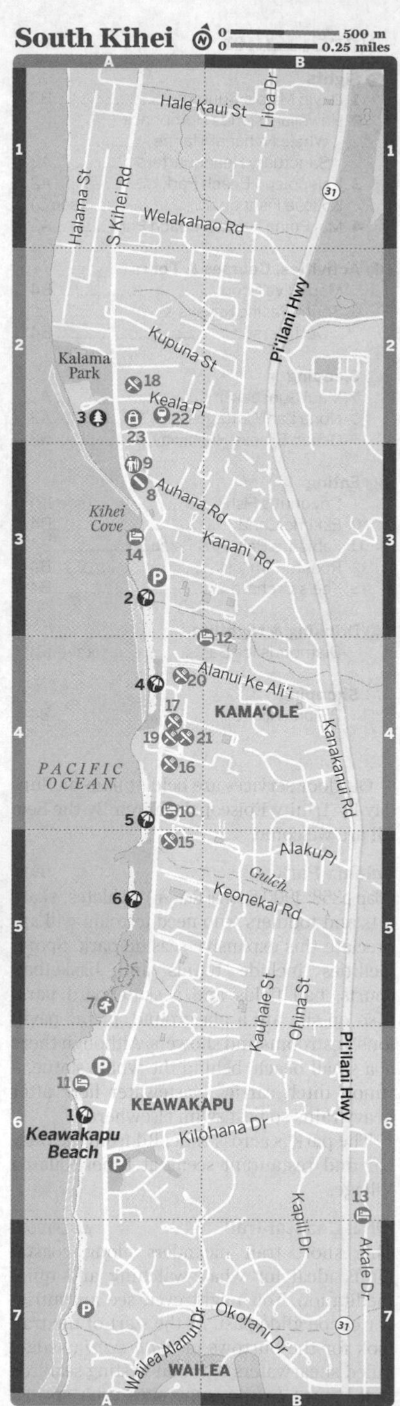

South Kihei

Top Sights

1 Keawakapu Beach A6

Sights

2 Charley Young Beach A3
3 Kalama Park A2
4 Kama'ole Beach Park I A4
5 Kama'ole Beach Park II A4
6 Kama'ole Beach Park III A5

Activities, Courses & Tours

7 Blue Water Rafting A5
8 Maui Dreams Dive Co A3
9 Maui Wave Riders A3
South Maui Bicycles .... (see 8)

Sleeping

10 Kihei Kai Nani A4
11 Mana Kai Maui A6
12 Maui Coast Hotel B4
13 Pineapple Inn Maui B6
14 Punahoa A3

Eating

808 Bistro .... (see 15)
15 808 Deli A5
16 Café O'Lei A4
17 Cafe@LaPlage A4
Da Kitchen Express .... (see 16)
18 Foodland A2
19 Hawaiian Moons Natural Foods A4
Kihei Caffe .... (see 23)
20 Kina'ole Grill A4
Local Boys Shave Ice .... (see 23)
21 Maui Thai Bistro A4
Sansei Seafood Restaurant & Sushi Bar .... (see 18)

Drinking & Nightlife

22 Dog & Duck A2
Five Palms .... (see 11)
South Shore Tiki Lounge .... (see 23)

Shopping

23 Kihei Kalama Village A2

The birds lay a single egg and remain until November, when the fledglings are large enough to head out to sea. The trail starts beyond the grassy lawn at the southern end of Kama'ole Beach Park III and winds half a mile south to Kihei Surfside condos, just beyond the Kihei Boat Ramp.

The path is made of packed gray gravel outlined in white coral. Curiously, when the trail was being built, a storm washed hundreds of yards of bleached coral onto the shore here. The coral was not originally planned for the trail construction, but the volunteers building the trail consulted with a Hawaiian kahuna (priest) and were told ancient trails were often outlined in white coral so they could be followed at night. The Hawaiian gods were thanked for the gift of coral, which was then incorporated into the trail.

Beaches

The further south you travel, the better the beaches. At the northern end of Kihei, swimming is not advised, but kayaking is good in the morning and windsurfers set off in the afternoon. The beaches following are listed geographically from north to south.

For a list of facilities at each of the county beaches, visit www.mauicounty.gov.

Mai Poina 'Oe Ia'u Beach Park BEACH

(Map p367; S Kihei Rd) This long sandy beach at the northern end of Kihei is a popular morning launch for outrigger canoes and kayaks. After the wind picks up in the afternoon, it's South Maui's main venue for windsurfing.

Kalepolepo Beach Park BEACH

(Map p367; S Kihei Rd at Ka'ono'ulu St;) This compact park beside the headquarters for the Humpback Whale National Marine Sanctuary is a nice spot for families with younger kids. A grassy lawn is fronted by the ancient **Ko'ie'ie Fishpond** (Map p367), whose stone walls create a shallow swimming pool with calm waters perfect for wading. There are also picnic tables, a grill and an outdoor shower.

Charley Young Beach BEACH

(Map p368; 2200 S Kihei Rd) On a side street, out of view of busy S Kihei Rd, this neighborhood beach is the least-touristed strand in Kihei. It's a real jewel in the rough: broad and sandy, and backed by swaying coconut palms. You're apt to find fishers casting their lines, families playing volleyball and someone strumming a guitar. It also has some of the better bodysurfing waves in Kihei.

Beach parking is on the corner of S Kihei Rd and Kaia'u Pl. To get to the beach, walk to the end of Kaia'u Pl.

Kama'ole Beach Parks BEACH

(S Kihei Rd) Kama'ole Beach is having so much fun, it just keeps rolling along. And along. And along. Divided into three sections by rocky points, these popular strands are known locally as **Kam I** (Map p368; 2400 S Kihei Rd), **Kam II** (Map p368; 2550 S Kihei Rd) and **Kam III** (Map p368; 2800 S Kihei Rd). All three are pretty, golden-sand beaches with full facilities and lifeguards. There's a volleyball court at Kam I and parking lots at Kam I and III.

Travelers with disabilities can access the ocean at Kam I using a sand beach chair. For details about ADA accessibility and the sand beach chair, check the Kamaole I listing at www.mauicounty.gov or call ☎808-270-6136.

Water conditions vary with the weather, but swimming is usually good. For the most part, these beaches have sandy bottoms with a fairly steep drop, which tends to create good conditions for bodysurfing, especially in winter.

For snorkeling, the southern end of Kama'ole Beach Park III has some nearshore rocks harboring a bit of coral and a few colorful fish, though it pales in comparison to the snorkeling at beaches further south.

★ **Keawakapu Beach** BEACH

(Map p368) From break of day to twilight, this sparkling stretch of sand is a showstopper. Extending from south Kihei to Wailea's Mokapu Beach, Keawakapu is set back from the main road and is less visible than Kihei's main roadside beaches just north. It's also less crowded, and is a great place to settle in and watch the sunset.

Wlth its cushiony soft sand, Keawakapu is also a favorite for sunrise yoga and wake-up strolls. The ocean is a perfect spot for an end-of-day swim. Mornings are best for snorkeling: head to the rocky outcrops that form the northern and southern ends of the beach. During winter look for humpback whales, which come remarkably close to shore here.

There are three beach access points, all with outdoor showers. To get to the southern end, drive south on S Kihei Rd until it dead-ends at a beach parking lot. Near the middle of the beach, there's a parking lot at the corner of Kilohana Dr and S Kihei Rd. At the northern end, beach parking can be found in a large unpaved access lot north of the Days Inn.

Activities

South Maui's top activities are water-based.

Stand-up paddle surfing (SUP) looks easy, and it is a learnable sport, but currents off Maui can carry you down the coast very quickly. Best to start with a lesson before renting a board.

Bicycling

South Maui Bicycles BICYCLE RENTAL

(Map p368; ☎808-874-0068; www.southmauibicycles.com; 1993 S Kihei Rd, Island Surf Bldg; per day $22-60, per week $99-250; ⏰10am-6pm Mon-Sat) Rents top-of-the-line Trek and Gary Fisher road bicycles, as well as basic around-town bikes. Bike lanes run along both the Pi'ilani Hwy and S Kihei Rd, but cyclists need to be cautious of inattentive drivers making sudden turns across lanes.

Diving & Snorkeling

Maui Dreams Dive Co DIVING, SNORKELING

(Map p368; ☎808-874-5332; www.mauidreamsdiveco.com; 1993 S Kihei Rd; shore dives $69-99, boat dives $129; ⏰7am-6pm) Maui Dreams is a first-rate, five-star PADI operation specializing in shore dives. With this family-run outfit, a dive trip is like going out with friends. Nondivers, ask about the introductory dive ($89), and to zoom around underwater, check out its scooter dive ($99 to $129).

Blue Water Rafting RAFTING, SNORKELING

(Map p368; ☎808-879-7238; www.bluewaterrafting.com; tours $39-135) In a hurry? Try the Molokini Express trip ($55) if you want to zip out to the crater, snorkel and be back within two hours.

An adventurous half-day trip heads southward on a motorized raft for snorkeling among sea turtles and dolphins at remote coves along Maui's lava-rock coast, which is beyond La Pe'rouse Bay. Trips depart from the Kihei Boat Ramp.

Maui Dive Shop DIVING, SNORKELING

(Map p367; ☎808-879-3388; www.mauidiveshop.com; 1455 S Kihei Rd; 2-tank dives $130-180, snorkel rentals per day $6-9; ⏰7am-9pm) This is a good spot to rent or buy water-sports gear, including boogie boards, snorkels and wetsuits. The company provides free transportation from South Maui resorts to tour departure points. This location also rents Jeep Wranglers.

Kayaking

South Pacific Kayaks & Outfitters KAYAKING

(Map p367; ☎808-875-4848; www.southpacifickayaks.com; kayak rental/tour from $45/69; ⏰rentals 6:45-11am, reservations 6am-8pm) This top-notch operation leads kayak-and-snorkel tours. It also rents kayaks for those who want to go off on their own, and will deliver them to Makena Landing by reservation. Surfing and SUP lessons are also available, as well as hiking trips.

Surfing & SUP

Stand Up Paddle Surf School SUP

(☎808-579-9231; www.standuppaddlesurfschool.com; 90min lesson $165) This SUP school is owned by champion paddle-surfer Maria Souza, who was also the first woman surfer to tow into the monster waves at Jaws. Small classes and safety are priorities, and the paddling location is determined by weather and water conditions. Classes fill quickly, so call a few days – or a week – ahead. Yoga SUP is also available.

Maui Wave Riders SURFING, SUP

(Map p368; ☎808-875-4761; www.mauiwaveriders.com; 2021 S Kihei Rd; surfing & SUP lessons from adult/child 8-12yr $65/55; ⏰lessons from 7:30am) In a brand-new shop in central Kihei, across the street from Kalama Park, Maui Wave Riders offers surfing and SUP lessons. Also rents surfboards, paddleboards and kayaks.

Festivals & Events

World Whale Day OUTDOOR FESTIVAL

(www.mauiwhalefestival.org; ⏰mid-Feb; 👪) Organized by the Pacific Whale Foundation, this family-friendly bash celebrates Maui's humpback whales with a parade (9am to 10am), crafts, live music, food booths and environmental displays. It's held at Kalama Park on a Saturday in mid-February.

Kihei First Friday CARNIVAL

(www.mauifridays.com) On the fourth Friday night of the month, between 6pm and 9pm, make your way to Azeka Mauka II Shopping Center for arts, crafts, live music, kiddie events and food trucks.

Sleeping

Condos are plentiful in Kihei, while hotels and B&Bs are few. Some condominium complexes maintain a front desk that handles bookings, but others are booked via rental agents. Be sure to ask about reservation fees, cleaning fees and cancellation policies, which vary. Traffic along S Kihei Rd can be noisy, so avoid rooms close to the road. Prices drop dramatically in the low season, which is typically April to mid-December.

★ **Pineapple Inn Maui** INN $$

(Map p368; ☎808-298-4403, 877-212-6284; www.pineappleinnmaui.com; 3170 Akala Dr; r $159-169, cottages $255; ❄📶🏊) The Pineapple Inn may be the best deal going in South Maui. This inviting boutique property offers style and functionality with a personal touch, and it's less than a mile from the beach. The four rooms, which have ocean-view lanai and private entrances, are as attractive as those at the exclusive resorts, but at a fraction of the cost. Rooms have kitchenettes, and the two-bedroom cottage comes with a full kitchen.

The complimentary welcome basket is a thoughtful – and tasty – touch. The inn is at the southern end of Kihei, bordering Wailea.

Ocean Breeze Hideaway B&B **$$**
(Map p367; ☎808-879-0657, 888-463-6687; www.hawaiibednbreakfast.com; 435 Kalalau Pl; r incl breakfast $105-119;) This welcoming hideaway is our favorite B&B in Kihei. Owners Bob and Sande have run Ocean Breeze for 15 years, and they are a treasure trove of insider tips. Their low-key home, located in an easy-to-access residential neighborhood, has two comfortable guest rooms, one with a queen bed and ceiling fan, the other with a king bed and air-con. Both have a private entrance and refrigerator.

The couple also rents a two-bedroom oceanfront condo ($200 per night; no breakfast; $125 cleaning fee).

Nona Lani Cottages COTTAGES **$$**
(Map p367; ☎808-879-2497; www.nonalanicottages.com; 455 S Kihei Rd; cottages $195;) Wooden cottages, lazy hammocks, picnic tables, swaying palms – this place looks like the tropical version of Camp Minnehaha. The eight retro cottages are compact but squeeze in a full kitchen, private lanai, living room with daybed and a bedroom with a queen bed, plus cable TV. Also offers four hotel-like cottage rooms ($195 per night). Wi-fi is available in the lobby area.

Kihei Kai Nani CONDO **$$**
(Map p368; ☎808-879-9088; www.kiheikainani.com; 2495 S Kihei Rd; 1br from $237;) Rooms and decor may be a little dated, but when it comes to amenities, this inviting low-rise condo is on par with more expensive properties. On-site are a large pool, a laundry room, shuffleboard, barbecue grills and picnic tables – all fringed by colorful tropical landscaping. All condos are one bedroom, and deluxe units have air-con. Kama'ole Beach Park II is across the street.

With about 160 rentable units, give these helpful folks a call if you've landed in Maui without reservations. They may have room or can suggest alternatives.

★**Punahoa** CONDO **$$$**
(Map p368; ☎808-879-2720; www.punahoabeach.com; 2142 Ili'ili Rd; studio $206, 1 bedroom $279-304, 2 bedroom $309;) Sip coffee, scan for whales, savor sunsets – it's hard to leave your lanai at Punahoa, a classy boutique condo where every unit has a clear-on ocean view. Tucked on a quiet side street, this 15-unit complex offers privacy and warm alohas. It's also next to a gorgeous strand of sand, Punahoa Beach, that's a favorite of turtles and surfers. Penthouse units have air-conditioning.

Cleaning fees from $90 per visit.

Mana Kai Maui CONDO **$$$**
(Map p368; ☎808-879-1561; www.manakaimaui.com; 2960 S Kihei Rd; r $250; 1/2 bedroom from $420/490;) From her throne overlooking Keawakapu Beach, Mana Kai Maui has much to admire in her seaside kingdom. Sunset views from the beach are some of the best in Kihei, and guests can swim and snorkel in the ocean right outside the door. The on-site rental company, with a front desk, manages hotel rooms (with microwaves and mini-refrigerators) and one- and two-bedroom condos. Decor varies.

Check the website for specials. Air-con in all hotel rooms and most condos. The full-service restaurant here, Five Palms (p374), is famous for its sunset happy hour.

Maui Coast Hotel HOTEL **$$$**
(Map p368; ☎808-874-6284; www.mauicoasthotel.com; 2259 S Kihei Rd; r $300-349, ste $325-379;) The snazzy Maui Coast has a lot going for it – sharp, modern rooms and a fun poolside bar – but the daily resort fee of $17.50 is off-putting. The property is not on the beach, and it's more hotel than traditional resort. The included local shuttle service is a nice touch. Overall, it's clean and comfortable, and its location back from the road keeps it quieter than other places on the strip.

The resort fee also includes parking and wi-fi.

Maui Sunseeker BOUTIQUE HOTEL **$$$**
(Map p367; ☎808-879-1261; www.mauisunseeker.com; 551 S Kihei Rd; r $239, ste $289-349;) After a no-holds-barred makeover on the Travel Channel's reality show *Hotel Impossible,* the Maui Sunseeker emerged sleeker, smarter and, dare we say, a bit more fun. Catering to gays and lesbians, this breezy property sprawls across five buildings in

north Kihei, across the street from Mai Poina 'Oela'u Beach. As for style, the low-key tropical decor outshines other places in this price range.

Watch the sunsets – or avoid tan lines – on the clothing-optional rooftop deck. The property is adults only.

Eating

808 Deli CAFE $
(Map p368; ☎808-879-1111; www.808deli.com; 2511 S Kihei Rd, Suite 102; breakfast $6-8, lunch $6-9; ⏰9am-5pm) With fresh breads, gourmet spreads and 19 different sandwiches and paninis, this tiny gourmet sandwich shop across from Kam II is the place to grab a picnic lunch. For a spicy kick, try the roast beef with pepper jack and wasabi aioli.

Kihei Caffe CAFE $
(Map p368; www.kiheicaffe.net; 1945 S Kihei Rd, Kihei Kalama Village; mains $6-13; ⏰5am-2pm) Maybe it's the sneaky birds on the patio, or the quick-to-arrive entrees, but dining at this Kihei institution is not exactly relaxing. But you know what? That's part of this busy joint's quirky charm. Order at the inside counter, fill your coffee cup at the thermos, snag a table on the patio then watch the breakfast burritos, veggie scrambles and *loco moco* flash by.

Solos, couples, families – everyone's here or on the way. Cash only.

Local Boys Shave Ice SWEETS $
(Map p368; www.localboysshaveice.com; 1941 S Kihei Rd, Kihei Kalama Village; shave ice from $4.25; ⏰10am-9pm) Load up on napkins at Local Boys, where they dish up hearty servings of shaved ice drenched in a rainbow of sweet syrups. We like it tropical (banana, mango and 'shark's blood') with ice cream, *kauai* cream and azuki beans. Cash only.

Cafe@LaPlage CAFE $
(Map p368; www.cafe-maui.com; 2395 S Kihei Rd, Dolphin Plaza; sandwiches $4-12; ⏰6:30am-5pm Mon-Sat, to 3pm Sun; 📶) They stack the sandwiches high at this small cafe and coffee shop. At breakfast, choose from five different bagel sandwiches or simply get your bagel slathered in cinnamon-honey butter. Lunchtime paninis include the Maui Melt, with turkey, bacon, pepper jack, avocados and jalapeños. Wi-fi is free, and there are computers in the front ($3 for the first 15 minutes, then 15¢ per minute).

Foodland SUPERMARKET $
(Map p368; ☎808-879-9350; www.foodland.com; 1881 S Kihei Rd, Kihei Town Center; ⏰24hr) Handy 24-hour supermarket.

Hawaiian Moons Natural Foods SUPERMARKET $
(Map p368; ☎808-875-4356; www.hawaiianmoons.com; 2411 S Kihei Rd, Kama'ole Beach Center; ⏰8am-9pm; 🌶) Pack a healthy picnic lunch or build a masterpiece at the salad bar.

Yee's Orchard FRUIT STAND $
(Map p367; 1165 S Kihei Rd; ⏰11am-5pm Tue-Thu, Sat & Sun) For out-of-this-world mangoes from May through summer, pull over for this 60-year-old fruit stand just north of Longs Drug.

★Roasted Chiles MEXICAN $$
(Map p367; ☎808-868-4351; www.hawaiiontv.com/roastedchiles; 1279 S Kihei Rd, Azeka Mauka II; lunch $11-16, dinner $15-22; ⏰9:30am-9pm) At most Mexican restaurants on Maui, the food is simply a buffer for the margaritas. But here? The margaritas are top-notch, but so is the authentic Mexican cuisine, which is thoughtfully seasoned and pleasantly presented. At this praised newcomer, start with fresh guacamole or *ono* ceviche then take your pick of savory traditional dishes and an array of sauces, from the complex chocolate *mole* to the creamy green sauce.

Attentive service ties it all together into a great night out.

★Café O'Lei HAWAII REGIONAL CUISINE $$
(Map p368; ☎808-891-1368; www.cafeoleimaui.com; 2439 S Kihei Rd, Rainbow Mall; lunch $8-16, dinner $17-27; ⏰10:30am-3:30pm & 4:30-9:30pm) This strip-mall bistro looks ho-hum at first blush. But step inside. The sophisticated atmosphere, innovative Hawaii Regional Cuisine, honest prices and excellent service knock Café O'Lei into the fine-dining big leagues. For a tangy treat, order the blackened mahimahi with fresh papaya salsa. Look for unbeatable lunch mains, with salads, for under $10, and a sushi chef after 4:30pm (Tuesday to Saturday). Famous martinis, too.

Da Kitchen Express HAWAIIAN $$
(Map p368; www.da-kitchen.com; 2439 S Kihei Rd, Rainbow Mall; breakfast $11-14, lunch & dinner $10-18; ⏰9am-9pm) Da Kitchen is da bomb. Come to this no-frills eatery for Hawaiian

WORTH A TRIP

KAHO'OLAWE

The sacred but uninhabited island of Kaho'olawe lies 7 miles southwest of Maui. It has long been central to the Hawaiian rights movement, and many consider the island a living spiritual entity, a *pu'uhonua* (refuge) and *wahi pana* (sacred place).

Yet for nearly 50 years, from WWII to 1990, the US military used Kaho'olawe as a bombing range. Beginning in the 1970s, liberating the island from the military became a rallying point for a larger resurgence of Native Hawaiian pride. Today, the bombing has stopped, the navy is gone and healing the island is considered both a symbolic act and a concrete expression of Native Hawaiian sovereignty. For a more detailed historic timeline for the island, visit www.kahoolawe.hawaii.gov.

The island (11 miles long and 6 miles wide) and its surrounding waters are now a reserve that is off-limits to the general public because of the unexploded ordnance. However, Protect Kaho'olawe 'Ohana (PKO; www.protectkahoolaweohana.org) conducts monthly visits to pull weeds, plant native foliage, clean up historic sites and honor the land. It welcomes respectful volunteers who are ready to work (not just sightsee). Visits last for four or five days during or near the full moon; volunteers pay a fee (four/five days $150/179), which covers food and transportation. You'll need your own sleeping bag, tent and personal supplies. For more details see Huaka'i on PKO's website. Note: these trips book up at least two years ahead.

plate lunches done right. The local favorite is Da Lau Lau Plate (with steamed pork wrapped in taro leaves), but you won't go wrong with any choice, from charbroiled teriyaki chicken to the gravy-laden *loco moco*. We particularly liked the spicy *kalua* pork.

Eskimo Candy SEAFOOD $$

(Map p367; ☎808-891-8898; www.eskimocandy.com; 2665 Wai Wai Pl; most mains $8-14; ⊙10:30am-7pm Mon-Fri; 👪) For top-notch fresh seafood served in a casual setting, come to this busy fishmarket with a takeout counter and a few tables. Fresh-fish fanatics should key in on the *poke,* ahi (yellowfin tuna) wraps and fish tacos. Parents will appreciate the under $8 kids' menu.

Fabiani's Bakery & Pizza ITALIAN, BAKERY $$

(Map p367; ☎808-874-0888; www.fabianis.com; 95 E Lipoa St; breakfast $3-9, lunch $8-16, dinner $11-18; ⊙7am-10pm) What puts the fab in Fabiani's? Definitely the prosciutto, mozzarella and arugula pizza with truffle oil. Or wait, maybe it's the linguini with sautéed clams. Or the chef-made pastries preening like celebrities as you walk in the door. Whatever your choice, you'll surely feel fabulous nibbling your meal inside this sparkling Italian eatery and pastry shop. There's also a rather nice bar. And Nutella fans – it sells a Nutella croissant.

Kina'ole Grill FOOD TRUCK $$

(Map p368; www.facebook.com/kinaolegrillfoodtruck; 11 Alanui Keali'i Dr; plate lunch $14; ⊙11am-7:30pm) Hawaiian-style seafood and meat plate lunches are the tasty specialties at this tropically bright food truck that parks on Alanui Keali'i Rd, not far from Kama'ole Beach Park I. Plates come with rice, mac and cheese, and greens. Cash only.

Coconut's Fish Cafe SEAFOOD $$

(Map p367; ☎808-875-9979; www.coconutsfishcafe.com; 1279 S Kihei Rd, Azeka Mauka II; mains $12-17; ⊙10am-9pm; 👪) For fresh, healthily prepared seafood in a family-friendly setting, try this chill spot in north Kihei. Order at the counter – we recommend the fish tacos – then settle in at one of the surfboard tables. All the fish is grilled, all ingredients are homemade (except the ketchup), staff are welcoming and service is quick. Dig in!

Maui Thai Bistro THAI $$

(Map p368; ☎808-874-5605; www.mauithaibistro.com; 2439 S Kihei Rd, Rainbow Mall; mains $13-19; ⊙11:30am-2:30pm & 4-9:30pm) Chef Prakong Tong, a partner in the famed 'Thai by Prakong/Thai by Pranee' eatery in Hana, known for its fresh and savory Thai fare, opened this restaurant in 2013. Come to these stylish digs for authentic Thai dishes, with seasonal menu changes. The noodles and curries are spiced just right.

Sansei Seafood Restaurant & Sushi Bar JAPANESE $$$

(Map p368; ☎808-879-0004; www.sanseihawaii.com; 1881 S Kihei Rd, Kihei Town Center; appetizers $3-15, mains $10-48; ⏲5:30-10pm, to 1am Thu-Sat) Maui is laid-back, but sometimes you have to plan ahead. Dinner at Sansei is one of those times – make a reservation or queue early for the sushi bar. The creative appetizer menu offers everything from a shrimp cake with ginger-lime chili butter to lobster-and-blue-crab ravioli. Fusion dishes include Japanese jerk chicken with garlic mashed potatoes and herb beurre fondue.

Between 5:30pm and 6pm all food is discounted 25%, and sushi is discounted 50% from 10pm to 1am Thursday through Saturday.

808 Bistro BISTRO $$$

(Map p368; ☎808-879-8008; www.808bistro.com; 2511 S Kihei Rd; breakfast $7-15, dinner $15-28; ⏲7am-noon & 5-9pm) This open-air eatery showcases comfort foods prepared with a gourmet spin – think short-rib pot pie and gorgonzola alfredo with shrimp. Kiss your diet goodbye at breakfast with the decadent whale pie with ham, hash browns, egg, cheese and gravy. The restaurant, owned by the maestros behind 808 Deli, is BYOB with a $5 corkage fee for the table.

Drinking & Nightlife

Most bars in Kihei are across the street from the beach and have nightly entertainment. Kihei Kalama Village, aka the Bar-muda Triangle (or just the Triangle), is packed with buzzy watering holes.

Dog & Duck PUB

(Map p368; ☎808-875-9669; www.theworldfamousdogandduck.com; 1913 S Kihei Rd, Kihei Kalama Village; ⏲8am-2am) This lively Irish pub with a welcoming vibe attracts a younger crowd. And yes, it has sports on TV, but it's not blaring from every corner. Decent pub grub goes along with the heady Guinness draft.

South Shore Tiki Lounge BAR

(Map p368; ☎808-874-6444; www.southshoretikilounge.com; 1913 S Kihei Rd, Kihei Kalama Village; ⏲11am-2am; 📶) The drink maestros at this cozy tropical shack regularly win annual *MauiTime Weekly* awards for best female and male bartenders. It's good for dancing too.

Five Palms COCKTAIL BAR

(Map p368; www.5palmsrestaurant.com; 2960 S Kihei Rd, Mana Kai Maui; ⏲8am-11pm, happy hour 3-7pm & 9-11pm) For sunset cocktails beside the beach, this is the place. Arrive an hour before the sun goes down because the patio, just steps from stunning Keawakapu Beach, fills quickly. Sushi is half-price during happy hour and mai tais and margaritas are $5.75.

Diamonds Ice Bar BAR

(Map p367; ☎808-874-9299; www.diamondsicebar.com; 1279 S Kihei Rd, Azeka Mauka II; ⏲8am-1:30am) We hear that the name of this place traces back to an unfulfilled plan to build the bar counter out of ice. We're not sure if that's true, but we can tell you this – Diamonds Ice loves its Jagermeister. So slurp your cold shot, get woozy, play pool then wait and see who's lured in by the bright neon lights. DJs and live music on the weekends.

Maui Brewing Co BREWERY

(☎808-213-3002; www.mauibrewingco.com; 605 Lipoa Pkwy; ⏲tasting room 11am-10pm) Maui Brewing opened its new brewery and taproom just as we were going to press. The tasting room is open daily, and tours ($10 per person) of the production facility are offered Monday through Saturday. A flight of four beers is included in the price. Check the website for tour times. Let us know what you think!

Shopping

Pi'ilani Village MALL

(Map p367; 225 Pi'ikea Ave; 📶) Kihei's largest shopping center has a wide range of stores. Flip through women's swimsuits at **Maui Waterwear** (www.mauiclothingcompany.com/mww.html) and Hawaiian-themed gifts at **Hilo Hattie** (www.hilohattie.com).

Kihei Kalama Village MARKET

(Map p368; ☎808-879-6610; 1941 S Kihei Rd; ⏲pavilion shops 10am-7:30pm) More than 40 shops and stalls are clustered at this central shopping arcade. For fashionable women's beachwear pop into **Mahina** (www.mahinamaui.com). Made-in-Hawaii jams and jellies are for sale in **Tutu's Pantry** (www.tutuspantry.com).

Information

Bank of Hawaii (☎808-879-5844; www.boh.com; 1279 S Kihei Rd, Azeka Mauka II; ⏲8:30am-4pm Mon-Thu, to 6pm Fri)

Kihei Police Station (☎808-244-6400; 2201 Pi'ilani Hwy)

Longs Drugs (☎808-879-2033; www.cvs.com; 1215 S Kihei Rd; ⏰24hr) This convenience store, with a pharmacy (8am to 10pm Monday to Friday, until 7pm Saturday and Sunday), has one aisle loaded up with rubbah slippers (flip flops, yo').

Post Office (Map p367; ☎808-879-1987; www.usps.com; 1254 S Kihei Rd; ⏰8:30am-4:30pm Mon-Fri, 9am-1pm Sat)

Urgent Care Maui Physicians (☎808-879-7781; 1325 S Kihei Rd; ⏰8am-7pm Mon-Thu & Sat, 8am-4pm Fri, 9am-4pm Sun) This clinic accepts walk-in patients.

Getting There & Around

TO/FROM THE AIRPORT

Almost everyone rents a car at the airport in Kahului. Otherwise, expect to pay about $26 to $33 for shuttle service or $33 to $55 for a taxi depending on your South Maui location.

BUS

The **Maui Bus** (www.mauicounty.gov) serves Kihei with two routes. One route, the Kihei Islander, connects Kihei with Wailea and Kahalui; stops include Kama'ole Beach Park III, Pi'ilani Village shopping center, and Uwapo at S Kihei Rds. The other route, the Kihei Villager, primarily serves the northern half of Kihei, with a half-dozen stops along S Kihei Rd and at Pi'ilani Village shopping center and Ma'alaea. Both routes operate hourly from around 6am to 8pm and cost $2.

CAR

Kihei Rent A Car (☎808-879-7257; www.kiheirentacar.com; 96 Kio Loop; per day/week from $35/175; ⏰7:30am-6pm Mon-Sat, 8am-5pm Sun) This family-owned company rents cars and 4WDs to those aged 21 and over, and includes free mileage. For the lowest rates consider one of the older-model cars (which can be well worn!). Provides Kahului Airport shuttle pickup for rentals over five days.

Wailea

POP 5938

The golden-sand beaches in Wailea are the stuff of daydreams, with phenomenal swimming, snorkeling and sunbathing adding to the appeal. Factor in the consistently sunny skies, and it's easy to see why Wailea is a hot spot for oceanfront resorts.

Beyond the beaches? With its tidy golf courses, protective privacy walls and discreet signage, Wailea looks like a members-only country club. Wailea is South Maui's most elite haunt, and it stands in sharp contrast to Kihei. Don't bother looking for gas stations or fast-food joints; this exclusive community is all about swank beachfront resorts and low-rise condo villas, with all the glitzy accessories.

If you're not staying here, say a loud *mahalo* (thank you) for Hawaii's beach-access laws that allow you to visit anyway, with dedicated public parking lots.

From Lahaina or Kahului, take the Pi'ilani Hwy (Hwy 31) to Wailea instead of taking S Kihei Rd, which is Kihei's stop-and-go main road. Once in Wailea, Wailea Alanui Dr turns into Makena Alanui Dr after Polo Beach and continues to Makena.

Beaches

Wailea's fabulous beaches begin at the southern end of Keawakapu Beach in Kihei and continue south toward Makena. All of the beaches that are backed by resorts have public access, with free parking, showers and restrooms. The beaches in this section are listed from north to south.

Mokapu & Ulua Beaches — BEACH

With the opening of the Andaz Maui, the scene has gotten busier at these two beaches, which are a few steps away from the resort. The lovely **Mokapu Beach** is behind the Andaz, on the northern side of a small point between the beaches. Snorkelers should head straight for **Ulua Beach** to the south of the point. The coral at the rocky outcrop on the right side of Ulua Beach offers Wailea's best easy-access snorkeling.

Not only is it teeming with brilliant tropical fish, but it's also one of the best spots for hearing humpbacks sing as they pass offshore. Snorkeling is best in the morning before the winds pick up and the masses arrive. When the surf's up, forget snorkeling – go bodysurfing instead. Beach access is just south of the Andaz Maui.

★Wailea Beach — BEACH

(👪) To strut your stuff celebrity-style, make a beeline to this sparkling strand, which fronts the Grand Wailea and Four Seasons resorts and offers a full menu of water activities. The beach slopes gradually, making it a good swimming spot. When it's calm, there's decent snorkeling around the rocky point on the southern end. Most afternoons there's a gentle shorebreak suitable for bodysurfing. Divers entering the water at Wailea Beach can follow an offshore reef that runs down to Polo Beach.

The beach access road is between the Grand Wailea and Four Seasons resorts.

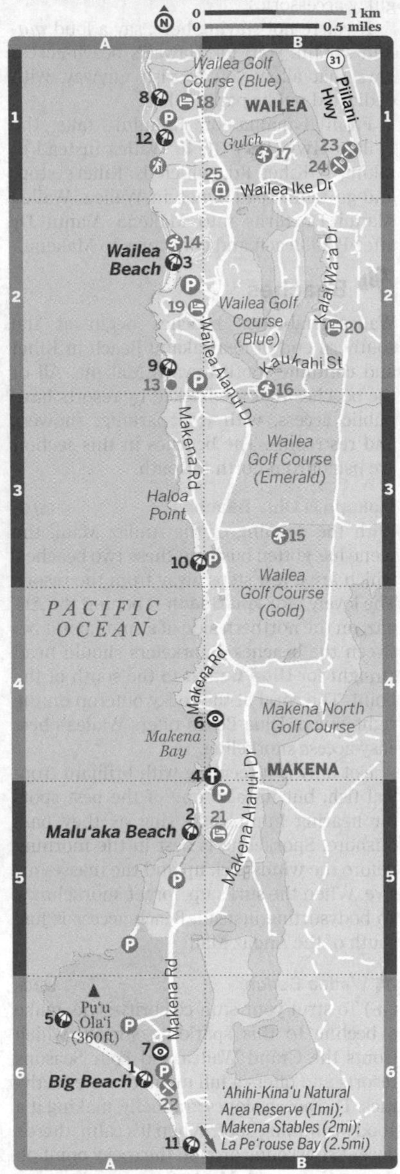

Wailea & Makena

Top Sights
1 Big Beach A6
2 Malu'aka Beach A5
3 Wailea Beach A2

Sights
4 Keawala'i Congregational Church B4
5 Little Beach A6
6 Makena Landing B4
7 Makena State Park A6
8 Mokapu Beach A1
9 Polo Beach A2
10 Po'olenalena Beach A3
11 Secret Cove A6
12 Ulua Beach A1

Activities, Courses & Tours
13 Hawaiian Sailing Canoe Adventures A2
14 Maui Ocean Activities A2
15 Wailea Golf Club B3
16 Wailea Old Blue Clubhouse B2
17 Wailea Tennis Club B1

Sleeping
18 Andaz Maui A1
19 Four Seasons Maui at Wailea A2
20 Hotel Wailea B2
21 Makena Beach & Golf Resort B5

Eating
Ferraro's ....(see 19)
22 Jawz Fish Tacos A6
Ka'ana Kitchen ....(see 18)
23 Monkeypod Kitchen B1
24 Pita Paradise B1
Waterfront Deli ....(see 25)

Drinking & Nightlife
Mulligan's on the Blue ....(see 16)
Red Bar at Gannon's ....(see 15)

Entertainment
Four Seasons Maui at Wailea ....(see 19)

Shopping
Blue Ginger ....(see 25)
Honolua Surf Co ....(see 25)
Martin & MacArthur ....(see 25)
Maui Waterwear ....(see 25)
25 Shops at Wailea B1

Polo Beach BEACH

In front of the Fairmont Kea Lani, Polo Beach is seldom crowded. When there's wave action, boogie boarders and bodysurfers usually find good shorebreaks here. When calm, the rocks at the northern end of the beach provide good snorkeling. At low tide, the lava outcropping at the southern end holds tide pools harboring spiny sea urchins and small fish. To find it, turn down Kaukahi St after the Fairmont Kea Lani and look for the beach parking lot on the right.

Po'olenalena Beach BEACH

This long and lovely crescent-shaped beach, south of the resorts, is a favorite with local families on the weekends. It's rarely crowded though, and the shallow, sandy bottom and calm waters make for excellent swimming. There's good snorkeling off both the southern and northern lava points. The parking lot is on Makena Alanui Rd, a half-mile south of its intersection with Makena Rd.

Activities

Wailea Golf Club GOLF

(808-875-7450; www.waileagolf.com; 100 Wailea Golf Club Dr; greens fee $119-235; 7am-5pm) There are three championship courses in Wailea. The **Emerald course** is a tropical garden that consistently ranks at the top; the rugged **Gold course** takes advantage of volcanic landscapes; and the **Old Blue course** (808-879-2530; 120 Kaukahi St) is marked by an open fairway and challenging greens.

For the cheapest fees, tee off in the afternoon (check times), when 'twilight' rates are in effect.

Wailea Beach Walk WALKING

For the perfect sunset stroll, take the 1.3-mile shoreline path that connects Wailea's beaches and the resort hotels that front them. The undulating path winds above jagged lava points and back down to the sandy shore.

In winter this is one of the best places in all of Maui for spotting humpback whales. On a good day you may be able to see more than a dozen of them frolicking offshore.

Some of the luxury hotels you'll pass along the walk are worth strolling through as well, most notably the Grand Wailea Resort, which is adorned with $30 million worth of artwork. In front of the Wailea Point condos you'll find the foundations of three Hawaiian house sites dating to AD 1300; this is also a fine spot to watch the sun drop into the sea.

Maui Ocean Activities WATER SPORTS

(808-357-8989; www.mauioceanactivities.com; 3850 Wailea Alanui Dr, Grand Wailea Resort; snorkel/boogie boards/kayak/stand-up paddleboard per hr $10/10/40/40; 7am-3pm) On the beach behind the Grand Wailea, Maui Ocean rents everything you need for watery fun.

Wailea Tennis Club TENNIS

(808-879-1958; www.waileatennis.com; 131 Wailea Ike Pl; per person $20, racket rental per day $10; 7am-6pm Mon-Fri, to 5pm Sat & Sun) Nicknamed 'Wimbledon West,' this award-winning complex has 11 Plexi-pave courts. Ninety-minute lessons are also available (clinic/private $35/140).

Tours

Hawaiian Sailing Canoe Adventures CANOEING

(808-281-9301; www.mauisailingcanoe.com; adult/child 5-12yr $99/79; tours 8am & 10am) Learn about native traditions on two-hour trips aboard a Hawaiian-style outrigger canoe. With a maximum of six passengers, it's able to accommodate requests – including stopping to snorkel with turtles. Tours depart from Polo Beach.

Festivals & Events

Maui Film Festival FILM

(www.mauifilmfestival.com; mid-Jun) Hollywood celebs swoop in for this five-day extravaganza in mid-June. Join the stars under the stars at various Wailea locations, including the open-air 'Celestial Theater' on a nearby golf course and the 'Toes-in-the-Sand Cinema' on Wailea Beach.

Sleeping

★ **Andaz Maui** RESORT HOTEL $$$

(808-573-1234; www.maui.andaz.hyatt.com; 3550 Wailea Alanui Dr; r/ste from $569/1144;) As you glide down the portico to the chic and airy lobby – complete with lounge chairs placed artfully in the sand – it feels as if you're beginning a grand adventure. The impression continues in the uncluttered rooms: low beds, simple wooden furniture, plantation shutters. It's basecamp for your cushy tropical expedition.

Here you can attend a lei-making class, paddle an outrigger canoe or craft your own lotion at 'Awili Spa & Salon's apothecary lounge. The resort is also home to the lauded Ka'ana Kitchen and the Japanese restaurant Morimoto Maui, the latest venture from Iron Chef Masaharu Morimoto. There is no resort fee, but valet-only parking is $30 per night.

Four Seasons Maui at Wailea RESORT HOTEL $$$

(808-874-8000; www.fourseasons.com/maui; 3900 Wailea Alanui Dr; r/ste from $619/1149; P) From the plush lobby lounge with its framed ocean views to the accommodating staff to the inclusive pricing (no resort fee), the joy is in the details and the warm aloha spirit at this impressive getaway. Standard rooms are midsized and furnished with understated tropical elegance, slightly more comfy than sophisticated. Marble-floored bathrooms have lots of counter space and a choice of piped-in music.

Children are welcome – there are fun pools plus the Kids for All Seasons program – but the resort feels more low-key than its neighbors. To relax, float in the adults-only serenity pool or enjoy a Hawaiian heated-stone face massage from a hut overlooking the sea. Parking is $27 per day.

Hotel Wailea HOTEL **$$$**
(808-874-0500, 866-970-4167; www.hotelwailea.com; 555 Kaukahi St; ste from $424;) With its hilltop perch, lush grounds and stovepipe lobby, the Hotel Wailea just needs a frame for artistic completion. The 72 roomy suites, fresh from a complete revamp, gleam with elegant but inviting beach-modern style, from the coral and limestone walls to the bleached oak floors and breezily stylish furnishings. Rooms come with microwaves and mini-refrigerators. Yoga classes offered four days per week.

The hotel is not on the ocean, but the $25 resort fee includes a shuttle to Wailea Beach where there is a beach concierge for guests.

Eating

Waterfront Deli DELI **$**
(808-891-2039; 3750 Wailea Alanui Dr, Shops at Wailea; sandwiches $7, mains under $9; store 7am-10:30pm, deli 7am-8pm) For a quick, inexpensive meal to-go, visit this deli inside the Whalers General Store at the back of the Shops at Wailea.

★ **Monkeypod Kitchen** PUB FOOD **$$**
(808-891-2322; www.monkeypodkitchen.com; 10 Wailea Gateway Pl, Wailea Gateway Center; lunch $14-26, dinner $14-37; 11:30am-11pm, happy hour 3-5:30pm & 9-11pm) The bar scene is convivial at Chef Peter Merriman's newest venture, where the staff, your fellow drinkers and the 36 beers on tap keep the alohas real. But microbrews are not the only draw. Gourmet pub grub takes a delicious Hawaiian spin and is typically sourced from organic and local ingredients, with Maui Cattle burgers and plenty of Upcountry veggies.

Wood-fired pizzas are $9 during happy hour – mmm, Hamakua wild mushrooms.

Pita Paradise MEDITERRANEAN **$$**
(808-879-7177; www.pitaparadisehawaii.com; 34 Wailea Gateway Pl, Wailea Gateway Center; lunch $9-24, dinner $17-30; 11am-9:30pm) Although this Greek taverna sits in a strip mall and lacks ocean views, the inviting patio, the townscape mural and the tiny white lights – not to mention the succulent Mediterranean chicken pita – banish any locational regrets. Owner John Arabatzis catches his own fish, which is served in everything from pita sandwiches at lunch to grilled kabobs at dinner.

★ **Ferraro's** ITALIAN **$$$**
(808-874-8000; www.fourseasons.com/maui; 3900 Wailea Alanui Dr, Four Seasons Maui at Wailea; lunch $19-26, dinner $24-46; 11:30am-9pm) No other place in Wailea comes close to this breezy restaurant for romantic seaside dining. Lunch strays into fun offerings like a seared ahi wrap with avocado and a lobster salad sandwich with garlic aioli. Dinner gets more serious, showcasing a rustic Italian menu, plus steak and seafood dishes.

Ka'ana Kitchen HAWAIIAN **$$$**
(808-573-1234; www.maui.andaz.hyatt; breakfast mains $16-25, breakfast buffet $28 & $56, dinner $17-56; breakfast 6:30am-11am, dinner 5:30-9pm) Maui's bounty is shared in high style – and with much aloha – at this much-lauded new restaurant at the Andaz Maui. At breakfast, the two buffets (one has a wider selection of entrees) will keep you nibbling fruit, bread, cheese, and cured fish and meats all morning. The dinner menu is arranged by local farm and food producers, with several ahi and rib-eye dishes looking especially enticing.

One quibble? The cured slab bacon. Thick, shiny, hard-to-cut and the opposite of delightful. One bit of praise? The $15 all-you-can-drink mimosas at breakfast.

Drinking & Entertainment

All of the Wailea hotels have some sort of live music, most often jazz or Hawaiian, in the evening.

Red Bar at Gannon's COCKTAIL BAR
(808-875-8080; www.gannonsrestaurant.com; 100 Wailea Golf Club Dr; 8:30am-9pm, happy hour 3-8:30pm) Everyone looks sexier when they're swathed in a sultry red glow. Come to this chic spot at happy hour for impressive food and drink specials, as well as attentive bartenders and stellar sunsets. The

bar is located inside Gannon's, Bev Gannon's restaurant at the Gold and Emerald courses' clubhouse.

Mulligan's on the Blue PUB
(☎808-874-1131; www.mulligansontheblue.com; 100 Kaukahi St; ⏰11am-1am Mon-Fri, 8:30am-1am Sat & Sun) Rising above the golf course, Mulligan's offers entertainment nightly, with anything from Hawaiian steel guitar to a lively magician. It's also a good place to quaff an ale while enjoying the distant ocean view, or catching a game on one of the 14 TVs.

Four Seasons Maui at Wailea LIVE MUSIC
(3900 Wailea Alanui Dr; ⏰5-11:30pm) The lobby lounge has Hawaiian music nightly from 5:30pm to 7:30pm, with hula performances from 5:30pm to 6:30pm.

Shopping

Shops at Wailea MALL
(☎808-891-6770; www.theshopsatwailea.com; 3750 Wailea Alanui Dr; ⏰9:30am-9pm) This outdoor mall has dozens of restaurants, galleries and stores, with most shops flashing designer labels such as Louis Vuitton and Gucci, but there are some solid island choices, too. Store hours may vary slightly from mall hours.

Blue Ginger CLOTHING
(☎808-891-0772; www.blueginger.com; 3750 Wailea Alanui Dr, Shops at Wailea) Women's clothing in cheery colors and tropical motifs.

Honolua Surf Co CLOTHING
(☎808-891-8229; www.honoluasurf.com; 3750 Wailea Alanui Dr, Shops at Wailea) Hip surfer-motif T-shirts, board shorts and aloha shirts.

Martin & MacArthur ARTS, CRAFTS
(☎808-891-8844; www.martinandmacarthur.com; 3750 Wailea Alanui Dr, Shops at Wailea) Museum-quality Hawaiian-made koa (Hawaiian timber tree) woodwork and accessories.

Maui Waterwear SWIMWEAR
(☎808-891-8669; www.mauiclothingcompany.com; 3750 Wailea Alanui Dr, Shops at Wailea) Tropical swimwear you'll love to flaunt. Flip through fun beach wear at the adjoining sister store Maui Clothing.

Information

Shops at Wailea (www.theshopsatwailea.com; 3750 Wailea Alanui Dr; ⏰9:30am-9pm) This outdoor mall has an ATM and public restrooms.

Getting There & Around

The **Maui Bus** (www.mauicounty.gov) operates the Kihei Islander between Wailea and Kahului hourly until 8:27pm. The first bus picks up passengers on Wailea Ike Dr (just east of the Shops at Wailea), at 6:27am, and runs north along S Kihei Rd before heading to the Pi'ilani Village shopping center and then to Kahului, with a final stop at Queen Ka'ahumanu Center. For Lahaina, pick up the Kihei Villager at Pi'ilani Village, which travels to Ma'alaea. There, transfer to the Lahaina Islander. Fare is $2 per bus ride.

Makena

POP 99

Makena may be home to an oceanfront resort and a well-manicured golf course, but the region still feels wild, like a territorial outpost that hasn't quite been tamed. It's a perfect setting for aquatic adventurers who want to escape the crowds, offering primo snorkeling, kayaking and bodysurfing, plus pristine coral, reef sharks, dolphins and loads of sea turtles.

The beaches are magnificent. The king of them all, Big Beach (Oneloa Beach), is an immense sweep of glistening sand and a prime sunset-viewing locale. The secluded cove at neighboring Little Beach is Maui's most popular nude beach you *will* see bare buns. Together these beaches form **Makena State Park**, but don't be misled by the term 'park,' as they remain in a natural state, with no facilities except for a couple of pit toilets and picnic tables. And those rumors about the nude Sunday evening drum circle? Well...

Beaches

The beaches here are listed north to south.

Makena Bay BEACH
Want to kayak along the coast? Then drop into this pretty bay. There's no better place on Maui for kayaking – as you might surmise from the collection of kayak-tour vans parked here every morning. When seas are calm, snorkeling is good along the rocks at the southern side of Makena Landing, the boat launch that's the center of the action. Makena Bay is also a good place for shore dives; divers should head to the north side of the bay.

Kayakers should paddle south along the lava coastline to Malu'aka Beach, where green sea turtles abound. Kayak-snorkel tour operators meet just south of the landing for trips. South Pacific Kayaks (p370) will deliver pre-reserved kayaks here for rental. There are no kayak shops on-site.

Makena Bay was once a busy port for livestock, pineapples and people, and *paniolo* used to herd cattle onto boats bound for Honolulu from here.

Heading south on Makena Alanui Rd, turn right onto Honoiki St then turn right onto Makena Landing Rd.

★Malu'aka Beach BEACH

Dubbed 'Turtle Beach,' this golden swath of sand behind Makena Beach & Golf Resort is popular with snorkelers and kayakers hoping to glimpse the surprisingly graceful sea turtles that feed along the coral here and often swim within a few feet of snorkelers. You'll find terrific coral about 100yd out, and the best action is at the southern end of the beach. Come on a calm day – this one kicks up with even a little wind, and when it's choppy you won't see anything.

Parking lots, restrooms and showers are at both ends of the beach. On the northern side, park at the lot opposite Keawala'i Congregational Church then follow the road a short distance south. If that lot is full, take the first right after the resort, where there's additional parking.

Little Beach BEACH

(Pu'u Ola'i Beach; www.hawaiistateparks.org) Those folks with the coolers and umbrellas, walking north from the sandy entrance to Big Beach? They're heading to Little Beach, which is part of Makena State Park. Also known as Pu'u Ola'i Beach, this cozy strand is *au naturel*. Nudity is officially illegal, though enforcement is at the political whim of the day. The beach is hidden by a rocky outcrop that juts out from Pu'u Ola'i, the cinder hill that marks the northern end of Big Beach. Take the short but steep trail over the outcropping and bam, there it is, bare buns city.

Little Beach fronts a sandy cove that usually has a gentle shorebreak ideal for bodysurfing and boogie boarding. When the surf's up, you'll find plenty of local surfers here as well. When the water's calm, snorkeling is good along the rocky point. For parking, use the northern lot at Big Beach.

★Big Beach BEACH

(Oneloa Beach; www.hawaiistateparks.org) The crowning glory of Makena State Park, this untouched beach is arguably the finest on Maui. In Hawaiian it's called Oneloa, literally, 'Long Sand.' And indeed the golden sands stretch for the better part of a mile and are as broad as they come. The waters are a beautiful turquoise. When they're calm you'll find kids boogie boarding here, but at other times the breaks belong to experienced bodysurfers, who get tossed wildly in the transparent waves. There is a lifeguard station here.

In the late 1960s this was the site of an alternative-lifestyle encampment nicknamed 'Hippie Beach.' The tent city lasted until 1972, when police finally evicted everyone. For a sweeping view of the shore, climb the short trail to the rocky outcrop just north, which divides Big Beach from Little Beach.

The turnoff to the main parking area is a mile beyond the Makena Beach & Golf Resort. There's a port-o-john here. A second parking area lies 440yd to the south. Thefts and broken windshields are a possibility, so don't leave valuables in your car in either lot.

Secret Cove BEACH

This lovely, postcard-size swath of sand, with a straight-on view of Kaho'olawe, is worth a peek – although it's no longer much of a secret. The cove is a 440yd after the southernmost Makena State Park parking lot. The entrance is through an opening in a lava-rock wall just south of house No 6900.

SUNSET DRUM CIRCLE AT LITTLE BEACH

One of the worst-kept secrets in Makena is the sunset drum circle on Sunday nights at Little Beach. How badly kept? Let's just say there's lots of online footage – and a photo from ABC News – of Aerosmith's Steven Tyler banging a drum on the sand here. He has a house nearby. The scene is pretty chill, but be warned: about 10% of the crowd is walking around naked. But most everyone is there for the same things: the surf, the sand and the sunset. And maybe some pot brownies. The fire dancing starts after the sun goes down. If you're feeling groovy, check it out. And bring a headlamp. The trail back, which twists over a lava outcrop, is short but it's also steep and rocky. So far, state authorities have kept a distance, but they could shut it all down at anytime. Walk this way...

Tours

Makena Landing is a popular starting point for kayak tours.

★ Aloha Kayaks KAYAKING
(☎808-270-3318; www.alohakayaksmaui.com; adult/child 5-9yr $75/55; ⏱tours 7:15am) For an eco-minded snorkel-kayak trip with an enthusiastic team of owner-operators, take a paddle with Aloha Kayaks. Owners Griff and Peter have about 10 years of guiding experience apiece. Their mission? To educate guests about the environment and to keep their operations sustainable – and to make sure you see marine life. Trips depart from Makena Landing. Wear a swimsuit and sandals.

Sleeping

★ Makena Beach & Golf Resort RESORT $$$
(☎808-874-1111; www.makenaresortmaui.com; 5400 Makena Alanui Dr; r/ste from $370/575; P ❄ @ ☎ ≋) The fortress-like exterior at this striking place isn't particularly inviting, but the aloha of the staff and the stunning Malu'aka Beach, which is just out back, vault this secluded retreat to the top of the heap. Rooms shine with simple but sophisticated style: white bedspreads, subdued tropical throws, granite countertops and cherrywood furniture. The kicker? No resort fee or parking fee.

The beach is a top launch pad for snorkelers and kayakers hoping to spy a green sea turtle or two. Golfers are shuttled, for no extra fee, to the Wailea golf courses, not the adjacent Makena course, which is now private.

Eating

Vendors with cold coconuts, pineapples and other fruit are sometimes found along Makena Alanui Dr opposite Big Beach.

Jawz Fish Tacos FOOD TRUCK $
(www.jawzfishtacos.com; Makena State Park; snacks $4-12; ⏱10:30am-5pm) Get your beach snacks – tacos, burritos, shave ice – at this food truck beside the northernmost Big Beach parking lot.

Beyond Makena

Makena Rd turns adventurous after Makena State Park, continuing for three narrow miles through the lava flows of 'Ahihi-Kina'u Natural Area Reserve before dead-ending at La Pe'rouse Bay.

'Ahihi-Kina'u Natural Area Reserve

Although scientists haven't been able to pinpoint the exact date, Maui's last lava flow probably spilled down to the sea here between AD 1480 and 1600, shaping 'Ahihi Bay and Cape Kina'u. Today, the jagged lava coastline and the pristine waters fringing it have been designated a reserve because of its unique marine habitat.

Thanks in part to the prohibition on fishing here, the snorkeling is incredible. Many head to the little roadside cove 175yd south of the first reserve sign – granted, it offers good snorkeling, but there is a better option. Instead, drive 350yd past the cove and look for a large clearing on the right. Park here and follow the coastal footpath south for five minutes to a black-sand beach with fantastic coral and clear water. Although this area, known as The Dumps, used to attract few visitors, the secret is out, so get here well before 9am to nab a decent parking spot – and maybe some solitude. Enter the water from the left side of the beach where access is easy; snorkel in a northerly direction and you'll immediately be over coral gardens teeming with an amazing variety of fish. Huge rainbow parrot fish abound here, and it's not unusual to see turtles and the occasional reef shark.

Large sections of the 1238-acre reserve are closed to visitors until July 31, 2016, which will allow the Department of Land and Resource Management (www.dlnr.hawaii.gov) to protect the fragile environment from tourist wear-and-tear and to develop a long-term protection plan. Visitation in the north is still permitted between 5:30am and 7:30pm.

La Pe'rouse Bay

Earth and ocean merge at La Pe'rouse Bay with a raw desolate beauty that's almost eerie. Historians originally thought that Maui's last volcano eruption occurred in 1790, but more recent analysis indicates that the lava flow occurred about 200 to 300 years earlier. Before the blast, the ancient Hawaiian village of Keone'o'io flourished here, and its remains – mainly house and heiau platforms – can be seen scattered among the lava patches.

In May 1786 the renowned French explorer Jean François de Galaup La Pérouse became the first Westerner to land on Maui. As he

PANIOLO ROOTS

Sitting beneath the slopes of Upcountry's 'Ulupalakua Ranch, Makena was once a *paniolo* (Hawaiian cowboy) village, home to Hawaiian cowboys who corralled cattle at the landing and loaded them onto barges bound for Honolulu slaughterhouses. To catch a glimpse of Makena's roots, stop at the **Keawala'i Congregational Church**, just south of Makena Landing. One of Maui's earliest missionary churches, its 3ft-thick walls were constructed of burnt coral rock. In the seaside churchyard take a look at the old tombstones adorned with cameo photographs of the Hawaiian cowboys laid to rest a century ago.

sailed into the bay that now bears his name, scores of Hawaiian canoes came out to greet him. A monument to the explorer is located at the end of the road at La Pe'rouse Bay.

From the volcanic shoreline look for pods of spinner dolphins, which commonly come into the bay early in the day. The combination of strong offshore winds and rough waters rule out swimming, but it's an interesting place to explore on land.

Activities

Makena Stables HORSEBACK RIDING

(Map p413; ☎808-879-0244; www.makenastables.com; Makena Rd; 1½-2½hr trail rides $155-190; ⏰8am-6pm) Located just before the road ends, this place offers a morning horseback ride across the lava flows. The sunset tour travels up the scenic slopes of 'Ulupalakua Ranch.

Hoapili Trail HIKING

From La Pe'rouse Bay, this section of the ancient King's Trail follows the coastline across jagged lava flows. The first part of the trail is along the sandy beach at La Pe'rouse Bay. Be prepared: wear hiking boots, bring plenty to drink, start early and tell someone where you're going. It's a dry area with no water and little vegetation, so it can get very hot.

Right after the trail emerges onto the lava fields, it's possible to take a spur trail for 0.75 miles down to the light beacon at the tip of Cape Hanamanioa. Alternatively, walk inland to the Na Ala Hele sign and turn right onto the King's Hwy as it climbs through rough *'a'a* lava inland for the next 2 miles before coming back to the coast to an older lava flow at Kanaio Beach. Although the trail continues, it becomes harder to follow and **Kanaio Beach** is the recommended turn-around point. If you don't include the lighthouse spur, the round-trip distance to Kanaio Beach is about 4 miles.

For more details and a very basic map, visit www.hawaiitrails.org, the state's trail and access website.

NORTH SHORE & UPCOUNTRY

This wild, lush and sometimes posh region of Maui is home to an extraordinary concentration of variety. In a half-hour drive, you can ascend from the beaches of the North Shore (including the world's windsurfing capital) through the jungle of the lower slopes, and break out into open Upcountry hills, where cowboys still roam the range, and farmers work the island's Garden Belt. Communities change accordingly. The hip surfer town of Pa'ia gives way to Makawao's Old West architecture, which dissolves into a handful of stores in mud-on-boots Keokea, after which the road pass rolls on to eternity – and maybe, we've heard, to Oprah's house.

The region begs for a lazy country drive, taking in athletic surfers, artsy shops, forest trails, mountain views and organic cafes at your own rate. For the adventurous, there's plenty of ziplining, paragliding and mountain biking.

Pa'ia

POP 2668

An eclectic mix of surfers and soul-seekers cluster in Pa'ia, also known as Maui's hippest burg. Once a thriving plantation town of 10,000 residents, it declined during the 1950s when the local sugar mill closed. Then, like some other well-known sugar towns (eg Hanapepe on Kaua'i, and Honoka'a on Hawai'i, the Big Island), Pa'ia successfully reinvented itself. First came an influx of paradise-seeking hippies attracted by low rents. Next came windsurfers attracted by Ho'okipa Beach. Then came the tourists. Today the town's aging wooden storefronts, splashed in bright colors, house a broad array of shops facing a constant stream of traffic. It still feels like a dusty outpost at times, but that's all part of the vibe.

Sights & Activities

Maui Dharma Center BUDDHIST SHRINE
(Map p387; ☎808-579-8076; www.mauidharmacenter.com; 81 Baldwin Ave; ⊙6:30am-6:30pm) Marked by its roadside stupa, this Tibetan Buddhist center offers daily, weekly and monthly prayer and meditation sessions, retreats and Dharma talks. Or just take a quick stroll around the stupa's prayer wheel. The stupa shrine was consecrated by the Dalai Lama in 2007.

Simmer WINDSURFING
(Map p387; ☎808-579-8484; www.simmerhawaii.com; 137 Hana Hwy; sailboards per day $60; ⊙10am-7pm) This windsurfing center handles everything from repairs to top-of-the-line gear rentals. Also sells stylish men's and women's beachwear.

Beaches

★Ho'okipa Beach Park BEACH
(Map p384; ⊙5:30am-7pm) Ho'okipa is to daredevil windsurfers what Everest is to climbers. It reigns supreme as the world's premier windsurfing beach, with strong currents, dangerous shorebreaks and razor-sharp coral offering the ultimate challenge. This is also one of Maui's prime surfing spots. Winter sees the biggest waves for board surfers, while summer has the most consistent winds for windsurfers. To prevent turf battles, surfers typically hit the waves in the morning and windsurfers in the afternoon.

While the action in the water is only suitable for pros, a lookout point on the eastern side of the park offers spectators a great view. In the fall the action includes green sea turtles laying eggs on the beach at dusk. Ho'okipa is just before the 9-mile marker.

HA Baldwin Beach Park BEACH
(Map p384; ⊙7am-7pm) Bodyboarders and bodysurfers take to the waves at this palm-lined county park about a mile west of Pa'ia, at the 6-mile marker. The wide sandy beach drops off quickly, and when the shorebreak is big, swimmers should beware of getting slammed. Calmer waters can be found at the eastern end, where there's a little cove shaded by ironwood trees. Showers, restrooms, picnic tables and well-used sports fields round out the facilities.

The park has a reputation for rowdy behavior after the sun sets, but it's fine in the daytime when there's a lifeguard on duty.

Tavares Beach BEACH
(Map p384) For a quiet stretch of sand during the week, try this unmarked beach, which is a short drive northeast from downtown. The place livens up on weekends when local families arrive with picnics, guitars, dogs and kids. A submerged lava shelf runs parallel to the beach about 25ft from the shore, shallow enough for swimmers to scrape over. Once you know it's there, however, the rocks are easy to avoid, so take a look before jumping in.

The beach parking lot is at the first shoreline access sign on the Hana side of the 7-mile marker. There are no facilities.

MAUI DOWNHILL

Biking from the summit of Haleakalā all the way down to seaside Pa'ia has become an island rite of passage. The 25-mile journey, a 10,000ft drop in elevation, offers tremendous views, a thrilling ride and Upcountry sightseeing, including Makawao. It's also easy – the bikes only have one gear – although you have to be careful to keep your speed down around some seriously sharp corners (yes, there have been accidents).

Two companies in Pa'ia do this well, albeit differently:

Maui Sunriders (Map p387; ☎808-579-8970; www.mauisunriders.com; 71 Baldwin Ave; online price per person $90; ⊙3am-4:30pm Mon-Fri) Offers a daily self-guided tour that begins in the wee hours (around 3:15am) with a van ride to the summit. After a beautiful sunrise, you're given a new Trek mountain bike, and off you go. You don't have to return the bike until 4:30pm, so you can sightsee at your own rate and make a day of it.

Tip: if you rent a bike for the day at Maui Sunriders ($30), the price includes a bike rack. Thus a travel companion could drop you and others off at the summit, saving $60 each.

Maui Easy Riders (Map p384; ☎808-344-9489; www.mauieasyriders.com; Baldwin Beach Park; per person $119) Offers a four-hour guided tour for groups of eight or less on comfy cruisers. Stops include Makawao and Pa'ia. Departs 9am and 1:30pm. Save $20 by booking online. They can arrange a sunrise viewing followed by the bike ride.

North Shore & Upcountry

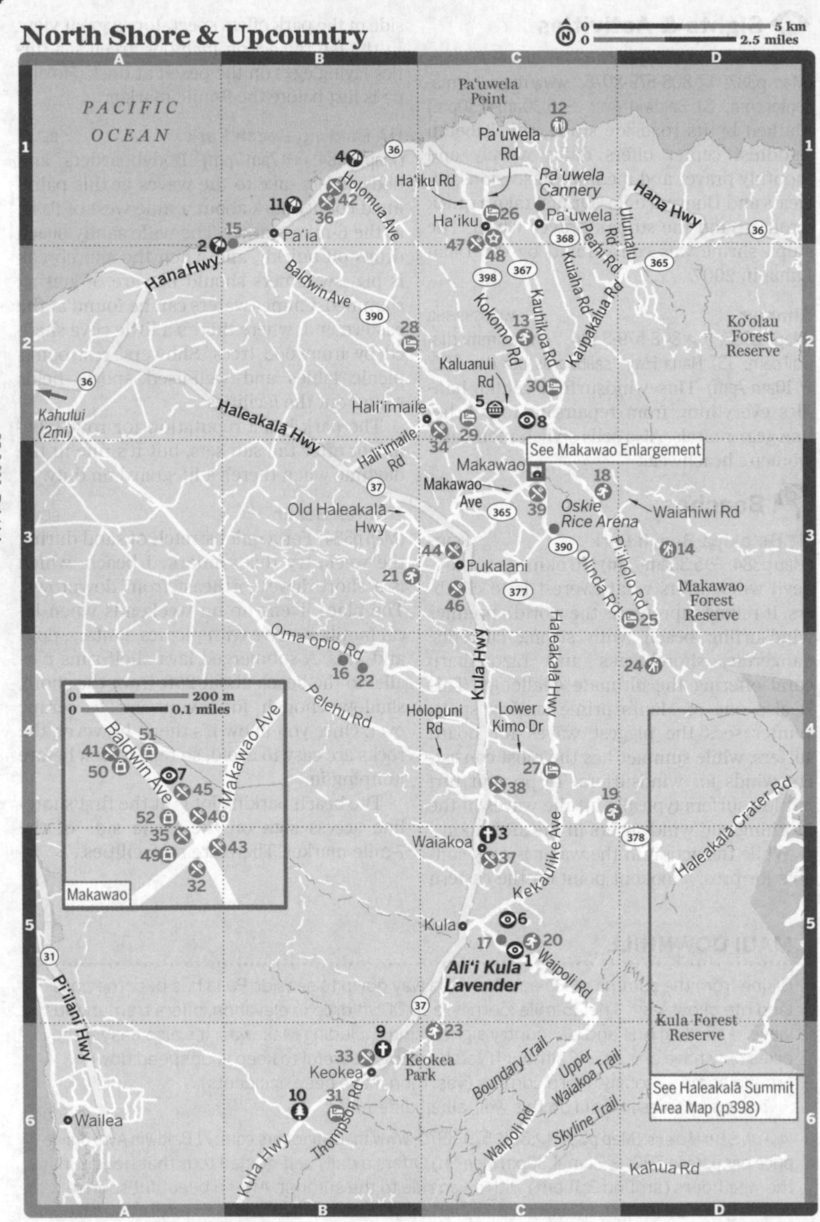

Sleeping

Nalu Kai Lodge HOTEL $$

(Map p387; 808-385-4344; www.nalukailodge.com; 18 Nalu Pl; r $135-150, studio $185;) Squeezed into a jungle-like block near downtown, this throwback to 1960s Hawaii kitsch offers 11 cute but tight rooms without much privacy. Interior bathrooms are closed off with a curtain. A stockade bamboo fence conceals a small garden, a tiki bar, and a waterfall so fake it fits right in.

North Shore & Upcountry

Top Sights
1 Ali'i Kula Lavender C5

Sights
2 HA Baldwin Beach Park A2
3 Holy Ghost Church C5
4 Ho'okipa Beach Park B1
5 Hui No'eau Visual Arts Center C2
6 Kula Botanical Garden C5
7 Makawao History Museum A4
8 Sacred Garden of Maliko C2
9 St John's Episcopal Church B6
10 Sun Yat-sen Park B6
11 Tavares Beach B1

Activities, Courses & Tours
12 Jaws C1
13 Kalakupua Playground C2
14 Makawao Forest Reserve Trails D3
15 Maui Easy Riders B1
16 Ocean Vodka Organic Farm & Distillery B4
17 O'o Farm C5
18 Pi'iholo Ranch Zipline C3
19 Pony Express C4
20 Proflyght Paragliding C5
21 Pukalani Country Club B3
Skyline Eco-Adventures .... (see 19)
22 Surfing Goat Dairy B4
23 Thompson Ranch C6
24 Waihou Spring Trail D4

Sleeping
25 Aloha Cottage D3
26 Ha'iku Plantation Inn C1
Inn at Mama's .... (see 42)
27 Kula Lodge C4
28 Lumeria Maui B2
29 Peace of Maui C2
30 Pilialoha C2
31 Star Lookout B6

Eating
32 Casanova Italian Restaurant & Deli A5
Colleen's .... (see 48)
33 Grandma's Coffee House B6
34 Hali'imaile General Store C2
35 Komoda Store & Bakery A5
36 Kuau Store B1
37 Kula Bistro C5
38 La Provence C4
39 Makawao Farmers Market C3
40 Makawao Garden Café A4
41 Makawao Steak House A4
42 Mama's Fish House B1
Nuka .... (see 47)
43 Polli's A5
44 Pukalani Superette C3
45 Rodeo General Store A4
Tuk Tuk Thai .... (see 48)
46 Upcountry Farmers Market C3
47 Veg Out C1

Drinking & Nightlife
Maui Kombucha .... (see 47)

Entertainment
48 Hana Hou Cafe C1

Shopping
Hot Island Glass .... (see 50)
Kula Marketplace .... (see 27)
49 Maui Hands A5
50 Viewpoints Gallery A4
51 Volcano Spice A4
52 Wertheim Contemporary A4

Rooms have mini-fridges but no hairdryers or TVs. Two rooms have air-con.

Parking can be tricky, with very tight spots along Nalu Pl.

★ Pa'ia Inn — BOUTIQUE HOTEL $$$

(Map p387; ☎808-579-6000; www.paiainn.com; 93 Hana Hwy; r $259-299, ste $359-899; ❄@📶) This classy boutique hotel, which has a brand-new bar in the works, offers the ultimate Pa'ia immersion: step out the front and the town is on your doorstep; step out the back and you're on a path to the beach. With 15 stylish rooms in five different categories, you'll find something to your liking.

Rooms in the historic main building can run on the small side. For a group, consider the captivating three-bedroom oceanfront beach house ($1999 per night).

Inn at Mama's — INN $$$

(Map p384; ☎808-579-9764; www.mamasfishhouse.com; 799 Poho Pl; cottage $175-575, ste $325; ❄📶) Maui's most famous seafood restaurant has a dozen accommodations divided between cottages (studio, one bedroom, two bedrooms) and luxurious junior suites (adults only). Four of the cottages are beachfront, the rest garden, while the spacious junior suites have an outdoor courtyard. All are uniquely designed and extremely well done, with the beachfront cottages enjoying idyllic views.

One caveat: ever-popular Mama's is not always the quietest of places.

Eating

Mana Foods — BAKERY $

(Map p387; ☎808-579-8078; www.manafoods-maui.com; 49 Baldwin Ave; sandwiches $7; ⏰8am-8:30pm; 🌿) Dreadlocked, Birkenstocked or just needing to stock up – everyone rubs shoulders at Mana, a health-food store, bakery and deli all wrapped into one. Once past the unassuming entrance, you'll find narrow aisles bursting with rare goodies, coffee galore, a great salad bar, and hot food to go. The mind of Pa'ia made visible.

Pa'ia Bay Coffee — CAFE $

(Map p387; ☎808-579-3111; www.paiabaycoffee.com; 43 Hana Hwy; sandwiches $3-10; ⏰7am-5:30pm; 📶) The lovely shaded garden is an inviting sanctuary on a hot day at this low-key coffee shop tucked on a busy downtown side street. Grab croissants to go or settle in at a table for Greek yogurt with berries and granola, an egg sandwich with goat cheese, or a smoked salmon and avocado sandwich.

Note: if you're not a local you will be checked out. Not a bad thing necessarily, just depends on your mood.

Kuau Store — DELI $

(Map p384; ☎808-579-8844; www.kuaustore.com; 701 Hana Hwy; mains $3-10; ⏰6:30am-7pm) Fuel up with coffee or a healthy juice before a drive on the Hana Hwy. Sandwiches are also available to go at this new general store and deli. Look for the photogenic surfboard fence about 1 mile east of downtown Pa'ia.

Anthony's Coffee Company — CAFE $

(Map p387; ☎808-214-5280; www.anthonyscoffee.com; 90 Hana Hwy; mains breakfast $4-13; ⏰5:30am-6pm; 📶) For fresh-ground organic coffee, a variety of goodies from pastries to lox Benedict, and picnic boxes for the drive to Hana ($13).

Ono Gelato — DESSERTS $

(Map p387; www.onogelatocompany.com; 115 Hana Hwy; cones $5; ⏰11am-10pm) Dishes up Maui-made organic gelato in island flavors such as guava, mango and Kula strawberry. For the ultimate treat, order the *liliko'i* quark, combining passion fruit and goat cheese.

★ Pa'ia Fish Market Restaurant — SEAFOOD $$

(Map p387; ☎808-579-8030; www.paiafishmarket.com; 100 Baldwin Ave; mains $10-21; ⏰11am-9:30pm; 👪) The communal picnic tables are perpetually packed inside this longtime favorite, where the fish is always fresh, tasty and affordable. The local favorite is *ono* fish and chips, but the menu includes plenty of other temptations, including charbroiled mahi, Cajun-style snapper, and a Hawaii classic, blackened ahi sashimi. As for those crowded picnic tables, don't worry, they turn over quick. Children's menu mains under $7.

Flatbread Company — PIZZA $$

(Map p387; ☎808-579-8989; www.flatbreadcompany.com; 89 Hana Hwy; pizzas $12-22; ⏰11am-10pm) 🍃 Wood-fired pizzas made with organic sauces, nitrate-free pepperoni, Maui pineapples – you'll never stop at a chain pizza house again. Fun combinations abound, from pure vegan to *kalua* pork with goat cheese.

Café des Amis — CAFE $$

(Map p387; ☎808-579-6323; www.cdamaui.com; 42 Baldwin Ave; breakfast under $11, lunch & dinner $4-18; ⏰8:30am-8:30pm) Grab a seat in the courtyard at this often-recommended eatery to dine on sweet or savory crepes and a variety of curries. You'll also find vegetarian offerings, creative breakfasts and a tempting array of drinks from fruit smoothies to fine wines. Note that the wraps may overpower the flavor of the fillings, and that service can be leisurely.

★ Mama's Fish House — SEAFOOD $$$

(Map p384; ☎808-579-8488; www.mamasfishhouse.com; 799 Poho Pl; mains $36-75; ⏰11am-3pm & 4:15-9pm) Mama's is a South Seas dream: superb food, top-notch service and a gorgeous seaside setting. The fish is literally fresh off the boat – they'll even tell you who caught it. The eclectic building successfully integrates everything from driftwood to sugarcane machinery. When the beachside tiki torches are lit at dinnertime, you'll swear you've entered a poster from South Pacific.

The only drawback is the eye-popping prices, which match the island's most expensive resorts. Yet no one seems to care. This is a magnet for honeymooners, or for anyone looking for that once-in-a-lifetime Hawaii experience. Located on Hana Hwy, 1.5 miles east of Pa'ia town. Reservations essential; holidays book out three months ahead.

Drinking & Nightlife

Milagros Food Company — BAR

(Map p387; ☎808-579-8755; www.milagrosfoodcompany.com; 3 Baldwin Ave; mains $10-16; ⏰11am-10pm) With sidewalk tables perched on Pa'ia's busiest corner, an island-style Tex-Mex menu and a variety of margaritas,

Pa'ia

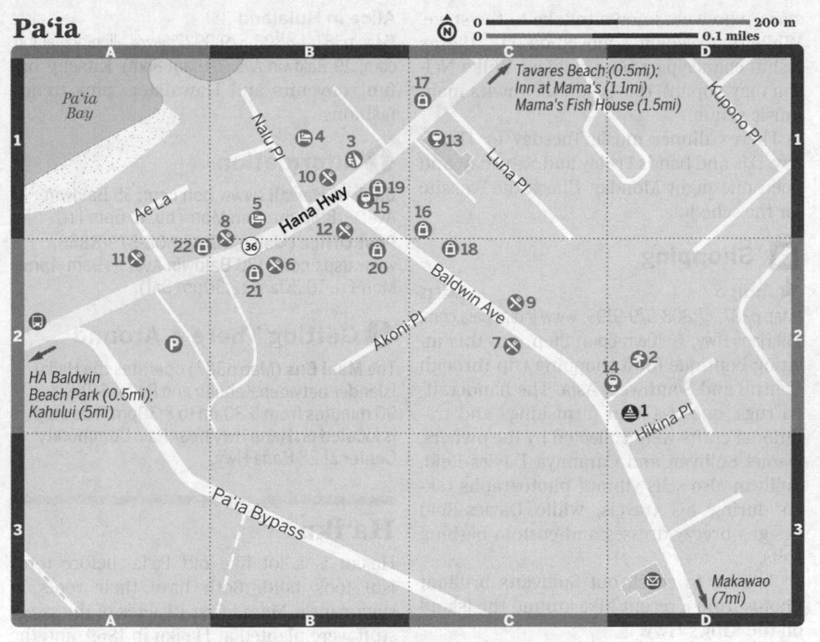

Pa'ia

Sights
1 Maui Dharma Center D2

Activities, Courses & Tours
2 Maui Sunriders D2
3 Simmer B1

Sleeping
4 Nalu Kai Lodge B1
5 Pa'ia Inn B1

Eating
6 Anthony's Coffee Company B2
7 Café des Amis C2
8 Flatbread Company B1
9 Mana Foods C2
10 Ono Gelato B1
11 Pa'ia Bay Coffee A2
12 Pa'ia Fish Market Restaurant B1

Drinking & Nightlife
13 Charley's C1
14 Dazoo D2
15 Milagros Food Company B1

Shopping
16 Alice in Hulaland C1
17 Indigo C1
18 Mandala Ethnic Arts C2
19 Maui Crafts Guild B1
20 Maui Girl B2
21 Maui Hands – Pa'ia B2
22 Wings Hawaii A2

this bar-restaurant is the perfect spot for a late-afternoon pit stop. Happy hour is from 3pm to 6pm.

Dazoo COCKTAILS
(Map p387; ☎808-579-9999; www.dazoomaui.com; 71 Baldwin Ave) Craft cocktails are the draw at new-on-the-scene Dazoo, a stylish place to sip drinks infused wth the flavors of Maui. For a taste of vodkas produced in the Upcountry, try the McLovin', made with Ocean Vodka and strawberry shrub, or stop by on the third Wednesday of the month when Pau Vodka from Hali'imaile Distilling Co takes the spotlight, with four specialty drinks.

The menu offers a Korean spin, with bibimbap and noodle dishes.

Charley's BAR
(Map p387; ☎808-579-8085; www.charleysmaui.com; 142 Hana Hwy; ⏰7am-10pm Sun-Thu, to 2am Fri & Sat) Pa'ia's legendary saloon has been slingin' suds and pub grub since 1969. In its heyday it was a magnet for visiting rock

stars, who were known to take to the stage. While that scene has moved on (OK, there's a slim chance part-time resident Willie Nelson may pop in), this is still the town's main music venue.

There's dinner music Tuesday to Thursday, DJs and bands Friday and Saturday, and open mic night Monday. Check the website for the schedule.

Shopping

★Indigo CRAFTS
(Map p387; ☎808-579-9199; www.indigopaia.com; 149 Hana Hwy; ⊙10am-6pm) Step into this inviting boutique for a shopping trip through Central and Southwest Asia. The handcrafted rugs, one-of-a-kind furnishings and traditional crafts were collected by the owners, Daniel Sullivan and Caramiya Davies-Reid. Sullivan also sells vibrant photographs taken during his travels, while Davies-Reid designs breezy dresses and custom bathing suits.

Be sure to check out Sullivan's brilliant photos from a recent hike around the island on the King's Hwy.

★Maui Crafts Guild ARTS, CRAFTS
(Map p387; ☎808-579-9697; www.mauicraftsguild.com; 120 Hana Hwy; ⊙10am-7pm, to 6pm Sep) Recently relocated to the corner of the Hana Hwy and Baldwin Ave, this long-standing artists' co-op sells everything from pottery and jewelry to hand-painted silks and natural-fiber baskets at reasonable prices.

Maui Hands – Pa'ia ARTS, CRAFTS
(Map p387; ☎808-579-9245; www.mauihands.com; 84 Hana Hwy; ⊙10am-7pm Mon-Sat, to 6pm Sun) Woodwork, jewelry and Maui-themed paintings.

Wings Hawaii CLOTHING, JEWELRY
(Map p387; www.wingshawaii.com; 69 Hana Hwy; ⊙9am-7pm Mon-Fri, 10am-7pm Sat & Sun) For truly unique clothing and jewelry – they call it beach boho chic – stop by this small shop for locally designed women's wear.

Mandala Ethnic Arts CLOTHING
(Map p387; 29 Baldwin Ave; ⊙10am-8pm) Lightweight cotton and silk clothing, Buddhas and Asian crafts.

Maui Girl CLOTHING
(Map p387; ☎808-579-9266; www.maui-girl.com; 12 Baldwin Ave; ⊙9am-6pm) Get your itty-bitty bikinis here.

Alice in Hulaland GIFTS
(Map p387; ☎808-579-9922; www.aliceinhulaland.com; 19 Baldwin Ave; ⊙9am-8pm) Kitschy but fun souvenirs and Hawaiiana, plus trendy fashions.

Information

Bank of Hawaii (www.boh.com; 35 Baldwin Ave; ⊙8:30am-4pm Mon-Thu, to 6pm Fri)

Post Office (Map p387; ☎808-579-8866; www.usps.com; 120 Baldwin Ave; ⊙9am-4pm Mon-Fri, 10:30am-12:30pm Sat)

Getting There & Around

The **Maui Bus** (Map p387) operates the Haiku Islander between Kahului and Pa'ia ($2) every 90 minutes from 5:30am to 8:30pm. The stop is located on Hana Hwy near Paia Community Center at 28 Hana Hwy.

Ha'iku

Ha'iku is a lot like old Pa'ia, before tourism took hold. Both have their roots in sugarcane – Maui's first 12 acres of the sweet stuff were planted at Ha'iku in 1869, and the village once had both a sugar mill and pineapple canneries. Thanks to its affordability and proximity to Ho'okipa Beach, it's also a haunt of pro surfers, who've helped rejuvenate the town. Nestled in greenery, this is a low-key place to stay, with many excellent accommodations and restaurants for its size.

Activities

Kalakupua Playground PARK
(Fourth Marine Division Memorial Park; Map p384; www.mauicounty.gov; Kokomo Rd, Mile 2;) Known as 'Giggle Hill,' the jungle gym and playground at this county park – complete with turrets, boardwalks and slides – is great for kids. At press time it was closed for safety upgrades, but local volunteers were hard at work to bring it up to standards. The park was the site of a marine training ground and camp during World War II.

Sleeping

★Pilialoha COTTAGE $$
(Map p384; ☎808-572-1440; www.pilialoha.com; 2512 Kaupakalua Rd; d $145;) A covenient basecamp for exploring the Upcountry, this sunny split-level cottage blends countryside charm with the comforts of home. But it's the warm hospitality and attention to detail – from the yoga mats to the Hawaiian music

collection and cozy quilts – that really stand out. Breakfast goodies for your first morning and coffee for the entire stay are provided.

Other perks include laundry facilities and fleece jackets for that Haleakalā sunrise.

Ha'iku Plantation Inn B&B $$
(Map p384; 808-575-7500; www.haikuleana.net; 555 Ha'iku Rd; r $144-169) Set in verdant surroundings on the edge of town, this large and lovingly restored plantation house, the former company doctor's residence, offers four rooms with private baths, high ceilings, clawfoot tubs, hardwood floors and oodles of easygoing charm, all at a reasonable price. Several acres loaded with tropical fruit trees ensure privacy when lounging on the classic porch. Gin, m'dear?

Three-night minimum but may be able to accommodate single-night stays.

Eating & Drinking

Veg Out VEGETARIAN $
(Map p384; 808-575-5320; www.veg-out.com; 810 Kokomo Rd, Ha'iku Town Center; mains $6-10, pizza $7-17; 10:30am-7:30pm Mon-Fri, 11:30am-7:30pm Sat & Sun;) Tucked inside a former warehouse, this rasta-casual vegetarian eatery serves up a dynamite burrito loaded with beans, hot tofu and jalapeños. Also right on the mark are the taro cheeseburgers and pesto-chèvre pizza.

Tuk Tuk Thai THAI $
(Map p384; 810 Ha'iku Rd, Ha'iku Marketplace; mains $10-14; 11am-8pm Tue-Sat) This psychedelic school bus (you'll know it when you see it) dishes out spicy, no-fuss Thai. Order at the window then find a seat under the canopy or in the sunshine. If it's raining, it may not open.

★ **Nuka** JAPANESE $$
(Map p384; 808-575-2939; www.nukamaui.com; 780 Ha'iku Rd; small plates $4-22, mains $15-18, rolls $8-19; 4:30-10pm) One of Maui's best dining options marries a traditional Japanese restaurant with a jazzy cafe, offering the classics, like sushi and tempura, alongside exotic rolls and *otsumami* (tapas). From the menus to the decor to the website, everything is presented with sophistication, and without inflated prices. And oh, that Nuka Roll…

No reservations.

Colleen's AMERICAN $$
(Map p384; 808-575-9211; www.colleensinhaiku.com; 810 Ha'iku Rd, Ha'iku Marketplace; breakfast $7-13, lunch $6-16, dinner $11-30; 6am-10pm) From morning to evening, this boisterous bistro is the Ha'iku hangout, for locals and visitors alike. Menu choices are straightforward – burgers, salads and build-your-own pizzas among them – but cooked to perfection, and supported by a wide range of craft beers. Excellent coffee and big breakfasts drag 'em in early.

Maui Kombucha TEAHOUSE
(Map p384; 808-575-5233; www.mauikombucha.com; 810 Kokomo Rd, Ha'iku Town Center; 12oz tea $4, mains $8-12; 8am-8pm) Welcome to 'The Booch,' home of Ha'iku's alternative drink, kombucha. Hidden behind the back of a strip mall, this hip hole-in-the-wall overflows with fermented tea (with bubbles!) and a lively crowd. The veggie fare changes daily, but expect wraps, salads and lots of fun. Located behind Ha'iku Town Center.

Entertainment

★ **Hana Hou Cafe** LIVE MUSIC
(Map p384; 808-575-2661; www.hanahoucafe.com; 810 Ha'iku Rd, Haiku Marketplace; 10:30am-9pm) While offering an interesting fusion of Hawaiian, Thai and Italian cuisine, this newcomer has rapidly become popular for high-quality live music (6pm to 9pm Monday and Wednesday to Saturday), particularly with more mature visitors, who also appreciate the indoor/outdoor seating. Whether it's bluegrass, blues or jazz, there's something for everyone. Reserve ahead Monday and Wednesday.

Information

Ha'iku has two gas stations, so you don't have to drive all the way back to Pa'ia.

Post Office (808-575-2614; www.usps.com; 770 Ha'iku Rd; 8:30am-3:30pm Mon-Fri, 9-11am Sat)

BIG WAVE SURFING

The North Shore harbors Maui's most famous big-wave surfing spot: **Jaws** (Pe'ahi; Map p384). When present, the mammoth swell reaches as high as a seven-story building. Surfers are towed in or even dropped by helicopter. Unfortunately for onlookers, there's no legitimate public access to the cliffs above, as the path crosses private land.

Hali'imaile

The tiny pineapple town of Hali'imaile is named for the sweet-scented maile plants – used in lei-making – that covered the area before pineapples took over. The heart of town is the old general store (c 1918) which has been turned into one of Maui's top restaurants.

At press time Hali'imaile Distilling Co (www.haliimailedistilling.com), which produces Pau Vodka and a rum developed by musician Sammy Hagar, was making plans to offer tastings and a tour.

Sleeping & Eating

Peace of Maui GUESTHOUSE $

(Map p384; ☎808-572-5045; www.peaceofmaui.com; 1290 Hali'imaile Rd; r with shared bathroom from $85, cottage $185; @ 📶) Upcountry's top budget sleep is in the middle of nowhere yet within an hour's drive of nearly everywhere, making it a central base for exploring the island. Spotlessly clean rooms are small but comfortable, with refrigerator and shared bath. There's also a guest kitchen and common area. A separate two-bedroom, one-bath cottage offers a covered deck with beautiful mountain views and extra room for kids.

★Hali'imaile General Store HAWAII REGIONAL CUISINE $$$

(Map p384; ☎808-572-2666; www.bevgannonrestaurants.com; 900 Hali'imaile Rd; lunch $14-26, dinner $32-44; ⏰11am-2:30pm Mon-Fri, 5:30-9pm daily; 🍷) The culinary sorceress behind this destination dining spot is Chef Bev Gannon, who was one of the original forces behind the Hawaii Regional Cuisine movement. A steady flow of in-the-know diners beat a track to this inviting outpost – the building was a general store during the plantation era – to feast on her fusion creations, such as sashimi pizza and Asian pear duck tostadas. At lunch, the kale salad with salmon is superb.

Makawao

POP 7184

Makawao is an attractive mélange of art haven and *paniolo* culture, with a twist of New Age sensibility. A ranching town since the 1800s, its false-front buildings and hitching posts look transported from the Old West. Today the surrounding hills still contain cattle pastures and the weekend rodeo, but also some expensive homes, as these cool and quiet uplands have become a choice residential area. Meanwhile, the town below has filled with attractive galleries and cafes. The main action is at the intersection of Baldwin Ave and Makawao Ave, where you can enjoy a few hours of browsing and a fine meal.

Sights

Hui No'eau Visual Arts Center ART GALLERY

(Map p384; ☎808-572-6560; www.huinoeau.com; 2841 Baldwin Ave; ⏰10am-4pm) FREE Occupying the former estate of sugar magnates Harry and Ethel Baldwin, Hui No'eau is a regal setting for a community arts center. In 1917 famed architect CW Dickey designed the main plantation house, which showcases the Hawaiian Regional architectural style he pioneered. You're welcome to visit the galleries, which exhibit the diverse works of island artists, and walk around the grounds, where you'll find stables converted into art studios.

The gift shop sells quality ceramics, glassware and prints created on-site. Pick up a walking-tour map at the front desk. The center is just north of the 5-mile marker.

Sacred Garden of Maliko GARDENS

(Map p384; ☎808-573-7700; www.sacredgardenmaui.com; 460 Kaluanui Rd; ⏰10am-5pm) FREE Up for a meditative moment? The nonprofit Sacred Garden of Maliko, a self-described healing sanctuary, has a pair of rock-garden labyrinth walks guaranteed to reset the harmony gauge. One's in an orchid greenhouse; the other's in a *kukui* (candlenut tree) grove beside Maliko Stream. It's a peaceful place, with sitting areas, to spend some time. Also sells plants and gifts.

From Baldwin Ave turn east onto Kaluanui Rd. After 0.8 miles you'll cross a one-lane bridge; 0.2 miles further look for a low stone wall – the garden is on the right just before a sharp S-curve in the road.

Makawao History Museum MUSUEM

(Map p384; ☎808-283-3732; 3643 Baldwin Ave) FREE Step into this tiny new museum for an overview of the town's cowboy past, with lots of ranching tools on display.

Activities

Makawao Forest Reserve Trails HIKING, MOUNTAIN BIKING

(Map p384; www.mauimountainbike.org; Kahakapau Rd, Makawao Forest Reserve; ⏰7am-7pm) The 2093-acre Makawao Forest Reserve offers a new, still-growing trail system popular with hikers and mountain bikers. The 5.75-mile multiuse Kahakapao Loop Trail is the primary trail, and it parallels a ravine before arcing back through cool upland forest. If dry, this is also a great running trail. You will pass two small pump tracks a short distance from the trailhead.

The trails are a joint effort between state agencies and the Maui Mountain Bike Coalition. At press time, trail maps and visitor information had not been added to state-run recreational websites. For a helpful map showing the various trails and their uses, visit www.mauimountainbike.org/kahakapao-recreation-area.

To reach Kahakapao Rd, head up Pi'iholo Rd for 1.5 miles, turn left on Waiahiwi Rd and turn right after 0.4 miles. Continue to the reserve.

Pi'iholo Ranch Zipline ZIPLINING

(Map p384; ☎800-374-7050; www.piiholozipline.com; 799 Pi'iholo Rd; zip tours $140-190, canopy tours $90-135; ⊙tours 9am-2:30pm, reservations 7am-7pm; 👪) This operation offers two options: a standard dual-line course of four/five lines ($140/190), the latter with a 2800ft finale that hits 600ft in altitude, and a three-/five-/six-line canopy course ($90/125/135). Allow one to three hours depending on length. There's a 60lb minimum weight. Helmet-mounted GoPro cams available ($40), or bring your own.

Waihou Spring Trail HIKING

(Map p384; www.hawaiitrails.ehawaii.gov) For a quiet walk in deep woods, take this cool, tranquil and easy trail, which begins 4.75 miles up Olinda Rd from central Makawao. A half-mile in you'll reach a loop trail, which brings you back where you started. A steep (and potentially muddy) offshoot descends to Waihou Spring, but for most the loop will be enough.

Festivals & Events

★Makawao Third Friday CARNIVAL

(www.mauifridays.com) On the third Friday of every month the center of Makawao turns into a pedestrian zone and laid-back street party from 6pm to 9pm, with food and live music.

Makawao Rodeo RODEO

(⊙Jul) Hundreds of *paniolo* show up at the Oskie Rice Arena on the weekend closest to Independence Day for Hawaii's premier rodeo, which celebrates its 60th anniversary in 2015. Qualifying roping and riding events occur all day on Thursday and Friday prior to the big prizes over the weekend. For thrills on Friday night, head up to the arena to see the bull-riding bash.

> **WORTH A TRIP**
>
> ### SCENIC OLINDA ROAD
>
> For a steep scenic drive with plenty of twists and turns, head into the hills above Makawao along Olinda Rd, which picks up in town where Baldwin Ave leaves off. Turn left onto Pi'iholo Rd near the top, and wind back down into town. The whole crazy loop takes about half an hour. Combine with Waihou Spring Trail for a cool midway break.

Paniolo Parade PARADE

(⊙9-11am) Held on the Saturday morning closest to July 4, this festive parade goes right through the heart of Makawao; park at Oskie Rice Arena and take the free shuttle to the town center.

Maui Polo Club POLO

(www.mauipoloclub.com; adult/child under 12yr $10/free; ⊙1:30pm, gates open 12:30pm) A friendly tailgating party surrounds these Sunday matches held behind Oskie Rice Arena, 1 mile above town on Olinda Rd, early September through mid-November; and at the Manduke Baldwin Polo Arena, 1.7 miles up Haleakalā Hwy from Makawao Ave, from early April to late June. Dress is casual to island dressy (ie your best aloha shirt).

Sleeping

Aloha Cottage COTTAGE $$

(Map p384; ☎808-575-9228; www.alohacottage.com; 1875 Olinda Rd; cottage $199-299, 4-night minimum, cleaning fee $100; 📶) This gated love nest, an octagonal cottage with one large room, sits on a bluff way up steep Olinda Rd, about 10 minutes from town. Surrounded by greenery, it assures privacy. There's a full kitchen, a laundry, vaulted ceilings, a king bed and a large lanai with hot tub. A perfect retreat. Rate varies based on length of stay.

As an alternative, try the A-framed and equally charming Thai Treehouse, a sister property on the same lush grounds (www.maui.cc/ThaiTreeHouse.html; from $179).

★ **Lumeria Maui** YOGA RETREAT $$$

(Map p384; ☎855-579-8877; www.lumeriamaui.com; 1813 Baldwin Ave; incl breakfast r $329-389, ste $489-539;) This spa for the soul starts working its magic the moment you pull into the hibiscus-lined drive. Set on tidy, garden-filled grounds on an upcountry slope between Pa'ia and downtown Makawao, Lumeria is a gorgeous place to nourish both mind and body. Farm-to-table breakfasts prime the spirit before days filled with yoga, garden strolls, hot stone massages and aromatherapy.

At night guests retreat to minimalist, Asian-inspired cottages that once served as dorms for plantation workers. A daily $25 resort fee covers a wide range of classes. To-go lunches and three-course dinners also available for an extra fee.

Eating

Komoda Store & Bakery BAKERY $

(Map p384; 3674 Baldwin Ave; 7am-5pm Mon, Tue & Thu-Sat) This homespun bakery, legendary for its mouthwatering cream puffs and guava-filled *malasadas* (Portuguese fried doughnuts), has been a Makawao landmark since 1916. Arrive early, as it often sells out by noon.

Makawao Garden Café CAFE $

(Map p384; ☎808-573-9065; www.makawaogardencafe.com; 3669 Baldwin Ave; mains under $10; 11am-3pm Mon-Sat) On a sunny day there's no better place in town for lunch than this outdoor cafe tucked into a courtyard at the northern end of Baldwin Ave. It's strictly sandwiches and salads, but everything's fresh, generous and made to order by the owner herself.

Rodeo General Store TAKEOUT $

(Map p384; 3661 Baldwin Ave; mains $4-9; 6:30am-8pm Sun-Thu, to 9pm Fri & Sat) The deli counter at this busy general store sells a variety of to-go meals, from salads and sandwiches to Hawaiian *poke* and plate lunches. The *kalua* pork is tender and oh-so tasty. Everything is made from scratch.

Makawao Farmers Market MARKET $

(Map p384; ☎808-280-5516; 200 Olinda Rd; 9am-2pm Wed) Upcountry gardeners gather to sell their homegrown veggies and fruit once a week at this small open-air market next to Po'okela Church.

★ **Casanova Italian Restaurant & Deli** ITALIAN $$

(Map p384; ☎808-572-0220; www.casanovamakawao.com; 1188 Makawao Ave; lunch $9-20, dinner $12-34; 11:30am-2pm Mon-Sat, 5-9:30pm daily) Classic Italian dishes. Juicy Maui-raised steaks. Innovative pizzas cooked in a kiawe-fired oven. It's hard to go wrong at this longtime Upcountry favorite. Casanova doubles as an entertainment venue, with a happening dance floor and live music on Wednesdays and weekends (9:30pm to 1am).

For a casual lunch, try one of the hearty sandwiches at the attached deli (7:30am to 5:30pm Monday to Saturday, 8:30am to 5:30pm Sunday).

Polli's MEXICAN $$

(Map p384; ☎808-572-7808; www.pollismexicanrestaurant.com; 1202 Makawao Ave; mains $10-24; 11am-10pm) Parked on the corner of Baldwin Ave and Makawao Ave, this friendly and reliable Tex-Mex restaurant is a longtime favorite. Have a cerveza at the small bar, or tackle sizzling fajitas in the nearby booths. Margaritas are $4 during happy hour (4pm to 5:30pm Monday to Friday).

Makawao Steak House STEAK $$$

(Map p384; ☎808-572-8711; www.cafeoleirestaurants.com; 3612 Baldwin Ave; mains $14-46; restaurant 5-9:30pm Tue-Sun, bar from 4:30pm Tue-Sun) What's a cowboy town without a steakhouse? Or a saloon? You get both here, along with a warm Upcountry atmosphere. Recently purchased by the Cafe O'Lei franchise, the varied menu offers something for everyone, including the kids. Five mains for $6 each on the children's menu.

Shopping

★ **Wertheim Contemporary** ART

(Map p384; ☎808-573-5972; www.wertheimcontemporary.com; 3660 Baldwin Ave; 11am-5pm) Showcases the extraordinary art of Andreas Nottebohm, who etches flat sheets of aluminum to create an illusion of depth. You won't believe your eyes.

Maui Hands ART

(Map p384; ☎808-572-2008; www.mauihands.com; 1169 Makawao Ave; 10am-6pm Mon-Sat, to 5pm Sun) A fascinating collection of high-quality Hawaii art, primarily from Maui, including photography, koa, ceramics, and a mix of traditional and contemporary paintings. Worth a stop.

Volcano Spice FOOD
(Map p384; 808-572-7729; www.volcanospicecompany.com; 3621 Baldwin Ave; 11am-5pm Mon-Sat) An enticing array of spicy rubs and hot sauces are sold in this tiny shop on Baldwin Ave. If you're a hot-sauce fiend, there are plenty to sample – just bring some water!

Viewpoints Gallery ART
(Map p384; 808-572-5979; www.viewpointsgallerymaui.com; 3620 Baldwin Ave; 10:30am-5pm) This classy gallery hosts a dozen of the island's finest artists, and feels like a museum.

Hot Island Glass ART
(Map p384; www.hotislandglass.com; 3620 Baldwin Ave; 9am-5pm) Watch artists in action at Maui's oldest handblown-glass studio from 10:30am to 4pm. Everything from paperweights with ocean themes to high-art decorative pieces are available.

Information

Post Office (808-572-0019; www.usps.com; 1075 Makawao Ave; 9am-4:30pm Mon-Fri, to 11am Sat)

Pukalani & Around

POP 7574

True to its name, which means Heavenly Gate, Pukalani is the gateway to the lush Upcountry. Most visitors just drive past Pukalani on the way to Kula and Haleakalā, unless they need food or gas (the last before the park).

To reach the business part of town, get off Haleakalā Hwy (Hwy 37) at the Old Haleakalā Hwy exit, which becomes Pukalani's main street.

Activities

Pukalani Country Club GOLF
(Map p384; 808-572-1314; www.pukalanigolf.com; 360 Pukalani St; greens fee with cart $63, with clubs $81; 7am-dusk) With its clubhouse in a mobile home, the Pukalani Golf Club doesn't present a pretty face, but the course is in excellent condition and one of the best deals on the island. Come after 2:30pm and golf the rest of the day for just $35 – cart included. Small clubhouse cafe on-site.

Tours

★ **Surfing Goat Dairy** FARM TOUR
(Map p384; 808-878-2870; www.surfinggoatdairy.com; 3651 Oma'opio Rd; store 9am-5pm Mon-Sat, to 2pm Sun;) 'Da' fetta mo betta' is the motto at this 42-acre farm, the source of all that luscious chèvre adorning the menus of Maui's top restaurants. There's a well-stocked store and various child-friendly 'ag tours.' Free samples of cheese provided to all visitors. Feel free to bring wine, order some cheese and enjoy the view at the outdoor seating area.

Tours include a frequent 20-minute dairy tour (10am to 3pm Monday to Saturday, to 1pm Sunday; adult/child under 12 years $12/8), an 'evening chores & milking' tour (3:15pm Monday to Saturday; adult/child under 12 years $15/12; reserve ahead) and the 2½-hour 'grand dairy' tour (9am Saturday; $25; call for dates).

★ **Ocean Vodka Organic Farm & Distillery** DISTILLERY TOUR
(Map p384; 808-877-0009; www.oceanvodka.com; 4051 Oma'opio Rd; adult/child under 12yr $10/free; tours 9:30am-4pm) From the sugarcane stalks to the bottling room to the end-of-tour tasting, the 45-minute guided tour at this family-run vodka distillery tells an interesting story about the organic roots of vodka production. As the name suggests, Ocean Vodka is made with deep ocean mineral water sourced off the coast of Hawai'i (Big Island). The company recently added organic rum to its product line.

Eating

Upcountry Farmers Market MARKET $
(Map p384; www.upcountryfarmersmarket.com; 55 Kiopaa St; 7-11:30am Sat) Several dozen local farmers – and a food truck or two – share fruit, vegetables and locally prepared fare at this market in the parking lot of Longs Drugs at the Kulamalu Shopping Center. Arrive by 9:30am for the best choices.

Pukalani Superette SUPERMARKET $
(Map p384; 808-572-7616; www.pukalanisuperette.com; 15 Makawao Ave; prepared meals $5-10; 5:30am-9pm Mon-Fri, 6:30am-9pm Sat, 7am-8pm Sun) A popular choice for prepared hot meals – *kalua* pork, chili chicken, Spam musubi etc.

Kula

POP 6452

It's cooler in Kula – refreshingly so. Think of this Upcountry heartland as one big garden, and you won't be far off. So bountiful is Kula's volcanic soil, it produces most of the onions, lettuce and strawberries grown in Hawaii and almost all of the commercially grown protea. The latest addition, sweet-scented lavender, is finding its niche, too. The magic is in the elevation. At 3000ft, Kula's cool nights and sunny days are ideal for growing all sorts of crops – making Kula synonymous with fresh veggies on any Maui menu.

Sights

★ Ali'i Kula Lavender — GARDENS

(Map p384; ☎808-878-3004; www.aklmaui.com; 1100 Waipoli Rd; admission per person $3; ⏲9am-4pm) Perched on a broad hillside with panoramic views of the West Maui Mountains and the central Maui coast, this charming lavender farm is a scenic place to relax. Distractions include fragrant pathways, a gift shop with lavender products, and a lanai with sweeping views where you can enjoy a scone and a cup of lavender tea.

To reach the parking area, proceed through the Kula Forest Reserve gates and follow the signs around the loop.

Kula Botanical Garden — GARDENS

(Map p384; ☎808-878-1715; www.kulabotanicalgarden.com; 638 Kekaulike Ave; adult/child 6-10yr $10/3; ⏲9am-4pm) A father-son team of nene – an endangered Hawaiian goose – hangs out at this well-kept and shady 9-acre garden. Walking paths wind through themed plantings, including native Hawaiian specimens and a 'taboo garden' of poisonous plants. Because a stream runs through it, the garden supports water-thirsty plants that you won't find in other Kula gardens. After a rain the whole place is an explosion of color.

DON'T MISS

UPCOUNTRY-GROWN TREATS

- Lunch tour, O'o Farm (p394)
- Mango chèvre, Surfing Goat Dairy (p393)
- Elk burgers, 'Ulupalakua Ranch Store (p396)
- Maui Splash wine, Maui's Winery (p396)
- Lavender scones, Ali'i Kula Lavender (p394)
- Maui-grown coffee, Grandma's Coffee House (p396)
- Distillery Tour, Ocean Vodka (p393)

Holy Ghost Church — CHURCH

(Map p384; 4300 Lower Kula Rd; ⏲8am-6pm) Waiakoa's hillside landmark, the octagonal Holy Ghost Church, was built in 1895 by Portuguese immigrants. The church features a beautifully ornate interior that looks like it came right out of the Old World, as indeed much of it did. The gilded altar was carved by renowned Austrian woodcarver Ferdinand Stuflesser and shipped in pieces around the Cape of Good Hope.

Activities

Pony Express and Skyline Eco-Adventures operate on land belonging to Haleakalā Ranch, a working cattle ranch that sprawls across the slopes beneath Haleakalā National Park. The businesses are adjacent to each other on Hwy 378, 2.5 miles up from Hwy 377.

Pony Express — HORSEBACK RIDING

(Map p384; ☎808-667-2200; www.ponyexpresstours.com; Haleakalā Crater Rd; ⏲reservations 7am-9pm) Offers a two-hour ride through the cattle country of Haleakalā Ranch ($125, 8am check-in), and a 1½-hour 'mauka ride' ($95, 11am and 1:30pm check-in), both with great views from 4000ft. Check website for discounts and reservations.

Skyline Eco-Adventures — ZIPLINING

(Map p384; ☎808-878-8400; www.zipline.com; Haleakalā Crater Rd; zipline tour $120; ⏲8:30am-3pm) Maui's first zipline has a prime location on the slopes of Haleakalā. The five lines are relatively short (100ft to 850ft) compared with the competition, although a unique 'pendulum zip' adds some spice at the end. Good for newbies.

Proflyght Paragliding — PARAGLIDING

(Map p384; ☎808-874-5433; www.paraglidemaui.com; Waipoli Rd; 1000ft paraglide $95, 3000ft $185; ⏲office 7am-7pm, flights 2hr after sunrise) Strap into a tandem paraglider with a certified instructor and take a running leap off the cliffs beneath Polipoli Spring State Recreation Area. The term 'bird's-eye view' will never be the same. Must be under 230lb.

Tours

O'o Farm — FARM TOUR

(Map p384; ☎808-667-4341; www.oofarm.com; Waipoli Rd; lunch tour adult/child 5-12yr $58/29; ⏲10:30am-2pm Mon-Thu) Whether a gardener or a gourmet, you're going to love a tour of famed Lahaina Chef James McDonald's organic Upcountry farm. Where else can you help harvest your own meal, turn the goodies over to a gourmet chef and feast on the bounty? BYO wine.

On the new 'Seed to Cup' Coffee Tour ($50 per person, 8:30am Tuesday and Wednesday), tour the fields where the coffee is grown, sip French-press coffee and savor a garden frittata along with jam and homemade bread.

Festivals & Events

Holy Ghost Feast PORTUGUESE FESTIVAL
(www.kulacatholiccommunity.org; May) This festival celebrates Kula's Portuguese heritage. Held at the Holy Ghost Church on the fourth Saturday and Sunday in May, it's a family event with games, craft vendors, a farmers market and a free Hawaiian-Portuguese lunch on Sunday.

Sleeping

Kula Lodge CABIN $$
(Map p384; 808-878-1535; www.kulalodge.com; 15200 Haleakalā Hwy; cabins $150-225;) These five rustic cabins are about 45 minutes from the summit of Haleakalā. All units come with lanai, coffeemakers and extra blankets, but no TVs or kitchenettes. Four have open lofts, which are great for kids, but offer no privacy. Wi-fi is available at the on-site restaurant.

Eating

★Kula Bistro ITALIAN $$
(Map p384; 808-871-2960; www.kulabistro.com; 4566 Lower Kula Rd; breakfast $9-17, lunch & dinner $12-39; 7:30am-10:30am & 11am-8pm) This superb family-owned bistro offers a friendly dining room, sparkling service and delicious home cooking, including fabulous pizza and huge servings of coconut cream pie (enough for two). BYOB wine from Morihara Store across the street. No corkage fee.

La Provence CAFE $$
(Map p384; 808-878-1313; www.laprovencekula.com; 3158 Lower Kula Rd, Waiakoa; pastries $2-5, lunch $11-14, crepes $4-13; 7am-9pm Wed-Sun) One of Kula's best-kept secrets, this little courtyard restaurant in the middle of nowhere is the domain of Maui's finest pastry chef. Popular offerings include ham-and-cheese croissants, chocolate-filled pastries and filled crepes. Weekends offer a brunch menu that draws patrons from far and wide. Try the warm goat cheese and Kula greens salad. Hours may fluctuate so call before making the drive.

Shopping

Kula Marketplace GIFTS
(Map p384; 808-878-2135; www.kulamarketplace.com; 15200 Haleakalā Hwy/Hwy 377; 7am-7pm) This rustic market perched on the side of the volcano acts as a clearinghouse for island vendors, with food and arts and crafts. Gourmet selections include wine, chocolate and homemade jams. Great for gifts. There's also fast food available if you've forgotten to load up.

Keokea

POP 1612

Blink-and-you'll-miss it Keokea is the last real town before Hana if you're swinging around the southern part of the island. The sum total of the town center consists of a coffee shop, an art gallery, a gas station and two small stores, the Ching Store and the Fong Store. The last two announce one of Hawaii's many immigrant populations. Drawn by rich soil, Hakka Chinese farmers migrated to this remote corner of Kula at the turn of the 20th century. Their influence is still found throughout the village.

But the village isn't entirely off the world's radar – media powerhouse Oprah Winfrey has a home and property in the area.

Sights

Sun Yat-sen Park PARK
(Map p384) For a time Sun Yat-sen, father of the Chinese nationalist movement, lived in Keokea. He's honored at Sun Yat-sen Park, found along the Kula Hwy (Hwy 37), 1.7 miles beyond Grandma's Coffee House. The park has picnic tables and is a great place to soak up the broad vistas that stretch clear across to West Maui.

St John's Episcopal Church CHURCH
(Map p384; services 8:30am Wed, 7:30am & 9:30am Sun) Built c 1907, this local landmark still bears its name in Chinese characters.

Activities

Thompson Ranch HORSEBACK RIDING
(Map p384; 808-878-1910; www.thompsonranchmaui.com; cnr Middle & Polipoli Rds; 2hr ride $100; tour 10am;) Join these folks for two-hour horseback rides across ranch land

in the cool Upcountry bordering Polipoli Spring State Recreation Area. At elevations of 4000ft to 6000ft, it's a memorable ride for those who enjoy mountain scenery. Reserve ahead. Located 1 mile up Polipoli Rd on the left.

Sleeping

Star Lookout COTTAGE $$
(Map p384; ☎907-250-2364; www.starlookout.com; 622 Thompson Rd; cottage $250) Starry skies, an outdoor hot tub and grounds so quiet you can hear the flowers bloom. Half a mile up a one-lane road from Keokea center, this two-bedroom cottage with a loft sleeps four comfortably, six in a pinch. There's also a full kitchen and wood-burning stove. What makes it spectacular? Its hillside perch overlooking 1000 acres of green pasture with sweeping views of Lana'i and West Maui.

Eating

★**Grandma's Coffee House** CAFE $
(Map p384; ☎808-878-2140; www.grandmascoffee.com; 9232 Kula Hwy; pastries $3, breakfast $5-16, sandwiches $8-10; ⊙7am-5pm, to 8pm Wed-Sat) Worthy of a Norman Rockwell painting, this charming island landmark with its creaking screen door and carved wooden tables grows its own coffee, dishes up deli lunches, and serves a varied dinner menu Wednesday to Saturday. Take your goodies out on the lanai and eat right under the coffee trees. Coffee is $1.50 – nice!

'Ulupalakua

The sprawling 18,000-acre 'Ulupalakua Ranch, which anchors this green landscape, is home to 2300 brood cattle, as well as a small herd of Rocky Mountain elk, which dot the hillside pastures. The ranch is still worked by *paniolo,* Hawaiian cowboys who have been here for generations. Most people stop by today to visit the bustling winery, which sits on 'Ulupalakua Ranch land, about 6 miles beyond Keokea.

Hwy 37 winds south through ranch country, offering good views of Kaho'olawe and the little island of Molokini. With a stop at the winery, it makes for a nice half-day drive. After the vineyard, it's another 25 dusty, bumpy miles to Kipahulu along the remote Pi'ilani Hwy.

Activities

Maui's Winery WINERY
(Map p413; ☎808-878-6058; www.mauiwine.com; Kula Hwy; ⊙10am-5pm, tours 10:30am & 1:30pm) Formerly Tedeschi Vineyards, Maui's sole winery offers free tastings in its historic stone cottage and twice-daily tours. It produces a noteworthy variety, from grape wines to novelty wines, using local fruit to great effect. Try the sweet Maui Splash, a light blend of pineapple and passion fruit, the robust 'Ulupalakua or the sophisticated dessert wine. Opposite the winery lie the remains of the Makee Sugar Mill, built in 1878.

To learn about the history of the ranch – which was established in the mid-1800s – step into the small exhibit room beside the tasting area.

Festivals & Events

'Ulupalakua Sunday Drive Event FESTIVAL
(www.mauiwine.com/events) Twice a year, 'Ulupalakua Ranch sponsors a fun bash on the lawn of Maui's Winery. In 2014 the first event was a chili cookout in July followed by a first-ever tree-lighting ceremony with Christmas carols in December. The festivals currently take place on a Sunday in December and July, but check ahead.

Eating

Bully's Burgers BURGERS $
(Map p413; ☎808-878-3272; www.triplelranchmaui.com; 15900 Pi'ilani Hwy, Triple L Ranch; burgers $7-12; ⊙11am-6:30pm winter, to 7pm summer) You've reached the end of the road. Or the beginning, if you wish. And what do you find but a burger shack – and we mean shack – decorated with cow skulls. No, Bully's has no Michelin stars, just one heck of a burger, thanks to the beef from Triple L Ranch and a few surprising twists, like the spicy chipotle sauce.

Located about 4 miles past Maui's Winery – or the end of the road from Hana. Before making a special trip, call to confirm it's open.

'Ulupalakua Ranch Store DELI $
(Map p413; www.ulupalakuaranch.com; burgers $9-14; ⊙store 9:30am-5pm, grill 11am-3pm) Sidle up to the life-size wooden cowboys on the front porch and say howdy. Then pop inside and check out the cowboy hats and souvenir T-shirts. If it's lunchtime, mosey over to the grill and treat yourself to an organic ranch-raised elk burger. Well yee-ha!

HALEAKALĀ NATIONAL PARK

To fully experience Maui – or at least peer into its soul – make your way to the summit of Haleakalā. Like a yawning mouth, the huge crater opens beneath you, in all its raw volcanic glory, caressed by mist and, in the experience of a lifetime, bathed in the early light of sunrise. Lookouts on the crater's rim provide breathtaking views of the moonscape below, and the many cinder cones marching across it.

The rest of this amazing park, which is divided into two distinct sections, is all about interacting with this mountain of solid lava, and the rare life-forms that live upon it, some of them found only here. You can hike down into the crater, follow lush trails on the slopes, or put your mountain bike through its paces. For the ultimate adventure, get a permit, bring a tent and camp overnight beneath the stars. However you do it, you will leave having touched something much, much larger than yourself.

Summit Area

Often referred to as the world's largest dormant volcano, the floor of Haleakalā is a colossal 7.5 miles wide, 2.5 miles long and 3000ft deep – nearly as large as Manhattan. In its prime, Haleakalā reached a height of 12,000ft before water erosion carved out two large river valleys that eventually merged to form Haleakalā crater. Technically, as geologists like to point out, it's not a true 'crater,' but to sightseers that's all nitpicking. Valley or crater, it's a phenomenal sight like no other in the US national park system.

Sights

Hosmer Grove FOREST

A pleasant half-mile loop trail winds through Hosmer Grove, which is home to non-native tree species – including pine, fir and eucalyptus – as well as native scrubland. The site is also popular with campers and picnickers. The whole area is sweetened with the scent of eucalyptus and alive with the red flashes and calls of native birds. Hosmer Grove sits on a side road just after the park's entrance booth.

Drive slowly on the road in, as this is one of the top places to spot nene, a rare goose that is also the state bird.

Waikamoi Preserve NATURE RESERVE

(☎808-572-4400; www.nature.org; ⏰hiking tour 8:45am Thu) This windswept native cloud forest supports one of the rarest ecosystems on earth. Managed by the Nature Conservancy, the 5230-acre preserve provides the last stronghold for 76 species of native plants and forest birds. You're apt to spot the *'i'iwi* and the *'apapane* (both honeycreepers with bright red feathers) and the yellow-green *'amakihi* flying among the preserve's koa and ohia trees. The only way to visit the area is to join the park service's weekly Waikamoi Preserve Hike.

This 3½-hour hiking tour currently departs Hosmer Grove campground on Thursdays at 8:45am. It's best to make reservations, which you can do up to one week in advance. The hike is moderately strenuous. Bring rain gear.

Leleiwi Overlook VIEWPOINT

For your first look into the crater, stop at Leleiwi Overlook (8840ft), midway between the Park Headquarters Visitor Center and the summit. The overlook also provides a unique angle on the ever-changing clouds floating in and out. You can literally watch the weather form at your feet. From the parking lot, it's a five-minute walk across a gravel trail to the overlook.

En route you'll get a fine view of the West Maui Mountains and the flat isthmus connecting the two sides of Maui.

Kalahaku Overlook VIEWPOINT

Don't miss this one. Kalahaku Overlook (9324ft), 0.8 miles beyond Leleiwi Overlook, offers a bird's-eye view of the crater floor and the ant-size hikers on the trails snaking around the cinder cones below. At the observation deck, plaques provide information on each of the volcanic formations that punctuate the crater floor. From the deck you'll also get a perfect angle for viewing both the Ko'olau Gap and the Kaupo Gap on the rim of Haleakalā.

Between May and October the *'ua'u* (Hawaiian dark-rumped petrel) nests in burrows in the cliff face at the left side of the observation deck. Even if you don't spot the birds, you can often hear the parents and chicks making their unique clucking sounds. Of about 20,000 *'ua'u* remaining today, most nest right here at Haleakalā, where they lay just one egg a year. These seabirds were thought to be extinct until sighted in the crater during the 1970s.

Haleakalā Summit Area

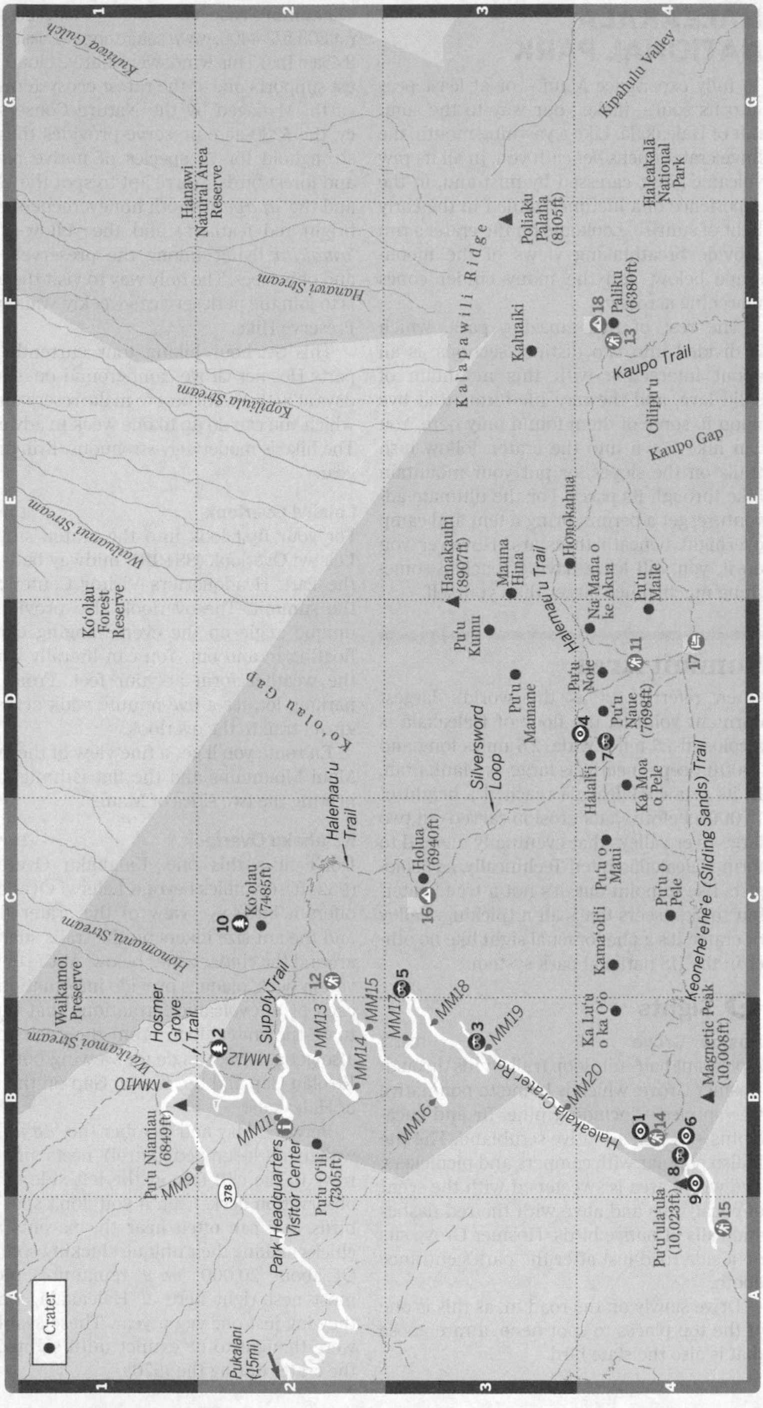

● Crater

2 km
1 miles

Waikamoi Preserve
Waikamoi Stream
Honomanu Stream
Ko'olau Forest Reserve
Wailuanui Stream
Kopiliula Stream
Hanawi Stream
Hanawi Natural Area Reserve
Kuhiwa Gulch
Pu'u Nianiau (6849ft)
MM9
MM10
Hosmer Grove Trail
2
378
Pukalani (15mi)
MM11
MM12
Supply Trail
10
Ko'olau (7485ft)
Ko'olau Gap
Park Headquarters Visitor Center
Pu'u O'ili (7305ft)
MM13
12
MM14
MM15
Halemau'u Trail
MM17
5
MM16
16
Holua (6940ft)
MM18
3
MM19
Silversword Loop
Hanakauhi (8907ft)
Pu'u Kumu
Kalapawili Ridge
Mauna Hina
Pu'u Mamane
Kaluaiki
Poliaku Palaha (8105ft)
Haleakalā Crater Rd
MM20
Halemau'u Trail
Honokahua
Ka Lu'u o ka O'o
Kama'oli'i
Pu'u o Maui
Halali'i
4
7
Pu'u Nole
Na Mana o ke Akua
Pu'u Naue (7698ft)
11
Pu'u Maile
18
13
Paliku (6380ft)
Kaupo Trail
Kipahulu Valley
1
14
Ka Moa o Pele
Oilipu'u
Kaupo Gap
Haleakalā National Park
Pu'u'ula'ula (10,023ft)
8
6
9
Pu'u o Pele
Keonehe'ehe'e (Sliding Sands) Trail
17
Magnetic Peak (10,008ft)
15

Haleakalā Summit Area

A short trail below the parking lot leads to a field of native *'ahinahina* (silversword), ranging from seedlings to mature plants.

This overlook is only accessible on the way down the mountain.

Haleakalā Visitor Center — CULTURAL CENTER, VIEWPOINT

(www.nps.gov/hale; sunrise-3pm) Perched on the rim of the crater at 9745ft, this visitor center is the park's main viewing spot. And what a magical sight awaits. The ever-changing interplay of sun, shadow and clouds reflecting on the crater floor creates a mesmerizing dance of light and color. The center has displays on Haleakalā's volcanic origins and details on what you're seeing on the crater floor 3000ft below.

Nature talks are given, books on Hawaiian culture and the environment are for sale, and there are drinking fountains and restrooms here. Hikers, note that it may be easier to fill a thermos at the water filling station at the Park Headquarters Visitor Center.

By dawn the parking lot fills with people coming to see the sunrise show, and it pretty much stays packed all day. Leave the crowds behind by taking the 10-minute hike up **Pa Ka'oao (White Hill)**, which begins at the eastern side of the visitor center and provides stunning crater views.

Pu'u'ula'ula (Red Hill) Overlook — VIEWPOINT

You may find yourself standing above the clouds while exploring Pu'u'ula'ula (10,023ft), Maui's highest point. The **summit building** provides a top-of-the-world panorama from its wraparound windows. On a clear day you can see Hawai'i (Big Island), Lana'i, Moloka'i and even O'ahu. When the light's right, the colors of the crater are nothing short of spectacular, with grays, greens, reds and browns.

An *'ahinahina* garden has been planted at the overlook, making this the best place to see these luminous silver-leafed plants in various stages of growth.

Magnetic Peak — MOUNTAIN

The iron-rich cinders in this flat-top hill, which lies immediately southeast of the summit building (the direction of Hawai'i, the Big Island), pack enough magnetism to play havoc with your compass. Modest as it looks, it's also – at 10,008ft – the second-highest point on Maui.

Science City — LANDMARK

(www.ifa.hawaii.edu) Science City is the nickname for the collection of domes just behind the summit. Managed by the University of Hawai'i, this area is unfortunately off-limits to visitors, as it houses some very interesting equipment – much of it studying the sun and outer space.

Pan-STARRS surveys the heavens for earth-approaching objects, both asteroids and comets, that might pose a danger to our planet. It is the most powerful survey system in the world in terms of combined field of view, resolution and sensitivity. The Air Force's Ground-Based Electro-Optical Deep Space Surveillance system performs a similar function. It is capable of identifying a basketball-size object 22,000 miles away. After years of delay, the Daniel K Inouye Solar Telescope is now under construction. When complete it will be the world's most powerful solar telescope. Operations are expected to begin in 2019.

The Institute for Astronomy at the University of Hawai'i holds monthly public talks at its office in Pukalani. For more information see www.ifa.hawaii.edu/haleakalanew. The website contains fascinating videos of past lectures.

Activities

Stop at the Park Headquarters Visitor Center to see what's happening. Free **ranger talks** on Haleakalā's unique natural history and Hawaiian culture are given at the Haleakalā Visitor Center and the Pu'u'ula'ula (Red Hill) Overlook; the schedule varies, but there are usually two or three each day.

Stargazing

On clear nights, stargazing is phenomenal on the mountain. You can see celestial objects up to the seventh magnitude, free of light interference, making Haleakalā one of the best places on the planet for a sky view.

Check the park's schedule of events to see if it is offering an evening star talk. Dependent on staffing, these one-hour talks typically occur between May and September, and sometimes in winter, at Hosmer Grove. Otherwise, pick up a free star map of the night sky for the current month at the Park Headquarters Visitor Center and have your own cosmic experience.

Hiking

There's a trail for every type of hiker in this otherworldly place, from short nature walks ideal for families to hardy two-day treks.

★ Keonehe'ehe'e (Sliding Sands) Trail — HIKING

Make time for this stunner, which starts at the southern side of the Haleakalā Visitor Center at 9740ft and winds down to the crater floor. If you take this hike after catching the sunrise, you'll walk directly into a gentle warmish wind and rays of sunshine. There is no shade, so bring water and a hat.

The path descends gently into an unearthly world of stark lava sights and ever-changing clouds. The first thing you'll notice is how quiet everything is. The only sound is the crunching of volcanic cinders beneath your feet. If you're pressed for time, just walking down 20 minutes will reward you with an into-the-crater experience and fabulous photo opportunities. Keep in mind that the climb out takes nearly twice as long.

The full trail leads 9.2 miles to the Paliku cabin and campground, passing the Kapalaoa cabin at 5.6 miles after roughly four hours. The first 6 miles follow the southern wall. There are great views, but virtually no vegetation. Four miles down, after an elevation drop of 2500ft, Keonehe'ehe'e Trail intersects with a spur that leads north into the cinder desert, where it connects with the Halemau'u Trail after 1.5 miles.

Continuing on Keonehe'ehe'e, you head across the crater floor for 2 miles to Kapalaoa. Verdant ridges rise on your right, giving way to ropy *pahoehoe* (smooth-flowing lava). From Kapalaoa cabin to Paliku, the descent is gentle and the vegetation gradually increases. Paliku (6380ft) is beneath a sheer cliff at the eastern end of the crater. In contrast to the crater's barren western end, this area receives heavy rainfall, with ohia forests climbing the slopes.

Halemau'u Trail — HIKING

With views of crater walls, lava tubes and cinder cones, the Halemau'u Trail down to the Holua campground and back – 7.4 miles round-trip – can be a memorable day hike. Just be sure to start early before the afternoon clouds roll in and visibility vanishes. The first mile is fairly level and offers a fine view of the crater with Ko'olau Gap to the east.

The trail then descends 1400ft along 2 miles of switchbacks to the crater floor and on to the Holua campground (6940ft). You'll

VOLUNTEER OPPORTUNITIES

Haleakalā National Park offers two different volunteer opportunities. One is a multiday trip sponsored by **Friends of Haleakalā National Park** (www.fhnp.org). This volunteer-led operation involves up to a dozen visitors, who hike into the wild and stay for two nights in cabins owned by the National Park Service. Volunteers perform one of a number of tasks ranging from cabin maintenance to native planting to invasive species removal.

The second opportunity is a day trip run by Pacific Whale Foundation (p365) as part of its **Volunteers on Vacation** (☎ ext 1 808-249-8811; www.volunteersonvacation.org; ⏲ reservations 6am-9pm) program, and occurs on the first and third Saturday of every month. Led by a certified naturalist and trained guide, volunteers work on projects that help protect Haleakalā National Park's ecosystem, such as removing invasive plants. There's also a short hike. Transportation is provided from Ma'alaea or Pukalani.

Both programs provide free admission into the park.

see impressive views of the crater walls rising a few thousand feet to the west. Several lava tubes are visible from the trail, but since endangered species use them for shelter, the Park Service has made them off-limits.

If you have the energy, push on just another mile to reach some colorful cinder cones, being sure to make a short detour onto the **Silversword Loop**, where you'll see these unique plants in various stages of growth. In summer, their tall stalks should be ablaze with hundreds of maroon and yellow blossoms. But be careful – half of all *'ahinahina* today are trampled to death as seedlings, mostly by careless hikers who wander off trails and inadvertently crush the plants' shallow, laterally growing roots. The trail continues another 6.3 miles to the Paliku cabin.

The trailhead to Halemau'u is 3.5 miles above the Park Headquarters Visitor Center and about 6 miles below the Haleakalā Visitor Center. There's a fair chance you'll see nene in the parking lot.

Cinder Desert Trails — HIKING

Two spur trails connect Keonehe'ehe'e (Sliding Sands) Trail, near Kapalaoa cabin, with the Halemau'u Trail between Paliku and Holua cabins. If you're camping you may have time to do them both, as the trails are not very long. The spur trail furthest west takes in many of the crater's most kaleidoscopic cones, and the viewing angle changes with every step.

If you prefer stark, black and barren, the other spur trail takes you through *'a'a* (rough, jagged lava) and *pahoehoe* (smooth-flowing lava) fields.

Both trails end up on the northern side of the cinder desert near **Kawilinau**, also known as the Bottomless Pit. Legend says the pit leads down to the sea, though the National Park Service says it's just 65ft deep. Truth be told, there's not much to see, as you can't really get a good look down the narrow shaft. The real prize is the nearby short loop trail, where you can sit for a while in the saddle of Pele's **Paint Pot Lookout**, the crater's most brilliant vantage point.

Kaupo Trail — HIKING

The most extreme of Haleakalā's hikes is the Kaupo Trail, which starts at the Paliku campground and descends to Kaupo on the southern coast. Be prepared for ankle-twisting conditions, blistered feet, intense tropical sun, torrential showers and a possibly hard-to-follow path. Your knees will take a pounding as you descend more than 6100ft over 8.6 miles.

> **PLAN AHEAD**
>
> Haleakalā National Park (p404) has two very different sections: the ethereal Summit Area and the coastal Kipahulu Area. There is no direct road connection between them. Thus travelers typically visit the summit on one day, and the Kipahulu Area on another (usually heading to or from Hana). One entrance ticket is good for both areas.

The first 3.7 miles of the trail drop 2500ft in elevation before reaching the park boundary. It's a steep rocky path through rough lava and brushland, with short switchbacks alternating with level stretches. From here you'll be rewarded with spectacular ocean views.

The last 4.9 miles pass through Kaupo Ranch property on a rough jeep trail as it descends to the bottom of Kaupo Gap, exiting into a forest where feral pigs snuffle about. Here trail markings become vague, but once you reach the dirt road, it's another 1.5 miles to the end at the eastern side of the Kaupo Store.

The 'village' of Kaupo is a long way from anywhere, with light traffic. Still, you'll probably manage a lift. If you have to walk the final stretch, it's 8 miles to the 'Ohe'o Gulch campground.

Because this is such a strenuous and remote trail, it's not advisable to hike it alone. No camping is allowed on Kaupo Ranch property, so most hikers spend the night at the Paliku campground and then get an early start.

Hosmer Grove Trail — HIKING

Anyone who is looking for a little greenery after hiking the crater will enjoy this shaded woodland walk, as will birders. The half-mile loop trail starts at Hosmer Grove campground, 0.75 miles south of the Park Headquarters Visitor Center, in a forest of lofty trees.

The exotics here were introduced in 1910 in an effort to develop a lumber industry in Hawaii. Species include fragrant incense cedar, Norway spruce, Douglas fir, eucalyptus and various pines. Although the trees adapted well enough to grow, they didn't grow fast enough at these elevations to make tree harvesting practical.

After the forest, the trail moves into native shrubland, with *'akala* (Hawaiian raspberry), mamane, pilo, kilau ferns and sandalwood. The *'ohelo,* a berry sacred to the volcano goddess Pele, and the *pukiawe,* which has red and white berries and evergreen leaves, are favored by nene.

Listen for the calls of the native *'i'iwi* and *'apapane;* both are fairly common here. The *'i'iwi* has a very loud squeaking call, orange legs and a curved salmon-colored bill. The *'apapane,* a fast-moving bird with a black bill, black legs and a white undertail, feeds on the nectar of bright red ohia flowers, and its wings make a distinctive whirring sound.

Cycling

Cycling downhill from the summit to the sea, via Makawao and Pa'ia, is a popular pursuit. There are companies that will lead a group tour, and others that will take you to the summit and let you ride down on your own. Many people combine this with sunrise, requiring a very early start.

Alternatively, you can arrange a bike and transportation on your own. This is not only cheaper, but less restrictive. Due to past problems, one-way downhill group cycle tours are not allowed to cycle within the park, but begin pedaling just below park boundaries. Individual cyclists are allowed to pedal without restriction. For rental equipment see Crater Cycles (p353) in Kahului, or Maui Sunriders (p383) in Pa'ia. Bike racks are available with the rental.

Mountain Biking

The **Skyline Trail**, a wild ride from Science City Access Rd down to Polipoli Spring State Recreation Area, was closed at press time due to damage from Hurricane Iselle. Check its status at www.hawaiitrails.org or one of the local bike shops.

Sleeping

Maui's best campgrounds are in Haleakalā National Park. To spend the night at Haleakalā is to commune with nature. All of the camping options are primitive; none have electricity or showers. Backcountry campgrounds have pit toilets and limited nonpotable water supplies that are shared with the crater cabins. Water needs to be filtered or chemically treated before drinking; conserve it, as water tanks occasionally run dry. Fires are allowed only in grills and in

THE SUNRISE EXPERIENCE

Haleakalā means 'House of the Sun.' So it's no surprise that since the time of the first Hawaiians people have been making pilgrimages up to Haleakalā to watch the sunrise. It's an experience that borders on the mystical. Mark Twain called it 'the sublimest spectacle' he'd ever witnessed.

Plan to arrive at the summit 90 minutes before the sunrise to guarantee a parking spot. Park at the summit or beside the crater at the Haleakalā Visitor Center. About 30 minutes later the night sky lightens and turns purple-blue, and the stars fade away. Ethereal silhouettes of the mountain ridges appear. The undersides of the clouds lighten first, accenting the night sky with pale silvery slivers and streaks of pink.

About 20 minutes before sunrise, the light intensifies on the horizon in bright oranges and reds. Turn around for a look at Science City, whose domes turn a blazing pink. For the grand finale, when the the sun appears, all of Haleakalā takes on a fiery glow. It feels like you're watching the earth awaken.

Come prepared – it's going to be c-o-l-d! However many layers of clothes you can muster, it won't be too many. Also bring a headlamp or flashlight to help you follow the short path to the summit shelter.

The best photo opportunities occur before the sun rises. Every morning is different, but once the sun is up, the silvery lines and the subtleties disappear.

Bring cash to feed into the automated fee machine (currently cash only), in case the entry kiosk is unattended in the wee hours. Cash and credit cards are accepted when the kiosk is manned.

One caveat: a rained-out sunrise is an anticlimactic event after tearing yourself out of bed in the middle of the night to drive up a pitch-dark mountain. So check the weather report the night before to calculate your odds of having clear skies.

If you just can't get up that early, sunsets at Haleakalā have inspired poets as well.

times of drought are prohibited entirely. You must pack in all your food and supplies, and pack out all your trash. Also be aware that during periods of drought you'll be required to carry in your own water.

Keep in mind that sleeping at an elevation of 7000ft is not like camping on the beach. You need to be well equipped – without a waterproof tent and a winter-rated sleeping bag, forget it.

Hosmer Grove Campground CAMPGROUND
(campsite free) Wake up to the sound of birdsong at Hosmer Grove, the only drive-up campground in the Summit Area section of Haleakalā National Park. On the slopes of the volcano, surrounded by towering trees and adjacent to one of Maui's best birding trails, this campground at an elevation of 6800ft tends to be a bit cloudy, but a covered picnic pavilion offers shelter if it starts to rain.

Camping is free on a first-come, first-served basis, with a limit of 50 people. No permit is required, though there's a three-day camping limit per month. It's busier in summer than in winter and is often full on holiday weekends. The campground is just after the park entrance booth, and has grills, toilets and running water. Since you're close to the summit, it's a cinch getting up for sunrise.

Backcountry Campgrounds CAMPGROUND
(campsite free) For hikers, two backcountry campgrounds lie in the belly of Haleakalā Crater. They are collectively called the Wilderness Campgrounds. The easiest to reach is at **Holua**, 3.7 miles down the Halemau'u Trail. The other is at **Paliku**, below a rainforest ridge at the end of Halemau'u Trail. Weather can be unpredictable at both. Permits are required.

Holua at 6940ft is typically dry after sunrise, until clouds roll back in the late afternoon. Paliku at 6380ft is in a grassy meadow, with skies overhead alternating between stormy and sunny. Wasps are present at both campsites, so take precautions if you're allergic to stings.

Unlike at Hosmer Grove, permits are required for backcountry camping in the crater. They are free and issued at the Park Headquarters Visitor Center on a first-come, first-served basis between 8am and 3pm up to one day in advance. Photo identification and a 10-minute orientation video are required. Camping is limited to three nights in the crater each month, with no more than two consecutive nights at either campground. Because only 25 campers are allowed at each site, permits can go quickly when larger parties show up, a situation more likely to occur in summer.

Haleakala Wilderness Cabins CABIN $
(☎808-572-4400, reservations 877-444-5777; www.recreation.gov; per cabin with 1-12 people $75) Three rustic cabins dating from the 1930s lie along trails on the crater floor at Holua, **Kapalaoa** and Paliku. Each has a wood-burning stove, a propane burner, 12 bunks with sleeping pads (but no bedding), pit toilets and a limited supply of water and firewood. There is no electricity.

Hiking distances to the cabins from the crater rim range from 4 to just over 9 miles. The driest conditions are at Kapalaoa, in the middle of the cinder desert off Keonehe'ehe'e (Sliding Sands) Trail. Those craving lush rainforest will find Paliku serene. Holua has unparalleled sunrise views. There's a three-day limit per month, with no more than two consecutive nights in any cabin. Each cabin is rented to only one group at a time.

The cabins can be reserved online up to six months in advance. A photo ID is required for the permittee, and all of those staying in the cabin must watch a 10-minute wilderness orientation video.

ℹ Information

Pack plenty of snacks, especially if you're going up for the sunrise. No food or bottled water is sold anywhere in the park. You don't want a growling stomach to send you back down the mountain before you've had a chance to see the sights.

Check out the current weather conditions at the summit by logging on to the crater webcam at Haleakalā Crater Live Camera (www.ifa.hawaii.edu/haleakalanew/webcams.shtml).

Bring extra layers of clothing. The temperature can drop dramatically at any point in the day.

Park Headquarters Visitor Center (☎808-572-4459; www.nps.gov/hale; ⏲8am-3:45pm) Less than a mile beyond the entrance, this visitor center is the place to pick up brochures and a trail map, buy nature books and get camping permits. It also has information on ranger talks and other activities being offered during your visit. If you're going hiking, you'll want to make sure your water bottles are filled before leaving here. Keep an eye out for nene wandering around the grounds; most nene deaths are the result of being hit by cars.

NENE WATCH

The native nene, Hawaii's state bird, is a long-lost cousin of the Canada goose. By the 1950s, hunting, habitat loss and predators had reduced its population to just 30. Thanks to captive breeding and release programs, it has been brought back from the verge of extinction and the Haleakalā National Park's nene population is now holding steady at about 250 to 300.

Nene nest in shrubs and grassy areas from 6000ft to 8000ft, surrounded by rugged lava flows with sparse vegetation. Their feet have gradually adapted by losing most of their webbing. The birds are extremely friendly and love to hang out where people do, anywhere from cabins on the crater floor to the Park Headquarters Visitor Center.

Their curiosity and fearlessness have contributed to their undoing. Nene don't fare well in an asphalt habitat and many have been run over by cars. Others have been tamed by too much human contact, so no matter how much they beg for your peanut butter sandwich, don't feed the nene. It only interferes with their successful return to the wild.

The nonprofit Friends of Haleakalā National Park runs an Adopt-a-Nene program. For $30 you get adoption papers, information about your nene, a certificate and postcard. The money funds the protection of nene habitat.

ENTRANCE FEES & PASSES

Haleakalā National Park (808-572-4400; www.nps.gov/hale; 3-day pass car/individual on foot, bicycle or motorcycle $10/5;) never closes, and the pay booth at the park entrance opens before dawn to welcome the sunrise crowd. The fee covers both sections of the park. If you're planning several trips, or are going on to Hawai'i (Big Island), consider buying an annual pass ($25), which covers all of Hawaii's national parks.

MAPS

A current hiking trail map can be downloaded from www.recreation.gov or the park's official website (www.nps.gov/hale). Other planning materials and books can be purchased online from the park's partner: www.hawaiipacificparks.org.

DANGERS & ANNOYANCES

This park can be a seriously dangerous place to drive, due to a combination of sheer drops with no guardrails, daily doses of thick mist, and strong wind. Exercise extra caution on winter afternoons, when a sudden rainstorm can add ice to the list.

Obey warning signs. They often mark a spot where a visitor has been hurt or killed by a fall, a flash flood or falling rocks.

The weather can change suddenly from dry, hot conditions to cold, windswept rain. Although the general rule is sunny in the morning and cloudy in the afternoon, fog and clouds can blow in at any time, and the windchill can quickly drop below freezing. Dress in layers and bring extra clothing.

At 10,000ft the air is relatively thin, so expect to tire more quickly, particularly if you're hiking. The higher elevation also means that sunburn is more likely.

Visitors rarely experience altitude sickness at the summit. An exception is those who have been scuba diving in the past 24 hours, so plan your trip accordingly. Children, pregnant women and those in generally poor health are also susceptible. If you experience difficulty breathing, sudden headaches and dizziness, or more serious symptoms such as confusion and lack of motor coordination, descend immediately. Sometimes driving down the crater road just a few hundred feet will alleviate the problem. Panicking or hyperventilating only makes things worse.

Getting There & Around

Getting to Haleakalā is half the fun. Snaking up the mountain it's sometimes hard to tell if you're in an airplane or a car – all of Maui opens up below you, with sugarcane and pineapple fields creating a patchwork of green on the valley floor. The highway ribbons back and forth, and in some places as many as four or five switchbacks are in view all at once.

Haleakalā Crater Rd (Hwy 378) twists and turns for 11 miles from Hwy 377 near Kula up to the park entrance, then another 10 miles to Haleakalā summit. It's a good paved road, but it's steep and winding. You don't want to rush, especially when it's dark or foggy. Watch out for cattle wandering freely across the road.

The drive to the summit takes about 1½ hours from Pa'ia or Kahului, two hours from Kihei and a bit longer from Lahaina. If you need gas, fill up the night before, as there are no services on Haleakalā Crater Rd.

On your way back downhill, be sure to put your car in low gear to avoid burning out your brakes.

Kipahulu Area ('Ohe'o Gulch)

There's more to Haleakalā National Park than the cindery summit. The park extends down the southeast face of the volcano all the way to the sea. The crowning glory of the Kipahulu section of the park is 'Ohe'o Gulch, with its magnificent waterfalls and wide pools, each one tumbling into the next one below.

Back in the 1970s 'Ohe'o Gulch was dubbed the 'Seven Sacred Pools' as part of a tourism promotion, but at the request of community elders, park staff use the traditional names for the stream and gulch. 'Seven pools' is a complete misnomer anyway since there are 24 pools in all, extending from the ocean to Waimoku Falls, and they were never sacred – but they certainly are divine.

The waters once supported a sizable Hawaiian settlement of farmers who cultivated sweet potatoes and taro in terraced gardens beside the stream. Archaeologists have identified the stone remains of more than 700 ancient structures at 'Ohe'o.

One of the expressed intentions of Haleakalā National Park is to manage its Kipahulu area 'to perpetuate traditional Hawaiian farming and *ho'onanea*' – a Hawaiian word meaning to pass the time in ease, peace and pleasure. So kick back and have some fun!

For drivers, note that there is no in-park access between the Summit Area and Kipahulu. For this reason you will most likely be visiting the two sections on different days.

Sights & Activities

Kipahulu Visitor Center CULTURAL CENTER
(Map p413; ☎808-248-7375; www.nps.gov/hale; 3-day pass per car $10, per person on foot, bicycle or motorcyle $5; ⏲park 24hr, visitor center 9am-5pm) Rangers here offer cultural history talks and demonstrations on the lives and activities of the early Hawaiians who lived in the area now within park boundaries. Guided hikes are also routinely given. Check the schedule of events on the park's website.

Kuloa Point Trail HIKING, SWIMMING
(Map p413) Even if you're tight on time, you've got to take this 20-minute stroll! The Kuloa Point Trail, a half-mile loop, runs from the visitor center down to the lower pools and back. A few minutes down, you'll come to a broad grassy knoll with a gorgeous view of the Hana coast. On a clear day you can see Hawai'i, the Big Island, 30 miles away across 'Alenuihaha Channel. This is a fine place to stop for a picnic.

The large freshwater pools along the trail are terraced one atop the other and connected by gentle cascades. They may look calm, but flash floods have taken several lives here, so the Park Service has closed the pools to swimming.

★Pipiwai Trail HIKING
(Map p413) Ready for an adventure? This fun trail ascends alongside the 'Ohe'o streambed, rewarding hikers with picture-perfect views of waterfalls and an otherworldly trip through a bamboo grove. The trail starts on the *mauka* (inland) side of the visitor center and leads up to Makahiku Falls (0.5 miles) and Waimoku Falls (2 miles). To see both falls, allow about two hours return. The upper section is muddy, but boardwalks cover some of the worst bits.

Along the path, you'll pass large mango trees and patches of guava before coming to an overlook after about 10 minutes. Makahiku Falls, a long bridal-veil waterfall that drops into a deep gorge, is just off to the right. Thick green ferns cover the sides of 200ft basalt cliffs where the water cascades – a very rewarding scene for such a short walk.

Continuing along the main trail, you'll walk beneath old banyan trees, cross Palikea Stream (killer mosquitoes thrive here) and enter the wonderland of the Bamboo Forest, where thick groves of bamboo bang together musically in the wind. Beyond them is Waimoku Falls, a thin, lacy 400ft waterfall dropping down a sheer rock face. When you come out of the first grove, you'll see the waterfall in the distance. Forget swimming under Waimoku Falls – its pool is shallow and there's a danger of falling rocks.

Wear your grippy water shoes for this one.

Tours

Kipahulu 'Ohana CULTURAL TOUR
(Map p413; ☎808-248-8558; www.kipahulu.org) Kipahulu was once a breadbasket, or more accurately a poi bowl, for the entire region. For fascinating insights into the area's past, join one of the ethnobotanical tours led by Kipahulu 'Ohana, a collective of Native Hawaiian farmers who have restored ancient taro patches within the national park. Some of these are in the most incredible places,

including high bluffs overlooking waterfalls. The tours include a sampling of Hawaiian foods and intriguing details on the native plants and ancient ruins along the way.

The two-hour outing ($49) includes about 2 miles of hiking, leaves at 10am and concentrates on the farm activities. The 3½-hour tour ($79) leaves at 12:30pm, covers 4.5 miles and adds on a hike to Waimoku Falls. Both tours leave from the Kipahulu Visitor Center; advance reservations required.

Sleeping

Kipahulu Campground CAMPGROUND

(Map p413; campsite free) This campground has an incredible setting on oceanside cliffs amid the stone ruins of an ancient Hawaiian village. Good mana here! This is a primitive campground. Facilities include pit toilets, picnic tables and grills. Drinking water is only available from the nearby visitor center restrooms. Camping is free and is first-come, first-served but limited to three nights within a 30-day period.

In winter you'll usually have the place to yourself, and even in summer there's typically enough space to handle everyone who shows up.

Bring mosquito repellent and gear suitable for rainy conditions. The campground is 440yd southeast of the Kipahulu Visitor Center.

Getting There & Around

The Kipahulu Area is on Hwy 31, 10 scenic miles south of Hana. There's no direct road access from here to the rest of Haleakalā National Park; the summit must be visited separately.

THE ROAD TO HANA

With its tumbling waterfalls, lush slopes, and rugged coasts, the Road to Hana is certainly beautiful. But it's the sense of earning the beauty that makes a drive on the road so special. Spanning the northeast shore of Maui, the legendary Hana Hwy ribbons tightly between jungle valleys and towering cliffs. Along the way, 54 one-lane bridges mark nearly as many waterfalls, some tranquil and inviting, others so sheer they kiss you with spray as you drive past. It's ravishingly gorgeous, but certainly not easy.

And there's more to the drive than beauty. When you're ready to get out and stretch your legs the real adventure begins: hiking trails climb into cool forests, short paths lead to Eden-like swimming holes, side roads wind down to sleepy seaside villages. If you've never tried smoked breadfruit, taken a dip in a spring-fed cave or gazed upon an ancient Hawaiian temple, set the alarm early – you've got a big day. As for rental cars, Jeeps and Mustangs look to be the ride of choice on the Hana Hwy.

Once you've left Pa'ia and Ha'iku behind, houses give way to thick jungle, and the scenery gets more dramatic with every mile. Then the road does a sleight-of-hand. After the 16-mile marker on Hwy 36, the Hana Hwy changes number to Hwy 360 and the mile markers begin again at zero.

Twin Falls

Just after the 2-mile marker a wide parking area with a fruit stand marks the start of the trail to Twin Falls. Local kids and tourists flock to the pool beneath the lower falls, about a 10-minute walk in. Twin Falls gets a lot of attention as being the 'first waterfall on the road to Hana.' It can get a bit crowded, but if you're traveling with kids or if you're up for a short, pleasant hike, this is a good one, with two photogenic falls and a swimming hole as your reward.

To get to the falls, follow the main trail across a stream. Turn left at the trail junction just ahead. Continue a short distance then climb over the aqueduct. The falls are straight ahead. You'll have to do a bit of wading to get there. Turn back if the water is too high.

We have seen smashed glass in the overflow parking area, so take valuables with you as a precaution.

Huelo

With its abundant rain and fertile soil Huelo once supported more than 50,000 Hawaiians, but today it's a sleepy, scattered community of farms and enviable cliffside homes.

The double row of mailboxes and green bus shelter, which come up after a blind curve 0.5 miles past the 3-mile marker, mark the start of the narrow road that leads into the village. The only sight, Kaulanapueo Church, is a half-mile down.

It's tempting to continue driving past the church, but not rewarding, as the road shortly turns to dirt and dead-ends at gated homes. There's no public beach access.

Sights & Activities

Kaulanapueo Church CHURCH

(Map p413) Constructed in 1853 of coral blocks and surrounded by a manicured green lawn, this tidy church remains the heart of the village. It has been built in early Hawaiian missionary style, with a spare interior and a tin roof topped with a green steeple. Swaying palm trees add a tropical backdrop. There are no formal opening hours, but the church is typically unlocked during the day.

Sleeping & Eating

Tea House COTTAGE $$

(Map p413; ☎800-215-6130; www.mauiteahouse.com; 370 Ho'olawa Rd; cottage $175; 📶) Built with walls recycled from a Zen temple, this one-of-a-kind cottage is so secluded it's off the grid and uses its own solar power. Yet it has everything you'll need, including a kitchen with gas burners and an open-air shower in a redwood gazebo.

The grounds also contain a Tibetan-style stupa with a spectacular cliff-top ocean view and a second cottage that rents for $100 per night. To get there follow Ulalama Loop, on the left after the 2-mile marker, to Ho'olawa Rd.

Huelo Lookout HEALTH FOOD $

(Map p413; ☎808-280-4791; www.huelolookout.coconutprotectors.com; 7600 Hana Hwy; snacks $5-12; ⏰7:30am-5pm) The fruit stand itself is tempting enough: drinking coconuts, smoothies, acai bowls and French crepes. But it doesn't stop there: take your goodies down the steps, where there's a shack selling waffles and sugarcane juice, and a table with a coastal panorama.

Ko'olau Forest Reserve & Around

This is where it starts to get wild! As the highway snakes along the edge of the Ko'olau Forest Reserve, the jungle takes over and one-lane bridges appear around every other bend. Ko'olau means 'windward,' and the upper slopes of these mountains squeeze a mighty 200in to 300in of rain from passing clouds annually, making for some awesome waterfalls.

After the 5-mile marker you'll pass through the village of **Kailua**. This little community of tin-roofed houses is largely home to employees of the East Maui Irrigation (EMI) Company. EMI operates the extensive irrigation system carrying water from the rainforest to the thirsty sugarcane fields in central Maui.

After leaving the village, just past the 6-mile marker, you'll be treated to a splash of color as you pass planted groves of **painted eucalyptus** with brilliant rainbow-colored bark. Roll down the windows and inhale the sweet scent of these majestic trees introduced from Australia.

Sights & Activities

Waikamoi Falls WATERFALL

(Map p413) There's only space for a few cars before the bridge at the 10-mile marker, but unless it's been raining recently don't worry about missing this one. The East Maui Irrigation Company diverts water from the stream, so the falls are usually a trickle. After the bridge, a green canopy of bamboo hangs over the road.

HANA TRIP TIPS

- Hundreds of cars are making the journey each day. To beat the crowd, get a sunrise start.
- Fill up the tank in Pa'ia or Ha'iku; the next gas station isn't until Hana, and the station there sometimes runs dry.
- Bring snacks and plenty to drink.
- Wear a bathing suit under your clothes so you're ready for impromptu swims.
- Bring shoes that are good for hiking as well as scrambling over slick rocks.
- Pull over to let local drivers pass – they're moving at a different pace.
- The drive can feel a bit rushed at times. If you want to slow down, consider spending one or two nights in Hana – you can visit the attractions you missed on the way back the next day.
- Leave valuables at home. Smash-and-grab thefts do occur.

Garden of Eden Arboretum GARDENS

(Map p413; www.mauigardenofeden.com; 10600 Hana Hwy; admission $15; ⏲8am-3pm) Why pay a steep $15 per person – not per carload, mind you – to visit an arboretum when the entire road to Hana is a garden? Well, it does offer a tamer version of paradise. The winding paths are neatly maintained, the flowers are identified, and the hilltop picnic tables sport gorgeous views, including ones of Puohokamoa Falls and Keopuka Rock, which was featured in the opening shot of *Jurassic Park*. A good choice for those not up for slippery jungle trails.

There's also a nifty art gallery, the **Fractal Gallery**, located within, its entrance guarded by peacocks. The arboretum is 0.5 miles past the 10-mile marker.

Puohokamoa Falls WATERFALL

Immediately after the 11-mile marker you'll pass Puohokamoa Falls. This waterfall no longer has public access, but you can get a glimpse of it from the bridge, or a bird's-eye view from the Garden of Eden Arboretum.

Haipua'ena Falls WATERFALL

For a secluded dip, Haipua'ena Falls, 0.5 miles past the 11-mile marker, provides a deep and serene pool. Since you can't see the pool from the road, few people know it's there. So it's not a bad choice if you *forgot* your bathing suit.

There's space for just a couple of cars on the Hana side of the bridge. To reach the falls, walk 50yd up the left side of the stream. Wild ginger grows along the path, and ferns hang from the rock wall beside the waterfall, creating an idyllic setting. Be aware of slippery rocks and flash floods.

Waikamoi Nature Trail HIKING

(Map p413) Put on your walking shoes and relish the majestic sights and spicy scents along this half-mile loop trail. At the start you're welcomed by a sign that reads 'Quiet. Trees at work' and a stand of grand reddish *Eucalyptus robusta*, one of several types of towering eucalyptus trees that grow along the path.

Once you reach the ridge at the top of the loop, you'll be treated to fine views of the winding Hana Hwy. At the turnoff to a spur, you'll enjoy great views of a huge green pincushion: a bamboo forest, facing you across the ravine. The spur leads up to a picnic area.

Look for the signposted trailhead 0.5 miles past the 9-mile marker, where there's a dirt pull-off wide enough for several cars.

★ **Rappel Maui** ADVENTURE SPORTS

(Map p413; ☎808-270-1500; www.rappelmaui.com; 10600 Hana Hwy, Garden of Eden Arboretum; per person $200; ⏲tours 8am & 11:30am) 'Are you insane?' That's the general reaction to telling people you are rappelling (abseiling) down the face of a waterfall. The magic of this new outfit is that it makes this way-out sport seem easy by the end, even if you have no previous experience.

After a 60ft instructional rappel down a dry cliff, you'll go straight down a 50ft waterfall, then a more difficult 30-footer, after which you'll swim to the finish line. This is real adventure, yet in the hands of the highly experienced and low-key Dave Black, it's also safe – and a compelling alternative to all those ziplines.

Kaumahina State Wayside Park

Kaumahina State Wayside Park PARK

(Map p413) Clean restrooms and a grassy lawn with picnic tables make this roadside park a family-friendly stop. The park comes up 350yd after the 12-mile marker and is open from 7am to 7pm. Take the short walk up the hill past the restrooms for an eye-popping view of coastal scenery.

For the next several miles, the scenery is absolutely stunning, opening up to a new vista as you turn round each bend. If it's been raining recently, you can expect to see waterfalls galore crashing down the mountains.

Honomanu Bay

This striking stream-fed bay comes into view at the 13-mile marker, where there's a roadside pull-off. This is the best stop on the first half of the Road to Hana. But you need to head down to the bay itself, via the inconspicuous road just after the 14-mile marker, to get the full effect.

Honomanu Bay's rocky black-sand beach is used mostly by local surfers and fishers. Surfable waves form during big swells, but the rocky bottom and strong rips make it dangerous if you're not familiar with the spot; there's no lifeguard here.

Honomanu Stream, which empties into the bay, forms a little pool just inland from the beach that's good for splashing around, and on weekends local families take the young 'uns here to wade in its shallow water. Walk to the end of the beach, look back up the stream, and take in the valley – ooh!

Sights

Kalaloa Point LOOKOUT

(Map p413) For a fascinating view of the coast stop at the pull-off on the ocean side of the highway 0.6 miles past the 14-mile marker. From the point you can look clear across Honomanu Bay and watch ant-size cars snaking down the mountain cliffs on the other side.

Ke'anae

What marks the halfway point on the drive to Hana? Dramatic landscapes and the friendliest seaside village on the route.

Starting way up at the Ko'olau Gap in the rim of Haleakalā Crater and stretching clear down to the coast, Ke'anae Valley radiates green, thanks to the 150in of rainfall that falls each year. At the foot of the valley lies Ke'anae Peninsula, created by a late eruption of Haleakalā that sent lava gushing all the way down Ke'anae Valley and into the ocean. Unlike its rugged surroundings, the volcanic peninsula is perfectly flat, like a leaf floating on the water.

You'll want to see the peninsula up close. But keep an eye peeled, as sights come up in quick succession. After passing the YMCA Camp 0.5 miles past the 16-mile marker, the arboretum pops up on the right and the road to Ke'anae Peninsula heads off to the left around the next bend.

Sights & Activities

★ Ke'anae Peninsula VILLAGE

(Map p413) This rare slice of 'Old Hawaii,' home to an 1860s church and a wild lava coast, is reached by taking Ke'anae Rd on the *makai* side of the highway just beyond Ke'anae Arboretum. Families have tended stream-fed taro patches here for generations.

Marking the heart of the village is **Ke'anae Congregational Church** (Lanakila 'Ihi'ihi o Iehova Ona Kaua; Map p413), built in 1860, and entered over the steps of the adjacent cottage. The church is made of lava rocks and coral mortar, uncovered by whitewash. It's a welcoming place with open doors and a guest book, although the roof has suffered storm damage (the community is taking up a collection to fix it). Note the cameo portraits in the adjacent cemetery.

Just past the church is **Ke'anae Beach Park** (Map p413; 8am-7pm), with its scenic coastline of jagged black lava and hypnotic white-capped waves. Forget swimming, as the water is rough and there's no beach. The rock islets you see off the coast – Mokuhala and Mokumana – are seabird sanctuaries. Turn around here, as there's a private residential area beyond with nothing else to see. There are public restrooms (open 8am to 7pm) across from the small parking area.

Ke'anae Peninsula Lookout VIEWPOINT

(Map p413) You'll get a superb bird's-eye view of the lowland peninsula and village, including the patchwork taro fed by Ke'anae Stream, by stopping at the paved pull-off just past the 17-mile marker on the *makai* side of the road. There's no sign, but it's easy to find if you look for the yellow tsunami speaker. If it's been raining lately, look to the far left to spot a series of cascading waterfalls.

Ke'anae Arboretum HIKING

(Map p413) Up for an easy walk that will introduce you to any array of tropical flora? Ke'anae Arboretum, 0.6 miles past the 16-mile marker, follows the Pi'ina'au Stream past magnificent shade trees and other plants, making for a lovely side trip that takes about 30 minutes total. Park opposite the entrance gate and follow the paved trail. It turns to dirt and finally grows in after you hit a fence.

Sleeping & Eating

YMCA Camp Ke'anae CABIN $

(Map p413; 808-248-8355; www.ymcacamp-keanae.org; 13375 Hana Hwy; campsite or van site s/f $20/35, cabin per person $20, apt $150) Reservations are your best bet, but if you need a last-minute place to sleep try the YMCA's beat-up cabins, which sit on a knoll overlooking the coast. Bunks are available in rustic, hostel-style dorms. Unless groups have rented the entire place, you can probably snag a bed. You'll need a sleeping bag, and cooking facilities are limited to simple outdoor grills. Another option is to pitch your tent on the grounds.

The location is superb, with great views across the bay to green sea cliffs cut by the highway. The great surprise is the duplex cottage down below, which is in much better shape and has spectacular ocean views. Each apartment has two bedrooms and a refrigerator, microwave and lanai. The camp is between the 16- and 17-mile markers.

★ Ke'anae Landing Fruit Stand HEALTH FOOD $

(Map p413; ☎808-248-7448; 210 Ke'anae Rd, Ke'anae Peninsula; banana bread $6, snacks $4-6; ⏰8:30am-2:30pm) 'Da best' banana bread on the entire road to Hana is baked fresh every morning by Aunty Sandy and her crew, and is so good you'll find as many locals as tourists pulling up here. You can also get fresh fruit and drinks at this stand, located in the village center just before Ke'anae Beach Park.

Ke'anae to Nahiku

Waterfalls are a highlight on this twisting stretch of the highway. Feeling hungry? Nahiku is a good place to pull over for a late lunch or afternoon snack.

Sights

Wailua Valley State Wayside VIEWPOINT

(Map p413) Just before the 19-mile marker, Wailua Valley State Wayside lookout comes up on the right, providing a broad view into verdant Ke'anae Valley, which appears to be 100 shades of green. You can see a couple of waterfalls (when they're running), and Ko'olau Gap, the break in the rim of Haleakalā crater, on a clear day. If you climb up the steps to the right, you'll find an outstanding view of Wailua Peninsula as well – don't miss this.

A word of caution: the sign for the wayside appears at the last moment, so be on the lookout.

Wailua Peninsula Lookout VIEWPOINT

(Map p413) For the most spectacular view of Wailua Peninsula, stop at the large paved pull-off on the ocean side of the road 0.25 miles past the 19-mile marker. There's no sign but it's not hard to find as two concrete picnic tables mark the spot. Grab a seat, break out your snack pack and ogle the taro fields and jungle vistas unfolding below.

★ Three Bears Falls WATERFALL

(Map p413) A real beauty, Three Bears takes its name from the triple cascade that flows down a steep rockface on the inland side of the road, 0.5 miles past the 19-mile marker. Catch it after a rainstorm and the cascades come together and roar as one mighty waterfall. There's limited parking up the hill to the left after the falls.

You can scramble down to the falls via a steep ill-defined path that begins on the Hana side of the bridge. The stones are moss-covered and slippery, so either proceed with caution or simply enjoy the view from the road.

Pua'a Ka'a State Wayside Park PARK

(Map p413) 🍃 The highway cuts right through this delightful park whose name, Pua'a Ka'a, means Rolling Pig. Some unlucky passersby see just the restrooms on the ocean side of the road and miss the rest. But you brought your beach towel, didn't you? Cross the highway from the parking area and head inland to find a pair of delicious waterfalls cascading into pools. The park is 0.5 miles after the 22-mile marker.

The best for swimming is the upper pool, which is visible just beyond the picnic tables. To reach it, you'll need to cross the stream, skipping across a few rocks. Be aware of the possibility of falling rocks beneath the waterfall and flash floods. To get to the lower falls, which drop into a shallow pool, walk back over the bridge and follow the trail upstream. And while you're at it, be sure to catch the view from the bridge.

Hanawi Falls WATERFALL

(Map p413) A waterfall with a split personality, Hanawi Falls sometimes flows gently into a quiet pool and sometimes gushes wildly across a broad rockface. No matter the mood it always invites popping out the camera and snapping a pic. The falls are 175yd after the 24-mile marker. There are small pull-offs before and after the bridge.

Makapipi Falls WATERFALL

(Map p413) Most waterfall views look up at the cascades, but this one offers a rare chance to experience an explosive waterfall from the top. Makapipi Falls makes its sheer plunge right beneath your feet as you stand on the ocean side of the Makapipi Bridge. You don't see anything from your car so if you didn't know about it, you'd never even imagine this waterfall was here. And sometimes it isn't, as it flows intermittently.

Makapipi Falls is 175yd after the 25-mile marker; you'll find pull-offs before and after the bridge.

Nahiku

The rural village of Nahiku is down near the coast, and cut by Nahiku Rd. Apart from an attractive lookout point, there's not much to tempt visitors. However, just before the 29-mile marker you'll find the Nahiku Marketplace. The jungle's best attempt at a strip mall, it ranges from a tent to a tin roof. Inside you'll find a fruit stand, and several small eateries with very flexible opening hours. If you're hungry, you'll want to stop. The food's tempting and this is the last place for a meal until you reach Hana.

Eating

Coconut Glen's ICE CREAM $

(Map p413; ☎808-979-1168; www.coconutglens.com; Hana Hwy, Mile 27.5; scoop of ice cream $5; ⏰10:30am-5:30pm;) From his inviting roadside shack Coconut Glen (aka Glen Simkins, who could double for Willy Wonka) is trying to 'change the world one scoop at a time.' Pull over here for his 100% vegan ice cream, served in a coconut shell with a coconut-shard for a spoon.

The ice cream comes in five flavors – try the chili chocolate – and is so tasty you won't even notice it's made from coconut milk, not cream.

Up In Smoke HAWAII REGIONAL CUISINE $

(Map p413; Hana Hwy, Nahiku Marketplace; mains $4-9; ⏰10am-5pm Sun-Wed) Hawaiian food never tasted so good. This bustling barbecue stand at the Nahiku Marketplace is *the* place to try kiawe-smoked breadfruit and *kalua* pig tacos.

'Ula'ino Road

'Ula'ino Rd begins at the Hana Hwy, just south of the 31-mile marker.

Sights & Activities

★Pi'ilanihale Heiau & Kahanu Garden HISTORIC SITE

(☎808-248-8912; www.ntbg.org; 650 'Ula'ino Rd; guided tour adult/child under 13yr $25/free, self-guided tour adult/child under 13yr $10/free; ⏰9am-2pm Mon-Sat) The most significant stop on the entire Road to Hana, this site combines a 294-acre ethnobotanical garden with the magnificent Pi'ilanihale Heiau, the largest temple in all of Polynesia. A must-do tour provides fascinating details of the extraordinary relationship between the ancient Hawaiians and their environment. This is perhaps the best opportunity in all of Hawaii to really feel what traditional Hawaiian culture was like prior to contact with the West. Amazingly, very few people visit.

Pi'ilanihale Heiau (Map p413) is an immense lava stone platform with a length of 450ft. The history of this astounding temple is shrouded in mystery, but there's no doubt that it was an important religious site. Archaeologists believe construction began as early as AD 1200 and continued in phases. The grand finale was the work of Pi'ilani (the heiau's name means House of Pi'ilani), the 14th-century Maui chief who is also credited with the construction of many of the coastal fishponds in the Hana area.

The temple occupies one corner of **Kahanu Garden** (Map p413), near the sea. An outpost of the National Tropical Botanical Garden (which also runs the Allerton and McBryde gardens on Kaua'i), Kahanu Garden contains the largest collection of breadfruit species in the world, with over 127 varieties. Breadfruit is significant because, as its name suggests, its nutritional value makes it a dietary pillar, and hence a weapon to combat global hunger. The garden also contains a living catalog of so-called canoe plants, those essentials of traditional life brought to Hawaii in the canoes of Polynesian voyagers, along with a hand-crafted canoe house that is another step back in time.

The very best way to unlock the relationship between the heiau, the plants, and their beautiful, park-like surroundings, where palms sway in the breeze, is to take a **guided tour**, something the entire family will enjoy. These are only given Saturdays, at 10am and 1pm, and last two hours. Advance online reservations required. The only other option is a self-guided tour by brochure. The site is located 1.5 miles down 'Ula'ino Rd from the Hana Hwy.

Hana Lava Tube CAVE

(Ka'eleku Caverns; Map p413; ☎808-248-7308; www.mauicave.com; 305 'Ula'ino Rd; admission $12; ⏰10:30am-4pm;) Who's afraid of the dark? Test yourself at the end of this underground walk by flipping off your flashlight. Eerie! One of the odder sights on the Road to Hana, this mammoth cave was formed by ancient lava flows. The lave tube is so large that it once served as a slaughterhouse – 17,000lb of cow bones had to be removed before it was opened to visitors!

Winding your way through the extensive cave, which reaches heights of up to 40ft, you'll find a unique ecosystem of dripping stalactites and stalagmites. The journey is well signed, takes about 45 minutes, and is a perfect rainy-day activity. Admission includes flashlights and hard hats. If you want to lose the kids, an adjoining **botanical maze** made from red ti plants is free. Hana Lava Tube is half a mile from the Hana Hwy.

Wai'anapanapa State Park

Swim in a cave, sun on a black-sand beach, explore ancient Hawaiian sites, use the public restrooms – this is one cool **park** (Map p413; www.hawaiistateparks.org; off Hana Hwy (Hwy 360)). A sunny coastal trail and a seaside campground make it a tempting place to dig in for a while. Honokalani Rd, which leads into Wai'anapanapa State Park, is just after the 32-mile marker. The road ends overlooking the park's centerpiece, the jet-black sands at Pa'iloa Bay. Go early and you'll have it all to yourself.

Sights & Activities

Lava Caves CAVE

(Map p413) A 10-minute loop path north from the beach parking lot leads to a pair of lava-tube caves. Their garden-like exteriors are draped with ferns and colorful impatiens, while their interiors harbor deep spring-fed pools with some resident fish. Wai'anapanapa means 'glistening waters' and the pools' crystal-clear mineral waters reputedly rejuvenate the skin. They certainly will invigorate – these sunless pools are refreshingly brisk!

Pi'ilani Trail HIKING

(Map p413) This gem of a coastal trail leads 3 miles south from Wai'anapanapa State Park to Kainalimu Bay, just north of Hana Bay. It offers a private, reflective walk on top of a raw lava field several meters above the sea, with refreshing views.

The trail, which follows an ancient footpath, packs a lot up front, so even if you just have time for the first mile, you won't regret it. In spots the loose gravel path skirts sheer, potentially fatal drops into the sea – exercise caution and leave the kids behind.

If you plan to hike the whole trail be sure to bring water, as it's unshaded the entire way, and good hiking shoes, as it gets rougher as you go along. The trail is indistinct sometimes, but as you are paralleling the coast the entire way it is impossible to get lost.

The route follows an ancient footpath known as the King's Trail that once circled the entire island. Some of the worn stepping-stones along the path date from the time of Pi'ilani, a king who ruled Maui in the 14th century. The trail begins along the coast just below the camping area and parallels the ocean along lava sea cliffs. Just a few minutes along you'll pass a burial ground, a natural sea arch and a blowhole that roars to life whenever there's pounding surf. This is also the area where you're most likely to see endangered Hawaiian monk seals basking onshore.

After 0.75 miles you'll view basalt cliffs lined up all the way to Hana, and ironwood encroaching the shoreline. Round stones continue to mark the way across lava and a grassy clearing, fading briefly on the way over a rugged sea cliff. A dirt road comes in from the right as the trail arrives at Luahaloa, a ledge with a small fishing shack. Inland stands of ironwood heighten the beauty of the scenic last mile of cliff-top walking to Kainalimu Bay. Stepping-stones hasten the approach to the bay ahead, as the trail dips down a shrubby ravine to a quiet, black-cobble beach. Dirt roads lead another mile from here south to Hana. Alternatively, you can walk inland to the asphalt road, and either walk or hitch back to Wai'anapanapa State Park.

Beaches

★Pa'iloa Beach BEACH

(Map p414) The small beach here is a stunner – hands down the prettiest black-sand beach on Maui. Walk on down, sunbathe, enjoy. But if you jump in, be very cautious. It's open ocean with a bottom that drops quickly and water conditions that are challenging, even for strong swimmers. Powerful rips are the norm (Pa'iloa means 'always splashing') and there have been several drownings here.

Sleeping

Wai'anapanapa Campground CAMPGROUND $

(Map p413; ☎808-984-8109; www.hawaiistateparks.org; Wai'anapanapa State Park; campsite $18) Fall asleep to the lullaby of the surf at this central campground, located on a shady lawn near the beach in Wai'anapanapa State Park. It's a great spot, but since this is the rainy side of the island, it can get wet at any time. State camping permit required. Reservations can be made by phone or online.

Wai'anapanapa Housekeeping Cabins CABIN $
(Map p413; ☎808-984-8109; www.hawaiistateparks.org; Wai'anapanapa State Park; cabin $90) Wai'anapanapa State Park has a dozen beat-up housekeeping cabins that are nonetheless extremely popular and may book up two to three months in advance. Each cabin sleeps six. They're located within walking distance of the parking area, facing the sea. Reservations can be made by phone or online.

HANA & EAST MAUI

Rugged and remote, East Maui is the go-to spot for Mauians looking to get away from it all. Instead of golf courses and beach resorts, you'll see a face that's hardly changed in ages. In slow-moving Hana you'll learn to talk story – l-o-n-g story – with people who take a personal approach to everything. Keep going and you'll reach sleepy Kipahulu, which makes Hana look urban. Then it's on to Kaupo, where the main street has one building. Finally you'll disappear into miles of open country on the back side of Haleakalā: one spectacular drive. From beginning to end you'll find off-the-grid farms, under-the-radar restaurants, secluded beaches and voices from the past.

Hana

POP 1235

Heavenly Hana. Is it paradise at the end of the rainbow or something a little bit different? Due to its history and its isolated location at the end of Hawaii's most famous drive, Hana has a legendary aura. But many travelers are disappointed when they arrive to find a sleepy hamlet, population 1235. But that is only because Hana takes more than an hour or two to understand.

Surprisingly, Hana does not try to maximize its benefit from the many day-trippers who arrive each afternoon. This is one of the most Hawaiian communities in the state, with a timeless rural character, and also home to many transplants willing to trade certain privations for a slow, thoughtful and personal way of life in a beautiful natural setting. Though 'Old Hawaii' is an oft-used cliché, it's hard not to think of Hana in such terms. Slow down, spend a night or two and enjoy it.

History

It's hard to imagine little Hana as the epicenter of Maui, but this village produced many of ancient Hawaii's most influential *ali'i* (chiefs). Hana's great 14th-century chief Pi'ilani marched from here to conquer rivals in Wailuku and Lahaina, and become the first leader of unified Maui.

The landscape changed dramatically in 1849 when ex-whaler George Wilfong bought 60 acres of land to plant sugarcane. Hana went on to become a booming plantation town, complete with a narrow-gauge railroad connecting the fields to the Hana Mill. In the 1940s Hana could no longer compete with larger sugar operations in Central Maui and the mill went bust.

Enter San Francisco businessman Paul Fagan, who purchased 14,000 acres in Hana in 1943. Starting with 300 Herefords, Fagan converted the cane fields to ranch land. A few years later he opened a six-room hotel as a getaway resort for well-to-do friends and brought his minor-league baseball team, the San Francisco Seals, to Hana for spring training. That's when visiting sports journalists gave the town its moniker, 'Heavenly Hana.'

Hana Ranch and the legendary Hana-Maui hotel (which changed hands many times) were the backbone of the local economy here for decades thereafter. In recent years, however, the hotel has been sold and transformed into Travaasa Hana. In 2014, sections of Hana Ranch's land holdings were in the process of being sold to various private and public entities.

Sights

Hana Cultural Center MUSEUM
(☎808-248-8622; www.hanaculturalcenter.org; 4974 Uakea Rd; $3 per person; ⊙10am-4pm Mon-Fri) FREE This down-home museum displays some interesting local artifacts. The best is an entire three-bench **courthouse** (c 1871). Although it looks like a museum piece, this tiny court is still used on the first Tuesday of each month when a judge shows up to hear minor cases, sparing Hana residents the need to drive all the way to Wailuku to contest a traffic ticket. Original paintings of Teddy Roosevelt and Admiral Dewey are a blast from the past.

Wananalua Congregational Church CHURCH
(cnr Hana Hwy & Hauoli St) On the National Register of Historic Places, this church (c 1838)

East Maui

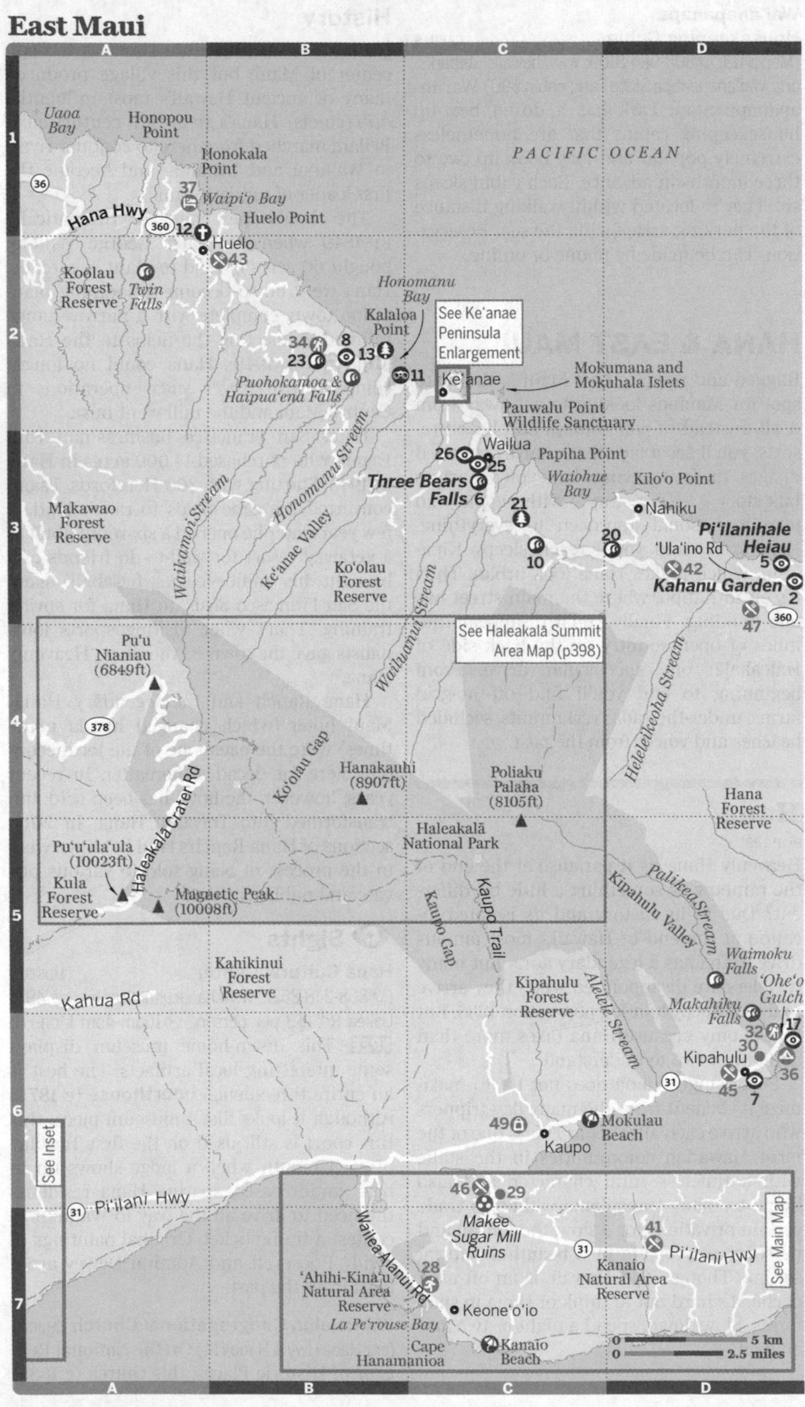

PACIFIC OCEAN
Uaoa Bay
Honopou Point
Honokala Point
Waipi'o Bay
Hana Hwy
Huelo Point
Huelo
Koolau Forest Reserve
Twin Falls
Honomanu Bay
Kalaloa Point
See Ke'anae Peninsula Enlargement
Puohokamoa & Haipua'ena Falls
Ke'anae
Mokumana and Mokuhala Islets
Pauwalu Point Wildlife Sanctuary
Wailua
Papiha Point
Three Bears Falls
Waiohue Bay
Kilo'o Point
Nahiku
Pi'ilanihale Heiau
'Ula'ino Rd
Kahanu Garden
Makawao Forest Reserve
Waikamoi Stream
Honomanu Stream
Ke'anae Valley
Ko'olau Forest Reserve
Wailuanui Stream
See Haleakalā Summit Area Map (p398)
Pu'u Nianiau (6849ft)
Ko'olau Gap
Hanakauhi (8907ft)
Poliaku Palaha (8105ft)
Haleakala Crater Rd
Pu'u'ula'ula (10023ft)
Haleakalā National Park
Kula Forest Reserve
Magnetic Peak (10008ft)
Heleleikeoha Stream
Hana Forest Reserve
Kipahulu Valley
Palikea Stream
Kaupo Trail
Kaupo Gap
Kahikinui Forest Reserve
Kipahulu Forest Reserve
Alelele Stream
Waimoku Falls
'Ohe'o Gulch
Makahiku Falls
Kipahulu
Kahua Rd
Mokulau Beach
Kaupo
See Inset
Pi'ilani Hwy
Makee Sugar Mill Ruins
Wailea Alanui Rd
Pi'ilani Hwy
See Main Map
Kanaio Natural Area Reserve
'Ahihi-Kina'u Natural Area Reserve
Keone'o'io
La Pe'rouse Bay
Cape Hanamanioa
Kanaio Beach
5 km
2.5 miles

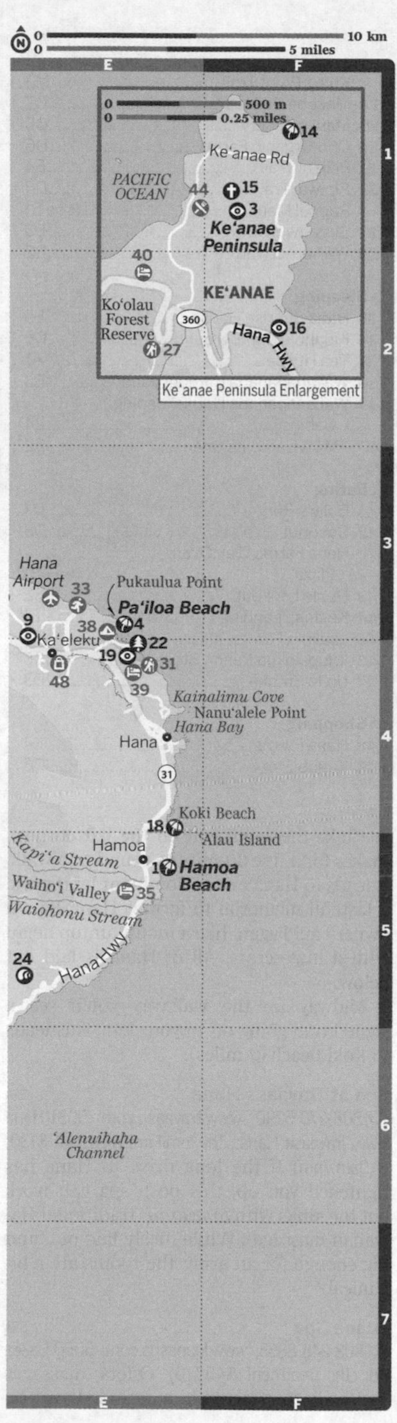

has such hefty walls it resembles an ancient Norman cathedral. The crumbling mausoleums in the cemetery, watched over by the draping arms of a massive banyan tree, are a poignant sight.

Hasegawa General Store HISTORIC SITE
(☎808-248-8231; 5165 Hana Hwy; ⏰7am-7pm Mon-Sat, 8am-6pm Sun) The Hasegawa family has operated a general store in Hana since 1910. The narrow aisles inside the tin-roof store are jam-packed with a little bit of everything. This icon of mom-and-pop shops is always crowded with locals picking up supplies and travelers stopping for snacks and the ATM.

Beaches

Kaihalulu Beach and Hana Beach Park are in downtown Hana. Hamoa Beach and Koki Beach sit alongside photogenic Haneo'o Rd, which loops for 1.5 miles off the Hana Hwy just south of town.

★ Hamoa Beach BEACH
(Map p413; Haneo'o Rd) With its clear water, white sand and scenic cove, this famous beach is a little gem; author James Michener once called it the only beach in the North Pacific that actually looked as if it belonged in the South Pacific. When the surf's up, surfers and bodyboarders flock here, though beware of rip currents. When it's calm, swimming is good in the cove.

Public access is down the steps just north of the hotel's bus-stop sign; there's parking for seven or eight cars opposite. Facilities include restrooms.

Koki Beach BEACH
(Map p413; Haneo'o Rd) This picturesque tan beach sits at the base of red cliffs with views toward tiny 'Alau Island. Bodysurfing is excellent, as it's shallow for quite a distance, but a rip current has been known to sweep people out to sea if they go too far. Shell-picking is good along the tide pools by the edge.

Hana Beach Park BEACH
Croquet by the beach? Why not? Welcome to Hana's version of the town plaza, a bayside park where children splash in the surf, picnickers enjoy the view from the rocky black-sand beach and musicians strum their ukuleles. And others play croquet. When water conditions are very calm, snorkeling and diving are good out past the pier. Currents can be strong, and snorkelers shouldn't

East Maui

Top Sights
1 Hamoa Beach ... E5
2 Kahanu Garden ... D3
3 Ke'anae Peninsula ... F1
4 Pa'iloa Beach ... E3
5 Pi'ilanihale Heiau ... D3
6 Three Bears Falls ... C3

Sights
7 Charles Lindbergh's Grave ... D6
8 Garden of Eden Arboretum ... B2
9 Hana Lava Tube ... E3
10 Hanawi Falls ... C3
11 Kalaloa Point ... B2
12 Kaulanapueo Church ... A1
13 Kaumahina State Wayside Park ... B2
14 Ke'anae Beach Park ... F1
15 Ke'anae Congregational Church ... F1
16 Ke'anae Peninsula Lookout ... F2
17 Kipahulu Visitor Center ... D6
18 Koki Beach ... E4
19 Lava Caves ... E4
20 Makapipi Falls ... D3
21 Pua'a Ka'a State Wayside Park ... C3
22 Wai'anapanapa State Park ... E4
23 Waikamoi Falls ... B2
24 Wailua Falls ... E5
25 Wailua Peninsula Lookout ... C3
26 Wailua Valley State Wayside ... C3

Activities, Courses & Tours
27 Ke'anae Arboretum ... E2
Kipahulu 'Ohana ... (see 36)
Kuloa Point Trail ... (see 36)
28 Makena Stables ... C7
29 Maui's Winery ... C6
30 Ono Organic Farms ... D6
31 Pi'ilani Trail ... E4
32 Pipiwai Trail ... D6
Rappel Maui ... (see 8)
33 Skyview Soaring ... E3
34 Waikamoi Nature Trail ... B2

Sleeping
35 Hana Sunrise House ... E5
36 Kipahulu Campground ... D6
37 Tea House ... A1
38 Wai'anapanapa Campground ... E3
39 Wai'anapanapa Housekeeping Cabins ... E4
40 YMCA Camp Ke'anae ... E2

Eating
41 Bully's Burgers ... D7
42 Coconut Glen's ... D3
Hana Farms Clay Oven Pizza ... (see 48)
43 Huelo Lookout ... B2
44 Ke'anae Landing Fruit Stand ... E1
45 Laulima Farms ... D6
46 'Ulupalakua Ranch Store ... C6
47 Up In Smoke ... D3

Shopping
48 Hana Farms ... E4
49 Kaupo Store ... C6

venture beyond the headland. Surfers head to **Waikoloa Beach** at the northern end of the bay.

Activities

★ Skyview Soaring GLIDING
(Map p413; ☎808-344-9663; www.skyviewsoaring.com; Hana Airport; 30min/1hr $160/300; ⏲by reservation) Haleakalā has excellent soaring conditions, and a sailplane is a unique, rewarding and safe way to see the mountain. After he cuts the engine, experienced pilot Hans Pieters will fly over the crater (weather permitting) and let you fly too, before gliding silently back to Hana Airport.

Call in advance for a reservation, or try your luck and visit the airport. Hans has clearly had his own share of luck, as he is one of the few people to have survived being struck by a propeller.

Lyon's Hill HIKING
(Ka'uiki Hill) This paved walkway up Ka'uiki Hill, behind the Travaasa Hana parking lot (take the small gate in the left corner), makes for a fine 30-minute round-trip walk. It leads to Hana's most dominant landmark, a tasteful memorial to former Hana Ranch owner Paul Fagan: like a mountaintop heiau with a huge cross. All of Hana is laid out below.

Midway up the walkway you'll see a signed trail going off to your left. This leads to Koki Beach (2 miles).

Spa at Travaasa Hana SPA
(☎808-270-5290; www.travaasa.com; 5031 Hana Hwy, Travaasa Hana; 1hr lomilomi massage $130; ⏲9am-7pm) If the long drive to Hana has tightened you up, this posh spa can work out the kinks with *lomilomi* (traditional Hawaiian massage). While nicely laid out, and big enough for an army, the rooms are a bit clinical.

Luana Spa SPA
(☎808-248-8855; www.luanaspa.com; 5050 Uakea Rd; 1hr treatment $45-170) Offers massages and body treatments in a secluded yurt on

Ka'uiki Hill, opposite Hana Ballpark. Lower office hidden next to Pranee's & Nucharee's Thai Food.

Tours

Hana-Maui Kayak & Snorkel SNORKELING
(808-264-9566; www.hanabaykayaks.com; Hana Beach Park; snorkel trip $89) If you're an inexperienced snorkeler, or want to snorkel out beyond Hana Bay, then Kevin Coates is your man. You'll paddle beyond the pier in Hana Bay and sample the reef before rounding the corner into open sea. Kevin's been doing this for 18 years, so has an endless number of stories to keep you entertained.

Travaasa Hana Stables HORSEBACK RIDING
(808-270-5276, reservations 808-359-2401; www.travaasa.com; 1hr ride $75; tours 9am & 10:30am) Enjoy a gentle trail ride along Hana's black-lava coastline. Riders must be at least nine years old.

Festivals & Events

★ **East Maui Taro Festival** CULTURAL
(www.tarofestival.org; Apr) Maui's most Hawaiian town throws its most Hawaiian party. If it's native, it's here – a taro pancake breakfast, poi making, hula dancing and a big jamfest of Hawaiian music. Held on the last weekend in April, it's Hana at its finest. Book accommodations well in advance.

Sleeping

There are cabins and tent camping at Wai'anapanapa State Park, just to the north of Hana, and camping at 'Ohe'o Gulch, about 10 miles south.

Bamboo Inn HOTEL $$
(808-248-7718; www.bambooinn.com; 4869 Uakea Rd; studio $195-210, ste $265;) The quiet Bamboo Inn, which overlooks black-pebble Waikoloa Beach, offers three quality suites, all with nice seaward lanai offering great sunrises and interesting views of the Waikoloa Peninsula. Two-person tubs are the place to end the day.

One two-story suite can further be divided into two studios with reduced rates. A central location, and a longtime owner steeped in Hawaiian history, makes for a very convenient stay.

Hale Ka'uiki YURT $$
(808-248-8855; www.luanaspa.com; 5050 Uakea Rd; d $170;) Perched on a secluded hill overlooking Hana Bay, this back-to-nature yurt at Luana Spa Retreat fuses outdoor living with indoor comforts, including a well-equipped kitchenette. Shower outdoors in a bamboo enclosure, enjoy spectacular stargazing over the bay – this is pure Hana.

Hana Kai-Maui CONDO $$
(808-248-8426; www.hanakaimaui.com; 4865 Uakea Rd; studio/1br from $210/220;) Hana's only condo complex is just a stone's throw from black-pebble Waikoloa Beach, comprising one ocean*front* building and an ocean*view* building behind it. Standard rooms have different owners and vary in decor; unit 1 has corner glass aimed straight down the beach. For $15 per person, staff will deliver breakfast to your door. Two-night minimum stay for oceanfront units.

★ **Hana Sunrise House** BUNGALOW $$$
(Map p413; 808-248-7556; www.hanasunrise.com; Kapia Rd; bungalow $250-275;) This split-level Balinese bungalow is absolute perfection. From the bamboo mats to the vaulted ceiling, the owner has lavished attention on every aspect to ensure a profound simplicity prevails. One entire wall can be removed to bring in the outdoors. Irresistible day beds will keep you contemplating the view for hours. Delicate *shōji* screens rule out children.

Travaasa Hana BOUTIQUE HOTEL $$$
(808-359-2401, 888-820-1043; www.travaasa.com; 5031 Hana Hwy; d from $400;) Oh Travaasa Hana, you leave us conflicted. This historic resort, under new ownership, was known for decades as Hotel Hana-Maui. It has left its roots behind in an effort to create a contemporary high-end resort experience – with prices to match. The country-club atmosphere is really not what Hana is about. But the big, breezy cottages, the gorgeous grounds and the multitude of activities – oh yes, we're liking those.

The hotel is divided between the upper garden cottages and the coastal Sea Ranch, which only accepts children during school breaks. All guests share an elegant heiau-like pool, the hotel's best feature. The resort shuttles guests to stunning Hamoa Beach.

If you just want a cottage, there are better rentals elsewhere at half the price. The limited, and expensive, dining options are also a drawback. Renovations were in progress during our visit.

Hana

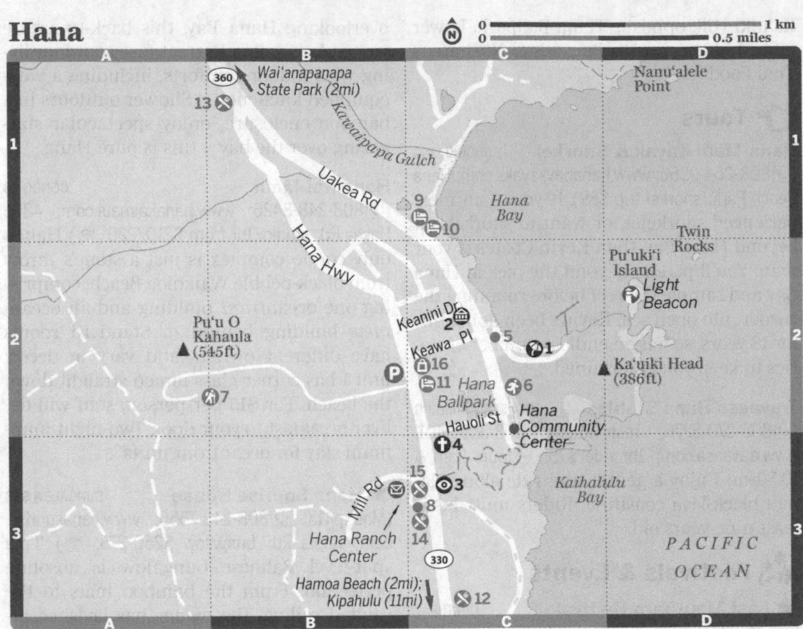

Hana

Sights

1 Hana Beach Park C2
2 Hana Cultural Center C2
3 Hasegawa General Store C3
4 Wananalua Congregational Church C3

Activities, Courses & Tours

5 Hana-Maui Kayak & Snorkel C2
6 Luana Spa C2
7 Lyon's Hill B2
Spa at Travaasa Hana .... (see 11)
8 Travaasa Hana Stables C3

Sleeping

9 Bamboo Inn C1
Hale Ka'uiki .... (see 6)
10 Hana Kai-Maui C1
11 Travaasa Hana C2

Eating

12 Bruddah Hutt's BBQ C3
13 Hana Fresh Market B1
Hasegawa General Store .... (see 3)
14 Ono Farmers Market C3
Pranee's & Nucharee's Thai Food .... (see 6)
15 Shaka Pops C3

Drinking & Nightlife

Paniolo Bar .... (see 11)

Shopping

16 Hana Coast Gallery C2

Eating

To the frustration of many visitors, there are only two restaurants open for dinner Sunday through Thursday (Travaasa Hana and Hana Ranch, which have the same owner) and both are pricey; the weekend adds the Hana Farms Clay Pizza Oven. Grocery stores are also limited and expensive, even by Hawaii standards. So if you're bothered by a $9 gallon of milk, do what the locals do: load up on food in Kahului before coming to Hana. Hana Ranch was closed for renovations at press time.

★ **Pranee's & Nucharee's Thai Food** THAI $
(5050 Uakea Rd; meals $10-15; ⏰10am-4pm) Hana's ever-popular Thai lunch stop is under one canvas roof, but changes identity depending on who's cooking: Nucharee (Tuesday to Friday) or Pranee (Saturday to Monday). Either way, you'll get one large and

tasty meal, including fiery curries and fresh stir-fried dishes. The opaka (red snapper) and mango salad is a house special. Located opposite Hana Ballpark.

★ Shaka Pops ICE CREAM $
(www.shakapopsmaui.com; 11am-4pm Mon-Sat) Life is a little brighter while slurping a Cocoa Hana Banana popsicle. These cool treats-on-a-stick come in a variety of fresh, tropical flavors. Locally made in small batches, they taste great and are definitely worth a lick. Look for the cart in front of the Hana Ranch Center.

Bruddah Hutt's BBQ BARBECUE $
(Hana Hwy; meals $8-13; 11am-3pm) This place is like a barbecue at your neighbor's house. Here, diners sit on folding chairs under a canvas awning while an extended family cooks away over gas grills. Favorites are the barbecued chicken and the fish tacos. Expect a crowd at noon, and don't take the closing time too seriously: it shuts down when the food runs out.

Hana Fresh Market HEALTH FOOD $
(808-248-7515; www.hanahealth.org; 4590 Hana Hwy; mains under $11; 7am-3pm Mon-Fri) This roadside stand in front of Hana Health sells organic produce grown on-site and healthy takeout plates featuring locally caught fish. Smoothies and yogurt bowls are also for sale.

Ono Farmers Market MARKET $
(www.onofarms.com; Hana Hwy; 10am-6pm) This is the place to pick up Kipahulu-grown coffee, jams and the most incredible array of fruit, from papaya to rambutan.

Hasegawa General Store SUPERMARKET $
(808-248-8231; 5165 Hana Hwy; 7am-7pm) This iconic mom-and-pop shop, with groceries and, well, a little bit of everything, has been a local fixture for a century.

★ Hana Farms Clay Oven Pizza PIZZA $$
(Map p413; 808-248-7371; www.hanafarmsonline.com; 2910 Hana Hwy; pizza $16-18; 4-8pm Fri & Sat) Located behind the Hana Farms stand, this little gem is *the* local choice on Friday and Saturday nights. Gourmet pizzas with toppings sourced from the farm come piping hot out of clay ovens. Gas lamps light picnic tables beneath thatched roofs. And the take-away pizza box is a folded palm leaf – a Hana classic. Pre-order by phone to avoid waiting.

Drinking & Nightlife

Paniolo Bar BAR
(808-248-8211; 5031 Hana Hwy, Travaasa Hana; restaurant 11:30am-9pm, bar open later) When it comes to Hana nightlife, this is the only game in town. But a great choice it is, with music nightly. On the liveliest nights enjoy a festive ambience that is uniquely Hana – with a touch of Rick's Cafe. Bar stays open until the crowd goes home – which could be early or 2am.

Shopping

★ Hana Coast Gallery ARTS, HANDICRAFTS
(808-248-8636; www.hanacoast.com; 5031 Hana Hwy; 9am-5pm) Even if you're not shopping, visit this gallery at the northern side of Travaasa to browse museum-quality wooden bowls, paintings and Hawaiian featherwork from about 100 different Hawaii artists.

Hana Farms FOOD
(Map p413; www.hanafarmsonline.com; 2910 Hana Hwy; 8:30am-7pm Sun-Thu, to 8pm Fri & Sat) This small 7-acre farm grows a large variety of tropical fruits, flowers and spices, and transforms them into interesting products. Its well-done roadside stand offers banana breads, exotic fruit preserves, tropical hot sauces, island candies, coffee and spices. A great place to find a unique and tasty gift.

Information

Hana Ranch Center (Mill Rd) is the commercial center of town.

Bank of Hawaii (808-248-8015; www.boh.com; Mill Rd; 3-4:30pm Mon-Thu, 3-6pm Fri) No ATM.

Hana Health (808-248-8294; www.hanahealth.org; 4590 Hana Hwy; 8am-5pm Mon-Wed & Fri, 8am-noon & 2-8pm Thu, 8am-noon

VOLUNTEER ON AN ORGANIC FARM

There are so many organic farms wanting volunteer labor in Hawaii that Worldwide Opportunities on Organic Farms (WWOOF), an organization that puts volunteers and organic farms together globally, runs a special Hawaii operation. In East Maui Hana Farms and Coconut Glen's (p411) are both sponsors, among others. For a full list of opportunities, see www.wwoofhawaii.org.

Sat) At the northern side of town. Physicians on-call for emergency care 24/7.

Post Office (1 Mill Rd, Hana Ranch Center; ⏲11am-4pm Mon-Fri)

Getting There & Around

There are two ways to get to Hana: rent a car and drive down the winding Hana Hwy (two hours from Pa'ia), or take a 20-minute prop-plane flight from Kahului with Mokulele Airlines ($74.30). Flights currently depart at 6:15am, 12:45pm and 5:41pm, returning at 6:51am, 1:20pm and 6:17pm. Passengers' weight cannot exceed 350lb. The Maui Bus doesn't serve East Maui.

Hana closes up early. The sole gas station in all of East Maui is **Hana Gas** (☎808-248-7671; cnr Mill Rd & Hana Hwy; ⏲7am-8pm Mon-Sat, to 6pm Sun), so plan accordingly.

Kipahulu

The lush drive south from Hana to Kipahulu brims with raw natural beauty. Between its twists and turns, one-lane bridges and drivers trying to take in all the sights, it's a slow-moving 10 miles, so allow yourself a half-hour just to reach Kipahulu.

Along the way you'll pass 'Ohe'o Gulch, your entry point to the Kipahulu section of Haleakalā National Park (p405). This is the undisputed highlight of the drive, offering fantastic falls, cool pools and tropical paths. Note: the rest of the park cannot be accessed from here by car.

The little village of Kipahulu lies less than a mile south of 'Ohe'o Gulch. It's hard to imagine, but this sedate community was once a bustling sugar-plantation town. After the mill shut down in 1922, most people left for jobs elsewhere. Today, mixed among modest homes, organic farms and back-to-the-landers living off the grid are a scattering of exclusive estates, including the former home of famed aviator Charles Lindbergh.

Sights

Wailua Falls WATERFALL

(Map p413) Before you reach Kipahulu, you'll see orchids growing out of the rocks, and jungles of breadfruit and coconut trees. Around 0.3 miles after the 45-mile marker, you'll come upon the spectacular Wailua Falls, which plunge a mighty 100ft just beyond the road. There's usually plenty of people lined up snapping photos.

Charles Lindbergh's Grave CEMETERY

(Map p413) Charles Lindbergh, the first man to fly across the Atlantic Ocean, moved to remote Kipahulu in 1968. After being diagnosed with terminal cancer, he decided to forgo treatment on the mainland and lived out his final days here. Following his death in 1974, Lindbergh was buried in the graveyard of **Palapala Ho'omau Congregational Church**. The church is also noted for its window painting of a Polynesian Christ draped in the red-and-yellow feather capes of Hawaii's highest chiefs.

Lindbergh's grave is a simple granite slab laid upon lava stones in the yard behind the church. The epitaph is a quote from the Bible: 'If I take the wings of the morning, and dwell in the uttermost parts of the sea.' Walk seaward and you'll find a viewpoint aimed at those uttermost parts.

To find the church, turn left 350yd south of the 41-mile marker and follow the road to the church.

Tours

★ **Ono Organic Farms** FARM

(Map p413; ☎808-248-7779; www.onofarms.com; Hana Hwy; 90min tours adult/child under 10yr $35/free; ⏲1:30pm Mon-Fri) This fascinating two-hour tour of a wildly exotic business begins with a delicious tasting of tropical fruit. The variety is amazing: ever tried Surinam cher-

THE OTHER SPECTACULAR DRIVE

The untamed Pi'ilani Hwy (Hwy 31) travels 25 ruggedly scenic miles between Kipahulu and 'Ulupalakua, skirting the southern flank of Haleakalā. This spectacular coastal drive starts out in lush jungle, with snaking bends through numerous gulches. Once it enters the dry side of the island, the road breaks out into magnificent, wide-open scenery, from the crashing sea to the volcano above. And hardly anyone is on it.

The road is subject to tall tales about its condition, particularly from rental-car companies. In reality it is rough and narrow in a few spots early on, with a series of unpaved sections, but easily driveable. The latter half has brand-new blacktop. There are no gas stations or other services along the way. Washouts sometimes close the road temporarily, so inquire about conditions at the Kipahulu Visitor Center (p405).

ries, rambutan, red bananas, santol or jaboticaba? The tour then heads into the fields of the 300-acre farm, of which 70 acres are planted.

The farm is well hidden on the inland side of the road just south of the national park; look for 'Ono' on the mailbox. If you can't make it here, sample the goods at Ono Farmers Market (p419) in Hana.

Eating

Laulima Farms MARKET $
(Map p413; ⏲9am-5pm) For hand-roasted coffee, veggies and fruit, fresh off the adjoining 13-acre farm. Located on Hana Hwy, between the 40- and 41-mile markers.

Kaupo

Leaving Kipahulu the road drops to parallel the edge of a rocky beach with breaking waves. At the 34-mile marker the open side of Haleakalā crater becomes visible. A mile later you'll reach Kaupo, a scattered community of *paniolo,* many of them fourth-generation ranch hands working at Kaupo Ranch.

As the only lowlands on this section of coast, Kaupo was once heavily settled and is home to several ancient heiau and two 19th-century churches. However, those days are gone: the sole commercial venture on the entire road is **Kaupo Store** (Map p413; ☎808-248-8054; ⏲10am-5pm Mon-Sat), which sells snacks and drinks. It's worth popping inside just to see the shelves, which are filled with vintage displays, including a camera collection dating to 1911.

A mile later **St Joseph Church** (1862) appears on the left. With its mountain backdrop, this is Kaupo's prettiest site, and prime for photography. From here you can see enormous waterfalls through **Kaupo Gap**, the great gash in the side of majestic Haleakalā. If you're passing through on Sunday you may also hear singing in Hawaiian.

Kaupo to 'Ulupalakua Ranch

Past Kaupo village, you enter the dry side of the island. Near the 31-mile marker, a short 4WD road runs down to **Nu'u Bay**, favored by locals for fishing and swimming. If you're tempted to hit the water, stay close to shore to avoid riptides.

Just east of the 30-mile marker you'll see two gateposts that mark the path to dramatic **Huakini Bay**. Park at the side of the highway and walk down the rutted dirt drive. It takes just a couple of minutes to reach this rock-strewn beach whipped by violent surf. After the 29-mile marker, keep an eye out for a natural lava **sea arch** that's visible from the road.

At the 19-mile marker the road crosses a vast **lava flow** dating from between AD 1480 and 1600, Haleakalā's last-gasp eruption. This flow, part of the Kanaio Natural Area Reserve, is the same one that covers the La Pe'rouse Bay area. It's still black and barren all the way down to the sea.

Just offshore is Kaho'olawe and on a clear day you can even see Hawai'i, the Big Island, popping its head up above the clouds. It's such a wide-angle view that the ocean horizon is noticeably curved. You'll wonder how anyone could ever have thought the world was flat!

As you approach 'Ulupalakua, eight graceful windmills, which started producing energy in 2012, mark the return of civilization. For lunch, keep an eye out for lonely Bully's Burgers (p396). Don't mind the cow skulls! From there it's 4 miles to Maui's Winery (p396), where you can toast the end of one spectacular drive.

Lana'i

Includes ➡

Best Places to Eat

- ➡ Lana'i City Grille (p429)
- ➡ Lana'i Ohana Poke Market (p428)
- ➡ Pele's Other Garden (p429)
- ➡ Nobu (p434)

Best Adventures

- ➡ Munro Trail (p430)
- ➡ Shipwreck Beach (p434)
- ➡ Road to Garden of the Gods (p435)
- ➡ Kaunolu (p435)

Why Go?

Although Lana'i is the most central of the Hawaiian Islands (on a clear day you can see five islands from here), it's also the least 'Hawaiian' of the islands. Now-closed pineapple plantations are its main historic legacy, and the locals are a mix of people descended from immigrant field workers from around the world.

Its signature (imported) Norfolk and Cook Island pines give the island a feel that could just as well come from a remote corner of the South Pacific. And therein lies the charm of Lana'i, a small island (at its widest point only 18 miles across) that's an off-the-beaten-path destination. Hidden beaches, archaeological sites, oddball geology and a sense of isolation let you get away from it all, without going far.

Of course, looming over Lana'i is billionaire owner Larry Ellison, who is determined to transform the island, even if the details change by the week.

When to Go

Lana'i City

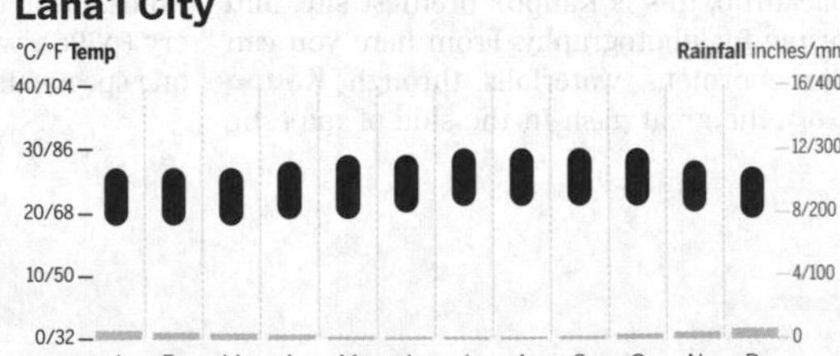

Nov–Mar Jackets are needed at night in lofty, temperate Lana'i City, while the beaches stay balmy.

Apr–Aug Winter rains have stopped and the entire island enjoys breezy tropical comfort.

Sep–Oct Lana'i City stays in the sunny 70s (°F), while Hulopo'e Beach is in the lovely low 80s.

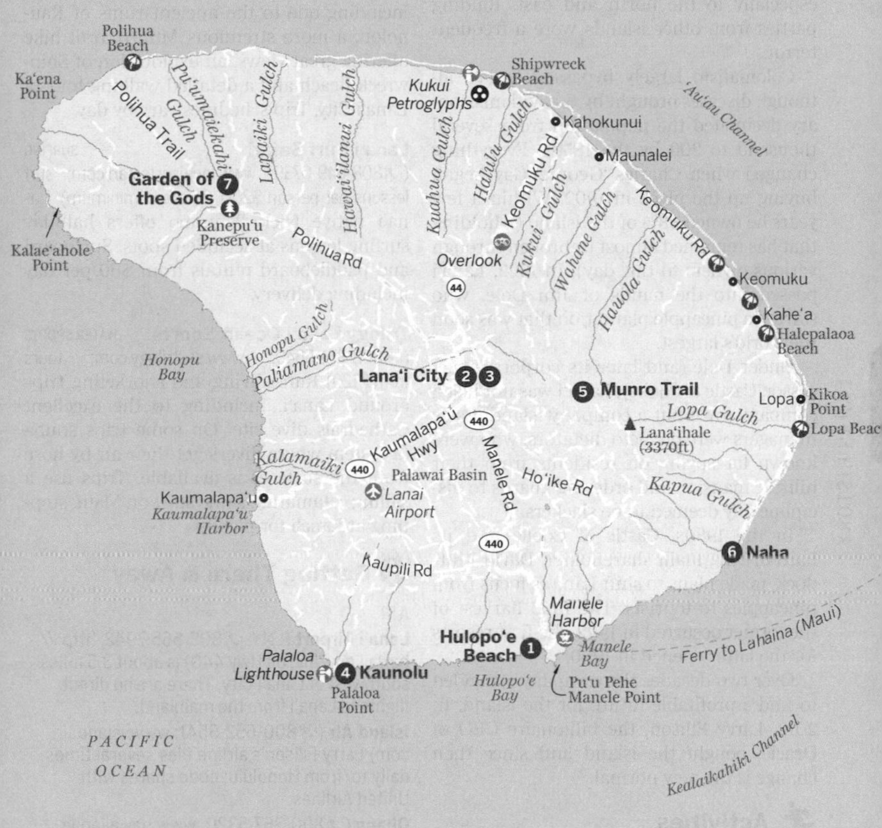

Lana'i Highlights

❶ Snorkel the protected reef at the island's best beach, **Hulopo'e Beach** (p430).

❷ Browse the choices, then enjoy simple but good food and drink at Lana'i City's many **cafes** (p428).

❸ Stroll the square at **Dole Park** (p425), picking up local gossip about the many changes sweeping the island.

❹ Explore the island's history, culture and natural beauty on one of the hikes offered by **Hike Lana'i** (p424).

❺ Hike the **Munro Trail** (p430) through the island's small but lush heart, stretching above Lana'i City.

❻ Get lost on the unpaved Keomuku Road to **Naha** (p435), where ancient fishponds lie offshore and idyllic beaches await discovery.

❼ Count the other islands from the otherworldly heights of the **Garden of the Gods** (p435), then ponder its weird rocks.

History

Evil spirits were thought to be the only inhabitants of Lana'i prior to about 1400, when settlers arrived from Maui. Little recorded history exists but there are traces of a thriving fishing culture along the coasts, especially to the north and east. Raiding parties from other islands were a frequent terror.

Colonialism largely bypassed Lana'i, although diseases brought by the odd missionary decimated the population from several thousand to 200 by the 1850s. Everything changed when Charles 'George' Gay began buying up the place in 1902. Within a few years he owned 98% of the island (a holding that has remained almost unbroken through various owners to this day). In 1922, Lana'i passed into the hands of Jim Dole, who started a pineapple plantation that was soon the world's largest.

Under Dole (and later its corporate successor, Castle & Cooke), Lana'i was not just a company town but a company island. Early managers were de facto dictators, who were known for spying on residents from their hillside mansion and ordering guards to discipline any deemed to be slackers.

In the 1980s, Castle & Cooke and its hard-driving main shareholder, David Murdock, made plans to shift Lana'i's focus from pineapples to tourists. The final harvest of the former occurred in 1992, the first resorts for the latter opened in 1990.

Over two decades the company struggled to find a profitable future for the island. In 2012, Larry Ellison, the billionaire CEO of Oracle, bought the island and since then change is the new normal.

Activities

Lana'i has no national, state or county parks, but its finest beach, Hulopo'e Beach, is run by the island's management as a free public park. The ridge that cuts across Lana'i's hilly interior offers good hiking opportunities with top-notch views from the Munro Trail.

★Hike Lana'i — HIKING

(☎808-258-2471; www.hikelanai.com; hikes $110-125) This creative outfit offers guided hikes, including one to the ancient ruins of Kaunolou, a more strenuous Munro Trail hike offering great views, an exploration of Shipwreck Beach and a detailed walking tour of Lana'i City. Trip schedules vary by day.

Lana'i Surf Safari — SURFING

(☎808-649-0739; www.lanaisurfsafari.com; surf lessons per person $200, 2-person minimum) Lana'i native Nick Palumbo offers half-day surfing lessons at secluded spots. Surfboard and paddleboard rentals from $60 per day including delivery.

Trilogy Lana'i Ocean Sports — WATER SPORTS

(☎808-874-5649; www.sailtrilogy.com; tours from $120) Runs diving and snorkeling trips around Lana'i, including to the excellent Cathedrals dive site. On some trips snuba (a system where divers get their air by hose from the surface) is available. Trips use a sailing catamaran; some start on Maui, stopping at Lana'i for pickups.

Getting There & Away

AIR

Lana'i Airport (LNY; ☎808-565-7942; http://hawaii.gov/lny; off Hwy 440) is about 3.5 miles southwest of Lana'i City. There are no direct flights to Lana'i from the mainland.

Island Air (☎800-652-6541; www.islandair.com) Larry Ellison's airline flies several times daily to/from Honolulu; code shares with United Airlines.

Ohana (☎800-367-5320; www.hawaiianairlines.com) The commuter carrier of Hawaiian Airlines serves Lana'i from Honolulu and Moloka'i.

LANA'I'S TOP ACTIVITIES

ACTIVITY	DESTINATION
Diving	Cathedrals (p431)
Hiking	Koloiki Ridge Trail (p426)
Snorkeling	Hulopo'e Bay (p430)
Swimming	Halepalaoa Beach (p435); Hulopo'e Bay (p430)

LANA'I IN...

One Day

Take the early morning **ferry** from Lahaina on Maui; keep an eye out for schools of dolphins as the boat approaches **Manele Bay**. Catch the shuttle into **Lana'i City** and pour your own coffee for breakfast at Blue Ginger Café before strolling the town's shops and superb Culture & Heritage Center. In the afternoon, snorkel at **Hulopo'e Beach** or dive at **Manele Bay** before heading back to Maui on the sunset ferry.

Three Days

With extra days, wander back into town and watch the sun set over the majestic Norfolk Island pines at **Dole Park**. Rent a mountain bike (virtually all places to stay can hook you up with bike rental) or put on your hiking boots and head up the **Munro Trail** for a sweeping view of everything Lana'i has to offer. Get a jeep and do some beachcombing along **Shipwreck Beach** and then explore the Keomuku Road to **Naha**.

SEA

Expeditions Maui-Lana'i Ferry (☎808-661-3756; www.go-lanai.com; adult/child 1 way $30/20) Worth it just for the ride, this ferry links Lahaina Harbor (Maui) with Manele Bay Harbor on Lana'i (one hour) several times daily. In winter there's a fair chance of seeing humpback whales; spinner dolphins are a common sight all year, especially on morning sails.

Hulopo'e Beach is near the dock; Lana'i tour and activity operators will meet the ferries if you call ahead. Day-trip packages from Maui are popular.

Getting Around

TO/FROM THE AIRPORT

The resorts provide a shuttle-van service that meets guests at the airport and ferry dock. Nonguests can use the shuttle for a fee ($10), or call a taxi (about $10 per person) in advance of your arrival.

CAR

Lana'i has one main car-rental firm; however, you can arrange for pricey rentals of upscale 4WDs such as Land Rovers through the hotels. The only gas station, **Lana'i City Service** (☎808-565-7227; 1036 Lana'i Ave; ⏲6:30am-10pm), sells pricey fuel – a hefty cost for the gas-guzzling 4WDs.

Dollar Rent-a-Car (☎808-565-7227; www.dollarlanai.com; 1036 Lana'i Ave, Lana'i City; 4WD per day $140-200; ⏲7am-6pm) The main car-rental office on the island is an affiliate of Dollar Rent-a-Car; however, it's best to make your reservations direct with this office. Having a monopoly on Lana'i translates into steep prices: heavily used 4WD Jeep Wranglers and Hummers – but not regular cars – are available.

The firm is owned by Lana'i City Service; note the firm's numerous restrictions on where you can drive your 4WD, confirm these in advance to avoid hefty fines.

Driving Distances & Times From Lana'i City

DESTINATION	MILES	TIME
Garden of the Gods	6	20min
Hulopo'e Beach	8	20min
Kaumalapa'u Harbor	7	20min
Keomuku	15	1hr
Lana'i Airport	3.5	10min

SHUTTLE

The hotels run a shuttle that links the hotels with the airport and ferry dock. Shuttles run about every 30 minutes throughout the day in peak season, hourly in the slower months. The first usually heads out about 7am, the last around 11pm. Fares may be included in the tariff for guests ($35 for unlimited use during your stay); others pay from $24 for a round-trip from the airport or ferry dock (credit cards only).

Lana'i City Shuttle (☎808-559-0230; rides from $10) Indie operator offers rides around the island, book in advance.

Lana'i City

POP 3100

Lana'i City's main square, **Dole Park**, is surrounded by tin-roofed houses and shops, with not a chain in sight. The architecture is little changed since the plantation days of the 1920s, although the gardening is much improved as Ellison's island management company, Pulama Lana'i, has been on a beautification kick. (Pulama means 'to care for' or 'cherish.')

Wander between the surprisingly rich collection of eateries and shops, all with a low-key appeal not found in more touristed places.

History

Lana'i is the only Hawaiian Island where the largest town is in the highlands and not on the coast. Lana'i City is, in fact, the only town on the island.

The village was built in the 1920s as a plantation town for the field workers and staff of Dole's Hawaiian Pineapple Company. The first planned city in Hawaii, Lana'i City was built in the midst of the pineapple fields, with shops and a theater surrounding the central park, rows of plantation houses lined up beyond that and a pineapple-processing plant on the edge of it all.

Sights

Lana'i City is laid out in a simple grid pattern, and almost all of the shops and services border Dole Park. The vaguely alien-looking Norfolk and Cook Island pine trees provide plenty of shade and you can enjoy the nascent buzz.

★ Lana'i Culture & Heritage Center — MUSEUM

(www.lanaichc.org; 111 Lana'i Ave; ⌚8:30am-3:30pm Mon-Fri, 9am-1pm Sat) FREE This engaging small museum has displays covering Lana'i's often mysterious history; photos and a timeline show its transformation into the world's pineapple supplier. The lives of the workers are shown in detail and facts such as this jaw-dropper abound: each worker was expected to plant up to 10,000 new pineapple plants per day.

Activities

Most tourist activities take place about a mile north of Dole Park at or near the Lodge at Koele (officially the 'Four Seasons Resort at Lana'i, the Lodge at Koele'). The Lana'i Culture & Heritage Center has some good hiking maps and brochures.

The once-impressive Koele golf course is closed pending an extensive redesign.

★ Koloiki Ridge Trail — HIKING

This 5-mile hike leads up to one of the most scenic parts of the Munro Trail. It takes about three hours (return) and offers sweeping views of remote valleys (where taro was once grown), Maui and Moloka'i.

The trail begins at the rear of the Lodge at Koele on the paved path that leads to the golf clubhouse. From there, follow the signposted path uphill past Norfolk Island pines until you reach a hilltop bench with a plaque bearing the poem 'If' by Rudyard Kipling. The heritage center publishes a map that makes following the route easy.

Follow the trail down through a thicket of guava trees until you reach an abandoned dirt service road and you'll intersect with the Munro Trail; after a few minutes you'll pass Kukui Gulch, named for the *kukui* (candlenut trees) that grow there. Continue along the trail until you reach a thicket of tall sisal plants; about 50yd after that bear right to reach Koloiki Ridge, where you'll be rewarded with panoramic views of much of the island.

Lana'i Western Adventures — ADVENTURE SPORTS

(☎808-563-9385; www.lanaigrandadventures.com; off Keomuku Rd; horseback rides from $125, UTV rides from $200; ⌚8am-5pm) If you would prefer to see Lana'i from a saddle, this operation, just west of the Lodge at Koele resort (within eyeshot), offers everything from a 1½-hour trail ride that takes in sweeping views of Maui to a four-hour private ride catered to your particular interest.

Festivals & Events

Pineapple Festival — CULTURAL

(⌚Jul) Lana'i's main bash, the Pineapple Festival, is held on or near July 4 and celebrates the island's pineapple past with games and live music at Dole Park (any pineapple you see is imported!).

Sleeping

With the status of the three Ellison-owned hotels in flux due to remodeling and closures, the smattering of rental rooms and houses are important. Check www.airbnb.com and www.homeaway.com for options; many are entire houses within the resort developments.

★ Hotel Lana'i — HOTEL $$

(☎808-565-7211; www.hotellanai.com; 828 Lana'i Ave; r $149-199, cottages $229; 📶) From 1923 to 1990 the Hotel Lana'i was the only hotel on the island. It seems little has changed here over the decades, other than the conversations that echo through the thin walls. The

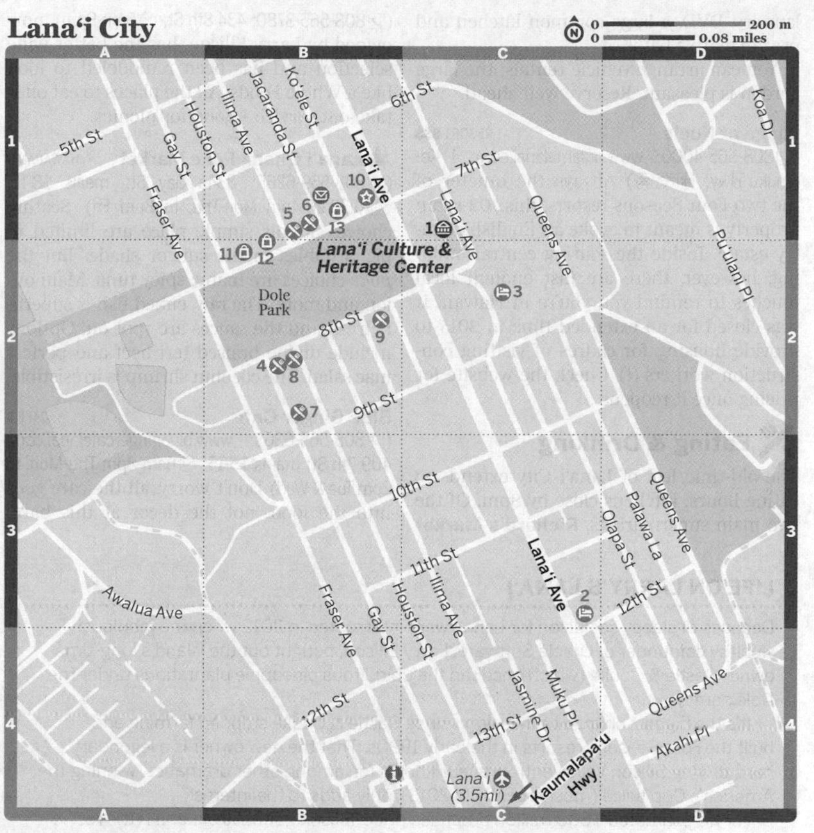

Lana'i City

Top Sights

1 Lana'i Culture & Heritage Center....C1

Sleeping

2 Dreams Come True....C3
3 Hotel Lana'i....C2

Eating

4 Anuenue Juice Bar & Cafe....B2
5 Blue Ginger Café....B1
6 Canoes Lana'i....B1
Lana'i City Grille....(see 3)
7 Lana'i Ohana Poke Market....B2
8 Pele's Other Garden....B2
9 Richard's Market....B2

Entertainment

10 Hale Keaka Lana'i Theater....B1

Shopping

11 Lana'i Arts & Cultural Center....B2
12 Local Gentry....B2
13 Mike Carroll Gallery....B1

10 renovated rooms have hardwood floors, antiques, pedestal sinks, patchwork quilts and more period pieces.

Go for a room with – appropriately – a lanai (a small porch) for viewing town, or opt for privacy and quiet in the detached cottage out back. A modest continental breakfast is provided.

Dreams Come True GUESTHOUSE **$$**
(☎808-565-6961; www.dreamscometruelanai.com; 1168 Lana'i Ave; r from $145; @📶) This spiffy plantation-style house was one of the first built in Lana'i City (1925). The four rooms have hardwood floors, and are furnished with a mixture of comfy antique and modern pieces. There are numerous amenities, including

laundry, DVD, a large common kitchen and private marble baths.

You can arrange vehicle rentals; the large garden is pleasant. Reserve well ahead.

Lodge at Koele RESORT $$$
(808-565-4000; www.pulamalanai.com; 1 Keomuku Hwy;) Always the quieter of the two Four Seasons resorts, this 102-room property is meant to evoke an English country estate. Inside the soaring central building, however, there are just enough local touches to remind you you're in Hawaii. It was closed for an extended time in 2015 to provide housing for cadres of visiting construction workers (!). Check the website for pricing once it reopens.

Eating & Drinking

The old-time feel of Lana'i City extends to eating hours: kitchens close by 8pm. Of the two main supermarkets, **Richard's Market** (808-565-3780; 434 8th St; 6am-9pm), now owned by Larry Ellison, has the better wine selection and has been remodeled to look like a Whole Foods. All the places to eat offer take-out service – good for picnics.

★Lana'i Ohana Poke Market HAWAIIAN $
(808-559-6265; 834a Gay St; meals $8-12; 10:30am-4pm Mon-Thu, to 8pm Fri) Seating choices at this simple place are limited to picnic tables in the sun or shade. But the *poke* choices are many: spicy tuna, Maui onion and more. The raw, cubed fish is superbly fresh and the sauces are spot on. Options include divine braised teri beef and perfect mac salad. The coconut shrimp is irresistible.

Blue Ginger Café CAFE $
(808-565-6363; www.bluegingercafelanai.com; 409 7th St; mains $5-15; 6am-8pm Thu-Mon, to 2pm Tue & Wed) Don't worry, all the care goes into the food, not the decor at this bare-

LIFE ON LARRY'S LANA'I

Decades of sleepy seclusion for Lana'i were interrupted in 2012 when the fabulously wealthy cofounder of Oracle Software, Larry Ellison, bought out the island's long-time owner Castle & Cooke (which once ran the ubiquitous pineapple plantations under the Dole name).

It's the biggest change to the island since Castle & Cooke stopped farming and built the Four Seasons resorts in the early 1990s. That the new owner is a legendary hard-driving Silicon Valley entrepreneur known for, among other dramatics, winning the America's Cup twice (most recently in 2013), only adds to the interest.

For his estimated $600 million purchase price, Ellison got 98% of Lana'i (the rest is private homes or government land) and a bevy of businesses, such as the resorts. Given that the island has struggled economically since the glory days of pineapples, Ellison's wide-ranging plans for his trophy are generating intense interest.

Under the guise of Pulama Lana'i, the company that manages the island, the changes have been many. One clear measure is that freight shipments to Lanai are up over 40% as building materials and supplies flow in. Among the notable events are the following:

➡ While the resorts were part of the original purchase, since then Ellison has hoovered up a bevy of businesses, including the Hotel Lana'i, Island Air, Richard's Market and more.

➡ Construction projects have proliferated, causing a shortage of workers and delays. Trying to ameliorate this, the Lodge at Koele has been closed to house workers. Meanwhile, the Manele Bay resort is undergoing a massive transformation, the theater has been turned into a state-of-the-art showplace, vast beautification schemes are underway across Lana'i City and historic old plantation homes are being torn down and replaced with new houses that ape the old.

➡ Ellison has discovered that just because you own an island doesn't mean you own the government. Regulatory hurdles have delayed projects including a reconstruction of the Experience at Koele golf course (it's gone to seed in the meantime) and a new beach resort at Halepalaoa.

For residents, life on Lana'i feels a bit like a soap opera as plans and schemes constantly surface and change. Ellison has said he wants the island to be economically self-sufficient, yet achieving this may be the biggest challenge of his life.

bones diner, where you can serve yourself a cup of coffee, grab a newspaper and settle back at a table outside. Muffins arrive warm from the bakery.

The long menu ranges from breakfasts and salads to burgers, delectable chicken katsu and more. It's been run by the same family for decades.

Anuenue Juice Bar & Cafe CAFE $
(☎808-250-0633; www.anuenuejuicebar.com; 338 8th St; meals $11-13; ⌚8am-4pm Tue-Sat; 📶) This recently opened place sells creative, organic smoothies for a price that was once a pineapple worker's daily wage: $8. The island's current owner has been spotted sipping fresh juice here. Food includes salads and wraps.

Canoes Lana'i CAFE $
(☎808-565-6537; 419 7th St; meals $5-12; ⌚7am-1pm) Breakfast is always on the menu at this old-time Hawaii cafe that is little changed since pineapple-pickers filled the tables. The best seller? *Loco moco* (rice, fried egg and hamburger topped with gravy). The omelets are good.

★Pele's Other Garden ITALIAN $$
(☎808-565-9628; cnr 8th & Houston Sts; lunch $5-9, dinner $10-24; ⌚kitchen 11am-2pm Mon-Fri, 5-8pm Mon-Sat, drinks until 9pm) More bistro than deli, this restored plantation house has tables inside and out. Owners Barb and Mark cook creatively Italian and serve up classic spaghetti and meatballs, crispy thin-crust pizza and some first-rate pesto. Salads are made with organic local greens; desserts are large but not extraordinary.

There's a fine beer list with 12 brews on tap. Watch for William Shatner, a regular when he beams down on holiday.

★Lana'i City Grille FUSION $$$
(☎808-565-7211; www.hotellanai.com; 828 Lana'i Ave, Hotel Lana'i; mains $28-42; ⌚5-9pm Wed-Sun) Famed Maui chef Bev Gannon designed the menu at the charming restaurant within the Hotel Lana'i. Sturdy 1930s schoolhouse furnishings give the wood-floored dining room a vintage air, while the menu combines fresh seafood with various meats in ways both familiar (a perfect rib-eye) and excellent (ahi *poke* tacos).

The small bar, which draws local movers and shakers (there are more every day), pours a fine highball, has a great wine list and is often open until 11pm! On Friday nights there's live Hawaiian music.

☆ Entertainment

Hale Keaka Lana'i Theater THEATER
(Lanai Theater; www.lanai96763.com; cnr Lana'i Ave & 7th St; adult/child $10/7; ⌚vary daily) The Edison-era projector at the old Lanai Theater (1926) showed its last film in the 1990s. Now, however, little of the past remains as Pulama Lana'i has spent millions to completely transform the building into a state-of-the-art multimedia facility with two theaters, a stage and a green room.

Shopping

Shops and galleries encircle Dole Park selling everything from flip-flops for locals to fine art for connoisseurs.

★Mike Carroll Gallery ART, BOOKS
(☎808-565-7122; www.mikecarrollgallery.com; cnr 7th & Ko'ele Sts; ⌚10am-5:30pm Mon-Sat, 9am-2pm Sun) Art-lovers enjoy Mike Carroll Gallery, where you can find the eponymous owner either creating a new work or busy displaying the work of another artist. It's a good source for local books plus Asian antiques (Larry loves Asian antiques!).

Lana'i Arts & Cultural Center ART
(www.lanaiart.org; cnr 7th & Houston Sts; ⌚10am-4pm Mon-Sat) Staffed by local artist volunteers, here you can choose from works in many mediums or learn how to create your own from the artists themselves. A great place to get *very* local recommendations.

Local Gentry CLOTHING
(☎808-565-9130; 363 7th St; ⌚10am-5pm Mon-Fri, to 6pm Sat, to 2pm Sun) Lovers of artful clothing flock to Local Gentry, a clothing store with color and flair that caters to visitors and locals alike.

ℹ Information

There's no local daily newspaper, but community notices, including rental-housing ads, are posted on bulletin boards outside the grocery stores. The monthly *Lana'i Today* covers local events.

Bank of Hawaii (www.boh.com; 460 8th St; ⌚8:30am-1pm & 2-4pm Mon-Thu, to 6pm Fri) Has a 24-hour ATM.

Lana'i Community Hospital (☎808-565-6411; 628 7th St; ⌚24hr) Offers emergency medical services.

Post office (620 Jacaranda St; ⌚9am-3pm Mon-Fri, 9:30-11:30am Sat)

Pulama Lana'i (☎808-565-3000; www.pulamalanai.com; 1311 Fraser Ave) The island's management company has two online sources of news and events: www.lanai96763.com and www.facebook.com/PulamaLanai. The main Pulama website has details on many of its projects.

Getting There & Around

The resort shuttle stops at Hotel Lana'i, the Lodge at Koele and pretty much anywhere else you ask including the Dollar Rent-a-Car office.

Munro Trail

This exhilarating 12-mile adventure through verdant forest can be hiked or mountain biked but not driven. For the best views, get an early start. Those hiking or biking should be prepared for steep grades and allow a whole day. Be aware that rains can turn the dirt path into a red swamp. Watch out for sheer drop-offs.

To start, head north on Hwy 44 from Lana'i City. About a mile past the Lodge at Koele, turn right onto the paved road that ends in half a mile at the island's **cemetery**. The Munro Trail starts left of the cemetery; passing through eucalyptus groves, it climbs the ridge and the path is studded with Norfolk Island pines. These trees, a species that draws moisture from the afternoon clouds and fog, were planted in the 1920s as a watershed by naturalist George Munro, after whom the trail is named.

The trail looks down on deep ravines cutting across the east flank of the mountain, and passes **Lana'ihale** (3370ft), Lana'i's highest point. On a clear day along the route you can see all the inhabited Hawaiian Islands except for distant Kaua'i and Ni'ihau. Stay on the main trail, which descends 6 miles to the central plateau. Keep the hills to your left and turn right at the big fork in the road. The trail ends back on Manele Rd (Hwy 440) between Lana'i City and Manele Bay.

Ask at the Lana'i Western Adventures (p426) about utility-task-vehicle (UTV) tours of the trail (from $200), which may be the best recourse for nonhikers.

CARRY WATER

Outside of Lana'i City there is nowhere to buy refreshments. So if you have a day planned of rural adventures to places such as the Keomuku Road, the Garden of the Gods or even Hulopo'e Beach, be sure to bring plenty of water and refreshments. This is especially important if you're embarking on hikes such as the Munro Trail.

Hulopo'e & Manele Bays

Lana'i's finest beach (and one of the best in Hawaii) is the golden crescent of sand at Hulopo'e Bay. Enjoy snorkeling in a marine preserve, walking to a fabled archaeological site or just relaxing in the shade of palms. Nearby, Manele Harbor provides a protected anchorage for sailboats and other small craft, just a 10-minute walk from Hulopo'e Beach.

Manele and Hulopo'e Bays are part of a marine-life conservation district that prohibits the removal of coral and restricts many fishing activities, all of which makes for great snorkeling and diving. Spinner dolphins seem to enjoy the place as much as humans. During wintertime *kona* (leeward) storms, strong currents and swells enliven the calm and imperil swimmers.

Beaches

★Hulopo'e Beach BEACH

(off Hwy 440; 🚻) The main beach on the island is kept looking beautiful thanks to the efforts of Panama Lana'i's legions of groundskeepers. Everybody loves this free, public beach – locals taking the kids for a swim, tourists on day trips from Maui and the many visitors who end up losing track of time here.

This gently curving golden-sand beach is long, broad and protected by a rocky point to the south. The Four Seasons resort sits on a low seaside terrace on the north side. But the beach is rarely crowded, except on weekends, when picnicking locals descend. Picnic tables shelter under palms and there are public restrooms with solar-heated showers. The ferry dock is an easy 10-minute walk.

For the best snorkeling, head to the left side of the bay, where there's an abundance of coral and reef fish. To the left, just beyond the sandy beach, you'll find a low lava shelf with tide pools worth exploring. Look for the protected shoreline splash pool, ideal for children.

Sights & Activities

★Pu'u Pehe NATURAL FEATURE

From Hulopo'e Beach, a path (of around 1320yd) leads south to the end of **Manele Point**, which separates Hulopo'e and Manele Bays. The point is actually a volcanic cinder cone that's sharply eroded on its seaward edge. The lava here has rich rust red colors with swirls of gray and black, and its texture is bubbly and brittle – so brittle that huge chunks of the point have broken off and fallen onto the coastal shelf below.

Pu'u Pehe is the name of the cove to the left of the point, as well as the rocky islet just offshore. This islet, which is also known as Sweetheart's Rock, has a tomblike formation on top that features in the Hawaiian legend of Pehe. According to the legend, Pehe was a beautiful maiden who was stashed away in a cave by her lover, lest any other young men on Lana'i set eyes upon her. One day when her lover was up in the mountains, a storm suddenly blew in and powerful waves drowned Pehe. The grief-stricken boy carried Pehe's body to the top of Pu'u Pehe, where he erected a tomb and laid her to rest. He then jumped to his death in the surging waters.

Manele Harbor HARBOR

(off Hwy 440) During the early 20th century, cattle were herded down to Manele Bay for shipment to Honolulu. These days the herds start in Maui, traveling on day trips to Lana'i on the ferry. There are a few picnic tables under a shelter and bathrooms. If you see a huge sailing yacht, it may be Larry's.

Cathedrals DIVING

Diving in and around the bay is excellent. Coral is abundant near the cliffsides, where the bottom quickly slopes off to about 40ft. Beyond the bay's western edge, near Pu'u Pehe rock, is Cathedrals, the island's most spectacular dive site, featuring arches and grottoes amidst a large lava tube that is 100ft in length.

Trilogy Lana'i Ocean Sports (p424) runs diving and snorkeling trips in the area.

Manele Golf Course GOLF

(☎808-565-2000; www.golfonlanai.com; Four Seasons Resort Lana'i at Manele Bay; guests/nonguests $210/225; ⏲7:30am-6pm;) This Jack Nicklaus–branded 7039yd course at the Four Seasons resort offers spectacular play along seaside cliffs. The 12th hole challenges golfers to hit across 200yd of ocean surf.

LANA'I SURF BEACHES & BREAKS

Lana'i has a paucity of surf breaks, but on the south shore the most consistent surf comes in around the Manele Point area, where the main break peels off the tip of Manele and into Hulopo'e Bay. Shallow reef and submerged rocks make this a dangerous spot at low tide or in smaller surf conditions (you're more likely to get ideal conditions on a double overhead swell, but check with locals to be safe).

Sleeping

Note that owners of the condos around Manele Bay are prevented from renting out their units to visitors.

★Hulopo'e Beach Camping CAMPGROUND $

(off Hwy 440; permit $30, plus per person per night $15) Rather pricey camping is allowed on the grassy expanse above Hulopo'e Beach. The permits are issued by staff in the park.

Four Seasons Resort Lana'i at Manele Bay RESORT $$$

(☎808-565-2000; www.fourseasons.com/manelebay; 1 Manele Bay Rd, off Hwy 440; r from $500;) With the closure of its sibling lodge, this resort is the premier destination on Lana'i. It has already been through several major changes during the relatively short time since Larry Ellison bought the place. Rooms and public spaces have been thoroughly revamped, with a minimalist Asian esthetic.

During 2015 the resort was closed for an extended time so that the pool area could be transformed. Three new pools with naturalistic features (and overall shallow depths), new poolside cafes and other delights are on the menu. New luxury suites are planned and the restaurants are likely to undergo another round of changes.

Unchanged are the views of the bay's azure waters.

Eating & Drinking

Other than the Four Seasons, where the food and drink options are in flux (although whatever is open should have fab water views), the closest sources for refreshments and picnics on Hulopo'e Beach are in Lana'i City.

Lana'i

Remote yet easily reached, Lana'i is in flux and rapid change is the new normal. Almost 98% of the island (formerly a vast pineapple plantation) is owned by a billionaire with big ideas. And while the resorts are being transformed, the wild to mild beaches and immense open spaces await discovery by the masses.

1

2

M.M. SWEET / GETTY IMAGES ©

4

QUINCY DEIN / ROBERT HARDING ©

1. Garden of the Gods (p435)
Weirdly shaped volcanic rocks are strewn about this stunning landscape.

2. Sunrise over the ocean
On a clear day, Lana'i, the most central of the Hawaiian Islands, has views to all five main islands on a clear day.

3. Malamalama Church (p434)
Originally built in 1903, Ka Lanakila o Ka Malamalama Church sits amongst the ruins of a sugarcane plantation.

4. Hulopo'e Bay (p430)
In this marine preserve snorkelers can swim alongside spinner dolphins.

3

JENNA SZERLAG / DESIGN PICS / GETTY IMAGES ©

★Nobu JAPANESE $$$

(☎808-565-2832; off Hwy 440, Four Seasons Resort Lana'i at Manele Bay; meals $30-100; ⏲6-9:30pm) The Four Seasons features a branch of the worldwide chain of very high-end Japanese sushi restaurants that just happen to be favorites of Larry Ellison. Created by chef Nobuyuki Matsuhisa, Nobu is known for ultrafresh and creative sushi and other Japanese dishes, in this case with Hawaiian elements.

Keomuku Road

The best drive on Lana'i, Keomuku Road (Hwy 44) heads north from Lana'i City into cool upland hills, where fog drifts above grassy pastures. Along the way, impromptu overlooks offer straight-on views of the undeveloped southeast shore of Moloka'i and its tiny islet Mokuho'oniki, in marked contrast to Maui's sawtooth high-rises in Ka'anapali off to your right.

The 8-mile road gently slopes down to the coast in a series of switchbacks through a mostly barren landscape punctuated by eccentrically shaped rocks. The paved road ends near the coast and you are in 4WD country. To the left, a dirt road leads to Shipwreck Beach, while turning right onto Keomuku Road takes the adventurous to Keomuku Beach or all the way to Naha.

Keep your eyes open – sightings of wild mouflon sheep on the inland hills are not uncommon. Males have curled-back horns, and dominant ones travel with a harem. You may also see white-spotted Axis deer.

Shipwreck Beach

Unlike many worldwide places named Shipwreck Beach, where the name seems fanciful at best, you can't miss the namesake wreck here. A large **WWII tanker** sits perched atop rocks just offshore. Unlike a metal ship (which would have dissolved decades ago), this one was part of a series made from concrete. It was dumped here by the navy after the war.

Start your beach exploration by taking the sandy road that runs 1.4 miles north from the end of Hwy 44, past some beach shacks. Park in the large clearing overlooking a rocky cove, which is known locally as Po'aiwa and has good **snorkeling** among the rocks and reef, as well as protected **swimming** over the sandy bottom. The wreck is about 440yd to the north, and you can stroll for at least 9 miles along the shore while looking for flotsam, other shipwrecks and taking in the Moloka'i and Maui views. Close to the parking area is the foundation of a former lighthouse on a lava-rock point.

Sights

Kukui Petroglyphs HISTORIC SITE

From the lighthouse foundation, trail markings lead directly inland about 100yd to the Kukui petroglyphs, a cluster of fragile carvings marked by a sign reading 'Do Not Deface.' The simple figures are etched onto large boulders on the right side of the path.

Kahokunui to Naha

Keomuku Road from Kahokunui to Naha is just the journey for those looking for real adventure on Lana'i. Overhanging kiawe trees shade long stretches of the dirt road, which varies from smooth to deeply cratered (and impossibly soupy after storms). This is where your 4WD will justify its daily fee, as you explore the ruins of failed dreams and discover magical beaches. If the road is passable, driving the entire length should take about an hour. The reef-protected shore is close to the road but usually not quite visible.

Sights

Maunalei HISTORIC SITE

Less than a mile from the end of paved Hwy 44 is Maunalei. An ancient heiau (stone temple) sat there until 1890, when the Maunalei Sugar Company dismantled it and used the stones to build a fence and railroad. Shortly after the temple desecration, the company was beset by misfortune, as saltwater filled the wells and disease decimated the workforce.

★Keomuku HISTORIC SITE

The center of the short-lived sugarcane plantation, Keomuku is 6 miles southeast of Maunalei. The highlight is the beautifully reconstructed **Ka Lanakila o Ka Malamalama Church**, which was originally built in 1903.

Look for ruins, including a steam locomotive and buildings and an old boat, towards the water.

Halepalaoa Landing HISTORIC SITE

Just under 2 miles southeast along the road from Keomuku, you reach Halepalaoa Landing, from which the sugar company planned to ship out its product. But little was accomplished during its short life (1899–1901), other than to shorten the lives of scores of Japanese workers, who are buried in a small **cemetery** that has a sign reading 'Japanese Memorial Shrine'.

On the ocean side, you'll see the remains of Club Lana'i, a 1970s failed recreation spot. There's a **pier** here that's maintained and which provides a good stroll out from the shore. Larry Ellison's plans for a new resort here are caught in a regulatory muddle.

Naha HISTORIC SITE
Four miles south of Halepalaoa brings you to Naha, which is both the end of the road and the site of ancient fishponds just offshore. With the wind whistling in your ears, this is a dramatic and desolate setting where the modern world seems very far away.

Beaches

★Halepalaoa Beach BEACH
Running southeast from the pier is the reef-protected and shaded Halepalaoa Beach, which seems to have come from desert-island central casting. In winter the number of whales breaching offshore may outnumber the humans basking on the sand.

Road to Garden of the Gods

Strange rock formations, views that would overexcite a condo developer and more deserted beaches are the highlights of northwestern Lana'i.

Reached via the unpaved Polihua Rd, the stretch leading to Kanepu'u Preserve and the Garden of the Gods is fairly good, although often dusty. It generally takes about 30 minutes from town. To travel onward to Polihua Beach, though, is another matter: depending on when the road was last graded, the trip could take anywhere from 20 minutes to an hour, as you descend 1800ft down to the coast.

Sights

Kanepu'u Preserve FOREST
(808-559-0120; Polihua Rd) The 590-acre Kanepu'u Preserve is the last native dryland forest of its kind across all Hawaii. Just 5 miles northwest of Lana'i City, the forest is home to 49 species of rare native plants, including the endangered *'iliahi* (Hawaiian sandalwood) and *na'u* (fragrant Hawaiian gardenia). Look for signs denoting a short new interpretive trail which covers the flora and fauna.

★Garden of the Gods NATURAL FEATURE
(Polihua Rd) The only fertilizer that might work in this garden is cement. Often weirdly shaped volcanic rocks are strewn about this seemingly Martian landscape. Multihued rocks and earth, with a palette from amber to rust to sienna, are stunning.

It's utterly silent up here and you can see up to four other islands across the white-capped waters. The colors change with the light – pastel in the early morning, rich hues in the late afternoon. Look for rocks oddly perched atop others.

Beaches

Polihua Beach BEACH
(Polihua Rd) This broad, 1.5-mile-long white-sand beach at the northwestern tip of the island takes its name from the green sea turtles that nest here (*polihua* means 'eggs in the bosom'). Although the beach itself is gorgeous, strong winds kicking up the sand and tiny shells often make it stingingly unpleasant; water conditions are treacherous.

Kaumalapa'u Highway

Kaumalapa'u Hwy (Hwy 440) connects Lana'i City to the airport before ending at Kaumalapa'u Harbor, the island's deepwater barge dock. The road itself is about as exciting as a can of pineapple chunks in heavy syrup, but it runs close to Lana'i's best archaeological site, at Kaunolu.

Kaunolu

Perched on a majestic bluff at the southwestern tip of the island, the ancient fishing village of Kaunolu thrived until its abandonment in the mid-19th century after missionary-transmitted disease had decimated the island. The waters of Kaunolu Bay were so prolific that royalty came here to cast their nets.

Now a registered National Historic Landmark, Kaunolu boasts the largest concentration of stone ruins on Lana'i. A gulch separates the two sides of the bay, with remnants of former house sites on the eastern side, obscured by thorny kiawe. The stone walls of **Halulu Heiau** at the western side of the gulch still dominate the scene. The temple once served as a *pu'uhonua* (place of refuge), where taboo-breakers fled to elude their death sentences. There are over 100 building sites here.

Northwest of the heiau, a natural stone wall runs along the perimeter of the sea cliff. Look for a break in the wall at the cliff's edge, where there's a sheer 63ft drop known as **Kahekili's Jump**. The ledge below makes diving into the ocean a death-defying thrill, but is recommended for professionals only. It's said that Kamehameha the Great would test the courage of upstart warriors by having them leap from this spot. More recently, it has been the site of cliff-diving championships.

To reach little-visited Kaunolu, follow Kaumalapa'u Hwy (Hwy 440) 1056yd past the airport, and turn left onto a partial gravel and dirt road that runs south through abandoned pineapple fields for 2.2 miles. A carved stone marks the turn onto a much rougher but still 4WD-capable road down to the sea. After a further 2.5 miles you'll see a sign for a short **interpretive trail**, which has well-weathered signs explaining the history of Kaunolu. Another 528yd brings you to a parking area amid the ruins.

Hike Lana'i (p424) offers excellent walking tours of the area. Note that your rental 4WD may be banned from driving here; check first.

Moloka'i

Includes ➡

Best Beaches

- ➡ Papohaku Beach (p467)
- ➡ Kawakiu Beach (p466)
- ➡ Twenty Mile Beach (p454)
- ➡ Halawa Beach (p455)

Best Adventures

- ➡ Kalaupapa by mule (p462)
- ➡ Halawa Valley hike (p455)
- ➡ Pepe'opae Trail (p457)
- ➡ Kayaking the coast (p456)

Why Go?

The popular local T-shirt proclaiming 'Moloka'i time is when I want to show up' sums up this idiosyncratic island perfectly: feisty and independent, while not taking life too seriously. The moniker 'Friendly Isle' means slowing waaay down and taking your sense of rhythm from the locals.

Moloka'i is often cited as the 'most Hawaiian' of the islands, and in terms of bloodlines this is true – more than 50% of the residents are at least part Native Hawaiian. But whether the island fits your idea of 'most Hawaiian' depends on your definition. If your idea of Hawaii includes great tourist facilities, forget it.

But if you're after a place that best celebrates the islands' geography and indigenous culture, then Moloka'i is for you. Ancient Hawaiian sites in the island's beautiful, tropical east are jealously protected and restored, and island-wide consensus eschews development of the often-sacred west.

When to Go

Kaunakaka

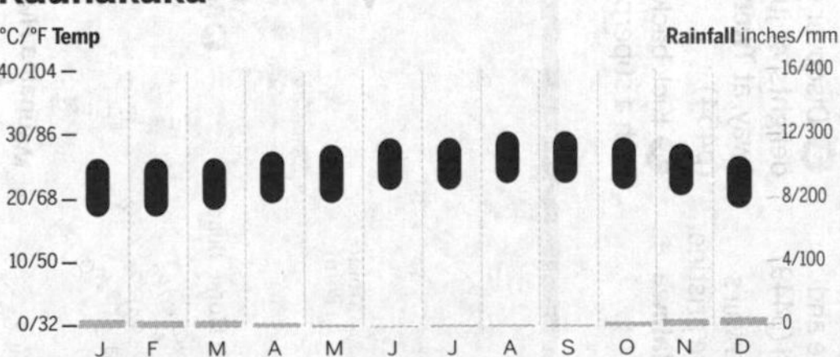

Nov–Mar Rain gear is needed in Kaunakakai and any place east; it's possibly chilly in the hills.

Apr–Aug Winter rains have stopped and the entire island enjoys breezy tropical comfort.

Sep–Oct Moloka'i enjoys lovely low 80s (°F) daytime temperatures; conditions are a little cooler up high.

Moloka'i Highlights

1. Explore the culture and beauty of **East Moloka'i** (p449).
2. Hear echoes of Hawaii's past while hiking in the pristine and deeply spiritual **Halawa Valley** (p455).
3. Discover underwater delights, or just laze the day away, at **Twenty Mile Beach** (p454).
4. Kick back at a picnic table with a superb plate lunch at **Mana'e Goods & Grindz** (p451) in Puko'o.
5. Follow in the footsteps of America's first saint on the **Kalaupapa Peninsula** (p461).
6. Make friends bust a nut by sending a **Post-a-Nut** (p460) from Ho'olehua.
7. Get your skin blasted clean on windswept and untrammeled **Papohaku Beach** (p467), on the west coast.
8. Relive plantation Hawaii wandering unrefined **Kaunakakai** (p445).

History

Moloka'i was possibly inhabited by the 7th century. Over the following years it was a vital locale within the Hawaiian Islands and played a key role in local culture. It was known for its warriors, and its chiefs held great sway in the ever-shifting alliances between O'ahu and Maui. Much of the population lived in the east, where regular rainfalls, fertile soil and rich waters ensured abundant food.

Some of the most amazing historical sites in the islands can be found here, including the enormous 'Ili'ili'opae Heiau and the series of fishponds just offshore.

At first European contact in 1786, the population was about 8000, close to today's total. Missionaries turned up in the east in the 1830s. Meanwhile, the possibilities of the vast western plains drew the interest of early capitalists and colonists. By the 1900s there were large plantations of sugarcane and pineapples as well as cattle ranches. All the big pineapple players – Libby, Dole and Del Monte – had operations here but had ceased all production by 1990. Given the large local population, relatively few immigrant laborers were brought to Moloka'i, one of the reasons the island population includes such a high proportion of Native Hawaiians.

Cattle were an important commodity during the 20th century. The Moloka'i Ranch owns much of the western third of the island, but changing investors coupled with some unsuccessful dabbles in tourism caused the ranch to shut down in 2008, throwing hundreds out of work.

Tourism plays a minor role in the local economy and, besides small-scale farming, the main employer now is Monsanto, which has experimental farms growing genetically modified (GM) seeds. Its low profile was shattered when it fought – and lost – an electoral initiative which banned GM farming in Maui County, of which Moloka'i is a part.

National, State & County Parks

The stunning Kalaupapa Peninsula, within Kalaupapa National Historical Park, and a tour of the leprosy settlement there are reason enough to visit Moloka'i. Verdant Pala'au State Park has views down to Kalaupapa and a range of attractions, from woodsy hikes to erotic rock formations.

The county's Papohaku Beach Park, which fronts one of Hawaii's longest and best beaches, is incentive enough to make the trek out west.

MOLOKA'I FOR CHILDREN

- Take a free sport-kite-flying lesson at the Big Wind Kite Factory (p465).
- Rent a house for running-around room, plus (usually) video entertainment and perhaps even a private beach.
- Explore under the sea in the shallow waters of Twenty Mile Beach (p454).

Activities

Moloka'i has wild ocean waters, rough trails, remote rainforests and the most dramatic oceanside cliffs in Hawaii. It's a perfect destination for adventure – just don't expect to be spoon-fed.

If you're considering action at sea, note that conditions are seasonal. During the summer you'll find waters are calm on the north and west shores, and made rough by the persistent trade winds on the south shore outside of the Pala'au Barrier Reef. Plan on getting out early, before the winds pick up. Winter storms make waters rough all around the island (outside of the reef, which runs the length of the south side of the island) but, even so, the calm days between winter storms can be the best times to get out on the water.

Moloka'i has plenty of wind – advanced windsurfers can harness it in the Pailolo and Ka'iwi Channels; however, you'll need your own gear.

ACTIVITY	BEST PLACES
Fishing	Penguin Banks
Kayaking	northeast coast
	south coast
Scuba Diving	Pala'au Barrier Reef
Snorkeling	Dixie Maru Beach (p468)
	Kawakiu Beach (p466)
	Twenty Mile Beach (p454)
Swimming	Dixie Maru Beach (p468)
	Twenty Mile Beach (p454)
Biking	island-wide
Hiking	Halawa Valley
	Kalaupapa Peninsula
	Kamakou Preserve

Moloka'i

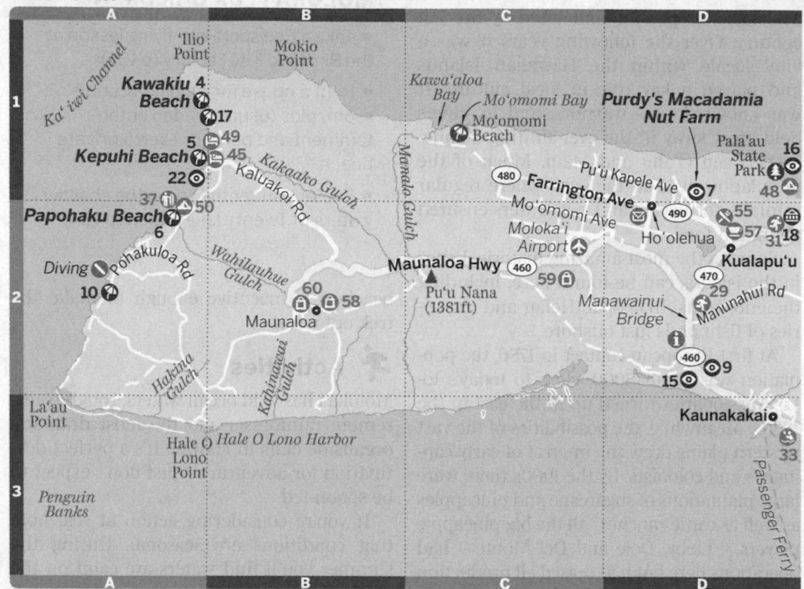

Among the activities operators and outfitters, there are three who pretty much handle every activity on the island and at times loosely work together.

Beach Break Moloka'i OUTDOORS
(808-567-6091; Holomua Jct, cnr Hwys 460 & 470; 10am-4pm Mon-Sat) This much-needed newcomer offers a wide range of surf gear and wear for sale. Surfboard rentals start at $20 per day and there are many kinds available, including stand-up paddle boards. Snorkeling sets are $9.50 per day and you can also rent beach gear including chairs, coolers and umbrellas. Sale items include yoga mats.

Moloka'i Fish & Dive OUTDOORS
(808-553-5926; www.molokaifishanddive.com; Ala Malama Ave, Kaunakakai; 2-tank boat dives incl equipment $165; 6am-7pm) This is really the Big Kahuna of activities on the island. It operates fishing trips and rents gear. If you have a vague notion of something you'd like to do, come here and see what they advise.

Part gas station, part shop (which is crammed with sporting gear and idiosyncratic souvenirs), its gear for rent includes mask and fins ($10/35 per day/week) and fishing poles ($13/35).

Moloka'i Outdoors OUTDOORS
(808-553-4477, 877-553-4477; www.molokai-outdoors.com; Hio Pl, Kaunakakai; SUP/kayak tour adult/child $68/35; hours vary) Moloka'i Outdoors can custom-design adventures and arrange activities. Paddling and stand-up paddleboarding (SUP) are its specialty and it also can arrange tours across the island. It is located off the road to the main pier, but it's best to call or email in advance.

Cycling & Mountain Biking

There are more than 40 miles of trails on Moloka'i that are good for mountain biking: the roads of the thick Moloka'i Forest Reserve are prime, as are trails on the arid West End, many with ocean views. As for cycling, pretty much all of Moloka'i's paved highways would make for a scenic ride, especially the trip to the Halawa Valley.

★ Moloka'i Bicycle BICYCLE RENTAL
(808-553-3931; www.mauimolokaibicycle.com; 80 Mohala St, Kaunakakai; bike rental per day/week from $25/75; 3-6pm Wed, 9am-2pm Sat & by appointment) This shop's owner, Phillip Kikukawa, has a great depth of knowledge about biking across the breadth of the island. He'll do pickups and drop-offs outside his opening hours. As well as offering repairs, parts and sales, he has a wide selection of bikes

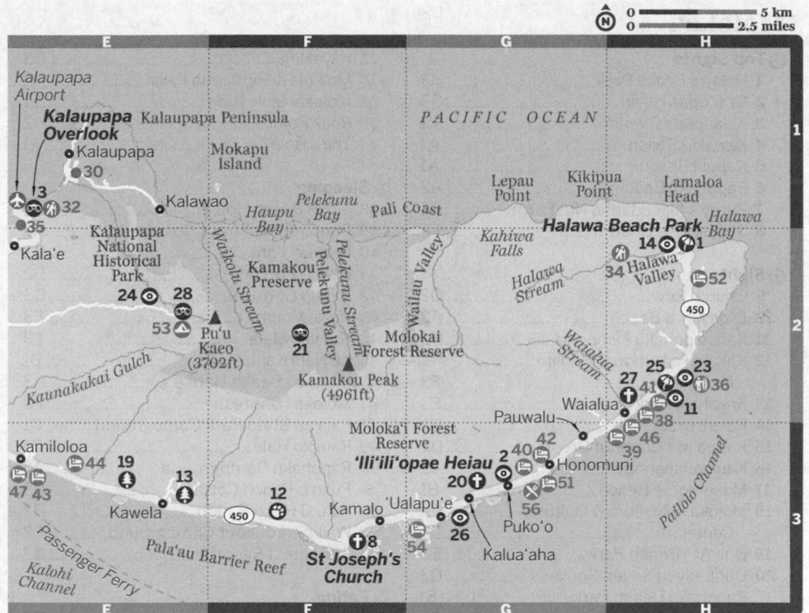

to rent, including mountain bikes. Prices include helmet, lock, pump, maps and much more.

Fishing

The sportfishing is excellent in the waters off Moloka'i, especially around the fish-filled Penguin Banks off the southwestern tip. Bait casting is good on the southern and western shores. Boats dock and leave from the Kaunakakai Wharf. Rates run at about $25 per person per hour with various time and passenger minimums (eg six-person, four-hour minimum would be $600). Close to shore expect to find large fish including *'omilu*, a type of trevally. Further out you'll find *a'u* (marlin) and the popular various species of ahi (yellowfin tuna).

Kayaking

Moloka'i Outdoors runs various kayak trips. Some are designed so that you paddle with the wind and then get a tow, or ride, back to the starting point.

Scuba Diving

Moloka'i's 32-mile Pala'au Barrier Reef – Hawaii's longest – lies along the south side of the island, promising top-notch snorkeling and excellent diving in uncrowded waters all year long, when conditions allow. To reach the good spots, you'll need a boat.

Check the boat charters, or go with Moloka'i Fish & Dive.

Whale-Watching

Witness the sudden drama of humpback whales breaching from December to April. Moloka'i Fish & Dive, Moloka'i Outdoors and the boat-charter operators all offer trips. Rates start at about $75. Also, during whale-watching season watch for whales along the coastal part of the drive to Halawa Valley after mile marker 20.

Tours

Tours on Moloka'i mirror the island's personality. Don't expect little buses to take you around with canned commentary and a stop for souvenirs. Rather, local tours concentrate on experiences you wouldn't be able to enjoy on your own, such as a trek up the Halawa Valley or down to Kalaupapa.

The activity operators offer various tours, including custom drives to pretty much any place on the island.

Much of Moloka'i's coastline is only accessible by boat. The wild beauty of the impenetrable Pali Coast, home to the world's tallest sea cliffs, is unforgettable. The activity

Moloka'i

Top Sights

1 Halawa Beach Park ... H2
2 'Ili'ili'opae Heiau ... G3
3 Kalaupapa Overlook ... E1
4 Kawakiu Beach ... A1
5 Kepuhi Beach ... A1
6 Papohaku Beach ... A2
7 Purdy's Macadamia Nut Farm ... D1
8 St Joseph's Church ... F3

Sights

9 Church Row ... D2
10 Dixie Maru Beach ... A2
11 Kahinapohaku Fishpond ... H2
12 Kakahai'a National Wildlife Refuge ... F3
13 Kakahaia Park ... E3
14 Kalani Pruet ... H2
15 Kapua'iwa Coconut Grove ... D2
16 Kauleonanahoa ... D1
17 Make Horse Beach ... B1
18 Moloka'i Museum & Cultural Center ... D2
19 One Ali'i Beach Park ... E3
20 Our Lady of Seven Sorrows ... G3
Papohaku Beach Park ... (see 6)
21 Pelekunu Valley Overlook ... F2
22 Pu'u o Kaiaka ... A1
23 Rock Point ... H2
24 Sandalwood Pit ... E2
25 Twenty Mile Beach ... H2
26 'Ualapu'e Fishpond ... G3
27 Waialua Congregational Church ... H2
28 Waikolu Lookout ... E2

Activities, Courses & Tours

29 Beach Break Moloka'i ... D2
30 Damien Tours ... E1
31 Ironwood Hills Golf Course ... D2
Kalaupapa Trail ... (see 32)
32 Kalaupapa Trailhead ... E1
33 Kayaking ... D3
34 Moa'ula & Hipuapua Falls ... H2
35 Molokai Mule Ride ... E1
36 Rock Point ... H2
37 Third Hole ... A1

Sleeping

38 Aloha Beach House ... H2
39 Dunbar Beachfront Cottages ... H3
40 Hale Lei Lani ... G3
41 Hale O Pu' Hala ... H2
42 Hilltop Cottage ... G3
43 Hotel Moloka'i ... E3
44 Ka Hale Mala ... E3
45 Ke Nani Kai ... B1
46 Moloka'i Beach House ... H3
47 Moloka'i Shores ... E3
48 Pala'au State Park Campground ... D1
49 Paniolo Hale ... B1
50 Papohaku Campground ... A2
51 Puko'o Beach Cottage ... G3
52 Pu'u O Hoku Ranch ... H2
53 Waikolu Lookout Campground ... E2
54 Wavecrest Resort ... G3

Eating

55 Kualapu'u Cookhouse ... D2
56 Mana'e Goods & Grindz ... G3

Drinking & Nightlife

57 Coffees of Hawaii ... D2

Entertainment

Hula Shores ... (see 43)

Shopping

58 Big Wind Kite Factory & Plantation Gallery ... B2
59 Kumu Farms ... C2
Kupu A'e ... (see 29)
60 Maunaloa General Store ... B2

operators and boat-charter operators all arrange trips that take the better part of a day, often including a stop for snorkeling. (These don't run in winter, lest storms send you to Gilligan's Island.)

Boat charters generally leave from Kaunakakai Wharf and, if you're traveling in a group, can be tailored to your desires. Rates start at about $100 per hour for whole-boat charters, with a four-hour minimum. Try one of the following personable outfits:

Alyce C Sportfishing Charters BOAT TOUR, FISHING
(☎808-558-8377; www.alycecsportfishing.com) Joe Reich has over 30 years of experience and, in addition to sportfishing charters, also does whale-watching jaunts and round-island runs on his 31ft boat.

Fun Hogs Sport Fishing BOAT TOUR, FISHING
(☎808-567-6789; www.molokaifishing.com) Fish your heart out on the *Ahi*, a 27ft sportfishing boat. Snorkeling and whale-watching are also offered. Mike Holmes is a legendary local long-distance canoeist.

Hallelujah Hou Fishing BOAT TOUR, FISHING
(☎808-336-1870; www.hallelujahhoufishing.com) Captain Clayton Ching runs all types of fishing trips, plus he's a real captain in the sense that he can marry you on ship *or* shore. He also organizes fly-fishing trips.

Moloka'i Ocean Tours BOAT TOUR, FISHING
(☎808-553-3299; www.molokaioceantours.com) Offers all types of fishing charters plus coastal tours, whale-watching and snorkeling trips.

Walter Naki CULTURAL TOUR, BOAT TOUR
(☎808-558-8184) Walter Naki, who is also known for his cultural tours and treks, offers deep-sea fishing, whale-watching and North Shore boat tours that include the Pali Coast.

Festivals & Events

If you're planning a visit during the island's culture-rich festivals, make sleeping reservations many months in advance. See www.visitmolokai.com for more details.

Ka Moloka'i Makahiki CULTURAL
(Kaunakakai; ⏲late Jan) The ancient makahiki festival was held after the year's main harvest was complete. Still celebrated on Moloka'i, it features traditional ceremonies, an Olympics-esque competition of ancient Hawaiian sports, crafts and activities.

Moloka'i Ka Hula Piko HULA
(www.kahulapiko.com; ⏲May) As Moloka'i is known as the birthplace of hula, its three-day hula festival has some profound roots. It opens with a solemn ceremony at 3am at Pu'u Nana (the site of Hawaii's first hula school), followed by a festival including performance, food and crafts. Confirm the dates in advance.

St Damien's Feast Day RELIGIOUS
(⏲May 10) There are various events held in honor of Moloka'i's first saint on his feast day. Plans call for a walk between the churches in the east that he built: St Joseph's (p450) and Our Lady of Seven Sorrows (p450).

Na Wahine O Ke Kai CANOE RACE
(www.nawahineokekai.com; ⏲Sep) Much the same as the Moloka'i Hoe, but with all-female teams. Best time (2008): five hours, 22 minutes, five seconds.

Moloka'i Hoe CANOE RACE
(www.molokaihoe.com; ⏲Oct) Grueling outrigger canoe race from remote Hale O Lono Point, with close to 200 six-person teams paddling furiously across the 41-mile Ka'iwi Channel to O'ahu. Best time (2011): four hours, 30 minutes, 54 seconds by the legendary Shell Va'a team. Considered the world championship of men's long-distance outrigger canoe racing.

Sleeping

Moloka'i's hotel choices are limited to one, in Kaunakakai. Almost everybody stays in a B&B, cottage, condo or house. Quality ranges from rustic to swank, with the best places having private grounds located right on the ocean. The nicest properties are usually in the verdant and coastal east. (With the closure of Moloka'i Ranch, condos in the west can seem desolate.) There are no hostels on the island; camping is limited to state and county parks.

Internet booking sites like www.homeaway.com and www.airbnb.com have dozens of listings for condos and houses. Good local sources of rental and accommodation information and reservations include the websites www.visitmolokai.com and www.molokai.com plus the following local agents:

Friendly Isle Realty ACCOMMODATION SERVICES
(☎808-553-3666; www.molokairesorts.com; 75 Ala Malama Ave, Kaunakakai; ⏲9am-5pm Mon-Sat) Books condos island-wide. Rates average $550 to $1000 per week.

Moloka'i Vacation Properties ACCOMMODATION SERVICES
(☎808-553-8334; www.molokai-vacation-rental.com; 8 Hio Pl, Kaunakakai; ⏲hours vary) Well respected local agent with houses and condos. The former cost an average of $175 to $300 per night.

Camping

Moloka'i's most interesting place to camp, in terms of setting and setup, is the county's **Papohaku Campground** (off Pohakuloa Rd) on the untrammeled West End. Camping at the county's One Ali'i Beach Park is not recommended.

County permits are issued by the **Department of Parks & Recreation** (☎808-553-3204; www.co.maui.hi.us; 90 Ainoa St, Mitchell Pauole Center, Kaunakakai; adult/child Mon-Thu $5/2, Fri-Sun $8/3; ⏲8am-1pm & 2:30-4pm Mon-Fri), by phone or in person. Permits are limited to three consecutive days in one park, with a yearly maximum of 15 days.

You can enjoy the views from Pala'au State Park and be ready for an early start on a visit to Kalaupapa from a peaceful camping area near the trailhead. For a true wilderness experience, consider the remote camping at Waikolu Lookout (p457). State permits are obtained from the **Division of State Parks** (☎808-567-6923;

www.hawaiistateparks.org; campsites per night resident/nonresident $12/18) via the website. Permits cannot be obtained on Moloka'i.

None of the campgrounds are near sources of food or drink. If you forget a piece of camping equipment, Moloka'i Fish & Dive (p440) has some supplies.

Eating

Foodie sensations have mostly passed Moloka'i by. In fact if you want a fancy dinner out, you'll have to leave the island. But for simple fare there are some fine choices, including a great lunch counter on the way to the Halawa Valley in Puko'o. Mostly, you'll be cooking for yourself – the stores and markets in Kaunakakai are well stocked and Moloka'i has some unique foods.

Getting There & Away

If you have time, taking the ferry from Maui is a more sociable and scenic experience than flying – the afternoon boat catches the sunset almost year-round, and in winter breaching whales are alone worth the trip.

AIR

Moloka'i Airport (MKK, Ho'olehua; ☎808-567-9660; http://hawaii.gov/mkk; Ho'olehua) is small: you claim your baggage on a long bench. Single-engine planes are the norm; sit right behind the cockpit area for spectacular views forward. Because of weight limits for individual bags (40lb), pack a small duffel bag in case you have to redistribute your belongings.

There is frequent service to Honolulu plus flights to Kahului on Maui and seasonal service nonstop to Lana'i and Kapalua on Maui. Unless you have a through ticket from the mainland, it's usually cheapest to buy direct from the carriers.

Makani Kai Air (☎877-255-8532, 808-834-1111; http://makanikaiair.com) Has scheduled and charter flights to Kalaupapa plus Honolulu (its fares on this route are often the cheapest).

Mokulele Airlines (☎866-260-7070; www.mokuleleairlines.com) A growing local carrier.

Ohana (☎800-367-5320; www.hawaiianairlines.com) The commuter carrier of Hawaiian Airlines.

SEA

Moloka'i Princess (☎808-667-6165; www.molokaiferry.com; Kaunakakai Wharf; adult/child one way $70/35) The ferry makes morning and late-afternoon runs between Lahaina on Maui (across from the Pioneer Inn) and Moloka'i's Kaunakakai Wharf. Buy tickets online, by phone or on the boat a half-hour before departure. Fares fluctuate with the price of fuel.

The 90-minute crossing through the Pailolo Channel (aka Pakalolo Channel for all the pot smuggling; *pakalolo* literally means 'crazy smoke') can get choppy; in fact, you can enjoy the thrill of a water park just by sitting on the top deck and getting drenched.

Getting Around

Renting a car is essential if you intend to fully explore the island or if you are renting a house or condo and will need to shop. All of Moloka'i's highways and primary routes are good, paved roads. The free tourist map, widely available on the island, is useful. James A Bier's *Map of Moloka'i & Lana'i* ($6) has an excellent index.

MOLOKA'I IN...

Two Days

After checking out **Kaunakakai**, drive the gorgeous 27 miles east to the **Halawa Valley** and hike out to the waterfall. Stop at Puko'o for lunch from the tasty lunch counter at **Mana'e Goods & Grindz**, then snorkel at **Twenty Mile Beach**. Wander around **Kaunakakai** gathering vittles for a dinner under the stars at your rental pad. On your second day let the sure-footed mules give you the ride of your life to the **Kalaupapa Peninsula** and crack open some fun at **Purdy's Macadamia Nut Farm**.

Four Days

Spend your third day in the ancient rainforests of **Kamakou Preserve**, followed by dinner at **Kualapu'u Cookhouse**. On the morning of day four, stop by Kaunakakai and pick up some island books at **Kalele Bookstore**, then head northwest to the culturally significant beaches of **Mo'omomi**, before finding the ultimate souvenirs at Maunaloa's **Big Wind Kite Factory**.

One Week

Add in lots of time to do nothing at all. You're on Moloka'i time.

TO/FROM THE AIRPORT & FERRY

If you arrive by ferry, you'll need to arrange pickup with your car-rental company.

A taxi from the airport costs around $30 to Kaunakakai and $60 to the West End.

BICYCLE

Moloka'i is a good place for cycling. The Kaunakakai bike shop Molokai Bicycle (p440) is a treasure.

BUS

MEO Bus (☎808-877-7651; bus trips free; ⌚Mon-Fri) This government economic development service runs a free shuttle bus around Moloka'i, roughly from 6am to 4pm. From a stop by Misaki's market in Kaunakakai, routes go east past the Hotel Moloka'i to Puko'o at mile marker 16, west to Maunaloa via the airport and to Kualapu'u.

The buses run roughly every two hours but it is essential that you confirm all details in advance and with the driver if you are hoping to make a round-trip. Stops are not marked.

CAR

Keep in mind that most rental cars are technically not allowed on unpaved roads. If you intend to explore remote parts of the island, such as Mo'omomi Bay, you'll at least need a vehicle with high clearance, probably a 4WD. Book well in advance, especially if planning a weekend visit. But if you're feeling lucky in low season, walk-up rates at the airport can be half that found online.

There are two gas stations in Kaunakakai. Expect sticker shock at the pump.

Average driving times and distances from Kaunakakai:

DESTINATION	MILES	TIME
Halawa Valley	27	1¼hr
Ho'olehua Airport	6.5	10min
Kalaupapa Trailhead	10	20min
Maunaloa	17	30min
Papohaku Beach	21.5	45min
Puko'o	16	20min
Twenty Mile Beach	20	40min

Alamo Rental Car (www.alamo.com; Moloka'i Airport, Ho'olehua) The rental agency with a desk at the airport; reserve well in advance. If you are arriving by ferry, first make a reservation, then call ☎808-567-6381 to arrange pickup from the wharf.

Molokai Car Rental (☎808-336-0670; www.molokaicars.com; off Ala Malama Ave, Kaunakakai; ⌚9am-3pm Mon-Fri, to noon Sat) This small local firm has a limited selection of cars and vans starting at about $40 per day. Cars are left for customer pickup at the airport and wharf.

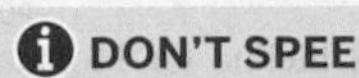

DON'T SPEED

One of Moloka'i's trademarks is the sign you see leaving the airport: 'Aloha. Slow down, this is Moloka'i. Mahalo.' Given the number of speeding tickets issued each day, this is truly friendly advice. Most posted speed limits are 35mph or less.

TAXI

Hele Mai Taxi (☎808-336-0967; www.molokaitaxi.com) Serves the entire island.

KAUNAKAKAI

POP 3400

View a photo of Moloka'i's main town from 50 years ago and the main drag won't look much different than it does today. Worn wood-fronted buildings with tin roofs that roar in the rain seem like refugees from a Clint Eastwood Western. But there's no artifice to Kaunakakai – it's the real deal. All of the island's commercial activities are here and you'll visit often – if nothing else, for its shops and services.

Walking around the town can occupy a couple of hours if you take time to get into the rhythm of things and do a little exploring. While there are stop signs, there are no stoplights. If possible, stop by on Saturday morning when the street market draws crowds.

Sights

Kaunakakai is an attraction in itself. Specifically look for gems of old buildings such as the **Moloka'i Library** (☎808-553-1765; Ala Malama Ave; ⌚9:30am-5pm Mon-Fri, noon-8pm Wed), which dates from 1937.

Kapua'iwa Coconut Grove HISTORIC SITE

(Maunaloa Hwy) As Moloka'i was the favorite island playground of King Kamehameha V, he had the royal 10-acre Kapua'iwa Coconut Grove planted near his sacred bathing pools in the 1860s. Standing tall, about a mile west of downtown, its name means 'mysterious taboo.' Be careful where you walk (or park) when you visit, because coconuts frequently plunge silently to the ground, landing with a deadly thump.

Kaunakakai Wharf PORT

The busy commercial lifeline for Moloka'i. OK, it's not that busy... A freight barge chugs in, skippers unload catches of mahimahi (white-fleshed fish also called 'dolphin') and a buff gal practices for a canoe race. A roped-off area with a floating dock provides a kiddie swim area.

Church Row HISTORIC SITE

(Maunaloa Hwy) Across from the coconut grove is Church Row. Any denomination that attracts a handful of members receives its own little tract of land. Religion in general is very popular on Moloka'i; there are many churches and some denominations – such as Catholicism – have more than one.

One Ali'i Beach Park PARK

(Maunaloa Hwy) Three miles east of town, this park is split into two parks. One side has a coconut-palm-lined shore, a playing field, a picnic pavilion and bathrooms, and although not especially attractive it's very popular with local families for huge weekend BBQs. The other side is a greener and more attractive picnic area. The water is shallow and silty.

Two memorials commemorate the 19th-century immigration of Japanese citizens to Hawaii.

Pacifica Hawai'i CRAFT PRODUCER

(808-553-8484; www.pacificahawaii.com; Kolapa Pl; by appointment) Much-lauded sea salt is produced close to the town center in the front yard of a house belonging to well-known (among salties) salt-maker Nancy Gove. Free tours (one hour, by appointment) reveal that there are more mysteries to making salt from ocean water than you'd imagine. The salt comes in various flavors – try the smoked.

FISHPONDS

Starting just east of Kaunakakai and continuing past mile marker 20 along Hwy 450 are dozens of *loko i'a* (fishponds), huge circular walls of rocks that are part of one of the world's most advanced forms of aquaculture. Monumental in size, backbreaking in creation, the fishponds operate on a simple principle: little fish swim in, big fish can't swim out. Some of the ponds are obscured and overgrown by mangroves, but others have been restored by locals anxious to preserve this link to their past. The Kahinapohaku Fishpond (p454), about half a mile past mile marker 19, is in excellent shape. Another good one is 'Ualapu'e Fishpond (p450) at mile marker 13.

Activities

While activities in Kaunakakai proper are limited, it is a good place to arrange island activities (p439).

Sleeping

Few travelers actually stay in Kaunakakai. The best places are further along the scenic east coast near the beaches and ocean.

Ka Hale Mala B&B $

(808-553-9009; www.molokai-bnb.com; Kamehameha V Hwy; apt $90, incl breakfast $100;) Enjoy the spaciousness of a 900-sq-ft, one-bedroom apartment with a fully equipped kitchen and living room with an exposed-beam ceiling. The two-story house is secluded by lush plantings, including trees laden with low-hanging fruit. The owners add to the bounty with organic vegetables and healthy breakfasts. Rates are for two people; extras (up to two) are $20 each.

It's about 5 miles east of Kaunakakai; the charming owners do airport and ferry pick-ups.

Moloka'i Shores CONDO $$

(808-553-5954, reservations 800-367-5004; www.castleresorts.com; Kamehameha V Hwy; condos from $180;) This 1970s condo development has 102 one- and two-bedroom units ranging from atrocious to charming, depending on the whims of the individual owners; choose your unit carefully. All have full kitchens, cable TV, lanai (verandah) and ceiling fans.

The grounds are the best feature and have a large pool, shuffleboard, BBQ areas and more. Like elsewhere on this stretch of coast, the water is shallow and muddy.

Hotel Moloka'i HOTEL $$

(808-553-5347; www.hotelmolokai.com; Kamehameha V Hwy; r $170-270;) Moloka'i's only hotel has a certain veteran feel about it and it's not especially alluring. It has quirky rooms with a faux-native design that gives them tunnel-like qualities, and compact grounds with a small pool and hammocks along the reef-protected limpid, silty shore. It may have a new restaurant later in 2015.

Kaunakakai

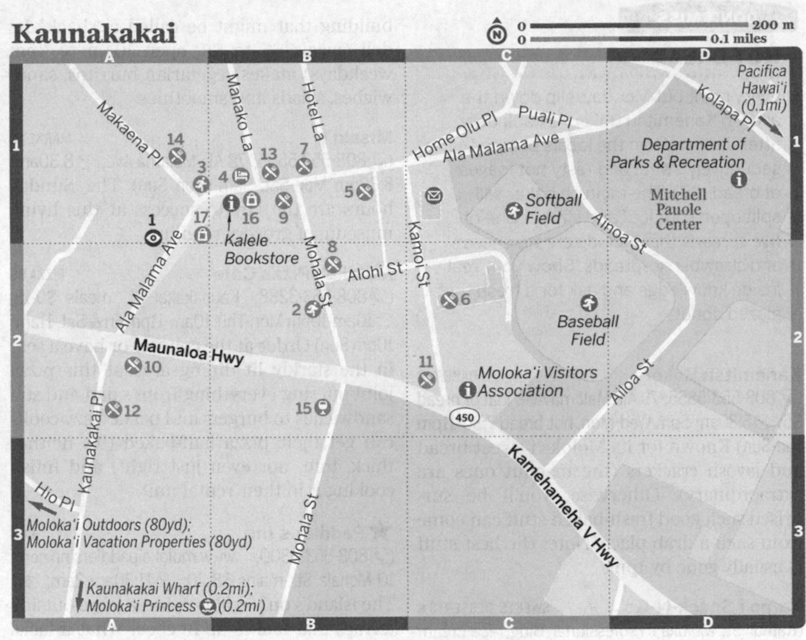

Upstairs rooms are slightly larger and brighter; some units have fridges and microwaves. Best of the lot are the four rooms with king-sized beds that face the water.

Eating & Drinking

The Saturday-morning market along Ala Malama Ave is a good source for local produce and prepared foods.

★ Maka's Korner CAFE $

(808-553-8058; cnr Mohala & Alohi Sts; meals $5-9; 7am-3pm & 5-9pm Mon-Fri, 9am-2pm Sat & Sun) A dead-simple corner location belies the fine yet basic fare here. Moloka'i's best burgers come with excellent fries, although many patrons are simply addicted to the mahimahi sandwich (go nuts and order it dressed with two shrimp tempura). Pancakes are served throughout the day. Sit at the tiny counter or at a picnic table outside.

Moloka'i Burger BURGERS $

(www.molokaiburger.com; 20 Kamehameha V Hwy; mains $5-9; 7am-9pm;) Moloka'i's only drive-through restaurant is a slick operation. The burgers come in many forms but are all thick and juicy. (Try a ramen burger, which is sandwiched between squares of fried noodles.) The dining room is unoffensive; the front terrace peacefully shady,

Kaunakakai

Sights

1 Moloka'i Library A1

Activities, Courses & Tours

2 Moloka'i Bicycle B2
3 Moloka'i Fish & Dive A1

Sleeping

4 Friendly Isle Realty B1

Eating

5 Friendly Market B1
6 Kamo'i Snack-N-Go C2
7 Kanemitsu Bakery B1
8 Maka's Korner B2
9 Misaki's B1
10 Moloka'i Burger A2
11 Moloka'i Drive-Inn C2
12 Moloka'i Pizza Cafe A2
13 Moloka'i Wines & Spirits B1
14 Outpost Natural Foods A1

Drinking & Nightlife

15 Paddler's Inn B2

Shopping

Kalele Bookstore & Divine Expressions .... (see 16)
16 Moloka'i Art from the Heart B1
17 Saturday Morning Market A1

DON'T MISS

HOT BREAD

Every night but Monday, slip down the alley to Kanemitsu Bakery's back door after dark and join the locals buying the seductively sweet and tasty hot loaves of bread ($7). The taciturn baker will split open your loaf and slather one of five spreads that include creme cheese and strawberry spreads. Show your real inside knowledge and ask for a fresh glazed donut.

Kanemitsu Bakery BAKERY $
(808-553-5855; 79 Ala Malama Ave; loaf of bread $5; 5:30am-5pm Wed-Mon, hot bread 7:30-11pm Tue-Sun) Known for its Moloka'i sweet bread and lavosh crackers (the macnut ones are extraordinary). Otherwise, you'll be surprised such good fresh-baked stuff can come from such a drab place. Note: the best stuff is usually gone by 1pm.

Kamo'i Snack-N-Go SWEETS, DESSERTS $
(Kamoi St, Moloka'i Professional Bldg; ice-cream scoops $2; 10am-9pm Mon-Fri, 9am-9pm Sat, noon-9pm Sun;) This candy store is loaded with sweets and, more importantly, Honolulu-made Dave's Hawaiian Ice Cream. The banana fudge is truly a treat.

Moloka'i Drive-Inn FAST FOOD $
(808-553-5655; Kamehameha V Hwy; mains $4-10; 6:30am-10pm;) Always popular, this barebones fast-food counter is best for plate lunches and simple local pleasures like teribeef sandwiches, omelets with Spam or Vienna lunch meat, and fried saimin noodles.

Moloka'i Wines & Spirits MARKET $
(Ala Malama Ave; 9am-7pm) Has many Hawaii and mainland microbrews plus inexpensive wines, upscale cheeses and deli items. This is the place to get all you need for silly tropical drinks. Fire up the blender!

Friendly Market SUPERMARKET $
(808-553-5595; 90 Ala Malama Ave; 8:30am-8:30pm Mon-Fri, to 6:30pm Sat) The best selection of any supermarket on the island. In the afternoon fresh fish from the wharf often appears.

Outpost Natural Foods HEALTH FOOD, DELI $
(808-553-3377; 70 Makaena Pl; 10am-6pm Mon-Fri, to 3pm Sun;) A smattering of organic produce, packaged and bulk health foods and various local fare sold from a building that might be called a 'shack.' Its deli (meals $5 to $8, open 10am to 3pm weekdays) makes vegetarian burritos, sandwiches, salads and smoothies.

Misaki's MARKET $
(808-553-5505; 78 Ala Malama Ave; 8:30am-8:30pm Mon-Sat, 9am-noon Sun) The Sunday hours are the key to success at this living museum of grocery retailing.

Moloka'i Pizza Cafe PIZZA $$
(808-553-3288; Kaunakakai Pl; meals $9-18; 10am-10pm Mon-Thu, 10am-11pm Fri & Sat, 11am-10pm Sun) Order at the counter or have a seat in the starkly lit dining area at this pizza joint offering everything from salad and sub sandwiches to burgers and pasta. Lazy cooks can get their pizza half-baked (it's neither thick, thin, nor even just right) and finish cooking it in their rental unit.

★ **Paddler's Inn** PUB
(808-553-3300; www.molokaipaddlersinn.com; 10 Mohala St; mains $8-20; 11:30am-2am;) The island's only real pub has a large outside terrace that makes up in cheer what it lacks in charm. The long menu is served until about 9pm. Regular items include deep-fried pub grub, burgers, steaks and simple pastas; however, there are many specials on various theme nights. Watch for live performances by local musicians many nights.

☆ Entertainment

Bring games, books and a gift for gab as nighttime fun is mostly DIY on Moloka'i.

★ **Hula Shores** LIVE MUSIC
(808-553-5347; Kamehameha V Hwy, Hotel Moloka'i; 4-6pm Fri) The Hotel Moloka'i's simple waterfront bar features local *kupuna* (elders) who gather at a long table to play Hawaiian music on 'Aloha Fridays.' The music always draws a crowd; the performers range from those with some languid and traditional hula moves to jam sessions with a ukulele.

It's a true community gathering with some of the people who are the heart and soul of local culture and who delight in showing off their traditional talents. Don't miss.

Shopping

★ **Kalele Bookstore & Divine Expressions** BOOKS
(808-553-5112; 64 Ala Malama Ave; 10am-5pm Mon-Fri, 9am-2pm Sat;) New and used

books, local artworks and loads of local culture and travel advice. Few locals walk past without dropping in to say hi.

Saturday Morning Market MARKET
(Ala Malama Ave; 8am-2pm Sat) This weekly market at the west end of Ala Malama Ave is the place to browse local crafts, try new fruits, stock up on organic produce and pick up some flowers. You'll find most of Moloka'i here before noon.

Moloka'i Art from the Heart ARTS
(808-553-8018; 64 Ala Malama Ave; 9:30am-5pm Mon-Fri, 9am-2:30pm Sat) Run by local artists, this small shop is packed with arts and crafts. Works in all mediums can be found here; quality ranges from the earnest to the superb. The T-shirts with local sayings are the real sleepers in the souvenir department.

Information

Bank of Hawaii (www.boh.com; Ala Malama Ave; 8:30am-1pm & 2-4pm Mon-Thu, to 6pm Fri) Has one of several 24-hour ATMs in town.

Kalele Bookstore (808-567-9094; 64 Ala Malama Ave; 10am-5pm Mon-Fri, 9am-2pm Sat;) A community treasure. Besides books, get free maps or enjoy a coffee and meet some locals out back on the shady terrace. Owner Teri Waros is a fount of all things Moloka'i. Make this one of your first stops.

Molokai Dispatch (www.themolokaidispatch.com) Free weekly published each Wednesday; watch the events calendar for local happenings.

Moloka'i Drugs (Kamoi St, Moloka'i Professional Bldg; 9am-5:45pm Mon-Fri, to 2pm Sat) Drugstore fare.

Moloka'i General Hospital (808-553-5331; 280 Homeolu Pl; 24hr) Emergency services.

Moloka'i Library (808-553-1765; Ala Malama Ave; 9:30am-5pm Mon, Tue, Thu & Fri, 12:30-8pm Wed;) Buy a library card for three months ($10) or five years ($25) and enjoy internet use (including wi-fi) and library privileges here and at 50 other branches statewide.

Moloka'i Mini Mart (Mohala St; 6am-11pm) Convenience store with internet access (10¢ per minute) and printing.

Moloka'i Visitors Association (MVA; 808-553-3876; www.gohawaii.com/molokai; 9am-noon Mon-Fri) This simple office can help with info about member businesses. Look for events updates on its Facebook page: facebook.com/MolokaiVisitorsAssociation.

Post office (Ala Malama Ave; 9am-4:30pm Mon-Fri, to 11am Sat) Most visitors prefer the fun-filled Ho'olehua post office (p460).

Visitmolokai.com (www.visitmolokai.com) Privately run website with encyclopedic links.

Getting There & Around

Kaunakakai is a walking town. **Rawlin's Chevron** (cnr Maunaloa Hwy/Hwy 460 & Ala Malama Ave; office 6:30am-8:30pm Mon-Sat, 7am-6pm Sun) has credit-card-operated pumps, making it the only round-the-clock gas station on the island.

EAST MOLOKA'I

The oft-quoted road sign 'Slow down, this is Moloka'i' really applies as you head east. Whether you are on the island for a day or a week, the 27-mile drive on Hwy 450 (aka Kamehameha V Hwy) from Kaunakakai to the Halawa Valley is simply a must.

Unlike the arid west, this is tropical Moloka'i, with palm trees arching over the road, and banana, papaya, guava and passion fruits hanging from the lush foliage, ripe for the picking. As you drive you'll catch glimpses of ancient fishponds, the neighboring islands of Lana'i and Maui, stoic old wooden churches, modest family homes, beaches and much more. But don't take your eye off the road for long or you'll run over a dog sleeping on the yellow line.

This being Moloka'i, the intoxicating drive is rarely crowded and cars tend to mosey. Of course for the final third, when the smoothly paved road narrows down to one sinuous lane, you have little choice but to slow down. But that's just as well, as each curve yields a new vista. The final climb up and over into the remote Halawa Valley is breathtaking.

On the practical side, bring gear so you can swim and snorkel at beaches that catch your fancy along the way. There's no gas east of Kaunakakai but there is an excellent small grocery and lunch counter about halfway, in Puko'o. Most of the choicest rentals are also found along this drive. Mile markers simplify finding things.

Kawela to Puko'o

Beginning about mile marker 5, the **Kakahai'a National Wildlife Refuge** (www.fws.gov/kakahaia) is a 44-acre refuge along the road. It includes freshwater marshland, with a dense growth of bulrushes and an inland freshwater fishpond that has been expanded to provide a home for endangered birds, including the Hawaiian stilt and coot. Look for the nene, the goose-like Hawaiian state bird. Most of it is closed to the public but it does give a taste of the green treats to come.

Just past mile marker 10, the road becomes sinuous and even more green. Kiawe trees and flowering bushes of all kinds line the road. The stunning views of Lana'i are gradually supplanted by views of Maui. The barely perceptible villages of **Kamalo** and **Kalua'aha** have picture-perfect churches built by Father Damien.

Although you need to get permission to visit first, the 'Ili'ili'opae Heiau, hidden off the road east of mile marker 15, is an island highlight.

Puko'o was once the seat of local government (complete with a courthouse, a jail, a wharf and a post office), but the center of island life shifted to Kaunakakai when the plantation folks built that more centrally located town. Nowadays, Puko'o is a sleepy, slow-paced gathering of a few structures just sitting on a bend in the road. But it has surprises, such as the cozy **beach** accessible just before the store, near mile marker 16. Take the short, curving path around the small bay, where fish leap out of the water, and you'll come to a stretch of sand with swimmable waters, backed by kiawe and ironwood trees.

Sights

The following sights are listed in order, running east from Kaunakakai.

Kakahaia Park PARK

Kakahaia Park is a grassy strip wedged between the road and sea in Kawela, just west of mile marker 6. It has a couple of picnic tables, and is a peaceful spot for a leg stretch or snack. This park is the only part of Kakahai'a National Wildlife Refuge open to the public.

★St Joseph's Church CHURCH

(Hwy 450, Kamalo; door usually open) Only two of the four Moloka'i churches that missionary and prospective saint Father Damien built outside of the Kalaupapa Peninsula are still standing. One of them is quaint little St Joseph's Church (the other is Our Lady of Seven Sorrows). This simple, one-room wooden church, dating from 1876, has a steeple and a bell, five rows of pews and some of the original wavy glass panes. It's just past mile marker 10.

There is also a lei-draped statue of Father Damien and a little cemetery beside the church.

'Ualapu'e Fishpond HISTORIC SITE

(Hwy 450) A half-mile beyond Wavecrest Resort condo development, at mile marker 13, you'll spot 'Ualapu'e Fishpond on the *makai* (seaward) side of the road. This fishpond, which is a National Historic Landmark, has been restored and restocked with mullet and milkfish, two species that were raised here in ancient times. It's a good place to ponder the labor involved in moving these thousands of large volcanic rocks.

Our Lady of Seven Sorrows CHURCH

(Hwy 450, Kalua'aha; doors usually open, service 7am Sun) The present Our Lady of Sorrows is a reconstruction from 1966 of the original wood-frame church, constructed in 1874 by the missionary Father Damien. It is just west of mile marker 15.

★'Ili'ili'opae Heiau HISTORIC SITE

(off Hwy 450) 'Ili'ili'opae Heiau is Moloka'i's biggest and best-known heiau, and is thought to be the second largest in Hawaii. It also might possibly be the oldest religious site in the state. The dimensions are astonishing: over 300ft long and 100ft wide, and about 22ft high on the eastern side, and 11ft high at the other end. The main platform is strikingly level. Historians believe the original heiau may have been three times its current size, reaching out beyond Mapulehu Stream.

Like the fishponds along this part of the island's coast, this heiau represents an extraordinary amount of labor by people with no real tools at their disposal.

Once a *luakini* (temple of human sacrifice), 'Ili'ili'opae is today silent except for the singing of birds. African tulip and mango trees line the trail to the site, a peaceful place

UNFORGIVING TRESPASSES

Exploring unmarked roads is not advisable. Folks aren't too keen on strangers cruising around on their private turf, and fair enough – trespassing is illegal. On the other hand, if there's a fishpond you want to see, and someone's house is between the road and the water, it's usually easy to strike up a conversation and get permission to cross. If you're lucky they might even share some local lore and history with you, particularly the old-timers.

filled with *mana* (spiritual essence), with stones that still seem to emanate vibrations of a mystical past. Remember: it's disrespectful to walk across the top of the heiau.

Visiting this heiau is a little tricky, since it's on private property. Call the owner, the delightful Pearl Hodgins (808-336-0378), for permission. Park on the highway (to avoid upsetting the neighbors) or, better yet, up the road near Mana'e Goods & Grindz and walk back west (about half a mile).

The trail is on the *mauka* (inland) side of the highway, just over half a mile past mile marker 15, immediately after Mapulehu Bridge. Look for the gated dirt track into the trees and a fire hydrant.

Walk up this dirt track, pass the roundabout around a patch of trees and continue up the rocky road. Soon after, you'll see a trail on the left-hand side, opposite a house, that will take you across a streambed. Head to the steps on the northern side of the heiau.

Sleeping & Eating

Puko'o Beach Cottage COTTAGE **$$**
(808-558-8442; http://beachhousemolokai.com; off Hwy 450; cottages from $180;) This apartment above a storage area is right on one of the nicest bits of beach in east Moloka'i. You can wander along the sand past a few neighboring houses and lull yourself to sleep to the sound of the surf. Coconut palms provide shade and you can ponder Maui from the terrace.

The apartment is comfortable and has one bedroom. The owners are long-time residents and can recommend other nearby options to stay. There's a three-night minimum and it is in a large private compound just east of Mana'e Goods & Grindz.

Hilltop Cottage COTTAGE **$$**
(808-357-0139; www.molokaihilltopcottage.com; off Hwy 450, Puko'o; cottages $150-180; @) Instead of sleeping down near the water, put your head in the clouds here. The wraparound lanai is almost as big as the living space and you can savor the views of the neighbor islands by day or the millions of stars (which would be drowned out by light in cities and suburbs) by night.

There's one nicely furnished bedroom, a full kitchen, laundry facilities and a two-night minimum stay.

Wavecrest Resort CONDO **$$**
(www.wavecrestaoao.com; off Hwy 450, 'Ualapu'e; per day/week 1 bedroom from $100/600, 2 bedrooms from $150/800;) With a striking view of green mountains rising up behind and the ocean lapping gently out front, the Wavecrest Resort is just off the main road and is as low-key as its host island. There is no beach, but the views are sweeping. Each unit is rented (and decorated) by the owner. Look for it east of mile marker 12.

All units have full kitchen, sofa bed, lanai or balcony, and use of the tennis court. Only some have internet access.

★**Hale Lei Lani** RENTAL HOUSE **$$$**
(415-457-3037; www.tranquilmolokai.com; off Hwy 450, Puko'o; main house/cottage from $265/320;) Perched partway up a hill near mile marker 16 (and more importantly, Mana'e Goods & Grindz), this contemporary home has sweeping views out to Maui and beyond. Two large bedrooms open off a great room and a kitchen that will inspire you to cook on your holiday.

A walled pool is outside the door and fruit trees drop their bounty in the gardens. There is also a slightly smaller two-bedroom cottage available.

★**Mana'e Goods & Grindz** HAWAIIAN **$**
(808-558-8186; Hwy 450; meals $5-13; kitchen 6:30am-4pm daily, store 6:30am-6pm Mon-Fri, to 4pm Sat & Sun;) Even if it wasn't your only option, you'd still want to stop here. The plate lunches are something of a local legend: tender yet crispy chicken katsu (deep-fried fillets), specials such as pork stew, and standards such as excellent teriyaki burgers and fresh fish sandwiches.

Sauces are homemade, the potato salad is superb and the mac salad is simply the island's best (it's not too gloopy). Many swear by the light and crispy shrimp tempura. Picnic tables are shaded by trees and there's a little garden. The store manages to pack an amazing amount of groceries, goods and a few DVDs into a small space.

Waialua

Waialua is a little roadside community found after a few bends in Hwy 450 along the increasingly rugged coast, just past the 19-mile marker. The attractive **Waialua Congregational Church** (Hwy 450) was built of stone in 1855. Onward north from there, the road is wafer-thin, winding its way along an undulating coast that's forlorn, mysterious and fronted by white-flecked turquoise surf.

Moloka'i

Fully half of this elongated island's population claim at least some Hawaiian ancestry and that's just part of a local pride that eschews the commercialism that drives the other islands. Sacred valleys, a stunner of a national park and appealing rental beach houses are some of the unglitzy lures.

2

WALTER BIBIKOW / GETTY IMAGES ©

4

DANITA DELMONT / GETTY IMAGES ©

1. *Pali* (ocean cliffs)
Moloka'i has wild ocean, remote rainforest and the most dramatic oceanside cliffs in Hawaii.

2. Kalaupapa beach (p461)
The isolated beaches of Kalaupapa Peninsula are spectacularly beautiful.

3. Pelekunu Bay
Sea kayaking is a popular way to see the dramatic coastline.

4. St Philomena Church (Father Damien's Church; p462)
Father Damien, the Belgian priest who cared for leprosy patients on Moloka'i, was canonized in 2009.

3

DOUGLAS PEEBLES / ROBERT HARDING ©

Sights

Twenty Mile Beach BEACH
(Murphy's Beach; Hwy 450) Well protected by a reef, the curve of fine sand fronts a large lagoon that is great for snorkeling. Near shore there are rocks and the water can be very shallow, but work your way out and you'll be rewarded with schools of fish, living sponges, octopuses and much more.

Kahinapohaku Fishpond HISTORIC SITE
(Hwy 450) Ongoing restoration efforts have made this the premier fishpond on the island. Tended by *konohiki* (caretakers) who live simply on-site, here you can see ancient fishing techniques in use today. It is a half-mile east of mile marker 19.

Sleeping

Some of Moloka'i's more popular rental houses are around Waialua. All offer your own little stretch of reef-protected beach, lots of privacy and nighttime views of the resorts, shops and traffic jams of Ka'anapali (Maui) flickering across the Pailolo Channel.

★ **Dunbar Beachfront Cottages** COTTAGE $$
(808-558-8153; www.molokai-beachfront-cottages.com; Hwy 450; cottages from $200;) The layout and furnishings are tidy and functional at these two vacation cottages just east of mile marker 18. Each cottage sleeps four people and comes with a fully equipped kitchen, TV, ceiling fans, laundry, lanai and BBQ grills. The Pu'unana unit sits on stilts, while Pauwalu is more grounded. Both have good views and a three-night minimum.

Hale O Pu' Hala RENTAL HOUSE $$
(800-367-2984; www.halabeachhouse.com; Hwy 450; house $175-275;) This modern home is right on its own narrow strip of sand and offers luxurious accommodation in three bedrooms. Features include a stylish interior, lavish kitchen and limestone bathrooms. Watch in the shallows for sea turtles. There is a three-night minimum. It is just east of mile marker 19.

Moloka'i Beach House RENTAL HOUSE $$$
(808-658-0344, 888-575-9400; www.molokaibeachhouse.com; Hwy 450; house from $270;) Like most of the houses in the east, this simple wooden affair holds a few surprises. Rooms follow one after another until you realize you've got three bedrooms and a huge living/family room. It's not posh but it's very relaxed. There's cable, plus the usual DVD, BBQ etc. The grassy yard backs up to a narrow, palm-shaded beach.

Aloha Beach House RENTAL HOUSE $$$
(888-828-1008; www.molokaivacation.com; Hwy 450; house $250-290; @) This modern house built in traditional plantation style has a breezeway linking the two bedrooms. The chef-friendly kitchen flows into the living room, which flows out onto the large covered porch, which flows out onto the lawn and the beach and... There's high-speed internet and lots of beach toys. It's just east of mile marker 19.

Waialua to Halawa

The pointy clutch of rocks sticking out as the road swings left before mile marker 21 is called **Rock Point** (aka Pohakuloa Point). This popular surf spot is the site of local competitions and it's the place to go if you're looking for east-end breaks. About 500yd beyond mile marker 21 is little **Sandy Beach**. Look for a taro farm back in a verdant notch in the coast near here. Offshore, you may well spot humpback whales breaching during winter.

After mile marker 22, Hwy 450 starts to wind upwards. It's a well-paved road, albeit very narrow. Take it slow and watch for other cars coming around the cliff-hugging corners; there's always a place to pull over so cars can pass.

The terrain is rockier and less verdant here than over the preceding miles. The road levels out just before mile marker 24, where there's a view of the spiky islet of **Mokuho'oniki**, a seabird sanctuary and natural photo spot. If you hear a boom, it's a hapless gull setting off one of the shells left over from WWII target practice.

As you crest the hill, the fenced grassland is part of **Pu'u O Hoku Ranch** (888-573-7775; www.puuohoku.com; off Hwy 450; 2-bedroom cottage from $225, 4-bedroom house from $300, minimum 2-night stay;), which at 14,000 acres is Moloka'i's second-largest ranch. Founded by Paul Fagan of Hana, the name means 'where hills and stars meet.' Guests can choose from several remote cottages, houses and even an entire lodge. There is an organic farm here and you can sometimes buy refreshments from a tiny store along the main road.

A hidden grove of sacred *kukui* (candlenut trees) on the ranch property marks the grave of the prophet Lanikaula, a revered

DON'T MISS

LOCAL TREATS

Fruit trees grow in profusion in the east end of Moloka'i; if you're lucky you'll have plenty to pick from your rental. Organic farms are sprouting as well and you'll find their produce at Kaunakakai's Saturday-morning market (p449). Other local foods to look for include the following:

Macadamia nuts from Purdy's farm (p460): probably the best you'll have anywhere

Coffees of Hawaii (p458): mostly grown and roasted on the island

Macadamia nut pesto from Kumu Farms (p460): buy it at the farm shop; superb and bursting with basil goodness

Lavosh crackers from Kanemitsu Bakery (p448): the macadamia-nut and taro varieties are crunchy and delicious

Sea salt from Pacifica Hawai'i (p446)

16th-century kahuna (priest, healer). One of the reasons the battling armies of Maui and O'ahu steered clear of Moloka'i for centuries was the powerful reputations of such kahuna, who were said to have been able to pray their enemies to death.

Past mile marker 25, the jungle closes in and the scent of eucalyptus fills the air. About 1.25 miles further on, you round a corner and the awesome panorama of the Halawa Valley sweeps into view. Depending on recent rains, the Moa'ula and Hipuapua Falls will either be thin strands or gushing white torrents back up the valley.

The road descends into the valley at a steep but manageable rate, crossing stone and wood bridges. Cyclists will love the entire ride, with the exception of having to stay alert for errant drivers in rental cars mesmerized by the views.

Halawa Valley

With stunningly gorgeous scenery, Halawa Valley enjoys end-of-the-road isolation, which residents guard jealously with gates and 'no trespassing' signs. It was an important settlement in precontact Moloka'i, with a population of more than 1000 and a complex irrigation system watering more than 700 taro patches. Little remains of its three heiau sites, two of which are thought to have been *luakini*, but you'll probably still feel the charge down here.

As late as the mid-19th century, the fertile valley still had a population of about 500 and produced most of Moloka'i's taro, as well as many of its melons, gourds and fruits. However, taro production came to an abrupt end in 1946, when a massive tsunami swept up the Halawa Valley, wiping out the farms and much of the community. A second tsunami washed the valley clean in 1957. Only a few families now remain.

Sights & Activities

Sunday services are still occasionally held in Hawaiian at the saintly little 1948 green-and-white **church**, where visitors are welcome anytime (the door remains open).

Kayaking from Halawa Beach is a popular way to see the northeastern shore and the world's tallest sea cliffs along the Pali Coast, although the logistics can be intimidating.

Kalani Pruet — FARM

(www.molokaiflowers.com; 10am-4pm Sun-Fri) Pruet runs a flower farm, offers waterfall hikes and makes a mean smoothie from fruit he gathers at this lush spread of land. You can self-tour his colorful gardens or arrange in advance for a waterfall hike. Walk the dirt road in from the church, straight for about 100ft until you reach the gate. Go around the gate continuing on another 100ft; the farm will be off to the right.

★Halawa Beach Park — BEACH

Halawa Beach was a favored surfing spot for Moloka'i chiefs and remains so today for local kids, although often you won't see a soul. The beach has double coves separated by a rocky outcrop, with the north side a bit more protected than the south.

When the water is calm, there's good swimming and folks launch sea kayaks here, but both coves are subject to dangerous rip currents when the surf is heavy.

Up from the beach, Halawa Beach Park has picnic pavilions, restrooms and nondrinkable running water. Throughout the valley, there's an eerie feel that you can't quite shake, as if the generations that came before aren't sure what to make of it all. Some locals aren't entirely welcoming of visitors.

★ **Moa'ula & Hipuapua Falls** HIKING

The hike and spectacle of the 250ft, twin Moa'ula and Hipuapua Falls, which cascade down the back of the lush Halawa Valley, are a highlight of many people's Moloka'i visit. They are reached via a straightforward 2-mile trail lined with historical sites. To protect these sites, and because the trail crosses private property, visiting the falls requires a hike with a local guide.

There are numerous cultural sites along the path. You'll pass through lush tropical foliage during the walk. Look for the bright-orange blossoms of African tulip trees and the brilliant green of beach heliotrope trees. Among the sights are a **burial ground** that may date to 650 AD and a **seven-tiered stone temple**.

Walks can easily take three to five hours. Expect muddy conditions and wear stout shoes so you can navigate over river boulders. Some of the river crossings may be especially perilous. Prepare for voracious mosquitoes, bring water and lunch and have plenty of sunscreen. Most people thrill to a bracing plunge into the pools at the bottom of the falls. Avoid days when small cruise ships visit Moloka'i as day-tripping crowds can lessen the experience. Rates are usually around $40 to $75 per person, depending on how long you wish to spend in the valley.

Sources for guides include Moloka'i Fish & Dive (p440), **Halawa Valley Falls Cultural Hike** (☎808-551-1055, 808-551-5538) and Kalani Pruet (p455). Local musician and lifelong native **Eddie Tanaka** (☎808-558-8396, 808-658-0191) will customize a hike – you can spend extra time on culture and lore.

Pali Coast

The world's tallest sea *pali* (cliffs) rise from the Pacific along an awe-inspiring 14-mile stretch of the Moloka'i coast from the Kalaupapa Peninsula east almost to Halawa Beach. The average drop of these sheer cliffs is 2000ft, with some reaching 3300ft. And these intimidating walls are not monolithic; vast valleys roaring with waterfalls cleave the dark rock faces. It's Moloka'i's most dramatic sight and also the most difficult to see. (Although it served as 'Skull Island' in the second – and less impressive – *King Kong*, from 1976.)

From land you can get an idea of the drama in the valleys from the remote Waikolu Lookout (p457) and the Pelekunu Valley Overlook (p457) in the Kamakou area.

But to really appreciate the cliffs, you won't want to settle for the backsides. From the Pacific you can get a full appreciation of their height. You can organize a boat tour or really earn your adventure cred by paddling yourself here in a kayak. In summer, when conditions allow, you can leave from Halawa Beach, but this is only for expert kayakers and will require a few days plus camping on isolated stone beaches. Check with Moloka'i Outdoors (p440) for advice as it can be hard to find kayaks to rent and rental companies don't allow kayaks on the roofs of cars.

A visit to Kalaupapa Peninsula also gives you an idea of the spectacle. Or you can appreciate the drama of the cliffs from the air. Many of Maui's helicopter tours include Moloka'i's Pali Coast. Moloka'i Fish & Dive (p440) can organize flight tours.

CENTRAL MOLOKA'I

Central Moloka'i is really two places. In the west there's the dry and gently rolling Ho'olehua Plains, which stretch from the remote and rare sand dunes of Mo'omomi Beach to the former plantation town and current coffee-growing center of Kualapu'u. To the east, the terrain rises sharply to the misty, ancient forests of Kamakou. Enjoy one of the island's great adventures here by going on a hike that takes you back in evolutionary time.

Moloka'i's second most popular drive (after the Halawa Valley drive in the east) runs from Kualapu'u up Hwy 470 to Pala'au State Park, site of the Kalaupapa Overlook (p459), where you'll find one of the island's most captivating views.

Kamakou Area

The best reason to rent a 4WD vehicle on Moloka'i is to enjoy the views from the Waikolu Lookout before discovering the verdant mysteries of the Nature Conservancy's Kamakou Preserve, where you'll find the island's highest peaks. Exploring this secret side of Moloka'i is pure adventure. Besides gazing down into two deep valleys on the island's stunning and impenetrable north coast, you'll explore a near-pristine rainforest that is home to more than 250 native plants (more than 200 endemic) and some of Hawaii's rarest birds. Although you can't quite reach the island's highest point, Kamakou Peak (4961ft), you'll still get your head in the clouds.

Orientation

The turnoff for the Kamakou Area is between mile markers 3 and 4 on Hwy 460, immediately south of the Manawainui Bridge. The paved turnoff is marked with a sign for the Homelani Cemetery. The pavement quickly ends and the road deteriorates into 4WD-only conditions.

About 5.5 miles from Hwy 460 and well past the cemetery, you'll cross into the Moloka'i Forest Reserve. After a further 1.5 miles, there's an old water tank and reservoir off to the left. Another 2 miles brings you to the Sandalwood Pit, and 1 mile past that to Waikolu Lookout and the boundary of the Kamakou Preserve.

Moloka'i Forest Reserve

As you climb and enter the Moloka'i Forest Reserve, the landscape starts off shrubby and dusty but then becomes filled with dark, fragrant woods of tall eucalyptus, with patches of cypress and Norfolk pines. Don't bother heading down the roads branching off Maunahui Rd, as the scenery will be exactly the same. Although there's no evidence of it from the road, the Kalamaula area (an old name for this general area) was once heavily settled. It was here that Kamehameha the Great (Kamehameha I) knocked out his two front teeth in grieving the death of a female high chief whom he had come to visit. Local lore says that women once traveled up here to bury their afterbirth in order to ensure that their offspring reached great heights.

Sights

Sandalwood Pit HISTORIC SITE

A grassy depression on the left side of the road marks the centuries-old Sandalwood Pit (Lua Na Moku 'Iliahi). In the early 19th century, shortly after the lucrative sandalwood trade began, the pit was hand-dug to the exact measurements of a 100ft-long, 40ft-wide and 7ft-deep ship's hold, and filled with fragrant sandalwood logs cleared from the nearby forest.

The *ali'i* (royalty) forced the *maka'ainana* (commoners) to abandon their crops and work the forest. When the pit was full, the wood was strapped onto the backs of the laborers, who hauled it down to the harbor for shipment to China.

Waikolu Lookout LOOKOUT

At 3600ft, Waikolu Lookout provides a breathtaking view into the steep Waikolu Valley and out to the ocean beyond. After rains, the white strands of numerous waterfalls accent the sheer cliffs and fill the valley with a dull roar. Morning is best for clear views, but if it's foggy, have a snack at the picnic bench and see if it clears.

The wide, grassy **Waikolu Lookout campground** (☎808-567-6923; www.hawaiistateparks.org; campsites per night resident/nonresident $12/18) is directly opposite the lookout. If you can bear the mist and cold winds that sometimes blow up from the canyon, this could make a base camp for hikes into the preserve. The site has a picnic pavilion. Bring water. No open fires are allowed and state camping permits are required.

Kamakou Preserve

Since 1982, the Nature Conservancy has managed the Kamakou Preserve, which includes cloud forest, bogs, shrubland and habitat for many endangered plants and animals. Its 2774 acres of native ecosystems start immediately beyond the Waikolu Lookout and feature over 230 native plant species.

Much of the preserve is forested with *'ohi'a lehua*, a native tree with fluffy red blossoms, the nectar of which is favored by native birds. It is home to the *'apapane* (bright-red Hawaiian honeycreeper), *'amakihi* (yellow-green honeyeater) and pueo (Hawaiian owl). Other treasures include tree ferns, native orchids and silvery lilies.

Activities

Pepe'opae Trail HIKING

The hike back through three million years of evolution on the Pepe'opae Trail is the star attraction of the Kamakou area. The trail ends at the **Pelekunu Valley Overlook**, where you'll enjoy a valley view of fantastic depth and, if it's not foggy, the ocean beyond.

You'll pass the **Pepe'opae Bog**, a Hawaiian montane bog that's a miniature primeval forest of stunted trees, dwarfed plants and lichens that feels like it's from the dawn of time. This bog receives about 180in of rain each year, making it one of the wettest regions in the Hawaiian Islands.

Almost the entire 1.5-mile-long trail is along an extremely narrow uphill boardwalk that feels at times like tightrope walking. It is covered with a coarse metal grating to prevent hikers from slipping, but you should still wear shoes with a good grip. At one point a trail seems to branch off to the left but ignore this and stay on the metal mesh.

The Pepe'opae Trail is 2.2 miles from Waikolu Lookout along a very rough road that is usually passable for 4WD, although after rains it may only be accessible by foot.

Visitors should sign in and out at the preserve's entrance. Look for entries in the logbook from others on everything from car breakdowns to trail conditions and bird sightings. Posted notices announce if any part of the preserve is closed. Bring rain gear, as the trails in Kamakou can be wet and muddy.

Tours

Excellent monthly Saturday hikes with the **Nature Conservancy** (808-553-5236; www.nature.org/hawaii; donation requested; Mar-Oct) explore the preserve's history and ecology. The hikes have an eight-person maximum and tend to book up several months in advance.

Local tour guide Walter Naki (p443) leads custom hikes in the lush areas outside the preserve.

Getting There & Away

Check driving and hiking conditions with the **Nature Conservancy** (808-553-5236; www.nature.org/hawaii; 23 Pueo Pl, Moloka'i Industrial Park, Kualapu'u; 9am-3pm Mon-Fri). The office has maps and a wealth of good information.

A 4WD vehicle is obligatory and even then the narrow, rutted track with its sheer edges and tendency to turn into a bog after rains is a challenge. The 10 miles from Hwy 460 to Waikolu Lookout takes about an hour to drive. Skilled mountain bikers will enjoy the trip.

Kualapu'u

Kualapu'u is the name of both a 1017ft hill and a nearby village. In a fact that only a booster could love, the world's largest rubber-lined reservoir lies at the base of the hill. Its 1.4 billion gallons of water are piped in from the rainforests of eastern Moloka'i and it is the only source of water for the Ho'olehua Plains and the dry West End.

In the 1930s the headquarters of the Del Monte pineapple plantation were located here and a company town grew. Pineapples ruled for nearly 50 years, until Del Monte pulled out of Moloka'i in 1982 and the economy crumbled.

While farm equipment rusted in overgrown pineapple fields, small-scale farming developed: watermelons, dryland taro, macadamia nuts, sweet potatoes, seed corn, string beans and onions. The soil is so rich here, some feel Moloka'i has the potential to be Hawaii's 'breadbasket.' In 1991 coffee saplings were planted on some formerly fallow pineapple fields.

Eating & Drinking

Kualapu'u Cookhouse HAWAIIAN $$
(Kamuela Cookhouse; 808-567-9655; Hwy 490; mains $5-33, cash only; 8am-8pm Tue-Sat, 9am-2pm Sun, 8am-4pm Mon) This old roadhouse serves good lunches and is the only place for meals west of Kaunakakai. Breakfasts feature huge omelets while plate-lunch options include good pork *tonkatsu*. The dinner menu is more ambitious and includes ribs, steak and spicy crusted ahi. Beer and wine can be purchased at the grocery across the street.

Coffees of Hawaii CAFE
(808-567-6830; www.coffeesofhawaii.com; cnr Hwys 470 & 490; cafe 7am-4pm, shop 10am-4pm Mon-Sat;) Coffees of Hawaii grows and roasts its own coffee on small plots around its attractive and easily reached setting. You can survey the scene from the verandah and enjoy a cup of the local coffee and a snack or modest meal.

At 10:30am on Tuesday and Thursday, the porch is the scene for the lilting tunes of Hawaiian traditional performers. The grande-sized gift shop, Blue Monkey, has a compelling selection of locally made goods. Besides books there is an intriguing selection of ukuleles.

Shopping

Kupu A'e GIFTS, CLOTHING
(808-646-0705; cnr Hwy 460 & Hwy 470; 10am-2pm Mon-Sat) A small but exquisite shop filled with locally made goods, including lovely batik, silk-screen clothes and various original Hawaiian clothing.

Kala'e

Rudolph Wilhelm Meyer, a German immigrant who had plans to make it big in the California gold rush, stopped off in Hawaii en route (he was going the long way around) and never left. He married a member of Hawaiian royalty who had huge tracts of land on Moloka'i and busied himself growing potatoes and cattle for export, serving as overseer of the Kalaupapa settlement and as manager of King Kamehameha V's ranch lands. In 1876, when a new treaty allowed Hawaii sugar planters to export sugar duty free to the US, Meyer turned his lands over to sugar and built a mill; it operated for only a decade until falling prices rendered it unviable.

Sights & Activities

Moloka'i Museum & Cultural Center MUSEUM
(808-567-6436; Hwy 470; adult/child $5/1; 10am-2pm Mon-Sat) The RW Meyer Sugar Mill has enjoyed a series of restorations over time. It now houses a museum and cultural center, which has a small but intriguing display of Moloka'i's history with period photos, cultural relics and a 10-minute video. Features of the mill include a 100-year-old steam engine, a mule-powered cane crusher and other working artifacts. Watch for special exhibits.

Ironwood Hills Golf Course GOLF
(808-567-6000; www.molokaigolfcourse.com; off Hwy 470; greens fee $18; 8am-5:30pm) The 'pro shop' in the modest trailer tells you everything you need to know about this casual nine-hole golf course, which was originally built for plantation managers in the 1920s. Fees: gas cart ($9) and club rental ($10).

Pala'au State Park

Soak in the views over the Kalaupapa Peninsula, listen to winds rustle through groves of ironwood and eucalyptus trees and witness sacred rocks that represent human genitals. This misty state park is at the end of Hwy 470, near the Kalaupapa trailhead. It's good for a picnic, some photos and possibly to increase your chances of falling pregnant.

Sights & Activities

★ Kalaupapa Overlook LOOKOUT
The Kalaupapa Overlook provides a scenic overview of the Kalaupapa Peninsula from the edge of a 1600ft cliff.

It's easy to get the lay of the land from up here and you'll get a good feel for just how far you'll travel if you descend the nearly 1700ft on the trail. Interpretive plaques identify significant landmarks below and explain Kalaupapa's history.

The village where all of Kalaupapa's residents live is visible, but Kalawao, the original settlement and site of Father Damien's church and grave, is not. Kalaupapa means 'flat leaf,' an accurate description of the lava-slab peninsula that was created when a low shield volcano poked up out of the sea, long after the rest of Moloka'i had been formed.

The dormant Kauhako Crater, visible from the overlook, contains a little lake that's more than 800ft deep. At 400ft, the crater is the highest point on the Kalaupapa Peninsula. The best light for photography is usually from late morning to mid-afternoon.

There's a vague trail of sorts that continues directly beyond the last plaque at the overlook. The path, on a carpet of soft ironwood needles, passes through diagonal rows of trees planted during a Civil Conservation Corps (CCC) reforestation project in the 1930s. Simply follow this trail for 20 minutes or so until it peters out.

Kauleonanahoa CULTURAL SITE
Kauleonanahoa (the penis of Nanahoa) is Hawaii's premier phallic stone, standing proud in a little clearing inside an ironwood grove, about a five-minute walk from the parking area. The legend goes that Nanahoa hit his wife Kawahuna in a jealous rage and when they were both turned to stone, he came out looking like a dick, literally. (The stone has been modified through the years to emphasize its appearance.)

Reputedly, women who come here with offerings of lei and stay overnight will soon get pregnant. There's no mention of what happens to men who might try the same thing with some nearby stones that have been carved into a female counterpart to the main rock.

Sleeping

Pala'au Campground CAMPGROUND $
(☎808-567-6923; www.hawaiistateparks.org; off Hwy 470; campsites per night resident/nonresident $12/18) Camping is allowed in a peaceful grassy field a quarter of a mile before the Pala'au overlook. There's a picnic pavilion and a portable toilet here (although there are good bathrooms near the main parking area). It rains a lot here and outside of the summer dry season, your tent will likely be drenched by evening showers.

Ho'olehua

Ho'olehua is the dry plains area that separates eastern and western Moloka'i. Here, in the 1790s, Kamehameha the Great trained his warriors in a yearlong preparation for the invasion of O'ahu.

Ho'olehua was settled as an agricultural community in 1924, although the locals were soon usurped by the pineapple giants Dole, Del Monte and Libby. Most were forced to lease their lands to the plantations.

Today the plantations are gone, but locals continue to plant small crops of fruits, vegetables and herbs. And Hawaiians continue to receive land deeds in Ho'olehua in accordance with the Hawaiian Homes Commission Act.

Sights

★Purdy's Macadamia Nut Farm FARM
(www.molokai-aloha.com/macnuts; Lihi Pali Ave; ⌚9:30am-3:30pm Tue-Fri, 10am-2pm Sat) FREE The tour here lets you take your pick of macadamia nuts as Tuddie Purdy takes you into his 80-year-old orchard and personally explains how the nuts grow without pesticides, herbicides or fertilizers.

Everything is done in quaint Moloka'i style: you can crack open macadamia nuts on a stone with a hammer and sample macadamia-blossom honey scooped up with slices of fresh coconut. Nuts (superb!) and honey are for sale. Linger and Purdy will go into full raconteur mode.

The farm is 528yd off Hwy 490.

Shopping

Kumu Farms FOOD
(☎808-351-3326; www.kumufarms.com; off Hwy 460; ⌚9am-4pm Tue-Fri) Part of a burgeoning organic farming scene on Moloka'i (in contrast to the GM fields of Monsanto), Kumu Farms grows bananas, papayas, herbs, tomatoes, lettuce and much more. At its attractive store you can enjoy various fresh treats at picnic tables and buy produce for your condo or vacation house. The pesto is extraordinary.

The farm store is southwest of the airport; look for the signs off Hwy 460.

Mo'omomi Beach

One of the few undisturbed, coastal sand-dune areas left in Hawaii is found on remote Mo'omomi Beach. Among its native grasses and shrubs are at least four endangered plant species that exist nowhere else on earth, including a relative of the sunflower. It is one of the few places in the populated islands where green sea turtles still breed. It also has over 1000 nests for the wedge-tailed

DON'T MISS

POST-A-NUT

Why settle for a mundane postcard or, worse, an emailed photo of you looking like a tan-lined git, when it comes to taunting folks in the cold climes you've left behind? Instead, send a coconut. Gary Lam, the world-class postmaster of the **Ho'olehua post office** (Pu'u Peelua Ave; ⌚8.30am-4pm Mon-Fri), has baskets of them for free. Choose from the oodles of markers and write the address right on the husk. Add a cartoon or two. Imagine the joy when a loved one waits in a long line for a parcel and is handed a coconut! Depending on the size of your nut, postage costs $11 to $20 and takes three to six days to reach any place in the US; other countries cost more and take longer – and you may run into quarantine issues.

If Lam, who takes the time to apply a panopoly of colored stamps to each coconut, was in charge of the postal service, its current financial woes would likely vanish. Should you want your nut made especially ornate, Teri Waros of Kalele Bookstore (p449) does custom paint jobs.

shearwater, which spend most of their life at sea searching for tuna.

Managed by Hawaiian elders as well as the Nature Conservancy, Moʻomomi is not lushly beautiful, but windswept, lonely and wild. From Hoʻolehua, follow Farrington Ave west, past the intersection with Hwy 480, until the paved road ends at what is often a richly red mud swamp. When passable (4WD only), it's 2.2 miles further along a dirt road that is in some areas quite smooth and in others deeply rutted.

The rocky eastern point, which protects Moʻomomi Bay, provides a fishing perch and further along the bluffs a sacred ceremony might be underway. There are toilets but no drinking water.

There is a broad, white-sand beach (often mistakenly called Moʻomomi) at Kawaʻaloa Bay, a 20-minute walk further west. The wind, which picks up steadily each afternoon, blows the dune sand into interesting ripples and waves. Swimming is dangerous.

The high hills running inland are actually massive sand dunes. The coastal cliffs, which have been sculpted into jagged abstract designs by wind and water, are made of sand that has petrified due to Moʻomomi's dry conditions.

Because of the fragile ecology of the dunes, visitors should stay along the beach and on trails only.

Tours

Nature Conservancy HIKING
(808-553-5236; www.nature.org/hawaii; donation requested; Mar-Oct) Nature Conservancy leads excellent monthly guided hikes of Moʻomomi. Transportation is provided to and from Moʻomomi. Reservations are required and spots fill up fast, up to six months advance.

KALAUPAPA NATIONAL HISTORICAL PARK

The spectacularly beautiful **Kalaupapa Peninsula** is the most remote part of Hawaii's most isolated island. The only way to reach this lush green peninsula edged with long, white-sand beaches is on a twisting trail down the steep *pali,* the world's highest sea cliffs, or by plane. This remoteness is the reason it was, for more than a century, where Hansen's disease patients were forced into isolation. From its inception until separation ended in 1969, 8000 patients were forced to come to Kalaupapa. Less than a dozen patients (respectively called 'residents') remain. They have chosen to stay in the only home they have ever known and have resisted efforts to move them away. The peninsula has been designated a national historical park and is managed by the Hawaii Department of Health and the **National Park Service** (www.nps.gov/kala).

While the state of Hawaii officially uses the term 'Hansen's disease' for leprosy, many Kalaupapa residents consider that to be a euphemism that fails to reflect the stigma they have suffered, and continue to use the old term 'leprosy.' The degrading appellation 'leper,' however, is offensive to all. 'Resident' is preferred.

State laws dating back to when the settlement was a quarantine zone require everyone who enters the settlement to have a 'permit.' The law is no longer necessary for health reasons but is enforced in order to protect the privacy of the residents. For this reason, all visitors must have a guide. Permits are issued by the tour operators. Because the exiled patients were not allowed to keep children if they had them, the residents made a rule that no one under the age of 16 is allowed in the settlement – this is strictly enforced, as are the permit requirements. Only guests of Kalaupapa residents are allowed to stay overnight.

The guided tour is Molokaʻi's most well-known attraction but, interesting as it is, the tour itself is not the highlight: this is one case where getting there truly is half the fun. Riding a mule or hiking down the steep trail, winding through lush green tropical forest, catching glimpses of the sea far below, is unforgettable.

History

Ancient Hawaiians used Kalaupapa as a refuge when caught in storms at sea. The peninsula held a large settlement at the time of early Western contact and the area is rich in archaeological sites. A discovery in 2004 indicated that Kalaupapa heiau may have ritual significance and possible astronomical purposes.

In 1835 doctors in Hawaii diagnosed the state's first case of leprosy, one of many diseases introduced by foreigners. Before modern medicine, leprosy manifested itself in horrible sores. Eventually patients experienced loss of sensation and tissue degeneration that could lead to small extremities becoming deformed. Blindness was common. Alarmed by the spread of the disease, King Kamehameha V signed a law that banished people with Hansen's disease to Kalaupapa Peninsula, beginning in 1866.

Hawaiian names for leprosy include *mai pake* (Chinese sickness) and *mai hoʻokaʻawale*, which means 'separating sickness,' a reference to how the disease tore families apart. All patients arrived at the peninsula in boats. There's no evidence that disease-fearing captains threw patients overboard to swim to land.

Once the afflicted arrived on Kalaupapa Peninsula, there was no way out, not even in a casket. The original settlement was in Kalawao, at the wetter eastern end of the peninsula. Early conditions were unspeakably horrible, with the strong stealing rations from the weak, and women forced into prostitution. Life spans were invariably short and desperate.

Father Damien arrived at Kalaupapa in 1873. He wasn't the first missionary to come, but he was the first to stay. What Damien provided, most of all, was a sense of hope and inspiration to others. Army vet Joseph Dutton arrived in 1886 and stayed 44 years. In addition to his work with the sick (he was often called 'Brother Joseph', although he never took vows), he was a prolific writer who kept the outside world informed about what was happening in Molokaʻi. Sister Marianne Cope arrived a year before Damien died. She stayed 30 years, helping to establish a girls' home and encouraging patients to live life to the fullest.

The same year that Father Damien arrived, a Norwegian scientist named Dr Gerhard Hansen discovered *Mycobacterium leprae*, the bacteria that causes leprosy, thus proving that the disease was not hereditary, as was previously thought. Indeed, Hansen's disease is one of the least contagious of all communicable diseases: only 4% of human beings are even susceptible to it.

In 1909 the US Leprosy Investigation Station opened at Kalawao. However, the fancy hospital was out of touch – requiring patients to live in seclusion for two years etc – so it attracted only a handful of patients and soon closed.

Since 1946 sulfa antibiotics have successfully treated and controlled leprosy, but the isolation policies in Kalaupapa weren't abandoned until 1969, when there were 300 patients here. The last arrived in 1965 and today the few remaining residents are all in their late 70s or older.

Sights & Activities

At the bottom of the park's near-vertical *pali* is a deserted **beach** with stunning views of the steep cliffs you've just descended. Mule riders and hikers should proceed past a parking area and wait at a row of benches near the mule stable for the mandatory bus tour.

The settlement is very quiet, and residents tend to stay indoors while the tour is going on. With their history of being persecuted and stigmatized, you can't blame them for avoiding curious tourists, but residents encourage visitation because it helps prevent their story from being forgotten. Restoration of village buildings is ongoing and the homes that have been restored are small and tidy, with covered lanai and clapboard siding. Other sights are mainly cemeteries, churches and memorials. Buy drinks and snacks at a small resident-run shop. There is a small museum and bookstore.

On the way to the east side of the peninsula is **St Philomena Church** (better known as Father Damien's Church), in **Kalawao**, which was built in 1872. The graveyard at the side contains Damien's gravestone and original burial site, although his body was exhumed in 1936 and returned to Belgium. In 1995 his right hand was reinterred here.

The tour pauses for lunch at Kalawao after a short drive through lush greenery dotted with colorful lantana plants. On the way, keep your eyes open for a heiau just past the water tanks; the remains of the ancient temple are on the same side as the wells.

The amazing view from Kalawao gives you a glimpse of Molokaʻi's dramatic Pali Coast.

Tours

★Molokai Mule Ride TOUR

(808-567-6088; www.muleride.com; Hwy 470; tour $200; Mon-Sat) A mule ride is the only way down the *pali* besides hiking, but be prepared – this is not an easy ride. You'll be sore afterwards, even if you're an experienced rider, and it's a safe bet that you've never experienced a ride like this one.

At some points the trail is only 2ft wide, nearly vertical in places, and yet the mules carefully pick their way down. The muleteers and sure-footed animals are very skilled, so settle back and enjoy a natural thrill ride.

MOLOKA'I'S SAINTS

Moloka'i was a key locale for two of the US' first saints in the Roman Catholic Church.

On October 11, 2009, Moloka'i (and the US) got its first saint. The story of Joseph de Veuster (better known as **Father Damien**), the Belgian priest who sacrificed everything to care for leprosy patients, has been the subject of many books and TV movies, few of which rise above the treacly clichés inherent in such a story. And yet Father Damien's story, once learned, makes the honor of sainthood seem like the bare minimum he deserves.

In 1873 the strong-willed priest traveled, at age 33, to the Kalaupapa Peninsula, the leprosy settlement he'd heard called 'the living tomb.' Once on this remote place of exile he found scores of people who'd been dumped ashore by a government not quite cruel enough to simply drown them at sea. Soon he had the residents helping him construct more than 300 houses, plant trees and much more. He taught himself medicine and gave his flock the care they desperately needed.

Father Damien contracted Hansen's disease in 1885, 12 years after he arrived, and died four years later at age 49, the only outsider ever to contract leprosy on Kalaupapa.

Meanwhile, in Syracuse, NY, **Sister Marianne Cope** was running a public hospital. In 1883 at age 45 she accepted a plea to treat leprosy patients in Hawaii after 50 other institutions had said no. After establishing hospitals in O'ahu and Maui, she moved to Kalaupapa in 1888 to care for Father Damien and the other patients. She remained here until her death from natural causes in 1918. She is widely considered to be the inspiration of the hospice movement.

Excitement over Moloka'i's saints is widespread locally. May 10, the feast day of Father Damien (formally known as Saint Damien of Moloka'i) is celebrated. Cope, whose feast day is January 23, was canonized in 2012 as Saint Marianne of Moloka'i.

You'll need to be quick with the camera if you want to get shots of the stunning views, because the mules don't stop for photo ops. (Hiking down would offer better chances for good pictures.) It takes about 45 minutes going down and one hour going up. Remember your mule's name so that the guides will put you back on the right one for the trip up! Tours include a short riding lesson from real *paniolo* (Hawaiian cowboys), the Damien Tours bus tour and lunch. Advance reservations for these popular rides are essential. Round-trip airport transfers are $32 per person (two-person minimum).

★Damien Tours BUS TOUR

(☎808-567-6171; tour $60; ⊙Mon-Sat) Everyone who comes to the Kalapaupa Peninsula is required to visit the settlement with this tour. If you didn't book through Molokai Mule Ride, reservations must be made in advance (call between 4pm and 8pm). Tours last 3½ hours, are done by bus and are accompanied by lots of stories about life in years past. If you're not on the mule ride or other packaged tour, bring your own lunch and a bottle of water. You must be 16 or over.

Getting There & Around

The trail from Pala'au down the *pali* is the only land route to the peninsula and can be taken either on foot or by the mule rides. It is possible to walk down and fly back up or you can fly to and from Kalaupapa.

AIR

The beauty of flying in on a small prop plane is the aerial view of the *pali* and towering waterfalls. Passengers need to first book a tour with Damien Tours before buying air tickets (unless your package includes this); otherwise you will be stuck at the landing strip if the day's tour is full.

If your flight gets you to the Kalaupapa landing strip before the 10am Damien Tours pickup, you'll have nothing to do but stand around admiring the view of the surf. If you are coming from another island, you may need to fly to Moloka'i the night before. Return trips 'topside,' as they say locally, to Ho'olehua are more convenient and usually allow for easy connections to Honolulu and Maui.

Makani Kai Air (☎877-255-8532, 808-834-1111; www.makanikaiair.com; round-trip tour package from Moloka'i/Honolulu $249/315) Runs regular flights from Ho'olehua on Moloka'i and Honolulu which are timed to allow for visits in a day. Packages include your place on Damien Tours. A package where you walk down, take the tour and fly back up topside is $149.

HOLY WATER

It's hot walking down the Kalaupapa trail, but it's far hotter walking back up. Instead of lugging a lot of water both ways, or even just bringing it back up with you, take extra containers and stash them behind rocks at the numbered switchbacks on your way down. Remember the numbers and retrieve your water on the way back up.

LAND

The Kalaupapa trailhead is on the east side of Hwy 470, just north of the mule stables, and marked by the Pala'au park sign and parked Kalaupapa employee cars. The very challenging 3.5-mile trail has 26 switchbacks, 1400 steps and drops 1664ft in elevation from start to finish.

It's best to begin hiking by 8am, before the mules start to go down, to avoid walking in fresh dung, though you have no choice on the return trip. Allow an hour and a half to descend comfortably. It can be quite an adventure after a lot of rain, though the rocks keep it from getting impossibly muddy. Many find walking sticks a help.

You can also hike down and fly back up.

WEST END

Seemingly deserted and just a couple of missed rainfalls from becoming a desert, Moloka'i's West End occupies a surprisingly significant place in Hawaii's history and culture. Pu'u Nana is the site of Hawaii's first-established hula school and the Maunaloa Range was once a center of sorcery. In recent decades much of the land has been controlled by the Moloka'i Ranch, and its fortunes – for better and more recently for much worse – have affected the entire island. Hale O Lono Harbor is the launching site for long-distance outrigger-canoe races, and the island's longest beach, Papohaku, dominates the west coast.

Given the economic woes of Moloka'i Ranch the atmosphere out west is a bit bleak. With the exception of one superlative store, Maunaloa might as well hold tumbleweed races, while the Kaluakoi Resort area is beset by financial troubles. Still, you can ignore all the earthly turmoil on one of the many fine beaches.

History

During the 1850s Kamehameha V acquired the bulk of Moloka'i's arable land and formed Moloka'i Ranch. Overgrazing eventually led to the widespread destruction of native vegetation and fishponds. Following his death, the ranch became part of the Bishop Estate (a huge estate created in 1884 by the will of Bernice Pauahi Bishop, the great-granddaughter of King Kamehameha the Great), which quickly sold it off to a group of Honolulu businesspeople in 1897.

An ambitious effort to grow sugarcane failed when supplies of fresh ground water were exhausted. Moloka'i Ranch then moved into honey production on such a large scale that at one point Moloka'i was the world's largest honey exporter, but in the mid-1930s an epidemic wiped out the hives and the industry. Strike two for the industrialists.

Meanwhile, efforts continued to find the crop for Moloka'i. Cotton, rice and numerous grain crops all took their turn biting Moloka'i's red dust. Finally pineapple took root as the crop most suited to the island's dry, windy conditions. Plantation-scale production began in Ho'olehua in 1920. Within 10 years Moloka'i's population tripled, as immigrants arrived to toil in the fields.

Citing overseas competition, Dole closed its operation in 1976; the other island giant, Del Monte, later followed suit. These closures brought hard times. Cattle raising, long a mainstay industry, was the next to collapse after an incidence of bovine tuberculosis. Moloka'i Ranch still owns some 64,000 acres – about 40% of the island – and more than half of the island's privately held lands. What will happen to these mostly disused lands is a perennial question.

Maunaloa

POP 180

In the 1990s the Moloka'i Ranch bulldozed the atmospheric old plantation town of Maunaloa, leveling all but a few buildings. New buildings mimicking old, plantation-style homes were erected, with the goal of creating a tourist attraction. This drove up rents and forced out some small businesses, provoking the ire of island residents.

Ironically, the new development is now all but closed: the hotel, the luxury beach campsite, the cinema and even the fast-food outlet are all shuttered.

Attractions are few, unless you're an urban planner doing research. However, there is one excellent reason to visit the quiet streets, one that will literally blow you away.

Shopping

★Big Wind Kite Factory & Plantation Gallery ARTS, CRAFTS
(☎808-552-2364; www.bigwindkites.com; 120 Maunaloa Hwy; ⏰8:30am-5pm Mon-Sat, 10am-2pm Sun) Big Wind custom-makes kites for high fliers of all ages. It has hundreds ready to go in stock or you can choose a design and watch production begin. Lessons are available, lest you have a Charlie Brown experience with a kite-eating tree.

There is a range of other goods to browse as well, including an excellent selection of Hawaii-themed books and artworks, clothing and crafts originating from everywhere, from just down the road to far-off Bali.

Maunaloa General Store MARKET
(Maunaloa Hwy; ⏰8am-6pm Mon-Sat) The Maunaloa General Store provides the village with basics. It has a limited selection of pricey groceries and alcohol.

RESISTING OUTSIDERS

Moloka'i has a long and tortured history with outside interests, even when they provide vital jobs.

Even before Moloka'i Ranch began efforts to develop its lands on the West End in the 1970s, local people weren't fond of the company. They resented the ranch for restricting access to land, which in turn restricted a number of traditional outdoor activities and visitation to sacred cultural and historical sites.

By 1975 tensions had mounted and people took to the streets, marching from Mo'omomi Beach to Kawakiu Beach to demand access to private, and heretofore forbidden, beaches on the West End. The protest was successful and convinced Moloka'i Ranch to provide public access to Kawakiu.

Beginning in 2001, the current owner of Moloka'i Ranch, the Singapore-based Moloka'i Properties, began a campaign to revitalize the holdings. It promoted plans to transfer the title to cultural sites and recreational areas amounting to 26,000 acres to a newly created Moloka'i Land Trust, essentially turning it into public land. It would also have given up the right to develop another 24,000 acres of its own lands.

But there was one small detail...what Moloka'i Properties wanted in return: the right to develop pristine La'au Point into a luxury enclave. Most locals opposed this and signs saying 'Save La'au Point' sprouted island-wide (and can still be seen). The plans were scuttled despite the promise of hundreds of resort and service jobs.

In 2008 the company essentially took its toys and went home. It pulled the plug on all its operations, laid off dozens, closed its hotel and golf course and furthered the ghost-town feel of Maunaloa and the Kaluakoi Resort area.

Since then, schemes to erect enormous power-generating windmills west of Maunaloa have run afoul of Moloka'i's fractious politics and strong preservation beliefs, while visits by small cruise ships to the island have drawn protests.

Rather surprisingly, however, a large segment of locals have supported Monsanto, which has experimental farms on the island where new lines of GMO seeds are developed (look for the fields of corn growing around central Moloka'i.).

Employing about 200 locals in full- and part-time plus seasonal jobs, Monsanto had kept a low profile on the island until 2014, when Maui County, of which Moloka'i is a part, held a referendum placing a moratorium on GMO crops. Monsanto and other GMO seed producers such as Dow Chemical spent almost $8 million to defeat the measure. However, they lost and the measure passed, leaving the future of Monsanto's operations in doubt pending the inevitable legal challenges.

Interestingly, a majority of voters on Moloka'i voted in support of Monsanto but were easily outnumbered by the votes against on Maui. While Monsanto is an outside interest, locals have also chafed under county rule by its wealthy island neighbor.

Kaluakoi Resort Area

You can almost picture this place when times were good: a low-key resort fronted a perfect crescent of sand while upscale condos lined the fairways of an emerald-green championship golf course.

Well, that was then (the 1980s) and the now is rather bleak. The resort was closed years ago and is in a state of advanced decay. The golf course died when Moloka'i Ranch pulled the plug in 2008. The fairways are now a sort of post-apocalyptic-desert spectacle. Meanwhile, the condo complexes do their best to put a good face on the situation as the individual owners try to play up the quiet aspects of the complex in their efforts to market their vacation rentals. Surrounding house lots have sold very slowly, although a few large mansions lurk behind walls along the beaches.

As with the rest of the west, you're best off bringing a picnic from Kaunakakai and enjoying the beautiful beaches. Everything is accessed from the paved Kalua Koi Rd that branches off Hwy 460 at mile marker 15 and curves its way down to the shore.

Beaches

★Kawakiu Beach BEACH

Kaluakoi's northernmost beach is also the best. Kawakiu Beach is a broad crescent beach of white sand and bright-turquoise waters. It's partially sheltered from the winds that can bedevil the beaches to the south, and when seas are calm, usually in summer, Kawakiu is generally safe for swimming.

When the surf is rough, there are still areas where you can at least get wet. On the southern side of the bay, there's a small, sandy-bottomed wading pool in the rocks; the northern side has an area of flat rocks over which water slides to fill up a shallow shoreline pool. Spindly kiawe trees provide shade. Outside of weekends, you may well have the place to yourself.

To get there, turn off Kaluakoi Rd onto the road to the Paniolo Hale condos, but instead of turning left to the condos, continue straight toward the former golf course. Where the paved road ends there's space to pull over and park. You'll come first to a rocky point at the southern end of the bay. Before descending to the beach, scramble around up here for a scenic view of the coast, south to Papohaku Beach and north to 'Ilio Point.

★Kepuhi Beach BEACH

You can see why they built the defunct Kaluakoi Hotel here: the beach is a rocky, white-sand dream. However, swimming here can be a nightmare. Not only can there be a tough shorebreak, but strong currents can be present even on calm days.

During winter, the surf breaks close to shore, crashing in sand-filled waves that can be a brutal exfoliant.

A five-minute hike up to the top of **Pu'u o Kaiaka**, a 110ft-high promontory at the southern end of the beach, is rewarded with a nice view of Papohaku Beach. At the top you'll find the remains of a pulley that was once used to carry cattle down to waiting barges for transport to O'ahu slaughterhouses. There was also a 40ft heiau on the hilltop until 1967, when the US army bulldozed it (and gave the superstitious another reason to ponder the local run of bad luck). There's plenty of parking in the resort's cracked parking lots.

Make Horse Beach BEACH

Make Horse Beach supposedly takes its name from days past when wild horses were run off the tall, dark cliff on its northern end; *make* (*mah*-kay) means 'dead.' This pretty, tiny white-sand cove is a local favorite and more secluded than Kepuhi further to the south.

It's a sublime spot for sunbathing and sunset, but usually not for swimming as the currents are fierce. On the calmest days, daredevils leap off the giant rock ledge at the beach's southern end.

To get here, turn off Kaluakoi Rd onto the road to the Paniolo Hale condos and then turn left toward the condo complex. You can park just beyond the condos and walk, or follow the dirt road heading off to the right for a quarter of a mile to a parking area. From there, follow the trail to the beach. In some of the distant reaches clothing has been deemed optional.

Sleeping & Eating

Units in the condominium complexes are rented either directly from the owners or through various agents. All units are decorated by the owners; facilities such as internet access vary. You'll need to shop in Kaunakakai, 20 miles distant, for all but a few convenience items that you can get up the hill at the Maunaloa General Store (p465) or in a small market in the closed resort. The closest restaurant is the Kualapu'u Cookhouse (p458), 15 miles east in Kualapu'u.

Although the two condo complexes listed here are maintaining their properties well, we need to again note that much of the rest of the area has a run-down and eerie feel. We can't recommend the Kaluakoi Resort, which has rental units in one wing of the failed resort: for one, its cooking facilities are meager and there's nowhere locally to eat.

Paniolo Hale CONDO $$
(www.paniolohale.org; Lio Pl; studios from $100, 1/2 bedrooms from $150/180;) Separated from the environs of the derelict resort by the arid expanse of the former golf course, this is an attractive option. Large trees shade this plantation-style complex, giving it a hidden, secluded air. Each unit has a long, screened-in lanai overlooking the quiet grounds; as always with condos, shop around to get one that's been recently renovated. It's a short walk to Make Horse Beach.

Ke Nani Kai CONDO $$
(858-679-2016; www.kenanikai.com; Kepuhi Pl; 1/2 bedrooms from $140/150;) This tidy operation should set an example to the rest of the complex. The 100-plus units are large and well maintained (though your interior-decor mileage may vary depending on the owner). The pool is big. Note that the ocean is not right outside, so the premium for 'ocean view' units is debatable.

Kepuhi and Papohaku Beaches are short walks away and you may have company from the local flock of wild turkeys. Weekly rates are often heavily discounted.

West End Beaches

Windy, isolated and often untrodden, the West End beaches define moody and atmospheric. Together with the beaches in the Kaluakoi Resort area, they can easily occupy a day or more of beachcombing and beach-hopping.

From this stretch of coast the hazy outline of O'ahu is just 26 miles away. Diamond Head is on the left, Makapu'u Point on the right. You can, reportedly, see the famous 'green flash' (the green color results from atmospheric refraction of the setting or rising sun) during sunset here. Also worth spotting are the green sea turtles that sometimes pass by.

During the calmer summer months the West End beaches are easily accessible, magical spots for snorkeling, with clear, flat waters.

To get to the West End beaches, take the turnoff for the Kaluakoi Resort Area at mile marker 15 and follow Kalua Koi Rd south.

Beaches

★Papohaku Beach BEACH
(off Kalua Koi Rd) Straight as a palm tree, the light-hued sands of Papohaku Beach run for an astounding 2.5 miles. The sand is soft and you can often stroll from one end to another without seeing another soul. Offshore, Third Hole is one of the island's most challenging surf breaks.

But just when you think you may have found the ultimate strand, consider a few leveling details. That intoxicating surf is

MOLOKA'I SURF BEACHES & BREAKS

What Moloka'i – one of the most breathtaking islands in Hawaii, if not the entire Pacific – possesses in beauty, it lacks in waves. Unfortunately, due to shadowing from the other islands, there just isn't much in the way of consistent surf. Yet when the surf's up, keep in mind that the Friendly Isle encompasses the ideals of 'old Hawaii' in which family remains the priority, so remember to smile a lot and let the locals have the set waves.

On the western end of Moloka'i, winter swells bring surf anywhere between 2ft and 10ft (and, very rarely, 15ft). The most exciting break on the island is **Third Hole**, just off Papohaku Beach at the West End. It's for advanced surfers only; in winter waves average 6ft to 8ft. Just north, Kawakiu Beach's winter waves are also best left to experts.

When it's breaking, the stretch from **Rock Point** to Halawa Beach (p455) on the east end and Kepuhi Beach on the West End are reliable spots and are more accessible to all skill levels. Stand-up paddlers enjoy the usually calm waters around the Kaunakakai Wharf.

Beach Break Moloka'i (p440) rents surfboards and other water-sports and beach gear. It's a good place for advice as well.

also a tangle of undertow and unpredictable currents. And there's no easy shade. You can bring an umbrella, but the often-strong winds may send it O'ahu-bound. Those same breezes kick up the fine sand, which can sting on blustery days. So come here for the solitude, but do so with your eyes figuratively, if not literally, wide open.

There are seven turnoffs from Kalua Koi Rd that access the beach and have parking. The first leads to **Papohaku Beach Park**, a grassy place with picnic facilities under gnarled ironwood and kiawe trees. Bathroom and shower facilities are rugged. You can camp (p443) here to the left of the restrooms as you face them from the parking lot, the 'no camping' sign only applies to the area to the right (be sure to read the signs that explain which areas are soaked by the automatic sprinklers on which days). See p443 for camping permit details. There are seldom any other campers here and the view of the stars at night and the sound of surf is mesmerizing. However, the park can be popular with rowdy folks young and old and occasionally some try to stay the night. Guards are meant to check permits but you may be happier here if you are not alone.

Dixie Maru Beach BEACH

(off Pohakuloa Rd) South of the long stretch of Papohaku Beach, there are small sandy coves surrounded by rocky outcrops. At the southern end of Pohakuloa Rd there's a parking lot with access to a narrow, round inlet, which the ancient Hawaiians knew as Kapukahehu.

It is now called Dixie Maru, after a ship that went down in the area long ago. It's the most protected cove on the west shore, and the most popular swimming and snorkeling area. The waters are generally calmer here than other West End beaches.

If you're up for just finding your way as you go, it's possible to hike south 3 miles along the coast to La'au Point and see what all the fuss was about. You'll pass a failed luxury camping resort and several utterly untouched beaches. So secluded is this area that the notoriously shy Hawaiian monk seals are often found enjoying the solitude.

Kaua'i

Includes ➡

Best Places to Eat

- ➡ Josselin's Tapas Bar & Grill (p547)
- ➡ Koloa Fish Market (p536)
- ➡ Kaua'i Community Market (p481)
- ➡ Tiki Tacos (p495)
- ➡ Hanalei Taro & Juice Co (p524)

Best Beaches

- ➡ Hanalei Bay (p517)
- ➡ Maha'ulepu Beach (p539)
- ➡ Kauapea (Secrets) Beach (p505)
- ➡ Kealia Beach (p502)
- ➡ Salt Pond Beach Park (p556)

Why Go?

On Kaua'i, the mana (spiritual essence) of the *'aina* (land) is palpable, and will hit you when you least expect it. It could descend as you round a corner and are gobsmacked by a velvety emerald mountain range. Or while navigating one of the island's spectacular trails into a lush interior kissed with endless rainbows and waterfalls. Or maybe when paddling down a sinuous red river.

For many visitors, bliss comes after diving, swimming, paddling or riding world-class waves in bays that are deep blue and life-affirming – where you can watch sea turtles, wild dolphins and whales, and contemplate endless Pacific horizons. On Kaua'i, your heart and mind cannot help but open wide. Even a short island-hop here could become an extended stay, which on the flight home may have you debating immediate relocation – that is, if you go home at all.

When to Go

Lihu'e

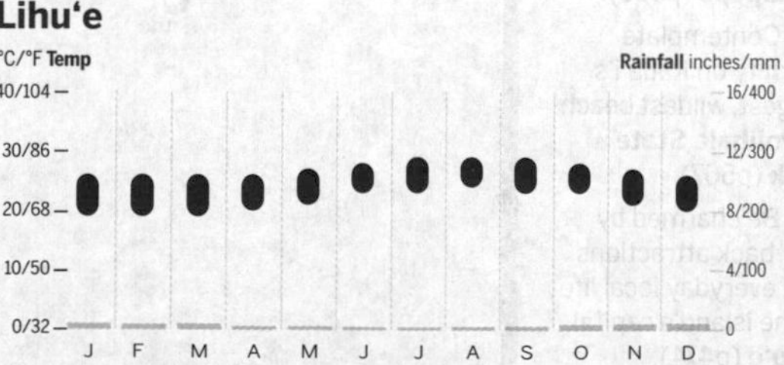

Jun–Sep Sunshine abounds, the ocean is calmer and days longer, with sunsets like splatters of paint.

Dec–Mar Whale-watching, sudden rainstorms and rainbows. Don't leave car windows down!

Apr–May Smallest crowds and best deals, and many festivals too.

Kaua‘i Highlights

❶ Take a sunset sail or test your strength by hiking or kayaking the **Na Pali Coast** (p531).

❷ Take in the grand vistas from roadside lookouts and wilderness trails in **Waimea Canyon** (p568).

❸ Paddle upstream to hidden jungle waterfalls in the sacred **Wailua River Valley** (p490).

❹ Laze on the beach or learn the ancient Hawaiian sport of surfing in idyllic **Hanalei Bay** (p517).

❺ Lace up your hiking boots for panoramic views or a journey into the otherworldly Alaka‘i Swamp at **Koke‘e State Park** (p570).

❻ Take the plunge and snorkel the South Shore around sunny **Po‘ipu** (p534).

❼ Go gallery-hopping, shopping and street-food-snacking on ‘Art Night’ in quirky **Hanapepe** (p556).

❽ Contemplate eternity on Kaua‘i’s biggest, wildest beach at **Polihale State Park** (p567).

❾ Be charmed by laid-back attractions and everyday local life in the island’s capital, **Lihu‘e** (p474).

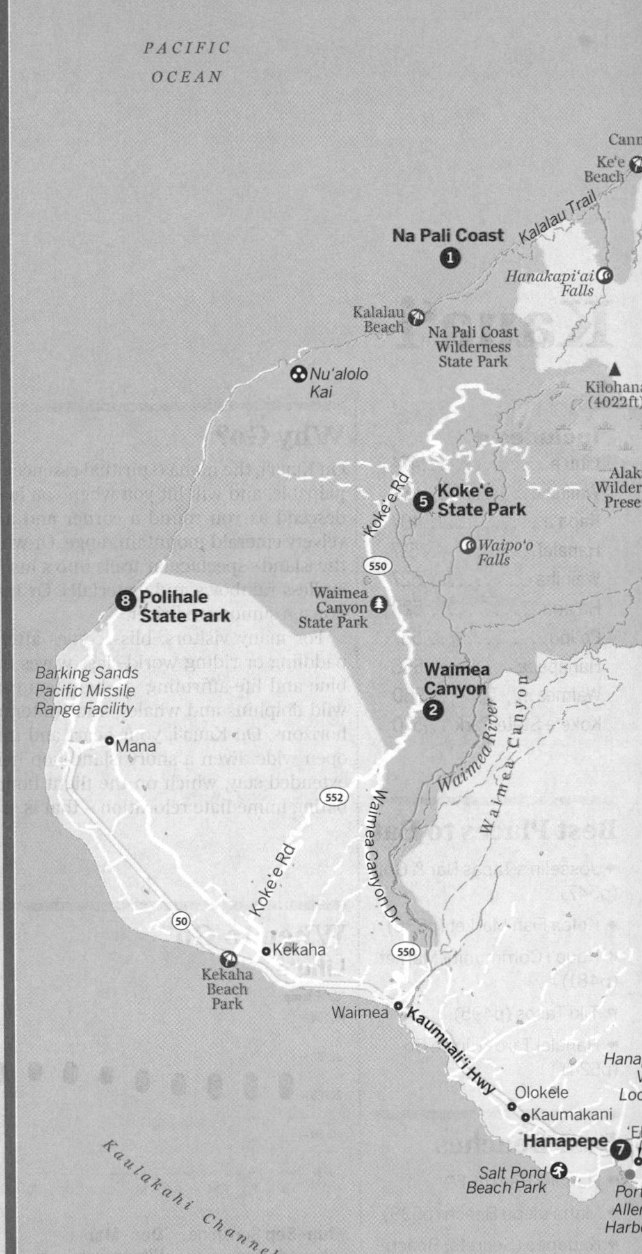

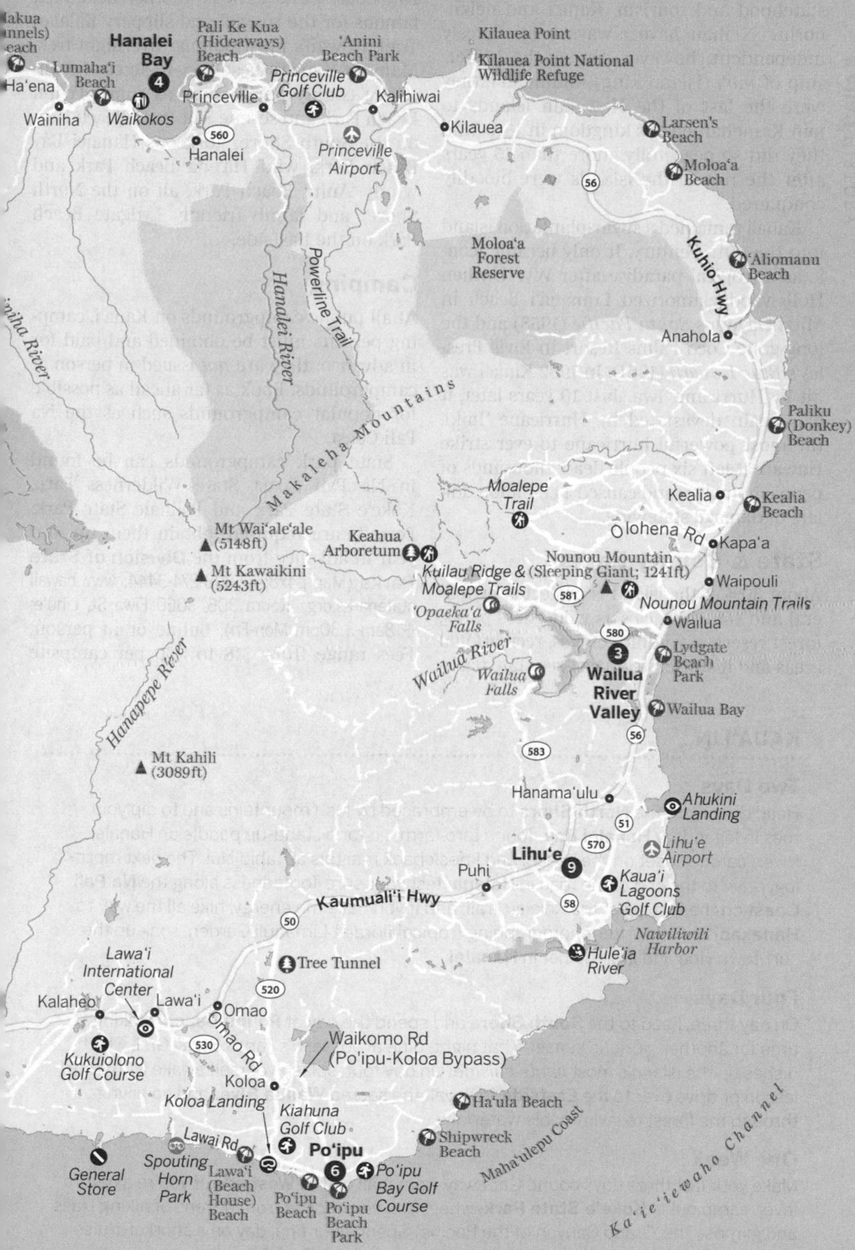

0 10 km
0 5 miles
Hanalei Bay
Pali Ke Kua (Hideaways) Beach
'Anini Beach Park
Kilauea Point
Kilauea Point National Wildlife Refuge
Lumaha'i Beach
Ha'ena
Wainiha
Waikokos
Princeville
Princeville Golf Club
Kalihiwai
Kilauea
Hanalei
560
Princeville Airport
Larsen's Beach
Moloa'a Beach
56
Moloa'a Forest Reserve
Kuhio Hwy
'Aliomanu Beach
Powerline Trail
Hanalei River
Anahola
Makaleha Mountains
Paliku (Donkey) Beach
Moalepe Trail
Kealia
Kealia Beach
Mt Wai'ale'ale (5148ft)
Keahua Arboretum
Olohena Rd
Kapa'a
Mt Kawaikini (5243ft)
Nounou Mountain (Sleeping Giant; 1241ft)
Kuilau Ridge & Moalepe Trails
581
Waipouli
'Opaeka'a Falls
Nounou Mountain Trails
Wailua
580
Hanapepe River
Wailua River
Lydgate Beach Park
Wailua Falls
Wailua River Valley
Wailua Bay
56
583
Mt Kahili (3089ft)
Hanama'ulu
Ahukini Landing
51
570
Lihu'e
Lihu'e Airport
Puhi
Kaua'i Lagoons Golf Club
Kaumuali'i Hwy
58
50
Nawiliwili Harbor
Hule'ia River
Lawa'i International Center
Tree Tunnel
520
Kalaheo
Lawa'i
Omao
Omao Rd
530
Waikomo Rd (Po'ipu-Koloa Bypass)
Kukuiolono Golf Course
Koloa
Koloa Landing
Ha'ula Beach
Kiahuna Golf Club
Mahaʻulepu Coast
Ka'ie'iewaho Channel
Lawai Rd
Shipwreck Beach
Po'ipu
General Store
Spouting Horn Park
Lawa'i (Beach House) Beach
Po'ipu Beach
Po'ipu Beach Park
Po'ipu Bay Golf Course

History

Like other Hawaiian Islands, Kaua'i saw a sea change in all aspects of life after the arrival of Captain Cook, sugar plantations, statehood and tourism. Kaua'i and neighboring Ni'ihau have always been fiercely independent, however. Under the leadership of *mo'i* (island king) Kaumuali'i, they were the last of the Hawaiian Islands to join Kamehameha I's kingdom in 1810, and they did so peacefully, more than 15 years after the rest of the islands were bloodily conquered.

Kaua'i remained a sugar-plantation island into the 20th century. It only became iconic as a tropical paradise after WWII, when Hollywood glamorized Lumaha'i Beach in Mitzi Gaynor's *South Pacific* (1958) and the long-gone Coco Palms Resort in Elvis Presley's *Blue Hawaii* (1961). In 1982 Kaua'i was hit by Hurricane 'Iwa. Just 10 years later, it was again devastated by Hurricane 'Iniki, the most powerful hurricane to ever strike Hawaii; it left six people dead, thousands of people homeless and caused $1.8 billion dollars of damage statewide.

State & County Parks

About 30% of the island is protected by federal and state agencies as wilderness parks, forest reserves, wildlife refuges, recreational areas and historic sites. Must-see state parks include the Westside's standout neighbors, Waimea Canyon and Koke'e, for awesome chasm views, steep clifftop hiking trails and native forests filled with wildlife. Na Pali Coast State Park is another headliner, famous for the rugged and slippery Kalalau Trail, Hawaii's most popular overnight trek. Many of Kaua'i's best easy-to-access beaches are county parks, such as sunny Po'ipu Beach Park and serene Salt Pond Beach Park on the South Shore; gorgeous Hanalei Bay Beach Park, wild Ha'ena Beach Park and windy 'Anini Beach Park, all on the North Shore; and family-friendly Lydgate Beach Park on the Eastside.

Camping

At all public campgrounds on Kaua'i, camping permits must be obtained and paid for in advance; they are *not* issued in person at campgrounds. Book as far ahead as possible for popular campgrounds such as the Na Pali Coast.

State park campgrounds can be found in Na Pali Coast State Wilderness Park, Koke'e State Park and Polihale State Park. Permits are required; obtain them up to a year in advance from the **Division of State Parks** (Map p478; ☎808-274-3444; www.hawaiistateparks.org; Room 306, 3060 Eiwa St, Lihu'e; ⌚8am-3:30pm Mon-Fri), online or in person. Fees range from $18 to $30 per campsite

KAUA'I IN...

Two Days

Head directly to the **North Shore** to be embraced by lush mountains and to dip your toes in legendary **Hanalei Bay**. Tour a taro farm; go for a stand-up paddle on Hanalei River; catch sunset on the beach; and knock back mai tais at Tahiti Nui. The next morning, drive to the end of the road in **Ha'ena**; test your sure-footedness along the **Na Pali Coast** on the first leg of the Kalalau Trail; and if you have the energy, hike all the way to **Hanakapi'ai Falls**. After photographing tropical flora at Limahuli Garden, soak up the surf-town vibe and grab dinner in **Hanalei**.

Four Days

On day three, head to the **South Shore** and spend the day at **Po'ipu Beach**, making time for another glorious sunset. That night, dine at Josselin's Tapas Bar & Grill, which dishes up the island's most *haute cuisine*. On day four, splash yourself awake with a surf lesson or drive over to the **Eastside** to kayak the sacred **Wailua River** and go hiking through the forest to swimmable waterfalls.

One Week

Make your last three days count. Get away from it all on the **Westside**. If you're a nature lover, camp out in **Koke'e State Park**, where you can choose from dozens of hiking trails and glimpse the 'Grand Canyon of the Pacific'. Spend your final day on a snorkel cruise up the Na Pali Coast – catamarans and rafts depart from **Port Allen**.

per night (or $20 per person per night on the Na Pali Coast); maximum-stay limits of three to five nights at each campground are enforced.

For remote backcountry camping on the Westside, the **Division of Forestry & Wildlife** (Map p478; ☎808-274-3433; http://dlnr.hawaii.gov/dofaw/; Room 306, 3060 Eiwa St, Lihu'e; ⊙8am-3:30pm Mon-Fri) issues permits for four sites in Waimea Canyon, three sites (Sugi Grove, Kawaikoi and Waikoali) in and around Koke'e State Park and the Wai'alae Cabin campsite near the Alaka'i Wilderness Preserve. Camping fees are the same as for state parks; maximum-stay limits also apply.

Of the seven county parks with campgrounds, the most pleasant are Ha'ena Beach Park, Black Pot Beach Park (Hanalei Pier) and 'Anini Beach Park on the North Shore, and Salt Pond Beach Park on the Westside. Campgrounds are subject to regular weekly closures (exact days vary by campground).

County camping permits cost $3 per night per nonresident adult camper (children under 18 years are free) and are issued by mail (at least one month in advance) or in person at the **Division of Parks & Recreation** (Map p478; ☎808-241-4463; www.kauai.gov; Suite 105, Lihu'e Civic Center, 4444 Rice St, Lihu'e; ⊙8am-4pm Mon-Fri). Permits can also be obtained in person at four satellite locations: **Hanapepe Neighborhood Center** (Map p554; ☎808-335-3731; 4451 Puolo Rd; ⊙8am-noon Mon Fri); **Kalaheo Neighborhood Center** (☎808-332-9770; 4480 Papalina Rd, Kalaheo; ⊙noon-4pm Mon-Fri); **Kapa'a Neighborhood Center** (☎808-822-1931; 4491 Kou St; ⊙10am-noon Mon, Wed & Fri, from 8am Tue & Thu); and **Kilauea Neighborhood Center** (☎808-828-1421; 2460 Keneke St; ⊙10am-noon Mon, Wed & Fri, 8am-4pm Tue & Thu). For mail-in permits, only cashier's checks or money orders are accepted for payment, not cash.

Getting There & Away

The vast majority of incoming flights from overseas and the US mainland arrive at Honolulu International Airport, where travelers can catch an interisland flight to Kaua'i. Airlines flying directly to Lihu'e Airport (p485) from the US mainland and Canada include Alaska Airlines, American Airlines, Delta Airlines, Hawaiian Airlines, United Airlines, US Airways and WestJet.

The only commercial passenger vessels docking at Nawiliwili Harbor in Lihu'e are cruise ships, mainly Norwegian Cruise Lines (p647) and Princess Cruises (p646).

Getting Around

TO/FROM THE AIRPORT

Book ahead for rental cars. Major car-rental agencies have booths outside the baggage-claim area, with complimentary shuttles to off-airport parking lots. Taxis wait curbside, or you can use an airport courtesy phone to call one. Average taxi fares from the airport include Lihu'e ($9 to $13), Po'ipu ($42 to $53) and Princeville ($89 to $119). For families or groups, it may be more economical to book an airport shuttle with **Speedi Shuttle** (☎877-242-5777; www.speedishuttle.com).

BICYCLE

Cycling all the way around the island isn't much fun, due to heavy traffic and narrow road shoulders. But it's a convenient way of getting around beach resorts, and the Eastside has a recreational paved bicycle path running through Kapa'a. Bicycles are rented in Waipouli, Kapa'a, Po'ipu and Hanalei.

BUS

The county's Kaua'i Bus (p485) stops approximately hourly on weekdays in towns along major highways, with limited services on Saturdays, Sundays and holidays. Routes run islandwide, but don't reach the Na Pali Coast Wilderness, Waimea Canyon or Koke'e State Parks. Schedules are available online. Check the website for where to buy monthly passes ($35).

KAUA'I'S TOP OUTDOOR ACTIVITIES

ACTIVITY	DESTINATION
Diving	South Shore, Ni'ihau, Makua (Tunnels) Beach
Hiking	Na Pali Coast, Koke'e State Park, Waimea Canyon State Park, Nounou Mountain (Sleeping Giant) Trails
Kayaking	Wailua River, Na Pali Coast, Hanalei River, Hule'ia River
Snorkeling	Po'ipu Beach Park, Lawa'i (Beach House) Beach, Koloa Landing, Makua (Tunnels) Beach
Surfing	Hanalei, Po'ipu, Kalapaki Beach

Buses are air-conditioned and equipped with bicycle racks and wheelchair ramps. A few caveats: drivers don't give change; surfboards (except for boogie boards), oversized backpacks and luggage aren't allowed on board; stops are marked but might be hard to spot; and schedules do not include a map.

CAR & MOTORCYCLE

Major international car-rental companies have booths at Lihu'e Airport, with free shuttle buses running to off-airport parking lots nearby. Locally owned rental agencies Kauai Car & Scooter Rental (p485) and Kaua'i Harley-Davidson (p485) are located in Lihu'e, while Rent a Car Kauai (p502), based in Kapa'a on the Eastside, offers free airport pickups and drop-offs. Arriving on the island without reservations usually subjects you to higher rates and limited availability. Rental cars may be entirely sold out during peak travel times, so book ahead.

Kaua'i has a belt road running three-quarters of the way around the island, from Ke'e Beach in the north to near Polihale State Park in the west.

Average driving distances and times from Lihu'e are as follows. Allow more time during morning and afternoon rush hours and on weekends.

DESTINATION	MILES	TIME
Anahola	14	25min
Hanalei	31	55min
Hanapepe	18	30min
Kapa'a	11	20min
Ke'e Beach	39	1¼hr
Kilauea	25	40min
Kokee State Park	42	1½hr
Po'ipu	14	25min
Port Allen	17	30min
Princeville	30	50min
Waimea	23	40min
Waimea Canyon	37	1¼hr

TAXI

The standard flag-fall fee is $3, plus 30¢ per additional 0.1 miles or up to 45 seconds of waiting; surcharges may apply for luggage, surfboards, wheelchairs and bicycles. Cabs line up at the airport during business hours, but they don't run all night or cruise for passengers. Elsewhere, you'll need to call ahead in advance. Most taxi companies operate islandwide, but it's usually faster to call one that's closer to your location.

Akiko's Taxi (☎808-822-7588, 808-651-1472; www.akikostaxikauai.com; ⏰5am-10pm) Based in Lihu'e.

Kauai Taxi Company (☎808-246-9554; http://kauaitaxico.com) Based in Lihu'e.

North Shore Cab (☎808-639-7829; www.northshorecab.com) Based in Kilauea.

Pono Taxi (☎808-634-4474; www.ponotaxi.com) Based in Lihu'e.

South Shore Cab (☎808-742-1525) Based in Po'ipu.

LIHU'E

The island's commercial center is strip-mall plain, but there's an abundance of economical eateries and shops along with a down-to-earth, workaday atmosphere that's missing in resort areas. While Kalapaki Beach is a charmer, Lihu'e is more a place to stock up on supplies after arrival at the airport before heading out on your island adventure.

Lihu'e arose as a plantation town back in 1849 when sugar was king, and its massive sugar mill (still standing south of town along Kaumuali'i Hwy) was Kaua'i's largest. The mill closed in 2001, ending more than a century of operations. It left behind an ethnic melting pot of Asian, European and Hawaiian traditions that make the town what it is today.

Beaches

Kalapaki Beach BEACH

(Map p476; 👪) This sandy beach and sheltered bay is tucked between a marina and the mountains. It's overlooked by the Marriott resort facing Kalapaki Bay and by an enviable collection of houses atop a rocky ridge to the east. Its easy-access location and versatility make it popular with families. Calmer waters toward the east are good for swimming, although a sandy bottom makes for poor snorkeling. Swells to the west draw bodyboarders and both novice and intermediate surfers.

For surfers, it's an easy paddle out of about 50yd to the reef, and there's no pounding shore break to get through. Most go right for a mellow, predictable wave, but there are more aggressive lefts, too.

Sights

★Wailua Falls WATERFALL

(Map p486; Ma'alo Rd) Made famous in the opening credits of *Fantasy Island,* these falls appear at a distance. When they are in full bloom and misting the surrounding tropical foliage, it's a fantastic photo op. While officially listed as 80ft, the falls have been repeatedly measured to have a far greater drop. Heed the sign at the top that warns: 'Slippery rocks at top of falls. People have been killed.' Many have fallen while trying to scramble down the steep path beyond.

To get here from Lihu'e, follow Kuhio Hwy (Hwy 56) north. Turn left onto Ma'alo Rd (Hwy 583), which ends at the falls after 4 miles. Expect crowds and difficult parking.

★Grove Farm HISTORIC SITE

(Map p476; ☎808-245-3202; http://grovefarm.org; 4050 Nawiliwili Rd; 2hr tour adult/child 5-12yr $20/10; ⏲tours 10am & 1pm Mon, Wed & Thu, by reservation only) History buffs adore this plantation museum, but kids may grow restless. Grove Farm once ranked among the most productive sugar companies on Kaua'i. George Wilcox, the Hilo-born son of Protestant missionaries, acquired the farm in 1864. The main house feels suspended in time, with rocking chairs sitting still on a covered porch and untouched books lining the library's shelves.

Call a week or more in advance to join a small-group tour, which includes cookies and mint tea served on the lanai (porch).

★Kaua'i Museum MUSEUM

(Map p478; ☎808-245-6931; www.kauaimuseum.org; 4428 Rice St; adult/child $10/2; ⏲10am-5pm Mon-Sat, tours 10:30am Tue-Fri) The island's largest museum is set in two buildings – one of which was built with lava rock in 1960. Come here for a quick grounding in Kaua'i's history and ecology, and in Hawaiian history and culture in general, which you'll gain especially if you take a free guided tour. A smattering of Asian art is also on display.

Admission is discounted on the first Saturday of the month.

Kilohana Plantation HISTORIC SITE

(Map p476; ☎808-245-5608; www.kilohanakauai.com; 3-2087 Kaumuali'i Hwy; admission free, attraction prices vary; ⏲10:30am-9pm Mon-Sat, to 3pm Sun) FREE If you're curious about how Kaua'i's powerful sugar barons lived,

KAUA'I'S SURF BEACHES & BREAKS

As a tourist in Hawaii, there are some places you go and there are some places you don't go. For many local families the beach parks are meeting places where generations gather to celebrate life under the sun. They're tied to these places by a sense of community and culture, and they aren't eager for outsiders to push them out of time-honored surf spots.

In the water, basic surf etiquette is vital. The person 'deepest,' or furthest outside, has the right of way. When somebody is already up and riding, don't take off on the wave in front of them. Also, remember you're a visitor out in the line-up, so don't expect to get every wave that comes your way. There's a definite pecking order and, frankly, as a tourist you're at the bottom. That said, usually if you give a wave, you'll get a wave in return.

The Garden Isle is one of Hawaii's most challenging islands for surfers. On the North Shore, a heavy local vibe is pervasive. With the Princeville resort overlooking the break, residents may be a bit more understanding of out-of-towners in the water at **Hanalei Bay** than at other North Shore spots, but surfing with respect is a must. Between localism and the inaccessibility of the Na Pali Coast, not to mention a sizable tiger shark population, you may want to pass on surfing the North Shore.

As a general rule, surf tourism is relegated to the South Shore around **Po'ipu**, which is perfect because there are some fun waves to be had there. Breaking best in the summer on south swells, spots such as **BK's**, **Acid Drop** and **Centers** challenge even advanced surfers. First-timers can get their feet wet at **Inside Po'ipu** near the Sheraton resort. Only bodyboarding and bodysurfing are permitted at **Brennecke's Beach** – no stand-up surfing.

On the Eastide, **Unreals** breaks at Anahola Bay. It's a consistent right point that can work well on easterly wind swell, when *kona* (leeward) winds are offshore.

Surfline (www.surfline.com) reports current conditions at the island's best-known surf breaks, or call the surf hotline (☎241-7873).

Lihu'e Area

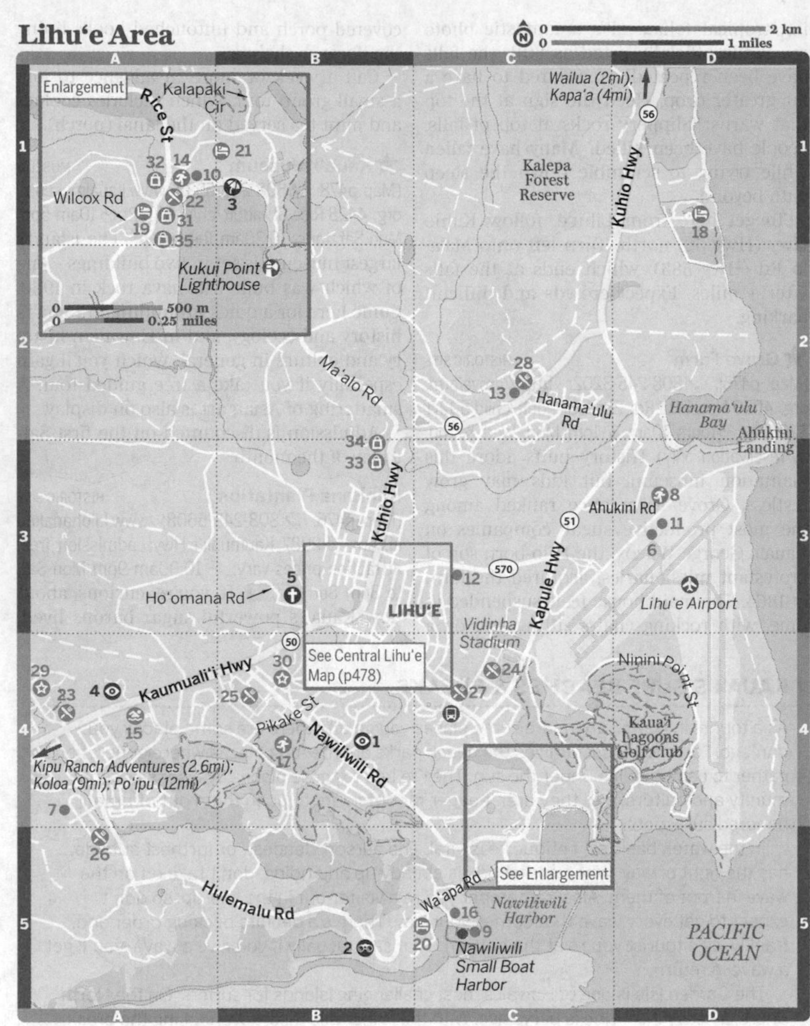

visit this historic plantation estate turned shopping complex, which also hosts a luau show (p483), the Kauai Plantation Railway (p480) and the Koloa Rum Company (p484). Plantation owner Gaylord Wilcox built the main house in 1936. Inside the 16,000-sq-ft Tudor-style mansion, antique-filled rooms and ornate carpets on hardwood floors lead past cases of poi pounders, koa bowls and other Hawaiiana to gallery shops.

Alekoko (Menehune) Fishpond Overlook VIEWPOINT
(Map p476; Hulemalu Rd) This roadside overlook offers an oft-photographed vista of the Hule'ia Valley, where the Hule'ia River winds beneath a ring of verdant peaks. The river is walled off at one bend to form a 39-acre *loko wai* (freshwater fishpond). Local legend attributes construction to *menehune,* the 'little people' of Hawaiian mythology. The best time to visit is just before sunset. It's about 0.5 miles west of the entrance to Nawiliwili Harbor.

Lihu'e Area

Top Sights

1	Grove Farm	B4

Sights

2	Alekoko (Menehune) Fishpond Overlook	B5
3	Kalapaki Beach	B1
	Kaua'i Society of Artists	(see 25)
4	Kilohana Plantation	A4
5	Lihu'e Lutheran Church	B3

Activities, Courses & Tours

6	AirVentures Hawaii	D3
7	Aloha Kaua'i Tours	A4
8	Blue Hawaiian Helicopters	D3
9	Captain Don's Sportfishing	C5
10	Island Adventures	A1
11	Island Helicopters	D3
12	Jack Harter Helicopters	C3
	Just Live	(see 31)
13	Kaua'i Backcountry Adventures	C2
14	Kauai Beach Boys	A1
15	Kauai Ohana YMCA	A4
	Kauai Plantation Railway	(see 4)
	Mauna Loa Helicopters	(see 32)
16	Outfitters Kauai	C5
17	Puakea Golf Course	B4

Sleeping

18	Aqua Kaua'i Beach Resort	D1
19	Garden Island Inn	A1
20	Kaua'i Inn	C5
21	Kaua'i Marriott	B1

Eating

	Duke's	(see 21)
	Feral Pig	(see 32)
	Gaylord's	(see 4)
22	Kalapaki Beach Hut	A1
23	Kaua'i Community Market	A4
24	Kaua'i Sunshine Market – Lihu'e	C4
25	Kukui Grove Center Farmers Market	B4
26	Right Slice	A5
27	Smiley's Local Grinds	C4
28	Sweet Marie's Hawaii	C2
	Times Supermarket	(see 25)

Drinking & Nightlife

	Duke's Barefoot Bar	(see 21)

Entertainment

29	Kaua'i Community College Performing Arts Center	A4
30	Kukui Grove Cinema 4	B4
	Luau Kalamaku	(see 4)

Shopping

31	Anchor Cove Shopping Center	A1
	Clayworks	(see 4)
	Da Life	(see 10)
32	Harbor Mall	A1
33	Kapaia Stitchery	B3
34	Koa Store	B3
	Koloa Rum Company	(see 4)
	Kukui Grove Center	(see 25)
	Longs Drugs	(see 25)
35	Tropic Isle Music & Gifts	A1

On the north side of the river lies the 240-acre **Hule'ia National Wildlife Refuge** (www.fws.gov/huleia), a breeding ground for endemic waterfowl. The refuge is closed to the public, except for guided kayaking tours.

Lihu'e Lutheran Church CHURCH
(Map p476; 4602 Ho'omana Rd; daily, services 8am & 10:30am Sun) Hawaii's oldest Lutheran church is a quaint clapboard house, with an incongruously slanted floor that resembles a ship's deck and a balcony akin to a captain's bridge. The building is a faithful 1983 reconstruction of the 1885 original (built by German immigrants) leveled by Hurricane 'Iwa. It's located just off Kaumuali'i Hwy (Hwy 50).

Kaua'i Society of Artists GALLERY
(KSA; Map p476; Kukui Grove Center, 3-2600 Kamauali'i Hwy; 11am-5pm Sat-Thu, to 8pm Fri) FREE Island artists share gallery space at the mall and exhibit thoughtful works in oils, pencil, watercolor, sculpture materials, mixed media and photography.

Activities

★ Just Live ADVENTURE TOUR
(Map p476; 808-482-1295; www.justlive.org; Anchor Cove Shopping Center, 3416 Rice St; zipline tours $79-125; tours daily, by reservation only) This adventure tour outfit stands above the rest – literally – by offering Kaua'i's only canopy-based zipping, meaning that you never touch ground after your first zip. The 3½-hour tour includes seven ziplines and four bridge crossings. Otherwise, there's a scaled-down 'Wikiwiki' zip tour. The 'Eco-Adventure' adds a climbing wall, a 100ft rappeling tower and a heart-stopping monster swing.

Participants must be at least nine years old and weigh between 70lb and 250lb.

Island Adventures ADVENTURE TOUR
(Map p476; 808-246-6333; www.islandadventureskauai.com; Da Life, 3500 Rice St; tours incl lunch adult/child 6-12yr $180/157; tours 8am Mon-Wed & Sat, 11am Fri, by reservation

Central Lihu'e

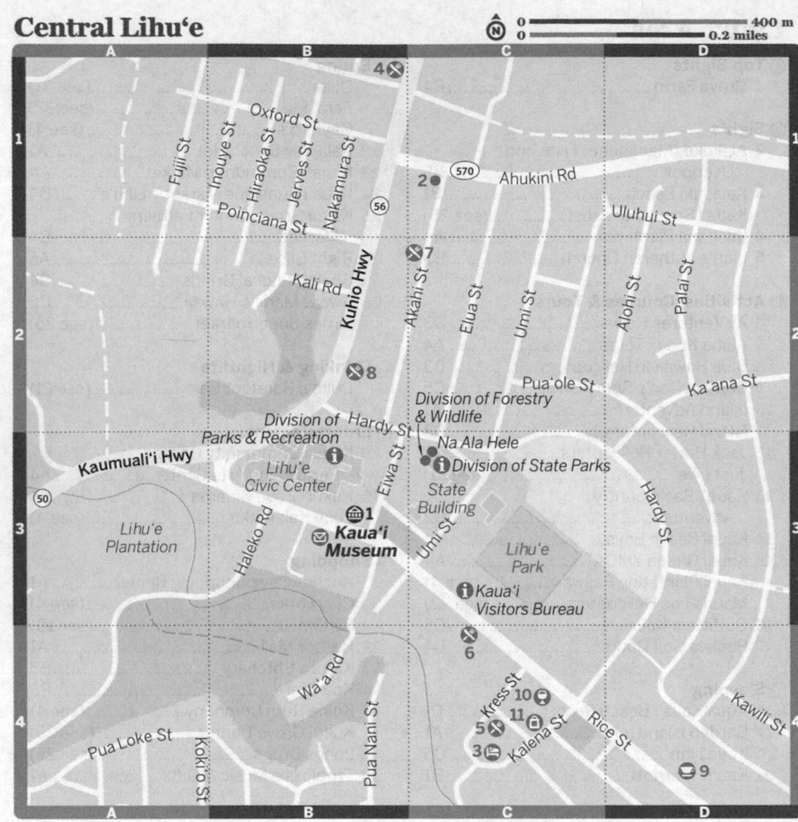

Central Lihu'e

Top Sights
1 Kaua'i Museum B3

Activities, Courses & Tours
2 Safari Helicopters C1

Sleeping
3 Kaua'i Palms Hotel C4

Eating
4 Fish Express B1
5 Hamura Saimin C4
6 Pho Kauai C4
7 Tip Top Cafe C2
8 Vim 'n Vigor B2

Drinking & Nightlife
9 Hā Coffee Bar D4
10 Kauai Beer Company C4

Shopping
Edith King Wilcox Gift Shop & Bookstore .... (see 1)
11 Flowers Forever C4

only) Jump on a 5½-hour tour into Hule'ia National Wildlife Refuge, where you'll paddle 2.5 miles in; hike to two waterfalls on private land; learn how to wet rappel up to 60ft down the side of a waterfall; and take a lazy swim followed by a picnic lunch.

Kaua'i Backcountry Adventures ADVENTURE TOUR
(Map p476; ☎808-245-2506, 888-270-0555; www.kauaibackcountry.com; 3-4131 Kuhio Hwy; 3hr tubing/zipline tours incl lunch $102/130; ⊙tours hourly 8am-2pm, by reservation only; 👪) This

3½-hour zipline tour features seven lines, which are elevated as high as 200ft above the ground and run as far as 900ft (almost three football fields). Afterward, you can refuel with a picnic lunch at the swimming pond. The family-friendly tubing tour (for ages five and up) floats through an old sugar plantation's ditch-and-tunnel irrigation system.

Zipliners must be at least 12 years old and weigh between 100lb and 250lb.

Outfitters Kauai ADVENTURE TOUR
(Map p476; ☎888-742-9887, 808-742-9667; www.outfitterskauai.com; Outfitters Kayak Shack, Nawiliwili Small Boat Harbor, 2494 Niumalu Rd; zipline tours adult/child 7-14yr from $116/106, 5hr SUP tours incl lunch adult/child 12-14yr $126/96; ⊙by reservation only;) Multi-activity tours at Kipu Ranch just outside town combine tandem ziplines with aerial bridges, hiking, and kayaking the Hule'ia River; the weight limit for zipliners is 250lb. Unique stand-up paddle surfing (SUP) river tours include short hikes, swimming and a motorized canoe ride back upstream.

Captain Don's Sportfishing FISHING, CRUISE
(Map p476; ☎808-639-3012; http://captaindonsfishing.com; Nawiliwili Small Boat Harbor, 2494 Niumalu Rd; half-/full-day shared charters per person $140/250, 2/4hr private charters for up to 6 passengers from $325/600; ⊙by reservation only) One of the many fishing charters departing from Nawiliwili Small Boat Harbor, Captain Don's gives guests creative freedom to design their own trip (fishing, whale-watching, snorkeling, a Na Pali Coast cruise) on the 34ft *June Louise*. Captain Don has decades of experience on Kaua'i's waters.

Kauai Beach Boys WATER SPORTS
(Map p476; ☎808-246-6333; http://kauaibeachboys.com; 3610 Rice St; 1hr sailboat cruises/lessons $39/140, 90min surfing or SUP lessons $75; ⊙8am-6pm, lesson hours vary) On Kalapaki Beach, this concessionaire rents snorkel gear, surfboards and stand-up paddle surfing (SUP) sets at reasonable prices, with 90-minute surfing and SUP lessons given several times daily. Call ahead for sailing lessons or to book a sailboat cruise on the bay.

Aloha Kaua'i Tours ADVENTURE TOUR
(Map p476; ☎808-245-6400, 800-452-8113; www.alohakauaitours.com; 1702 Haleukana St; half-day tours adult/child 5-12yr $80/63) Specializes in 4WD trips on backroads, including a half-day trip (minimum four people, weekdays only) that rumbles through the gate used in filming *Jurassic Park* and ends with a 3-mile round-trip hike to a waterfall pool fed by a stream from mighty Mt Wai'ale'ale. Book at least 24 hours in advance.

Kipu Ranch Adventures ADVENTURE TOUR
(☎808-246-9288; www.kiputours.com; Kipu Rd; tours adult/child from $125/94; ⊙daily tour hours vary, by reservation only) This outfit's most popular all-terrain vehicle (ATV) tour takes you on a three-hour scenic journey around a private ranch used for filiming *Raiders of the Lost Ark* and *The Descendants*. The four-hour tour includes a short hike to a waterfall for swimming and a picnic lunch.

Kauai Lagoons Golf Club GOLF
(☎808-241-6000, 800-634-6400; 3351 Ho'olaule'a Way, Kaua'i Marriott Resort; green fees incl cart rental $135-205) Designed by Jack Nicklaus, the recently redone 18-hole, par-72 Kiele Course is tucked into the mountains by the coast. Book tee times up to 90 days in advance; discounts are offered to hotel guests. Club and shoe rentals available.

Puakea Golf Course GOLF
(Map p476; ☎808-245-8756, 866-773-5554; www.puakeagolf.com; 4150 Nuhou St; green fees incl cart rental $35-99) The lush cliffs of Mt Ha'upu serve as a backdrop to this Robin Nelson-designed public course. Club rentals are available. Book tee times up to three months ahead.

Kauai Ohana YMCA SWIMMING
(Map p476; ☎808-246-9090; www.ymcaofkauai.org; 4477 Nuhou St; day pass member/nonmember $5/10; ⊙5:30am-9am & 11am-7pm Mon-Fri, 10am-5:30pm Sat & Sun) Lap swimmers, get your fix at this open-air, Olympic-sized pool. A small weights/cardio workout room is also available, but towels and padlocks for lockers aren't provided. US mainland YMCA members should bring their card from home.

☞ Tours

Most 'flightseeing' tours depart from Lihu'e Airport. Book ahead online for major discounts.

★AirVentures Hawaii SCENIC FLIGHTS
(Map p476; ☎808-651-0679, 866-464-7864; https://kauaiairtour.com; Lihu'e Airport, 3651 Ahukini Rd; 1hr tours $245; ⊙tours Mon-Fri, by reservation only) When it comes to fixed-wing

KIPU FALLS

Once famous for its cliff jump and rope swing involving slippery rocks and water contaminated by leptospirosis, these falls are no longer legally accessible, let alone advisable to explore. Several tourists have been seriously injured or have died here.

aircraft, there's nothing like an open-cockpit biplane. This outfit's gorgeous YMF-5 Super can seat two people up front. Visibility may not be the same as by helicopter, but the roar of the engine and the wind makes for a memorable experience. You'll even get to don an old-fashioned cloth aviator's hat and goggles.

Kauai Plantation Railway GUIDED TOUR
(Map p476; ☎808-245-7245; www.kilohanakauai.com; Kilohana Plantation, 3-2087 Kaumuali'i Hwy; 40min train rides adult/child 3-12yr $18/14, 4hr train & walking tours $75/60; ⊙hourly departures 10am-2pm, guided tours 9:30am Mon-Fri; 👪) If you crave a bit of history and agricultural education, hop on this vintage-style train for a scenic 40-minute ride through a working plantation. The four-hour train and walking tour combo will get you into the fields and orchards, where you can pluck tropical fruit straight from the tree and feed the sheep, goats and wild pigs. Luau packages are available.

Island Helicopters SCENIC FLIGHTS
(Map p476; ☎808-245-8588, 800-829-8588; www.islandhelicopters.com; 50/75min tours $297/371) Pilots with this long-running helicopter tour company have perfect safety records, and they only fly AStar helicopters, equipped with floor-to-ceiling windows. The 'Jurassic Falls' tour includes an exclusive 25-minute landing at 350ft-high Manawaiopuna Falls, hidden deep in Hanapepe Valley.

Mauna Loa Helicopters SCENIC FLIGHTS
(Map p476; ☎808-652-3148; www.helicopter-tours-kauai.com; Harbor Mall, 3501 Rice St; 1hr tours from $275) Highly qualified pilots don't skimp on full 60-minute private tours for up to three passengers. Small groups allow for more-personalized interaction between pilot and passengers. You can choose to have the doors on or off, and all seats are window seats.

Safari Helicopters SCENIC FLIGHTS
(Map p478; ☎808-246-0136, 800-326-3356; www.safarihelicopters.com; 3225 Akahi St; 60/90min tours $229/279) Flies AStar helicopters on the standard circle-island tour. The longer 'eco-tour' includes a 40-minute stop at Robinson Ranch's wildlife refuge overlooking Okolele Canyon.

Jack Harter Helicopters SCENIC FLIGHTS
(Map p476; ☎808-245-3774, 888-245-2001; www.helicopters-kauai.com; 4231 Ahukini Rd; 60-65min tours $269) This pioneering outfit (operating since 1962) offers a standard enclosed, six-passenger AStar or a doors-off, four-passenger Hughes 500 helicopter. Longer doors-on tours are also offered.

Blue Hawaiian Helicopters SCENIC FLIGHTS
(Map p476; ☎808-245-5800, 800-745-2583; www.bluehawaiian.com/kauai/tours; 3651 Ahukini Rd; 55min tours $240) Flies high-end Eco-Star choppers, offering more space, glass and comfort with less noise due to quiet, enclosed tail rotors. Grab a souvenir DVD of your flight for an extra $25.

Festivals & Events

For an up-to-date, comprehensive calendar of events, check www.kauaifestivals.com online.

★May Day Lei Contest CULTURAL
(www.kauaimuseum.org; ⊙May; 👪) FREE Established in 1981, the Kaua'i Museum's annual lei contest in early May brings out legendary floral art, with do-it-yourself workshops, live music and an auction.

Fourth of July Concert in the Sky CULTURAL
(www.kauaihospice.org; adult/child $15/7; ⊙4 Jul; 👪) Enjoy island food, live entertainment and the grand finale fireworks show set to music at Vidinha Stadium.

Kaua'i County Farm Bureau Fair FAIR
(www.kauaifarmfair.org; ⊙Aug; 👪) Old-fashioned family fun happens at Vidinha Stadium in late August. The fair brings carnival rides and games, livestock shows, a petting zoo, hula performances and lots of local food.

Kaua'i Composers Contest & Concert MUSIC
(www.maliefoundation.org/composers.html; ⊙Sep) The signature event of the Kaua'i Mokihana Festival, this musical competition

showcases homegrown musical talent in mid- to late September.

Kaua'i Mokihana Festival Hula Competition CULTURAL, DANCE
(808-822-2166; www.maliefoundation.org; Sep) Three days of serious hula competitions are staged at the Aqua Kaua'i Beach Resort in mid- to late September. Both *kahiko* (ancient) and *'auana* (modern) styles enchant.

★ **Garden Island Range & Food Festival** FOOD
(www.kauaifoodfestival.com; adult/child $35/18; Nov) This annual foodie gathering at Kilohana Plantation in mid-November spotlights local chefs, as well as the farmers and ranchers who provide their Kaua'i-grown ingredients. Future dates and the location of this festival are subject to change.

★ **Hawaiian Slack Key Guitar Festival** MUSIC
(http://slackkeyfestival.com; Nov) This opportunity to see master slack key guitarists is not to be missed. It's usually staged at the Aqua Kaua'i Beach Resort in mid-November.

Lights on Rice Parade PARADE
(http://lightsonrice.org; Dec;) A charming parade of illuminated floats takes over Rice St on the first Friday evening of December.

Sleeping

Accommodations range from Marriott's beachfront resort to no-frills motels in the town center.

Kaua'i Palms Hotel MOTEL $
(Map p478; 808-246-0908; www.kauaipalmshotel.com; 2931 Kalena St; r from $79; office 7am-9pm;) One of two motels in central Lihu'e, this is easily the more appealing. Inside a two-story, open-air building, the 28 rooms are small but tidy, with refrigerators and cable TV. Air-con and kitchenettes cost extra. It's at the end of an industrial road downtown.

Aqua Kaua'i Beach Resort RESORT $$
(Map p476; 808-954-7419, 866-536-7976; www.kauaibeachresorthawaii.com; 4331 Kaua'i Beach Dr; r from $105;) Set on its own thin ribbon of sand (no swimming), this sprawling resort sports 350 renovated boutique-on-a-budget rooms, four pools, nightly lounge entertainment and a full-service spa. You'll pay more for a room with a view. It's just north of town and the airport.

Garden Island Inn HOTEL $$
(Map p476; 808-245-7227, 800-648-0154; http://gardenislandinn.com; 3445 Wilcox Rd; r from $105;) This two-story hotel across the street from Kalapaki Beach holds its own for value and friendliness. Rooms are bright but kitschy, with murals splashed on the walls, tropical bamboo and wood furnishings, and kitchenettes. Free beach gear and DVDs to borrow.

Kaua'i Inn HOTEL $$
(Map p476; 808-245-9000, 800-808-2330; www.kauai-inn.com; 2430 Hulemalu Rd; r from $100;) This large inn, just west of the harbor, offers a simple home base away from traffic and crowds. The 48 plain rooms each have a refrigerator and microwave. Ground-floor rooms come with back porches; those on the 2nd floor are larger but sans lanai.

★ **Kaua'i Marriott** RESORT $$$
(Map p476; 808-245-5050, 800-220-2925; www.marriott.com; 3610 Rice St; r from $279;) Anyone looking for a classic Hawaii resort experience won't be disappointed here. The hotel has Kalapaki Beach, a top golf club, the island's liveliest oceanfront restaurant and a gargantuan pool for all-day entertainment. Hawaiian artifacts are displayed along the gleaming corridors. Room decor and amenities are contemporary chain-hotel standard; oceanfront units are worth it for the lanai views.

Eating

Lihu'e has two small farmers markets each week: **Kukui Grove Center Farmers Market** (Map p476; www.kukuigrovecenter.com; Kukui Grove Center, 3-2600 Kamuali'i Hwy; from 3pm Mon;) in the Kmart parking lot at the Kukui Grove Center and **Kaua'i Sunshine Market** (Map p476; www.kauai.gov; Vidinha Stadium, Ho'olako St; from 3pm Fri;) at the Vidinha Stadium parking lot.

★ **Kaua'i Community Market** MARKET $
(Map p476; 808-855-5429; www.kauaicommunitymarket.org; Kauai Community College, 3-1901 Kaumuali'i Hwy; 9:30am-1pm Sat;) One of the island's biggest and best farmers markets, in partnership with the Kaua'i County Farm Bureau, brings a bonanza of locally grown, often organic fruits and vegetables; free-range eggs and local dairy cheeses; island-grown coffee and flowers; hand-harvested honey and sea salts; Hawaiian plate lunches and

poi; and fresh smoothies, juices, popsicles and baked goods. Don't miss it!

★Right Slice BAKERY $

(Map p476; ☎808-212-8320; http://rightslice.com; Puhi Industrial Park, 1543 Haleukana St; slices from $5; ⏰11am-6pm Mon-Sat) The amazing pie vendor who graces farmers markets across the island has a commercial bakeshop. Order an hour ahead for your savory pot pie baked fresh, or swipe a sweet pie – blueberry piña colada, anyone? – by the slice or whole.

Kalapaki Beach Hut AMERICAN, LOCAL $

(Map p476; ☎808-246-6330; www.kalapakibeachhut.com; 3474 Rice St; mains $7-10; ⏰7am-8pm; 👪) This rubbah-slippah spot raises the bar for beach-shack cuisine. Order 100% Kaua'i grass-fed beef burgers with taro fries, catch-of-the-day fish sandwiches or gravy-licious *loco moco* (rice, egg and hamburger patty topped with gravy), with fresh coconuts or shave ice to top it all off.

Hamura Saimin LOCAL $

(Map p478; ☎808-245-3271; 2956 Kress St; dishes $3-8; ⏰10am-10:30pm Mon-Thu, to midnight Fri & Sat, to 9:30pm Sun; 👪) An island institution, Hamura's is a hole-in-the-wall specializing in homemade saimin (local-style noodle soup). At lunchtime, expect crowds slurping noodles elbow-to-elbow at retro, U-shaped lunch counters. Save room for the other (and much more beloved) specialty, *liliko'i* (passion fruit) chiffon pie.

Pho Kauai VIETNAMESE $

(Map p478; ☎808-245-9858; Rice Shopping Center, 4303 Rice St; mains $7-12; ⏰10am-9pm Mon-Sat) Hidden in a strip mall, this no-frills Vietnamese noodle shop serves steaming bowls of decent pho (noodle soup). Choose from meat or vegetable toppings, such as beef brisket, grilled shrimp, snow peas or eggplant.

Tip Top Cafe LOCAL, DINER $

(Map p478; 3173 Akahi St; mains $6-12; ⏰6:30am-2pm Tue-Sun; 👪) The stark white building might give you pause, but inside this retro diner teems with locals filling up on good, ol'-fashioned eats. The main draws are its famous banana-macnut (macadamia nut) pancakes, oxtail soup and *loco moco*.

Times Supermarket SUPERMARKET $

(Map p476; www.timessupermarkets.com; Kukui Grove Center, 3-2600 Kaumuali'i Hwy; ⏰6am-11pm) Swing by this grocery store, which sells to-go salads, sandwiches, plate lunches and sushi. It has a smoothie bar and a *poke* (cubed raw fish mixed with *shōyu*, sesame oil, salt, chili pepper, ground candlenuts or other condiments) station with 30 varieties made fresh daily.

Vim 'n Vigor HEALTH FOOD $

(Map p478; ☎808-245-9053; 3-3122 Kuhio Hwy; sandwiches around $6; ⏰9am-7pm Mon-Fri, to 5pm Sat; 🌶) Stocks healthy snacks, bulk staples and gluten-free and dairy-free products, but not much produce. Vegetarian and vegan sandwiches sell out fast.

Feral Pig PUB FOOD $$

(Map p476; ☎808-246-1100; www.theferalpigkauai.com; Harbor Mall, 3501 Rice St; mains $8-13; ⏰7:30am-9pm Wed-Mon) Across from Kalapaki Beach, this sports bar with a strong local following keeps Hawaii-brewed beers on tap and in bottles. Breakfasts and 'beermosas' are popular, but let's be honest: it's the massive namesake burger of island-raised beef topped with a slab of pork belly that wins. It's not on the menu, so ask for it.

Fish Express SEAFOOD $$

(Map p478; ☎808-245-9918; 3343 Kuhio Hwy; mains $7-12; ⏰10am-6pm Mon-Sat, grill until 3pm) Fish lovers, this is almost a no-brainer. Order chilled deli items, from fresh ahi *poke* to green seaweed salad, or try a plate lunch of blackened ahi (yellowfin tuna) with guava-basil sauce or a gourmet *bentō* (Japanese boxed meal). Get there early before the best *poke* runs out.

Smiley's Local Grinds LOCAL $$

(Map p476; ☎808-245-4772; 4100 Rice St; meals $8-15; ⏰10:30am-1:30pm & 5-8:30pm Mon-Sat) Every workaday island town has its locals' favorite plate-lunch kitchen. 'Mini' plates will leave you stuffed with crispy pork *katsu* (cutlets), Korean-spiced chicken, Hawaiian kalua pig or even *laulau* (bundle made of pork or chicken and salted butterfish, wrapped in taro and *ti* leaves and steamed). Contrary to the name, service can be curt.

Sweet Marie's Hawaii BAKERY $$

(Map p476; ☎808-823-0227; www.sweetmarieshawaii.com; 3-4251 Kuhio Hwy; items from $2, mains $11-15; ⏰8am-2pm Tue-Sat) A gluten-free bakery operating out of a cute storefront delivers macaroons, cookies, brownies and a host of muffins and cakes, as well as a few breakfast and lunch dishes.

Gaylord's HAWAII REGIONAL CUISINE $$$

(Map p476; ☎808-245-9593; www.kilohanakauai.com; Kilohana Plantation, 3-2087 Kaumuali'i Hwy;

mains lunch $12-18, dinner $26-36, Sun brunch buffet adult/child 5-12yr $30/15; ⌚11am-2:30pm & 5-9pm Mon-Sat, 9am-2pm Sun) There is no doubt that the historic Wilcox home at Kilohana Plantation provides a handsome setting, particularly on the veranda. Amid manicured lawns and white tablecloths in an open-air dining room, you can daydream as you fork into a local field-greens salad, sesame-seared ahi with tempura avocado or banana-coconut cream pie. Sunday's brunch buffet has a Bloody Mary bar. Make reservations.

Duke's FUSION **$$$**
(Map p476; ☎808-246-9599; www.dukeskauai.com; Kaua'i Marriott, 3610 Rice St; bar mains $11-17, restaurant $23-34; ⌚restaurant 5-10pm, bar from 11am) You won't find an evening spot more fun and lively than Duke's, which offers a classic view of Kalapaki Beach. The steak-and-seafood menu is none too innovative, but fish tacos served in the downstairs Barefoot Bar are a fave, especially on cheaper 'Taco Tuesdays.' Hula Pie, a mound of macnut ice cream in a chocolate-cookie crust, satisfies a touristy crowd. Complimentary valet parking.

Drinking

★Duke's Barefoot Bar BAR
(Map p476; www.dukeskauai.com; Kaua'i Marriott, 3610 Rice St; ⌚11am-11pm) For a convivial, Waikiki-style tropical bar with live music every night, hurry and grab a beachside table before the nonstop evening queue. Happy hour runs from 4pm to 6pm daily.

Kauai Beer Company BREWERY
(Map p478; ☎808-245-2337; http://kauaibeer.com; 4265 Rice St; ⌚3-8pm Wed-Sat) Kaua'i's only microbrewery has a friendly bar downtown, where everyone kicks back with a honeyed IPAloha 2.0, a Lihu'e Lager or a rotating seasonal or nitrogenated brew. Some nights food trucks pull up right outside, while other nights the kitchen is open, serving pub grub such as poutine, Bavarian pretzels and taro avocado *poke*.

Hā Coffee Bar CAFE
(Map p478; www.hacoffeebar.com; 4180 Rice St; ⌚6:30am-5pm Mon-Sat; 📶) Coffee hipsterdom has hit Kaua'i at this airy, high-ceilinged cafe, where retro island travel prints and local art hang on the walls. Locally baked maple macnut cinnamon rolls, focaccia sandwiches, gluten-free treats and teas round out the menu.

Entertainment

★Luau Kalamaku LUAU
(Map p476; ☎877-622-1780; http://luaukalamaku.com; Kilohana Plantation, 3-2087 Kaumuali'i Hwy; adult/child 5-11yr/youth 12-16yr $100/40/60; ⌚5-8:30pm Tue & Fri; 👪) Skip the same-old commercial luau and catch this dinner theater-in-the-round with a dash of Cirque du Soleil (think lithe dancers, flashy leotards and pyrotechnics) thrown in. The stage play about one family's epic voyage to Hawaii features hula and Tahitian dancing, and show-stopping, nail-biting Samoan fire dancing. The buffet dinner is above average, despite the audience size (maximum 1000 people).

Kaua'i Concert Association MUSIC
(☎808-245-7464; www.kauai-concert.org; tickets from $25) Stages the annual Red Clay Jazz Festivals and classical, jazz and world-music concerts at the **Kaua'i Community College (KCC) Performing Arts Center** (Map p476; ☎245-8311; http://kauai.hawaii.edu/pac/; 3-1901 Kaumuali'i Hwy), where past performers include Berklee College of Music and the Harlem String Quartet.

Kukui Grove Cinema 4 CINEMA
(Map p476; ☎808-245-5055; www.kukuigrovecinema.com; 4368 Kukui Grove St; tickets $6-9; 👪) Standard fourplex shows mainstream first-run Hollywood movies.

Shopping

Lihu'e's biggest mall is the aging, open-air **Kukui Grove Center** (Map p476; ☎808-245-7784; www.kukuigrovecenter.com; 3-2600 Kaumuali'i Hwy; ⌚9:30am-7pm Mon-Thu & Sat, to 9pm Fri, 10am-6pm Sun; 📶), home to department stores, sporting-goods and electronics shops, banks and more. Near Nawiliwili Harbor, the busy, low-slung **Anchor Cove Shopping Center** (Map p476; 3416 Rice St) and emptier two-story **Harbor Mall** (Map p476; ☎808-245-6255; www.harbormall.net; 3501 Rice St) draw mainly tourists from cruise ships and the nearby Marriott.

★Edith King Wilcox Gift Shop & Bookstore BOOKS, GIFTS
(Map p478; ☎808-246-2470; www.kauaimuseum.org; Kaua'i Museum, 4428 Rice St; ⌚10am-5pm Mon-Sat) 🍃 The Kaua'i Museum's gem of a gift shop carries a variety of genuine Hawaiian crafts, such as Ni'ihau shell jewelry, koa woodwork and *lauhala* (a type of traditional Hawaiian leaf weaving) hats, along with collectible contemporary artworks and

plenty of Hawaiiana books. Enter the shop, free of charge, through the museum lobby.

★Koloa Rum Company DRINK
(Map p476; 808-246-8900; www.koloarum.com; Kilohana Plantation, 3-2087 Kaumuali'i Hwy; store 9:30am-5pm Mon, Wed & Sat, 9:30am-9pm Tue & Fri, 9:30am-6:30pm Thu, 9:30am-3pm Sun, tasting room 10am-3:30pm Mon, Wed & Sat, 10am-7:30pm Tue & Fri, 10am-5pm Thu, 10am-2pm Sun) Kaua'i's own rum label is a relatively new brand, which means it doesn't have a fine aged rum yet, but its dark and spiced versions win awards. Learn how to mix a classic mai tai during a free rum tasting, starting every 30 minutes daily.

Koa Store GIFTS, SOUVENIRS
(Map p476; 808-245-4871, 800-838-9264; www.thekoastore.com; 3-3601 Kuhio Hwy; 10am-6pm) Other galleries carry high-end masterpieces, but here you'll find more affordable and functional pieces, such as picture frames and jewelry boxes. Many items come in three grades, from the basic straight-grain koa to premium 'curly' koa. All woodcraft are genuine – they're not the cheap fakes sold at tourist traps. There's another location in Koloa.

Flowers Forever GIFTS
(Map p478; 808-245-4717, 800-646-7579; www.flowersforeverhawaii.com; 2679 Kalena St; 8am-5pm Mon-Thu, to 6pm Fri, to 4pm Sat) Voted 'Best Kaua'i Flower Shop' for 12 years running, Forever Flowers strings together a multitude of flower, maile, *ti*-leaf and more unusual specialty lei. It will ship tropical flowers, plants and lei to the mainland too.

Kapaia Stitchery ARTS & CRAFTS
(Map p476; www.kapaia-stitchery.com; 3-3551 Kuhio Hwy; 9am-5pm Mon-Sat) A quilter's heaven, this longtime shop features countless tropical-print cotton fabrics, as well as island-made patterns and kits. Stop here also for handmade gifts and apparel, including children's clothing and aloha shirts.

Clayworks ARTS & CRAFTS
(Map p476; 808-246-2529; www.clayworksatkilohana.com; Kilohana Plantation, 3-2087 Kaumuali'i Hwy; 10am-6pm Mon-Fri, 11am-2pm Sat & Sun) A hidden pottery studio and gallery overflows with colorful vases, mugs, bowls and tiles. Potters also offer tutelage at the throwing wheel, and you'll get to take home your *raku*-fired, glazed masterpiece. Call ahead for lessons.

Da Life OUTDOOR EQUIPMENT
(Map p476; 808-246-6333; www.livedalife.com; 3500 Rice St; 9am-5pm Mon-Fri, 10am-4pm Sat & Sun) This outdoor outfitter and booking agent's retail shop is stuffed with sports gear for all manner of land and sea adventures on Kaua'i. If you forgot to pack it, Da Life probably stocks it.

Tropic Isle Music & Gifts SOUVENIRS, MUSIC
(Map p476; www.tropicislemusic.com; Anchor Cove Shopping Center, 3416 Rice St; 10am-8pm) This tiny shop is crammed with a huge selection of Hawaiiana books, CDs, DVDs, bath and body products, home décor, island-made foodstuffs – you name it. Here you can avoid mistakenly buying mass-produced knock-offs imported from Asia.

Longs Drugs SOUVENIRS, FOOD
(Map p476; 808-245-8871; www.cvs.com; Kukui Grove Center, 3-2600 Kaumuali'i Hwy; 7am-10pm) So much more than a drugstore, Longs is an inexpensive place to shop for a wide selection of Hawaii-made products, from children's books to macnuts and crack-seed candy.

Information

EMERGENCY

Police, Fire & Ambulance (911)

Police Station (808-241-1638; www.kauai.gov; 3990 Kaana St) For nonemergencies and incident reporting.

MEDICAL SERVICES

Kaua'i Urgent Care (808-245-1532; www.wilcoxhealth.org; 4484 Pahe'e St; 8am-7pm Mon-Fri, to 4pm Sat & Sun) Walk-in clinic for nonemergencies.

Longs Drugs (808-245-8871; Kukui Grove Center, 3-2600 Kaumuali'i Hwy; store 7am-10pm, pharmacy to 9pm Mon-Fri, to 6pm Sat & Sun) Full-service pharmacy.

Wilcox Memorial Hospital (808-245-1100; www.wilcoxhealth.org; 3-3420 Kuhio Hwy) Kaua'i's only major hospital has a 24-hour emergency room.

MONEY

American Savings Bank (808-246-8844; www.asbhawaii.com; Kukui Grove Center, 3-2600 Kaumuali'i Hwy) Convenient shopping-mall branch with a 24-hour ATM.

Bank of Hawaii (808-245-6761; www.boh.com; 4455 Rice St) Downtown bank with a 24-hour ATM.

POST

Lihu'e Post Office (Map p478; ☎808-245-1628; www.usps.com; 4441 Rice St; ⏰8am-4pm Mon-Fri, 9am-1pm Sat) Kaua'i's main post office.

TOURIST INFORMATION

Kaua'i Visitors Bureau (Map p478; ☎808-245-3971, 800-262-1400; www.gohawaii.com/kauai; Suite 101, 4334 Rice St; ⏰8am-4:30pm Mon-Fri) Comprehensive web resources for visitors, with free vacation-planning kits downloadable online.

Getting There & Away

AIR

Lihu'e Airport (LIH; ☎808-274-3800; http://hawaii.gov/lih; 3901 Mokulele Loop) Only 2 miles from downtown, this small airport handles all commercial interisland, US mainland and Canada flights.

BUS

Kaua'i Bus (Map p476; ☎808-246-8110; www.kauai.gov; 3220 Ho'olako St; one-way fare adult/senior & child 7-18yr $2/1) As the hub for Kaua'i Bus, Lihu'e has service to all major island regions, including Hanalei, the Eastside and the Westside. Most routes run hourly or so on weekdays, with limited service on Saturdays, Sundays and holidays. Check the website for current schedules.

CAR & MOTORCYCLE

Kauai Car & Scooter Rental (☎808-245-7177; www.kauaimopedrentals.com; 3148 Oihana St; ⏰8am-5pm) Locally owned agency rents older economy-size island cars from $25 per day, and scooters or mopeds from $35 per day, with additional taxes and fees. Younger drivers (over 21 years) and debit cardholders welcome. Book in advance; free airport pickups available.

Kaua'i Harley-Davidson (☎808-212-9469, 808-212-9495, 888-690-6233; www.kauaiharley.com; 3-1878 Kaumuali'i Hwy; ⏰8am-5pm) It'll cost up to $200 per day, plus a $1000 minimum security deposit, but if you want a hog in paradise, you've got one.

Getting Around

TO/FROM THE AIRPORT

To pick up rental cars, check in at agency booths outside the baggage-claim area, then catch a complimentary shuttle bus to the agency's parking lot. Or go straight to the rental-car lot, where there may be less of a queue.

Taxicabs are infrequently used because most visitors rent cars, but you'll usually find them waiting curbside outside the baggage-claim area. If not, use the courtesy phones to call one.

BUS

Kaua'i Bus serves Lihu'e with a shuttle that runs hourly from about 6am until 9pm. Stops include Kukui Grove Center, Lihu'e Airport (no large backpacks or luggage allowed), Vidinha Stadium and Wilcox Memorial Hospital. There's also a lunchtime shuttle within central Lihu'e that runs at 15-minute intervals between approximately 10:30am and 2pm.

CAR & MOTORCYCLE

Most businesses have free parking lots for customers. Metered street parking is pretty easy to find.

HIGHWAY NICKNAMES

Locals call highways by nickname rather than by number.

HIGHWAY NUMBER	NICKNAME
Hwy 50	Kaumuali'i Hwy
Hwy 51	Kapule Hwy
Hwy 56	Kuhio Hwy
Hwy 58	Nawiliwili Rd
Hwy 520	Maluhia Rd (Tunnel of Trees)
Hwy 530	Koloa Rd
Hwy 540	Halewili Rd
Hwy 550	Waimea Canyon Dr and Koke'e Rd
Hwy 560	Kuhio Hwy (continuation of Hwy 56)
Hwy 570	Ahukini Rd
Hwy 580	Kuamo'o Rd
Hwy 581	Kamalu Rd and Olohena Rd
Hwy 583	Ma'alo Rd

KAPA'A & THE EASTSIDE

If you look past the strip malls and highway traffic, the Eastside fascinates. Its geography runs the gamut, from mountaintop forests to pounding surf and a majestic river. In ancient times, the Wailua River was sacred and Hawaiian royalty lived along its fertile banks. Kapa'a's historic town center echoes another bygone era of sugar plantations.

Kaua'i's population is concentrated here. Stretching from Wailua to Kapa'a, the 'Coconut Coast' has a busy, workaday vibe, as opposed to the swankier resorts of Princeville

Eastside

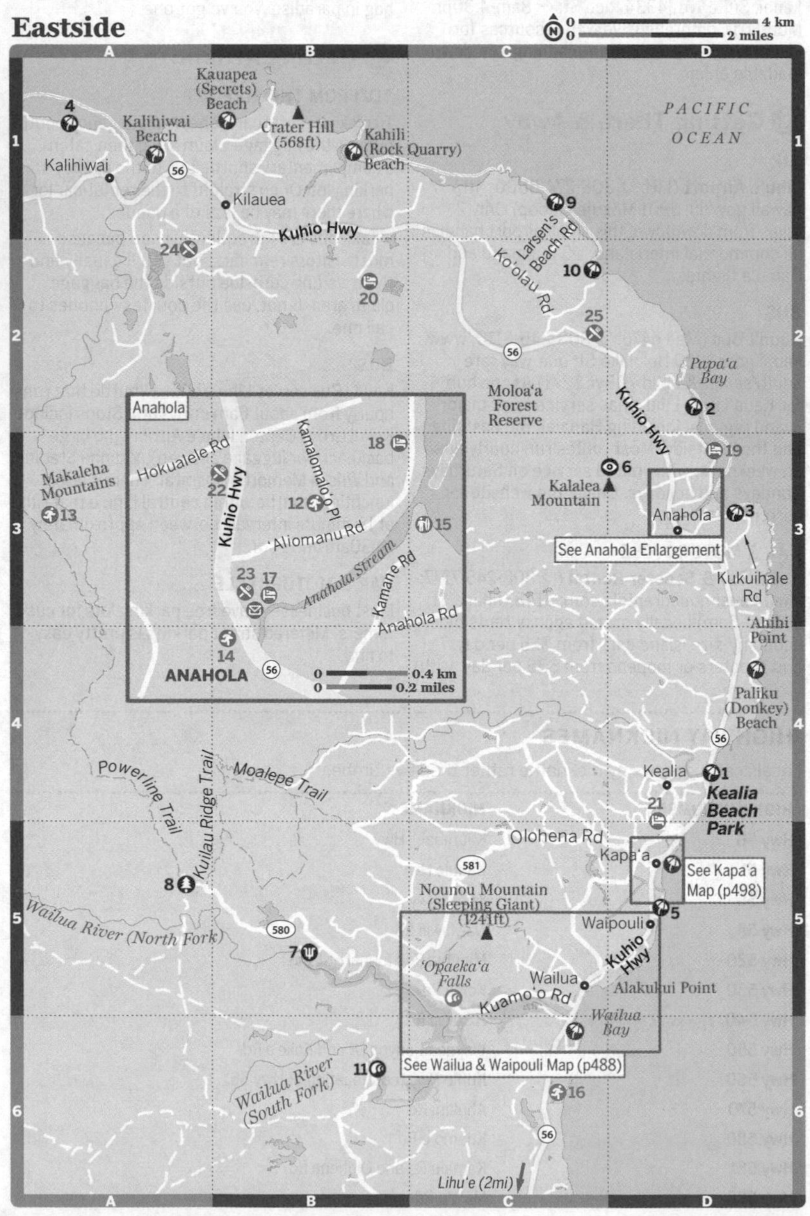

and Po'ipu. Traffic can grind to a painful halt at any time of day here, however. Further north and hidden away from the hubbub is down-home Anahola – a fishing and farming village where Hawaiians make up about half of all residents.

Wailua

Wailua has two sides to it. The coast belongs to strip-mall businesses and package tourists, who are packed into oceanfront condos and hotels like happy slices of a pie chart. But if you're after that wild-palm-grove nature magic for which Kaua'i is famous, you can find that here too. Just head to the languid Wailua River – the only navigable river in the state – or follow hiking trails that wind high into lush forested mountains.

Beaches

★Lydgate Beach Park BEACH
(www.kamalani.org;) A narrow stretch of windswept blond sand strewn with driftwood can entertain restless kids of all ages, all afternoon. There's generally safe swimming to be found in two pools inside a protected breakwater, and beginner snorkeling too. Other amenities include two big playgrounds, game-sized soccer fields, a paved recreational path, picnic tables and pavilions, restrooms, outdoor showers, drinking water and lifeguards.

To get here, turn *makai* (seaward) on Kuhio Hwy between mile markers 5 and 6.

At the park's northern end, multifeatured **Kamalani Playground** is a massive 16,000-sq-ft wooden castle with swings, a volcano slide, mirror mazes, an epic suspension bridge and other kid-pleasing contraptions.

Beware of the open ocean beyond the protected pool – it can be rough and dangerous, with strong currents, huge waves, sharp coral and slippery rocks.

Sights

Take a virtual tour of the **Wailua Heritage Trail** (www.wailuaheritagetrail.org) for an overview of historical sights and natural attractions, with a downloadable map.

★Kaua'i's Hindu Monastery HINDU TEMPLE
(Map p486; ☎808-822-3012, 888-735-1619; www.himalayanacademy.com; 107 Kaholalele Rd; ⏲9am-noon, inner gate open after 10:30am) FREE Serious pilgrims and curious sightseers are welcome at this Hindu monastery, set in 363 acres of verdant forest above the Wailua River. Amid bountiful gardens, the Kadavul Temple, Ganesha and Nandi statues and other structures are all devoted to the god Shiva. While visitors can access a limited area on their own daily, free guided tours are offered once a week – call or check the website for details. Modest dress required: no shorts, T-shirts, tank tops or short dresses.

The **Kadavul Temple** contains a rare single-pointed quartz crystal, a 50-million-year-old, six-sided *shivalingam* (representation of the god Shiva) that weighs 700lb and stands over 3ft tall. In the temple (which visitors may not enter except to attend a 9am daily worship service), monks have performed a *puja* (prayer ritual) every three hours around the clock since the temple was established in 1973.

Eastside

Top Sights
1 Kealia Beach Park ... D4

Sights
2 'Aliomanu Beach ... D2
3 Anahola Beach Park ... D3
4 'Anini Beach Park ... A1
5 Fujii Beach ... D5
6 Hole in the Mountain ... D3
7 Kaua'i's Hindu Monastery ... B5
8 Keahua Arboretum ... A5
9 Larsen's Beach ... C1
10 Moloa'a Beach ... C2
11 Wailua Falls ... B6

Activities, Courses & Tours
12 Angeline's Mu'olaulani ... B3
13 Powerline Trail ... A3
14 TriHealth Ayurveda Spa ... B4
15 Unreals ... C3
16 Wailua Municipal Golf Course ... C6

Sleeping
17 Hale Kiko'o ... B3
18 'Ili Noho Kai O Anahola ... B3
19 Kaleialoha ... D3
20 Kauai Vacation Cottages ... B2
21 No Ka Oi ... D4

Eating
22 Anahola Farmers Market ... B3
23 Duane's Ono Char-Burger ... B3
24 Garden Cafe ... A2
25 Moloa'a Sunrise Juice Bar ... C2

Wailua & Waipouli

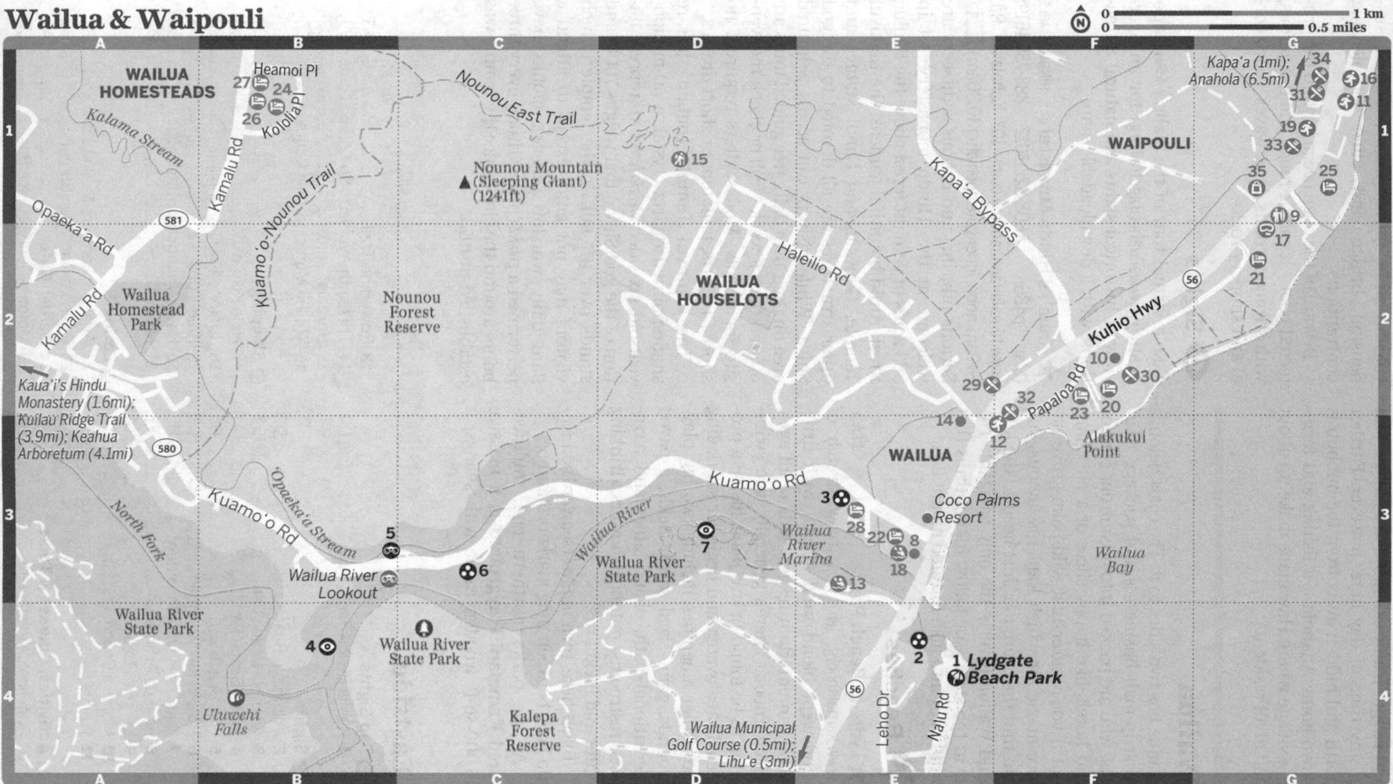

Wailua & Waipouli

Top Sights
1 Lydgate Beach Park ... E4

Sights
2 Hikina'akala Heiau ... E4
3 Holoholoku Heiau ... E3
4 Kamokila Hawaiian Village ... B4
5 'Opaeka'a Falls Lookout ... B3
6 Poli'ahu Heiau ... C3
7 Smith's Tropical Paradise ... D3

Activities, Courses & Tours
8 Ali'i Kayaks & Water Sports ... E3
9 Ambrose's Kapuna Surf Gallery ... G1
10 Kaua'i Cultural Center ... F2
11 Kauai Cycle ... G1
12 Kauai Water Ski Co ... F3
13 Kayak Kaua'i ... E3
14 Kayak Wailua ... E3
15 Nounou Mountain Trail ... D1
16 Seasport Divers ... G1
Smith's Motor Boat Service ... (see 13)
17 Snorkel Bob's ... G2
18 Wailua Kayak & Canoe ... E3
19 Yoga House ... G1

Sleeping
20 Aston Islander on the Beach ... F2
21 Courtyard by Marriott Kauai at Coconut Beach ... G2
22 Fern Grotto Inn ... E3
23 Kauai Shores ... F2
24 Lani Keha ... B1
25 Outrigger Waipouli Beach Resort & Spa ... G1
26 Rosewood Kaua'i ... B1
27 Sleeping Giant Cottage ... B1
28 Surf & Ski Cottage ... E3

Eating
29 Caffè Coco ... E2
Coconut Marketplace ... (see 10)
Foodland ... (see 35)
30 Hukilau Lanai ... F2
31 Kaua'i Pasta ... G1
Kilauea Fish Market ... (see 20)
32 Kintaro ... F2
Monico's Taqueria ... (see 12)
Oasis on the Beach ... (see 25)
33 Papaya's Natural Foods ... G1
Safeway ... (see 33)
34 Shrimp Station ... G1
Tiki Tacos ... (see 34)
Tropical Dreams ... (see 33)

Entertainment
Coconut Marketplace Hula Show ... (see 10)
Smith's Garden Luau ... (see 7)
Trees Lounge ... (see 20)

Shopping
Marta's Boat ... (see 9)
Mint & Sea ... (see 29)
Moloa'a Bay Coffee ... (see 34)
Nani Moon Meadery & Tasting Room ... (see 31)
35 Waipouli Town Center ... G1

If you're not dressed properly, you can borrow sarongs to cover up with at the entrance.

'Opaeka'a Falls Lookout VIEWPOINT

While not a showstopper, these 150ft-high waterfalls make for an easy roadside stop, less than 2 miles up Kumao'o Rd. For the best photographs, go in the morning. Don't be tempted to try trailblazing to the base of the falls. These steep cliffs are perilous and have caused fatalities. Cross the road for a fantastic photo op of the Wailua River.

Kamokila Hawaiian Village CULTURAL CENTER

(808-823-0559; http://villagekauai.com; 5443 Kuamo'o Rd; village admission adult/child 3-12yr $5/3, outrigger canoe tours adult/child $30/20; 9am-5pm;) While not a must-see, it's a pleasant diversion, especially for kids. Along the Wailua River, the 4-acre site includes reproductions of traditional Hawaiian structures amid thriving gardens of guava, mango and banana trees. Kamokila also offers canoe rentals and guided **outrigger canoe tours**, leaving hourly, which include paddling, hiking and waterfall swimming.

Turn south from Kuamo'o Rd, opposite 'Opaeka'a Falls. The half-mile road leading to the village is steep and narrow.

Smith's Tropical Paradise GARDENS

(808-821-6895; www.smithskauai.com; adult/child 3-12yr $6/3; 8:30am-4pm;) Other gardens might have fancier landscaping, but you can't beat Smith's for value. Take a leisurely stroll along a mile-long loop trail past a serene pond, grassy lawns and island-themed gardens. The setting can seem Disney-esque, with an Easter Island *moai* statue replica, but it's appealingly unpretentious.

Keahua Arboretum PARK

(Map p486) FREE Sitting at the top of Kuamo'o Rd, this arboretum has grassy fields, a gurgling stream and groves of rainbow

THE SOURCE: MT WAI'ALE'ALE

Nicknamed the Rain Machine, Mt Wai'ale'ale (translated as 'rippling water' or 'overflowing water') averages more than 450in of rainfall annually. With a yearly record of 683in in 1982, it's widely regarded as one of the wettest places on earth. Its steep cliffs cause moist air to rise rapidly and focus rainfall in one area. Believed by ancient Hawaiians to be occupied by the god Kane, it's located in the center of the island, representing Kaua'i's *piko* (navel). It's the source of the Wailua, Hanalei and Waimea Rivers, as well as almost every visible waterfall on the island.

eucalyptus and other towering trees. Locals come here to picnic and to swim in the freshwater stream and pools, but beware that the water is infected with leptospira bacteria.

Activities

★Wailua Municipal Golf Course GOLF

(Map p486; ☎808-241-6666; www.kauai.gov/golf; 3-5350 Kuhio Hwy; nonresident green fees $48-60) This 18-hole, par-72 course, designed by former head pro Toyo Shirai, is one of Hawaii's top-ranked municipal golf courses. Plan ahead because morning tee times are sometimes reserved a week in advance. After 2pm, the green fee drops by half and it's first-come, first-served. Cart and club rentals available.

Kaua'i Cultural Center COURSE

(☎808-651-0682; http://kauaiculturalcenter.com; Coconut Marketplace, 4-484 Kuhio Hwy; 1hr class from $5; 👪) Inside a shopping mall, this tiny community center is run by Leilani Rivera Low, a respected *kumu* hula (hula teacher). Take a beginner's hula, Tahitian dance or ukulele lesson, or learn how to make a *ti*-leaf skirt or flower lei. Call a day ahead to reserve a spot or drop by to ask about walk-in space.

Check the website for a schedule of upcoming classes, workshops and events.

Kauai Water Ski Co WATER SPORTS

(☎808-822-3574, 808-639-2829; www.kauaiwaterskiandsurf.com; Kinipopo Shopping Village, 4-356 Kuhio Hwy; per 30/60min $75/140; ⏰9am-5pm Mon-Fri, to noon Sat) Hawaii's only non-ocean water-skiing happens on the Wailua River. Rates are per trip, not per person (maximum number of riders varies by skill level; beginners welcome), and include water-skiing or wakeboarding equipment and a professional instructor as your driver. Reservations are required.

Powerline Trail MOUNTAIN BIKING

(Map p486) While this trail (which covers more than 11 miles between Wailua and Princeville) is used mainly by hunters, it's a decent ride for die-hard mountain bikers. Hikers might find the trek too long, too exposed and, especially toward the north end, too monotonous. Beware of steep drop-offs hidden in dense foliage, and expect to slog through mud and puddly ruts.

The southern trailhead is at the end of Kuamo'o Rd. Beyond the Keahua Arboretum parking lot, you must cross water – not recommended with a standard car, especially in rainy weather.

Kayaking

Majestic and calm, the 20-mile-long **Wailua River** is fed by two streams originating on Mt Wai'ale'ale. It's the only navigable river across the Hawaiian Islands, and kayaking it has become a visitor must-do. Fortunately, the paddle is a doable 5 miles for all ages.

Tours usually paddle 2 miles up the river's north fork, which leads to a mile-long hike through dense forest to **Uluwehi Falls** (Secret Falls), a 100ft waterfall. The hike crosses a stream and scrambles over rocks and roots, and if muddy it will probably cause some slippin' and slidin'. Wear sturdy, washable, nonslip watersports sandals.

Most tours last four to five hours, departing in the morning or early afternoon (call ahead for exact check-in times). The maximum group size is 12, with paddlers going out in double kayaks. The pricier tours include lunch, but on budget tours, you can store your own food in coolers or waterproof bags. Bring a hat, sunscreen and insect repellent.

Experienced paddlers might want to rent individual kayaks and go out on their own. Note that not all tour companies are also licensed to rent individual kayaks, and no kayak tours or rentals are allowed on Sundays. Kayaking outfitters are based in Wailua or Kapa'a.

★**Kayak Wailua** KAYAKING, HIKING
(☎808-822-3388; www.kayakwailua.com; 4565 Haleilio Rd; 4½hr tours $50) This small, family-owned company specializes in Wailua River tours. It keeps its boats and equipment in tip-top shape; shuttles you to the marina launch site; and provides dry bags for your belongings and a nylon cooler for your own food.

Ali'i Kayaks & Water Sports KAYAKING, HIKING
(☎808-241-7700, 877-246-2544; www.aliikayaks.com; 174 Wailua Rd; kayak tours $40, SUP rental per 2hr/day $30/45, SUP lessons $60) Right on the Wailua River, this outfitter specializes in kayak-and-hike tours. You can also experience the river another way by stand-up paddle surfing (SUP). No kayak rentals.

Kayak Kaua'i KAYAKING
(☎808-826-9844, 800-437-3507; www.kayakkauai.com; Wailua River Marina; double kayak rental per day $64, 4½hr tours $60-85) This reputable island-wide operator offers Wailua River tours and kayak rentals (small surcharge for dry bags and coolers). If you're renting, you'll have to transport the kayak a short distance atop your car.

Wailua Kayak & Canoe KAYAKING, HIKING
(☎808-821-1188; https://wailuariverkayaking.com; 169 Wailua Rd; single/double kayak rental $50/85, tours $65-90; 👪) Located at the boat ramp on the north bank of the Wailua River, this outfit is very convenient for individual rentals (no need to transport the kayak), but service is minimal and prices have skyrocketed.

Hiking

Most Eastside hiking trails ascend into Kaua'i's tropical-jungle interior. Expect humidity, red dirt (or mud) and slippery patches after rains.

★**Kuilau Ridge & Moalepe Trails** HIKING
Just more than 2 miles long each way, the **Kuilau Ridge Trail** is recommended for its sheer beauty: emerald valleys, dewy bushes, thick ferns and glimpses of misty Mt Wai'ale'ale in the distance. After 1 mile, you'll reach a grassy clearing with a picnic table. Continue north on descending switchbacks until you meet the mountain-view **Moalepe Trail** (2.25 miles one way).

Both of these moderate hikes are among the most visually rewarding on Kaua'i. Remember, the trails don't complete a circuit

THE SACRED WAILUA RIVER

To ancient Hawaiians, the Wailua River was among the most sacred places across the islands. The river basin, near its mouth, was one of the island's two royal centers (the other was Waimea) and home to the high chiefs. Here you can find the remains of many important heiau (ancient stone temples), together now as a national historic landmark.

The **Hikina'akala Heiau** (Rising of the Sun Temple) sits south of the Wailua River mouth, which is today the north end of Lydgate Beach Park. In its heyday, the long, narrow temple (built around AD 1300) was aligned directly north to south, but only a few remaining boulders outline its original massive shape. Neighboring **Hauola Pu'uhonua** (meaning 'the place of refuge of the dew of life') is marked by a bronze plaque. Ancient Hawaiian *kapu* (taboo) breakers were assured safety from persecution if they made it inside.

Believed to be the oldest *luakini* (temple dedicated to the war god Ku, often a place for human sacrifice) on the island, **Holoholoku Heiau** is located a quarter-mile up Kuamo'o Rd on the left. It's believed to be Kaua'i's oldest heiau. Toward the west, against the flat-backed birthstone marked by a plaque reading **Pohaku Ho'ohanau** (Royal Birthstone), queens gave birth to future royals. Only a male child born here could become king of Kaua'i.

Perched high on a hill overlooking the meandering Wailua River, well-preserved **Poli'ahu Heiau**, another *luakini*, is named after the snow goddess Poli'ahu, one of the sisters of the volcano goddess Pele. The heiau is immediately before **'Opaeka'a Falls Lookout**, on the opposite side of the road.

Although Hawaiian heiau were originally imposing stone structures, most now lie in ruins, covered with scrub. But they are still considered powerful vortices of *mana* (spiritual essence) and should be treated with respect. For a compelling history of the Wailua River's significance to ancient Hawaiians, read Edward Joesting's *Kauai: the Separate Kingdom*.

so you must retrace your steps (8.5 miles round-trip). You might want to skip the final mile of the outbound leg, which crosses the treeless pastureland of Wailua Game Management Area.

The Kuilau Ridge Trail starts at a marked trailhead on the right just before Kuamo'o Rd crosses the stream at the Keahua Arboretum, 4 miles above the junction of Kuamo'o Rd and Kamalu Rd. The Moalepe Trail trailhead is at the end of Olohena Rd in the Wailua Homesteads neighborhood.

Nounou Mountain Trail HIKING

Climbing Nounou Mountain (Sleeping Giant), you'll ascend over 1000ft for panoramic views of Kaua'i's Eastside. Approach the mountain on the Nounou East Trail (2 miles), on the Nounou West Trail (1.5 miles) or from the south on the Kuamo'o-Nounou Trail (2 miles). The trails meet near the center (all distances given are one way).

Most visitors prefer the exposed **Nounou East Trail** because it offers sweeping views of the ocean and distant mountains. The well-maintained trail is moderately strenuous and steep, with switchbacks almost to the ridge. At the three-way junction near the top, take the left fork, which leads to the summit, marked by a picnic shelter. Now atop the giant's chest, only his head prevents you from getting a 360-degree view. Climbing further is extremely risky and not recommended.

Do this hike early in the morning, when it's relatively cool and you can witness daylight spreading across the valley. The hard-packed dirt trail is exceedingly slippery when wet; look for a walking stick, which hikers sometimes leave near the trailhead. The trail starts at a parking lot a mile up Haleilio Rd in the Wailua Homesteads neighborhood. When the road curves left, look for telephone pole 38 with the trailhead sign.

The **Nounou West Trail** ascends faster, but it's better if you prefer a cooler, shadier forest trail. There are two ways to access the trailhead: from Kamalu Rd, near telephone pole 11, or from the end of Lokelani Rd, off Kamalu Rd. Walk through a metal gate signed as a forestry right-of-way.

The **Kuamo'o-Nounou Trail** runs through groves of trees planted in the 1930s by the Civilian Conservation Corps; it connects with the Nounou West Trail. Marked by a brown-and-yellow Na Ala Hele sign, the trailhead is right on Kuamo'o Rd between mile markers 2 and 3.

Kaua'i Nature Tours HIKING

(808-742-8305, 888-233-8365; www.kauainaturetours.com; tours adult/child 7-12yr from $130/105) For guided hikes, the gold standard is geoscientist Chuck Blay's company, which offers a full-day tour – snacks, drinks and transportation included. Guided hikes also hit the North Shore's Na Pali Coast, Po'ipu, and Waimea Canyon and Koke'e State Parks.

Tours

Steelgrass Farm WALKING TOUR

(808-821-1857; www.steelgrass.org; 3hr tour adult/child under 12yr $60/free; 9am-noon Mon, Wed & Fri;) Learn more about diversified agriculture, cacao growing and the owners' intriguing family history at this working chocolate farm. The farm's other main crops are bamboo and vanilla, and additionally hundreds of tropical species can also be seen on these 8 acres. Advance reservations for the (overpriced) tours are required; you'll be given driving directions after booking.

Smith's Motor Boat Service BOAT TOUR

(808-821-6892; www.smithskauai.com; Wailua Marina; 80min tour adult/child $20/10; departures at 9:30am, 11am, 2pm & 3:30pm) If you're curious to see the once legendary Fern Grotto, this covered boat ride is hokey but homespun. Bear in mind that since heavy rains and rockslides in 2006, visitors cannot enter the grotto – which looks a bit parched, frankly – but must stay on the wooden platform quite a distance from the shallow cave.

THE SLEEPING GIANT

Take a look at Nounou Mountain. What do you see?

Islanders see a sleeping giant. According to legend, an amicable giant fell asleep on the hillside after gorging at a luau. His *menehune* (little people) friends tried to rouse him by throwing stones. But the stones bounced from his full belly into his open mouth and lodged in his throat. He died in his sleep and turned into rock.

Now he rests, stretched with his head in Wailua and his feet in Kapa'a. At an elevation of almost 1250ft, the giant's forehead is the highest point on the ridge.

Festivals & Events

Taste of Hawaii FOOD
(www.tasteofhawaii.com; Jun) On the first Sunday in June, the Rotary Club of Kapa'a hosts the 'Ultimate Sunday Brunch' at Smith's Tropical Paradise, where you can indulge in gourmet samples by 40 chefs from around Hawaii. Dance it off to more than 10 live-music acts. For discounts, buy tickets online in advance.

Sleeping

Many condos, B&Bs and inns require a three-night minimum stay and charge a one-time cleaning fee. Some are located not by the coast but inland in residential areas.

Rosewood Kaua'i INN $
(808-822-5216; www.rosewoodkauai.com; 872 Kamalu Rd; r with shared bath $75-85;) Budget travelers will be spoiled by these meticulously tidy, if small, private rooms, each with bunk beds or a king-sized loft bed, a built-in kitchenette and lots of light. Bathrooms and a gazebo-enclosed outdoor shower are all shared. Expect a cleaning fee ($45).

For a step up, inquire about Rosewood's cottages, vacation homes and condo rentals.

Sleeping Giant Cottage COTTAGE $
(505-401-4403; www.wanek.com/sleepinggiant; 5979 Heamoi Pl; 1-bedroom cottage $99;) Surrounded by tropical foliage and open-air lanai, this plantation-style bungalow makes a private and spacious retreat. It's pleasantly appointed with hardwood floors, a full kitchen, washer/dryer, a king-sized bed, BBQ grills and a huge screened patio facing a backyard garden. There's free beach gear to borrow. Cleaning fee $50.

Surf & Ski Cottage COTTAGE $
(808-822-3574; http://kauaiwaterskiandsurf.com/cottage; Ohana St; cottage per night/week $85/550;) Suitable for solos or couples looking for something serene but convenient, this tastefully decorated studio features a more-than-functional kitchenette, a queen bed and a Hawaiian *palapa* with a waterproof thatched roof. It's located a few steps from the Wailua River and has a private kayak launch.

Lani Keha COTTAGE $
(808-822-1605; www.lanikeha.com; 848 Kamalu Rd; s/d from $55/65;) Solo travelers and sociable types will appreciate the low-key, communal atmosphere at this simple guesthouse. It's nothing fancy, just three rooms with *lauhala*-mat flooring, king or twin beds and well-worn but clean furnishings. The shared kitchen is stocked with breakfast fixings. It doesn't always rent rooms, so call ahead. No credit cards.

Fern Grotto Inn INN $$
(808-821-9836; www.ferngrottoinn.com; 4561 Kuamo'o Rd; cottages $135-195, 3-bedroom house $250;) Charmingly retro yet remodeled, these early-20th-century plantation-style cottages vary in size. All have hardwood floors, tasteful furnishings and a kitchen or a kitchenette. A prime location near the Wailua River dock reduces the need to drive, and there is a kayak and bikes to borrow. Friendly owners go the extra mile to ensure guests' comfort. Cleaning fee $75 to $125.

Kauai Shores HOTEL $$
(808-822-4951, 866-970-4169; www.kauaishoreshotel.com; 420 Papaloa Rd; r $85-240; @) Recently renovated by Hawaii's boutique-hotel chain Aqua, this coastal property has tidy little rooms splashed with sunny modern panache. The mandatory 'hospitality fee' ($15 plus tax per night) covers continental breakfast, morning yoga and DVDs, video games, and beach chairs and towels for borrowing

Courtyard by Marriott Kauai at Coconut Beach HOTEL $$
(808-822-3455, 877-997-6667; www.marriotthawaii.com; 650 Aleka Loop; r $110-290; @) This polished, 300-plus-room beachside hotel has been fully renovated, from a soaring lobby full of plush seating to an ocean-view pool. Business-class suites pamper guests with deep soaking tubs and kitchenettes. More than half of the regular rooms have cinnamon-wood plantation shutters opening onto private lanai. The mandatory resort fee ($20 per night) covers parking and two mai tais.

Aston Islander on the Beach HOTEL $$
(808-822-7417, 877-977-6667; www.astonislander.com; 440 Aleka Pl; r $175-230;) It's not a resort, so don't expect too many frills. Yet the rooms inside these low-rise beachfront buildings are contemporary and upscale, with teak furnishings, granite countertops, flat-screen TVs, microwaves and mini fridges. A mandatory amenity fee ($18 plus tax per night) covers parking plus DVD and video-game rentals. Deep discounts often available online.

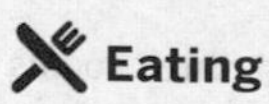

Eating

Waipouli and Kapa'a have loads of eating options just a couple of miles north.

Coconut Marketplace FAST FOOD $
(www.coconutmarketplace.com; 4-484 Kuhio Hwy; snacks from $2, mains $6-12) A tiny farmers market is held at this mall on Tuesday and Thursday mornings from 9am until noon. Outside of this, you'll find a few snack bars, fish-and-chips and burger stands, and ice-cream and shave ice stalls here (hours vary).

★ **Kilauea Fish Market** SEAFOOD, LOCAL $$
(☎808-822-3474; 440 Aleka Pl; mains $9-19; ⏰11am-8pm Mon-Sat; 👪) Bringing their time-tested skills and recipes down from the original North Shore location, this kitchen makes *broke da mout* (delicious) ahi wraps, fresh *poke,* grilled fish plates, salads with local greens, and more. Get take-out for a picnic on the beach.

Monico's Taqueria MEXICAN $$
(☎808-822-4300; http://monicostaqueria.com; Kinipopo Shopping Village, 4-356 Kuhio Hwy; mains $12-15; ⏰11am-3pm & 5-9pm Tue-Sun) Everything made by this Oaxaca-born chef tastes fresh and authentic, from stuffed burritos and fish taco plates to the freshly made chips, salsa and sauces. It's worth the wait.

Hukilau Lanai HAWAII REGIONAL CUISINE $$
(☎808-822-0600; www.hukilaukauai.com; Kaua'i Coast Resort at the Beachboy, 520 Aleka Loop; mains $18-32; ⏰5-9pm Tue-Sun; 👪) An upgrade from the typical T-shirt–casual joint, this laid-back spot hosts live music nightly. Although the menu doesn't always live up to its promise, it showcases top local ingredients, from Kilauea goat's cheese to Kailani Farms greens. Book a table for before 5:45pm if you want to try the early-bird happy hour tasting menu ($32; with wine pairings $50).

Gluten-free and kids' menus available.

Caffè Coco FUSION $$
(☎808-822-7990; www.restauranteur.com/caffecoco; 4-369 Kuhio Hwy; mains $13-21; ⏰11am-2pm Tue-Fri, 5-9pm Tue-Sun; 🌶) At this rustic little hideaway, Asian, Middle Eastern and other 'exotic' flavors infuse into healthful dishes to delight the *Yoga Journal* crowd. Moroccan-spiced ahi is a standout, served with banana chutney rice and a curried veggie samosa. There's live music nightly in the garden, where voracious mosquitoes attack.

Kintaro JAPANESE $$
(☎808-822-3341; 4-370 Kuhio Hwy; small plates $3-15, mains $12-26; ⏰5:30-9:30pm Mon-Sat) Night after night, this locals' favorite sushi bar packs 'em in, despite high prices and slowed-down service. From thick slices of sashimi to tempura combos, the dishes shine in quantity, but only glimmer in quality. The house specialty is sizzling *teppanyaki* service, with chefs showing off at tableside grills. Make reservations.

☆ Entertainment

Coconut Marketplace Hula Show DANCE, MUSIC
(☎808-822-3641; www.coconutmarketplace.com; Coconut Marketplace, 4-484 Kuhio Hwy; admission free; ⏰usually 5pm Wed, 1pm Sat; 👪) While touristy, the Coconut Marketplace's free hula show is nevertheless fun and features Leilani Rivera Low and her hula *halau* (school). She's the daughter of famous Coco Palms entertainer Larry Rivera, who occasionally performs Hawaiian music here and talks story at the mall's Kaua'i Cultural Center (p490).

Smith's Garden Luau LUAU
(☎808-821-6895; www.smithskauai.com; Smith's Tropical Paradise, Wailua Marina; adult/child 7-13yr/child 3-6yr $88/30/19; ⏰4:45pm or 5pm Mon, Wed & Fri; 👪) It's a Kaua'i institution, attracting droves of tourists yet run with aloha spirit by four generations at the family's riverside gardens. Surprisingly, the highlight is the buffet food, including a roasted pig unearthed from an *imu* (underground oven). The multicultural Polynesian show of Hawaiian hula, Tahitian drum dances and Samoan fire dancing is less than exciting.

Prebook online for discounts.

Trees Lounge LIVE MUSIC
(☎808-823-0600; www.treesloungekauai.com; 440 Aleka Pl; ⏰5-11pm Mon-Sat) For those seeking a live-music fix, this venue hosts two happy hours most nights. Headliner acts range from melt-your-face-off rock to mellow acoustic, jazz and traditional Hawaiian sounds. Occasionally a DJ spins. It's behind the Coconut Marketplace.

Shopping

Mint & Sea CLOTHING
(☎808-822-7946; http://instagram.com/mintandseahawaii; 4-369 Kuhio Hwy; ⏰10am-4pm Mon-Thu, to 6pm Fri & Sat) This fresh-faced, breezy women's boutique is stocked with goodies

for women who've outgrown the teenage surfer-chick look. Drapey knit tops, tropical-print shorts, knitted tanks and platform sandals are chic and affordable.

Information

Longs Drugs (808-822-4918; www.cvs.com; 645 Aleka Loop; store 7am-10pm daily, pharmacy 8am-9pm Mon-Fri, 9am-5pm Sat & Sun) Pharmacy has an ATM and also sells beach gear, snacks, drinks and souvenirs.

Getting There & Away

Don't look for a town center. Most attractions are scattered along coastal Kuhio Hwy (Hwy 56) or Kuamo'o Rd (Hwy 580) heading *mauka* (inland). Driving north, Kapa'a Bypass runs from just north of the Wailua River to beyond Kapa'a, completely skipping the traffic jams of Waipouli and Kapa'a.

Waipouli

Waipouli (dark water) and its gentle lagoons served as a departure point for ancient Hawaiians setting sail for Tahiti and other islands of Polynesia. Nowadays Waipouli is less a town than a cluster of restaurants, grocery stores and miscellaneous businesses in strip malls. It's a convenient place to stock up on supplies or grab a bite to eat.

Activities

Bear in mind that rental outlets in Wailua are located at a distance from the activities themselves.

Ambrose's Kapuna Surf Gallery SURFING, SUP
(808-822-3926; www.ambrosecurry.com; 770 Kuhio Hwy; per hr $40; by reservation only) Don't miss the chance to meet surf guru Ambrose Curry, who offers to 'take people surfing' (or stand-up paddling), not to 'give surf lessons'. If you're baffled, then you have much to learn from this longtime surfer-philosopher. Originally from California, Curry has lived on Kaua'i since 1968 and is also an artist and board shaper.

Yoga House YOGA
(808-823-9642; www.bikramyogakapaa.com; 4-885 Kuhio Hwy; drop-in class $17) Come find your yogic bliss in this superheated studio. Classes are offered daily, so there's plenty of opportunity to get centered. To build some serious *prana,* get the all-you-can-bend-in-a-week deal ($55). Go online for current schedules.

Kauai Cycle CYCLING
(808-821-2115; www.kauaicycle.com; 4-934 Kuhio Hwy; bicycle rental per day from $20; 9am-6pm Mon-Fri, to 4pm Sat) Kauai Cycle sells, services and rents all kinds of models – cruisers, hybrids, and road and mountain bikes – that are maintained by experienced cyclists, who also do repairs. Rental prices include a helmet and lock.

Snorkel Bob's SNORKELING, SURFING
(808-823-9433; www.snorkelbob.com; 4-734 Kuhio Hwy; snorkel-set rental per week adult/child under 13yr from $25/22, wetsuit/bodyboard rental per week from $20/26; 8am-5pm) The cool thing about this place is that if you're island-hopping you can rent snorkel gear on Kaua'i and return it on the Big Island, O'ahu or Maui.

Sleeping

Waipouli is sandwiched between Wailua and Kapa'a, which both have more accommodations options.

Outrigger Waipouli Beach Resort & Spa RESORT **$$**
(808-822-6000, 800-688-7444; www.outriggerwaipouli.com; 4-820 Kuhio Hwy; studio/1-/2-bedroom condo from $165/225/275;) The surrounding strip malls and traffic belie the Outrigger's cachet as the Eastside'sánciest condo complex. Units are law-firm handsome with big flat-screen TVs, kitchenettes or full kitchens, and washer-dryers. There's no swimmable beach, but a saltwater 'river pool' and sand-bottom hot tubs compensate somewhat. Outrigger represents nearly half of the almost 200 rental units, but also check www.vrbo.com.

Outrigger's mandatory resort fee ($12 per night) covers parking and internet access; one-time cleaning fee $95 to $195.

Eating

★**Tiki Tacos** MEXICAN **$**
(808-823-8226; www.facebook.com/tikitacos; Waipouli Complex, 4-961 Kuhio Hwy; mains $5-8; 11am-8:30pm) Riding the wave of an island-wide taco craze, this laid-back place with a reggae soundtrack offers authentic *taquería* gravitas right down to the house-made tortillas. Tacos come with chicken, fish, chorizo, shrimp, beef, pork, spicy vegetables or tofu, and they'reha piled high with island-grown cabbage, *queso fresco* (fresh cheese), sour cream and onion. Our fave? The 'surfing pig' taco with pork and fish.

Papaya's Natural Foods HEALTH FOOD $
(☎808-823-0190; www.papayasnaturalfoods.com; Kauai Village, 4-831 Kuhio Hwy; ⊙8am-8pm Mon-Sat, 10am-5pm Sun, cafe closes 1hr earlier;) Kaua'i's biggest health-food store carries local and organic produce, plus other island specialties such as Kilauea honey and goat's cheese. Deli fixings and the salad bar make for a quick, healthy meal, while the cafe grills taro burgers, blends fresh fruit smoothies and sells shots of Hawaiian *noni* juice (a type of mulberry with smelly yellow fruit used medicinally).

Shrimp Station SEAFOOD $
(☎808-821-0192; 4-985 Kuhio Hwy; dishes $8-14; ⊙11am-8:30pm Sun-Wed, to 9pm Thu-Sat;) This offshoot of Waimea's original Shrimp Station serves recipes that have stayed in the family. With seasonings such as garlic, Cajun and Thai on their shrimp tacos, burgers and plate meals, it's hard to shoot and miss here. Some claim it has the 'Best Coconut Shrimp on the Planet.' Whaddya know?

Tropical Dreams ICE CREAM $
(http://tropicaldreamsicecream.com; 4-831 Kuhio Hwy; snacks from $4; ⊙noon-9pm Sun-Thu, to 10pm Fri & Sat) A tiny taste of ice-cream heaven, this only-in-Hawaii chain rotates through scores of premium flavors crafted almost entirely from Hawaii-harvested ingredients. It does soft serve as well as old-fashioned scoops. Cash only.

Foodland SUPERMARKET $
(☎808-822-7271; www.foodland.com; Waipouli Town Center, 4-771 Kuhio Hwy; ⊙6am-11pm) Groceries stocked here include local produce and artisanal foods, as well as select gourmet and health-conscious brands. Scoop up some fresh *poke* from the deli.

Safeway SUPERMARKET $
(☎808-822-2464; www.safeway.com; Kaua'i Village, 4-831 Kuhio Hwy; ⊙store 24hr, pharmacy 8am-8pm Mon-Fri, 9am-6pm Sat & Sun) Caters to mainland tourists through familiar national brands and an American-style deli, bakery, pizza station and sushi bar.

Oasis on the Beach HAWAII REGIONAL CUISINE $$
(☎808-822-9332; www.oasiskauai.com; Outrigger Waipouli Beach Resort, 4-820 Kuhio Hwy; mains lunch & brunch $11-18, dinner $15-35; ⊙11:30am-9pm Mon-Sat, from 10am Sun) This is truly on the beach, like the name says, with unmatched ocean views, a romantic atmosphere and sophisticated cuisine featuring star local ingredients. It's perfect for sharing elevated fusion dishes or hitting up one of Kaua'i's better happy hours (4pm to 6pm daily). Sunday brunch spikes the *loco moco* with cognac and the eggs Benedict with Sriracha sauce. Make reservations for dinner. Expect slow service.

Kaua'i Pasta ITALIAN $$
(☎808-822-7447; www.kauaipasta.com; 4-939b Kuhio Hwy; mains $12-24; ⊙11am-9pm, lounge to midnight Mon-Sat, to 10pm Sun;) Your ticket to surprisingly good Italian food is this strip-mall bistro. Colorful salads meld peppery arugula, creamy goat's cheese and sweet tomatoes, and hot focaccia sandwiches, classic homemade pastas and spinach-artichoke dip pass muster even with finicky foodies. Gluten-free menu available.

Shopping

Waipouli's two pedestrian shopping malls are **Waipouli Town Center** (4-771 Kuhio Hwy) and **Kaua'i Village** (4-831 Kuhio Hwy).

Nani Moon Meadery & Tasting Room WINE
(☎808-651-2453; www.nanimoonmead.com; 4-939 Kuhio Hwy; ⊙noon-5pm Tue-Sat) Nani Moon makes and pours tropical honey wine, which is arguably the oldest alcoholic beverage on earth – humans have been drinking it for 6000 years or more. It crafts a half dozen flavors of mead using only locally sourced ingredients, including tropical fruit and ginger. Most are surprisingly dry, food-forward and 'best enjoyed under moonlight.'

Moloa'a Bay Coffee DRINK, FOOD
(☎808-821-8100; http://moloaabaycoffee.com; 943 Kipuni Way; ⊙8am-noon Mon-Fri) If you miss sampling this North Shore estate-grown coffee at Kaua'i's top farmers markets, stop by the retail shop on weekday mornings to taste the hand-picked, small-batch roasted brews. Unusually, it also makes flavored teas from dried coffee-fruit husks.

Marta's Boat CLOTHING, JEWELRY
(☎808-822-3926; www.martasboat.com; 4-770 Kuhio Hwy; ⊙10am-6pm Mon-Sat) This unique boutique delights 'princesses of all ages' with original block and screen prints on silks and other soft and flowing fabrics, and some funky, fab jewelry. A quirky art-love philosophy is at work in this jewel box. Expect big-city prices.

Information

There are ATMs inside Foodland in Waipouli Town Center and, just a minute north, inside Safeway in the Kaua'i Village shopping center, where you'll also find free wi-fi at Starbucks.

Kapa'a

Kapa'a is the only walkable town on the Eastside, and it has its charms. Although it's not Kaua'i, even at its most beautiful, sunny Kapa'a has a more down-to-earth disposition than other tourist towns, and its eclectic population of old-timers, new transplants, new-age hippies and budget travelers coexists happily. A paved recreational path for cyclists and pedestrians runs along the part-sandy, part-rocky coast, the island's best vantage point for sunrises. Kapa'a's downfall? It sits right along the highway – try walking across the road during rush hour!

Beaches

Kapa'a Beach Park BEACH
(pool 808-822-3842; park dawn-dusk, pool 7:30am-3:45pm Tue-Fri, 10am-4:30pm Sat, noon-4:30pm Sun;) From the highway, you'd think that Kapa'a is beachless. But along the coast is a mile-long ribbon of beach that's very low-key. While the whole area is officially a county park called Kapa'a Beach Park, that name is commonly used only for the northern end, where there's a grassy field, picnic tables and a public **swimming pool**. The best sandy area is at the south end, informally called **Lihi Beach**, where you'll find locals hanging out and talking story.

Further to the south is **Fujii Beach** (Map p486), nicknamed 'Baby Beach' because an offshore reef creates a shallow, placid pool of water that's perfect for toddlers. Located in a modest neighborhood that attracts few tourists, this is a real locals' beach, so be respectful.

A good starting point for the paved coastal path is the footbridge just north of Lihi Beach. To get there, turn *makai* (seaward) on Panihi Rd from the Kuhio Hwy.

Activities

★ **Kapa'a Beach Shop** WATER SPORTS, CYCLING
(www.kapaabeachshop.com; 4-1592 Kuhio Hwy; bike rental per day $5-15, snorkel set rental per day/week $6/12, boogie board $7/20, surfboard $20/50; 8am-6pm Sun-Fri;) Located along the coastal path, this shop has loads of affordable rental options, including cruiser, hybrid comfort and kids' bikes, snorkel and beach gear, boogie boards, surfboards, scuba equipment and even fishing poles. The helpful owners will gladly point enthusiasts in the right direction for whatever adventure they seek, and they also guide shore dives.

Online reservations available.

Coconut Coasters CYCLING
(808-822-7368; www.coconutcoasters.com; 4-1586 Kuhio Hwy; bike rental per day from $20; 9am-6pm Tue-Sat, to 4pm Mon & Sun;) Conveniently located in the heart of Kapa'a town, this outfit rents beach cruiser bikes, tandem bicycles, hybrid comfort bikes, kids' bikes and tow trailers. The shop, which also does repairs, is right by the bike path.

Wailua Kayak Adventures KAYAKING, HIKING
(808-822-5795, 808-639-6332; www.kauaiwailuakayak.com; 1345 Ulu St; single/double kayak rental per day $25/50, 4½hr tours $50-85) Offers good-value individual kayak rentals, but you'll have to transport kayaks to Wailua River yourself on top of your car. Budget-friendly guided kayak tours include

KAPA'A'S COASTAL PATH

The Eastside's **Ke Ala Hele Makalae** (The Path That Goes by the Coast) is a paved shared-use path reserved for pedestrians, cyclists and other nonmotorized modes of transportation. Also known as the Kauai Path (www.kauaipath.org) or Kapa'a Bike Path, it has jump-started locals into daily fitness: walking, running, cycling, rollerblading and, perhaps, forgoing the habit of driving everywhere.

In Kapa'a, the path currently starts at **Lihi Boat Ramp** at the south end of Kapa'a Beach Park and ends just past Paliku (Donkey) Beach at **Ahihi Point**, a 5-mile stretch. The ambitious plan calls for a path eventually extending more than 16 miles all the way from Lihu'e's Nawiliwili Harbor to Anahola Beach Park.

While a loud minority has complained about pouring concrete along the coast, most appreciate the easy-access path. Sunrise walks are brilliant. And for an added kick, you can head out on a cruiser bike rented in Kapa'a or Waipouli.

Kapa'a

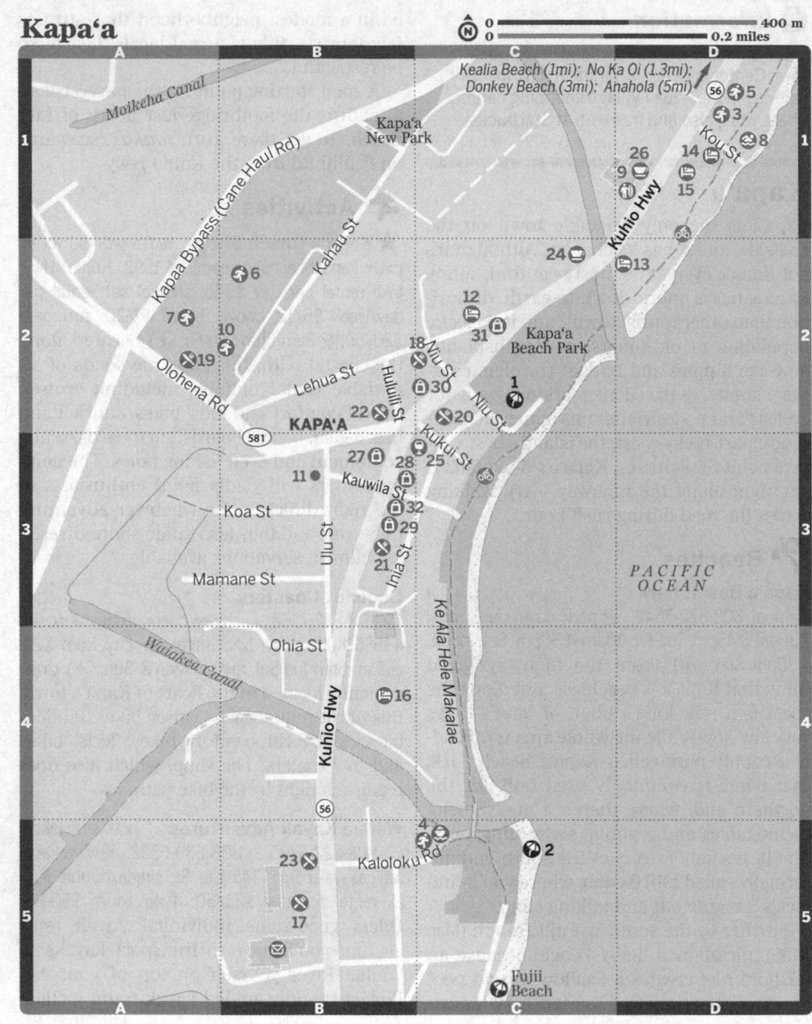

generous snacks at your paddle-and-hike waterfall destination.

Kauai Yoga on the Beach YOGA

(☎808-635-6050; www.kauaiyogaonthebeach.com; 4-885 Kuhio Hwy; drop-in classes incl mat rental $20) What could be better than doing your sun salutations on the sand as the sun actually rises (or maybe just a little later in the morning)? Classes are held on the beach in Kapa'a and Waipouli, as well as on the North and South Shores. Check the website for current schedules and meet-up locations.

Seasport Divers WATER SPORTS

(☎808-823-9222, 800-685-5889; www.seasportdivers.com; 4-976 Kuhio Hwy; dives $90-235) Eastside waters are less protected by reefs and choppier due to easterly onshore winds, so diving and snorkeling are very limited here. Still, this small branch of a Po'ipu-based outfit rents diving and snorkeling gear, boogie boards and surfboards, and offers seasonal dive trips to the North Shore.

Hawaiian Style Fishing FISHING

(☎808-635-7335; www.hawaiianstylefishing.com; Kalokolu Rd; 4hr trips per person $140, half-/full-day

Kapa'a

Sights

1	Kapa'a Beach Park	C2
2	Lihi Beach	C5

Activities, Courses & Tours

3	Coconut Coasters	D1
4	Hawaiian Style Fishing	C5
5	Kapa'a Beach Shop	D1
6	Kapa'a New Park	B2
7	Skateboarding Park	A2
8	Swimming Pool	D1
9	Tamba Surf Company	D1
10	Tennis Courts	B2
11	Wailua Kayak Adventures	B3

Sleeping

12	Honuea Hostel	C2
13	Hotel Coral Reef	D2
14	Kapa'a Neighborhood Center	D1
15	Kauai Beach House Hostel	D1
16	Pono Kai Resort	B4

Eating

17	Big Save	B5
	Coconut Cup Juice Bar & Cafe	(see 13)
18	Hoku Foods	C2
19	Kapa'a Farmers Market	A2
20	Mermaids Cafe	C2
21	Pono Market	B3
	Rainbow Living Foods	(see 20)
22	Sushi Bushido	B2
23	Verde	B5

Drinking & Nightlife

24	Art Cafe Hemingway	C2
	Java Kai	(see 20)
25	Olympic Cafe	C3
26	Small Town Coffee Co	D1

Shopping

27	Garden Isle Bath & Body	B3
28	Hula Girl	B3
29	Kamoa Ukulele Company	B3
30	Orchid Alley Kauai	C2
31	Root	C2
32	Vicky's Fabrics	B3

private charter $600/1050) Join gregarious Captain Terry, who shares the catch with you. Shared and private charters (six-passenger maximum) depart from Lihi Boat Ramp at the end of Kaloloku Rd. Book a week or more in advance.

Tamba Surf Company SURFING
(☎808-823-6942; www.tambasurfcompany.com; 4-1543 Kuhio Hwy; bodyboard/surfboard rental per day from $10/25; ⌚9am-5pm Mon Sat) Along with board rentals, this small shop with local attitude sells surf clothing, and new and used boards. Surf fans may recognize the name as seen on the boards, hats and T-shirts of many pro surfers, past and present, who hail from Kaua'i.

Kapa'a New Park TENNIS, SKATEBOARDING
(www.kauai.gov; 4536 Olehana Rd) You'll find free tennis courts, soccer and baseball fields, and a skateboarding park here.

Tours

Kapa'a Town Walking Tour WALKING TOUR
(☎808-822-1651, 808-245-3373; http://kauaihistoricalsociety.org; 90min tours adult/child $20/10; ⌚by reservation only) Knowledgeable local guides will point out landmarks, describe the history of Kapa'a's sugar and pineapple plantation days and, best of all, tell stories and answer questions.

Festivals & Events

★**Kapa'a Art Walk** ART, CULTURAL
On the first Saturday of every month from 5pm to 8pm, town businesses open up their doors in celebration, showcasing island artists, live music and food. Locals and visitors alike come together in high spirits, and after-parties often keep going past 9pm. Parking is crowded, so arrive early or expect to walk into town. Bring cash.

Garden Isle Artisan Fair ART, MUSIC
(www.gardenislandarts.org; ⌚Mar, Aug & Nov) Held three times each year in mid-March (in Po'ipu) and in mid-August and mid-November (in Kapa'a), this fair brings out handcrafted items, live Hawaiian music and local food.

Heiva I Kaua'i Ia Orana Tahiti DANCE, CULTURAL
(www.heivaikauai.com; ⌚Aug; 👪) In early August, dance troupes from as far away as Tahiti, Japan and the US mainland join groups from around Hawaii at Kapa'a Beach Park for this Tahitian dancing and drumming competition.

★**Coconut Festival** FOOD, CULTURAL
(www.kbakauai.org; ⌚Oct; 👪) Celebrate all things coconut at this free two-day festival at Kapa'a Beach Park. Held the first weekend in early October, it brings coconut-pie-eating

contests, a coconut cook-off, cooking demonstrations, live music, hula dancing, Polynesian crafts and local food.

Sleeping

If you're seeking accommodations right in town, pickings are slim. Kapa'a has only one hotel, one timeshare resort and two hostels. Most B&Bs and inns are situated *mauka* (inland) in residential areas, too far away to walk into town.

Honuea Hostel
HOSTEL $

(808-823-6142; http://kauaihostel.com; 4532 Lehua St; dm from $30, r with shared/private bath from $65/70;) Despite lax management, this is the better of Kapa'a's two hostels. Semiprivate rooms set off mural-painted dorms share bathrooms. Private rooms have access to the communal kitchen and TV room after hours, as well as a private bathroom. Borrow snorkel gear and kayaks for free. Check-in is after 1pm, but you can drop off your bags anytime after 11am.

Kauai Beach House Hostel
HOSTEL $

(808-652-8162; www.kauaibeachhouse.net; 4-1552 Kuhio Hwy; dm/r with shared bath from $33/75;) Not the cleanest of hostels, what with the ramshackle bunks and courtyard, and the pervasive hippy vibe. Private rooms tend to be better maintained than dorms, but they also share bathrooms. On the plus side, there's a communal kitchen and the hostel is lazily located right on the beach.

★Kaua'i Country Inn
INN $$

(808-821-0207; www.kauaicountryinn.com; 6440 Olohena Rd; ste incl breakfast from $169; office 8am-11am Mon-Fri, 9am-10:30pm Sat & Sun;) With gleaming hardwood floors and upscale furnishings, this inn is one class act. Four spacious suites each have cable TV, a DVD player, en-suite computer and a kitchen or kitchenette. The inland location (read: 10-minute drive to the beach) lends itself to serene surroundings and breezy nights. Complimentary continental breakfast provided. Cleaning fee $35 (waived with four-night minimum stay).

Beatles fans, don't miss the chance to gawk at the owner's astounding collection of memorabilia.

No Ka Oi
APARTMENT $$

(Map p486; 808-651-1055, 808-822-0223; www.vrbo.com/125884; 4691 Pelehu Rd; studio apt $120;) Wake up to sunshine in this California king-bedded studio with a full kitchen and a wraparound lanai overlooking Kapa'a and the distant coast. Avid surfers themselves, your hosts know all the local beaches and surf breaks, and lend boogie boards and beach gear for free. There's a three-night minimum stay; weekly and monthly discounts available. Cleaning fee $75.

Hotel Coral Reef
HOTEL $$

(808-822-4481, 800-843-4659; www.hotelcoralreefresort.com; 4-1516 Kuhio Hwy; r/ste from $125/175;) Kapa'a's sole hotel has one major advantage: an oceanfront location. True, it's a basic hotel, but it's also a stone's throw from the ocean and a short stroll into town. Quality-wise, you get what you pay for, with the budget rooms covering the basics and the pricier rooms affecting mock luxury. Book online for discounts.

Pono Kai Resort
RESORT $$

(808-822-9831; http://ponokairesort.com; 4-1250 Kuhio Hwy; studio/1-/2-bedroom condo from $125/155/179;) An aging three-star condo complex dominates the middle stretch of Kapa'a beach. The units are not especially well maintained, offering outdated bathrooms and electronics, but they're spacious. Outside there are BBQ grills, shuffleboard and tennis courts. Cleaning and reservation fees, which vary by rental agency, typically total more than $150.

Eating

Roadside restaurants abound, none terrible, but some terribly touristy.

★Kapa'a Farmers Market
MARKET $

(www.kauaigrown.org; Kapa'a New Town Park, Kahau Rd & Olohena Rd; 3-5pm Wed;) One of the island's biggest and best-attended farmers markets, this weekly outdoor gathering is the spot to pick up local produce such as mangoes, star fruit, ginger and even fresh coconuts. Many of the vendors own organic North Shore farms.

★Pono Market
DELI, MARKET $

(808-822-4581; 4-1300 Kuhio Hwy; meals $6-12; 6am-6pm Mon-Fri, to 4pm Sat) Line up for local *grinds* (food) at this longtime hole-in-the-wall serving generous plate lunches, homemade sushi rolls, spicy ahi *poke* bowls, savory seafood delicacies such as smoked marlin and traditional Hawaiian dishes including pork *laulau*. Bite into *manju* (Japanese sweet bean-filled pastries) for dessert.

Coconut Cup Juice Bar & Cafe HEALTH FOOD $
(808-823-8630; www.coconutcupjuicebar.com; Hotel Coral Reef, 4-1516 Kuhio Hwy; items $3-10; 8am-5pm;) Almost hidden, this roadside kitchen (slowly) makes big ol' sandwiches, salads and smoothies. Wash down your 'Pineapple Express' veggie wrap or island-style Waldorf salad with a passion-fruit smoothie or a green shot of kale juice.

Hoku Foods HEALTH FOOD $
(808-821-1500; www.hokufoods.com; 4585 Lehua St; 10am-6pm;) This small back-street grocery store is ideal for health-conscious types who seek a wide assortment of organic, gluten-free and raw foods. Stocks locally grown produce and convenient snacks and drinks for hiking or the beach.

Big Save SUPERMARKET $
(808-822-4971; www.timessupermarkets.com; Kapa'a Shopping Center, 4-1105 Kuhio Hwy; 6am-11pm) Great for self-caterers, this local supermarket chain has a deli that mixes up fresh *poke*. It also stocks more locally grown produce and Hawaii-made food products than any of its competition.

Verde MEXICAN, FUSION $$
(808-821-1400; www.verdehawaii.com; Kapa'a Shopping Center, 4-1101 Kuhio Hwy; mains $9-17; 11am-9pm;) Chef Joshua Stevens' Mexican, New Mexican and California-style cooking might take whatever fish tacos you've been eating back home and put them to shame. Be sure to save room for the sopaipillas drizzled with honey or the cinammon churro fries for dessert. Excellent cocktails.

Mermaids Cafe FUSION $$
(808-821-2026; www.mermaidskauai.com; 4-1384 Kuhio Hwy; mains $10-14; 11am-9pm;) 'No shirt, no shoes, no worry' is the slogan at this walk-up counter that makes humongous burritos, wraps and Asian-style curry and stir-fry plates. Get the ahi nori wrap with brown rice and wasabi cream sauce, and you'll return every day thereafter to repeat the experience – maybe adding a coconut-milk Thai ice tea.

Sushi Bushido JAPANESE $$
(808-822-0664; www.sushibushido.com; 4504 Kukui St; mains $13-28; 4-9pm Mon-Thu, to 9:30pm Fri, 5-9:30pm Sat, 5-9pm Sun) This locals' favorite sushi stop sets up in a funky corner of the Dragon Building. It has pop art on the walls and serves imaginative fusion sushi, such as the yellowtail 'lollipop' roll drizzled with sweet sauce. Prices are high, portions small and waits excruciatingly long, but the social atmosphere and extensive sake list make it a fun night out.

Rainbow Living Foods HEALTH FOOD $$
(808-821-9759; http://rainbowlivingfood.com; 4-1384 Kuhio Hwy; mains $12-14; 10am-5pm Mon-Fri, to 3pm Sat;) Absolutely everything is vegan, organic, raw and both gluten- and dairy-free. Portions can be too limited for the price, but Rainbow's integrity – utilizing local organic farms and serving an abundance of superfoods with inventive preparations – helps justify the expense. The entrance is around back, off Inia St.

Drinking

★ Java Kai CAFE
(808-823-6887; www.javakaihawaii.com; 4-1384 Kuhio Hwy; 6am-10pm Mon-Sat, to 6pm Sun;) Always busy, this Kaua'i-based micro-roastery is best for grabbing a cup of joe or a fruit smoothie to go. The muffins, scones, banana bread and coconut-macnut sticky rolls are baked fresh, and the salads are tossed with Kailani Farms greens. Another highlight is the selection of Blair Estate shade-grown organic coffee, grown just a few minutes up the road.

Small Town Coffee Co CAFE
(www.smalltowncoffee.com; 6am-4pm) This indie coffeehouse brews organic, fair-trade coffee for the hippie-boho crowd, which also enjoys fresh kombucha and chai tea. Good tunes perpetually play at their temporary location, a big red bus in the former Kojima's parking lot.

Olympic Cafe BAR
(808-822-5825; www.olympiccafekauai.com; 4-1354 Kuhio Hwy; 6am-9pm Sun-Thu, to 10pm Fri & Sat) People pack into this spacious 2nd-floor sports bar to enjoy perched views of the Coconut Coast's reefs. With a full bar, copious draft beers and decent island-style bar food, it's a popular place to grab a drink, especially during happy hour.

Art Cafe Hemingway CAFE
(www.art-cafe-hemingway.com; 4-1495 Kuhio Hwy; 8am-2pm & 6-9pm Wed-Sun;) This quaint cafe offers all the caffeine and croissants you crave downstairs, while putting on local art exhibitions upstairs.

Shopping

Kuhio Hwy is chock full of beachwear boutiques and assorted vintage and antiques shops worth a browse.

★Kamoa Ukulele Company MUSIC

(Larry's Music; ☎808-652-9999; http://kamoaukulelecompany.com; 4-1310 Kuhio Hwy; ⏲11am-4pm Mon-Fri, to 2pm Sat) This high-quality uke dealer offers starters for under $100 and vintage and high-end ukes costing $1000 to $5000. All come with the manufacturer's warranty. Inquire with any questions about ukuleles and expect a warm and thorough response from the musically talented folks doing the sales.

Orchid Alley Kauai FLOWERS

(☎808-822-0486; www.orchidalleykauai.com; 4-1383 Kuhio Hwy; ⏲10am-5pm Mon-Sat) A certified orchid nursery that even grows its own award-winning hybrid plants. It'll ship whatever you buy back to the mainland for you, or pack it for you to take on the plane. Take deep breaths of the scented air as you browse.

Hula Girl CLOTHING, GIFTS

(☎808-822-1950; 4-1340 Kuhio Hwy; ⏲9am-6pm Mon-Sat, 10am-5:30pm Sun) This family-run shop is a standout for contemporary Hawaiiana clothing and gifts – shirts, dresses, jewelry, souvenirs and more. Aloha-shirt aficionados can find a wide selection of quality, name-brand shirts here. Feel the silky-soft Tori Richard line or admire the retro looks of the Paradise Found label.

Vicky's Fabrics HANDICRAFTS, SOUVENIRS

(☎808-822-1746; www.vickysfabrics.com; 4-1326 Kuhio Hwy; ⏲9am-5pm Mon-Sat) Established in the early 1980s, this simple storefront stocks a wide selection of Hawaiian, Japanese and batik print fabrics for quilters and crafters. Longtime owner and seamstress Vicky also sells some handmade Hawaiian quilts and bags.

Garden Isle Bath & Body BEAUTY, GIFTS

(☎808-639-6351; www.gardenislebathandbody.com; 4-1353 Kuhio Hwy; ⏲9am-5pm Mon-Sat) Hurting from a beach sunburn? Don't sweat it. Swing by this family-run shop to sample island-made aloe lotions or the coconut-macdamia nut body butter, which even some Hollywood stars swear by.

Root CLOTHING

(☎808-823-1277; http://shoptheroot.com; 4-1435 Kuhio Hwy; ⏲9am-7pm Mon-Sat, noon-5:30pm Sun) Caters to women looking for hip, contemporary fashions including svelte bikinis, flowing maxi dresses, yoga threads, flowery beach hats and jewelry. Second location in Hanalei.

Blue House Booksellers BOOKS

Attached to Small Town Coffee Co (p501). What better way to browse for a new beach read in this book-nook than with a fresh cup of java in hand?

Information

First Hawaiian Bank (☎808-822-4966; www.fhb.com; 4-1366 Kuhio Hwy; ⏲8:30am-4pm Mon-Thu, to 6pm Fri) Has a 24-hour ATM.

Kapa'a Post Office (☎808-822-0093; www.usps.com; 4-1101 Kuhio Hwy; ⏲9am-4pm Mon-Fri, to 1pm Sat)

Samuel Mahelona Memorial Hospital (☎808-822-4961; www.smmh.hhsc.org; 4800 Kawaihau Rd) Basic 24-hour emergency care. Serious cases are transferred to Lihu'e's Wilcox Memorial Hospital (p484).

Getting There & Around

Kapa'a is 8 miles north of the airport (in Lihu'e).

To avoid the paralyzing crawl to and from Wailua, take the Kapa'a Bypass road.

Kaua'i Bus (p485) runs north and south through Kapa'a approximately hourly from 6am to 10pm on weekdays (limited weekend service).

Downtown Kapa'a is walkable. To get to nearby beaches and some outlying sights, rent a bike from Kapa'a Beach Shop (p497) or Coconut Coasters (p497).

Family firm **Rent A Car Kauai** (☎808-822-9272; www.rentacarkauai.com; 4-1101 Kuhio Hwy) has great customer service and is a good choice for renting economy-sized cars to 4WD SUVs and pickup trucks. Most vehicles are older models that have racked up a lot of miles. Five-day minimum rental required; free pickups and drop-offs at Lihu'e Airport.

Kealia Beach

Blessed with a wild, near-pristine location, a laid-back vibe and easy access via car or the coastal path, scenic **Kealia Beach** (Map p486) is the Eastside's best beach, bar none. Isolated from residential development, the beach begins at mile marker 10 as you head north on the Kuhio Hwy and continues for more than a mile.

WORTH A TRIP

PALIKU (DONKEY) BEACH

Once unofficially known as a nude spot, this beach is scenic but rarely swimmable. It's a place where you can escape the cars on the highway and instead amble along on foot, with rocks scattered at the water's edge, windswept ironwood trees and *naupaka* and *'ilima* flowers adding dashes of color.

Summer swells might be manageable, but stay ashore if you're an inexperienced ocean swimmer. From October to May, dangerous rip currents and a powerful shore break take over. Stick to sunbathing or sunrise beach strolls at that time.

The beach is accessible by two ways. You can cycle or walk north along Kapa'a's coastal path and turn *makai* (toward the ocean). Or you can drive the Kuhio Hwy to a parking lot with restrooms about halfway between mile markers 11 and 12. Look for the small brown parking and hiking sign.

The beach-access footpath cuts through a 300-acre planned community called **Kealia Kai** (www.kealiakai.com). Public nudity is illegal in Hawaii and the developer has cracked down on folks baring all.

The sandy bottom slopes offshore very gradually, making it possible to walk out far to catch long rides back. But the pounding barrels can be treacherous and are definitely not recommended for novices; it's a crushing shore break. A breakwater protects the north end, so swimming and snorkeling are occasionally possible there.

Outdoor showers, restrooms, lifeguards, picnic tables and ample parking are available. Natural shade is not, so sunscreen is a must.

Anahola

Most travelers don't even stop in sleepy Anahola, a Hawaiian fishing and farming village with rootsy charm and a stunning coastline. Pineapple and sugar plantations once thrived here, but today the area is mainly residential, with subdivisions of Hawaiian Homestead lots. The few who spend the night will find themselves in rural seclusion among longtime locals.

Grouped at the side of Kuhio Hwy, just south of mile marker 14, Anahola's tiny commercial center includes a **post office** (Map p486; ☎808-822-4710; www.usps.com; 4-4350 Kuhio Hwy; ⏰10am-1:30pm & 2-3:30pm Mon-Fri, 9:30-11:30am Sat) and a convenience store.

Beaches

Anahola Beach Park BEACH
(Map p486; 👪) Despite having no sign from the highway, this locals' beach is an easy getaway. Backed by pines and palms, it's blessed with excellent swimming thanks to a wide, sandy bay with a sheltered cove on the south end. At the beach's choppy northern end is the surf break **Unreals** (Map p486).

Because this county park sits on Hawaiian Home Lands, you'll probably share the beach with Hawaiian families, especially on weekends. Remember, it's their beach: respect the locals.

There are two ways to get here: for the south end, turn off Kuhio Hwy onto Kukuihale Rd at mile marker 13, drive a mile down and then turn onto the dirt beach road. For the north end, take 'Aliomanu Rd at mile marker 14 and park in the sandy lot.

'Aliomanu Beach BEACH
(Map p486) Secluded 'Aliomanu Beach is a spot frequented primarily by locals, who pole- and throw-net fish and gather *limu* (seaweed). It's a mile-long stretch of beach, with grittier golden sand, a few rocks in the shallows and crystalline water.

You can get to the beach's pretty northern end by turning onto the second 'Aliomanu Rd, just past mile marker 15 on the Kuhio Hwy. Turn left onto Kalalea View Dr, then drive around 0.5 miles and hang a right at the beach-access sign.

Sights & Activities

Hole in the Mountain LANDMARK
(Map p486) Ever since a landslide altered this once-obvious landmark, the *puka* (hole) in Pu'u Konanae has been a mere sliver. From slightly north of mile marker 15 on Hwy 56, look back at the mountain, down to the right of the tallest pinnacle: on sunny days, light shines through a slit in the rock face.

Legend says that the original hole was created when a warrior threw his spear through the mountain, causing the water stored within to gush forth as waterfalls.

★ Angeline's Mu'olaulani SPA
(Map p486; ☎808-822-3235; www.angelineslomikauai.com; Kamalomalo'o Pl; massage treatments $160; ⏰9am-2pm Mon-Fri, by appointment only) Experience authentic four-handed *lomilomi* (traditional Hawaiian massage; literally 'loving hands') at this longstanding bodywork center run by a Hawaiian family. With its outdoor shower, open-air deck and simple sarongs for covering up, it's a refreshingly rustic contrast to plush resort spas. Treatments include a steam, a sea salt–clay scrub and a Hawaiian *oli* (chant). Last appointment at noon.

TriHealth Ayurveda Spa SPA
(Map p486; ☎808-828-2104; www.trihealthayurvedaspa.com; Kuhio Hwy; treatments $140-325; ⏰by appointment only) In a simple bungalow just off the highway, you can sample traditional ayurvedic therapies, practiced by therapists trained both locally and in India. Kudos if you can withstand a full-body (head and all) session in that horizontal steamer.

Sleeping & Eating

Oceanfront camping is allowed (except on Thursday nights) at Anahola Beach Park (p503) with an advance county camping permit.

Hale Kiko'o INN $
(Map p486; www.halekikoo.com; 4-4382b Kuhio Hwy; s/d incl tax from $85/110; 📶) Along an unnamed, unpaved lane are these two charming, modern studios, each with a kitchenette. The bigger downstairs unit features slate floors, a garden patio and an outdoor shower. The upstairs unit is brighter, with windows aplenty and a sunny deck. There's beach gear to borrow and surfboards to rent. Three-night minimum stay; cleaning fee $100 to $125.

'Ili Noho Kai O Anahola B&B $
(Map p486; ☎808-821-0179; anahola@kauai.net; 'Aliomanu Rd; r with shared bath incl breakfast $100; 📶) This simple guesthouse fronting Anahola Beach has four compact but tidy rooms (sharing two bathrooms) surrounding a central lanai, where guests talk story and fill up on home-cooked breakfasts (vegetarians welcome) made by the musical hosts – both Native Hawaiian activists. Weekly and monthly rates available.

Kaleialoha RENTAL HOUSE $$
(Map p486; ☎888-311-5252; www.kauaialoha.com; 4934 'Aliomanu Rd; d $100-225; 📶) Set on the north end of the Anahola Beach area, these romantic, wooden houses are sprinkled in a lovely quiet neighborhood fronting the beach. Some have a kitchenette or full kitchen, but there's no telephone. Ask about weekly discounts.

Anahola Farmers Market LOCAL $
(Map p486; Kuhio Hwy; meals around $10; ⏰9am-dusk Fri-Sun) More of a permanent weekend market than a traditional farmers market. Stop by for wild boar plate lunches, *huli-huli* (rotisserie-grilled) chicken and fresh-baked mango bread.

Duane's Ono Char-Burger FAST FOOD $
(Map p486; ☎808-822-9181; 4-4350 Kuhio Hwy; items $3-9; ⏰10am-6pm Mon-Sat, from 11am Sun; 👪) If you're a fan of In-N-Out and Dairy Queen, you'll go nuts over this drive-in. Try the 'old fashioned' (cheddar, onions and sprouts) or the 'local girl' (Swiss cheese, pineapple and teriyaki sauce). Burgers come slathered in mayo, just FYI. Add a side order of crispy onion rings and a milkshake.

Ko'olau Road

Ko'olau Rd is a peaceful, scenic loop drive through rich green pastures dotted with white cattle egrets and bright wildflowers. It makes a nice diversion and it's the way to reach untouristed beaches (no facilities). Ko'olau Rd connects with the Kuhio Hwy about 0.5 miles north of mile marker 16 and again just south of mile marker 20.

Beaches

★ Larsen's Beach BEACH
(Map p486) This long, loamy, golden-sand beach, named after L David Larsen (former manager of C Brewer's Kilauea Sugar Company), is stunning, raw and all-natural, with a scrubby backdrop offering afternoon shade. Although it's shallow, snorkeling can be good when the waters are calm – usually only in the summer. Beware of a vicious current that runs westward along the beach and out through a channel in the reef.

To get here, turn onto Ko'olau Rd from whichever end (ie where it intersects either Kuhio Hwy or Moloa'a Rd); go just over a mile then turn toward the ocean on a dirt road (it should be signposted) and take the immediate left. It's about a mile to the parking area and then a five-minute walk downhill to the beach.

Moloa'a Beach BEACH

(Map p486;) Off the tourist radar, this classically curved bay appeared in the pilot for *Gilligan's Island*. There's a shallow protected swimming area good for families at the north end; to the south, the waters are rougher but there's more sand. When the surf's up, stay dry and safe – go beach walking instead.

To get here, follow Ko'olau Rd and turn onto Moloa'a Rd, which ends about 0.75 miles down at a few beach houses and a little parking area.

Eating & Drinking

Moloa'a Sunrise Juice Bar CAFE $

(Map p486; 808-822-1441; www.moloaasunrisejuicebar.com; 6011 Ko'olau Rd; items $3-11; 7:30am-5pm Mon-Sat, 8am-4pm Sun;) A roadside shack sells fresh tropical fruit and unforgettably tasty smoothies, healthful multigrain-bread sandwiches, fish tacos, garden salads and addictive chocolate-chip and macadamia-nut cookies.

HANALEI & THE NORTH SHORE

Forget Eden. Arguably the most pristine part of the island, the North Shore's quilted green slopes and valleys are unbelievably fertile. Somewhere between Hanalei Valley and the 'end of the road,' the seemingly untouched landscape makes it easy to imagine what life must have been like for ancient Hawaiians. Swim through the turquoise sea, bite into juicy fresh-picked guava or nap away the afternoon on warm, sugary sand. With the nearest traffic light almost 20 miles away, the North Shore runs on 'island time.' To be sure, this sleepy little enclave is a treasure: it's the island within the island.

Kilauea

For many visitors, this former sugar-plantation town is a quick stop to gas up, grab lunch and take a few photos. But perhaps they're a little too hasty. Kaua'i's northernmost point offers lush vegetation, a wildlife refuge surrounding a century-old lighthouse, sustainable farms, peaceful accommodations and arguably the island's best beach.

Beaches

As all of Kilauea is perched several hundred feet above the ocean, reaching its beaches takes a bit of effort. But rest assured that effort will be rewarded. Car break-ins are common, so don't leave any valuables behind.

★Kauapea (Secrets) Beach BEACH

Obviously a 'secret' no longer, these powdery white sands extend along massive cliffs for more than a mile, wrapping around two rock reefs, all the way to Kilauea Point. There's a sandy ocean floor and sea shells galore, with crystal-clear seas that are the domain of bait balls and occasionally dolphins. Alas, the swimming isn't always safe, thanks to a massive shore break, with frequent close-outs and tremendously strong currents that flow along the entirety of the beach.

Swimming is especially hazardous during big swells (common in winter), which is why it's popular for surfing. This is a local spot, so mind your manners. Nudists also dig it, although technically they're breaking the law.

If you can handle such, ahem, sights, don't mind dirt roads or steep trails, adore virginal beaches and savor sunsets, you'll think Secrets is absolutely magical. However, if the swells are even a little bit big or rough, do not go out into even knee-high water and don't clamber on the rocky outcrops, as people have drowned here.

Turn *makai* (seaward) at Kalihiwai Rd (about 0.5 miles north of the gas station) and take a right on the first dirt road just after the initial bend. Drive toward the end of the road, park and find the steep trail down to the beach starting in plum trees.

Kahili (Rock Quarry) Beach BEACH

This scenically rugged stretch of beach is tucked away between two densely vegetated cliffs where Kilauea Stream meets the ocean. There's no protective barrier reef, so when surf's up, waves can pound. Calm summer days are best for swimming, but beware the rip current from the stream's outflow. Public access is via Wailapa Rd, which begins at the Kuhio Hwy midway between mile markers 21 and 22. Follow Wailapa Rd north for less than 0.5 miles, then turn left onto the unmarked dirt road (4WD recommended) beginning at a bright-yellow water valve.

North Shore

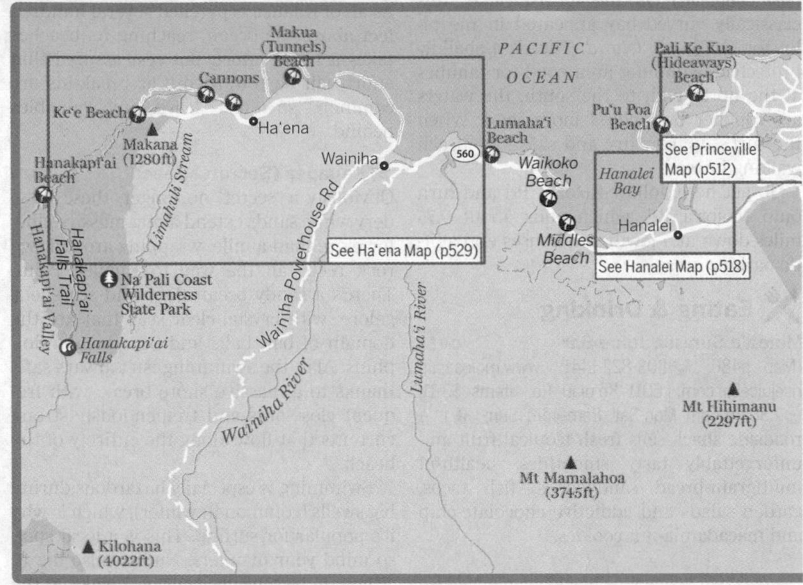

Sights

★Kilauea Point National Wildlife Refuge
WILDLIFE RESERVE

(☎808-828-1413; www.fws.gov/kilaueapoint; Kilauea Rd; adult/child under 16yr $5/free; ⏲10am-4pm Tue-Sun, closed federal holidays) Home to some of Hawaii's endangered wildlife, this refuge claims sweeping views from atop the sea cliffs, where you'll also find a 1913 **lighthouse**. You can occasionally glimpse breaching whales in winter and spinner dolphins year-round offshore. Red-footed boobies, Pacific golden plovers, red-tailed and white-tailed tropic birds and Laysan albatrosses are among the birds spotted here, along with nene, the endangered Hawaiian goose. You'll also spy **Moku'ae'ae Island**, which is teeming with more protected wildlife.

To get here, turn seaward onto Kolo Rd, then take a left onto Kilauea (Lighthouse) Rd and follow it for about 2 miles through town to the end.

Na 'Aina Kai Botanical Gardens & Sculpture Park
GARDENS

(☎808-828-0525; http://naainakai.org; 4101 Wailapa Rd; tours $35-85; ⏲tours 9am, 9:30am & 1pm Tue-Thu, 9am Fri;) In a somewhat over-the-top approach, this husband-and-wife operation pays tribute to Hawaiian culture on 240 acres of botanical gardens. Also on the grounds are a beach, a bird-watching marsh and a forest of exotic hardwood trees. Tour reservations are highly recommended.

To get here, turn right onto Wailapa Rd, between mile markers 21 and 22 on the Kuhio Hwy, and look for signs.

Activities

Kauai Mini Golf & Botanical Gardens
GOLF

(☎808-828-2118; www.kauaiminigolf.com; 5-2723 Kuhio Hwy; adult/child under 5yr/5-10yr $18/free/10; ⏲11am-8pm, last entry 7:30pm;) Part mini-golf, part botanical gardens, this is one environmentally educational round of putt-putt. Winding past Native Hawaiian, Polynesian, plantation-era and East Asian plants, each hole offers a first-hand experience of exquisite flora. It gets busy on weekends, when there may be a wait.

Wai Koa Loop Trail
HIKING, CYCLING

(☎808-828-2118; http://anainahou.org; 5-2723 Kuhio Hwy; ⏲11am-9pm, closed Mon Sep-May) This 5-mile loop trail leads through the greater Namahana Plantation property, starting from Anaina Hou Community Park (also home to Kauai Mini Golf). Along the way you'll traverse a stream and walk through fruit orchards past signs explaining the

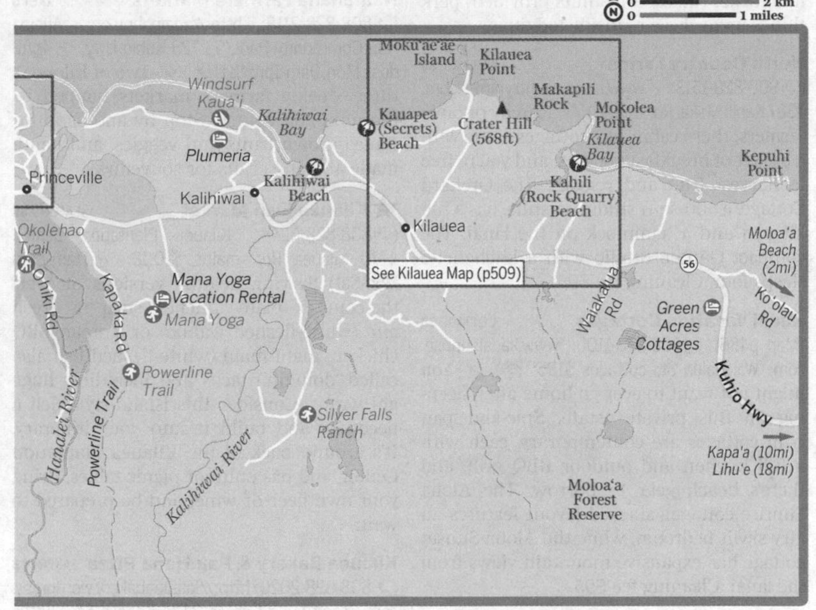

plantation's history. Hike for free or rent a mountain bike ($25 for up to six hours).

Hikers must sign a waiver, available at the on-site Namahana Cafe, before hitting the trail.

Kauai Fresh Farms ECOTOUR
(☎808-651-1191; www.kauaifreshfarms.com; 5545 Kahiliholo Rd; 2hr tours incl lunch $45; ⏲tours 10am Tue, Wed & Fri, by reservation only) The farm-curious might enjoy this sustainable farm tour on Wai Koa Plantation. Learn about hydroponically grown fruits, veggies and herbs, and experience the beauty of the world's largest mahogany plantation before a farm-to-fork lunch. Reservations required.

Metamorphose Yoga Studio YOGA
(☎808-828-6292; http://metamorphoseyoga.com; Kilauea Plantation Center, 4720 Kilauea Rd; drop-in classes $15) This studio nestled in the heart of Kilauea town is sure to redefine the phrase 'going on a bender' with its Vinyasa flow and restorative yoga classes. Go online for current schedules.

Pineapple Yoga YOGA
(☎808-652-9009; www.pineappleyoga.com; 2518 Kolo Rd; drop-in classes/weekly pass $20/90; ⏲usually 7:30-9:30am Mon-Sat) Mysore-style Ashtanga yoga links the breath with 'moving meditation' to create heat throughout the body and sweat (lots of sweat) that detoxifies muscles and organs. The studio is in the parish house of Christ Memorial Church.

Sleeping

Sleepy Kilauea has a handful of unique B&Bs. What they lack in ocean views, they make up for with quiet, rural farm settings.

Anahata Spa & Sanctuary GUESTHOUSE $
(☎808-652-3698; www.anahatasanctuary.net; 4356 Kahili Makai St; r with shared/private bath from $80/145; P 📶) Stay over in this uplifting home owned by a hospitable couple. The great room features wood floors, an open kitchen and gorgeous leafy views. The outdoor shower is a stunner too. All rooms open onto a common lanai with a Balinese daybed for catching a sunrise.

Green Acres Cottages INN $
(☎808-828-0478, 866-484-6347; www.greenacrescottages.com; 5-0421c Kuhio Hwy; d $75-90; P 📶) The 'cottages' are really just kitchenette rooms with grandmotherly decor in the back wing of someone's house. But mornings spent picking fresh bananas and avocados, a communal hot tub and an old-school

nutcracker (macadamia nuts provided) perk things up at these roadside lodgings.

North Country Farms COTTAGE **$$**
(808-828-1513; www.northcountryfarms.com; 4387 Kahili Makai Rd; d $160) Run by organic farmers, these cabin-like cottages come with a basket of breakfast goodies, and you're free to harvest fruit and veggies. The Orchard Cottage, a 500-sq-ft studio on stilts, has a full kitchen and a hammock on the lanai. The compact Garden Studio with a kitchenette sleeps four. Cleaning fee $95.

Kauai Vacation Cottages COTTAGE **$$**
(Map p486; 808-828-1100; www.kauaisunrise.com; Waiakalua St; cottages $185;) You might not want to ever go home after sleeping on this private estate. Spic-and-span twin cottages are contemporary, each with a full kitchen and outdoor BBQ grill, and there's beach gear to borrow. The Aloha Sunrise cottage's stacked layout features an airy skylit bedroom, while the Aloha Sunset cottage has expansive mountain views from the lanai. Cleaning fee $95.

Eating

Healthy Hut Market & Cafe HEALTH FOOD **$**
(808-828-6626; www.healthyhutkauai.com; 4480 Ho'okui Rd; 7:30am-9pm;) All of the gluten-free, dairy-free and all-natural groceries, snacks and supplies you'll need, and some you'll just want for your high-end, healthy lifestyle. Much of what this place carries is grown or made on Kaua'i. Thumbs up for the juice and smoothie bar, and organic coffee and espresso drinks.

For omnivores on a budget, tasty local food trucks (hours vary) are permanently parked outside by the picnic tables.

Kilauea Sunshine Market MARKET **$**
(Kilauea Neighborhood Center, 2460 Keneke St; 4:30-6:30pm Thu;) It's a modest market with a friendly hippie vibe. A dozen or so local, often organic farmers show up to sell mangoes, papaya, cucumbers, tomatoes, salad greens, fresh coconuts and more.

Banana Joe's Fruitstand MARKET **$**
(808-828-1092; www.bananajoekauai.com; 5-2719 Kuhio Hwy; items $4-8; 9am-5:30pm Mon-Sat;) Inside this tin-roofed shack they're making pineapple-banana frosties (dairy-free) that are worth pulling over for. Have you heard of *atemoya* or *mamey sapote*? Here's your chance to try these exotic fruits.

Namahana Farmers Markets MARKET **$**
(808-828-2118; http://anainahou.org; Anaina Hou Community Park, 5-2723 Kuhio Hwy; 4pm-dusk Mon, 9am-1pm Sat;) Two of Kilauea's three weekly farmers markets happen by the mini-golf course. Stop by and shop for Kaua'i-grown fruits and veggies, and handmade arts and crafts for souvenirs.

★Kilauea Fish Market SEAFOOD **$$**
(808-828-6244; Kilauea Plantation Center, 4270 Kilauea Rd; mains $10-18; 11am-8pm Mon-Sat) Serving healthy versions of over-the-counter plate lunches such as fresh *ono* (white-fleshed wahoo) or Korean BBQ chicken, mahi mahi (white-fleshed fish also called 'dolphin') tacos and incredibly huge ahi wraps. Consider this island-style deli a necessity and build it into your itinerary. It's around back of the Kilauea Plantation Center, and has outdoor picnic tables. Bring your own beer or wine, and be prepared to wait.

Kilauea Bakery & Pau Hana Pizza BAKERY **$$**
(808-828-2020; http://kilaueabakery.wordpress.com; Kong Lung Center, 2484 Keneke St; snacks & drinks from $3, pizzas $15-33; 6am-9pm, pizza from 10:30am;) Kilauea's go-to comfort food and social hub, this bakery has an impressive array of hearty soups, baked goods and pizzas (try the 'Billie Holliday' with smoked *ono* and goronzola), although not everything is satisfying. That said, the espresso and chai tea are brewed fresh and the people-watching is superb. Don't expect smiles from the harried staff.

Bistro HAWAII REGIONAL CUISINE **$$**
(808-828-0480; www.lighthousebistro.com; Kong Lung Center, 2484 Keneke St; mains lunch $10-17, dinner $17-26; noon-2:30pm & 5:30-9pm) The tasteful, shabby-chic ambience works; the wine list is terrific; and it does burgers, fish sandwiches, salads, seafood and other carnivorous mains, but not equally well. The best dish in the house? Fish rockets (seared ahi wrapped in lumpia dough, fried with furikake – Japanese rice seasoning – and served with wasabi aioli). Live music happens some nights.

Garden Cafe CAFE **$$**
(Map p486; 808-828-2192; http://commongroundlife.com; 4900 Kuawa Rd; mains $12-18; 9am-3pm Tue-Sun) Situated inland from the highway is the sustainability motivated Common Ground complex. Its nature-chic cafe menu rotates, but always includes salads,

Kilauea

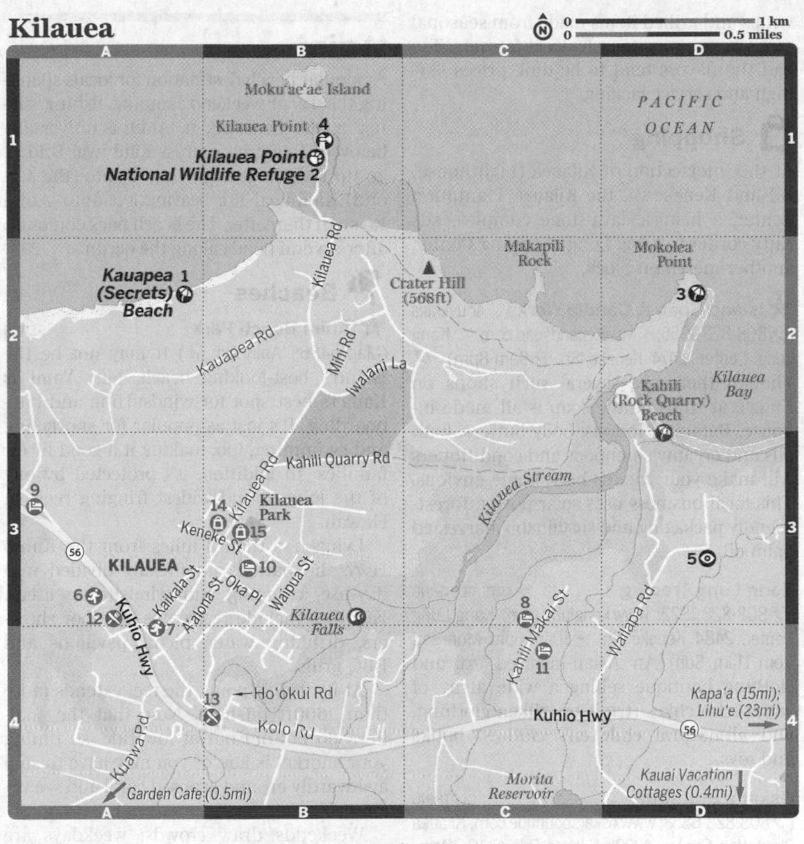

Kilauea

Top Sights
1 Kauapea (Secrets) Beach A2
2 Kilauea Point National Wildlife Refuge B1

Sights
3 Kahili (Rock Quarry) Beach D2
4 Kilauea Lighthouse B1
5 Na 'Aina Kai Botanical Gardens & Sculpture Park D3

Activities, Courses & Tours
Kauai Fresh Farms .... (see 6)
6 Kauai Mini Golf & Botanical Gardens A3
Metamorphose Yoga Studio .... (see 14)
7 Pineapple Yoga A4
Wai Koa Loop Trail .... (see 6)

Sleeping
8 Anahata Spa & Sanctuary C3
9 Bamboo A3
10 Kilauea Neighborhood Center B3
11 North Country Farms C4

Eating
12 Banana Joe's Fruitstand A3
Bistro .... (see 15)
13 Healthy Hut Market & Cafe B4
Kilauea Bakery & Pau Hana Pizza .... (see 15)
Kilauea Fish Market .... (see 14)
Kilauea Sunshine Market .... (see 10)
Namahana Farmers Markets .... (see 6)

Shopping
Banana Patch Studio .... (see 15)
Cake Nouveau .... (see 15)
Island Soap & Candle Works .... (see 15)
14 Kilauea Plantation Center B3
15 Kong Lung Center B3
Kong Lung Trading .... (see 15)
Oskar's Boutique .... (see 14)

wraps and grilled items made from seasonal crops grown on-site or by local farmers. Too bad the flavors tend to be dull, prices sky-high and service lacking.

Shopping

At the intersection of Kilauea (Lighthouse) Rd and Keneke St, the Kilauea Plantation Center, a historic lava-stone complex, sits catty-corner to Kong Lung Shopping Center, another merchant block.

★Island Soap & Candle Works SOUVENIRS
(☎808-828-1955; www.islandsoap.com; Kong Lung Center, 2474 Keneke St; ⏲9am-8pm) Though there are several such shops on Kaua'i, at this one the soap is all made in-house. Botanical lotions, body butters, bath oils and creamy shampoos and conditioners will make your friends back home envious. This local business uses solar power, forest-friendly packaging and sustainably harvested palm oil.

Kong Lung Trading ARTS, CLOTHING
(☎808-828-1822; www.konglung.com; Kong Lung Center, 2484 Keneke St; ⏲10am-6pm Mon-Sat, from 11am Sun) An Asian-inspired art and clothing boutique selling a wide array of artful tchotchkes (trinkets), silken clothing, and all-natural children's clothes, books and toys.

Oskar's Boutique CLOTHING
(☎808-828-6858; www.oskarsboutique.com; Kilauea Plantation Center, 4270b Kilauea Rd; ⏲10:30am-6pm Mon-Fri, from noon Sat;) On the racks are some unique, island-inspired casual and beach wear for men, women and children, including pieces created by island fashion designers and jewelry makers.

Banana Patch Studio SOUVENIRS
(☎808-828-6522; www.bananapatchstudio.com; Kong Lung Center, 2474 Keneke St; ⏲9am-5pm Mon-Sat, 10am-4pm Sun) This is a fun place to pick up touristy 'Hawaiian-style' souvenirs bearing local phraseology. Popular items include custom-designed ceramic tiles and Hawaiiana art.

Cake Nouveau CLOTHING
(☎808-828-6412; Kong Lung Center, 2484 Keneke St; ⏲10am-6pm) The closest you'll come in town to an LA-meets-Polynesia-inspired selection of women's boutique-style clothes and accessories – perfect for those with a hot date coming up.

'Anini

A popular beach destination for locals spending the day or weekend camping, fishing, diving or just 'beaching' it, 'Anini is universally beloved. To get here, cross Kalihiwai Bridge, go up the hill and turn right onto (the second) Kalihiwai Rd, bearing left onto 'Anini Rd soon thereafter. The beach park comes up after several bends along the ocean.

Beaches

★'Anini Beach Park BEACH
(Map p486; 'Anini Rd;) It may not be the island's best-looking beach, but 'Anini is Kaua'i's best spot for windsurfing and kite-boarding. It's just as popular for snorkeling and swimming, too, making it a good fit for families. In addition, it's protected by one of the longest and widest fringing reefs in Hawaii.

Lying less than 3 miles from the Kuhio Hwy, the park is unofficially divided into day-use, camping and windsurfing areas. Facilities include restrooms, outdoor showers, drinking water, picnic pavilions and BBQ grills.

At its widest point, the reef extends more than 1600ft offshore. Note that the shallows do bottom out at low tide, so timing your snorkel is key, or you may have to step awkwardly around exposed coral and sea urchins on your way in.

Weekends draw crowds; weekdays are low-key.

Activities

Windsurf Kaua'i WINDSURFING
(☎808-828-6838; www.windsurf-kauai.com; 'Anini Beach Park; 2hr lessons $100, board & sail rental per hr $25; ⏲by appointment only) Learn what it's like to glide on water with Celeste Harvel. With 30 years of windsurfing experience, she guarantees you'll be sailing in your first lesson. Lessons are by appointment only, usually at 10am and 1pm on weekdays. Advanced lessons can be arranged (call for pricing).

Na Pali Sea Breeze SNORKELING, CRUISE
(☎808-828-1285; www.napaliseabreezetours.com; charter per person $135-195) The only tour leaving out of 'Anini, this aims for a personable experience. The pretrip rendezvous location is usually at the captain's house (except during winter, when departures are from Lihu'e's Nawiliwili Harbor). Ocean conditions permitting, sea cave exploration is a

WORTH A TRIP

KALIHIWAI VALLEY

Sandwiched between Kilauea and 'Anini, Kalihiwai ('water's edge' in Hawaiian) is a hidden treasure that's easy to pass by. Most venture here to **Kalihiwai Beach**, an ideal frolicking spot for sunbathing, sandcastle building and, swells permitting, swimming, bodyboarding and surfing along the cliff on the east side.

Kalihiwai Rd was at one point a road that passed Kalihiwai Beach, connecting with the highway at two points. A tidal wave in 1957 washed out the old Kalihiwai Bridge. The bridge was never rebuilt, and now there are two Kalihiwai Rds, one on each side of the river. To get here, take the easternmost Kalihiwai Rd, about 0.5 miles northwest of Kilauea's gas station.

Kalihiwai Stream offers an ideal spot for a short kayak jaunt if you don't feel like paddling the more crowded Wailua or Hanalei Rivers. Launch at the beach and into Kalihiwai Valley, where you should keep eyes peeled for **Kalihiwai Falls**. The closest outfit that will allow unsupervised rentals on Kalihiwai Stream is Kayak Kaua'i (p491) in Wailua, a 30-mile drive away.

Kalihiwai Falls are on land leased by Princeville Ranch Stables. Athough all navigable waterways in Hawaii are public property, exiting the kayak and stepping foot on land (even land covered by water) is trespassing. To go for a swim in one of the valley's waterfalls, take a jaunt on horseback at animal-friendly **Silver Falls Ranch** (808-828-6718; www.silverfallsranch.com; Kamo'okoa Rd; rides $99-139; by appointment only;), where **Esprit de Corps Riding Academy** (808-822-4688; http://kauaihorses.com; tours per person from $99) also gives guided tours.

highlight, along with an hour of snorkeling and lunch.

Inquire about whale-watching and fishing charters.

Sleeping

High-end vacation rentals abound in 'Anini. Camping at the justifiably popular 'Anini Beach Park is another option. The campground, which hosts a mix of frugal travelers and long-term 'residents,' is generally safe. All campers must vacate the park on Tuesday nights.

Bamboo APARTMENT $$
(808-828-0811; www.surfsideprop.com; 3281 Kalihiwai Rd; 1-bedroom apt per night/week $200/1300;) Overlooking the Kalihiwai Valley and a 10-minute walk to the beach, this airy getaway is attached to the owners' larger house. The private entrance stairs are steep, leading to a cozy but well-appointed apartment with a full kitchen, living-room lanai and spa tub in the bathroom. Cleaning fee $150.

Plumeria RENTAL HOUSE $$$
(808-828-0811; www.surfsideprop.com; 3585 'Anini Rd; 3-bedroom house per night/week $375/2500;) A unique abode that's both comfortable and chic, Plumeria has an enviable location – it's such a short walk to the beach. Expect modest luxury, Hawaii-style, with a finely polished wood interior, sweeping views, and indoor and outdoor showers. Add to this amicable caretakers and complimentary beach and snorkel gear, kayaks and bicycles to borrow. Cleaning fee $175.

Princeville

Princeville (dubbed 'Haolewood') is a methodically landscaped resort community that is about as carefully controlled (and protected) as a film set – which it sometimes actually is. Comprising high-end resorts, finely manicured golf courses and a mixture of cookie-cutter residences, vacation rentals and even some working-class condo complexes, what Princeville lacks in personality it makes up for in convenience.

History

Princeville traces its roots to Robert Wyllie, a Scottish doctor who became foreign minister to King Kamehameha IV. In 1853 Wyllie aquired land for a sugar plantation in Hanalei. When the king and his wife, Queen Emma, came to visit in 1860, Wyllie named his plantation and the surrounding lands Princeville to honor their two-year-old son, Prince Albert, who died only two years later. The plantation later became a cattle ranch.

Princeville

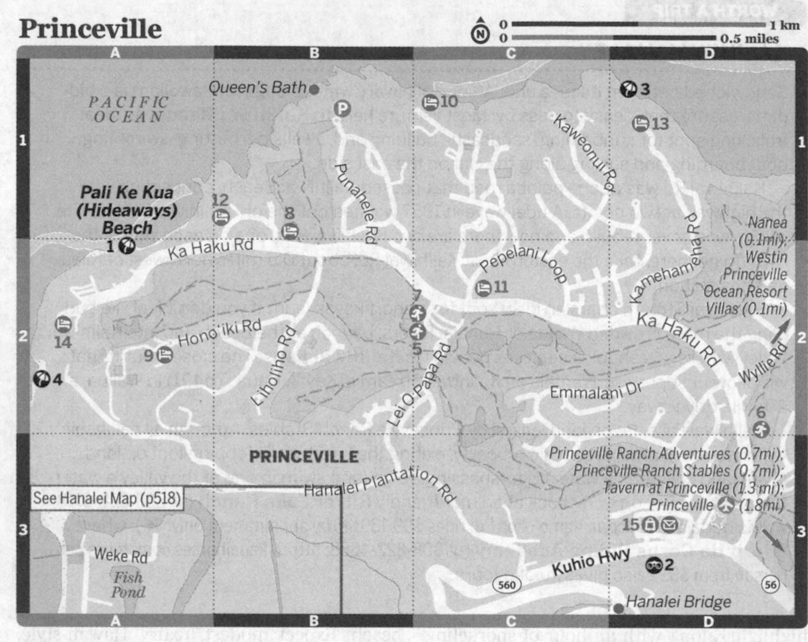

Princeville

Top Sights
1 Pali Ke Kua (Hideaways) Beach ... A2

Sights
2 Hanalei Valley Lookout ... D3
3 Honu Cove ... D1
4 Pu'u Poa Beach ... A2

Activities, Courses & Tours
Halele'a Spa ... (see 14)
5 Makai Golf Club ... C2
6 Prince Golf Course ... D2
Princeville Yoga ... (see 15)
7 Tennis at the Makai Club ... C2

Sleeping
8 Emmalani Court ... B1
9 Hanalei Bay Resort ... A2
10 Holly's Kauai Condo ... C1
11 Nihilani ... C2
12 Pali Ke Kua ... B1
13 Sealodge ... D1
14 St Regis Princeville ... A2

Eating
Federico's FreshMex Cuisine ... (see 15)
Foodland ... (see 15)
Kaua'i Grill ... (see 14)
Lappert's Hawaii ... (see 15)
Lei Petite Bakery & Coffee Shop ... (see 15)
North Shore General Store & Café ... (see 15)
Tavern at Princeville ... (see 6)
Tiki Iniki Bar & Restaurant ... (see 15)

Drinking & Nightlife
St Regis Bar ... (see 14)

Shopping
Magic Dragon Toy & Art Supply Co ... (see 15)
15 Princeville Center ... D3

Beaches

★ Pali Ke Kua (Hideaways) Beach — BEACH

A cove notched in the cliffs, Hideaways has a short strand of golden sand and turquoise shallows. It's an ideal snorkel and swim spot (when it's calm), with a teeming reef just off the beach. Be wise and don't get caught out when the tide comes in.

Park at the tiny, always-crowded lot past the St Regis gatehouse, where a path between two fences followed by a steep railing- and rope-assisted scramble leads down to the beach.

A path to the left of the gatehouse takes you to **Pu'u Poa Beach**. Although public, it sits below and adjacent to the St Regis resort and serves as its on-campus beach.

Honu Cove BEACH
Beloved by locals but best visited only on calm days, this secret cove awaits at the end of Kamehameha Rd. Simply take the first right past the Westin, follow it all the way to the end and keep left. From the parking area, you'll see a trail that hugs the cliffs. At the bottom of the trail, stay left along the cliffs and you'll find a beach with good snorkeling and green sea turtles. Come at high tide.

Sights

Hanalei Valley Lookout VIEWPOINT
Take in views of farmland that's been cultivated for more than 1000 years, including broad brushstrokes of valley, river and taro. Park opposite Princeville Center and take care to watch for other pedestrians when pulling out onto the busy highway.

Activities

★Halele'a Spa SPA
(808-826-9644; www.stregisprinceville.com; St Regis Princeville, 5520 Ka Haku Rd; treatments from $165; 9am 7pm, by appointment only) Translated as 'house of joy', this 11,000 sq ft palatial escape offers massages, replete with couples and VIP treatment rooms. The interior incorporates native Hawaiian woods and natural fibers, and treatments are based upon a foundation of traditional Hawaiian medicine, using botanical and ocean resources such as taro clay and seaweed-leaf body wraps. Spa treatments include complimentary fitness-center access.

★Princeville Ranch Stables HORSEBACK RIDING
(808-826-7669; http://princevilleranch.com; Kuhio Hwy at Kapaka St; tours $99-135; Mon-Sat, by appointment only;) Offering a beautiful ride, even for beginners, the pleasant 3½-hour trip to Kalihiwai Falls includes picnicking and a swim. Find the stables between mile markers 26 and 27 on the Kuhio Hwy, across from the Prince Golf Course. Wear jeans and bring sunblock and insect repellent. Minimum ages for riders is eight to 10 years old; maximum weight limits vary.

★Makai Golf Club GOLF
(808-826-1912; www.makaigolf.com; 4080 Lei O Papa Rd; green fees incl car rental $159-239, 9-hole round from $55) The St Regis Princeville resort's golf club is divided into three 9-hole courses designed by Robert Trent Jones Jr. Each has its own distinctive personality and scenic flavor. The **Ocean Course** runs out to the magnificent coastline and offers a signature par 3 overlooking Hanalei Bay. The Ocean and Lakes Courses link up for traditional 18-hole play.

The **Lakes Course** winds around serene lakes, while the **Woods Course** – the cheapest and gentlest – meanders through native woodlands.

Club and shoe rentals available.

Prince Golf Course GOLF
(808-826-5001; www.princeville.com; 5-3900 Kuhio Hwy; green fees $165-250) Most call it difficult. Tiger Woods is rumored to have called it 'unfair.' Regularly ranked among the USA's best, this Robert Trent Jones Jr–designed, links-style golf course offers breathtaking vistas. It's as humbling as it can be rewarding – you best bring your A-game, and possibly extra sleeves of balls. Club and shoe rentals available.

Princeville Ranch Adventures ADVENTURE TOUR
(808-826-7669; http://princevilleranch.com; Kuhio Hwy at Kapaka St; tours $99-145; by reservation only;) This family-oriented enterprise can bring out your adventurous side, whether it's for a waterfall hike, a zipline ride, an off-road buggy drive or a kayak tour to a secluded swimming hole. Age and weight requirements vary. Reservations required.

Powerline Trail MOUNTAIN BIKING
Measuring more than 11 miles each way, this bike ride presents challenging steep

QUEEN'S BATH

This deadly spot – formed by a sharp lava-rock shelf – has pools that provide a natural and rather inviting-looking swimming hole. Often hit by powerful waves, it's notorious for pulling visitors out to sea, as happens annually. Though the surf at times splashes softly, what many visitors don't realize is that waves come in sets, meaning that a 15-minute flat period could be followed by a 15ft wave that seemingly comes out of nowhere. People die here every year, most commonly by walking along the ledge used to access the pool. For safety, we recommend staying away.

climbs, deep ruts and even deeper puddles (bike-tire deep) before finishing near Wailua's Keahua Arboretum (p489). The scenery doesn't measure up to the sheer audacious wild beauty of other island trails, however. The trail starts about 2 miles down Kepaka St, the road to Princeville Stables.

Look for the Na Ala Hele trailhead sign just past an obvious water tank, where the road turns to red dirt.

Tennis at the Makai Club TENNIS
(☎808-826-1912; www.makaigolf.com; 4080 Lei O Papa Rd; hourly court rental per person $25;) Newly remodeled, rust-tinted outdoor hard courts host lessons offered daily by the local pro, and also pickup games. Call up to a week in advance for reservations. Racket rental available.

Princeville Yoga YOGA
(☎808-826-6688; www.princevilleyogakauai.com; Princeville Center, 5-4280 Kuhio Hwy; drop-in classes $15, 3-class pass $40) In Bikram style, a skilled team of yogis lead classes for any and all willing to practice in a room heated to between 95°F and 100°F. Mat and towel rentals available. Go online for current class schedules.

Mana Yoga YOGA
(☎808-652-3823; www.manayoga.com; 3812 Ahonui Pl; classes $20, 4-class pass $60; usually 8:30-10am Mon & Wed) Michaelle Edwards has created her own version of yoga that may straighten even the most unruly of spines. Combining massage and yoga, it heals with natural poses rather than contortionistic ones.

Tours

★Island Sails Kaua'i SAILING
(☎808-212-6053; www.islandsailskauai.com; Pu'u Poa Beach; 90min cruises adult/child from $99/60; by reservation only) Whether snorkeling in the morning, cruising in the afternoon or catching a sunset, this is your chance to ride in a traditional Polynesian sailing canoe. The red-painted *Ku'upa'aloa* pulls right on the beach in front of the St Regis Princeville resort.

Sunshine Helicopters SCENIC FLIGHTS
(☎808-270-3999, 866-501-7738; www.sunshinehelicopters.com; 45min tours $245-295) Leaving out of Princeville airport, Sunshine Helicopters offers convenience if you're on the North Shore. Flights buzz along the Na Pali Coast and over Waimea Canyon. First-class seating with extra leg room next to the pilot costs extra.

Sleeping

Princeville has an abundance of vacation rentals, though the overly planned country-club atmosphere isn't for everyone. But with a central position on the North Shore and an elevated tropical milieu, many who end up staying here – whether for a day, a week or a month – count themselves lucky.

Sealodge CONDO $
(www.hestara.com; 3700 Kamehameha Rd; 1-/2-bedroom condo from $95/125;) These condos are wooden shingled affairs with gorgeous cliffside perches. Some units are in better shape than others and not all interiors are wonderful, so insist upon pictures prior to online booking through local rental agencies. Nonetheless, the setting will not disappoint. Cleaning fee $95 to $115.

★Mana Yoga Vacation Rental APARTMENT $$
(☎808-826-9230; http://kauainorthshorevacationrentals.com; 3812 Ahonui Pl; studio/2-bedroom apt from $85/135;) Situated next to the serene Mana Yoga Center, the larger apartment features all natural wood details, teak cabinets and a tile floor. The lanai has vast 180-degree mountain views for contemplation. Though more compact, the studio nevertheless has a king-sized bed and private lanai. Farm-fresh eggs, coconuts and an orchard seal the deal. Cleaning fee $40.

Three-night minimum stay; ask about weekly discounts.

Holly's Kauai Condo CONDO $$
(☎480-831-0061; www.hollyskauaicondo.com; Ali'i Kai Resort, 3830 Edward Rd; 2-bedroom condo $195;) Perched cliffside with nothing but water between you and Alaska, this 1200 sq ft, two-bedroom, two-bath unit is a real deal. Wintertime offers guaranteed whale sightings – basically from your bed – and the remodeled interior comes with HDTV, bamboo furnishings and a top-of-the-line kitchen. Three-night minimum stay; cleaning fee $135. Book far in advance.

Pali Ke Kua CONDO $$
(☎808-826-6585, 800-222-5541; www.oceanfrontrealty.com; 5300 Ka Haku Rd; 1-/2-bedroom condo from $175/225;) Situated cliffside, some condos here get both ocean and mountain views. Easy alternative access to Pali Ke Kua (Hideaways) Beach is on the property. Oceanfront Realty charges fees for reservations ($50) and cleaning ($130). Many other agencies also handle bookings here, so search online for the best quotes.

Nihilani CONDO $$
(☎808-987-3502, 877-877-5758; www.alohacondos.com; 4919 Pepelani Loop; 3-bedroom townhouse $139-209; P❄📶🏊) This manicured Princeville condo complex is not cliffside nor does it have sea views, but it's built with a certain Cape Cod panache. Townhouses show off louvered awnings and shutters, while an up-to-date pool area and outdoor BBQ grills make it ideal for family vacations. Cleaning fee $200.

Hanalei Bay Resort RESORT $$
(☎808-826-6522, 877-344-0688; www.hanaleibayresort.com; 5380 Hono'iki Rd; r from $149; 🏊) Location is the name of the game. Suites are steeply priced, but you might see deals pop up at this timeshare property. Units vary drastically in quality and not all have the same amenities, so ask for details and photos before booking.

Emmalani Court CONDO $$
(☎808-742-2000, 800-325-5701; www.parrishkauai.com; 5250 Ka Haku Rd; 1-/2-bedroom condo from $125/175; ❄🏊) Adjacent to the Makai Golf Club, these remodeled units are located in a quieter part of town. They're roomy and well kept, and some afford ocean views. There's a small, tiled outdoor swimming pool. Five-night mimimum stay; cleaning fee $175 to $225.

★ **St Regis Princeville** RESORT $$$
(☎808-826-9644, 866-716-8140; www.stregisprinceville.com; 5520 Ka Haku Rd; d from $500; ❄@📶🏊) The Oz at the end of the road overlooks Hanalei Bay. More than 250 rooms range from merely opulent to 'what do I do with myself' extravagant. Decorated in upscale tropical fashion, all have custom-designed furniture, electronically controlled windows and marble bathrooms. A 5000-sq-ft infinity pool with multiple hot tubs sits oceanside, with Pu'u Poa Beach just steps away.

Westin Princeville Ocean Resort Villas CONDO $$$
(☎808-827-8700, 866-837-4254; www.westinprinceville.com; 3838 Wyllie Rd; studio/1-bedroom condo from $275/400; ❄@📶🏊) Take advantage of this comparatively inexpensive Starwood property. Situated cliffside, the views are expansive, and from November to March whale sightings may only require you to gaze out at the ocean. Condo-like 'villas' boast full kitchens, flat-screen TVs and a washer-dryer, while studio units have kitchenettes. The resort's mutilevel pool complex is kid-friendly.

PRINCEVILLE RENTAL AGENCIES

The following companies handle bookings for condos and vacation rentals in and around Princeville:

Kauai Vacation Rentals (☎866-922-5642; www.kauai-vacations-ahh.com)

Parrish Collection Kaua'i (☎800-325-5701; www.parrishkauai.com)

Princeville Vacations (☎808-828-6530, 800-800-3637; www.princeville-vacations.com)

Eating

Just a few miles down the road, Hanalei has many more eateries to match all budgets.

Foodland SUPERMARKET $
(☎808-826-9880; www.foodland.com; Princeville Center, 5-4280 Kuhio Hwy; ⏰6am-11pm) The North Shore's biggest supermarket has an abundance of fruits and vegetables, freshly prepared sushi and *poke,* wine, beer and a better selection overall than the Big Save in Hanalei.

Lappert's Hawaii ICE CREAM $
(www.lappertshawaii.com; Princeville Center, 5-4280 Kuhio Hwy; ⏰10am-9pm; 👪) The sweet smell of waffle cones beckons, as do scoops of island flavors such as Kauai Pie (Kona coffee ice cream with coconut flakes and macadamia nuts).

North Shore General Store & Café AMERICAN $
(☎808-826-1122; Princeville Center, 5-4280 Kuhio Hwy; items $2-10; ⏰6am-8pm Mon-Fri, 7am-8pm Sat, 7am-6pm Sun) A greasy-spoon minimarket that's also a coffee bar serving up bagel sandwiches, breakfast burritos, grass-fed Princeville beef burgers, plate lunches and more. It's inside the gas station.

Federico's FreshMex Cuisine MEXICAN $
(☎808-826-7177; Princeville Center, 5-4280 Kuhio Hwy; mains $5-12; ⏰10:30am-8pm Mon-Sat; 👪) Just your standard strip-mall Mexican joint, but with relatively reasonable prices for fueling up on, say, shrimp ceviche tostadas and chipotle fish tacos.

Lei Petite Bakery & Coffee Shop CAFE $
(808-826-7277; Princeville Center, 5-4280 Kuhio Hwy; items $2-8; 6am-4pm;) Princeville's prime people-watching can be found at this caffeine station dishing up acai bowls and fruit scones. Expect long lines in the morning.

Tiki Iniki Bar & Restaurant AMERICAN $$
(808-431-4242; www.tikiiniki.com; Princeville Center, 5-4280 Kuhio Hwy; mains lunch $10-14, dinner $14-32; 11:30am-midnight;) With a faux thatched roof and memorabila from the long-gone Coco Palms Resort, this place nails the retro Hawaiiana vibe. It's more suited to sipping tropical cocktails such as mai tais or the 'Hanalei Sling' than eating, although there are some satisfying plates of burgers, wraps, seafood, pasta and salads on the menu. They also serve later than anywhere else in Princeville.

Dinner reservations advised.

★**Kaua'i Grill** HAWAII REGIONAL CUISINE $$$
(808-826-2250; www.kauaigrill.com; St Regis Princeville, 5520 Ka Haku Rd; mains $35-72; 5:30-9:30pm Tue-Sat) An offshoot of the internationally venerated executive chef Jean-Georges Vongerichten, Kaua'i Grill is where the cuisine is sophisticated and the views extend for miles. Rice-cracker-crusted ahi in citrus-chili sauce and sautéed Kona lobster are some of the star cast, while black-truffle cheese fritters and mushroom spring rolls play well-crafted supporting roles. Wine pairings encouraged. Vegetarian and gluten-free menus available. Advance reservations essential.

Nanea HAWAII REGIONAL CUISINE $$$
(800-827-8808; www.westinprinceville.com; Westin Princeville Ocean Resort Villas, 3838 Wylie Rd; mains lunch $12-18, dinner $20-45; 7-10:30am, 11am-2:30pm & 5:30-9:30pm Mon-Sat, 8:30am-12:30pm & 5:30-9:30pm Sun;) Nanea's Hawaii fusion dishes are elegant, but are not always quite worth the price tag. Alaska-born executive sous chef Eric Purugganan – whose family has roots on O'ahu – cut his culinary teeth at award-winning restaurants in the Pacific Northwest. His menu integrates locally caught seafood and island-grown greens, goat's cheese and honey. Lunch is definitely the better value. Reservations recommended.

Tavern at Princeville AMERICAN $$$
(808-826-8700; www.tavernbyroy.com; 5-3900 Kuhio Ave; mains lunch $13-24, dinner $18-46; 11am-4pm & 5-9:30pm) Don't let the golf-clubhouse location fool you: this eatery is the offspring of star chef Roy Yamaguchi. The atmosphere can feel hollow, but service is enthusiastic. Complimentary popcorn and a creative drinks menu set the stage for an ambitious array of dishes that are at the very least original, such as baby back ribs with guava-*liliko'i* barbecue sauce.

Drinking & Entertainment

★**St Regis Bar** LOUNGE
(808-826-9644; www.stregisprinceville.com; St Regis Princeville, 5520 Ka Haku Rd; 3:30-11pm) Don't let the elegance or the enormous crystal raindrop chandelier intimidate you. The lobby bar is for any and all wanting to take a load off. The vibe is a step more welcoming than the chichi surroundings, so relax and enjoy the ultimate location for a sunset cocktail and unforgettable views of Hanalei Bay.

Some nights serenade imbibers with live jazz music.

Shopping

Princeville Center MALL
(8080-826-9497; www.princevillecenter.com; 5-4280 Kuhio Hwy) If you're staying in Princeville, you'll inevitably wind up at this assortment of island and luxury lifestyle shops. There's live local entertainment in the food court from 6pm to 8pm nightly.

Magic Dragon Toy & Art Supply Co TOYS
(808-826-9144; Princeville Center, 5-4280 Kuhio Hwy; 9am-6pm;) A wonderland of whirling, colorful and inspired toys, from kites and beach gear to watercolors and puppets, all packed into a tiny imaginative storefront. Prices aren't cheap, though.

Information

Bank of Hawaii (808-826-6551; Princeville Center, 5-4280 Kuhio Hwy; 8:30am-4pm Mon-Thu, to 6pm Fri) Has a 24-hour ATM.

Chevron Gas Station (Princeville Center, 5-4280 Kuhio Hwy; usually 6am-10pm Mon-Sat, to 9pm Sun) The last fuel option before the end of the road.

First Hawaiian Bank (808-826-1560; www.fhb.com; Princeville Center, 5-4280 Kuhio Highway; 8:30am-4pm Mon-Thu, to 6pm Fri) Has a 24-hour ATM.

Princeville Mail Service Center (808-826-7331; Princeville Center, 5-4280 Kuhio Hwy; per 15min $3; 9am-5pm Mon-Fri) Internet computer workstations available.

Princeville Post Office (☎808-828-1721; www.usps.com; Princeville Center, 5-4280 Kuhio Hwy; ⏰10:30am-2:30pm Mon-Fri, to noon Sat)

Getting There & Around

Princeville is great for walking, running or bicycle cruising. The one main arterial road (Ka Haku Rd) runs through the middle with an adjacent paved recreational path.

The Kaua'i Bus (p485) between Lihu'e and Hanalei stops near Princeveille Center on the Kuhio Hwy approximately hourly on weekdays (limited weekend service).

Hanalei

There are precious few towns on this sweet earth with the majestic natural beauty and barefoot soul of Hanalei. The bay is the thing, of course. Its half-dozen surf breaks swell to well above triple overhead and are the stuff of legend, partly because local surf gods such as the late Andy Irons cut their teeth here. But even if you aren't here for waves, the beach, with its wide sweep of cream-colored sand and magnificent jade mountain views, will demand your loving attention.

When beach time is done, stroll around the pint-sized town, take a yoga class, snack on sushi or duck into a grass-shack tiki dive bar. It's true that Hanalei has more than its fair share of adults with Peter Pan syndrome and kids with seemingly Olympian athletic prowess. You'll see as many men in their 60s waxing their surfboards as you will groms with 'guns' (ie big-wave surfboards). Which begs the query: why grow up at all when you can grow old in Hanalei?

Beaches

Well-known for being filmed in *The Descendants,* **Hanalei Bay** is easily Kaua'i's most famous beach and for good reason. Really one long beach that's divided into several sections with different names, there's something for almost everyone here: sunbathing, swimming, snorkeling, kayaking, bodyboarding and surfing. The winter months can make this stretch of water an expert spot for board riders only (no swimming or snorkeling). In summer, the water is sometimes so calm it's hard to distinguish between sky and sea, except for a smattering of yachts bobbing on the horizon.

★Black Pot Beach Park (Hanalei Pier) — BEACH

This small section of Hanalei Bay near the Hanalei River mouth usually offers the calmest surf among the wild North Shore swells. Also known as Hanalei Pier for its unmistakable landmark, this stretch of sand shaded by ironwood trees is popular mainly with surfers. In summer, swimming and snorkeling are decent, as is kayaking. Use extreme caution during periods of high surf because dangerous shore breaks and rip currents are common.

The sandy-bottomed beach slopes gently, making it safe for beginning surfers. Lessons are typically taught just west of the pier, where you'll find surf schools galore. At the park's eastern end, where the Hanalei River empties onto the beach, is a small boat ramp where kayakers launch for trips upriver.

Facilities include restrooms and outdoor showers, and there are lifeguards.

Hanalei Beach Park — BEACH

With its sweeping views, this makes a great place for a picnic, sunset or lazy day at the beach. Ideally located, its downside is the parking, which can be a challenge. Park along Weke Rd if you have to, as the public lot gets crowded. Facilities include restrooms and outdoor showers. Camping is allowed only with an advance county permit.

Hanalei Pavilion Beach Park — BEACH

Toward the middle of Hanalei Bay, you'll find this scenic beach park that possesses a white-sand crescent made for strolling. Waters are typically not as calm as further east by the pier, but swimming and stand-up paddle surfing are possible during the calmest summer months. Facilities include restrooms and outdoor showers.

Wai'oli (Pine Trees) Beach Park — BEACH

Offering respite from the sun, this park is equipped with restrooms, outdoor showers and picnic tables. Winter months are when the North Shore is at its highest surf-wise and locals dominate the surf spot here known as **Pine Trees**. The shore break is harder here than any other spot on Hanalei Bay and swimming is dangerous, except during the calmest summer surf.

Middles Beach — BEACH

At mile marker 4 on the *makai* (ocean) side of the road is a small, scrubby parking area. Walk along the beach or look out to

Hanalei

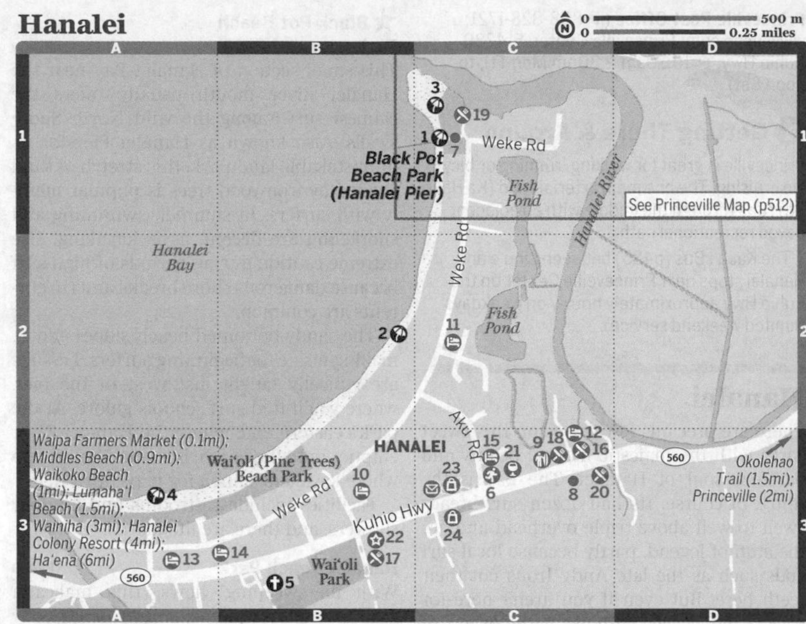

the ocean to see three surf breaks; from left to right, they are **Waikokos**, **Middles** and **Chicken Wings**.

This beach is informally known as Middles because of the break. The highway bridge just past the parking area crosses over Waikoko Stream, so the shoreline from the bridge onward is known as Waikoko Beach.

Waikoko Beach BEACH

Protected by a reef on the western bend of Hanalei Bay, this sandy-bottomed beach with no facilities offers shallower and calmer waters than the middle of the bay. Local surfers call this break **Waikokos** (literally, 'blood water'); look for them in the water and you'll see where the break is.

Sights

Wai'oli Hui'ia Church & Wai'oli Mission House CHURCH

(☎808-826-6253; www.hanaleichurch.org; 5-5363a Kuhio Hwy) A popular site for quaint church weddings, the original Wai'oli Hui'ia Church was built by Hanalei's first missionaries, William and Mary Alexander, who arrived in 1834 in a double-hulled canoe. Today the church, hall and mission house remain in the middle of town, set on a huge manicured lawn with a beautiful mountain backdrop.

The green American Gothic–style wooden **church** that passersby can see today was donated in 1912 by three sons of Abner Wilcox, another island missionary. The doors remain open during the day, and visitors are welcome. A 19th-century bible printed in Hawaiian is displayed on top of the old organ. The church choir sings hymns in Hawaiian at the 10am Sunday service.

Guided tours of the historic **mission house** are currently available for walk-in visitors (no reservations) between 9am and 3pm on Tuesdays, Thursdays and Saturdays. Check the Grove Farm website (http://grovefarm.org) for details.

Activities

Less crowded than the Eastside's Wailua River, Hanalei River offers roughly 6 miles of tranquil scenery, ideal for kayaking or stand-up paddle surfing.

★**Ho'opulapula Haraguchi Rice Mill & Taro Farm Tours** GUIDED TOUR

(☎808-651-3399; www.haraguchiricemill.org; tours incl lunch adult/child 5-12yr $87/52; ⏱tours usu-

Hanalei

ally 9:45am Wed, by reservation only) Learn all about cultivating taro on Kaua'i at this sixth-generation family-run, nonprofit farm and rice mill (the last remaining one in the Hawaiian Islands). On farmer-guided tours, which take you out into the *lo'i kalo* (wet taro fields), you'll also get a glimpse of the otherwise inaccessible Hanalei National Wildlife Refuge and learn about Hawaii's immigrant history.

Tours meet by Hanalei Taro & Juice Co (p524) food truck on Kuhio Hwy. A Hawaiian plate lunch is included in the price.

Titus Kinimaka's Hawaiian School of Surfing SURFING

(☎808-652-1116; www.hawaiianschoolofsurfing.com; 5-5088 Kuhio Hwy; 90min lessons from $65, board rental per hour/day/week $10/30/75; ⌚by appointment only) Call in advance for a lesson with legendary pro big-wave surfer Titus Kinimaka or, more likely, with one of his minions, who line up the boards daily on the beach or at the pier. No more than three students per instructor. Bonus: they'll let you use the boards for a couple of hours of practice after the lesson.

Kayak Hanalei WATER SPORTS

(☎808-826-1881; http://kayakhanalei.com; Ching Young Village, 5-5070a Kuhio Hwy; kayak/SUP set rental per day from $35/40, 2hr surfing or SUP lessons $90, kayak tours adult/child 5-12yr $105/95; ⌚8am-4:30pm) This long-standing, family-run outfitter rents SUP sets and surfboards at the in-town store, and kayaks at the river dock. Beginners surfing and SUP lessons are available daily except Sunday (reservations advised).

Hawaiian Surfing Adventures WATER SPORTS

(☎808-482-0749; www.hawaiiansurfingadventures.com; 5-5134 Kuhio Hwy; 90min group surfing or SUP lessons $65, surfboard/SUP rental per day $20/50; ⌚store 8am-3:30pm, last lesson starts 2pm) Surfing lessons for novices include 30 minutes on land, and one hour in the water. SUP lessons could even get you doing yoga poses atop your board. The company is owned by local Hawaiian surfer Mitch Alepa and his family.

Pedal 'n Paddle ADVENTURE SPORTS

(☎808-826-9069; www.pedalnpaddle.com; Ching Young Village, 5-5190 Kuhio Hwy; ⌚9am-6pm) This full-service rental shop is conveniently located and offers some of the best rates in town for renting snorkel sets, boogie boards, SUP sets, kayaks, bicycles and almost all the camping gear you could need for trekking the Na Pali Coast. Daily and weekly rental rates available.

Fathom Five Divers DIVING

(☎808-742-6991, 800-972-3078; http://fathomfive.com; dives $90-155; ⌚by reservation only Mar-Oct) The PADI-certified Fathom Five outfit in Koloa also gears up for a North Shore dive at the reef off Makua (Tunnels) Beach. In summer, dare a night dive.

Kauai Island Experience WATER SPORTS

(☎808-346-3094; www.kauaiexperience.com; 1½hr group/private surfing lessons $80/160, surfboard rental per day $20; 👪) Waterman Mike Rodger's team will teach you to surf, stand-up paddle, snorkel, fish, paddle a traditional Hawaiian canoe and more.

Hanalei Surf Company SURFING

(☎808-826-9000; www.hanaleisurf.com; Hanalei Center, 5-5161 Kuhio Hwy; 2hr group/private lessons $65/160, snorkel set/surfboard rental per day $5/20; ⌚8am-9pm) Pro surf instructors are especially suited for advanced surfers. If you're really serious, Russell Lewis has coached many of the pro surfers coming out of Kaua'i.

Kauai Outrigger Adventures SURFING, SUP

(☎808-212-5692; www.kauaioutriggeradventures.com; Hanalei Pier; surfboard/SUP rental from $20/40, SUP, outrigger canoe & surfing lessons from $75; ⌚usually 8am-5pm) The North Shore's only company for outrigger canoe surfing lessons and tours also offers surf and SUP lessons near the pier, near a Hanalei River put-in.

Yoga Hanalei YOGA

(☎808-826-9642; www.yogahanalei.com; Hanalei Center, 5-5161e Kuhio Hwy; drop-in classes $10-15) Instructors were all students of Bhavani Maki, who leads this Ashtanga-based studio. Classes tend to flow vinyasa or hatha style, except the ropes-wall class, which is for dangling. For something mellower, come later in the day.

Okolehao Trail HIKING

(Ohiki Rd) This 4.6-mile round-trip trail affords panoramic views of Hanalei's taro fields, the start of the Na Pali Coast and, on a clear day, Kilauea Lighthouse. It's rumored to be named for 'moonshine,' referring to distilled liquor made from the roots of *ti* plants. The visual spoils are worth the pain of the steep, sweaty uphill climb through the forest.

The first half-mile is a quad burner, which means few other hikers on what is a fairly quiet hike (except for your heavy breathing). After the initial vista at the power-line tower, the trail continues gradually upward,

HOMAGE TO KALO

According to Hawaiian cosmology, Papa (earth mother) and Wakea (sky father) gave birth to Haloa, a stillborn brother to man. Haloa was planted in the earth, and from his body came taro, or *kalo,* a plant that has long sustained the Hawaiian people and been a staple for oceanic cultures around the world.

Kalo is still considered a sacred food, full of tradition and spirituality for Hawaiians. Hanalei is home to the largest taro-producing farm in the state, Ho'opulapula Haraguchi Rice Mill & Taro Farm (p518), where the purple, starchy potato-like plant is grown in *lo'i kalo* (wet taro fields). Rich in nutrients, *kalo* is often boiled and pounded into poi, an earthy, starchy and somewhat sweet and sticky pudding-like food.

Families enjoy poi, defined by some Hawaiians as the 'staff of life,' in different ways. Some prefer it fresh, while others prefer sour poi, or *'awa'awa* (bitter) poi, possibly derived from the method in which poi used to be served – often it sat in a bowl on the table for quite some time.

All traditional Hawaiian households show respect for taro: when the bowl of poi sits on the table, one is expected to refrain from arguing or speaking in anger. That's because any bad energy is *'ino* (evil) – and can spoil the poi.

offering photo opportunities before ending 1250ft above the slow shuffle of Hanalei. Bring plenty of water.

Coming from Hanalei, veer right immediately before the Hanalei Bridge, between the river and the taro fields. Go down the road about 0.5 miles to a parking area on the left. The trail starts across the road.

North Shore Divers DIVING
(808-828-1223, 877-688-3483; www.northshoredivers.com; dives $79-149; by reservation only Mar-Oct) If you're already a certified diver, a night dive (during summer only) is an unforgettable experience. All dives take place at the reef off Makua (Tunnels) Beach.

Snorkel Depot WATER SPORTS
(808-826-9983; 5-5075 Kuhio Hwy; snorkel gear rental per day/week $5/20; 8am-5pm) This little stand in the Hanalei Trading Co building rents budget-priced, well-used snorkel gear, SUP sets and boogie boards.

Tours

Na Pali Catamaran BOAT TOUR
(808-826-6853, 866-255-6853; www.napalicatamaran.com; Ching Young Village, 5-5190 Kuhio Hwy; 4hr tours $180) This exceptional outfit has been running tours for 35 years, offering comfy catamaran cruises along the Na Pali Coast from Hanalei Bay. Depending on ocean conditions and the time of year, you might venture into some sea caves. Remember, though, the surf can pound and there's no reprieve from the elements. Minimum age five years.

Na Pali Explorer BOAT TOUR
(808-338-9999; www.napaliexplorer.com; 4½hr tours adult/child $139/89;) Take a coastal snorkeling trip on a rigid-hull inflatable raft, which is hard-bottomed and gives a smoother ride than all-inflatable Zodiacs. The longer 49ft raft, which carries up to 36 passengers, has a restroom and a canopy for shade. Tours run out of Hanalei Bay. Minimum age for participants is five to eight years, depending on the boat.

Captain Sundown BOAT TOUR
(808-826-5585; https://captainsundown.com; 6hr tours $185) This outfit is based out of Lihu'e most of the year, so take the advantage and board this sailing catamaran (17 passengers max) for a coastal snorkeling tour when it's here during the summer. A true character, Captain Bob has four decades of experience. No kids under seven years old.

Bali Hai Tours BOAT TOUR
(808-634-2317; www.balihaitours.com; 3½hr cruises adult/child $165/95;) Explore the Na Pali Coast in a 20ft Zodiac (maximum six passengers) and splash your way to pure nature bliss. Cruise for up to four hours among humpbacks, dolphins and flying fish, and explore sea caves (weather permitting). Departs from Hanalei Pier.

Festivals & Events

Music & Mango Festival MUSIC, FOOD
(http://waipafoundation.org; mid-Aug;) A late summer celebration of locally harvested food and live music happens at the nonprofit Waipa Foundation's farmlands on the outskirts of Hanalei.

Hawaii Sand Festival ART, MUSIC
(http://hawaiisandcastle.com; mid-Aug;) Magnificent sand castles and art sculptures are built on the sands of Hanalei Bay, with free lessons and live music.

★ **Kalo Festival** FOOD, CULTURAL
(http://waipafoundation.org; Dec;) In early December Halulu Fish Pond is host to demonstrations on growing taro and pounding poi, traditional Hawaiian games for kids, local food vendors and live music.

Sleeping

Though it requires getting an advance county permit, camping at Black Pot Beach Park (Hanalei Pier; p517) is fun and safe. Amenities are limited to restrooms, picnic tables and cold-water outdoor showers. Camping is allowed on Fridays, Saturdays and holidays only.

Garden Surf Cottage COTTAGE $$
(808-346-4371; 5278 Malolo Pl; 1-bedroom cottage $169;) Slumber inside this rustic wooden surf shack that has terracotta floors, a tiny kitchen with a two-burner stovetop, flat-screen TV and a BBQ grill out on the patio by the hammock. The location is quiet, yet right in the center of the action: you can stroll to downtown in one direction and the beach in the other. Cleaning fee $80.

Hanalei Vacation House APARTMENT $$
(808-826-0006; www.hanaleivacationhouse.com; 4483 Aku Rd; studio/1-/2-bedroom apt $115/125/149;) Not far from the beach, and just a quick stroll from the river, this relaxed vacation rental is a no-fuss alternative to Hanalei's pricier lodging options. Tiled floors,

Kaua'i

From the legendary surf swells of Hanalei to the Na Pali Coast's stunning treks, this island offers laidback adventures for all. Kayak in Wailua, then snorkel off Po'ipu; venture to the rim of magnificent Waimea Canyon, dripping with waterfalls, and hit the trail in Koke'e State Park – it's all here waiting.

2

STEVE OGLE / GETTY IMAGES ©

4

VISUALS UNLIMITED, INC./PATRICK SMITH / GETTY IMAGES ©

1. Makua (Tunnels) Beach (p528)
Named for the underwater caverns in its reef, this is one of the best snorkeling spots on Kaua'i.

2. Kalalau Trail (p532)
The trail winds for 22 miles along the coastal cliffs, offering views over pristine valleys.

3. Nounou Mountain Trail (p492)
With sweeping views of the ocean and lush forest to explore, this trail can be strenuous but rewarding.

4. Black Pot Beach Park (Hanalei Pier; p517)
This small section of Hanalei Bay offers calmer surf than is usually found among the wild North Shore swells.

3

MATTHEW MICAH WRIGHT / GETTY IMAGES ©

knotty wood walls and old-fashioned kitschy furnishings give it a cabin-like atmosphere. Noise-sensitive types might want to look elsewhere, due to the next-door parking lot. Cleaning fee $75 to $85.

Hanalei Inn INN $$
(808-826-9333, 877-769-5484; www.hanaleiinn.com; 5-5468 Kuhio Hwy; r $149-159;) Despite being a bit on the shabby side, these four studios – each with a kitchenette or full kitchen, HDTV, private lanai and classic retro Hawaiiana furniture – are in an ideal locale. On-site manager Bill works side by side with the resident cats and chickens to maintain a simple country atmosphere. Daily maid services cost extra.

Hale Reed RENTAL HOUSE $$
(415-662-1086; www.hanalei-vacation.com; 4441 Pilikoa Rd; 5-bedroom house $245;) Approximately 89 paces from the white sand of Hanalei Bay, Hale Reed's location is key. The ground-floor, two-bedroom apartment has a full kitchen and a patio for barbecuing on. The airier upstairs unit has three bedrooms and a loft, along with a wraparound lanai. Boards and beach gear come with the territory. Three-night minimum stay; cleaning fee $150 to $250.

The apartment and upstairs can be rented separately, but only by the week.

★Hanalei Dolphin Cottages COTTAGE $$$
(808-826-1675; www.hanaleicottages.com; 5-5016 Kuhio Hwy; 2-bedroom cottage $260;) Launch a canoe, kayak or stand-up paddleboard right from your backyard on the Hanalei River. A lazy walk from the heart of Hanalei town, each cottage is styled similarly, with bamboo furniture, a full kitchen, BBQ grill, private outdoor (and indoor) showers, front-of-house bedrooms and airy quasi-lounge areas facing the river. Cleaning fee $130.

Hanalei Surfboard House INN $$$
(808-651-1039; www.hanaleisurfboardhouse.com; 5459 Weke Rd; ste $325;) A work of art built with recycled and salvaged materials, this stylish surfer's haven is a one-minute walk to the beach. The two suites each feature unique vintage Hawaiiana decor, have a kitchenette and share a backyard lanai with a BBQ grill. The ever-mellow owner, a former globetrotting music executive, sets the mood at this adults-only property. Cleaning fee $95.

Eating

With a captive audience of day-trippers, Hanalei's eateries tend to be overpriced and underwhelming, but there are a few good-value exceptions to this rule.

★Hanalei Taro & Juice Co HAWAIIAN $
(808-826-1059; www.hanaleitaro.com; 5-5070a Kuhio Hwy; items $1.50-6, meals $9-11; 11am-3pm Mon-Sat;) Find this roadside trailer for a taste of poi, the traditional Hawaiian staple food, made right on the family farm in Hanalei Valley. It does tropical taro smoothies, taro hummus, taro burgers, taro mochi cakes and Hawaiian plate lunches too. If you miss the truck in Hanalei, look for the booth at farmers markets in Kapa'a (p500) and Lihu'e (p481).

★Hanalei Farmers Market MARKET $
(808-826-1011; www.halehalawai.org; Kuhio Hwy; 9:30am-noon Sat;) One of the island's most popular farmers markets happens on the sports fields in front of the community center, Hale Halawai 'Ohana 'O Hanalei. Locals line up before the market opens, then literally run to their favorite farmers' booths. Don't miss a coconut-and-chocolate-covered banana from Kunana Dairy. North Shore artisans sell crafts, jewelry and tropical soaps, perfect for gifts or souvenirs.

Waipa Farmers Market MARKET $
(808-826-9969; www.waipafoundation.org; Kuhio Hwy; 2-4pm Tue;) Set on the Waipa Foundation's old Hawaiian *ahupua'a* (land division), just over the one-lane bridge from Hanalei proper on the way to Ha'ena, this market is small but still ample, with tropical fruit, leafy greens, flowers and handicrafts.

To learn how to make poi as a hands-on volunteer on Thursday mornings, visit the website for details.

Pink's Creamery ICE CREAM, SANDWICHES $
(808-824-9134; 4489d Aku Rd; items $4-9; 11am-9pm;) A side-street ice-cream shop scoops tropical flavors such as banana-macnut brittle, mango and an unreal *haupia* (coconut pudding). It also whips up *liliko'i* and lychee sorbet, tropical fruit popsicles, date shakes, and absurdly tasty grilled cheese sandwiches on island-style sweet bread with munster cheese, *kalua* pork (cooked in the traditional method in an underground pit) and pineapple.

Harvest Market MARKET $
(808-826-0089; http://harvestmarkethanalei.com; Hanalei Center, 5-5161 Kuhio Hwy; 9am-7pm Mon-Sat, to 6pm Sun;) If you like to treat your body well, pick up organic and all-natural snacks, groceries and produce with a locavore touch. Put together a beach picnic from the salad bar, smoothie station and weighable bulk-foods section (dried fruit, nuts and such), but beware that prices can sneak up on you.

Pat's Taqueria MEXICAN, AMERICAN $
(parking lot near Hanalei Pier; items $2-9; noon-3pm;) If you're by the pier and heading to the beach, a couple of *kalua* pork tacos or a mahimahi burrito with beans and rice on the side won't set you back too much. Kids menu (mini burritos, quesadillas etc) available. Cash only.

Village Snack Shop & Bakery BAKERY, DELI $
(808-826-6841; www.facebook.com/VillageSnackShopBaker; Ching Young Village, 5-5190 Kuhio Hwy; mains $6-9; 6:30am-4pm Mon-Sat, to 3pm Sun;) Just your basic mom-and-pop storefront, perfect for stuffing yourself with macnut pancakes before hiking the Na Pali Coast. Show up later in the day for heaping plate lunches and chocolate *haupia* (coconut) pie.

Big Save SUPERMARKET $
(808-826-6652; www.timessupermarkets.com; Ching Young Village, 5-5172 Kuhio Hwy; 7am-10pm;) For any basic grocery items and beach, hiking or road-tripping snacks and drinks you need.

★ **Hanalei Dolphin Restaurant & Sushi Lounge** SEAFOOD, MARKET $$
(808-826-6113; www.hanaleidolphin.com; 5-5016 Kuhio Hwy; mains lunch $12-16, dinner $25-40; restaurant 11:30am-9pm, market 10am-7pm) At one of Hanalei's oldest restaurants (more than 30 years), the slow-roasted menu is abundant and the sushi chefs will play culinary jazz with their daily fresh fish if decision-making is not your forte. Lunch is served riverside and the sushi bar seating fills up quickly. Wander around back to the fish market for take-out and DIY meals for grilling.

The fish market not only sells fish by the pound, but also assorted sushi rolls, *poke* bowls, a daily fresh-catch sandwich and a chunky seafood chowder.

Hanalei Gourmet CAFE, DELI $$
(808-826-2524; www.hanaleigourmet.com; Hanalei Center, 5-5161 Kuhio Hwy; dinner mains $10-29; 8am-10:30pm;) At this lively sit-down spot, the best bets are huge sandwiches on house-baked bread. Meals – creatively skipping from a sampler of lox-style smoked Hawaiian fish to crunchy macadamia-nut fried chicken – are tasty and unpretentious, even if more mainstream American than local. Twice-weekly musical acts and happy hour (3:30pm to 5:30pm daily) are more good reasons to swing by.

Chicken in a Barrel BARBECUE $$
(808-826-1999; www.chickeninabarrel.com; Ching Young Village, 5-5190 Kuhio Hwy; meals $10-15; 11am-8pm Mon-Sat, to 3pm Sun;) Using a custom-made, 50-gallon barrel drum smoker, this island BBQ joint is all about the bird. Grab a heaping plate of chicken or a hoagie sandwich with chili cheese fries. You won't have to eat again all day. Second location in Kapa'a.

★ **BarAcuda Tapas & Wine** MEDITERRANEAN $$$
(808-826-7081; www.restaurantbaracuda.com; Hanalei Center, 5-5161 Kuhio Hwy; shared plates $7-26; 5:30-10pm, kitchen closes at 9:30pm) A trendy wine and tapas bar presents ornately plated food that's noteworthy, but pricey. Pluses include inventive sustainability-driven uses of local products, such as North Shore honeycomb, goat's cheese and mizuna greens. A seductive 'see and be seen' atmosphere, service that's impeccable from start to finish and a groovy soundtrack all perpetuate the illusion that you're in a movie. Reservations essential.

Postcards Café FUSION $$$
(826-1191; http://postcardscafe.com; 5-5075 Kuhio Hwy; mains $19-38; 6-9pm;) With innocent charm, this riverside cottage could just as easily be found in the New England countryside. Vegan-friendly and seafood dishes, although hit and miss, often have an appealing world-fusion twist such as the wasabi-crusted ahi or *ono* in curried coconut broth. A genteel atmosphere will induce nostalgia like a Robert Redford film. Reservations recommended for groups of four or more.

Drinking & Entertainment

★ **Tahiti Nui** BAR
(808-826-6277; http://thenui.com; 5-5134 Kuhio Hwy; 11:30am-midnight Mon-Sat, from 2pm Sun) Usually crowded from mid-afternoon onward, the legendary Nui (which made a

cameo appearance in *The Descendants*) can get rollicking with live Hawaiian music and quite rowdy on weekends, when it's really the only place open past 10pm. It's a tiki dive bar with heart and history. On Wednesday nights, the **luau** (per adult/child $75/45) is a modest all-you-can-eat dinner show.

For luau reservations, call ☎808-482-4829.

Hanalei Coffee Roasters CAFE
(☎808-826-6717; www.hanaleicoffeeandteacompany.com; Hanalei Center, 5-5183 Kuhio Hwy; ⊙6:30am-6pm;) The caffeine isn't the only thing buzzing here. Coffee infusions are strong and waffles are sweetly topped with coconut syrup. The mellow vibes and lazy front porch will soothe strung-out psyches.

Hawaiian Slack Key Guitar Concerts LIVE MUSIC
(☎808-826-1469; www.hawaiianslackkeyguitar.com; Hanalei Community Center, Malolo Rd; adult/child 6-17yr $20/15; ⊙4pm Fri, 3pm Sun) Slack key guitar and ukulele concerts are performed by longtime musicians Doug and Sandy McMaster year-round in a refreshingly informal atmosphere.

Shopping

Hanalei's handful of boutiques sell everything from tourist kitsch to beach chic. Most are at the old-guard **Ching Young Village** (www.chingyoungvillage.com; 5-5190 Kuhio Hwy) and the more upscale **Hanalei Center** (5-5161 Kuhio Hwy).

★ **Kauai Nut Roasters** FOOD
(☎808-826-7415; www.kauainutroasters.com; Ching Young Village, 5-5190 Kuhio Hwy; ⊙10am-6:30pm Mon-Sat, to 5pm Sun) Some of the most delicious treats you can find on the island are found here in these unassuming little packages, bursting with unusual flavors. Coconut, wasabi, lavender, sesame, butterscotch and praline rank tops. Also in Kilauea and Koloa.

Hanalei Surf Company CLOTHING, OUTDOOR EQUIPMENT
(www.hanaleisurf.com; Hanalei Center, 5-5161 Kuhio Hwy; ⊙8am-9pm) Surf, surf, surf is this outfit's MO. Surfer-girl earrings, bikinis and rashies, as well as guys' boardshorts, flip-flops and all the gear you might need for hitting the surf: wax, shades and even the board itself. Their **Backdoor** (www.hanaleisurf.com; Ching Young Village, 5-5190 Kuhio Hwy; ⊙8am-9pm) store is across the street.

Havaiki ARTS
(☎808-826-7606; www.havaikiart.com; Hanalei Center, 5-5161 Kuhio Hwy; ⊙10am-5pm) This hidden shop sells traditional, hand-crafted Polynesian art hand-picked by the owners, from inexpensive tchotchkes to museum-quality artworks. Keep an eye out for more exotic pieces such as penis gourds.

On the Road to Hanalei CLOTHING, GIFTS
(☎808-826-7360; Ching Young Village, 5-5190 Kuhio Hwy; ⊙10am-6pm) Vibrant batik-print dresses and pareus, hand-crafted silver jewelry and Japanese teapots are just a few of the treasures inside this rustic wooden-floored shop.

Bikini Room CLOTHING
(☎808-826-9711; www.thebikiniroom.com; 4489 Aku Rd; ⊙10am-6pm Mon-Sat, 11am-5pm Sun) They're itsy bitsy and teeny weenie, but they show off a variety of wild, vibrant prints from Brazil instead of the said polka dots.

I Heart Hanalei CLOTHING
(☎808-826-5560; www.shopihearthanalei.com; 5-5106 Kuhio Hwy; ⊙11am-9pm) At one of Hanalei's cutest beachy boutiques, you can peruse racks of stylish bikinis, beach cover-ups, sun hats, shorts and yoga wear.

aFeinberg Gallery ARTS
(☎808-634-7890; www.afeinbergphotography.com; Ching Young Village, 5-5190 Kuhio Hwy; ⊙noon-7pm) Photographer Aaron Feinberg captures international award-winning landscapes of Kaua'i and beyond.

Information

Hanalei has no bank, but there are ATMs at the Hanalei Liquor Store and Big Save supermarket.

Hanalei Post Office (☎808-826-1034; www.usps.com; 5-5226 Kuhio Hwy; ⊙10am-4pm Mon-Fri, to noon Sat) On the *makai* (seaward) side of the road, just west of Big Save supermarket.

Getting There & Around

There's one road into and one road out of Hanalei. During heavy rains (common in winter), the Hanalei Bridge occasionally closes due to flooding, and those on either side are stuck until it reopens.

Parking in town can be a headache, and absent-minded pedestrians even more so. Everything in Hanalei is walkable. Otherwise, do as locals do and hop on a bicycle.

Pedal 'n Paddle (☎808-826-9069; www.pedalnpaddle.com; Ching Young Village, 5-5105

DRIVING WITH ALOHA

Lauded as one of the most scenic and breathtaking drives on the island, the drive to the 'end of the road' is impossibly beautiful. However, though you might want to pull over for that must-have photograph, please do so safely as accidents occur when drivers stop suddenly or in a bad place to snap a photo. If you're heading to the road's end (Ke'e Beach), take it slowly and enjoy the crossing of each of the seven one-lane bridges, the first of which is in Hanalei.

When crossing these bridges, do as the locals do:

➡ When the bridge is empty and you reach it first, you can go.

➡ If there's a steady stream of cars already crossing as you approach, then simply follow them.

➡ When you see cars approaching from the opposite direction, yield to the entire queue of approaching cars for at least five cars, if not all.

➡ Give the *shaka* sign ('hang loose' hand gesture, with index, middle and ring fingers downturned) as thanks to any drivers who have yielded from the opposite direction.

Kuhio Hwy; ⏲9am-6pm) Rents cruisers (per day/week $15/60) and hybrid road bikes ($20/80), all including helmets and locks.

Around Hanalei

On turning out of Hanalei Bay the highway immediately plunges into dramatic coastal contour. It winds around cliffside points that offer glimpses of what's ahead, leading all who follow towards the grand finale of the Na Pali Coast. Between mountains and the ocean, there's a sliver of beach and just enough road space for traffic in both directions to squeeze by.

Lumaha'i Beach

Countless Kaua'i locals consider this their absolute favorite beach on an island blessed with dozens of choices. It's so damn cinematic that it's where the famous scene was shot for the 1958 movie *South Pacific* in which Mitzi Gaynor declared her intent to 'wash that man' right out of her hair.

The beach, though beautiful, is known on-island as one of the most dangerous. Too many visitors have drowned trying to swim at this beguiling spot, dubbed 'Luma-die' for its rough rip currents and powerful waves. The inlet lacks barrier reefs and breaks, so swimming here is very risky. Instead, stay dry and take a stroll (which still requires being water savvy).

There are two ways onto Lumaha'i Beach. The first and more scenic is a three-minute walk that begins at the parking area 0.75 miles past mile marker 4 on the Kuhio Hwy. The trail slopes to the left at the end of the retaining wall. On the beach, the lava-rock ledges are popular for sunbathing and photo ops, but beware: bystanders have been washed away by high surf and rogue waves.

The other way to access Lumaha'i is along the road at sea level at the western end of the beach, just before crossing the Lumaha'i River Bridge. The beach at this end is lined with ironwood trees.

Wainiha

Between Ha'ena and Hanalei rests this little spot marked by the 'Last Chance' Wainiha General Store. Steeped in ancient history, the narrow, green recesses of Wainiha Valley were the last hideout of the *menehune*, the legendary little people of the islands.

Today the valley remains as it did in the old days: a holdout for Hawaiians, though some vacation rentals have encroached onto the area. An unwelcoming vibe is not uncommon. When the locals stare you down, don't take it personally.

Sleeping & Eating

Coco Cabana Cottage COTTAGE $$

(☎808-821-9836; www.vrbo.com/153703; 4766 Ananalu Rd; d $175-190; 📶) The hot tub, chirping birds, airy ambience and swimmable Wainiha River nearby make for a lovely secluded stay. This cute little cottage is perfectly suited to a couple wanting privacy and coziness, and so is the two-person outdoor jungle shower. Four-night minimum stay; cleaning fee $125.

Riverhouse at River Estate RENTAL HOUSE $$$

(☎808-826-5118, 800-390-8444; www.riverestate.com; 5-6691 Kuhio Hwy; d from $295; ❄📶) Resting on stilts 30ft above the Wainiha River, this enchanting abode is fit for honeymooners or a family. Brazilian hardwood floors and marble countertops are deluxe, while a screened-in lanai allows for no-mosquito barbecues and soaks in the mini hot tub. Weekly rates are available. Cleaning fee from $275.

Guesthouse at River Estate RENTAL HOUSE $$$

(☎808-826-5118, 800-390-8444; www.riverestate.com; 5-6691 Kuhio Hwy; d from $275; ❄📶) This place is pricey, but one look and you'll see why. Airy, huge and open, set on jungly grounds, this vacation home features a master bedroom with a king bed, a second room with a queen bed, a decked-out kitchen, a wraparound lanai, beach gear to borrow and almost anything else you could need. Weekly rates available. Cleaning fee from $250.

Sushigirl Kauai SUSHI $$

(www.sushigirlkauai.fish; 5-6607b Kuhio Hwy; mains $12-15; ⏲11am-7pm Mon-Sat, to 4pm Sun) A roadside kitchen delivers generous *maki* (hand) rolls, *poke* bowls drizzled with *ponzu* (Japanese citrus) sauce and sushi burritos made with 'yum yum' sauce, organic local veggies and heaps of TLC.

Shopping

7 Artists ARTS

(5-6607 Kuhio Hwy; ⏲11am-5pm) Local painters, photographers, ceramic artists, jewelers, puka-shell-lei and beach-glass-mosaic makers staff this co-op gallery.

Wainiha General Store MARKET

(5-6607 Kuhio Hwy; ⏲10am-dusk) If you've left Hanalei and need a few items, don't panic. The 'Last Chance' store sells last-minute beach essentials, including snorkel gear, drinks and snacks. Service can be eccentric.

Ha'ena

Remote, resplendent and idyllic, this is where the road ends amid lava-rock pinnacles, lush wet forest and postcard-perfect beaches. It's also the site of controversy, as many of the luxury homes on the point were built atop *'iwi kupuna* (ancient Hawaiian burial grounds). No Kaua'i adventure is complete without a drive to the end of road and at least a short hike along the roadless Na Pali Coast.

Beaches

Makua (Tunnels) Beach BEACH

One of the North Shore's almost-too-beautiful beaches, named for the underwater caverns in and among the near-shore reef, this is among the best snorkel spots on the island. It's also the North Shore's most popular dive site. Although the area is more suitable for the summer months, as the reef is adjacent to the beach, winter snorkelling may be possible. Always use caution and check with locals or lifeguards before heading into the water. Beware of a regular current flowing west toward the open ocean.

If you can't score a parking spot at one of the two unmarked lots down short dirt roads, then park at Ha'ena State Park and walk.

Ha'ena Beach Park BEACH

Not ideal for swimming in winter, because of the regular pounding shore break that creates a strong undertow, this beach is nevertheless good for taking in some sun. During the summer months, the sea is almost always smooth and safe. Ask lifeguards about conditions before going in, especially between October and May. To the left is **Cannons**, an expert local surf break.

Facilities include restrooms, outdoor showers, picnic tables and a pavilion.

Sights & Activities

★Limahuli Garden GARDENS

(☎808-826-1053; http://ntbg.org/gardens/limahuli.php; 5-8291 Kuhio Hwy; self-guided/guided tours $20/40; ⏲9:30am-4pm Tue-Sat, guided tours 10am; 👪) 🌿 About as beautiful as it gets for living education, this garden offers a pleasant overview of endemic botany and ancient Hawai'i's *ahupua'a* (land division) system of management. Self-guided tours take about 1½ hours, allowing you to meditate on the scenery along a 0.75-mile loop trail; in-depth guided tours (minimum age 10 years, reservations required) last 2½-hours.

Volunteer service projects in native ecosystem restoration give ecotourists a glimpse into the entire 985-acre preserve.

Ha'ena

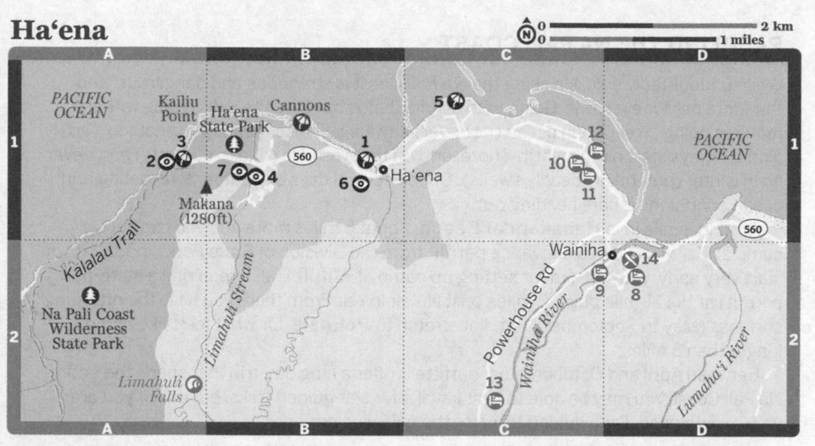

Ha'ena

Sights
1 Ha'ena Beach Park B1
2 Kaulu Paoa Heiau A1
3 Ke'e Beach A1
4 Limahuli Garden B1
5 Makua (Tunnels) Beach C1
6 Maniniholo Dry Cave B1
7 Wet Caves B1

Activities, Courses & Tours
Hanalei Day Spa .... (see 12)

Sleeping
8 Coco Cabana Cottage D2
9 Guesthouse at River Estate C2
10 Hale Ho'o Maha C1
11 Hale Oli C1
12 Hanalei Colony Resort C1
13 River House C2
Riverhouse at River Estate .... (see 9)

Eating
Mediterranean Gourmet .... (see 12)
14 Sushigirl Kauai D2

Shopping
7 Artists .... (see 14)
Na Pali Art Gallery .... (see 12)
Wainiha General Store .... (see 14)

To get here, turn inland just before the stream that marks the boundary of Ha'ena State Park.

Maniniholo Dry Cave CAVE

Directly across from Ha'ena Beach Park, Maniniholo Dry Cave is deep, broad and high enough to explore. A constant seep of water from the cave walls keeps the dark interior dank. Drippy and creepy, the cave is named after the head fisherman of the *menehune* who, according to legend, built ponds and other structures overnight.

Hanalei Day Spa SPA

(☎808-826-6621; www.hanaleidayspa.com; Hanalei Colony Resort, Kuhio Hwy; ⊙9am-6pm Mon-Sat) If you're tired or need to revitalize, this friendly, though modest spa offers some of the island's more competitively priced massages (including Hawaiian *lomilomi*) and body treatments.

Sleeping & Eating

Ha'ena Beach Park, a popular and beautiful camping spot (closed on Monday nights), is a base for exploring the North Shore, including the Na Pali Coast. Advance county camping permits are required.

There is an abundance of vacation rentals in Ha'ena, although some have recently fallen through legal cracks.

Hale Ho'o Maha B&B $$

(☎808-826-7083, 800-851-0291; http://halemaha.com; 7083 Alamihi Rd; r incl breakfast $220; @ 📶) Though the word 'communal' is applicable, don't let it turn you off this quirky, four-room home. You'll share everything with your hosts, including an ozonated hot tub, high-end kitchen, an enormous flat-screen HDTV, a guest-use computer and even an elevator. Each suite has its own lanai.

PADDLING THE NA PALI COAST

While undoubtedly epic, kayaking the Na Pali Coast is strenuous and dangerous, and therefore not for everyone. Going with a guide helps mitigate the risks; going without requires being an expert in ocean (not river) kayaking. It also means you shouldn't go alone. Always start on the North Shore, end on the Westside (due to currents) and never go in winter (potentially deadly swells). Check several days of weather forecasting and ocean conditions before heading out.

Around a mile in is **Hanakapi'ai Beach**. About 6 miles more and you can set up camp at **Kalalau** (with an advance permit from the Division of State Parks; p532). If you start very early, you can aim for setting up camp at **Miloli'i** (also requiring a state-park permit) at the 11-mile point, 2 miles past Nu'alolo Kai. From there you have the often surf-less (May to September), hot, flat stretch to **Polihale**, for what feels like much longer than 3 miles.

Between April and October, most outfitters offer a long day-trip that spans the entire Na Pali Coast. You may be able to rent kayaks for self-guided treks, but only if you are very experienced. For a guided tour, try the following options:

Na Pali Kayak (☎808-826-6900; www.napalikayak.com; 5-5075 Kuhio Hwy, Hanalei) The Na Pali Coast trip is the only tour these folks lead, and their guides have over a decade of experience. Guided overnight camping trips start at $400 per person; a one-day trip costs from $225.

Kayak Kaua'i (p491) The original Na Pali kayaking outfitter's 'Odyssey' ($240) paddles the entire stretch from Ke'e to Polihale in one long day.

River House RENTAL HOUSE **$$$**
(☎808-826-7272, 800-715-7273; www.napaliprop.com; 5121 Powerhouse Rd; house & cottage per night $325-350) It's got a jungle paradise feel, just a mile from Tunnels Beach and close to the Kalalau Trail. Avocados, lychees, bananas, papayas and mountain apples abound. The sandalwood-floored main house comes with a queen bed, soaking tub and full kitchen. A separate cottage and a screened-in sleeping gazebo called the Bird's Nest are part of the rental. Cleaning fee $290.

Hale Oli RENTAL HOUSE **$$$**
(☎808-826-6585; www.oceanfrontrealty.com; 7097 Alimihi Rd; 2-bedroom house per night/week from $300/1800; ☎) Perched on stilts, this place boasts nothing but greenery between its front lanai and Ha'ena's jutting mountains. Inside it's Hawaiiana-meets-Zen decor. The bedrooms each have a queen-sized bed, and the kitchen is full-sized. On the back lanai, a spacious hot tub provides starry and foamy nights and a sliver of an ocean view. One-time rental ($50) and cleaning ($185) fees apply.

Hanalei Colony Resort HOTEL **$$$**
(☎808-826-6235, 800-628-3004; www.hcr.com; 5-7130 Kuhio Hwy; 2-bedroom ste from $255; @☎☎) It'd be difficult to find a more knock-out location for a resort than this spot, the only resort west of Princeville. While the decor often looks dated, the property is waterfront and about as reclusive as it gets. Condos are scattered in several exceedingly charmless stucco out-buildings that arc alongside an exquisite beach and bay. No TVs or phones.

Mediterranean Gourmet MEDITERRANEAN **$$**
(☎808-826-9875; www.kauaimedgourmet.com; Hanalei Colony Resort, 5-7130 Kuhio Hwy; mains lunch $12-17, dinner $26-37; ⊙noon-3:45pm & 4-8pm Mon & Wed-Sun, noon-3pm Tue) A taste of the Mediterranean literally on the Pacific (if the windows weren't there, you'd get salty ocean mist on your face), this fish out of water offers an eclectic range of Euro-inspired dishes such as rosemary rack of lamb and pistachio-crusted ahi. Food quality and service both tend toward mediocre, but there's live music on Saturday and Sunday evenings.

Shopping

Na Pali Art Gallery ARTS, CRAFTS
(☎808-826-1844; www.napaligallery.com; Hanalei Colony Resort, 5-7130 Kuhio Hwy; ⊙7am-5pm Mon-Sat, to 3pm Sun; ☎) Peruse a quality array of local artists' paintings, woodworking, sculptures, ceramics, art glass and jewelry such as coveted Ni'ihau shell necklaces. Skip the coffeehouse's weak brews.

Ha'ena State Park

Wind-beaten Ha'ena State Park is sculpted into the narrow lava-rich coastline and burns with allure, mystique and beauty. Pele (the Hawaiian goddess of fire) is said to have overlooked the area as a home because of the water percolating through its wet and dry caves. Today this 230-acre park remains home to the 1280ft cliff commonly known in the tourism industry as 'Bali Hai,' its name in the film *South Pacific*. Its real name is Makana (gift). Rather apt, for sure.

 Beaches & Sights

Ke'e Beach BEACH

Memorable North Shore sunsets happen at this spiritual spot, where ancient Hawaiians came to practice hula. In summer, the beach offers a refreshing dip after hiking the nearby Kalalau Trail. But beware that Ke'e Beach may appear calm when it is, in fact, otherwise. Vicious currents have sucked some through a keyhole in the reef out into the open sea.

Facilities include outdoor showers and restrooms. Car break-ins are common in the parking lot, so don't leave any valuables.

Wet Caves CAVE

Two wet caves lie within the boundaries of Ha'ena State Park. Formed by the constant pounding of waves many years ago, the massive cavern of **Waikapala'e Wet Cave** is as enchanting as it is spooky. It's on the opposite side of the street, a short walk from the visitor-overflow parking area. **Waikanaloa Wet Cave** is a little further down on the south side of the highway.

Though some enter the water to experience the sunlight's blue reflection in Waikapala'e's deeper chamber, note the water may be contaminated with leptospira bacteria; the rocks are slippery; and there's nothing to hold onto once you're in the water.

Kaulu Paoa Heiau TEMPLE

The roaring surf was a teacher to those who first practiced the spiritual art of hula, chanting and testing their skills against nature's decibel levels. Ke'e Beach is the oceanfront site of a cherished heiau (ancient stone temple) dedicated to Laka, the goddess of hula. It's also where the volcano goddess Pele fell in love with Lohiau.

Lei and other sacred offerings found on the ground should be left as is. Enter the heiau through its entryway; don't be disrespectful by crossing over the temple walls.

Na Pali Coast Wilderness State Park

Roadless, pristine and hauntingly beautiful, this 22-mile-long stretch of stark cliffs, white-sand beaches, turquoise coves and gushing waterfalls links the island's northern and western shores. It's arguably Kaua'i's most magnificent natural sight. While fit trekkers tackle the exposed, undulating, slippery trail from Ha'ena to Kalalau Valley, it's also possible to experience the coastline by kayak, raft or catamaran. Kalalau, Honopu, Awa'awapuhi, Nu'alolo and Miloli'i are the five major valleys along the coast, each seemingly more stunning than the last.

History

Based on excavation of ancient weapons and hunting tools in the area, archaeologists maintain that in the extreme, remote Nu'alolo Valley, a sophisticated civilization dating back more than a thousand years once lived. Irrigation ditches and agricultural terraces suggest that Kalalau Valley was formerly home to one of the most advanced communities in the Hawaiian Islands.

In the mid-19th century, missionaries established a school in Kalalau, the largest of the valleys along the coast, and registered the valley population at about 200. Influenced by Western ways, people gradually began moving to towns, and by century's end the valleys were largely abandoned.

Sights & Activities

For epic views of the Na Pali Coast, hiking the 11-mile coastal Kalalau Trail or sea kayaking all the way to Polihale State Park are adventures sure not to disappoint. You can

> **HANAKAPI'AI BEACH WARNING!**
>
> Made evident by the knife-etched tally before the descent, Hanakapi'ai Beach has ended many a vacation – and life – too soon. Heed this warning. The waters in Hawaii are as powerful as anywhere on the planet and can catch many a toe-dipper off guard in the blink of an eye. Strong undertows can sweep even the most experienced swimmers off their feet and out to sea in a matter of seconds.

also get inspiring clifftop views of the valleys by hiking the trails inside Koke'e State Park on the Westside.

Kalalau Trail

Winding along *nā pali* (literally, 'the cliffs') offers glimpses of Kaua'i's most pristine valleys, with deep, riveting pleats. This trail is without a doubt the best way to connect directly with the elements, though keep in mind that the trek – if you opt to complete the full 22-mile round trip – is a steep, rough hike with some dangerously eroded sections.

The hike's three segments are Ke'e Beach to Hanakapi'ai Beach, Hanakapi'ai Beach to Hanakapi'ai Falls, and Hanakapi'ai Beach to Kalalau Valley. There are hunters who can do the entire trail in and out in one day, but most people will opt for either a day hike to Hanakapi'ai Beach or Hanakapi'ai Falls or will bring camping gear for an overnight backpack all the way to Kalalau Beach.

Take safety concerns seriously along this trail. In winter trails can become rivers, streams can become impassable and the beaches will disappear in high surf. Give this slippery trail a second thought before heading out on a rainy day. Always use extreme caution when swimming at the beaches, especially Hanikapi'ai Beach, where numerous people have drowned over the years.

The Division of State Parks (p472) office in Lihu'e can provide a Kalalau Trail brochure with a map. Even if you're not planning to camp, a camping permit is legally required to day-hike beyond Hanakoa. Camping permits ($20 per person per night for nonresidents) are available from **Hawaii State Parks** (http://hawaiistateparks.

Kalalau Trail

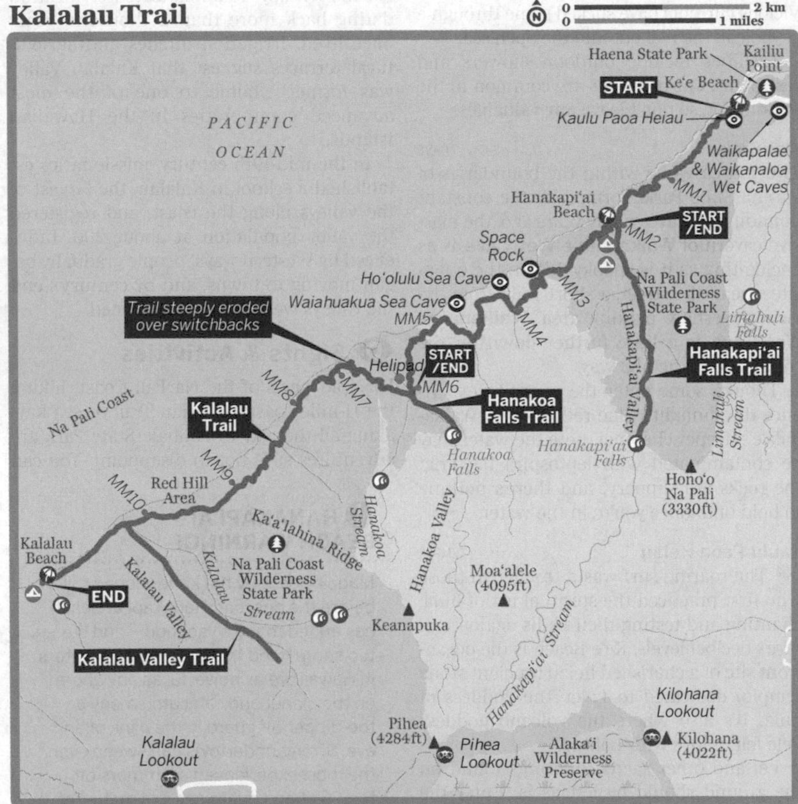

SAFE HIKING ON THE KALALAU TRAIL

The Kalalau Trail is *very* rugged, and hiking its entire length is not for everyone. Only fit, experienced backpackers need apply. Being prepared is critical: you won't want to pack too much but you will need to stay hydrated, prepped for rain, and you *must* pack out your trash. You may see hikers with machetes, walkie-talkies, climbing rope and reef shoes, but even trekkers with the most impressive gear should know not to expect a rescue by emergency responders. These precipices are to be taken seriously, and your safety is ultimately your own responsibility. Anyone with a police scanner can tell you 'plenty story' about the braggart from the mainland who was warned by friends, family or an onlooker, but said something along the lines of these famous last words: 'Nah, I'm from the Rockies. This is nothing.' Finally, mosquitoes here are bloodthirsty and the sun can ravage, so always wear insect repellent and sunblock.

org/camping) online or in person at the Lihu'e office. There's a five-night maximum per trip, with camping allowed only at Hanakoa (maximum one night) and at Kalalau. Book permits as far in advance as possible, up to a year ahead.

Ke'e Beach to Hanakapi'ai Beach

It shouldn't take more than a few hours to complete this 4-mile (round-trip) trek. It's easy to see why it's so popular: it's a perfect mini–Na Pali experience that passes through small hanging valleys and over trickling streams, offering panoramic views down the entire coast. You'll end this hike at white-sand **Hanakapi'ai Beach** at the bottom of Hanikapi'ai Valley.

Never turn your back on the ocean, especially near the river mouth. Swimming at this beach is not only dangerous but prohibited (see p531).

Hanakapi'ai Beach to Hanakapi'ai Falls

For a longer day hike, cross Hanakapi'ai Stream and follow the trail 2 miles up the valley. Hanakapi'ai Falls is spectacular, falling 300ft into a wide pool that's gentle enough for swimming. Directly under the falls, the cascading water forces you back from the rock face – a warning from nature, as falling rocks are common. The setting is idyllic, though not very sunny near the falls because of the incredible steepness.

On this 4-mile round-trip detour, you'll see the remains of age-old taro fields, and step through wild guava groves before the canyon narrows, framed by mossy rock walls. The streamside trail, which ascends gradually and repeatedly crosses the stream, gets washed out periodically. Be particularly careful of your footing on the rocky upper part of the trail, where some of the rocks are covered with slick algae – worse than walking on ice. When it rains, flash floods are likely in this narrow valley, so hike only in fair weather.

Hanakapi'ai Beach to Kalalau Beach

Going past Hanakapi'ai means you've got 9 miles left, and that you've committed to the whole 22-mile round-trip hike. **Hanakoa Valley** marks the almost halfway point and is a rest stop or campground for hikers – depending how you choose to break up the trail. It's also the turnoff for the 0.6-mile round-trip trail to **Hanakoa Falls** (no swimming).

Past Hanakoa the trail gets noticeably drier and more exposed, and the blue Pacific waters at the base of the cliff taunt you that much more. Hiking poles are helpful along the entire trail, but especially along these rocky ledges. Near the end, the trail takes you across the front of Kalalau Valley, where you can feel dwarfed by 1000ft lava-rock cliffs before proceeding to the campsites on the beach, just west of the valley.

Tours

Kaua'i Nature Tours GUIDED TOUR
(808-742-8305, 888-233-8365; www.kauainaturetours.com; 10hr tours adult/child 7-12yr $150/115; by reservation only) Geologist Chuck Blay's company guides an excellent 8-mile (round-trip) hike to Hanakapi'ai Falls. All-day tours depart by shuttle van from Po'ipu Beach Park on the South Shore.

Getting There & Away

The parking lot nearest the Kalalau Trail head at Ke'e Beach is quite large, but fills quickly. By mid-morning and during the jam-packed summer months, you may well find yourself out of luck. Break-ins are rampant; some people advise leaving your car empty and unlocked to prevent damage such as window smashing. Overnight hikers should consider parking at Ha'ena Beach Park (free, but not patrolled) or possibly at private **YMCA Camp Naue** (808-246-9090; http://www.ymcaofkauai.org/YMCA/CampNaue.html; Kuhio Hwy; per night $5) instead.

PO'IPU & THE SOUTH SHORE

Tourists adore Po'ipu, and it's no surprise why: sun, surf and sand. The quintessential elements of a beach vacation are guaranteed here, where the weather's less rainy and the waves are less changeable than on the North Shore. Since the 1970s, condos and resort hotels have mushroomed along this coastline.

The South Shore also has two world-renowned botanical gardens, as well as the undeveloped Maha'ulepu Coast, where lithified sand-dune cliffs and pounding surf make for an unforgettable walk. You're bound to stop at least once in Koloa, a former plantation town that's now the South Shore's lively little commercial hub.

Koloa

The district of Koloa revolves around a historic sugar plantation town of quaint painted cottages, now filled with tourist shops, restaurants and galleries. Known today as **Old Koloa Town**, it was founded in 1835 by New England missionaries turned sugarcane entrepreneurs.

Coming from Lihu'e, take Maluhia Rd (Hwy 520), which leads through the enchanting **Tree Tunnel**, a mile-long canopy of towering eucalyptus trees. Pineapple baron Walter McBryde planted them as a community project in 1911, using leftover trees from his estate.

Sights

Koloa Jodo Mission TEMPLE
(808-742-6735; www.koloajodo.com; 3480 Waikomo Rd; services usually 10:30am Sun) Serving the local Japanese community for more than a century, this sect of Buddhism practices a form of chanting meditation. The temple on the left is the original, which dates back to 1910, while the larger temple on the right is used for a weekly service followed by a Dharma talk – everyone is welcome. For a guided tour, call ahead.

Check the website for the dates of summer Obon festivities, which feature Japanese drumming, folk dancing and more.

Koloa History Center MUSEUM
(www.oldkoloa.com; Koloa Rd; 9am-9pm) FREE This tiny open-air museum traces the town's history through old photos and historic artifacts such as old barber chairs and kerosene dispensers, plows, yolks, saws and sewing machines. In effect, the entire town is part of this museum, as many buildings have placards describing their history.

Sugar Monument (Old Mill) HISTORIC SITE
(Koloa Rd) The sugar industry, once Hawaii's largest, began here in 1835. This memorial stands on the site of the first mill. There's little left besides a foundation, an old stone chimney and a bronze sculpture depicting the ethnically diverse laborers of Hawaii's plantation era.

Activities & Tours

★ Fathom Five Ocean Quest Divers DIVING
(808-742-6991, 800-972-3078; http://fathomfive.com; 3450 Po'ipu Rd; dives $75-350) Considered Kaua'i's best dive outfit, Fathom Five offers a full range of options, from Ni'ihau boat dives to certification courses and enticing night dives. Newbies can expect reassuring hand-holding during introductory shore dives. Groups max out at six people, and mixing skill levels is avoided. Scuba and snorkel gear are rented at the full-service shop. Book well in advance.

Koloa Zipline ADVENTURE TOUR
(808-742-2894, 877-707-7088; www.koloazipline.com; 3477a Weliweli Rd; tours $145-185; tours daily, by reservation only) Take the plunge and zip upside down as you enjoy superlative views from the longest (measured in feet, not minutes) zipline tour on the island, and the only one to allow tandem zipping. Try to book at least two weeks ahead, or call the day before to ask about last-minute openings. Minimum age is seven years; maximum weight is 270lbs.

Snorkel Bob's WATER SPORTS
(808-742-2206, 800-262-7725; www.snorkelbob.com; 3236 Po'ipu Rd; 8am-5pm) The king of snorkel gear rents and sells enough styles and sizes to assure a good fit. Wetsuits, flotation devices and boogie boards are all rented here. You can return snorkel gear to any location on Kaua'i, O'ahu, Maui or the Big Island.

Boss Frog's Dive, Surf & Bike WATER SPORTS
(808-742-2025, 888-700-3764; www.bossfrog.com; 3414 Po'ipu Rd; 8am-5pm) This outfit rents well-used snorkel gear pretty darn cheaply. You can even return snorkel gear to their Maui or Big Island shops. Rental boogie boards, surfboards, underwater cameras, beach chairs and umbrellas are also available (but no bikes).

Kauai Z Tourz BOAT TOUR
(808-742-7422; http://kauaiztours.com; 3417e Po'ipu Rd; tours adult/child 5-12yr from $99/84) The 'z' is for Zodiac boat, which whisks you off on a snorkeling tour of the South Shore. Options include reefs off Spouting Horn, Prince Kuhio Park and Allerton Gardens. You may wish to avoid sites you can reach from shore yourself. Winter boat trips go out dolphin- and whale-watching (no snorkeling).

Festivals & Events

★Koloa Plantation Days Celebration CULTURAL, MUSIC
(808-652-3217; www.koloaplantationdays.com; Jul;) In mid- to late July, the South Shore's biggest annual celebration spans nine days of family-friendly fun with a gamut of attractions (many free), including a parade, *paniolo* (Hawaiian cowboy) rodeo, traditional Hawaiian games, Polynesian dancing, a craft fair, film nights, live music, guided walks and hikes, a beach party and plenty of 'talk story' about the old days.

Sleeping

Most accommodations are vacation rentals in Lawa'i or the Koloa and Omao Rd residential neighborhoods.

Yvonne's B&B B&B $
(808-742-2418; yvonne.e.johnson@gmail.com; 3857 Omao Rd; s/d with shared bath $89/99, incl breakfast $99/119;) World traveler, collector of oddities and teller of hilarious stories, Yvonne makes this homey B&B sing. Guests will enjoy a good chat on the charming veranda and showers of kindness. Her two rooms are decorated with Hawaiiana artifacts, retro furnishings and original art. While the bathroom is shared, only one room is typically rented at a time. Three-night minimum stay.

KOLOA HERITAGE TRAIL

The **Koloa Heritage Trail** (www.koloaheritagetrail.info) is a 10-mile walk, bike ride or drive with 14 stops highlighting the archaeology, culture and history of the South Shore. Some stops are little more than bronze plaques, while others, such as Spouting Horn and Po'ipu Beach Parks, are popular sights. If you want to combine fresh air and exercise with an overview of the region, it'll do the trick. Download a free trail guide online or drop by the Poipu Beach Resort Association (p550) for a free brochure.

Boulay Inn APARTMENT $
(808-742-1120; www.boulayinn.com; 4175 Omao Rd; 1-bedroom apt $85;) This airy apartment in quiet residential Omao sits atop a garage, but has its own wraparound lanai, full kitchen, high ceilings, washer-dryer and complimentary use of beach gear. There's a sofabed in the living room, so you can bring the kids or another adult. Fresh flowers and a breakfast basket welcome your arrival. Three-night minimum stay; cleaning fee $50.

★Kaua'i Banyan Inn INN $$
(888-786-3855; www.kauaibanyan.com; 3528b Mana Hema Pl, Lawa'i; ste incl breakfast $155-230;) Perched on a lush hillside in Lawa'i, this inn is chic enough for even the most discerning guests. Each impeccable suite features polished hardwood floors, a kitchenette (or full kitchen), vaulted ceilings, private lanai and quality wood furnishings. The top suite (Ali'i) has mountain and (distant) ocean views. Guests make their own breakfast from food provided. Cleaning fee $45.

★Marjorie's Kaua'i Inn B&B $$
(808-332-8838, 800-717-8838; www.marjorieskauaiinn.com; Hailima St, Lawa'i; r incl breakfast $150-215;) After a long day's adventures, relax at this class-act B&B with a 50ft saltwater lap pool and great views over Lawa'i Valley. The three rooms are tastefully furnished (one with a hot tub), and each

WORTH A TRIP

LAWA'I INTERNATIONAL CENTER

Spiritual. Stirring. Enchanting. Such words are often used to describe the quiet **Lawa'i International Center** (tour reservations 808-639-4300; www.lawaicenter.org; 3381 Wawae Rd, Lawa'i; admission by donation; 2nd & last Sun of the month, tours depart 10am, noon & 2pm) FREE. Originally it was the site of a Hawaiian heiau; however, Japanese immigrants placed 88 miniature Shingon Buddhist shrines, each about 2ft tall and made of wood and stone, along a steep hillside path here in 1904. It symbolizes the famous 88 pilgrimage shrines of Shikoku, Japan.

For years, island pilgrims would journey here to meditate upon these shrines, but the site was abandoned by the 1960s, and half of the shrines were scattered in shards. In the late 1980s, a crew of volunteers formed a nonprofit group, acquired the 32-acre property and embarked on a back-breaking project to repair or rebuild the shrines.

Today, all 88 are beautifully restored, and there is a newly built wooden temple, the Hall of Compassion. Leisurely tours include a detailed history and a hillside trail walk that amounts to a mini pilgrimage. Everyone is welcome, since the center is a non-denominational sanctuary.

comes with a kitchenette and a private lanai. Friendly innkeepers throw in many vacation perks for free: beach and snorkel gear, shared washer-dryer, outdoor BBQ grill and more.

Hale Kipa O Koloa COTTAGE $$
(808-651-4493; www.vrbo.com/68868; 1-bedroom cottage per night/week $135/810;) This plantation-style house is a walkable half-mile to Old Koloa Town and affords much privacy. With one queen and three twin beds, a full kitchen and a washer-dryer, a family can settle in and have plenty of room. The inland location can be hot, but the cottage has high ceilings and cool tile floors. Free beach gear to borrow.

Eating & Drinking

★ **Koloa Fish Market** SEAFOOD, LOCAL $
(808-742-6199; 5482 Koloa Rd; meals $7-11; 10am-6pm Mon-Fri, to 5pm Sat) Line up with those in the know at this hole-in-the-wall. It serves outstanding *poke* in all kinds of flavors (spicy kimchi is the hands-down winner), Japanese-style *bentō* (boxed meals), sushi rolls, seaweed salads and both Hawaiian and local plate lunches grilled to order. Thick-sliced, perfectly seared ahi and rich slabs of homemade *haupia* (coconut) or sweet-potato pie are quite addictive.

★ **Fresh Shave** DESSERT $
(www.thefreshshave.com; 3540 Koloa Rd, Lawa'i; shave ice from $5.50; 11am-3pm Wed-Fri, to 5pm Sat;) Out of a shiny vintage Aristocrat trailer comes the best shave ice on the island, made using fresh, organic and often local ingredients such as apple, bananas and coffee. Opening hours vary, but be forewarned that this roadside pit stop is always mobbed with neighborhood moms and kids after school in the afternoon.

Koloa Farmers Market MARKET $
(www.kauai.gov; Knudsen Park, Maluhia Rd; noon-2pm Mon;) Vendors sell mostly flowers and produce, including exotic fruit – try drinking the milk from a whole coconut. Bring small bills and change, and show up on time, as competition is fierce once the whistle blows.

Koloa Mill Ice Cream & Coffee CAFE $
(808-742-6544; http://koloamill.ahez.com; 5424 Koloa Rd; items from $3; 7am-9pm) Homemade cotton candy, Kaua'i coffee and nothing but the best Maui-made Roselani Tropics ice cream are always served with a smile. If you're indecisive, start with the Kona coffee, macadamia nut or 'Pauwela Sunrise' containing pineapple chunks.

Sueoka Snack Shop AMERICAN $
(808-742-1112; www.sueokastore.com; 5392 Koloa Rd; items $2-5, meals around $7; 9am-5pm or 6pm Tue-Sun) Next door to Sueoka's grocery store, this little yellow take-out window is the smart place to order that picnic lunch, be it teriyaki burgers, fish and chips or mixed plates. For better or worse, all the food tastes home-cooked. It's as inexpensive a meal as you'll find anywhere on Kaua'i. Cash only.

Chalupa's MEXICAN $
(808-634-4016; www.chalupaskauai.com; 3477 Weliweli Rd; items $3-10, meals $10-13; 10am-7pm Mon-Fri, 11am-4pm Sat & Sun) Hailing from Veracruz, this Mexican chef and his food truck is worth seeking out behind the shops. Fish tacos and shrimp (garlic, Cajun or spicy *diabla*) plates are what everyone's chowing down on at the picnic tables. BYOB.

Big Save SUPERMARKET $
(808-742-1614; www.timessupermarkets.com; 5516 Koloa Rd; 6am-11pm) Fill up the kitchen of your vacation rental at this local chain supermarket; this is one of its best branches, and it stocks some locally grown produce. Pick up the value-priced ahi *poke*.

Sueoka Store SUPERMARKET $
(808-742-1611; www.sueokastore.com; 5392 Koloa Rd; 6:30am-8:30pm Mon-Sat, from 7:30am Sun) Located on the town's main drag, this small local grocery store holds its own by stocking the basics, plus pre-packaged Japanese snacks and Kaua'i-made Taro Ko (p558) chips.

La Spezia ITALIAN, AMERICAN $$
(808-742-8824; www.laspeziakauai.com; 5492 Koloa Rd; mains breakfast $8-14, dinner $14-22; 7:30-11am Mon, Tue & Thu-Sat, 8:30-11am Wed, 8am-1pm Sun, 5:30-10pm daily) A step up in sophistication from everywhere else in town, this Italian *ristorante*, with polished wooden floors and a wine bar, crafts flatbreads, crunchy crostini and housemade sausage and pasta. Surprisingly, it doubles as a creative breakfast spot – turn up for stuffed French toast and Bloody Marys at Sunday brunch.

Yanagi Sushi FUSION $$
(5371 Koloa Rd; mains $12-15; 11am-3pm Mon-Thu) Look for the 'Dragon Wagon' parked at the old mill site, across the street from the main shopping strip. The enthusiastic, superfriendly, Kaua'i-born sushi guru is creative and generous in his plating of fusion rolls. Show up too late and you might find everyone has gone surfing, brah.

Pizzetta ITALIAN, AMERICAN $$
(808-742-8881; www.pizzettakauai.com; 5408 Koloa Rd; mains $12-20, pizzas $17-25; 11am-9:30pm) More than the pasta bowls it's the baked pizzas, with toppings such as *kalua* pig, Hawaiian BBQ chicken or spinach with goat's cheese, that are the draw at this casual spot. Nab a patio table out back.

Shopping

Island Soap & Candle Works BEAUTY, GIFTS
(808-742-1945, 888-528-7627; www.kauaisoap.com; 5428 Koloa Rd; 9am-9pm) The aromas wafting out of this shop are enough to turn your head. Wander in and sample the all-natural Hawaii botanical bath and body products, including lip balms, soaps, lotions and tropically scented candles. Some of the products are made on-site at the back of the store, which was established in 1984.

Pohaku T's CLOTHING
(808-742-7500; www.pohaku.com; 3430 Po'ipu Rd; 10am-6pm Mon-Sat, to 5pm Sun) Spot the Kaua'i-made clothing hanging out on the lanai (when it's not raining), including unique aloha shirts, and a grab bag of souvenirs indoors. Stonewashed (*pohaku* means stone in Hawaiian) T-shirt designs are printed with Hawaiian themes such as petroglyphs, Polynesian carvings and navigational maps.

Art House ARTS & CRAFTS
(808-742-1400; www.arthousehawaii.com; 3440 Po'ipu Rd; 11am-6pm) Local artists show their plein-air paintings, mixed media and groovy handicrafts such as sweet silver jewelry and art boxes at this brightly lit gallery. Owner Julie Berg's acrylic images shine with an unusual additive: surfboard resin.

Information

First Hawaiian Bank (808-742-1642; www.fhb.com; 3506 Waikomo Rd; 8:30am-4pm Mon-Thu, to 6pm Fri) Has a 24-hour ATM.
Koloa Post Office (808-742-1319; www.usps.com; 5485 Koloa Rd; 9am-4pm Mon-Fri, to 11am Sat) Serves both Koloa and Po'ipu.

Getting There & Away

Kaua'i Bus (p485) stops in Koloa on its route between Po'ipu and Kalaheo; the latter has onward connnections to Lihu'e and the Westside.

Po'ipu

Often sunnier and drier than the North Shore, Po'ipu (which ironically translates as 'completely overcast' – don't worry, it isn't) is renowned for its beaches, some of which are hidden and so gorgeously wild that they rival the island's best scenery. The quality of Po'ipu sunsets is reflected in the dizzy smiles of awe-drunk tourists, weaving and leaning against one another on the sand.

Po'ipu

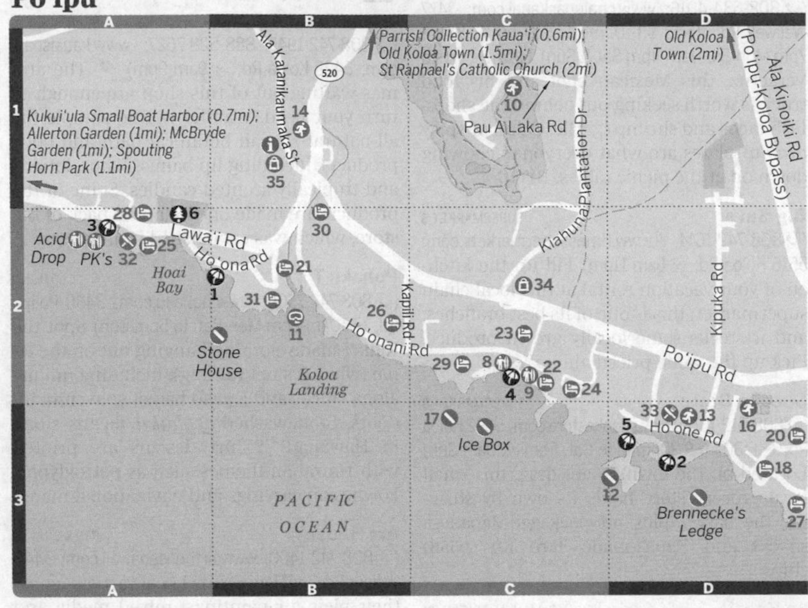

Po'ipu is a simply pleasant resort area, with condos galore and two sprawling hotels. But it's all done in good taste, with no building taller than a palm tree. It's ideal for families – especially those with young children, as several of the beaches are sheltered, with calm waters. Po'ipu has no town center, so most of the tourist activity revolves around two open-air shopping and dining complexes.

Beaches

Po'ipu has two different beach areas: the in-town beaches, which front resorts and condos, and the wild beaches along the Maha'ulepu Coast. The former are popular and crowded, the latter unspoiled and surprisingly private.

In-Town Beaches

Po'ipu Beach Park BEACH

(👪) At the South Shore's most popular beach, there are no monster waves or idyllic solitude, but it's a go-to spot with something for everyone. Patrolled by resident *honu* (sea turtles) in the shallows, the beach is protected by a rocky reef that attracts fish of all kinds.

The beach spills into two separate bays connected by the reef outside and bisected by a sandbar. Add in lifeguards, picnic tables, toilets and outdoor showers, and you have one safe, family-friendly beach.

At the end of Ho'owili Rd, there's parking located right across from the beach. There are also three nearby surf breaks and a grassy lawn connecting to Brennecke's Beach just east.

Brennecke's Beach BEACH

With a sandbar bottom and a notch of sand and sea wedged between two lava rock outcrops, this little beach attracts a cadre of bodyboarders, bobbing in the water, waiting for the next set at any time of day or year. No surfboards are allowed near shore, so bodyboarders rule. Tourists sit on the roadside stone wall, gawking at the action.

The beach flanks the eastern edge of Po'ipu Beach Park. Check with lifeguards there before venturing out.

Po'ipu Beach BEACH

Although it's nicknamed Sheraton Beach or Kiahuna Beach, this long swath of sand is not private. It merely fronts these hotel and condo complexes, both of which scored big-time with their location here, lying west of Po'ipu Beach Park.

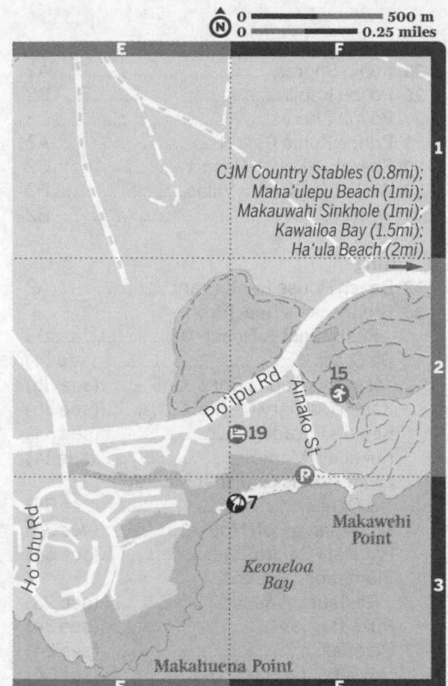

The waters are often too rough for kids, although an offshore reef tames the waves enough for strong ocean swimmers and snorkelers. To get to the beach, drive to the end of Hoʻonani Rd.

Experienced surfers and bodyboarders can attempt the breaks near the Sheraton, but those waters are famous for sneaker sets (rogue waves that appear out of nowhere) and the rocky coast makes it difficult to get offshore and back.

Shipwreck Beach BEACH

Unless you're an expert surfer, bodyboarder or bodysurfer, keep your feet dry at 'Shipwrecks.' Instead, come for an invigorating walk along the half-mile crescent of light-gold sand. You'll have some company, as the Grand Hyatt overlooks much of the beach along Keoneloa Bay. Row after row of waves crash close to shore, giving this beach a rugged, untamed feel.

To the east of the bay looms **Makawehi Point**, a gigantic lithified sand dune. Beware that cliff-jumpers (or those who accidentally fall due to erosion) have been seriously injured and have even died. To the west is **Makahuena Point**, the southernmost tip of Kauaʻi, a rocky cliff overlooking crashing waves that is covered with condos.

Baby Beach BEACH

(👪) Introduce tots to the ocean at this beach, where the water is barely thigh high. The sandy shore runs behind a row of beach homes on Hoʻona Rd west of Koloa Landing. Access is easy but parking is limited (don't block any driveways). Look for the beach-access sign that marks the path down to the beach.

Don't confuse this Baby Beach with the one in Kapaʻa on the island's Eastside.

Lawaʻi (Beach House) Beach BEACH

For such a tiny beach, this snorkeling and surfing spot gets lots of attention. Almost adjacent to Lawaʻi Rd, just west of the landmark Beach House Restaurant, it's not especially scenic or sandy. But during calm surf, the waters are rich snorkel turf, especially for novices. Expect a crowd of vacationers from nearby timeshares and condos.

Restrooms, outdoor showers and a smidgen of public parking are found across the street from the beach.

Mahaʻulepu Coast Beaches

The windswept Mahaʻulepu Coast resembles no other on Kauaʻi: lithified sand-dune cliffs, pounding surf, secluded coves, and three outstanding beaches with very few people on them. Swimming can be dicey, even in summer, so use your best judgment.

★Mahaʻulepu Beach BEACH

(Gillin's Beach; http://malama-mahaulepu.org) You feel like you're sitting on the reef in this secluded spot, so it's no surprise that there's excellent snorkeling. To get here, hike the Mahaʻulepu Heritage Trail (p541) from Shipwreck Beach or drive 1.5 miles on the dirt road that begins after the Grand Hyatt, turning right where it dead-ends at a gate (open 7:30am to 6pm daily, to 7pm in summer, and strictly enforced). Continue to the parking area, where a trail leads to the beach.

Look out for the sole house on the entire coast, the **Gillin Beach House**, originally built in 1946 by a civil engineer with the Koloa Sugar Plantation.

Kawailoa Bay BEACH

The beach at Kawailoa Bay has sand dunes at one end and cliffs at the other. The reliable breeze here makes it a popular spot for windsurfing and kitesurfing, while the ironwood trees bordering the beach create an impromptu picnic area. It's also a local

Po'ipu

Sights

1 Baby Beach ... B2
2 Brennecke's Beach ... D3
3 Lawa'i (Beach House) Beach ... A2
Moir Pa'u a Laka ... (see 23)
4 Po'ipu Beach ... C2
5 Po'ipu Beach Park ... D3
6 Prince Kuhio Park ... A2
7 Shipwreck Beach ... F3

Activities, Courses & Tours

Anara Spa ... (see 19)
8 Garden Island Surf School ... C2
Kauai Down Under ... (see 29)
9 Kaua'i Surf School ... C2
10 Kiahuna Golf Club ... C1
11 Koloa Landing ... B2
12 Nukumoi Point ... D3
13 Nukumoi Surf Shop ... D3
14 Outfitters Kauai ... B1
15 Po'ipu Bay Golf Course ... F2
16 Poipu Kai Tennis Club ... D3
Po'ipu Surf ... (see 35)
Seasport Divers ... (see 14)
17 Sheraton Caverns ... C3
Spa at Koa Kea ... (see 24)

Sleeping

18 Aikane Po'ipu Beach Houses ... D3
Castle Resorts ... (see 23)
19 Grand Hyatt Kauai Resort & Spa ... F2
20 Hideaway Cove Poipu Beach ... D3
21 Kaua'i Cove ... B2
22 Kiahuna Beachside ... C2
23 Kiahuna Plantation ... C2
Kiahuna Plantation Resort Kauai by Outrigger ... (see 23)
24 Koa Kea Hotel & Resort ... C2
25 Kuhio Shores ... A2
26 Po'ipu Kapili ... B2
27 Po'ipu Shores ... D3
28 Prince Kuhio Resort ... A2
29 Sheraton Kaua'i Resort ... C2
30 Waikomo Stream Villas ... B2
31 Whalers Cove ... B2

Eating

32 Beach House Restaurant ... A2
33 Brennecke's Beachfront Restaurant & Beach Deli ... D3
Da Crack ... (see 14)
Josselin's Tapas Bar & Grill ... (see 35)
Kaua'i Culinary Market ... (see 35)
Keoki's Paradise ... (see 34)
Kukui'ula Market ... (see 14)
Living Foods Gourmet Market & Café ... (see 35)
Merriman's Fish House ... (see 35)
Papalani Gelato ... (see 34)
Plantation Gardens Restaurant & Bar ... (see 23)
Puka Dog ... (see 34)
Red Salt ... (see 24)
Roy's Po'ipu Bar & Grill ... (see 34)
Tortilla Republic ... (see 35)

Drinking & Nightlife

Seaview Terrace ... (see 19)

Entertainment

'Auli'i Luau ... (see 29)
Havaiki Nui Luau ... (see 19)

Shopping

Malie Organics Boutique ... (see 35)
34 Po'ipu Shopping Village ... C2
35 Shops at Kukui'ula ... B1

fishing spot. Coming from Maha'ulepu Beach, continue down the coastal Maha'ulepu Heritage hiking trail on foot or follow the inland dirt road by car until you run into Kawailoa Bay.

★ Ha'ula Beach BEACH

Ha'ula is an isolated bay and pocket beach nestled into the shoreline. You'll feel like Robinson Crusoe here, particularly when swinging in a hammock made from a washed-up fishing net. If you're lucky, you might see a monk seal hauling out on the beach. *Kokua* (please) stay back at least 50yd to avoid disturbing these critically endangered marine mammals. The beach is a 15-minute walk beyond Kawailoa Bay along the coast, past a rusty fence.

Sights

★ Allerton Garden GARDENS

(808-742-2623; www.ntbg.org; 4425 Lawa'i Rd; 2½hr tours adult/child 6-12yr $40/15; visitor center 8:30am-5pm, tours by reservation only) An extraordinary tour of this garden, part of the multi-site National Tropical Botanical Garden, wanders deep into Lawa'i Valley. Robert Allerton, a wealthy Chicago transplant, spent three decades modifying this beautiful tropical valley, which has its own jungle river and ocean beach, by adding stone walkways, pools, sculptures, waterfalls, gazebos and a tremendous variety of plants. Book ahead for all tours.

Tour guides are knowledgeable and enthusiastic as they leisurely lead groups through the meticulously landscaped grounds. Highlights include otherworldly Moreton Bay fig trees (as seen in *Jurassic Park*), golden bamboo groves, a pristine lagoon and valley walls blanketed with purple bougainvillea during summer. More expensive three-hour sunset tours peek inside Allerton's historic home, where drinks and appetizers are civilly served on the lanai.

McBryde Garden GARDENS
(808-742-2623; www.ntbg.org; 4425 Lawa'i Rd; self-guided tours adult/child 6-12yr $20/10; visitor center 8:30am-5pm, tours by reservation only;) This garden showcases palms, flowering and spice trees, orchids and rare endemic species, plus a pretty stream and a waterfall. For budget travelers, the self-guided tour allows you to wander in the vast grounds without watching the clock. Advance reservations are required, however.

Spouting Horn Park VIEWPOINT
A concrete walkway and a grassy picnic area sit just above two blowholes in the lava-rock reef where the surf juts through like a mini geyser. The waves can be unpredictable, so you might need to wait for some action. Eruptions are typically less than 30ft and last only seconds, but they can reach twice that height during big surf.

To get here, turn right off Po'ipu Rd onto Lawa'i Rd and continue along the coast for less than 2 miles.

Moir Pa'u a Laka GARDENS
(808-742-6411; www.outrigger.com; Kiahuna Plantation, 2253 Po'ipu Rd; sunrise-sunset) FREE On the grounds of Outrigger's Kiahuna Plantation condo complex, this historical cactus and exotic flower garden is a diverting, if modest, collection interspersed with winding paths, a koi pond and colorful shocks of orchids. Established in the 1930s by Hector Moir, manager of Koloa Sugar Plantation, and his wife Alexandra, the gardens were once far better known than they are today.

St Raphael's Catholic Church CHURCH
(808-742-1955; www.st-raphael-kauai.org; 3011 Hapa Rd) Kaua'i's oldest Catholic church is the burial site of some of Hawaii's first Portuguese immigrants. The original 1854 church was made of lava rock and coral mortar with walls 3ft thick – a type of construction visible in the ruins of the adjacent rectory. When the church was enlarged in 1936 it was plastered over, giving it a more typical, whitewashed appearance. Church service hours vary, but you can poke around the old cemetery during daylight.

Activities

★Maha'ulepu Heritage Trail HIKING
(www.hikemahaulepu.org) This outstanding coastal hike runs for 2 miles each way between Shipwreck Beach and Ha'ula Beach. Leaving from Shipwreck Beach, park in the Grand Hyatt lot at the end of Ainako St; from the beach, head east through the ironwood trees. Windblown and mostly deserted, the trail offers tremendous variety: stark cliffs, pounding seas, secluded bays and beaches, heiau ruins, tidepools and more.

If you want to shorten the hike, start from Maha'ulepu Beach, or simply turn back at any time. For an interpretive trail guide and map, visit the website or the Poipu Beach Resort Association (p550) office.

Outfitters Kauai KAYAKING, SNORKELING
(808-742-9667, 888-742-9887; www.outfitterskauai.com; Po'ipu Plaza, 2827a Po'ipu Rd; full-day tours adult/child 12-14yr $156/126; guided tours usually 7am-3pm Tue & Thu mid-Sep–mid-May, by reservation only) Take a unique kayaking tour of the Po'ipu coastline, and go snorkeling and surfing at beaches only accessible by boat. Tandem, open-cockpit kayaks or sit-on-top, self-bailing kayaks with pedal rudders make it easy for novices, but if you get seasick, think twice. Make tour reservations in advance. No nonswimmers or children under 12 years old.

CJM Country Stables HORSEBACK RIDING
(808-742-6096; www.cjmstables.com; off Po'ipu Rd; 2hr group rides $110-140, private rides from $140; rides usually 9:30am & 2pm Mon-Sat, 1pm Wed & Fri;) The Maha'ulepu Coast is a perfect landscape to see by horse. CJM offers two gentle tours of the purely nose-to-tail walking variety suitable for the whole family. More experienced riders may opt for a private ride.

Anara Spa SPA
(808-742-1234; www.anaraspa.com; Grand Hyatt Kaua'i Resort & Spa, 1571 Po'ipu Rd; by appointment only) The Grand Hyatt does everything grandly, and this 45,000-sq-ft spa, embellished with tropical gardens and waterfalls, is no exception. Spa treatments inspired by Hawaiian healing arts are given in private garden-view rooms. Don't miss the lava-rock showers. Access to the lap pool and a fitness

DON'T MISS

SOUTH SHORE SNORKELING SPOTS

Take the plunge at these top-rated South Shore snorkeling areas with handy beach access:

Koloa Landing Once Kaua'i's largest port, this site is known for the best shore diving, with a quick drop-off to 45ft. The edge is also great for advanced snorkeling. Expect to see large schools of fish, eels and the usual turtles. Avoid the sandy middle ground.

Lawa'i (Beach House) Beach (p539) If you don't mind the crowds, you'll find good coral, lots of reef fish and sea turtles, all within a depth of 3ft to 12ft. There are restrooms and outdoor showers on shore.

Maha'ulepu Beach (p539) Though often overlooked because of its seclusion, this near-shore reef is perhaps the best of the lot, though you'll need calm wind and water.

Po'ipu Beach Park (p538) Ranging from 3ft to 12ft, this shallow protected bay is great for families, although experts will enjoy it as well. Snorkeling is best on the left side as you enter. Facilities include lifeguards, outdoor showers and restrooms.

Prince Kuhio Park Directly across the street from this grassy park, ocean waters ranging from 3ft to 21ft deep appeal to both beginners and advanced snorkelers. There's a rocky shoreline, but the bay is protected.

center offering yoga and wellness classes is complimentary with a minimum 50-minute treatment. Reservations required.

Po'ipu Bay Golf Course GOLF

(808-742-8711, 800-858-6300; www.poipubaygolf.com; 2250 Ainako St; green fees incl cart rental $130-255) Known for its magnificent views of mountains and sea, this 18-hole, par-72 course designed by Robert Trent Jones Jr hosted the PGA Grand Slam for 13 years. It sports 85 bunkers, multiple water hazards and unpredictable winds. Rates drop dramatically in the afternoons. Club and shoe rentals available.

Kiahuna Golf Club GOLF

(808-742-9595; www.kiahunagolf.com; 2545 Kiahuna Plantation Dr; green fees incl cart rental $75-110) A relatively inexpensive and forgiving 18-hole, par-70 course designed by Robert Trent Jones Jr, interestingly incorporating some archaeological ruins. The scenery is excellent, with some ocean views, although the course is often windy. Rental clubs available.

Poipu Kai Tennis Club TENNIS

(808-742-8706; www.poipukai.org/tennis.html; 1775 Po'ipu Rd; per person per day $20, racket rental $5; 8am-noon & 2-6pm) Rent one of six hard courts or two artificial grass courts with ocean views at this resort racquet club. It has tennis clinics and round-robin tourneys. You can either make a reservation or just show up.

Spa at Koa Kea SPA

(808-828-8888; www.koakea.com; Koa Kea Hotel & Resort, 2251 Po'ipu Rd; by appointment only) A boutique spa with just five treatment rooms (including one for couples) that puts a variety of massage styles on the menu. Choose from Hawaiian *lomilomi* and *pohaku* (hot stone), as well as body scrubs and treatments utilizing island-sourced ingredients such as *kukui* (candlenut) and coconut oils, Kaua'i coffee and red clay. Book ahead.

Diving

The Po'ipu coast offers the majority of the island's best dive sites, including **Sheraton Caverns**, a series of partially collapsed lava tubes, with shafts of glowing sunlight illuminating their dim, atmospheric interior; **General Store**, with sharks, octopuses, eels and the remains of an 1892 shipwreck; and **Nukumoi Point**, a shallow site as well as habitat for green sea turtles.

Dive boats and catamaran cruises typically depart from **Kukui'ula Small Boat Harbor** (Lawa'i Rd).

★ **Seasport Divers** DIVING

(808-742-9303, 800-685-5889; www.seasportdivers.com; Po'ipu Plaza, 2827 Po'ipu Rd; shore/boat dives from $90/135; by reservation only) This leading outfit schedules a variety of dives from shore or by boat, including twice-daily South Shore boat trips, and a rare and wonderful three-tank dive to Ni'ihau, available twice-weekly from late spring through early fall. All dives are guided by instructor-level dive masters; any group with noncertified divers includes an additional instructor. Rental equipment available. Book in advance.

Kauai Down Under DIVING
(☎808-742-9534; www.kauaidownunderscuba.com; Sheraton Kauai Resort, 2440 Ho'onani Rd; boat dives incl equipment rental from $159; ⊙by reservation only) With one instructor per four guests, personal attention is guaranteed. This outfit offers introductory noncertified one-tank dives, two-tank scooter dives, and night dives for the truly adventurous. It also has a multitude of classes including the recommended pre-arrival online academic portion of the certification for those wanting to maximize playtime while on the island. Make reservations in advance.

Surfing & Stand-Up Paddleboarding

Po'ipu's killer breaks and year-round waves make it a popular spot for surfing lessons and rentals.

★Kaua'i Surf School SURFING, SUP
(☎808-651-6032; www.kauaisurfschool.com; Ho'onani Rd; 2hr group/private surfing lessons $75/175; ⊙by reservation only; 👪) With 90 minutes of teaching, 30 minutes of free practice, and only four students per instructor, you get your money's worth. Ages four and up are welcome in group lessons as long as they can swim; alternatively, book a special one-hour private lesson for kids. Ask about surf clinics, surf camps, private surf coaches and SUP lessons.

Kauai Stand-up Paddle & Surf SUP, SURFING
(☎808-652-9979; www.kauaisurfandsup.com; 2hr group/private surfing lessons $75/120, 2hr SUP lessons $85, surfing & SUP tours $120-150; 👪) This locally owned, small-group outfitter runs kids' surf camps in summer, offers family discounts and has 30 years of experience to bring to the table. It's also the only one to offer custom SUP tours island-wide.

Surf Lessons by Margo Oberg SURFING
(☎808-332-6100; www.surfonkauai.com; 2hr group/semiprivate/private surfing lessons $68/90/125; ⊙by appointment only) Owned and operated by a seven-time world champ, one of the longest-running surf schools on Kaua'i has a fine rep. Group classes can include up to six people.

Garden Island Surf School SURFING, SUP
(☎808-652-4841; www.gardenislandsurfschool.com; Po'ipu Beach; 2hr group/private surfing lessons $75/150, 80min SUP lessons $65, outrigger canoe tours $50; ⊙by reservation only) Group surfing lessons include just one hour with an instructor and an hour of free surfing. For a unique experience, surf the waves while paddling a Hawaiian outrigger canoe. Reservations required.

Po'ipu Surf SURFING
(☎808-742-8797; http://poipusurf.com; Shops at Kukui'ula, 2829 Ala Kalanikaumaka St; surfboard/SUP rental per day from $20/40; ⊙9am-9pm) Local surf and skate shop renting beginner and performance surfboards and SUP sets at competitive rates. Weekly discounts are available.

Nukumoi Surf Shop WATER SPORTS
(☎808-742-8019; www.nukumoi.com; 2100 Ho'one Rd; snorkel set & boogie board/surfboard/SUP rental per day from $6/25/60; ⊙8am-sunset) For surfboard, snorkel and SUP rentals, this shop is right across from Po'ipu Beach Park. Check your gear carefully before heading out.

Tours

Captain Andy's Sailing Adventures BOAT TOUR
(☎808-335-6883, 800-535-0830; www.napali.com; Kukui'ula Small Boat Harbor; 2hr tours adult/child 2-12yr $79/59; ⊙departs 4pm or 5pm Sat) If you're dreaming of a scenic sunset cruise down the Maha'ulepu Coast by catamaran, Captain Andy is a real pro. Cross your fingers to spot whales between December and April. Tours, which depart only once a week, include appetizers, cocktails and live music. Book at least three days ahead.

Festivals & Events

★Prince Kuhio Celebration of the Arts CULTURAL, ART
(http://princekuhio.net; ⊙Mar) The South Shore hosts this two-week celebration in mid- to late March. Events include hula dancing and slack key guitar music, a rodeo, canoe racing, 'talk story' time, an artisan fair (p499) and Hawaiian cultural presentations on *kapa* (bark cloth), lei and poi making, stone and wood carving, and much more.

Sleeping

The **Po'ipu Beach Resort Association** (www.poipubeach.org/places-to-stay/condominium-resorts/) website gives a good overview of condo complexes with helpful photos. Condo owners tend to offer better prices, while a rental agency can help connect you with the right property and assist with any problems during your stay.

On-site property management agencies include **Outrigger** (808-742-6411, 866-733-0587; http://outriggerkiahunaplantationcondo.com) and **Castle Resorts** (808-742-2200, 877-367-1912; www.castleresorts.com), but **Kiahuna Beachside** (808-742-2200, 800-937-6642; www.kiahuna.com) manages some of the best (and most expensive) oceanfront units.

Prince Kuhio Resort CONDO **$**
(888-747-2988; www.prince-kuhio.com; 5061 Lawa'i Rd; studio/1-/2-bedroom condo from $75/125/275;) This 72-unit complex has an enviable location across from Lawa'i Beach. Although varying in quality and amenities, most condos here have views across the road to the ocean. All have full kitchens and lanai. The pool is no slouch, and the grounds are well kept. A last-minute rental here can be great value. Cleaning fee $85 to $150.

★**Kuhio Shores** CONDO **$$**
(www.kuhioshores.net; 5050 Lawa'i Rd; 1-/2-bedroom condos from $175/275) Set on a grassy outcrop jutting into the sea opposite Prince Kuhio Park, this three-story oceanfront complex claims the most stunning vistas in Po'ipu. Privately owned condos each spill out onto a patio or lanai. That makes them perennially popular, even though some units are showing their age and amenities vary. Book well ahead. Cleaning fee $95 to $150.

Hideaway Cove Poipu Beach CONDO **$$**
(808-635-8785, 866-849-2426; www.hideawaycove.com; 2307 Nalo Rd; studio/1-/2-/3-bedroom condos from $185/215/275/425;) Near Po'ipu Beach Park, these impeccable, modern and professionally managed units that come with concierge services are a cut above their peers. All condos feature private lanai, hardwood flooring, genuine art and antiques, name-brand appliances, whirlpool tubs and 50in flat-screen HDTVs, making them feel like private homes. Air-con is only in the bedrooms. Cleaning fee $140 to $325. Complimentary concierge services and loaner beach gear.

Kaua'i Cove COTTAGE, INN **$$**
(808-742-2562, 800-624-9945; www.kauaicove.com; 2672 Pu'uholo Rd & 2367 Ho'ohu Rd; r/ste from $129/159, cottage $149-229;) In a low-key neighborhood near Koloa Landing, this trio of lodgings deftly blends modern amenities with a tropical bungalow feel. In the private studio cottage, an efficient layout allows for a bamboo canopy bed, vaulted ceilings and a fully loaded kitchenette. Add tastefully exotic decor, lustrous hardwood floors and parking right outside your doorstep. Cleaning fee $50 to $75.

Beach gear is free to borrow, and guests have access to a nearby pool and hot tub.

Kiahuna Plantation CONDO **$$**
(808-742-6411, 800-542-4862; www.outrigger.com; 2253 Po'ipu Rd; 1-/2-bedroom condo from $115/235;) This aging beauty is still a hot property because it's among the rare Po'ipu accommodations flanking a swimmable beach. Buildings are spread around a tidy oceanfront park. Comfy units have fully equipped kitchens and large lanai, but vary in quality. Guests can use the Poipu Beach Athletic Club fitness center and pool across the road. Cleaning fee $35 to $175.

Waikomo Stream Villas CONDO **$$**
(808-742-2000, 800-325-5701; www.parishkauai.com; 2721 Po'ipu Rd; 1-/2-bedroom condos from $135/165) Because it's neither beachfront nor oceanfront, this condo can be a steal. The 60 units vary in decor but are huge, with full kitchens, washer-dryers and lanais (an unlucky few look onto the parking lot and Po'ipu Rd roundabout). The split-level, two-bedroom units soar with vaulted ceilings and an upstairs sleeping loft. Cleaning fee $135 to $165.

Sheraton Kaua'i Resort RESORT **$$**
(808-742-1661, 866-716-8109; www.sheraton-kauai.com; 2440 Ho'onani Rd; r from $209; @) While it can't compete with top resorts such as the Hyatt, the Sheraton has one enviable advantage: a prime stretch of sandy, swimmable, sunset-perfect beach, ideal for families. Rooms are unmemorable, however. The hotel's open-air design highlights its ocean setting, yet the cheapest garden-view and partial ocean-view rooms are flung across the street, where they feel like a different hotel. Mandatory per-night resort fee $30.

Complimentary activities, including yoga, hula and lei-making classes, guided tidepool tours and introductory surfing and snorkel lessons, make it fun.

★**Grand Hyatt Kauai Resort & Spa** RESORT **$$$**
(808-742-1234, 888-591-1234; www.grandhyattkauai.com; 1571 Po'ipu Rd; r from $309; P@) Po'ipu's glamour girl is 600-rooms strong and loves to show off, with a soaring lobby, tropical gardens, a huge spa, a world-renowned golf course, oceanfront restaurants

MORE PO'IPU CONDO & VACATION RENTALS

Aikane Po'ipu Beach Houses (www.kauaivacationproperties.com/poipu.htm) Dreamy beach houses near Brennecke's Beach and Po'ipu Beach. Rentals are handled by private owners.

Ocean Kaua'i Vacation Rental Condos (☎888-747-2988; www.kauai-vacation-rental-condos.com) Reasonable rates on privately owned condos at Prince Kuhio Resort.

Parrish Collection Kaua'i (☎808-742-2000, 800-325-5701; www.parrishkauai.com; 3176 Po'ipu Rd, Koloa) Top-rated rental agency for condos and vacation homes not just in Po'ipu, but also on the North Shore and the Westside. Professional staff is friendly and accommodating.

Po'ipu Connection Realty (☎808-742-2233, 800-742-2260; www.poipuconnection.com; 5488 Koloa Rd, Koloa) A variety of condo rentals at decent rates (mostly at Prince Kuhio Resort), plus personalized service.

and meandering 'river pools.' Rooms are simple yet elegant with tropical wood crown mouldings, marble entryways and baths, and rain showerheads. Adjacent Shipwreck Beach is a natural wonder. Mandatory per-night resort fee $25.

There's plenty to do here, with saltwater lagoons you can kayak around or even scuba dive in, tennis courts, and Camp Hyatt for kids. Guests can learn Hawaiian crafts or watch cultural demonstrations in the hotel atrium or sign up for volunteering with local nonprofit organizations.

Whalers Cove CONDO **$$$**
(☎808-742-7571, 800-225-2683; www.whalerscoveresort.com; 2640 Pu'uholo Rd; 1-/2-bedroom condos from $360/500;) These luxury condos with private check-in and daily maid service will suit discriminating travelers. Although somewhat impersonal, the units are palatial (1300 sq ft on average), elegantly appointed and immaculate, with outstanding ocean views. Prized koa wood has been used on some doors and furnishings. Mandatory nightly resort fee is $15, but no cleaning fee.

Koa Kea Hotel & Resort HOTEL **$$$**
(☎808-828-8888, 888-898-8958; www.koakea.com; 2251 Po'ipu Rd; r from $369;) This romantic boutique hotel occupies a unique niche in Po'ipu. It's a bold exploration of design instead of the Hawaiiana lei motif of so many other hotels. With 121 rooms, it's intimate and inwardly focused: the U-shaped building opens onto the beach, leaving many rooms looking across the central pool at each other. Mandatory nightly resort fee ($26) includes valet parking.

Po'ipu Shores CONDO **$$$**
(☎808-742-7700, 877-367-1912; www.poipushores.com; 1775 Pe'e Rd; 2-/3-bedroom condos from $450/525; @) Location, location, location. This seemingly ordinary 39-unit condo sidles up to the coast, overlooking lava rock and pounding surf. Although there's no sandy beach, guests can swim in a heated pool. Search online for much lower rates offered by local rental agencies and private owners.

Po'ipu Kapili CONDO **$$$**
(☎808 742-6449, 800-443-7714; www.poipukapili.com; 2221 Kapili Rd; 1-/2-bedroom condos from $255/385;) This 60-unit complex features landscaped grounds and spacious condos with lots of hardwood, big plush beds, extra bathrooms, tech electronics and air-con in some bedrooms. With tennis and pickleball courts, BBQ grills and a saltwater pool, the property is walking distance to the beach. One-bedroom units can have iffy views, however.

Eating

In Po'ipu, some top restaurants rely on ocean views and ambience to get you through an average dinner – which you pay heavily for. Budget travelers should look for the few restaurants that are split-level, offering separate menus on each floor that target two different price ranges.

★**Kaua'i Culinary Market** MARKET **$**
(☎855-742-9545; http://kukuiula.com; Shops at Kukui'ula, 2829 Ala Kalanikaumaka St; ⌚3:30-6pm Wed;) An upscale take on the traditional island farmers market features not only a couple dozen local farmers and food

WORTH A TRIP

MAKAUWAHI SINKHOLE

You may well think this enormous sinkhole is a lost world. The only way in is by squeezing through a tiny opening in a rock wall. Suddenly you find yourself in a beautiful, open-air atrium, with palm trees dwarfed by high cliffs and an enormous cave system beneath.

While this is arguably the richest fossil site in the Hawaiian Islands, very few people seem to know about it. Since 1996 it has been excavated by scientists with the help of students, volunteers and visitors, yielding fascinating results. The site has provided evidence for the widespread extinction of species in Hawaii following human settlement. Paleontologist David Burney's well-written book *Back to the Future in the Caves of Kaua'i* tells this cautionary tale.

Makauwahi Cave (808-634-0605, 808-212-1710; www.cavereserve.org; guided tours 9am-2pm Wed, Fri, Sat & Sun) FREE is located at the western end of Maha'ulepu Beach (p539), but is best approached from above by car, then on foot. Trail guides are usually available in a self-serve box, or downloadable online. The sinkhole is currently open to visitors for free guided tours (no reservations). Check the website for up-to-date tour times and directions.

vendors, but also free live music, cooking demonstrations by South Shore chefs and *pau hana* (happy hour) drinks in an outdoor beer and wine garden.

Papalani Gelato ICE CREAM $
(808-742-2663; www.papalanigelato.com; Po'ipu Shopping Village, 2360 Kiahuna Plantation Dr; scoop $4; 11am-9:30pm;) Deliciously sweet treats are all made on-site. You can't go wrong with classic pistachio, but for local flavor, get a scoop of macadamia-nut butter or coconut gelato, or guava, *liliko'i* or lychee sorbet. Second location at the Anchor Cove Shopping Center (p483) in Lihu'e.

Da Crack MEXICAN, AMERICAN $
(808-742-9505; www.dacrack.com; Po'ipu Plaza, 2827 Po'ipu Rd; mains $5-10; 11am-8pm Mon-Sat, to 4pm Sun;) A guilty pleasure, this taco shop (literally, it's a hole in the wall) cooks up tacos, burritos and rice-and-beans bowls overstuffed with batter-fried fish, *carnitas* (braised pork), shredded chicken or chipotle shrimp. Expect to wait.

Kukui'ula Market SUPERMARKET $
(808-742-1601; Po'ipu Plaza, 2827 Po'ipu Rd; 8am-8:30pm Mon-Fri, to 6:30pm Sat & Sun) Locally owned grocery store stocking almost everything a vegan, vegetarian or gluten-free DIY eater needs, and it has a sushi bar too. A juice bar at the back makes smoothies and acai bowls until 4pm on weekdays, 3pm on weekends.

Puka Dog FAST FOOD $
(808-742-6044; www.pukadog.com; Po'ipu Shoping Village, 2360 Kiahuna Plantation Dr; hot dogs $7-8; 10am-8pm;) Popular with tourists more than locals, these specialty hot dogs come with a toasty Hawaiian sweet bread bun, a choice of Polish sausage or a veggie dog, a 'secret' sauce and tropical fruit relish (mango and pineapple, yum).

Keoki's Paradise HAWAII REGIONAL CUISINE $$
(808-742-7534; www.keokisparadise.com; Po'ipu Shopping Village, 2360 Kiahuna Plantation Dr; bar mains $11-20, restaurant dinner mains $22-35; restaurant 4:45-9:30pm, bar 11am-10:30pm) Natural woods, tiki torches and water features combine to form a warm jungle-lodge atmosphere. The higher-priced dining room offers grilled meats and seafood, while the Bamboo Bar is all about tropical *pupu* (snacks) and pub grub. Throw in a great selection of draft beers and nightly live music, and Keoki's is a winner.

Brennecke's Beachfront Restaurant & Beach Deli AMERICAN $$
(808-742-7588; www.brenneckes.com; 2100 Ho'one Rd; deli sandwiches $6-10, restaurant mains lunch $11-20, dinner $14-30; deli 7am-9pm, restaurant 11am-10pm, bar 10am-close;) Part sports bar, part restaurant, this institution across from Po'ipu Beach Park has served up endless plates of ribs, steak, fresh fish, pasta, burgers and tacos for three decades, along with tropical cocktails and cold brewskis. The downstairs deli is the only breakfast burrito or club sandwich within range of your beach towel.

Tortilla Republic MEXICAN $$
(808-742-8884; http://tortillarepublic.com/hawaii; Shops at Kukui'ula, 2829 Ala Kalanikaumaka St;

dinner mains bar $11-21, restaurant $14-32; ⌚ restaurant 5:30-9pm Sun-Thu, to 10pm Fri & Sat, bar 8am-1pm Mon-Fri, from 9am Sat & Sun) In a plantation-style building with two levels, you'll find a buzzing margarita bar and taqueria downstairs, and a dining room upstairs that's intriguingly decorated with an onyx bar top, metalwork sculpture and carved wooden doors from Guadalajara. While the food is just as artfully designed, with some new takes on old favorites, portions are awfully small for these prices.

Living Foods Gourmet Market & Café MARKET, CAFE $$
(📞808-742-2323; http://shoplivingfoods.com; Shops at Kukui'ula, 2829 Ala Kalanikaumaka St; mains $10-18; ⌚7am-9pm;) High-priced even by island standards, the often organic, gluten-free and/or all-natural groceries sold here include cheeses, meats and imported wines, along with a selection of local produce and artisanal foodstuffs such as Kaua'i-made juices, nuts, honey, salts, coffee and cookies.

★ Josselin's Tapas Bar & Grill HAWAII REGIONAL CUISINE $$$
(📞808-742-7117; www.josselins.com; Shops at Kukui'ula, 2829 Ala Kalanikaumaka St; shared plates $11-32; ⌚5-9pm or 10pm) Heading up the restaurants at the Shops at Kukui'ula is this creative take on tapas by revered chef Jean-Marie Josselin. His Asian-influenced food is culinary high art, yet somehow still understated and approachable, with explosions of unexpected flavor combinations that leave you contemplating a second go at duck confit tacos or a deconstructed ahi roll.

There's always a lively, multigenerational crowd here, yet the low lighting and decor are stylish enough for dates. Table service begins with the sangria cart rolling up – try the lychee flavor – but the creative cocktails are even better. Reservations are strongly recommended.

Roy's Po'ipu Bar & Grill HAWAII REGIONAL CUISINE $$$
(📞808-742-5000; www.royshawaii.com/roys-poipu.html; Po'ipu Shopping Village, 2360 Kiahuna Plantation Dr; mains $28-42; ⌚5:30-9:30pm;) Popular with everyone from tourists to longtime locals, bustling Roy's continues to deliver above-average dishes such as miso-marinated *misoyaki* (butterfish), blackened ahi and pesto-steamed monchong. The prix-fixe menu ($50) comes with an appetizer sample and Roy's signature dark chocolate soufflé for dessert. Set in a shopping mall, it manages not to suffer much for it. Make reservations.

Red Salt FUSION $$$
(📞808-828-8888; www.koakea.com; Koa Kea Hotel & Resort, 2251 Po'ipu Rd; mains $29-39; ⌚restaurant 6-10pm, lounge 5:30pm-midnight) At this romantic hideaway, fusion dishes such as pan-seared *opah* (moonfish) with king crab and a sake-spiked coconut broth or vanilla bean-seared mahimahi elevate the culinary game. Seafood appetizers, sushi and strong cocktails are served in the svelte lounge, and there's always that root beer float with warm macnut cookies or *liliko'i*-ginger crème brûlée for dessert. Valet parking is complimentary.

Beach House Restaurant SEAFOOD $$$
(📞808-742-1424; www.the-beach-house.com; 5022 Lawa'i Rd; mains lunch $10-19, dinner $20-48; ⌚11am-10pm;) There are many oceanfront restaurants in Po'ipu, but only one iconic spot for sunset dining and special occasions such as weddings, birthdays and anniversaries. The focus of the Pacific Rim cuisine is fresh fish – island fishers are identified by name on the menu – but sauces are heavy. For sunset dining, reserve a 'first seating' weeks in advance. Vegan and gluten-free menus available.

Merriman's Fish House HAWAII REGIONAL CUISINE $$$
(📞808-742-8385; www.merrimanshawaii.com; Shops at Kukui'ula, 2829 Ala Kalanikaumaka St; bar mains $11-17, restaurant dinner mains $24-40; ⌚bar 11:30am-10pm, restaurant 5-9pm) Upstairs is a breezy surf-and-turf dining room, where 90% of all menu ingredients are locally caught or grown, and the fusion cuisine is designed by a famous chef. Sunset views are excellent from the plantation house's upper lanai, so book ahead. Downstairs is a family-friendly spot for burgers and pizza (happy hour 3:30pm to 5:30pm daily).

Plantation Gardens Restaurant & Bar HAWAII REGIONAL CUISINE $$$
(📞808-742-2121; http://pgrestaurant.com; Kiahuna Plantation, 2253 Po'ipu Rd; mains $24-37; ⌚restaurant 5:30-9pm, bar from 5pm) Set in a historic plantation house, this longstanding favorite is known more for its ambience than its food. The open-air setting in tropical gardens is lovely, particularly when illuminated

PAPAHĀNAUMOKUĀKEA MARINE NATIONAL MONUMENT

In a ground-breaking move, the Northwestern Hawaiian Islands became the USA's first Marine National Monument in 2006. Encompassing almost 140,000 sq miles of ocean, Papahānaumokuākea Marine National Monument (PMNM) is the world's largest protected marine area and the USA's first Unesco World Heritage site designated for both natural and cultural reasons.

PMNM begins more than 150 miles northwest of Kaua'i and stretches for 1200 miles. It's composed of 10 island clusters, which contain atolls (low sandy islands formed on top of coral reefs) and some single-rock islands. From east to west, the clusters are Nihoa Island, Mokumanamana (Necker Island), French Frigate Shoals, Gardner Pinnacles, Maro Reef, Laysan Island, Lisianski Island, Pearl and Hermes Atoll, Midway Atoll and Kure Atoll.

PMNM's total land area is less than 6 sq miles. Human history on the islands began when the first Polynesian voyagers arrived in the Hawaiian archipelago (Papahānaumokuākea is the Hawaiian 'earth mother'). In modern times, the most famous place has been Midway Atoll; it's normally the only island open to visitors.

Preserving an Ecological Balance

PMNM contains the USA's largest and healthiest coral-reef system, home to more than 7000 marine species. About one quarter of all species found here are endemic to Hawaii, with new ones discovered on every scientific voyage. This is a rare 'top predator-dominated ecosystem,' in which sharks, groupers, jacks and others make up more than 54% of the biomass (compared with around 3% in the main Hawaiian Islands). PMNM also supports more than 14 million tropical seabirds, and is the primary breeding ground for endangered green sea turtles and Hawaiian monk seals.

However, the islands are not pristine. Ocean currents bring more than 50 tons of debris to the islands annually, and cleanups have removed more than 750 tons of entangled fishing nets, plastic bottles and trash so far.

Today, the monument is jointly managed by the National Oceanic & Atmospheric Administration (NOAA), the US Fish & Wildlife Service (FWS) and the state of Hawaii. The monument's 15-year management plan has raised concerns among some Hawaiians and environmental groups such as the Sierra Club. The plan exempts from its regulations the US military (which conducts missile tests and Navy training exercises in the area) and allows for increasing visits to Midway and trips for scientific research – all of which could damage areas the monument is charged with preserving.

Nihoa & Mokumanamana

Nihoa and Mokumanamana, the two tiny islands closest to Kaua'i, were home to Hawaiians from around AD 1000 to 1700. More than 135 archaeological sites have been identified, including temple platforms, house sites, agricultural terraces, burial caves and carved stone images. As many as 175 people may have once lived on Nihoa and paddled over to Mokumanamana for religious ceremonies.

That anyone could live at all on these rocks is remarkable. Nihoa is only 1 sq km in size, and Mokumanamana is one-sixth that size. Nihoa juts from the sea steeply, like a broken tooth; it's the tallest of the Northwestern Hawaiian Islands, with 900ft sea cliffs. Two endangered endemic land birds live on Nihoa. The Nihoa finch, which, like the Laysan finch, is a raider of other birds' eggs, has a population of a couple of thousand. The Nihoa millerbird, related to the Old World warbler family, numbers fewer than a thousand.

French Frigate Shoals

Surrounded by more than 230,000 acres of coral reef, these islets contain the monument's greatest variety of coral. They're also where most of Hawaii's green sea turtles and Hawaiian monk seals breed. The 67-acre reef forms a classic comma-shaped atoll on top of an eroded volcano, in the center of which 120ft-high La Pérouse Pinnacle rises like a ship. Small, sandy Tern Island is dominated by an airfield, which was built as a refueling stop during WWII. Today, Tern Island has a US Fish & Wildlife Service (FWS) field station housing scientific researchers and volunteers.

Laysan Island

Not quite 1.5 sq miles, Laysan is PMNM's second-biggest land mass. The grassy island has the most bird species in the monument, and to see the huge flocks of Laysan albatross, shearwaters and curlews – plus the endemic Laysan duck chasing brine flies around a supersalty inland lake – you'd never know how close this island came to becoming a barren wasteland.

In the late 19th century, humans began frequenting Laysan to mine *guano* (bird droppings) to use as fertilizer. Poachers also killed hundreds of thousands of albatross for their feathers (to adorn hats) and took eggs for albumen, a substance used in photo processing. Albatross lay just one egg a year, so poaching could destroy an entire year's hatch.

Traders also built structures and brought pack mules and, oddly enough, rabbits for food. The rabbits ran loose and multiplied, and within 20 years their nibbling mostly extirpated the island's 26 endemic plant species. Without plants, at least three endemic land birds – the Laysan rail, Laysan honeycreeper and Laysan millerbird – became extinct. Laysan finches and the last dozen Laysan ducks seemed doomed to follow.

In 1909, public outcry led President Theodore Roosevelt to create the Hawaiian Islands Bird Reservation, and the island has been under some kind of protection ever since. By 1923 every last rabbit was removed from Laysan, and ecological rehabilitation began. With weed-abatement assistance, endemic plantlife recovered, and so did the birds. The Laysan finch is again common, and the Laysan duck numbers about 600 (a smaller population has been established on Midway).

Nearly the same sequence of events unfolded on nearby Lisianski Island; together, these islands are a stunning success story.

Midway Atoll

Midway Atoll was an important naval air station during WWII. It's best known as the site of a pivotal battle in June 1942, when US forces surprised an attacking Japanese fleet and defeated it. This victory is credited with turning the tide in the war's Pacific theater. Midway later became a staging point for Cold War air patrols and an underwater listening post to spy on Soviet submarines.

By 1996 the military transferred jurisdiction to the FWS. Before leaving, it conducted an extensive clean-up program to remove debris, environmental contaminants, rats and non-native plants. Midway was then developed for tourism: barracks became hotel rooms, the mess hall a cafeteria, and a beachfront restaurant and bar were added. A gym, movie theater, bowling alley and library were part of the original military facility. On Sand and Eastern Islands, various military structures have been designated National Historical Landmarks.

The ecological highlight at Midway is the more than two million seabirds that nest here, including the world's largest colony of Laysan albatross, which are so thick between November and July that they virtually blanket the ground. Midway's coral reefs are unusually rich and are frequented by Hawaiian monk seals and green sea turtles.

Visiting & Learning More

All tourist facilities on Midway Islands are managed by the **US Fish & Wildlife Service** (FWS; www.fws.gov/refuge/Midway_Atoll/), which issues permits only to organized groups. As of 2015, Midway was temporarily closed to visitors due to federal funding cutbacks. Check the website to see if it has since reopened and for a list of approved tour operators, then book your trip as far in advance as possible (normally at least a year).

If you can't make the trip in person, you can virtually visit **Papahānaumokuākea Marine National Monument** (www.papahanaumokuakea.gov) and Midway Atoll's Sand Island online (www.fws.gov/refuge/Midway_Atoll/sand_island_tour/); drop by Hilo's Mokupapapa Discovery Center (p272) on the Big Island; or read Pamela Frierson's riveting first-hand reports in *The Last Atoll: Exploring Hawai'i's Endangered Ecosystems*.

by tiki torches. The mostly seafood menu is mercifully concise and features local ingredients. However, the taste just isn't there with many dishes. Book ahead.

Drinking & Entertainment

★ Seaview Terrace BAR

(☎808-240-6456; http://kauai.hyatt.com; Grand Hyatt Kauai Resort & Spa, 1571 Po'ipu Rd; ⊙5:30-11am & 4:30-10pm) Don't miss Po'ipu's grandest and most memorable ocean view. In the morning, this stepped terrace is an espresso and pastry cafe. Later in the day, a torch-lighting ceremony announces sunset, with live music and occasionally hula dancing before 9pm. Show up early for a prime viewing table (no reservations). Head directly through the hotel lobby and atrium toward the sea.

'Auli'i Luau LUAU

(☎808-634-1499; http://auliiluau.com; Sheraton Kaua'i Resort, 2440 Ho'onani Rd; adult/child 3-12yr/youth 13-17yr from $101/49/74; ⊙6pm Mon & Thu Mar-Sep, 5:30pm Mon & Thu Oct-Feb) The Sheraton's luau banks on its oceanfront setting. The Polynesian revue and dinner buffet are both pretty standard. Beware: the jokester emcee demands audience participation. When it rains, the luau happens in a hotel ballroom – not fun.

Havaiki Nui Luau LUAU

(☎808-240-6456; www.grandhyattkauailuau.com; Grand Hyatt Kaua'i Resort & Spa, 1571 Po'ipu Rd; adult/child/teen $109/70/97; ⊙5:15-8pm Thu & Sun) The Havaiki Nui Luau is a well-oiled pan-Polynesian production befitting the Grand Hyatt's beachfront setting. But the price is too steep, especially when the show takes place indoors instead of outside in the resort's gardens.

Shopping

Shops at Kukui'ula MALL

(☎808-742-9545; http://kukuiula.com/theshops; 2829 Ala Kalanikaumaka St; ⊙10am-9pm) An upscale outdoor shopping mall conveniently located at the Po'ipu roundabout offers more than 30 restaurants and designer shops, including fine-art galleries such as cutting-edge Galerie 103 and aFeinberg Gallery (p526) from Hanalei, a few high-end jewelry stores and some only-in-Hawaii fashion boutiques such as Mahina and Blue Ginger.

Po'ipu Shopping Village MALL

(☎808-742-2831; http://poipushoppingvillage.com; 2360 Kiahuna Plantation Dr; ⊙most shops 9am-9pm Mon-Sat, 10am-7pm Sun) A small-scale outdoor mall sports affordable, vacation-centric shops (think aloha wear, T-shirts, swimwear and souvenirs) such as the beachy boutique Sand People; Honolua Surf Co and Honolua Wahine for surf-style fashions; and By the Sea for a huge variety of 'rubbah slippah' (flip-flops).

Malie Organics Boutique BEAUTY, GIFTS

(☎808-332-6220, 866-767-5727; www.malie.com; Shops at Kukui'ula, 2829 Ala Kalanikaumaka St; ⊙10am-9pm) *Kukui* nuts, mangoes, coconuts and vanilla are just a few of the island plant 'essences' utilized by this homegrown bath and body products company. It stocks Kaua'i's high-end resorts with its sprays, soaps, body creams and candles, but this is its only retail outlet.

Allerton Garden Gift Shop BOOKS, GIFTS

(☎808-742-2623; www.ntbg.org; 4425 Lawa'i Rd; ⊙8:30am-5pm) Stocks an excellent array of books (especially nature and Hawaiiana titles), as well as quality nature-themed gifts and souvenirs.

Information

Poipu Beach Resort Association (☎808-742-7444, 888-744-0888; www.poipubeach.org; Shops at Kukui'ula, 2829 Ala Kalanikaumaka St; ⊙9:30am-2pm Mon-Fri) Go online for general visitor information about Po'ipu and the entire South Shore, including beaches, activities, accommodations, dining, shopping and events.

Getting There & Around

Navigating is easy, with just two main roads: Po'ipu Rd (along eastern Po'ipu) and Lawa'i Rd (along western Po'ipu). You'll need a car, scooter or bike to go anywhere here besides the beach. It's possible to walk along the roads, but the vibe is more suburbia than surf town.

The Kaua'i Bus (p485) runs through Koloa into Po'ipu, stopping along Po'ipu Rd at the turnoff to Po'ipu Beach Park and also by the Hyatt. It's an option for getting here from other towns, but not very useful as transport around the resort area.

Outfitters Kauai (☎808-742-9667, 888-742-9887; www.outfitterskauai.com; Po'ipu Plaza, 2827a Po'ipu Rd; bicycle rental per day $25-45; ⊙9am-4:30pm) Perhaps because of the lack of bike lanes, cyclists are scarce in Po'ipu. However, you can rent bikes here, including road, mountain and hybrid models. Rates include a helmet and lock. Phone reservations recommended.

Kalaheo

Kalaheo is a one-stoplight cluster of eateries and little else. But along the back roads, this neighborly town offers peaceful accommodations away from the tourist crowd. If you plan to hike at Waimea Canyon and Koke'e State Parks but also want easy access to Po'ipu beaches, Kalaheo's central location is ideal.

Sights

★ Kaua'i Coffee Company FARM
(808-335-0813, 800-545-8605; http://kauaicoffee.com; 870 Halewili Rd; 9am-5:30pm Jun-Aug, to 5pm Sep-May, guided tours usually 10am, noon, 2pm & 4pm daily) A short drive east of town on Hwy 540, the island's biggest coffee estate is planted with more than four million trees, producing about 60% of the state's entire crop. Around the back of the plantation store and visitor center, you can glimpse the roasting process, peruse historical photographs and sample estate-grown coffees including a robust peaberry and flavored chocolate macadamia nut. Afterward, take a quick self-guided walking tour of the farm, or join a free guided tour (check current schedules online).

The rolling seaside plantation, where coffee berries are cooled by tradewinds, is 100% powered by renewable energy.

Hanapepe Valley Lookout VIEWPOINT
Popping up shortly after mile marker 14, this lookout offers a view deep into Hanapepe Valley, where the red-clay cliffs are topped by wild green sugarcane. This sight is but a teaser for the dramatic vistas awaiting at Waimea Canyon.

While the sugar business has faded, Hanapepe Valley remains an agriculture stronghold with grazing cattle and local farmers growing taro. Look *makai* (seaward) across the highway and you'll see the region's cash crop: coffee.

Kukuiolono Park PARK
(854 Pu'u Rd; 6:30am-6:30pm) Unless you're staying in Kalaheo, you'll miss this little park with a nine-hole golf course, modest **Japanese garden**, sweeping views and grassy grounds for strolling or running. Kukuiolono means 'light of Lono,' referring to the torches that Hawaiians once placed on this hill to help guide canoes safely to the shore.

To get here, turn left onto Papalina Rd from Kaumuali'i Hwy (heading west).

Activities

Kukuiolono Golf Course GOLF
(808-332-9151; Kukuiolono Park, 854 Pu'u Rd; green fees $9; 6:30am-6:30pm, last tee time 4:30pm) There are only nine holes, but they come with spectacular ocean and valley views and zero attitude. The course was built in 1927 by Walter McBryde (think McBryde Garden) and later donated to the public. McBryde clearly loved golf: he's buried by the eighth hole. The driving range and cart and club rentals are about as cheap as the green fees.

Kalaheo Yoga YOGA
(808-652-3216; www.kalaheoyoga.com; 4427 Papalina Rd; per class $18, 3-/4-class pass $48/62) A bright, harmonious yoga space one block from the highway teaches a few classes daily, including gentle, restorative and vinyasa flow. Pre-register for classes online.

Sleeping

Hale Ikena Nui INN $
(808-332-9005, 800-550-0778; www.kauaivacationhome.com; 3957 Uluiali'i St; d $75-95;) Located at the end of a cul-de-sac, this spacious in-law apartment (1000 sq ft) includes a living area with a queen-sized sofa bed, a full kitchen and washer-dryer. There's a three-night minimum stay. The B&B room is less private, but has its own bathroom and rates include breakfast.

Sea Kauai APARTMENT $
(808-332-9744; www.seakauai.com; 3913 Uluali'i St; d $75-95;) Choose between two comfortable ground-floor units with Japanese *shōji* (rice-paper sliding doors) and sunset ocean views. The one-bedroom suite has a full kitchen, separate living and dining areas and beds for four (one king and two twins). The compact studio, with a kitchenette, is a steal. Free beach gear to borrow. Three-night minimum stay.

Kalaheo Inn INN $
(808-332-6023; www.kalaheoinn.com; 4444 Papalina Rd; r & ste $88-119;) Like most plain Janes, this one is dependable, low-key and quiet (except it has thin walls). Resembling a typical motel, it best suits budget travelers looking for kitchenette studios. For couples and families, the one- and two-bedroom suites are decent, but you could do better.

All have basic furnishings, TV/DVD combos and access to BBQ grills and beach gear.

Hale O Nanakai B&B $$
(☎808-652-8071; www.nanakai.com; 3726 Nanakai Pl; s $75-85, d $115-175, most incl breakfast; 📶) A sky-blue family house turned five-room B&B has plush wall-to-wall carpeting, beamed ceilings and spectacular sea views. Rooms range in size, yet all but the cheapest digs have similar amenities including HDTVs and queen- or full-sized beds with high-end mattresses. The tiny Maile Room has but a single bed for the wandering nomad. Cleaning fee $40 to $45.

Eating

Kalaheo Farmers Market MARKET $
(www.kauai.gov; Kalaheo Neighborhood Center, 4480 Papalina Rd; ⏲3-5pm Tue; 👪) Just a straightforward, small-town produce market. It's one of the county-wide Sunshine Markets, so no shopping allowed before the whistle blows.

Lanakila Kitchen LOCAL $
(☎808-332-5500; www.lanakilapacific.org/services/lanakila-kitchen/; 2-3687 Kaumuali'i Hwy; meals $8-10; ⏲6:30am-2:30pm Mon-Fri) A local's haunt, this tiny cafe with a cause serves a steam table of meat and fish dishes, which you can pick and mix for plate lunches, such as chicken *laulau,* teriyaki fish, tofu stir-fry and more. It also does *ono* fish burgers, ahi *poke* bowls, soups, salads and pies. Proceeds benefit an employment program for people with disabilities.

Kauai Kookie Bakery & Kitchen CAFE, BAKERY $
(☎808-332-0821; 2-2436 Kaumuali'i Hwy; mains $5-11, meals $8-13; ⏲5:30am-4pm) Stop at this roadside diner for simple but filling breakfasts, *bentō,* and Asian and island-style fusion dishes served as plate lunches to an almost exclusively local customer base. It does an authentic oxtail soup too. For a bigger selection of the famous cookies, visit the Hanapepe factory store (p560).

★Kalaheo Café & Coffee Co CAFE, BREAKFAST $$
(☎808-332-5858; www.kalaheo.com; 2-2560 Kaumuali'i Hwy; mains breakfast & lunch $5-15, dinner $16-28; ⏲6:30am-2:30pm Mon-Sat, to 2pm Sun, 5-8:30pm Tue-Thu, to 9pm Fri & Sat) Adored by locals and visitors alike, this always-busy cafe has a spacious dining room and brews strong coffee. Order egg scrambles with grilled cornbread for breakfast, or a deli sandwich (*kalua* pork with guava BBQ sauce, yum) and a salad of local greens for lunch. Weightier dinner plates include hoisin-glazed fresh catch and salt-rubbed ribs.

Expect a long wait at breakfast time. The parking lot gets crowded, so consider parking on the highway shoulder.

Shopping

Collection at the Cafe ARTS, GIFTS
(☎808-332-5858; 2-2560 Kaumuali'i Hwy; ⏲9am-3pm) An airy walk-though gallery displaying ever-changing works by local artists, including oil paintings, watercolors and prints, hand-crafted shell jewelry and more.

WAIMEA CANYON & THE WESTSIDE

Kaua'i doesn't get more local than the Westside, where revered traditions and family pride reign. Here, you're more likely to hear fluent Hawaiian, spot real-life *paniolo* (Hawaiian cowboys) and see fishers sewing their nets than anywhere else on the island. Deep, riveting red canyons and a seemingly infinite expanse of ocean create the widest range of ecosystems found anywhere on Kaua'i. The least touristy and the most tried and true, the Westside isn't for everyone. It's good like that.

Port Allen & Around

The island's next biggest harbor after Lihu'e, Port Allen centers on a mini mall packed with charter companies and wedged into a largely industrial port area. The majority of the island's Na Pali Coast tours leave from Port Allen and, depending on the season, there are a variety of ways to experience the spectacular seascape – from snorkeling in summer to whale-watching in winter. The small Port Allen Airport faces the harbor from across the bay, but is adjacent to Hanapepe, not 'Ele'ele, the town closest to the port.

Beaches

Glass Beach BEACH
(Map p554) Trash as art – many a visitor has pored through the colorful well-worn remnants of glass spread along the shoreline here. Glass 'pebbles,' along with abandoned

OFF THE BEATEN TRACK

NU'ALOLO KAI: A LAST PARADISE?

On the remote, rugged Na Pali Coast and accessible only from the sea, Nu'alolo Kai is perhaps the ultimate end-of-the-earth location. Its beach is trapped between two soaring cliffs, framing an empty ocean that goes on for thousands of miles. The site is blessed by a fringing reef that is teeming with fish and shellfish.

Nu'alolo Kai was once linked by a precarious cliffside path to Nu'alolo 'Aina, a terraced valley whose fertile soil was planted with taro, and whose walls held burial caves. This isolated paradise was inhabited by about 100 people for 600 years, until 1919. They lived in thatched pole houses, commuting between reef and fields, completely self-sufficient. Men did most of the fishing, while women and children harvested seaweed and shellfish. They weren't entirely cut off from the rest of the island, however. There was once a trail here from Koke'e (now washed away), and their beach was the safest stop for Hawaiians canoeing between Hanalei and Waimea.

Today all that is left is the stone foundations of various structures, but it's enough to get you thinking. To help preserve Nu'alolo Kai, just three companies currently have landing rights: Kaua'i Sea Tours and Captain Andy's Sailing Adventures provide guided tours of the archaeological site, while Waimea-based Na Pali Explorer (p562) only lands on the beach. Weather usually restricts boat landings to between mid-April and late October only.

metals (some with newfound patina, some not so much), are washed up from an old dumpsite nearby.

To get to the little cove, take Aka'ula St (the last left before entering the Port Allen wharf) past the fuel storage tanks, then curve to the right down a bumpy dirt road about 100yd to the beach.

Activities & Tours

A number of companies offer very similar Na Pali Coast snorkeling, sunset and dinner tours. Book ahead online for discounts. Beware that motion sickness is common, especially on the Zodiac rafts, which offer little respite from the waves and sun. The journey may be less rough departing from Waimea's small boat harbor instead.

★Captain Andy's Sailing Adventures BOAT TOUR
(Map p554; ☎808-335-6833, 800-535-0830; www.napali.com; Port Allen Marina Center, 4353 Waialo Rd; tours adult/child from 2-12yr $119/89) This outfit offers a high-end sailing experience aboard the *Southern Star* – its 65ft flagship luxury catamaran – and a more rugged, adrenaline-addled Zodiac raft tour of the sea caves and secluded beaches of the Na Pali Coast. Six-hour raft trips include a beach landing at Nu'alolo Kai (weather permitting, April to October only), along with snorkeling and easy hiking.

Sunset dinner cruises add an awesome sky to the coast's bewitching cliffs, as well as a chef-prepared meal washed down with a 'sneaky tiki.'

Kaua'i Sea Tours BOAT TOUR
(Map p554; ☎808-826-7254, 800-733-7997; www.kauaiseatours.com; Port Allen Marina Center, 4353 Waialo Rd; tours adult/child under 13yr/child 13-17yr from $115/75/105) Take a seat on the 60ft catamaran *Lucky Lady* for a snorkel or sunset dinner cruise, or clamber aboard a rigid-hull inflatable raft for a more adventurous Na Pali trip. Six-hour raft tours add a beach landing and a guided walking tour of Nu'alolo Kai (weather permitting, between April and October only), along with sea cave and waterfall explorations.

Holo Holo Charters BOAT TOUR
(Map p554; ☎808-335-0815, 800-848-6130; www.holoholocharters.com; Port Allen Marina Center, 4353 Waialo Rd; tours adult/child 5-12yr from $115/99) Holo Holo's 50ft sailing catamaran and rigid-hull inflatable rafts happily do Na Pali snorkeling tours and sunset sails that include food and drinks. The power cat takes you on a longer, 3½-hour sunset tour serving substantial appetizers and cocktails, or the marathon seven-hour Ni'ihau and Na Pali Coast snorkeling combo that includes continental breakfast and a buffet lunch.

Blue Dolphin Charters BOAT TOUR
(Map p554; ☎808-335-5553; http://bluedolphinkauai.com; Port Allen Marina Center, 4353 Waialo Rd; tours adult/child 5-11yr/child 12-17yr from $117/90/106) Sailing 65ft catamarans, this

Westside

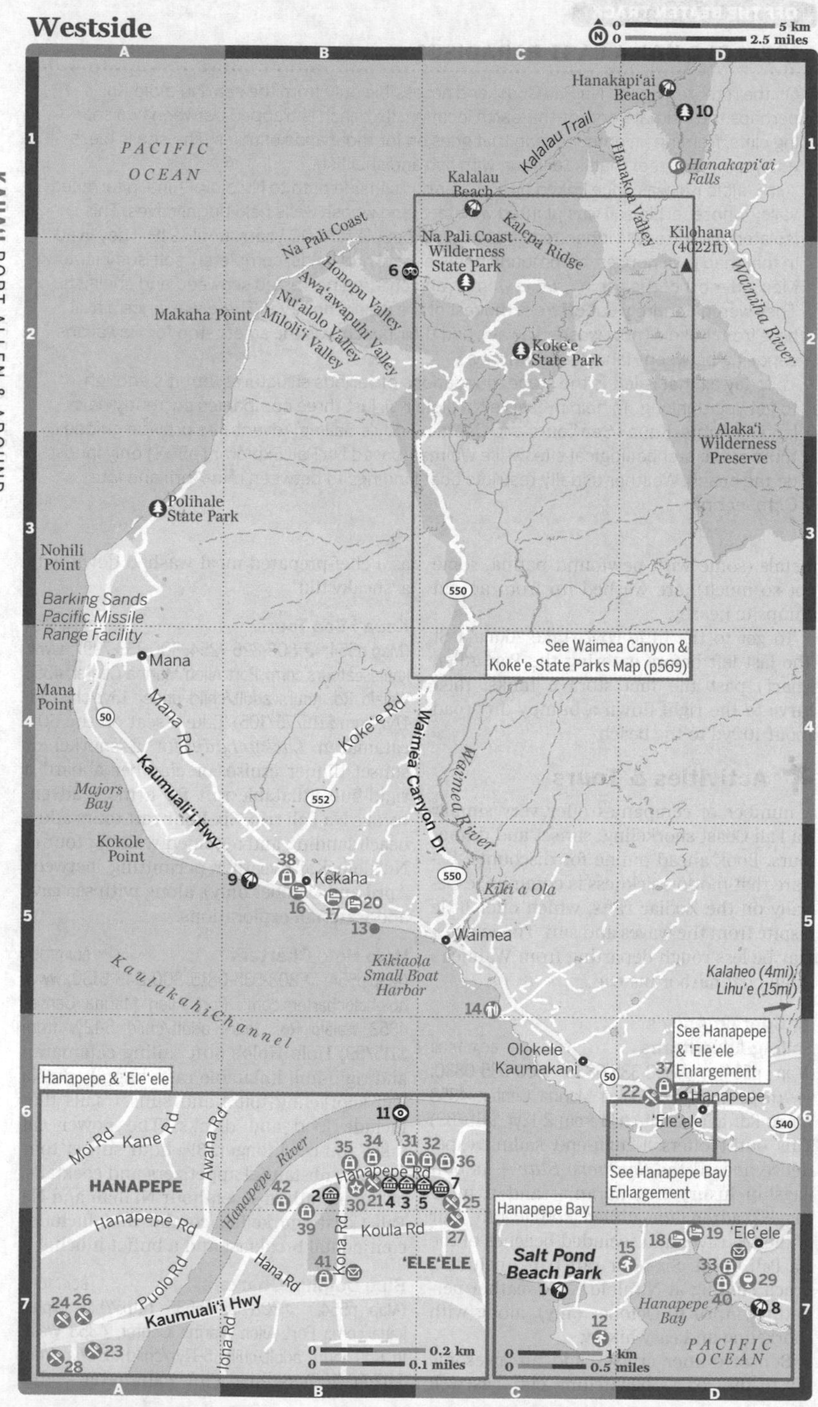

PACIFIC OCEAN
Hanakapi'ai Beach
10
Kalalau Trail
Hanakoa Valley
Hanakapi'ai Falls
Kalalau Beach
Na Pali Coast
Kalepa Ridge
Na Pali Coast Wilderness State Park
Kilohana (4022ft)
Wainiha River
6
Honopu Valley
Awa'awapuhi Valley
Nu'alolo Valley
Miloli'i Valley
Makaha Point
Koke'e State Park
Alaka'i Wilderness Preserve
Polihale State Park
Nohili Point
Barking Sands Pacific Missile Range Facility
550
See Waimea Canyon & Koke'e State Parks Map (p569)
Mana
Mana Point
50
Mana Rd
Koke'e Rd
Waimea Canyon Dr
Waimea River
Kaumuali'i Hwy
Majors Bay
552
Kokole Point
9
38
Kekaha
16
17
20
550
Kiki a Ola
13
Waimea
Kaulakahi Channel
Kikiaola Small Boat Harbor
Kalaheo (4mi); Lihu'e (15mi)
14
See Hanapepe & 'Ele'ele Enlargement
Olokele
Kaumakani
50
37
22
Hanapepe
'Ele'ele
540
See Hanapepe Bay Enlargement
Hanapepe & 'Ele'ele
11
Moi Rd
Kane Rd
Awana Rd
Hanapepe River
35
34
31
32
36
Hanapepe Rd
HANAPEPE
42
2
21
4
3
5
7
25
30
Hanapepe Rd
39
Koula Rd
27
Kona Rd
Hana Rd
41
'ELE'ELE
Puolo Rd
24
26
Kaumuali'i Hwy
Iona Rd
23
28
0.2 km
0.1 miles
Hanapepe Bay
18
19
'Ele'ele
Salt Pond Beach Park
15
33
1
29
Hanapepe Bay
40
8
12
1 km
0.5 miles
PACIFIC OCEAN
5 km
2.5 miles

Westside

Top Sights
1 Salt Pond Beach Park C7

Sights
2 Amy-Lauren's Gallery B6
3 Angela Headley Fine Art & Island Art Gallery B6
4 Arius Hopman Gallery B6
5 Art of Marbling & Robert Bader Wood Sculpture C6
6 Awa'awapuhi Lookout B2
7 Bright Side Gallery C6
Dawn Traina Gallery .... (see 4)
8 Glass Beach D7
9 Kekaha Beach Park B5
10 Na Pali Coast State Wilderness Park D1
11 Swinging Bridge B6

Activities, Courses & Tours
12 Birds in Paradise C7
Blue Dolphin Charters .... (see 40)
Captain Andy's Sailing Adventures .... (see 40)
Catamaran Kahanu .... (see 40)
Holo Holo Charters .... (see 40)
Kaua'i Sea Tours .... (see 40)
13 Na Pali Explorer B5
14 Pakalas C5
15 Skydive Kauai D7

Sleeping
16 Hale La B5
17 Hale Makai B5
18 Hanapepe Neighborhood Center D7
19 Hanapepe Riverside D7
20 Mindy's B5

Eating
21 Bobbie's B6
Da Imu Hut Café .... (see 33)
Grinds Café .... (see 33)
22 Hanapepe Farmers Market D6
23 Kaua'i Pupu Factory A7
Kauai Ramen .... (see 33)
24 Lappert's Hawaii A7
25 Little Fish Coffee C6
26 Paco's Tacos A7
27 Taro Ko Chips Factory C7
28 Wong's Restaurant & Omoide Bakery A7

Drinking & Nightlife
29 Kauai Island Brewery & Grill D7
Port Allen Sunset Grill & Bar .... (see 40)

Entertainment
30 Storybook Theatre of Hawaii B6

Shopping
31 Aloha Spice Company B6
32 Banana Patch Studio C6
33 'Ele'ele Shopping Center D7
34 Jacqueline on Kaua'i B6
35 JJ Ohana B6
Kauai Chocolate Company .... (see 40)
36 Kauai Fine Arts C6
37 Kauai Kookie Company D6
38 Kekaha Farmers Market B5
39 Machinemachine B7
Original Red Dirt Shirt .... (see 29)
40 Port Allen Marina Center D7
41 Puahina B7
Salty Wahine .... (see 37)
42 Talk Story Bookstore B6

outfit offers a standard array of tours, including a seven-hour Na Pali and Ni'ihau snorkel trip and a four-hour sunset dinner cruise. Uniquely, it'll take you on a one-tank dive – even if it's your first time scuba diving – and the Zodiac rafts are equipped with hydrophones for listening underwater to whales in winter. Inquire about sportfishing charters.

Catamaran Kahanu BOAT TOUR
(Map p554; ☎808-645-6176, 888-213-7711; www.catamarankahanu.com; Port Allen Marina Center, 4353 Waialo Rd; tours adult/child from $79/60) This small-group catamaran affords a more personal experience, whether you take a Na Pali snorkel trip or a sunset dinner or winter whale-watching cruise. The superfriendly captain and his crew talk story about Hawaiian culture and marine traditions on your way out to sea. Big discounts for online bookings.

Eating & Drinking

Da Imu Hut Café CAFE $
(Map p554; ☎808-335-0200; 'Ele'ele Shopping Center, 4469 Waialo Rd; meals $7-11; ⏰10am-1:30pm & 5-8pm Mon-Fri) Try specials such as the teriyaki fried chicken, traditional-style *kalua* pig or any of the Hawaiian plates (especially the fried saimin), which change daily. If you don't want to intrude on the mostly local vibe, meals are also great to order in advance and take out for a picnic.

Kauai Ramen ASIAN, FUSION $
(Map p554; ☎808-335-9888; 'Ele'ele Shopping Center, 4469 Waialo Rd; mains $7-11; ⏰11am-10pm; 👪) A hot bowl of spicy seafood ramen with grilled *gyoza* (pork dumplings) and fried rice on the side might just be what your tummy needs after being rollicked by the waves on a Na Pali Coast boat tour. The bargain-priced menu is nominally

Japanese, but with Chinese and local island-style dishes rolled in.

Grinds Café DINER $$

(Map p554; ☎808-335-6027; www.grindscafe.net; 'Ele'ele Shopping Center, 4469 Waialo Rd; mains $8-20; ⏲5:30am-9pm Mon & Fri-Sun, 6am-3pm Tue-Thu,) This family restaurant in a barn-like building is good for a hearty meal with the locals. It's strong on sandwiches, salads and specialty pizzas, and big breakfasts are served all day. Dinners aren't particularly cheap, however.

Kauai Island Brewery & Grill BREWERY

(Map p554; ☎808-335-0006; www.kauaiislandbrewing.com; 4350 Waialo Rd; ⏲11am-9:30pm) The founder of the once beloved, now defunct brewery in Waimea is still brewing in Port Allen. Sample the hoppy, high-alcohol IPAs, the lauded Pakala Porter, South Pacific Brown or light *liliko'i*-infused ale. Drinks and decent pub grub are discounted during happy hour (3:30pm to 5:30pm daily).

Port Allen Sunset Grill & Bar BAR

(Map p554; ☎808-335-3188; http://portallensunsetgrillandbar.com; Port Allen Marina Center, 4353 Waialo Rd; ⏲11am-10pm) This is the place to hang out while you are waiting for your tour to start or if you want to grab a bite afterwards. Located at the water end of the Port Allen Marina Center, it has a small bar and covered outdoor seating area. Popular bar-food picks include the macnut-crusted calamari steak.

Shopping

Kauai Chocolate Company FOOD

(Map p554; ☎808-335-0448; www.kauaichocolate.us; Port Allen Marina Center, 4341 Waialo Rd; ⏲10am-6pm Mon-Fri, 11am-5pm Sat, noon-3pm Sun) Sample the fudge and truffles with creamy ganaches, mousses and delicate creams of papaya, *liliko'i*, coconut, guava, Kaua'i coffee or sugarcane. The chocolate *'opihi* (limpet) is the biggest seller, followed by handmade chocolate bars chock full of macnuts.

Original Red Dirt Shirt CLOTHING

(Map p554; ☎800-717-3478; www.dirtshirt.com; 4350 Waialo Rd; ⏲8am-6pm) With punny sayings such as 'Older than Dirt' and 'Life's Short, Play Dirty,' these shamefully touristy T-shirts can be useful if you're planning on hiking, since most of Kaua'i's dirt wants to destroy your clothing and dye your shoes permanently red.

Information

'Ele'ele Post Office (Map p554; ☎808-335-5338; www.usps.com; 4485 Waialo Rd; ⏲9am-noon & 1-4pm Mon-Fri)

Hanapepe

Sleepy Hanapepe is a historic farming and port town that prospered during Hawaii's sugar plantation days. Although taro, a touch of cane and other crops are still grown in this wide, red earth valley accessed by a sinuous riverside road and hemmed in by craggy cliffs on both sides, downtown has been the domain of art galleries for decades. More recently, groovy young entrepreneurs have moved in, and in their hands Kaua'i's 'biggest little town' may soon become the island's hippest, most creative place. It's a town where quirk is cool, and where young, brainy locals who have trouble identifying with the island-dominant surf culture can feel at home. Most visitors turn up on Friday's Art Night (p558), which is absolutely the best time to see Hanapepe.

Beaches

★**Salt Pond Beach Park** BEACH

(Map p554; 👪) Named for its saltwater flats, where seawater is still drained and harvested for reddish-pink sodium crystals, this crescent-shaped beach is great for lounging. With a shallow (but not too shallow) swimming area accessible from the sand and sheltered by a rock reef, it's popular with local families. Full facilities include BBQ grills, outdoor showers, restrooms, lifeguards and camping.

Turn *makai* (seaward) onto Lele Rd, off the Kuhio Hwy just west of Hanapepe, then hang a right on Lokokai Rd.

Stronger swimmers and snorkelers may venture through the narrow keyhole in the reef and swim further west where the water clarifies and fish gather along a rugged coast defined by lava jagged cliffs. But beware of ocean conditions, because currents and tides can shift in a blink. Check with the lifeguards before venturing out.

Sights

Swinging Bridge LANDMARK

(Map p554) Built in 1911 and rebuilt after the 1992 hurricane, this narrow wood and cable suspension bridge spans the Hanapepe River just before it snakes inland between stark red-earth cliffs. It does swing and moan a bit in the wind. It's tucked behind the Aloha Spice Company. No diving!

Angela Headley Fine Art & Island Art Gallery GALLERY
(Map p554; ☎808-335-0591; http://islandartkauai.com; 3876 Hanapepe Rd; ⏰11am-5pm Mon-Sat, plus 6-9pm Fri) Make this your first stop in Hanapepe for contemporary Hawaiian art: reverse acrylic paintings and giclée prints on wood and metal that are luminous blends of color. It's a somewhat more adventurous gallery than the rest, but it also sells a few baubles, bracelets and foodstuffs.

Amy-Lauren's Gallery GALLERY
(Map p554; ☎808-335-2827; www.amylaurensgallery.com; 4545 Kona Rd; ⏰11am-5pm Mon-Thu, to 9pm Fri, noon-5pm Sat) Here's a chance to buy (or at least gaze upon) an original instead of a giclée print. This boutique gallery invites passersby inside with vibrantly colored oil paintings, photography and mixed media.

Art of Marbling & Robert Bader Wood Sculpture GALLERY
(Map p554; ☎808-335-3553; 3890 Hanapepe Rd; ⏰10am-5pm Sat-Thu, to 9pm Fri) Becky J Wold's original marbled silk scarves and sarongs hang from bamboo poles alongside her husband's wooden bowls and sculpture, making this a unique gallery experience.

Arius Hopman Gallery GALLERY
(Map p554; ☎808-335-0227; www.hopmanart.com; 3840c Hanapepe Rd; ⏰10am-2pm Mon-Fri, plus 6-9pm Fri) Art photography and plein-air watercolors spotlight Kaua'i's tropical landscapes, flora and fauna, from mango and banana trees to sunrise breaking over the Na Pali Coast.

Dawn Traina Gallery GALLERY
(Map p554; ☎808-335-3993; 3840b Hanapepe Rd; ⏰6-9pm Fri or by appointment) Traditional Hawaiian themes come to life in many different media, including oil paintings, limited-edition giclées and scratchboards (hard-panel carving reminiscent of scrimshaw).

Bright Side Gallery GALLERY
(Map p554; ☎808-634-8671; www.thebrightsidegallery.com; 3890 Hanapepe Rd; ⏰11am-4pm Mon-Fri, plus 6-9pm Fri) Representing both island and US mainland artists, this fun, whimsical space never takes itself too seriously. Surf themes show up in many of the oils, acrylics and giclées.

Activities

Skydive Kauai ADVENTURE SPORTS
(Map p554; ☎808-335-5859; www.skydivekauai.com; Lele Rd, Port Allen Airport; per person from $239; ⏰by reservation only) For a real adrenaline rush, jump out of an airplane (in tandem with an instructor) and freefall back down to earth with this adventure tour company. The experience may seem expensive, but considering it includes a free 25-minute flightseeing tour on the way up, it's not such a bad deal.

Birds in Paradise SCENIC FLIGHTS
(Map p554; ☎808-822-5309; www.birdsinparadise.com; 3666 Kuiloko Rd, Port Allen Airport) Take a flying lesson in an ultralight plane: a 25-minute flight allows you to see the Westside from above, while 50-minute flights glide into Waimea Canyon and along the Na Pali Coast; 80-minute flights may get you around the entire island. At the time of research, flights were on temporary hiatus; call ahead for reservations, updated schedules and pricing.

STARRY ISLAND NIGHTS

Minimal light pollution makes Kaua'i's Westside ideal for taking in the night sky. **Kaua'i Education Association for Science & Astronomy** (KEASA; ☎808-332-7827, 808-652-2373; www.keasa.org) holds free monthly 'Starwatches' on Saturdays closest to the new moon. Educators share both their gear and insights with the public, beginning at sunset.

Bring a light jacket, a lawn chair, insect repellent, and a small flashlight preferably covered with red cellophane.

Follow Hwy 50 west past Hanapepe. After mile marker 18, turn right at the fork to Kaumakani School. Follow the signs to the sports field, and remember to turn off your headlights when approaching.

Prepare to have your mind blown. Space: it goes on forever.

Festivals & Events

★ Art Night

ART, FOOD

(www.hanapepe.org; 6-9pm Fri) On any given Friday night, Hanapepe comes to life and gives everyone an extended peek into its art world. Galleries stay open later and the town's main drag is transformed by musicians and street vendors. Visitors and locals come to stroll, browse and snack streetside on everything from barbecue to hot, sugary *malasadas* (Portuguese fried dough, served warm and sugar-coated).

During this weekly event, galleries hold open houses, and artists often make themselves available. On egalitarian display are island-inspired originals, Hawaiiana vintage, pure kitsch and the works of Sunday dabblers to fine-art photography, watercolors and a sampling of Asian art.

Sleeping

Salt Pond Beach Park (p556) offers convenient camping; an advance county camping permit is required. There are hardly any other accommodations in Hanapepe.

Hanapepe Riverside

APARTMENT $

(Map p554; 808-635-7860; 4466 Puolo Rd; 1-bedroom apt $85;) This one-bedroom cottage on stilts faces the Hanapepe River on a residential street. It has a full kitchen, a shared washer-dryer, a king-sized bed, a living room and an amiable upper deck for morning coffee. The decor needs sprucing up but the cottage is near town, and the price is right. Three-night minimum stay; cleaning fee $85.

Eating & Drinking

★ Taro Ko Chips Factory

LOCAL $

(Map p554; 808-335-5586; 3940 Hanapepe Rd; per small bag $4-5; 8am-5pm) Thinly sliced *kalo* (taro) that's been seasoned with garlic salt, slathered with oil and tortured in a deep wok makes for some crispy, slightly sweet but mostly salty crunching. The farmer who grows the taro is also the chef, so show aloha.

Lappert's Hawaii

ICE CREAM $

(Map p554; 808-335-6121; www.lappertshawaii.com; 1-3555 Kaumuali'i Hwy; scoops from $4; 10am-6pm) The famed ice-cream chain started operations right here along the highway in 1983 at this quaint little roadside shop and factory. The business is way too big for Hanapepe-based production now, but this humble shop still scoops the goodness of tropical flavors such as 'Kauai Pie' (Kona coffee ice cream, chocolate fudge, macadamia nuts, coconut flakes and vanilla cake crunch). Deadly.

Kaua'i Pupu Factory

LOCAL, HAWAIIAN $

(Map p554; 808-335-0084; 1-3566 Kaumuali'i Hwy; mains $7-10; 9am-5:30pm Mon-Fri, to 3pm Sat) A down-home-style deli is your source for fresh *poke* – try a scoop of *tako* (octopus) or ahi with *limu* (seaweed) – and Hawaiian plate lunches with bundles of *laulau* and *lomilomi* salmon. If you've got a big group, get enough for everyone, pack a cooler and head to the beach.

Bobbie's

LOCAL $

(Map p554; 808-334-5152; 3824 Hanapepe Rd; meals $9-12; 10am-3pm & 5-8pm Mon-Wed, 10am-2:30pm Thu-Sat, plus 5-8:30pm Fri) In a small storefront, this humble lunch counter makes huge plate lunches of local faves such as *loco moco* and chicken katsu (deep-fried fillets), as well as BBQ chicken and ribs on Friday nights. It's not good-for-you food, but it certainly tastes darn good.

Little Fish Coffee

CAFE $

(Map p554; 808-335-5000; www.facebook.com/LittleFishCoffee; 3900 Hanapepe Rd; items $3-11; 6:30am-5pm Mon-Thu & Sat, to 9pm Fri;) The colorful chalkboard menu at this cute coffee shop lures you with espresso drinks, fruit smoothies, granola bowls, homemade soups, garden salads and bagel and panini sandwiches. Sit inside amid the retro artwork and music, or on the back patio splashed with both sun and shade.

Hanapepe Farmers Market

MARKET $

(Map p554; Hanapepe Town Park; 3-5pm Thu) One of the county-wide Sunshine Markets. Small-scale farmers truck in the goods themselves and locals line up before the whistle blows just to score the best produce.

Wong's Restaurant & Omoide Bakery

CHINESE, LOCAL $

(Map p554; 808-335-5066; www.wongsomoide.com; 1-3543 Kaumuali'i Hwy; mains $8-12; 8am-9pm Tue-Sun) A popular diner that serves up local plantation-style fare such as saimin noodle soup with pork or a whole roasted duck. But the real reason to stop by is the *liliko'i* chiffon pie.

Paco's Tacos

MEXICAN $

(Map p554; 808-335-0454; 4505 Puolo Rd; mains $4-16; 10am-8pm Mon-Sat) Grab takeout or sit at picnic tables outside this Baja-style roadside shack offering all the usual suspects, including *carne asada* (grilled meat) tacos, shrimp burritos and enchilada platters.

☆ Entertainment

Storybook Theatre of Hawaii THEATER
(Map p554; ☎808-335-0712; www.storybook.org; 3814 Hanapepe Rd; 90min walking tour per individual/couple/family $18/25/30; ⊙tours depart 9:30am Tue & Thu;) The Storybook Theatre, which tours Hawaii with puppets who 'talk story', has been around for 35 years. Schedules vary, but it's worth a peek on Art Night, when it sometimes hosts kids' activities. Book ahead to join one of its historical walking tours of Hanapepe (no puppets, sorry!), which finishes with a relaxing Chinese herbal tea served in the garden.

Shopping

Talk Story Bookstore BOOKS, MUSIC
(Map p554; ☎808-335-6469; www.talkstorybookstore.com; 3785 Hanapepe Rd; ⊙10am-5pm Mon-Thu, to 9:30pm Fri, noon-5pm Sat) The USA's westernmost bookstore is a funky indie bookseller's paradise, the kind that may even fill e-reader enthusiasts with musty page-turning nostalgia. New books by local authors are stocked up front, but it's mostly used fare here, with more than 40,000 books (organized by both genre and, curiously, author gender), vintage Hawaiian sheet music and vinyl records.

Machinemachine CLOTHING
(Map p554; www.machinemachineapparel.com; 3800 Hanapepe Rd; ⊙5:30-9pm Fri) Shannon Hiramoto, a fifth-generation Kaua'i-born designer, scours flea markets and thrift stores for aloha wear and other tossed-out fashions, which she upcycles into funky, elegant dresses, skirts and cloth-covered journals. She has a devoted cult following, and does most of the sewing out of her Hanapepe workshop.

Puahina CLOTHING
(Map p554; ☎808-335-9771; 4141 Kona Rd; ⊙11am-4pm Mon-Thu, 11am-4pm & 6-8:30pm Fri, Sat & Sun by appointment) Bold designs set this small boutique apart. You'll find wearable keepsakes that fuse traditional motifs with contemporary styles here. Look for original-design shirts, skirts and tops adorned by native ferns, as well as unusual shell jewelry. The shop also carries Maui-made Hana Lima Soap Co bath and body products with alluring tropical scents.

Jacqueline on Kaua'i CLOTHING
(Map p554; ☎808-335-5797; 3837 Hanapepe Rd; custom shirts $60-200; ⊙9am-6pm Mon-Thu, Sat & Sun, to 9pm Fri) Friendly Jacqueline makes her mark with aloha shirts custom-made while you wait (usually one to two hours), including children's sizes, and with coconut buttons no less. You choose the fabric, and she does the rest. Place an order at the beginning of Art Night and you're good to go by the end.

Banana Patch Studio ARTS & CRAFTS
(Map p554; ☎808-335-5944, 800-914-5944; www.bananapatchstudio.com; 3865 Hanapepe Rd; ⊙10am-4:30pm Mon-Thu, to 9pm Fri, to 4pm Sat) This studio puts out functional crafts rather than fine art – koi watercolors, wooden tiki bar signs, pottery with tropical flowers, souvenir ceramic tiles and coasters – but there's plenty to behold in this crowded little space, which is usually packed with shoppers. Also in Kilauea on the North Shore.

Salty Wahine FOOD
(Map p554; ☎808-378-4089; http://saltywahine.com; 1-3529 Kaumuali'i Hwy; ⊙9am-5pm) Beside the highway on the outskirts of town, this factory shop is a smorgasbord of salt and spice-blends with island flavors, from herbs to fruit. 'Black Lava' and *kiawe* (Hawaiian mesquite) sea salt, coconut-infused cane sugar and *li hing mui* maragarita salt are bestsellers.

JJ Ohana GIFTS, SOUVENIRS
(Map p554; ☎808-335-0366; www.jjohana.com; 3805b Hanapepe Rd; ⊙8am-6pm Mon-Thu, to 9pm Fri, to 5pm Sat & Sun) There aren't many places where you can find both $2.50 comfort food and a $7000 necklace. This family-run spot offers affordable daily food specials (such as chili and rice) and high-quality, Hawaii-made crafts and souvenirs, such as koa wood bowls, coral and abalone-shell jewelry, and Ni'ihau shell lei.

Aloha Spice Company FOOD
(Map p554; ☎808-335-5960, 800-915-5944; www.alohaspice.com; 3857 Hanapepe Rd; ⊙10am-4:30pm Mon-Thu, to 9pm Fri, to 4pm Sat) You can smell the savory, smoky goodness as soon as the bells on the swinging front door announce your presence. In addition to local spices, this place also sell sauces and jams,

lotions and oils, nuts and chocolate, teas and Kaua'i-made tropical-fruit popsicles.

Kauai Fine Arts ARTS
(Map p554; ☎808-335-3778; 3751 Hanapepe Rd; ⏲9:30am-4:30pm Mon-Thu & Sat, to 9pm Fri) If you want to get your hands on a unique piece of memorabilia, step inside to peruse fossilized shark teeth, antique and newer tiki carvings, prints of old Pan Am ads, old-world maps and vintage botanical prints.

Kauai Kookie Company FOOD
(Map p554; ☎808-335-5003; www.kauaikookie.com; 1-3529 Kaumuali'i Hwy; ⏲8am-5pm Mon-Fri, from 10am Sat & Sun) Though some say it's more novelty than delicious, Kauai Kookie has a local following rivaling that of Girl Scout cookies. Classic tastes sold at the factory warehouse shop include Kona coffee and chocolate chip–macadamia nut.

Information

American Savings Bank (☎808-335-3118; www.asbhawaii.com; 4548 Kona Rd; ⏲8am-5pm Mon-Thu, to 6pm Fri) Has a 24-hour ATM.

Bank of Hawaii (☎808-335-5021; www.boh.com; 3764 Hanapepe Rd; ⏲8:30am-4pm Mon-Thu, to 6pm Fri) Has a 24-hour ATM.

Hanapepe Post Office (Map p554; ☎808-335-5433; www.usps.com; 3817 Kona Rd; ⏲9am-1:30pm & 2-4pm Mon-Fri)

Getting There & Around

Veer *mauka* (inland) onto Hanapepe Rd, the main drag, at the 'Kaua'i's Biggest Little Town' sign on the Kuhio Hwy.

Waimea

One of several Waimeas in Hawaii, this is not O'ahu's legendary surf spot nor is it the Big Island's upscale cowboy town. But in some ways, Kaua'i's Waimea is equally intriguing. Part Hawaiian hamlet, part big-dollar agriculture stronghold, it's the original landing spot of Captain Cook and the jumping-off point for visiting spectacular Waimea Canyon and Koke'e State Parks.

Waimea means 'reddish-brown water,' which refers to the river that picks up salt from the canyon and colors the ocean red. Sugar plantations played a role in the town's development, and the skeleton of the old mill can still be seen amid the tech centers that house both defense contractors working at the nearby Pacific Missile Range Facility and an even more controversial presence: multinational chemical companies that develop genetically modified seeds for worldwide crop cultivation.

Beaches

Waimea State Recreational Pier BEACH
(www.hawaiistateparks.org; La'au Rd) This wide black beach, flecked with microscopic green crystals called olivine, stretches between two scenic rock outcroppings and is bisected by the namesake fishing pier. It's especially beautiful at sunset.

Facilities include restrooms, picnic areas and drinking water.

Sights

★West Kaua'i Technology & Visitor Center MUSEUM
(☎808-338-1332; www.westkauaivisitorcenter.org; 9565 Kaumuali'i Hwy; ⏲12:30-4pm Mon, 9:30am-4pm Tue & Wed, 9:30am-12:30pm Fri; FREE) Orient yourself historically to the Westside with modest exhibits on Hawaiian culture, Captain Cook, sugar plantations and the US military. The gift shop sells locally made artisan crafts, including rare Ni'ihau shell lei.

This complex doubles as a visitor center and offers a free, three-hour historic Waimea walking tour at 9:30am Mondays (call to register by noon on the previous Friday).

Waimea Town Center ARCHITECTURE
Surprisingly, Waimea offers some interesting architecture, including the neoclassical First Hawaiian Bank (p566; 1929), the art-deco Waimea Theater (p566; 1938), and a historic church, the crushed coral-covered **Waimea United Church of Christ** (Makeke Rd), first built during the early missionary era and faithfully reconstructed after Hurricane 'Iniki.

Russian Fort Elizabeth State Historical Park HISTORIC SITE
(www.hawaiistateparks.org; off Kaumuali'i Hwy; ⏲dawn-dusk) FREE A Russian fort in Hawaii? Yes, it's true. Constructed in 1817 and named after the Empress of Russia, Fort Elizabeth commanded the entrance to Waimea River. The octagonal design ranges from 350ft to 450ft across. In addition to a cannon, it once harbored a Russian Orthodox chapel. Apart from impressive walls, some 20ft high, there is little else to see nowadays.

Captain Cook Monument MONUMENT
(Hofgaard Park, cnr Waimea Rd & Kaumuali'i Hwy) Captain James Cook changed the course of

Waimea

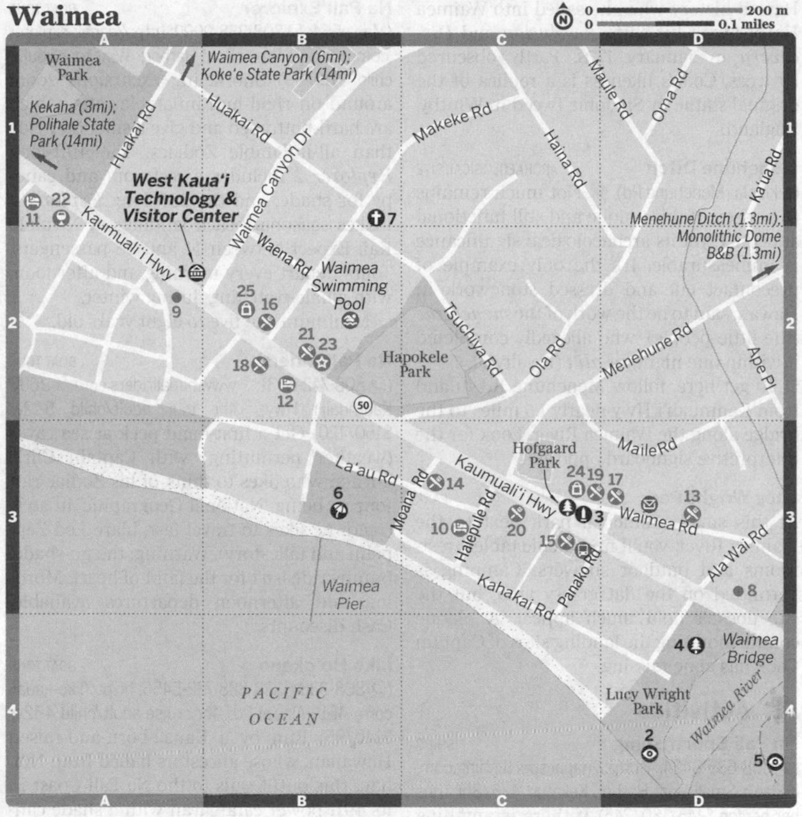

Waimea

Top Sights

1 West Kaua'i Technology & Visitor Center A2

Sights

2 Captain Cook Landing Site D4
3 Captain Cook Monument C3
4 Lucy Wright Park D4
5 Russian Fort Elizabeth State Historical Park D4
6 Waimea State Recreational Pier B3
7 Waimea United Church of Christ B1

Activities, Courses & Tours

8 Liko Ho'okano D3
9 Na Pali Riders A2

Sleeping

10 Inn Waimea C3
11 Waimea Plantation Cottages A1
12 West Inn B2

Eating

13 Da Booze Shop D3
14 G's Juicebar C3
15 Ishihara Market C3
16 Island Taco B2
17 Jo-Jo's Anuenue Shave Ice & Treats D3
18 Shrimp Station B2
19 Super Duper Two C3
20 Wrangler's Steakhouse C3
21 Yumi's B2

Drinking & Nightlife

22 Kalapaki Joe's A1

Entertainment

23 Waimea Theater B2

Shopping

24 Aunty Lilikoi Passion Fruit Products C3
25 Kaua'i Granola B2

Hawaii history when he sailed into Waimea Harbor with his ships *Resolution* and *Discovery* in January 1778. Partly obscured by trees, Cook's likeness is a replica of the original statue by Sir John Tweed in Whitby, England.

Menehune Ditch ARCHAEOLOGICAL SITE

(Kikiaola; Menehune Rd) Not much remains to be seen of this unique and still functional aqueduct, yet its archaeological significance is immeasurable. It's the only example of precontact cut and dressed stonework in Hawaii, said to be the work of the *menehune* (the little people), who allegedly completed it within one night for *ali'i* (royalty).

To get here, follow Menehune Rd inland from Kaumuali'i Hwy nearly 1.5 miles to the bridge along the Waimea River. Look for the interpretive signboard opposite.

Lucy Wright Park PARK

At this small municipal park next to the Waimea River, you'll find picnic tables, restrooms and outdoor showers. Camping is permitted on the flat grassy area, but the site doesn't hold much appeal. A plaque commemorating the landing sites of Captain Cook has gone missing.

Activities

Na Pali Sportfishing FISHING

(808-635-9424; http://napalisportfishing.com; Kikiaola Small Boat Harbor, Kekaha; 4/6/8hr trips per person $145/180/245) If there is anything to upend a deep-sea fishing trip, it's hanging green over the side. This outfit has lessened that risk with a 34ft catamaran, which makes for a much steadier platform. Standard catch includes yellowfin, skipjack, marlin, mahimahi and wahoo. All gear supplied.

Pakalas SURFING

(Infinities; Map p554; Kaumuali'i Hwy) Between mile markers 21 and 22 on Kaumuali'i Hwy, you'll notice cars parked on the side of the highway in an area known as Makaweli. It's the access point to Pakalas (Infinities), an experts-only surf break said to offer the 'longest lefts' anywhere on the island. Conflicts between locals and nonlocals are common here, so leave this break alone.

Tours

Taking Na Pali Coast tours that start from Kekaha's Kikiaola Small Boat Harbor (instead of Port Allen near Hanapepe) means the journey isn't as rough.

Na Pali Explorer BOAT TOUR

(Map p554; 808-338-9999; http://napali-explorer.com; Kikiaola Small Boat Harbor; 4½hr tour adult/child $119/99) Snorkeling excursions zoom around on rigid-hull inflatable rafts, which are hard-bottomed and give a smoother ride than all-inflatable Zodiacs. The 49ft-long *Explorer 2* includes a restroom and canopy for shade, and the 26ft-long *Explorer 1* makes seasonal beach landings at Nu'alolo Kai. Expect between 14 and 36 passengers. Tours depart every morning and afternoon, with whale-watching during winter.

Minimum age five to eight years old.

Na Pali Riders BOAT TOUR

(808-742-6331; www.napaliriders.com; 9600 Kaumuali'i Hwy; 4hr tour adult/child 5-12yr $150/120) Get a first-hand peek at sea caves (weather permitting) with Captain Chris Turner, who likes to think of his Zodiac raft tour as being 'National Geographic' in style (read: he likes to travel fast, blare Led Zeppelin and talk story). Warning: the no-shade, bumpy ride isn't for the faint of heart. Morning and afternoon departures available. Cash discounts.

Liko Ho'okano BOAT TOUR

(808-338-0333, 888-732-5456; http://liko-kauai.com; 4516 Alawai Rd; 4hr cruise adult/child 4-12yr $140/95) Run by a Kaua'i-born-and-raised Hawaiian, whose ancestors hailed from Ni'ihau, this outfit sails to the Na Pali Coast in its 49ft power catamaran with a shade canopy and forward-facing padded seats. Tours go as far as Ke'e Beach during summer. Snorkel gear provided.

Festivals & Events

★ **Waimea Town Celebration** CULTURAL

(www.waimeatowncelebration.com; Feb;) Free fun in mid-February includes a *paniolo* (Hawaiian cowboy) rodeo; storytelling; canoe, SUP and surf-skiing races; local food vendors; carnival games; an arts-and-crafts fair; and lei-making and ukulele-playing contests.

Sleeping

Monolithic Dome B&B B&B $

(808-651-7009; Menehune Rd; r $95;) Constructed by the hard-working owner herself, this unique concrete creation – looking like a spaceship getting ready to blast off – rises above the neighbors on a residential street. The private studio apartment can be hot and a tad buggy, but it has modern conveniences: a bathroom with painted walls, a queen bed with memory-foam mattress, a kitchenette and a lanai. Three-night minimum. Cleaning fee $75.

Coco's Kaua'i B&B B&B $$
(808-338-0722, 808-639-1109; http://cocoskauai.com; ste $120-140;) An off-the-grid retreat on sprawling ranch lands is run by one of the descendants of the Robinson family, who own the island of Ni'ihau. With its own private entrance, the suite offers a king bed, kitchenette, outdoor BBQ grill and cowboys riding by on horses. There's free beach gear to borrow and seasonal tropical fruit for snacking. Two-night minimum stay. Address given upon booking. Book well ahead.

Inn Waimea INN $$
(808-338-0031; www.innwaimea.com; 4469 Halepule Rd; r & ste $110-120, cottages $150;) This inn feels like a family summer house that has seen the passing of many generations. In the heart of town, the suites feature clawfoot tubs and other vintage-style furnishings, while the king-bedded Taro Room is ADA-compliant with a roll-in shower. The inn's two-bedroom cottages are even more quaint (the Ishihara Cottage is the better pick).

There's a three-night minimum stay in the cottages. A $25 surcharge applies for one-night stays in the room or suites.

West Inn INN $$
(808-338-1107; http://thewestinn.com; 9690 Kaumauli'i Hwy; r from $200;) Across from Waimea Theater, this feels like a budget chain hotel but isn't one. Some buildings have been recently renovated with spacious rooms that have king or double beds, high ceilings, granite countertops, flat-screen TVs, microwaves and mini fridges. More expensive suites are equipped with full kitchens. The decor won't win any awards, though, and rates are comparatively overpriced.

Waimea Plantation Cottages INN $$$
(808-338-1625, 800-992-4632; www.waimea-plantation.com; 9400 Kaumuali'i Hwy; d from $199;) These rebuilt plantation cottages from the 1930s and 1940s once housed sugarcane laborers. The 57 tin-roofed, clapboard, pastel-painted sweethearts with wide porches and rattan seating are scattered over a wide lawn, studded with golden bamboo, swaying palm groves and a cathedral banyan tree. The only downsides are poor upkeep of some of the arguably too-rustic cottages and spotty wi-fi.

Oceanside yoga classes, massages and spa services are priced à la carte.

Eating

★ Ishihara Market SUPERMARKET, DELI $
(808-338-1751; 9894 Kaumuali'i Hwy; 6am-7:30pm Mon-Thu, to 8pm Fri & Sat, to 7pm Sun) It's an ad-hoc lesson in local cuisine shopping at this historic market (c 1934) with deli. Trusty take-out meals (get here before the lunch rush) include sushi, spicy ahi *poke* and smoked marlin. Daily specials and marinated ready-to-go meats are available for those wanting to barbecue. The parking lot is often full – it's that popular.

Yumi's DINER $
(808-338-1731; 9691 Kaumuali'i Hwy; mains $5-10; 7:30am-2:30pm Tue-Thu, 7am-1pm & 6-8pm Fri, 8am-1pm Sat) Friendly, filling and reasonably priced sums up this local institution, where you can get a plate lunch with some chicken katsu or teriyaki beef, a burger, a mini *loco moco* or a special bowl of saimin. Be sure to order a slice of coconut pie or the pumpkin crunch for dessert.

G's Juicebar HEALTH FOOD $
(808-634-4112; 4492 Moana Rd; snacks from $7; 7am-6pm Mon-Fri, 9am-5pm Sat) Your quest for Kaua'i's top acai bowl might reach the finish line inside this Rastafarian corner shack. A Marley bowl comes with kale and bee pollen, and the Kauai Bowl with mango juice and shaved coconut. Fresh tropical juice smoothies and yerba mate tea will quench your thirst.

Super Duper Two ICE CREAM $
(808-338-1590; 9889 Waimea Rd; snacks from $3; noon-9pm Mon-Thu, to 10pm Fri & Sat) Across the street from Captain Cook's statue, this place lives up to its moniker. Stop in for tropically flavored shakes, sundaes, floats or old-fashioned scoops of Roselani ice cream (made on Maui) in crispy handmade waffle cones.

Island Taco MEXICAN $
(808-338-9895; www.islandfishtaco.com; 9643 Kaumuali'i Hwy; mains $6-13; 11am-5pm) At this island fusion taqueria, tortillas are stuffed with wasabi-coated or Cajun-dusted seared ahi, fresh cabbage and rice. Have the same trick done with mahimahi, tofu, shrimp with papaya seeds or *kalua* pork with spinach instead. Wet burritos and taco salads round out the menu.

NI'IHAU

Only 72 sq miles, Ni'ihau is the smallest and flattest of the inhabited Hawaiian Islands. Nicknamed the 'Forbidden Island,' Ni'ihau lies west of Kaua'i and remains an intriguing mystery due to its private ownership and unique isolation. Accessible only to its owners, Native Hawaiian residents, government officials, occasional US Navy personnel and invited guests, Ni'ihau is the last bastion of traditional Hawaiian culture.

Captain Cook anchored off Ni'ihau on January 29, 1778, less than two weeks after 'discovering' Hawaii. Cook noted in his log that the island was lightly populated and largely barren – a description still true today. His visit was short, but it had a lasting impact. Cook gave two things to Ni'ihau that would quickly change the face of Hawaii: he left goats, the first of the grazing animals that would devastate the island's native flora and fauna; and his men introduced syphilis, the first of several Western diseases that would strike down Hawaiians.

In 1864 Elizabeth Sinclair, a Scottish widow who was moving from New Zealand to Vancouver when she got sidetracked in Hawaii, bought Ni'ihau from King Kamehameha V for $10,000 in gold. He originally tried to sell her the 'swampland' of Waikiki, but she passed it up for the 'desert island.' Interestingly no two places in Hawaii could today be further apart, either culturally or in land value. Mrs Sinclair brought the first sheep to Ni'ihau from New Zealand and started the island's longstanding, but now defunct, ranching operation.

Today the island is owned by Mrs Sinclair's great-great-grandsons Keith and Bruce Robinson, brothers who also own a vast expanse of land on Kaua'i, where they live. The Robinsons are outdoorsmen and are fluent in Hawaiian. Keith, who worked for years in ranching and fishing, is often found in red-dirt-covered jeans, driving a beat-up pickup or doing heavy labor to save endangered plants. Bruce, whose wife Leiana is Ni'ihauan, holds top management positions in the family businesses – while also leading efforts to safeguard Ni'ihau's monk seals.

Population & Lifestyle

Ni'ihau's residents are predominantly Native Hawaiian. Over the years the island's population has dropped from more than 250 in 1960, to 160 in the 2000 census. Today Ni'ihau's population is a mere 130, and it is the only island where the primary language is still Hawaiian. Business is conducted in Hawaiian, as are Sunday church services. Inside a solar-powered schoolhouse, teachers hold classes from kindergarten through 12th grade; courses are taught solely in Hawaiian up to the fourth grade, and students learn English as a second language.

Residents are known for being humble, generous and mellow, and most live in Pu'uwai (heart), a village on the dry leeward coast. Their lifestyle is extremely rustic, with no sense of hurry. The island has no paved roads, no airport, no phones and no plumbing or running water. Rainwater is collected in catchments, and toilets are in outhouses. While there is no island-wide electricity, homes have generators and solar power. Alcohol and guns are banned, and a code of ethics advocates honesty and monogamy. It all sounds utopian.

Despite their isolation, residents are not unacquainted with the outside world. Ni'ihau residents are permitted to go to Kaua'i or even Las Vegas to shop, drink a few beers or just hang out. However, there are restrictions on Ni'ihauans bringing friends from other islands back home with them. If Ni'ihauans marry people from other islands, or if the Robinsons view particular residents as undesirable, they are rarely allowed to return.

While the Robinsons consider themselves protectors of Ni'ihau's isolation and its people, and most Ni'ihauans point out that their traditional Hawaiian lifestyle isn't possible on any other island, some outsiders have been critical. Some Hawaiians on other islands see the Robinsons as colonialists and believe that Ni'ihau's inhabitants should be granted their own land and the right to self-determination.

Geography & Environment

Ni'ihau is the smallest of the inhabited Hawaiian Islands: 18 miles long and 6 miles at the widest point, with 45 miles of coast. The island is around 18 miles west of Kaua'i. The climate is warm, windy and semiarid, with a relatively extreme temperature range, from 42°F to more than 110°F. Ni'ihau rainfall averages a scant 20in annually because the island is in Kaua'i's rain shadow. Its highest peak, Paniau, is only 1280ft tall and cannot generate the trade-wind-based precipitation that is prevalent on the main Hawaiian Islands, notably Kaua'i.

Ni'ihau's 820-acre Halali'i Lake is the largest in Hawaii, but even during the rainy winter season it's only a few feet deep. In summer it sometimes dries up to a mud pond.

Between 50 and 100 endangered Hawaiian monk seals live on Ni'ihau, and many endangered *'alae ke'oke'o* (Hawaiian coots) breed here and on crescent-shaped, uninhabited Lehua Island, a state seabird sanctuary less than a mile offshore. Back on Ni'ihau, introduced animals proliferate: wild boar; feral sheep, goats and turkeys; and exotic antelope translocated from the former Moloka'i Ranch. Ni'ihau's waters have suffered depletion by sport and commercial fishers who sail in to fish and pick *'opihi* (edible limpets) from the island's shore breaks.

Economy & Politics

The island economy long depended on Ni'ihau Ranch, the sheep and cattle business owned by the Robinsons. But it was always a marginal operation on windy Ni'ihau, with droughts devastating the ranch's herds. In 1999 the ranch ceased operations, putting most of the island's residents on federal welfare. A few artisans make a living by hand-crafting highly valued Ni'ihau shell lei, which can sell for thousands of dollars each.

Historically the Robinsons diverted funds from their (now defunct) sugar company on Kaua'i to provide Ni'ihauans with subsidized housing, food staples, medical care and education.

Since 1999 the US Navy has leased sites on the uninhabited southern end of the island for remotely operated radar surveillance and periodic, small-scale training maneuvers. The Robinsons have also pushed for Ni'ihau's participation in major Navy missile testing, which they consider less invasive and damaging (both to the physical land and to the preservation of Ni'ihau's culture and privacy) than tourism.

Apart from the income derived from military operations, the only other realistic option is tourism, which is why the Robinsons started offering helicopter and hunting safari tours. Neither is a booming moneymaker, probably due to the steep tour prices as well as the Robinsons' ambivalence about opening the island to tourists.

Politically, Ni'ihau falls under the jurisdiction of Kaua'i County.

Visiting Ni'ihau

Although outsiders are not allowed to visit Ni'ihau independently, the Robinsons offer helicopter flights and hunting excursions, and several dive outfits on Kaua'i offer scuba-diving tours to the waters around Ni'ihau and Lehua Islands (a typical three-tank dive costs around $350). Book all tours well in advance.

Ni'ihau Helicopters (☎877-441-3500; www.niihau.us; per person $385) The pilot flies over much of Ni'ihau (but avoids the population center of Pu'uwai) and lands beachside for snorkeling. Lunch, snacks and drinks are included; five-person minimum required.

Ni'ihau Safaris (☎877-441-3500; www.niihau.us; per hunter from $1750) Provides everything you'll need (air transportation, guide, preparation and shipping of trophies) to hunt Polynesian boar and feral sheep, mostly, but also wild eland, Barbary sheep and wild oryx. Organizers promote this as 'useful harvesting of game' (due to overpopulation and overgrazing) and obey the norms of free-chase hunting.

Jo-Jo's Anuenue Shave Ice & Treats DESSERTS **$**
(9899 Waimea Rd; snacks from $3; 10am-5:30pm;) Now in a new location, this shack delivers icy flavor: all syrups are homemade without additives and won't knock you out with sweetness. The superstar item is the *halo halo* (Filipino-style mixed fruit) with coconut.

Shrimp Station SEAFOOD **$**
(808-338-1242; 9652 Kaumuali'i Hwy; mains $8-12; 11am-5pm;) Want shrimp? Whether sautéed scampi-style, coconut- or beer-battered, in taco form or ground up into a 'shrimp burger,' crustaceans is what this roadside chow hut is all about. Look for the flamingo-pink sign out front.

Da Booze Shop LOCAL **$**
(808-338-9953; 9883 Waimea Rd; mains $5-10; 10:30am-9pm Mon-Sat, to 5pm Sun) For down-home burgers, box lunches, BBQ ribs and plates full of artery-clogging local faves such as *katsu loco moco* covered in gravy, step inside this family-owned storefront deli and grill. Ironically, no alcohol is served.

Wrangler's Steakhouse STEAK **$$**
(808-338-1218; www.innwaimea.com/wranglers.html; 9852 Kaumuali'i Hwy; lunch meals around $10, dinner mains $18-30; 11am-8:30pm Mon-Thu, 4-9pm Fri & Sat, 4-8:30pm Sun;) Yes, it's touristy, but this Western-style saloon dishes up plantation lunches in authentic *kaukau* (food) tins full of shrimp and vegetable tempura, teriyaki steak, rice and kimchi. Sizzling dinner steaks are decent, but the seafood and soup-and-salad bar less so. Save room for peach cobbler. There's atmospheric seating on the front lanai or back porch.

Drinking & Entertainment

Kalapaki Joe's SPORTS BAR
(808-338-1666; http://kalapakijoes.com; Waimea Plantation Cottages, 9400 Kaumuali'i Hwy; 11am-10pm) Calling itself the USA's westernmost sports bar, this outpost of the Lihu'e original inhabits a charming plantation building with a full bar, ceiling fans, ocean-view verandas and local music some nights. Take your pick of two dozen beers on tap, including made-in-Hawaii brews. Skip the pub grub, except for happy-hour specials (from 3pm to 6pm daily).

Waimea Theater CINEMA
(808-338-0282; www.waimeatheater.com; 9691 Kaumuali'i Hwy; adult/child 5-10yr $8/6) This art deco movie theater is the place to head for shelter on a rainy day or for an early-evening reprieve from sun and sea. Kaua'i is a little behind with new releases and movie schedules are erratic, but since this is one of only two functioning cinemas on the island (the other is in Lihu'e), no one's complaining.

Shopping

Aunty Lilikoi Passion Fruit Products FOOD, GIFTS
(808-338-1296, 866-545-4564; www.auntylilikoi.com; 9875 Waimea Rd; 10am-6pm) Find something for almost any occasion: award-winning passion fruit–wasabi mustard, passion-fruit syrup (great for banana pancakes), massage oil (the choice for honeymooners) and a tasty lip balm (ideal for après surf), all made with at least a kiss of, you guessed it, *liliko'i*.

Kaua'i Granola FOOD
(808-338-0121; www.kauaigranola.com; 9633 Kaumuali'i Hwy; 10am-5pm Mon-Sat) Before you head up to Waimea Canyon and Koke'e State Parks, drop by this island bakery for snacks such as trail mix, macadamia-nut cookies, chocolate-dipped coconut macaroons and tropically flavored granola.

Information

First Hawaiian Bank (808-338-1611; www.fhb.com; 4525 Panako Rd; 8:30am-4pm Mon-Thu, to 6pm Fri) Has a 24-hour ATM.

Waimea Post Office (808-338-9973; www.usps.com; 9911 Waimea Rd; 9am-1pm & 1:30-4pm Mon-Fri, 9-11am Sat)

Waimea Public Library (808-338-6848; 9750 Kaumuali'i Hwy; noon-8pm Mon & Wed, 9am-5pm Tue, Thu & Fri;) Free wi-fi; online computer terminals are available for use with temporary nonresident library card ($10).

West Kauai Medical Center (808-338-9431; www.kvmh.hhsc.org; 4643 Waimea Canyon Dr) Basic 24-hour emergency services.

West Kaua'i Technology & Visitor Center (808-338-1332; www.westkauaivisitorcenter.org; 9565 Kaumuali'i Hwy; 12:30-4pm Mon, 9:30am-4pm Tue & Wed, 9:30am-12:30pm Fri) Free internet computer access.

Kekaha

Kekaha is an old working-class sugar town, and today it's home to many military families. There's no town center here, but Kekaha Beach Park offers one of the most beautiful sunsets on the island. If you're looking for a scenic beach near the base of Waimea Canyon, staying here is an option. Most visitors will find it too remote, however.

Beaches

Kekaha Beach Park BEACH
(Map p554) Kaua'i's Westside is known for its unrelenting sun and vast beaches. Just west of Kekaha town, this long stretch of sand is best for beachcombing and catching sunsets. Before jumping in, find a lifeguard and make sure it's okay to swim, since the beach lacks reef protection. In high surf, the currents are extremely dangerous. Under the right conditions, however, it's good for surfing and bodyboarding.

Facilities include outdoor showers, restrooms and picnic tables.

Sleeping

For more vacation rental homes and beach cottages, contact **Kekaha Oceanside** (☎800-351-4609; www.kekahaoceansidekauai.com).

Mindy's APARTMENT $
(Map p554; ☎808-337-9275; 8842 Kekaha Rd; ste from $95; 📶) Featuring a private lanai, this second-story, fan-cooled apartment, with a full-sized bed and a kitchen, feels large and open. There's free beach gear to borrow, and complimentary fruit and coffee in the mornings.

Hale Makai RENTAL HOUSE $$
(Map p554; ☎760-492-7583; www.vrbo.com/135835; 4635 Palila Loop; 2-bedroom house $180-200; ❄📶) Children are welcome at this two-bedroom house, a short walk inland from the beach. Polished wooden floors, a full kitchen, two en-suite bedrooms (one king, one queen), a screened-in lanai and a private hot tub are among many welcome amenities. Minimum four-night stay. Cleaning and reservation fees $150.

Hale La RENTAL HOUSE $$$
(Map p554; ☎808-652-6852; www.kekahakauaisunset.com; 8240a Elepaio Rd; 3-bedroom house $395; ❄📶) This modern, green-painted, oceanside house offers three suites with cherrywood and bamboo furnishings, and two with private lanai and ocean views. Watch whales breach off the beach in winter. One hiccup: traffic noise. Three-night minimum stay. Cleaning fee $250.

Shopping

Kekaha Farmers Market MARKET
(Map p554; Kekaha Neighborhood Center, 8130 Elepaio Rd; ⏲9-11am Sat) A handful of local farmers and flower growers gather every Saturday morning just off the Kaumuali'i Hwy.

Getting There & Around

The Kaumuali'i Hwy borders the coastline. Kekaha Rd, the town's main drag, lies parallel and a few blocks inland. All you'll find in town are a post office and a couple of stores. Further east toward Waimea, Kekaha Rd and Kaumuali'i Hwy meet near the Kikiaola Small Boat Harbor.

Barking Sands

Between Kekaha Beach Park and Polihale State Park, the Westside's biggest beach stretches for around 15 miles. Much of it is taken up by the US Navy's **Barking Sands Pacific Missile Range Facility**, which is closed to the public. Established during WWII, it has the world's largest instrumented underwater listening range (more than 1100 sq miles) and controls more than 40,000 sq miles of airspace.

Polihale State Park

A wide, loamy beach curls into dunes that climb into bluffs, set by a turquoise bay that thrashes against the looming majesty of the Na Pali cliffs. Sunsets are epic here.

Here's the catch: the beach is only accessible by a rutted 5-mile dirt road from Mana village off the Kaumuali'i Hwy. This road takes a beating from harsh conditions, but it's usually passable in the absence of severe flooding. Most rental-car companies legally prohibit you from driving on it, however.

The **park** (www.hawaiistateparks.org; ⏲dawn-dusk) has restrooms, outdoors showers and a picnic area, but no lifeguards – exercise caution if you go swimming, and only enter the water during calm conditions. Camping is allowed with an advance state-park permit.

Waimea Canyon State Park

Of all Kaua'i's unique wonders, none can touch Waimea Canyon for grandeur. On this tropical island, few would expect to find a gargantuan chasm of ancient lava rock, 10 miles long and more than 3500ft deep, popularly nicknamed the 'Grand Canyon of the Pacific.' Flowing through the canyon is the Waimea River, Kaua'i's longest, which is fed by tributaries that bring reddish-brown waters from the mountaintop bog of Alaka'i Swamp.

Waimea Canyon was formed when Kaua'i's original shield volcano, Wai'ale'ale, slumped along an ancient fault line, which was followed by millennia of erosion by the Waimea River and heavy annual rainfall. The horizontal striations along the canyon walls represent successive volcanic eruptions. The red colors indicate where water has seeped through the rocks, creating mineral rust from the iron ore inside.

Drives here on a clear day are phenomenal. But don't be disappointed by rain, as that's what makes the waterfalls gush. Sunny days following rain are ideal for prime views, though slick mud makes hiking a challenge at these times.

Sights & Activities

Waimea Canyon Lookout — VIEWPOINT

This breathtaking vista is about 0.3 miles north of mile marker 10, at an elevation of 3400ft. The canyon running in an easterly direction off Waimea Canyon is Koai'e Canyon, an area accessible to backcountry hikers.

Waipo'o Falls — WATERFALL

This 800ft waterscape can be seen from a couple of small unmarked lookouts before mile marker 12 and then from a lookout opposite the picnic area shortly before mile marker 13. The picnic area has restrooms and drinking water.

Pu'u Hinahina Lookout — VIEWPOINT

A majestic canyon lookout (elevation 3640ft) showing the river glistening in the distance and giving panoramic views down to the ocean. There are two lookouts near the parking lot at a marked turnoff between mile markers 13 and 14.

★Waimea Canyon Drive — DRIVING TOUR

(Hwy 550) This spectacular drive, the best on the island, follows the entire length of Waimea Canyon into Koke'e State Park, ascending 19 miles from the coast to Pu'u o Kila Lookout. It begins as Waimea Canyon Dr by Waimea's West Kaua'i Technology & Visitor Center, then merges into and becomes Koke'e Rd. You can stop at scenic lookouts and take short hikes during the drive. There are no gas stations along the way, but major signposted lookouts have restrooms.

Hiking

For experienced hikers, several rugged trails lead deep into Waimea Canyon. Keep in mind these trails are shared with pig hunters and are busiest on weekends and holidays. Trail maps are available at the Koke'e Museum (p571) in Koke'e State Park.

Hiking poles or a sturdy walking stick will ease the steep descent into the canyon. Note the time of sunset and plan to return well before dark, as daylight will fade inside the canyon long before sunset. Beware of rain, which creates hazardous conditions in the canyon: red-dirt trails quickly become slick and river fords rise to impassable levels.

While packing light is recommended, take enough water for your entire trip, especially the uphill return journey. Do not drink fresh water found along the trails without treating it.

Cell phones will not work here. If possible, hike with a companion or at least tell someone your expected return time. Wear brightly colored clothing to alert hunters of your presence.

Iliau Nature Loop — HIKING

(https://hawaiitrails.ehawaii.gov; off Waimea Canyon Dr) This easy, mostly flat 0.3-mile nature loop is a good leg-stretcher for those itching to get out of the car but who are ill-equipped for a big trek. *Iliau,* a plant endemic to Kaua'i's Westside, grows along the route and produces stalks up to 10ft high. The marked trailhead comes up shortly before mile marker 9 on Hwy 550.

For a top-notch panorama of Waimea Canyon and its waterfalls, you only have to walk for about three minutes past the bench on your left.

Kukui Trail — HIKING

(http://hawaiitrails.ehawaii.gov; off Waimea Canyon Dr) This narrow switchbacking trail drops 2000ft in elevation over 2.5 miles without offering much in the way of sweeping views, though there's a river at the bottom. The climb back out of the canyon is for seriously

Waimea Canyon & Koke'e State Parks

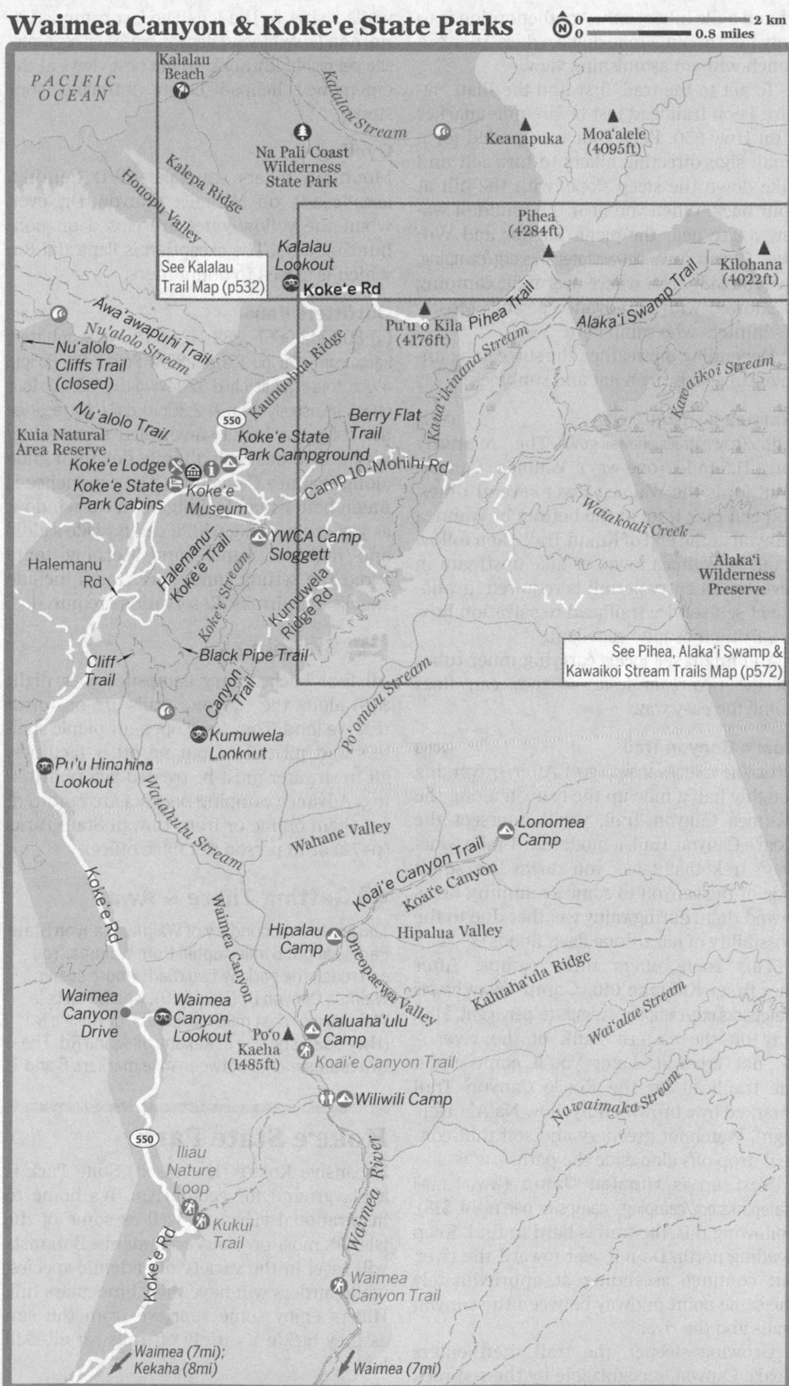

fit and agile hikers only. Another option is to only hike about a mile down, where there's a bench with an astonishing view.

To get to the trail, first find the Iliau Nature Loop trailhead just before mile marker 9 on Hwy 550. Keep your eyes peeled for a small sign directing hikers to turn left and hike down the steep slope, with the hill at your back. When you hear the sound of water, you're near the picnic shelter and **Wiliwili Camp** (www.hawaiistateparks.org/camping; per night $18) area, where overnight camping is allowed with an advance permit. Mostly it's hunters who camp here.

Depending on weather, the sun can be unrelenting, so bring a hat and sunblock.

Waimea Canyon Trail HIKING
(http://hawaiitrails.ehawaii.gov) The relatively flat, 11.5-mile (one-way) Waimea Canyon Trail fords the Waimea River several times. You can pick it up at the bottom of Waimea Canyon at the end of Kukui Trail, then follow it out to Waimea town, or hike upstream in reverse. An entry permit is required (available at self-service trailhead registration boxes). Bring mosquito repellent.

You might see locals carrying inner tubes on the upstream hike, so they can float home the easy way.

Koai'e Canyon Trail HIKING
(http://hawaiitrails.ehawaii.gov) After traversing roughly half a mile up the canyon along the Waimea Canyon Trail, you'll intersect the Koai'e Canyon Trail, a moderate 3-mile (one-way) trek that takes you down the south side of the canyon to some swimming holes (avoid them during rainy weather due to the possibility of hazardous flash floods).

This route offers three camps. After the first, **Kaluaha'ulu Camp** (www.hawaiistateparks.org/camping; campsite per night $18), stay on the eastern bank of the river – do not cross it. Later you'll come upon the trailhead for the Koai'e Canyon Trail (marked by a brown-and-yellow Na Ala Hele sign). Watch for greenery and soil that conceal drop-offs alongside the path.

Next up is **Hipalau Camp** (www.hawaiistateparks.org/camping; campsite per night $18). Following this, the trail is hard to find. Keep heading north. Do not veer toward the river, but continue ascending at approximately the same point midway between the canyon walls and the river.

Growing steeper, the trail then enters Koai'e Canyon, recognizable by the red-rock walls rising to the left. The last camp is **Lonomea** (www.hawaiistateparks.org/camping; campsite per night $18). Soak up the best views at the emergency helipad before retracing your steps.

Cycling

Mountain bikers can take 4WD hunting-area roads off Waimea Canyon Dr, even when the yellow gates are closed on nonhunting days. The exception is Papa'alai Rd, which is closed to nonhunters.

Outfitters Kauai CYCLING
(☎808-742-9667, 888-742-9887; www.outfitterskauai.com; Po'ipu Plaza, 2827a Po'ipu Rd, Po'ipu; 4½hr tours adult/child 12-14yr $106/86; ⏲tour check-in usually 6am & 2:30pm daily, by reservation only) For lazy two-wheeled sightseeing, it's hard to beat this 13-mile downhill glide along Waimea Canyon Dr. The experience is much better than looking out a car window, as you cruise along with a comfy, wide saddle and high-rise handlebars. Morning tours avoid the setting sun's glare. Tours include snacks and drinks. Reservations required.

Sleeping

All four backcountry campsites (per night $18) along the canyon's trails are on forest reserve land. They have open-air picnic shelters and pit toilets, but no other facilities; all freshwater must be treated before drinking. Advance camping permits are required; get them online or from Hawaii State Parks (p472) or in person at Lihu'e office.

Getting There & Away

The southern boundary of Waimea Canyon State Park is about 6 miles uphill from Waimea. You can reach the park by two roads: more scenic Waimea Canyon Dr (Hwy 550), which starts in Waimea just past mile marker 23, or Koke'e Rd (Hwy 552), starting in Kekaha off Mana Rd. The two routes merge between mile markers 6 and 7.

Koke'e State Park

Expansive Koke'e (ko-*keh*-eh) State Park is a playground for ecotourism. It's home to inspirational views, as well as some of the island's most precious ecosystems. Botanists will revel in the variety of endemic species, while birders will have their binoculars full. Hikers enjoy some reprieve from the sun as they tackle a variety of trails for all skill levels.

ALAKA'I SWAMP

Nothing provides an out-of-the-ordinary hiking experience the way **Alaka'i Swamp** does. Designated a wilderness preserve in 1964, this soggy paradise has a hiking trail that is almost completely lined with wooden planks, mainly to discourage off-trail trekking. The state started laying these planks around 1989, and it was a time-consuming process that was delayed when Hurricane 'Iniki hit in 1992. There are still ambitions to cover part of the Pihea Trail, but the Alaka'i Swamp Trail already has some planks missing.

Nevertheless, you'll traverse truly fantastic terrain on this hike, including misty bogs with knee-high trees and tiny, carnivorous plants. On a clear day, you'll get outstanding views of the Wainiha Valley and the distant ocean from Kilohana Lookout. If it's raining, don't fret: search for rainbows and soak up the eerie atmosphere. Queen Emma was said to have been so moved by tales from this spiritual place that she sojourned here while chanting in reverence.

The swamp has its own unique biological rhythms, and there are far more endemic birds than introduced species here – elsewhere in Hawaii the opposite is true. Many of these avian species are endangered, some with fewer than 100 birds remaining today.

The rainy season lasts from October through May, although you might need a waterproof layer at any time of year. The park's elevation (2000ft to 4000ft above sea level) necessitates some light insulation – bring a fleece jacket, or a heavier one if you are camping in winter, when temperatures can dip below 40ºF (4ºC). Although one of the park's charms is its bumpy 4WD roads, the state has paved the main road from beginning to end.

Sights

Koke'e Museum MUSEUM

(808-335-9975; www.kokee.org; donation $1; 9am-4:30pm;) Inside this two-room museum you'll find detailed topographical maps, exhibits on flora and fauna, and local historical photographs. It also has botanical sketches of endemic plants and taxidermic representations of some of the wildlife that calls Koke'e home.

The gift shop sells a handy fold-out map of the park and its hiking trails, as well as a self-guiding brochure for the short nature trail out back.

Kalalau Lookout VIEWPOINT

At mile marker 18, the Kalalau Lookout stands up to the ocean, sun and winds with brave, severe beauty. Hope for a clear day for views of Kalalau Valley, but know that even on a rainy day, the clouds could quickly blow away to reveal gushing waterfalls and, of course, rainbows.

Though it might be hard to imagine due to the extremity of the terrain, as late as the 1920s Kalalau Valley was home to many residents who farmed rice. The only way into the valley nowadays is via the North Shore's Kalalau Trail or by sea kayaking.

Pu'u o Kila Lookout VIEWPOINT

The paved park road (subject to periodic closures) heads a mile beyond the Kalalau Lookout before it dead-ends at a parking lot. The views of Kalalau Valley are similarly spectacular to those at Kalalau Lookout, but usually less crowded. Pu'u o Kila is also the trailhead for the Pihea Trail.

Activities

Koke'e's sheer size can make it tough to nail down where to start. The 4WD roads that access many trailheads complicate things more. Be prepared for wet, cold weather anytime. For trail information, stop at the Koke'e Museum and consult the **Na Ala Hele** (Map p478; http://hawaiitrails.ehawaii.gov) website.

In total, this state park boasts 45 miles of trails that range from swampy bogs to wet forest to red-dirt canyon rim with clifftop views that can cause vertigo even in wannabe mountain goats. Hiking here offers chances to spy endemic species of animals and plants, including Kaua'i's rare, endangered forest birds.

Halemanu Rd, just north of mile marker 14 on Koke'e Rd, is the starting point for several scenic hikes. Whether or not the road is passable in a non-4WD vehicle depends on recent rainfall. Note that many rental-car agreements forbid any off-road driving.

Pihea, Alaka'i Swamp & Kawaikoi Stream Trails

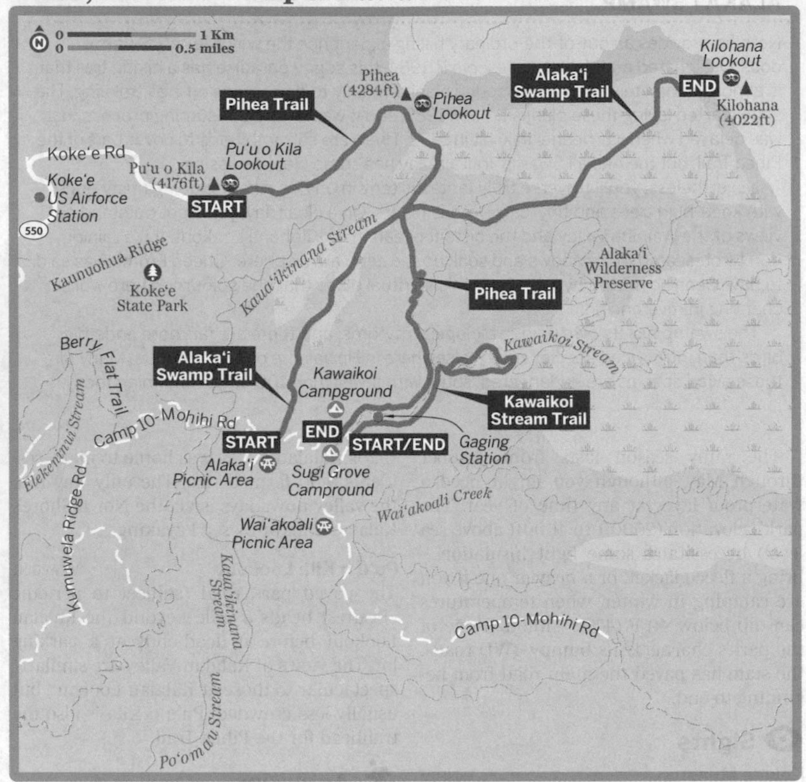

★**Cliff & Canyon Trails** HIKING

(👪) The 0.1-mile **Cliff Trail** is a relatively easy walk with rewarding canyon views. Keep going on the 1.7-mile **Canyon Trail**, a steep forested trail that descends before opening up to a vast red-dirt promontory with cliffs to one side and charming log-steps to guide you further. Shortly thereafter it'll take some huff-and-puff climbing to get to **Waipo'o Falls**.

If it's getting to be too much, you could turn around at the falls. Otherwise, follow the trail across the stream to the canyon rim. The trail ends at **Kumuwela Lookout**, where you can rest at a picnic table before backtracking to Halemanu Rd.

For an alternate return route, make a right at the signed intersection with the **Black Pipe Trail** at the top of the switch-back where you leave the canyon rim. This 0.5-mile alternative trail stops at the 4WD road, where you turn left (downhill) and walk back to where you started.

To get to the trailhead for the Cliff and Canyon Trails, walk down Halemanu Rd over 0.5 miles. Keeping Halemanu Stream on your left, turn right onto a footpath leading to the Cliff and Canyon Trails. At the next junction, the Cliff Trail veers right and uphill to a viewpoint.

★**Awa'awapuhi & Nu'alolo Trails** HIKING

The **Awa'awapuhi Trail** (3.2 miles one way) and more challenging **Nu'alolo Trail** (3.8 miles) are the best of Koke'e. Both ultimately afford unforgettable vistas of 2000ft cliffs rising above the Na Pali Coast. If you're undecided as to which trail to take, Awa'awapuhi is much less technical and Nu'alolo is steeper, though each require a good amount of endurance.

The Awa'awapuhi Trail sees more people, and there are some steep steps where you might find yourself hugging a tree. At the trail's end you'll arrive at a breathtaking view of the cliffs below **Awa'awapuhi Lookout** (Map p554).

Perhaps nothing is more exhilarating than the connecting **Nu'alolo Cliffs Trail** (2.1 miles), where you'll sometimes feel like more of a rock climber or makeshift acrobat than a hiker. As of 2014, this trail was closed indefinitely, however, due to erosion and a washout.

The trailhead for the Nu'alolo Trail is just south of the Koke'e Museum. The Awa'awapuhi Trail begins off Koke'e Rd, about 1.5 miles uphill past the museum.

Pihea Trail to Alaka'i Swamp Trail HIKING

This rugged, strenuous 7.5-mile round-trip trek begins off Koke'e Rd at Pu'u o Kila Lookout (p571). A mere mile in, **Pihea Lookout** appears. After a short scramble downhill, the boardwalk begins. About 1.8 miles later, you'll come to a crossing with the **Alaka'i Swamp Trail**. Taking a left at this crossing puts you on the trail toward **Kilohana Lookout**.

Continuing straight on the Pihea Trail will take you to Kawaikoi Campground instead. Most hikers begin this trip at Pu'u o Kila Lookout because it's accessible via the paved road.

Both of these trails may be muddy and not recently maintained. The stretch between Alaka'i Crossing and Kilohana Lookout includes hundreds of steps, which can be hell on your knees.

Halemanu–Koke'e Trail HIKING

This trail starts off Halemanu Rd, along from the Cliff and Canyon Trails. A gentle recreational nature hike, the 1.2-mile trip passes through a native forest of koa and ohia trees, which provide habitat for endemic birds. The trail ends near YWCA Camp Sloggett, about 0.5 miles from Koke'e Lodge.

One common trailside plant is banana poka, a member of the passion-fruit family and a serious invasive pest. It has pretty pink flowers, but it drapes the forest with its vines and chokes out less-aggressive native plants.

Kawaikoi Stream Trail HIKING

This easy, 1.8-mile loop trail initially follows Kawaikoi Stream through a grove of Japanese cedar and California redwood trees, rises up on a bluff, then loops back down to the stream before returning to where you started. Find the trailhead upstream from Sugi Grove Campground on Camp 10–Mohihi Rd (4WD only).

Festivals & Events

Banana Poka Round-Up ART, MUSIC

(www.kokee.org; May;) This unique festival in late May strips Koke'e of an invasive pest from South America, the banana poka vine, then weaves baskets from it. Come for live music, a rooster-crowing contest and the 'Pedal to the Meadow' bicycle race.

★ **Eo e Emalani I Alaka'i** DANCE, MUSIC

(www.kokee.org; Oct) A one-day outdoor dance festival at the Koke'e Museum in early October, commemorating Queen Emma's 1871 journey to Alaka'i Swamp. The festival includes a royal procession, hula dancing, live music and more.

Sleeping & Eating

Koke'e State Park Campground CAMPGROUND $

(www.hawaiistateparks.org/camping; campsite $18-30) The most accessible camping area is **Koke'e State Park Campground**, which is north of the meadow, just a few minutes' walk from Koke'e Lodge. The campsites sit in a grassy area beside the woods and have picnic tables, drinking water, restrooms and outdoor showers. There's a five-night maximum stay. Book online in advance.

Kawaikoi & Sugi Grove CAMPGROUND $

(www.hawaiistateparks.org/camping; campsites $18-30) FREE About 4 miles east of Koke'e Lodge, off the 4WD-only Camp 10–Mohihi Rd, these primitive campgrounds have pit toilets, picnic shelters and fire pits. There's no water source, so you'll need to bring your own or treat the stream water. Three-night maximum stay; advance camping permits required.

Koke'e State Park Cabins CABIN $

(808-335-6061; www.thelodgeatkokee.net; Koke'e Rd; cabin incl taxes $115) Minimally maintained, these dozen cabins are for folks seeking a remote, bare-bones experience – pretend you're reliving college dorm life (without a phone or TV). All cabins have a double bed and twin beds with sagging mattresses, a kitchen, hot shower, wood-burning stove (your only heating source), linens and blankets. There's a small cleaning fee, depending on how long you stay.

YWCA Camp Sloggett CAMPGROUND, CABIN $
(☎808-245-5959; www.campingkauai.com; campsite $15, cottage, lodge or bunkhouse $120-200) Choose basic cottage, lodge or bunkhouse accommodations, or camp on the grass; all have hot showers available. The cottage has a king-sized bed, kitchen and wood-burning fireplace, while the bunkhouse and lodge are outfitted for large groups, with a kitchen or kitchenette. Bring sleeping bags and towels. No reservations typically needed for camping, but call ahead to check. These facilities are extremely rustic, even run-down.

To get here, turn right off Koke'e Rd, just past the lodge, at the YWCA sign and follow that dirt road for around 0.5 miles.

Koke'e Lodge AMERICAN $
(☎808-335-6061; Koke'e Rd; mains $5-8; ⊙cafe 9am-2:30pm, takeout until 3pm; 👪) This summer camp–style restaurant's strong point is convenience. And that goes a long way in Koke'e, where you're a 30-minute drive from any other dining options. Pancakes, salads, sandwiches, burgers and booze are served. The gift shop, which stays open until 3:30pm or 4pm daily, sells sundries, souvenirs, snacks and drinks.

ℹ Information

The park's southern boundary lies beyond Pu'u Hinahina Lookout on Koke'e Rd. After mile marker 15, you'll pass the park's cabins, restaurant, museum and campground. The nearest place for provisions and gas is Waimea, 15 miles away.

Koke'e Museum (☎808-335-9975; www.kokee.org; Koke'e Rd) Sells inexpensive trail maps and provides basic information on trail conditions. You can call for real-time mountain weather reports.

Understand Hawaii

Hawaii Today

The state motto, 'Ua Mau ke Ea o ka 'Āina i Ka Pono' (The life of the land is perpetuated in righteousness), is not just an idealistic catchphrase. Hawaii's modern sovereignty movement, eco-sustainability initiatives and antidevelopment activism are rooted in *aloha 'aina* (literally, love and respect for the land), a traditional Hawaiian value deeply felt by almost everyone who calls Hawaii home. This belief has nurtured widespread cooperation and commitment to overcoming the 21st-century challenges facing these ancient islands today.

Best on Film

The Descendants (2011) Contemporary island life, with all of its heartaches and blessings.

From Here to Eternity (1953) Classic WWII-era drama leading up to the Pearl Harbor attack.

Blue Crush (2002) Cheesy, but a local favorite for its surf cinematography.

50 First Dates (2004) Silly rom-com shot on gorgeous Windward O'ahu beaches.

Blue Hawaii (1961) Romp poolside with a ukulele-playing Elvis during Hawaii's tiki-tacky tourism boom.

Best in Print

Shark Dialogues (1994) Kiana Davenport's multigenerational family saga, stretching from ancient times into the plantation era.

Wild Meat and the Bully Burgers (1996) Lois-Ann Yamanaka's short-story novel about growing up local and speaking Hawaiian pidgin.

Hotel Honolulu (2001) Paul Theroux' satirical tale about a washed-up writer managing a Waikiki hotel.

'Olelo Noe'au (1997) *Kupuna* (elder) Mary Kawena Pukui's bilingual collection of Hawaiian proverbs and sayings, illustrated by Dietrich Varez.

Staying Hawaiian

Evolving from ancient Polynesian traditions, Hawaiian culture was attacked and suppressed in the two centuries after first Western contact with Captain Cook in 1778. But beginning with the Hawaiian Renaissance in the 1970s, a rebirth of Native Hawaiian cultural and artistic traditions, as well as the Hawaiian language, has taken hold. For more than three decades, there have been Hawaiian-language immersion programs in public schools, and Hawaiian-culture-focused charter schools have been popping up all over the islands.

Today Hawaiian culture is about much more than just melodic place names and luau shows. Traditional arts like *lauhala* (pandanus leaf) weaving, *kapa* (pounded-bark cloth) making, and gourd and wood carving are all experiencing a revival. Healing arts like *lomilomi* (loving touch) massage and *la'au lapa'au* (plant medicine) are being shared with students – both within and beyond the Native Hawaiian community. Ancient *heiau* (temples) and fishponds are being restored, native forests replanted and endangered birds bred and released back into the wild.

Being Hawaiian remains an important part of the identity of the islands, reflected in ways both large and small – in spontaneous hula dancing at a concert, an *oli* (chant) sung before important occasions such as political inaugurations or development ground-breakings, the *lomilomi* treatments given at spas, or listening to the word of the day in *'ōlelo Hawai'i* (the Hawaiian language) on local radio stations.

Although few island residents can agree on what shape the fragmented Hawaiian sovereignty movement should take (or even if it should exist at all), its grassroots political activism has achieved some tangible results. Decades of protests and a federal lawsuit filed by sovereignty activists finally pressured the US military into returning the island of Kaho'olawe, which had been used for bombing practice since WWII, to the state in 1994. Sovereignty activists also helped spur the US federal government's official 1993 apology for its role in the unjust overthrow of the Kingdom of Hawai'i exactly a century before.

Seeking Sustainability

Before the 19th-century arrival of foreign whalers, traders and Christian missionaries, the population of the Hawaiian Islands was somewhere between 200,000 and a million people – around the population of O'ahu today. It's mind-boggling to think about how all of those ancient people were sustainably supported using natural-resource management practices and without metal or technology. As modern-day Hawaii's population swells – which it did by almost 200,000 between 2000 and 2014 – new housing developments sprawl, stretching the state's water resources, transportation systems, public schools and landfills.

Hawaii is less stable today than it was before first Western contact. That's because the islands have become wholly dependent on the outside world. Fully 80% of Hawaii's consumer goods, including up to a staggering 90% of its food, are imported. Despite being in a place blessed with a wealth of natural energy sources, nearly 95% of Hawaii's power still comes from carbon-based fuels. In fact, the state spends around $5 billion a year on oil and coal, all of it imported. Public transportation is limited or nonexistent on the islands except O'ahu, resulting in an average of one registered motor vehicle for each man, woman and child living here.

The future is far from decided, however. Hawaii is striving to become a pioneer in clean energy. In 2008 the Hawaii Clean Energy Initiative (HCEI) set the statewide goal of generating 40% of the state's energy locally by 2030. Public government and private industry are pursuing every renewable and clean energy option available – wind farms on Maui, for example, geothermal and biomass plants on the Big Island, algae-based biofuels and ocean thermal energy conversion (OTEC) on O'ahu and Kaua'i, and solar power on Moloka'i and Lana'i. In addition the state is modernizing its electricity grid and embarking on its most ambitious – and politically controversial – project yet: building a light-rail system for Honolulu that will cost over $5 billion.

Diversifying the Economy

Hawaii is dependent on the outside world not only for its food and fuel, but for nearly its entire economy. After losing sugar and pineapple plantations to cheap imports from the developing world, Hawaii's eggs were pretty much left in one economic basket: tourism. When a recession tanked the national economy in 2008, Hawaii's tourism went with it. By year's end state revenue shortfalls soared to nearly $2 billion and

POPULATION: **1.4 MILLION**

GROSS STATE PRODUCT: **$68.9 BILLION**

MEDIAN ANNUAL HOUSEHOLD INCOME: **$67,116**

UNEMPLOYMENT: **5.2%**

if Hawaii were 100 people

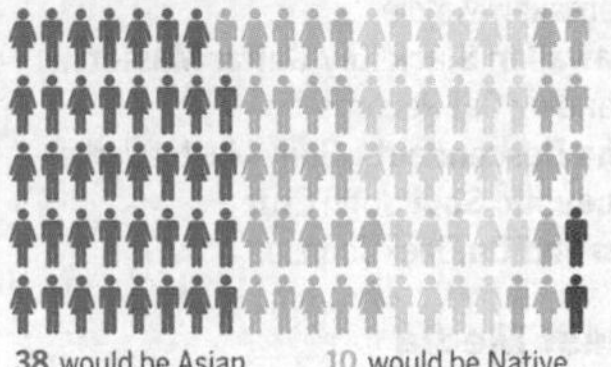

38 would be Asian
24 would be White
17 Two or More Races
10 would be Native Hawaiian
9 would be Latino
2 would be Black

belief systems

(% of population)

Protestant Other/None Catholic

Buddhist Mormon Hindu

population per sq mile

HONOLULU HAWAII USA

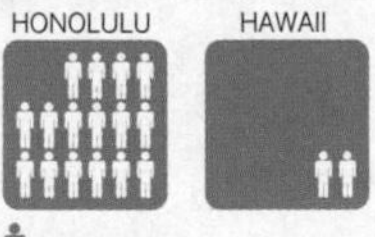

≈ 100 people

Best on TV

Hawaii Five-0 Rebooted crime drama now shot entirely on O'ahu.

Magnum, P.I. Dated as it is, locals still watch it (if only to pick out the locations).

Rap's Hawaii Rap Reiplinger was a local '70s comedy icon – his skit 'Room Service' is timeless.

Frank De Lima Pidgin-speaking comic whose parody songs and commercials crack locals up – just search YouTube.

Best Music Albums

Facing Future, Israel (Iz) Kamakawiwo'ole

Hawaiian Slack Key Guitar Masters, Dancing Cat Records

The Descendants, Sony Masterworks

Acoustic Soul, John Cruz

On and On, Jack Johnson

Best Media

Honolulu Star-Advertiser (p101) Daily statewide newspaper covering news, politics, entertainment and more.

Ka Wai Ola (www.oha.org/kwo) Office of Hawaiian Affairs' newspaper on cultural and political topics; free downloadable issues online.

Hawaii Public Radio (www.hawaiipublicradio.org) Local and national news and talk shows; live web streaming and episode archives online.

OC16 (www.oc16.tv) Oceanic Cable channel 16 – 24-hour, all-local programming.

'Ōiwi TV (www.oiwi.tv) Native Hawaiian television programming, including documentaries, all free to watch online.

then-governor Linda Lingle imposed extremely harsh budget cuts, including furloughs for state employees and shortened schedules for public schools.

Since 2011 Hawaii's economy has rebounded. In terms of statistical measures like unemployment and outstanding debt, Hawaii is now in better shape than some US mainland states that have long been economic powerhouses. The state's push toward energy independence and food security (aka 'food sovereignty') includes supporting small farmers and encouraging consumers to 'buy local,' to mitigate Hawaii's dependency on imports and also tourism.

Tourism will likely be Hawaii's bread and butter for the foreseeable future, even though it comes at a price. Almost eight million visitors land on the islands each year – more than five times the resident population – overcrowding roads and beaches and driving up the price of real estate, not to mention fueling community resistance to new resort developments. Some locals feel inundated by Hawaii's 'unofficial' residents, including part-time retirees and military personnel. Feelings can be mixed toward both tourism and the continued US military presence.

Many of those who live here acknowledge that Hawaii's current economic model is both unstable and unsustainable. Today the islands stand at a crossroads – Hawaii can either suffer the side effects of its dependence on tourism, imported goods and fossil fuels, or boldly move toward securing a more secure homegrown future.

History

Hawaii's discovery and colonization is one of humanity's great epic tales, starting with ancient Polynesians who found their way to these tiny islands – the world's most isolated – in the midst of Earth's largest ocean. Almost a millennium passed before Western explorers, whalers, missionaries and entrepreneurs arrived on ships. During the tumultuous 19th century, global immigrants came to work on Hawaii's plantations before the kingdom founded by Kamehameha the Great was overthrown, making way for US annexation.

Polynesian Voyagers

To ancient Polynesians, the Pacific Ocean was a passageway, not a barrier, and the islands it contained were connected, not isolated. Between AD 300 and 600, they made their longest journey yet and discovered the Hawaiian Islands. This would mark the northern reach of their migrations, which were so astounding that Captain Cook – the first Western explorer to take their full measure – could not conceive of how the Polynesians did it, settling 'every quarter of the Pacific Ocean' and becoming one of the most widespread nations on earth.

Although the discovery of Hawaii may have been accidental, subsequent journeys were not. Polynesians were highly skilled seafarers, navigating over thousands of miles of open ocean without maps, and with only the sun, stars, wind and waves to guide them. In double-hulled wooden canoes, they imported to the islands over two dozen food plants and domestic animals, along with their religious beliefs and social structures. What they didn't possess is equally remarkable: no metals, no wheels, no alphabet or written language, and no clay to make pottery.

Almost nothing is known about the first wave of Polynesians (likely from the Marquesas Islands) who settled Hawai'i, except that the archaeological record shows they were here. A second wave of Polynesians from the Tahitian Islands began arriving around AD 1000, and they conquered the first peoples and obliterated nearly all traces of their history and culture. Later Hawaiian legends of the *menehune* – an ancient race of little people who mysteriously built temples and great stoneworks overnight – may refer to the islands' original human inhabitants.

The paintings of acclaimed artist, historian and Polynesian Voyaging Society co-founder Herb Kawainui Kane give a glimpse into Hawaii's mythic and historical past, including in his illustrated book *Voyagers* (2005). Several dozen of his artworks are on display at King Kamehameha's Kona Beach Hotel on the Big Island.

TIMELINE

30 million BC

The first Hawaiian island, Kure, rises from the sea, appearing where the Big Island is today. Borne by wind, wing and wave, plants, insects and birds colonize the new land.

AD 300–600

The first wave of Polynesians, most likely from the Marquesas Islands, voyage by canoe to the Hawaiian Islands – at least a century before Vikings leave Scandinavia to plunder Europe.

1000–1300

Sailing from Tahiti, a second wave of Polynesians arrives. Their tools are made of stone, shells and bone, and they bring taro, sweet potato, sugarcane, coconut, chickens, pigs and dogs.

Ancient Hawai'ian Society

When for unknown reasons trans-Pacific voyages from Polynesia stopped around AD 1300, ancient Hawaiian culture kept evolving in isolation, but retained a family resemblance to cultures found throughout Polynesia. Hawaiian society was highly stratified, ruled by a chiefly class called *ali'i* whose power derived from their ancestry: they were believed to be descended from the gods. In ancient Hawai'i, clan loyalty trumped individuality, elaborate traditions of gifting and feasting conferred prestige, and a pantheon of shape-shifting gods animated the natural world.

Several ranks of *ali'i* ruled each island, and life was marked by frequent warfare as they jockeyed for power. The largest geopolitical division was the *mokupuni* (island), presided over by a member of the *ali'i nui* (kingly class). Each island was further divided into *moku* (districts), wedge-shaped areas of land running from the ridge of the mountains

The community website www.hawaiihistory.org offers an interactive timeline of Hawaii's history and essays delving into every aspect of ancient Hawaiian culture, with evocative images and links.

HAWAII'S WAYFARING TRADITIONS REBORN

In 1976, a double-hulled wooden canoe and her crew set off from O'ahu's Windward Coast, aiming to re-create the journey of Hawaii's first human settlers and to do what no one had done in over 600 years – sail 2400 miles to Tahiti without benefit of radar, compass, satellites or sextant. Launched by the Polynesian Voyaging Society, this modern reproduction of an ancient Hawaiian long-distance seafaring canoe was named *Hokule'a* (Star of Gladness).

The canoe's Micronesian navigator, Mau Piailug, still knew the art of traditional Polynesian wayfaring at a time when such knowledge had been lost to Hawaiian culture. He knew how to use horizon or zenith stars – those that always rose over known islands – as a guide, then evaluate currents, winds, landmarks and time in a complex system of dead reckoning to stay on course. In the mind's eye, the trick is to hold the canoe still in relation to the stars while the island sails toward you.

Academic skeptics had long questioned whether Hawaii's early settlers really were capable of journeying back and forth across such vast, empty ocean. After 33 days at sea, the crew of the *Hokule'a* proved those so-called experts wrong by reaching their destination, where they were greeted by 20,000 Tahitians. This historic achievement helped spark a revival of interest in Hawaii's Polynesian cultural heritage.

Since its 1976 voyage, the *Hokule'a* has served as a floating living-history classroom. The canoe has made 10 more trans-oceanic voyages, sailing throughout Polynesia and to the US mainland, Canada, Micronesia and Japan. Its current voyage, which began in 2014, will circumnavigate the globe, visiting over 26 countries, and travel more than 45,000 nautical miles before returning to Hawaii in 2016 or 2017. Learn more at www.hokulea.com.

1778–79

Captain Cook, the first foreigner known to reach the islands, visits Hawai'i twice. After being warmly welcomed, Cook loses his temper over a stolen boat and is killed by Hawaiians.

1810

Kamehameha the Great negotiates to take control of Kaua'i, uniting the islands into one kingdom for the first time. His royal court moves from Lahaina, Maui to Honolulu, O'ahu.

1819

Kamehameha I dies. A few months later, his son, the new king Liholiho, breaks the kapu (taboo) on eating with women, dramatically – and publicly – violating the Hawaiian religion.

1820

The first Christian missionaries arrive in Hawai'i at Kailua-Kona. King Liholiho eventually allows missionary leader Hiram Bingham to establish the mission's headquarters in Honolulu.

to the sea. Smaller, similarly wedge-shaped *ahupua'a* comprised each *moku;* they were mostly self-sustaining and had local chiefs.

Ranking just below *ali'i,* kahuna (experts or masters) included priests, healers and skilled craftspeople such as canoe makers and navigators. Also beneath the chiefs were the *konohiki,* who supervised natural resource management on land and sea within an *ahupua'a;* they collected taxes from the *maka'ainana* (commoners), who did most of the physical labor. Occupying the lowest tier was a small class of outcasts or untouchables called *kaua,* who were a source of *pua'a waewae loloa* – 'long-legged pigs,' a euphemism for human sacrificial victims.

A culture of mutuality and reciprocity infused what was essentially a feudal agricultural society. Chiefs were custodians of their people, and humans custodians of nature, all of which was sacred – the living expression of mana (spiritual essence). Everyone played a part through work and ritual to maintain the health of the community and its comity with the gods. Ancient Hawaiians also developed rich traditions in art, music, dance and competitive sports.

Captain Cook & First Western Contact

Starting in 1778, everything changed. It was the archetypal clash of civilizations: the British Empire, the most technologically advanced culture on the planet, sent an explorer on a mission. The Hawai'i he stumbled upon was, to his eyes, a place inhabited by heathens stuck in prehistoric times; their worship of pagan gods and human sacrifice seemed anathema to the Christian world view. But Hawai'i's strategic geographic position and wealth of natural resources ensured these islands would quickly become a target of the West's civilizing impulse.

Captain James Cook had spent a decade traversing the Pacific over the course of three voyages. He sought the fabled 'Northwest Passage' linking the Pacific and Atlantic, but his were also voyages of discovery. He sailed with a complement of scientists and artists to document what they found. On the third voyage in 1778, and quite by accident, Cook sailed into the main Hawaiian Island chain. Ending nearly half a millennium of isolation, his arrival irrevocably altered the course of Hawaiian history.

Cook dropped anchor off O'ahu and, as he had elsewhere in the Pacific, bartered with the indigenous people for fresh water and food. While Cook was already familiar with Polynesians, Hawaiians knew nothing of Europeans, nor of the metal, guns and diseases their ships carried. Hawaiians thought of the natural world as inseparable from the spiritual realm, while Cook embodied Enlightenment philosophy, in which God ruled in heaven and only humans walked the earth.

When Cook returned to the islands almost a year later, he sailed around before eventually anchoring at Kealakekua Bay on the Big Island.

Restored Hawaiian Temples

- *Pu'uhonua o Honaunau National Historical Park, Hawai'i, the Big Island*
- *Pi'ilanihale Heiau, Maui*
- *Pu'ukohola Heiau National Historic Site, Hawai'i, the Big Island*
- *Ahu'ena Heiau, Hawai'i, the Big Island*

1826

Missionaries formulate an alphabet for the Hawaiian language and set up the first printing press. It's said that Queen Ka'ahumanu learned to read in five days.

1828

Missionary Sam Ruggles plants the first coffee tree in the Big Island's Kona district as a garden ornamental. Coffee doesn't succeed as a commercial crop until the 1840s.

1830

To control destructive herds of feral cattle (introduced by British sea captain George Vancouver), Hawaiians recruit Spanish-Mexican cowboys, dubbed *paniolo,* who bring guitars with them.

1831

Lahainaluna Seminary, the first secondary school west of the Rocky Mountains, opens in Lahaina. Its press later prints Hawai'i's first newspaper and first paper currency.

Cook's ships were greeted by a thousand canoes, and Hawaiian chiefs and priests honored him with rituals and deference. Cook had landed at an auspicious time during the makahiki, a time of festival and celebration in honor of the god Lono, and some have theorized that the Hawaiians mistook Cook for the god. The Hawaiians were so unrelentingly gracious, in fact, that Cook and his men felt safe to move about unarmed.

Cook set sail some weeks later, but storms forced him to turn back. The mood in Kealakekua had changed, however. The makahiki had ended: no canoes met the Europeans, and suspicion replaced welcome. A small series of minor conflicts, including the theft of a boat by some Hawaiians, provoked Cook into leading an armed party ashore to capture local chief Kalaniopu'u. When the Englishmen disembarked, they were surrounded by angry Hawaiians. In an uncharacteristic fit of pique, Cook shot and killed a Hawaiian man. Hawaiians immediately mobbed Cook, killing him on February 14, 1779.

Reign of Kamehameha the Great

In the years following Cook's death, a steady number of exploring and trading ships sought out the Kingdom of Hawai'i as a resupply spot. With the discovery of a deepwater anchorage in Honolulu (sheltered bay) in 1794, Hawai'i became the new darling of trans-Pacific commerce, first in the fur trade involving China, New England and the Pacific Northwest. The main commodity in the islands – salt – happened to be useful for curing hides. For Hawaiian chiefs, the main items of interest were firearms, which the Europeans willingly traded.

In *Blue Latitudes: Boldly Going Where Captain Cook Has Gone Before*, Tony Horwitz examines the controversial legacy of Captain Cook's South Seas voyages, weaving amusing real-life adventure tales together with bittersweet oral history.

Bolstered with muskets and cannons, Kamehameha, a chief from the Big Island, began a campaign in 1790 to conquer all of the Hawaiian Islands. Other chiefs had tried and failed, but Kamehameha had Western guns; not only that, he was prophesied to succeed and possessed an unyielding determination and exceptional personal charisma. Within five years he united – albeit bloodily – the main islands, except for Kaua'i (which eventually joined peacefully). The dramatic final skirmish in his campaign, the Battle of Nu'uanu, took place on O'ahu in 1795.

Kamehameha was a singular figure who reigned over the most peaceful era in Hawaiian history. A shrewd politician, he configured multi-island governance to mute competition among *ali'i*. A savvy businessman, he created a profitable monopoly on the sandalwood trade in 1810 while protecting the trees from overharvesting. He personally worked taro patches as an example to his people, and his most famous decree – Kanawai Mamalahoe, or 'Law of the Splintered Paddle' – established a kapu (taboo) to protect travelers from harm. Today it is interpreted more broadly for the protection of human rights – you'll even see the symbolic crossed paddles on the badges of Honolulu police officers.

1843

The Kingdom of Hawai'i's only foreign invasion occurs when British naval officer George Paulet seizes O'ahu for five months; his illegal actions are disavowed by the British government.

1846

At the peak of the Pacific whaling era, a record 736 whaling ships stop over in the islands. Four of Hawai'i's 'Big Five' sugar-plantation companies get started supplying whalers.

1848

King Kamehameha III institutes the Great Mahele, a land redistribution act. Two years later, further legislation allows commoners and foreigners to own land in Hawai'i for the first time.

1852

The first indentured sugar-plantation laborers arrive from China; most are single men who, upon completing their contracts, often chose to stay in Hawai'i, starting businesses and families.

Most importantly, Kamehameha I absorbed growing foreign influences while fastidiously honoring Hawai'i's indigenous customs. He did the latter even despite widespread doubts among his people about the justice of Hawaii's kapu system and traditional Hawaiian ideas about a divine social hierarchy. When Kamehameha died in 1819, he left the question of how to resolve these troubling issues to his son and heir, 22-year-old Liholiho. Within the year, Liholiho had broken with the traditional religion in one sweeping, stunning act of repudiation.

Of Hawai'i's eight ruling monarchs, only King Kamehameha I begat children who eventually inherited the throne. His dynasty ended less than a century after it began with the death of Kamehameha V in 1872.

Breaking Kapu & Destroying the Temples

One purpose of the kapu system Kamehameha I upheld was to preserve mana. Mana could be strong or weak, won or lost; it expressed itself in one's talents and the success of a harvest or battle. The kapu system kept *ali'i* from mingling with commoners and men from eating with women; it also kept women from eating pork or entering *luakini heiau* (sacrificial temples). Chiefs could declare temporary kapu to preserve their mana, and thus enhance their power.

However, foreigners arriving in Hawai'i weren't accountable to the kapu system, and lesser *ali'i* saw they could possess power without following its dictates. Women saw that breaking kapu – for example, by dining with sailors – didn't incur the gods' wrath. Kamehameha the Great's most powerful wife, Ka'ahumanu, chafed under the kapu, as it kept women from becoming leaders equal to men. Eventually even Hawai'i's highest-ranking kahuna (priest), Hewahewa, couldn't defend the system.

Soon after Kamehameha's death, Hewahewa conspired with Kamehameha's favorite wife Ka'ahumanu, who ruled as *kahuna nui* (coregent) with her stepson Liholiho, and Keopulani, who possessed more mana than any of Kamehameha's other royal wives. The trio arranged a feast where Liholiho would eat with women, thereby breaking the kapu.

A PLACE OF REFUGE

In ancient Hawai'i, a very strict code – called the kapu (taboo) system – governed daily life. If a commoner dared to eat *moi*, a type of fish reserved for *ali'i*, for example, it was a violation of kapu. Penalties for such transgressions could be harsh, including death. Furthermore, in a society based on mutual respect, slights to honor – whether of one's chief or extended family – could also not be abided.

Although ancient Hawai'i could be a fiercely uncompromising place, it was also forgiving at times. Anyone who had broken kapu or been defeated in battle could avoid the death penalty by fleeing to a *pu'uhona* (place of refuge). At the heiau (temple), a kahuna (priest) would perform purification rituals, lasting a few hours up to several days. Absolved of their transgressions, kapu breakers were free to return home in safety.

1864

Scottish widow Elizabeth Sinclair buys Ni'ihau from King Kamehameha V for $10,000 in gold. Her descendants still own it, restricting access to almost everyone except the predominantly Native Hawaiian residents.

1868

The first Japanese contract laborers arrive to work the sugar plantations. The eruption of Mauna Loa volcano on the Big Island causes an estimated magnitude-8 earthquake, Hawai'i's largest ever.

1873

Belgian Catholic priest Father Damien arrives at Moloka'i's leprosy colony. He stays for 16 years, dying of leprosy (now called Hansen's disease) in 1889. He is sainted in 2009.

1879

King Kalakaua lays the cornerstone for 'Iolani Palace, an ornate four-story building with a throne room, running water and electric lights. Costing more than $350,000, it's completed in 1882.

This act – effectively ending Hawai'i's religion – was nearly beyond the young king. He delayed for months, and drank himself into a stupor the day before.

Then to the shock of the gathered *ali'i* at the feast, Liholiho helped himself to food at the women's table. Hewahewa, signaling his approval, noted that the gods could not survive without kapu. 'Then let them perish with it!' Liholiho is said to have cried. For months afterward, Ka'ahumanu and others set fire to the temples and destroyed *ki'i* (deity images). Many Hawaiians were relieved to be free from kapu, but some continued to venerate the old gods and secretly preserved *ki'i*.

In *Legends and Myths of Hawaii*, King David Kalakaua (1836–91) captures the nature of ancient Hawaiian storytelling by seamlessly mixing history (of Kamehameha, Captain Cook, the burning of the temples) with living mythology.

Missionaries & Whalers Come Ashore

After Cook's expedition sailed back to Britain, news of his 'discovery' of Hawai'i soon spread throughout Europe and the Americas, opening the floodgates to seafaring explorers and traders. By the 1820s, whaling ships began pulling into Hawai'i's harbors for fresh water and food, supplies, liquor and women. To meet their needs, ever more shops, taverns and brothels sprang up around busy ports, especially at Honolulu on O'ahu and also Lahaina on Maui. By the 1840s the islands had become the unofficial whaling capital of the Pacific.

To the ire of 'dirty-devil' whalers, Hawai'i's first Christian missionary ship sailed into Honolulu's harbor on April 14, 1820, carrying staunch Calvinists who were set on saving the Hawaiians from their 'heathen ways.' Their timing could not have been more opportune, as Hawai'i's traditional religion had been abolished the year before, leaving Hawaiians in a spiritual vacuum. Both missionaries and the whalers hailed from New England, but soon were at odds: missionaries were intent on saving souls, while to many sailors there was 'no God west of the Horn.' Sailors repeatedly clashed, sometimes violently, with the missionaries, because they craved all the pleasures that the Calvinists censured.

In the 19th century, New England missionaries needed six months to sail from Boston around Cape Horn to Hawai'i. Early-20th-century Matson steamships embarking from San Francisco took just five days to reach Honolulu.

The missionaries arrived expecting the worst of Hawai'i's indigenous 'pagans,' and in their eyes, that's what they found: public nudity, 'lewd' hula dancing, polygamy, gambling, drunkenness and fornication with sailors. To them, kahuna were witch doctors and Hawaiians hopelessly lazy. Because the missionaries' god was clearly powerful, Christianity attracted Hawaiian converts, notably Queen Ka'ahumanu. But many of these conversions were not deeply felt; Hawaiians often quickly abandoned the church's teachings, reverting to their traditional lifestyles.

The missionaries found one thing that attracted avid, widespread interest: literacy. The missionaries formulated an alphabet for the Hawaiian language, and with this tool, Hawaiians learned to read with astonishing speed. In their oral culture, Hawaiians were used to prodigious feats of memory, and *ali'i* understood that literacy was a key to accessing Western

1882

Macadamia trees are imported from Australia to the Big Island by William Purvis, who plants them as an ornamental. The nuts aren't grown commercially in Hawaii until the 1920s.

1884

The first pineapple plants are introduced to Hawai'i by Captain John Kidwell, but the industry doesn't take off until James Dole incorporates his O'ahu pineapple plantation in 1901.

1893

On January 17 the Hawaiian monarchy is overthrown by a group of US businessmen supported by military troops. Queen Lili'uokalani acquiesces under protest; not a shot is fired.

1895

Robert Wilcox leads a failed counter-revolution to restore Hawaii's monarchy. The deposed queen, charged with being a co-conspirator, is placed under house arrest at 'Iolani Palace.

DEFYING THE VOLCANO GODDESS

One of Christianity's early champions in Hawai'i was a chief from the Kona side of the Big Island. Her name was Kapi'olani (not to be confused with Queen Kap'iolani). People living near Kilauea volcano, many of whom had experienced its deadly 1790 eruption, were less enthusiastic about worshiping the Christian god, however. They feared that if they failed to propitiate Pele, the Hawaiian goddess of volcanoes and fire, the consequences might be dire.

When missionaries toured Kilauea in 1823, Hawaiians were astonished to see them flagrantly violate kapu by exploring the crater and eating *'ohelo* berries (a food reserved for Pele) with impunity. This primed the ground for chief Kapi'olani to challenge Pele directly and to prove that the Christian god was more powerful.

In 1824, the story goes, she walked about 60 miles from her home to the brink of the steaming crater and, dismissing pleas from her people and defying curses from the priests of Pele, descended into the vent at Halema'uma'u. Surrounded by roiling lava, Kapi'olani ate consecrated *'ohelo* berries, read passages from the Bible and threw stones into the volcano without retribution, demonstrating Pele's impotence before the missionaries' god.

The epic scene has become legendary, and it has been the subject of artwork such as Herb Kane's painting *Kapi'olani Defying Pele*. While the story is likely to have been embellished over the years, you can still appreciate how profound Kapi'olani's confidence in the new religion must have been to test the power of a goddess who was all too real to most ancient Hawaiians.

culture and power. By the mid-1850s, Hawai'i had a higher literacy rate than the USA and supported dozens of Hawaiian-language newspapers.

The Great Mahele: Losing the Land

Amid often conflicting foreign influences, some Hawaiian leaders decided that the only way to survive in a world of more powerful nations was to adopt Western ways and styles of government. Hawai'i's absolute monarchy had previously denied citizens a voice in their government. Traditionally, no Hawaiian ever owned land, but the *ali'i* managed it in stewardship for all. None of this sat well with resident US expatriates, many of whose grandparents had fought a revolution for the right to vote and to own private property.

Born and raised in Hawai'i after Western contact, King Kamehameha III (Kauikeaouli) struggled to retain traditional Hawaiian society while developing a political system better suited to foreign, frequently American tastes. In 1840 Kauikeaouli promulgated Hawai'i's first constitution, which established a constitutional monarchy with limited

1898

On July 7 President McKinley signs the resolution annexing Hawaii as a US territory; this is formalized by the 1900 Hawaiian Organic Act, which forms a territorial government.

1900

A fire set to control an outbreak of bubonic plague in Honolulu's Chinatown blazes out of control. Meanwhile, the territory's Hawaiian population drops to its lowest point.

1909

In Hawaii's first major labor strike, 7000 Japanese plantation workers protest low pay and harsh treatment compared with other ethnic workers. The strike fails, winning no concessions.

1912

Duke Kahanamoku wins gold and silver medals in swimming at the Stockholm Olympics. He goes on to become an ambassador of Hawaiian surfing around the world.

citizen representation. Given an inch, foreigners pressed for a mile, so Kauikeaouli followed up with a series of revolutionary land reform acts beginning with the Great Mahele (Great Division) of 1848.

It was hoped the Great Mahele would create a nation of small freeholder farmers, but instead it was a disaster – for Hawaiians, at least. Confusion reigned over boundaries and surveys. Unused to the concept of private land and sometimes unable to pay the necessary tax, many Hawaiians simply failed to follow through on the paperwork to claim titles to the land they had lived on for generations. Many of those who did – perhaps feeling that a taro farmer's life wasn't quite the attraction it once was – immediately cashed out, selling their land to eager and acquisitive foreigners.

Many missionaries ended up with sizable tracts of land, and more than a few left the church to devote themselves to their new estates. Within 30 to 40 years, despite supposed limits, foreigners owned fully three-quarters of the kingdom, and Hawaiians – who had already relinquished so much of their traditional culture so quickly during the 19th century – lost their sacred connection to the land. As historian Gavan Daws wrote, 'So the great division became the great dispossession.'

LEPROSY ON MOLOKA'I

For more than a century beginning in 1866, Moloka'i's Kalaupapa Peninsula was a place of involuntary exile for those afflicted with leprosy (now called Hansen's disease). In *The Colony: The Harrowing True Story of the Exiles of Moloka'i*, John Tayman tells the survivors' stories with dignity, compassion and unflinching honesty.

King Sugar & the Plantation Era

Ko (sugarcane) arrived in Hawai'i with the early Polynesian settlers. But it wasn't until 1835 that Bostonian William Hooper saw a business opportunity to establish Hawaii's first sugar plantation. Hooper persuaded Honolulu investors to put up the money for his venture and then worked out a deal with Kamehameha III to lease agricultural land at Koloa on Kaua'i. The next order of business was finding an abundant supply of low-cost labor, which was needed to make sugar plantations profitable.

The natural first choice for plantation workers was Hawaiians, but even when willing, they were not enough. Due to introduced diseases like typhoid, influenza, smallpox and syphilis, the Hawaiian population had steadily and precipitously declined. By some estimates around 800,000 indigenous people lived on the islands before Western contact, but by 1800 that had dropped by two-thirds, to around 250,000. By 1860 Hawaiians numbered fewer than 70,000.

Wealthy plantation owners began to look overseas for a labor supply of immigrants accustomed to working long days in hot weather, and for whom the low wages would seem like an opportunity. In the 1850s wealthy sugar-plantation owners began recruiting laborers from China, then Japan and Portugal. After annexing Hawaii in 1898, US restrictions on Chinese and Japanese immigration made O'ahu's plantation owners turn to Puerto Rico, Korea and the Philippines for laborers. Different immigrant groups, along with the shared pidgin language they developed,

1916

The US National Park Service is created by Congress; Hawai'i National Park is established, initially encompassing Haleakalā on Maui, and Kilauea and Mauna Loa on the Big Island.

1921

The Hawaiian Homes Commission Act sets aside 200,000 acres for homesteading by Hawaiians with 50% or more Native Hawaiian blood, granting 99-year leases costing $1 a year.

1922

A distant cousin to one of Hawaii's most powerful missionary families, James Dole becomes the sole landowner of 98% of the island of Lana'i. He starts a pineapple plantation that becomes the world's largest.

1925

The first US military seaplane lands safely in Hawaii. Commercial flights start over a decade later when Pan Am offers the first passenger flights to the islands in 1936.

created a unique plantation community that ultimately transformed Hawaii into the multicultural, multiethnic society it is today.

During California's Gold Rush and later the US Civil War, sugar exports to the mainland soared, making plantation owners wealthier and more powerful. Five sugar-related holding companies, known as the Big Five, came to dominate all aspects of the industry: Castle & Cooke, Alexander & Baldwin, C Brewer & Co, American Factors (today Amfac, Inc), and Theo H Davies & Co. All were run by haole (Caucasian) businessmen, many the sons and grandsons of missionaries, who eventually reached the same conclusion as their forebears: Hawaiians could not be trusted to govern themselves. So, behind closed doors, the Big Five developed plans to relieve Hawaiians of the job.

Farm-born and raised, Gerald Kinro brings personal insight and scholarship to *A Cup of Aloha*, an oral-history portrait of Kona's coffee industry. *Hawai'i's Pineapple Century* by Jan K Ten Bruggencate is another highly readable account of plantation life in Hawaii.

COFFEE

Downfall of the Merrie Monarch

King Kalakaua, who reigned from 1874 to 1891, fought to restore Hawaiian culture and indigenous pride. He resurrected hula and its attendant arts from near extinction. Along with his fondness for drinking, gambling and partying, this earned him the nickname 'the Merrie Monarch' – much to the dismay of Christian missionaries. Foreign businessmen considered his pastimes to be follies, but worse, Kalakaua was a mercurial decision-maker given to replacing his entire cabinet on a whim.

Kalakaua spent money lavishly, piling up massive debts. Wanting Hawai'i's monarchy to equal any in the world, he commissioned 'Iolani Palace, holding an extravagant coronation there in 1883. He also saw Hawai'i playing a role on the global stage, and in 1881 embarked on a trip to meet foreign heads of state and develop stronger ties with Japan especially. When he returned to Hawai'i later that year, he became the first king to have traveled around the world.

Even so, the days of the Hawaiian monarchy were numbered. The 1875 Treaty of Reciprocity, which had made Hawai'i-grown sugar profitable, had expired. Kalakaua refused to renew, as the treaty now contained a provision giving the US a permanent naval base at Pearl Harbor – a provision that Native Hawaiians regarded as a threat to the sovereignty of the kingdom. A secret anti-monarchy group called the Hawaiian League, led by a committee of mostly American lawyers and businessmen, 'presented' Kalakaua with a new constitution in 1887.

This new constitution stripped the monarchy of most of its powers, reducing Kalakaua to a figurehead, and it changed the voting laws to exclude Asians and allow only those who met income and property requirements to vote – effectively disenfranchising all but wealthy, mostly white business owners. Kalakaua signed under threat of violence, earning the document the moniker the 'Bayonet Constitution.' Soon the US got its base at Pearl Harbor, and foreign businessmen consolidated their power.

1927

The $4-million Royal Hawaiian hotel, dubbed the 'Pink Palace,' opens in Waikiki. The arrival of the SS *Malolo* (Flying Fish) luxury liner inaugurates a new era of steamship tourism.

1941

On December 7 Pearl Harbor is attacked by Japanese forces, catapulting the US into WWII. The sinking of the battleship USS *Arizona* kills all 1177 crew members aboard.

1946

On April 1 the most destructive tsunami in Hawaii history (generated by an earthquake in Alaska) kills 159 people across the islands and causes $26 million in property damage.

1949

Dockworkers stage a 177-day strike that halts all shipping to and from Hawaii; this is accompanied by plantation-worker strikes that win concessions from the 'Big Five' companies.

Hawaii's Last Queen & US Annexation

When Kalakaua died while visiting San Francisco, CA, in 1891, his sister and heir, Lili'uokalani, ascended the throne. The queen fought against foreign intervention and control, and she secretly drafted a new constitution to restore Hawaiian voting rights and the monarchy's powers. However, in 1893, before Lili'uokalani could present this, a hastily formed 'Committee of Safety' put in motion the Hawaiian League's long-brewing plans to overthrow the Hawaiian government.

Part political statement, part historical treatise, *To Steal a Kingdom: Probing Hawaiian History* by Michael Dougherty takes a hard look at the legacy of Western colonialism and the lasting impacts of missionary culture on the islands.

First, the Committee of Safety requested support from US Minister John Stevens, who allowed American marines and sailors to come ashore in Honolulu Harbor 'only to protect American citizens in case of resistance.' The Committee's own militia then surrounded 'Iolani Palace and ordered Lili'uokalani to step down. With no standing army and wanting to avoid bloodshed, the last Hawaiian monarch acquiesced under protest.

Immediately after the coup, the Committee of Safety formed a provisional government and requested annexation by the US. Much to the committee's surprise, US President Grover Cleveland refused: he condemned the coup as illegal, conducted under false pretext and against the will of the Hawaiian people, and he requested Lili'uokalani be reinstated. Miffed but unbowed, the Committee instead established their own government, the short-lived Republic of Hawai'i.

For the next five years, Queen Lili'uokalani pressed her case (for a time while under house arrest at 'Iolani Palace), but to no avail. In 1898, spurred by a new US president, William McKinley, Congress annexed the republic as a US territory. In part, the US justified this act of imperialism because the ongoing Spanish-American War had showed the strategic importance of the islands as a Pacific military base. Indeed, some feared that if America didn't take Hawaii, another Pacific Rim power – say, Japan – just might.

Shoal of Time: A History of the Hawaiian Islands by Gavan Daws is an in-depth look at Hawaiian history, from Captain Cook's precipitous arrival in 1778 through the end of the Hawaiian monarchy and post-WWII statehood.

Matson Ships & Waikiki Beachboys

In 1901 WC Weedon, the owner of Waikiki Beach's first resort hotel, the Moana, went on a promotional tour of San Francisco with a stereopticon and daguerreotypes of palm-fringed beaches and smiling 'natives.' Just two years later, 2000 visitors a year were making the nearly five-day journey to Honolulu by sea. Travelers departed San Francisco aboard the Matson Navigation Company's white-painted steamships, inaugurating the so-called 'White Ship Era' that continued until the mid-1930s, when flying made travel by ship passé. By the beginning of WWII, more than 30,000 visitors were landing in Hawaii each year.

1959

Hawaii becomes the 50th US State. Hawaii's Daniel Inouye is the first Japanese American elected to the US Congress, which he serves in continuously until his death in 2012.

1961

Elvis Presley stars in the musical *Blue Hawaii*. Along with *Girls! Girls! Girls!* and *Paradise, Hawaiian Style,* Elvis' on-screen romps set the mood for Hawaii's post-statehood tourism boom.

1962

John Burns is elected governor as Democrats take control of all three branches of state government (including Hawaii's House and Senate), a grip on power they hold until 2002.

1968

Hawaii Five-O begins its 12-year run, becoming one of American TV's longest-running crime dramas. The iconic theme song returns when the prime-time TV series relaunches in 2010.

The Hawaii of popular imagination – lei-draped visitors mangling the hula at a beach luau, tanned beachboys plying the surf in front of Diamond Head, the sounds of *hapa haole* (Hawaiian music with predominantly English lyrics) – was relentlessly commodified. More hotels sprouted along the strand at Waikiki, which had until the late 19th century been a wetland where the *ali'i* retreated for relaxation. The 1927 opening of the Royal Hawaiian Hotel, nicknamed the 'Pink Palace,' transformed Waikiki into a jet-setting tropical destination for the rich and famous, including celebrities of the day: Groucho Marx, Bing Crosby, Bette Davis, Clark Gable and even Shirley Temple.

This was also the era of Duke Kahanamoku, Olympic gold-medal swimmer, master waterman, movie star and Hawaii's unofficial 'ambassador of aloha.' He introduced the world beyond Hawaii's shores to the ancient sport of *he'e nalu* (wave sliding), more familiarly called surfing. Duke was named after his father, who had been christened by Hawaiian princess Bernice Pauahi Bishop in honor of a Scottish lord. Duke Jr grew up swimming and surfing on Waikiki Beach, where he and his 'beachboys' taught tourists to surf, including heiress Doris Duke, who became the first woman to surf competitively.

Pearl Harbor & the 'Japanese Problem'

In the years leading up to WWII, the US government became obsessed with the Territory of Hawaii's 'Japanese problem.' What, they wondered, were the true loyalties of 40% of Hawaii's population, the *issei* (first-generation Japanese immigrants), who had been born in Japan? During a war, would they fight for Japan or defend the US? Neither fully Japanese nor American, their children, island-born *nisei* (second-generation Japanese immigrants), also had their identity questioned.

On December 7, 1941, a surprise Japanese force of ships, submarines and aircraft bombed and attacked military installations across O'ahu. The main target was Pearl Harbor, the USA's most important Pacific naval base. This devastating attack, in which dozens of ships were damaged or lost and more than 3000 military and civilians were killed or injured, instantly propelled the US into WWII. In Hawaii, the US Army took control, martial law was declared and civil rights were suspended.

A coalition of forces in Hawaii resisted immense federal government pressure, including from President Roosevelt, to carry out a mass internment of Japanese on the islands, similar to what was being done on the US West Coast. Although around 1250 people were unjustly detained in internment camps on O'ahu, the majority of Hawaii's 160,000 Japanese citizens were spared incarceration – although they did suffer racial discrimination and deep suspicions about their loyalties. Hawaii's multiethnic society emerged from WWII severely strained, but not broken.

HAWAII CALLS

The popular radio program *Hawaii Calls* introduced the world to Hawaiian music. It broadcast from the banyan tree courtyard of Waikiki's Moana hotel between 1935 and 1975. CD compilations are available through www.mele.com.

1971

The Merrie Monarch hula festival, begun in 1964, holds its first competitive hula competition; part of a Hawaiian cultural renaissance, it becomes a proving ground for serious hula practitioners.

1976

Native Hawaiian sovereignty activists illegally occupy the island of Kaho'olawe. The *Hokule'a* – a reproduction of an ancient Polynesian voyaging canoe – sails to Tahiti and back.

1978

The 1978 Constitutional Convention establishes the Office of Hawaiian Affairs (OHA), which holds the Hawaiian Home Lands in trust to be used for the benefit of Native Hawaiians.

1983

Kilauea volcano begins its current eruption cycle, now the longest in recorded history; eruptions have destroyed the entire village of Kalapana, various residential subdivisions and a coastal road.

In 1943 the federal government was persuaded to reverse itself and approve the formation of an all-Japanese combat unit, the 100th Infantry Battalion. Thousands of *nisei* volunteers were sent, along with the all-Japanese 442nd Regimental Combat Team, to fight in Europe, where they became two of the most decorated units in US military history. By the war's end, Roosevelt proclaimed these soldiers were proof that 'Americanism is a matter of mind and heart; Americanism is not, and never was, a matter of race or ancestry.' The 1950s and '60s would test this noble sentiment.

In *Strangers from a Different Shore,* Ronald Takaki tells the story of the USA's Asian immigrant communities, from Hawaii's plantation laborers to the effects of WWII on racial discrimination and modern attitudes toward multiculturalism.

A Long, Bumpy Road to Statehood

The end of WWII brought Hawaii closer to the center stage of American culture and politics. Three decades had passed since Prince Jonah Kuhio Kalaniana'ole, Hawaii's first delegate to the US Congress, introduced a Hawaii statehood bill in 1919, which received a cool reception in Washington, DC. Despite its key role in WWII, Hawaii was viewed as too much of a racial melting pot for many US politicians to support statehood.

After WWII and during the Cold War, Southern Democrats in particular raised the specter that Hawaiian statehood would leave the US open not just to the 'Yellow Peril' (embodied, as they saw it, by imperialist Japan), but also to Chinese and Russian communist infiltration through Hawaii's labor unions. Further, they feared that Hawaii would elect Asian politicians who would seek to end racial segregation, then legal on the US mainland. Conversely, proponents of statehood for Hawaii increasingly saw it as a necessary civil rights step to prove that the US actually practiced 'equality for all.'

In the late 1950s Alaska narrowly beat out Hawaii to be admitted as the 49th state. With more than 90% of island residents voting for statehood, Hawaii finally became the USA's 50th state on August 21, 1959. A few years later, surveying Hawaii's relative ethnic harmony, President John Kennedy pronounced, 'Hawaii is what the rest of the world is striving to be.' In the 1960s Hawaii's two Asian American senators – WWII veteran and *nisei* Daniel Inouye and Honolulu-born Hiram Fong – helped secure the passage of America's landmark civil rights legislation.

For a history of Hawaii you can finish on the flight over, *A Concise History of the Hawaiian Islands* by Phil Barnes captures a surprising amount of nuance in fewer than 90 pages.

Statehood had an immediate economic impact and Hawaii's timing was remarkably fortuitous. The decline of sugar and pineapple plantations in the 1960s – due in part to the labor concessions won by Hawaii's unions – left the state scrambling economically. But the advent of the jet airplane meant tourists could become Hawaii's next staple crop. Tourism exploded, which led to a decades-long cycle of building booms. By 1970 over one million tourists each year were generating $1 billion annually for the state, surpassing both agriculture and federal military spending.

1990

After much litigation and more than a decade of grassroots Hawaiian activism, the US Navy is forced to stop bombing Kaho'olawe. Control over that island isn't officially returned to the state of Hawaii until 2003.

1992

On September 11 Hurricane 'Iniki slams into Kaua'i, demolishing almost 1500 buildings and damaging 5000, causing $1.8 billion in damage. Miraculously, only a few people are killed.

1993

On the 100-year anniversary of the Hawaiian monarchy being overthrown, President Clinton signs the 'Apology Resolution,' which acknowledges the US government's role in the kingdom's illegal takeover.

2000

US Senator Daniel Akaka first introduces the Native Hawaiian Government Reorganization Act (the 'Akaka Bill'), asking for federal recognition of Native Hawaiians as indigenous people.

Hawaiian Renaissance & Sovereignty Movement

By the 1970s Hawaii's rapid growth meant new residents (mostly mainland 'transplants') and tourists were crowding island beaches and roads, and runaway construction was rapidly transforming resorts such as Waikiki almost beyond recognition. The relentless peddling of 'aloha' got some island-born and -raised *kama'aina* wondering: what did it mean to be Hawaiian? Some Native Hawaiians turned to *kapuna* (elders) to recover their heritage, and in doing so became more politically assertive.

In 1976 a group of activists illegally occupied Kaho'olawe, aka 'Target Island,' which the US government had taken during WWII and used for bombing practice ever since. During another protest occupation attempt in 1977, two activist members of the Protect Kaho'olawe 'Ohana (PKO) – George Helm and Kimo Mitchell – disappeared at sea, instantly becoming martyrs. Saving Kaho'olawe became a rallying cry, and it radicalized a nascent Native Hawaiian rights movement that continues today.

When the state held its landmark Constitutional Convention in 1978, it passed several amendments of special importance to Native Hawaiians. For example, it made Hawaiian the official state language (along with English) and mandated that Hawaiian culture be taught in public schools. At the grassroots level, the islands were simultaneously experiencing a revival of Hawaiian culture, with a surge in residents – of all ethnicities – joining hula *halau* (schools), learning to play Hawaiian music and rediscovering traditional island crafts such as feather lei-making.

Today, asking the US federal government to recognize Native Hawaiians as an indigenous people, which would give them similar legal status as Native American tribes, is widely supported in Hawaii. But there is great controversy over what shape Hawaiian sovereignty should take and who exactly qualifies as Native Hawaiian. Even so, the issue of Hawaiian sovereignty, as retired US senator Daniel Akaka said, 'is important for all people of Hawaii…to finally resolve the longstanding issues from a dark period in Hawaii's history, the overthrow of the Kingdom of Hawai'i.'

To keep in touch with contemporary issues that are important to the Hawaiian community, both in the islands and in the global diaspora, browse the independent news and culture magazine *Mana* (www.welivemana.com).

2002

Partly as a voter response to Democratic Party corruption scandals, mainland-born Linda Lingle is elected Hawaii's first Republican governor in 40 years. She is re-elected in 2006.

2006

Papahanaumokuakea Marine National Monument, protecting the rich yet fragile reef ecosystem of the remote Northwestern Hawaiian Islands, is established. It's designated a World Heritage Site in 2010.

2012

Born and raised on O'ahu, US President Barack Obama is re-elected. Just as in the 2008 presidential election, Obama wins over 70% of the vote in Hawaii, more than in any other state.

2013

After much public debate and extended hearings before the state legislature in Honolulu, Hawaii joins a growing number of US states to legalize same-sex marriage.

Hawaii's People

Whatever your postcard tropical idyll might be – a paradise of white sandy beaches, emerald cliffs and azure seas; of falsetto-voiced ukulele strummers, bare-shouldered hula dancers and sun-bronzed surfers – it exists somewhere on these islands. But beyond the frame-edges of that magical postcard is a startlingly different version of Hawaii, a real place where a multicultural mixed plate of everyday people work and live.

Mary Kawena Pukui's *Folktales of Hawai'i* (1995), illustrated by island artist Sig Zane, is a delightful bilingual collection of ancient teaching stories and amusing tall tales.

Island Life Today

Hawaii may be a Polynesian paradise, but it's one with shopping malls, landfills and industrial parks, cookie-cutter housing developments and sprawling military bases. In many ways, it's much like the rest of the USA. A first-time visitor stepping off the plane may be surprised to find a thoroughly modern place where interstate highways and McDonald's look pretty much the same as back on 'da mainland.'

Underneath the veneer of consumer culture and the tourist industry is a different world, defined by – and proud of – its separateness, its geographic isolation and its unique blend of Polynesian, Asian and Western traditions. While those cultures don't always merge seamlessly in Hawaii, there are few places in the world where so many ethnicities, with no single group commanding a majority, get along.

Perhaps it's because they live on tiny islands in the middle of a vast ocean that Hawaii residents strive to treat one another with aloha, act politely and respectfully, and 'make no waves' (ie be cool). As the Hawaiian saying goes, 'We're all in the same canoe.' No matter their race or background, residents share a common bond: an awareness of living in one of the planet's most bewitchingly beautiful places.

Local vs Mainland Attitudes

Hawaii often seems overlooked by the other 49 states (except maybe by Alaska, the mainland's other oddball younger sibling), yet it's protective of its separateness. This has both advantages and disadvantages. On the up side, there's a genuine appreciation for Hawaii's uniqueness. On the down side, it reinforces an insider-outsider mentality that in its darkest moments manifests as exclusivity or, worse, blatant discrimination.

What does it mean to be Hawaiian today? Read Sally-Jo Bowman's *The Heart of Being Hawaiian* (2008), a moving collection of reflections, articles and interviews that explore this question with unsentimental tenderness.

Mainland transplants tend to stick out, even after they've lived in the islands for some time. For example, as a rule, loud assertiveness is discouraged in Hawaii, where it's better to avoid confrontation and 'save face' by keeping quiet. In a stereotype that's often true, the most vocal and passionate speakers – say, at a community meeting or a political rally – may be mainland activists who just moved in. No matter how long they live here, those folks will never be considered 'local.'

Locals take justifiable umbrage at outsiders who presume to know what's good for Hawaii better than they do. To get anywhere in Hawaii, it's better to show aloha – and a bit of deference – toward people who were island-born and raised, popularly called *kama'aina*.

WHO'S WHO ON THE ISLANDS

Hawaiian A person of Native Hawaiian ancestry. It's a faux pas to call just any Hawaii resident 'Hawaiian' (as you would a Californian or Texan), thus semantically ignoring the islands' indigenous people.

Local A person who grew up in Hawaii. Locals who move away retain their local 'cred,' at least in part. But transplant residents never become local, even once they've lived in the islands for many years. To call a transplant 'almost local' is a compliment, despite its emphasis on an insider-outsider mentality.

Malihini 'Newcomer,' someone who's just moved to Hawaii and intends to stay.

Resident A person who lives, but might not have been born and raised, in Hawaii.

Haole White person (except local Portuguese people); further subdivided as 'mainland' or 'local' haole. Can be insulting or playful, depending on the context.

Hapa A person of mixed ancestry; *hapa* is Hawaiian for 'half.' A common racial designation is *hapa haole* (part white and part other, such as Hawaiian and/or Asian).

Kama'aina Literally a 'child of the land.' A person who is native to a particular place, eg a Hilo native is a *kama'aina* of Hilo, not Kona. The term connotes a deep connection to a place. In a commercial context, *kama'aina* discounts apply to any resident of Hawaii (ie anyone with a Hawaii driver's license).

Island Identity

Honolulu is 'the city,' not only for those who live on O'ahu but for all of Hawaii. Far slower paced than NYC or LA, Hawaii's capital can still be surprisingly cosmopolitan, technologically savvy and fashion-conscious. Rightly or wrongly, Honoluluans see themselves at the center of everything; they have sports stadiums, the state's premier university and actual (if relatively tame) nightlife. Kaua'i, Maui, Hawai'i (the Big Island), Lana'i and especially Moloka'i are considered 'country.' That said, in a landscape as compressed as Hawaii, 'country' is a relative term. Rural areas tend not to be too far from the urban or suburban, and there are no vast swaths of uninterrupted wilderness like on the US mainland.

Neighbor Island residents tend to dress more casually and speak more pidgin. Status isn't measured by a Lexus but by a lifted pick-up truck. *'Ohana* (extended family and friends) is important everywhere, but on the islands it's often the center of one's life. When locals first meet, they usually don't ask 'What do you do?' but 'Where you wen' grad?' (Where did you graduate from high school?). Like ancient Hawaiians comparing genealogies, locals often define themselves not by their accomplishments but by the communities to which they belong: island, town, high school.

In *Folks You Meet in Longs and Other Stories* (2005), local newspaper columnist, novelist and playwright Lee Cataluna captures the flavor and the voice of working-class Hawaii in side-splittingly funny, exquisitely real monologues.

Regardless of where they're from within the state, when two locals happen to meet each other outside Hawaii, there's often an automatic bond based on mutual affection and nostalgic longing for their island home – wherever they go, they belong to Hawaii's all-embracing *'ohana*.

Diversity & Values

During the 2012 US presidential election, island residents were thrilled that someone from Hawaii was re-elected president (*'Hana hou*!' read the front-page headline in the *Honolulu Star-Advertiser* newspaper, meaning 'bravo' or 'encore'). Barack Obama, who spent most of his boyhood in Honolulu, was embraced by local voters because his calm demeanor and respect for diversity represent Hawaii values. It also didn't hurt that he can bodysurf, and, more importantly, that he displayed true devotion to his *'ohana*. His grandmother, who lived in Honolulu, died one day before the 2008 election – Obama suspended his campaign to visit her before she passed. To many locals, these are the things that count.

What didn't matter to Hawaii is what the rest of the country seemed fixated on: his race. That Obama is of mixed-race parentage was barely worth mentioning. *Of course* he's mixed race – who in Hawaii isn't? One legacy of the plantation era is Hawaii's unselfconscious mixing of ethnicities. Cultural differences are freely acknowledged, even carefully maintained, but they don't normally divide people. For residents, the relaxed lifestyle and inclusive cultural values are probably the most defining, best-loved aspects of island life. Depending on your perspective, Honolulu is either America's most Asian city or Polynesia's most American city.

To learn more about *mahu* in Polynesian culture and their experience in modern Hawaii, read Andrew Metzner's collection of spoken narratives, *'O Au No Keia: Voices from Hawai'i's Mahu and Transgender Communities* (2001).

Among the older generation of locals, plantation-era stereotypes still inform social hierarchies and interactions. During plantation days, whites were the wealthy plantation owners, and for years after minorities would joke about the privileges that came with being a haole *luna* (Caucasian boss). But in a growing generational divide, Hawaii's youth often dismiss these distinctions even as they continue to speak pidgin. As intermarriage increases, racial distinctions become even more blurred. It's not uncommon nowadays to meet locals who can rattle off four or five different ethnicities in their ancestry – Hawaiian, Chinese, Portuguese, Filipino and Caucasian, for example.

Hawaii is as ethnically diverse as California, Texas or Florida – and more racially intermixed – but it's noticeably missing the significant African American and Latino populations that help define those other states and most multiculturalism on the mainland. Politically, the majority of

HAOLE

Depending upon the context, the Hawaiian word haole can be merely descriptive, warm or insulting. Originally it meant 'foreigner,' anything (person or object) exotic to the islands, but later it came to denote Caucasian people.

No one's sure why ancient Hawaiians used this word to describe Captain Cook and his crew or what they meant by it. A popular explanation is that the British explorer didn't *honi* (share breath) with Hawaiians. In ancient Polynesia and still today, Hawaiians often greet one another by touching noses and breathing together. Breath (*hā* in Hawaiian) is considered an expression of life force, and exchanging it is a gesture of respect and welcome. Instead the British kept their distance, shaking hands; thus it's reasoned the Hawaiians called them 'haole,' meaning 'without breath' – somewhat of an insult. Another explanation is that the British would speak after praying, saying 'amen,' rather than breathing three times after *pule* (prayer) as Hawaiians would.

Other experts challenge these explanations on linguistic grounds. In Hawaiian, glottal stops and long vowels are critical to a word's meaning. The word for 'without breath' is 'hā'ole,' not 'haole.' Transcriptions of ancient chants indicate that 'haole' meant 'foreign,' and that the word was used before the British arrived.

Regardless of how it happened, today haole means 'white person,' particularly one of European descent (excluding local Portuguese, who were part of Hawaii's plantation labor force). If you're called haole, don't automatically let your lily-white skin turn red with anger; in many cases, it's a completely neutral descriptive term, as in 'See that haole guy over there?' Sometimes it's playful, as in 'Howzit haole boy/girl!' Some local white people describe themselves as haole, often with self-deprecating humor. But if someone calls you a 'stupid haole,' you can be reasonably sure they meant to insult both your intelligence and your race.

Much less ambiguous is the phrase to 'act haole.' This describes people of any color who are condescending, presumptuous or demanding – deriving from islanders' experiences with pushy visitors and transplants. If someone tells you to 'stop acting haole,' you'd better dial it down a notch.

Hawaii residents are middle-of-the-road Democrats who vote along party, racial/ethnic, seniority and local/nonlocal lines. As more mainland transplants arrive, conservative Republican candidates – such as Hawaii's former governor Linda Lingle – stand a better chance.

Ethnic Tensions

In Hawaii, tensions among ethnicities, while they exist, are typically more benign and rarely violent compared with racial strife on the mainland. Among locals, island stereotypes are the subject of affectionate humor, eg talkative Portuguese, stingy Chinese, goody-goody Japanese and know-it-all haoles. Hawaii's comedians often use such stereotypes to hilarious comic effect. When racial conflict occurs, it's usually incidental to some other beef – if a white surfer cuts off a Hawaiian on a wave, the Hawaiian might curse the 'f'n haole.' But rarely is anyone insulted or attacked merely *because* of their race.

Things shift when nonlocals enter the picture, because they aren't always sensitive to Hawaii's colonial history and may not appreciate island ways. For instance, while the legitimacy of Hawaiian pidgin as a language has many challengers, the loudest critics are often mainlanders who don't speak it. In general, tourists and transplants are welcomed in the islands but have to earn trust by being *pono* – respectful and proper.

Religion & Sexual Orientation

Hawaii's values of tolerance and acceptance extend beyond race – they apply also to religion and sexual orientation. The overwhelming majority of locals are Christian, but there are also substantial Buddhist communities as well as small populations of Jews, Muslims and Hindus. Mutual respect and acceptance among islanders of different faiths is the rule, not the exception. Even for devout Christians, religion often isn't a matter of rigid orthodoxy; many Hawaiians combine indigenous beliefs and ancient practices with modern Christianity.

Until the state legislature passed the Hawaii Marriage Equality Act legalizing same-sex marriage in 2013, Hawaii was politically behind the curve in its treatment of gay, lesbian and transgendered people, but in practice there is little visible discrimination. In fact, in traditional Hawaiian culture, the *mahu* (a transgendered or cross-dressing male) has been regarded as a figure of power and mystery.

LIFE EXPECTANCY

What makes Hawaii *no ka 'oi*, or 'the best'? Maybe it's that Hawaii residents have the longest life expectancy in the US: 81 years, compared with the national average of 78.

Island Style

'On the islands, we do it island style,' sings local musician John Cruz in his slack key guitar anthem to life in Hawaii. While he doesn't say explicitly what 'island style' means, he doesn't have to; every local understands. Island style is easygoing, low-key, casual; even guitar strings are more relaxed. Islanders take pride in being laid-back – that everything happens on 'island time' (a euphemism for taking things slow or being late), that aloha shirts are preferred over suits and that a *tutu* (grandmother) will hold up a line to chat with the checkout person at Longs Drugs (and that no one waiting seems to mind). 'Slow down! This ain't da mainland!' reads one popular bumper sticker.

Even in urban Honolulu, the 54th largest US city, with a population of almost 350,000, there's something of a small-town vibe. Shave ice, surfing, 'talking story,' ukulele, hula, baby luau, pidgin, broken-down 'rubbah slippah' (flip-flops) and particularly *'ohana* – these are touchstones of everyday life, which tends to be family-oriented. School sporting events are packed with eager parents plus the gamut of aunties and uncles (whether they're actual relatives or not). Working overtime is uncommon, and weekends are saved for playing and potlucks at the beach.

DOS & DON'TS FOR ISLAND VISITORS

➡ Don't try to speak pidgin – unless you're *really* good at it.

➡ Do liberally wave the *shaka* (Hawaii's hand greeting sign).

➡ Do take off your shoes when entering a home (most residents wear rubbah slippah partly for this reason – easy to slip on and off, no socks required).

➡ Don't overdress. For example, you'll see male executives wear Tori Richard aloha shirts and slacks to high-power business meetings.

➡ Do ask permission before you pick fruit or flowers from trees on private property.

➡ Don't be pushy. You'll get what you want (this time), but you'll get no aloha with it.

➡ Do drive slowly. Locals rarely have far to go, and they drive that way. In fact, do everything slowly.

➡ Unless you're about to hit someone, don't honk your car horn. That's a sure way to attract 'stink eye.'

➡ Don't refer to Maui, Kaua'i, Moloka'i, Lana'i and Hawai'i (the Big Island) as 'outer islands,' which is O'ahu-centric. They're called 'Neighbor Islands.'

➡ Do try to correctly pronounce Hawaiian place names and words. Even if you fail, the attempt is appreciated. If you aren't sure how to say it, ask. Even long names aren't that hard with a little practice.

➡ Don't grumble about high prices. You're (probably) not being gouged by the local business owner: 80% of Hawaii's consumer goods must be shipped in, which adds significantly to the cost. If you're miffed about paying $8 for a gallon of milk, think about how residents feel.

➡ Do visit a farmers market. It's an awesome way to interact with locals and try some delicious local produce – some of which might be new to you.

➡ Don't freak out at every gecko and cockroach. It's the tropics. There are critters.

➡ Don't collect (or even move) stones at sacred sites. If you're not sure whether something's sacred, consider that in Hawaiian thinking, *everything* is sacred, especially in nature.

➡ Don't stack rocks or wrap them in *ti* leaves at waterfalls, heiau (temples) etc. This is a bastardization of the Hawaiian practice of leaving *ho'okupu* (offerings) at sacred sites – and it's littering the islands' fragile environment.

Health, Wealth & Homelessness

By most social indicators, life is good. In 2014 Hawaii was ranked the healthiest state in the nation, with high immunization rates and lower than average rates of smoking. Over 90% of residents have graduated from high school, and nearly 30% have a bachelor's degree or higher (both above the national average). Unemployment, which dropped to 4.3% in mid-2014, and violent crime rates are also lower than the national average. Despite the mass quantities of Spam consumed in the islands, Hawaii had the second-lowest obesity rate in the US in 2013 – only Colorado, another outdoors-oriented lifestyle state, did better. In 2012 Hawaii's median annual household income ($66,259) ranked sixth and its poverty rate (11.6%) was seventh lowest among US states.

Those last statistics, however, gloss over glaring inequity in the distribution of wealth. There are a large number of wealthy locals and mainland transplants with magnificent estates and vacation homes skewing the average, while a much larger number of locals, particularly Pacific Islanders, struggle with poverty and all the social challenges that come with it. The state is currently trying to control one of the highest rates of ice (crystal methamphetamine) abuse in the US, a problem that leads to illness, unemployment, robberies and violent crimes.

Homelessness remains another serious concern: on average, more than 6300 people are homeless statewide. Most telling about the cost of living in Hawaii is the following statistic: up to 42% of its homeless people are employed, but still can't make ends meet. Sprawling tent communities have popped up at beach parks and other public areas. Every now and then police disperse them, but the problem is never solved – only moved. Hale o Malama, the state's new strategic plan for ending homelessness, aims to more closely coordinate among city, county, state and federal agencies that offer emergency housing, medical services and social support to Hawaii's homeless population. At the same time, the state is giving free plane tickets to some homeless people in Waikiki so that they can fly back to wherever they came from on the mainland – a proposal that is politically controversial, not to mention expensive.

Costs of Living & Commuting

Honolulu has the third-highest cost of living among US cities (behind New York City's Manhattan and Brooklyn boroughs). Utility bills average almost double those on the mainland, and grocery bills are also exorbitant because over 85% of all food is imported. Limited land area (especially in a place where 20% of the land is controlled by the US military) has led to sky-high real-estate prices, and many locals are unable to buy a home. In 2013 the median price of a single-family home in Hawaii was $665,000, compared with $257,000 nationally. One study found that renters and homeowners in Hawaii spend almost 25% of their income on housing, which is significantly higher than the US average. The most affordable housing isn't close to the majority of jobs, which are near tourist resort areas, and this results in long commutes and nightmarish traffic jams. After years of controversy and delays, Honolulu's multibillion-dollar light-rail system, which is expected to begin service in 2018, should help relieve at least some traffic congestion on O'ahu.

Hawaii almost leads the nation in shared housing: 28% of young adults live with parents or relatives, compared with 24% nationally. So don't be surprised by how many pairs of rubbah slippah are left by the front door at the next island home you visit!

Hawaiians, Locals & Tourism

Hawaiians are still struggling with the colonial legacy that has marginalized them in their own homeland. They constitute a disproportionate number of Hawaii's homeless (over one-third) and impoverished residents. Their children lag behind state averages in reading and math and are more likely to drop out of school. Hawaiian charter schools were created in part to address this problem and they have demonstrated some remarkable success using alternative, culturally relevant approaches. However, many Hawaiians feel that some form of political sovereignty is necessary to correct these deeply entrenched inequities.

The socioeconomic stresses of everyday life – along with having to deal with a constant flow of tourists purchasing temporary paradise at resorts that many locals could never afford – can sap the aloha of residents. For many locals and Hawaiians in particular, tourism is a Faustian bargain at best; with it comes jobs and economic stability, but many question whether it's worth the cost.

Yet whatever difficulties arise, finding someone who'd prefer to live somewhere else is hardest of all. No matter what comes, locals say, 'Lucky you live Hawaii.'

Hawaii's Cuisine

Forget pineapple-topped pizza: Hawaii's cuisine is no cliché. It's a multicultural flavor explosion, influenced by the Pacific Rim and rooted in the islands' natural bounty. The first Polynesians brought nourishing staples such as *kalo* (taro) and *niu* (coconut). Later, plantation-era immigrants imported rice, *shōyu* (soy sauce), chilies and more. Over time, all these wildly different flavors fused to become 'local,' which you can taste in a heaping island-style plate lunch.

The Island 'Diet'

Edible Hawaiian Islands (www.ediblehawaiianislands.com), a colorful quarterly magazine, focuses on Hawaii's locavore movement and foodie trends. It's available free at many local restaurants, gourmet food shops and natural-foods grocery stores.

Before human contact, the only indigenous island edibles were ferns and *ohelo* berries. In their wooden canoes, Polynesians brought *kalo, niu, 'ulu* (breadfruit), *'uala* (sweet potato), *mai'a* (banana) and *ko* (sugarcane), as well as chickens, pigs and dogs for meat, and they harvested an abundance of seafood from the ocean.

Starting in the 18th century, European explorers dropped off cattle and goats, while later American missionaries imported the tropical fruits, such as pineapple, that have come to symbolize Hawaii. When the sugar industry rose in the late 19th century – bringing waves of immigrants from China, Japan, Portugal, Puerto Rico, Korea and the Philippines – Hawaii's cuisine developed an identity all of its own. It mixed in imported ingredients, especially from around Asia, but never abandoned Hawaiian staples such as *kalua* pork and *poi* (steamed, mashed taro).

What does all this mean for visitors? Always sample the unknown during your trip, take another bite and travel the world on a single plate. Hawaii isn't a place to diet – it's a *broke da mout* (delicious) reward.

Local Food

Cheap, tasty and filling, local food is the stuff of cravings and comfort. A classic example of Hawaii's ubiquitous plate lunch would be chunky layers of tender *kalua* pork, a dollop of smooth, creamy macaroni salad and two hearty scoops of white rice. Of course, the pork can be swapped for just about any other protein, maybe Korean-style *kalbi* short ribs, Japanese *mochiko* (rice flour batter-fried) chicken or *furikake*-encrusted mahimahi. Health-conscious eaters can often substitute tossed greens and brown rice for the sides. A favorite breakfast combo is fried eggs with Portuguese sausage or Spam and, always, two-scoop rice.

Sticky white rice is more than a side dish in Hawaii. It's a culinary building block, an integral partner in everyday meals. Without rice, Spam *musubi* would just be a slice of canned meat. The *loco moco* (rice, fried egg and hamburger patty topped with gravy or other condiments) would be nothing more than an egg-covered hamburger. And without two-scoop rice, the plate lunch would be just a ho-hum conversation between meat and macaroni salad. Just so you know, sticky white rice means exactly that. Not fluffy rice. Not wild rice. And definitely *not* instant.

Snacks & Sweets

Pupu is the local term used for all kinds of snacks, munchies and appetizers. Especially on bar menus, *pupu* often represent the ethnic diversity of the islands, for example, boiled peanuts flavored with Chinese star anise or salted Japanese edamame (boiled fresh soybeans in the pod). Not to be missed is *poke,* a savory dish of bite-sized, cubed raw fish – ahi (yellowfin or bigeye tuna) is perennially popular. Although *poke* comes in a huge variety of flavors, it's traditionally seasoned with *shōyu,* sesame oil, green onion, chili-pepper flakes, sea salt, *ogo* (seaweed) and/or *'inamona,* a Hawaiian condiment made of roasted, ground *kukui* (candlenut).

An old-fashioned, locally made candy is mouth-watering Chinese crack seed. It's preserved fruit (typically plum, cherry, mango or lemon) that, like Coca-Cola or curry, is impossible to describe. It can be sweet, sour, salty or licorice-spicy. Sold prepackaged at supermarkets, convenience stores and pharmacies, like Longs Drugs, or dished out by the pound at specialty shops, crack seed is mouthwatering and addictive.

On a hot day, nothing beats shave ice. It's *not* just a snow cone: the ice is shaved as fine as powdery snow, packed into a paper cup and drenched with sweet flavored syrups in an eye-popping rainbow of hues. For decadence, add a scoop of ice cream, sweet red azuki beans or soft *mochi* (Japanese pounded-rice cakes) underneath, or maybe *haupia* coconut cream, a dusting of powdered *li hing mui* (salty dried plums) or *halo halo* (Filipino-style mixed fruit) on top.

Best Shave Ice

Matsumoto's, O'ahu

Ululani's Hawaiian Shave Ice, Maui

Anuenue, Hawai'i (Big Island)

Waiola Shave Ice, O'ahu

Fresh Shave, Kaua'i

Original Big Island Shave Ice Co, Inc. Hawai'i (Big Island)

Hawaiian Traditions

With its earthy flavors and Polynesian ingredients, Hawaiian cooking is like no other. *Kalua* pig is traditionally roasted whole underground in an *imu,* a pit of red-hot stones layered with banana and *ti* leaves. Cooked this way, the pork is smoky, salty and succulent. Nowadays *kalua* pork is typically oven-roasted and seasoned with salt and liquid smoke. At commercial luau, a pig placed in an *imu* is usually only for show (it couldn't feed 300-plus guests anyway).

Poi – a purplish paste made of pounded taro root, often steamed and fermented – was sacred to ancient Hawaiians. Taro is highly nutritious, low in calories, easily digestible and versatile to prepare. Tasting bland to mildly tart or even sour, *poi* is usually not eaten by itself, but as a starchy counterpoint to strongly flavored dishes such as *lomilomi* salmon (minced, salted salmon with diced tomato and green onion).

SPAM-TASTIC!

Hawaii may be the only place in the USA where you can eat Hormel's iconic canned meat with pride. Here in the nation's Spam capital, locals consume almost seven million cans per year.

Of course, Spam looks and tastes different in Hawaii. It is always eaten cooked (typically fried to a light crispiness in sugar-sweetened *shōyu*), not straight from the can, and often served as a tasty breakfast dish with eggs and rice.

A pork-based meat product, Spam was first canned in 1937 and introduced to Hawaii during WWII, when the islands were under martial law. During that period fresh meat imports were replaced by this standard GI ration. By the time the war ended, Hawaiians had developed an affinity for the fatty canned stuff.

One common preparation is Spam *musubi:* a block of rice with a slice of cooked Spam on top (or in the middle), wrapped with nori (Japanese dried seaweed). Created in the 1960s, it has become a classic, and thousands of *musubi* are sold daily at island grocers, lunch counters and convenience stores.

Check out Honolulu's Waikiki Spam Jam (p115) festival in late April or early May. For Spam trivia, recipes, games and more, go to www.spam.com.

A common main dish is *laulau*, a bundle of pork or chicken and salted butterfish wrapped in taro or *ti* leaves and steamed until it has a soft sautéed spinach-like texture. Other traditional Hawaiian fare includes baked *'ulu* (breadfruit), with a mouthfeel similar to a potato; *'opihi*, tiny mollusks called limpets that are picked off reefs at low tide; *pipi kaula* (beef jerky); and *haupia*, a coconut-cream custard thickened with arrowroot or cornstarch.

Hawaii Regional Cuisine

Hawaii was once considered a culinary backwater. That is, until the early 1990s, when a handful of island chefs – including Alan Wong, Roy Yamaguchi, Sam Choy, Bev Gannon and Peter Merriman, all of whom still have their own popular island restaurants – created a new cuisine, borrowing liberally from Hawaii's multiethnic heritage. These chefs partnered with island farmers, ranchers and fishers to highlight fresh, local ingredients, and transformed childhood favorites into gourmet Pacific Rim masterpieces. Suddenly macadamia-nut-crusted mahimahi, miso-glazed butterfish and *liliko'i* (passion fruit) anything were all the rage.

Learn about local agriculture, farm tours, farmers markets and more on the Hawaii Organic Farming Association (HOFA) website, www.hawaiiorganic.org.

This culinary movement was dubbed 'Hawaii Regional Cuisine' and its 12 pioneering chefs became celebrities. Back then HRC was rather exclusive, found only at high-end dining rooms. Its hallmarks included Eurasian fusion flavors, gastronomic techniques and elaborate plating. In the early 21st century, the focus began shifting toward island-grown, organic, seasonal and handpicked ingredients. Upscale restaurants are still the mainstay for star chefs, but now you'll find neighborhood bistros and even plate-lunch food trucks serving dishes inspired by Hawaii Regional Cuisine, with island farms lauded like designer brands on menus.

Hawaii's Locavore Movement

A whopping 85% to 90% of Hawaii's food is imported. Now, a growing number of small-scale farmers are trying to shift the agriculture industry away from corporate-scale, industrialized monocropping (eg sugar, pineapple) enabled by chemical fertilizers, pesticides and herbicides. Instead,

HAWAII'S HOME-GROWN BOUNTY

Today, outstanding island farms are lauded like designer brands on local restaurant menus. There are way too many notables to name, but here are a few:

Hawai'i, the Big Island Hamakua Coast mushrooms and vanilla; tomatoes and salad greens from Hamakua Springs Country Farms; *kampachi* (yellowtail) from Kampachi Farms and Big Island Abalone from the Kona coast; Kona-grown coffee and chocolate; Mauna Kea Tea; Tea Hawaii & Company in Volcano; and Ka'u coffee and oranges.

Kaua'i Goat cheese from the North Shore's Kaua'i Kunana Dairy; grass-fed beef from Medeiros Farm and Kauai Coffee Company coffee from Kalaheo; Kilauea honey and Kolo Kai Organic Farm's fresh ginger; Hanalei-grown taro; Salty Wahine sea salts; Yoshii Farms' tropical fruit; Taro Ko Chips from Hanapepe; pork from Kaneshiro Farms; and red-fleshed Sunrise papayas.

Maui Grass-fed beef from Maui Cattle Co; Surfing Goat Dairy cheese, 'Ulupalakua Ranch elk meat and Kula Country Farms' strawberries and onions, all from the Upcountry; Maui Brand natural cane sugar; and Ka'anapali Estate's MauiGrown Coffee.

Moloka'i Organic fruit, veggies and herbs from Kumu Farms; coffee from Coffees of Hawaii; Pacifica Hawai'i sea salt; Moloka'i Meli honey; and macadamia nuts from Purdy's.

O'ahu Salad greens from Nalo Farms in Waimanalo; grass-fed beef from North Shore Cattle Co; tomatoes from North Shore Farms; Wailalua coffee, vanilla and chocolate; Manoa honey; sweet corn from Kahuku; 'Ewa-grown melons; and orange-flesh Kamiya papayas.

family farms around the islands are growing diverse crops for high-end restaurants and also for sale locally, including at busy farmers markets.

Many scientific and state government reports suggest, unsurprisingly, that an increase in production and consumption of locally grown food will benefit Hawaii in four areas: food security (popularly called 'food sovereignty'), the regional economy, the vitality of the land and water, and community pride. Furthering these goals is a grassroots political campaign to label GMOs (genetically modified organisms) and possibly exclude them from the islands' food supply chain.

But convincing consumers isn't always easy. Locals tend to buy whatever is cheapest and often balk at paying for fruit they see falling off neighborhood trees. And supermarket chains typically prefer to stock blemish-free Sunkist oranges and California grapes. A notable exception is the Big Island's KTA Superstore, a mini-chain that carries 200 products – including milk, beef, produce and coffee – from dozens of local vendors labeled with its Mountain Apple Brand.

Island Drinks

Fruit trees thrive in Hawaii, so you'd expect to find fresh juices everywhere. Alas, most supermarket cartons contain imported purees or sugary 'juice drinks' like POG (passion fruit, orange and guava). Look for real, freshly squeezed or blended juices at health food stores, farmers markets, specialty juice bars and roadside fruit stands – but even then, don't assume the fruit is locally grown.

Bear in mind that ancient Hawaiians never tasted such exotic species as succulent mango or tangy pineapple. Hawaii's original intoxicants were plant-based Polynesian elixirs: *'awa,* a mild, mouth-numbing sedative made from the roots of the kava plant, and *noni* (Indian mulberry), which some consider a cure-all. Both of those natural ingredients are pungent in smell and taste, so they're often mixed with other juices.

Coffee: Kona & Beyond

Hawaii was the first US state to grow coffee. Kona coffee is now world-famous for its mellow flavor that has no bitter aftertaste. The upland slopes of Mauna Loa and Hualalai in the Big Island's Kona district offer the ideal climate (sunny mornings and afternoon clouds with light seasonal showers) for coffee cultivation. While 100% Kona coffee has the most cachet, crops from Ka'u (the Big Island's southernmost district) have won accolades and impressed many aficionados, as have small-farm and estate-grown coffees from Maui, Kaua'i and Moloka'i.

Craft Beer, Island-Style

Once a novelty, microbreweries are now firmly established on Hawaii's biggest islands. Brewmasters claim that the mineral content and purity of Hawaii's water makes for excellent-tasting beer. Another hallmark of local craft beers is added hints of tropical flavor, such as Kona coffee, honey or *liliko'i*.

Most island microbreweries have lively brewpubs and tasting rooms, where you can try these popular pours: Longboard Island Lager and Pipeline Porter by Kona Brewing Company, on the Big Island (p191) and O'ahu (p132); Coconut Porter and Big Swell IPA by Maui Brewing Company (p342); Belgian-style Golden Sabbath strong ale and White Mountain Porter by the Big Island Brewhaus (p247); honeyed IPAloha 2.0 and Lihu'e Lager from Kauai Beer Company (p483); Mehana Brewing Company's Mauna Kea Pale Ale and Belgian-style Southern Cross Double Red Ale, both made by Big Island-based **Hawai'i Nui Brewing** (808-934-8211; http://hawaiinuibrewing.com; 275 E Kawili; 10am-6pm Mon-Fri) FREE; and IPAs and unfiltered pale ales at Honolulu Beerworks (p95) on O'ahu.

On O'ahu's North Shore, Waialua Soda Works (www.waialuasodaworks.com) bottles old-fashioned soda pop that's naturally flavored by tropical *liliko'i*, mango and pineapple, as well as Hawaii-grown vanilla and sugarcane.

CHEERS FOR HAWAII'S GREEN BEER

Maui Brewing Company and Kona Brewing Company beers aren't literally turning green, but the folks who brew them have implemented ingenious eco-conscious practices.

At Maui Brewing Company, vegetable oil used in the brewpub is converted to biodiesel fuel, which powers the cars of owners Garrett Marrero and Melanie Oxley as well as the delivery truck. Spent grain, yeast and hops from the solar-powered production facility is given to local ranchers for composting, and the brewery's retail beers are sold in recyclable cans. Cans over glass? Yep, cans aren't breakable, so they're less of a threat on the beach. They also stop light exposure and oxidation from affecting the beer's taste.

Kona Brewing Company hopped on the green bandwagon back in 2010 by installing a solar-energy generating system at its Big Island brewery and brewpub, as well as by producing the state's first certified green beer, Belgian-style Oceanic Organic Saison. The brewery also donates spent grain to local cattle ranches – that is, whatever it doesn't reuse as an ingredient in its certified-green brewpub's pizza dough and bread!

Wine, Spirits & Cocktails

Hawaii isn't known for its wineries and vineyards. Upscale restaurants cater to connoisseurs looking to complement their meals with bottles from California, Europe and elsewhere. Maui's Winery (p396) is known for its unique pineapple wines and Kaua'i's Nani Moon Meadery (p496) for its honey wines, while the Big Island's Volcano Winery (p301) makes equally unusual guava-grape and macadamia-nut-honey concoctions – they're not to everyone's taste, however.

Every beachfront and hotel bar mixes zany tropical cocktails topped with a fruit garnish and a little toothpick umbrella. Hawaii's legendary mai tai is a mix of dark and light rum, orange curaçao, orgeat and a simple syrup with orange, lemon, lime and/or pineapple juices – learn how to mix a simplified version yourself at Kaua'i's Koloa Rum Company (p484) tasting room. Microdistilleries are popping up on other islands too, including Maui's Ocean Vodka (p393) and **Hali'imaile Distilling Company** (☎808-633-3609; www.haliimailedistilling.com; 841 Hali'imaile Rd) and Kaua'i's Nani Moon Meadery (p496).

Island Cookbooks

- *Roy's Feasts from Hawaii, by Roy Yamaguchi*
- *Hali'imaile General Store Cookbook, by Beverly Gannon*
- *Aloha Cuisine, by Sam Choy*
- *What Hawaii Likes to Eat, by Muriel Muria and Betty Shimabukuro*

Celebrating with Food & Drink

Whether it's a 200-guest wedding or an intimate birthday party, a massive spread is almost mandatory in Hawaii. Most gatherings are informal, held at parks and beaches or in backyards, featuring a potluck buffet of homemade dishes. On major US holidays, mainstream mainland foods appear (eg Thanksgiving turkey) alongside local favorites such as rice (instead of mashed potatoes), sweet-potato tempura (instead of yams) and hibachi-grilled teriyaki beef (instead of roast beef).

Luau

In ancient Hawaii, a luau commemorated auspicious occasions, such as births, war victories or successful harvests. Modern luau celebrations, typically for weddings or a baby's first birthday, are often large banquet-hall gatherings of the *'ohana* (extended family and friends). The menu might be daring – including Hawaiian delicacies such as raw *'a'ama* (black crab) and *'opihi* (limpet) – but the entertainment is low-key.

Hawaii's commercial luau began in the 1970s. Today these dinner shows offer the elaborate Hawaiian feast and Polynesian dancing and fire eaters that folks expect. Expect an all-you-can-eat buffet with some luau standards including *kalua* pig, but also other dishes toned down for visitors' palates, such as steamed mahimahi and teriyaki chicken. Most commercial luau are overpriced and touristy, but one stands out for authenticity and aloha: Maui's Old Lahaina Luau (p328).

Festivals & Events

Festivals in Hawaii often showcase island-grown crops, such as the Big Island's Kona Coffee Cultural Festival and Ka'u Coffee Festival, Hana's East Maui Taro Festival, the Maui Onion Festival in Ka'anapali, Kapa'a's Coconut Festival on Kaua'i, the Big Island Chocolate Festival on the Kohala Coast, and the Pineapple Festival on Lana'i. Beer drinkers should mark their calendars with the Big Island's Kona Brewers Festival. And only in Hawaii will you find the Waikiki Spam Jam, held on O'ahu.

Gourmet culinary events are hot tickets across the islands. On O'ahu, Restaurant Week Hawaii brings dining-out deals and special menus. The Hawai'i Food & Wine Festival lets star chefs and island farmers shine on both O'ahu and Maui. Maui also hosts the Kapalua Wine & Food Festival for gourmands. Kaua'i's Spring Gourmet Gala in Lihu'e and Taste of Hawaii in Wailua bring top chefs to that island, while the Garden Island Range & Food Festival at Kilohana Plantation showcases local cattle ranchers and farmers. On the Big Island, A Taste of the Hawaiian Range agricultural festival happens at the Hilton Waikoloa Village resort; the Kohala 'Aina Festival opens the makahiki harvest season with 100% Hawaii-grown feasting; and the Puna Culinary Festival celebrates farm-to-fork eating with tours, tastings and chefs' demos.

Star Chefs' Tables

Alan Wong's, O'ahu

Roy's Waikiki, O'ahu

Merriman's, Hawai'i (Big Island)

Hali'imaile General Store, Maui

Josselin's Tapas Bar & Grill, Kaua'i

Where to Eat & Drink

The dining scene in Honolulu, with its seemingly endless, multiethnic variety and famous chefs, is a lot different than on the Neighbor Islands. On Kaua'i, you can count the number of Japanese restaurants on your fingers, while on O'ahu they number in the hundreds, from impeccable sushi bars and house-made noodle shops to trendy *izakaya* (Japanese pubs serving tapas-style food). The Big Island and, especially, Maui are closer to O'ahu as trendsetters, with farm-to-table dishes whipped up at food trucks, casual cafes and high-end dining rooms alike.

Across the islands, you'll find similar types of restaurants. For sit-down meals, there's a big divide between highbrow restaurants that could rival mainland counterparts and family-style restaurants that serve local fare and are beloved for their generous portions. Keep in mind that at oceanfront resort restaurants, you're probably paying for the view, not the food.

If calories are no concern, go for true local *grinds* (food) at '70s-style drive-ins serving plate lunches, *loco moco* and the like. Ideal for picnics are *okazu-ya* (island-style Japanese take-out delicatessens); these are

ONLY IN HAWAII: MUST-TRY TASTES

Leonard's (p122) *Malasadas* – sugar-coated Portuguese fried doughnuts (no hole), often filled with flavored custard – are made around Waikiki on O'ahu.

KCC Farmers Market (p130) Food growers and artisanal producers of everything from Hawaiian sea salt to coffee gather near Diamond Head on O'ahu.

Kanaka Kava (p193) Thirst-quenching kava, brewed from certified-organic *'awa* grown on the Big Island, in Kailua-Kona.

Hanalei Taro & Juice Co (p524) Taro-based smoothies, *mochi* cakes and hummus on Kaua'i's North Shore.

Aunty Lilikoi (p566) Sweet syrups, spicy mustards and (inedible) massage oil, all made with *liliko'i* (passion fruit), on Kaua'i's Westside.

often the best places to find good, authentic Hawaiian food too. Commercial luau buffets include all the notable Hawaiian dishes but the quality can be mediocre and tastes often watered down for tourists.

Outside of Honolulu and Waikiki, especially on the Neighbor Islands, restaurants typically close early (say, by 9pm). For late-night dining, you'll have to seek out bars or the rare 24-hour coffee shop or diner.

Although it's now an island staple, salmon is not native to local waters. It's an imported fish, first introduced to Hawaii by whaling ships during the 19th century.

Self-Catering & Saving Money

In Hawaii, most groceries are imported. The everyday price of food averages 30% more than on the US mainland, so you may not save much money by cooking your own meals. But you will find fantastic prices on fresh seafood at local fish markets. Local produce is surprisingly pricey and hard to find except at farmers markets, roadside stands and some locally owned supermarkets. Many residents and tourists cannot resist the bulk-food deals at members-only Costco warehouses on the bigger main islands; their deli-fresh *poke* gets props from locals.

EATING HAWAII'S FISH

Locals eat twice as much seafood as the per-capita national average. Ahi is the local favorite, but mahimahi and *ono* are also very popular. Browse the Hawaii Seafood website, www.hawaii-seafood.org, to find out more about wild local fish, including sustainability, fishing methods, seasonality, nutrition and cooking tips, or to sign up for Saturday morning tours of Honolulu's fish auction ($25, reservations required).

The free *Seafood Watch* (www.seafoodwatch.org) guide, published by the Monterey Bay Aquarium, provides at-a-glance information about ocean-friendly seafood, including sustainability specifics for Hawaii's fish. Download the free smartphone app or print a pocket guide from the website.

In Hawaii, most fish go by their Hawaiian names, but Japanese names are often used as well. Fish species commonly eaten in the islands include the following:

ahi yellowfin or bigeye tuna; red flesh, excellent raw or rare

aku skipjack tuna; red flesh, strong flavor; *katsuo* in Japanese

'ama'ama striped mullet; delicate white flesh

awa milkfish; tender white flesh

hebi shortbill spearfish; soft, white to pinkish flesh, mild flavor

kajiki Pacific blue marlin; firm white to pinkish flesh; *a'u* in Hawaiian

mahimahi dolphinfish or dorado; firm pink flesh

moi Pacific threadfish; flaky white flesh, rich flavor; reserved for royalty in ancient times

monchong sickle pomfret; mild flavor, firm pinkish-white flesh

nairagi striped marlin; firm flesh, colored pink to deep red-orange; *a'u* in Hawaiian

'o'io bonefish

onaga long-tail red snapper; soft and moist

ono wahoo; white-fleshed and flaky

opah moonfish; firm and rich flesh, colored pink, orange, white or dark red

'opakapaka pink snapper; delicate flavor, firm flesh

'opelu mackerel scad; pan-sized, delicious fried

papio jack fish; also called *ulua*

shutome swordfish; succulent and meaty, white to pinkish flesh

tako octopus; chewy texture; *he'e* in Hawaiian

tombo albacore tuna; light flesh, mild flavor, silky texture

If you're not cooking for yourself, favorite budget eating picks include island bakeries, diners, drive-ins, delis, food trucks and plate-lunch takeout joints. At top-end dining rooms inside oceanfront hotels and golf-course clubhouses and at resort shopping centers, stop by the bar during *pau hana* (happy hour), when *pupu* and drinks are discounted.

Vegetarians & Vegans

Many restaurant menus in Hawaii include a few meatless selections, such as grilled vegetables, garden salads and pastas. Hawaii's Asian kitchens ensure plenty of vegetable and tofu dishes, as well as options for anyone who can't tolerate gluten or lactose. Healthy dishes are increasingly available at casual local joints, including meal-sized salads and grilled-vegetable or tofu sandwiches and wraps, often served on whole-wheat bread or with brown rice.

Finding an exclusively vegetarian restaurant isn't easy in Hawaii. Vegans especially will have to look hard; soups and sauces usually contain broth made from chicken or fish or other meat. The most economical way to avoid eating meat and animal-sourced ingredients is to forage at farmers markets, or graze the hot-and-cold takeout food bars at natural-foods stores, which also stock groceries for special diets (eg gluten-free).

Best Plate Lunches

- *Ted's Bakery, O'ahu*
- *Super J's, Hawai'i (Big Island)*
- *Umeke, Hawai'i (Big Island)*
- *Kilauea Fish Market, Kaua'i*
- *Da Kitchen, Maui*
- *Cafe 100, Hawai'i (Big Island)*

Habits & Customs

When entertaining at home, locals typically serve meals potluck-style with a spread of flavorful dishes that may seem ridiculously clashing to the uninitiated palate. Locals may be laid-back, but they're punctual when it comes to meals. If you're invited to a local home, show up on time, bring dessert (ideally from a local bakery) and remove your shoes at the door. Locals are generous with leftovers and might insist that you take a plate (along with fresh fruit from the backyard) home with you.

Meals are early and start on the dot in Hawaii: typically 6am breakfast, noon lunch and 6pm dinner. Restaurants are jammed around these habitual mealtimes, but they clear out an hour or two later, as locals are not lingerers. Locals also tend to consider quantity as important as quality, and portion sizes reflect this attitude; feel free to split a meal or ask for a box for leftovers.

Compared with the mainland, restaurant dress codes are relaxed (it's called 'island casual'), with no jackets or ties normally required for men. Tourists can get away with an aloha shirt and neat khaki or golf shorts at most resorts, although locals usually don casual slacks when dining out.

Smoking is not allowed inside any restaurants in Hawaii.

Food Glossary

Hawaii cuisine is multiethnic and so is the lingo.

adobo Filipino chicken or pork cooked in vinegar, *shōyu*, garlic and spices
'awa kava, a Polynesian plant used to make a mildly intoxicating drink
bentō Japanese-style box lunch
broke da mout delicious; literally 'broke the mouth'
char siu Chinese barbecued pork
chirashizushi assorted sashimi served over rice
crack seed Chinese-style preserved fruit; a salty, sweet and/or sour snack
donburi Japanese-style large bowl of rice topped with a protein (eg pork *katsu*)
furikake catch-all Japanese seasoning or condiment, usually dry and sprinkled atop rice; in Hawaii, sometimes mixed into *poke*
grind to eat
grinds food (usually local)
guava fruit with green or yellow rind, moist pink flesh and lots of edible seeds
haupia coconut-cream custard, often thickened with arrowroot or cornstarch
hulihuli chicken rotisserie-cooked chicken with island-style barbecue sauce

imu underground earthen oven used to cook *kalua* pig and other luau food
'inamona roasted, ground *kukui* (candlenut), used as a condiment (eg mixed into *poke*)
izakaya Japanese pub serving tapas-style dishes
kalbi Korean-style grilled meats, typically marinated short ribs
kalo Hawaiian word for taro, often pounded into *poi*
kalua Hawaiian method of cooking pork or other luau food, traditionally in an *imu*
kare-kare Filipino oxtail stew
katsu Japanese deep-fried cutlets, usually pork or chicken
kaukau food
laulau bundle of pork or chicken and salted butterfish, wrapped in taro and *ti* leaves and steamed
li hing mui sweet-salty preserved plum, a type of crack seed; also refers to the flavor powder
liliko'i passion fruit
loco moco hearty dish of rice, fried egg and hamburger patty topped with gravy or other condiments
lomilomi salmon minced, salted salmon with diced tomato and green onion
luau Hawaiian feast
mai tai tiki-bar drink typically containing rum and tropical fruit juices
malasada sugar-coated, fried Portuguese doughnut (no hole), often filled with flavored custard
manapua Chinese *bao* (baked or steamed buns) with *char siu* or other fillings
manjū Japanese steamed or baked cake, often filled with sweet bean paste
miso red, yellow or white Japanese fermented soybean paste
mochi Japanese pounded-rice cake, sticky and sweet
musubi Japanese *onigiri* (rice ball or triangle) wrapped in *nori*
noni type of mulberry with smelly yellow fruit, used medicinally by Hawaiians
nori Japanese seaweed, usually dried
ogo crunchy seaweed, sometimes added to *poke; limu* in Hawaiian
okazu-ya Japanese take-out delicatessen, often specializing in home-style Hawaiian and local dishes
'ono delicious
'ono kine grinds good food
pau hana happy hour (literally 'stop work')
pipi kaula Hawaiian beef jerky
poha gooseberry
poi staple Hawaiian starch made of steamed, mashed taro (*kalo*)
poke cubed, marinated raw fish
ponzu Japanese citrus sauce
pupu snacks or appetizers
saimin local-style noodle soup
shave ice cup of finely shaved ice doused with sweet syrups
shōyu soy sauce
star fruit translucent green-yellow fruit with five extended parts, like the points of a star, and sweet, juicy pulp
taro plant with edible corm used to make *poi* and with edible leaves to wrap around *laulau; kalo* in Hawaiian
teishoku Japanese set meal
teppanyaki Japanese style of cooking with an iron grill
uni sea urchin

MANAPUA

Manapua, the local version of Chinese *bao* (steamed or baked filled bun), probably derives from either of two Hawaiian phrases: *mea 'ono pua'a* (good pork thing) or *mauna pua'a* (mountain of pork).

Hawaii's Arts & Crafts

Contemporary Hawaii is a vibrant mix of cultural traditions, with the state capital of Honolulu being a hybrid of East and West. Underneath it all beats a Hawaiian heart, pounding with an ongoing revival of Hawaii's indigenous language, artisan crafts, music and the hula. *E komo mai* (welcome) to these unique Polynesian islands, where storytelling and slack key guitar are among the sounds of everyday life.

Hula

Ancient Stories

In ancient Hawai'i, hula sometimes was a solemn ritual, in which *mele* (songs, chants) were an offering to the gods or celebrated the accomplishments of *ali'i* (chiefs). At other times hula was lighthearted entertainment, in which chief and *kama'aina* (commoner) danced together, including at annual festivals such as the makahiki held during harvest season. Most importantly, hula embodied the community – telling stories of and celebrating itself.

Can't resist the rhythms of the hula? Look for low-cost (or even free) introductory dance lessons at resort hotels, shopping malls and local community centers and colleges. No grass skirt required!

Traditionally, dancers trained rigorously in *halau* (schools) under a *kumu* (teacher), so their hand gestures, facial expressions and synchronized movements were exact. In a culture without written language, chants were important, giving meaning to the movements and preserving Hawaii's oral history, anything from creation stories about gods to royal genealogies. Songs often contained *kaona* (hidden meanings), which could be spiritual, but also slyly amorous, even sexual.

Modern Revival

One can only imagine how hard Hawaii's earliest Christian missionaries blushed at the hula, which they disapproved of as licentious. Missionary efforts to suppress hula were aided by Christian convert Queen Ka'ahumanu, who banned public hula performances in 1830.

The tradition might have been lost forever were it not for King Kalakaua. The 'Merrie Monarch' revived hula dancing in the 1880s, saying famously, 'Hula is the language of the heart, therefore the heartbeat of the Hawaiian people.' After he died, the monarchy was soon overthrown, and hula faded again, until a Hawaiian cultural renaissance beginning in the 1960s and '70s brought it back for good.

Today, hula *halau* run by revered *kumu* hula are thriving, as hula competitions blossom and some islanders adopt hula as a life practice.

Celebrating Hula

In hula competitions today, dancers vie in *kahiko* (ancient) and *'auana* (modern) categories.

Kahiko performances are raw and elemental, accompanied only by chanting and thunderous gourd drums; costumes are traditional, with *ti*-leaf lei, *kapa* skirts or wraps, primary colors and sometimes lots of skin showing.

Western contemporary influences – English-language lyrics, stringed instruments, innovative costumes, sinuous arm movements and smiling faces – may appear in *'auana* dances. Some hula troupes even flirt with postmodern dance styles.

Hawaii's Olympics of hula is the Big Island's Merrie Monarch Festival (p274), but authentic hula competitions and celebrations happen year-round on all the main islands. At touristy commercial luau, vigorously shaking hips and Vegas showgirl–style headdresses might be entertaining, but they're closer to Tahitian dance than to hula.

Browse classic and contemporary Hawaiian recordings online – including those by Na Hoku Hanohano award-winning musicians – at Mountain Apple Company (www.mountainapplecompany.com) and Mele (www.mele.com).

Island Music

Hawaiian music is rooted in ancient chants. Foreign missionaries and sugar-plantation workers introduced new melodies and instruments, which were incorporated and adapted to create a unique local musical style. *Leo ki'eki'e* (falsetto, or 'high voice') vocals, sometimes just referred to as soprano for women, employs a signature *ha'i* (vocal break, or split-note) style, with a singer moving abruptly from one register to another. Contemporary Hawaiian musical instruments include the steel guitar, slack key guitar and ukulele.

But if you tune your rental-car radio to today's island radio stations, you'll hear everything from US mainland hip-hop beats, country-and-western tunes and Asian pop hits to reggae-inspired 'Jawaiian' grooves. A few Hawaii-born singer-songwriters, most famously Jack Johnson, have achieved international stardom. To discover new hit-makers, check out this year's winners of the Na Hoku Hanohano Awards (www.nahokuhanohano.org), Hawaii's version of the Grammys.

TOP 10 HAWAIIAN HIT ALBUMS

Ideally, any list like this would come bundled with a CD and a ukulele. Here's our take on the essential Hawaiian albums, past and present:

➡ Israel Kamakawiwo'ole, *Facing Future* (1993) – 'Braddah Iz' touched Hawaii's soul with songs such as 'Hawai'i '78,' while his version of 'Somewhere Over the Rainbow' has become world-famous. When Braddah Iz died in 1997, his body lay in state at the Capitol in Honolulu, an honor never before bestowed on a musician.

➡ *The Descendants* (2011) – Keola Beamer, Gabby Pahinui and other slack key and steel guitar masters are showcased in this Hollywood movie soundtrack.

➡ Genoa Keawe, *Party Hulas* (1965) – Ukulele player 'Aunty Genoa' and her *ha'i* (voiced register-break singing technique) epitomized old-school Hawaiian hula music, and this sets the standard.

➡ Brothers Cazimero, *Some Call It Aloha...Don't Tell* (2004) – After kicking off the Hawaiian renaissance in Peter Moon's band Sunday Manoa, the dynamic duo of Robert and Roland blended melodic vocals with 12-string guitar and bass rhythms.

➡ Gabby Pahinui, *Gabby* (1972) – No self-respecting slack key music collection is complete without this seminal 1970s album.

➡ Dennis and David Kamakahi, *'Ohana* (1999) – Father Dennis and son David harmonize their musical gifts on Hawaiian slack key guitar and ukulele, respectively.

➡ Ledward Ka'apana, *Black Sand* (2000) – From a multi-talented master of the ukulele and slack key and steel guitars comes soothing instrumentals that evoke the islands' natural beauty.

➡ Keali'i Reichel, *Ke'alaokamaile* (2003) – Charismatic vocalist and *kumu* hula Reichel combines ancient chanting and soulful ballads in Hawaiian and English.

➡ HAPA, *In the Name of Love* (1997) – Founded by a New Jersey slack key guitarist and a Hawaiian vocalist, HAPA's contemporary pop-flavored fusion has universal appeal.

➡ John Cruz, *Acoustic Soul* (1996) – An O'ahu-born singer-songwriter crafting modern, blues-tinged riffs, most famously the hit song 'Island Style.'

Cowboy Heritage

Spanish and Mexican cowboys introduced the guitar to Hawaiians in the 1830s. Fifty years later, O'ahu-born high-school student Joseph Kekuku started experimenting with playing a guitar flat on his lap while sliding a pocket knife or comb across the strings. His invention, the Hawaiian steel guitar *(kika kila),* lifts the strings off the fretboard using a movable steel slide, creating a signature smooth sound.

In the early 20th century, Kekuku and others introduced the islands' steel guitar sounds to the world. The steel guitar later inspired the creation of resonator guitars such as the Dobro, now integral to bluegrass, blues and other genres, and country-and-western music's lap and pedal steel guitar. Today Hawaii's most influential steel guitarists include Henry Kaleialoha Allen, Alan Akaka, Bobby Ingano and Gregory Sardinha.

The 'Jumping Flea'

Heard all across the islands is the ukulele, derived from the *braguinha,* a Portuguese stringed instrument introduced to Hawaii in 1879. Ukulele means 'jumping flea' in Hawaiian, referring to the way players' deft fingers swiftly move around the strings. The ukulele is enjoying a revival as a young generation of virtuosos emerges, including teenaged Nick Acosta, who plays with just one hand, and genre-bending rockers led by Jake Shimabukuro, whose album *Grand Ukulele* (2012) reached number two on Billboard's world music chart.

Both the ukulele and the steel guitar contributed to the lighthearted *hapa haole* (Hawaiian music with predominantly English lyrics) popularized in the islands after the 1930s, of which 'My Little Grass Shack' and 'Lovely Hula Hands' are classic examples. For better or for worse, *hapa haole* songs became instantly recognizable as 'Hawaiian' thanks to Hollywood movies and the classic *Hawaii Calls* radio show, which broadcast worldwide from the banyan-tree courtyard of Waikiki's Moana hotel from 1935 until 1975.

Slackin' Sounds

Since the mid-20th century, the Hawaiian steel guitar has usually been played with slack key *(ki ho'alu)* tunings, in which the thumb plays the bass and rhythm chords, while the fingers play the melody and improvisations, in a picked style. Traditionally, slack key tunings were closely guarded secrets among *'ohana* (extended family and friends).

The legendary guitarist Gabby Pahinui launched the modern slack key guitar era with his first recording of 'Hi'ilawe' in 1946. In the 1960s, Gabby and his band the Sons of Hawai'i embraced the traditional Hawaiian sound. Along with other influential slack key guitarists such as Sonny Chillingworth, they spurred a renaissance in Hawaiian music that continues to this day. The list of contemporary slack key masters is long and ever growing, including Keola Beamer, Ledward Ka'apana, Martin and Cyril Pahinui and Ozzie Kotani.

SLACK KEY GUITAR

To find out more about slack key guitar, visit George Winston's Dancing Cat music label website, www.dancingcat.com, to listen to sound clips, browse bios of celebrated island guitarists and download a free ebook.

Traditional Hawaiian Crafts

In the 1970s, the Hawaiian renaissance sparked interest in artisan crafts. The most beloved traditional craft is lei-making, stringing garlands of flowers, leaves, berries, nuts or shells. More lasting souvenirs include wood carvings, woven baskets and hats, and Hawaiian quilts. All of these have become so popular with tourists that cheap imitation imports from across the Pacific have flooded into Hawaii, so shop carefully and always buy local.

Hawaii's Arts & Crafts

The beauty of the Hawaiian Islands will reawaken your senses with the flowing gestures of hula dancers and the melodious sounds of slack key guitars and ukuleles. The delicate artistry of a flower lei sets the soul in harmony with the natural world.

1

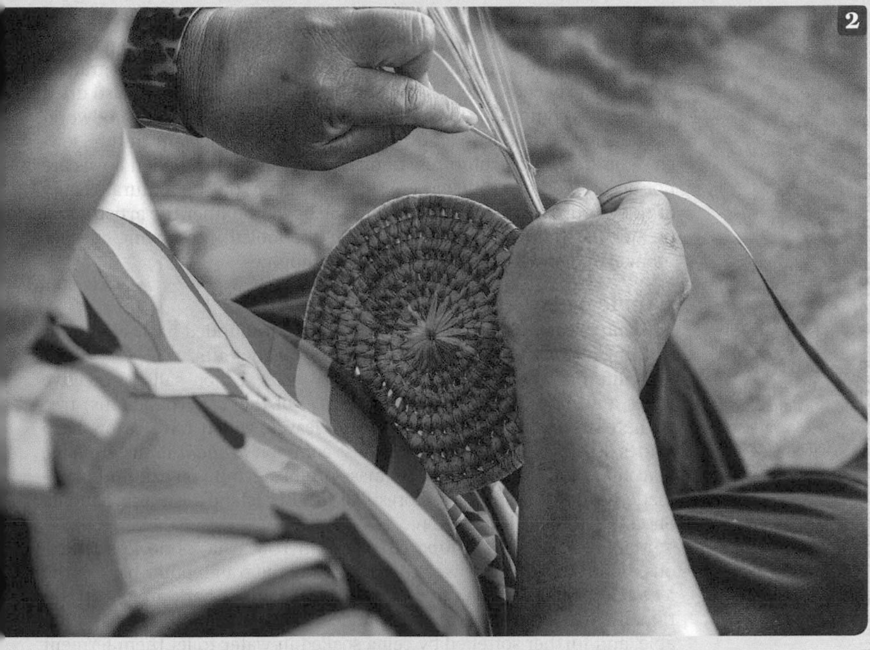

PETE RYAN / GETTY IMAGES ©

LONELY PLANET / GETTY IMAGES ©

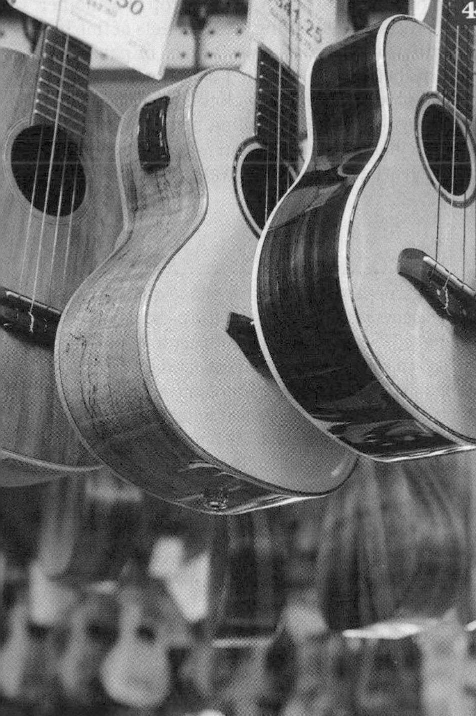

1. Lei making (p615)
Traditional lei makers sew, wind or braid flowers, feathers, nuts, shells, seeds, seaweed, vines and leaves.

2. Basket weaving (p612)
Weaving *lau* (leaves) to make baskets, floor mats and hats is a traditional Hawaiian craft.

3. Hawaiian fabric
Bright and colorful Hawaiian prints are used for everything, including the iconic aloha shirt.

4. Ukuleles at Bounty Music (p356)
Ukulele means 'jumping flea' in Hawaiian, referring to swift movements of players' fingers across the strings.

EMILY RIDDELL / GETTY IMAGES ©

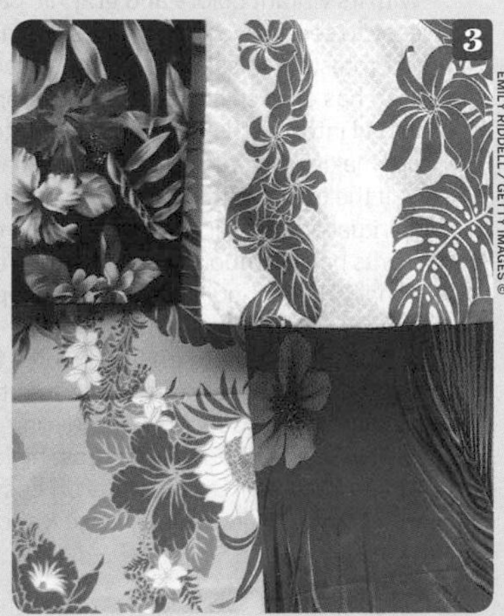

Woodworking

Ancient Hawaiians were expert woodworkers, carving canoes out of logs and hand-turning lustrous bowls from a variety of beautifully grained tropical hardwoods, such as koa and milo. *Ipu* (gourds) were also dried and used as containers and as drums for hula. Contemporary woodworkers take native woods to craft traditional bowls, exquisite furniture, jewelry and free-form sculptures. Traditionally, Hawaiian wooden bowls are not decorated or ornate, but are shaped to bring out the natural beauty of the wood. The thinner and lighter the bowl, the finer the artistry and greater the value – and the price. Don't be fooled into buying cheaper monkeypod bowls imported from the Philippines.

Fabric Arts

Kapa Hawaii (www.kapahawaii.net) celebrates the art of *kapa* with photo essays, news about workshops and events, and how-to tips for making, displaying and caring for this handmade fabric.

Lauhala weaving and the making of *kapa* (pounded-bark cloth) for clothing and artworks are two ancient Hawaiian crafts.

Traditionally *lauhala* served as floor mats, canoe sails, protective capes and more. Weaving the *lau* (leaves) of the *hala* (pandanus) tree is the easier part, while preparing the leaves, which have razor-sharp spines, is messy work. Today the most common *lauhala* items are hats, placemats and baskets. Most are mass-produced, but you can find handmade beauties at specialty stores like the Big Island's Kimura Lauhala Shop (p200) near Kailua-Kona.

Making *kapa* (called *tapa* elsewhere in Polynesia) is no less laborious. First, seashells are used to scrape away the rough outer bark of the *wauke* (paper mulberry) tree. Strips of softer inner bark are cut (traditionally with shark's teeth) and pounded with mallets until thin and pliable, and further softened by being soaked in water to let them ferment between beatings. Softened bark strips are then layered atop one another and pounded together in a process called felting. Large sheets of finished *kapa* are colorfully dyed with plant materials and stamped or painted by hand with geometric patterns before being scented with flowers or oils.

In ancient times, *kapa* was worn as everyday clothing by both sexes, and used as blankets for everything from swaddling newborns to burying the dead. Today authentic handmade Hawaiian *kapa* cloth is rarely seen outside of museums, fine-art galleries and private collections.

QUILTING A HAWAIIAN STORY

With its vibrant colors and graphic patterns, the appeal of Hawaiian appliqué quilting is easy to see. But look more closely and you'll discover the story behind the beauty.

Protestant missionaries introduced quilting to Hawaii in the early 19th century, but the craft has evolved since then. Traditional quilts typically have a solid color fabric, which is folded into fourths or eighths, cut into a repeating pattern derived from nature (remember making snowflakes in school?), and then appliquéd onto neutral foundation cloth.

If the quilt's center, or *piko* (navel), is open, it's said to be a gateway between the spiritual and physical worlds; a solid core embodies the strength of family. Fruits and plants have symbolic meaning, too: *'ulu* (breadfruit) represents prosperity and is traditionally the first quilt made, a pineapple signifies hospitality, taro equates to strength, and a mango embodies wishes granted.

Don't look for human figures on a traditional quilt, though; they might come alive at night. Each original design is thought to contain the very spirit of the crafter. To prevent their creators' souls from wandering, early Hawaiian quilts were buried with their makers.

The *'ohana* of one of the most highly regarded traditional Hawaiian quilters, the late Althea Poakalani Serrao, runs an encyclopedic website (www.poakalani.net) about Hawaiian quilting, including classes, shops, patterns, history and more.

Lisa Dunford

Island Writings

From Outsiders' to Insiders' Views

Until the late 1970s, Hawaii's literature was dominated by nonlocal Western writers observing these exotic-seeming islands from the outside. Globetrotters such as Mark Twain and Isabella Bird wrote the earliest travelogues about the islands. Best-selling modern titles include James Michener's historical saga, *Hawaii* (1959), and Paul Theroux's caustically humorous *Hotel Honolulu* (2001). More recently, Hawaii-centered historical fiction written by non-residents includes *The Last Aloha* (2009), by Gaellen Quinn, and *Bird of Another Heaven,* by James Houston (2007).

Meanwhile, contemporary locally born writers have created an authentic literature of Hawaii that evokes island life from the inside. Leading this has been Bamboo Ridge Press (www.bambooridge.com), which for over 35 years has published contemporary local fiction and poetry in an annual journal and has launched the careers of many Hawaii writers. The University of Hawai'i Press (www.uhpress.hawaii.edu) and Bishop Museum Press (www.bishopmuseum.org/press) have also made space for local writers to air their voices, especially with insightful nonfiction writings about Hawaiian culture, history, nature and art.

Hawaiian Folktales, Proverbs & Poetry

Folktales of Hawai'i, illustrated by Sig Zane

'Olelo No'eau, illustrated by Dietrich Varez

Obake Files, by Glen Grant

Pidgin Beyond Plantations

In 1975, *All I Asking for Is My Body,* by Milton Murayama, vividly captured sugar plantation life for Japanese *nisei* (second-generation immigrants) around WWII. Murayama's use of pidgin opened the door to an explosion of vernacular literature. Lois-Ann Yamanaka has won widespread acclaim for her poetry (*Saturday Night at the Pahala Theatre,* 1993) and stories (*Wild Meat and the Bully Burgers,* 1996), in which pidgin embodies her characters like a second skin.

Indeed, redeeming pidgin – long dismissed by academics and disparaged by the upper class – has been a cultural and political cause for some. The hilarious stories (*Da Word,* 2001) and essays (*Living Pidgin,* 2002) of Lee Tonouchi, a prolific writer and playwright whose nickname is 'Da Pidgin Guerrilla,' argue that pidgin is not only essential to understanding local culture, but is also a legitimate language. Another great introduction to pidgin is *Growing Up Local* (1998), an anthology of poetry and prose published by Bamboo Ridge Press.

More than a pidgin dictionary, *Pidgin to Da Max,* by Douglas Simonson (aka Peppo), Pat Sasaki and Ken Sakata, is a side-splitting primer on local life that has knocked around forever because it (and its sequels) are so funny.

New Voices

Other influential Hawaii writers who found their voices toward the end of the 20th century include Nora Okja Keller, whose first novel, *Comfort Woman,* won the 1998 American Book Award, and Kiana (born Diana) Davenport, whose *Shark Dialogues* (1994), *Song of the Exile* (2000) and *House of Many Gods* (2007) are sweeping multigenerational family tales entwined with Hawaii's own history.

Other contemporary Hawaii writers, especially women, abound. Some, such as Mia King (*Sweet Life,* 2008), eschew purely ethnic or Hawaii-centered narratives, while others – such as Kaui Hart Hemmings (*House of Thieves,* 2005) and Marie Hara (*An Offering of Rice,* 2007) – explode the 'paradise myth' as they explore conflicted issues of race and class. Hemmings' novel *The Descendants* (2007) has a dissolute Southern Gothic air, as the troubled *'ohana* of haole plantation owners and a Hawaiian princess almost lose their inheritance and their way.

Hawaii on Screen

Nothing has cemented the paradisaical fantasy of Hawaii in the popular imagination as firmly as Hollywood. Today, Southern California's 'dream factory' continues to peddle variations on a South Seas genre that first swept movie theaters in the 1930s. Whether the mood is silly or serious, whether Hawaii is used as a setting or a stand-in for someplace else, the story's familiar tropes rarely change, updating the original tropical castaways soap opera and often romantically glossing over the islands' history of colonization.

Hawaii has been the home of many modern painters, and scores of visiting artists have drawn inspiration from the islands' rich cultural heritage and landscapes. *Encounters with Paradise: Views of Hawaii and Its People, 1778–1941*, by David Forbes, is a vivid art-history tour.

Hollywood arrived in Hawaii in 1913, a little more than a decade after Thomas Edison first journeyed here to make movies that you can still watch today at Lahaina's Wo Hing Museum (p320) on Maui. By 1939, dozens of Hollywood movies had been shot in Hawaii, including the musical comedy *Waikiki Wedding* (1937), in which Bing Crosby crooned the Oscar-winning song 'Sweet Leilani.' Later favorites include the WWII–themed drama *From Here to Eternity* (1953), the musical *South Pacific* (1958), and Elvis Presley's goofy postwar *Blue Hawaii* (1961).

Today, Hawaii actively encourages and supports a lucrative film industry by maintaining state-of-the-art production facilities and providing tax incentives. Hundreds of feature films have been shot in the state, including box-office hits *Raiders of the Lost Ark* (1981), *Jurassic Park* (1993), *Pearl Harbor* (2001), *50 First Dates* (2004), *Pirates of the Caribbean: On Stranger Tides* (2011), *The Hunger Games: Catching Fire* (2013) and *Godzilla* (2014). Kaua'i is the most prolific island 'set' and has appeared in more than 70 films. Avid fans can tour movie sites all over Kaua'i and on O'ahu at Kualoa Ranch (p147).

Hawaii has hosted dozens of TV series since 1968, when the original *Hawaii Five-O*, an edgy cop drama unsentimentally depicting Honolulu's gritty side, debuted. In 2010 *Hawaii Five-O* was rebooted as a prime-time drama, filmed on O'ahu. That island also served as the location for the hit series *Lost*, which, like *Gilligan's Island* (the pilot of which was filmed on Kaua'i), is about a group of island castaways trying to get home. To find *Lost* filming locations, visit www.lostvirtualtour.com.

For a complete filmography and a list of hundreds of TV episodes filmed here, including what's currently being shot around the islands, check the Hawaii Film Office website, http://filmoffice.hawaii.gov.

Lei

Greetings. Love. Honor. Respect. Peace. Celebration. Spirituality. Good luck. Farewell. A Hawaiian lei – a handcrafted garland of fresh tropical flowers – can signify all of these meanings and many more. Lei-making may be Hawaii's most sensuous and transitory art form. Fragrant and ephemeral, lei embody the beauty of nature and the embrace of *'ohana* (extended family and friends) and the community, freely given and freely shared.

The Art of the Lei

In choosing their materials, lei makers express emotions and tell a story, since flowers and other plants may embody Hawaiian places and myths. Traditional lei makers may use feathers, nuts, shells, seeds, seaweed, vines, leaves and fruit, in addition to more familiar fragrant flowers. The most common methods of making lei are by knotting, braiding, winding, stringing or sewing the raw natural materials together.

Above Braiding flowers to make a lei

Worn daily, lei were integral to ancient Hawaiian society. In the islands' Polynesian past, they were part of sacred hula dances and given as special gifts to loved ones, as healing medicine to the sick and as offerings to the gods, all practices that continue today. So powerful a symbol were they that on ancient Hawaii's battlefields, a lei could bring peace to warring armies.

Today, locals wear lei for special events, such as weddings, birthdays, anniversaries and graduations. It's no longer common to make one's own lei, unless you belong to a hula *halau* (school). For ceremonial hula, performers are often required to make their own lei, even gathering raw materials by hand.

Does an airport lei greeting to surprise your *ipo* (sweetheart) sound like fun? Several companies offer this service, including **Greeters of Hawaii** (from US mainland 800-366-8559, in Hawaii 888-523-4487; www.greetersofhawaii.com), which has been in the business of giving aloha since 1957.

Modern Celebrations

For visitors to Hawaii, the tradition of giving and receiving lei dates back to the 19th-century steamships that brought the first tourists to the islands. Later, disembarking cruise-ship passengers were greeted by vendors who would toss garlands around the necks of *malihini* (newcomers).

In 1927, the poet Don Blanding and Honolulu journalist Grace Tower Warren called for making May 1 a holiday to honor lei. Every year, Lei Day is still celebrated across the islands with Hawaiian music, hula dancing, parades, and lei-making workshops and contests.

The tradition of giving a kiss with a lei began during WWII, allegedly when a hula dancer at a USO club was dared by her friends to give a military serviceman a peck on the cheek when offering him a flower lei.

Lei Dos & Don'ts

- Do not wear a lei hanging directly down around your neck. Instead, drape a closed (circular) lei over your shoulders, making sure equal lengths are hanging over your front and back.
- When presenting a lei, bow your head slightly and raise the lei above your heart. Do not drape it with your own hands over the head of the recipient because this isn't respectful; let them do it themselves.

ISLAND LEI TRADITIONS

Lei are a universal language in Hawaii, but some special lei evoke a particular island.

O'ahu The yellow-orange *'ilima* is the island's official flower, and a symbol of Laka, the Hawaiian goddess of hula dancing. Once favored by royalty, an *'ilima* lei may be made of up to a thousand small blossoms strung together.

Hawai'i, the Big Island Lei made from lehua, the pom-pom flowers of the ohia plant, are most often red or pink. According to legend, the first lei was made of lehua and given by Hi'iaka, goddess of healing, to her sister Pele, goddess of fire and volcanoes.

Maui The *lokelani* (pink damask rose, or 'rose of heaven') is a soft, velvety and aromatic flower. It was imported by 19th-century Christian missionaries for their gardens in Lahaina. Today it's Maui's official flower, the only exotic flora so recognized in Hawaii.

Lana'i A yellowish-orange vine, *kauna'oa* is traditionally gathered from the island's windward shores, then twisted into a lei. One traditional Hawaiian chant sings of this plant growing on Lana'i like a feathered cape lying on a strong chief's shoulders.

Moloka'i *Kukui* (candelnut) lei are either made from the laboriously polished, dark-brown nuts of Hawaii's state tree (in which case, they're usually worn by men) or the tree's white blossoms, which are Moloka'i's official flower.

Kaua'i On the 'Garden Island,' leathery, anise-scented *mokihana* berries are often woven with strands of glossy, green maile vines. *Mokihana* trees thrive on the rain-soaked western slopes of Mt Wai'ale'ale.

Floral lei

➡ Don't give a closed lei to a pregnant woman for it may bring bad luck; choose an open (untied) lei or *haku* (head) lei instead.

➡ Resist the temptation to wear a lei intended for someone else. That's bad luck.

➡ Never refuse a lei, and do not take one off in the presence of the giver.

➡ When you stop wearing your lei, don't throw it away. Untie the string, remove the bow and return the lei's natural elements to the earth (eg scatter flowers in the ocean, bury seeds or nuts).

On O'ahu, it's a tradition for passengers to throw their lei into the sea as their departing ship passes Diamond Head. If the flowers of their lei float back toward the beach, it's said that they'll return to Hawaii someday.

Shopping for Lei

A typical Hawaiian lei costs anywhere from $10 for a single strand of orchids or plumeria to thousands of dollars for a 100% genuine Ni'ihau shell lei necklace. Beware that some *kukui* (candelnut) and *puka* shell lei are just cheap (even plastic) imports.

When shopping for a lei, ask the florist or shopkeeper for advice about what the most appropriate lei for the occasion is (eg for a bride, pick a string of pearl-like *pikake* jasmine flowers), and indicate if you're giving the lei to a man or a woman.

Land & Sea

It has been said that if Darwin had arrived first in Hawaii, a remote archipelago with spectacularly varied wildlife, he would have developed his theory of evolution in just weeks instead of years. On the other hand, few places have felt humanity's heavy footprint as deeply as Hawaii, which today holds the ignominious title of being the 'endangered species capital of the world' while facing some serious environmental challenges.

Kilauea's ongoing eruption, which began in 1983, is the most voluminous outpouring of lava onto the volcano's east rift zone in 500 years. It has added 500 acres of new land to the Big Island – so far.

Earth's Most Remote Paradise

Many people think of the Hawaiian Islands as tiny rafts of white sand and tiki bars sailing westward inch-by-inch to Japan. In fact, these islands are the palm-fringed tops of the planet's largest mountain range, something whales may appreciate more than humans do.

For 80 million years, a 'hot spot' beneath the earth's mantle has operated like a volcanic conveyor belt here, manufacturing a 1500-mile string of shield volcanoes that bubble out of the sea in the most geographically isolated spot on the planet, almost 2000 miles from the closest continent. This profound isolation has created a living textbook of evolution, with incredible biodiversity unmatched by anywhere else in the US.

A Hot Spot for Volcanoes

The Hawaiian archipelago embraces more than 50 volcanoes (and 137 islands and atolls), part of the larger, mostly submerged Hawaiian-Emperor Seamount chain that extends 3600 miles across the ocean. Hawaii's volcanoes are created by a rising column of molten rock – a 'hot spot' – under the Pacific Plate. As the plate moves northwest a few inches each year, magma pierces upward through the crust, creating volcanoes.

Each new volcano slowly creeps northwest past the hot spot that created it. As each volcanic island moves off the hot spot, it stops erupting and instead of adding more new land, it starts eroding. Wind, rain and waves add geologic character to the newly emerged islands, cutting deep valleys, creating sandy beaches and turning a mound of lava into a tropical paradise.

At the far northwestern end of the chain, the Hawaiian Islands have receded back below the ocean surface to become seamounts. Moving eastward from Kure Atoll, the islands get progressively taller and

HAWAII BY THE NUMBERS

- Hawaii comprises 6423 sq miles of total land area, less than 0.2% of the total US landmass.
- Within the state, there are eight main islands, but only seven are populated.
- Beyond Kaua'i, the minuscule Northwestern Hawaiian Islands stretch for 1200 miles.
- On the Big Island, Ka Lae (South Point) is the USA's southernmost point, 18°55'N of the equator.

younger until you reach Hawai'i, aka the Big Island, the still-growing, 500,000-year-old baby of the Hawaiian group.

Straddling the hot spot today, the Big Island's Kilauea is the world's most active volcano. All Hawaiian volcanoes are shield volcanoes that erupt with effusive lava to create gently sloped, dome-shaped mountains, but they can also have a more explosive side, as Kilauea dramatically reminded onlookers and scientists in 2008.

Under the sea about 20 miles southeast of the Big Island, a new undersea volcano is erupting – Lo'ihi Seamount. Although you can't see it today, stick around: in 10,000 years or so, it will emerge from the water to become the newest island in the Hawaiian chain.

Wildlife in Hawaii

In the Beginning

Born of barren lava flows, the Hawaiian Islands were originally populated only by plants and animals that could traverse the Pacific – for example, seeds clinging to a bird's feather or fern spores that drifted thousands of miles through the air. Most species that landed here didn't survive. Scientists estimate that successful species were established maybe once every 70,000 years – and these included no amphibians, no browsing animals, no mosquitoes and only two mammals: a bat and a seal.

Hawaii is the northernmost point of the triangle of Pacific islands known as Polynesia (many islands); the other points are New Zealand and Rapa Nui (Easter Island).

However, the flora and fauna that did succeed thrived on an unusually rich, diverse land, containing nearly every ecological or life zone. Without predators or much competition, new species dropped their defensive protections: thorns, poisons and strong odors disappeared. This evolutionary process accounts for why more than 90% of native species are endemic, or unique to the islands, and why they fare so poorly against modern invaders and artificial environmental changes.

Humans Invade

When the first Polynesians arrived, they introduced new animals and plants, including pigs, chickens, rats, coconuts, bananas, taro and about two dozen other plants, not to mention people. These 'Polynesian introductions' caused the first wave of species extinctions, including an estimated 50-plus birds that had disappeared by the time Captain Cook dropped off goats and melon, pumpkin and onion seeds in 1778. Later European, Asian and American sea captains and immigrants imported more exotic (or 'alien') species, such as cattle that foraged at will, invasive ground covers and ornamental plants.

The endangered *'ope'ape'a* (Hawaiian hoary bat), one of Hawaii's two endemic mammals, has reddish-brown or grey fur with white tinges, making it appear 'hoary' (grayed by age). With a foot-wide wingspan, these tree-dwellers exist predominantly around forests on the leeward sides of the Big Island and Kaua'i.

Today, Hawaii is the extinction capital of the USA, accounting for 75% of the nation's documented extinctions. More than two-thirds of Hawaii's known birds and half of its endemic plant species are already extinct. Recently the islands have become a unique laboratory in the global scientific effort to discover sustainable methods of conservation – preserving a diversity of wildlife, and by extension our own skins.

Animals

In modern times, nearly every animal introduced to the islands – whether rabbits, goats, sheep, pigs or horses – has led to environmental devastation. Some, like Maui's axis deer and the Big Island's cattle, were 'gifts' to Hawaiian kings that spun off out-of-control feral populations. The ubiquitous mongoose was originally introduced to control sugarcane rats, but has become a worse plague than the rats. Feral animals are one of the most destructive ecological forces in Hawaii today, and getting rid of them is central to re-establishing native landscapes and saving endangered species.

HAWAII'S ANGRY BIRDS VS FERAL PIGS

How delicately interdependent are Hawaiian ecosystems? Consider how pigs are driving Hawaiian birds to extinction. Not directly, but the chain of cause and effect is undeniable.

Feral pigs, most likely descended from domestic pigs brought by early Europeans, have caused widespread devastation to the islands' native forests. At Hawaii's national parks, pigs are considered public enemy number one, and the subject of federally sponsored eradication and fencing programs. Outside national parks, eradication efforts are few, and it's estimated that there may be one feral pig for every 33 human residents in the state.

Pigs trample and kill native fauna, destroy the forest understory and spread the seeds of invasive plants far and wide. Pigs love native tree-fern stems, knocking them over and eating the plants' tender insides; the bowl-like cavities left behind catch rainwater and create ideal breeding pools for mosquitoes.

Common mosquitoes – presumed to have arrived in Hawaii in water casks aboard whaling ships in 1826 – pick up avian malaria and avian pox (also introduced from the European continent) and spread it to native birds, particularly honeycreepers, who have lost their natural immunity to these diseases.

It's a simple equation: no feral pigs, far fewer mosquitoes, far fewer avian diseases, and far more honeycreepers. What's not so simple is how to make that a reality.

Island Birds

Many of Hawaii's birds are spectacular examples of adaptive radiation. For instance, all 56 species of endemic Hawaiian honeycreepers most likely evolved from a single finch ancestor. Today, only 18 of these brightly colored birds survive, and six are considered critically endangered. Two-thirds of all native birds are already extinct, the victims of more aggressive, non-native birds, predatory feral animals (such as mongooses and pigs) and infectious avian diseases against which they have no natural immunity.

The endangered nene, Hawaii's state bird, is a long-lost cousin of the Canada goose. Nene usually nest in sparse vegetation on rugged lava flows, to which their feet have adapted by losing most of their webbing. While eight other species of Hawaiian geese (now extinct) became flightless, nene remain strong flyers. There were once as many as 25,000 nene on all of the Hawaiian Islands, but by the 1950s there were only 30 left. Captive breeding and release programs have raised their numbers to around 2500 on the Big Island, Maui, Kaua'i and Moloka'i today. In 2014 a breeding pair of nene hatched goslings on O'ahu for the first time in three centuries.

The only hawk native to Hawaii, the *'io* was a symbol of royalty and often an *'aumakua* (protective deity). They are known to breed only on the Big Island, where their numbers have held steady at more than 3000 for the last decade. In 2008 the *'io* was proposed for delisting from the endangered species list, but a decision is still pending.

Hawaii for Birders

- *Papahānau mokuākea Marine National Monument*
- *Haleakalā National Park*
- *Koke'e State Park*
- *James Campbell National Wildlife Refuge*
- *Kealia Pond National Wildlife Refuge*

Marine Mammals

Up to 10,000 migrating North Pacific humpback whales come to Hawaiian waters for calving each winter, and whale-watching is a major attraction. The world's fifth-largest whale, the endangered humpback can reach lengths of 45ft and weigh up to 50 tons. Other whales (such as rarely seen blue and fin whales) also migrate through. By federal law, no one may approach a whale in Hawaiian waters closer than 100yd.

Hawaii is also home to a number of dolphins, most famously the spinner dolphin, named for its leaps from the water. These acrobats are nocturnal feeders that come into sheltered bays during the day to rest. Because they are extremely sensitive to human disturbance, federal guidelines recommend that swimmers do not approach any wild dolphins closer than 50yd.

One of the Pacific's most endangered marine creatures is the Hawaiian monk seal, named for both the monastic cowl-like fold of skin at its neck and its solitary habits. Having migrated to the islands more than 10 million years ago, the Hawaiian monk seal has evolved into a unique species that has been called a 'living fossil.' The Hawaiian name for the animal is *'ilio holo kai,* meaning 'the dog that runs in the sea.' Adults are more than 7ft long and 500lb of toughness, some with the scars to prove they can withstand shark attacks. Once nearly driven to extinction, their population today numbers just over 1000.

Although monk seals once bred primarily in the remote Northwestern Hawaiian Islands, recently they have begun hauling out on beaches on the main islands. According to the National Oceanic and Atmospheric Administration (NOAA), people are now the biggest threat to the survival of Hawaiian monk seals. Humans who disturb seals that have hauled out on beaches to rest, molt or breed are driving down an already endangered population. Federal guidelines advise staying back at least 50yd and avoiding all human-seal interactions. Areas of the beach around a hauled-out seal are often roped off to prevent close approach.

Hawaii Books for Nature Lovers

A World Between Waves, edited by Frank Stewart

Hawaii: The Islands of Life by the Nature Conservancy with Gavan Daws

Tropical Fish

Hawaii's coral reefs constitute 84% of all US reefs, and they are home to more than 500 fish species, of which more than 20% are endemic. Protected coral reefs teem with vast numbers of tropical fish: bright yellow tangs, striped butterfly fish and Moorish idols, silver needlefish, and gape-mouthed moray eels. Neon-colored wrasse, which have more species than any other Hawaiian reef fish, change sex (and color) as they mature.

The contrast between the variety and numbers of fish in the main islands and Papahānaumokuākea Marine National Monument is stunning. For instance, the weight of fish per acre in the Northwestern Hawaiian Islands is 2000lb, but it's 600lb in the main islands; meanwhile, predators like sharks and jacks are 15 times as numerous in the monument's shallow reefs.

SACRED HONU

Hawaiians traditionally revere the green sea turtle, called *honu*. Often considered a personal *'aumakua* (protective deity), its image appears in petroglyphs (and today in tattoos). For ancient Hawaiians, sea turtles were a delicious and prized source of food, but their capture and consumption were typically governed by strict religious and traditional codes.

As with Hawaii's other two native species of sea turtles – the hawksbill and the leatherback – *honu* are endangered and protected by federal law. Adults can grow more than 3ft long and weigh more than 200lb. Young turtles are omnivorous, but adults become strict vegetarians (unique among sea turtles). Eating sea grasses and algae turns their fat green – hence their name.

Green sea turtles can be seen throughout the Hawaiian Islands, often spotted while they are feeding in shallow lagoons, bays and estuaries. Their main nesting site is French Frigate Shoals in remote Papahānaumokuākea Marine National Monument. Up to 700 female turtles (90% of the total population) come to lay their eggs there each year.

If you spot a sea turtle hauled out on a beach in Hawaii, federal guidelines advise keeping back at least 20ft to avoid disturbing the animal or interfering with its natural activities. Always leave turtles a clear path from the beach back into the water and never touch, feed, chase or otherwise attempt to interact with them.

Land & Sea

In Hawaii, what's going on underwater – where rainbow-colored tropical fish and sea turtles swim, migratory whales sing and monk seals dive – is just as thrilling as what awaits on land: fiery lava flowing into the Pacific and skyscraping mountain summits giving star-studded glimpses of the Milky Way.

1

2

DAVE FLEETHAM / DESIGN PICS / GETTY IMAGES ©

4

MATTHEW MICAH WRIGHT / GETTY IMAGES ©

1. Observatory on Mauna Kea (p249)
The observatories on Mauna Kea comprise the greatest collection of telescopes on earth – they are all here for the for the ideal views of the heavens.

2. Hawaiian monk seal (p621)
With a population of just over 1000, this is one of the Pacific's most endangered marine creatures.

3. *'Ohi'a* (p624) growing in lava flow
The *'ohi'a's* tufted flowers are considered sacred to Pele, goddess of fire and volcanoes.

4. Na Pali Coast (p531)
The pristine 22-mile stretch of cliffs, white-sand and turquoise coves is a magnificent sight.

3

RON DAHLQUIST / DESIGN PICS / GETTY IMAGES ©

Plants

Mile for mile, Hawaii has the highest concentration of ecological zones on earth. Whether you're in tropical rain forests or dry forests, high-altitude alpine deserts or coastal dunes, wetland marshes or grassy plains, extravagantly diverse flora occupies every island niche.

Of course, what you'll see today is not what the first Polynesians or ancient Hawaiians saw. Most 'Hawaiian' agricultural products started as exotic imports – including papayas, pineapples, mangoes, bananas, macadamia nuts and coffee. Over half of Hawaii's native forests are now gone, mainly due to logging, conversion to agriculture and invasive plants. Of Hawaii's nearly 1300 endemic plant species, more than 100 are already extinct and more than 300 remain endangered.

Exotic & Endangered Flora

The classic hibiscus is native to Hawaii, but many varieties have also been introduced, so that now hundreds of varieties grow on the islands. Sadly, it's perhaps fitting that Hawaii's state flower, the *pua aloalo* (yellow hibiscus), was added to the endangered species list in 1994. The *koki'o ke'oke'o,* a native white shrub or small tree that can grow up to 30ft high, is one of the only known hibiscus in the world with a fragrance.

The Last Atoll: Exploring Hawai'i's Endangered Ecosystems, by Pamela Frierson, narrates fascinating explorations of the most remote points of the Hawaiian archipelago. It's the next best thing to sailing to Midway Island yourself.

Strangely enough, while Hawaii's climate is ideal for growing orchids, there are only three native species. In the 19th century, Asian immigrants began importing orchids and today they're a thriving industry. Hawaii also blooms with scores of introduced ornamental and exotic tropical flowers, including blood-red anthurium with heart-shaped leaves, brilliant orange-and-blue bird-of-paradise and myriad heliconia.

Notable exotic trees include ironwood, a non-native conifer with drooping needles, which acts as a natural windbreak and prevents erosion from beaches; majestic banyan trees, which have a canopy of hanging aerial roots with trunks large enough to swallow small children; and towering monkeypods, a common shade tree that has dark glossy green leaves, powder-puff pink flowers and longish seed pods.

Native Trees, Flowers & Ferns

Perhaps the most bewitching of native Hawaiian trees is the koa, growing more than 50ft high and nowadays found only at higher elevations. This rich hardwood has been used to make canoes, surfboards and even ukuleles. Endemic *wiliwili* is a lightweight wood also popular for making surfboards and canoes. Hawaii was once rich in fragrant *'iliahi (*sandalwood) forests, but these were almost entirely sold off to foreign traders in the 19th century.

Ancient Hawaiians didn't have metals and never developed pottery, so plants fulfilled most of their needs. Ethnobotanist Beatrice H Krauss delves into this fascinating history in her books *Plants in Hawaiian Culture* and *Plants in Hawaiian Medicine.*

The widespread and versatile *'ohi'a* is one of the first plants to colonize lava flows. Its distinctive tufted flowers (*lehua*), consisting of petalless groups of red, orange, yellow, pink and white stamens, are considered sacred to Pele, goddess of fire and volcanoes. Native forests of *'ohi'a* and *hapu'u* (tree ferns) are vital, endangered habitats. Brought by early Polynesian settlers, the *kukui* (candlenut tree) has light silver-tinged foliage that stands out brightly in the forest; the oily nuts from Hawaii's state tree can be burned like candles and are used for making lei and lotions.

Flowering native coastal plants include *pohuehue* (beach morning-glory), with its glossy green leaves and pink or purple flowers, found just above the wrack line; beach *naupaka,* a shrub with oval green leaves and small pinkish-white, five-petaled flowers that look as if they've been torn in half (by a broken-hearted lover, according to Hawaiian legend); and *'ilima* (a yellow flowering ground-cover that is the island of O'ahu's official flower), its delicate yellow-orange blossoms strung into lei.

Hawaii's Parks & Preserves

Hawaii has two national parks: Haleakalā National Park on Maui and Hawai'i Volcanoes National Park on the Big Island (www.nps.gov/state/HI/). Both have volcanoes as centerpieces, contain an astonishing range of environments and provide some of the best hiking in the islands. A Unesco World Heritage Site since 1987, the latter welcomes more than 1.5 million visitors a year, making it the state's most visited attraction.

HAWAII'S TOP 15 NATURAL AREAS

PROTECTED AREA	FEATURES	ACTIVITIES	WHEN TO VISIT
O'ahu			
Hanauma Bay Nature Preserve	enormous coral reef in a volcanic ring	snorkeling, swimming, diving	year-round
Malaekahana State Recreation Area	sandy beach, offshore bird sanctuary	swimming, snorkeling, camping, birding	May–Oct
Hawai'i, the Big Island			
Hawai'i Volcanoes National Park	lava tubes, volcanic craters, fern forests, petroglyphs	hiking, camping, backpacking, caving, birding	year-round
Kealakekua Bay State Historical Park	calm waters, coral reefs, sea caves	snorkeling, diving, kayaking	year-round
Mauna Kea	Hawaii's highest peak, ancient Hawaiian sites	hiking, stargazing	year-round
Maui			
Haleakalā National Park (Kipahulu area)	bamboo forest, waterfalls, cascading pools	hiking, swimming	year-round
Haleakalā National Park (summit area)	cloud forest, eroded volcanic summit, nene	hiking, camping, birding, backpacking, cabins	year-round
Wai'anapanapa State Park	black-sand beach, caves	hiking, camping, cabins	year-round
Lana'i			
Hulopo'e Bay	white-sand beach, spinner dolphins	swimming, snorkeling, diving	year-round
Moloka'i			
Kalaupapa National Historical Park	remote peninsula, steep sea cliffs, historic sites	hiking, mule riding, guided tours	year-round
Kamakou Preserve	rain forest, montange bog, striking valley vistas	hiking, birding	May–Oct
Kaua'i			
Koke'e State Park	clifftop vistas, waterfalls, swamp, rain forest	scenic lookouts, hiking, birding	May–Oct
Na Pali Coast State Park	waterfalls, beaches, Hawaii's most famous trekking route	hiking, backpacking, camping, swimming, snorkeling	May–Oct
Waimea Canyon State Park	unbeatable views of the 'Grand Canyon of the Pacific'	scenic lookouts, hiking, cycling, mountain biking	May–Oct
Papahānaumokuākea Marine National Monument			
Midway Atoll	Laysan albatross colony, rich coral reefs, marine wildlife, WWII history	birding, snorkeling, kayaking, photography, guided tours	Nov–Jul

In addition, the islands have six national historical parks, sites, trails and memorials, most of which help to preserve Hawaiian culture. Four are on the Big Island, the most popular of which is Pu'uhonua O Hōnaunau (Place of Refuge) National Historical Park. On Moloka'i, Kalaupapa National Historical Park is a unique living-history interpretive site. O'ahu claims the USS *Arizona* Memorial at Pearl Harbor, part of the larger WWII Valor in the Pacific National Monument. Hawaii also has nine national wildlife refuges (www.fws.gov/pacific/refuges) on the main islands that protect endangered waterbirds and plants.

Incredibly, Hawaii has more than 50 state parks, historic sites, monuments and recreational areas (www.hawaiistateparks.org). These diverse natural areas include stunners such as Waimea Canyon on Kaua'i and Diamond Head on O'ahu. Each island also has county-managed beaches and parks, as well as privately run botanical gardens, zoos and aquariums.

Environmental Report Card

Keeping Hawaii Wild

Among the most dire environmental problems facing Hawaii right now are feral exotic animals and the uncontrolled proliferation of invasive, habitat-modifying plants and insects that are continually being introduced from overseas. Even on Hawaii's protected public lands, budget cuts hamper eradication and rehabilitation efforts.

Hawaii wildlife conservation reports can be depressing reading, but success stories prove that with enough effort and the right conditions, nature can rehabilitate itself. The nonprofit **Nature Conservancy** (www.nature.org/hawaii) is deeply involved in Hawaii – read its biodiversity conservation plan (www.hawaiiecoregionplan.info) online.

Land Development

Since the 1960s, mass tourism has posed challenges to Hawaii's natural environment, with the rampant development of land-hungry resorts and water-thirsty golf courses. Sprawling subdivisions also strain Hawaii's limited watershed and nearly full landfills. Meanwhile, ongoing construction often uncovers and disturbs archaeological sites such as heiau (temples), petroglyphs and burial grounds. Protecting these important Hawaiian cultural sites and repatriating *iwi kupuna* (human remains) can delay road building and construction for years.

Mainland tech billionaire Larry Ellison, who bought 98% of the island of Lana'i in 2012, has announced plans to turn that island into a 'laboratory for sustainability.' But so far ambitious plans for solar energy, ocean water desalination and organic farms have gone nowhere, while improving infrastructure for affluent tourists has been a priority. Lana'i's previous owner, David Murdock, retains rights to develop a controversial wind farm on the former pineapple plantation island. Wind-farm opposition group Friends of Lana'i (http://friendsoflanai.org) argues that some environmentally and culturally sensitive areas of the island would be destroyed, that wildlife would be endangered and that there are better renewable energy alternatives for such a small island.

Future development of the sacred volcanic summits of Mauna Kea and Haleakalā is another hot-button topic. Many environmental and Hawaiian groups adamantly oppose building any new astronomical or solar observatories on either peak. In 2013 the state's Board of Land and Natural Resources renewed the University of Hawai'i's long-term lease atop Mauna Kea, paving the way for building the new Thirty Meter Telescope (www.tmt.org) near its summit on the Big Island. One year earlier the board granted a construction permit for the world's largest optical/infrared solar telescope (http://dkist.nso.edu) atop Haleakalā on Maui.

ENVIRONMENT HAWAI'I

Curious about Hawaii's environmental health? Get the lowdown from Environment Hawai'i (www.environment-hawaii.org), a watchdog group that publishes a monthly newsletter on a wide range of topics, from wildlife conservation to development. Browse top stories and recent issues online.

MARINE WILDLIFE 911

➡ Report Hawaiian monk seal sightings to the Fisheries Service of the National Oceanic and Atmospheric Administration (NOAA) by calling ☎808-220-7802.

➡ If you notice an entangled or injured seal or dolphin, or a whale or dolphin swimming in very shallow ocean water, stay back and call the NOAA hotline: ☎888-256-9840.

➡ If you spot an obviously sick or injured, stranded or dead sea turtle, keep your distance and call ☎808-983-5730, or ☎808-288-5685 outside of normal business hours.

Farm & Military Cleanup

Vast tracts of Hawaii's native forest were long ago cleared to make way for the monocrop industries of sugarcane and pineapple. In the past, corporate agribusiness in Hawaii has been found guilty of violating Environmental Protection Agency (EPA) guidelines regarding soil and groundwater contamination on the islands. In 2010 – almost 15 years after being added to the EPA's Superfund national priority list – O'ahu's Del Monte Corp plantation was finally cleaned up. Some other former agricultural land has been successfully placed under conservation easement protections for future generations. Statewide issues yet to be resolved include water pollution caused by agricultural runoff and debates over whether GMOs (genetically modified organisms) should be outlawed.

Long-standing friction over the US military presence also continues, especially on O'ahu. Unfortunately, the military has not always fully complied with environmental regulations, and some military training maneuvers have had a negative impact on Hawaiian cultural sites and local communities. For example, in 2002 it was discovered that the army dumped tons of conventional weapons off the Wai'anae Coast in western O'ahu; it took almost a decade for 'Ordnance Reef,' littered with military munitions, to be cleaned up.

Sustainable Fishing & Shores

Overfishing is a major concern, as three-quarters of Hawaii's reef fish have been depleted during the last century. Unsurprisingly, the species most in danger are those fish popular for aquariums or for eating. To help fish stocks recover, the state has almost completely banned laying gill nets. Sustainable fishing practices are growing, including through community partnerships with **Hawaii Fish Trust** (www.conservation.org/projects/Pages/hawaii-fish-trust.aspx).

Hawaii's shorelines are still in danger. The threat of rising seas due to global warming and persistent beach erosion are raising alarm bells. Scientific studies have found that 25% of beaches on O'ahu and Maui have been lost in the last 50 years. Meanwhile, if sea levels rise 1ft to 3ft by the end of this century as predicted, half of Waikiki's hotels will find themselves standing in the ocean.

Plastic pollution can be an issue on- and offshore. In 2014 Hawaii became the first US state to ban plastic store bags. These and other plastic items can be easily mistaken for jellyfish and eaten by endangered sea turtles. Further out in the ocean surrounding Hawaii, the density of floating debris is ever increasing, and some scientists estimate that the 'Great Pacific Garbage Patch' may now be larger than Texas.

A multicultural grassroots environmental alliance, **Kahea** (http://kahea.org), tackles a wide range of Hawaiian ecological, developmental and cultural issues. Check for action alerts online.

Green Hawaii

Hawaii is a Polynesian paradise with astoundingly varied natural environments – from *mauka* (toward the mountains) to *makai* (toward the sea). It's also a high-profile test case of whether humans can achieve a sustainable relationship with nature. With a renaissance of Hawaiian traditions, *aloha 'aina* (respect and love for the land) runs strong. Conservation efforts, both state funded and grassroots, are gaining strength; ecotourism is growing; and environmentally responsible businesses are sprouting statewide.

The **Hawaii Ecotourism Association** (HEA; www.hawaiiecotourism.org) runs an ecotour certification program and publishes a free online directory of member 'green' businesses, including outdoor outfitters and hotels.

The Islands Go Green

Hawaii breathes green. From volcano summits and verdant cloud forests to the ocean depths where whales sing, the natural beauty of this place swallows you up. Green is also a way of thinking and living on these islands, where residents spend many of their waking hours outdoors. It's fair to say that nearly everyone who lives here feels a close personal connection to the land and to the sea.

Environmental concerns are entangled in just about every major issue facing Hawaii. Development is almost always a contentious issue, due to the negative impacts that tourism, the military and agribusiness have had on Hawaii's natural environment and indigenous culture. While the state's economy would not survive without these industries, some residents are asking what kind of jobs they really bring, and at what cost? Tourism and a growing human population are intensifying the pressures on Hawaii's watershed, energy resources and landfills.

How to achieve a more diversified, 'greener' economy and sustainable growth for the future is the question on almost everyone's minds. Hawaii residents have repeatedly shown their support, although not unanimously, for 'green' initiatives at the ballot box, including renewable-energy initiatives. Meanwhile, islanders of all backgrounds have become environmental activists – from Hawaiians restoring ancient fishponds to volunteers working to clean up beaches and uproot invasive plants.

Travel More Sustainably

More than eight million tourists land in Hawaii every year – they outnumber residents five to one. But with a few simple, sustainable travel practices, you can help to keep these islands a paradise for years to come.

HAWAII IN 2050

'Living sustainably is part of our daily practice,' decided the ambitious **Hawai'i 2050** (www.hawaii2050.org) sustainability plan. This statewide program combined community input with a governmental task force to formulate economic, social and environmental policies that focus on renewable energy, living sustainably within the bounds of the islands' natural resources and striking a balance between profitable tourism and Hawaiian cultural preservation. A tall order, but as the plan itself admitted, this is 'not an academic or political exercise; it is a matter of the survival of Hawai'i as we know it.'

Eat, Drink & Shop Locally

Keep in mind that everything not grown or raised in Hawaii has to be shipped long-distance to the islands by boat or plane, which results in increased greenhouse-gas emissions, not to mention higher prices. It's no wonder that even the state government has started encouraging residents to buy more food grown and raised on the islands. Get a taste of the goodness at weekly farmers markets on any of the main islands.

When shopping at grocery stores and choosing restaurants in Hawaii, look for places that feature locally grown produce and sustainably caught seafood. Takeout food containers and disposable silverware and chopsticks are a nightmare for Hawaii's limited landfills. Try to patronize places that use biodegradable takeout-ware, even if it costs you a bit extra. Bottled water may be convenient, but tap water is perfectly fine to drink in Hawaii, so bring along your own refillable container.

Buying island-made products as souvenirs supports the local economy and the survival of traditional Hawaiian arts and crafts, and it often helps sustain the environment too. Beware of mass-produced 'Hawaiian' quilts, shell lei and other fakes and knockoffs made cheaply overseas, often in the Philippines. Look for official seals on island-made products on Kaua'i (see http://kauaimade.net) and Maui (see www.madeinmaui.org); on Hawai'i, visit Honoka'a's Big Island Grown (p259) shop.

A new crop of small, family-owned organic farms are growing in Hawaii, and you can sample their bounty at farmers markets statewide. Plug into the local food scene, including farmers markets and farm-to-table restaurants, with the magazine *Edible Hawaiian Islands* (http://hawaiianislands.ediblefeast.com).

Sleeping Green

A number of hotels in Hawaii have yet to embrace many sustainable business practices. Even such simple eco-initiatives as switching to bulk soap dispensers and offering recycling bins are rare. Check the hotel or resort's website for 'green' policies before booking your stay.

Once you've checked in, you can help save energy by turning off all lights, electronics and air-conditioning units whenever you leave your hotel room. Hang-dry and reuse your towels, and display the card provided to request that linens not be changed daily. Bring your own toiletries in refillable containers instead of using plastic mini bottles of shampoo, conditioner etc.

Consider camping while you're in Hawaii or staying at an ecofriendly, locally owned B&B or guesthouse. Renting a condo, apartment, cottage or vacation home with a kitchen can also reduce your environmental impact, including by saving the water expended on daily housekeeping, the energy consumed by round-the-clock services and the surplus food that gets thrown out by restaurants at Hawaii's hotels and resorts.

Recycle, Reduce & Reuse

Recycling bins are not common at hotels or on the streets outside of major tourist areas such as Waikiki on O'ahu, but you'll find them at many beaches, public parks and some museums and tourist attractions on the main islands. Each county also has public recycling drop-off collection bins, often located at garbage transfer stations.

Plastic shopping bags were banned statewide in 2014. You can help cut down on landfill waste by reusing your own cloth bags when shopping. Sold at supermarkets, convenience stores and tourists shops, these reusable bags also make colorful aloha-print souvenirs of your trip.

Alternative Transportation

Avoid driving if you can walk, cycle or take public transportation. Public buses run limited, mostly commuter-focused routes on Maui, Kaua'i, the Big Island and Moloka'i. On O'ahu, bus routes are more comprehensive, frequently running to many of the same places that visitors want to go. Look for a new bike-sharing program, Bikeshare Hawaii (www.bikesharehawaii.org), to be operational in Honolulu as soon as 2016.

SUSTAINABLE ICON

It seems like everyone's trying to be 'green' these days, but how can you know which Hawaii businesses are actually ecofriendly and which are simply jumping on the sustainable bandwagon? Lonely Planet's sustainable icon (🌿) indicates listings that have proven to contribute to a greener future for Hawaii. Some are involved in environmental education and wildlife conservation, while others help preserve Hawaiian cultural traditions and historical sites or support the local food economy.

If you need to rent your own wheels during your trip, try to choose the most fuel-efficient vehicle. Book in advance for hybrid or biofueled cars, now offered by some major international car-rental agencies as well as local independent businesses that maintain small fleets of Toyota Priuses, biodiesel VW Beetles, Smart cars etc.

Looking for a carbon-offsetting program for your airline flights? ClimateCare (www.climatecare.org) funds pro-environment projects in the developing world.

Focused on Hawaii's natural and cultural beauty, the website **Alternative Hawaii** (www.alternative-hawaii.com) offers hundreds of ecofriendly tourism listings, from accommodations and restaurants to tours and events.

Tread Lightly

So many travelers come to enjoy Hawaii's gorgeous scenery and myriad wildlife that only strict protections keep certain mega-popular places – such as O'ahu's Hanauma Bay – from being loved to death. But many equally scenic and fragile areas have fewer regulations, or little oversight, and the question becomes: just because you can do something, should you?

Every step you take on the islands has an impact, but you can minimize the effects by being conscious of your surroundings. What are the best ways to experience Hawaii's natural beauty without harming it in the process? For some outdoor activities, there isn't a single definitive answer, but here are some universal guidelines and best practices to follow:

Coral-reef etiquette When snorkeling or diving, never touch the coral reef. It's that simple. Coral polyps are living organisms, and broken pieces can create wounds and openings for infection and disease. Watch your fins; avoid stirring up clouds of sand, which can settle on and damage reef organisms. Don't feed fish.

Dive etiquette Practice proper buoyancy control to avoid hitting the reef. Don't use reef anchors or ground boats over coral. Limit your time in caves, as air bubbles can collect on roofs and leave organisms high and dry.

Encountering sea turtles and marine mammals Federal and state laws protect all wild marine mammals and turtles from 'harassment.' Legally, this usually means approaching them closer than 50yd (100yd for whales, or 20ft for turtles) or doing anything that disrupts their behavior. The most important actions to avoid are pursuing or touching wild dolphins, and disturbing monk seals or sea turtles that have 'hauled out' and are resting on beaches.

Cruises Choose a sailboat over a motor-propelled cruise. Riding with the wind is more ecofriendly, and sailboats can often get closer (although not too close!) to marine life that would otherwise be repelled by the noise of motors. Look for tour companies that adhere to strict environmental practices and don't discharge waste into the ocean.

Hiking Scrub the soles of your shoes and wipe down your backpack and any outdoor gear *before* landing in Hawaii to avoid inadvertently importing invasive species via stray seeds. Prevent erosion by staying on marked hiking and mountain-biking trails. Respect all 'No Trespassing – Kapu' and 'Private Property' signs, unless a trustworthy local resident says it's actually OK.

Helicopter rides Some places in Hawaii you can't reach except by air. However, as air tours increase, aircraft noise disturbs visitors and island residents on the ground, and it stresses bird populations. If you do fly, pick the most fuel-efficient helicopter possible, and consider carbon offsetting your flight.

4WDs & ATVs Always stay on the road, track or pre-established trail. Off-roading, even on private land, can cause scars on the land that may take decades to heal. Better yet, consider mountain biking or hiking as an alternative, low-impact way of exploring the landscape.

Volunteering on Vacation

Volunteering provides an experience you'll never get by just passing through a place, and also lets you give something back to the local community during your trip. In Hawaii, there's almost always some kind of volunteer project for visitors to get involved in – for instance, cleaning up public beaches, restoring forest and mountain trails, or pulling invasive exotic plants – even if it's for just an afternoon.

To find volunteer opportunities, ask your hotel concierge; check alternative local newspapers and websites such as Volunteer Match (www.volunteermatch.org) and Craigslist (http://honolulu.craigslist.org); or contact nonprofit organizations working on the islands directly, including the following:

Conservation Connections (www.conservationconnections.org) Browse a variety of drop-in, eco-conscious volunteer opportunities on all of the main islands.

Habitat for Humanity (www.habitat.org) Build affordable housing in Hawaii's low-income communities.

Haleakalā National Park (p404) Day and overnight wilderness conservation trips in Maui's national park.

Hawaii Food Bank (www.hawaiifoodbank.org) Help feed the hungry on O'ahu and Kaua'i.

CLOSE ENCOUNTERS: DOLPHIN SWIMS

Signing up for a 'dolphin encounter' in Hawaii deserves careful consideration. Although many programs claim to be educational and ecofriendly, the effects of human-dolphin interaction are complex. Due to animal-welfare and human-safety concerns, a few countries – including Brazil, Italy and the UK – have completely banned interactive programs with marine mammals. Widely reported concerns in Hawaii include the following:

➡ In the wild, acrobatic spinner dolphins are nocturnal feeders that come into sheltered bays during the day to rest; they are sensitive to human disturbance, and federal guidelines recommend that swimmers don't approach within 50yd. Some tour boats allow swimmers to approach the dolphins much closer than this.

➡ According to marine biologists, encountering humans can exhaust wild dolphins, leaving them without enough critical energy to feed or defend themselves later. Repeated encounters with humans have driven some dolphins out of their natural habitats to seek less-safe resting places, where they may be predated upon.

➡ In captivity, dolphins are trained to perform for humans using a variety of techniques, ranging from positive behavioral training to food deprivation. They may also be exposed to human-borne illnesses and bacteria when touched or kissed by people. Some dolphins kept in captivity have had their dorsal fins damaged by human swimmers.

➡ The US National Marine Fisheries Service has reported that 'dolphin encounter' programs tend to make captive animals act more aggressively, especially if the human participants are nervous. Injuries to human participants, such as broken arms and ribs, have occurred. Dolphin encounters can be particularly dangerous for children.

➡ The Oscar-winning documentary *The Cove,* featuring an ex–dolphin trainer turned animal-welfare activist, looks at the 'dolphinarium' biz and the global industry that profits from keeping dolphins in captivity. Learn more at www.thecovemovie.com.

For more easy ideas about how to make your trip more sustainable and ecofriendly, pick up *50 Simple Things You Can Do to Save Hawai'i* by environmental studies professor Gail Grabowsky.

Hawaii Nature Center (www.hawaiinaturecenter.org) Trail maintenance, gardening, environmental restoration and special events on O'ahu and Maui.
Hawaii State Parks Partners (www.hawaiistateparks.org/partners) Natural and cultural resource preservation on all of the main islands.
Hawai'i Volcanoes National Park (p289) Reforestation and invasive-plant-removal projects, sea-turtle monitoring and more.
Hawai'i Wildlife Fund (http://wildhawaii.org) Turtle conservation and beach and marine-debris cleanup on Maui and the Big Island.
Hawaiian Islands Humpback Whale National Marine Sanctuary (p366) Annual migratory whale counts and year-round volunteer opportunities on Maui, O'ahu and Kaua'i.
Kaho'olawe Island Reserve Commission (KIRC; http://kahoolawe.hawaii.gov) Restoring the island's natural environment and important Hawaiian cultural sites.
Koke'e Resource Conservation Program (www.krcp.org) Eradicating invasive exotic plants ('weed busting') in Kaua'i's native forests.
Pacific Whale Foundation (www.volunteersonvacation.org) Lists short- and long-term volunteer projects from *mauka* to *makai* all around Maui.
Sierra Club (http://www.hi.sierraclub.org/kauai/) Educational volunteer service trips on Maui and the Big Island are all-inclusive working vacations for club members (annual membership from $15).
Surfrider Foundation (p48) Individual island chapters sponsor family-friendly coastal-cleanup and habitat-restoration days.

Survival Guide

Directory A–Z

Accommodations

Peak vs Off-Peak Times

- During high season – mid-December through March or April, and June through August – lodgings are more expensive and in demand.
- Major holidays and special events command premium prices, and lodgings can book up a year ahead.
- In low or shoulder seasons, expect discounts and easier booking. Polite bargaining may be possible.
- Unless otherwise noted, all lodgings are open year-round.

Reservations

Reservations are recommended year-round, especially during high season. A reservation guarantees your room, but most reservations require a deposit. If you cancel your reservation after a certain date, your money may not be refunded. Ask about cancellation policies and other fine-print restrictions before making a deposit.

Amenities

- Accommodations offering online computer terminals for guests are designated with the internet icon. An hourly fee may apply (eg at hotel business centers).
- In-room internet access at hotels is sometimes wired (not wireless); a daily fee may apply.
- The wi-fi icon (wi-fi) indicates that wireless internet access is offered. Look for free wi-fi hot spots in common areas (eg hotel lobbies, poolside).
- The swimming icon (swimming) appears where an indoor or outdoor pool is available.
- The air-conditioning icon (air-con) indicates where air-con is a standard amenity at hotels and resorts. At some hotels, condos, hostels, B&Bs and vacation rentals only fans may be provided.
- At the few properties where smoking rooms are available, you must specifically request them. At many hotels, resorts and condo complexes, smoking is prohibited everywhere on the property, even outdoors; expect high penalty fees for noncompliance.

BOOK YOUR STAY ONLINE

For more accommodations reviews by Lonely Planet authors, check out http://lonelyplanet.com/hotels/. You'll find independent reviews, as well as recommendations on the best places to stay. Best of all, you can book online.

B&Bs & Vacation Rentals

B&B accommodations in Hawaii vary from spare bedrooms in residential homes to pull-out-all-the-stops romantic hideaways. Often family-run operations, B&Bs can provide more personal experiences than hotels, but offer fewer services.

Despite their name, only some B&Bs offer breakfast or stock supplies – usually coffee, juice, fruit and bread or pastries – in guests' accommodations. Without a state-approved restaurant kitchen, B&Bs can be fined if caught making hot meals for guests.

B&Bs discourage unannounced drop-ins, so they sometimes do not appear on maps. Same-day reservations are hard to get. Always try to book B&Bs in advance, because they tend to fill up weeks or even months ahead of time. Many B&Bs have minimum-stay requirements of a few nights, although some will waive this if you pay a surcharge.

Typically, a vacation rental means renting an entire duplex, condo or house (with no on-site manager and no breakfast provided), but many B&Bs also rent standalone cottages and often all these kinds of properties are handled by the same rental agencies. Ask about any mandatory cleaning fees (minimum $50), which are common for stays of less than five nights.

Sometimes B&Bs and vacation rentals will refuse credit cards, instead requiring payment by cash, traveler's checks or a personal check drawn on a US bank account.

For B&B and vacation rental listings statewide, try the following:

Airbnb (www.airbnb.com)

Affordable Paradise (☎808-261-1693; www.affordable-paradise.com)

FlipKey (www.flipkey.com)

Hawaii's Best B&Bs (☎808-885-4550; www.bestbnb.com)

HomeAway (www.homeaway.com)

Pacific Islands Reservations (☎808-262-8133, 800-429-5711; www.pacificislandsreservations.com)

Purple Roofs (http://purpleroofs.com)

VRBO (www.vrbo.com)

Camping & Cabins

Hawaii has almost no full-service private campgrounds. The best public camping facilities are in national parks; next best are state parks; and typically the least well cared for are county parks. Campgrounds are less busy during the week than on weekends, when they tend to fill up with local families.

NATIONAL PARKS

Hawaii's two national parks – Maui's Haleakalā National Park and the Big Island's Hawai'i Volcanoes National Park – have drive-up campgrounds that are first-come, first-served and usually free (except for the Big Island's Namakanipaio Campground). Typically these drive-up campgrounds are just grassy dispersed areas with minimal amenities.

Permits, which are required for backcountry camping, are almost always available same-day for walk-up visitors. Advance reservations are strongly recommended for all cabin rentals.

STATE PARKS

➡ The five largest Hawaiian Islands offer camping at state parks (usually $18 to $30 per site per night, or $12 to $20 for Hawaii residents).

➡ State park campgrounds typically have picnic tables, BBQ grills, drinking water, toilets and outdoor cold-water showers.

➡ Some state parks also rent basic housekeeping cabins ($50 to $90 per night, or $30 to $60 for Hawaii residents).

➡ Obtain camping and cabin permits in person from any **Division of State Parks** (www.hawaiistateparks.org) office or book ahead online up to one year in advance. Permits are *not* available in person at campgrounds.

➡ On O'ahu, the **Division of State Parks (DSP) Headquarters** (☎808-587-0300; www.hawaiistateparks.org; room 310, 1151 Punchbowl St, Honolulu; ⏰8am-3:30pm Mon-Fri) handles camping reservations for all islands. Hours may vary, so call ahead.

COUNTY PARKS

Some county parks are wonderful, with white-sand beaches and good facilities, while others are run-down and dangerous. Keep in mind that just because you *can* camp somewhere doesn't necessarily mean you'll *want* to. Check out the campground in person or ask around before committing.

Each county has its own camping regulations, fees and reservation procedures; consult the government website for the latest details. Most counties don't allow you to show up without reservation and pay for a campsite in person at the campground. Usually you must reserve and pay for a camping permit in advance.

Condominiums

Usually more spacious than hotel rooms, condos are privately owned apartments furnished with almost everything a visitor needs, including a kitchen(ette). They're often less expensive than all but the cheapest hotel rooms, especially if you're traveling with family or friends.

➡ Most condo units have a multinight minimum stay requirement (five days is average), especially in high season.

SLEEPING PRICE RANGES

The following price ranges refer to a double room with private bath in high season. Unless otherwise stated, breakfast and taxes of almost 14% are not included.

$ less than $100

$$ $100 to $250

$$$ more than $250

SAFE CAMPING IN HAWAII

For safety reasons, a few county and state park campgrounds are not recommended because they are either very isolated or late-night carousing spots. Theft and violence aimed at campers is uncommon, but you should still choose your campgrounds carefully. Check our reviews, then ask locals and park staff for advice.

- The weekly rental rate is often six times the daily rate, and the monthly rate three times the weekly.
- Ask about mandatory cleaning fees, a surcharge that depends on the length of stay (usually $50 or more).
- To save money, try booking condos directly first, then go through rental agencies.
- Search online for condo-rental classified ads at **HomeAway** (www.homeaway.com), **VRBO** (www.vrbo.com), **FlipKey** (www.flipkey.com), **Airbnb** (www.airbnb.com) and **Craigslist** (http://honolulu.craigslist.org).

Hostels

Hawaii has only two hostels associated with **Hostelling International USA** (☎240-650-2100; www.hiusa.org), both of which are in Honolulu. All of the main islands have a small selection of private hostels, usually in larger towns and cities. A few are friendly and well kept, but the majority are aimed at backpackers or seasonal surfers and can be well-worn crash pads. Most are spartan, offering a common kitchen, internet access, bulletin boards and lockers. Dorm beds average $20 to $40 nightly, semiprivate or private rooms $50 to $100.

Hotels

It's common for hotels, particularly chains, to discount their published rack rates, typically by offering advance-purchase internet booking discounts. Otherwise rooms may be discounted by the season, week or day, depending on demand. Ask about special promotions and vacation packages when booking.

Be aware that descriptors such as 'oceanfront' and 'oceanview' are liberally used, though a periscope may be required to spot the surf. An ocean view can easily cost 50% to 100% more than a parking-lot view (which is sometimes euphemistically called a 'garden view' or 'mountain view').

Resorts

Hawaii's resorts are tropical pleasure palaces designed to anticipate your every need and provide 'the best' of everything (to keep you on the property every minute of the day). Expect myriad dining options, bars with live entertainment, multiple swimming pools, children's activity programs, and modern fitness and business centers. Mandatory daily resort fees may be charged; inquire when booking.

Courses

Some resort hotels and shopping centers offer free or low-cost Hawaiian arts and cultural classes, and workshops in hula dancing, lei making and the like. These introductory classes are mostly just for fun, and not for serious study. Schedules are sporadic, so keep your eyes and ears open and ask your hotel concierge about what's going on.

You can also learn how to surf, kayak, scuba dive or go stand-up paddleboarding (SUP) at most popular tourist beaches and resort areas on the main islands. Try to sign up for classes at least a couple of days in advance.

Road Scholar (☎800-454-5768; www.roadscholar.org) Top-notch educational programs, usually designed for those aged 50 or over, focus on Hawaii's people, traditional culture, wildlife and the natural environment. Programs last for one to three weeks and cost from $1500 to $6000, including accommodations, meals, classes, activities and interisland flights, but not airfare to/from Hawaii.

Customs Regulations

Currently, each international visitor is allowed to bring into the USA duty-free:

- 1L of liquor (if you're over 21 years old)
- 200 cigarettes (1 carton) or 100 (non-Cuban) cigars (if you're over 18 years old)

Amounts higher than $10,000 in cash, traveler's checks, money orders and other cash equivalents must be declared. For more detailed, up-to-date information, check with **US Customs and Border Protection** (www.cbp.gov).

Most fresh fruits and plants are restricted from entry into Hawaii (to prevent the spread of invasive species), and customs officials strictly

PRACTICALITIES

- **Electricity** 110/120V, 50/60Hz
- **Newspapers** *Honolulu Star-Advertiser* (www.staradvertiser.com) is Hawaii's major daily.
- **Radio** Hawaii has about 50 radio stations; National Public Radio (NPR) is at the lower end of the FM dial.
- **TV & DVDs** All major US TV networks and cable channels, plus 24-hour tourist information; DVDs coded region 1 (US and Canada only).
- **Time** Hawaii-Aleutian Standard Time (HST) is GMT-10. Hawaii doesn't observe Daylight Saving Time (DST). 'Island time' means taking things at a slower pace or being late.
- **Weights & Measures** Imperial (except 1 US gallon = 0.83 gallon)

enforce these regulations. Because Hawaii is a rabies-free state, the pet quarantine laws are draconian. Questions? Contact the **Hawaii Department of Agriculture** (http://hdoa.hawaii.gov).

All checked and carry-on bags leaving Hawaii for the US mainland, Alaska or Guam must be checked by an agricultural inspector at the airport using an X-ray machine. Make sure that any fresh food, produce or flowers in your baggage have been commercially packaged and approved for travel, or else you'll be forced to surrender those pineapples and orchids at the airport. For more information, call the **USDA Honolulu Office** (☎808-834-3240).

Discount Cards

Free visitor magazines packed with discount coupons are widely available at airports, hotels and tourist hot spots. However, you may find better deals on activities and tours by booking online directly with the company, preferably in advance.

Children, students, seniors, active and retired military personnel, and Hawaii residents usually receive discounts at museums and other sights; all but children need to present valid photo ID proving their status.

American Association of Retired Persons (AARP; www.aarp.org) Advocacy group for Americans aged 50 years and older offers member discounts (usually 10%) on hotels, car rentals and more; an annual membership costs $16.

American Automobile Association (AAA; ☎808-593-2221, from Neighbor Islands 800-736-2886; www.aaa.com; 1130 N Nimitz Hwy, Honolulu; ⊙Honolulu office 9am-5pm Mon-Fri, to 2pm Sat) Members of AAA and its foreign affiliates (eg CAA) qualify for small discounts (usually 10%) on car rentals, hotels, attractions and tours; an annual membership starts at $57.

ISIC Association (International Student Identity Card; www.isic.org) Offers savings on airline fares, travel insurance and more for full-time students (ISIC) and for nonstudents under 26 years of age (IYTC). Cards are issued by student unions, hostelling organizations and youth-oriented budget travel agencies.

Electricity

Food

The following price ranges refer to an average main course at dinner in a restaurant (lunch is cheaper, usually half-price) or a meal at a casual take-out joint. Unless otherwise stated, taxes and tips are not included in the price.

$ less than $12

$$ $12–$30

$$$ more than $30

See p598 for more information on Hawaiian cuisine.

Gay & Lesbian Travelers

The state of Hawaii has strong minority protections and a constitutional guarantee of privacy that extends to sexual behavior between consenting adults. Same-sex couples have the right to marry.

Locals tend to be private about their personal lives, so you will not see much public hand-holding or open displays of affection, either same-sex or opposite-sex. Everyday LGBTQ life is low-key – it's more about picnics and potlucks, not nightclubs. Even in Waikiki, the laid-back gay scene comprises just a half dozen or so bars, clubs and restaurants.

That said, Hawaii is a popular destination for LGBTQ travelers, who are served by a small network of gay-owned and gay-friendly B&Bs, guesthouses and hotels. Monthly free magazine *Odyssey* (www.odysseyhawaii.com), free at gay-friendly businesses throughout Hawaii, covers the islandwide scene, as does *eXpression!* magazine (www.expression808.com).

For more information on LGBTQ Hawaii, including recommended places to stay, beaches, events and more, check these community resources:

Out in Hawaii (www.outinhawaii.com) Somewhat dated website, but with active online discussion boards and listings of gay-friendly businesses on Oʻahu, Hawaiʻi, Maui and Kauaʻi.

Out Traveler (www.outtraveler.com) Gay-oriented Hawaii travel articles are free online.

Pacific Ocean Holidays (www.gayhawaiivacations.com) Personalized vacation packages for gay and lesbian travelers.

Pride Guide Hawaii (www.gogayhawaii.com) Online news, events calendar and free visitor guides to each island for gay-friendly activities, dining, nightlife, shopping, weddings and more.

Purple Roofs (http://purpleroofs.com) Online directory of gay-owned and gay-friendly B&Bs, vacation rentals, guesthouses and hotels.

Health

➡ For emergency medical assistance anywhere in Hawaii, call ☎911 or go directly to the emergency room (ER) of the nearest hospital. For nonemergencies, consider an urgent-care center or walk-in medical clinic.

➡ Some insurance policies require you to get preauthorization for medical treatment from a call center before seeking help. Keep all medical receipts and documentation for claims reimbursement later.

Marine Animals

Marine spikes, such as those found on sea urchins, scorpionfish and lionfish, can cause severe localized pain. If this occurs, immediately immerse the affected area in hot water (as hot as can be tolerated). Keep topping up with hot water until the pain subsides and medical care can be reached. Do the same for cone shell stings.

Stings from jellyfish and Portuguese man-of-war (aka bluebottles) also occur in Hawaii's tropical waters. Even touching a bluebottle hours after it's washed up onshore can result in burning stings. Jellyfish are often seen eight to 10 days after a full moon, when they float into Hawaii's shallow near-shore waters, often on the islands' leeward shores. If you are stung, douse the affected area in vinegar, or carefully peel off the tentacles with a gloved hand, then rinse the area well in sea water (not freshwater or urine), followed by rapid transfer to a hospital; antivenoms are available.

Leptospirosis

➡ Leptospirosis is acquired by exposure to untreated water or soil contaminated by the urine of infected animals, especially rodents.

➡ Outbreaks often occur after flooding, when overflow contaminates water sources downstream from livestock or wild animal habitats.

➡ Initial symptoms, which resemble a flu, usually subside uneventfully in a few days, but a minority of cases involve potentially fatal complications.

➡ Diagnosis is through urine and/or blood tests and treatment is with antibiotics.

➡ Minimize your risk by staying out of bodies of freshwater (eg pools, streams, waterfalls); avoid these entirely if you have open cuts or sores.

➡ On hiking trails, take warning signs about leptospirosis seriously. If you're camping, water purification and good hygiene are essential.

Giardiasis

➡ Symptoms of this parasitic infection of the small intestine include nausea, bloating, cramps and diarrhea and may last for weeks.

➡ To protect yourself, don't drink from untreated water sources (eg waterfalls, ponds, streams, rivers), which may be contaminated by animal or human feces.

➡ Giardiasis is diagnosed by a stool test and treated with antibiotics.

Dengue Fever

➡ In Hawaii the last dengue fever outbreak was in 2002; for updates, consult the **Hawaii State Department of Health** (http://health.hawaii.gov).

➡ Dengue is transmitted by aedes mosquitoes, which bite preferentially during the daytime and breed primarily in artificial water containers.

➡ Dengue usually causes flu-like symptoms, including fever, muscle aches, joint pains, severe headaches, nausea and vomiting, often followed by a rash.

➡ If you suspect you've been infected, do not take

VOG

Vog, a visible haze or smog caused by volcanic emissions from the Big Island, is often (but not always) dispersed by trade winds before it reaches other islands. On the Big Island, vog can make sunny skies hazy in West Hawaiʻi, especially in the afternoons around Kailua-Kona.

Short-term exposure to vog is not generally hazardous; however, high sulfur-dioxide levels can create breathing problems for sensitive groups (eg anyone with respiratory or heart conditions, pregnant women, young children and infants). Avoid vigorous physical exertion outdoors on voggy days.

INTERNATIONAL VISITORS

Entering Hawaii

➡ Double-check current visa and passport requirements *before* coming to the USA.

➡ For current information about entry requirements and eligibility, check the visa section of the **US Department of State** (http://travel.state.gov) and the travel section of the **US Customs & Border Protection** (www.cbp.gov) websites.

➡ Upon arrival in the USA, most foreign citizens (excluding for now, many Canadians, some Mexicans, all children under age 14 and seniors over age 79) must register with the **Department of Homeland Security** (DHS; www.dhs.gov), which entails having electronic (inkless) fingerprints and a digital photo taken.

Passports

➡ A machine-readable passport (MRP) is required for all foreign citizens to enter the USA.

➡ Your passport must be valid for six months beyond your expected dates of stay in the USA.

➡ If your passport was issued/renewed after October 26, 2006, you need an 'e-passport' with a digital photo and an integrated chip containing biometric data.

Visas

➡ Currently, under the US Visa Waiver Program (VWP), visas are not required for citizens of 38 countries for stays up to 90 days (no extensions).

➡ Under the VWP program you must have a return ticket (or onward ticket to any foreign destination) that's nonrefundable in the USA.

➡ All VWP travelers must register online at least 72 hours before arrival with the Electronic System for Travel Authorization (ESTA; https://esta.cbp.dhs.gov/esta/esta.html), which currently costs $14. Once approved, registration is valid for two years (or until your passport expires, whichever comes first).

➡ Canadian citizens are generally admitted visa-free for stays up to 182 days; they do not need to register with the ESTA.

➡ All other foreign visitors who don't qualify for the VWP and aren't Canadian citizens must apply for a tourist visa. The process costs a nonrefundable fee (minimum $160), involves a personal interview and can take several weeks, so apply early.

➡ www.usembassy.gov has links for all US embassies and consulates abroad. You're better off applying for a visa in your home country rather than while on the road.

Embassies & Consulates

Hawaii has no foreign embassies. O'ahu has a few consulates in Honolulu, including the following:

Australia (☎808-529-8100; 1000 Bishop St)

Japan (☎808-543-3111; 1742 Nu'uanu Ave)

Korea (☎808-595-6109; 2756 Pali Hwy)

New Zealand (☎808-595-2200; 3929 Old Pali Rd)

Post

➡ The **US Postal Service** (USPS; ☎800-275-8777; www.usps.com) is inexpensive and reliable. Mail delivery to/from Hawaii usually takes slightly longer than on the US mainland.

➡ To send urgent or important letters and packages internationally, try **Federal Express** (☎800-463-3339; www.fedex.com) or **United Parcel Service** (UPS; ☎800-742-5877; www.ups.com), which both offer door-to-door delivery.

aspirin or NSAIDs (eg ibuprofen), which can cause hemorrhaging. See a doctor for diagnosis and monitoring; severe cases may require hospitalization.

Staphylococcus

➡ Hawaii leads the nation in antibiotic-resistant staphylococcus infections. Staph infections are caused by bacteria, which often enter the body through an open wound.

➡ To prevent infection, practice good hygiene (eg wash your hands thoroughly and frequently; shower or bathe daily; wear clean clothing). Apply antibiotic ointment (eg Neosporin) to any open cuts or sores and keep them out of recreational water; if cuts or sores are on your feet, don't go barefoot, even on sand.

➡ If a wound becomes painful, looks red, inflamed or swollen, leaks pus or causes a rash or blisters, seek medical help immediately.

Insurance

Getting travel insurance to cover theft, loss and medical problems is highly recommended. Some insurance policies do not cover 'risky' activities such as scuba diving, trekking and motorcycling, so read the fine print. Make sure your policy at least covers hospital stays and an emergency flight home.

Some insurance policies require you to get preauthorization before receiving medical treatment – contact their call center. Keep your medical receipts and documentation for claims reimbursement later.

Paying for your airline ticket or rental car with a credit card may provide limited travel accident insurance. For car-rental insurance information, see p647. If you already have private US health insurance or a homeowners or renters policy, find out what those policies cover and only get supplemental insurance. If you have prepaid a large portion of your vacation, trip cancellation insurance may be a worthwhile expense.

Worldwide travel insurance is available at www.lonelyplanet.com/bookings. You can buy, extend and claim online any time – even if you're already on the road.

Internet Access

➡ Most accommodations, many coffee shops and a few bars, restaurants and other businesses offer public wi-fi hot spots (sometimes free only for paying customers). In-room internet access at Hawaii's hotels is sometimes wired, not wireless.

➡ Cities and larger towns usually have cybercafes or business centers offering pay-as-you-go internet terminals (typically $6 to $12 per hour) and sometimes wi-fi (free or fee-based).

➡ Hawaii's **public libraries** (www.librarieshawaii.org) provide free internet access via computer terminals if you get a temporary nonresident library card ($10). A few library branches also offer free wi-fi (no card required).

Language

Hawaii has two official languages: English and Hawaiian. While Hawaiian's multisyllabic, vowel-heavy words may look daunting, the pronunciation is actually quite straightforward and with a little practice, you'll soon get the hang of it. There's also an unofficial vernacular, pidgin (formerly referred to as Hawai'i Creole English), which has a laid-back, lilting accent and a colorful vocabulary that permeates everyday speech.

Legal Matters

If you are arrested, you have the right to an attorney; if you can't afford one, a public defender will be provided for free. The **Hawaii State Bar Association** (☎808-537-9140; http://hawaiilawyerreferral.com; ⏲8:30am-4:30pm Mon-Fri) makes attorney referrals. International visitors may want to call their nearest consulate or embassy for advice; police will provide the telephone number upon request.

Alcohol & Drugs

➡ Bars, clubs and liquor stores may require photo ID to prove you're of legal age (21 years) to buy alcohol.

➡ Drinking alcohol anywhere other than at a private residence or licensed premises (eg bar, restaurant) is illegal, which puts parks and beaches off-limits.

➡ The possession of marijuana and nonprescription narcotics is illegal. Foreigners convicted of a drug offense face immediate deportation.

HAWAI'I VS HAWAII

The *'okina* punctuation mark (') is the Hawaiian language's glottal stop, which determines the pronunciation and meaning of words. In this guide, Hawai'i (with the *'okina*) refers to the island of Hawai'i (the Big Island), to ancient Hawai'i and to the Kingdom of Hawai'i pre-statehood. Hawaii (without the *'okina*) refers to the US territory that became a state in 1959.

Driving

➡ If you are stopped by the police while driving, be courteous. Don't get out of the car unless asked. Keep your hands where the officer can see them at all times.

➡ Anyone driving with a blood alcohol level of 0.08% or higher is guilty of driving 'under the influence' (DUI), a serious offense that may incur heavy fines, a suspended driver's license, jail time and other penalties.

➡ Police can give roadside sobriety checks to assess if you've been drinking or using drugs. Refusing to be tested is considered legally the same as if you had taken and failed the test.

➡ It's illegal to carry open containers of alcohol inside a motor vehicle, even if they're empty. Unless containers are still sealed and have never been opened, store them inside the trunk.

Smoking

➡ Smoking is prohibited statewide inside all public buildings, including airports, restaurants, bars and nightclubs, as well as fully or semi-enclosed shopping malls and hotel and resort common areas.

➡ Not allowed at restaurants, even on outdoor patios or at sidewalk tables.

➡ Allowed at some hotels in specially requested smoking rooms only. Note that some properties are entirely nonsmoking by law, with high penalty fees for noncompliance.

➡ Banned at all county beaches and parks on O'ahu, Maui and the Big Island.

Other Laws

➡ Public nudity (as at beaches) and hitchhiking are both illegal in Hawaii, but sometimes are ignored by police. Hitching is never entirely safe, and we don't recommend it. Travelers who hitch should understand that they are taking a small but potentially serious risk.

➡ Due to security concerns about terrorism, never leave your bags unattended, especially at airports.

TIPPING

Tipping is *not* optional; only withhold tips in cases of outrageously bad service.

Airport and hotel porters $2 per bag, minimum $5 per cart

Bartenders 15% to 20% per round, minimum $1 per drink

Concierges Nothing for simple information, up to $10 for securing last-minute restaurant reservations etc

Housekeeping staff $2 to $4 per night, left under the card provided; more if you're messy

Parking valets At least $2 when your keys are returned

Restaurant servers and room service 18% to 20%, unless a gratuity is already charged (common for groups of six or more)

Taxi drivers 10% to 15% of metered fare, rounded up to the next dollar

Maps

Franko's Maps (www.frankosmaps.com) publishes a series of colorful, laminated and waterproof ocean sports and island sightseeing maps, including *Obama's O'ahu Guide* and *Pearl Harbor: Then and Now Historical Guide*. These maps are sold at many bookstores and outdoor outfitters.

Map geeks and backcountry hikers can buy topographical maps from bigger bookstores and national park visitor centers. Alternatively, download printable **US Geological Survey** (www.usgs.gov) maps for free online, or order printed maps for a fee. Pay attention to Hawaiian Island topo map dates, since some were drawn decades ago.

GPS navigation devices are handy, but cannot be relied upon 100% of the time, especially in more remote and rural areas.

Money

Hawaii has a 4.17% state sales tax tacked onto virtually everything, including meals, groceries and car rentals (which also entail additional state and local tax surcharges). Accommodations taxes total 13.96%.

ATMs

➡ ATMs are available 24/7 at banks, shopping malls, airports and grocery and convenience stores.

➡ Expect a minimum surcharge of around $3 per transaction, in addition to any fees charged by your home bank.

➡ Most ATMs are connected to international networks (Plus and Cirrus are common) and offer decent exchange rates.

Credit Cards

➡ Credit cards are widely accepted and often required for car rentals, hotel reservations etc. Some B&Bs and vacation rentals refuse them (pay in US dollar traveler's checks, personal checks or cash instead) or else add a 3% surcharge.

➡ Visa, MasterCard and American Express are most commonly accepted, followed by Discover and JTB.

Moneychangers

➡ Exchange foreign currency at Honolulu International Airport or the main branches of bigger banks, such as the **Bank of Hawaii** (www.boh.com) or **First Hawaiian Bank** (www.fhb.com).

➡ Outside of cities and larger towns, exchanging money may be impossible, so make sure you carry enough cash and/or a credit card.

Traveler's Checks

Traveler's checks have pretty much fallen out of use. That said, traveler's checks in US dollars are still accepted like cash at many tourist-oriented businesses in Hawaii, such as hotels, resorts and higher-end restaurants. Smaller businesses like grocery stores and fast-food chains usually refuse them.

Opening Hours

Standard opening hours year-round are as follows:

Banks	8:30am–4pm Mon–Fri; some open to 6pm Fri and 9am–noon or 1pm Sat
Bars & clubs	noon–midnight daily; some open to 2am Thu–Sat
Businesses (general) & government offices	8:30am–4:30pm Mon–Fri; some post offices open 9am–noon Sat
Restaurants	breakfast 6–10am, lunch 11:30am–2pm, dinner 5–9:30pm
Shops	9am–5pm Mon–Sat, some also open noon–5pm Sun; shopping malls keep extended hours

Public Holidays

On the following national holidays, banks, schools and government offices (including post offices) close, and museums, transportation and other services operate on a Sunday schedule. Holidays falling on a weekend are usually observed the following Monday.

New Year's Day January 1

Martin Luther King Jr Day Third Monday in January

Presidents' Day Third Monday in February

Prince Kuhio Day March 26

Good Friday Friday before Easter Sunday in March/April

Memorial Day Last Monday in May

King Kamehameha Day June 11

Independence Day July 4

Statehood Day Third Friday in August

Labor Day First Monday in September

Columbus Day Second Monday in October

Veterans Day November 11

Thanksgiving Fourth Thursday in November

Christmas Day December 25

Safe Travel

Hawaii is generally a safe place to visit. If you become the victim of a crime or have an accident while vacationing, the **Visitor Aloha Society of Hawaii** (VASH; ☎808-926-8274; www.visitoralohasocietyofhawaii.org) provides nonmonetary emergency aid. To qualify for VASH assistance, you must have a round-trip ticket back to the US mainland or abroad and be staying in Hawaii for less than 60 days.

Scams

The main scams directed toward visitors in Hawaii involve fake activity-operator booths and timeshare booths. Salespeople at the latter will offer you all sorts of deals, from free luaus to sunset cruises, if you'll just come to hear their 'no obligation' pitch. *Caveat emptor.*

Theft & Violence

The islands are notorious for thefts from parked cars, especially rentals (which are obviously tagged with bar-code stickers). Thieves can pop a trunk or pull out a door-lock assembly within seconds. They strike not only at trailheads when you've gone for a hike, but also at crowded beach and hotel parking lots where you'd expect safety in numbers.

As much as possible, do not leave anything valuable in your parked car, ever. If you must do so, then pack all valuables out of sight *before* arriving at your destination; thieves may be hanging out just waiting to see what you put in the trunk. Some locals leave their car doors unlocked with the windows rolled down to discourage break-ins and avoid costly damages (eg broken windows).

Stay attuned to the vibe on any beaches at night, even where police patrol (eg Waikiki), and in places like campgrounds and roadside county parks, where drunks, drug users and gang members sometimes hang out. In rural areas of the islands, there may be pockets of resentment against tourists, so be respectful as you explore off the beaten path.

Flash Floods & Waterfalls

No matter how dry a streambed looks or how sunny the sky above is, a sudden rainstorm miles away can cause a flash flood in minutes, sending down a huge surge of debris-filled water that sweeps away everything in its path. Always check the weather report before setting out on a hike; this is crucial if you're planning on hiking

KNOW BEFORE YOU GO: HAZARDS & TRESPASSING

Flash floods, rock falls, tsunami, earthquakes, volcanic eruptions, shark attacks, jellyfish stings and, yes, even possibly getting brained by a falling coconut – the potential dangers of traveling in Hawaii might seem alarming at first. But like the old saying goes, statistically you're more likely to get hurt crossing the street at home.

Of course, that's not to say that you shouldn't be careful. It's best to educate yourself first about potential risks to your health and safety. This advice becomes even more important when you're engaged in outdoor activities in a new and unfamiliar natural environment, whether that's an island snorkeling spot, a jungle waterfall, a high-altitude mountain or an active (and thus unpredictable) volcanic eruption zone.

Wherever you choose to explore on the islands, remember to mind your manners and watch your step. Hawaii has strict laws about trespassing on both private land and government land not intended for public use. Trespassing is always illegal, no matter how many other people you see doing it. As a visitor to the islands, it's important to respect all 'Kapu' or 'No Trespassing' signs. Always seek explicit permission from the land owner or local officials before venturing onto private or government-owned land that is closed to the public, regardless of whether it is fenced or signposted as such. Doing so not only respects the *kuleana* (rights) of residents and the sacredness of the land, but also helps ensure your own safety.

through any narrow canyons or swimming in waterfalls or natural pools. Swimming underneath waterfalls is always risky due to the danger of falling rocks.

Tell-tale signs of an impending flash flood include sudden changes in water clarity (eg the stream turns muddy), rising water levels and/or floating debris, and a rush of wind, the sound of thunder or a low, rumbling roar. If you notice any of these signs, immediately get to higher ground (even a few feet could save your life). Don't run downstream or down-canyon – you can't beat a flash flood.

Tsunami

On average, tsunami (incorrectly called tidal waves – the Japanese term *tsunami* means 'harbor wave') occur only about once a decade in Hawaii, but they have killed more people statewide than all other natural disasters combined. Hawaii's tsunami warning system is tested on the first working day of each month at 11:15am for less than one minute, using the yellow speakers mounted on telephone poles around the islands. If you hear tsunami warning sirens at any other time, head for higher ground immediately; telephone books have maps of evacuation zones. Turn on the radio or TV for news bulletins. For more information, visit **Hawaii State Civil Defense** (www.scd.hawaii.gov) and **Pacific Disaster Center** (www.pdc.org) online.

Telephone

Cell Phones

Check with your service provider about using your phone in Hawaii. Among US providers, Verizon and AT&T have the most extensive networks; Sprint and T-Mobile are more limited. Cellular coverage is best on O'ahu, sometimes spotty outside major towns on the Neighbor Islands and nonexistent in many rural areas, on hiking trails and at remote beaches.

International travelers need a multiband GSM phone in order to make calls in the USA. With an unlocked multiband phone, popping in a US prepaid rechargeable SIM card is usually cheaper than using your own network. SIM cards are available at any telecommunications or electronics store. If your phone doesn't work in the USA, these stores also sell inexpensive prepaid phones, including some airtime.

Dialing Codes

- All Hawaii phone numbers consist of a three-digit area code (☎808) followed by a seven-digit local number.
- To call long-distance from one Hawaiian Island to another, dial ☎1 + ☎808 + local number.
- Always dial 1 before toll-free numbers (☎800, ☎888 etc). Some toll-free numbers only work within Hawaii or from the US mainland (and possibly Canada).
- To call Canada from Hawaii, dial ☎1 + area code + local number (international rates still apply).
- For all other international calls from Hawaii, dial ☎011 + country code + area code + local number.
- To call Hawaii from abroad, the international country code for the USA is ☎1.

Useful Numbers

- Emergency (police, fire, ambulance) ☎911

➡ Local directory assistance ☎411

➡ Long-distance directory assistance ☎1-808-555-1212

➡ Toll-free directory assistance ☎1-800-555-1212

➡ Operator ☎0

Payphones & Phonecards

➡ Payphones are a dying breed, usually found at shopping centers, hotels and public places (eg beaches, parks).

➡ Some payphones are coin-operated (local calls usually cost 50¢), while others only accept credit cards or phonecards.

➡ Private prepaid phone cards are available from convenience stores, newsstands, supermarkets and pharmacies.

Tourist Information

There are staffed tourist-information desks in the airport arrivals areas. While you're waiting for your bags to appear on the carousel, you can peruse racks of free tourist brochures and magazines, which contain discount coupons for activities, tours, restaurants etc.

For pretrip planning in several languages, browse the information-packed website of the **Hawaii Visitors & Convention Bureau** (www.gohawaii.com).

Travelers with Disabilities

➡ Bigger, newer hotels and resorts in Hawaii have elevators, wheelchair-accessible rooms (reserve these well in advance) and TDD-capable phones.

➡ Telephone companies provide relay operators (TTY/TDD dial ☎711) for the hearing-impaired.

➡ Many banks provide ATM instructions in Braille.

➡ Traffic intersections in cities and some towns have dropped curbs and audible crossing signals.

➡ Guide and service dogs are not subject to the same quarantine requirements as other pets, but must enter the state at Honolulu International Airport. Contact the Department of Agriculture's **Animal Quarantine Station** (☎808-483-7151; http://hdoa.hawaii.gov/ai/aqs/animal-quarantine-information-page) before arrival.

Transportation

➡ Where available on the islands, public transportation is wheelchair-accessible. Buses will usually 'kneel' if you're unable to use the steps – let the driver know you need the lift or ramp.

➡ Some major car-rental agencies offer hand-controlled vehicles and vans with wheelchair lifts; reserve these well in advance.

➡ If you have a disability parking placard from home, bring it with you and hang it from your rental vehicle's rearview mirror when using designated disabled-parking spaces.

Wheelchair Getaways (☎800-638-1912; www.wheelchairgetaways.com) Rents wheelchair-accessible vans on Hawai'i (Big Island), Maui and Kaua'i.

Wheelers Van Rentals (☎800-456-1371; www.wheelersvanrentals.com) Wheelchair-accessible van rentals on O'ahu, Hawai'i (Big Island), Maui and Kaua'i.

Helpful Resources

Access Aloha Travel (☎808-545-1143, 800-480-1143; www.accessalohatravel.com) Local travel agency that can help book wheelchair-accessible accommodations, rental vans and sightseeing tours.

Disability & Communication Access Board (☎808-586-8121; http://health.hawaii.gov/dcab/) Online 'Traveler Tips' brochures provide info about airports, accessible transportation, all-terrain beach wheelchairs, and medical and other support services on O'ahu, Hawai'i (Big Island), Maui and Kaua'i.

Work

US citizens can pursue work in Hawaii as they would in any other state – the problem is finding a job. International visitors in the USA on tourist visas are strictly prohibited from taking employment. To work legally, foreigners must secure sponsorship from an employer or international work-exchange program and apply for a visa before leaving home.

Joining the waitstaff of tourist restaurants and bars is the most likely short-term employment opportunity. If you have foreign-language, guiding or outdoor activity (eg scuba diving) skills, seek employment with outdoor outfitters. Most entry-level service jobs, such as housekeeping, at hotels and resorts go to locals.

In addition to notice boards at hostels, coffee shops and natural-foods stores, check the classified ads online at **Craigslist** (http://honolulu.craigslist.org).

Transportation

GETTING THERE & AWAY

Roughly 99% of visitors to Hawaii arrive by air. Flights, cars and tours can be booked online at lonelyplanet.com/bookings.

Air

All checked and carry-on bags leaving Hawaii for the US mainland, Alaska and Guam must be inspected by a US Department of Agriculture (USDA) x-ray machine at the airport.

Airports

The majority of incoming flights from overseas and the US mainland arrive at **Honolulu International Airport** (HNL; ☎808-836-6411; http://hawaii.gov/hnl; 300 Rodgers Blvd, Honolulu) on O'ahu. Flights to Lana'i and Moloka'i usually originate from Honolulu or Maui.

The main Neighbor Island airports include the following:

Hilo International Airport (ITO; ☎808-961-9300; http://hawaii.gov/ito; 2450 Kekuanaoa St) East Hawai'i (Big Island).

Kahului International Airport (OGG; ☎808-872-3830; http://hawaii.gov/ogg; 1 Kahului Airport Rd, Kahului) Maui.

Kona International Airport at Keahole (KOA; ☎808-327-9520; http://hawaii.gov/koa; 73-200 Kupipi St) West Hawai'i (Big Island).

Lana'i Airport (LNY; ☎808-565-7942; hawaii.gov/lny; off Hwy 440) Lana'i.

Lihu'e Airport (LIH; ☎808-274-3800; http://hawaii.gov/lih; 3901 Mokulele Loop, Lihu'e) Kaua'i.

Moloka'i Airport (MKK, Ho'olehua; Map p440; ☎808-567-9660; http://hawaii.gov/mkk; Ho'olehua) Moloka'i.

Tickets

Hawaii is a competitive market for US domestic and international airfares, which vary tremendously by season, day of the week and demand. Competition is highest among airlines flying to Honolulu from major US mainland cities, especially between Hawaiian Airlines and Alaska Airlines, while Allegiant Air serves smaller US regional airports.

The 'lowest fare' fluctuates constantly. In general, return fares from the US mainland to Hawaii cost from $400 (in low season from the West Coast) to $800 or more (in high season from the East Coast). **Pleasant Holidays** (☎800-742-9244; www.pleasantholidays.com) offers competitive vacation packages from the US mainland.

Sea

Most cruises to Hawaii include stopovers in Honolulu and on Maui, Kaua'i and the

CLIMATE CHANGE & TRAVEL

Every form of transport that relies on carbon-based fuel generates CO_2, the main cause of human-induced climate change. Modern travel is dependent on airplanes, which might use less fuel per mile per person than most cars but travel much greater distances. The altitude at which aircraft emit gases (including CO_2) and particles also contributes to their climate change impact. Many websites offer 'carbon calculators' that allow people to estimate the carbon emissions generated by their journey and, for those who wish to do so, to offset the impact of the greenhouse gases emitted with contributions to portfolios of climate-friendly initiatives throughout the world. Lonely Planet offsets the carbon footprint of all staff and author travel.

Big Island. Cruises typically last two weeks, with fares starting around $100 per person per night, based on double occupancy; airfare to/from the departure point costs extra.

Popular cruise lines include the following:

Holland America (☎877-932-4259; www.hollandamerica.com) Departures from San Diego and Vancouver, British Columbia.

Princess Cruises (☎800-774-6237; www.princess.com) Departures from Los Angeles, San Francisco and Vancouver, British Columbia.

Royal Caribbean (☎866-562-7625; www.royalcaribbean.com) Departures from Vancouver, British Columbia.

GETTING AROUND

Most interisland travel is by plane, although limited ferry services connect Maui with Moloka'i and Lana'i. Rent a car if you want to really explore; on Lana'i and Hawai'i (Big Island), a 4WD vehicle may come in handy for off-the-beaten-track adventures. Public transportation exists on the bigger islands, but you'll probably find it time-consuming and difficult to get around if only using public buses, except on O'ahu.

Air

Hawaii's major interisland carrier – reliable Hawaiian Airlines – offers frequent interisland flights in jet planes, as well as turboprop service through its new subsidiary brand, 'Ohana by Hawaiian. Two smaller, commuter-oriented airlines – Mokulele Airlines and Island Air – provide scheduled service daily in turboprop planes.

Smaller turboprop planes fly so low that their flights almost double as sightseeing excursions – fun! The only drawback to turboprop planes is that carry-on baggage limitations are usually much more strict, so you may end up paying extra to check all of your bags.

Expect further schedule changes and possible shake-ups in the interisland flight biz. Interisland airfares vary wildly, from $50 to $190 one way. Round-trip fares are typically double the price without any discounts. Usually the earlier you book, the cheaper the fare.

While it's often possible to walk up and get on a flight among the four biggest islands (particularly to/from Honolulu), advance reservations are recommended, especially at peak times.

Airline regulations concerning surfboards, bicycles and other oversized baggage vary and can be restrictive, not to mention expensive – ask before booking.

Airlines in Hawaii

Hawaiian Airlines (☎800-367-5320; www.hawaiianairlines.com) Flies nearly 200 daily routes between Honolulu, Kaua'i, Maui and the Big Island, with limited flights to Moloka'i and Lana'i. Flying between two Neighbor Islands often requires changing planes in Honolulu.

Island Air (☎800-388-1105; www.islandair.com) Flies turboprop jet planes directly from its Honolulu hub to Kahului, Maui; Lana'i City, Lana'i; and Lihu'e, Kaua'i.

Mokulele Airlines (☎866-260-7070; www.mokuleleairlines.com) Flies turboprop planes to Honolulu and Kalaeloa on O'ahu; Kona and Waimea (Kamuela) on Hawai'i (Big Island); Kahului, Kapalua and Hana on Maui; Ho'olehua on Moloka'i; and Lana'i City on Lana'i.

Bicycle

Cycling around the islands is a great, nonpolluting way to travel. As a primary mode of transportation, however, cycling can be a challenge. All islands have narrow roads, dangerous traffic and changeable weather. Long-distance cycling is best done with a tour group, but if you're adventurous and in good shape, it can be done on your own. Smaller islands such as Kaua'i and Moloka'i are generally better suited to cycle touring.

Rental

➡ Tourist resort areas and specialty bicycle shops rent beach cruisers, hybrid models and occasionally high-end road and mountain bikes. In Waikiki, **EBikes Hawaii** (☎808-722-5454; www.ebikeshawaii.com; 3318 Campbell Ave; 4/7hr $40/50) rents electric bicycles.

➡ Rental rates average $20 to $40 per day (easily double that for high-tech road or mountain bikes). Multiday and weekly discounts may be available, so ask.

➡ Some B&Bs, guesthouses and hostels rent or loan bicycles to guests.

➡ In Honolulu, Bikeshare Hawaii (www.bikesharehawaii.org) stations are expected to start operating in 2016.

Road Rules

➡ Generally, bicycles are required to follow the same rules of the road as cars. Bicycles are prohibited on freeways and sidewalks.

➡ State law requires all cyclists under the age of 16 to wear helmets.

➡ For more bicycling information, including downloadable cycling maps, search the website of the **Hawaii Department of Transportation** (http://hidot.hawaii.gov/highways).

Transporting Bicycles

➡ Bringing your own bike to Hawaii costs $100 or more on flights from the US mainland, while interisland flights charge $35 and up to transport your bike.

➡ You can usually check your bicycle at the airline counter, the same as any baggage. It needs to be in a box or hard-sided case with the handlebars fixed sideways and the pedals removed or enclosed in plastic foam.

➡ Many island buses are equipped with front-loading two-bicycle racks. Let the driver know *before* loading your bicycle on or off the rack. If the bicycle rack is already full, you may have to wait until the next bus comes along (which can be problematic on the Big Island, Maui and Kaua'i, but not usually on O'ahu).

Boat

Interisland ferry service is surprisingly limited in Hawaii. Currently only Moloka'i and Lana'i have regular, passenger-only public ferry service to/from Lahaina, Maui.

Norwegian Cruise Line (NCL; ☎877-397-1504; www.ncl.com) Operates a seven-day cruise between the four biggest Hawaiian Islands that starts and ends in Honolulu; fares start at $899 per person based on double occupancy.

Bus

By using **TheBus** (☎808-848-5555; www.thebus.org), O'ahu is the easiest island to get around without a car. Schedules are frequent; service is reliable; and fares are inexpensive. That said, TheBus doesn't go everywhere – for example, to most hiking trailheads.

Public bus systems on the larger Neighbor Islands are more geared toward resident commuters; service is infrequent and limited to main towns, sometimes bypassing tourist destinations entirely.

➡ After O'ahu, the next best system is **Maui Bus** (☎808-871-4838; www.mauicounty.gov/bus), but it doesn't run to Hana or Haleakalā National Park.

➡ The Big Island's **Hele-On Bus** (☎808-961-8744; www.heleonbus.org; fare $2) will get you around (albeit slowly, and sometimes not on Sundays) to many island towns, but schedules are too limited for sightseeing. It stops at Hawai'i Volcanoes National Park's main visitor center.

➡ **Kaua'i Bus** (☎808-246-8110; www.kauai.gov) can take visitors between the main island towns (limited weekend service), but not to the Na Pali Coast, Waimea Canyon or Koke'e State Park.

➡ On Moloka'i, the free **MEO Bus** (☎808-877-7651; bus trips free; ⏲Mon-Fri) trundles east and west of Kaunakakai every couple of hours, but call in advance to confirm schedules.

Car

Most visitors to Hawaii rent their own vehicles, particularly on the Neighbor Islands. If you're just visiting Honolulu and Waikiki, a car may be more of a hindrance than a help. Free parking is usually plentiful outside of cities and major towns. Some hotels and resorts, especially in Waikiki, may charge $30 or more for overnight parking.

Automobile Associations

American Automobile Association (AAA; ☎808-593-2221, from Neighbor Islands 800-736-2886; www.hawaii.aaa.com; 1130 N Nimitz Hwy, Honolulu; ⏲9am-5pm Mon-Fri, to 2pm Sat) Members are entitled to discounts on select car rentals, hotels, sightseeing and attractions, as well as free road maps and travel-agency services. For emergency roadside assistance and towing, members can call ☎800-222-4357. AAA has reciprocal agreements with automobile associations in other countries (eg CAA). Bring your membership card from home.

Driver's License

➡ US citizens with a driver's license from another state can legally drive in Hawaii if they are at least 18 years old.

➡ International visitors can legally drive in Hawaii with a valid driver's license issued by their home country (minimum age 18).

➡ Car-rental companies will generally accept foreign driver's licenses written in English with an accompanying photo. Otherwise, be prepared to present an International Driving Permit (IDP), obtainable in your home country, along with your foreign driver's license.

Fuel

➡ Gasoline (petrol) is readily available everywhere except along remote roads (eg Saddle Road on the Big Island, Hana Hwy on Maui).

➡ Gas prices in Hawaii are the highest in the country, currently averaging $3.90 per US gallon.

Insurance

➡ Required by law, liability insurance covers any people or property that you might hit. For damage to the rental vehicle, a collision damage waiver (CDW) costs an extra $15 to $20 a day.

➡ If you decline CDW, you will be held liable for any damages up to the full value of the car.

➡ Even with CDW, you may be required to pay the first $100 to $500 for repairs; some agencies will also charge you for the rental cost of the car during the time it takes to be repaired.

➡ If you have vehicle insurance at home, it might cover damages to car rentals; ask your insurance agent before your trip.

➡ Some credit cards offer reimbursement coverage for collision damages if you rent the car with that card; check on this in advance.

- Most credit-card coverage isn't valid for rentals over 15 days or for 'exotic' models (eg convertibles, 4WD Jeeps).

Rental

AGENCIES

- Most rental companies require that you be at least 25 years old, possess a valid driver's license and have a major credit card, not a debit or check card.
- A few major companies will rent to drivers between the ages of 21 and 24, typically for an underage surcharge of around $25 per day; call ahead to check.
- Without a credit card, many agencies simply won't rent you a vehicle, while others require prepayment by cash, traveler's checks or debit card with an additional refundable deposit of $500 per week, proof of return airfare and more.
- When picking up your vehicle, most agencies will request the name and phone number of the place where you're staying. Some agencies are reluctant to rent to visitors who list a campground as their address; a few specifically add 'No Camping Permitted' to car-rental contracts.
- Most islands have a couple of independent car-rental agencies, and these are worth checking out. On Maui, it's the only way to rent a biofueled car, and on O'ahu it's the only way to rent a Smart car. On Hawai'i (Big Island), it's the only way to rent a 4WD that's allowed to drive to Mauna Kea's summit. Independent agencies are more likely to rent to drivers under 25 and offer deals, especially on 4WDs.

Major car-rental agencies in Hawaii (some of which may offer ecofriendly 'green' hybrid and electric models) that have branches on the four biggest islands include the following:

Advantage (☎800-777-5500; www.advantage.com) On O'ahu, Maui and Kaua'i.

Alamo (☎877-222-9075; www.alamo.com) On Moloka'i as well as Hawai'i (Big Island), O'ahu, Maui and Kaua'i.

Avis (☎800-633-3469; www.avis.com)

Budget (☎800-218-7992; www.budget.com)

Dollar (☎800-800-4000; www.dollar.com) On Lana'i as well as Hawai'i (Big Island), O'ahu, Maui and Kaua'i.

Enterprise (☎800-261-7331; www.enterprise.com)

Hertz (☎800-654-3131; www.hertz.com)

National (☎877-222-9058; www.nationalcar.com)

Thrifty (☎800-847-4389; www.thrifty.com)

RATES

- The daily rate for renting a small car usually ranges from $35 to $75, while typical weekly rates are $150 to $300.
- When getting quotes, always ask for the full rate including all taxes, fees and surcharges, which can easily add $10 or more per day.
- Rental rates usually include unlimited mileage.
- If you belong to an automobile club or airline frequent-flyer or hotel rewards program, you may be eligible for discounts when booking car rentals.
- For more discounts and possibly cheaper rates from local car-rental companies, search **Hawaii Discount Car Rental** (http://discounthawaiicarrental.com) and **Car Rental Express** (www.carrentalexpress.com).

RESERVATIONS

Always reserve rental cars in advance. With most car-rental companies there's little or no cancellation penalty if you change your mind before arrival. Walking up to the airport counter without a reservation will subject you to higher rates, and during busy periods it's not uncommon for all cars to be rented out, even in Honolulu. Joining the rental-car company's rewards program in advance can help you shortcut long lines at the airport.

If you need them, reserve child safety seats (rentals from $10 per day) when booking your car.

Road Conditions & Hazards

- The main hazards are drunk drivers and narrow, winding and/or steep roads that wash out or flood after heavy rains. In rural areas, watch for livestock and wildlife.
- On narrow, unpaved or potholed roads, locals may hog both lanes and drive over the middle stripe until an oncoming car approaches.
- Don't drive your standard car on dirt and/or 4WD roads, which is usually prohibited by rental companies and will void insurance coverage. Ask your rental-car company about additional driving and road restrictions.

HAWAII'S HIGHWAY ADDRESSES

Street addresses on some island highways may seem random and overly long, but there's a pattern. For hyphenated numbers, such as 4-734 Kuhio Hwy, the first part of the number identifies the tax zone and section, while the second part identifies the street address. Thus, it's possible for 4-736 to be followed by 5-002; you've just entered a new zone, that's all.

➡ If you get into trouble with your car, towing is prohibitively expensive in Hawaii – avoid it at all costs.

Road Rules

Slow, courteous driving is the rule in Hawaii. Locals usually don't honk (unless they're about to crash), don't follow close (ie tailgate) and let other drivers pass and merge. Do the same, and you may get an appreciative *shaka* (Hawaiian hand greeting sign) from other drivers.

➡ Drive on the right-hand side of the road.

➡ Speed limits are posted and enforced. If you're stopped for speeding, expect a ticket, as police rarely just give warnings.

➡ Turning right on red is allowed (unless a sign prohibits it), but island drivers often wait for the green light.

➡ At four-way stop signs, cars proceed in order of arrival. If two cars arrive simultaneously, the one on the right has the right of way. When in doubt, politely wave the other driver ahead.

➡ For one-lane-bridge crossings, one direction of traffic usually has the right of way while the other must obey the posted yield sign.

➡ Downhill traffic must yield to uphill traffic where there is no sign.

➡ Diamond-marked carpool lanes are reserved for high-occupancy vehicles during morning and afternoon rush hours.

➡ When emergency vehicles (ie police, fire or ambulance) approach from either direction, carefully pull over to the side of the road.

Safety Laws

➡ Talking or texting on a handheld device (eg cell phone) while driving is illegal.

➡ Driving under the influence (DUI) of alcohol or drugs is a serious criminal offense. It's illegal to carry open containers of alcohol (even if they're empty) inside a car. Unless the containers are still sealed and have never been opened, store them in the trunk instead.

➡ The use of seat belts is required for the driver, front-seat passengers and all children under age 18.

➡ Child safety seats are mandatory for children aged three and younger. Those aged four to seven must ride in a booster seat, unless they are over 4ft 9in tall, in which case they must be secured by a lap-only belt in the back seat.

Moped, Scooter & Motorcycle

Moped and motorcycle rentals are not common in Hawaii, but are available in some tourist resort areas. Surprisingly, they can be more expensive to rent than cars. Rental mopeds cost from $35 per day and $175 per week, while scooters start around $85 and motorcycles around $100 per day; a hefty credit-card deposit is usually required.

Road Rules

➡ You can legally drive a moped in Hawaii with a valid driver's license issued by your home state or country. Motorcyclists and scooter drivers need a valid US state motorcycle license or a specially endorsed International Driving Permit (IDP).

➡ The minimum age for renting a moped is 16; for a motorcycle it's 21.

➡ State law requires mopeds to be ridden by one person only and prohibits their use on sidewalks and freeways.

➡ Mopeds must always be driven in single file and may not be driven at speeds above 30mph.

Safety Tips

➡ Helmets are not legally required for anyone 18 years or older, but rental agencies often provide them for free – use 'em.

➡ Riding on the rainy windward sides of the islands may require foul-weather gear.

Taxi

➡ The main islands have taxis with metered fares based on mileage, although a few drivers may offer flat rates.

➡ Taxi rates vary, as they're set by each county, but average more than $3 at flagfall, then $3 or more per additional mile (luggage and airport surcharges may apply).

➡ Taxis are readily available at airports and many hotels and resorts, but otherwise you'll probably need to phone a taxi company dispatcher.

➡ Most cab companies serve only a limited area, and won't drive islandwide. On the Neighbor Islands, taxis may only be available in major towns and tourist resorts.

Tours

Several local companies offer half- and full-day island sightseeing tours by bus or van. Specialized adventure tours, such as whale-watching cruises and snorkeling trips, are available on all the main islands. Helicopter tours are especially popular on Hawai'i (the Big Island), Kaua'i and Maui. Most tours can be booked after arrival in Hawaii, but if your schedule is tight or you're visiting during peak travel times, reserve ahead.

Roberts Hawaii (☎808-539-9400, 800-831-5541; www.robertshawaii.com) If you want to visit another island while you're in Hawaii but only have a day to spare, consider an island-hopping tour.

Glossary

'a'a – type of lava that is rough and jagged

ae'o – Hawaiian black-necked stilt

'ahinahina – silversword plant with pointed silver leaves

ahu – stone cairns used to mark a trail; an altar or shrine

ahupua'a – traditional land division, usually in a wedge shape that extends from the mountains to the sea (smaller than a *moku*)

'aina – land

'akala – Hawaiian raspberry or thimbleberry

'akohekohe – Maui parrotbill

'alae ke'oke'o – Hawaiian coot

'alae 'ula – Hawaiian moorhen

'alauahio – Maui creeper

ali'i – chief, royalty

ali'i nui – high chiefs, kingly class

aloha – the traditional greeting meaning love, welcome, good-bye

aloha 'aina – love of the land

'amakihi – small, yellow-green honeycreeper; one of the more common native birds

anchialine pool – contains a mixture of seawater and fresh-water

'apapane – bright red native Hawaiian honeycreeper

a'u – swordfish, marlin

'aumakua – protective deity or guardian spirit, deified ancestor

'awa – see *kava*

'awa'awa – bitter

azuki bean – often served as a sweetened paste, eg as a topping for shave ice

braguinha – a Portuguese stringed instrument introduced to Hawaii in the late 19th century from which the ukulele is derived

e komo mai – welcome

'elepaio – Hawaiian flycatcher; a brownish native bird with a white rump

hā – breath

ha'i – voiced register-break technique used by women singers

haku – head

hala – pandanus tree; the leaves *(lau)* are used in weaving mats and baskets

hale – house

Haloa – the stillborn son of Papa and Wakea, Hawaiian earth mother and sky father deities

haole – Caucasian; literally, 'without breath'

hapa – portion or fragment; person of mixed blood

hapa haole – Hawaiian music with predominantly English lyrics

hapu'u – tree fern

hau – indigenous lowland hibiscus tree whose wood is often used for making canoe outriggers (stabilizing arms that jut out from the hull)

he'e nalu – wave sliding, or surfing

heiau – ancient stone temple; a place of worship in Hawaii

holua – sled or sled course

honi – to share breath

honu – turtle

ho'okipa – hospitality

ho'okupu – offering

ho'olaule'a – celebration, party

ho'onanea – to pass the time in ease, peace and pleasure

hukilau – fishing with a *seine*, involving a group of people who pull in the net

hula – Hawaiian dance form, either traditional or modern

hula 'auana – modern hula, developed after the introduction of Western music

hula halau – hula school or troupe

hula kahiko – traditional and sacred hula

'i'iwi – scarlet Hawaiian honeycreeper with a curved, salmon-colored beak

'iliahi – Hawaiian sandalwood

'ilima – native plant, a ground cover with delicate yellow-orange flowers; O'ahu's official flower

'ilio holo kai – 'the dog that runs in the sea'; Hawaiian monk seal

'io – Hawaiian hawk

ipo – sweetheart

ipu – spherical, narrow-necked gourd used as a hula implement

issei – first-generation immi-grants to Hawaii who were born in Japan

kahili – a feathered standard, used as a symbol of royalty

kahuna – knowledgeable person in any field; commonly a priest, healer or sorcerer

kahuna lapa'au – healer

kahuna nui – high priest(ess) or royal co-regent

kalo lo'i – taro fields

kama'aina – person born and raised, or a longtime resident, in Hawaii; literally, 'child of the land'

kane/Kane – man; if capitalized, the name of one of four main Hawaiian gods

kapa – see *tapa*

kapu – taboo, part of strict ancient Hawaiian social and religious system

kapuna – elders

kaua – ancient Hawaiian lower class, outcasts

kaunaoa – a yellowish- orange vine used in Lana'i lei

kava – a mildly narcotic drink (*'awa* in Hawaiian) made from the roots of *Piper methysticum*, a pepper shrub

keiki – child

ki – see *ti*

ki ho'alu – slack key

kiawe – a relative of the mesquite tree introduced to Hawaii in the 1820s, now very common; its branches are covered with sharp thorns

kika kila – Hawaiian steel guitar

ki'i – see *tiki*

ki'i akua – temple images, often carved wooden idols

kilau – a stiff, weedy fern

kipuka – an area of land spared when lava flows around it; an oasis

ko – sugarcane

koa – native hardwood tree often used in making Native Hawaiian crafts and canoes

koki'o ke'oke'o – native Hawaiian white hibiscus tree

kokua – help, cooperation

koloa maoli – Hawaiian duck

kona – leeward side; a leeward wind

konane – a strategy game similar to checkers

konohiki – caretakers of *ahupua'a*

ko'olau – windward side

Ku – Polynesian god of many manifestations, including god of war, farming and fishing (husband of Hina)

kukui – candlenut, the official state tree; its oily nuts were once burned in lamps

kuleana – rights

kumu hula – hula teacher

Kumulipo – Native Hawaiian creation story or chant

kupuna – grandparent, elder

ku'ula/Ku'ula – a stone idol placed at fishing sites, believed to attract fish; if capitalized, the god of fishers

la'au lapa'au – plant medicine

lanai – veranda; balcony

lau – leaf

lauhala – leaves of the *hala* plant, used in weaving

lei – garland, usually of flowers, but also of leaves, vines, shells or nuts

leptospirosis – a disease acquired by exposure to water contaminated by the urine of infected animals, especially livestock

limu – seaweed

lokelani – pink damask rose, or 'rose of heaven'; Maui's official flower

loko i'a – fishpond

loko wai – freshwater pond

lolo – stupid, feeble-minded, crazy

lomi – to rub or soften

lomilomi – traditional Hawaiian massage; known as 'loving touch'

Lono – Polynesian god of harvest, agriculture, fertility and peace

loulu – native fan palms

luakini – a type of *heiau* dedicated to the war god Ku and used for human sacrifices

luau – traditional Hawaiian feast

luna – supervisor or plantation boss

mahalo – thank you

mahele – to divide; usually refers to the Great Mahele land reform act of 1848

mahu – a transgendered or cross-dressing male

mai ho'oka'awale – leprosy (Hansen's disease); literally, 'the separating sickness'

mai'a – banana

maile – native plant with twining habit and fragrant leaves; often used for lei

maka'ainana – commoners; literally, 'people who tend the land'

makaha – a sluice gate, used to regulate the level of water in a fishpond

makahiki – traditional annual wet-season winter festival dedicated to the agricultural god Lono

makai – toward the sea; seaward

make – to die

malihini – newcomer, visitor

mamo – a yellow-feathered bird, now extinct

mana – spiritual power

mauka – toward the mountains; inland

mele – song, chant

menehune – 'little people' who, according to legend, built many of Hawaii's fishponds, heiau and other stonework

milo – a native shade tree with beautiful hardwood

moa – jungle fowl

mokihana – a tree with leathery berries that faintly smell of licorice, used in *lei*

moku – wedge-shaped areas of land running from the ridge of the mountains to the sea

mokupuni – low, flat island or atoll

mo'i – king

mo'o – water spirit, water lizard or dragon

muumuu – a long, loose-fitting dress introduced by the missionaries

na keiki – children

na'u – fragrant Hawaiian gardenia

naupaka – a native shrub with delicate white flowers

Neighbor Islands – the term used to refer to the main Hawaiian Islands except for O'ahu

nene – a native goose; Hawaii's state bird

nisei – second-generation Japanese immigrants

niu – coconut palm

no ka 'oi – the best

'ohana – family, extended family; close-knit group

'ohi'a lehua – native Hawaiian tree with tufted, feathery, pom-pom-like flowers

'olelo Hawai'i – the Hawaiian language

oli – chant

olona – a native shrub

'ope'ape'a – Hawaiian hoary bat

'opihi – an edible limpet

pahoehoe – type of lava that is quick and smooth- flowing

pakalolo – marijuana; literally, 'crazy smoke'

palaka – Hawaiian-style plaid shirt made from sturdy cotton

pali – cliff

paniolo – cowboy

Papa – earth mother

pau – finished, no more

pa'u – traditional horse riding, in which lei-bedecked women in flowing dresses ride for show (eg in a parade)

pau hana – 'stop work'; happy hour

Pele – goddess of fire and volcanoes; her home is in Kilauea Caldera

pidgin – distinct local language and dialect, originating from Hawaii's multiethnic plantation immigrants

pikake – jasmine flowers

piko – navel, umbilical cord

pili – a bunchgrass, commonly used for thatching traditional *hale* and *heiau*

pohaku – rock

pohuehue – beach morning glory (a flowering plant)

pono – righteous, respectful and proper

pua aloalo – yellow hibiscus

pua'a waewae loloa – 'long-legged pigs,' an ancient Hawaiian euphemism for human sacrificial victims

pueo – Hawaiian owl

puka – any kind of hole or opening; puka shells are small, white and strung into necklaces

pukiawe – native plant with red and white berries and evergreen leaves

pule – prayer, blessing, incantation or spell

pulu – the silken clusters encasing the stems of tree ferns

pupu – snack or appetizer; also a type of shell

pu'u – hill, cinder cone

pu'uhonua – place of refuge

raku – a style of Japanese pottery characterized by a rough, handmade appearance

rubbah slippah – flip-flops

sansei – third-generation Japanese immigrants

shaka – hand gesture used in Hawaii as a greeting or sign of local pride

shōji – translucent paper-covered wooden sliding doors

stink-eye – dirty look

taiko – Japanese drumming

talk story – to strike up a conversation, make small talk

tapa – cloth made by pounding the bark of paper mulberry, used for Native Hawaiian clothing (*kapa* in Hawaiian)

ti – common native plant; its long shiny leaves are used for wrapping food and making hula skirts (*ki* in Hawaiian)

tiki – wood- or stone-carved statue, usually depicting a deity (*ki'i* in Hawaiian)

tutu – grandmother or grandfather; also term of respect for any member of that generation

'ua'u – dark-rumped petrel

ukulele – a stringed musical instrument derived from the *braguinha*, which was introduced to Hawaii in the 1800s by Portuguese immigrants

'uli'uli – gourd rattle containing seeds and decorated with feathers, used as a hula implement

'ulu – breadfruit

'ulu maika – ancient Hawaiian stone bowling game

wahi pana – sacred or legendary place

Wakea – sky father

warabi – bracken fern

wauke – paper mulberry, used to make *tapa*

wiliwili – the lightest of the native woods

zendo – communal Zen meditation hall

Behind the Scenes

SEND US YOUR FEEDBACK

We love to hear from travelers – your comments keep us on our toes and help make our books better. Our well-traveled team reads every word on what you loved or loathed about this book. Although we cannot reply individually to your submissions, we always guarantee that your feedback goes straight to the appropriate authors, in time for the next edition. Each person who sends us information is thanked in the next edition – the most useful submissions are rewarded with a selection of digital PDF chapters.

Visit **lonelyplanet.com/contact** to submit your updates and suggestions or to ask for help. Our award-winning website also features inspirational travel stories, news and discussions.

Note: We may edit, reproduce and incorporate your comments in Lonely Planet products such as guidebooks, websites and digital products, so let us know if you don't want your comments reproduced or your name acknowledged. For a copy of our privacy policy visit lonelyplanet.com/privacy.

OUR READERS

Many thanks to the travelers who used the last edition and wrote to us with helpful hints, useful advice and interesting anecdotes:

Caroline Drake, Dan Berger, Janire Echevarri, Jayne Lucock, Jennifer Lam, Jim Beveridge, Lena Schulze, Lisa Wilkie, Mark Sharwood, Rhea Wimpenny and Richard Valkering

AUTHOR THANKS

Sara Benson

Thanks to Alex Howard for ace editorial problem-solving skills and project leadership, and to my Hawaii co-authors for their research tips and expert input. Thanks also to all of the travelers, locals and long-time residents who shared insider spots, savvy advice and more. Without Jai's help, this trip to Kaua'i would never have happened in the middle of two tropical storms – *shukriyaa*.

Amy C Balfour

Maholo to Alex Howard for entrusting me with this awesome assignment, coordinating author Sara Benson for skillfully leading the way, and my talented co-authors. Big thanks to Beckee Morrison, Libby Fulton and family and the whole BBQ gang, Matt Talbot, Torrie Nohara, Kevin Cooney, Craig Lowell and Kennon Savage.

Adam Karlin

Mahalo: J Alayna Kilkuskie, for advice, a place to crash and insight into the Big Island; the many Big Island residents who helped me at every step of the way; Alexander Howard for manning the editor's desk; Sara Benson for directing the *Hawaii* 12 ship of state; my co-authors for being an excellent team; Gizmo, for warming my lap whenever I write; Mom and Dad, for constant support; Rachel, my wonderful travelling companion, who always helps me see the world anew, and the best it can offer; and my Sanda, for being there with us, even if in a womb, on the first of many, many adventures.

Craig McLachlan

A huge thanks to my on-the-road assistant and exceptionally beautiful wife, Yuriko! And cheers to Paul and Nezia, Phil and Liwei and everyone else who helped us out.

Ryan Ver Berkmoes

Teri Waros on Moloka'i was a delight, as was Topside-visiting Leanna Lang. On Lana'i kudos to the unnamed many who shared their insight into a rapidly changing island. And big thanks to Mark Zigmond who showed me that a hint of sweet plum makes everything more lickable.

ACKNOWLEDGMENTS

Climate map data adapted from Peel MC, Finlayson BL & McMahon TA (2007) 'Updated World Map of the Köppen Geiger Climate Classification', *Hydrology & Earth Systems Sciences*, 11, 163344.

Cover photograph: Big-wave surfing at Jaws, Maui; Ron Dahlquist/Corbis ©

THIS BOOK

This 12th edition of Lonely Planet's *Hawaii* guidebook was written by Sara Benson, Amy C Balfour, Adam Karlin, Craig McLachlan and Ryan Ver Berkmoes. Sara, Amy, Adam and Ryan also worked on the previous edition, along with Adam Skolnick and Paul Stiles.

This guide was produced by the following:

Destination Editor Alexander Howard

Product Editors Briohny Hooper, Kate Mathews

Senior Cartographer Anthony Phelan

Book Designer Jennifer Mullins

Assisting Editors Carolyn Boicos, Melanie Dankel, Andrea Dobbin, Kate James, Anne Mulvaney, Charlotte Orr, Kirsten Rawlings, Susan Paterson

Cartographer Alison Lyall

Cover Researcher Naomi Parker

Thanks to Elizabeth Jones, Claire Naylor, Karyn Noble, Martine Power, Ellie Simpson, Tony Wheeler, Tracy Whitmey

Index

Map Pages **000**
Photo Pages **000**

C

Map Pages **000**
Photo Pages **000**

Map Pages **000**
Photo Pages **000**

Map Pages **000**
Photo Pages **000**

N

O

P

Map Pages **000**
Photo Pages **000**

W

Y

Z

Map Legend

Sights
- Beach
- Bird Sanctuary
- Buddhist
- Castle/Palace
- Christian
- Confucian
- Hindu
- Islamic
- Jain
- Jewish
- Monument
- Museum/Gallery/Historic Building
- Ruin
- Shinto
- Sikh
- Taoist
- Winery/Vineyard
- Zoo/Wildlife Sanctuary
- Other Sight

Activities, Courses & Tours
- Bodysurfing
- Diving
- Canoeing/Kayaking
- Course/Tour
- Sento Hot Baths/Onsen
- Skiing
- Snorkeling
- Surfing
- Swimming/Pool
- Walking
- Windsurfing
- Other Activity

Sleeping
- Sleeping
- Camping

Eating
- Eating

Drinking & Nightlife
- Drinking & Nightlife
- Cafe

Entertainment
- Entertainment

Shopping
- Shopping

Information
- Bank
- Embassy/Consulate
- Hospital/Medical
- Internet
- Police
- Post Office
- Telephone
- Toilet
- Tourist Information
- Other Information

Geographic
- Beach
- Hut/Shelter
- Lighthouse
- Lookout
- Mountain/Volcano
- Oasis
- Park
- Pass
- Picnic Area
- Waterfall

Population
- Capital (National)
- Capital (State/Province)
- City/Large Town
- Town/Village

Transport
- Airport
- BART station
- Border crossing
- Boston T station
- Bus
- Cable car/Funicular
- Cycling
- Ferry
- Metro/Muni station
- Monorail
- Parking
- Petrol station
- Subway/SkyTrain station
- Taxi
- Train station/Railway
- Tram
- Underground station
- Other Transport

Note: Not all symbols displayed above appear on the maps in this book

Routes
- Tollway
- Freeway
- Primary
- Secondary
- Tertiary
- Lane
- Unsealed road
- Road under construction
- Plaza/Mall
- Steps
- Tunnel
- Pedestrian overpass
- Walking Tour
- Walking Tour detour
- Path/Walking Trail

Boundaries
- International
- State/Province
- Disputed
- Regional/Suburb
- Marine Park
- Cliff
- Wall

Hydrography
- River, Creek
- Intermittent River
- Canal
- Water
- Dry/Salt/Intermittent Lake
- Reef

Areas
- Airport/Runway
- Beach/Desert
- Cemetery (Christian)
- Cemetery (Other)
- Glacier
- Mudflat
- Park/Forest
- Sight (Building)
- Sportsground
- Swamp/Mangrove

Ryan Ver Berkmoes
Lana'i & Moloka'i. Ryan first visited Moloka'i in 1987 and remembers being intoxicated by lush, rural scenery on the drive east (or maybe it was the fumes from the heaps of mangos fermenting along the side of the road). He's been back often, usually renting a beachside house where, between novels, he looks without envy at the busy lights of Maui across the channel. For this edition of *Hawaii*, Ryan wheedled the latest gossip out of tight-lipped locals on Larry Ellison's Lana'i.

OUR STORY

A beat-up old car, a few dollars in the pocket and a sense of adventure. In 1972 that's all Tony and Maureen Wheeler needed for the trip of a lifetime – across Europe and Asia overland to Australia. It took several months, and at the end – broke but inspired – they sat at their kitchen table writing and stapling together their first travel guide, *Across Asia on the Cheap*. Within a week they'd sold 1500 copies. Lonely Planet was born.

Today, Lonely Planet has offices in Franklin, London, Melbourne, Oakland, Beijing and Delhi, with more than 600 staff and writers. We share Tony's belief that 'a great guidebook should do three things: inform, educate and amuse'.

OUR WRITERS

Sara Benson

Coordinating Author, Kaua'i & Ni'ihau After graduating from college, Sara jumped on a plane to California with just one suitcase and $100 in her pocket. She then hopped across the Pacific to Japan, followed by time spent living on Maui, O'ahu and the Big Island, and tramping all around Kaua'i, Moloka'i and Lana'i. Sara is an avid hiker, backpacker, paddler and outdoors enthusiast who has worked for the National Park Service and as a volunteer at Hawai'i Volcanoes National Park. The author of more than 65 travel and nonfiction books, Sara is also the lead author of Lonely Planet's *California* and *USA's Best Trips* guides. Follow her latest adventures online at www.indietraveler.blogspot.com, www.indietraveler.net, @indie_traveler on Twitter and indietraveler on Instagram.

Amy C Balfour

Maui Amy first visited Hawaii as a toddler. These days she returns annually to tackle new adventures – and return to old favorites. For this edition, she wandered the Makawao Forest Reserve, sampled organic vodka in the Upcountry and dug into healthy new culinary creations from Wailea to Wailuku. Amy has authored or co-authored 26 books for Lonely Planet, including *Discover Maui*, *Hawaii*, *California*, *Southwest USA* and *USA*.

Adam Karlin

Hawai'i, the Big Island How great is Hawai'i? Adam has written over 40 guidebooks for Lonely Planet, but he'd never seriously considered finding a vacation cabin somewhere until he reached the Big Island. It's a magical micro-continent, and Adam spent a lovely time researching there amidst the tropical fish, flowing lava, excellent sushi and burgers, pounding waves and generally awe-inspiring beauty of creation. When not exploring the tropics for Lonely Planet, Adam calls New Orleans home.

Craig McLachlan

O'ahu A Kiwi from the southern end of the Polynesian triangle, Craig is a regular on O'ahu and has an MBA from the University of Hawai'i at Manoa. Other Lonely Planet titles he has worked on range from *Greece* to *Japan* to *Rarotonga, Samoa & Tonga*. Craig considers himself a 'freelance anything' and jobs have included pilot, karate instructor, photographer, tour leader, hiking guide, novelist and Japanese interpreter. He once set the record for climbing Japan's 100 Famous Mountains! See www.craigmclachlan.com.

Published by Lonely Planet Publications Pty Ltd
ABN 36 005 607 983
12th edition – September 2015
ISBN 978 1 74321 675 0

10 9 8 7 6 5 4 3 2 1
Printed in China